FEDERAL INCOME TAXATION

ASPEN PUBLISHERS

FEDERAL INCOME TAXATION

Fifteenth Edition

WILLIAM A. KLEIN
Maxwell Professor of Law Emeritus
University of California, Los Angeles

JOSEPH BANKMAN
Ralph M. Parsons Professor of Law and Business
Stanford University

DANIEL N. SHAVIRO
Wayne Perry Professor of Taxation
New York University School of Law

KIRK J. STARK
Professor of Law
University of California, Los Angeles

Wolters Kluwer
Law & Business

AUSTIN   BOSTON   CHICAGO   NEW YORK   THE NETHERLANDS

Aspen Publishers
Attn: Permissions Department
76 Ninth Avenue, 7th Floor
New York, NY 10011-5201

To contact Customer Care, e-mail customer.care@aspenpublishers.com, call 1-800-234-1660, fax 1-800-901-9075, or mail correspondence to:

Aspen Publishers
Attn: Order Department
PO Box 990
Frederick, MD 21705

Printed in the United States of America.

1 2 3 4 5 6 7 8 9 0

ISBN 978-0-7355-7809-8

Library of Congress Cataloging-in-Publication Data

Federal income taxation / William A. Klein ... [et al.].–15th ed.
    p. cm.
    Rev. ed of: Federal income taxation / William A. Klein, Joseph Bankman, Daniel N. Shaviro. 14th ed. c2006.
    Includes index.
    ISBN 978-0-7355-7809-8
1. Income tax — Law and legislation — United States — Cases. I. Klein, William A. II. Klein, William A. Federal income taxation.

KF6369.F4238 2009
343.7305′2 — dc22

2009007843

About Wolters Kluwer Law & Business

Wolters Kluwer Law & Business is a leading provider of research information and workflow solutions in key specialty areas. The strengths of the individual brands of Aspen Publishers, CCH, Kluwer Law International and Loislaw are aligned within Wolters Kluwer Law & Business to provide comprehensive, in-depth solutions and expert-authored content for the legal, professional and education markets.

CCH was founded in 1913 and has served more than four generations of business professionals and their clients. The CCH products in the Wolters Kluwer Law & Business group are highly regarded electronic and print resources for legal, securities, antitrust and trade regulation, government contracting, banking, pension, payroll, employment and labor, and health-care reimbursement and compliance professionals.

Aspen Publishers is a leading information provider for attorneys, business professionals and law students. Written by preeminent authorities, Aspen products offer analytical and practical information in a range of specialty practice areas from securities law and intellectual property to mergers and acquisitions and pension/benefits. Aspen's trusted legal education resources provide professors and students with high-quality, up-to-date and effective resources for successful instruction and study in all areas of the law.

Kluwer Law International supplies the global business community with comprehensive English-language international legal information. Legal practitioners, corporate counsel and business executives around the world rely on the Kluwer Law International journals, loose-leafs, books and electronic products for authoritative information in many areas of international legal practice.

Loislaw is a premier provider of digitized legal content to small law firm practitioners of various specializations. Loislaw provides attorneys with the ability to quickly and efficiently find the necessary legal information they need, when and where they need it, by facilitating access to primary law as well as state-specific law, records, forms and treatises.

Wolters Kluwer Law & Business, a unit of Wolters Kluwer, is headquartered in New York and Riverwoods, Illinois. Wolters Kluwer is a leading multinational publisher and information services company.

SUMMARY OF CONTENTS

CONTENTS

2

SOME CHARACTERISTICS OF INCOME   47

3

PROBLEMS OF TIMING   211

4

PERSONAL DEDUCTIONS, EXEMPTIONS, AND CREDITS   351

5

ALLOWANCES FOR MIXED BUSINESS AND PERSONAL OUTLAYS   419

6

DEDUCTIONS FOR THE COSTS
OF EARNING INCOME

511

7

THE SPLITTING OF INCOME   621

8

CAPITAL GAINS AND LOSSES   695

PREFACE

Boris Bittker, who single-handedly wrote the first few editions of this book, had a unique gift for presenting complex material in an easy-to-understand way. We have tried to preserve that quality, despite the unceasing efforts of Congress (aided at times by taxpayers, their advisors, and the courts) to make the tax law incomprehensible. In this fifteenth edition, we have maintained the approachable style that is the legacy of this book while also keeping it up to date in an era of perpetual change.

This edition features a handful of new judicial opinions and other illustrative legal authorities, including a recent IRS Chief Counsel memorandum concerning the taxation of same-sex partners and a private letter ruling on a like-kind exchange involving a conservation easement. We have also expanded the discussion of several important topics, such as the earned income tax credit and the deduction for state and local taxes. A revised section on constructive sales incorporates an excerpt from the legislative history of section 1259, along with a problem designed to highlight lingering ambiguity in that provision and the tax lawyer's role in giving advice in the face of legal uncertainty.

In addition to these changes, the fifteenth edition also features a few innovations. For the first time, we have included images of the Form 1040, along with several of its accompanying schedules. Rather than simply reproducing the forms, we have chosen to include the most recent federal income tax return of America's first family. In addition, we have included throughout the book several new shaded passages under the heading Comparative Focus. These are brief descriptions of how other countries have approached particular tax policy issues in the design of their income taxes.

As with each of the prior editions, the overall objective has been to give students a basic framework for understanding federal income tax law and policy. While tax may be a field famous for its ever-changing legal details, our hope is that this book will help students develop a durable and adaptive knowledge base that will serve them well beyond future amendments to the tax code.

William A. Klein
Joseph Bankman
Daniel N. Shaviro
Kirk J. Stark

March 2009

EDITORIAL NOTICE

The original author of this casebook was Boris I. Bittker of Yale Law School, who has earned the admiration and affection of generations of teachers and students. Much of his original structure and choice of materials remains in the current edition. Bittker was joined in later editions by Lawrence M. Stone, who kept the book current and added important ideas and materials. Neither Bittker nor Stone has been involved in recent revisions, but the current authors are deeply indebted to them for the many wise choices and valuable insights that have survived.

All omissions from cases and other materials, except omissions of footnotes, are indicated either by substitution of new material in brackets or, more often, by an ellipsis (. . .). Thus, omissions of citations, as well as omissions of text, are generally indicated by the insertion of the ellipsis. Citations have been excised ruthlessly on the theory that for the most part they are of no use to students and that the rare student who might have some interest in them can easily look them up in the original report. There is no notation of omitted footnotes, and all footnotes, including those in cases and other materials, are numbered consecutively from the beginning of each chapter.

FEDERAL INCOME TAXATION

1

INTRODUCTION

Taxation is eternally lively; it concerns nine-tenths of us more directly than either smallpox or golf, and has just as much drama in it.

—H.L. Mencken

No other branch of law touches human activities at so many points.

—Justice Robert H. Jackson

Welcome to the world of taxation. If you are like most law students, chances are that the course for which you are reading this book marks your first formal introduction to tax law. Most law students show up for their first tax class thinking it's going to be dull and dry, dense and difficult. We would like to use the first few paragraphs of this introductory chapter to offer an alternative view of tax as a field of study in order to lay the groundwork for what follows.

Taxation is an age-old phenomenon, one that predates the invention of money and even government. In the earliest times, taxes were collected in kind—in the form of food grains, furs, and other valuables—and delivered to priest-kings on the backs of animals or through other primitive means.[1] These items were then put to whatever use the king deemed appropriate. In today's modern democracies, of course, we think of taxation very differently, but it is useful to remember that the basic problem is the same. Stated in the most general terms, taxation is about how to allocate the burdens of collective activities. How should we share the cost of civilized society? What (if anything) do we owe each other? What (if anything) are we entitled to keep for ourselves?

These are big, important questions at the heart of the social contract. It is no surprise that tax has been a central preoccupation of political theorists across the ages. From Hobbes and Locke to Rawls and Nozick, philosophers have debated the morality of taxation and its implications for the relationship between the individual and the broader community. But more importantly, these same questions regularly stoke debate among ordinary citizens at kitchen tables, barbershops, and sidewalk cafés from Pacoima to Hoboken.

---

1. Carolyn Webber & Aaron Wildavsky, A History of Taxation and Expenditure in the Western World 38-92 (1986).

1

Everyone has an opinion about taxes. Are they too high? Are they too low? Who pays too much? Who pays too little? It is for good reason that taxes stir up so much controversy. Tax has always been, and will always be, a key source of intellectual, social, economic, and political conflict.

Our hope is that this book will assist you in developing an insider's expertise on tax law and policy. This expertise will serve you in many different ways. For example, as many commentators have noted, an understanding of a society's tax system can offer important insights into that society's core values. Which life choices do we favor? Which do we discourage? Who is deserving? Who is not? At some fundamental level, therefore, a detailed study of U.S. tax law is also an in-depth examination of American society. It is also the case, however, that an understanding of tax is central to understanding a society's *legal* system. Justice Jackson's admonition—that "no other branch of law touches human activities at so many points"—rings even truer today than it did when he penned it more than sixty years ago. Every lawyer, from the toxic tort litigator to the real estate attorney, should have at least a basic understanding of this essential pillar of America's legal structure. No matter what sort of legal career you ultimately pursue, a knowledge of tax will make you a better lawyer.

What follows in the remaining pages of this introduction is an abbreviated overview of some of the key data, issues, and concepts relevant to the study of the U.S. tax system. The idea in these initial pages is to give you some sense of the history, background, and structure of the U.S. federal income tax, as well as some of the overarching themes that will recur throughout the book. As in every law school course or casebook, there will be times during your study of tax when you will feel as though you have lost sight of the forest by having focused so intensely on the trees. At those moments, we encourage you to return to these first few pages in order to readjust your perspective.

We also encourage you to use the time you are studying tax to undertake your own independent field research in this area. Discuss the topics you learn about with your parents, your classmates, your co-workers. Surf the web for the latest news stories about tax, and try to follow legal and policy developments in Washington and your state capitol. Identify your most liberal and most conservative friends and have them debate the pros and cons of the latest proposal for fundamental tax reform. In short, use this opportunity not just to learn the law of taxation, but also to develop an appreciation for tax as a site for excavating some of the polity's deepest moral commitments. With that sort of approach, we're confident that, like Mencken, you'll find taxation to be eternally lively, with maybe even more drama than smallpox or golf.

A.   THE IMPORTANCE OF INCOME TAXES

1.   Some Data on Taxes and the Distribution of Income

Income taxes dominate the American tax structure. As can be seen from Table 1-1 below, for 2009, income taxes, corporate and individual, are expected to produce 60 percent of total federal revenues.[2] If one removes social insurance taxes and contributions and looks only at the so-called general revenues, income taxes exceed 90 percent of the total. Income taxes are also an important source of revenue for state governments. In 2007, of a total of $750 billion in tax collections at this level, the individual income tax produced 35 percent, and the corporate income tax produced 7.1 percent.[3]

TABLE 1-1
Sources of Federal Revenue for 2009 (estimated)

Source	Amount (billions)	Percentage of total
Individual income taxes	$1,259	47
Corporation income taxes	339	13
Social insurance taxes and contributions	950	35
Excise taxes	69	2
Other	83	3
Total	$2,700	100

Nearly all individuals will at some time file a federal income tax return — the infamous Form 1040. Take a moment to review the Form 1040 that appears on the opposite page. You may recognize the filers.

In 2005, approximately 134 million individual income tax returns were filed. Of these, approximately 53 million returns were joint returns filed by married couples, while 59 million returns were filed by single individuals. The remaining 22 million returns consist of those who filed as head of household, surviving spouse, or married persons filing separate returns. As discussed further below, these are all filing options for individuals subject to the U.S. income tax, but the most common filing statuses are consistently "unmarried individual" and "married individuals filing a joint return."

The average "adjusted gross income" (a defined term discussed in greater detail below) for all individual income tax returns filed in 2005 was $55,238. However, not all filers owed income tax. Of the 134 million returns filed for 2005, about two-thirds reported positive income tax liability for the year. These "taxable returns" reported an average AGI of $75,687 for the year and an average tax paid of $10,319. Thus, the average effective income tax rate for all taxable returns for 2005 (i.e., tax owed as a percentage of AGI) was 13.6 percent. The remaining one-third of individual tax returns filed for 2005 reported income low enough that no tax was due. Individuals filing these "nontaxable returns" reported an average AGI of $12,923 per return; however, their income tax liability was eliminated by the application of certain

2. The Budget for Fiscal Year 2009, Historical Tables, available at www.gpoaccess.gpo.gov/usbudget.
3. U.S. Census Bureau, State Government Tax Collections: 2007 (February 29, 2008), http://www.census.gov/govs/statetax/0700usstax.html.

Form **1040**	U.S. Individual Income Tax Return	**2007**			IRS Use Only - Do not write or staple in this space.		

OMB No. 1545-0074

Label
(See instructions on page 12.)
Use the IRS label.
Otherwise, please print or type.

L A B E L

H E R E

For the year Jan. 1-Dec. 31, 2007, or other tax year beginning   , 2007, ending   , 20

Your first name and initial — **BARACK H.** | Last name — **OBAMA**
Your social security number

If a joint return, spouse's first name and initial — **MICHELLE L.** | Last name — **OBAMA**
Spouse's social security number

Home address (number and street). If you have a P.O. box, see page 12.   Apt. no.

You must enter ▲ your SSN(s) above. ▲

City, town or post office, state, and ZIP code. If you have a foreign address, see page 12.
CHICAGO, IL 60615

Checking a box below will not change your tax or refund.

Presidential Election Campaign ► Check here if you, or your spouse if filing jointly, want $3 to go to this fund (see page 12) ►   [X] You   [X] Spouse

Filing Status

Check only one box.

1 ☐ Single
2 [X] Married filing jointly (even if only one had income)
3 ☐ Married filing separately. Enter spouse's SSN above and full name here. ►
4 ☐ Head of household (with qualifying person). If the qualifying person is a child but not your dependent, enter this child's name here. ►
5 ☐ Qualifying widow(er) with dependent child (see page 14)

Exemptions

6a [X] Yourself. If someone can claim you as a dependent, **do not** check box 6a ....
b [X] Spouse ....

Boxes checked on 6a and 6b **2**

c **Dependents:**

(1) First name Last name	(2) Dependent's social security number	(3) Dependent's relationship to you	(4) ✓ if qualifying child for child tax credit (see page 15)
MALIA A OBAMA	-	DAUGHTER	X
NATASHA M OBAMA		DAUGHTER	X

No. of children on 6c who:
● lived with you **2**
● did not live with you due to divorce or separation (see page 16)

Dependents on 6c not entered above

If more than four dependents, see page 15.

d   Total number of exemptions claimed ....

Add numbers on lines above ► **4**

Income

Attach Form(s) W-2 here. Also attach Forms W-2G and 1099-R if tax was withheld.

If you did not get a W-2, see page 19.

Enclose, but do not attach, any payment. Also, please use Form 1040-V.

7	Wages, salaries, tips, etc. Attach Form(s) W-2		7	260,735.
8a	Taxable interest. Attach Schedule B if required		8a	1,442.
b	Tax-exempt interest. Do not include on line 8a	8b	45,851.	
9a	Ordinary dividends. Attach Schedule B if required		9a	
b	Qualified dividends (see page 19)	9b		
10	Taxable refunds, credits, or offsets of state and local income taxes STMT 1 STMT 3		10	6,167.
11	Alimony received		11	
12	Business income or (loss). Attach Schedule C or C-EZ		12	3,972,821.
13	Capital gain or (loss). Attach Schedule D if required. If not required, check here ► ☐		13	-3,000.
14	Other gains or (losses). Attach Form 4797		14	
15a	IRA distributions	15a	b Taxable amount	15b	
16a	Pensions and annuities	16a	b Taxable amount	16b	
17	Rental real estate, royalties, partnerships, S corporations, trusts, etc. Attach Schedule E		17	
18	Farm income or (loss). Attach Schedule F		18	
19	Unemployment compensation		19	
20a	Social security benefits	20a	b Taxable amount (see page 24)	20b	
21	Other income. List type and amount (see page 24)		21	
22	Add the amounts in the far right column for lines 7 through 21. This is your **total income** ►		22	4,238,165.

Adjusted Gross Income

23	Educator expenses (see page 26)	23	
24	Certain business expenses of reservists, performing artists, and fee-basis government officials. Attach Form 2106 or 2106-EZ	24	
25	Health savings account deduction. Attach Form 8889	25	
26	Moving expenses. Attach Form 3903	26	
27	One-half of self-employment tax. Attach Schedule SE	27	53,200.
28	Self-employed SEP, SIMPLE, and qualified plans	28	45,000.
29	Self-employed health insurance deduction (see page 26)	29	
30	Penalty on early withdrawal of savings	30	
31a	Alimony paid b Recipient's SSN ►	31a	
32	IRA deduction (see page 27)	32	
33	Student loan interest deduction (see page 30)	33	
34	Tuition and fees deduction. Attach Form 8917	34	
35	Domestic production activities deduction. Attach Form 8903	35	

36	Add lines 23 through 31a and 32 through 35	36	98,200.
37	Subtract line 36 from line 22. This is your **adjusted gross income** ►	37	4,139,965.

710001
11-05-07

LHA For Disclosure, Privacy Act, and Paperwork Reduction Act Notice, see page 83.   Form **1040** (2007)

Form 1040 (2007) BARACK H. & MICHELLE L. OBAMA Page 2

Tax and Credits	38	Amount from line 37 (adjusted gross income)	38	4,139,965.
Standard Deduction for -	39a	Check if: You were born before January 2, 1943, ☐ Blind. Spouse was born before January 2, 1943, ☐ Blind. Total boxes checked ▶ 39a		
● People who checked any box on line 39a or 39b **or** who can be claimed as a dependent.	b	If your spouse itemizes on a separate return or you were a dual-status alien, see page 31 and check here ▶ 39b ☐		
	40	Itemized deductions (from Schedule A) or your **standard deduction** (see left margin)	40	374,008.
	41	Subtract line 40 from line 38	41	3,765,957.
	42	If line 38 is $117,300 or less, multiply $3,400 by the total number of exemptions claimed on line 6d.		
● All others:		If line 38 is over $117,300, see the worksheet on page 33	42	4,532.
Single or Married filing separately, $5,350	43	**Taxable income.** Subtract line 42 from line 41. If line 42 is more than line 41, enter -0-	43	3,761,425.
	44	**Tax.** Check if any tax is from: a ☐ Form(s) 8814 b ☐ Form 4972 c ☐ Form(s) 8889	44	1,288,705.
Married filing jointly or Qualifying widow(er), $10,700	45	**Alternative minimum tax.** Attach Form 6251	45	0.
	46	Add lines 44 and 45 ▶	46	1,288,705.
	47	Credit for child and dependent care expenses. Attach Form 2441	47	
Head of household, $7,850	48	Credit for the elderly or the disabled. Attach Schedule R	48	
	49	Education credits. Attach Form 8863	49	
	50	Residential energy credits. Attach Form 5695	50	
	51	Foreign tax credit. Attach Form 1116 if required	51	298.
	52	Child tax credit (see page 39). Attach Form 8901 if required	52	
	53	Retirement savings contributions credit. Attach Form 8880	53	
	54	Credits from: a ☐ Form 8396 b ☐ Form 8859 c ☐ Form 8839	54	
	55	Other credits: a ☐ Form 3800 b ☐ Form 8801 c ☐ Form	55	
	56	Add lines 47 through 55. These are your **total credits**	56	298.
	57	Subtract line 56 from line 46. If line 56 is more than line 46, enter -0- ▶	57	1,288,407.
Other Taxes	58	Self-employment tax. Attach Schedule SE	58	106,399.
	59	Unreported social security and Medicare tax from: a ☐ Form 4137 b ☐ Form 8919	59	
	60	Additional tax on IRAs, other qualified retirement plans, etc. Attach Form 5329 if required	60	
	61	Advance earned income credit payments from Form(s) W-2, box 9	61	
	62	Household employment taxes. Attach Schedule H	62	1,966.
	63	Add lines 57 through 62. This is your **total tax** ▶	63	1,396,772.
Payments	64	Federal income tax withheld from Forms W-2 and 1099	64	59,090.
	65	2007 estimated tax payments and amount applied from 2006 return	65	277,856.
If you have a qualifying child, attach Schedule EIC.	66a	Earned income credit (EIC)	66a	
	b	Nontaxable combat pay election ▶ 66b		
	67	Excess social security and tier 1 RRTA tax withheld (see page 59)	67	
	68	Additional child tax credit. Attach Form 8812	68	
	69	Amount paid with request for extension to file (see page 59)	69	
	70	Payments from: a ☐ Form 2439 b ☐ Form 4136 c ☐ Form 8885	70	
	71	Refundable credit for prior year minimum tax from Form 8801, line 27	71	
	72	Add lines 64, 65, 66a, and 67 through 71. These are your **total payments** ▶	72	336,946.
Refund Direct deposit? See page 59 and fill in 74b, 74c, and 74d, or Form 8888.	73	If line 72 is more than line 63, subtract line 63 from line 72. This is the amount you **overpaid**	73	
	74a	Amount of line 73 you want **refunded to you.** If Form 8888 is attached, check here ▶ ☐	74a	
	b	Routing number ▶ c Type: ☐ Checking ☐ Savings d Account number ▶		
	75	Amount of line 73 you want **applied to your 2008 estimated tax** ▶	75	
Amount You Owe	76	**Amount you owe.** Subtract line 72 from line 63. For details on how to pay, see page 60 ▶	76	1,059,826.
	77	Estimated tax penalty (see page 61)	77	0.

Third Party Designee Do you want to allow another person to discuss this return with the IRS (see page 61)? ☒ **Yes.** Complete the following. ☐ No

Designee's name ▶ PREPARER   Phone no. ▶   Personal identification number (PIN) ▶

Sign Here Under penalties of perjury, I declare that I have examined this return and accompanying schedules and statements, and to the best of my knowledge and belief, they are true, correct, and complete. Declaration of preparer (other than taxpayer) is based on all information of which preparer has any knowledge.

Joint return? See page 13. Keep a copy for your records.

Your signature | Date 4/13/08 | Your occupation US SENATOR | Daytime phone number

Spouse's signature. If a joint return, both must sign. *Michelle Obama* | Date 4/13/08 | Spouse's occupation HOSPITAL ADMINISTRATOR

Paid Preparer's Use Only

Preparer's signature ▶ | Date 4/16/08 | Check if self-employed ☐ | Preparer's SSN or PTIN

Firm's name (or yours if self-employed), address, and ZIP code | WINEBERG SOLHEIM HOWELL & SHAIN, PC 180 N LASALLE ST, STE 2200 CHICAGO, IL 60601 | EIN | Phone no.

710002 11-05-07

deductions and tax credits, most notably the earned income tax credit, a wage subsidy designed to supplement the earnings of low-income workers.[4]

A strikingly high percentage of total income tax receipts comes from those in the upper income brackets. In 2005, individuals reporting adjusted gross income of $200,000 or more for the year—about 3.5 million returns, representing 2.7 percent of all returns—accounted for 29.2 percent of adjusted gross income reported on all returns and paid 51.3 percent of total individual income taxes.[5] Stated very roughly, one might say that the top 3 percent earned just under one-third of all income and paid more than half of all income taxes. These taxpayers had an average taxable income of about $530,000 and paid an average income tax of about $135,000, resulting in average tax rate of just over 25 percent. To put these figures in perspective, note that median household income as reported by the U.S. Census Bureau for 2005 was about $48,000.

The fact that the rich pay a high proportion of total income taxes is in part attributable to the system of progressive marginal tax rates set forth in section 1 of the Internal Revenue Code. In 2008, statutory tax rates ranged from a low of 10 percent to a high of 35 percent. But the high proportion of income taxes paid by the rich is also due to the fact that their incomes represent a large and growing share of the total. Over the past forty years, pretax income inequality has increased significantly in the United States, with the top 10 percent increasing their share of total income from roughly one-third to one-half. Much of that change is due to gains within the top percentile. From 1968 to 2006, the top 1 percent of earners increased their share of total income from 12 percent to just under 23 percent.[6]

These figures offer policy advocates of all stripes ample support for their tendentious claims. Conservatives point to the rising share of income taxes paid by the rich (true) and argue for tax cuts shifting the relative burden downward. Liberals cite dramatic increases in income inequality (also true) and assert that the rich should be paying more. Lurking behind these arguments is usually a set of unstated assumptions regarding the moral legitimacy of pretax market outcomes. Any discussion of tax policy, including arguments over the nitty-gritty details of seemingly obscure code provisions, is bound to bump into these meta-issues sooner or later. However one feels about these matters, it bears emphasizing that the tax structure has only a modest effect on the concentration of income and wealth. For 2005, the bottom quintile increased its share of income from 4.1 percent before taxes to 4.9 percent after taxes, while the top quintile's share fell from 53.5 percent before taxes to 50.1 percent after taxes.[7]

4. Kyle Mudry & Justin Bryan, Individual Income Tax Rates and Shares, 2005, IRS Statistics of Income Bulletin, Winter 2008.

5. See Internal Revenue Service, Statistics of Income, available at www.irs.gov/taxstats.

6. Emmanuel Saez, Striking It Richer: The Evolution of Top Incomes in the United States, Pathways (Winter 2008), available at http://www.stanford.edu/group/scspi/pdfs/pathways/winter_2008/Saez.pdf. For the data, see http://elsa.berkeley.edu/~saez/TabFig2006prel.xls.

7. For a thorough and valuable presentation of data on concentration of income and wealth, drawing on various sources such as the Census Bureau, the Congressional Budget Office, and the Internal Revenue Service, see Martin J. McMahon, Jr., The Matthew Effect and Federal Taxation, 45 B.C. L. Rev. 993 (2004).

2. Impact on the Practice of Law

The income tax is important not only because of its central role in financing government but also, and of special interest to lawyers, because of the ways in which it affects so many other branches of law. The tax lawyer, perhaps above all else, is a planner — a person who advises clients on how to structure transactions so as to ensure compliance with the tax laws and minimize tax liability. Lawyers who do not specialize in tax law must know at least enough about it to recognize when a tax specialist must be consulted. Tax considerations may play a key role in transactions ranging from the sale, lease, or encumbrance of property; to the dissolution of a marriage; to the choice between the partnership and the corporate form of business organization; to the form of compensation in an employment agreement; to the settlement of a claim for damages for personal injuries; and so on. By the same token, the practitioner or the legal scholar who wants to understand economic and legal institutions such as the sale and leaseback method of financing the purchase of property, the family-controlled charitable foundation, or the use of limited partnerships must understand the tax reasons for the use of such devices. For good or ill, the federal income tax has played a role in legal history ranking in importance with the invention of the trust and the corporation and the development of the doctrine of respondeat superior.

The income tax has had this kind of impact not just because of the amount of money involved but also because it is a complex system of rules that presents many opportunities for adjustment of conduct to achieve desirable tax results. The state and local property tax and general sales tax raise more than $500 billion a year. That is about 35 percent of the federal and state income taxes. Yet because sales and property taxes are generally based on simpler concepts and rules, they produce far less business for lawyers, relative to the amounts involved, than the income tax.

3. Economic Consequences

The income tax has also had a substantial effect on the allocation of resources in our economy. Economists typically describe the effects of taxes by reference to *income effects* and *substitution effects*. Income effects are changes in behavior induced by the fact that the tax reduces the money available to the taxpayer. All taxes have income effects, in theory leading taxpayers to work more to make up for the lost income. Substitution effects are changes in behavior that arise from a change in the relative attractiveness of different commodities or activities. For example, if the government imposes a 50 percent tax on red apples without a corresponding tax on green apples, those who are otherwise indifferent between apple types are likely to shift from Fujis to Granny Smiths. A tax on labor income (by far the most significant component of the income tax base) should have a similar effect, inducing people to substitute untaxed leisure for taxable labor income — in other words, to work less and play more.

In theory, income taxes should have both income and substitution effects. On the basis of theory alone, however, it is impossible to know which effect predominates, though it seems likely that the combined effect would vary by individual. Empirical studies have shown that the effect of income taxes on labor supply is the weakest among men in their prime working years (ages 20-60). By contrast, some studies have shown the labor supply of married women to be very responsive to income taxes, though the effect varies by income class.

The current U.S. income tax has many consequences for individual behavior far beyond the decision regarding whether or how much to work. Many of these economic effects are attributable to specific provisions in the law that favor a particular type of activity or investment. For example, the deductions for home mortgage interest and for property taxes and the non-taxation of imputed income encourage people (especially those with high incomes) to buy homes rather than rent apartments. At one time, very substantial tax breaks benefited the oil industry, thereby encouraging the production of oil and reducing the price of gasoline; even today, the tax laws treat the oil industry more favorably in some respects than other industries. It is by no means implausible to suppose that these tax provisions played an important role in encouraging the shift of populations to the suburbs and in the problems of pollution and of energy management. Other kinds of tax provisions may have had effects that most people would view as more benign. For example, the deduction for charitable contributions seems to have played a significant role in raising the level of support for private colleges and universities, museums and symphony orchestras, as well as religious organizations.

Much of the complexity of the present tax laws is attributable to provisions designed to encourage particular kinds of economic activity. Even when the use of the tax system in this way is less effective than direct government expenditure, politicians and voters often prefer it to direct expenditure because it looks different. Suppose that a company is paying income taxes of $10 million per year, and that someone proposes a subsidy for a particular type of investment that will give that company $6 million a year. Using the tax system to deliver the subsidy permits its advocates to label it a "tax cut" rather than a "spending increase." This may be politically advantageous even though the company's net payment to the government is $4 million either way. In part for this reason, the tax system is used to deliver an enormous range of incentive provisions for different kinds of business investment. Whether this is good or bad policy, it contributes substantially to the complexity of the law and to the need for tax advice in planning business and other activities.

B. HISTORY

The current federal income tax is a creature of the twentieth century. From the time of the Jefferson administration until the Civil War, tariffs (whose burden Jefferson thought was borne by the rich) were the backbone of the federal tax system. Tariffs not only produced revenues but also protected developing industries, mostly in the North. Congress levied the country's first income tax in 1861 at the outset of the Civil War with a single rate of 3 percent on all incomes over $800 per year. Initially, Treasury Secretary Salmon Chase did little to enforce or even collect the tax. As the war progressed, however, the demand for revenue escalated dramatically. Faced with financial calamity and widespread calls for the rich to sacrifice more for the war effort following the New York draft riots, Congress in 1864 amended the rate structure to impose a tax of 5 percent on income from $600 to $5,000, 7.5 percent on income from $5,000 to $10,000, and 10 percent on income above $10,000. By comparison with the present law, the statute then was almost unbelievably short and simple. The Confederacy also employed an income tax.

After the Civil War, the federal income tax was repealed and tariffs again became the most important source of federal revenue, supplemented by excises on tobacco and liquor. Throughout the 1870s and 1880s, agrarian and labor groups called for reductions in the tariff and for a revival of the income tax. Leading the opposition were Eastern businessmen, for whom the income tax meant "confiscation," "spoliation," and "communism." Throughout this period the Republican Party was able to hold the fort, but the task became more difficult as the Democratic Party gradually emerged from its handicap as the party of secession and finally became impossible when the Populist movement gained strength from the panic of 1893.

In 1894, during Grover Cleveland's second administration, a federal income tax, based largely on the Civil War statute, was passed by Congress after a bitter struggle, a notable feature of which was the oratory of William Jennings Bryan. A tax of 2 percent was imposed on individual incomes over $4,000 and on the entire income of business corporations. In 1894, eggs sold for twenty cents a dozen and round steak for twelve cents a pound,[8] and the average annual earnings of nonfarm employees was $420.[9] Adjusted to take account of inflation (by applying the Consumer Price Index[10]) the $4,000 threshold of 1894 would have been about a $100,000 threshold in 2005. Thus, the income tax was a tax on the well-to-do.

The victory of the Democrats and the Populists was soon to be snatched away, however, by the Supreme Court. The tax became law on August 28, 1894, to take effect as of January 1, 1895, and by January 29, 1895, the Supreme Court had agreed to hear a test case challenging its constitutionality. Pollock v. Farmers' Loan & Trust Co., 157 U.S. 429, aff'd on rehearing, 158 U.S. 601 (1895). The attack was based on the theory that a tax on rental income and on dividends and interest was in effect a tax on the underlying property interest and because it was not levied on states in proportion to population, violated the prohibition on unapportioned "direct" taxes in

---

8. See U.S. Department of Commerce, Historical Statistics of the United States, Colonial Times to 1970, at 213 (1975).

9. Id. at 165.

10. See id. at 210-211.

Article I, section 9, clause 4, of the Constitution. ("No Capitation, or other direct, Tax shall be laid, unless in Proportion to the Census or Enumeration herein before directed to be taken.") The Court heard argument, involving several notable attorney-orators, for five days. The public interest was intense. After a rehearing, the Court, in a five-to-four decision, sustained the constitutional challenge to the imposition of the tax on rents, dividends, and interest and further held that since the provisions taxing those receipts were inseparable from the other provisions of the law, the entire income tax law was invalid.

After Pollock v. Farmers' Loan & Trust Co., advocates of an income tax turned their efforts to amendment of the Constitution. Those efforts bore fruit in 1913 with the adoption of the Sixteenth Amendment, which provides: "The Congress shall have the power to lay and collect taxes on incomes, from whatever source derived, without apportionment among the several States, and without regard to any census or enumeration."

Congress reacted quickly, adopting in 1913 a tax law modeled after the 1894 act. Like its 1894 predecessor, the 1913 tax was imposed only on the well-to-do, but the rates were modest. There was an exemption of $3,000 for an individual and of an additional $1,000 for a married person living with his or her spouse.[11] The rate was 1 percent with a "surtax" ranging from 1 percent on net income from $20,000 to $50,000 up to 6 percent on that part of net income exceeding $500,000. The revenue needs created by World War I led to dramatic expansion of the tax, however, leading to "the discovery of how easily and quickly large sums or revenue could be raised through the income tax."[12] The reach of the tax was broadened by reducing personal exemptions and its impact was increased by raising rates, with individual rates reaching a maximum of 77 percent in 1918. The tax rates had become significantly progressive.[13] Despite the lowering of exemptions, the major burden of the tax fell on people with high incomes. "For the years 1917 to 1919, although less than 1 percent of the returns reported income over $20,000, that group paid an average of 70 percent of the income taxes."[14]

Following World War I, as federal expenditures declined and budget surpluses arose, rates were gradually reduced, reaching a maximum individual rate of 24 percent. During World War II, the income tax became, and since then has remained, a mass tax (that is, one imposed on people across a broad range of the income spectrum), although, as noted above, high-income individuals continue to pay a substantial share of the total tax. Maximum marginal rates have gone as high as 91 percent (for some forms of income, in the early 1960s), back down to 28 percent in 1986, and gradually back up to

11. Since 1894, the Consumer Price Index had risen by only about 14 percent, and average annual earnings of fully employed employees was still only $663.

12. See J. Witte, The Politics and Development of the Federal Income Tax 81 (1985). This book is an excellent source of facts and analysis and is relied on heavily in the account that follows in text.

13. A progressive rate structure is one under which rates rise as income rises. Thus, high-income taxpayers pay a higher *proportion* of their income as taxes than do lower-income taxpayers. See discussion infra page 20-22.

14. Witte, supra note 15, at 86.

about 40 percent by the end of the twentieth century. In 2003 the top marginal tax rate on capital gains and dividends was reduced to 15 percent and the top marginal rate on other forms of income was reduced to 35 percent. In 2001 there had been tax reductions for lower-income taxpayers, including an increase in the child credit and a new 10 percent bracket (the previous low bracket having been 15 percent). During the same era, however, increasing numbers of middle-class taxpayers became subject to the Alternative Minimum Tax (AMT), which imposes a tax at a rate of 26 percent or 28 percent on income more broadly calculated than under the regular tax, subject to an exemption amount, if that alternative tax is greater than the regular tax. The rate structure is discussed further in Chapter 7 and at pages 20-22, infra.

C. THEORY AND POLICY

1. Taxation and "Ability to Pay"

There are many different ways in which the federal government could distribute tax burdens. Perhaps the simplest approach would be to levy a "head tax" — a tax of an equal dollar amount on everyone, or at least each person above a certain age. A simpler tax system is hard to imagine. Imposing a lump-sum levy would eliminate the need for tax returns, tax lawyers, or tax planning (apart from finding money with which to pay the tax). Moreover, a head tax would be highly efficient, in the sense that it would not distort economic behavior. After all, the same amount would be owed regardless of hours worked, money spent, etc.

Yet despite the ostensible advantages of a head tax, most people would regard a tax system that charged everyone the same amount as unfair, even unthinkable. Unpacking the intuition behind that natural reaction goes a long way toward explaining the allure of income taxes. At bottom, most people believe that a highly compensated CEO should pay more tax than a schoolteacher, who in turn should pay more tax than someone who is unable to find work. The reason for this belief is usually that those with higher earnings are thought to be "better off" and therefore have a greater "ability to pay."

Tax scholars have long used the term "ability to pay" to describe the attribute that might justify requiring some people to pay more tax than others. But what does it mean? While the phrase might superficially imply convenience in paying, with relative tax burdens turning on the availability of cash or other liquid assets, a moment's reflection reveals the shortcomings of such an approach. Among other things, it would encourage people to lower their tax bills by accepting payment in illiquid assets, like artwork or real estate, arguably to no good purpose. As we will see, taxpayer liquidity has sometimes influenced the development of our tax rules; however, most commentators view this as a concession to administrative practicalities rather than a determination regarding taxpayers' relative abilities.

A broader view of ability to pay looks to people's material well-being without regard to liquidity. Under this view, those with higher levels of material well-being, regardless of the form it takes, are considered to be "better off" and thus should bear greater tax burdens. The view that the rich should pay more than the average tax, and the poor less or none at all, might rest on a notion of declining marginal utility of income — i.e., the wealthier you are, the less each dollar lost to the tax collector diminishes your well-being. We suspect that this approach might resonate with your intuitions about how to allocate tax burdens. But again, further reflection might lead us to question even this seemingly reasonable approach. As an example, compare Dora, who works fifty hours per week and brings home a $1,000 weekly paycheck, to Felix, who works ten hours per week for the same $1,000 paycheck but spends forty hours per week fishing, golfing, and taking leisurely walks on the beach as the sun disappears into the ocean. Their tax returns will show identical annual wages of $52,000, but do Felix and Dora have identical levels of well-being? Those inclined to answer no may be sensing that we have yet to identify an adequate conception of ability to pay.

An even broader view might encompass what economists sometimes call "endowment" or "wage rate" (the rate at which one can earn money) — the *opportunity* to earn wealth whether or not exercised (and indeed whether or not developed through education and experience). In the example above, one might note that Dora's wage rate is $20 per hour while Felix's is $100 per hour. Should these differences be taken into account in allocating tax burdens? While few would claim that the tax system either could or should cast quite so broad a net, the basic argument for taxing endowment is similar to that for moving beyond a simple liquidity-based view of ability to pay. Taxing people only if they exercise their earning power may discourage such exercise (presumably not a deliberate goal of the tax system) and mistakenly classify people who earn and spend at a given level as "better off" than those who have the same opportunities but just happen to prefer to work and spend less.

2.   What Should We Tax?

Once one accepts that some variant of ability to pay ought to serve as the touchstone for allocating tax burdens, the question becomes how to implement it. Since the thing we really want to tax may not be directly observable, we must rely on some proxy measure. There are numerous possibilities. Historically, the main contenders have been income, consumption, and wealth, although one could imagine a host of other alternatives, such as an amalgam based on looks, height, schooling, intelligence, and family connections. It is important to keep in mind that the argument for taxing any of these alternatives depends on its properties as indirect evidence or a signal of what we really care about in distributing tax burdens.

A key issue in choosing among income, consumption, and wealth as tax bases concerns the choice of time frame for evaluating ability to pay. For "snapshot" comparisons of how well off people are at a given moment, wealth may seem the most appropriate measure. The ease with which one can pay tax at a given moment may depend on one's entire bank account (and other assets), not just the interest income that the account earned during the current year, or the year's spending out of the account to pay for currently consumed market goods and services. However, the use of a lifetime perspective to compare individuals' well-being may make consumption seem the better measure, so that people's decisions to hold wealth before consuming it do not end up increasing their tax burdens any more than the choice between liquid and illiquid assets. The income tax can be viewed as an intermediate option and best reconciled with supporting at least a limited degree of wealth taxation.

It is worth emphasizing that there is a great deal of overlap in these alternative tax bases. For example, consider income taxes and consumption taxes. To illustrate the difference between these two tax bases, tax scholars sometimes use the following equation:

$$Y = C + S$$

where Y is income, C is consumption, and S is saving (or investment). The idea presented here — admittedly oversimplified though analytically useful — is that people can do one of two things with their income, spend it or save it. Among other things, this simple formula reveals that an income tax contains within it a consumption tax. Indeed, for those who spend exactly what they earn, there is no difference. Thus, the chief difference between the two taxes concerns those amounts that are not spent — i.e., those amounts that are saved and invested. In other words, the debate between an income tax and a consumption tax is principally a debate about the proper tax treatment of savings and investment.

At one time, many experts thought that a consumption tax would be hopelessly difficult to administer because of problems of measuring consumption outlays. In an article published in 1974, however, Professor William D. Andrews of Harvard Law School demonstrated that this fear was unfounded both conceptually and practically and that, apart from other possible virtues, a consumption tax could even (depending on the form it took) be *easier* to compute than an income tax.[15] Working from the insight conveyed by the formula above, Andrews showed that a consumption tax is simply an income tax with a deduction for savings and with the inclusion in the tax base of amounts drawn down from savings and used for consumption, as well as amounts borrowed for current consumption. The type of consumption tax Andrews had in mind is sometimes called a "cash-flow consumption tax."

The practical operation of a cash-flow consumption tax is best illustrated by reference to a feature added to our present law in 1981, the *individual retirement account* (IRA). Amounts set aside in an IRA for retirement are currently deductible in computing the amount subject to taxation and amounts

---

15. Joint Committee on Taxation, Estimates of Federal Tax Expenditures for Fiscal Years 2005–2009 (JCS-1-05), January 12, 2005. Table 1-2 at page 17, infra, is a substantially reduced version of the original on which it is based.

withdrawn from the IRA account are included in income in the year of withdrawal. For example, if a taxpayer earns $40,000 each year and contributes $4,000 to an IRA, the amount subject to income taxation is $36,000 (assuming no other deductions). Later, if the taxpayer earns $10,000 and withdraws from the IRA a retirement benefit of, say, $5,000, the amount subject to income taxation is $15,000. This is entirely consistent with a consumption tax and entirely inconsistent with a straightforward income tax. If one simply imagines a vastly expanded IRA account, with no limits on the amount or purpose of contributions to the account and with no limits on the time of or reasons for withdrawal, one has a consumption tax. In 1995, Senators Sam Nunn and Pete Domenici proposed a variation of such a tax, which they called a "U.S.A." (unlimited savings allowance) tax.

One feature that income, consumption, and wealth taxation share is the use of a relatively objective measure of ability to pay. All tend to measure cash flows or else the market value of specific items. This tends to reduce government officials' discretion, which could potentially be abused if all factors pertinent to "ability to pay" were legally relevant, as well as the costs of running a more subjective and personalized system. A preference for relying on observable transactions has always led, and in all likelihood always will lead, to the disregard of what economists call "imputed income," or the value of goods and services one provides to oneself. Examples include living in one's own home rather than paying rent, raising one's own children rather than paying for childcare, and enjoying leisure rather than working for a wage. Here at the beginning of the book, you may well be wondering how on earth any sane person could ever entertain the idea of including in taxable income the value of goods and services provided to oneself. While your apprehension is understandable, we urge you to keep an open mind about these things. As we hope to illustrate in the following chapter, our failure to tax imputed income — however understandable — has concrete economic consequences for society, not all of them favorable.

3.   What Do We Tax?

Given the title of this book, the answer to the question "What do we tax?" might seem completely obvious: income. By the time you reach the end of the book, however, we suspect you may have some doubts that the U.S. "income" tax truly deserves that label. After all, just calling something an income tax doesn't make it so. As a first approximation, one might note that "income" means something like the accounting concept of net income (receipts less allowances for the costs of producing those receipts). In the legal and economic literature, the prevalent "Haig-Simons" definition of income calls it the sum of the taxpayer's consumption plus change in net worth, each defined in terms of market value, during some specified accounting period (such as a taxable year). See H. Simons, Personal Income Taxation 50 (1938). The Haig-Simons definition of income is considerably broader than any that has ever been implemented or even seriously proposed. For example, beyond potentially including whatever imputed income was thought to have a discernible market value, it would include unrealized appreciation (the increase in value of one's assets such as a home or shares of corporate stock) and the value of government services.

COMPARATIVE FOCUS: Global vs. Schedular Approaches to Designing Income Taxes

It is sometimes observed that income taxes can be designed either as either "global" or "schedular." Under a global approach, income from all sources is combined and taxed under a rate schedule that applies to the taxpayer's entire income, net of any allowable losses or deductions. By contrast, under a schedular system a separate rate schedule applies to several different categories of income and losses within each category are allowed only with respect income from that category. The two approaches can be understood as occupying opposite extremes of a spectrum. Most countries' income tax systems fall somewhere in between these two extremes, featuring characteristics of both systems.

The schedular approach is illustrated by reforms adopted in the four Nordic countries (Denmark, Finland, Norway, and Sweden) between 1987 and 1992. Although the reforms vary in their details, each country established a separate rate schedule for earned income and capital income. Detailed rules specify the circumstances in which a taxpayer's negative capital income (due to investment losses) can be used as an offset against earned income. Note that receipts not meeting the definition of earned or capital income, such as unexpected windfalls, are simply not taxed under a schedular approach.

The references to income "from whatever source derived" in both the Sixteenth Amendment and section 61 of the Internal Revenue Code suggest that the U.S. follows a global approach to income taxation. Over the years, however, Congress has incorporated various schedular features in the U.S. income tax, including, for example, preferential tax rates for capital gains and dividend income and limitations on the deductibility of capital losses and passive activity losses. In addition, taxpayers calculate certain of these items on separate "schedules" attached to their tax returns (e.g., Schedule D for capital gains and losses), leading some commentators to view the U.S. income tax as a global system built on a schedular foundation.

Even if accepted as describing what income "really" means, a definition in terms of receipts minus the expenses of producing them, or consumption plus change in net worth, merely begins, rather than ends, the process of identifying income in practice. For example, does "consumption" include the cost of dinner with a business client who is also a friend? Should it include medical expenses incurred to recover from an illness? What about the cost of a gift to a charity or a family member? Surely the answer to such questions is not a matter of parsing dictionary definitions, but rather of deciding how we want to allocate tax burdens, based on ability to pay (however defined) and all other relevant considerations.

In practice, U.S. federal income tax liability depends on the statutory concept of "taxable income," rather than on any abstract definition. This concept, in turn, reflects a welter of competing objectives, and myriad compromises between them. Yet both the design of the tax laws, and their interpretation by the Internal Revenue Service and the courts in ambiguous cases, are strongly influenced by the notion of ability to pay and its implementation via the notion of "income." Reflection on the meaning of "income" and its commonly identified components can therefore have practical value for tax lawyers.

4. The Tax Expenditure Budget

Tax scholars and policymakers often refer to a concept called the "tax expenditure budget," under which certain tax benefits are equated with direct subsidies. The general approach is to identify various exclusions (such as interest on state and local bonds), deductions (such as the deduction for charitable contributions), deferrals (such as for employer payments to pension plans), and credits (such as the child-care credit or the credit for investment in new equipment) that are seen as departures from a neutral concept of income taxation; then to figure out the cost of these special provisions; and then to attribute these costs to various budget functions. The government now regularly publishes tax expenditure data. See Table 1-2.[16] You cannot expect at the beginning of the study of the income tax law to understand many of the individual references in this table, but you may be able to gain some sense of how the law has developed and you should be aware of the availability of the data so that you can go back to it later.

The tax expenditure budget depends on the notion that there is a natural, neutral, or normal income tax and that it is possible to identify departures without great difficulty or dissent. That proposition is not beyond debate. For example, it is not clear why the deduction for medical expenses is regarded as an expenditure for health and welfare while the deduction for alimony is not an expenditure for marriage or divorce; or why neither the exclusion for scholarships nor the nontaxation of the benefit of an education at a public university is on the list; or why imputed income from home ownership is not included; or why the deduction for contributions to educational institutions is a subsidy to education while the deduction for contributions to churches is not a subsidy to religion. Clearly, then there is much legitimate debate over and genuine

---

16. The tax expenditure budget wholly ignores features of the current income tax that are arguably less favorable to taxpayers than a "pure" income tax—for example, the failure to make inflation adjustments, and the "double tax" on corporate income, which may be taxed at both the corporate and shareholder levels, thus in some cases tax-penalizing it relative to investment by individual proprietors or partnerships.

TABLE 1-2
Tax Expenditure Estimates by Budget Function: 2009
[In billions of dollars; includes both individual and corporate tax.]

Description	Amount
National defense:	
Exclusion of benefits and allowances to Armed Forces personnel	3.3
International affairs:	
Exclusion of income earned abroad by United States citizens	4.2
Commerce and housing:	
Exclusion of interest on life insurance and annuity contracts	27.5
Reduced rates of tax on dividends and long-term capital gains	131.0
Exclusion of capital gains on sales of principal residences	30.1
Deductibility of—	
Mortgage interest on owner-occupied homes	85.2
Property tax on owner-occupied homes	14.2
Exclusion of capital gains at death	57.5
Reduced rates on the first $10,000,000 of corporate incomes	3.5
Education and social services:	
Deductibility of—	
Charitable contributions (education)	7.3
Charitable contributions other than education and health	37.2
Credit for child and dependent care expenses	2.6
Tax credit for children under age 17	44.8
Health:	
Exclusion of employer contributions for health care, health insurance premiums, and long-term care insurance premiums	126.0
Deductibility of medical expenses and long-term care expenses	10.8
Exclusion of interest on state and local debt for private nonprofit health facilities	2.0
Social Security and railroad retirement:	
Exclusion of certain Social Security and railroad retirement benefits	24.0
Medicare:	
Exclusion of untaxed Medicare benefits:	
Hospital insurance	23.5
Supplementary medical insurance	16.3
Prescription drug insurance	6.0
Income security:	
Exclusion of workers' compensation benefits	2.7
Net exclusion of pension contributions and earnings:	
Employer plans	120.4
Individual Retirement Accounts	18.5
Keogh plans	10.6
Exclusion of other employee benefits:	
Premiums on group term life insurance	2.7
Premiums on accident and disability insurance	3.0
Additional exemption for elderly and blind	1.7
Veterans' benefits and services:	
Exclusion of veterans disability compensation	3.5
General purpose fiscal assistance:	
Exclusion of interest on public purpose state and local debt	22.5
Deduction of nonbusiness state and local government income, sales and personal property taxes	29.6

uncertainty about the proper contours of an income tax; the tax expenditure budget largely ignores the debate and denies the uncertainty. What is more, one could challenge the use of any variety of the income tax as a "reference tax base" to measure tax expenditures. For example, suppose one preferred consumption taxation and thus thought that interest income in general should not be taxed. This presumably would suggest zeroing out the "tax expenditures" pertaining to municipal bonds, and instead treating the imposition of income taxes on other interest income as involving a "tax penalty."[17]

Despite all the debate, there does seem to be substantial agreement that most of the items on the published lists deserve to be there — that they aim at some purpose unrelated to measuring ability to pay. And it does seem clear that the tax expenditure budget has proved to be an extremely valuable tool in exposing tax policy issues. In particular, it somewhat counters the tendency to distinguish unduly between direct government spending and the use of the tax system to serve the same objectives.

5.   Tax Incidence

Tax policy analysts typically use the term "incidence" to describe the ultimate economic burden of a tax. It is important to note that the person bearing the ultimate economic burden of a tax may not be the same person that remitted the tax to the government. For example, if a tax is imposed on the manufacture of refrigerators and the manufacturer is able to raise prices and pass the tax on to consumers, then it is said that the tax has been shifted and the incidence is on consumers rather than on manufacturers. To determine the incidence of a tax, or the burden or effect of particular provisions of a tax system, one must compare the world with the tax or provision and the world without it. This is a difficult (perhaps too difficult) task, even for the best economists. Detailed discussion of incidence-related issues is not appropriate in this book; however, some basic observations may be useful.

It is generally assumed that the burden of the individual income tax, so far as it falls on income from wages, salaries, and other earnings from services, is, for the most part, not shifted from the individuals on whom it is imposed. There is much less consensus as to the incidence of the tax on corporate income and on individual income from investments.

To the extent that the tax system favors one type of investment over another, money and other resources will be shifted from the unfavored type of investment to the favored type. This kind of important economic effect is easy to predict and to observe. Moreover, as resource allocations shift in response to tax incentives, before-tax rates of return will be altered. For example, because of the exemption from taxation of interest on state and local bonds, the rate of return on these bonds is less than the rate of return on taxable bonds. The individual who invests in tax-exempt bonds accepts a lower rate of before-tax

---

17. For example, if taxable bonds yield 10 percent and tax-exempt bonds of comparable quality yield 7 percent, a person investing $1,000 in tax-exempts earns $70 per year and forgoes an additional $30 that could have been earned by investing in taxable bonds. The forgone $30 is the putative tax.

return because that return is not subject to tax. The before-tax reduction in return on the investment in tax-exempt bonds — that is, the difference between the return on tax-exempt bonds and the higher return on taxable bonds that the taxpayer might have bought — is a form of self-imposed tax, often called an implicit or *putative tax*.[18] This is a widespread phenomenon.

To the extent that before-tax rates of return fall in response to the effects of a tax provision, and a putative tax arises, any lack of fairness (horizontal equity) associated with treating one source or use of income better than another is reduced or eliminated. For example, if a person buys tax-exempt bonds and pays a putative tax, that implicit or putative burden should be taken into account before asserting that the person has been treated more favorably than other people with income that is directly taxed.

6. Inflation

Inflation makes it difficult to levy the right amount of tax on investment income. To illustrate, suppose a taxpayer purchases property for $100 on January 1. The inflation rate during the year is 5 percent and the property is sold on January 1 the following year for $105. The property transaction does not leave the taxpayer any wealthier: The $105 sales proceeds purchase the same basket of goods that cost $100 a year earlier. A tax imposed only on real increase in economic well-being would not measure gain or loss by the difference in investment cost (or basis) and sales proceeds. Instead, such a tax would increase basis, or investment cost, by the inflation rate. Here, that would require an increase in the $100 cost by 5 percent, to give an inflation-adjusted cost of $105. If that were done, no gain would be recognized on the sale of the property for $105. (The same result could be reached by leaving investment cost at $100 but reducing the sales proceeds by the inflation rate, to $100.) This adjustment would also be required in other areas. For example, suppose the taxpayer had loaned out her $100 and received that sum back, plus $5 interest. The transaction would leave the taxpayer no wealthier. The taxpayer receives $5 characterized as interest but there is no real economic (or inflation-adjusted) profit on the loan transaction. Increasing the taxpayer's investment in the loan by the inflation rate, to $105, yields the correct result. Now the entire $105 can be treated as tax-free recovery of investment. Unfortunately, the tax system does not allow this cost or basis adjustment and as a result systemically overtaxes investment income.

Inflation also poses a problem in determining the proper rate at which to tax income. To illustrate, suppose that our tax law initially provides that at an income of $25,000 a person's marginal rate of taxation (see infra page 20-22) is 15 percent and that at an income of $50,000 the marginal rate is 30 percent. Now suppose that ten years pass and inflation reduces the value of money by half. A person currently earning $50,000 is in the same real economic position as a person earning $25,000 ten years earlier. There will be many more people earning $50,000 now than earlier. (The higher we go on the real

---

18. All section references are to the Internal Revenue Code of 1986, unless otherwise noted.

income ladder, the fewer people we find.) If there is no automatic adjustment that lowers the rates to take account of the economic reality, then even without any increase in real (that is, inflation-adjusted) income, people will be paying higher percentages of their real incomes as taxes. Government revenues will increase (in real terms) with none of the unpleasant political consequences associated with explicit increases in rates. In 1981, Congress added §1(f) and §151(f),[19] which require increases in the standard deduction, in the deduction for personal exemption, and in the rate schedule dollar-amount brackets, to reflect increases in the Consumer Price Index.

D.   AVERAGE VERSUS MARGINAL TAX RATES

One of the most controversial features of any tax system is the extent to which it redistributes income or otherwise requires some people to pay more than others. As we have already seen, tax burdens can vary widely depending on the choice of tax base. Another way to vary tax burdens is through the use of differential tax rates.

A *progressive* income tax is one with average tax rates that rise as income rises. Under a progressive rate structure the tax on a person with a high income is not just a greater *amount* than the tax on a person with a lower income; it is a greater *proportion of* income. This is why we use the term "average tax rate" (sometimes also called "effective tax rate") in the first sentence of this paragraph; it refers to the taxpayer's total income tax burden expressed as a percentage of his or her total income. Thus, a taxpayer who pays $30,000 in taxes on $100,000 of income has an average tax rate of 30 percent. A *regressive* income tax is one where average tax rates decline with income. The table below shows the distribution of tax burdens in three different income tax systems — one with proportional rates (System A), one with progressive rates (System B), and one with regressive rates (System C). Note that in each system the *amount* of tax owed increases with income.

| Taxpayer | Income | Type of Tax and Total Tax Owed (Average Tax Rate) | | |
		System A: Proportional	System B: Progressive	System C: Regressive
Akira	$20,000	$2,000 (10%)	$2,000 (10%)	$5,000 (25%)
Benito	$50,000	$5,000 (10%)	$10,000 (20%)	$10,000 (20%)
Cora	$100,000	$10,000 (10%)	$30,000 (30%)	$15,000 (15%)

19. A Consumption-Type or Cash Flow Personal Income Tax, 87 Harv. L. Rev. 1113. See also J. Pechman, ed., What Should Be Taxed: Income or Expenditure? (1980); Klein, Timing in Personal Taxation, 6 J. Legal Studies 461 (1977); Warren, Would a Consumption Tax Be Fairer Than an Income Tax?, 89 Yale L.J. 1081 (1980); Warren, Fairness and a Consumption-Type or Cash Flow Personal Income Tax, 88 Harv. L. Rev. 931 (1975); Andrews, Fairness and the Personal Income Tax: A Reply to Professor Warren, 88 Harv. L. Rev. 947 (1975).

Overall, the U.S. federal tax system (including all taxes, not just income taxes) generally features progressive average tax rates, though the degree of progression varies depending on the tax. A study published by the Congressional Budget Office in December 2007 reports overall effective tax rates for 2005 for the lowest and second quintiles of 4.3 and 9.9 percent, respectively, and a rate of 14.1 percent for the middle quintile. The study reports effective tax rates of 17.3 and 25.2 percent for the fourth and top quintiles, respectively. Disaggregating these data into the separate taxes reveals that the individual and corporate income taxes are quite progressive (with negative effective rates for the bottom two quintiles), while payroll taxes — for Social Security and Medicare — and excise taxes are regressive (with the top quintile subject to the lowest effective rate).

Within the individual income tax, progression is accomplished primarily by a schedule of rates with increasing *marginal tax rates* — that is, with increases in rates that apply only to increments in income. For example, suppose the rates are 15 percent on the first $20,000 of income and 25 percent on all income above that amount. A person with income of $30,000 would pay 15 percent on the first $20,000, or $3,000, plus 25 percent on the next $10,000, or $2,500, for a total of $5,500. The marginal rate for such a person is 25 percent; it is the rate applicable to the last, and the next, increment of income. Progression is also accomplished by exempting a certain amount of income from taxation (in effect applying a zero rate to that amount), as well as by limiting the availability of certain deductions and credits to persons with income below some threshold amount.

During most of the history of the income tax in this country, the rate structure for individuals was characterized by a large number of rates and a big difference between the highest and the lowest rate. For example, in 1986, for married couples there were fourteen rates applicable to various levels of income, with a range from 11 percent to 50 percent (plus a zero rate on income that is not subject to taxation because of personal exemptions, the zero bracket amount (now the standard deduction), and a credit for earned income). As of 2006, the number of brackets had been reduced, nominally, to six ranging from 10 percent to 35 percent. Moreover, the benefits of the personal exemption and certain itemized deductions are phased out as adjusted gross income exceeds a certain threshold amount. See §§68, 151(d). These phaseouts have the effect of increasing marginal tax rates, since the taxpayer loses a tax benefit (and thus pays more tax) for each additional dollar earned above the threshold amount. The significance of the phaseouts depends on the number of personal exemptions and itemized deductions claimed.

It is important to recognize that it is the marginal rate that is relevant for purposes of tax planning and for understanding incentive effects. For example, suppose a couple with an income of $50,000 and a marginal rate of 15 percent contemplates a gift of $1,000 to charity. As you will learn (or perhaps already knew), taxpayers are generally permitted to deduct such gifts in calculating the amount of their income subject to taxation. By making the gift they would reduce their taxable income by $1,000 and save $150 in taxes. In other words, the net cost to the couple of making the gift would not be $1,000, but rather $850. By contrast, for a couple with a taxable income of $150,000 and a marginal rate of 30 percent, the net cost of a $1,000 gift is $700. As these examples illustrate, the bottom line value of a deduction depends on the marginal tax rate at which the taxpayer's income would have been taxed.

In addition, it is the taxpayer's marginal rate that is relevant for purposes of evaluating the incentive effects of the income tax. For example, it is commonly argued that the income tax discourages work by taxing people on their labor income. Consider a taxpayer, Neela, who currently earns $80,000 and is subject to a marginal tax rate of 25 percent. Should Neela work Saturday afternoons to earn an additional salary of $10,000 per year? In making her decision, Neela will of course want to think about how she would otherwise spend her Saturday afternoons and what value that activity has to her. But she shouldn't compare her subjective value of that experience to $10,000 but rather to her after-tax wage, which would be $7,500 after accounting for the income taxes she will owe on the additional earnings.

E.   THE TAXABLE UNIT AND THE MARRIAGE PENALTY

Among tax theorists, "taxable unit" means that individual, or group of individuals, who is, or are, treated as a taxpaying unit in the sense that they must aggregate their income for purposes of calculating the tax payable. Theorists have examined at length the question whether the unit should be the individual; husband and wife; husband, wife, and children; all people in the household; or some other possibility. While that kind of inquiry seems meaningful for some purposes, it is unfortunately not one that is properly framed for a person seeking to understand the present rules of the federal income tax. Those rules do not reflect the kind of logical, coherent approach implicit in the notion of a taxable unit. To some significant extent, the present rules can be understood only by reviewing their history. The historical development is presented later in this book. (See Chapter 7.A, infra.) For the present, it is enough to recognize that the rules governing how taxes are affected by the relationships of people to one another are reflected in the four rate schedules and in the rules for applying them[20] and, to a lesser extent, in the exemptions[21] and certain other provisions.[22] We will see that the rate-schedule rules produce a "marriage penalty" and a seemingly perverse work incentive for married "secondary" workers.

Married people[23] are permitted to file a "joint return," which means a return on which they aggregate their income and deductions so that it does

---

20. §1.
21. §151.
22. For example, see §21 (child-care credit); §71 (alimony).
23. "Marriage" has a special statutory definition. §143.

not matter who earned what. The rate schedule for such returns provides the lowest rates of the four schedules provided in the Internal Revenue Code. This rate schedule is also available to "surviving spouses"[24] but not to single-sex couples, who might wish to marry but are not permitted to do so.

Another rate schedule is for "heads of households"[25] and is somewhat less favorable than the one for married couples. Very roughly, a head of household is an unmarried person with a dependent living with him or her. The thought behind the semifavorable rate schedules is that a head of household has financial burdens similar to those of married couples and should get part of the benefits available to them.

Next is the schedule for "unmarried individuals,"[26] commonly referred to as single people. The rate schedule for such people is less favorable than the one for heads of households.

Finally, there is the least favorable schedule of all, for married people filing separate returns. For reasons explained in Chapter 7B, there is a special rate schedule for married persons filing separate returns. With this rate schedule, the filing of separate returns generally will result in increased aggregate taxes and only rarely will result in reduced aggregate taxes.[27]

Apart from married people who file jointly (as almost all do) and who aggregate their income, taxpayers are not required to include in their income the income of relations, dependents, or members of their households. In other words, the taxable unit is the individual, except that we take account of a deceased spouse (in the provision for a surviving spouse), of dependents (in the provision for heads of households), and various other family attributes. To demonstrate the significance of the basic rule that each individual is a separate taxpayer, consider a hypothetical family consisting of a husband, a wife, and a fifteen-year-old daughter. Suppose that the daughter is entitled each year to the income of $25,000 from a trust set up for her by her grandmother. The child would file her own return. The parents' return would not reflect the $25,000 income of the child (except possibly if some of that income were used to discharge their obligation of support). Moreover, if all the $25,000 were put aside for the child and the parents supplied more than half her support, they would be entitled to claim a deduction for her as a dependent[28] and they could deduct her medical expenses,[29] to the extent allowable.[30]

The relationship between the rate schedules for married people, heads of households, single people, and married people filing separately, and the rules relating to their availability, produce two important effects. First, married single-earner couples are better off than they would be under a system with one schedule for all, since they have the advantage of the most favorable rate.

---

24. Defined in §2(a).
25. Defined in §2(b).
26. This is a residual category — that is, one including anyone who is not married, a surviving spouse, or a head of household. §1(c).
27. Even if filing separately would increase total liability, the spouses might want to do so if, for example, they are separated and cannot find one another or are unable to cooperate in filing jointly.
28. §151.
29. §213.
30. §213(a).

This is sometimes called the "marriage bonus." On the other hand, two-earner married couples may be worse off than if they had remained single because of the requirement that they file jointly (or use the unfavorable schedule for separate returns of married people). This is true because if they were single each would use a less-favorable rate schedule, but since they would be filing two returns they would get two separate starts at the bottom of the rate schedule. Married couples filing jointly have only one start at the bottom of their rate schedule, albeit that is a more favorable schedule. The result is so-called marriage penalty — that is, the added tax paid by two people who have roughly the same earnings and who marry one another. In 2003, the Code was amended to reduce the marriage penalty by doubling the 10 and 15 percent brackets for married couples filing jointly.

A final point worth noting about the rate-structure rules is that the secondary worker in a married couple is subject to marginal tax rates determined by the income of the primary worker. The "secondary worker" is the person whose income is lower and whose attachment to the labor force is generally weaker than that of the primary worker. In the United States, the secondary worker has historically been the wife rather than the husband, though these labor force patterns have shifted considerably in recent years. For most couples, the secondary worker's income will be thought of as the marginal income, since it is more likely that the couple would consider sacrificing this income than the income of the primary worker. Thus, the marginal rates that must be taken into account by married secondary workers are the relatively high rates resulting from the fact that the primary worker's income uses up the lower rates. This effect is magnified by the fact that the secondary worker's alternative of providing services in the home, rather than working outside the home, results in "imputed" income, which is not taxed at all. Also, one must bear in mind that for secondary workers the Social Security tax is a significant burden.[31]

Both the marriage penalty and the disincentive for secondary workers would be eliminated by a system featuring a single tax rate (i.e., no progressive marginal rates) and a rule making each individual taxable on his or her own income.

F. COMPLIANCE AND ADMINISTRATION

1. Self-Assessment, Audits, and Tax Litigation

Our income tax relies on initial self-assessment, which means that once each year each individual or entity subject to the tax makes a calculation of the

---

31. For further discussion and citations of economic studies of the effects on labor-force participation, see Gann, Abandoning Marital Status as a Factor in Allocating Tax Burdens, 59 Tex. L. Rev. 1, 39-46 (1980). For an earlier presentation of similar observations, see Blumberg, Sexism in the Code: A Comparative Study of Income Taxation of Working Wives and Mothers, 21 Buffalo L. Rev. 49 (1971). But recall the prior discussion of the barriers to studies of incidence and economic effects.

amount of tax owed. The calculation is based on information supplied by the taxpayer on forms, sometimes called tax "returns," devised and provided by the Internal Revenue Service. The Internal Revenue Service, often called the Service, or the IRS, is a branch of the Treasury Department, is headed by a person called the Commissioner of Internal Revenue, and is responsible for the administration of the tax laws. The Service makes available some limited amount of assistance in preparing returns, but no government approval or other involvement is required before a return is filed. Before the taxpayer files the annual return, some amount approximating the tax owed will probably have been paid to the government either through withholding from wages by an employer[32] or by special quarterly returns for estimated taxes for people whose income is from sources not subject to withholding (like income from self-employment) or for whom the amount withheld is less than the amount of tax that will be payable.[33] When the annual return is filed, the taxpayer takes a credit against the tax computed on that return for any taxes paid by withholding or as estimated tax and will be entitled to a refund of any overpayment or must pay the amount of any shortfall.

A person who fails to file an income tax return may be subject to both civil and criminal penalties.[34] There is no statutory limit on the time within which the civil penalties must be sought[35] and a six-year limitation on criminal prosecution.[36] The risk of being caught for failure to file is high, in large part because employers and other payors of income are required to file "information" returns,[37] reporting wages, dividends, and interest, and various other kinds of payments and benefits.

The Service reviews all income tax returns for computational error and selects a relatively small number of them for a more complete review, called an audit. Some returns are selected for audit at random, but most are selected on the basis of some evidence, either in the return itself or from some other source (e.g., information returns), indicating a greater-than-average probability of error. The Service ordinarily has three years to assert a "deficiency"[38] — that is, to assert that the taxpayer owes more tax by virtue of an error in the return. The amount owed is called an "underpayment," and the taxpayer must pay interest on all underpayments.[39] The interest rate is set quarterly and is equal to the rate on U.S. Treasury short-term obligations plus 3 percent.[40]

If a taxpayer's return is audited and the taxpayer and the employee who initially reviews the return for the IRS cannot agree on one or more items, there are opportunities for review at higher levels within the IRS. Most disputes are ultimately settled within the IRS, often after considerable bargaining and with

---

32. §3402.
33. §§6015, 6153.
34. The basic provisions are §6651(a) (civil) and §7201 (criminal).
35. §6501(c)(3).
36. §6531.
37. §§6031-6058.
38. §6501(a). The period is extended to six years if the taxpayer omits from gross income more than "25 percent of the amount of the gross income stated in the return." §6501(e). See also §6229(c)(2) (similar rule for partnerships).
39. §6601.
40. §6621.

compromise on both sides. If the taxpayer and the IRS cannot reach agreement, the IRS will order the taxpayer to pay the deficiency, plus interest and any applicable penalties, and the taxpayer must either do so or go to court.

Three different options are available to the taxpayer for judicial review. One option is to decline to pay the tax and file a petition for review with the *Tax Court*[41] (formerly the Board of Tax Appeals). The Tax Court is available only if the tax has not been paid as of the date of the petition. (The tax can be paid thereafter to stop the running of interest.) Tax Court judges typically have tax backgrounds and try only tax cases. There are no jury trials in the Tax Court. Tax Court judgments are reviewable by the federal circuit courts of appeals in the circuit where the taxpayer resides[42] and ultimately by the Supreme Court (but only on certiorari). If the taxpayer loses, the tax must be paid with interest to the date of payment, so an important factor in deciding whether to follow the Tax Court route is the current interest rate charged by the government on deficiencies, as compared with what the taxpayer must pay or can earn elsewhere.

The second option is to pay the tax and sue for a refund in the federal *district court* where the taxpayer resides.[43] The judge in the district court is not likely to be a tax expert and a jury trial is available. Appeal is, as usual, to the circuit courts of appeals, with the possibility of review by the Supreme Court on certiorari.

The final option is to pay the tax and sue for a refund in the United States Court of Federal Claims.[44] Its decisions are reviewable by the United States Court of Appeals for the Federal Circuit[45] and by the Supreme Court (on certiorari). If an issue is first litigated by a taxpayer who obtains a favorable legal ruling in the Claims Court, and that ruling is upheld on appeal, all other taxpayers may then take their cases to that court and foreclose the possibility of a conflict among the circuits. By contrast, if a taxpayer wins a favorable ruling in a court of appeals in a circuit other than the Federal Circuit, the government is free to litigate that issue with other taxpayers in other circuits.[46]

2. Penalties for Noncompliance

In a tax system based on self-assessment, policymakers may find it necessary to provide incentives for taxpayers to comply with the law. In the U.S. income

41. §6662(a), (c).

42. Asimow, Civil Penalties for Inaccurate and Delinquent Tax Returns, 23 UCLA L. Rev. 637, 650 (1976).

43. §6662(a), (d).

44. See Regs. §1.6661-3(a)(2), stating that "a position with respect to the tax treatment of an item that is arguable but is *fairly unlikely* to prevail in court would satisfy a reasonable basis standard [applicable to the imposition of a negligence penalty under §6653(a)], but not the substantial authority standard." (Emphasis supplied.) What, if anything, does "fairly" add to "unlikely"?

45. §6662(d)(2)(B). For items "attributable to a tax shelter," however, for noncorporate taxpayers, the disclosure exception does not apply and the substantial authority exception applies only to taxpayers who "reasonably believed that the tax treatment of [the] item . . . was more likely than not" proper. §6662(d).

46. §6664(c).

tax, these incentives take the form of penalties for noncompliance. Taxpayers must pay a penalty equal to 20 percent of the amount of any underpayment due to negligence,[47] but "the sort of conduct typically found subject to the negligence penalty is reckless and intentional."[48] A penalty equal to 20 percent of the amount of any underpayment is levied on taxpayers who substantially understate their income tax.[49] A substantial understatement is one that exceeds the greater of 10 percent of the proper tax or $5,000 ($10,000 for corporations), but the amount of the understatement is reduced by amounts attributable to treatment for which there was "substantial authority"[50] or amounts "with respect to which the relevant facts affecting the item's tax treatment are adequately disclosed . . . and [for which] there is a reasonable basis."[51] The penalty "may" be waived by the Service if the taxpayer demonstrates "reasonable cause" and "good faith."[52] An underpayment that fits within more than one category (for example, an understatement that is substantial and negligent) is subject to only one 20 percent penalty. There is also a penalty of 5 percent per month, not to exceed 25 percent, for failure to file a return and 0.5 percent per month, not to exceed 25 percent, for failure to pay a tax shown on a return when it is due or for failure to pay, within ten days, a tax assessed and demanded by the IRS.[53] Notwithstanding the seemingly inclusive array of penalty provisions, in the ordinary case of underpayment, all the taxpayer stands to lose, in addition to the amount of the tax owed, is interest on that amount.

An error may be attributable to what is loosely referred to as "fraud." An underpayment attributable to fraud subjects the taxpayer to a civil penalty of 75 percent of the amount of the fraudulent underpayment.[54] While fraud seems to be a familiar concept and one that could sensibly be applied to a large number of taxpayer returns, in fact the courts have developed a narrow definition and even the civil penalty is imposed only in "cases of highly flagrant behavior."[55] Criminal fraud, or, to be more precise, any "willful attempt

47. §6651(a). The penalty percentages for failure to file are increased to 15 percent and 75 percent if the failure is "fraudulent." §6651(f).

48. §6663.

49. Asimow, supra note 42, at 645.

50. §7201.

51. Asimow, supra note 42, at 646.

52. §§6501(c)(2), 6671.

53. §6531.

54. §102.

55. In 1965, the ABA Standing Committee on Ethics and Professional Responsibility, in Formal Opinion 65-314, adopted a standard under which a lawyer could advise a client to take any position for which there was a "reasonable basis." In 1985, in Formal Opinion 85-352, the ABA replaced this standard with the current standard, "some realistic possibility of success":

[A] lawyer may advise reporting a position on a return even where the lawyer believes the position probably will not prevail, there is no "substantial authority" in support of the position, and there will be no disclosure of the position in the return. However, the position to be asserted must be one which the lawyer in good faith believes is warranted in existing law or can be supported by a good faith argument for an extension, modification or reversal of existing law. This requires that there is *some realistic possibility of success if the matter is litigated*. In addition, in his role as advisor, the lawyer should refer to potential penalties and other legal consequences should the client take the position advised. (Emphasis supplied.)

In the Report of the Special Task Force on Formal Opinion 85-352, 39 Tax Law. 635, 638 (1986), it is said that "a position having only a 5% or 10% likelihood of success, if litigated, should not meet the new standard."

to evade or defeat any tax imposed by this title or the payment thereof,"[56] is a felony carrying a penalty of not more than $100,000 ($500,000 for corporations) or five years in prison, or both. As with civil fraud, however, criminal

---

Also of importance to lawyers and other people such as accountants who practice before the IRS is the Treasury's Circular 230. Section 10.33 of these rules (31 C.F.R. §10.33) sets forth "best practice" standards, including clear communication about the client's "expected purpose and use of the [lawyer's] advice," establishing facts and their relevance, and "[a]cting fairly and with integrity." Under §10.34, a practitioner may not sign a return as preparer that "contains a position" or advise a client to take a position on a return unless the position:

(a)   has "a realistic possibility of being sustained on its merits"; or
(b)   "is not frivolous and is adequately disclosed to the Service."

The "realistic possibility" test is amplified as follows (emphasis supplied):

A position is considered to have a realistic possibility of being sustained on its merits if a reasonable and well-informed analysis by a person knowledgeable in the tax law would lead such a person to conclude that the position has *approximately a one in three, or greater, likelihood of being sustained on its merits.*

Violation of the proposed standard subjects a practitioner to disbarment or suspension from practice before the Service. The force of the rules may be diminished by a provision that "only violations of this section that are willful, reckless, or a result of gross incompetence will subject a practitioner to suspension or disbarment."

The Treasury has published a proposed revision of Circular 230. Proposed §10.34 (31 C.F.R. Part 10, 72 Fed. Reg. 54621, 2007 WL 2778177) reads as follows:

§10.34 Standards with respect to tax returns and documents, affidavits and other papers.
(a) *Tax returns.* A practitioner may not sign a tax return as a preparer unless the practitioner has a reasonable belief that the tax treatment of each position on the return would more likely than not be sustained on its merits (the more likely than not standard), or there is a reasonable basis for each position and each position is adequately disclosed to the Internal Revenue Service. A practitioner may not advise a client to take a position on a tax return, or prepare the portion of a tax return on which a position is taken, unless—
(1) The practitioner has a reasonable belief that the position satisfies the more likely than not standard; or
(2) The position has a reasonable basis and is adequately disclosed to the Internal Revenue Service.
* * *
(e) *Definitions.* For purposes of this section—
(1) *More likely than not.* A practitioner is considered to have a reasonable belief that the tax treatment of a position is more likely than not the proper tax treatment if the practitioner analyzes the pertinent facts and authorities, and based on that analysis reasonably concludes, in good faith, that there is a greater than fifty-percent likelihood that the tax treatment will be upheld if the IRS challenges it. The authorities described in 26 CFR 1.6662-4(d)(3)(iii), or any successor provision, of the substantial understatement penalty regulations may be taken into account for purposes of this analysis.
(2) *Reasonable basis.* A position is considered to have a reasonable basis if it is reasonably based on one or more of the authorities described in 26 CFR 1.6662-4(d)(3)(iii), or any successor provision, of the substantial understatement penalty regulations. Reasonable basis is a relatively high standard of tax reporting, that is, significantly higher than not frivolous or not patently improper. The reasonable basis standard is not satisfied by a return position that is merely arguable or that is merely a colorable claim. The possibility that a tax return will not be audited, that an issue will not be raised on audit, or that an issue will be settled may not be taken into account.
(3) Frivolous. A position is frivolous if it is patently improper.

---

56. For a fascinating and valuable treatment of some of the issues, see Cooper, The Avoidance Dynamic: A Tale of Planning, Tax Ethics, and Tax Reform, 80 Colum. L. Rev. 1553 (1980). See generally B. Wolfman, J. Holden & D. Schenk, Ethical Problems in Federal Tax Practice (3d ed. 1995).

fraud penalties are used only to "punish highly culpable conduct . . . [in] cases involv[ing] large amounts of income and deficiencies, patterns of conduct stretching over several years, and particularly reprehensible forms of concealment."[57] There is no statutory limit on the time within which the civil fraud penalties may be sought.[58] For criminal prosecution the statute of limitations is six years.[59]

Despite these penalty provisions, the odds are heavily in favor of aggressive taxpayer reporting postures — that is, in favor of reliance on any favorable position for which there is a "reasonable basis." This is true largely because of the "audit lottery" — the fact that because of the limited enforcement resources of the IRS, the chances of an audit of the return and of a challenge to the item in question are small. In addition, the consequences of losing are, in many situations, by no means onerous. This situation has led one scholar[60] to conclude:

> The most surprising fact that emerges from the theoretical models and the relevant tax law is that anyone complied with the income tax law in the past decade whenever fraud penalties could have been avoided. The most rudimentary cost-benefit analysis . . . reveals [that] . . . if the sanction structure is to have any deterrent effect, a probability of punishment of less than 100 percent requires that the sanction must be greater than the amount of the cheater's benefit. During the past decade, while aggregate audit probabilities were typically closer to 2 percent than 100 percent, interest rates on understated tax liabilities were often less than market rates.

What if the taxpayer files a return thinking that it is correct and later discovers a mistake? If the mistake is one that becomes evident only because of events that have occurred after the close of the year for which the return was filed, the remedy is to make an adjustment in the year in which the true facts appear. If, however, the mistake was plainly an error at the time of reporting — in other words, if, on the basis of the facts existing at the time the return was filed, the return was in error — then the remedy is to file an amended return. An amended return is simply a new version of the original return, changed to correct the error. Claims for refunds of overpayments, made by an amended return or otherwise, must be filed within the general three-year statute of limitations period.[61] Naturally, if the error is in the favor of the government and the taxpayer is entitled to a refund, he or she can refrain from claiming the refund, but is unlikely to do so if the amount is significant. That leaves the question whether the taxpayer is obligated to file an amended return if the error is in his or her favor and the tax paid was less than what was owed. We assume here that we are talking about errors — sometimes redundantly called "innocent" errors — and not about willful misrepresentation.

57. Graetz, Can the Income Tax Continue to Be the Major Revenue Source?, in J. Pechman, ed., Options for Tax Reform 39, 58 (1984).
58. §6511(a).
59. But see Regs. §§1.451-1(a), 1.461-1(a) (taxpayer "should" file amended return to report items of income and expense erroneously reported in prior year).
60. §§6213, 7441.
61. §7482(b).

There is no explicit statutory penalty for failure to file an amended return.[62] It may be that the only legal consequence of failing to file an amended return is that, if the error is later discovered and payment made, the taxpayer will owe greater interest on the underpayment. On the other hand, it can be argued that the amount owed is a debt and that taxpayers have as much moral obligation to pay their debts to the government (that is, to their fellow citizens) as they have to pay their just debts to anyone else (even though the creditor may not realize that the amount is due).

G. OPINION PRACTICE AND THE MARKET FOR TAX ADVICE

Many tax lawyers are involved in "tax controversy" work, representing taxpayers or the government in the administrative process or actual litigation over a disputed legal question. Even more commonly, however, tax lawyers give advice to their clients regarding the tax consequences of alternative courses of action. When representing individuals, this advice may concern matters such as the acquisition of real estate, the tax consequences of marriage or divorce, or perhaps the structure of a compensation package. In the business context, a tax attorney's advice is likely to relate to more sophisticated issues, such as the choice of business entity (e.g., corporation versus partnership), the tax consequences of bankruptcy, or the optimal structure for a cross-border merger or acquisition.

In many cases, the tax lawyer will be asked to render an "opinion" specifying the federal income tax treatment of a particular transaction or transactions. Although the law may be clear in some instances, chances are that if a client is willing to retain a lawyer for professional advice the "correct" tax treatment of the proposed transaction is open to question. Often the client will want to know not only which course of action produces the best tax result, but also the likelihood of prevailing on the merits in the event that the return is audited and the question litigated in court. The client may also want some assurances regarding penalty exposure in the event that the return position is successfully challenged. Thus, when offering a professional opinion, the tax attorney must be equipped with a vocabulary for expressing legal uncertainty.

Tax opinions are often expressed in terms of varying levels of confidence regarding the likely outcome of litigation if a return position is challenged. These "confidence levels" in turn derive principally from the penalty provisions discussed above. In general, tax opinion confidence levels include the standards set forth below, with ballpark percentages (indicating the likelihood of prevailing on the merits) noted in parentheses:

• The taxpayer has a "reasonable basis" for the position (15-30 percent).[63]

---

62. §7422; 28 U.S.C. §§1346(a)(1), 1402(a)(1).
63. §6662(d)(2)(B)(i), §6694(a)(2)(C) (ii).

- The taxpayer's position is supported by "substantial authority" (30-50 percent).[64]
- The taxpayer is "more likely than not" to prevail if the position is challenged in litigation (more than 50 percent).[65]
- The taxpayer "should" prevail if if the position is challenged in litigation (70 percent and higher).[66]

While it is quite common for tax attorneys to think of these confidence levels in terms of the percentage figures listed above, it bears noting that uncertainty regarding the outcome of legal disputes is rarely susceptible to such precision. The idea is not to put an exact number on the likelihood of prevailing on the merits, but rather to equate an otherwise vague legal standard (e.g., "reasonable basis") with some range of probability. One benefit of this approach is that it gives practitioners a common vocabulary for articulating their professional opinions regarding legal uncertainty. As might be expected, tax lawyers often disagree about the strength or validity of legal authority for some proposed transaction. These disagreements form the basis of an ongoing professional dialogue in the hallways of law firms' tax departments, at meetings of the Tax Section of the American Bar Association, and in the pages of the profession's leading periodicals.

We encourage you to keep the foregoing framework in mind when considering the various open-ended legal questions posed throughout the book. In many cases, the questions will not have clear-cut answers. For example, a "gift" is not includable in income[67] and need not be reported on one's tax return, but tips and other such payments in recognition of the performance of services are includable. Suppose that a surgeon performs a life-saving operation and the grateful patient presents to her a gift certificate for $1,000. What are the obligations of the surgeon and of his or her lawyer? Answering this question requires not only an evaluation of relevant legal authorities to advise the client, but also a judgment regarding the lawyer's professional responsibilities.

Often it is said that taxpayers are entitled to call the close ones in their own favor; that there is no obligation to bring the decision to exclude to the attention of the Service; and that all the taxpayer needs is a reasonable basis for his or her decision. It may be more accurate to say that if there is a reasonable basis for the taxpayer decision, the taxpayer who decides an issue in his or her own favor is not guilty of a crime, even though the taxpayer knows that the government would undoubtedly dispute the taxpayer's decision if it became aware of it and would probably prevail if the issue were tested in court. It bears noting that in crafting legal advice for a client, the lawyer must assume that the matter will be litigated in a court of law; the percentages discussed above do not and should not incorporate the likelihood of an audit.

---

64. §6662(d)(2)(B).
65. §6694(a)(2)(B).
66. See Jasper L. Cummings, Jr., The Range of Legal Tax Opinions, with Emphasis on the "Should" Opinion, Tax Notes, February 17, 2003, p. 1125.
67. 28 U.S.C. §1491.

If the decision is close to fraud, the government's basis for asserting fraud may be undercut if the taxpayer "red flags" the issue (that is, voluntarily makes some note of the issue as part of the return). A lawyer cannot countenance criminal conduct on the part of a client, even if the client is willing to run the risk of criminal prosecution. In addition, a lawyer should never advise a client to take a tax position that would not be defensible if all the facts were known; in other words, a lawyer cannot countenance lying or concealment, no matter how remote the chance of detection. But a lawyer is not barred by any canon of ethics from advising a client of the possibilities for making claims based on weak but "reasonable" grounds.[68] Of course, just as a lawyer is not required to represent murderers, rapists, or drug traffickers, he or she is not required to represent or assist those taxpayers who seek always to take the most aggressive possible position—who seek always to shift as much as possible of the tax burden from their own shoulders to the shoulders of those who, for one reason or another, are unwilling to push to the limits.

Problems of professional responsibility in tax practice are more subtle and complex than the foregoing remarks might suggest,[69] but it does seem clear that clients are entitled to know the consequences of their actions and to make their own decisions if they want to.

H. SOME TAX TERMINOLOGY AND CONCEPTS

As is true for most law school courses, especially those that survey an entire field of law, the basic federal income tax class effectively requires you to learn a new language. Some of the terminology will already be familiar to you, though much of will not. In tax, the learning curve is made somewhat steeper by virtue of the fact that many of the underlying concepts may not be familiar to you. Set forth below is a brief introduction to some of the most important terminology.

1. The Tax Base and Calculation of the Tax Payable

Tax base is not part of the specialized vocabulary of the Internal Revenue Code. It refers to a general concept used by lawyers and economists to describe the amount that is to be taxed under whatever system of taxation one adopts—that is, the amount to which the appropriate tax rate is applied. Under a sales tax the base is sales; under a consumption tax the base is consumption or expenditure. Under general theories of income taxation the base is, of course, income or perhaps, at a somewhat higher level of sophistication, disposable income, meaning the amount available to pay taxes after

---

68. 28 U.S.C. §1295.
69. See 4 B. Bittker, Federal Taxation of Income, Estates, and Gifts ¶115.7, at 115-142 (1981).

appropriate allowances for the basic costs of staying alive and well. Under the present tax, which, of course, is the subject of this book, the tax base is a specialized, technically defined amount called *taxable income*, a statutory[70] term that is narrower than one would expect if one started with the notion that disposable income is the appropriate base. The narrowness is in large part attributable to Code provisions that treat favorably various actions such as making gifts to charity or acquiring and holding buildings, machinery, and other assets for profit-making purposes.

Taxable income, then, is the bottom line. However, the term "taxable income" is itself defined by reference to certain other statutory terms of art. The starting point is the taxpayer's *gross income*. Gross income is defined by an elaborate set of rules found in the Internal Revenue Code, the case law, and other sources of tax law. The statutory centerpiece is §61. Take a look at it, if you haven't already. You will see that it consists of a general, all-inclusive description of what is to be included ("all income from whatever source derived"), plus a list of nonexclusive exemplars. For most individuals the major items covered will be wages, salaries, interest, dividends, and rents. Note that item 2 on the list is "gross income derived from a business." This is a bit misleading. It is understood to mean amounts received by a taxpayer ("gross receipts") after subtraction of the cost of any goods that had been acquired by the taxpayer and ultimately sold (possibly after some transformation) to generate those returns. Sections 71 to 85 list various items that are included in gross income but require special treatment. These sections also, however, identify certain receipts, such as child-support payments,[71] that are excluded from gross income. Sections 101 to 127 exclude from gross income a number of receipts such as interest on state and local bonds[72] and tort recoveries for personal injuries.[73]

The result of the various statutory and other exclusions is that there is a substantial difference between any generally accepted economic concept of gross income and the tax concept. Chapter 2 is devoted to an elaboration of the tax concept. The table of contents for that chapter provides some sense of the kinds of issues that will be considered.

Once a taxpayer's gross income has been determined, the next step is to calculate *adjusted gross income*, or *AGI*, another statutorily defined term that is arrived at by deducting (subtracting) from gross income a set of items listed in §62. At this point you should give §62 a once-over-lightly reading. Most of what is listed will be, at best, barely comprehensible. It's like reading a foreign language. That is a problem in any field that has developed its own terminology; even though the words are familiar, their meaning in the specialized context is not. You will become familiar with tax terminology as you work your way through this book. If the §62 list seems to you to lack coherence, don't worry; you may be right. Certainly the items lack any clear relationship to each other. The most important item on the list is the first, which may be thought of

---

70. §63.
71. §71(b).
72. §103.
73. §104(a)(2).

as the costs of producing business income. These allowances must be made in order to move from total receipts to net income.

The next step is to move from AGI to *taxable income*. This involves deducting (a) the amount of the personal exemptions of the taxpayers and their dependents, if any, plus (b) either (i) the standard deduction or (ii) "itemized" deductions. The deduction for personal exemptions was $3,500 for 2008 tax returns; it is adjusted annually for inflation.[74] The standard deduction for 2008 tax returns (after the annual adjustment for inflation) was $10,900 for a married couple or surviving spouse, $8,000 for a head of household, and $5,450 for a single person, with an extra amount — $1,050 or $1,350 — for taxpayers over age 65.[75] The function of the standard deduction is to relieve people with modest incomes of the nuisance of keeping track of outlays covered by the itemized deduction, and of filing a somewhat complex return, and to ensure that people with incomes below a certain level pay no tax. Itemized deductions, which may be claimed only by taxpayers who forgo the standard deduction, include mortgage interest, state income and property taxes, casualty losses above 10 percent of AGI, medical expenses above 7.5 percent of AGI, charitable contributions, and certain other expenses (most notably unreimbursed employee business expenses) to the extent that they exceed 2 percent of AGI.[76]

The net figure arrived at by deducting from AGI the personal exemptions and either the standard deduction or the itemized deductions is, as previously stated, called taxable income. It is this figure that is used in the rate schedule to arrive at the amount of the tax. The rate schedules are set forth in §1 of the Code. By applying these rates to taxable income, taxpayers will arrive at an amount of tax that they owe. That is almost the end of the process, but not quite. The final step is to offset the tax with any credits that may be available and to determine whether a minimum tax must be paid. A credit is a direct offset to the tax. It is to be contrasted with a deduction, which reduces taxable income and thereby reduces the tax payable by the amount of the deduction multiplied by the relevant rate of tax. For example, there is a credit for "expenses for household and dependent care services necessary for gainful employment," sometimes referred to (somewhat inaccurately) as the

---

74. §151.

75. §63. The standard deduction replaces the zero bracket amount (ZBA) that had been in effect for a number of years and accomplished the same objectives in a confusing way. For a person who may be claimed as a dependent by another taxpayer, the standard deduction is limited to the greater of $500 or the person's earned income. §63(c)(5). In 1999, with the inflation adjustment, the standard deduction had increased to $7,200 for married couples and $4,300 for single persons.

76. The concept of AGI has three functions. First, AGI is used to separate those deductions that can be claimed by all taxpayers, regardless whether they claim the standard deduction, from those that cannot. Essentially, one must choose between the standard deduction and certain other deductions (mostly personal) but not between the standard deduction and those deductions allowable in arriving at AGI. Second, AGI is for some tax policy purposes considered a better measure of income than is taxable income. Thus, it is used in shaping the rule for deduction of medical expenses, where the amount deductible is the excess of such expenses over 7.5 percent of AGI. §213(a). Similarly, AGI is used in calculating the maximum amount that can be deducted for contributions to charity. §170(b). Third, people using tax statistics in analysis of tax and economic policy issues find AGI to be more useful for many purposes than taxable income, since AGI corresponds more closely to economic income.

child-care credit.[77] Other credits are found at §§21 to 41. The most important, and most obviously appropriate, is the credit for the amount of tax withheld from wages.[78]

Finally, there is an alternative minimum tax for individuals, the details of which are set forth in §§55 et seq.[79] The tax is imposed on a special base at a rate of 26 percent of the first $175,000 and 28 percent on amounts above $175,000. The special base is AGI plus various "preferences" and exclusions, reduced, for individuals, by certain non-§62 deductions. This tax is in lieu of, and is payable only if it is greater than, the tax computed under the normal rules. There is also a counterpart for corporations: a 20 percent minimum tax on tax preferences.

2. Capital Gain and Dividend Income

During most of the history of our income tax, capital gain was taxed at a lower rate than was other income. The preferred treatment was eliminated by the 1986 act but was reintroduced in attenuated form by the 1990 act. Currently most forms of capital gain of noncorporate taxpayers are subject to a nominal maximum rate of 15 percent — 20 percentage points less that the maximum rate on other forms of income, though the effective rate may be higher in certain income ranges because of the alternative minimum tax (AMT). The definition of capital gain depends on a large and complex body of law; efforts to transform gain from ordinary income into capital gain gave rise to an even larger and more complex body of law. Capital losses can be used only to offset capital gain, except that individuals may use up to $3,000 of capital losses to offset ordinary income. This means that it is important in some instances to be able to distinguish between capital gain and loss and ordinary gain and loss. The distinction is explored in detail in Chapter 8. Briefly, capital gain or loss is gain or loss from the "sale or exchange of a capital asset."[80] "Capital asset" is statutorily defined as "property," with a number of exceptions — most notably for "inventory" or "property held by the taxpayer primarily for sale to customers in the ordinary course of his trade or business."[81] For example, a person who invests in a corporation, like IBM or AT&T, by buying common stock or bonds issued by the corporation, has acquired a capital asset. Gain on the sale of a capital asset held for one year or less is short-term capital gain. Gain from the sale of a capital asset held for more than a year is long-term capital gain. After a netting process, only "net capital gain" (i.e., the excess of net long term capital gain over net short term capital loss) is subject to the preferential rate.

---

77. §21.
78. §31.
79. For further discussion of §55, see Chapter 6.I.7, infra.
80. §1222.
81. §1221.

Most forms of dividend income are taxed at the same rate as net capital gain (i.e., a maximum rate of 15 percent) or a somewhat higher rate for certain taxpayers who are subject to the alternative minimum tax.

3.   Tax Accounting

Methods. The rules of accounting for income tax purposes follow the basic approaches of nontax accounting, though they differ in some important respects. The two basic methods of tax accounting, which are familiar to nontax accounting, are the *cash receipts and disbursements method*, or *cash method*, and the *accrual method*. Under the cash method, speaking very generally, amounts are treated as income when received in cash (or cash equivalent) and are deductible when paid. Under the accrual method, subject to some important exceptions, items are included in gross income when earned, regardless whether payment has been received, and items of expense are deductible when the obligation to pay is incurred, regardless when payment is made. For example, suppose that an accountant, *A*, performs services in connection with the law practice of a lawyer, *L*. The services are performed on December 5, 2003; three days later *L* receives a bill for $500; *L* does not dispute his obligation to pay the full amount but does not pay until January 10, 2004. If *A* and *L* both use the cash method, *L* is entitled to a deduction (if otherwise allowable) in 2004, and *A* should report the item as income in the same year, since 2004 is the year of payment by *L* and of receipt by *A*. If both *A* and *L* used the accrual method, *L* would be entitled to the deduction in 2003, when the obligation was incurred, and *A* would include the $500 in income in 2003, when it was earned.[82] Most individuals use the cash method (because it is simple), and most businesses use the accrual method (because it more accurately reflects economic realities).

Capital expenditures. An important limitation on the cash method is that the costs of capital investments may not be deducted when the cash outlay is made, but only as the asset is used or when it is sold, exchanged, or abandoned. For example, suppose a farmer who uses the cash method buys forty acres of farm land, to be used in his farming business, for $40,000. The $40,000, which is called a capital expenditure, may not be deducted at the time of the purchase. Generally speaking, capital expenditures are amounts spent for assets that have a useful life of more than a year. In the case of land, a record is kept of the cost and gain or loss is computed, and reported for tax purposes, on disposition of the land. Suppose the farmer buys a tractor for $10,000. Again, the $10,000 outlay is a capital expenditure and cannot be treated as a current expense. Instead, a record is kept of the amount of the outlay and a portion is deducted each year as the tractor is used. The annual

---

82. Under rules added to the Code in 1984, the deduction for *L* in 2003 would be allowed under the accrual method, but the result would depend not only on principles of accrual accounting but also on the fact that the obligation meets the requirements of §461(h)(4) (the "all events" test) and §461(h)(2)(a)(i) (the "economic performance" test).

deduction is called depreciation of — under the present tax law — the ACRS (accelerated cost recovery system) deduction.

Annual accounting. Tax liabilities are computed on an annual, as opposed to a transactional, basis. To illustrate, suppose that a business firm, *F*, performs work under a contract in 2000 and in doing so incurs current expenses of $50,000. Suppose further that there is a substantial dispute as to whether *F* is entitled to any payment for its work, so no income is accrued in 2000. In 2001, the work is completed (at no further cost), the dispute is settled, and *F* collects $50,000. The proper accounting for tax purposes, even for an accrual method taxpayer, is to deduct all the expenses in 2000, when incurred, and to report all the income in 2001. The deduction in 2000 may do the firm no good if it has no other income. That does not matter. The point is that each year must be closed out for tax accounting purposes at the end of the year on the basis of the information then available. The firm must report the entire $50,000 as income in 2001,[83] even though the transaction as a whole produced no profit and regardless whether the deduction in 2000 produced a tax benefit. If the deduction produced no tax benefit in 2000, this system of accounting obviously produces an unfair outcome.[84] There are provisions of the Code that give relief from this unfairness (here, most notably, a provision for carrying forward the loss from 2000 to 2001),[85] but these are relief provisions; they leave in place the general principle of annual accounting.

4. Realization and Recognition

Realization and recognition are important terms of art in tax law. A gain or loss is said to be realized when there has been some change in circumstances such that the gain or loss *might be* taken into account for tax purposes. A gain or loss is said to be recognized when the change in circumstances is such that the gain or loss is taken into account. Thus, where there is realization there may or may not be recognition, but where there is recognition there must have been realization. For example, suppose a taxpayer, T, buys shares of common stock (that is, a portion of the ownership interest) in ABC Corporation for $1,000 and the value of the ABC shares (which, let us assume, are publicly traded at prices regularly reported in the newspapers) rises to $2,500. The gain of $1,500 is not realized. Now suppose that ABC Corporation is acquired by XYZ Corporation in a transaction in which T receives shares of XYZ stock in return for the ABC shares, and that the XYZ shares received by T are worth $2,500. As a result of the exchange of the ABC shares for the XYZ shares, T will have realized a gain of $1,500. That gain must be recognized unless the

---

83. For tax purposes, the $50,000 is not considered to have been earned in 2000 because of the uncertainty about entitlement.

84. The hypothetical facts are based on Burnet v. Sanford & Brooks Co., 282 U.S. 359 (1931) (see Chapter 2.E.1), in which the taxpayer argued unsuccessfully that the outcome was not constitutionally permissible under the Sixteenth Amendment, since the transaction did not produce any net gain.

85. §172.

two corporations have taken advantage of special provisions of the Code[86] under which recognition can be avoided (until the XYZ shares are sold).

5.   Recovery of Cost, Depreciation, and Basis

Suppose T is a retail seller of widgets. In a particular year, T buys 1,000 widgets for $10 each and sells them all for $15 each. Obviously T has a profit (assuming no expenses other than the cost of the widgets) of $5,000, which is arrived at simply by deducting her cost of $10,000 from her receipts of $15,000. Since the federal income tax is a tax on the net income of $5,000, not on the gross receipts of $15,000, T must be allowed to recover her cost of $10,000 in arriving at the taxable amount.

Now suppose T decides to manufacture widgets and buys widget-making machinery at a cost of $100,000. Assume that there are no other expenses. T makes the widgets and starts selling them. For tax purposes, how does she take account of the cost incurred in buying the machinery? One possibility would be to provide that the proceeds of sales are not taxable until T has taken in $100,000 and all proceeds thereafter are fully taxable as profit. That would be a very extreme form of "cash method" accounting. It is not allowed. What T must do instead is recover her investment by taking a deduction (against gross receipts) traditionally called *depreciation*,[87] but now called (in the Code) the *accelerated cost recovery system* (ACRS) amount or, more simply, cost recovery.[88] Under ACRS, the cost of the machine is spread out over a number of years (less than the expected life) according to formulas provided in the Code. The effect of the formulas is to bunch the deductions in the early years of the use of the machine.[89] This treatment is accelerated in comparison with normal methods of accounting, under which the amount of the allowance is designed to correspond better to the actual decline in the value of the asset and under which costs are spread out over a period roughly equivalent to the expected useful life of the asset. Often these normal methods of accounting are used by publicly owned corporations in reporting profits to investors even though accelerated methods have been used for tax purposes. The reason is simple: The tax method produces a larger deduction and a correspondingly smaller profit, a profit that is less than the realistic amount in most cases.

6.   Entities

A *sole proprietor* is a person who owns a business solely and directly — no partners or other co-owners and no use of a corporation or other such legal device. All items of income and expense of the business are treated for tax purposes as items of income and expense of the sole proprietor. There are

---

86. See §354.
87. See §167.
88. §168.
89. See Chapter 6D infra.

separate forms on which these items may be netted out, but the use of these forms does not negate the direct relationship between the sole proprietor and each and every one of the transactions occurring in his or her business.

A *partnership* is a combination of two or more people who have agreed to carry on a business for profit as co-owners. The partnership is to some extent reified for tax purposes: "It" files a tax return. (That is, some person files a tax return covering the joint activities of the partners.) On the partnership tax return, income and expenses are netted out, but the partnership pays no tax. (That is, the partners' jointly held funds are not used to pay a tax.) Instead, the partners report on their individual tax returns their pro rata share of whatever net profit or loss was calculated by the partnership. This treatment of partners and partnerships is sometimes called *pass-through* taxation. The partnership is also sometimes referred to as a *conduit* for tax purposes. The pass-through feature is critical to groups of people who pool their resources to invest in *tax shelters*, which are investments that, because of special tax accounting rules (like the ACRS deductions), produce a loss for tax purposes even though profitable in an economic sense. The loss is passed through to the partner/investors and is used by them to offset income from other sources (such as a medical practice or an acting career).

A *trust* is a legal device by which one person, the trustee, holds and invests property for the benefit of another person, the beneficiary. The rules for taxation of trusts are too complex for development here. It is enough for now to say that the general effect is to achieve a pass-through or conduit result, but since there may be a delay between the time income is earned and the time when a beneficiary becomes entitled to it, and since the identity of the beneficiary may be undetermined, the trust may be required to pay a tax, which is generally treated like a withholding tax paid by an employer on the wages of an employee but is sometimes the final tax on the income.

Corporations, which are legal devices for organizing economic activity, are treated as separate taxpaying entities. They compute the amount of their income, for the most part, according to the same rules as those applicable to the business activities of individuals and pay a tax based on a special rate schedule with rates of 15 percent on the first $50,000, 25 percent on the next $25,000, 34 percent on amounts above $75,000, and 35 percent on amounts in excess of $10 million, but with a phaseout of the benefits of the lower rates as income rises.[90] Payments of income by a corporation to its shareholders are called dividends[91] and are treated as income of the shareholders.[92] Thus, distributed income is doubly taxed, once at the corporate level and again at the individual level, while income that is retained is subject only to the corporate tax. When a corporation retains income, if the amount is wisely invested, the value of the corporation and of its common shares should rise (all other things equal). Thus, retained income should result in an increase in

---

90. §11.

91. See §316.

92. §61(a)(7). Technically, income (or, to be more precise, "earnings and profits," a statutory concept similar to income) is an accounting concept, not a medium of payment, and a dividend is that portion of any payment (normally in cash) that does not exceed income.

shareholder wealth in the form of increased share values. Such gain is not realized; it is not taxed until the shares are sold. Shareholders, unlike partners, cannot take into account their pro rata share of corporate losses. Losses can be used only by the corporation to offset income in other years.[93]

I.   DEFERRAL AND ITS VALUE

In recent years, as interest rates have risen, taxpayers have found it increasingly advantageous to find ways to defer their tax liability to future years. The advantage of deferral is simple: A tax liability deferred from the present to the future gives the taxpayer the use in the interim of the amount that would otherwise have been paid presently in taxes. The advantage of deferral is far greater than the untutored may suspect (except for those who, from grammar school years, may recall the miracle of compound interest). Consider this illustration:

T is a high-income taxpayer subject to a marginal rate of 40 percent. Assume that he is permitted to set aside from his income, in a retirement fund, $10,000, without paying any tax on that amount and that, in addition, the earnings on that $10,000 from the present to whenever it is drawn out on retirement are not taxed. In other words, T has received the income, in cash; he has the cash to use, but taxation is deferred until retirement on both the $10,000 and the earnings on it. Suppose T invests the $10,000 for ten years at 10 percent, compounded annually, and then retires. By that time, the $10,000 will have increased to $25,937. If T then pays a tax at the rate of 40 percent, he will have $15,562 left to spend. In contrast, suppose that the law is different, that there is no special provision for deferral and that T must pay taxes on any money that he earns and wants to set aside for retirement as well as on the earnings on the amount set aside. In other words, assume normal current taxation rather than deferral. The $10,000 would be reduced by taxes to $6,000 and that $6,000, if invested to produce interest at the rate of 10 percent per year, would earn, after tax, only 6 percent. At the end of ten years, at 6 percent, the $6,000 would have increased to $10,745. This amount would be tax paid and fully spendable, but it is still only 69 percent of what is available with deferral. As the number of years of deferral increases, the gap between the two amounts becomes even more dramatic. If the number of years to retirement is twenty rather than ten, the relative after-tax amounts are $40,365 with deferral and $19,243 without.

Another way of looking at deferral is to calculate the present value of a future payment. Suppose, for example, that your client, C, wants to know what is saved by pushing a tax of $10,000 five years into the future, assuming a tax

---

93. Certain corporations are permitted to elect, under Subchapter S of the Code (§§1361 to 1379), to be taxed on a conduit or pass-through basis, in which case the corporation pays no tax and all net gains and losses are taken into account pro rata by the shareholders on their individual returns. In other words, the tax treatment of these corporations is essentially the same as that of partnerships.

rate of 40 percent. One way to approach answering that question is to ask what amount must be set aside today to pay $10,000 in five years, assuming some reasonable rate of return on the amount set aside. Suppose *C* tells you she can earn 8 percent after tax (compounded annually) on her investments. With this interest rate, the amount to be set aside is $6,805. This means that a tax of $10,000 to be paid five years hence is financially equivalent to a tax of $6,805 to be paid today. That $6,805 is the *present value* of the $10,000 future amount, at 8 percent.

The process of calculating the present value of a future amount is called *discounting to present value* and the present value is sometimes redundantly called the discounted present value.[94]

Table 1-3 gives relationships between present and future amounts. Present values can be derived by multiplying the future amount by the appropriate number. Thus, for the present value of $1 ten years hence, at 10 percent, the multiplier is 0.386. The present value of $10,000 ten years hence, at 10 percent, is 0.386 ($10,000) or $3,860. The present value of $25,907 ten years hence, at 10 percent, is 0.386 ($25,907) or about $10,000. (These figures are slightly inaccurate because of rounding off in the table.)

The same table can be used to calculate future amounts, simply by dividing by the appropriate number rather than multiplying by it. For example, the future value of $10,000 ten years hence, at 10 percent, is $10,000 ÷ 0.386, which equals $25,905 (again slightly inaccurate due to rounding).

In case you want to make some rough calculations of present or future amounts or figure out interest rates, and don't have access to a table or a pocket calculator, you can use a convenient rule of thumb — the "rule of 72." This rule holds that (roughly) an amount doubles within the number of years determined by dividing 72 by the interest rate. Thus, at 12 percent, compounded annually, $1 will be worth $2 in six years (72 ÷ 12). By the same token, if the interest rate is 12 percent, the right to receive $2 six years from now is presently worth $1. And if $1 invested today yields $2 in six years, the return is 12 percent per year.

As the materials in this book unfold, it will become clear just how important is an understanding of the relationships between present and future value. Deferral is a major phenomenon in tax analysis.

---

94. The algebraic formulas for the relationships between present and future value are simple. For computing future value,

$$FV = PV(1 + r)^n,$$

where *FV* is future value (or future amount), *PV* is present value (or amount), *r* is the interest rate, and *n* is the number of years. Thus, in the first example, in which $10,000 is invested at 15 percent for ten years,

$$FV = \$10,000(1.15)^{10} = \$40,456.$$

To determine present value, we do a minor transposition, and the formula is

$$PV = FV/(1 + r)^n$$

Thus, using the same numbers,

$$PV = \$40,456/(1.15)^{10} = \$10,000.$$

TABLE 1-3
Present Value of $1: What a Dollar at End of Specified Future Year Is Worth Today

Year	3%	4%	5%	6%	7%	8%	10%	12%	15%	20%	Year
1	.971	.962	.952	.943	.935	.926	.909	.893	.870	.833	1
2	.943	.925	.907	.890	.873	.857	.826	.797	.756	.694	2
3	.915	.889	.864	.840	.816	.794	.751	.712	.658	.579	3
4	.889	.855	.823	.792	.763	.735	.683	.636	.572	.482	4
5	.863	.822	.784	.747	.713	.681	.620	.567	.497	.402	5
6	.837	.790	.746	.705	.666	.630	.564	.507	.432	.335	6
7	.813	.760	.711	.665	.623	.583	.513	.452	.376	.279	7
8	.789	.731	.677	.627	.582	.540	.467	.404	.327	.233	8
9	.766	.703	.645	.592	.544	.500	.424	.361	.284	.194	9
10	.744	.676	.614	.558	.508	.463	.386	.322	.247	.162	10
11	.722	.650	.585	.527	.475	.429	.350	.287	.215	.135	11
12	.701	.625	.557	.497	.444	.397	.319	.257	.187	.112	12
13	.681	.601	.530	.469	.415	.368	.290	.229	.163	.0935	13
14	.661	.577	.505	.442	.388	.340	.263	.205	.141	.0779	14
15	.642	.555	.481	.417	.362	.315	.239	.183	.123	.0649	15
16	.623	.534	.458	.394	.339	.292	.218	.163	.107	.0541	16
17	.605	.513	.436	.371	.317	.270	.198	.146	.093	.0451	17
18	.587	.494	.416	.350	.296	.250	.180	.130	.0808	.0376	18
19	.570	.475	.396	.331	.277	.232	.164	.116	.0703	.0313	19
20	.554	.456	.377	.312	.258	.215	.149	.104	.0611	.0261	20
25	.478	.375	.295	.233	.184	.146	.0923	.0588	.0304	.0105	25
30	.412	.308	.231	.174	.131	.0994	.0573	.0334	.0151	.00421	30
40	.307	.208	.142	.0972	.067	.0460	.0221	.0107	.00373	.000680	40
50	.228	.141	.087	.0543	.034	.0213	.00852	.00346	.000922	.000109	50

J.   THE SOURCES OF FEDERAL TAX LAW IN A NUTSHELL

Taxes are imposed only by statute. Although the lawyer who fails to look beyond the statute will often err, the statute should almost always be the starting point.

At the same time, some parts of federal tax law, especially where statutory pronouncements were absent, vague, or confused, have been influenced by judicial doctrines of a common law character, created by the courts as case after case came before them. In these areas, the lawyer must be attuned to the judiciary's signals even more than to those of Congress. Moreover, the detail of the statute is often deceptive, since the courts may exercise their traditional power to disregard form for substance and to hold that an arrangement that complies with the literal terms of the statute is not within its spirit, just as a deed absolute on its face may be shown to be a mortgage. One of the fascinations of federal tax law is the interplay between the detail of a statute and the creative spirit of the courts; and even the tax attorney who cannot pause to enjoy this interplay must understand it to survive.

The statute is, of course, the Internal Revenue Code of 1986. The prior Codes were enacted in 1939 and in 1954 and were frequently amended.

Although the congressional debates ordinarily do not illuminate technical problems of federal taxation, there are occasional exceptions, and then recourse to the Congressional Record is necessary. The committee reports, on the other hand, are frequently helpful, and it is common for the courts to rely heavily on them.[95] They are prepared by technicians on the staff of the Joint Committee on Taxation. That committee is composed of representatives of the House Ways and Means Committee and the Senate Finance Committee, who are assisted by a kind of legislative civil service of tax experts.[96] Because of the profusion of technical detail and because some members of the committee may know little of the content of the committee's reports (and this is a fortiori true of the members of Congress who do not serve on the tax committees), it might be said that the reports are not evidence of the "intent" of Congress unless we apply the doctrine of respondeat superior. However, the same might be said of the statutes themselves (as well as many other complex

95. Since 1939, the reports of the House Ways and Means Committee, the Senate Finance Committee, and the conference committees have been reprinted in the Internal Revenue Bulletin, which is published weekly by the Internal Revenue Service and compiled into semiannual volumes. The congressional reports for the period 1913-1939 were reprinted together in a separate number of the bulletin: 1939-1 (Part 2) C.B.

96. The preparation of the committee report is described as follows in R. Blough, The Federal Taxing Process 75-76 (1952):

> Preparation of the Committee report is ordinarily in the hands of the Chief of Staff of the Joint Committee [on Taxation] and his staff members. The report is customarily divided into two parts. The first is a discussion in non-technical language of the need for the legislation, what the bill provides, and the anticipated impact on various groups of taxpayers. Among the tax staffs this section of the report is referred to as the "guff." Despite this derisive label, the section is very important. The latter part of the Committee report is a technical explanation of what each section of the bill provides. The Legislative Counsel [of the Treasury] and the Treasury tax staff participate in the preparation of the technical section.

In recent years, the Joint Committee Staff has published a General Explanation of tax acts after their enactment. This is a compilation of the various committee reports — House, Senate, and Conference — into one report that reflects the final legislation. The General Explanation is an interesting and useful document, nicely described in the following passage from Michael Livingston, Congress, the Courts, and the Code: Legislative History and the Interpretation of Tax Statutes, 69 Tex. L. Rev. 819, 884-885 (1991) (footnotes omitted):

> A notable example of post-enactment legislative history is the General Explanation, commonly known as the "Blue Book" [because its cover is blue], written by the Joint Committee on Taxation staff after a major tax bill [has been enacted]. While primarily a collation of the previous committee reports, the Blue Book also contains some materials not found in the committee reports. These materials are not officially part of the legislative history, and a debate persists as to their authority. Courts have cited the Blue Book on various occasions. . . . The consensus appears to be that the Blue Book has some authority, but less than the actual committee reports.
>
> I am not so sure. If the legislative history is largely an exercise in writing regulations, are the staff's later efforts necessarily worse than their earlier ones? . . .
>
> I recommend that the Blue Book be treated in a manner similar to the committee reports themselves. Where the Blue Book adds explanatory material, it should be as persuasive as similar material in the committee reports. (This is a relatively rare occurrence.) Where the Blue Book specifies detailed applications of the statute, it should be entitled to a presumption of correctness, but should not be followed if it is inconsistent with the underlying provision. This would discourage the use of the Blue Book to "strong-arm" interpretations not otherwise supported by the statute.
>
> In taking this position, I am aware of the constitutional difficulties in consulting post-enactment history.

statutes), since many members of Congress, including some on the tax committees, do not understand the technical detail of the statutes and instead rely on the representations of the "technicians" regarding the contents of the statute and the committee reports. The importance of the committee reports increases with the complexity of the statute, since difficult drafting problems frequently are "taken care of" in the committee report.[97]

Occasionally, though more rarely, the courts refer to the hearings before the House and Senate Committees as an aid to construction. Although some of the oral testimony is quite diffuse, interested public and private individuals and groups often present closely reasoned memoranda in support of their positions. If a proposal is accepted, modified, or rejected by the committee after it has been explained by testimony or memorandum, the presentation may be a clue to the meaning of the committee's action and, by extension, to the meaning of the action of Congress. The hearings are printed by the committees in limited quantities, however, and are to be found in only a few libraries.[98]

Second only to the statute and the legislative materials in importance are the Treasury Regulations. Code §7805 authorizes the Secretary of the Treasury or his delegate to prescribe "all needful rules and regulations for the enforcement" of the Code. In addition, the secretary is authorized to issue regulations to cover more specific areas—e.g., under §3 to prescribe tax tables for individuals, and under §472 to set rules governing use of the last-in-first-out method of accounting for inventories. Perhaps most interesting are §§1501 to 1505, giving to the Treasury the authority to prescribe by regulations the conditions under which consolidated returns may be filed by one or more affiliated corporations and pursuant to which virtually a separate tax code has been promulgated by regulation. Regulations issued under these sections are of a quasi-legislative character; Congress has chosen to delegate to the Treasury authority it might have exercised itself. Other regulations interpret the statute for the guidance of the taxpayers and the staff of the Internal Revenue Service. During recent years the Congress has increasingly intervened in the Treasury's regulation function. Regulations or rulings dealing with fringe benefits, travel and entertainment, deduction of expenses of commuting to work, treatment of deferred compensation, and imputed interest on related party transactions have been blocked either by formal legislation or by agreement with congressional committees.[99] Whatever their function or origin, regulations are issued from time to time in the form of Treasury Decisions (T.D.), which are compiled at irregular intervals as a systematic series of regulations.

97. Occasionally, the Committee Report is used to direct the Treasury to modify, institute, or abandon a regulation or other administrative practice. Often these directions, the result of understandings between Treasury staff and the committees, are followed by the Internal Revenue Service. Some view this as abuse of the process, others as an efficient way of doing business.

98. On use by the judiciary of inaccessible legislative history as an aid to the construction of statutes, see Justice Jackson, concurring, in United States v. Public Utilities Commission, 345 U.S. 295, 319 (1953).

99. See Parnell, Congressional Interference in Agency Enforcement: The IRS Experience, 89 Yale L.J. 1360 (1980).

The current regulations bear the key numeral "1" if related to the income tax provisions of the Code; "20" or "25" if related to the estate or gift tax provisions, respectively. Thus, "Regs. §1.170-1" denotes a regulation having to do with §170 (income tax consequences of charitable contributions); "Regs. §20.2041-1" is concerned with §2041 (estate tax treatment of powers of appointment). There are other series for more specialized subjects. Changes in the regulations are issued as Treasury Decisions. The Administrative Procedure Act requires proposed regulations (with certain exceptions) to be published in the Federal Register to permit interested parties to file their objections or suggestions for consideration before adoption.[100] The proposed regulations are prepared by the Service in consultation with the Treasury staff.

Regulations, whether of a legislative or an interpretive character, can serve a useful function only if both administrators and taxpayers can rely on them. Seldom are regulations, of either kind, overturned by the courts, but occasionally a regulation, especially one of the interpretive type, is invalidated. It is impossible to generalize beyond saying that a regulation that was issued soon after enactment of the statute it interprets and that has been adhered to consistently by the government will command great respect from the courts, but that if contemporaneity and consistency are lacking, the courts will be less constrained to accept the regulation. Reenactment of a statute may carry an implication of congressional approval of an interpretive regulation.[101] Another problem in this area is whether a proper interpretive regulation in time takes on the force of law so that only Congress, and not the Treasury, may alter it. The Treasury may ordinarily amend an interpretive regulation if the new interpretation is to be given prospective force only, and there may also be power to apply it retroactively. Retroactive application may be withheld by the Treasury itself, however, as wise administration, pursuant to its power, conferred by §7805(b), to prescribe the extent to which regulations and rulings shall be applied prospectively only.

In addition to the regulations, which are issued by authority of the Secretary of the Treasury, a steady supply of rulings, instructions, releases, and other lesser pronouncements flows from the Internal Revenue Service. Not bearing the imprimatur of the secretary, these documents are less authoritative than the regulations, but they are of great importance in the day-to-day administration of the tax laws, and often they are persuasive to the courts. The most important are Revenue Rulings (Rev. Rul.) and Revenue Procedures (Rev. Proc.). Revenue Rulings are opinions on matters of law arising in particular fact settings. Often they are based on requests by taxpayers for advice about a specific legal issue with which they are confronted. Revenue Procedures are statements describing procedures affecting the rights or duties of taxpayers or other information. Both Revenue Rulings and Revenue Procedures are published by the government currently in the weekly Internal Revenue Bulletin

---

100. 5 U.S.C. §553.

101. It is hard to assess the importance of the reenactment rule in this area. It may be only a handkerchief covering something already covered by a blanket if the court would have upheld the regulation whether the statute had been reenacted or not; but it may be crucial if the court thinks the regulation when issued was either debatable or demonstrably wrong but that it gained authority as a result of silent acquiescence by Congress.

(I.R.B.) and permanently (every six months) in the Cumulative Bulletins (Cum. Bull.). Also of importance is advice given to taxpayers in "private letter rulings" (Ltr. Rul.), sometimes referred to as "private rulings" or "letter rulings." These rulings are issued (in letter form) to taxpayers in response to requests for advice about their own specific fact situations. Some of these ultimately are developed into Revenue Rulings, which set forth the official position of the IRS on which all taxpayers are entitled to rely. In the case of a letter (private) ruling that has not become a Revenue Ruling, the government is not bound to follow the legal position that it adopts except as it is applied to the individual taxpayer to whom the advice is directed. Letter rulings are published by commercial publishers.[102] While letter rulings lack precedential force,[103] they are useful to practitioners in determining the position the IRS has adopted.

As we have seen, tax litigation may begin in the Tax Court, in the various federal district courts, or in the Claims Court. The opinions of the Tax Court fall into two categories: "regular" decisions, which are published by the court itself, and "memorandum" decisions, which are not officially reported but are published commercially by Research Institute of America and by Commerce Clearing House.

When the service loses a case in the Tax Court, it often announces, in the Internal Revenue Bulletin, whether it acquiesces (acq. or A) or does not acquiesce (nonacq. or NA) in the decision. Acquiescence operates as advice to the staff of the Service on whether to rely on the decision in the disposition of other cases. Nonacquiescence indicates that the Service, whether it appeals the decision or not, will not accept the principle enunciated in it in disposing of other cases (though of course the decision is binding as to the taxpayer in the case itself, unless reversed on appeal), and that it may litigate the same issue when it arises again. Because decisions of the Tax Court are reviewed by thirteen courts of appeals, the government may eventually succeed in obtaining a reversal of the Tax Court, even though the decision in the non-acquiesced case was affirmed by a court of appeals; indeed, the principal way for the Treasury to get a conflict among the circuits (as a basis for a petition for certiorari) when the Tax Court decides in favor of the taxpayer is to stick to its guns and relitigate the same issue in one or more other cases. After announcing its nonacquiescence, the Treasury may be discouraged by a series of losses in the courts of appeals, or it may reconsider its views for other reasons and substitute an acquiescence for nonacquiescence.[104]

---

102. Letter rulings first became public information in 1976 with the adoption of §6110.

103. Section 6110(j)(3). See Rev. Proc. 79-45, 1979-2 C.B. 508, §17.01.

104. The Tax Court will normally apply the rule of the Court of Appeals with jurisdiction over an appeal in the particular case before it even if it disagrees with the Court of Appeals. Golsen v. Commissioner, 54 T.C. 742 (1970).

2

SOME CHARACTERISTICS OF
INCOME

What is income? Chances are that you already have some well-developed intuitions about the answer to that question. For example, when you read the opening pages of Harper Lee's novel, *To Kill a Mockingbird*, you probably weren't stumped by the sentence, "Atticus derived a reasonable income from the law." Like most people, you probably imagined Atticus Finch receiving cash from his clients for the various legal services he rendered. For the most part, you will find that your everyday intuitions about what is and isn't income are a useful guide in thinking about the meaning of the term for legal purposes as well.

At times, however, your intuition may not be enough. Take the case of Walter Cunningham, the poor Maycomb County farmer Atticus helped in connection with an entailment on his land. What "income" was there when Cunningham, lacking cash, instead left a sack of hickory nuts and turnip greens at the Finches' back door in partial satisfaction of his legal fees? Does it make any difference to Finch or to Cunningham that payment was made in kind rather than in cash? Would it matter if Finch's usual fee for legal work far exceeded the value of the hickory nuts and turnip greens? What if Finch had accepted an ownership interest in Cunningham's land instead? At the risk of spoiling one of America's greatest novels with talk of federal taxes, we'd like to suggest that intuition alone may not have equipped you to offer professional tax guidance on these questions. One of the objectives of this chapter, therefore, is to provide you with a framework for thinking about the definition of income from a legal perspective.

So, what is income? As a legal matter, the short answer is: whatever the Internal Revenue Code is authoritatively (and constitutionally) interpreted to say that it is. Although this initial response may seem curt and not particularly helpful, the fact is that some aspects of how the tax laws define income resist abstract explanation. For example, no simple or intuitive conception of income could yield the result that interest earned on bonds issued by a State (or any political subdivision thereof), unlike other interest, is excludable from the bondholder's gross income. Similarly, no amount of logic, intuition, or other abstract reasoning will reveal that income does not include gain from the sale of one's principal residence, but only to the extent that such gain does not exceed $250,000 ($500,000 in the case of married couples filing a joint return) and only if the taxpayer has owned and occupied the residence for at least two out of the last five years.

Clearly these rules derive not from logic or intuition, but rather from the fact that the U.S. Congress, in accordance with the powers conferred upon it by Article I and the Sixteenth Amendment of the U.S. Constitution, approved legislation defining income in this manner. Nonetheless, we would like to suggest that a general understanding or theory of the term "income" still has considerable legal significance. For example, the Internal Revenue Code defines "gross income" through the (at first glance) inscrutably circular statement that it "means *all income* from whatever source derived" (§ 61(a)) (emphasis added). Moreover, before listing some of the most obvious sources of income (wages, interest, etc.), the statute indicates that the term is "not limited to" the enumerated items. Thus, from the very outset, the statutory language strongly implies that the term "income" has some meaning beyond that which Congress has expressly given it. In addition, both courts and the Internal Revenue Service — in some cases, with explicit statutory encouragement — may regard accurate measurement of "income" as among the principles that should guide interpretive and interstitial decisions when there is no persuasive authority on point. Again, the implication is that the term "income" has some general, common meaning to which we can turn. But what is that meaning? And where does it come from?

Judicial opinions provide some guidance. An early Supreme Court decision, Eisner v. Macomber, 252 U.S. 189, 207 (1920) (infra page 213), drew on contemporary dictionaries to define income as "the gain derived from capital, from labor, or from both combined." As we will see, this is a narrow definition. Among other things, it excludes windfalls, so that a person who works to earn money is taxed on it, while a person who stumbles across the same amount lying in the street would not be. One could criticize this narrowness as producing unfairness (because people with similar ability to pay are not taxed similarly) or inefficiency (because some kinds of gain-producing activities are favored over others). In any event, by 1955 the Supreme Court had developed a much broader understanding of the term, concluding instead that "Congress applied no limitations as to the source of taxable receipts, nor restrictive labels as to their nature" (Commissioner v. Glenshaw Glass, 348 U.S. 426, 429-430 (1955) (infra page 85).

Support for an even broader definition of income can be found in the economics literature. This approach, often called the Haig-Simons definition in honor of two early proponents, provides as follows:

> Personal income may be defined as the algebraic sum of (1) the market value of rights exercised in consumption and (2) the change in the value of the store of property rights between the beginning and the end of the period in question.

H. Simons, Personal Income Taxation 50 (1938).

With its reference to algebra and the market value of rights, this definition sounds at once both precise and capacious. Yet a moment's reflection reveals that the Haig-Simons approach, if fully implemented, would likely encounter some political resistance, as well as some practical problems of implementation. Among other things, it would require taxation of such items as unrealized asset appreciation, imputed income from the ownership of homes and other assets, and the value of government services such as education at a state-supported low-tuition university. Even the value of leisure might be included (although Simons did not take this view), on the ground that its market value is the wage one could have earned. Moreover, the Haig-Simons approach would not countenance the use of the tax system to reward or penalize activities thought by Congress to merit special treatment. In the Internal Haig-Simons Revenue Code, there would be no exemption for interest on state and local bonds and no special exclusion for gain from the sale of a principal residence.

Of course, no one thinks that the Haig-Simons definition either could or should be fully implemented by Congress, although that hardly means that it is irrelevant. Over the history of the U.S. income tax, reformers have advocated moving toward it, usually by championing certain "base-broadening" reforms. Ever present in the design of real-world tax systems, however, are practical concerns of implementation. Administrative considerations are thought to require relying most of the time on observable market transactions, such as the actual sale of an asset, not just its appreciation; or the actual earning of a wage, not just the opportunity to earn a wage. In practice, therefore, even those who favor a Haig-Simons approach concede the importance of workable accounting rules that emphasize observable inflows and outflows of cash and other valuable assets. As a result, key design questions arise at the implementation stage regarding how to account for a given inflow or outflow. Should a particular item be included or deducted at all, rather than ignored? Should inclusion or deduction occur now or later? As is almost always the case in tax, the devil is in the details.

A final point to keep in mind about the definition of income (at least for background interpretive purposes) is that it ought to reflect what we actually want to tax, not just a search for internal logical consistency. If, as discussed in Chapter 1, the reason for having an income tax is that we think income is a valuable proxy for "ability to pay," then perhaps the real question at the heart of all "Is it income?" questions should be, "How does our treatment of a particular item or receipt affect ability to pay?" Does requiring inclusion (or allowing exclusion) of a particular item get us closer to, or move us further away from, a tax system that properly reflects taxpayers' relative ability to pay? How well-off is an individual who did thing X, or to whom thing Y happened, compared to individuals whose circumstances are similar except that they did not share experiences of this kind? Remember that, in the final analysis, designing a tax system is about deciding how to share burdens. So keep in mind that every decision about what is or isn't income is ultimately a decision about who should be treated the same and who should be treated differently.

A. NONCASH BENEFITS

Our investigation of the contours of the term "income" begins in what may seem to be, at least initially, an unlikely place: the income tax treatment of *noncash* benefits. It bears noting that the reason for starting here is not because of the overall significance of noncash benefits to the federal revenue structure. In fact, the vast majority of total U.S. income tax receipts comes from taxes on various types of cash payments, most notably cash salaries and wages. By focusing on noncash benefits, however, we hope to instill in you, at the earliest possible stage, one of the most admirable habits of mind engendered by a sustained interaction with the tax law—namely, the tendency to evaluate transactions on the basis of economic substance rather than form. We have already seen that the Internal Revenue Code, in its definition of "gross income" as "all income from whatever source derived," makes no distinction whatsoever between cash and noncash transactions. Likewise, under long-standing Treasury regulations, "[g]ross income includes income realized in any form, whether in money, property, or services." Regs. § 1.61-1(a). For example, "if services are paid for in property, the fair market value of the property taken in payment must be included in income as compensation." Regs. § 1.61-2(d)(1). Thus, what matters is not the form that one's income takes but rather the fact that the taxpayer has received an economic benefit.

Some may find these rules troubling. After all, payment of taxes must be made in cash, check, money order, or by other "commercially acceptable means" (such as electronic funds transfers) deemed appropriate by the Internal Revenue Service. § 6311(a). However, one can easily appreciate the need to include noncash benefits in income if the outcomes under a contrary rule are imagined. Although not all taxpayers could readily barter work for noncash benefits, many could—for example, a lawyer might draft a will for a carpenter in exchange for work on her home, or the employees of a supermarket might accept part of their pay in groceries. To the extent that some people could take advantage of such arrangements more freely than others, tax burdens to some degree would, at least initially, fall in a haphazard manner, depending on the practicality of compensation in kind in a particular kind of activity. That might reduce fairness. As people responded by moving to tax-favored jobs, the wages in such jobs would tend to fall. Industries providing such jobs would, for no good reason, tend to benefit as compared with industries that did not. That might reduce efficiency. Moreover, people would be encouraged to take compensation in the form of goods and services instead of taking it in cash and spending the cash on goods and services that they might value more highly; again, that might reduce efficiency—it would be wasteful.

On the other hand, taxing noncash benefits raises problems of administrative feasibility or practicality. Often it is difficult to know whether a noncash benefit (e.g., life insurance or free air travel) has any significant value to the taxpayer and, if so, how much. Sometimes it may be best, for reasons of practicality, to wait until some later time to impose the tax (e.g., where the benefit consists of an item of property that will not be sold until some time in the future and whose present value is uncertain). Sometimes it may be difficult to separate the business from the personal aspects of such noncash benefits as the use of a well-furnished office or a company limousine.

The cases and other materials that follow in this section reveal how the law has reacted to the competing dictates of fairness, efficiency, and practicality. One background factor must be kept in mind: Use of noncash benefits may make enforcement difficult. The amounts involved tend to be modest; the Service (IRS) has bigger fish to fry. Cheating is often difficult to detect. Taxpayers begin to realize that they can get away with certain kinds of cheating—for example, with not reporting the value of the personal use of a company car. They may rely on that disturbing but common defense, "everyone is doing it." The Service must ever be alert to the dangers inherent in enforcement policies that tend to encourage such attitudes, not so much because the amounts may grow over time (if they do, the Service can crack down), but because of adverse effects on general taxpayer morale and because, after a sufficiently long period of nonenforcement, taxpayers may begin to rely on, and to feel that they are entitled to continue to enjoy, the tax benefits they have claimed; and Congress may agree. One should always be careful, however, to distinguish between cheating that one can get away with (and that the Service knows people are getting away with) and permissible conduct. Tax cheating may not be a mortal sin. It's certainly not as serious a moral transgression as murder or robbery. But it is cheating; it is contrary to law; and it does mean that the cheaters shift their legally mandated share of the total burden to honest taxpayers.

1. Meals and Lodging Provided to Employees

Suppose that, for federal income tax purposes, a worker's gross income from a job consisted solely of the amount of all paychecks received during the year. Employers and workers would find that they could generate substantial tax savings by changing the form of their transactions, without making any change (the use of the tax savings aside) in how much the employer paid or what the employee got.

Example 1

Alice is a computer programmer who works for Unitek. Ignoring tax planning considerations, Unitek would pay her a salary of $5,000 per month ($60,000 per year). Every month she would spend $1,000 of this amount on rent.

Suppose (counterfactually) that Alice's gross income under § 61 from working for Unitek included only the amount of her paycheck. Alice and Unitek could agree that it would directly pay her only $4,000 per month, but that it would also pay her rent. It would still be paying $5,000 per month, and she would still have $4,000 per month left before tax after payment of her rent. Thus, in a sense nothing would have changed. Yet her income for tax purposes would have declined by $1,000 per month, or $12,000 per year.

Assuming a marginal tax rate of 28 percent, she would potentially have reduced her annual federal income tax liability by $3,360.

If this worked, perhaps the next step would be for Unitek to reduce Alice's paycheck still more, substituting payments to grocery stores, restaurants, dry cleaners, health clubs, and the like that she patronizes, to be credited to her account in these establishments. Suppose Unitek and Alice could work out a way to convert an additional $2,500 per month of her compensation into this indirect form, without any change in her patronage of these establishments. Thus, her paycheck would be down to $1,500 per month ($18,000 per year). She would be taxed like someone who was really making that amount annually, rather than like someone who was really making the same $60,000 but had not structured the cash flows as cleverly.

NOTES AND QUESTIONS

1. Why would Unitek agree to such a deal? Might Alice and Unitek end up splitting the tax savings? What would this involve?

2. If Unitek pays Alice's rent of $1,000 per month, do we have any evidence that the value of the apartment to Alice is at least equal to the amount that Unitek pays? Tax considerations aside, what should Alice and Unitek do if the apartment is not worth that much to her?

3. To allow Alice's rent to be excluded from her income when Unitek pays it has the same effect as permitting her a deduction if she pays it. Thus, suppose that rent were deductible from income. Alice's income would be the same, $4,000, whether (a) Unitek directly paid her $5,000, and she paid and deducted $1,000 of rent; or (b) Unitek paid $4,000 to her and $1,000 to the landlord, and she were permitted to exclude the latter amount.

4. Why doesn't it make sense to let Alice and Unitek reduce her income tax liability through these arrangements?

5. Under longstanding income tax law, Alice would in fact have income in the amount of Unitek's rental (and other) payments on her behalf. The leading case is Old Colony Trust Co. v. Commissioner, 279 U.S. 716, 729 (1929), holding that an employer's payment of federal income taxes on behalf of its employee constituted income to the employee. The Court found it "immaterial that the taxes were directly paid over [by the employer] to the Government. The discharge by a third person of an obligation to him is equivalent to receipt by the person taxed." This case preceded the adoption of federal income tax withholding. Due to withholding, it is now routine for the employer to make federal (along with state and local) income tax payments on the employee's behalf, and yet for these payments to be included in the employee's gross income.

Example 2

Unitek also makes a single $10,000 payment to an insurance company that accepts in return the obligation, when Alice reaches the age of 70, to pay her

$50,000. Her legal rights to this money are fully vested. That is, she will get it at age 70 even if Unitek fires her or goes bankrupt in the interim. She is not entitled to receive any cash payment until she reaches age 70. If she dies before reaching this age, her estate or heirs become entitled to the money on the date when she would have reached age 70. As it turns out, Alice lives to age 70 and receives the $50,000 payout from the insurance company.

QUESTIONS

1. Under *Old Colony*, the Internal Revenue Service argues that Alice has $10,000 of taxable income in the year Unitek paid that amount to the insurance company. In the absence of specific statutory rules concerning retirement benefits, are the issues here identical to those presented by Example 1?

2. What should be Alice's taxable income upon receiving the $50,000 distribution if the $10,000 employer contribution was included in her income? If it was not?

3. If Alice's overall taxable income from this transaction is $50,000 whether or not she includes $10,000 up front, does it make any difference whether this early inclusion is required? Why or why not?

4. Each year, as Alice grows older, the value of her right to receive the $50,000 increases. How, if at all, should this economic gain be reflected on her annual income tax returns?

Example 3

Same as Example 1, except that Unitek happens to be Alice's landlord. Thus, it provides her with in-kind compensation (the free use of an apartment that rents for $1,000 per month) instead of indirect compensation from paying a third-party landlord. The apartment's rental value is known, despite the lack of an observed payment for it, because a dozen identical apartments on the same floor rent for $1,000 per month to tenants who do not work for Unitek. In addition, living in the apartment has no effect on Alice's ability to provide services to Unitek.

NOTES AND QUESTIONS

1. Is Example 3 relevantly different than Example 1? Note that, if the rental value in Example 3 is not taxed, Alice and Unitek may be able in Example 1 to evade *Old Colony* by having Unitek go into the rental housing business (along, perhaps, with the grocery and dry cleaning businesses, among others). How significant is this concern?

2. The *Old Colony* principle of including indirect and in-kind benefits is potentially quite broad. It can suggest that, absent specific statutory provision to the contrary, a worker's income includes not only her paycheck but the value of any and all benefits that the employer provides by any means. This principle has no obvious built-in limit. Might it require including in income

the value to Alice of a nice corner office with a window? A prestigious title? A short commute? A meal with a client in a fancy restaurant?

3. One important point about Example 3 was that it did not involve a valuation problem. The free apartment's rental value of $1,000 per month was assumed to be known. In practice, however, as we will see beginning with the *Benaglia* case right below, in-kind benefits often present severe valuation problems. It can be hard to tell how much an item is worth in cash to the recipient. In considering such problems, one should keep in mind the question: How ought the tax system respond to such uncertainty in general? By avoiding overvaluation (and thus overtaxation of the recipient) at all costs? By attempting "rough justice" under the premise that overvaluation and undervaluation (with resulting undertaxation of the recipient) are equally regrettable?

BENAGLIA v. COMMISSIONER
36 B.T.A. 838 (1937), acq. 1940-1 C.B. 1

FINDINGS OF FACT

The petitioners are husband and wife, residing in Honolulu, Hawaii, where they filed joint income tax returns for 1933 and 1934.

The petitioner has, since 1926 and including the tax years in question, been employed as the manager in full charge of the several hotels in Honolulu owned and operated by Hawaiian Hotels, Ltd., a corporation of Hawaii, consisting of the Royal Hawaiian, the Moana and bungalows, and the Waialae Golf Club. These are large resort hotels, operating on the American plan. Petitioner was constantly on duty, and, for the proper performance of his duties and entirely for the convenience of his employer, he and his wife occupied a suite of rooms in the Royal Hawaiian Hotel and received their meals at and from the hotel.

Petitioner's salary has varied in different years, being in one year $25,000. In 1933 it was $9,625, and in 1934 it was $11,041.67. These amounts were fixed without reference to his meals and lodging, and neither petitioner nor his employer ever regarded the meals and lodging as part of his compensation or accounted for them.

OPINION

STERNHAGEN, J.

The Commissioner has added $7,845 each year to the petitioner's gross income as "compensation received from Hawaiian Hotels, Ltd.," holding that this is "the fair market value of rooms and meals furnished by the employer." In the deficiency notice he cites article 52 [53], Regulations 77,[1] and holds

---

1. ["Where services are paid for with something other than money, the fair market value of the thing taken in payment is the amount to be included as income. . . . When living quarters such as camps are furnished to employees for the convenience of the employer, the ratable value need not be

inapplicable Jones v. United States, 60 Ct. Cls. 552; I.T. 2232; G.C.M. 14710; and G.C.M. 14836. The deficiency notice seems to hold that the rooms and meals were not in fact supplied "merely as a convenience to the hotels" of the employer.

From the evidence, there remains no room for doubt that the petitioner's residence at the hotel was not by way of compensation for his services, not for his personal convenience, comfort or pleasure, but solely because he could not otherwise perform the services required of him. The evidence of both the employer and employee shows in detail what petitioner's duties were and why his residence in the hotel was necessary. His duty was continuous and required his presence at a moment's call. He had a lifelong experience in hotel management and operation in the United States, Canada, and elsewhere, and testified that the functions of the manager could not have been performed by one living outside the hotel, especially a resort hotel such as this. The demands and requirements of guests are numerous, various, and unpredictable, and affect the meals, the rooms, the entertainment, and everything else about the hotel. The manager must be alert to all these things day and night. He would not consider undertaking the job and the owners of the hotel would not consider employing a manager unless he lived there. This was implicit throughout his employment and when his compensation was changed from time to time no mention was ever made of it. Both took it for granted. The corporation's books carried no accounting for the petitioner's meals, rooms, or service.

Under such circumstances, the value of meals and lodging is not income to the employee, even though it may relieve him of an expense which he would otherwise bear. In Jones v. United States, supra, the subject was fully considered in determining that neither the value of quarters nor the amount received as commutation of quarters by an Army officer is included within his taxable income. There is also a full discussion in the English case of Tennant v. Smith, H.L. (1892) App. Cas. 150, III British Tax Cases 158. A bank employee was required to live in quarters located in the bank building, and it was held that the value of such lodging was not taxable income. The advantage to him was merely an incident of the performance of his duty, but its character for tax purposes was controlled by the dominant fact that the occupation of the premises was imposed upon him for the convenience of the employer. The Bureau of Internal Revenue has almost consistently applied the same doctrine in its published rulings.

The three cases cited by the respondent, Ralph Kitchen, 11 B.T.A. 855; Charles A. Frueauff, 30 B.T.A. 449; and Fontaine Fox, 30 B.T.A. 451, are distinguishable entirely upon the ground that what the taxpayer received was not shown to be primarily for the need or convenience of the employer. Of course, as in the *Kitchen* case, it can not be said as a categorical proposition of law that, where an employee is fed and lodged by his employer, no part of the value of such perquisite is income. If the Commissioner finds that it was received as

---

added to the cash compensation of the employees, but where a person receives as compensation for services rendered a salary and in addition thereto living quarters, the value to such person of the quarters furnished constitutes income subject to tax." — EDS.]

compensation and holds it to be taxable income, the taxpayer contesting this before the Board must prove by evidence that it is not income. In the *Kitchen* case the Board held that the evidence did not establish that the food and lodging were given for the convenience of the employer. In the present case the evidence clearly establishes that fact, and it has been so found.

The determination of the Commissioner on the point in issue is reversed.

Reviewed by the Board.

Judgment will be entered under Rule 50.

MURDOCK, J., concurs only in the result.

ARNOLD, J., dissenting.

I disagree with the conclusions of fact that the suite of rooms and meals furnished petitioner and his wife at the Royal Hawaiian Hotel were entirely for the convenience of the employer and that the cash salary was fixed without reference thereto and was never regarded as part of his compensation.

Petitioner was employed by a hotel corporation operating two resort hotels in Honolulu — the Royal Hawaiian, containing 357 guest bed rooms, and the Moana, containing 261 guest bed rooms, and the bungalows and cottages in connection with the Moana containing 127 guest bed rooms, and the Waialae Golf Club. His employment was as general manager of both hotels and the golf club.

His original employment was in 1925, and in accepting the employment he wrote a letter to the party representing the employer, with whom he conducted the negotiations for employment, under date of September 10, 1925, in which he says:

> Confirming our meeting here today, it is understood that I will assume the position of general manager of both the Royal Waikiki Beach Hotel (now under construction) and the Moana Hotel in Honolulu, at a yearly salary of $10,000.00, payable monthly, together with living quarters, meals, etc., for myself and wife. In addition I am to receive $20.00 per day while travelling, this however, not to include any railroad or steamship fares, and I [am] to submit vouchers monthly covering all such expenses.

While the cash salary was adjusted from time to time by agreement of the parties, depending on the amount of business done, it appears that the question of living quarters, meals, etc., was not given further consideration and was not thereafter changed. Petitioner and his wife have always occupied living quarters in the Royal Hawaiian Hotel and received their meals from the time he first accepted the employment down through the years before us. His wife performed no services for the hotel company.

This letter, in my opinion, constitutes the basic contract of employment and clearly shows that the living quarters, meals, etc., furnished petitioner and his wife were understood and intended to be compensation in addition to the cash salary paid him. Being compensation to petitioner in addition to the cash salary paid him, it follows that the reasonable value thereof to petitioner is taxable income. Cf. Ralph Kitchen, 11 B.T.A. 855; Charles A. Frueauff, 30 B.T.A. 449.

Conceding that petitioner was required to live at the hotel and that his living there was solely for the convenience of the employer, it does not follow that he was not benefited thereby to the extent of what such accommodations were reasonably worth to him. His employment was a matter of private contract. He was careful to specify in his letter accepting the employment that he was to be furnished with living quarters, meals, etc., for himself and wife, together with the cash salary, as compensation for his employment. Living quarters and meals are necessities which he would otherwise have had to procure at his own expense. His contract of employment relieved him to that extent. He has been enriched to the extent of what they are reasonably worth.

The majority opinion is based on the finding that petitioner's residence at the hotel was solely for the convenience of the employer and, therefore, not income. While it is no doubt convenient to have the manager reside in the hotel, I do not think the question here is one of convenience or of benefit to the employer. What the tax law is concerned with is whether or not petitioner was financially benefited by having living quarters furnished to himself and wife. He may have preferred to live elsewhere, but we are dealing with the financial aspect of petitioner's relation to his employer, not his preference. He says it would cost him $3,600 per year to live elsewhere.

It would seem that if his occupancy of quarters at the Royal Hawaiian was necessary and solely for the benefit of the employer, occupancy of premises at the Moana would be just as essential so far as the management of the Moana was concerned. He did not have living quarters or meals for himself and wife at the Moana and he was general manager of both and both were in operation during the years before us. Furthermore, it appears that petitioner was absent from Honolulu from March 24 to June 8 and from August 19 to November 2 in 1933, and from April 8 to May 24 and from September 3 to November 1 in 1934—about 5 months in 1933 and 3½ months in 1934. Whether he was away on official business or not we do not know. During his absence both hotels continued in operation. The $20 per day travel allowance in his letter of acceptance indicates his duties were not confined to managing the hotels in Honolulu, and the entire letter indicates he was to receive maintenance, whether in Honolulu or elsewhere, in addition to his cash salary.

At most the arrangement as to living quarters and meals was of mutual benefit, and to the extent it benefited petitioner it was compensation in addition to his cash salary, and taxable to him as income.

The Court of Claims in the case of Jones v. United States, relied on in the majority opinion, was dealing with a governmental organization regulated by military law where the compensation was fixed by law and not subject to private contract. The English case of Tennant v. Smith, involved the employment of a watchman or custodian for a bank whose presence at the bank was at all times a matter of necessity demanded by the employer as a condition of the employment.

The facts in both these cases are so at variance with the facts in this case that they are not controlling in my opinion.

SMITH, TURNER, and HARRON agree with this dissent.

NOTES AND QUESTIONS

1. Why should it matter whether the reason for giving Benaglia free room and board was the "convenience of the employer"? Wasn't paying him a cash salary also convenient for the employer, since otherwise he would have declined to take the job? Should the court have focused on the value to Benaglia of the free room and board?

2. How does the "convenience of the employer" claim undermine the government's position that the room and board were worth their market price of $7,845? Does it support arguing that the free room and board had zero value to Benaglia?

3. Judge Arnold's dissent notes that Benaglia "says it would cost him $3,600 per year to live elsewhere." Would this provide a good measure of the value of the room and board in this case? In future cases? What about the cost to the employer (including opportunity costs if other paying customers were turned away?) of providing the meals and lodging to Benaglia? What if there had been credible evidence either that Benaglia disliked hotel accommodations notwithstanding his choice of career or that he had written a letter to the employer during the wage negotiations in which he offered to find housing within a few blocks of the hotel if his salary were increased by $5,000?

4. Even if one agreed that Benaglia's free room and board should be excluded from income, what about that provided to his wife? Since there is no claim that she was providing hotel management services, should some amount have been included in the Benaglias' income for the benefits to her?

STATUTORY AFTERMATH TO BENAGLIA

Section 119, enacted in 1954, ended the common law realm of "convenience of the employer" cases such as *Benaglia* by adopting a specific version of their general approach. You can see this by reading § 119(a), which states a general rule quite close to the outcome in *Benaglia* (although not resting on the parties' intent). The rest of § 119 provides additional detail, including an array of special rules for particular taxpayers, such as employees of educational institutions (§ 119(d)).

While § 119(a) may look simple on its face, it stands as a good example of how a seemingly minor provision, in terms of revenue and general applicability, can foster an inordinate amount of judicial interpretation and administrative complexity, not to mention repeated congressional intervention. (It has been amended four times since the beginning of 1978.) A key part of the problem is that even, or perhaps especially, a simple English word such as "meal" or "employee" can be ambiguous in practice. Here are some of the terms in § 119(a) that a good tax lawyer might immediately spot as potentially ambiguous, followed by a brief account of their litigation history:

(a) *"Meals."* While this term may initially appear unambiguous, what about groceries that the employee selects in the employer's commissary and takes home? Tougher v. Commissioner, 51 T.C. 737 (1969), aff'd per curiam, 441 F.2d 1148 (9th Cir.), cert. denied, 404 U.S. 856 (1971), held that groceries were not within the term "meals." On the other hand, Jacob v. United States, 493 F.2d 1294 (3d Cir. 1974), held that groceries were within the meals exclusion, and also held toilet tissue, soap, and other nonfood items to be excludable under § 119 as an integral part of meals and lodging.

(b) *"Furnished."* Is a meal "furnished" by the employer if the employer provides cash to purchase it rather than directly (i.e., through the use of its employees) supplying the food? In Commissioner v. Kowalski, 434 U.S. 77 (1977), the Court, resolving a conflict among the circuits, held that meal allowance payments to state highway patrol troopers were not excludable under § 119 due to failure to satisfy the "furnished" requirement. Thus, in effect, to meet the terms of the statute, the state would need to open its own version of McDonald's or Pizza Hut at various convenient points along the highway, rather than relying on the private sector to supply its troopers with fast food.

One might have supposed that *Kowalski* would have settled the controversy over cash versus in-kind benefits. In Sibla v. Commissioner, 611 F.2d 1260 (9th Cir. 1980), however, the court allowed a fireman to exclude from his income the amounts he paid (about $3 a day) to participate in an obligatory organized mess at the station house. The court distinguished *Kowalski* on the ground that in that case the taxpayer received cash that he was free to spend wherever he wished or not to spend at all. The court conceded that its language was inconsistent with the "language" of *Kowalski* (more precisely, its expressed rationale), but argued that the Supreme Court could not have meant what it said, only what it held.

Inconsistent treatment of this less than scintillating issue has since continued. See, e.g., Ron Phillips v. Commissioner, T.C. Mem. 1986-503 (holding costs of firefighters' meals nondeductible where the firefighters' union, rather than the employer as in *Sibla*, organized the mess); Christey v. United States, 841 F.2d 809 (8th Cir. 1988) (upholding, as not clearly erroneous, a district court finding that state troopers' meal expenses under *Kowalski*-like circumstances of limited choice were "ordinary and necessary" business expenses under 162(a)).

(c) *"Convenience of the employer."* This term presumably refers to business reasons other than tax advantages for having the employee accept free or below-cost meals and lodging. The difficulty lies in determining how strong the nontax motives must be and how they are to be demonstrated. Section 119(b)(1) sheds some light by stating that "the provisions of an employment contract . . . shall not be taken as determinative of whether the meals or lodging are intended as compensation." Thus, one cannot satisfy the standard simply by adding a contract clause that says, in effect, "Take this free room and board, please," although such a clause may still be legally relevant. In practice, the requisite employer's convenience is most often established by proof that the employee is "on call" outside of business hours. See Rev. Rul. 71-411, 71-2 C.B. 103.

(d) *"Business premises of the employer."* The circuits have split on what constitutes "business premises of the employer" for state police. United States v. Barrett, 321 F.2d 911 (5th Cir. 1963), held that every state road and highway, and evidently adjacent restaurants as well, constitute the business premises of their employer, the state. Accord: United States v. Keeton, 383 F.2d 429 (10th

Cir. 1967); United States v. Morelan, 356 F.2d 199 (8th Cir. 1966). Contra: Wilson v. United States, 412 F.2d 694 (1st Cir. 1969). In *Kowalski*, supra, the Supreme Court did not reach the "business premises" issue because it was able to dispose of the case on the basis of the "furnished" language.

In Lindeman v. Commissioner, 60 T.C. 609 (1973), acq., the business premises of a beachfront hotel were held to include a house across the street from it occupied by the hotel's manager and his family. But in Commissioner v. Anderson, 371 F.2d 59 (6th Cir. 1966), cert. denied, 387 U.S. 906 (1967), a house that was two blocks away from the employer's motel and was occupied by its manager was held not to be part of the employer's business premises. Official residences of the governors of the states, and presumably the White House, also qualify under § 119. Rev. Rul. 75-540, 1975-2 C.B. 53. Taking the idea a step further, the Court of Claims permitted exclusion for the "White House" of the U.S. Jaycees (U.S. Junior Chamber of Commerce v. United States, 334 F.2d 660 (1964)) and the Tokyo residence of the president of a Japanese subsidiary of Mobil Oil (Adams v. United States, 585 F.2d 1060 (1977)).

(e) *"Employee."* Section 119's exclusion is for "an employee," which rules out self-employed persons such as farmers who own and operate their own farms, or those who are classified as independent contractors (such as a lawyer who does work for various clients). But a person may be treated as the employee of a corporation even if she or he owns all the shares of that corporation, and thus in a practical (as opposed to a legal) sense appears to be self-employed. And since corporations are themselves taxpayers, they can potentially deduct the costs of providing meals and lodging to owner-employees who receive these benefits tax-free.

In J. Grant Farms, Inc. v. Commissioner, 49 T.C.M. 1197 (1985), Mr. Grant had since 1949 owned and operated a farm. In 1976 he formed a corporation, all of whose shares were owned by himself and his wife. Mr. Grant transferred or leased to the corporation all of the assets used in the farming business and the corporation formally became the operator of the farm. The corporation hired Mr. Grant as its employee in the role of manager of the farm, and he continued to manage and operate the farm as he had been doing in the past. One of the assets transferred to the corporation was the house in which the Grants and their children lived; the house thus became a business asset of the corporation instead of a personal asset of the Grants. The corporation (remember, it was owned and controlled by the Grants) required Mr. Grant to live in the house as a condition of his employment, and the Tax Court found that there were sound business reasons for this requirement. Accordingly, the corporation was allowed deductions for depreciation and utility costs for the house (which had not previously been allowable to anyone), and Mr. Grant was not required to include any amount in his gross income by virtue of its use by himself and his family.

2. Other Fringe Benefit Statutes

Meals and lodging are only two examples of fringe benefits, or noncash benefits that are provided at no charge, or at a below-market price, by an employer to an employee. Among the most important of such benefits are life insurance, medical insurance and payments, discounts on merchandise, parking, company cars, airline travel, club memberships, and tuition remissions. In many cases these benefits are a substitute for cash; they relieve employees of expenses they would otherwise incur and are intended as compensation. Yet often they have not been taxed, which explains in part why it is that over the years they became an increasingly important part of employee compensation. Fringe benefits raise problems of valuation, of enforcement, and of political acceptance.

The problems of valuation are similar to those we have already examined in this chapter. The value of a particular benefit to the person receiving it may depend on the circumstances of that person. Consider, for example, airline employees who are permitted to fly free, or at reduced cost, on their employers' flights. Is it fair to include in income the amount that ordinary passengers would be required to pay for the same flight? Even if employees are required to fly on a standby basis? Or what about life insurance supplied to a single person with no dependents? Or a government-owned limousine that drives the Commissioner of Internal Revenue from home to the office in the morning, to meetings around town during the day, and back home at night? Is it relevant that the limousine has a reading lamp and a telephone?

Problems of enforcement are associated with the fact that the individual items are often small and the information on which the tax outcome depends is easy to falsify. For example, suppose an employer supplies an employee with the free use of a car. The employee is supposed to include in income the value of his or her personal use of the car. Until recently, many employees simply ignored the matter; they reported no income at all. Others relied on unrealistic claims that their personal use was a small part of the total use. The Service, understandably concerned about deployment of limited resources, was lax in enforcement. As word of this reality got around, abuse increased. Ultimately it became clear that some action was required. Revenue was being lost. Perhaps more important was the effect on the morale of taxpayers who were compensated in cash and paid for their cars out of after-tax dollars and even on the morale of those who were cheating (on the "don't be dumb, everyone's doing it" theory) but felt uncomfortable about it. But there was resistance to change: No matter how unjustified a tax break may be, if people have relied on it for long enough they will resent giving it up and, if asked to do so, will complain to their representatives in Congress about how they are being unjustly treated, about the adverse economic effects of the proposed change and, in general, about how nobody respects or appreciates them. This is the problem of political acceptance.

Through the years, some fringe benefits were excluded as a result of the Service's inaction (e.g., parking supplied or paid for by an employer and air travel by airline employees) or acquiescence (e.g., tuition remission). Others were excluded by express statutory provisions, including $50,000 worth of group term life insurance (§ 79), medical insurance and payments (§§ 105(b), 106), and dependent care assistance (§ 129). Finally, in 1984 Congress enacted § 132, providing comprehensive coverage of fringe benefits. We next discuss certain statutory exclusions, followed by the state of the law where no such exclusion applies.

SECTION 132 FRINGE BENEFITS

The basic approach taken in § 132 was to offer taxpayers and the Internal Revenue Service a "ceasefire in place": statutory exclusion for well-established taxpayer practices (or those supported by significant political clout), in exchange for forestalling further expansion of such practices. To the latter end, § 61(a)(1), specifying that gross income includes compensation for services, was amended to include a specific mention of fringe benefits. The main fringe benefits that § 132 presently makes excludable are:

(1) "no-additional cost services," such as free seating for airline employees on flights that would not otherwise have sold out (§ 132(b));

(2) "qualified employee discounts," such as when a department store permits its employees to purchase at a modest discount items that are sold to customers (§ 132(c));

(3) "working condition fringes," such as the business use of a company car, or a free subscription to a magazine that relates to the employee's job (e.g., where a brokerage house buys a financial publication for its brokers) (§ 132(d));

(4) "de minimis fringes," or those of sufficiently low value to make accounting for them "unreasonable or administratively impractical" (§ 132(e)(1)). A special rule extends the reach of this provision to certain eating facilities (§ 132(e)(2)), without regard to whether they would otherwise qualify;

(5) "qualified transportation fringes," such as employer-provided parking or mass transit passes (§ 132(f));

(6) "qualified moving expense reimbursement" (§ 132(g));

(7) "qualified retirement planning services" (§ 132(m)); and

(8) certain "on-premises gyms and other athletic facilities" (§ 132(j)(4)).

No-additional cost services and qualified employee discounts, but not the other items on this list, are subject to two further restrictions. First, in order to claim either exclusion, one must work in a line of business of the employer in which the item at issue is ordinarily offered for sale to customers (§§ 132(b)(1) and (c)(4)). Thus, if the same corporation operated both an airline and a department store, airline workers would be taxed on receiving discount department store goods, and department store workers would be taxed on receiving free airline flights. Second, neither of these two exclusions applies to "highly compensated employees" if the employer discriminates in favor of such employees in determining to whom a given fringe benefit is available (§ 132(j)(1)).

"No additional cost services" and "qualified employee discounts," as well as "qualified tuition reduction" (§ 117(d)), may be provided tax free to an employee's spouse, surviving spouse, or dependent children (§ 132(h)) but not to others such as same-sex domestic partners. See Private Letter Ruling 200137041.

QUESTIONS

1. Suppose that an airline offers free seating to its employees on a standby basis (i.e., only for seats that are not sold as of boarding time), qualifying for

exclusion as a no-additional-cost service. Can the exclusion be defended on the ground that, if the employees were taxed on the value of the seating, they would simply decline to go, leading to pointless waste as the seats stayed vacant and the Commissioner got no revenue from attempting to impose a tax? Or is the point simply that overvaluation, like undervaluation, can result in mismeasuring ability to pay and/or distorting economic decisions?

2. Why limit tax-free no-additional-cost services and qualified employee discounts to employees in the line of business of the employer in which the item at issue is ordinarily offered for sale to customers?

3. Why deny the exclusion for a no-additional-cost service or a qualified employee discount to highly compensated employees when the employer discriminates in favor of such employees in determining to whom the item is available? Even if the employer disdains its rank-and-file employees, is its self-interest served by offering them these benefits if excludable?

4. Review the various subsections of § 132 that include "special rules" for air transportation (e.g., § 132(h)(3), § 132(j)(5)). Can you think of any principled reason why the exclusion of a no-additional-cost service should extend to the parents of employees in the airline industry (§ 132(h)(3)) but not to the parents of those employed in other industries? Although the Internal Revenue Code is a highly technical compendium of rules, it is important to keep in mind that it is, at bottom, a political document. When reviewing this and other provisions of the tax code, be on the lookout for "special rules" like these. If you do a little independent digging, you will find that each one has its own unique political history. But before joining the chorus of critics who decry the extension of special interest favors for the well-connected, ask yourself whether some other provision that you like would have been enacted without the political "grease" furnished by these "special rules." Then decide — are you a tax code purist or a political realist? Can you be both?

COMPARATIVE FOCUS:
The Australian Fringe Benefits Tax

Every tax system that attempts to tax wage income must contend with the nettlesome problem of employer-provided fringe benefits. As noted in the text above, failing to tax these benefits creates problems of fairness and efficiency, but taxing them raises several practical administrative problems with respect to valuation and record-keeping. There is no perfect solution.

In 1986, the Commonwealth of Australia enacted the "Fringe Benefits Tax Assessment Act" in an effort to address these concerns. The Act imposes a tax of 46.5 percent on all "reportable fringe benefits." The Australian Tax Office describes a fringe benefit to which the tax applies as "a benefit provided in respect of employment," including situations such as when an employer:

- allows an employee to use a work car for private purposes,
- gives an employee a cheap loan,

- pays an employee's gym membership,
- provides entertainment by way of free tickets to concerts, or
- pays an employee's green fees at golf days.

Economically, there should be little difference between a fringe benefits tax that is imposed on employers versus one that is imposed on employees, assuming that the base is defined in the same manner. As a political matter, however, it may be easier to secure approval for a tax on employers. Moreover, to the extent that tax rates vary between employers and employees, the total amount of revenue (as well as the overall effect on wage levels) may also vary. This appears to be the case with respect to the Australian tax. Those interested in learning more about the Australian Fringe Benefits Tax may wish to review the comprehensive guide available on the website of the Australian Tax Office.

FURTHER NOTES ON FRINGE BENEFITS

1. *Valuation: the regulations.* The Treasury has published detailed regulations on fringe benefits. Regs. § 1.61-21 and § 1.132-1 to -8. These regulations include rules for valuation of certain fringe benefits, most significantly the personal use of employer-provided aircraft and automobiles. The basic valuation rule is that the amount to be included is "fair market value." Regs. § 1.61-21(b). Special optional "safe-harbor" valuation formulas are provided, however, for aircraft and automobiles, and it can be expected that most employers and employees will use these formulas. For automobiles there is a table that provides an "annual lease value" based on the value of the automobile. Regs. § 1.61-21. There is a special rule for situations in which the personal use of the automobile is commuting and "for bona fide non-compensatory reasons, the employer requires the employee to commute to and/or from work in the vehicle" (e.g., so that the vehicle can be used on emergency calls at night or to keep the vehicle safe from thieves and vandals). In this situation, the value is treated as $3 per round trip. Regs. § 1.61-21(f). For aircraft, the formula consists of the Standard Industry Fare Level (SIFL), plus a terminal charge, multiplied by a factor based on the weight of the aircraft. Regs. § 1.61-21(g). The regulations respond to the particular circumstances of a variety of employment situations and contain myriad special rules for those circumstances. While the rules are lengthy and detailed, individual employers and employees will generally be able to focus on the relatively few rules relevant to them. A reading of the regulations will provide a good sense of the interplay between the need to impose fair tax burdens and prevent tax avoidance and the need to have common-sense, workable rules.

2. *Cafeteria plans.* A "cafeteria plan" is a plan under which an employee may choose among a variety of noncash nontaxable benefits or may choose to take cash (which is, of course, taxable). In other words, an employee may

in effect elect to reduce his or her taxable salary and take noncash benefits instead. This makes it possible for an employer to provide nontaxable fringe benefits to those employees who want them without disfavoring employees who have no need for them. For example, suppose an employer has two employees, each earning $35,000 a year. One employee has children and pays $5,000 a year to babysitters while he is at work. The other employee has no children. Under a cafeteria plan, the employer can allow the employee with children to take his compensation in the form of $30,000 worth of taxable salary and $5,000 worth of child-care payments (nontaxable under § 129). Meanwhile, the other employee can elect to take the entire $35,000 in salary; all of this is taxable, but he is no worse off than he would be if there were no cafeteria plan. The employer is allowed to deduct the full $35,000 for each employee.

Section 125 expressly authorizes cafeteria plans. Were it not for that provision, the doctrine of constructive receipt would result in an employee being taxed on the cash that he or she could have taken, even if a nontaxable benefit were chosen instead. In other words, without § 125, cafeteria plans in which there was an option to take cash would not be tax effective. (It would still be possible to have plans under which the only alternatives were various nontaxable fringe benefits.) Section 125 greatly increases the potential use of nontaxable fringe benefits by removing the element of employee envy that would restrain an employer from offering fringe benefits for which some employees have no use.

Section 125 limits the fringe benefits that can be included in a cafeteria plan and imposes a nondiscrimination rule. The permissible benefits include group-term life insurance (up to $50,000) (§ 79), dependent care assistance (§ 129), adoption assistance (§ 137), excludable accident and health benefits (§ 105 and § 106(a)), and elective contributions under a qualified cash or deferred arrangement under § 401(k).

One interesting and important aspect of cafeteria plans is the so-called use-it-or-lose-it rule. See § 125(d)(2)(A) and Proposed Regs. § 1.125-1. Under this rule, if, for example, an employee elects at the beginning of the year to take $5,000 worth of child-care reimbursement instead of the same amount of cash compensation or other benefits, any part of the $5,000 not used for child care will be lost to the employee. The unused portion cannot at the end of the year be paid out to the employee as additional taxable compensation or carried forward to the next year. There is an exception allowing a change in election of benefits or cash during the year on account of, and consistent with, a change in family status (e.g., marriage, divorce, or death of a child). The rationale offered by the Treasury in support of the use-it-or-lose-it rule is that nontaxable benefits under cafeteria plans are supposed to be in the nature of insurance. Why so? There is some evidence in testimony by Treasury officials before Congress of concern about the substantial loss of revenue associated with increasing use of cafeteria plans.

The use-it-or-lose-it rule presents a good example of how the income tax laws often try to limit the extent to which taxpayers can take advantage of favorable planning opportunities. The rule imposes burdens on taxpayers that in some respects seem pointless and wasteful. In order to get the maximum benefit from the exclusion, employees must engage up front in relatively precise forecasting and planning of their expected expenses. If they aim too high, they risk losing some of their salary for the year. Or, they may end up purchasing medical or other covered services at year's end that they do not really need or value very highly. Health care providers, among others, have found that § 125 is great for business in December!

The use of § 125 therefore bears a practical price that will tend to reduce the extent to which employees utilize it, thus reducing its revenue cost. However, if its revenue cost needs to be limited, why not simply lower the dollar ceilings without imposing indirect burdens of this sort? Thus, taxpayers, with or without limitation to employees whose employers offered qualifying plans, might simply be permitted to deduct, up to a stipulated dollar ceiling, all amounts spent for child care and the other benefits available under cafeteria plans. Is there any good argument against such a change in the law? Why isn't it done this way?

3. *Frequent flyer credits.* Most airlines now have "frequent flyer" programs, under which passengers can earn credits that can be accumulated and traded in for tickets or for upgrades. (Credits may also be earned from hotel stays and car rentals.) When these credits are earned from personal travel they can best be thought of as reductions in the price of the flights (or hotel stays or car rentals) from which they are earned — as if the ticket cost consists of a package of a flight plus credits — and there should be, and is, no tax consequence. For business trips, however, clearly there is a tax issue. Suppose, for example, that Ada, an employee of Baker Co., takes a flight for Baker Co.'s business purposes, with Baker Co. paying for the ticket but with Ada receiving the frequent flyer credits in her own name. Baker Co.'s cost for the ticket plainly should be, and is, a deductible business expense. If Ada flies frequently enough to accumulate entitlement to a free ticket and if she uses the free ticket for a business flight, Baker Co. is not properly chargeable with taxable gain. Again, the free ticket is just a reduction in Baker Co.'s cost of earlier tickets.

Suppose, however, that Ada uses the credits for a ticket, or for an upgrade, for a purely personal trip (with or without Baker Co.'s acquiescence). Ada has plainly received a benefit and most tax experts would agree that she has income in some amount. But how much? Generally there are limitations on the use of frequent flyer credits; often, for example, they cannot be used during peak travel periods. Moreover, for all we know, if Ada had not had the credit she might not have taken the flight or the upgrade. And, given the fact that airlines charge many different fares for the same flight, who knows what Ada's ticket would have cost? Beyond that, she may have used credits from a combination of personal trips for which she paid and business trips for which Baker Co. paid. Keeping track of the relative amounts might be difficult. What is more, treating the use of the business-derived credits as income would impose significant administrative costs on the IRS.

For many years the IRS, though well aware of the tax issue, made no effort to impose tax liability, despite some criticism (largely from academics and other spoilsports). Business travelers became accustomed to using the credits for personal purposes without including any amount in income. Finally, in

2002, the IRS officially threw in the towel, issuing Announcement 2002-18 (2002-10 I.R.B. 621), which stated:

> Consistent with prior practice, the IRS will not assert that any taxpayer has understated his federal tax liability by reason of the receipt or personal use of frequent flyer miles or other in-kind promotional benefits attributable to the taxpayer's business or official travel. . . .
>
> This relief does not apply to travel or other promotional benefits that are converted to cash, to compensation that is paid in the form of travel or other promotional benefits, or in other circumstances where these benefits are used for tax avoidance purposes.

If you had been Commissioner of Internal Revenue would you have authorized the issuance of this Announcement? Bear in mind that as Commissioner you would be a high-level political appointee, probably from private tax practice. You might want to think about the fact that members of Congress are frequent flyers.

Suppose that a respected member of your staff had proposed that, rather than adopt a policy of no taxation, the Announcement should impute a value of $100 per flight (round trip) for free tickets received by an employee using miles earned from travel for the employer. The $100 value would presumably be lower than the fair market value of the flight and lower than the value placed upon the flight by nearly all frequent fliers. What would your reaction be? Which of the problems mentioned above would be eliminated?

4. *Employer deduction.* One of the barriers to taxing employees on fringe benefits is that often the value to each employee is small and difficult to determine — for example, the value of meals supplied to employees at a company cafeteria. One way to respond to this problem is to ignore the income to the employees but deny the employer a deduction for the amount of the subsidy — that is, the amount by which the cost of the meals exceeds the payments received from employees. The effect is to treat the employer, for taxpaying purposes, as a surrogate for the employees. Another possibility is to impose a special tax on the amount of the subsidy, using a rate intended to approximate the rate at which the employees would be taxed. One problem with this approach is that it may be difficult to explain to people why one person should be denied a deduction, or pay a tax, because another person may have income. Another is that the denial of a deduction is ineffective when the employer is not taxable (either because it shows a loss for tax purposes or because it is a governmental, charitable, or other nontaxable entity).

5. *Benefits from other than employer.* Suppose that a school principal receives unsolicited sample books from the publishers. Even if the books could be sold, it would not seem proper to include the value of the books in the gross income of the principal. After all, they are not items for personal consumption, nor do they provide the wherewithal to acquire consumption items, except by trade or barter. And even if the value of the books were included in income, an offsetting deduction for the same amount, as a business expense (§ 162), might seem appropriate. Accordingly, exclusion seems sensible. On the other hand, if the books are sold, the proceeds surely should be included in income. If the

taxpayer gives the books to a charity (e.g., the school's library) and claims their value as a deduction, it is as if they had been sold and the proceeds given to charity. Any amount allowed as a charitable deduction should be included in income. It was so held in Haverly v. United States, 513 F.2d 224 (7th Cir.), cert. denied, 423 U.S. 912 (1975). In Rev. Rul. 70-498, 1970-2 C.B. 6, the Service ruled that sample books (received by a book reviewer for a newspaper) would be taxable only if the taxpayer donated them to charity and claimed a deduction for that donation.

QUESTIONS

What tax treatment is required by § 132 in each of the following situations?

1. F, a flight attendant in the employ of A, an airline company, and F's spouse decide to spend their annual vacation in Europe. A has a policy whereby any of its employees, along with members of their immediate families, may take a number of personal flights annually for a nominal charge, on a standby basis. F and F's spouse take advantage of this policy and fly to and from Europe.

2. P is the president of C, a corporation that has its executive offices situated in New York City. P is planning a week-long business trip to Los Angeles and will fly there and back on C's corporate jet. P's spouse intends to accompany P on the round-trip flight for personal reasons.

3. B is an officer in the employ of C, a manufacturing company. C provides personalized financial planning services to all of its officers without charge.

4. S, a senior vice president of D, a retail department store, purchases a refrigerator from D's appliance department. D has a policy whereby all employees are entitled to a 20 percent discount from the ticketed sales price of any item sold by the store so long as the resulting sales price, on average, approximately covers D's costs. See § 132(c), Regs. § 1.132-3(c).

5. The facts are the same as in Question 4 except that D's profit margin on ticketed items is only 10 percent, so the resultant sales price does not cover D's costs.

6. The facts are the same as in Question 4 except that the discount is available only to S and other officers of D.

7. A, an assistant manager in the employ of D, a department store, is occasionally required to work overtime to help mark down merchandise for special sales. On those occasional instances, D pays for the actual cost of A's evening meal. Such payment is pursuant to company policy whereby D will pay the actual, reasonable meal expense of a management-level employee when such an expense is incurred in connection with the performance of services either before or after such an employee's regular business hours.

8. S, a senior partner of L, a law firm, is provided free parking by the law firm. This benefit is provided by L to all partners, associates, and other employees. The parking privilege has a value of $75 per month. See § 132(f)(5)(E).

9. The facts are the same as in Question 8 except that it now pertains to A, an associate at L, and that L offers all partners, associates, and other

employees at L a choice of whether to accept parking or $75 a month and A accepts the parking.

10. The facts are the same as in Question 9 except that L offers no cash option and provides parking only to partners and associates of the law firm.

11. A is an associate in the employ of L, a prominent law firm located in a large city. In order to encourage participation in community activities and local society, L pays its associates' membership fees for various local clubs and organizations. A, taking advantage of this policy, joins a prestigious country club.

12. A, an attorney in the employ of C, a corporation, works at C's national headquarters. C maintains an on-site gymnasium that is available to all employees during normal business hours. A uses the gymnasium each working day.

3. Health Insurance

Probably the most important of all employee noncash benefits is health insurance. Under current law, employers are allowed to deduct the cost of medical insurance that they buy for their employees. At the same time, the benefits received by employees are excluded from their gross income. § 106(a). The exclusion extends to an employee's spouse or dependents. See Regs. § 1.106-1. According to the Joint Committee on Taxation, the revenue cost of this provision for 2008 is $116.5 billion. A similar benefit is extended to self-employed taxpayers (at a cost of $4.4 billion for 2008) by allowing them a deduction for the cost of medical care (including insurance premiums) as a business expense under § 162(1). No comparable tax benefit is available to employees who do not receive employer coverage.

Thus, consider three taxpayers, Emily (an employee with employer coverage), Sam (self-employed), and Nina (an employee with no employer coverage). Emily receives a salary of $70,000 plus health insurance worth $5,000. The $70,000 is included in her gross income but the $5,000 is not. Sam earns $75,000 and pays $5,000 for health insurance. He deducts the $5,000, so his adjusted gross income is reduced to $70,000. Nina receives a salary of $75,000, with no health benefits and buys her own health coverage for $5,000. She pays tax on the full $75,000. This disparity in treatment is difficult to rationalize.

Nina's relative maltreatment could be eliminated by allowing her a deduction like Sam's. In fact, there is a deduction for medical expenses, including the cost of health insurance (see § 213, covered in Chapter 4.C); however, this deduction is limited to expenses in excess of 7.5 percent of adjusted gross income. In Nina's case, the threshold for deduction is thus $5,625, so her $5,000 insurance premium would not be deductible. In effect, Congress says to Nina, "tough luck, we have better claims to tax reductions." Do you agree? (Even if Nina's medical expenses did exceed the 7.5 percent threshold, they might do her no good because of the operation of the dreaded Alternative Minimum Tax, which increases the threshold to 10 percent. See Chapter 6.I.7.)

The combination of the exclusion of employer-provided health insurance and the threshold for deduction of medical expenses creates a tax disincentive for health coverage policies or plans choosing employer-provided health insurance plans that have higher deductibles. Plans with higher deductible amounts may be cheaper before-tax, because they induce covered individuals to be more cost-conscious regarding routine medical care, but they are less favorable from a tax standpoint since the amounts paid by the consumer out-of-pocket may not be deductible.

In part to address these concerns, President George W. Bush in 2007 proposed repealing § 106 and replacing it with a flat $7,500 deduction ($15,000 for families). The deduction would be available to anyone obtaining qualifying health insurance but would not vary according to the cost of the insurance. The idea was to give individuals an incentive to purchase insurance while also encouraging them to economize on its cost. Congress never acted on the Bush proposal. Would you support such a proposal?

4. Economic Effects: An Example

Suppose an employer is willing to provide employees with parking during working hours at the place of employment, which costs the employer $50 per month. Suppose further that the parking is worth only $40 per month to a particular employee (who would take the bus or join a carpool if a payment of more than $40 were required). Suppose, finally, that the employer is willing either to provide the parking or pay the employee $50 per month. Either way, the employer will spend and will be able to deduct $50, so even after tax effects are accounted for, the employer is indifferent concerning the two options. The question is, what are the economic effects of a tax system under which the employee is taxed on the cash payment but not on the noncash benefit (the parking)?

First, assume that there is no income tax at all; assume, that is, a no-tax world. Plainly the employee would choose the $50 cash, with which he or she could buy goods or services worth that amount to him or her. If the employer were to provide the parking, it would be paying $50 for a benefit worth only $40 to the employee. There would be a waste of $10. But that won't happen.

Next assume that we have an income tax system under which the cash payment is taxable but parking is not, and suppose that the combined state and federal marginal tax rate of the employee is 40 percent. Now, if the employee takes the cash, he or she will pay a tax of $20 and will have only $30 left. If, on the other hand, the employee takes the parking, there will be no tax; the net benefit will be the $40 value of the parking. So the employee will take the parking, worth only $40 to him or her, despite the fact that it costs the employer $50 to provide it. There appears to be a waste of $10. Economists call this a "deadweight loss."

So far we have established that a tax system with an exclusion of the value of the parking seems to produce a perverse outcome. The next question is, what about a tax system that taxes the employee on the employer's cost of the parking? Suppose, then, that there is an income tax but that the employer's cost of the parking is included in the employee's income. In this situation there will be no distortion (no deadweight loss). The employee can take either the parking or the cash. Either way, the tax will be $20. So we can forget about the tax; it is a constant. Since the tax is a constant, the employee will take the cash. There will be no deadweight loss.

Another way of arriving at the same result is to observe that if both cash and parking are taxed, the employee can take the parking (worth $40, but valued for tax purposes at $50) and pay a tax of $20, leaving a net benefit of $20, or take the cash ($50) and pay the tax of $20, leaving a net benefit of $30. The employee will choose cash and the employer will not supply a noncash benefit whose cost is higher than its value to the employee.

Finally, suppose that the employee is taxed only on the $40 value of the parking, rather than its cost of $50. If that is the rule, again the result is no distortion, but the demonstration gets a bit more difficult. If the employee takes the parking, the value of the benefit is $40 and the tax is $16. The net benefit is $24. If the cash is taken, the benefit is $50 and the tax is $20 for a net benefit of $30. The cash will be chosen and there will be no distortion. To put that another way, if the cash is taken, the tax rises by $4 but the value of the benefit rises by $10. The relative difficulty of analysis arises from the fact that two variables change at the same time. But the result is the same.

Of course, Congress might decide, despite all this, that parking benefits should be tax free because it wants to encourage commuting by private automobile (perhaps as an aid to the automobile industry), because it wants to encourage the use of land for parking lots, or for some other such reason. Comparison of the world with taxes with an imaginary world without taxes may be helpful in identifying and describing the economic consequences of taxes, but it is an unreliable guide to tax policy. What is important is that members of Congress and their advisors be clear in their own minds about what they are doing with the tax system. In the case of parking, it is reasonable to suppose that under the present rule (excluding the value of parking from the employee's income) employees whose parking is free may use parking space that is worth less to them than its market value (that is, its value to others) and that this would not happen under a rule that treats the value of the parking as income subject to taxation. We can also expect that under the rule excluding the value of parking there will be greater use of private automobiles for commuting to work than there would be under a rule including that value. It is difficult to imagine that in this era of concern for traffic congestion, air pollution, and energy conservation Congress would consciously adopt a provision with that kind of economic incentive.[2] What we see, then, is a good example of how rules with presumably undesirable economic effects can become part of our tax law unless we are alert to those effects.

2. The federal government has, however, provided most of the funds for construction of urban freeways, and local governments have in various ways encouraged development of both the suburbs and (more recently) of downtown shopping and business areas, actions that seem to have encouraged the use of private automobiles.

The possibility of undesirable economic effects of employer-provided free parking is not just the idle speculation of ivory-tower intellectuals. Professor Donald C. Shoup presents the following data:

> When it comes to commuters, cars, and free parking in the United States, all percentages are in the nineties. Ninety-one percent of all commuters drive to work. Ninety-two percent of all cars driven to work have only one occupant. Ninety-five percent of all commuters who drive to work receive free parking. . . . Most commuters park free even in the central business districts (CBDs) of the largest cities. For example, a survey of commuters to the Los Angeles CBD found that 53 percent of motorists received employer-paid parking. A survey of trans-Hudson commuters found that 54 percent of auto drivers bound for the Manhattan CBD during the morning peak received employer-paid parking.

Evaluating the Effects of Cashing Out Employer-Paid Parking: Eight Case Studies, 4 Transport Policy 201 (1997).

In other work, Professor Shoup has surveyed research concerning the behavioral effects of employer-paid parking. One study compared two similar groups of employees in suburban Los Angeles and found that among the group that paid for parking, 46 percent drove to work alone, while in the group that did not pay, 90 percent did so. Another study found that in Ottawa, Canada, when the government stopped providing free parking to its employees the number driving to work alone fell by 20 percent. In short, Shoup concludes, employer-paid parking provides an "almost irresistible invitation to drive to work alone," which in turn generates potentially adverse effects on the transportation system, urban form, air quality, fuel consumption, and fairness. In part because of Shoup's work, Congress amended § 132 in 1998 (see § 132(f)(4)) to remove a disincentive employers had previously faced for offering cash payments in lieu of free parking. This statutory change, along with the incorporation of transit passes and vanpools in § 132(f), may help to counterbalance the tax law's longstanding subsidy for employer-provided parking.

One final point deserves mention. The critique of § 132's exclusion for employer-provided parking rests in part on an unstated assumption that the choice of whether to drive to work and pay for parking or take mass transit (or carpool) is a personal rather than a business decision. That assumption is not free from doubt. Maybe parking should be considered a cost of earning income and, as such, as a proper deduction in arriving at net income. If so, exclusion of free parking would be the correct treatment and taxation would be considered a burden or penalty. Suppose that an associate in a law firm drives to work and thereafter uses her automobile to drive to court and that the firm pays for the parking near the court building. Should that free parking be treated as part of the associate's income? If, so, should there be an offsetting deduction as a business expense? Suppose we know that if the value of the parking near the court building were included in the associate's income, with no offsetting deduction, she would take public transportation. Would you characterize a rule excluding the value of the parking from income as a "subsidy" or "encouragement" to the use of private transportation? When a manufacturer is allowed to deduct the cost of raw materials, is that a "subsidy" to the use of those raw materials? What, if anything, is different about the use of an automobile by our hypothetical associate?

5. Another Approach to Valuation

As the prior four sections showed, the employment setting has mainly been characterized by an all-or-nothing approach to including in-kind benefits. Items tend either to be wholly excludable (as under §§ 119 and 132), or else included at their fair market value without regard to any argument that they were worth less to the taxpayer. The following case adopts a different approach in the setting of a quiz show award.

TURNER v. COMMISSIONER
13 T.C.M. 462 (1954)

MEMORANDUM FINDINGS OF FACT AND OPINION

The Commissioner determined a deficiency of $388.96 in the income tax of the petitioners for 1948. The only question for decision is the amount which should be included in income because of the winning by Reginald of steamship tickets by answering a question on a radio program.

FINDINGS OF FACT

The petitioners are husband and wife who filed a joint return for 1948 with the collector of internal revenue for the District of North Carolina. They reported salary of $4,536.16 for 1948.

Reginald, whose name had been selected by chance from a telephone book, was called on the telephone on April 18, 1948 and was asked to name a song that was being played on a radio program. He gave the correct name of the song and then was given the opportunity to identify a second song and thus to compete for a grand prize. He correctly identified the second song and in consideration of his efforts was awarded a number of prizes, including two round trip first-class steamship tickets for a cruise between New York City and Buenos Aires. The prize was to be one ticket if the winner was unmarried, but, if he was married, his wife was to receive a ticket also. The tickets were not transferable and were good only within one year on a sailing date approved by the agent of the steamship company.

The petitioners reported income on their return of $520, representing income from the award of the two tickets. The Commissioner, in determining the deficiency, increased the income from this source to $2,220, the retail price of such tickets.

Marie was born in Brazil. The petitioners had two sons. Reginald negotiated with the agent of the steamship company, as a result of which he surrendered his rights to the two first-class tickets, and upon payment of $12.50

received four round trip tourist steamship tickets between New York City and Rio de Janeiro. The petitioners and their two sons used those tickets in making a trip from New York City to Rio de Janeiro and return during 1948.

The award of the tickets to Reginald represented income to him in the amount of $1,400.

OPINION

Persons desiring to buy round trip first-class tickets between New York and Buenos Aires in April 1948, similar to those to which the petitioners were entitled, would have had to pay $2,220 for them. The petitioners, however, were not such persons. The winning of the tickets did not provide them with something which they needed in the ordinary course of their lives and for which they would have made an expenditure in any event, but merely gave them an opportunity to enjoy a luxury otherwise beyond their means. Their value to the petitioners was not equal to their retail cost. They were not transferable and not salable and there were other restrictions on their use. But even had the petitioner been permitted to sell them, his experience with other more salable articles indicates that he would have had to accept substantially less than the cost of similar tickets purchased from the steamship company and would have had selling expenses. Probably the petitioners could have refused the tickets and avoided the tax problem. Nevertheless, in order to obtain such benefits as they could from winning the tickets, they actually took a cruise accompanied by their two sons, thus obtaining free board, some savings in living expenses, and the pleasure of the trip. It seems proper that a substantial amount should be included in their income for 1948 on account of the winning of the tickets. The problem of arriving at a proper fair figure for this purpose is difficult. The evidence to assist is meager, perhaps unavoidably so. The Court, under such circumstances, must arrive at some figure and has done so.

NOTES AND QUESTIONS

1. The court's decision seems to imply that $2,200 was the price for tickets that were identical to the taxpayers' but transferable. Suppose there had been evidence that nonrefundable, nontransferable tickets, precisely identical to those awarded to the Turners had a retail price of $1,900. Would this have made it an open-and-shut case, with $1,900 clearly the amount includible? Or would the Turners' argument that the tickets' value to them was less than the retail price have remained as relevant as in the actual case?

2. Why exactly could the Turners argue (persuasively, as it turned out) that the tickets' value to them was less than the retail price? Should it have mattered that they were able to exchange two first-class tickets to Buenos Aires for four tourist-class tickets to Rio de Janeiro, thus permitting them to take their children and visit the country where Mrs. Turner was born?

3. How do you think the court determined that the value of the tickets to the Turners was $1,400? Might it have averaged the opposing "bids"

($520 + $2,220 = $2,740/2 = $1,370) and then rounded off this number to the nearest $100 increment?

4. It is useful to keep in mind exactly what matters about the arbitrariness of the court's precise finding as to value. Despite the lack of any evident basis for the court's precise determination, the $1,400 value that it selected may conceivably have come closer to measuring the tickets' value accurately than either the Commissioner's or the taxpayer's position (although, how would one know this?). The problem with the arbitrariness of the court's determination is less that it was unlikely to be exactly correct, than that it provided little guidance as to what value taxpayers should report in similar circumstances in the future.

5. Another subjective valuation case is McCoy v. Commissioner, 38 T.C. 841 (1962), acq., in which the taxpayer won a new Lincoln car in a sales contest. The car's cost to the employer ($4,453) was more than half of the taxpayer's income for the year (about $7,500), and he did not own another car. He drove the Lincoln for ten days and then traded it in for a Ford station wagon (with a dealer's price of $2,600) plus $1,000 cash. The court, exercising its "best judgment" where the "evidence adduced does not permit of an exact determination of . . . fair market value," held that the amount includible in income was $3,900 (38 T.C. at 844). On the other hand, in Rooney v. Commissioner, 88 T.C. 523 (1988), the court required members of an accounting firm who had reluctantly accepted payment in the form of goods and services in payment of fees to include these items at their market prices. The court approvingly quoted the following language from an earlier case: "[T]he use of any such subjective measure of value as is suggested is contrary to the usual way of valuing either services or property, and would make the administration of the tax laws in this area depend upon a knowledge by the Commissioner of the state of mind of the individual taxpayer. We do not think that tax administration should be based upon anything so whimsical" (88 T.C. at 528).

6. Carla, a contestant on a game show, wins a new car. The show's producer received the car free from the manufacturer because of the advertising value of its use on the show. The ordinary dealer cost of the car is $20,000 and the "sticker" price is $25,000. Carla tries to sell the car, but the best offer she gets is $16,000 and she decides to keep it even though the value to her is more like $12,000. She hires you for professional tax advice concerning the amount, if any, that she must include as income on her federal income tax return. Her exact words to you are "Just tell me the answer." What sort of advice should you give her? How should you frame your response? In thinking about how you'll approach the situation, assume that you'll be up for partner next year at your law firm and that Carla owns a business that could provide lots of fees for the firm.

Taxing the Mets Fan Who Caught the Historic Home Run Ball

On August 7, 2007, Barry Bonds hit his 756th career home run in the bottom of the fifth inning against the Washington Nationals, making him baseball's all-time career home run leader. Matt Murphy, a 21-year old

New York Mets fan who had extended a layover in San Francisco to attend the game before leaving for Australia, emerged from a scrum of screaming fans with possession of the ball. "I kept yelling, 'I got it! I got it!,'" Murphy recounted, "'And get the bleep off of me, get the bleep off of me!' The San Francisco Police Department saved my life." Asked how he felt after catching the ball, Murphy told reporters that he was banged up and bruised but otherwise felt like he had won the lottery. Murphy had indeed struck it rich. News reports the next day cited estimates of the ball's value ranging from $400,000 to $500,000. In fact, Murphy sold ball in an online auction on September 15, 2007 for $752,467.20 to fashion designer Mark Ecko. Two weeks later, Washington Wizards point guard Gilbert Arenas announced on his blog that he would be willing to pay Ecko $800,000 for the ball.

1. Did Murphy have taxable income upon catching the ball in August? Upon selling it in September? What about Ecko? Should the tax system take account of his opportunity to sell the ball for $800,000, even if he doesn't accept the offer?

2. Would it make any difference to Murphy's taxability if he had immediately given the ball to Bonds? If so, on what ground? What tax consequences if the San Francisco Giants had given Murphy season tickets worth $5,000 in exchange for his giving the ball to Bonds, and Murphy accepted this offer in lieu of selling the ball for cash because he felt that selling it to the highest bidder was wrong?

3. Would Bonds have taxable income upon receiving the ball from Murphy? Upon receiving it from a stadium usher on behalf of the team, if that individual, rather than Murphy, had caught the ball?

Similar issues were raised in 1998 in connection with the historic home run balls of Mark McGwire and Sammy Sosa, who were in a heated race to break the record of 61 home runs in a single season held by Roger Maris. After the fan who caught McGwire's 61st home run ball handed it over to the slugger, an IRS spokesman was quoted as saying that the fan might owe federal gift taxes on the transfer. The statement did not mention federal income tax consequences, but arguably they followed as well from viewing the events as significant for tax purposes. Various commentators noted that McGwire's upcoming 62nd home run ball, which would set the new single-season record, was likely to be worth at least $1 million.

Congressional critics of the IRS had a field day. Senate Finance Committee Chair Roth called "even the possibility of Mark McGwire's historic 62nd baseball being taxed . . . a prime example of what is wrong with our current tax code." Senator Christopher Bond demanded corrective legislation and said: "If the IRS wants to know why they are the most hated federal agency in America, they need look no further than this assault on America's baseball fans."

The IRS promptly backed off, issuing a press release in which it stated that a fan who catches and returns a home run ball does not have taxable income "based on an analogy to principles of tax law that apply when someone immediately declines a prize or returns unsolicited merchandise." It cautioned that the tax implications "may be different" if the fan retained the ball for sale. As it turned out, McGwire's 62nd home run ball was retrieved by a groundskeeper at the stadium, rather than a fan. The groundskeeper promptly (and arguably in his capacity as a baseball team employee) gave it to McGwire. The IRS apparently decided not to explore the possibility that McGwire had taxable income from the transfer.

Traditionally, the IRS has not sought to tax the income of commercial fishermen, big game hunters, prospectors, miners, and salvors who raise sunken treasure from ships until they turn their bounty into cash (or its equivalent). However, this practice seemingly contradicts Regs. § 1.61-14, which states: "Treasure trove, to the extent of its value in United States currency, constitutes gross income for the taxable year in which it is reduced to undisputed possession."

B. IMPUTED INCOME

People may use their property or their own services to provide benefits directly to themselves or to members of their households — for example, when they occupy houses that they own, when they care for their own children, or when they prepare their own tax returns. The benefits they derive are not part of any commercial transaction. Experts refer to these kinds of benefits as "imputed income." That terminology may cause some confusion since the ordinary person probably does not think of the benefits as "income" and generally they are not in fact treated as income for tax purposes. Nonetheless, it can be demonstrated that failure to include these benefits in income produces serious problems of fairness and economic rationality. As one might guess, the reason why we seem to be stuck with these problems is that inclusion of the benefits in the calculation of individual income is assumed to be impractical.

1. Property Other Than Cash

(a) The best and most significant example of imputed income from property is the owner-occupied home. The imputed income is simply the rental value of that home. It is the same kind of benefit that we examined in *Benaglia* (supra page 54, involving the manager of the Royal Hawaiian Hotel). An illustration will reveal this similarity and will uncover a complexity arising from the fact that a home in this era is not just a source of personal benefit but an investment as well.

To begin, imagine that there are two taxpayers, *A* and *B*, each earning $50,000 per year. Each inherits $100,000, which is received tax-free. § 102(a). *A* invests the $100,000 in U.S. Treasury bonds that pay her $8,000 per year. She continues to live in a house that she rents. Her income will be $58,000; there is no deduction for rent, since it is a personal expense. See § 262. *B* uses his $100,000 to buy a virtually identical house next door to *A*'s. He figures that in the first year he will earn a return of $5,000 in the form of the rent that he saves plus $3,000 from the increase in value he expects. His return, like *A*'s, will be 8 percent. But his income for tax purposes will be only his $50,000 salary. The $8,000 return on the investment in the house will escape taxation. The $5,000 rental value is imputed income. It is never taxed. The other $3,000, the increase in value of the house, is unrealized income (see infra page 206) and is taxed only on ultimate sale of the house, if at all (see § 121).

This may be considered unfair to A. B's and A's economic positions are essentially the same; each has essentially the same ability to pay. But A is taxed on $58,000 while B is taxed on only $50,000. To the extent of the $5,000 imputed rental income, this unfairness is associated with the failure to include the $5,000 rental value in B's income — or to allow A a deduction for her rental payment. So far, however, the facts are unrealistic in one important respect. A earns an 8 percent taxable return, while B earns an 8 percent untaxed return. People like A will soon awaken to reality and will begin to emulate B. They will buy houses, which will drive up the price and drive down the rate of return. As this happens, the after-tax return to people like B will fall. The after-tax difference between people like A and B will diminish. Moreover, any claim of unfairness by A can be blunted by pointing out that she was entirely free to make the same kind of investment made by B — or to make some other tax-favored investment. Even if fairness is not a problem, however, we will find that we have encouraged investment in owner-occupied housing — without any prior conscious, deliberate consideration of the wisdom of doing so.

(b) While A may be free to pursue the tax advantage seized by B, there are others who may not have the same option unless they borrow. For example, imagine a taxpayer, C, with a salary of $58,000 and no inheritance. Suppose that C is able to borrow $100,000 to buy a house just like B's, at an interest rate of 8 percent or $8,000 per year. If C is allowed to deduct the amount of interest paid, her position will be the same as B's. Her income subject to taxation will be $50,000 ($58,000 less the $8,000 interest payment), and she will have imputed income of $5,000 plus unrealized gain of $3,000. But then A may have further cause for complaint of unfairness. Both B and C now are treated better than A (though, again, only because A has not had the wit to engage in effective tax planning). Or perhaps the effect of the tax incentives on investment behavior will tend to eliminate any unfairness, but only at the cost of questionable economic effects. Many economists have argued that the trouble with our economy is in part attributable to the fact that the tax system has induced people to invest in housing when they should invest instead in the tools of production. "Sound farfetched? A tortured argument by someone pushing a tax reform scheme? Not a bit. Merely a way of showing the effect of the tax system on behavior." Baldwin, Where Will the Money Come From?, Forbes, Sept. 14, 1981, at 150, 153.

(c) Often it is asserted that the treatment of homeowners (the deductibility of interest, plus the deductibility of property tax, and the nontaxation of imputed income) discriminates against renters. It is worth noting, however, that the tax system may, in some circumstances, provide significant tax benefits to landlords, mainly in the form of deductions for "cost recovery" that may be unrelated to economic reality (see infra page 565). Presumably these tax benefits to some significant degree are passed through to tenants in the form of lower rents (though to some significant extent the tax benefits may simply drive up the price of land and existing buildings). The result may be to increase the tax system's bias in favor of investment in homes rather than other assets, while reducing (or even eliminating) the bias in favor of home ownership relative to rental.

(d) The reason people usually give for not taxing imputed income from home ownership is that it would be impractical to do so because of problems of valuation. What would be wrong with including in income an amount equal to a percentage of the value of the house? The critical issue then would be the value of the house itself rather than its rental value. In most states, houses are valued for purposes of local property taxes and we seem to think that the results are tolerable despite all the obvious problems.

(e) It should be clear that the kind of benefit that people derive from their investments in their principal residences will also be derived from their investments in vacation homes, in yachts, and in a wide variety of consumer durables. If one were intent on taxing the imputed income from ownership of principal residences, would it follow that we must also tax the imputed income from all these other investments, or at least those of any significant size? Where would you draw the line?

(f) A phenomenon of some importance in the marketing and ownership of resort developments is the "time share." There are many variations, but essentially what happens in time-sharing is that a number of individuals buy shares in a particular unit (an apartment, condominium apartment, hotel room, or what have you), with each owner entitled to use the unit for a given period of time. For example, a particular unit at a resort might be divided into fifty shares, with fifty separate owners each entitled to use the unit for one week (and two weeks set aside for maintenance). It is interesting to speculate on why this kind of arrangement might be attractive to an investor as compared with simply renting a unit when it is wanted. The time-share approach may produce economies to users by virtue of the fact that there are no vacancies or rental costs. A disadvantage of traditional time shares is that the owner is pinned down to a particular place and time year after year. Many time-share programs have eliminated this disadvantage by allowing flexibility as to time and, even more importantly, by creating programs that facilitate the exchange of time shares at one location for time shares at various other locations (sometimes even in different countries). Taking this a step or two further, some promoters now sell vacation "points." The buyer pays a substantial initial amount (ranging upward from around $10,000), plus a much smaller annual fee, for a given number of points, which can be used each year for lodging (the more points, the better the accommodations and the available dates) or for airline tickets, rental cars, or other vacation items.

It would be difficult at best to know how important tax considerations are in the rise of time shares. It does seem plain, however, that ownership of a time share provides on a reduced level the kinds of imputed income available in greater amount to the more affluent people who can afford to own the year-round use of vacation homes.

(g) A point made in connection with the initial discussion of owner-occupied housing deserves emphasis. The person who borrows to invest in a personal residence relies on a combination of two tax rules: (1) the nontaxation of imputed income and (2) the deductibility of the interest payment. On the tax return, the favored tax position shows up simply as the interest deduction, and much of the discussion of the tax bias in favor of home ownership focuses on this aspect of the phenomenon. But the bias could be ended by taxing the imputed income. If the imputed income were taxed, the interest deduction would be entirely justified since the interest would be the cost of producing taxable income. Thus, the tax benefit at issue in the case of debt-financed personal residences is part of a broader category of benefits achieved by taxpayers who borrow money to invest in tax-favored investments. For all such debt-financed investments, one must ask whether it would be appropriate to disallow the interest deduction and thereby limit the advantages of the tax-favored investment to those taxpayers who can afford to acquire them without borrowing.

2. Services

(a) Suppose that a nurse works overtime to earn enough money so he can afford to hire someone to paint his house. Obviously, the nurse will pay income tax on the amount earned in the overtime work. If, on the other hand, the nurse decides to forgo the overtime work and stay home and paint his own house, the value of the time he devotes to the project will not count as income. The benefit of the services that one performs for oneself is called imputed income, and the failure to tax that benefit produces the same kinds of problems encountered in connection with imputed income from home ownership. First, there is unfairness: The nurse who performs services for others, as a nurse, and uses his wages to hire housepainting services will pay more tax than an otherwise similar person who does not work overtime and instead performs housepainting services for himself. Second, there is economic distortion or misallocation: The nurse may put in time as a housepainter even though, disregarding taxes, his time is more valuable when he works as a nurse and even though he would rather work overtime as a nurse than paint his house. The tax system reduces the value to him (though not to others) of his time as a nurse but does not similarly reduce the value to him of his time as a housepainter (for himself), which means that he may choose to paint his house even though his productivity as a nurse is greater than his productivity painting his house.[3]

This does not mean that we should tax the imputed income. Indeed, overwhelming considerations of practicality, privacy, public comprehension,

---

3. Suppose for example that the nurse can earn $20 per hour as a nurse; that is the value that society places on his services. If his tax rate is, say, 40 percent, he nets only $12 per hour. Suppose that a housepainter would charge $15 per hour, which is, again, the value that society places on those services. Assume that the nurse can do the housepainting job just as efficiently as the housepainter and has no aversion to the work (or at least no more aversion than to overtime nursing). The nurse will be better off to do his own housepainting than to work as a nurse and hire a housepainter, and will presumably wind up doing the housepainting job for himself. Thus, a $20-per-hour person performs a $15-per-hour job even though there is ample demand for the $20-per-hour services. There is a $5-per-hour deadweight loss.

and enforcement make any suggestion that we tax such benefits seem patently unsound. But to conclude that the benefit should not be taxed is not to deny that nontaxation offends principles of fairness and of economic rationality.

(b) It may be difficult to take seriously problems arising from such services as painting one's house, shining one's shoes, or filling one's gas tank. There is, however, another set of services that cannot be dismissed so readily: the services performed essentially full time for the members of one's household, usually by women — in other words, the services of homemakers. These services raise an important tax issue because they are of substantial value and are not evenly distributed among households. Again, we find problems both of fairness and of unfortunate economic effects. Imagine, for example, two couples, each with two children. With the first couple, one spouse works and earns $40,000 while the other stays at home and performs services in caring for the children, cleaning the house, preparing the meals, etc. With the second couple, both spouses work, with one earning $40,000 and the other earning $10,000, and a housekeeper is hired at a cost of $8,000. The second couple has a true economic advantage over the first of only $2,000, but for tax purposes its income is greater by $10,000. To the extent that it is taxed on the extra $8,000, the second couple is treated unfairly as compared with the first. And the effect may be to induce the secondary worker in the second household to stay home and provide services to the household rather than take a job where his or her services may be more valuable to society. One solution to this set of problems would be to tax the imputed income of the first couple, but that possibility is universally dismissed as impractical. A second possibility is to allow a deduction for the second couple for the costs of hiring household services from outsiders. Section 21 (the credit for child and household care) moves in this direction, as does § 129 (allowing tax-free employer reimbursement for child-care expenses), combined with § 125 (allowing employers to offer employees a choice between tax-free benefits and cash). See supra page 65. Deductions and credits for child-care services are considered more fully in Chapter 5.C.

(c) Another important source of imputed income from services has received relatively little attention from tax experts but has begun to be more widely recognized in the context of marital dissolution. This is the value of services that one performs for oneself in creating "human capital." A good example is that of the person who devotes many years to the study of medicine. During the period of training, such a person forgoes income that could have been earned in some other activity in order to develop a skill of considerable financial value. The prospective doctor is not wasting time; the time is being used in a valuable way. The return is the ultimate ability to practice medicine, which is an intangible asset whose value can far exceed that of tangible assets. (For further discussion of the tax issues associated with marital dissolution, see Chapter 3.G.)

3. Psychic Income and Leisure

Closely related to the phenomenon of imputed income is that of psychic income and leisure. Imagine, for example, two taxpayers with the same salary.

One enjoys playing chess, engaging in intellectual discourse, reading, and bird-watching. The other is happy only while sailing a yacht or traveling abroad. Both manage to enjoy life to the same degree; their "psychic income" is the same. But the cost of achieving similar happiness is higher for the second taxpayer than for the first. The tax system does not, and obviously cannot, take account of the possible difference in the two taxpayers' ability to pay.

Similarly, imagine two taxpayers with the same incomes, one who earns that income working two days a week and another who works six. Apart from the possibility of taxing the first person's untapped ability to pay, one might think it appropriate, in the interests of fairness, to take account of the value of the first person's leisure or the psychic income it produces. Since we do not, the tax system distorts economic choice: It taxes earnings but does not tax the benefit of the leisure that one "buys" by not working.

The idea of taxing leisure may sound like the worst sort of ivory-tower theorizing, but note that the distortion here is no different from that created by differential taxation of any two choices or commodities, such as a higher tax on red apples than on green apples. To the extent that we find these distortions problematic, we might consider tax policies designed to reduce them. For example, we might consider designing wage taxes to interfere as little as possible with the labor-leisure tradeoff, perhaps by imposing higher rates on those likely to work no matter what (e.g., primary earners in their peak earning years) and lower rates on those more likely to be on the fence about working (e.g., secondary earners deciding whether to enter the labor force). In effect, such an approach recognizes that different people value leisure differently and that the distortions created by the tax system could be reduced by taking account of these differences.

QUESTIONS

1. Which, if any, of the following raise issues of imputed income?
(a) buying a car
(b) buying a tuxedo
(c) renting a tuxedo
(d) buying a washing machine
(e) repairing one's own car
(f) enjoyment of leisure
(g) enjoyment of work
2. In what way does the nontaxation of imputed income from housing create problems of fairness? Of economic efficiency?
3. Is a rent deduction for people who do not own their own homes a good solution to the problems created by the nontaxation of the imputed income from owner-occupied housing?
4. Suppose the tax rate on earned income is lowered and a special tax is added to the price of leisure-time activities such as sporting events, concerts, movies, and nonbusiness travel. Would these two changes be a sensible way to reduce the problems caused by the nontaxation of the psychic value of leisure?

4. Drawing the Line

The Revenue Ruling produced below is concerned with a problem of economic benefit, or noncash benefit, rather than with a problem of imputed income. Its function at this point in the book is to permit exploration of the distinction between imputed income and noncash benefits. The taxpayers in the ruling perform services for strangers, not themselves or members of their households. But the difference may not be so clear in other situations.

REVENUE RULING 79-24
1979-1 C.B. 60

FACTS

Situation 1. In return for personal legal services performed by a lawyer for a housepainter, the housepainter painted the lawyer's personal residence. Both the lawyer and the housepainter are members of a barter club, an organization that annually furnishes its members a directory of members and the services they provide. All the members of the club are professional or trades persons. Members contact other members directly and negotiate the value of the services to be performed.

Situation 2. An individual who owned an apartment building received a work of art created by a professional artist in return for the rent-free use of an apartment for six months by the artist.

LAW

The applicable sections of the Internal Revenue Code of 1954 and the Income Tax Regulations thereunder are 61(a) and 1.61-2, relating to compensation for services.

Section 1.61-2(d)(1) of the regulations provides that if services are paid for other than in money, the fair market value of the property or services taken in payment must be included in income. If the services were rendered at a stipulated price, such price will be presumed to be the fair market value of the compensation received in the absence of evidence to the contrary.

HOLDINGS

Situation 1. The fair market value of the services received by the lawyer and the housepainter are includible in their gross incomes under section 61 of the Code.

Situation 2. The fair market value of the work of art and the six months fair rental value of the apartment are includible in the gross incomes of the apartment-owner and the artist under section 61 of the Code.

QUESTIONS

1. Suppose that Betty owns the right, under a time share (see supra page 79), to the use of an apartment at the beach for a week in July and exchanges that right for the right of another time-share owner, Stan, to the use of an apartment at a ski resort for a week in December. Should each person report income by virtue of the exchange?

2. Suppose that two couples exchange babysitting services on weekends. Should both report income? Code § 6045 requires information reporting by any "barter exchange." Regs. § 1.6045-1(a)(4) provides that "the term 'barter exchange' . . . does not include arrangements that provide solely for the informal exchange of similar services on a noncommercial basis."

3. Suppose that one couple joins a cooperative day care center that maintains a limited professional staff and requires each parent to supply two hours of day care a week. Parents who do not wish to supply day care may buy out of the obligation for $50 a month. However, parents are encouraged to provide child care and not buy their way out of the obligation. Should parents who provide child care pay tax on $50 of monthly income?

4. Attorney Ann joins a barter club. In return for services as an attorney, Ann receives credits that she can use to obtain other professional services, such as carpentry or dentistry. Taxable? See Rev. Rul. 80-52, 1980-1 C.B. 100, holding people taxable on credits earned in a barter club. As noted above, § 6045 requires information returns to the IRS from "barter exchanges."

5. One hundred people pool their resources and buy land in Colorado, where they set up a commune. They perform various tasks for each other according to their skills. Any income for tax purposes?

6. A bank offers its customers the option of earning interest on the money in their checking accounts or of receiving free checking services. Any income to the customers who take the free checking services? The Service has never sought to tax the value of such services. Would you concur in that practice if you were Commissioner?

C. WINDFALLS AND GIFTS

1. Punitive Damages

The case that follows, Commissioner v. Glenshaw Glass, Inc., is one of the most famous and important Supreme Court opinions in the tax field. We suspect, however, that you may find its holding to be somewhat unremarkable. To fully appreciate its significance requires an understanding of its historical context; we'll have more to say about that in the notes following the case. For now, we'd like to draw your attention to the reference in the first paragraph of Chief Justice Warren's opinion to the fact that the taxpayers prevailed in both the Tax Court and the U.S. Court of Appeals. Both of those tribunals based their holdings on a much earlier Supreme Court opinion, Eisner v. Macomber

(1920), which, as you will recall from the Introduction, narrowly defined the term "income" as "the gain derived from capital, from labor, or from both combined." In many ways, *Glenshaw Glass* is less about punitive damages than about the continuing vitality of Eisner v. Macomber, as well as the Supreme Court's role in policing the contours of the term "income."

COMMISSIONER v. GLENSHAW GLASS CO.
348 U.S. 426 (1955)

Mr. Chief Justice WARREN delivered the opinion of the Court.

This litigation involves two cases with independent factual backgrounds yet presenting the identical issue. The two cases were consolidated for argument before the Court of Appeals for the Third Circuit and were heard en banc. The common question is whether money received as exemplary damages for fraud or as the punitive two-thirds portion of a treble-damage antitrust recovery must be reported by a taxpayer as gross income under § 22(a) of the Internal Revenue Code of 1939 [the predecessor of § 61 of the 1954 Code]. In a single opinion, 211 F.2d 928, the Court of Appeals affirmed the Tax Court's separate rulings in favor of the taxpayers. . . .

The facts of the cases were largely stipulated and are not in dispute. So far as pertinent they are as follows:

Commissioner v. Glenshaw Glass Co. The Glenshaw Glass Company, a Pennsylvania corporation, manufactures glass bottles and containers. It was engaged in protracted litigation with the Hartford-Empire Company, which manufactures machinery of a character used by Glenshaw. Among the claims advanced by Glenshaw were demands for exemplary damages for fraud and treble damages for injury to its business by reason of Hartford's violation of the federal antitrust laws. In December 1947, the parties concluded a settlement of all pending litigation, by which Hartford paid Glenshaw approximately $800,000. Through a method of allocation which was approved by the Tax Court, 18 T.C. 860, 870-872, and which is no longer in issue, it was ultimately determined that, of the total settlement, $324,529.94 represented payment of punitive damages for fraud and antitrust violations. Glenshaw did not report this portion of the settlement as income for the tax year involved. The Commissioner determined a deficiency claiming as taxable the entire sum less only deductible legal fees. As previously noted, the Tax Court and the Court of Appeals upheld the taxpayer.

Commissioner v. William Goldman Theatres, Inc. William Goldman Theatres, Inc., a Delaware corporation operating motion picture houses in Pennsylvania, sued Loew's, Inc., alleging a violation of the federal antitrust laws and seeking treble damages. After a holding that a violation had occurred, William Goldman Theatres, Inc. v. Loew's, Inc., 150 F.2d 738, the case was remanded to the trial court for a determination of damages. It was found that Goldman had suffered a loss of profits equal to $125,000 and was entitled to treble damages in the sum of $375,000. William Goldman Theatres, Inc. v. Loew's, Inc., 69 F. Supp. 103, aff'd, 164 F.2d 1021, cert. denied, 334 U.S. 811. Goldman reported only $125,000 of the recovery as gross income and claimed that the $250,000 balance constituted punitive damages and as such was not taxable. The Tax Court agreed, 19 T.C. 637, and the Court of Appeals, hearing this with the Glenshaw case, affirmed. 211 F.2d 928.

It is conceded by the respondents that there is no constitutional barrier to the imposition of a tax on punitive damages. Our question is one of statutory construction: Are these payments comprehended by § 22(a)?

The sweeping scope of the controverted statute is readily apparent:

Sec. 22.   Gross Income

(a) *General Definition*. "Gross income" includes gains, profits, and income derived from salaries, wages, or compensation for personal service . . . of whatever kind and in whatever form paid, or from professions, vocations, trades, businesses, commerce, or sales, or dealings in property, whether real or personal, growing out of the ownership or use of or interest in such property; also from interest, rent, dividends, securities, or the transaction of any business carried on for gain or profit, *or gains or profits and income derived from any source whatever*. . . .

(Emphasis added.)

This Court has frequently stated that this language was used by Congress to exert in this field "the full measure of its taxing power." Helvering v. Clifford [309 U.S. 331]; Helvering v. Midland Mutual Life Ins. Co., 300 U.S. 216, 223; Douglas v. Willcuts, 296 U.S. 1, 9; Irwin v. Gavit, [268 U.S. 161]. Respondents contend that punitive damages, characterized as "windfalls" flowing from the culpable conduct of third parties, are not within the scope of the section. But Congress applied no limitations as to the source of taxable receipts, nor restrictive labels as to their nature. And the Court has given a liberal construction to this broad phraseology in recognition of the intention of Congress to tax all gains except those specifically exempted. . . . Thus, the fortuitous gain accruing to a lessor by reason of the forfeiture of a lessee's improvements on the rented property was taxed in Helvering v. Bruun [infra page 226]. Cf. Robertson v. United States, 343 U.S. 711; Rutkin v. United States, 343 U.S. 130; United States v. Kirby Lumber Co. [infra page 161]. Such decisions demonstrate that we cannot but ascribe content to the catchall provision of § 22(a), "gains or profits and income derived from any source whatever." The importance of that phrase has been too frequently recognized since its first appearance in the Revenue Act of 1913 to say now that it adds nothing to the meaning of "gross income."

Nor can we accept respondents' contention that a narrower reading of § 22(a) is required by the Court's characterization of income in Eisner v. Macomber, 252 U.S. 189, 207 [infra page 213], as "the gain derived from capital, from labor, or from both combined."[4] The Court was there endeavoring to determine whether the distribution of a corporate stock dividend

---

4. The phrase was derived from Stratton's Independence, Ltd. v. Howbert, 231 U.S. 399, 415, and Doyle v. Mitchell Bros. Co., 247 U.S. 179, 185, two cases construing the Revenue Act of 1909, 36 Stat. 11,112. Both taxpayers were "wasting asset" corporations, one being engaged in mining, the other in lumbering operations. The definition was applied by the Court to demonstrate a distinction between a return on capital and "a mere conversion of capital assets." Doyle v. Mitchell Bros. Co., supra, at 184. The question raised by the instant case is clearly distinguishable.

constituted a realized gain to the shareholder, or changed "only the form, not the essence," of his capital investment. Id. at 210. It was held that the taxpayer had "received nothing out of the company's assets for his separate use and benefit." Id. at 211. The distribution, therefore, was held not a taxable event. In that context — distinguishing gain from capital — the definition served a useful purpose. But it was not meant to provide a touchstone to all future gross income questions. . . .

Here we have instances of undeniable accessions to wealth, clearly realized, and over which the taxpayers have complete dominion. The mere fact that the payments were extracted from the wrongdoers as punishment for unlawful conduct cannot detract from their character as taxable income to the recipients. Respondents concede, as they must, that the recoveries are taxable to the extent that they compensate for damages actually incurred. It would be an anomaly that could not be justified in the absence of clear congressional intent to say that a recovery for actual damages is taxable but not the additional amount extracted as punishment for the same conduct which caused the injury. And we find no such evidence of intent to exempt these payments. . . .

Reversed.

Mr. Justice DOUGLAS dissents.

Mr. Justice HARLAN took no part in the consideration or decision of this case.

NOTES AND QUESTIONS

1. *Why is this case important?* As previously indicated (supra page 48), the thrust of the Court's opinion is in the language, "But Congress applied no limitations as to the source of taxable receipts, nor restrictive labels as to their nature." The significance of this statement derives not so much from its conclusion regarding whether Congress applied "limitations" or "restrictive labels" in the definition of income, but rather from its premise that it is *Congress* that decides how narrow or broad "income" should be. In this regard, *Glenshaw Glass* marks a complete and final repudiation of the Supreme Court's earlier approach, which had characterized much of the first four decades of the modern U.S. income tax. During that earlier era, courts had actively scrutinized legislative and regulatory decisions for consistency with their views regarding the meaning of "income" under the Sixteenth Amendment. That approach, typified by the famous decision in Eisner v. Macomber (1920), viewed the Supreme Court as the ultimate arbiter of the scope of legislative power, thus sharing a jurisprudential heritage with famous nontax cases like Lochner v. New York (1905). As with the "Lochner era," the Court's "Macomber era" began to pass with the advent of the New Deal Court in the late 1930s. *Glenshaw Glass* was the final nail in the coffin. Should the Court's abandonment of its Sixteenth Amendment jurisprudence be celebrated? Or does it mark an abdication of the Court's responsibility to interpret the U.S. Constitution? Now that more than a half-century has passed, is it time for the Supreme Court to put a nail in the coffin of the *Glenshaw Glass* era?

2. Glenshaw Glass *and the modern (broad) conception of income.* In many ways, Chief Justice Warren's opinion in *Glenshaw Glass* is consistent with the broad definition of income that is reflected in the Simons formulation (supra page 48) and is favored by most modern tax experts. The facts of the case nicely illustrate the appeal of that definition. As the Court argues, it would be anomalous indeed to tax a recovery of lost profits but not a treble-damages windfall arising from the same events. Similarly, it would offend one's sense of fairness to tax wages a person earns by hard work but not money a person happens to find lying on the street. See Cesarini v. United States, 296 F. Supp. 3 (N.D. Ohio 1969), aff'd per curiam, 428 F.2d 812 (6th Cir. 1970), holding that $4,467 in old currency discovered in a piano, which had been bought for $15 at an auction, was income in the year it was discovered. See Regs. § 1.61-14. Is there any argument in principles of taxation other than fairness for excluding windfalls? Are windfalls "income" as that word is normally used outside the tax system?[5] Examine the language of § 22(a) of the 1939 Code, quoted in the Court's opinion. Can you make a "strict constructionist" or "plain language" argument for exclusion? Bear in mind, this is a tax code that we interpret, not a constitution. Is there virtue in a "government of laws," even if the laws produce results we would not otherwise find appealing?

3. *Taxation and antitrust policy.* The punitive portion of an antitrust treble-damages award is intended to encourage private actions of the sort initiated by the plaintiffs in *Glenshaw Glass*. Should the punitive portions of the awards be excluded from gross income in order to promote, or avoid undercutting, the policies of the antitrust laws? If the punitive award is not a large enough incentive, would it be preferable to increase it and make the enlarged amount taxable, or retain the current amount and make it tax free? To focus the issue, think about an award of $1 million as the punitive portion of damages received (under the present system, without augmentation for tax effects) by two different corporations, *A* Corp., which is taxable at a rate of 35 percent, and *B* Corp., which is not taxable (because of losses carried forward from earlier years or because it is a not-for-profit corporation).

4. *Personal injury recoveries.* In a footnote, the Court attempts to reconcile its holding with the rule that damages for personal injury had been excluded, for many years, by administrative rulings. The implications of the current law, which largely incorporates these rulings, are considered further infra. It does seem plain, however, that the administrative rulings are consistent with the Eisner v. Macomber definition of income, on which the earlier ones expressly relied.

2. Gift: The Basic Concept

What should be the income tax consequences of receiving a gift? In the words of *Glenshaw Glass*, an outright gift — say, of cash with no strings

---

5. Suppose that last year you earned $20,000 as a law clerk and won $5,000 in a lottery and someone now asks you, "How much did you earn last year?" What would you say? Suppose the question is, "What was your income last year?"

attached—would appear to be an "undeniable accession to wealth, clearly realized, and over which the [recipient] has complete dominion." Even if it is a gift of some sort of property, such as a birthday gift of an item of clothing, one would think that only its value to the recipient (which might conceivably be less than its cost or market price), as opposed to whether it is income to begin with, could seriously be contested.

Nonetheless, gifts have always been excluded from taxable income under what is presently section 102. What is more, this exclusion extends to gifts (such as cash) that involve no valuation difficulty, and is not simply a de minimis rule of administrative convenience; it applies to large gifts as well as small.[6] To understand why this rule might be considered reasonable, even by advocates of broadly applying the *Glenshaw Glass* principle, it is important to consider both sides of the gift transaction—that is, the income tax treatment of the donor as well as the donee.

Example

Donna earns $100,000 per year, and her adult son Edward earns nothing. Out of love, Donna gives Edward $30,000 per year. Nothing else with federal income tax consequences happens to either of them. There would appear to be three main ways in which the federal income tax could treat them in light of the gift transaction:

(a) income to Edward, deduction to Donna. Thus, Edward's annual taxable income would be $30,000 and Donna's would be $70,000.

(b) income to Edward, no deduction to Donna. Thus, Edward's annual taxable income would be $30,000 and Donna's would be $100,000.

(c) no income to Edward, no deduction to Donna. This is the rule that the federal income tax actually follows, and under it Edward's taxable income is zero and Donna's is $100,000.

NOTES AND QUESTIONS

1. What do you think of the hypothetical rule in (a) above? Does it inappropriately permit Donna a deduction for a voluntary personal consumption expense akin to buying food? What tax planning opportunities would this rule open up for related parties, such as Donna and Edward, who are in different income tax rate brackets?

2. What do you think of the hypothetical rule in (b) above? Note that it describes the actual tax treatment that would apply if Edward were Donna's employee rather than (or in addition to being) her son, and received $30,000

---

6. Gifts in excess of $10,000 per year by a given donor to a given donee may give rise to gift tax liability. Essentially, the gift tax is a backup to the estate tax, since the latter would be too easy to avoid if transfers before one died were excluded. However, if one believes that both the income tax and the estate and gift tax should be levied, then taxing a transaction under one system presumably should not rule out taxing it under the other system.

for rendering nondeductible personal services such as cooking, cleaning, mowing the lawn, and so forth. What, if anything, makes the gift case relevantly different from the case of compensation for personal services?

3. Rule (c), which the federal income tax actually follows, has administrative advantages even apart from whether it levies the right amount of tax on the participants in a gift transaction. Under it, there is generally no need under the income tax to report gift transactions or determine the value of property received as a gift. On the other hand, it requires determining whether a given transfer, received by the taxpayer from another person, constitutes a gift under § 102 and thus can be excluded from taxable income. As the following case shows, such determinations can be particularly difficult when transfers arguably constituting gifts occur in a commercial rather than a family setting.

COMMISSIONER v. DUBERSTEIN
363 U.S. 278 (1960)

Mr. Justice BRENNAN delivered the opinion of the Court.

These two cases concern [§ 102(a)] which excludes from the gross income of an income taxpayer "the value of property acquired by gift." . . .

No. 376, Commissioner v. Duberstein. The taxpayer, Duberstein, was president of the Duberstein Iron & Metal Company, a corporation with headquarters in Dayton, Ohio. For some years the taxpayer's company had done business with Mohawk Metal Corporation, whose headquarters were in New York City. The president of Mohawk was one Berman. The taxpayer and Berman had generally used the telephone to transact their companies' business with each other, which consisted of buying and selling metals. The taxpayer testified, without elaboration, that he knew Berman "personally" and had known him for about seven years. From time to time in their telephone conversations, Berman would ask Duberstein whether the latter knew of potential customers for some of Mohawk's products in which Duberstein's company itself was not interested. Duberstein provided the names of potential customers for these items.

One day in 1951 Berman telephoned Duberstein and said that the information Duberstein had given him had proved so helpful that he wanted to give the latter a present. Duberstein stated that Berman owed him nothing. Berman said that he had a Cadillac as a gift for Duberstein, and that the latter should send to New York for it; Berman insisted that Duberstein accept the car, and the latter finally did so, protesting however that he had not intended to be compensated for the information. At the time Duberstein already had a Cadillac and an Oldsmobile, and felt that he did not need another car. Duberstein testified that he did not think Berman would have sent him the Cadillac if he had not furnished him with information about the customers. It appeared that Mohawk later deducted the value of the Cadillac as a business expense on its corporate income tax return.

Duberstein did not include the value of the Cadillac in gross income for 1951, deeming it a gift. The Commissioner asserted a deficiency for the car's value against him, and in proceedings to review the deficiency the Tax Court affirmed the Commissioner's determination. It said that "The record is significantly barren of evidence revealing any intention on the part of the payor to make a gift. . . . The only justifiable inference is that the automobile was intended by the payor to be remuneration for services rendered to it by Duberstein." The Court of Appeals for the Sixth Circuit reversed. 265 F.2d 28.

No. 506, Stanton v. United States. The taxpayer, Stanton, had been for approximately 10 years in the employ of Trinity Church in New York City. He was comptroller of the Church corporation, and president of a corporation, Trinity Operating Company, the church set up as a fully owned subsidiary to manage its real estate holdings, which were more extensive than simply the church property. His salary by the end of his employment there in 1942 amounted to $22,500 a year. Effective November 30, 1942, he resigned from both positions to go into business for himself. The Operating Company's directors, who seem to have included the rector and vestrymen of the church, passed the following resolution upon his resignation:

> *BE IT RESOLVED* that in appreciation of the services rendered by Mr. Stanton . . . a gratuity is hereby awarded to him of Twenty Thousand Dollars, payable to him in equal installments of Two Thousand Dollars at the end of each and every month commencing with the month of December, 1942; provided that, with the discontinuance of his services, the Corporation of Trinity Church is released from all rights and claims to pension and retirement benefits not already accrued up to November 30, 1942.

The Operating Company's action was later explained by one of its directors as based on the fact that,

> Mr. Stanton was liked by all of the Vestry personally. He had a pleasing personality. He had come in when Trinity's affairs were in a difficult situation. He did a splendid piece of work, we felt. Besides that . . . he was liked by all of the members of the Vestry personally.

And by another:

> [W]e were all unanimous in wishing to make Mr. Stanton a gift. Mr. Stanton had loyally and faithfully served Trinity in a very difficult time. We thought of him in the highest regard. We understood that he was going in business for himself. We felt that he was entitled to that evidence of good will.

On the other hand, there was a suggestion of some ill-feeling between Stanton and the directors, arising out of the recent termination of the services of one Watkins, the Operating Company's treasurer, whose departure was evidently attended by some acrimony. At a special board meeting on October 28, 1942, Stanton had intervened on Watkins' side and asked reconsideration of the matter. The minutes reflect that "resentment was expressed as to the 'presumptuous' suggestion that the action of the Board, taken after long deliberation, should be changed." The Board adhered to its determination that Watkins be separated from employment, giving him an opportunity to resign rather than be discharged. At another special meeting two days later it was revealed that Watkins had not resigned; the previous resolution terminating his services was then viewed as effective; and the Board voted the payment of six months' salary to Watkins in a resolution similar to that quoted in regard to Stanton, but which did not use the term "gratuity." At the meeting, Stanton announced that in order to avoid any such embarrassment or question at any time as to his willingness to resign if the Board desired, he was tendering his resignation. It was tabled, though not without dissent. The next week, on November 5, at another special meeting, Stanton again tendered his resignation which this time was accepted.

The "gratuity" was duly paid. So was a smaller one to Stanton's (and the Operating Company's) secretary, under a similar resolution, upon her resignation at the same time. The two corporations shared the expense of the payments. There was undisputed testimony that there were in fact no enforceable rights or claims to pension and retirement benefits which had not accrued at the time of the taxpayer's resignation, and that the last proviso of the resolution was inserted simply out of an abundance of caution. The taxpayer received in cash a refund of his contributions to the retirement plans, and there is no suggestion that he was entitled to more. He was required to perform no further services for Trinity after his resignation.

. . . The trial judge, sitting without a jury, made the simple finding that the payments were a "gift," and judgment was entered for the taxpayer. The Court of Appeals for the Second Circuit reversed. 268 F.2d 727. . . .

The exclusion of property acquired by gift from gross income under the federal income tax laws was made in the first income tax statute passed under the authority of the Sixteenth Amendment, and has been a feature of the income tax statutes ever since. The meaning of the term "gift" as applied to particular transfers has always been a matter of contention. Specific and illuminating legislative history on the point does not appear to exist. Analogies and inferences drawn from other revenue provisions, such as the estate and gift taxes, are dubious. . . . The meaning of the statutory term has been shaped largely by the decisional law. With this, we turn to the contentions made by the Government in these cases.

First. The Government suggests that we promulgate a new "test" in this area to serve as a standard to be applied by the lower courts and by the Tax Court in dealing with the numerous cases that arise.[7] We reject this invitation. We are of opinion that the governing principles are necessarily general and have already been spelled out in the opinions of this Court, and that the problem is one which, under the present statutory framework, does not lend itself to any more definitive statement that would produce a talisman for the solution of concrete cases. The cases at bar are fair examples of the settings in which the problem usually arises. They present situations in which payments have been made in a context with business overtones — an employer making a payment to a retiring employee; a businessman giving something of value to another businessman who has been of advantage to him in his business. In this context, we review the law as established by the prior cases here.

7. [The government's test would have generally ruled out gift treatment for transfers from employers to employees. — EDS.]

The course of decision here makes it plain that the statute does not use the term "gift" in the common-law sense, but in a more colloquial sense. This Court has indicated that a voluntary executed transfer of his property by one to another, without any consideration or compensation therefor, though a common-law gift, is not necessarily a "gift" within the meaning of the statute. For the Court has shown that the mere absence of a legal or moral obligation to make such a payment does not establish that it is a gift. Old Colony Trust Co. v. Commissioner, 279 U.S. 716, 730. And, importantly, if the payment proceeds primarily from "the constraining force of any moral or legal duty," or from "the incentive of anticipated benefit" of an economic nature, Bogardus v. Commissioner, 302 U.S. 34, 41, it is not a gift. And, conversely, "[w]here the payment is in return for services rendered, it is irrelevant that the donor derives no economic benefit from it." Robertson v. United States, 343 U.S. 711, 714. A gift in the statutory sense, on the other hand, proceeds from a "detached and disinterested generosity," Commissioner v. LoBue, 351 U.S. 243, 246; "out of affection, respect, admiration, charity or like impulses." Robertson v. United States, supra, at 714. And in this regard, the most critical consideration, as the Court was agreed in the leading case here, is the transferor's "intention." Bogardus v. Commissioner, 302 U.S. 34, 43. "What controls is the intention with which payment, however voluntary, has been made." Id., at 45 (dissenting opinion).

The Government says that this "intention" of the transferor cannot mean what the cases on the common-law concept of gift call "donative intent." With that we are in agreement, for our decisions fully support this. Moreover, the *Bogardus* case itself makes it plain that the donor's characterization of his action is not determinative — that there must be an objective inquiry as to whether what is called a gift amounts to it in reality. 302 U.S., at 40. It scarcely needs adding that the parties' expectations or hopes as to the tax treatment of their conduct in themselves have nothing to do with the matter. . . .

Second. The Government's proposed "test," while apparently simple and precise in its formulation, depends frankly on a set of "principles" or "presumptions" derived from the decided cases, and concededly subject to various exceptions; and it involves various corollaries, which add to its detail. Were we to promulgate this test as a matter of law, and accept with it its various presuppositions and stated consequences, we would be passing far beyond the requirements of the cases before us, and would be painting on a large canvas with indeed a broad brush. The Government derives its test from such propositions as the following: That payments by an employer to an employee, even though voluntary, ought, by and large, to be taxable; that the concept of a gift is inconsistent with a payment's being a deductible business expense; that a gift involves "personal" elements; that a business corporation cannot properly make a gift of its assets. The Government admits that there are exceptions and qualifications to these propositions. We think, to the extent they are correct, that these propositions are not principles of law but rather maxims of experience that the tribunals, which have tried the fact of cases in this area have enunciated in explaining their factual determinations. Some of them simply represent truisms: it doubtless is, statistically speaking, the exceptional payment by an employer to an employee that amounts to a gift.

Others are overstatements of possible evidentiary inferences relevant to a factual determination on the totality of circumstances in the case: it is doubtless relevant to the over-all inference that the transferor treats a payment as a business deduction, or that the transferor is a corporate entity. But these inferences cannot be stated in absolute terms. Neither factor is a shibboleth. The taxing statute does not make nondeductibility by the transferor a condition on the "gift" exclusion; nor does it draw any distinction, in terms, between transfers by corporations and individuals, as to the availability of the "gift" exclusion to the transferee. The conclusion whether a transfer amounts to a "gift" is one that must be reached on a consideration of all the factors.

Specifically, the trier of fact must be careful not to allow trial of the issue whether the receipt of a specific payment is a gift to turn into a trial of the tax liability, or of the propriety, as a matter of fiduciary or corporate law, attaching to the conduct of someone else. . . . The major corollary to the Government's suggested "test" is that, as an ordinary matter, a payment by a corporation cannot be a gift, and, more specifically, there can be no such thing as a "gift" made by a corporation which would allow it to take a deduction for an ordinary and necessary business expense. As we have said, we find no basis for such a conclusion in the statute; and if it were applied as a determinative rule of "law," it would force the tribunals trying tax cases involving the donee's liability into elaborate inquiries into the local law of corporations or into the peripheral deductibility of payments as business expenses.[8]

Third. Decision of the issue presented in these cases must be based ultimately on the application of the fact-finding tribunal's experience with the mainsprings of human conduct to the totality of the facts of each case. The nontechnical nature of the statutory standard, the close relationship of it to the data of practical human experience, and the multiplicity of relevant factual elements, with their various combinations, creating the necessity of ascribing the proper force to each, confirm us in our conclusion that primary weight in this area must be given to the conclusions of the trier of fact. . . .

This conclusion may not satisfy an academic desire for tidiness, symmetry and precision in this area, any more than a system based on the determinations of various fact-finders ordinarily does. But we see it as implicit in the present statutory treatment of the exclusion for gifts, and in the variety of forums in which federal income tax cases can be tried. If there is fear of undue uncertainty or overmuch litigation, Congress may make more precise its treatment of the matter by singling out certain factors and making them determinative of the matter, as it has done in one field of the "gift" exclusion's former application, that of prizes and awards. Doubtless diversity of result will tend to be lessened somewhat since federal income tax decisions, even those in tribunals of first instance turning on issues of fact, tend to be reported, and since there may be a natural tendency of professional triers of fact to follow

---

8. Justice Cardozo once described in memorable language the inquiry into whether an expense was an "ordinary and necessary" one of a business: "One struggles in vain for any verbal formula that will supply a ready touchstone. The standard set up by the statute is not a rule of law; it is rather a way of life. Life in all its fullness must supply the answer to the riddle." Welch v. Helvering, 290 U.S. 111, 115. The same comment well fits the issue in the cases at bar.

one another's determinations, even as to factual matters. But the question here remains basically one of fact, for determination on a case-by-case basis.

One consequence of this is that appellate review of determinations in this field must be quite restricted. Where a jury has tried the matter upon correct instructions, the only inquiry is whether it cannot be said that reasonable men could reach differing conclusions on the issue. . . . Where the trial has been by a judge without a jury, the judge's findings must stand unless "clearly erroneous." Fed. Rules Civ. Proc., 52 (a). . . .

Fourth. A majority of the Court is in accord with the principles just outlined. And, applying them to the *Duberstein* case, we are in agreement, on the evidence we have set forth, that it cannot be said that the conclusion of the Tax Court was "clearly erroneous." It seems to us plain that as trier of the facts it was warranted in concluding that despite the characterization of the transfer of the Cadillac by the parties and the absence of any obligation, even of a moral nature, to make it, it was at bottom a recompense for Duberstein's past services, or an inducement for him to be of further service in the future. We cannot say with the Court of Appeals that such a conclusion was "mere suspicion" on the Tax Court's part. To us it appears based in the sort of informed experience with human affairs that fact-finding tribunals should bring to this task.

As to *Stanton,* we are in disagreement. To four of us, it is critical here that the District Court as trier of fact made only the simple and unelaborated finding that the transfer in question was a "gift." To be sure, conciseness is to be strived for, and prolixity avoided, in findings; but, to the four of us, there comes a point where findings become so sparse and conclusory as to give no revelation of what the District Court's concept of the determining facts and legal standard may be. . . . Such conclusory, general findings do not constitute compliance with Rule 52's direction to "find the facts specially and state separately . . . conclusions of law thereon." While the standard of law in this area is not a complex one, we four think the unelaborated finding of ultimate fact here cannot stand as a fulfillment of these requirements. It affords the reviewing court not the semblance of an indication of the legal standard with which the trier of fact has approached his task. For all that appears, the District Court may have viewed the form of the resolution or the simple absence of legal consideration as conclusive. While the judgment of the Court of Appeals cannot stand, the four of us think there must be further proceedings in the District Court looking toward new and adequate findings of fact. In this, we are joined by Mr. Justice Whittaker, who agrees that the findings were inadequate, although he does not concur generally in this opinion.

Accordingly, in No. 376, the judgment of this Court is that the judgment of the Court of Appeals is reversed, and in No. 546, that the judgment of the District Court of Appeals is vacated, and the case is remanded to the District Court for further proceedings not inconsistent with this opinion.

It is so ordered.

Mr. Justice HARLAN, concurs in the result in No. 376. In No. 546, he would affirm the judgment of the Court of Appeals for the reasons stated by Mr. Justice Frankfurter.

Mr. Justice WHITTAKER, agreeing with Bogardus that whether a particular transfer is or is not a "gift" may involve "a mixed question of law and fact," 302 U.S., at 39, concurs only in the result of this opinion.

Mr. Justice DOUGLAS dissents, since he is of the view that in each of these two cases there was a gift under the test which the Court fashioned nearly a quarter of a century ago in Bogardus v. Commissioner, 302 U.S. 34.

[Mr. Justice BLACK concurred in *Duberstein* and dissented in *Stanton*, on the ground that the trial court's finding in each case was "not clearly erroneous."]

[Mr. Justice FRANKFURTER said that "in the two situations now before us the business implications are so forceful that I would apply a presumptive rule placing the burden upon the beneficiary to prove the payment wholly unrelated to his services to the enterprise" and that the Court's emphasis on the fact-finding tribunal's "experience with the mainsprings of human conduct" would set them "to sail on an illimitable ocean of individual beliefs and experiences." He concluded that Duberstein was properly taxed, and that Stanton's payment should have been taxed because it was not "sheer benevolence but in the nature of a generous lagniappe, something extra thrown in for services received though not legally nor morally required to be given."]

NOTES AND QUESTIONS

1. *Aftermath.* (a) On the remand of the *Stanton* case, the district court made detailed findings of fact and again concluded that the payments to Stanton were gifts. 186 F. Supp. 393 (E.D.N.Y. 1960). On appeal the Court of Appeals affirmed on the ground that the findings were not "clearly erroneous," Chief Judge Lumbard concurring because of the restricted character of appellate review, although he thought a "contrary inference should have been drawn from the undisputed basic facts." 287 F.2d 876, 877 (2d Cir. 1961).

(b) Section 102(c), added in 1986, alters the result in *Stanton* by a categorical rule precluding gift treatment in the case of any transfer by an employer to an employee. There is, however, a modest and carefully circumscribed exclusion for "employee achievement awards." See § 74(c).

2. *Analysis.* (a) The Court says that it cannot find any "specific and illuminating legislative history." Accordingly, it interprets "gift" in the "colloquial sense." In other words, it adopts a "plain language" approach to the statute. From there, it defines "gift" by reference to a state of mind. What is the required state of mind? In a case like *Stanton*, whose state of mind counts? How does the trier of fact find that state of mind?

(b) Can a part of the message that the Supreme Court was really sending in *Duberstein* be fairly summarized as follows: "We don't ever want to review another gift case, so within limits finders of fact can do whatever they like"?

(c) The Court refuses to accept as a "shibboleth" that "nondeductibility by the transferor [is] a condition on the 'gift' exclusion" (supra page 94). How can a transfer simultaneously proceed from the "detached and disinterested generosity" of the transferor and yet generate a business deduction on the ground that it was a cost of earning income?

(d) Is the Court letting itself off too easily when it concludes that its broad focus on "the mainsprings of human conduct" will not satisfy "a desire for academic tidiness"? What would happen to the career of a law firm associate who, when asked to provide helpful guidance regarding whether a given transfer qualified as a gift, replied, quoting Justice Cardozo from the Court's approving footnote, that "[l]ife in all its fullness must supply the answer to the riddle"?

3. *Business versus family transfers.* (a) Would an inquiry into the policy reasons for excluding gifts from gross income have been useful? Henry Simons argued that gifts ought to be included in income because "surely it is hard to defend exclusion of certain receipts merely because one has done nothing or given nothing in return." Personal Income Taxation 135 (1938). Simons would not have allowed a deduction for the donor. Id. at 136. Thus, Simons would have followed Rule (b) from the Example that precedes *Duberstein*. Simons' position has been criticized on two main grounds: for insufficient sensitivity to notions of the family or household as an economic unit, and for overly harsh treatment of socially desirable altruistic transfers. Does this perspective on the gift exclusion shed any light on what the outcome ought to be under the *Duberstein* and *Stanton* facts?

(b) People who are supported by members of their family do not have gross income in the amount of the support they receive. This rule is without express statutory authority; it is simply part of the accepted definition of "income" and has never been questioned by the Service or by tax theorists. Often it may be difficult to distinguish between support payments and gifts—for example, where a parent buys an automobile for his or her child. Does this help explain the gift exclusion? If so, how does it bear on the decision in *Duberstein*?

4. *Congressional reaction and the payor's deduction for business gifts.* Section 274(b), added in 1962, allows persons such as Berman, in the *Duberstein* case, to deduct as an ordinary and necessary business expense the first $25 of any business gift. That section seems to accept implicitly the notion that there can be "business gifts"—that is, transfers that, though business motivated for the transferor, are gifts to the transferee. Of course, if the business motivation is strong enough, the transfer will not be a gift, the transferee will be required to treat the value of the item received as an addition to adjusted gross income, and § 274(b)'s limitation will not operate to deny a deduction to the transferor. Where the item is treated as a gift to the transferee and, under § 274(b) the deduction is denied to the transferor, the net effect can be thought of as a form of surrogate taxation, where the tax burden of one person (here, the transferor) is increased to offset what is regarded as an improper tax benefit to another person (here, the payee).

In a case like *Duberstein*, for example, suppose you start with the notion that Berman's cost in presenting the Cadillac to Duberstein is properly regarded as a business expense for Berman and income to Duberstein. Suppose the cost was $10,000 and that both Berman and Duberstein pay tax at a rate of 40 percent. Berman should be entitled to a deduction of $10,000, which will reduce his tax liability by $4,000. Duberstein should have income of $10,000, which will increase his tax liability by $4,000. Now suppose that for some reason we decide that we cannot tax Duberstein on the value of the automobile. Duberstein's tax payments will decline by $4,000 (compared with what we think to be the correct result). We might then deny a deduction to Berman. His tax payments will then increase by $4,000 (compared with the correct result). The Treasury then comes out whole. Duberstein escapes taxation, but Berman is taxed as his surrogate. Berman might claim that he has been treated unfairly, but one's sympathy for this claim may be diminished by the knowledge that he can adjust the amount of the benefit he is willing to confer on Duberstein to take account of the tax detriment to himself and the tax benefit to Duberstein. Surrogate taxation may be especially appealing where an employer supplies a benefit that is particularly difficult to allocate among employees (e.g., the use of athletic facilities). But note the importance of the relative tax rates of the person who should be taxed and the surrogate. Consider, for example, what the surrogate would be in the *Stanton* case. The net effect of surrogate taxation is that the Treasury will collect the proper amount of tax, or close to the proper amount, in most, but not all, cases. To achieve the proper tax result in all cases, one must tax the proper person (a result now achieved under § 102(c) for transfers like those in *Stanton*, involving transfers from employers to employees).

5. *Later development: § 83.* Section 83 was adopted after the decision in *Duberstein*, with different, more sophisticated kinds of transactions in mind. Would it make a difference in a case like *Duberstein*? Under the decision in *Duberstein* is it possible for a transfer of property to be a "gift" within the meaning of § 102 and still be made "in connection with the performance of services" within the contemplation of § 83? If so, which provision governs?

6. While away from home on a business trip, Ellen eats at an airport coffee shop. Ellen knows that she is unlikely to ever eat at the coffee shop again. Nonetheless, after lunch, Ellen leaves a $5 tip for the waiter, who happens to be your best friend Rakesh. Rakesh asks for your professional opinion regarding whether or not he must include tips like these in income. What sort of advice would you give Rakesh?

UNITED STATES v. HARRIS
942 F.2d 1125 (7th Cir. 1991)

ESCHBACH, Senior Circuit Judge.

David Kritzik, now deceased, was a wealthy widower partial to the company of young women. Two of these women were Leigh Ann Conley and Lynnette Harris, twin sisters. Directly or indirectly, Kritzik gave Conley and Harris each more than half a million dollars over the course of several years. For our purposes, either Kritzik had to pay gift tax on this money or Harris and Conley had to pay income tax. The United States alleges that, beyond reasonable doubt, the obligation was Harris and Conley's. In separate criminal trials, Harris and Conley were convicted of willfully evading their income tax obligations regarding the money,[9] and they now appeal....

---

9. Harris was sentenced to ten months in prison, to be followed by two months in a halfway house and two years of supervised release. She was also fined $12,500.00 and ordered to pay a $150.00

INSUFFICIENCY OF THE EVIDENCE AS TO CONLEY

Conley was convicted on each of four counts for violating 26 U.S.C. § 7203, which provides,

> Any person . . . required . . . to make a [tax] return . . . who willfully fails to . . . make such return . . . shall, in addition to other penalties provided by law, be guilty of a misdemeanor. . . .

Conley was "required . . . to make a return" only if the money that she received from Kritzik was income to her rather than a gift. Assuming that the money was income, she acted "willfully," and so is subject to criminal prosecution, only if she knew of her duty to pay taxes and "voluntarily and intentionally violated that duty." Cheek v. United States 498 U.S. 192 (1991). The government met its burden of proof if the jury could have found these elements beyond a reasonable doubt, viewing the evidence in the light most favorable to the government.

The government's evidence was insufficient to show either that the money Conley received was income or that she acted in knowing disregard of her obligations. "Gross income" for tax purposes does not include gifts, which are taxable to the donor rather than the recipient. §§ 61, 102(a), 2501(a). In Commissioner v. Duberstein, 363 U.S. 278 (1960), the Supreme Court stated that in distinguishing between income and gifts the "critical consideration . . . is the transferor's intention." A transfer of property is a gift if the transferor acted out of a "detached and disinterested generosity, . . . out of affection, respect, admiration, charity, or like impulses." Id. By contrast, a transfer of property is income if it is the result of "the constraining force of any moral or legal duty, constitutes a reward for services rendered, or proceeds from the incentive of anticipated benefit of an economic nature."

Regarding the "critical consideration" of the donor's intent, the only direct evidence that the government presented was Kritzik's gift tax returns. On those returns, Kritzik identified gifts to Conley of $24,000, $30,000, and $36,000 for the years 1984-6, respectively, substantially less than the total amount of money that Kritzik transferred to Conley. This leaves the question whether Kritzik's other payments were taxable income to Conley or whether Kritzik just under-reported his gifts. The gift tax returns raise the question, they do not resolve it.[10]

---

special assessment. Conley was sentenced to five months in prison, followed by five months in a halfway house and one year supervised release. She was also fined $10,000.00 and ordered to pay a $100.00 assessment.

10. Our discussion assumes that the gift tax returns were admissible as evidence because the parties have not raised the issue. We note, however, that the returns appear on their face to be hearsay. The government used the returns (out of court statements) to prove that Kritzik's gifts were the amount that he reported (that is, to prove the truth of the matter asserted). . . .

Along these lines, the United States tried to present direct evidence of Kritzik's intent in the form of an affidavit that he provided IRS investigators before his death. In the affidavit, Kritzik stated that he regarded both Harris and Conley as prostitutes. But Kritzik had an obvious motive to lie to the investigators — he could have been subject to civil or criminal penalties for failure to pay gift taxes if he failed to shift the tax burden to the sisters. The District Court was correct to exclude this affidavit under the hearsay rule and under the confrontation clause. In general, evidentiary difficulties such as this will often be insurmountable in trying to prove a willful tax violation that hinges on the intent of a dead person. The civil remedies available to the IRS will almost always lead to surer justice in such cases than criminal prosecution.

This failure to show Kritzik's intent is fatal to the government's case. . . .

The government's remaining evidence consisted of a bank card that Conley signed listing Kritzik in a space marked "employer" and testimony regarding the form of the payments that Conley received. The bank card is no evidence of Kritzik's intent and even as to Conley is open to conflicting interpretations — she contends that she listed Kritzik as a reference and no more. As to the form of payments, the government showed that Conley would pick up a regular check at Kritzik's office every week to ten days, either from Kritzik personally or, when he was not in, from his secretary. According to the government, this form of payment is that of an employee picking up regular wages, but it could just as easily be that of a dependent picking up regular support checks.

We will "not permit a verdict based solely upon the piling of inference upon inference." United States v. Balzano, 916 F.2d 1273, 1284 (7th Cir. 1990). . . .

THE ADMISSIBILITY OF KRITZIK'S LETTERS

Harris was convicted of two counts of willfully failing to file federal income tax returns under § 7203 (the same offense for which Conley was convicted) and two counts of willful tax evasion under § 7201. At trial, Harris tried to introduce as evidence three letters that Kritzik wrote, but the District Court excluded the letters as hearsay. The District Court also suggested that the letters would be inadmissible under Fed. R. Evid. 403 because the possible prejudice from the letters exceeded their probative value. We hold that the letters were not hearsay because they were offered to prove Harris' lack of willfulness, not for the truth of the matters asserted. We further hold that the critical nature of the letters to Harris' defense precludes their exclusion under Rule 403, and so reverse her conviction.

The first of the letters at issue was a four page, handwritten letter from Kritzik to Harris, dated April 4, 1981. In it, Kritzik wrote that he loved and trusted Harris and that, "so far as the things I give you are concerned — let me say that I get as great if not even greater pleasure in giving than you get in receiving." Def. Ex. 201, p.2. He continued, "I love giving things to you and to see you happy and enjoying them." Id. In a second letter to Harris of the same date, Kritzik again wrote, "I . . . love you very much and will do all that I can to make you happy," and said that he would arrange for Harris' financial security. Def. Ex. 202, p.3. In a third letter, dated some six years later on May 28, 1987, Kritzik wrote to his insurance company regarding the value of certain jewelry that he had "given to Ms. Lynette Harris as a gift." Kritzik forwarded a copy of the letter to Harris.

These letters were hearsay if offered for the truth of the matters asserted — that Kritzik did in fact love Harris, enjoyed giving her things, wanted to take care of her financial security, and gave her the jewelry at issue as a gift. But the letters were not hearsay for the purpose of showing what Harris believed, because her belief does not depend on the actual truth of the matters asserted in the letters. Even if Kritzik were lying, the letters could have caused Harris to believe in good faith that the things he gave her were intended as gifts. . . .

This good faith belief, in turn, would preclude any finding of willfulness on her part. . . .

The Tax Treatment of Payments to Mistresses

Our conclusion that Harris should have been allowed to present the letters at issue as evidence would ordinarily lead us to remand her case for retrial. We further conclude, however, that current law on the tax treatment of payments to mistresses provided Harris no fair warning that her conduct was criminal. Indeed, current authorities favor Harris' position that the money she received from Kritzik was a gift. We emphasize that we do not necessarily agree with these authorities, and that the government is free to urge departure from them in a *non*criminal context. But new points of tax law may not be the basis of criminal convictions. For this reason, we remand with instructions that the indictment against Harris be dismissed. Although we discuss only Harris' case in this section, the same reasoning applies to Conley and provides an alternative basis for dismissal of the indictment against her.

Again, the definitive statement of the distinction between gifts and income is in the Supreme Court's *Duberstein* decision, which applies and interprets the definition of income contained in § 61. But as the Supreme Court described, the *Duberstein* principles are "necessarily general." It stated, "'One struggles in vain for any verbal formula that will supply a ready touchstone. The standard set up . . . is not a rule of law; it is rather a way of life. Life in all its fullness must supply the answer to the riddle.'" Id., quoting Welch v. Helvering, 290 U.S. 111 (1933). Along these lines, Judge Flaum's concurrence properly characterizes *Duberstein* as "eschew[ing] . . . [any] categorical, rule-bound analysis" in favor of a "case-by-case" approach.

Duberstein was a civil case, and its approach is appropriate for civil cases. But criminal prosecutions are a different story. These must rest on a violation of a clear rule of law, not on conflict with a "way of life." If "defendants [in a tax case] . . . could not have ascertained the legal standards applicable to their conduct, criminal proceedings may not be used to define and punish an alleged failure to conform to those standards." United States v. Mallas, 762 F.2d 361, 361 (4th Cir. 1985). . . .

We do not doubt that *Duberstein*'s principles, though general, provide a clear answer to many cases involving the gift versus income distinction and can be the basis for civil as well as criminal prosecutions in such cases. We are equally certain, however, that *Duberstein* provides no ready answer to the taxability of transfers of money to a mistress in the context of a long term relationship. The motivations of the parties in such cases will always be mixed. The relationship would not be long term were it not for some respect or affection. Yet, it may be equally clear that the relationship would not continue were it not for financial support or payments. . . .

The most pertinent authority lies in several civil cases from the Tax Court, but these cases *favor* Harris' position. At its strongest, the government's case against Harris follows the assertions that Harris made, but now repudiates, in a lawsuit she filed against Kritzik's estate. According to her sworn pleadings in that suit, "all sums of money paid by David Kritzik to Lynette Harris . . . were made . . . in pursuance with the parties' express oral agreement." Government Exhibit 22, p.4. As Harris' former lawyer testified at her trial, the point of this pleading was to make out a "palimony" claim under the California Supreme Court's decision in Marvin v. Marvin, 18 Cal. 3d 660, 134 Cal. Rptr. 815, 557 P.2d 106 (1976). Yet, the Tax Court has likened *Marvin*-type claims to amounts paid under antenuptial agreements. Under this analysis, these claims are *not* taxable income to the recipient:

> In an antenuptial agreement the parties agree, through private contract, on an arrangement for the disposition of their property in the event of death or separation. *Occasionally, however, the relinquishment of marital rights is not involved. These contracts are generally enforceable under state contract law. See* Marvin v. Marvin, 18 Cal. 3d 660 [134 Cal. Rptr. 815], 557 P.2d 106 (1976). Nonetheless, transfers pursuant to an antenuptial agreement are generally treated as gifts between the parties, because under the gift tax law the exchanged promises are not supported by full and adequate consideration, in money or money's worth.

Green v. Commissioner, T.C. Memo 1987-503 (emphasis added).[11] We do not decide whether *Marvin*-type awards or settlements are or are not taxable to the recipient. The only point is that the Tax Court has suggested they are not. Until contrary authority emerges, no taxpayer could form a willful, criminal intent to violate the tax laws by failing to report *Marvin*-type payments. Reasonable inquiry does not yield a clear answer to the taxability of such payments.

Other cases only reinforce this conclusion. Reis v. Commissioner, T.C. Memo 1974-287 is a colorful example. The case concerned the tax liability of Lillian Reis, who had her start as a 16-year-old nightclub dancer. At 21, she met Clyde "Bing" Miller when he treated the performers in the nightclub show to a steak and champagne dinner. As the Tax Court described it, Bing passed out $50 bills to each person at the table, on the condition that they leave, until he

---

11. [The Court's use of the *Green* decision may be misleading. Note that the last sentence of the excerpt from the case refers to the gift tax, not the income tax. It is settled that the definition of "gift" is different for gift-tax purposes than for income-tax purposes. For nine years, taxpayer Green, and a man named Richmond, who was a stockbroker, had been "inseparable." Among other things, Green had traveled with Richmond on his business trips and had "watched his diet and health, cared for him when he was ill, kept track of his appointments and concerned herself with his personal needs." Though he declined to marry Green, Richmond promised to leave his large estate to her. He died without having kept the promise and Green sued the estate, under a theory of quantum meruit, for the value of services rendered. After Green was successful at trial, the suit was settled for a payment of $900,000 by the estate to her. The Tax Court sustained the IRS's determination that the settlement amount was income to Green. The court, in rejecting Green's effort to analogize her rights to a claim under an antenuptial agreement, stated that there was in fact no antenuptial agreement and that, in her state-court action, Green had relied on a theory of quantum meruit — that is, on claimed entitlement to payment for services rendered.

On the other hand, in Reynolds v. Commissioner, T.C. Memo. 1999-62, the court concluded that cash payments received by a woman were nontaxable compensation for relinquishment of her interests in property (consisting mainly of a house and a large boat). The man and woman had lived together for 25 years, unmarried but in a marriage-like relationship. Despite the fact that the property had been bought by the man and was held solely in his name, the court accepted the woman's claim that the man had given her an interest in the property, as gifts, during their years together. The court emphasized that although the woman, in the legal action filed against the man, had referred to various household services that she had provided, she had not made any claim based on those services. — EDS.]

was alone with Reis. Bing then offered to write a check to Reis for any amount she asked. She asked for $1,200 for a mink stole and for another check in the same amount so her sister could have a coat too.

The next day the checks proved good; Bing returned to the club with more gifts; and "a lasting friendship developed" between Reis and Bing. For the next five years, she saw Bing "every Tuesday night at the [nightclub] and Wednesday afternoons from approximately 1:00 p.m. to 3:00 p.m. . . . at various places including . . . a girl friend's apartment and hotels where [Bing] was staying." He paid all of her living expenses, plus $200 a week, and provided money for her to invest, decorate her apartment, buy a car, and so on. The total over the five years was more than $100,000. The Tax Court held that this money was a gift, not income, despite Reis' statement that she "earned every penny" of the money. Similarly, in Libby v. Commissioner, T.C. Memo 1969-184 (1969), the Tax Court accorded gift treatment to thousands of dollars in cash and property that a young mistress received from her older paramour. And in Starks v. Commissioner, T.C. Memo 1966-134, the Tax Court did the same for another young woman who received cash and other property from an older, married man as part of "a very personal relationship."

The Tax Court did find that payments were income to the women who received them in Blevins v. Commissioner, T.C. Memo 1955-211, and in Jones v. Commissioner, T.C. Memo 1977-329. But in *Blevins*, the taxpayer was a woman who practiced prostitution and "used her home to operate a house of prostitution" in which six other women worked. Nothing suggested that the money at issue in that case was anything other than payments in the normal course of her business. Similarly in *Jones*, a woman had frequent hotel meetings with a married man, and on "*each* occasion" he gave her cash (emphasis added). Here too, the Tax Court found that the relationship was one of prostitution, a point that was supported by the woman's similar relationships with other men.

If these cases make a rule of law, it is that a person is entitled to treat cash and property received from a lover as gifts, as long as the relationship consists of something more than specific payments for specific sessions of sex. What's more, even in *Blevins*, in which the relationship was one of raw prostitution, the Tax Court rejected the IRS' claim that a civil fraud penalty should be imposed. Nor was a fraud penalty applied in *Jones*, the other prostitution case, although there the issue apparently was not raised. The United States does not allege that Harris received specific payments for specific sessions of sex, so *Reis*, *Libby*, and *Starks* support Harris' position. . . .

Besides Harris' prior suit, the United States also presented evidence regarding the overall relationship between Harris and Kritzik. Testimony showed that Harris described her relationship with Kritzik as "a job" and "just making a living." She reportedly complained that she "was laying on her back and her sister was getting all the money," described how she disliked when Kritzik fondled her naked, and made other derogatory statements about sex with Kritzik.

This evidence still leaves Harris on the favorable side of the Tax Court's cases. Further, this evidence tells us only what Harris thought of the relationship. Again, the Supreme Court in *Duberstein* held that the *donor's* intent is the "critical consideration" in determining whether a transfer of money is a gift or income. Commissioner v. Duberstein, 363 U.S. 278, 285 (1960). If Kritzik viewed the money he gave Harris as a gift, or if the dearth of contrary evidence leaves doubt on the subject, does it matter how mercenary Harris' motives were? *Duberstein* suggests that Harris' motives may not matter, but the ultimate answer makes no difference here. As long as the answer is at least a close call, and we are confident that it is, the prevailing law is too uncertain to support Harris' criminal conviction. . . .

In short, criminal prosecutions are no place for the government to try out "pioneering interpretations of tax law." United States v. Garber, 607 F.2d 92, 100 (5th Cir. 1979) (en banc). The United States has not shown us, and we have not found, a single case finding tax liability for payments that a mistress received from her lover, absent proof of specific payments for specific sex acts. Even when such specific proof is present, the cases have not applied penalties for civil fraud, much less criminal sanctions. The broad principles contained in *Duberstein* do not fill this gap. Before she met Kritzik, Harris starred as a sorceress in an action/adventure film. She would have had to be a real life sorceress to predict her tax obligations under the current state of the law.[12]

CONCLUSION

For the reasons stated, we reverse Harris and Conley's convictions and remand with instructions to dismiss the indictments against them.

FLAUM, Circuit Judge, concurring.

The majority has persuasively demonstrated why Leigh Ann Conley's conviction is infirm and why the district court abused its discretion in excluding the Kritzik letters. I therefore join that portion of its opinion.

I further agree that Lynnette Harris' conviction must be reversed as well. . . .

---

12. Harris and Conley have already served most of the sentences under the convictions that we now reverse. This is an injustice, and requires at least a brief explanation.

To be released pending appeal of a criminal conviction, a defendant must show "by clear and convincing evidence that the person is not likely to flee or pose a danger to the safety of any other person" *and* "that the appeal is not for the purpose of delay and raises a substantial question of law or fact likely to result in reversal or an order for a new trial." 18 U.S.C. § 3143(b).

This is an exacting standard. Harris and Conley's counsel performed well, but failed in their petitions for release pending appeal to draw the Court's attention to the unique nature of Harris and Conley's convictions under the prevailing tax cases. In Orders dated September 25, 1990 and October 26, 1990, the Court denied those petitions. We vacated those Orders on May 10, 1991, the day after oral argument, and ordered Harris and Conley's immediate release.

In the future, counsel who believe that the Court should have granted a petition for release can assist the Court by renewing the petition in their main appellate briefs. Also, this Court's warnings to counsel against the "buckshot" approach of raising as many issues as possible . . . are particularly applicable to motions for release pending appeal. Finally, the district courts can assist us by stating in detail their reasons for denying a petition for release pending appeal, especially in a case like the present one in which the defendants posed no danger to the community and apparently negligible threat of flight. Necessarily, a district court's thorough knowledge of the merits of a case puts it in a better position to evaluate petitions for release than our Court, at least until the issues have been fully presented to the Court through briefing and oral argument.

I am troubled, however, by the path the majority takes to reach this result, and thus concur only in the court's judgment with respect to the reversal of Harris' conviction. I part company with the majority when it distills from our gift/income jurisprudence a rule that would tax only the most base type of cash-for-sex exchange and categorically exempt from tax liability all other transfers of money and property to so-called mistresses or companions.... Consider the following example. *A* approaches *B* and offers to spend time with him, accompany him to social events, and provide him with sexual favors for the next year if *B* gives her an apartment, a car, and a stipend of $5,000 a month. *B* agrees to *A*'s terms. According to the majority, because this example involves a transfer of money to a "mistress in the context of a long-term relationship," *A* could never be charged with criminal tax evasion if she chose not to pay taxes on *B*'s stipend. I find this hard to accept; what *A* receives from *B* is clearly income as it is "in return for services rendered." 363 U.S. at 285. To be sure, there will be situations — like the case before us — where the evidence is insufficient to support a finding that the transferor harbored a "cash for services" intent; in such cases, criminal prosecutions for willful tax evasion will indeed be impossible as a matter of law. That fact does not, however, condemn as overly vague the analysis itself.

I am thus prompted to find Harris' conviction infirm because of the relative scantiness of the record before us, not because mistresses are categorically exempt from taxation on the largess they receive....

NOTES

1. *The stakes in* Harris. A government victory in *Harris* would have increased income tax revenue by the amount of tax due on the income; there would have been no offsetting deduction for the payor, Kritzik. (A government victory would, however, lessen the gift tax liability due the government from Kritzik's estate.) In contrast, cases involving business-related transfers usually involve a trade-off for the government. If the transfers do not constitute gifts, they are taxable to the recipient but generally deductible by the payor. As noted supra page 97, if the two parties are in the same tax bracket, tax revenues will not be affected by whether the transfer is characterized as a gift or a business payment.

2. *Criminal tax evasion.* Harris is a criminal tax case; it is the only such case in this casebook. The statutes under which Harris was convicted, § 7201 and § 7203, apply to "willful" failures to pay tax or file a return, respectively. In order to obtain a conviction, the government had to prove not only that the transfers constituted income to Harris but that Harris *knew* the transfers constituted income and willfully failed to file returns or pay tax due. The mens rea requirement for the crime is knowledge or intent. Note that there is no mens rea required for civil tax liability. (Or, to put the matter somewhat differently, the tax law is in general a strict liability statute.) An individual who receives income is liable for tax on that income regardless of whether she realizes she has income or, for that matter, realizes she must pay tax on that income.

Would the court have reached a similar decision if the issue had been solely one of civil tax liability?

3. *Transfers in and out of marriage.* Had Kritzik and Harris married, the transfers of money to Harris would have been tax free under § 1041, discussed in Chapter 3.G. The tax law would not inquire as to the motives for the marriage or the transfers. Because Kritzik and Harris were not married, the taxability of the transfers hinged on the application of the "detached and disinterested generosity" test of *Duberstein*.

4. *Taxes and morality.* Relationships like the one in *Harris* may be inherently exploitative. It may be that the tax law does not want to make it easy for couples to structure this kind of relationship in a tax-favored manner. Certainly, at the extreme, the tax law would not want to exempt wages from prostitution.

On the other hand, transfers may be made between two same-sex individuals who live in a committed relationship and cannot legally marry, or between two individuals in a committed relationship who choose not to marry. Assume the low-wage earner in the couple wants to assure himself the right to support payments in the event the relationship ends. He cannot rely on alimony: It is reserved for transfers incident to the breakup of a marriage. He could perhaps establish a right to "palimony" by insisting on a contract that assured him support in the event of a breakup. The consideration for the contract might include the services he provides to the relationship. Would the receipt of property pursuant to such a contract be taxable? Should it be taxable?

3. Gift: Some Applications

The scope of the gift exclusion, and the taxability of various gratuitous transfers even if they do not constitute gifts under § 102, has varied over time and with the type of transfer involved. Here are some of the main areas in which the issue has arisen:

1. *Ordinary tips.* Ordinary tips are includable in income on the theory that they are payments for services rendered. See Regs. § 1.61-2(a)(1). The problem with tips is enforcement. Section 6053, enacted in 1982, contains complex and stiff rules requiring employer information returns on actual or putative tip income in the case of restaurants and cocktail lounges employing more than ten persons. The apparent burdensomeness of the reporting requirement is testimony to the seriousness of the Service's enforcement problems.

More unusual payments, analogous (at least) to tips, have led to clever, but unsuccessful, arguments. For example, United States v. McCormick, 67 F.2d 867 (2d Cir. 1933), cert. denied, 291 U.S. 662 (1934), holds that "contributions" received by a city clerk after marriage ceremonies from bridegrooms who were fearful of being accused of stinginess were taxable; and see Regs. § 1.61-2(a)(1), to the effect that "marriage fees and other contributions received by a clergyman for services" are taxable.

In Olk v. United States, 536 F.2d 876 (9th Cir.), cert. denied, 429 U.S. 920 (1976), the court required inclusion of money given to a craps dealer in a casino by gamblers who the trial court determined were acting out of "impulsive generosity or superstition." The court rejected as a mere conclusion of law the trial court's further finding of "detached and disinterested generosity." It deemed this conclusion to be erroneous because of the gamblers' hope of a benefit of some sort.

2. *Surviving spouses.* Poyner v. Commissioner, 301 F.2d 287 (4th Cir. 1962), referred to by the court in *Olk*, was one of many cases involving payments by corporations to the surviving spouses of deceased executives, with the recipient claiming gift and the corporation claiming a deductible expense. Relying on the wording of the corporate resolution authorizing the payment, which resolution began "in recognition of the services," the Tax Court had ruled that the payment was not a gift. The Court of Appeals reversed, relying on pre-*Duberstein* Tax Court precedent (301 F.2d at 291-292):

> The clearest formulation appears in Florence S. Luntz, 29 T.C. 647, 650 (1958) where the Tax Court listed the following as the five factors to be considered:
>
>> (1) the payments had been made to the wife of the deceased employee and not to his estate; (2) there was no obligation on the part of the corporation to pay any additional compensation to the deceased employee; (3) the corporation derived no benefit from the payment; (4) the wife of the deceased employee performed no services for the corporation; and (5) the services of her husband had been fully compensated.
>
> The stipulated facts directly respond to every one of the five factors, and in each instance the response is favorable to the widow. This being so, we see no justification for the Tax Court's finding that "there is no solid evidence that they [the directors authorizing the payments] were motivated in any part by the widow's needs or by a sense of generosity or the like." . . . The only evidence on which the Tax Court specifically relies for its contrary finding is the wording of the authorizing corporate resolutions. . . .
>
> The Supreme Court in *Duberstein* did not destroy the authority of the earlier Tax Court cases and the guides enunciated in them for discovering motivation.

The appeal of this kind of benefit was reduced considerably by the adoption, in 1962, of § 274(b), which limits the deduction for gifts to $25. Would it still be possible for separate triers of fact to find a gift in the case of a surviving spouse and nongift in the case of the corporate payor? How would you advise a corporate client on the drafting of a resolution authorizing a payment to a surviving spouse, assuming that management is determined to assure the corporation a deduction?

3. *Prizes, awards, scholarships, and fellowships.* Before 1954, the forerunner of § 102 was relied on by the courts and the Service to provide a broad exclusion for scholarships and fellowships and a limited exclusion for prizes and awards. The 1954 act added provisions that modified and attempted to clarify the existing law in this area but, at least in the case of scholarships and fellowships, left enough uncertainty to generate a seemingly endless stream of litigation (e.g., over whether a graduate student's or an intern's stipend was compensation for services rather than a fellowship). The 1986 act excised that portion of the provision relating to prizes and awards (§ 74) that allowed a limited

exclusion. In doing so it left in place a rule requiring inclusion of such benefits in gross income (with a few minor exceptions relating to charitable contributions).[13]

The 1986 act also drastically modified the provision relating to scholarships and fellowships (§ 117), leaving only a limited exclusion for scholarships provided to degree candidates. The limited exclusion is for that portion of a scholarship that is required to be used for tuition, fees, books, and supplies and for equipment required for courses. The new law retained the previous rule that the exclusion does not apply to any portion of a scholarship that represents payment for teaching, research, or other services. This rule has given rise to disputes between students (who proved to be an exceptionally litigious lot) and the Service in the past and will no doubt continue to do so in the future, but the stakes will be much smaller (because the exclusion is more limited). Does the distinction between a "pure" scholarship and one that requires the performance of services seem to you to be consistent with sound principles of taxation? Why should there be any exclusion at all for scholarships? Are they like gifts? (And if so, so what?) Or does the exclusion reflect the notion that a tuition remission has no significant value? If it is fair to exclude tuition scholarships from gross income, should students who work their way through school, and pay full tuition, be allowed a deduction for their tuition payments? Should students who pay relatively low tuition at state universities and colleges be required to include in income the value of the subsidy they receive? What about the argument that scholarship students generally receive barely enough for survival and therefore should not be expected to pay taxes?

4. *Bequest.* Under § 102, bequests are excluded from income along with gifts. Problems have arisen in distinguishing between bequests and belated compensation for services rendered to the decedent during his or her lifetime. In Wolder v. Commissioner, 493 F.2d 608 (2d Cir.), cert. denied, 419 U.S. 828 (1974), a "bequest" to a lawyer pursuant to a formal agreement under which he rendered legal services without charge was held to be income. On the other hand, in McDonald v. Commissioner, 2 T.C. 840 (1943), a bequest "in appreciation" of services as the decedent's nurse, dietitian, secretary, and driver during his declining years was held to be excluded under § 102.

A payment received in settlement of a will contest by a person claiming rights as an heir has been held to be a bequest within the contemplation of § 102. Lyeth v. Hoey, 305 U.S. 188 (1938).

5. *Welfare.* Traditional welfare payments and various other government payments, such as those for relief of disaster (Rev. Rul. 76-144, 1976-1 C.B. 17) and for victims of crime (Rev. Rul. 74-74, 1974-1 C.B. 18), have long been treated by the Service as excludable not under § 102 but rather as not within the contemplation of § 61. The label attached has been payments "for the general welfare," or something similar. Unemployment payments were also excluded (Rev. Rul. 76-63, 1976-1 C.B. 14), but now, under § 85, are fully includable.

---

13. The 1986 act also added § 74(c), which provides a narrowly circumscribed exclusion for certain noncash awards to employees for length of service or for safety achievements.

In 1996 Congress replaced the basic federal welfare program, Aid to Families with Dependent Children (AFDC), with a program called Temporary Assistance for Needy Families (TANF). TANF places a substantially increased emphasis on forcing welfare recipients to perform "work services"—essentially by imposing time limits to cut off benefits of people who do not perform such services. The program thus gave prominence to a difficult tax issue—how to distinguish between excludable welfare payments and taxable pay for work. The type of work services contemplated by TANF as a condition for continued entitlement to benefits included unsubsidized private sector employment, subsidized public sector employment, on-the-job training, community service, and certain school attendance. Most benefit recipients will not earn enough to reach the threshold for paying income taxes, but some might do so if, for example, they had a good job before qualifying for benefits or got a good job after doing so. More importantly, compensation for work, unlike welfare benefits, is subject to Social Security taxes and may entitle the worker to receive payments from the § 32 Earned Income Tax Credit (EITC).

In Notice 99-3, 1999-1 C.B. 271, the IRS offered the following guideline:

> In cases where the following three conditions are satisfied, TANF payments will be treated as made for the promotion of the general welfare and therefore will not be includible in an individual's gross income; will not be earned income for EIC purposes; and will not be wages for employment tax purposes:
>
> (1) The only payments received by the individual with respect to the work activity are received directly from the state or local welfare agency (for this purpose, an entity with which a state or local welfare agency contracts to administer the state TANF program on behalf of the state will be treated as the state or local welfare agency);
>
> (2) The determination of the individual's eligibility to receive any payment is based on need and the only payments received by the individual with respect to the work activity are funded entirely under a TANF program (including any payments with respect to qualified state expenditures (as defined in § 409(a)(7)(B)(i)(1) of the Social Security Act) and the Food Stamp Act of 1977)); and
>
> (3) The size of the individual's payment is determined by the applicable welfare law, and the number of hours the individual may engage in the work activity is limited by the size of the individual's payment (as determined by applicable welfare law) divided by the higher of the federal or state minimum wage.

Is there a sound policy argument for drawing a distinction between wages and welfare benefits for purposes of imposing an income tax (assuming total income above the exemption threshold)? For purposes of imposing a Social Security (FICA) tax, with a corresponding right to receive benefits at retirement age or upon permanent and total disability? If so, what is it? If not, which way would you go: tax both or tax neither? Would your answer to these questions be different under the old AFDC law, which had much weaker provisions for inducing benefit recipients to go to work (or prepare to go to work)?

6. *Social Security.* Before 1983, the entire amount of social security retirement benefits was excluded from income, by longstanding IRS fiat. See Rev.

Rul. 70-217, 1970-1 C.B. 13. Under current law, the treatment of social security benefits depends on the taxpayer's adjusted gross income, augmented by one-half the benefits received, tax-exempt interest and other items. § 86. Married couples filing joint returns with adjusted gross income (augmented by items stated above) less than $32,000 may continue to exclude social security benefits from taxation. Married couples with adjusted gross income in excess of $32,000 but below $44,000 must take into income the lesser of one-half of social security benefits or one-half the amount by which adjusted gross income exceeds $32,000. The treatment of benefits received by married couples with adjusted gross income between $44,000 and about $60,000 is computationally somewhat complex. Essentially, as adjusted gross income rises above $44,000, the couple must take into income 85 percent of the amount of social security benefits. The intent behind all this complexity is to phase out the exclusion as income rises. As is the case when any benefit is phased out as income rises, this approach ensures substantially higher effective marginal tax rates (and corresponding disincentives to work) for taxpayers over a certain income range.

7. *Alimony versus gift.* The special rules relating to alimony, child support, and property settlement payments are considered later (Chapter 3.G). Generally, alimony payments are deductible by the payor and taxable to the recipient, while child support and property settlement payments are not deductible by the payor and are not income to the payee. Under the law of many states, the obligation to pay alimony terminates on the remarriage of the person entitled to receive such payments. Rev. Rul. 82-155, 1982-2 C.B. 36, considers two situations in which alimony payments were continued despite the fact that the recipient had remarried and the payor's legal obligation to make those payments had terminated. In one situation, the payor was unaware of the remarriage; the ruling holds that the payment is taxable to the recipient under § 61 but the payor is not entitled to a deduction. In the other situation, the payor knew of the termination of the legal obligation and decided to continue payments anyway; the ruling holds that those payments were excludable from the income of the recipient under § 102.

QUESTIONS

1. (a) Orthopedic surgeon Sandy successfully performs a difficult operation on accident victim Wendy. Therapist Teresa helps Wendy recover the full use of her damaged muscles. Wendy pays her bill and then, unexpectedly, offers both Sandy and Teresa free use of her ski condominium. Sandy and Teresa each accept Wendy's offer and each spends two weeks at the condominium. Suppose that Sandy and Teresa ask your advice on whether they must, or should, report the value of their use of the condominium as income. What do you say?

(b) The facts are the same as in Question 1(a) except that instead of giving the use of the condominium, Wendy gives Sandy and Teresa each a check for $2,000. Are Sandy and Teresa taxable on the amounts they received? Is it important to know whether Wendy claimed a deduction for the payments as medical expenses? Suppose Wendy did deduct the payments as medical expenses, that the deduction was challenged by the IRS, and that the Tax Court, after observing that Wendy's opinion about the nature of the payments is irrelevant, upheld the IRS's denial of the deduction. Would these additional facts relating to the deduction by Wendy strengthen or weaken Sandy's and Teresa's claim that the payments were gifts?

2. Phyllis is a wealthy woman who grew up in a small town. She learns that the factory that is the principal employer in the town pays wages so low that its employees can eke out only a meager existence. She wants to help these hardworking people and enters into an arrangement with the factory owner under which each employee receives at Christmas a bonus equal to 25 percent of the wages he or she earned in the preceding twelve months. Is the bonus excludable from gross income under § 102? What if the same bonus is paid every year for ten years?

4. Transfer of Unrealized Gain by Gift While the Donor Is Alive

The following case is not part of our examination of gifts and windfalls as they affect the concept of income for tax purposes. Instead, it illustrates the effects of a gift transaction. The principal purpose of putting the case here is to introduce the concept of basis, which we will examine at various points in these materials and which is vital to an understanding of income taxation. But the case may also be thought of as an illustration of what might be called a "surrogate" taxpayer — a person who is taxed on the income of another person. As such, the case is another example of the conflict between fairness (which argues in this setting for taxing the person to whom the income accrued) and practicality (which argues here for taxing the person who realizes the income).

The present statutory background of the case is this: Section 61(a)(3) includes in gross income "gains from dealings in property." Section 1001 provides that the amount of the gain is the "excess of the amount realized . . . over the adjusted basis." The adjusted basis is the basis, defined under § 1012 as "cost" (with certain exceptions), "adjusted as provided in section 1016." However, there is an exception in § 1015 for property acquired by gift. Generally, the donee's basis (which word is used in § 1015 to refer to adjusted basis) is the same as the donor's basis — in other words, the donee takes a "transferred basis" (§ 7701(a)(43)) from the donor. (Tax experts often use the word "basis" to refer to the original or cost basis or the adjusted basis, whichever is appropriate, and commonly use the phrase "carryover basis" to refer to what the code now calls "substituted basis.") There is, however, an exception: If at the time of the gift the donor's basis is greater than the fair market value of the property (so the donor would have a loss if he or she sold the property), then for purposes of computing the donee's loss (but not gain) on any subsequent sale, the donee's basis is the fair market value at the time of the gift. This rule was added to the statute in 1934.

The same basic statutory scheme (minus the 1934 revision) was in effect at the time the case arose. The taxpayer challenged its application on constitutional grounds.

TAFT v. BOWERS

278 U.S. 470 (1929)

Mr. Justice MCREYNOLDS delivered the opinion of the Court. . . .
Abstractly stated, this is the problem:

> In 1916 *A* purchased 100 shares of stock for $1,000, which he held until 1923 when the fair market value had become $2,000. He then gave them to *B* who sold them during the year 1923 for $5,000. The United States claim that under the Revenue Act of 1921 *B* must pay income tax upon $4,000, as realized profits. *B* maintains that only $3,000—the appreciation during her ownership—can be regarded as income; that the increase during the donor's ownership is not income assessable against her within intendment of the Sixteenth Amendment.

The District Court ruled against the United States; the Circuit Court of Appeals held with them. . . .

We think the manifest purpose of Congress expressed in [§ 1015] was to require the petitioner to pay the enacted tax.[14]

The only question subject to serious controversy is whether Congress had power to authorize the exaction.

It is said that the gift became a capital asset of the donee to the extent of its value when received and, therefore, when disposed of by her no part of that value could be treated as taxable income in her hands.

The Sixteenth Amendment provides—

> The Congress shall have power to lay and collect taxes on incomes from whatever source derived, without apportionment among the several States, and without regard to any census or enumeration.

Income is the thing which may be taxed—income from any source. The Amendment does not attempt to define income or to designate how taxes may be laid thereon, or how they may be enforced.

Under former decisions here the settled doctrine is that the Sixteenth Amendment confers no power upon Congress to define and tax as income without apportionment something which theretofore could not have been properly regarded as income.

Also, this Court has declared—"Income may be defined as the gain derived from capital, from labor, or from both combined, provided it be understood to include profit gained through a sale or conversion of capital assets." Eisner v. Macomber, 252 U.S. 189, 207 [infra page 213]. The "gain derived from capital," within the definition, is "not a gain accruing to capital, nor a growth or increment of value in the investment, but a gain, a profit, something of exchangeable value proceeding from the property, severed from the capital however invested, and coming in, that is, received or drawn by the claimant for

---

14. [Before the enactment of the predecessor of § 1015, the Service had ruled that the basis to the donee of property received by gift was its fair market value at the time of the transfer. In 1921 the House Committee on Ways and Means reported: "This rule has been the source of serious evasion and abuse. Taxpayers having property which has come to be worth far more than it cost give such property to wives or relatives by whom it may be sold without realizing a gain unless the selling price is in excess of the value of the property at the time of the gift." To cure this practice, Congress enacted what is now the first clause of § 1015(a). At the same time, it endorsed the administrative rule for pre-1921 gifts. § 1015(c). See H.R. Rep. No. 350, 67th Cong., 1st Sess., 1939-1 (Pt. 2) C.B. 175.—EDS.]

his separate use, benefit and disposal." United States v. Phellis, 257 U.S. 156, 169.

If, instead of giving the stock to petitioner, the donor had sold it at market value, the excess over the capital he invested (cost) would have been income therefrom and subject to taxation under the Sixteenth Amendment. He would have been obliged to share the realized gain with the United States. He held the stock — the investment — subject to the right of the sovereign to take part of any increase in its value when separated through sale or conversion and reduced to his possession. Could he, contrary to the express will of Congress, by mere gift enable another to hold this stock free from such right, deprive the sovereign of the possibility of taxing the appreciation when actually severed, and convert the entire property into a capital asset of the donee, who invested nothing, as though the latter had purchased at the market price? And after a still further enhancement of the property, could the donee make a second gift with like effect, etc.? We think not.

In truth the stock represented only a single investment of capital — that made by the donor. And when through sale or conversion the increase was separated therefrom, it became income from that investment in the hands of the recipient subject to taxation according to the very words of the Sixteenth Amendment. By requiring the recipient of the entire increase to pay a part into the public treasury, Congress deprived her of no right and subjected her to no hardship. She accepted the gift with knowledge of the statute and, as to the property received, voluntarily assumed the position of her donor. When she sold the stock she actually got the original sum invested, plus the entire appreciation and out of the latter only was she called on to pay the tax demanded.

The provision of the statute under consideration seems entirely appropriate for enforcing a general scheme of lawful taxation. . . .

The power of Congress to require a succeeding owner, in respect of taxation, to assume the place of his predecessor is pointed out by United States v. Phellis, 257 U.S. 156, 171:

> Where, as in this case, the dividend constitutes a distribution of profits accumulated during an extended period and bears a large proportion to the par value of the stock, if an investor happened to buy stock shortly before the dividend, paying a price enhanced by an estimate of the capital plus the surplus of the company, and after distribution of the surplus, with corresponding reduction in the intrinsic and market value of the shares, he was called upon to pay a tax upon the dividend received, it might look in his case like a tax upon his capital. But it is only apparently so. In buying at a price that reflected the accumulated profits, he of course acquired as a part of the valuable rights purchased the prospect of a dividend from the accumulations — bought "dividend on," as the phrase goes — and necessarily took subject to the burden of the income tax proper to be assessed against him by reason of the dividend if and when made. He simply stepped into the shoes, in this as in other respects, of the stockholder whose shares he acquired, and presumably the prospect of a dividend influenced the price paid, and was discounted by the prospect of an income tax to be paid thereon. In short, the question whether a dividend made out of company profits constitutes income of the stockholder is not affected by antecedent transfers of the stock from hand to hand.

There is nothing in the Constitution which lends support to the theory that gain actually resulting from the increased value of capital can be treated as taxable income in the hands of the recipient only so far as the increase occurred while he owned the property. And Irwin v. Gavit, 268 U.S. 161, 167, is to the contrary.

The judgments below are affirmed.

NOTES AND QUESTIONS

1. *Gift versus compensation.* The stock received by the taxpayer in this case was plainly a gift. As such it was excluded from income under § 102(a). If the transfer had been compensatory, the basis rule would have been different. For example, suppose that L (a lawyer) performs services for C (a client) and bills C for $2,000. C admits she owes the $2,000 but offers to pay by transferring to L shares of stock of IBM that C had bought for $1,000 and that presently are worth $2,000. L accepts, and the shares are transferred. L has income of $2,000, and her basis for the shares is $2,000. The basis is arrived at under § 1012, which refers to "cost"; "cost" has a special meaning for tax purposes. The results are, as they should be, the same as they would be if C had paid L $2,000 cash and L had used the cash to buy the shares. If L subsequently sells the shares for $5,000, she will have a gain for tax purposes of $3,000. By virtue of the transfer of the shares to L, C has a taxable gain of $1,000, just as if she had sold the shares and paid L cash. Would it be better in this situation to follow the approach used in the case of gifts? That is, would it be sensible to ignore the gain on the stock at the time of the transfer from C to L and tax L on $4,000 gain at the time of sale? Would your answer be different if the property transferred were not shares of stock of a publicly traded corporation but rather property that was difficult to value (for example, a work of art)?

2. *Pity the donee?* The taxpayer made the following argument (278 U.S. at 474): "The person acquiring property can never tell what liability he assumes in the way of income tax if any basis entirely foreign to him can be arbitrarily adopted for determining his gain." How would you respond? Is it relevant that Ms. Taft, the donee, happened to be the daughter of the donor? Is this relationship a surprising element in the case? Why should the donee's basis not be zero?

3. *Estoppel?* The Court says that Ms. Taft "accepted the gift with knowledge of the statute." Would the result be different in another case if the taxpayer were able to prove total ignorance of the statute? What if the taxpayer were six months old at the time of the gift?

4. *Tax the donor?* Would it be better to tax the gain (or allow a deduction for the loss) on property at the time of a transfer by gift? In other words, should such a transfer be a recognition event? See § 84, treating the transfer of appreciated property to a political organization as a sale. See also § 644, taxing a trust at the donor's rates where property is sold by the trust within two years of the transfer to it.

5. *Broader implications.* In *Taft*, the taxpayers (there were two cases, consolidated) relied heavily on Eisner v. Macomber's definition of income, but

they lost. See infra page 112. This case therefore can be seen as a limitation on, or partial rejection of, the concept of income for which *Macomber* is authority and symbol. (Note, by the way, that where a tax case is to be referred to by one of two names in its caption, the name used should be that of the taxpayer, e.g., Macomber, not that of the tax collector, e.g., Eisner, since the tax collector's name is likely to appear in many cases.)

6. *Adjustment for gift tax.* Section 1015(d) provides an upward adjustment of the donee's basis to reflect any federal gift tax paid by the donor.[15] For gifts made before 1977 the adjustment is for the entire amount of the gift tax paid by the donor, but the basis as adjusted may not exceed the value of the property at the time of the gift. For post-1977 gifts, the adjustment is limited to the gift tax attributable to the net appreciation in the value of the gift property. § 1016(d)(6). The congressional rationale for the adjustment is that the gift tax is part of the cost of the property. The post-1977 rule reflects a sense that the prior rule was too generous, but, in any event, the congressional rationale is unsatisfactory. See 2 B. Bittker, Federal Income, Estate and Gift Taxation ¶41.3.23 (1981). The adjustment perhaps reflects the fact that the gift tax may have been excessive since that tax is based on the full value of the property instead of the value reduced by the liability for a future income tax. See discussion of the § 691 adjustment for estate taxes, infra page 116.

5. Transfers at Death

1. *Inherited property.* Under § 1014, the basis of property acquired by reason of death is the fair market value on the date of death or, at the election of the executor or administrator under § 2032, on the optional valuation date (six months after death).[16] For simplicity we will, as most practitioners do, sometimes use "date-of-death" value to refer to whichever date is applicable. The effect of § 1014 is that the basis is either "stepped up" or "stepped down" from the decedent's basis to the date-of-death value. What we encounter in practice is mostly stepped-up basis, because of inflation and because holders of property will find it profitable to sell their loss property before death, to take advantage of a deduction for the loss, and to retain their gain property, enabling their heirs to take advantage of the step-up.

What principle of tax policy justifies this extraordinary rule? It is true, of course, that the full value of the property may be subject to an estate tax. However, this tax (which reaches only large estates) applies without regard to previously unrealized appreciation. Thus, a person who sells property before death pays an income tax on any gain plus an estate tax on the property

---

15. The gift tax is a tax on the act of transfer by gift and is imposed on the donor with secondary liability on the donee if the donor does not pay. For the most part, the gift tax, and the estate tax (which is a tax on the act of transfer by reason of death), should be thought of as entirely separate from, and not relevant to, the income tax.

16. In community-property states, the basis of the entire amount of property held by husband and wife as community property is stepped up (or down) (see § 1014(b)(6)), whereas in common-law property states, there is a basis step up (or down) for only half of property held in joint tenancy. Under either property-law regime, the basis of the separate property of the decedent spouse is stepped up (or down), but not that of the survivor.

remaining in the estate after payment of the tax. An otherwise identical person who holds on to the property until death pays only the estate tax, though on a larger amount, because the estate has not been reduced by the income tax. In any event, legislation enacted in 2001 would repeal the estate tax — though not the related gift tax — in 2010.

The effect of § 1014 is to encourage people to hold on to appreciated property until death, which results in some degree of immobility of capital, which economists find troubling. The fact that a person must hold on to the property until death does not necessarily mean that that person will be unable to enjoy the benefit of its increased value. Often, the owner will be able to borrow against the appreciation, and loans do not result in recognition of gain, even when they exceed basis. (See infra page 159.) The proceeds of the loan can be used for any purpose, including consumption, and the property can be sold to pay off the loan after death has produced a stepped-up basis, so that the sale will not generate taxable income. At the same time, the loan obligation will reduce the value of the estate for estate tax purposes.

In 1970, Stanley Surrey (Harvard Law School professor and, from 1961 to 1969, Assistant Secretary of the Treasury for Tax Policy) and Jerome Kurtz (tax practitioner, formerly Tax Legislative Counsel and later Commissioner of Internal Revenue) wrote (perhaps with hyperbole) that "the failure of the income tax to reach the appreciation in value of assets transferred at death" is "the most serious defect in our federal tax structure today." Reform of Death and Gift Taxes: The 1969 Treasury Proposals, The Criticisms, and a Rebuttal, 70 Colum. L. Rev. 1365, 1381. In 1976 Congress enacted § 1023, which provided for a substituted basis for property acquired by reason of death; however, this provision proved to be surprisingly complicated and (perhaps more important, from a political perspective) was extremely unpopular. In response to these complaints, Congress postponed the effective date of the new substituted basis rule and then ultimately repealed it, with a grandfather clause to protect reliance interests.

In a more limited fashion, Congress may now be heading down the § 1023 route all over again (with enactment followed by repeal before the effective date). Under the 2001 legislation repealing the estate tax in 2010 (but then restoring it when the entire 2001 Act expires in 2011), a "modified carryover basis regime" will be in effect for 2010 only. Under this rule (in new § 1022), recipients of assets acquired from decedents will generally take a basis that is the lesser of the decedent's adjusted basis or the fair market value of the assets. However, the decedent's executor will be allowed to allocate as much as $1.3 million of additional basis to the basis of eligible appreciated assets, so long as no asset's basis is increased to more than its fair market value. These complicated rules, which entail significant administrative difficulty, may never take effect given the uncertain political prospects for retention of the 2001 Act's deferred repeal of the estate tax.

2. *Income in respect of a decedent.* Although § 1014(a) relieves from taxation income or gain that had not been realized at the time of decedent's death, under § 691, income or gain that had been *earned*, in an accrual accounting sense, before death is subject to a different set of rules. See § 1014(c). Such income is called "income in respect of a decedent," a term that is used in § 691 but is not defined anywhere in the Code. The application of § 691 may be

illustrated as follows. In 1986, *L*, a lawyer, bills a client $10,000 for services but, before collecting, dies. *L*'s executor collects the $10,000 for the estate in 1987. Three tax returns must be considered. First, there is the final income tax return of the decedent *L* for 1986. Second, there is the estate tax return — that is, the return on which the amount of the estate tax is calculated. Third, there is the income tax return of the estate for 1987.

If *L* were an accrual-method taxpayer (which would be unusual), the $10,000 fee would be reported on his 1986 return. Suppose that his marginal tax rate is 40 percent. The tax would be $4,000. Since the $10,000 was reported as income on *L*'s 1986 return, it would not be treated as income of the estate when collected by it in 1987, so it would not affect the 1987 income tax return of the estate. For estate tax purposes, the right to collect the $10,000 would be an asset of the estate, but it would be offset by the tax liability of $4,000, so the item would increase the size of the estate by only $6,000. Suppose that the estate tax marginal rate is 30 percent. The estate tax attributable to the item would be $1,800. The total of the income tax ($4,000) and the estate tax ($1,800) would be $5,800. As applied to these facts, accrual accounting is an accurate method of accounting and the result, with a total tax of $5,800, is the accurate (though to some people perhaps distasteful) result, given the basic rules embodied in the income tax and the estate tax.

Now suppose (more realistically) that *L* is a cash-method taxpayer. For purposes of his 1986 tax return, his executor is permitted to continue to use the cash method. Consequently, *L*'s 1986 income tax return will not include the $10,000 item of earned income. Under § 691, however, that item must be reported as income by the estate, on its 1987 income tax return. But the estate must also include the full value of the item — $10,000 — in the estate for the purpose of computing the estate tax. Assume again that the marginal estate tax rate for the estate is 30 percent. It will pay an estate tax of $3,000 on the item. This $3,000 becomes a deduction on the income tax return of the estate. § 691(c). Thus, the net amount by which the item increases the income of the estate, for purposes of its income tax return, is $7,000. If the income tax rate of the estate is the same as *L*'s rate, 40 percent, the tax attributable to the item will be $2,800. The total taxes paid by the estate will be the $3,000 estate tax and the $2,800 income tax, or $5,800. This is the same as the result arrived at under the "accurate" method. The identity of result depends, however, on the fact that the income tax rate of the estate was hypothesized to be the same as the income tax rate of the decedent.

Instead of collecting the $10,000 itself, the estate might, in certain circumstances, assign that right to a beneficiary of the estate. In that case, the beneficiary would include the $10,000 in his or her income in the year of collection, with a deduction for the amount of the estate tax attributable to the item.

Income in respect of a decedent is not limited to items of income from the performance of services or to items of ordinary income. Suppose, for example, that before his death *L* had contracted to sell a piece of property but that delivery and payment had not occurred at the date of death. Any gain realized on the transaction would be taxed under the same system of rules applicable to the $10,000 income from performance of services, except that the gain would be capital gain.

Income in respect of a decedent does not, however, include gain on assets owned by the decedent and not subject to any contract for sale at the date of death; if it did, there would be nothing left of the § 1014 stepped-up basis at death. Suppose, for example, that at the time of his death in 1986, L owned a house, in which he lived, with a basis of $10,000. Suppose that in 1987 L's executor sells the house for $115,000. Here § 1014(a) controls. The basis of the house for the purpose of determining gain or loss on sale by the executor in 1987 is the fair market value at the date of death (or alternative valuation date). Suppose that that value was $100,000. In that case, the executor, on the income tax return of the estate for 1987, would report a capital gain of $15,000.

QUESTIONS

1. Suppose A purchases stock for $1,000 and gives the stock to his son, B, at a time when the fair market value of the stock is $2,500.
  (a) How much gain does B recognize if he sells the stock for $3,500?
  (b) How much gain does B recognize if he sells the stock for $1,500?
2. Suppose C purchases stock for $2,000 and gives the stock to her daughter, D, at a time when the fair market value of the stock is $1,000. What amount of gain or loss (if any) is recognized by D on a sale for the following amounts?
  (a) $2,500
  (b) $500
  (c) $1,500
3. During the next four years, Ernesto's daughter, Ana, will require $80,000 for college tuition and expenses. In each of the following settings, advise Ernesto as to the best means of transferring wealth to his daughter so that she may go to college. Ernesto is in the maximum marginal tax bracket and Ana has no income.
  (a) Ernesto has a single asset, stock with a basis of $20,000 and a fair market value of $80,000.
  (b) Ernesto has a single asset, stock with a basis of $120,000 and a fair market value of $80,000.
  (c) Ernesto has stock with a basis of $20,000 and a fair market value of $80,000, plus $80,000 in a savings account.
  (d) Ernesto has stock with a basis of $20,000 and a fair market value of $80,000, plus stock with a basis of $120,000 and a fair market value of $80,000.
  (e) The facts are the same as in (a) except that Ernesto is 88 years old and is in poor health.

COMPARATIVE FOCUS: Canada's Approach of "Deemed Disposition" for Gifts and Bequests

Recall that under U.S. law, the transfer of property by gift does not trigger gain or loss to the transferor and the transferee generally takes a basis in the property equal to that of the transferor. § 1015. For property transferred by bequest, again there is no gain or loss for the transferor, but the transferee takes a basis equal to the property's fair market value. § 1014.

The Canadian approach is entirely different. Canada began taxing capital gain in 1972, following the recommendation of the Royal Commission on Taxation (the "Carter Commission"). In addition to making this change, Canada also chose to follow the Commission's recommendation to tax not only gain arising from the sale of property, but also imputed gain arising from the transfer of property by gift or bequest. Under Canadian law, taxpayers who transfer property by gift or bequest must recognize gain equal to the excess of the fair market value of the property over transferor's cost. The transferee then takes a basis in the property equal to its fair market value.

Three important points about the Canadian approach deserve mention. First, Canada generally requires taxpayers to include only one-half of capital gain in income. Second, deemed realization does not apply to transfers by gift or bequest to one's spouse and a carryover basis regime applies for such transfers. Third, Canada's decision to tax capital gains, including those arising from deemed realizations, was coupled with a repeal of the Canadian estate and gift tax.

D. RECOVERY OF CAPITAL

Income includes interest, rents, dividends, and other returns *on* one's capital or cost or investment. It also includes gains from the sale (or other disposition) of that capital. But it does not include returns or recoveries *of* one's capital. The materials in this section are concerned with the recovery-of-capital exclusion, which has always been a part of fundamental tax doctrine. The rules tend to reflect the ever-present conflict between practicality and accuracy.

If a taxpayer buys one hundred shares of common stock of a corporation for $1,000 and later sells forty of those shares for $700, the tax calculation is simple. Since the shares are homogeneous, the total cost is allocated equally among them. Thus, the cost of the forty shares that were sold is $400, and the gain for tax purposes is $300. But suppose that the taxpayer buys one hundred acres of land for $1,000, that forty acres are wooded and sixty acres are tillable, and that the forty wooded acres are sold for $700. It is not reasonable to assume that the value of wooded acres is necessarily the same as the value of tillable acres. An allocation of the total cost will require judgment based on experience. Despite the difficulties, an allocation of cost will be required. Suppose, for example, that experts determine that at the time of purchase, the wooded acres had been worth $450 and the tillable acres had been worth $550. The gain on the sale of the wooded acres for $700 would then be $250. See Regs. § 1.61-6 and cases cited in Heiner v. Mellon, 304 U.S. 271, 275 n.3 (1938).

1.   Sale of Easements

INAJA LAND CO. v. COMMISSIONER
9 T.C. 727 (1947), acq. 1948-1 C.B. 2

[In 1928 the taxpayer paid $61,000 for 1,236 acres of land on the banks of the Owens River in Mono County, California, together with certain water rights, for use primarily as a private fishing club. In 1934, the City of Los Angeles constructed a tunnel nearby and began to divert "foreign waters" into the Owens River upstream from the taxpayer's property. These foreign waters contained "concrete dust, sediment, and foreign matter," which adversely affected the fishing on taxpayer's preserve and, by substantially increasing the flow of water, caused flooding and erosion. In 1939, after the taxpayer threatened legal action, a settlement was reached under which the city paid the taxpayer $50,000 to "release and forever discharge" the city from any liability for the diversion and for an easement to continue to divert foreign waters into the Owens River. In settling its claim, the taxpayer incurred attorneys' fees and costs of $1,000.]

LEECH, Judge.

The question presented is whether the net amount of $49,000 received by petitioner in the taxable year 1939 under a certain indenture constitutes taxable income under [§ 61(a)], or is chargeable to capital account. The respondent contends: (a) That the $50,000, less $1,000 expenses incurred, which petitioner received from the city of Los Angeles under the indenture of August 11, 1939, represented compensation for loss of present and future income and consideration for release of many meritorious causes of action against the city, constituting ordinary income; and, (b) since petitioner has failed to allocate such sum between taxable and nontaxable income, it has not sustained its burden of showing error. Petitioner maintains that the language of the indenture and the circumstances leading up to its execution demonstrate that the consideration was paid for the easement granted to the city of Los Angeles and the consequent damage to its property rights; that the loss of past or future profits was not considered or involved; that the character of the easement rendered it impracticable to attempt to apportion a basis to the property affected; and, since the sum received is less than the basis of the entire property, taxation should be postponed until the final disposition of the property. . . .

Upon this record we have concluded that no part of the recovery was paid for loss of profits, but was paid for the conveyance of a right of way and easements, and for damages to petitioner's land and its property rights as riparian owner. Hence, the respondent's contention has no merit. Capital recoveries in excess of cost do constitute taxable income. Petitioner has made no attempt to allocate a basis to that part of the property covered by the easements. It is conceded that all of petitioner's lands were not affected by the easements conveyed. Petitioner does not contest the rule that, where property is acquired for a lump sum and subsequently disposed of a portion at a time, there must be an allocation of the cost or other basis over the several units and gain or loss computed on the disposition of each part, except where apportionment would be wholly impracticable or impossible. . . . Petitioner argues that it would be impracticable and impossible to apportion a definite basis to the easements here involved, since they could not be described by metes and bounds; that the flow of the water has changed and will change the course of the river; that the extent of the flood was and is not predictable; and that to date the city has not released the full measure of water to which it is entitled. In Strother v. Commissioner, 55 Fed.(2d) 626, the court says: ". . . A tax-payer . . . should not be charged with gain on pure conjecture unsupported by any foundation of ascertainable fact." See Burnet v. Logan [infra Chapter 3.E].

This rule is approved in the recent [case of] Raytheon Prod. Corp. [v. Commissioner, 144 F.2d 110 (1st Cir.), cert. denied, 323 U.S. 779 (1944)]. Apportionment with reasonable accuracy of the amount received not being possible, and this amount being less than petitioner's cost basis for the property, it can not be determined that petitioner has, in fact, realized gain in any amount. Applying the rule as above set out, no portion of the payment in question should be considered as income, but the full amount must be treated as a return of capital and applied in reduction of petitioner's cost basis. Burnet v. Logan [supra].

Reviewed by the Court.

NOTES AND QUESTIONS

1. *All or nothing at all?* Given the difficulty of allocating basis or cost, why not treat the entire $49,000 as gain? What about some sort of arbitrary rule of allocation? What justification, if any, is there for in effect allocating the entire basis, up to the amount received, to the interest conveyed? Rev. Rul. 70-510, 1970-2 C.B. 104, covering a situation remarkably similar to that in *Inaja*, follows the same allocation-of-basis rule. No explanation is given.

2. *Drawing the line.* The 1,236 acres owned by the taxpayer included 419 acres of "rocky hill lands." Suppose that this part of the property had been sold for $2,000. How would gain or loss be determined? See Introductory Note supra page 119. See also Williams v. McGowan, infra page 783 (taxpayer selling hardware business is treated as selling various individual assets, not one aggregate asset, and must allocate price among the various components to determine tax consequences, where the sale of some assets produces ordinary gain or loss and the sale of others produces capital gain or loss).

3. *Effect in later years.* Suppose that in a later year Inaja sells the entire property for $25,000. What tax consequences? Suppose that in 1939 the city had paid Inaja $65,000 instead of $49,000 (net). What tax result in that year and in a later year when the entire property is sold for $25,000?

4. *The foregone income issue.* (a) What characteristics of the transaction justify treatment of the $50,000 as payment for part of the taxpayer's property rather than rent or the like? Is it possible for a payment to be for "loss of profits" and still be proceeds from the sale of a capital asset?

(b) Suppose that negotiations between the city and Inaja had reached a point where the city offered to pay a fee of $2,500 a year forever for the discharge and easement, but Inaja was more interested in a lump-sum payment. Suppose that at this point a financial expert pointed out that for an annual interest cost of $2,500 the city could issue a bond for $50,000 and use the proceeds to pay off Inaja and that an agreement was thereupon reached under which Inaja received the $50,000 instead of the $2,500 per year. Plainly, the $2,500 per year would have been fully taxable — there would be no recovery-of-cost offset. Does it follow that the $50,000 should be fully taxable? Why?

2. Life Insurance

Basic analysis. Section 101(a) excludes "amounts received . . . under a life insurance contract, if such amounts are paid by reason of the death of the insured." This exclusion applies to all types of life insurance policies. As to some of these, the exclusion results in a reasonably accurate reporting of income in the aggregate (as explained below), though not in individual cases. As to others, the result is a substantial underreporting in the aggregate as well as inaccuracy in individual cases. To understand these tax effects one must understand the two basic elements of life insurance policies — (1) mortality protection or "pure" insurance and (2) savings — and how they work.

Let us begin with the pure insurance element — the simple protection against mortality losses. One example of this kind of insurance is trip insurance covering air travel. These policies pay off if the insured dies as a result of an airplane crash. Suppose that a person pays $5 for $50,000 of such coverage. If the plane crashes and the insured dies, the beneficiary receives the $50,000, which can be thought of as consisting of a $5 recovery of cost plus a mortality gain of $49,995. The entire amount is excluded under § 101(a). On the other hand, if the plane arrives safely at its destination, the insured loses his or her gamble with the insurance company. There is a $5 mortality loss, for which there is no deduction. In this lottery with life there will be those who gain, financially, and those who do not. In individual cases, where death occurs, large gains will escape taxation. In the aggregate, however, the amounts paid out will equal the amounts paid in (disregarding the amounts diverted to cover the costs and profits of the insurer). Since the premiums are not deductible, the tax effect in the aggregate is roughly accurate: In the aggregate, the amount received is a recovery of capital and no gain escapes taxation (assuming that we disregard the value of the peace of mind acquired by the purchase of the policies).

The same analysis applies to other types of "term" insurance, under which a premium is paid in return for protection against death for a defined, relatively short, term or period of time. For example, depending on age, a person might be able to buy $50,000 worth of protection for one year for, say, $1,000. Again, if the person dies during the year, there is a mortality gain — in this case $49,000 — that is excluded under § 101(a). If the person lives out the year, there is a mortality loss of $1,000, which is not deductible. If the insurance company sells enough policies and makes the proper calculations of life expectancy, it will be subject to virtually no risk. Assuming a large enough number of insured people, the number of deaths should be such that the amount collected in premiums will cover the amounts paid out in benefits, plus the company's cost of operation and its profit. This observation is a reflection of the idea previously expressed — that in the aggregate there is no gain or loss (disregarding the insurance company's costs and profits) and that consequently the tax effect is accurate in the aggregate but not in individual cases (except in an expected, or ex ante, sense). Individual policies of one-year term insurance are widely sold. Far more common are one-year term policies for groups of people such as employees of a particular firm; these policies are called group-term life insurance.

So far, however, we have seen only part of the picture. We have ignored the savings element that is found in many forms of life insurance and the exclusion from taxation of the accumulated earnings on that savings element. An extreme example of a savings element is found in the single-premium life insurance policy. Suppose, for example, that an insurance policy calls for a single initial payment of $25,000 by the insured in return for a payment by the insurance company of $100,000 at death, whenever it occurs. Here, both in the aggregate, and in individual cases, the amounts paid out will be four times the amounts paid in. How can the insurance company afford to do that? Obviously, because it is able to invest the $25,000 and earn enough to make the required payments (plus covering its costs and profits). The returns on investment earned by the insurance company essentially benefit the people who have bought the policies. The insurance company is not required to pay a tax on such returns, on the theory that they are set aside as reserves for payment to policyholders. Nor are those returns taxed to the policyholders. While this kind of policy has a large savings element, it also includes protection against mortality risk. For insureds who die early there will be a mortality gain (to the beneficiary) and for those who outlive their life expectancies there will be a mortality loss. Even for those in the latter category, there will be an overall gain; the proceeds will still be $100,000 on an investment of $25,000. But the mortality loss reduces what would otherwise be a larger investment gain.[17] In any event, if we wanted to tax returns on the savings element while preserving the rule that mortality gains and losses were to be ignored, we would be confronted with the difficult task of separating the two elements of the proceeds.

17. Suppose that there are three people, Alice, Bob, and Carol, each of whom has a life expectancy of 14.5 years and each of whom buys, for $25,000, a single-premium life insurance policy with a death benefit of $100,000. The interest rate at which $25,000 grows to $100,000 in 14.5 years is 10 percent. Suppose that Alice dies exactly at the end of 14.5 years. For her, the $100,000 proceeds includes her $25,000 plus an investment gain of $75,000. There is no mortality gain or loss. Bob dies the day after he buys his policy. The $100,000 paid on his policy includes a mortality gain of $75,000 and no investment gain. Carol lives twenty-five years. If she had invested her $25,000 at 10 percent for that time it would have grown to $271,000. Since she collects only $100,000 on the policy, she has an investment gain of $246,000 and a mortality loss of $171,000. The numbers may be summarized as follows:

	Life span	Investment grows to	Death benefit	Investment gain or loss	Mortality gain or loss
Alice	14.5 yrs	$100,000	$100,000	$ 75,000	-0-
Bob	-0-	25,000	100,000	-0-	$ 75,000
Carol	25 yrs	271,000	100,000	246,000	(171,000)

The single-premium policy is, as previously suggested, just an extreme example. Other forms of insurance also have substantial savings elements, and the result is that the amounts paid out, in the aggregate, will exceed the amounts paid in as premiums. These other policies have many names, such as whole life, ordinary life, endowment, and level-premium term. They are all varying combinations of term insurance and a savings element.[18] The greater the savings element, the greater the aggregate tax avoidance. Consider, for example, a level-premium term policy. For a simple one-year term policy the premium will rise each year as the insured gets older and the probability of death increases. Suppose that a policy is offered that provides for a level yearly premium for ten years. In order to be able to afford to offer such a level premium, an insurance company obviously must charge a premium that exceeds the one-year pure term cost in the early years of the policy. The excess over true cost is the savings element, or reserve, which is used, in effect, to help meet the higher costs in the later years of the policy. If the premium is to remain level not just for ten years but for the entire life of a young insured, the savings element in the early years will have to be even greater. As with the single premium policy, proceeds in individual cases will include mortality gains and losses plus returns on the savings element. In the aggregate, the amounts paid out will exceed the amounts paid in. Yet because of § 101(a), nothing will be taxed. Note that in all cases some return on savings will escape taxation. It is true that people who live long enough may pay more in premiums than their beneficiaries receive in proceeds. This may suggest that in such cases there has been no gain for tax purposes, but that is not so. All that will have happened is that the mortality loss has exceeded the investment gain. The investment gain has still provided a benefit: lower total premiums than would have been paid with simple one-year renewable term insurance. Even though total premiums over time exceed total proceeds, if a savings element has decreased the amount that would otherwise have been paid in premiums, a return on investment will have escaped tax. Where premiums exceed proceeds, this kind of escape from taxation does not depend on § 101(a). There is no tax even if the policy is of the sort that not only pays the covered amount at death, but also, in lieu of the payment at death, pays the covered amount at some specified age (e.g., 65), if the insured lives to that age. See § 72(e)(1)(B).[19]

18. For a good description of various types of insurance policies, see Joint Committee on Taxation, Tax Reform Proposals: Taxation of Insurance Products and Companies (September 20, 1985).

19. Suppose, for example, that at age 45 Edith buys an "endowment" policy for which the premium is $500 per year for twenty years (until she is age 65). Suppose the policy provides that if she dies at any time during the twenty-year term of the policy, her beneficiary is to receive $10,000, but if she is still alive at the end of the twenty years, she is entitled to a cash payment of $10,000 (the endowment). Suppose it turns out that she lives for twenty years and collects the $10,000. No tax will be payable. This result ignores the value of the insurance on Edith's life during the twenty-year term of the policy. Actuaries can readily figure out the relative amounts of each annual premium allocable to current life insurance and to the endowment (the savings element). (If they could not, insurance companies could not sell such policies and stay in business for long.) Suppose that the cost of the insurance element over the twenty years was $6,000 and the amount allocated to the savings element was $4,000. In this case, Edith has had a gain of $6,000 on her savings account with the insurance company and should be taxed on it at some time. She has also spent $6,000 on life insurance, but that is not a deductible outlay, any more than it would have been if she had separately bought term insurance and put money aside in a savings account.

Policy questions. Why is it that Congress allows returns on investments with insurance companies to escape taxation while investments with banks or in mutual funds are taxed? Consider the two elements of tax avoidance—the deferral and the ultimate exemption—in the case of the single-premium policy. Each year, as the insured gets older, the policy increases in value. Would it be appropriate to tax this annual increment or allocate the insurance company's investment income each year to policyholders based on the company's calculations of amounts required for necessary reserves for future payments? Is the policyholder's gain more like the increase in the value of farm land held for investment or like the annual interest earned on a savings account? (Note that, because of commissions and other costs, if a life insurance policy is cashed in too soon after its purchase, the insured person generally will lose money. Life insurance is not a good short-term investment.) If annual taxation of policyholders is not sensible, would it be appropriate to tax the insurance company on the investment returns set aside for policyholders? What about the exclusion at death?

Assuming that the annual increments in the value of a life insurance policy should not be taxed each year, is the gain like the gain that escapes taxation under § 1014 or like the gain that is taxable under § 691? (See supra pages 115-118.)

Life insurance might also be compared with qualified pension plans. When an employer has adopted a qualified pension plan and sets aside money that is to be used to pay a pension to an employee, the employer deducts the amount set aside. In effect, that money is treated as if it had been paid as a salary or as wages to the employee. The employee, however, is not required to report the amount as income. That exclusion is equivalent to the receipt and simultaneous deduction of the amount by the employee. In other words, it is as if the employee had earned income and had received a deduction by putting it into a pension trust. Thereafter, the employee is not taxed on amounts earned by the pension trust, but amounts ultimately received as pension payments are fully taxed. In short, from the perspective of the employee, the system is, in effect, one of deduction of the investment, tax-free buildup, and taxation on ultimate receipt. But the financial result of this system is equivalent to that of a system in which there is no initial deduction, but the income earned on the investment is entirely free of tax (both as it accumulates and when it is received), and that is the tax treatment of the savings element in life insurance. So one way to think about how life insurance should be taxed is to ask whether there are reasons to afford it the same favorable tax treatment as we afford qualified pension plans.

Tax planning (avoidance) implications. The single-premium insurance policy, as we have just seen, is obviously a good device for avoiding taxes on the returns on one's investment. But suppose that the taxpayer lacks the $25,000. Such a taxpayer is analogous to the person who observes that his or her neighbor is enjoying tax-free imputed income from home ownership but lacks the money to buy a house. The solution that this analogy suggests is to borrow the $25,000. Assuming that the interest on the loan is deductible, the effect is to reduce income subject to tax by the amount of that interest. Meanwhile, the gain generated by the investment of the borrowed funds in the insurance policy is tax free. Taxable income is transformed into tax-free gain, in a process sometimes called "tax arbitrage." For example, suppose that a woman wants to buy $100,000 worth of coverage for the benefit of her child; that the cost of a single-premium $100,000 policy for a woman her age is $25,000; and that her marginal tax rate (combined state and federal) is 40 percent. She might borrow the $25,000 (perhaps from the insurance company) at an interest cost of, say, 10 percent. If her $2,500 annual interest payment is deductible, her after-tax cost is only $1,500. Essentially, she will have transformed a nondeductible payment of an insurance premium into a deductible payment of interest; the government will pay 40 percent of the cost of her coverage. Her insurance policy will increase in value each year (by more than the $1,500 net cost, if she chooses policies wisely), but that gain will be tax free if she holds the policy until death.[20]

Does that sound too good to be true? In its simplest form, it is. Congress caught on many years ago and provided in § 264(a)(2) that the interest paid on indebtedness "incurred or continued to purchase or carry a single premium life insurance, endowment, or annuity contract" is not deductible. The barrier presented by § 264(a)(2) can be avoided (though not completely) by use of policies with relatively large savings elements that avoid categorization as "single premium" policies. See § 264(b) and (c). Since 1987, however, tax avoidance has been constrained by the disallowance, in § 163(h), of deductions for "personal" interest (see infra Chapter 4.E).

Employee coverage. Suppose that a corporation buys one-year term insurance on the life of one of its key executives, with itself as the beneficiary. Here the premium seems to be part of the cost of doing business and should be deductible like any other business expense (under § 162). But § 264(a)(1) expressly denies the deduction. Correspondingly, the proceeds, if any, are excluded under § 101(a). On the other hand, if the beneficiary under the policy on the life of the executive were his or her spouse, or if the corporation were to buy group-term life insurance for its employees, § 264(a)(1) would not apply and the premiums would be deductible (as a form of compensation to such employees). The premiums would be taxable to the executive or other employees, except for the portion allocable to the first $50,000 of group-term coverage. See § 79.

Transferees. The exclusion in § 101(a)(1) generally is not available to a person who acquired the policy for valuable consideration. For many such people there will be no statutory basis for deduction of premiums and for some, even if there is such a basis in § 162, deduction will be barred by § 264(a)(1). The congressional rationale for the § 101(a)(2) limitation was that the

---

20. If, as this example assumes, the loan is still outstanding at the time of death, the insurance company will subtract the loan amount from the proceeds otherwise due and pay the beneficiary the net amount of $75,000. The fact that the beneficiary receives only the net amount of coverage would not mitigate the tax advantage: The policy has combined tax-free interest buildup with tax-deductible interest payments.

exclusion might "result in abuse by encouraging speculation on the death of the insured." S. Rep. No. 1622, 83d Cong., 2d Sess. 14 (1954). Consistently with this rationale, certain policies that were transferred for consideration remain eligible for the exclusion—policies transferred to a person with a substituted, or carryover, basis (e.g., a successor corporation in a tax-free merger or a corporation resulting from a tax-free incorporation of a partnership) and transfers to the insured or to his or her partner, partnership, or corporation. Both these exceptions were enacted to overrule adverse judicial decisions. No exemption from the "transfer for valuable consideration" restriction is needed for transfers of insurance policies by gift or bequest, since no consideration is paid for such transfers.

Accelerated benefits for the terminally ill and chronically ill. If a life insurance policy is sold to an authorized "viatical settlement provider" by a person who is "chronically ill" (as defined in § 7702B(c)(2)) or "terminally ill" (as defined in § 101(g)(4)(A)), the payments received are treated as having been received by reason of the death of the insured and are excluded from gross income under § 101(a). See § 101(g).

3. Annuities and Pensions

Basic analysis: annuities. Traditionally, an "annuity" was a contract requiring the payment of a specified amount at specified regular intervals (generally, monthly or yearly), often for the lifetime of the person entitled to the payments (the "annuitant"). In the current era, the term "annuity" is widely used to refer to a contract with an insurance company under which the annuitant makes a current payment in return for the promise of a single larger payment by the insurance company in the future. These newer types of annuity contracts are vehicles by which individuals can invest their funds and achieve the substantial tax advantage of deferral of tax on their investments, as explained immediately below; they are essentially tax avoidance devices. Despite this modern development, it is useful to focus on the nature, and tax treatment, of a traditional annuity.

To illustrate, suppose that A is 62 years old, has just retired, and has $100,000 to invest. She goes to an insurance company seeking a fixed payment from it for as long as she lives. Her life expectancy is about twenty years. See Regs. § 1.72-9. What should an insurance company be willing to pay her each year? Because the insurance company will have the $100,000 to invest, plainly it can afford to pay more than $5,000 per year ($100,000 divided by twenty years). How much more depends on how much it expects to earn on the $100,000. Suppose that it calculates that it can afford to pay $9,000 per year (which implies an interest rate of about 6.4 percent). If A lives her life expectancy, no more and no less, she will collect $180,000. The question is, how do we tax the $9,000 annual payment that she receives?

One possibility, an investment-first rule, would be to treat each payment as a tax-free recovery of capital until the entire $100,000 investment is recovered and then treat all payments as income. That is the approach of the *Inaja Land*

Co. case, supra page 120, and of Burnet v. Logan, infra page 268. It would be the best *A* could hope for. It was once allowed generally, but is too favorable and is permitted now only for unsecured promises by individuals to pay so-called private annuities (see Lloyd v. Commissioner, 33 B.T.A. 903 (1936)). At the opposite pole, under an income-first rule, all payments could be treated as income to the extent of any income set aside for the policyholder by the insurance company in its policyholder reserves. Thus, the early payments would be largely income;[21] as time passed, more and more of each payment would be a recovery of capital; for people who lived out their life expectancies exactly, capital would be fully recovered at death and all income would be taxed; for others there would be mortality gains and losses. This approach would be roughly consistent with the treatment of distributions by corporations (all distributions are dividend income to the extent of accumulated earnings and profits) and trusts (all distributions are income to the extent of previously undistributed accumulations of income). See supra pages 658-667. It might still be more favorable than the treatment of amounts held in a savings account, where interest is taxed as earned, without regard to whether it is withdrawn. Again, however, the income-first rule has not been adopted in the Code. Which of the two possibilities seems fairer?

In fact, the rule under § 72 requires the calculation of an "exclusion ratio." § 72(b). The ratio is simply the investment in the contract (here, $100,000) divided by the expected return ($180,000), or 55.55 percent. This ratio is applied to each payment received. Thus, of each $9,000, 55.55 percent, or $5,000, would be treated as a nontaxable recovery of investment and the remaining $4,000 would be treated as income. If *A* dies before twenty years pass, she will not recover, for tax purposes, the entire amount of her investment. In that case, she is entitled, in her final income tax return, to a deduction for the portion of her investment not recovered by the time of her death through the operation of the exclusion ratio. § 72(b)(3). If she lives more than twenty years, she will have recovered her entire investment in the contract and after that has occurred the entire amount of each $9,000 payment received is included in gross income. § 72(b)(2). This is the rule for

---

21. The position of the policyholder would be comparable to that of a bank that has loaned $100,000 on a long-term loan to finance the purchase of a home and will receive fixed monthly payments throughout the term of the loan to cover interest and to "amortize" (that is, pay off in increments) the principal amount. In the early years of such a loan, most of each payment is interest, but some is principal. As the principal sum of the debt is slowly reduced, the amount of interest owed is reduced correspondingly, and for each succeeding payment the interest portion declines and the principal portion rises until the loan is finally repaid.

Thus, assuming payments of $9,000 per year for twenty years, the amounts of interest and principal are as follows:

Year	Interest	Principal	Balance
1	$6,395	$2,605	$97,395
2	6,228	2,772	94,623
3	6,051	2,949	91,674
—	—	—	—
18	1,527	7,473	16,410
19	1,049	7,951	8,459
20	541	8,459	-0-

annuities whose payments begin after December 31, 1986. For annuities whose payments began before that date, the rule (from the law as it stood before the 1986 act) is that the exclusion ratio applies for as long as the payments last, even if that means total exclusions of more than the investment in the contract. Correspondingly, if death occurs, and payments end, before recovery of the investment in the contract, there is no deduction for the unrecovered basis. In recent years deferred annuities, because of their substantial tax advantage, have become an important product for insurance companies and an important tax-reduction tool for individuals. Insurance companies have enhanced the attraction of deferred annuities by designing them so that investors can choose the type of investment (for example, a choice from among a number of different mutual funds, including common stock funds, bond funds, etc.) and, thus, can choose a "variable" return, or buildup in value, dependent on their investment choice. Moreover, investors can be allowed to change their minds from time to time (for example, switching from one type of mutual fund to another).

Suppose that A had paid the $100,000 to the insurance company long before her retirement and, thus, long before any payments to her were called for under the contract. Under this arrangement, called a "deferred annuity," the insurance company would have had the benefit of investment of the $100,000 for a longer period of time, and it could afford to make larger payments beginning on A's retirement at age 62. The increase in value before A's retirement would not be taxed to A before retirement, so that increase would not affect her investment in the contract for tax purposes (which would, therefore, still be $100,000). For example, if the $100,000 had been paid to the insurance company twelve years before retirement and if it had grown in value at the rate of 6 percent a year, it would roughly double, to $200,000, by the time of retirement. Thus, the insurance company could afford to double the annual payment, to $18,000. The expected return would then be $360,000, and the exclusion ratio would be 27.77 percent ($100,000 divided by $360,000). The treatment of deferred annuities is obviously favorable to taxpayers: The value of the annuitant's investment increases each year as the payment dates approach, but tax on that increase is deferred until the payments are received.

The favorable rules governing annuities have given rise to a number of tax planning strategies. For example, a taxpayer might invest in a deferred annuity and then borrow the increase in value of the annuity. In the past, such loans did not trigger recognition of gain except to the extent that the amount of the loan exceeded the investment in the contract. If the amount of the loan did not exceed the investment, no tax would be due on the loan or on the increase in the value of the investment until payments began. Today, under § 72(e), a taxpayer who receives a loan against an annuity policy will recognize income equal to the lesser of the amount of the loan or the increase in the value of the policy. Moreover, under § 72(q), taxpayers who are under the age of 59½ generally must pay a penalty tax equal to 10 percent of the amount of the income otherwise recognized.

Section 72(q) applies not just to amounts received by loan but to any "premature distribution." A premature distribution includes any distribution that is not part of a series of substantially equal periodic payments for life. Absent § 72(q), a taxpayer might purchase a deferred annuity that did not pay out for the annuitant's lifetime but that instead provided only a few annual payments beginning at a designated future date. Such an annuity would offer tax-deferred savings and a quick withdrawal of the investment at maturity; it would be much like a bond issued by a corporation or certificate of deposit issued by a bank. Under § 72(q), unless the recipient is age 59½ or older, the distributions on such nonperiodic annuities are subject to the 10 percent penalty tax. For people over 59½, and for younger people who do not need access to their savings until they reach that age, the deferred annuity offers a tax-favored alternative to direct investment in a mutual fund or savings account. The tax advantage cannot be achieved without some cost. The insurance companies that sell annuities charge fees for their services. Still, in many situations deferred annuities will produce better long-run returns than will direct investments that are essentially identical except for tax considerations. The annuity with an underlying investment in a mutual fund and a direct investment in the same mutual fund are, financially, "perfect substitutes," with different tax characteristics. Taxpayers are therefore encouraged to select the tax-favored investment over the direct investment as long as the tax saving exceeds the fees paid to achieve that tax saving. A question that emerges from these observations is, if Congress is willing to allow people to escape tax on their investments, why not let them do so directly so they can save the administrative costs of an intermediary? The answer to that question may have more to do with the exercise of political influence by insurance companies and their agents than criteria for good tax rules.

Pensions. The tax treatment of "pensions" (technically, "qualified employer retirement plans") is essentially the same as the tax treatment of annuities, except that the exclusion for one's investment (basis) is determined by a "simplified" method under which the investment in the contract is divided by the number of "anticipated payments," specified in the Code according to the annuitant's age at the starting date (unless there is a specified number of payments, in which case that number is used). See § 72(d). In applying § 72 to pensions one must remember, however, that amounts contributed toward the pension by the employer and not treated at the time of the contribution as income of the employee are not part of the employee's "investment in the contract" for purposes of the § 72(b) exclusion ratio. For example, suppose that an employer sets up a "qualified" pension plan (described more fully infra page 290), and each year for ten years contributes $5,000 to the trustee of the plan. This $5,000 is not treated as income to the employee because of the special rules applicable to qualified plans. (Despite the nontaxation of the employee, the employer is entitled to deduct the $5,000 as compensation. See § 404(a). And all earnings on amounts invested and held by the pension plan trustee are nontaxable.) Suppose that in addition to the employer contribution of $5,000 per year, the employer withholds from the employee's wages and transfers into the plan an additional $3,000. This is usually called an employee "contribution" even though the employee is given no choice. This

$3,000 contribution would be treated as taxable to the employee.[22] At the end of the ten years suppose the employee retires and starts to collect her pension. Her investment in the contract is $30,000, the amount on which she has already been taxed. The $50,000 contributed by the employer was not taxed to her and is therefore not an amount that she is, or should be, entitled to recover tax-free.

As is perhaps obvious, employee contributions are not treated as favorably as employer contributions. The best explanation (though not an excuse) for plans that require mandatory employee contributions seems to be money illusion. Employers may feel that employees are attracted by higher nominal salaries even though part of the wage or salary is withheld for a pension. Suppose, for example, that the employee's salary is $53,000 and that $3,000 is withheld for the employee's "contribution" to the pension plan. The employee would be better off financially if the employer reduced the salary to $50,000 and paid the $3,000 into the plan as an employer contribution. But employers may fear that employees will fail to understand this and will seek other jobs where the nominal salary is higher.[23]

Variable annuities. "Normal" annuities call for payments that are fixed at the time of issuance of the contract and in effect reflect a fixed rate of interest guaranteed by the company. The Code also expressly provides for a form of annuity, called a variable annuity, under which the payments to the annuitant depend on the investment experience of a "segregated assets account" held by the company for such policyholders. § 801(g).

4. Gains and Losses from Gambling

The basic rule. By definition, every bet that has a winner also has a loser. Thus, in a economy-wide sense, monetary gains from gambling transactions must always equal monetary losses, leading to net financial income of zero. Under the federal income tax, however, we tax more than aggregate "income" in this financial sense: All gains are taxable, but losses (both for professional and amateur gamblers) are deductible only to the extent of gains from the same taxable year. See § 165(d). Thus, in theory, although, one suspects, not very often in practice, if two friends bet $50 on the outcome of the Super Bowl and make no other bets for the year, the winner has $50 of taxable income while the loser has no deduction.

---

22. Neither the employee contribution nor the employer contribution is subject to Social Security (FICA) tax. Nor are amounts received as a pension. See § 3121(a)(2)(A), (5).

23. Another possibility that achieves the same tax objective as the $8,000 employer contribution with a salary reduction to $50,000 has been available since 1980 under § 401(k): The employer can leave the salary at $53,000, contribute $5,000 to the plan, and give the employee an option to reduce his or her salary by $3,000 and have that amount contributed to the plan on his or her behalf. Without § 401(k) the employee would be taxable on the $3,000 that could have been taken in cash, under the doctrine of constructive receipt (see infra page 276). Under § 401(k), the $3,000 employee contribution is excluded from the employee's gross income, so the employee is taxed on $50,000.

It may be that this seemingly adverse treatment of gambling transactions reflects a moral condemnation of them, although for lawful betting and in particular state-sponsored lotteries this position seems difficult to defend. There is another possible rationale, however. Consider gambling at a casino, racetrack, or other organized consumer business that provides gambling opportunities to its patrons as a form of entertainment for which they are willing to pay. One typically knows, or at least ought to know, that on average one is likely to lose. If one gambles anyway, this may be due to the fun and excitement of the process along with the special satisfaction that winning would provide. How is a night at the casino that on average costs, say, $100 any different than (nondeductibly) spending $100 on dinner and a movie?

From this perspective, one could in theory have taxable income reflect the undeniable fact that someone who gambles and wins is better off than someone who gambles and loses, without having to allow the deduction of consumption expenditures. The way to do this would be to treat the expected cost of one's gambling (given the amount wagered and the odds) as a nondeductible consumption expense, with an inclusion or deduction to the extent one did better or worse than this. Thus, suppose that someone "ought" to have lost $100 given her bets. If she actually lost $150, she would deduct $50; if she broke even she would have taxable income of $100.

Obviously, this approach is utterly impractical. One could also question whether it correctly characterizes all gamblers' motivation as one of engaging in a costly consumption activity. To some purchasers of lottery or "numbers" tickets, their purchases may be a substitute for conventional saving: the only way the person has any reasonable likelihood (from setting aside the occasional winnings) of accumulating enough money for a costly item of consumption or a truly meaningful binge of some sort.

The actual statutory approach of allowing gambling losses to be deducted only against gambling gains is an example of an approach that could be called "basketing" and that is quite common in the tax law. In effect, gambling transactions are placed in a separate "basket" from all of the taxpayer's other transactions to ensure that no net loss from the "basket" will be deductible. Other prominent "basketing" rules that cause particular deductions to be allowable only against related income and that are discussed infra pertain to investment interest (§ 163(d)), capital losses (§ 1211), personal casualty losses (§ 165(h)), hobby losses (§ 183), and passive losses (§ 469).

Whatever their overall merits, "basketing" rules give unfortunate prominence to the question of which transactions fit in the basket. Thus, in Boyd v. United States, 762 F.2d 1369 (9th Cir. 1985), the manager of a poker room at a casino unsuccessfully argued that his losses from playing poker there were business expenses rather than gambling losses because he played in order to attract customers. He also lost his alternative argument, that compensation in the form of a part of the house's take from poker games constituted gambling income against which he could deduct these losses if they were from gambling. In Jasinski v. Commissioner, 37 T.C.M. 1 (1978), the taxpayer had bought risky subordinated corporate debentures — "junk bonds" in common parlance — that yielded interest income but an eventual loss. The court gave short shrift to the taxpayer's argument that the entire high-risk transaction amounted to gambling and that the loss should therefore be deductible against the interest income instead of being treated as a capital loss. Precisely what is the difference between a person who legally bets the horses (but only after many hours studying all available information) and one who trades in the commodities market?

Enforcement. Since gambling is a cash business, enforcement is a problem. For relatively large transactions, § 3402(q) requires that the race track or other payor withhold taxes at a rate of 20 percent. Withholding is not required for most gambling winnings of lesser amounts, though the payor is often required to send the payee and the IRS an information return indicating the amount won. In general, this information reporting obligation is only triggered for winnings of $600 or more, leading some gamblers to believe that the law allows individuals to receive up to $600 in gambling winnings tax-free. This is of course not true (all gambling winnings are taxable; the $600 refers only to the reporting threshold), but it illustrates the importance of reporting obligations to public perceptions regarding tax rules.

Recall that gambling losses are deductible to the extent of gambling winnings. How would a taxpayer prove losses to offset such her gambling winnings? In Parchutz v. Commissioner, 1988-327 T.C. Memo, the court had this to say about evidence of race-track gambling losses:

> Gambling loss tickets are of slight, if any, evidentiary weight where no cor-roboration is offered of petitioner's own testimony that each ticket was pur-chased by him. . . . In the instant case, petitioner offered only his own uncorroborated testimony that the losing tickets were his. We have no way of knowing whether petitioner purchased these tickets or received them from acquaintances at the track or acquired them by resorting to stooping, i.e., stooping down and picking up the discarded stubs of other bettors. . . . More-over, the credibility of petitioner's testimony that he purchased each of the losing tickets has been undermined since some of the losing tickets were pur-chased during a two-week period within the first two months of 1982, when he was confined to a hospital and unable to go to the track.

The preceding cases and materials on recovery of cost have focused on judicial and legislative reactions to problems of practicality. The case that follows is concerned with the somewhat more perplexing question of what we mean, for tax purposes, by a "recovery of capital."

5. Recovery of Loss

CLARK v. COMMISSIONER
40 B.T.A. 333 (1939), acq. 1957-1 C.B. 4

LEECH, J.

This is a proceeding to redetermine a deficiency in income tax for the calendar year 1934 in the amount of $10,618.87. The question presented is whether petitioner derived income by the payment to him of an amount of

$19,941.10, by his tax counsel, to compensate him for a loss suffered on account of erroneous advice given him by the latter. The facts were stipulated and are so found. The stipulation, so far as material, follows:

3. The petitioner during the calendar year 1932, and for a considerable period prior thereto, was married and living with his wife. He was required by the Revenue Act of 1932 to file a Federal Income Tax Return of his income for the year 1932. For such year petitioner and his wife could have filed a joint return or separate returns.

4. Prior to the time that the 1932 Federal Income Tax return or returns of petitioner and/or his wife were due to be filed, petitioner retained experienced tax counsel to prepare the necessary return or returns for him and/or his wife. Such tax counsel prepared a joint return for petitioner and his wife and advised petitioner to file it instead of two separate returns. In due course it was filed with the Collector of Internal Revenue for the First District of California.

5. Thereafter on or about the third day of February, 1934, a duly appointed revenue agent of the United States audited the aforesaid 1932 return and recommended an additional assessment against petitioner in the sum of $34,590.27, which was subsequently reduced to $32,820.14. This last mentioned sum was thereafter assessed against and was paid by petitioner to the Collector of Internal Revenue for the First District of California.

6. The deficiency of $32,820.14 arose from an error on the part of tax counsel who prepared petitioner's 1932 return. The error was that he improperly deducted from income the total amount of losses sustained on the sale of capital assets held for a period of more than two years instead of applying the statutory limitation required by Section 101(b) of the Revenue Act of 1932.

7. The error referred to in paragraph six above was called to the attention of the tax counsel who prepared the joint return of petitioner and his wife for the year 1932. Recomputations were then made which disclosed that if petitioner and his wife had filed separate returns for the year 1932 their combined tax liability would have been $19,941.10 less than that which was finally assessed against and paid by petitioner.

8. Thereafter, tax counsel admitted that if he had not erred in computing the tax liability shown on the joint return filed by the petitioner, he would have advised petitioner to file separate returns for himself and his wife, and accordingly tax counsel tendered to petitioner the sum of $19,941.10, which was the difference between what petitioner and his wife would have paid on their 1932 returns if separate returns had been filed and the amount which petitioner was actually required to pay on the joint return as filed. Petitioner accepted the $19,941.10.

9. In his final determination of petitioner's 1934 tax liability, the respondent included the aforesaid $19,941.10 in income.

10. Petitioner's books of account are kept on the cash receipts and disbursements basis and his tax returns are made on such basis under the community property laws of the State of California.

The theory on which the respondent included the above sum of $19,941.10 in petitioner's gross income for 1934, is that this amount constituted taxes paid for petitioner by a third party and that, consequently, petitioner was in receipt of income to that extent. The cases of Old Colony Trust Co. v. Commissioner, 279 U.S. 716; United States v. Boston & Maine Railroad, 279

U.S. 732, are cited as authority for his position. Petitioner, on the contrary, contends that this payment constituted compensation for damages or loss caused by the error of tax counsel, and that he therefore realized no income from its receipt in 1934.

We agree with petitioner. The cases cited by the respondent are not applicable here. Petitioner's taxes were not paid for him by any person — as rental, compensation for services rendered, or otherwise. He paid his own taxes.

When the joint return was filed, petitioner became obligated to and did pay the taxes computed on that basis. . . . In paying that obligation, he sustained a loss which was caused by the negligence of his tax counsel. The $19,941.10 was paid to petitioner, not qua taxes . . . , but as compensation to petitioner for his loss. The measure of that loss, and the compensation therefor, was the sum of money which petitioner became legally obligated to and did pay because of that negligence. The fact that such obligation was for taxes is of no moment here.

It has been held that payments in settlement of an action for breach of promise to marry are not income. . . . Compromise payments in settlement of an action for damages against a bank on account of conduct impairing the taxpayer's good will by injuring its reputation are also not taxable. . . . The same result follows in the case of payments in settlement for injuries by libel and slander. . . . Damages for personal injury are likewise not income. . . .

The theory of those cases is that recoupment on account of such losses is not income since it is not "derived from capital, from labor or from both combined." . . . And the fact that the payment of the compensation for such loss was voluntary, as here, does not change its exempt status. . . . It was, in fact, compensation for a loss which impaired petitioner's capital.

Moreover, so long as petitioner neither could nor did take a deduction in a prior year of this loss in such a way as to offset income for the prior year, the amount received by him in the taxable year, by way of recompense, is not then includable in his gross income. . . .

Decision will be entered for the petitioner.

CURRENT LEGAL STATUS OF CLARK

The apparent ultimate ground for the holding in *Clark*, that the payment the taxpayer received from his tax counsel was not "derived from capital, from labor, or from both combined," is no longer good law. See Glenshaw Glass Co. v. Commissioner, supra page 85. Nonetheless, the holding in *Clark* remains good law, as shown by its occasional invocation in private letter rulings issued by the Internal Revenue Service in response to taxpayer requests for advice about their own specific fact situations. According to the Internal Revenue Service, *Clark* does not apply to a reimbursement by one's tax advisor unless it compensates one for having paid more than the minimum amount of tax that was actually due given all relevant facts. For example, there is no exclusion if, in connection with a business transaction, Sam tells Betty that her tax will be $100 and it turns out that Betty is required to pay $110 (the true amount payable) and recovers $10 from Sam. Similarly, there is no exclusion if Sam pays Betty $10 because he told her to structure a business transaction one way, resulting in tax liability of $110, and it turns out that if only he had given her better advice regarding how to structure the transaction she could, at zero practical inconvenience, have been in a position to owe only $100 of tax.

NOTES AND QUESTIONS

1. The problem presented by *Clark* is more subtle and puzzling than it may initially appear. The core of the dilemma that it poses can be shown through the following hypothetical:

Suppose that in Year 1 Tom, Dick, and Harry all have identical economic circumstances (and thus would have had the same taxable income and income tax liabilities) except that, of the tax accountants they hire to prepare their federal income tax returns, only Harry's is competent. As a result, for Year 1 Tom and Dick end up paying $5,000 more of federal income tax than does Harry. As in *Clark*, suppose that the error cannot be corrected by filing an amended return for Year 1.

Plainly, once the dust has settled Harry is $5,000 better off than Tom and Dick. His bank account is that much higher after paying the tax, and their circumstances otherwise remain the same. It is not as if Tom and Dick received an extra $5,000 of valuable government services by reason of paying more tax. However, because federal income tax payments are nondeductible, the difference in economic well-being is ignored in the measurement of their respective taxable incomes (except insofar as, in future years, Harry has more income due to investing the $5,000).

Now suppose that, before the end of Year 2, Tom receives a $5,000 payment from his tax accountant as compensation for the error that resulted in his overpaying by that amount in Year 1. Dick, however, learns that no compensation will be forthcoming at any time from *his* accountant, who has permanently moved to Patagonia to search for dinosaur fossils. This changes the three taxpayers' relative positions as follows: Rather than Harry's being $5,000 better off than Tom and Dick, Tom and Harry are $5,000 better off than Dick. In other words, Tom has moved up from the "Dick" level to the "Harry" level of relative well-being.

Should Tom's $5,000 recovery be taxed? If we compare him to Dick, the answer is clearly yes. He is $5,000 better off than Dick due to the recovery, and this ought to be recognized in an income tax that aims to apportion tax liability based on a measure of people's relative well-being. By contrast, if we compare Tom to Harry, the answer is clearly no. Recovering the $5,000 that he needlessly overpaid merely places him on a par with Harry, and thus should not result in his having $5,000 *more* of taxable income (as would result from including the recovery).

Accordingly, the question posed by *Clark* is, in effect, whether Tom should be undertaxed relative to Dick via exclusion of the recovery, or overtaxed relative to Harry via its inclusion. We cannot avoid committing one or the other of these two "errors" (of the overall tax system, not the decision maker) given that Dick and Harry are not being taxed correctly relative to each other. The court in *Clark* chose to impose the first error rather than the second.

2. How would you resolve this unavoidable dilemma and decide the *Clark* case?

3. How did the court determine how the unavoidable dilemma was best resolved? Perhaps the best clue, apart from its now-dated theorizing about what the payment was "derived from," is its statement that the taxpayer merely received "compensation for a loss which impaired [his] capital." In short, in organizing the facts, it seems (perhaps quite logically) to have conceived of an overall "transaction" in which *Clark* first needlessly overpaid federal income tax and then was reimbursed for the overpayment. It then determined that a transaction yielding no overall gain should have no overall income tax consequences. What, if anything, makes this "transactional" view an appealing one?

4. In effect, the court in *Clark* treats the taxpayer as having a kind of partial or quasi-basis as a result of the nondeductible tax overpayment of $19,941.10. In general, an asset's true or full basis can be used to offset inclusion of amounts realized when it is sold or loss. For example, if you buy an acre of land for $20,000, it has a $20,000 basis. Thus, if you sell it for $25,000 you will deduct the basis from the amount realized and report only $5,000 of gain. The overpayment in *Clark* seems to work the same way. Thus, had the tax-payer's counsel made his apology even fuller by throwing in an extra $5,000 and paying Clark $24, 941.10, the extra $5,000 would presumably have been taxable income.

True or full basis, however, can often (although with important exceptions and qualifications) be deducted when it turns out to be unrecoverable. For example, if the acre of land that you bought for $20,000 turns out to contain a toxic waste dump and you therefore transfer it for zero consideration, then, subject to various special rules that we can ignore for now, you could deduct the $20,000 loss from the transaction. By contrast, in a *Clark* situation the taxpayer gets no deduction for the overpayment if there is no recovery.

HYPOTHETICAL

Suppose that on December 29, 2008, Tom picks up his pay envelope containing $300. When he arrives home he finds that there is a hole in his pocket and no pay envelope. He retraces his steps and cannot find it. He reports his loss to the police but they offer him no encouragement. He checks with the police again on December 31 and still there is no encouragement.

1. What are the income tax consequences for 2008? (a) Is the $300 exclud-able from income? (b) May Tom deduct the $300 as a loss? (See § 165(c)(3); disregard the limitations in § 165(h).)

2. Assume that Tom was entitled to and claimed a deduction of $300 in 2008 but that in 2009 he once more retraces his steps and, by a stroke of remarkable good fortune, finds his lost pay envelope with the $300 still in it. (a) Should he file an amended return for 2008? (b) Assuming that it would not be appropriate to file an amended return for 2008, should he treat the $300 as

income in 2009? Your intuition no doubt tells you that he should. That intuition is sound and is consistent with rules referred to as the "tax benefit doctrine," which is considered later in this chapter.

3. Assume again that in 2009, he finds his lost pay envelope with the $300, but that in 2008 he had not been entitled to and did not claim a loss deduction. How should he treat the $300 in 2009? The *Clark* case provides the answer to this question. Is that answer correct? Is it not clear that Tom is better off than an otherwise identical person who does not find his pay envelope in 2009? To achieve fairness, if Tom can exclude the $300, should that other person not be allowed a deduction? When?

4. Assume, as in Note 3, that Tom was not entitled to and did not claim a deduction in 2008 and in 2009 he finds a pay envelope with $300 but it is someone else's rather than his own. Assume further that efforts to find the owner prove unavailing and Tom is advised by a lawyer in 2009 that he is entitled to treat the $300 as his own. Must he report that amount as income? See *Glenshaw Glass*, supra page 85. Can you reconcile your answer to this question with your answer to the questions in Note 3? What would Henry Simons (see supra page 48) say?

5. Suppose that Tom was entitled to a deduction in 2008 but neglected to claim it. (a) He finds his $300 in 2009. Should he include it in income? (b) He finds his $300 in 2013, after the statute of limitations has run on 2008. Now, how should he treat the $300?

E.   ANNUAL ACCOUNTING AND ITS CONSEQUENCES

The issues and principles to be examined in this section have traditionally been thought of as stemming from problems of "accounting," and because of the tradition it is convenient to accept the categorization. Otherwise, these issues and principles might have been treated as part of the broader problems of recovery of cost (or capital or investment) that we have just examined or as part of the still broader problems of timing and recognition that are taken up later.

1.   The Use of Hindsight

BURNET v. SANFORD & BROOKS CO.
282 U.S. 359 (1931)

Mr. Justice STONE delivered the opinion of the Court. . . .

From 1913 to 1915, inclusive, respondent, a Delaware corporation engaged in business for profit, was acting for the Atlantic Dredging Company in carrying out a contract for dredging the Delaware River, entered into by that company with the United States. In making its income tax returns for the years 1913 and 1916, respondent added to gross income for each year the payments made under the contract that year, and deducted its expenses paid that year in performing the contract. The total expenses exceeded the payments received by $176,271.88. The tax returns for 1913, 1915, and 1916 showed net losses. That for 1914 showed net income.

In 1915 work under the contract was abandoned, and in 1916 suit was brought in the Court of Claims to recover for a breach of warranty of the character of the material to be dredged. Judgment for the claimant, 53 Ct. Cls. 490, was affirmed by this Court in 1920. . . . It held that the recovery was upon the contract and was "compensatory of the cost of the work, of which the government got the benefit." From the total recovery, petitioner received in that year the sum of $192,577.59, which included the $176,271.88 by which its expenses under the contract had exceeded receipts from it, and accrued interest amounting to $16,305.71. Respondent having failed to include these amounts as gross income in its tax returns for 1920, the Commissioner made the deficiency assessment here involved, based on the addition of both items to gross income for that year.

The Court of Appeals ruled that only the item of interest was properly included, holding, erroneously as the government contends, that the item of $176,271.88 was a return of losses suffered by respondent in earlier years and hence was wrongly assessed as income. Notwithstanding this conclusion, its judgment of reversal and the consequent elimination of this item from gross income for 1920 were made contingent upon the filing by respondent of amended returns for the years 1913 to 1916, from which were to be omitted the deductions of the related items of expenses paid in those years. Respondent insists that as the Sixteenth Amendment and the Revenue Act of 1918, which was in force in 1920, plainly contemplate a tax only on net income or profits, any application of the statute which operates to impose a tax with respect to the present transaction, from which respondent received no profit, cannot be upheld.

If respondent's contention that only gain or profit may be taxed under the Sixteenth Amendment be accepted without qualification, . . . the question remains whether the gain or profit which is the subject of the tax may be ascertained, as here, on the basis of fixed accounting periods, or whether, as is pressed upon us, it can only be net profit ascertained on the basis of particular transactions of the taxpayer when they are brought to a conclusion.

All the revenue acts which have been enacted since the adoption of the Sixteenth Amendment have uniformly assessed the tax on the basis of annual returns showing the net result of all the taxpayer's transactions during a fixed accounting period, either the calendar year, or, at the option of the taxpayer, the particular fiscal year which he may adopt. . . .

That the recovery made by respondent in 1920 was gross income for that year within the meaning of these sections cannot, we think, be doubted. The money received was derived from a contract entered into in the course of respondent's business operations for profit. While it equalled, and in a loose sense was a return of, expenditures made in performing the contract, still, as the Board of Tax Appeals found, the expenditures were made in defraying the expenses incurred in the prosecution of the work under the contract, for the purpose of earning profits. They were not capital investments, the cost of which, if converted, must first be restored from the proceeds before there is a capital gain taxable as income. . . .

That such receipts from the conduct of a business enterprise are to be included in the taxpayer's return as a part of gross income, regardless of whether the particular transaction results in net profit, sufficiently appears from the quoted words of § 213(a) and from the character of the deductions allowed. Only by including these items of gross income in the 1920 return would it have been possible to ascertain respondent's net income for the period covered by the return, which is what the statute taxes. The excess of gross income over deductions did not any the less constitute net income for the taxable period because respondent, in an earlier period, suffered net losses in the conduct of its business which were in some measure attributable to expenditures made to produce the net income of the later period. . . .

But respondent insists that if the sum which it recovered is the income defined by the statute, still it is not income, taxation of which without apportionment is permitted by the Sixteenth Amendment, since the particular transaction from which it was derived did not result in any net gain or profit. But we do not think the amendment is to be so narrowly construed. A taxpayer may be in receipt of net income in one year and not in another. The net result of the two years, if combined in a single taxable period, might still be a loss; but it has never been supposed that that fact would relieve him from a tax on the first, or that it affords any reason for postponing the assessment of the tax until the end of a lifetime, or for some other indefinite period, to ascertain more precisely whether the final outcome of the period, or of a given transaction, will be a gain or a loss.

The Sixteenth Amendment was adopted to enable the government to raise revenue by taxation. It is the essence of any system of taxation that it should produce revenue ascertainable, and payable to the government, at regular intervals. Only by such a system is it practicable to produce a regular flow of income and apply methods of accounting, assessment, and collection capable of practical operation. It is not suggested that there has ever been any general scheme for taxing income on any other basis. The computation of income annually as the net result of all transactions within the year was a familiar practice, and taxes upon income so arrived at were not unknown, before the Sixteenth Amendment. . . . It is not to be supposed that the amendment did not contemplate that Congress might make income so ascertained the basis of a scheme of taxation such as had been in actual operation within the United States before its adoption. While, conceivably, a different system might be devised by which the tax could be assessed, wholly or in part, on the basis of the finally ascertained results of particular transactions, Congress is not required by the amendment to adopt such a system in preference to the more familiar method, even if it were practicable. It would not necessarily obviate the kind of inequalities of which respondent complains. If losses from particular transactions were to be set off against gains in others, there would still be the practical necessity of computing the tax on the basis of annual or other fixed taxable periods, which might result in the taxpayer being required to pay a tax on income in one period exceeded by net losses in another. . . .

NOTES AND QUESTIONS

1. *Relationship with recovery-of-cost principles.* How can the decision in this case be reconciled with the decision in Clark v. Commissioner, supra page 133?

2. *Implications. Sanford & Brooks* is often cited for the proposition that our income tax system uses annual, as opposed to transactional, accounting. Transactional accounting as a general proposition would present the practical problem of separating out the costs of and returns from separate transactions. For example, in *Sanford & Brooks* it would require allocation of the taxpayer's general overhead cost (e.g., the salary of its president and the costs of its headquarters facilities) among all of its projects. At the time of the decision in *Sanford & Brooks* such allocation would probably have been considered a daunting task. In the current era accountants are more familiar with the re-quired techniques. In fact, allocations of overhead and other such costs among various projects are now required for the purpose of determining the costs of assets that a taxpayer produces for itself. See § 263A, which is described infra page 519.

3. *Relief from harshness: whose job?* The Court's insistence on strict application of annual accounting produces a harsh, basically unfair outcome in this case. Should the Court have figured out some device for providing relief? Or is the problem one that should be left to Congress? Consider the forms of relief from the harshness of annual accounting that are discussed in the rest of this section.

4. *"Refundable" or negative taxes.* The reason annual accounting produced such harsh results in this case is that losses do not result in negative taxes. That is, the tax on income of, say, negative $1 million, or for that matter negative $100 million, like the tax on income of zero, is zero. Under an income tax system that provided for negative taxes (sometimes called a "refundable" system), negative taxable income would trigger payments from the govern-ment, perhaps using the same rate tables as those used to determine positive tax liability on positive taxable income. Thus, if the tax on income of positive $1 million were $400,000, then the government might pay $400,000 to tax-payers with a loss of $1 million. In practice, this would mainly matter to businesses (including but not limited to those that are operated in corporate form), since one who is primarily a wage-earner generally will not have income much below zero.

Why aren't losses refundable in this way under the federal income tax? Would the case for refundability be strengthened if we were more confident that taxable income roughly equalled economic income, and thus that gov-ernment payments were not going to taxpayers who had merely engaged in clever tax planning to generate noneconomic tax losses? How might non-refundability influence a taxpayer's decision whether to enter a risky business (one that might either make a lot or lose a lot of money)?

5. *Loss carryovers.* The harshness of annual accounting is mitigated by the provision in § 172 for net operating loss (NOL) carryovers. ("Carryover" includes carryback to earlier years and carryforward to later years.) The losses that may be carried over are primarily losses incurred in a trade or business. There is a separate provision for carryover of capital losses, in § 1212. In

United States v. Foster Lumber Co., 429 U.S. 32, 42 (1976), the Supreme Court described the policy objectives of § 172 as follows:

> [In Libson Shops v. Koehler, 353 U.S. 382, 386 (1957)] the Court said that the net operating loss carryover and carryback provisions
>
>> were enacted to ameliorate the unduly drastic consequences of taxing income strictly on an annual basis. They were designed to permit a taxpayer to set off its lean years against its lush years, and to strike something like an average taxable income computed over a period longer than one year.
>
>> There were, in fact, several policy considerations behind the decision to allow averaging of income over a number of years. Ameliorating the timing consequences of the annual accounting period makes it possible for shareholders in companies with fluctuating as opposed to stable incomes to receive more nearly equal tax treatment. Without loss offsets, a firm experiencing losses in some periods would not be able to deduct all the expenses of earning income. The consequence would be a tax on capital, borne by shareholders who would pay higher taxes on net income than owners of businesses with stable income. Congress also sought through allowance of loss carryovers to stimulate enterprise and investment, particularly in new businesses or risky ventures where early losses can be carried forward to future more prosperous years.

Under the original version of § 172, enacted in 1918, the NOL could be carried over to the one immediately preceding year and the one immediately succeeding year. Over time, the carryover period has bit by bit been extended. The period ordinarily is two years back and twenty years forward. For individuals, the losses that can be carried over are primarily business losses, as distinguished from losses attributable to investments, unused non-§ 62 deductions, and deductions for personal dependency exemptions. In general, § 172 fulfills the policy objectives stated by the Court in *Foster Lumber*. However, § 172 contains some technical provisions that produce results inconsistent with those objectives.

6. *Accounting for long-term contracts*. Taxpayers who perform work under long-term contracts for construction or the manufacture of property must account for profit under the percentage-of-completion method. See § 460. Under this method, a portion of the gross contract price is included in income as work progresses, with the portion determined on the basis of cost of work performed. See Regs. § 1.451-3.

7. *Capital expenditures*. If a taxpayer buys a barge or a truck, the cost is treated as a capital expenditure. Such costs are spread out over the years and are recovered through ACRS or, in earlier times, the depreciation deduction. See supra page 38. The outlays at issue in *Sanford & Brooks*, by contrast, are not capital expenditures; they were not the cost of acquiring an asset that is expected to contribute to generating income over future years. The income in *Sanford & Brooks* was generated — it was *earned* (though payment was not received) — in the year in which the outlays occurred. Ordinarily an accrual method taxpayer reports income in the year in which it is earned and this results in a matching of income and expenses. In *Sanford & Brooks*, however, the taxpayer did not use the accrual method. Moreover, because of the uncertainty about collection, even if the taxpayer had used the accrual method, the amount earned probably would not have been accrued (that is, treated as

current income and reported on that year's tax return). Nonetheless, in a situation like that in *Sanford & Brooks* the accounting theory is that matching is achieved, if at all, not by holding off on deducting the expenses but by accruing the income. The holding of the case is that if the taxpayer suffers as a result of the fact that matching does not occur in this way, it is just tough luck for the taxpayer.

PROBLEMS

1. Aerospace Corp. was formed in 1999, and in the same year was awarded a ten-year government contract, which was its only source of business. At the end of 1999, its books showed a loss on the contract of $30,000 and a net taxable loss of the same amount. In 2000, Aerospace Corp. showed a profit on the contract of $30,000 (still its only source of business) and a net taxable income of the same amount. Aerospace Corp. did not elect or qualify for the special accounting methods for long-term contracts. Must Aerospace Corp. pay tax on the $30,000 income in 2000? See § 172(b)(1)(A)(ii), (c).

2. Would your answer to Problem 1 change if Aerospace's $30,000 net income in 2000 were attributable to sales to other companies, rather than to profits on the government contract?

3. In 2009, Bob earned a salary of $60,000 as an associate of a large law firm and had no other income. He had a deduction for personal exemptions of $4,000 and itemized nonbusiness deductions of $16,000, so his taxable income for 2009 was $40,000. In 2010, Bob again earned $60,000 as an associate in the law firm, but also suffered an ordinary (that is, noncapital) loss of $80,000 from his wholly owned business. His deduction for personal exemptions was $6,000 and his itemized nonbusiness deductions were $15,000. How much, if any, of the 2010 loss can Bob carry back against his 2009 income? (Assume Bob had no income in 2007 and 2008 so that no portion of the 2010 loss could be carried back to those years.) See § 172(c), (d)(3) and (4).

4. Xenon Corp.'s adjusted taxable income for the years 2005-2010, before the application of § 172, is shown below:

2005	2006	2007	2008	2009	2010
$400	$700	($3,000)	$700	$700	$600

The $3,000 loss for 2007 is a net operating loss. Disregarding any special elections, how is the 2007 NOL allocated to the other years?

2. Claim of Right

NORTH AMERICAN OIL CONSOLIDATED v. BURNET
286 U.S. 417 (1932)

Mr. Justice BRANDEIS delivered the opinion of the Court.

The question for decision is whether the sum of $171,979.22 received by the North American Oil Consolidated in 1917, was taxable to it as income of that year.

The money was paid to the company under the following circumstances. Among many properties operated by it in 1916 was a section of oil land, the legal title to which stood in the name of the United States. Prior to that year, the Government, also claiming the beneficial ownership, had instituted a suit to oust the company from possession; and on February 2, 1916, it secured the appointment of a receiver to operate the property, or supervise its operations, and to hold the net income thereof. The money paid to the company in 1917 represented the net profits which had been earned from that property in 1916 during the receivership. The money was paid to the receiver as earned. After entry by the District Court in 1917 of the final decree dismissing the bill, the money was paid, in that year, by the receiver to the company. United States v. North American Oil Consolidated, 242 Fed. 723. The Government took an appeal (without supersedeas) to the Circuit Court of Appeals. In 1920, that Court affirmed the decree. 264 Fed. 336. In 1922, a further appeal to this Court was dismissed by stipulation. 258 U.S. 633.

The income earned from the property in 1916 had been entered on the books of the company as its income. It had not been included in its original return of income for 1916; but it was included in an amended return for that year which was filed in 1918. Upon auditing the company's income and profits tax returns for 1917, the Commissioner of Internal Revenue determined a deficiency based on other items. The company appealed to the Board of Tax Appeals. There, in 1927, the Commissioner prayed that the deficiency already claimed should be increased so as to include a tax on the amount paid by the receiver to the company in 1917. The Board held that the profits were taxable to the receiver as income of 1916; and hence made no finding whether the company's accounts were kept on the cash receipts and disbursements basis or on the accrual basis. 12 B.T.A. 68. The Circuit Court of Appeals held that the profits were taxable to the company as income of 1917, regardless of whether the company's returns were made on the cash or on the accrual basis. 50 F.(2d) 752. This Court granted a writ of certiorari. 284 U.S. 614.

It is conceded that the net profits earned by the property during the receivership constituted income. The company contends that they should have been reported by the receiver for taxation in 1916; that if not returnable by him, they should have been returned by the company for 1916, because they constitute income of the company accrued in that year; and that if not taxable as income of the company for 1916, they were taxable to it as income for 1922, since the litigation was not finally terminated in its favor until 1922.

First. The income earned in 1916 and impounded by the receiver in that year was not taxable to him, because he was the receiver of only a part of the properties operated by the company. Under Sec. 13(c) of the Revenue Act of 1916 [and its successors], receivers who "are operating the property or business of corporations" were obliged to make returns "of net income as and for such corporations," and "any income tax due" was to be "assessed and collected in the same manner as if assessed directly against the organization of whose business or properties they have custody and control."[24] The

___

24. [The current equivalent of this provision is § 6012(b)(3). — EDS.]

regulations of the Treasury Department have consistently construed these statutes as applying only to receivers in charge of the entire property or business of a corporation; and in all other cases have required the corporations themselves to report their income. . . . That construction is clearly correct. The language of the section contemplates a substitution of the receiver for the corporation; and there can be such substitution only when the receiver is in complete control of the properties and business of the corporation. Moreover, there is no provision for the consolidation of the return of a receiver of part of a corporation's property or business with the return of the corporation itself. It may not be assumed that Congress intended to require the filing of two separate returns for the same year, each covering only a part of the corporate income, without making provision for consolidation so that the tax could be based upon the income as a whole.

Second. The net profits were not taxable to the company as income of 1916. For the company was not required in 1916 to report as income an amount which it might never receive. See Burnet v. Logan [infra page 268]. Compare Lucas v. American Code Co., 280 U.S. 445, 452; Burnet v. Sanford & Brooks Co. [supra page 138]. There was no constructive receipt of the profits by the company in that year, because at no time during the year was there a right in the company to demand that the receiver pay over the money. Throughout 1916 it was uncertain who would be declared entitled to the profits. It was not until 1917, when the District Court entered a final decree vacating the receivership and dismissing the bill, that the company became entitled to receive the money. Nor is it material, for the purposes of this case, whether the company's return was filed on the cash receipts and disbursements basis, or on the accrual basis. In neither event was it taxable in 1916 on account of income which it had not yet received and which it might never receive.

Third. The net profits earned by the property in 1916 were not income of the year 1922 — the year in which the litigation with the Government was finally terminated. They became income of the company in 1917, when it first became entitled to them and when it actually received them. If a taxpayer receives earnings under a claim of right and without restriction as to its disposition, he has received income which he is required to return [that is, report on his or her tax return], even though it may still be claimed that he is not entitled to retain the money, and even though he may still be adjudged liable to restore its equivalent. . . . If in 1922 the Government had prevailed, and the company had been obliged to refund the profits received in 1917, it would have been entitled to a deduction from the profits in 1922, not from those of any earlier year. . . .

Affirmed.

NOTES AND QUESTIONS

1. *The stakes.* While ordinarily the taxpayer seeks to defer the taxation of income, here the taxpayer argues for taxation in the earliest possible year. The explanation is that in 1916 the tax rate was 2 percent; in 1917 it was 6

percent plus an excess profits tax ranging from 20 percent to 60 percent; and in 1922 it was 12.5 percent, with no excess profits tax.

2. *The receivership.* The Court viewed the receiver, appointed in 1916, as a custodian of funds and not as a substitute operator of the business. Such a receiver, who is not in control of the taxpayer's entire business, was not required to file a return for the taxpayer. (For the present rule, which is to the same effect, see § 6012(b)(3).) What, if anything, would be wrong with taxing the receiver? If the receiver had invested the funds and earned interest on the investment, how should that interest have been treated?

3. *The proper taxable year.* (a) There was no finding as to whether the taxpayer was on the cash or the accrual method of accounting. Under § 446(a), "taxable income shall be computed under the method of accounting on the basis of which the taxpayer regularly computes his income in keeping his books." Section 446(b) provides an exception where the method used by the taxpayer "does not clearly reflect income." Assume that the taxpayer was on the accrual method. (For a brief description, see supra page 36.) What was it that stood in the way of taxation in 1916, the dispute or the receivership?

(b) If the latter, can the result be reconciled with principles of accrual accounting?

(c) If the former, why was the receipt taxable in 1917, when the dispute was still alive?

(d) Could the taxpayer have protected itself from liability in 1917 by treating the receipt as a trust fund pending outcome of the appeal — for example, by depositing it in a special account and labeling it as a trust fund on its books? No, per Commissioner v. Alamitos Land Co., 112 F.2d 648 (9th Cir.), cert. denied, 311 U.S. 679 (1940), and Rev. Rul. 55-137, 1955-1 C.B. 215. See also Commissioner v. Brooklyn Union Gas Co., 62 F.2d 505 (2d Cir. 1933), acq. (amount under dispute but received before final judicial determination taxable despite the fact that taxpayer was required to post bond to secure repayment if dispute ultimately were resolved against it).

4. *The "claim of right" doctrine.* (a) *North American Oil* is often cited for its statement (in the final paragraph of the opinion) of the "claim-of-right" doctrine:

> If a taxpayer receives earnings under a claim of right and without restriction as to its disposition, he has received income which he is required to return [i.e., report], even though it may still be claimed that he is not entitled to retain the money, and even though he may still be adjudged liable to restore its equivalent.

(b) In Illinois Power Co. v. Commissioner, 792 F.2d 683 (7th Cir. 1986), the taxpayer, an electric company, was ordered by the Illinois Commerce Commission to raise its rates. The Commission made it clear, however, that its purpose was to discourage the consumption of electricity and that the taxpayer would not be allowed to keep the extra revenue resulting from the increase, or any interest on it. The money was not, however, kept in any separate account or trust. The IRS argued that the money was taxable under *North American Oil.* The court, in rejecting this position, likened the taxpayer to "a custodian, . . . with no greater beneficial interest in the revenues collected than a bank has in the money deposited with it." Generalizing, the court stated, "The underlying principle is that the taxpayer is allowed to exclude from his [sic] income money received under an unequivocal contractual, statutory, or regulatory duty to repay it, so that he really is just the custodian of the money." Thus, in this case there was no dispute; the taxpayer never claimed a right to the funds at issue. Note that during the time the power company held the money, it earned interest on that money. How should that interest be taxed?

UNITED STATES v. LEWIS
340 U.S. 590 (1951)

Mr. Justice BLACK delivered the opinion of the Court.

Respondent Lewis brought this action in the Court of Claims seeking a refund of an alleged overpayment of his 1944 income tax. The facts found by the Court of Claims are: In his 1944 income tax return, respondent reported about $22,000 which he had received that year as an employee's bonus. As a result of subsequent litigation in a state court, however, it was decided that respondent's bonus had been improperly computed; under compulsion of the state court's judgment he returned approximately $11,000 to his employer. Until payment of the judgment in 1946, respondent had at all times claimed and used the full $22,000 unconditionally as his own, in the good faith though "mistaken" belief that he was entitled to the whole bonus.

On the foregoing facts the Government's position is that respondent's 1944 tax should not be recomputed, but that respondent should have deducted the $11,000 as a loss in his 1946 tax return. . . . The Court of Claims, however, relying on its own case, Greenwald v. United States, 102 Ct. Cl. 272, 57 F. Supp. 569, held that the excess bonus received "under a mistake of fact" was not income in 1944 and ordered a refund based on a recalculation of that year's tax. 117 Ct. Cl. 336, 91 F. Supp. 1017. We granted certiorari, 340 U.S. 903, because this holding conflicted with many decisions of the courts of appeals, see, e.g., Haberkorn v. United States, 173 F.2d 587, and with principles announced in North American Oil v. Burnet [supra page 143].

In the *North American Oil* case we said:

> If a taxpayer receives earnings under a claim of right and without restriction as to its disposition, he has received income which he is required to return, even though it may still be claimed that he is not entitled to retain the money, and even though he may still be adjudged liable to restore its equivalent.

286 U.S. at 424. Nothing in this language permits an exception merely because a taxpayer is "mistaken" as to the validity of his claim. Nor has the "claim of right" doctrine been impaired, as the Court of Claims stated, by Freuler v. Helvering, 291 U.S. 35, or Commissioner v. Wilcox, 327 U.S. 404. The Freuler case involved an entirely different section of the Internal Revenue Code, and its holding is inapplicable here. 291 U.S. at 43. . . .

Income taxes must be paid on income received (or accrued) during an annual accounting period. Cf. [§§ 441, 451(a), and 446(a)]; and see Burnet v. Sanford & Brooks Co. [supra page 138]. The "claim of right" interpretation of the tax laws has long been used to give finality to that period, and is now deeply rooted in the federal tax system. . . . We see no reason why the Court should depart from this well-settled interpretation merely because it results in an advantage or disadvantage to a taxpayer.[25]

Reversed.

Mr. Justice DOUGLAS, dissenting.

The question in this case is not whether the bonus had to be included in 1944 income for purposes of the tax. Plainly it should have been because the taxpayer claimed it as of right. Some years later, however, it was judicially determined that he had no claim to the bonus. The question is whether he may then get back the tax which he paid on the money.

Many inequities are inherent in the income tax. We multiply them needlessly by nice distinctions which have no place in the practical administration of the law. If the refund were allowed, the integrity of the taxable year would not be violated. The tax would be paid when due; but the Government would not be permitted to maintain the unconscionable position that it can keep the tax after it is shown that payment was made on money which was not income to the taxpayer.

NOTES AND QUESTIONS

1. *Claim of right and amended returns.* The *Lewis* decision is consistent with the objective of according "finality" to tax returns, an objective that, at least superficially, seems to promote administrative efficiency and may be thought of as an attribute of annual accounting. Amended returns are used to claim refunds of overpayments for earlier years. Such returns may be filed only to correct mistakes about facts that were, or reasonably should have been, known before the end of the earlier year, and then may be filed only if the statute of limitations (generally three years) has not run. See supra page 29. What, then, is the relevance of the "claim of right" doctrine? In a situation like the one in *Lewis*, how weighty would be the administrative burden of allowing the taxpayer to file an amended return for the year in which the overpayment was received?

2. *Equity consideration.* Why did Justice Douglas think that an adjustment for 1944 would be more equitable? After all, the taxpayer did receive the full $22,000 in 1944. In 1946 he discovered that he was $11,000 less well off than he had thought. Why is his economic setback any different from an investment loss or a casualty loss in 1946?

---

25. It has been suggested that it would be more "equitable" to reopen respondent's 1944 tax return. While the suggestion might work to the advantage of this taxpayer, it could not be adopted as a general solution because, in many cases, the three-year statute of limitations would preclude recovery. [§ 6511(a).]

3. *Scope of the doctrine.* Suppose a bank erroneously credits your account with interest on December 31. You discover this on January 1 of the following year and have the bank make the correction. Must you include the erroneous interest in income for the first year and take a deduction in the later year? What if you withdraw the interest on December 31 of the first year (with or without knowledge of the error) and repay it in the following year?

4. *Congressional reaction: § 1341.* (a) Congress apparently agreed that the result in cases like *Lewis* was inequitable and provided relief in § 1341. It retained the notion that the proper starting point was a deduction in the year of repayment rather than a reopening of the earlier year. But it provided that if the deduction exceeds $3,000, the tax is the lesser of the amount determined by claiming a deduction in the ordinary manner or by forgoing the deduction and claiming a credit in the year of repayment for the tax that would have been saved by excluding the item in the earlier year. The effect of the latter alternative is the same as allowing the taxpayer to reopen the earlier year, except for the interest on the overpayment. If § 1341 had been the law in 1946, Lewis would have reduced his tax bill for 1946 by the "tax cost" of including the item in 1944. Why is the taxpayer allowed to choose the better of two alternatives? A taxpayer who paid little or no tax when the item was included in gross income is permitted, under § 1341, to deduct it from the later year's income, even though the tax saving from the deduction in that later year exceeds the tax cost of the earlier inclusion. Would Justice Douglas have found that unconscionable?

(b) While Congress's objective in enacting § 1341 may have been to achieve equity, it was not content simply to provide the courts with a broad, vague mandate to accomplish that objective. The statute applies to items as to which it *appeared* that the taxpayer had an *unrestricted right* in one year and as to which a repayment is made in a subsequent year "because it was *established* after the close of such prior taxable year" that the taxpayer did not have such an unrestricted right (emphasis added). The IRS has ruled that restorations do not qualify under § 1341 if based on "mere errors," such as in arithmetic, or on "subsequent events," such as a refund pursuant to a contractual right. Rev. Rul. 68-153, 1968-1 C.B. 371. Nor does it believe that the repayment by an embezzler of his embezzled gains qualifies. Rev. Rul. 65-254, 1965-2 C.B. 50. The rulings are based on the theory that § 1341 applies only where amounts are held under a "semblance" of a right—i.e., a claim that is somewhere between "absolutely no right" (embezzled funds) and a situation where the repayment is made to the payee based on a "non-challengeable" obligation to make such repayment (e.g., a refund based on a contractual right merely contingent upon subsequent events). The ruling that an embezzler cannot invoke § 1341 because he or she does not have an "unrestricted right" to the embezzled funds was upheld in McKinney v. United States, 574 F.2d 1240 (5th Cir. 1978), cert. denied, 439 U.S. 1072 (1979), and in Yerkie v. Commissioner, 67 T.C. 388 (1976). In each of these cases the taxpayer restored part of the embezzled funds when the embezzlement was discovered. The IRS did not dispute the taxpayer's right to a deduction for the restoration but denied the right to invoke § 1341(a)(5)(B). As an alternative to their claims for relief under § 1341, the taxpayers sought unsuccessfully to establish that they were in the trade or business of embezzlement and therefore should be entitled to carry the undeducted portion of the losses back to earlier years under § 172. This position was rejected, even though, in McKinney's case, the taxpayer established that he had devoted about half of his working time to the embezzlement scheme and that the one in question was his third.

5. *Fluctuating tax rates and fluctuating income.* The problem addressed by § 1341 arises because taxpayers often find themselves in different marginal rate brackets in different taxable years. This can happen either because Congress changes the rate structure from year to year or, under our system of graduated marginal rates, because the taxpayer has more overall income in one year than in another. The "claim of right" cases that § 1341 covers involve only one narrow instance of this phenomenon, however.

For example, suppose that in Year 1 the marginal rate for all taxpayers above a certain income level is 40 percent, but that for Year 2 Congress either raises this rate to 50 percent or else lowers it to 30 percent. Suppose that Bob and Judy, both of whom are above this income level for both years, each receive a $100,000 fee that is includable upon receipt, but that Bob is paid in December of Year 1 while Judy is paid in December of Year 2. Does it make sense that, while Bob will pay $40,000 of tax on his fee, Judy, whose circumstances are scarcely different, will pay either $30,000 or $50,000, depending on the direction of the rate change?

Now suppose that, for both Year 3 and Year 4, the marginal tax rate is 0 percent on one's first $50,000 of taxable income, and 50 percent on all income above that amount. Wayne earns $50,000 each year and thus pays no tax, while Jenna earns $100,000 in Year 3 and zero in Year 4, and thus pays $25,000 of tax (50 percent of the excess over $50,000 in Year 3). How much sense does this make?

What could be done about rate swing problems such as these? If nothing is done about them in general, how does that affect the desirability of addressing the "claim of right" problems that fall within the reach of § 1341?

3. The Tax Benefit Rule

In claim of right cases, the taxpayer includes something in income in an earlier year and then has an offsetting deduction (or more valuable credit under § 1341) in a later year when the income is lost. What are called "tax benefit" cases involve the opposite problem. The taxpayer claims a deduction in an earlier year, and then in a later year the deducted amount is in some sense recovered or regained. This may happen, for example, where there have been deductions for bad debts, taxes, losses by theft, worthless assets, expropriation losses, or other calamities and later, to the surprise and delight of the taxpayer, there is a recovery of part or all of the amount written off. As it turns out, the tax benefit doctrine has two aspects, one exclusionary and one inclusionary.

Exclusionary aspect of the tax benefit rule. Suppose initially that the taxpayer received no tax benefit (in the sense of a reduction of tax liability) for any year by reason of the earlier year's deduction. Thus, in the year when the deduction arose, the taxpayer may have had negative taxable income even without regard to this deduction, and thus owed the same tax of zero with it as without it. Or the deduction may simply have increased the taxpayer's net capital loss for the year that was disallowed under § 1211 (discussed in Chapter 8). However, since excess deductions that create net operating losses, excess capital losses, and the like typically give rise to carryovers that can be deducted in other taxable years, the possibility of tax benefit from a given deduction cannot be foreclosed until any such carryovers have expired.

Under § 111, if (or to the extent that) a deduction did not reduce the taxpayer's tax liability for any year *and* any loss carryovers resulting from it have expired without being used, the recovery of the amount deducted need not be included in income. In effect, § 111 protects the taxpayer against adverse marginal tax rate swings that result from, in effect, claiming the deduction at a zero percent rate and then including the recovery at a positive rate. Unlike § 1341 in claim of right cases, however, it does not protect the taxpayer against adverse marginal rate changes more generally. Thus, suppose that (under a hypothetical rate structure) a taxpayer deducted $100 when his marginal rate was 1 percent (thus saving $1 of tax), and then included the recovery when his marginal rate was 99 percent (thus paying $99 of tax). Section 111, unlike § 1341 in the reverse case of an inclusion at 99 percent followed by a deduction at 1 percent, would not apply or provide any relief. Both statutes permit the taxpayer to gain from favorable rate swings, such as when $100 is in one year deducted at a 99 percent rate, and in another year included at a 1 percent rate.

Inclusionary aspect of the tax benefit rule. The distinct "inclusionary" aspect of the tax benefit rule arises when the taxpayer has indeed received a tax benefit from a deduction, and the includability or amount of the subsequent offsetting gain is not otherwise clear-cut. Under these circumstances, the rule requires that income in the amount of the prior deduction be included, thus moving toward transactional rather than strict annual accounting.

In illustration, in Alice Phelan Sullivan Corp. v. United States, 381 F.2d 399 (Ct. Cl. 1967), the taxpayer had made a charitable gift of property subject to the condition that the property be used for either a religious or educational purpose, and claimed a charitable deduction that it used in full. Nearly twenty years later, the charity decided not to so use the property, and therefore returned it to the taxpayer. This recovery was held to generate taxable income in the amount of the earlier deduction, as distinct from, say, the value of the property in the year when it was returned.

The most difficult cases for determining the applicability of the inclusionary aspect of the tax benefit rule are those where the event that "matches" the earlier deduction is not a "recovery" of property in the most direct and literal sense. In Hillsboro National Bank v. Commissioner, 460 U.S. 370 (1983), the Supreme Court considered two such cases (*Hillsboro* itself and the consolidated case of United States v. Bliss Dairy, Inc.). In *Hillsboro*, a corporation had been allowed, under § 164(e), to deduct certain state taxes that were imposed on its shareholders but that it paid. (Without § 164(e), such payments would be treated as nondeductible dividends to the shareholders whose state tax liabilities were thereby satisfied.) However, due to a state law dispute about whether the taxes were lawfully imposed, the payments went to a state-administered escrow fund. The taxes were subsequently struck down under state law, whereupon state authorities repaid the contested payments to the shareholders rather than to the bank itself. The Commissioner claimed that the bank had taxable income by reason of the refund, even though it had not literally recovered the amounts paid, on the ground that payment of the disputed amount to the shareholders was "inconsistent" with the earlier deduction, which had been premised on the view that a state tax liability was owed. The taxpayer argued that a literal recovery was necessary in order for inclusion to be mandated by the tax benefit rule.

In *Bliss Dairy*, a corporation had deducted the cost of buying cattle feed, under since-repealed rules permitting farming businesses to use the cash method of accounting. In a later year, however, rather than using the cattle feed in its operations, the corporation liquidated and distributed its assets, including the unused cattle feed, to its shareholders. Here again, the government argued that inclusion by the corporation was required by the tax benefit rule under its "inconsistent event" theory, while the taxpayer pointed to the lack of a literal "recovery" of the deducted cattle feed by the liquidating corporation.

The Supreme Court began by rejecting the taxpayer's view of the tax benefit rule:

> An examination of the purpose and accepted applications of the tax benefit rule reveals that a "recovery" will not always be necessary to invoke the tax benefit rule. The purpose of the rule is not simply to tax "recoveries." On the contrary, it is to approximate the results produced by a tax system based on transactional rather than annual accounting. . . . It has long been accepted that a taxpayer using accrual accounting who accrues and deducts an expense in a tax year before it becomes payable and who for some reason eventually does not have to pay the liability must then take into income the amount of the expense earlier deducted. . . . The bookkeeping entry canceling the liability, though it increases the balance sheet net worth of the taxpayer, does not fit within any ordinary definition of "recovery." Thus, the taxpayers' formulation of the rule neither serves the purpose of the rule nor accurately reflects the cases that establish the rule. Further, the taxpayer's proposal would introduce an undesirable formalism into the application of the tax benefit rule. . . . Imposition of a requirement that there be a recovery would, in many cases, simply require the Government to cast its argument in different and unnatural terminology, without adding anything to the analysis.

However, the Court also rejected the Government's proposed test, which it described as "requir[ing] the inclusion of amounts previously deducted if later events are inconsistent with the deductions," on the following ground:

> The basic purpose of the tax benefit rule is to . . . protect the Government and the taxpayer from the adverse effects of reporting a transaction on the basis of assumptions that an event in a subsequent year proves to have been erroneous. Such an event, unforeseen at the time of an earlier deduction, may in many cases

require the application of the tax benefit rule. We do not, however, agree that this consequence invariably follows. Not every unforeseen event will require the taxpayer to report income in the amount of his earlier deduction. On the contrary, the tax benefit rule will "cancel out" an earlier deduction only when a careful examination shows that the later event is indeed *fundamentally* inconsistent with the premise on which the deduction was initially based. (Emphasis added.)

The Court then decided, on somewhat confusing and technical grounds, that the tax benefit rule required inclusion in *Bliss Dairy* but not in *Hillsboro*.

NOTES AND QUESTIONS

1. By applying solely when the marginal tax rate in the year of the deduction was in effect zero, does § 111 do too little to address tax rate differences between the year of deduction and of recovery? Or does it do too much? Does it matter to the merits of this rule that the government gets no relief in cases where the taxpayer received a tax benefit from the deduction but gets no "tax detriment" (in the form increased tax liability for any year) from including the recovery?

2. Can the inclusionary aspect of the tax benefit rule reduce the amount that a taxpayer must include in income? Consider *Alice Phelan Sullivan Corp.* where the taxpayer received back property that it had contributed to a charity. Is it possible, in the absence of the tax benefit rule, that the taxpayer would have had income in the full amount of the property's value, rather than the amount of the earlier deduction? In the words of *Glenshaw Glass*, supra, could one argue that this was taxable as an "undeniable accession to wealth, clearly realized, and over which the taxpayer had complete dominion"?

Does it matter in this regard that the taxpayer in *Alice Phelan Sullivan* technically had never given away the right to hold the property if it ceased to be used for religious or educational purposes? If so, does it matter that the taxpayer had claimed a charitable deduction for the property's full value at the time of the gift, rather than treating itself as having made only a partial gift (akin to a term interest) through its retention of a valuable, albeit conditional, right of reversion?

3. The Supreme Court in *Hillsboro* declined to broaden the term "recovery" to cover all cases where the inclusionary aspect of the tax benefit rule ought to apply, on the ground that this would "simply require the Government to cast its argument in different and unnatural terminology, without adding anything to the analysis." In retrospect, might such an approach have provided greater clarity than what the Court actually did? For example, the Court could perhaps have developed a notion of "constructive" or "equitable" recovery, to cover at least two types of cases: (a) those where assets are converted from deductible to nondeductible use and (b) cases where the recovery is by parties closely related to the taxpayer, such as a corporation's shareholders or an individual taxpayer's children. How would the *Hillsboro* and *Bliss Dairy* cases come out under such a rule?

F.   RECOVERIES FOR PERSONAL AND BUSINESS INJURIES

1.   The Basic Rules

Tax lawyers often are asked to describe the treatment of amounts received as damages for injuries of one kind or another. For taxpayers other than individuals, the tax treatment is straightforward. Damage awards for lost profits are taxed in the year received. See Burnet v. Sanford & Brooks Co., supra page 138; North American Oil Consolidated v. Burnet, supra page 143. Thus a company that sues and recovers for lost profits is taxed on the amount received just as if it had earned that amount as profit in the year the recovery is made. Punitive damages are also taxed in the year received. See *Glenshaw Glass,* supra page 85. Suppose a company recovers damages in recompense for destroyed or damaged property. The recovery is taxable in the year received to the extent it exceeds the basis of the property. However, § 1033 allows a taxpayer to defer taxation provided the amounts are reinvested in similar or related in use. To understand the treatment of amounts received for damaged or destroyed property, suppose a company's building is destroyed by a contractor's negligence. The building has a basis of $600,000 and a fair market value of $700,000. The company sues and in the same year collects $700,000. The company is taxable on $100,000 — just as if it had sold the building for $700,000.[26] However, the tax will be deferred if the company uses the proceeds to build or buy a similar building. In the above examples, the awards were court ordered. The result would be the same if the recoveries were received through settlement or through insurance.

In the case of individual taxpayers, awards (or settlements or insurance proceeds) are generally tax-free — provided the payment is attributable to a personal injury. § 104. The tax-free treatment does not extend, however, to punitive damages arising out of a personal injury. § 104(a)(2). In recent years, a surprising amount of litigation has arisen concerning the definition of "personal injury." The term clearly encompasses physical injuries, but what about amounts received for nonphysical injuries, such as libel or discrimination? The issue led to two Supreme Court decisions, and scores of lower court decisions and controversies, before Congress finally resolved the issue in late 1996. Section 104(a)(2) now excludes only amounts arising from personal physical injuries or sickness.

In some cases, the nontaxation of recoveries on account of physical injuries is arguably correct. Suppose, for example, someone is hit by a car and recovers amounts for uninsured medical expenses, pain, and suffering. The victim may seem to be no better off (at least if the court got the award right) after the

---

26. The result would be different if the company had deducted the $600,000 as a loss in one year and then did not recover the amount until a subsequent year. In that case, the so-called tax benefit rule, described supra at page 150, would require the taxpayer to treat the entire amount as gain in the year received. In effect, the taxpayer would not only recognize the $100,000 income but also have to "give back" the $600,000 loss that, in retrospect, was erroneously deducted.

award than prior to the accident. If this is the comparison (the same individual prior to the accident and after the award) nontaxation seems appropriate. There simply has not been an increase in well-being. Nontaxation also seems appropriate if we compare the victim after the award to those who did not suffer an accident. Again, the combination of accident and award have not produced an increase in wealth. (Note, however, that the individual after the award will be better off than someone who suffers from the same accident and does not recover. If this is the most relevant comparison, and we do not allow a deduction for the victim who does not recover, nontaxation seems incorrect. See *Clark*, supra page 135.)

We could, in theory, treat the damage to the individual from the accident in the same manner as damage to business property — taxable to the extent that the award exceeds basis. That approach, however, would require us to attribute basis to the human body or treat the entire award as taxable. For obvious reasons, no one has ever seriously suggested such treatment. In other cases, the nontaxation of physical injuries seems flawed. For example, suppose an individual is hit by a car and misses a month of work. Some portion of her recovery is attributable to lost wages. The wages would be taxed, why not the amounts received in lieu of the wages?

Suppose an individual receives an award for a nonpersonal injury. In that case, the treatment described above, for taxpayers other than individuals, applies. Amounts received in recompense for lost profits are taxed as profits in the year received. Amounts received as damages to property are taxed to the extent such amounts exceed basis. Thus, an individual who recovers $200,000 for the destruction of property with a basis of $150,000 is taxed on $50,000. As in the case of business taxpayers, special nonrecognition rules will allow deferral of gain if the proceeds are reinvested in similar property.

Consider, finally, the effect of the 1996 legislation that limited personal injury to physical injuries. *A* is injured in an automobile accident and recovers $100,000 for pain and suffering; *B* recovers the same amount for damages to reputation from libel, or perhaps as compensation for emotional distress. *A*'s recovery is tax free. *B*'s recovery is taxed in its entirety. How, if at all, can this difference in outcome be justified? *A*'s exclusion is justified on the grounds that she is simply being made whole. At an intuitive level, the $100,000 recovery seems to constitute "income" no more than the $7.01 change you get after giving the cashier a $20 bill for a $12.99 DVD. But doesn't the same argument apply to *B*? If so, then what business does Congress have applying an "income" tax to *B*'s recovery? More precisely, does Congress even have the constitutional authority to impose a tax on *B* and others receiving compensatory damages outside of the scope of § 104?

In a decision issued in 2006, Murphy v. United States, the D.C. Circuit Court of Appeals addressed precisely this question. The case involved a taxpayer, Marrita Murphy, who recovered "damages totaling $70,000, of which $45,000 was for 'emotional distress or mental anguish,' and $25,000 was for 'injury to professional reputation.'" The government asserted that Murphy's recovery was not excludable by virtue of the statutory limitation of the exclusion to "physical" injuries and "physical" sickness. Chief Judge Douglas Ginsburg agreed with the government's statutory argument, but contended that the statute was unconstitutional under the Sixteenth Amendment. Ginsburg began with the following statement:

> At the outset, we reject the Government's breathtakingly expansive claim of congressional power under the Sixteenth Amendment—upon which it founds the more far-reaching arguments it advances here. The Sixteenth Amendment simply does not authorize the Congress to tax as "incomes" every sort of revenue a taxpayer may receive. As the Supreme Court noted long ago, the "Congress cannot make a thing income which is not so in fact." Burk-Waggoner Oil Ass'n v. Hopkins, 269 U.S. 110, 114 (1925). Indeed, because the "the power to tax involves the power to destroy," McCulloch v. Maryland, 17 U.S. (4 Wheat.) 316, 431 (1819), it would not be consistent with our constitutional government, and the sanctity of property in our system, merely to rely upon the legislature to decide what constitutes income.[27]

Ginsburg's opinion concludes by noting that "Albert Einstein may have been correct that '[t]he hardest thing in the world to understand is the income tax,' ... but it is not hard to understand that not all receipts of money are income." Accordingly, the court determined that "insofar as § 104(a)(2) permits the taxation of compensation for a personal injury, which compensation is unrelated to lost wages or earnings, that provision is unconstitutional."[28]

The *Murphy* decision was one of the most controversial tax opinions in recent years, with commentators throughout the blogosphere describing it as a "bombshell," a "momentous" and "epochal" decision that was "utterly stunning and unexpected." The case even drew the attention of the mainstream media, with coverage from several major news outlets. One leading tax law scholar said, "It is impossible to overstate the potential damage caused by this decision. In my 15 plus years in this business, this decision takes the cake for judicial mischief."[29] Reactions like these may have played a role in prompting the court to vacate its original decision, which it did on December 22, 2006. The court took the highly unusual step of rehearing the case and issuing a new opinion that reversed its earlier holding. The new *Murphy* decision, issued in 2007, concluded that the tax on Murphy, even if not an "income tax" within the meaning of the Sixteenth Amendment still "passes constitutional muster" as an excise tax that is not subject to the apportionment requirement of Article 1, section 9 of the Constitution.[30]

The *Murphy* case is unusual for many reasons, one of which is its focus on constitutional law. Tax law is not typically thought of as a branch of constitutional law, but in fact for the first forty-some years following the adoption of the Sixteenth Amendment the courts played an active role in policing the contours of the term "income." As noted earlier in this chapter, that era came to an end with the Court's 1955 opinion in *Glenshaw Glass*. The original *Murphy* decision raised the possibility of a new era of tax law as constitutional law. Had the court's 2006 opinion not been vacated, it likely would have

---

27. 460 F.3d 79 (D.C. Cir. 2006).
28. Id.
29. Paul Caron, *Murphy* a Boon for Protestors, Critics Say, Tax Notes, Sept. 4, 2006.
30. 493 F.3d 170 (D.C. Cir. 2007), cert. denied, 553 U.S. _____ (2008).

spawned other litigation, with taxpayers claiming that other types of receipts were not "income" within the meaning of the Sixteenth Amendment. The New York Times cited tax law experts who predicted "challenges to the taxation of other money, including some insurance proceeds, gambling winnings and windfalls like found money."[31] Of course with the court's new opinion, these predictions never came to pass.

Leaving aside the constitutional arguments, do you agree with the final outcome of the *Murphy* litigation as a policy matter? Should Congress tax individuals on recoveries for nonphysical injuries? Is the taxation of damages received on account of nonphysical injuries consistent with *your* understanding of the proper scope of an income tax?

2. Deferred Payments and Structured Settlements

In 1983, Congress codified an earlier revenue ruling and added to § 104(a)(2) the language that reads "and whether as a lump sum or periodic payments." Under that provision, as amended, a tort victim who is able to defer current payment in return for a series of later payments can exclude the entire amount of the later payments as recovery for personal injury. The complete exclusion is available even though the deferred payments will invariably contain an interest component.

The nontaxation of the interest component creates an incentive for tort victims to structure settlements to provide deferred periodic payments. After all, if one received a lump-sum payment and invested it, the interest returns would presumably be taxable.

In many circumstances, the tax advantage to the tort victim may be offset by a disadvantage to the tortfeasor. Suppose, for example, that the tortfeasor is an individual who cannot deduct the amount to be paid. If the tortfeasor retains for a while a portion of the principal that is due to the victim, she presumably will earn taxable interest income, and receive no deduction for whatever payments of principal plus interest she ultimately makes. The arrangement may, however, reduce the overall tax paid on the interest income if the tortfeasor pays tax for the relevant period at a lower marginal tax rate than the tort victim.

Now suppose that the tortfeasor is a business firm and is allowed to deduct the payment, although not until it is made. Once again, the tax advantage to the tort victim from delaying the transfer of the funds may be offset by a disadvantage to the tortfeasor, since deduction of the loan principal is deferred until the payment is made. Deferral of the deduction can be avoided, however, if the business tortfeasor enters into a somewhat complex set of transactions with an insurance company, which in turn transacts with another company that specializes in "structured settlements" (that is, settlements providing for deferred payments). Consequently, deferred payments are now commonly used to settle tort cases involving large sums of money. The victim

31. Ruling May Open Tax Law to More Challenges, N.Y. Times, Aug. 24, 2006.

might prefer to take an immediate payment and invest it herself or himself, but the tax advantage of deferred payment—the ability to avoid tax on interest earned on the lump-sum amount—provides a powerful incentive to use the somewhat complex, costly, and restrictive structured settlement technique.

3.   Medical Expenses and Other Recoveries and Benefits

Medical expenses, including premiums paid for medical insurance, are deductible only to the extent that in the aggregate they exceed, for the taxable year, 7.5 percent of adjusted gross income. § 213. Recoveries under an individual's medical insurance policy are excluded, even if those recoveries exceed the cost of medical care (for example, where the insured has two policies covering the same outlay and is permitted to recover under both). See § 104(a)(3). Assuming that the premium was not deducted (as part of expenses in excess of 7.5 percent of adjusted gross income), this rule of no deduction of premiums/ no income from payments is consistent with the rule for taxation of life insurance; in the aggregate, disregarding insurance company costs and profits, nondeductible payments equal nontaxable benefits. There is an exception for payments received in reimbursement of expenses previously deducted. See § 104(a), initial flush language. This rule simply takes account of the fact that in retrospect the deduction was unjustified. It is a kind of tax benefit rule.

Where an employer pays the premiums on the employee's medical insurance, the amount is deductible by the employer but is not included in the employee's income. See §§ 106 and 162. Similarly, if an employer does not take out insurance and instead adopts a plan under which it pays or reimburses employee medical expenses itself, the payments (or reimbursements) are not taxable to the employee. § 105(b). Again, there is an exception for reimbursements of amounts previously deducted. Thus, if an employer pays an employee, say, $28,500 per year in salary and the employee uses $3,500 of that money to buy medical insurance, the full $28,500 received by the employee will be included in his or her income, and there will be no offsetting deduction for the outlay for insurance except to the extent that it (together with other medical-expense outlays for the year) exceeds 7.5 percent of adjusted gross income. If the employer pays only $25,000 as salary to the employee and uses the extra $3,500 to buy medical insurance for that employee, the $3,500 does not enter into the employee's income. This opportunity for paying for medical insurance (and medical expenses) out of before-tax dollars is not available to the self-employed, but self-employed people are allowed to deduct part of their health insurance outlays, in various percentages rising to 100 percent in 2007.

The exclusion for employer-provided medical care extends to an employee's spouse or dependents. See Regs. § 1.106-1. The definition of *dependent* is set forth in § 152 (discussed infra Chapter 4.G.) The exclusion does not apply to coverage that might be offered by an employer to a nondependent partner in an unmarried couple.

The opportunity to pay for employee medical insurance with before-tax dollars presumably increases the amounts that are spent on this benefit and may help doctors maintain a tolerable standard of living (in the short run) or provide opportunities for more people to make a living as doctors (in the longer run). If the tax system is to provide benefits for doctors, what about lawyers? They were late getting into the act, but in 1976 Congress enacted § 120, excluding employer payments for benefits under any "group legal services plan." As originally enacted, this provision would have expired at the end of 1981, at which point reconsideration, based on experience, was supposed to occur, but in 1981 the provision was extended through 1984. After further extensions in 1985 and 1986, it was extended through 1988, but with a limitation of $70 worth of insurance per year. After two more extensions, the provision finally expired on June 30, 1992.

What about plumbers? Alas, they have been ignored. Why so? Are medical and legal services more vital to individual welfare than indoor plumbing?

Section 104(a)(1) excludes workers' compensation. Section 105(c) excludes certain payments from employer insurance (or plans) for permanent physical injuries. No matter how misguided these exclusions may be, they are at least rules of general application. Far more troublesome are the exclusions for members of special groups such as veterans of the armed forces, the Coast and Geodetic Survey, and the Public Health Service. § 104(a)(4), (b). Recoveries under disability insurance policies financed by taxpayer (rather than employer) payments are excluded under § 104(a)(3); but the premiums are not deductible.

G.   TRANSACTIONS INVOLVING LOANS AND "INCOME FROM DISCHARGE OF INDEBTEDNESS"

The ideas presented in this section relate to an aspect of tax doctrine often referred to as "income from discharge of indebtedness." See § 61(a)(12). We will see that the issues are more disparate than that simple phrase seems to suggest, but there is enough of a nexus to justify deference to the traditional rubric.

1.   Loan Proceeds Are Not Income

The rule. Before examining the rules relating to income from the discharge of indebtedness, we must take notice of another basic rule of tax law (which is not spelled out in any express provision of the Code) — namely, that loan proceeds are not included in gross income and loan repayments are not deductible. This rule applies both to recourse loans (that is, loans on which the borrower is personally liable) and to nonrecourse loans (as to which the lender's only recourse in case of default is against the property pledged as security for the loan). The rule also applies without regard to the nature and tax attributes of the property used as security for the loan.[32]

---

32. But see § 72(e)(4)(A), treating loans against annuity policies as income to the extent of earned increments in the value of the policy. See supra page 129. See also § 77, giving the taxpayer an election to treat crop loans from the Commodity Credit Corporation as income.

The rationale. The rationale usually given for the exclusion of loan proceeds is that they do not improve one's economic condition because they are offset by a corresponding liability; in other words, the loan does not increase net worth. This rationale requires exclusion regardless of the security for the loan, the probable source of repayment, or the use of the funds. Is the rationale sound? Examine the following hypotheticals. Do you think that in any or all of them gain should be recognized when the loan proceeds are received, bearing in mind that if the proceeds are included in income, any repayment should be a deductible outlay?

(a) *A* earns a good salary and over the years is able to save, out of her after-tax earnings, $50,000. She invests this $50,000 in common stock of IBM. At a time when the stock is still worth $50,000, she decides to take a trip around the world and borrows $25,000, nonrecourse, pledging the IBM shares as security for the loan.

(b) *B* saves $25,000 out of after-tax earnings and uses this, together with $75,000 borrowed from a bank, to buy for $100,000 a house that he occupies as a personal residence. The house is mortgaged to secure the loan.

(c) *C* saves $10,000 out of after-tax earnings and invests it in the common stock of XYZ Computer Co. The stock rises in value to $100,000, at which point *C* borrows $50,000 from a bank, nonrecourse, pledging the stock as collateral. What if the loan were with recourse?

(d) *D* has just completed a surgical residency and is about to begin her practice, in which she expects that she will soon be earning over $100,000 a year. She borrows $25,000 from a bank and uses it to pay the initial expenses of establishing her practice (rent, wages paid to assistants, telephone bills, stationery, etc.).

(e) *E*'s circumstances are the same as *D*'s except that *E* uses the $25,000 for a trip around the world with her husband.

(f) *F* owns property with a basis of $10,000 and a highly uncertain fair market value. He is able to convince a financier to lend him $50,000, for one year, nonrecourse, on the security of the property. He believes the property is worth only $40,000 and does not expect to repay the loan when it is due, though he retains a glimmer of hope that the property will rise in value and that it will be worth his while to repay the loan, when due, so as to retain the property, sell it, and increase his gain.

2. True Discharge of Indebtedness

The notion that a person can have income from the discharge of indebtedness may not be intuitively obvious to a person who is not versed in tax law, but as a matter of pure tax logic it is not debatable. The task of the student is to master the logic — a task that becomes especially challenging in contexts in which the loan transaction is tied to an investment in and disposition of property.

Suppose that *T* borrows $50,000 for three years, at 8 percent per year, and uses the money to finance a trip around the world. He returns from his trip six months later and finds that interest rates have risen drastically in his absence.

In the meantime, he has inherited some money and offers to pay off the loan for $45,000. The bank accepts, since it can lend the $45,000 at a rate higher than the 8 percent that it is entitled to receive from *T*. *T* received $50,000 and paid no tax on that amount. He now repays only $45,000. He is $5,000 ahead on the loan transaction and must pay tax on that gain. Think about what his situation would have been if he had not paid off the loan early. He would have held onto his $45,000 and could have invested it. Presumably he could have earned more than the 8 percent he would have been required to pay on his loan. The difference could be thought of as his profit from having borrowed money on terms that turned out to be favorable. This profit would have been realized over the remaining term of the loan. Instead, when *T* pays off the loan, the profit from the favorable loan is realized in a lump sum without waiting.

One's intuition may be misled by the fact that in settling the debt *T* laid out $45,000. It is easy to forget the $50,000 that was previously received and not treated as income. But the net cash flow is clear: $50,000 in, $45,000 out, leaving a net gain of $5,000. What has *T* to show for it? Presumably memories of a $50,000 trip around the world. He saved $5,000 not because the trip was worth less than $50,000 (though it may have been) but rather because he entered into a loan transaction that turned out well for him. For tax purposes one should separate the loan transaction from the transaction in which the proceeds of the loan were used. The tax consequences of the use of the funds should be accounted for independently, according to the requirements of annual accounting. Thus, if the $50,000 had been embezzled by *T*'s travel agent and *T* had never taken the trip, the loss presumably would be deductible, at least in part, in the year in which it occurred, according to rules affecting the use of the funds, not the source of the funds. See § 165(c)(3), discussed infra page 355. For purposes of tax accounting, this is a separate item from the income from discharge of the indebtedness. Unfortunately, the leading case on discharge of indebtedness (*Kirby Lumber*, presented immediately below) distinguished, instead of rejecting outright, an earlier case (*Kerbaugh-Empire*) that mistakenly applied a transactional approach, tying the treatment of the loan discharge to a loss on the use of the proceeds.

UNITED STATES v. KIRBY LUMBER CO.
284 U.S. 1 (1931)

Mr. Justice HOLMES delivered the opinion of the Court.

In July, 1923, the plaintiff, the Kirby Lumber Company, issued its own bonds for [$12,000,000] for which it received their par value.[33] Later in the same year it purchased in the open market [$1,000,000 face amount] of the same bonds at [$862,000], the difference of price being [$138,000]. The

---

33. [Generally, it has been assumed these proceeds were cash. The bonds were in fact issued in exchange for Kirby Lumber Co.'s outstanding preferred stock that had large dividend arrearages on them. Bittker, Income from Cancellation of Indebtedness: A Historical Footnote to the *Kirby Lumber case*, 4 J. Corp. Tax. 124 (1977). — EDS.]

question is whether this difference is a taxable gain or income of the plaintiff for the year 1923. By the Revenue Act of 1921, gross income includes "gains or profits and income derived from any source whatever" [§ 61(a), 1954 Code] and by the Treasury Regulations . . . that have been in force through repeated reenactments, "If the corporation purchases and retires any of such bonds at a price less than the issuing price or face value, the excess of the issuing price or face value over the purchase price is gain or income for the taxable year." . . . We see no reason why the Regulations should not be accepted as a correct statement of the law.

In Bowers v. Kerbaugh-Empire Co., 271 U.S. 170, the [taxpayer] had borrowed money repayable in marks or their equivalent for an enterprise that failed. At the time of payment the marks had fallen in value, which so far as it went was a gain for the [taxpayer] and it was contended by the [Service] that the gain was taxable income. But the transaction as a whole was a loss, and the contention was denied. Here there was no shrinkage of assets and the taxpayer made a clear gain. As a result of its dealings it made available [$138,000 worth of] assets previously offset by the obligation of bonds now extinct. We see nothing to be gained by the discussion of judicial definitions. The [taxpayer] has realized within the year an accession to income, if we take words in their plain popular meaning, as they should be taken here. Burnet v. Sanford & Brooks Co. [supra page 138].

Judgment reversed.

NOTES AND QUESTIONS

1. *Theory.* *Kirby Lumber* and its progeny are aptly described in the following passages from 1 B. Bittker, Federal Taxation of Income, Estates and Gifts ¶¶ 6-31 to 6-32 (1981):

> A particularly troublesome legacy of the above passage has been the tendency of some courts to read *Kirby Lumber* as holding that the *freeing of assets* on the cancellation of indebtedness, rather than the cancellation itself, results in a taxable gain. In actuality, income results from the discharge of indebtedness because the taxpayer has received more than is paid back, not because assets are freed of offsetting liabilities on the balance sheet. . . .
>
> Since borrowed funds are obviously worth their face amount and assets acquired on credit in an arm's-length transaction are also worth what the buyer agrees to pay, a taxpayer who ultimately pays back less than he received enjoys a financial benefit whether the funds were invested successfully, lost in a business venture, spent for food and clothing, or given to a charity. Were we blessed with perfect foresight, it would be possible to exclude borrowed funds from gross income only to the extent of the ultimate repayment and to tax at the outset the amount that will not be repaid. In the absence of perfect prevision, however, a second-best solution is required. One alternative would be to tax the entire amount borrowed and to allow deductions only when, as, and if the debt is repaid. But since most loans are in fact paid in full and taxing the receipt would impose a heavy front-end burden on debt financing of investment projects, a better alternative is the existing system of excluding the borrowed funds from

gross income when received and requiring the taxpayer to account for any gain if he succeeds in settling the debt for less than the amount due.

[T]he tax treatment of below-face debt discharges would have been much simplified if it had been based at the outset on the fact that borrowed funds are excluded from gross income because of the assumption that they will be repaid in full and on the simple corollary that a tax adjustment is required when this assumption proves erroneous, regardless of the use to which the taxpayer put the borrowed funds. Unfortunately, *Kerbaugh-Empire* linked the tax treatment of the debt discharge to the fate of the borrowed funds, and *Kirby Lumber* carried forward this idea by distinguishing rather than repudiating *Kerbaugh-Empire*, seeming thereby to sanction an open-ended inquiry into the debtor's financial history in order to determine whether the discharge of the debt generated a "clear gain."

In Vukosovich, Inc. v. Commissioner, 790 F.2d 1409 (9th Cir. 1986), the taxpayer, relying on *Kerbaugh-Empire*, argued that it was not required to recognize income from discharge of indebtedness because it had suffered a loss on the transaction in which the borrowed funds had been invested. The government conceded that if *Kerbaugh-Empire* were still good law, the taxpayer's argument had merit, but argued that the case had in effect been overruled by later Supreme Court decisions. The Ninth Circuit agreed with the government, citing United States v. Kirby Lumber (supra), Commissioner v. Tufts (infra page 188), and Burnet v. Sanford & Brooks (supra page 138) (rejecting transactional accounting).

2. *Child support and other obligations.* Does a noncustodial parent realize income from discharge of indebtedness when he or she fails to make legally required child-support payments? If so, when? What about a person who fails to pay a judgment in a personal injury case? Should it matter that the debtor in these situations never received cash or other property as a consequence of incurring the debt? Or is it enough that such a person is better off than a similarly situated person who pays the debt?

3. Relief Provision

Insolvent debtors. Section 108 contains elaborate rules relating to discharge of the indebtedness of insolvent debtors. Generally, these rules reflect the notion, previously embodied in judicially developed doctrine, that one should not hit a person who is down, or cannot squeeze blood from a turnip, or both. If, at the time of discharge, taxpayer was insolvent or was the debtor in a proceeding under the Bankruptcy Act, the income from discharge of indebtedness is excluded, but certain tax attributes (e.g., the net operating loss carryover) must be reduced so that in effect the income will show up later if all goes well and the taxpayer has profits that would otherwise escape taxation. See § 108(b).

Solvent farmers. The relief provided under § 108 for insolvent debtors is also available to solvent farmers for "qualified farm indebtedness," which is debt incurred in the operation of a farm by a person who, during the three preceding taxable years, derived more than 50 percent of his or her annual gross receipts from farming. § 108(g). This relief for farmers is a vestige of a general relief provision for solvent debtors that was repealed by the 1986 act.

Adjustment of purchase money debt. Section 108(e)(5) provides that the reduction of debt incurred to purchase property and owed to the seller is treated as a reduction in sale price, rather than income to the purchaser.

Student loan forgiveness. Section 108(f)(2) excludes from income any cancellation or repayment of a student loan, provided the cancellation or repayment is contingent upon work for a charitable or educational institution.

Mortgage forgiveness. Section 108(h), enacted in late December 2007, provides relief for taxpayers who would otherwise recognize income from the discharge of indebtedness when mortgage lenders foreclose on the taxpayer's principal residence. In addition to foreclosure situations, the exclusion applies to mortgage workouts where the lender renegotiates the terms of the taxpayer's mortgage indebtedness in such a manner that would normally result in the recognition of income from the discharge of indebtedness. The statute provides for an exclusion of up to $2,000,000 of forgiven "qualified principal residence indebtedness." The taxpayer must reduce her basis in the principal residence (but not below zero) by the amount excluded. The reduction in basis would normally increase the likelihood that the taxpayer would recognize gain on a subsequent disposition of the property. Where the property is the taxpayer's principal residence, however, any subsequent gain may be excluded up to $250,000 ($500,000 for married couples filing a joint return) (see § 121).

4.   Misconceived Discharge Theory

Suppose that *X* borrows $10,000 from her parents to finance her law school education and that on graduation, in a spirit of love, affection, and pride, they cancel the debt. That might be thought of as a discharge of debt, but the benefit to *X* is not income for tax purposes because it was received as a gift. See § 102(a).

Suppose that *Y* borrows $10,000 from a bank to finance her law school education and that on her graduation, her proud, loving parents pay the debt for her. As with *X*, there is no income for tax purposes because of § 102(a). Moreover, although from *Y*'s perspective the debt has, in a sense, been canceled, from the perspective of the bank it has been paid in full. This is not a true discharge of debt case, or at least it is not the same kind of case as *Kirby Lumber*, where a debt was discharged for less than the amount that was owed. The best way to grasp the tax consequences of the transaction is to compare it with a gift of $10,000 cash to *Y* from her parents and use of that money by *Y* to pay the debt.

Finally, suppose that *Z* borrowed $10,000 to finance her law school education and that her employer pays the debt on her behalf as a Christmas bonus for her good work during the few months following her graduation. *Z* plainly has income of $10,000. Again, however, "discharge of indebtedness" does not seem to be an apt theory, since the debt has been paid in full. The transaction should be viewed for tax purposes as if the employer had paid *Z* a cash bonus of $10,000 and she had used her money to pay her debt. The tax should be imposed under § 61(a)(1), not § 61(a)(12). "Indirect payment" or "economic benefit" might best capture the essence of the transaction. Regardless of the theory, or semantics, the correct tax result should be clear. But the theory might be relevant to other issues, such as the availability of relief under § 108. See supra page 163.

ZARIN v. COMMISSIONER
916 F.2d 110 (3d Cir. 1990)

COWEN, Circuit Judge.

David Zarin ("Zarin") appeals from a decision of the Tax Court holding that he recognized $2,935,000 of income from discharge of indebtedness resulting from his gambling activities, and that he should be taxed on the income. . . . After considering the issues raised by this appeal, we will reverse.

I

Zarin was a professional engineer who participated in the development, construction, and management of various housing projects. A resident of Atlantic City, New Jersey, Zarin occasionally gambled, both in his hometown and in other places where gambling was legalized. To facilitate his gaming activities in Atlantic City, Zarin applied to Resorts International Hotel ("Resorts") for a credit line in June, 1978. Following a credit check, Resorts granted Zarin $10,000 of credit. Pursuant to this credit arrangement with Resorts, Zarin could write a check, called a marker,[34] and in return receive chips, which could then be used to gamble at the casino's tables.

Before long, Zarin developed a reputation as an extravagant "high roller" who routinely bet the house maximum while playing craps, his game of choice. Considered a "valued gaming patron" by Resorts, Zarin had his credit limit increased at regular intervals without any further credit checks, and was provided a number of complimentary services and privileges. By November, 1979, Zarin's permanent line of credit had been raised to $200,000. Between June, 1978, and December, 1979, Zarin lost $2,500,000 at the craps table, losses he paid in full.

Responding to allegations of credit abuses, the New Jersey Division of Gaming Enforcement filed with the New Jersey Casino Control Commission a complaint against Resorts. Among the 809 violations of casino regulations alleged in the complaint of October, 1979, were 100 pertaining to Zarin. Subsequently, a Casino Control Commissioner issued an Emergency Order, the effect of which was to make further extensions of credit to Zarin illegal.

---

34. A "marker" is a negotiable draft payable to Resorts and drawn on the marker's bank.

Nevertheless, Resorts continued to extend Zarin's credit limit through the use of two different practices: "considered cleared" credit and "this trip only" credit.[35] Both methods effectively ignored the Emergency Order and were later found to be illegal.[36]

By January, 1980, Zarin was gambling compulsively and uncontrollably at Resorts, spending as many as sixteen hours a day at the craps table.[37] During April, 1980, Resorts again increased Zarin's credit line without further inquiries. That same month, Zarin delivered personal checks and counterchecks to Resorts which were returned as having been drawn against insufficient funds. Those dishonored checks totaled $3,435,000. In late April, Resorts cut off Zarin's credit.

Although Zarin indicated that he would repay those obligations, Resorts filed a New Jersey state court action against Zarin in November, 1980, to collect the $3,435,000. Zarin denied liability on grounds that Resort's claim was unenforceable under New Jersey regulations intended to protect compulsive gamblers. Ten months later, in September, 1981, Resorts and Zarin settled their dispute for a total of $500,000.

The Commissioner of Internal Revenue ("Commissioner") subsequently determined deficiencies in Zarin's federal income taxes for 1980 and 1981, arguing that Zarin recognized $3,435,000 of income in 1980 from larceny by trick and deception. After Zarin challenged that claim by filing a Tax Court petition, the Commissioner abandoned his 1980 claim, and argued instead that Zarin had recognized $2,935,000 of income in 1981 from the cancellation of indebtedness which resulted from the settlement with Resorts.

Agreeing with the Commissioner, the Tax Court decided, eleven judges to eight, that Zarin had indeed recognized $2,935,000 of income from the discharge of indebtedness, namely the difference between the original $3,435,000 "debt" and the $500,000 settlement. Zarin v. Commissioner, 92 T.C. 1084 (1989). Since he was in the seventy percent tax bracket, Zarin's deficiency for 1981 was calculated to be $2,047,245. With interest to April 5, 1990, Zarin allegedly owes the Internal Revenue Service $5,209,033.96 in additional taxes. Zarin appeals the order of the Tax Court.

II

The sole issue before this Court is whether the Tax Court correctly held that Zarin had income from discharge of indebtedness.[38] Section 108 and section

---

35. Under the "considered cleared" method, Resorts would treat a personal check as a cash transaction, and would therefore not apply the amount of the check in calculating the amount of credit extended Zarin. "This trip only" credit allows Resorts to grant temporary increases of credit for a given visit, so long as the credit limit was lowered by the next visit.

36. On July 8, 1983, the New Jersey Casino Control Commission found that Resorts violated the Emergency Order at least thirteen different times, nine involving Zarin, and fined Resorts $130,000.

37. Zarin claims that at the time he was suffering from a recognized emotional disorder that caused him to gamble compulsively.

38. Subsequent to the Tax Court's decision, Zarin filed a motion to reconsider, arguing that he was insolvent at the time Resorts forgave his debt, and thus, under section 108(a)(1)(B), could not have income from discharge of indebtedness. He did not, however, raise that issue before the Tax Court

61(a)(12) of the Code set forth "the general rule that gross income includes income from the discharge of indebtedness." § 108(e)(1). The Commissioner argues, and the Tax Court agreed, that pursuant to the Code, Zarin did indeed recognize income from discharge of gambling indebtedness.

Under the Commissioner's logic, Resorts advanced Zarin $3,435,000 worth of chips, chips being the functional equivalent of cash. At that time, the chips were not treated as income, since Zarin recognized an obligation of repayment. In other words, Resorts made Zarin a tax-free loan. However, a taxpayer does recognize income if a loan owed to another party is cancelled, in whole or in part. I.R.C. §§ 61(a)(12), 108(e). The settlement between Zarin and Resorts, claims the Commissioner, fits neatly into the cancellation of indebtedness provisions in the Code. Zarin owed $3,435,000, paid $500,000, with the difference constituting income. Although initially persuasive, the Commissioner's position is nonetheless flawed for two reasons.

III

Initially, we find that sections 108 and 61(a)(12) are inapplicable to the Zarin/Resorts transaction. Section 61 does not define indebtedness. On the other hand, section 108(d)(1), which repeats and further elaborates on the rule in section 61(a)(12), defines the term as any indebtedness "(A) for which the taxpayer is liable, or (B) subject to which the taxpayer holds property." § 108(d)(1). In order to bring the taxpayer within the sweep of the discharge of indebtedness rules, then, the IRS must show that one of the two prongs in the section 108(d)(1) test is satisfied. It has not been demonstrated that Zarin satisfies either.

Because the debt Zarin owed to Resorts was unenforceable as a matter of New Jersey state law,[39] it is clearly not a debt "for which the taxpayer is liable." § 108(d)(1)(A). Liability implies a legally enforceable obligation to repay, and under New Jersey law, Zarin would have no such obligation.

---

until after it rendered its decision. The Tax Court denied the motion for reconsideration. By reason of our resolution of this case, we do not need to decide whether the Tax Court abused its discretion in denying Zarin's motion.

39. The Tax Court held that the Commissioner had not met its burden of proving that the debt owed Resorts was enforceable as a matter of state law. *Zarin*, 92 T.C. at 1090. There was ample evidence to support that finding. In New Jersey, the extension of credit by casinos "to enable [any] person to take part in gaming activity as a player" is limited. N.J. Stat. Ann. § 5:12-101(b) (1988). Under N.J. Stat. Ann. § 5:12-101(f), any credit violation is "invalid and unenforceable for the purposes of collection. . . ." In Resorts Int'l Hotel, Inc. v. Salomone, 178 N.J. Super. 598, 429 A.2d 1078 (App. Div. 1981), the court held that "casinos must comply with the Legislature's strict control of credit for gambling purposes. Unless they do, the debts reflected by players' checks will not be enforced. . . ." Id. at 607, 429 A.2d at 1082.

With regards to the extension of credit to Zarin after the Emergency Order of October, 1979, was issued, Resorts did not comply with New Jersey regulations. The Casino Control Commission specifically stated in 1983 "that Resorts was guilty of infractions, violations, improprieties, with the net effect that [Zarin] was encouraged to continue gambling long after, one, his credit line was reached, and exceeded; two, long after it became apparent that the gambler was an addicted gambler; three, long after the gambler had difficulty in paying his debts; and four, Resorts knew the individual was gambling when he should not have been gambling." Appendix at 325-326. It follows, therefore, that under New Jersey law, the $3,435,000 debt Zarin owed Resorts was totally unenforceable.

Moreover, Zarin did not have a debt subject to which he held property as required by section 108(d)(1)(B). Zarin's indebtedness arose out of his acquisition of gambling chips. The Tax Court held that gambling chips were not property, but rather, "a medium of exchange within the Resorts casino" and a "substitute for cash." Alternatively, the Tax Court viewed the chips as nothing more than "the opportunity to gamble and incidental services. . . ." Zarin, 92 T.C. at 1099. We agree with the gist of these characterizations, and hold that gambling chips are merely an accounting mechanism to evidence debt.

Gaming chips in New Jersey during 1980 were regarded "solely as evidence of a debt owed to their custodian by the casino licensee and shall be considered at no time the property of anyone other than the casino licensee issuing them." N.J. Admin. Code tit. 19k, § 19:46-1.5(d) (1990). Thus, under New Jersey state law, gambling chips were Resorts' property until transferred to Zarin in exchange for the markers, at which point the chips became "evidence" of indebtedness (and not the property of Zarin).

Even were there no relevant legislative pronouncement on which to rely, simple common sense would lead to the conclusion that chips were not property in Zarin's hands. Zarin could not do with the chips as he pleased, nor did the chips have any independent economic value beyond the casino. The chips themselves were of little use to Zarin, other than as a means of facilitating gambling. They could not have been used outside the casino. They could have been used to purchase services and privileges within the casino, including food, drink, entertainment, and lodging, but Zarin would not have utilized them as such, since he received those services from Resorts on a complimentary basis. In short, the chips had no economic substance.

Although the Tax Court found that theoretically, Zarin could have redeemed the chips he received on credit for cash and walked out of the casino, Zarin, 92 T.C. at 1092, the reality of the situation was quite different. Realistically, before cashing in his chips, Zarin would have been required to pay his outstanding IOUs. New Jersey state law requires casinos to "request patrons to apply any chips or plaques in their possession in reduction of personal checks or Counter Checks exchanged for purposes of gaming prior to exchanging such chips or plaques for cash or prior to departing from the casino area." N.J. Admin. Code tit. 19k, § 19:45-1.24(s) (1979) (currently N.J. Admin. Code tit. 19k, § 19:45-1.25(o) (1990) (as amended)). Since his debt at all times equalled or exceeded the number of chips he possessed, redemption would have left Zarin with no chips, no cash, and certainly nothing which could have been characterized as property.

Not only were the chips non-property in Zarin's hands, but upon transfer to Zarin, the chips also ceased to be the property of Resorts. Since the chips were in the possession of another party, Resorts could no longer do with the chips as it pleased, and could no longer control the chips' use. Generally, at the time of a transfer, the party in possession of the chips can gamble with them, use them for services, cash them in, or walk out of the casino with them as an Atlantic City souvenir. The chips therefore become nothing more than an accounting mechanism, or evidence of a debt, designed to facilitate gambling in casinos where the use of actual money was forbidden. Thus, the chips which Zarin held were not property within the meaning of § 108(d)(1)(B).

In short, because Zarin was not liable on the debt he allegedly owed Resorts, and because Zarin did not hold "property" subject to that debt, the cancellation of indebtedness provisions of the Code do not apply to the settlement between Resorts and Zarin. As such, Zarin cannot have income from the discharge of his debt.

Instead of analyzing the transaction at issue as cancelled debt, we believe the proper approach is to view it as disputed debt or contested liability. Under the contested liability doctrine, if a taxpayer, in good faith, disputed the amount of a debt, a subsequent settlement of the dispute would be treated as the amount of debt cognizable for tax purposes. The excess of the original debt over the amount determined to have been due is disregarded for both loss and debt accounting purposes. Thus, if a taxpayer took out a loan for $10,000, refused in good faith to pay the full $10,000 back, and then reached an agreement with the lendor that he would pay back only $7000 in full satisfaction of the debt, the transaction would be treated as if the initial loan was $7000. When the taxpayer tenders the $7000 payment, he will have been deemed to have paid the full amount of the initially disputed debt. Accordingly, there is no tax consequence to the taxpayer upon payment.

The seminal "contested liability" case is N. Sobel, Inc. v. Commissioner, 40 B.T.A. 1263 (1939). In *Sobel*, the taxpayer exchanged a $21,700 note for 100 shares of stock from a bank. In the following year, the taxpayer sued the bank for recision, arguing that the bank loan was violative of state law, and moreover, that the bank had failed to perform certain promises. The parties eventually settled the case in 1935, with the taxpayer agreeing to pay half of the face amount of the note. In the year of the settlement, the taxpayer claimed the amount paid as a loss. The Commissioner denied the loss because it had been sustained five years earlier, and further asserted that the taxpayer recognized income from the discharge of half of his indebtedness.

The Board of Tax Appeals held that since the loss was not fixed until the dispute was settled, the loss was recognized in 1935, the year of the settlement, and the deduction was appropriately taken in that year. Additionally, the Board held that the portion of the note forgiven by the bank "was not the occasion for a freeing of assets and that there was no gain. . . ." Id. at 1265. Therefore, the taxpayer did not have any income from cancellation of indebtedness.

There is little difference between the present case and *Sobel*. Zarin incurred a $3,435,000 debt while gambling at Resorts, but in court, disputed liability on the basis of unenforceability. A settlement of $500,000 was eventually agreed upon. It follows from *Sobel* that the settlement served only to fix the amount of debt. No income was realized or recognized. When Zarin paid the $500,000, any tax consequence dissolved.[40]

Only one other court has addressed a case factually similar to the one before us. In United States v. Hall, 307 F.2d 238 (10th Cir. 1962), the taxpayer owed an unenforceable gambling debt alleged to be $225,000. Subsequently, the

---

40. Had Zarin not paid the $500,000 dollar settlement, it would be likely that he would have had income from cancellation of indebtedness. The debt at that point would have been fixed, and Zarin would have been legally obligated to pay it.

taxpayer and the creditor settled for $150,000. The taxpayer then transferred cattle valued at $148,110 to his creditor in satisfaction of the settlement agreement. A jury held that the parties fixed the debt at $150,000, and that the taxpayer recognized income from cancellation of indebtedness equal to the difference between the $150,000 and the $148,110 value affixed to the cattle. Arguing that the taxpayer recognized income equal to the difference between $225,000 and $148,000, the Commissioner appealed.

The Tenth Circuit rejected the idea that the taxpayer had any income from cancellation of indebtedness. Noting that the gambling debt was unenforceable, the Tenth Circuit said, "The cold fact is that taxpayer suffered a substantial loss from gambling, the amount of which was determined by the transfer." Id. at 241. In effect, the Court held that because the debt was unenforceable, the amount of the loss and resulting debt cognizable for tax purposes were fixed by the settlement at $148,110. Thus, the Tenth Circuit lent its endorsement to the contested liability doctrine in a factual situation strikingly similar to the one at issue.[41]

The Commissioner argues that *Sobel* and the contested liability doctrine only apply when there is an unliquidated debt; that is, a debt for which the amount cannot be determined. . . . Since Zarin contested his liability based on the unenforceability of the entire debt, and did not dispute the amount of the debt, the Commissioner would have us adopt the reasoning of the Tax Court, which found that Zarin's debt was liquidated, therefore barring the application of *Sobel* and the contested liability doctrine. *Zarin*, 92 T.C. at 1095 (Zarin's debt "was a liquidated amount" and "[t]here is no dispute about the amount [received].").

We reject the Tax Court's rationale. When a debt is unenforceable, it follows that the amount of the debt, and not just the liability thereon, is in dispute. Although a debt may be unenforceable, there still could be some value attached to its worth. This is especially so with regards to gambling debts. In most states, gambling debts are unenforceable, and have "but slight potential. . . ." United States v. Hall, 307 F.2d 238, 241 (10th Cir. 1962). Nevertheless, they are often collected, at least in part. For example, Resorts is not a charity; it would not have extended illegal credit to Zarin and others if it did not have some hope of collecting debts incurred pursuant to the grant of credit.

Moreover, the debt is frequently incurred to acquire gambling chips, and not money. Although casinos attach a dollar value to each chip, that value, unlike money's, is not beyond dispute, particularly given the illegality of

41. The Commissioner argues that the decision in *Hall* was based on United States Supreme Court precedent since overruled, and therefore *Hall* should be disregarded. Indeed, the *Hall* court devoted a considerable amount of time to Bowers v. Kerbaugh-Empire Co., 271 U.S. 170 (1926), a case whose validity is in question. We do not pass on the question of whether or not *Bowers* is good law. We do note that *Hall* relied on *Bowers* only for the proposition that "'a court need not in every case be oblivious to the net effect of the entire transaction.'" United States v. Hall, 307 F.2d at 242, quoting Bradford v. Commissioner, 233 F.2d 935, 939 (6th Cir. 1956). *Hall*'s reliance on *Bowers* did not extend to the issue of contested liability, and even if it did, the idea that "Courts need not apply mechanical standards which smother the reality of a particular transaction," Id. at 241, is hardly an exceptional concept in the tax realm. See Commissioner v. Tufts, 461 U.S. 300 (1983); Hillsboro Nat'l Bank v. Commissioner, 460 U.S. 370 (1983).

gambling debts in the first place. This proposition is supported by the facts of the present case. Resorts gave Zarin $3.4 million dollars of chips in exchange for markers evidencing Zarin's debt. If indeed the only issue was the enforceability of the entire debt, there would have been no settlement. Zarin would have owed all or nothing. Instead, the parties attached a value to the debt considerably lower than its face value. In other words, the parties agreed that given the circumstances surrounding Zarin's gambling spree, the chips he acquired might not have been worth $3.4 million dollars, but were worth something. Such a debt cannot be called liquidated, since its exact amount was not fixed until settlement.

To summarize, the transaction between Zarin and Resorts can best be characterized as a disputed debt, or contested liability. Zarin owed an unenforceable debt of $3,435,000 to Resorts. After Zarin in good faith disputed his obligation to repay the debt, the parties settled for $500,000, which Zarin paid. That $500,000 settlement fixed the amount of loss and the amount of debt cognizable for tax purposes. Since Zarin was deemed to have owed $500,000, and since he paid Resorts $500,000, no adverse tax consequences attached to Zarin as a result.

In conclusion, we hold that Zarin did not have any income from cancellation of indebtedness for two reasons. First, the Code provisions covering discharge of debt are inapplicable since the definitional requirement in I.R.C. section 108(d)(1) was not met. Second, the settlement of Zarin's gambling debts was a contested liability. We reverse the decision of the Tax Court and remand with instructions to enter judgment that Zarin realized no income by reason of his settlement with Resorts.

STAPLETON, Circuit Judge, dissenting.

I respectfully dissent because I agree with the Commissioner's appraisal of the economic realities of this matter.

Resorts sells for cash the exhilaration and the potential for profit inherent in games of chance. It does so by selling for cash chips that entitle the holder to gamble at its casino. Zarin, like thousands of others, wished to purchase what Resorts was offering in the marketplace. He chose to make this purchase on credit and executed notes evidencing his obligation to repay the funds that were advanced to him by Resorts. As in most purchase money transactions, Resorts skipped the step of giving Zarin cash that he would only return to it in order to pay for the opportunity to gamble. Resorts provided him instead with chips that entitled him to participate in Resorts' games of chance on the same basis as others who had paid cash for that privilege.[42] Whether viewed as a one or two-step transaction, however, Zarin received either $3.4 million in cash or an entitlement for which others would have had to pay $3.4 million.

---

42. I view as irrelevant the facts that Resorts advanced credit to Zarin solely to enable him to patronize its casino and that the chips could not be used elsewhere or for other purposes. When one buys a sofa from the furniture store on credit, the fact that the proprietor would not have advanced the credit for a different purpose does not entitle one to a tax-free gain in the event the debt to the store is extinguished for some reason.

Despite the fact that Zarin received in 1980 cash or an entitlement worth $3.4 million, he correctly reported in that year no income from his dealings with Resorts. He did so *solely* because he recognized, as evidenced by his notes, an offsetting obligation to repay Resorts $3.4 million in cash. . . . In 1981, with the delivery of Zarin's promise to pay Resorts $500,000 and the execution of a release by Resorts, Resorts surrendered its claim to repayment of the remaining $2.9 million of the money Zarin had borrowed. As of that time, Zarin's assets were freed of his potential liability for that amount and he recognized gross income in that amount. . . .[43]

The only alternatives I see to this conclusion are to hold either (1) that Zarin realized $3.4 million in income in 1980 at a time when both parties to the transaction thought there was an offsetting obligation to repay or (2) that the $3.4 million benefit sought and received by Zarin is not taxable at all. I find the latter alternative unacceptable as inconsistent with the fundamental principle of the Code that anything of commercial value received by a taxpayer is taxable unless expressly excluded from gross income.[44] Commissioner v. Glenshaw Glass Co., 348 U.S. 426 (1955); United States v. Kirby Lumber Co., supra. I find the former alternative unacceptable as impracticable. In 1980, neither party was maintaining that the debt was unenforceable and, because of the settlement, its unenforceability was not even established in the litigation over the debt in 1981. It was not until 1989 in this litigation over the tax consequences of the transaction that the unenforceability was first judicially declared. Rather than require such tax litigation to resolve the correct treatment of a debt transaction, I regard it as far preferable to have the tax consequences turn on the manner in which the debt is treated by the parties. For present purposes, it will suffice to say that where something that would otherwise be includable in gross income is received on credit in a purchase money transaction, there should be no recognition of income so long as the debtor continues to recognize an obligation to repay the debt. On the other hand, income, if not earlier recognized, should be recognized when the debtor no longer recognizes an obligation to repay and the creditor has released the debt or acknowledged its unenforceability.

In this view, it makes no difference whether the extinguishment of the creditor's claim comes as a part of a compromise. Resorts settled for 14 cents on the dollar presumably because it viewed such a settlement as reflective of

43. This is not a case in which parties agree subsequent to a purchase money transaction that the property purchased has a value less than thought at the time of the transaction. In such cases, the purchase price adjustment rule is applied and the agreed-upon value is accepted as the value of the benefit received by the purchaser; see e.g., Commissioner v. Sherman, 135 F.2d 68 (6th Cir. 1943); N. Sobel, Inc. v. Commissioner, 40 B.T.A. 1263 (1939). Nor is this a case in which the taxpayer is entitled to rescind an entire purchase money transaction, thereby to restore itself to the position it occupied before receiving anything of commercial value. In this case, the illegality was in the extension of credit by Resorts and whether one views the benefit received by Zarin as cash or the opportunity to gamble, he is no longer in a position to return that benefit.

44. As the court's opinion correctly points out, this record will not support an exclusion under § 108(a) which relates to discharge of debt in an insolvency or bankruptcy context. Section 108(e)(5) of the Code, which excludes discharged indebtedness arising from a "purchase price adjustment" is not applicable here. Among other things, § 108(e)(5) necessarily applies only to a situation in which the debtor still holds the property acquired in the purchase money transaction. Equally irrelevant is § 108(d)'s definition of "indebtedness" relied upon heavily by the court. Section 108(d) expressly defines that term solely for the purposes of § 108 and not for the purposes of § 61(a)(12).

the odds that the debt would be held to be enforceable. While Zarin should be given credit for the fact that he had to pay 14 cents for a release, I see no reason why he should not realize gain in the same manner as he would have if Resorts had concluded on its own that the debt was legally unenforceable and had written it off as uncollectible.[45]

I would affirm the judgment of the Tax Court.

NOTES

1. The dissent in *Zarin* and the majority opinion in the Tax Court decision in that case treated the forgiveness of Zarin's debt as income under the holding of *Kirby Lumber*, supra page 161. The majority in *Zarin* ruled for the taxpayer on the basis of a judicially created "contested liability" doctrine, under which the amount of a disputed debt is held to be the amount for which the debt is settled. In the majority's view, there was never a valid debt for $2,935,000, so there could be no relief from cancellation of indebtedness income when the debt was settled for $500,000.

Central to the majority's holding in *Zarin* was the fact that New Jersey law cast doubt on the enforceability of debts incurred by compulsive gamblers such as Zarin. Suppose that such debts were clearly enforceable under state law. Is it clear then that Zarin would have recognized income equal to the difference between the debt incurred and the settlement amount? Does someone who borrows approximately $3.4 million from a casino, loses the sum in a matter of hours, and settles the debt for $500,000 have $2,900,000 of income? The Tax Court opinion indicated that at the time the debt was incurred, Zarin was gambling twelve to sixteen hours a day, seven days a week, and wagering $15,000 on each roll of the dice. Is that relevant? Why do you suppose the casino allowed Zarin to gamble with its money (or chips)?

2. One of the dissents in the Tax Court case held that Zarin qualified for the exclusion from relief from indebtedness income under § 108(e)(5). That provision treats the reduction of debt incurred to purchase property as a reduction in the purchase price of property. This argument was rejected by the majority of the judges in both the Tax Court and the Third Circuit on the grounds that the chips did not represent property. Is there any good reason why § 108(e)(5) should not cover debt incurred to purchase services?

3. Zarin's losses occurred in 1980 and he settled with Resorts in 1981. Code § 165(d) provides, "Losses from wagering transactions shall be allowed only to the extent of the gains from such transactions." Regs. § 1.165-10 provides, "Losses sustained during the taxable year on wagering transactions shall be allowed as a deduction but only to the extent of the gains *during the taxable year* from such transactions" (emphasis supplied). If Zarin had settled with Resorts

---

45. A different situation exists where there is a bona fide dispute over the amount of a debt and the dispute is compromised. Rather than require tax litigation to determine the amount of income received, the Commission treats the compromise figure as representing the amount of the obligation. I find this sensible and consistent with the pragmatic approach I would take.

in 1980, could he have prevailed on the ground that any gain from cancellation was offset by his losses from gambling? If so, what is your view of the Regulation limiting offsets to the current year?

DIEDRICH v. COMMISSIONER
457 U.S. 191 (1982)

Chief Justice BURGER delivered the opinion of the Court.

We granted certiorari to resolve a circuit conflict as to whether a donor who makes a gift of property on condition that the donee pay the resulting gift tax receives taxable income to the extent that the gift tax paid by the donee exceeds the donor's adjusted basis in the property transferred. 454 U.S. 813 (1981). The United States Court of Appeals for the Eighth Circuit held that the donor realized income. 643 F.2d 499 (1981). We affirm.

I

In 1972 petitioners Victor and Frances Diedrich made gifts of approximately 85,000 shares of stock to their three children, using both a direct transfer and a trust arrangement. The gifts were subject to a condition that the donees pay the resulting federal and state gift taxes. There is no dispute concerning the amount of the gift tax paid by the donees. The donors' basis in the transferred stock was $51,073; the gift tax paid in 1972 by the donees was $62,992. . . .

II

A

Pursuant to its Constitutional authority, Congress has defined "gross income" as income "from whatever source derived," including "[i]ncome from discharge of indebtedness." § 61 (1976).[46] This Court has recognized that "income" may be realized by a variety of indirect means. In Old Colony Tr. Co. v. Commissioner, 279 U.S. 716 (1929), the Court held that payment of an employee's income taxes by an employer constituted income to the employee. Speaking for the Court, Chief Justice Taft concluded that "[t]he payment of the tax by the employer was in consideration of the services rendered by

---

46. The United States Constitution provides that Congress shall have the power to lay and collect taxes on income "from whatever source derived." Art. I, § 8, cl. 1; Amendment XVI.

In Helvering v. Bruun [infra page 226], the Court noted: "While it is true that economic gain is not always taxable as income, it is settled that the realization of gain need not be in cash derived from a sale of an asset. Gain may occur as a result of exchange of property, *payment of the taxpayer's indebtedness, relief from a liability*, or other profit realized from the completion of a transaction." (Emphasis supplied.)

the employee and was a gain derived by the employee from his labor." Id., at 729. The Court made clear that the substance, not the form, of the agreed transaction controls. "The discharge by a third person of an obligation to him is equivalent to receipt by the person taxed." Ibid. The employee, in other words, was placed in a better position as a result of the employer's discharge of the employee's legal obligation to pay the income taxes; the employee thus received a gain subject to income tax. . . .

B

The principles of *Old Colony* . . . control.[47] A common method of structuring gift transactions is for the donor to make the gift subject to the condition that the donee pay the resulting gift tax, as was done in each of the cases now before us. When a gift is made, the gift tax liability falls on the donor under § 2502(d).[48] When a donor makes a gift to a donee, a "debt" to the United States for the amount of the gift tax is incurred by the donor. Those taxes are as much the legal obligation of the donor as the donor's income taxes; for these purposes they are the same kind of debt obligation as the income taxes of the employee in *Old Colony*, supra. Similarly, when a donee agrees to discharge an indebtedness in consideration of the gift, the person relieved of the tax liability realizes an economic benefit. In short, the donor realizes an immediate economic benefit by the donee's assumption of the donor's legal obligation to pay the gift tax.

An examination of the donor's intent does not change the character of this benefit. Although intent is relevant in determining whether a gift has been made, subjective intent has not characteristically been a factor in determining whether an individual has realized income. Even if intent were a factor, the donor's intent with respect to the condition shifting the gift tax obligation from the donor to the donee was plainly to relieve the donor of a debt owed to the United States; the choice was made because the donor would receive a benefit in relief from the obligation to pay the gift tax.[49]

47. Although the Commissioner has argued consistently that payment of gift taxes by the donee results in income to the donor, several courts have rejected this interpretation. . . .

It should be noted that the *gift* tax consequences of a conditional gift will be unaffected by the holding in this case. When a conditional "net" gift is given, the gift tax attributable to the transfer is to be deducted from the value of the property in determining the value of the gift at the time of transfer. . . .

48. "The tax imposed by section 2501 shall be paid by the donor."

Section 6321 imposes a lien on the personal property of the donor when a tax is not paid when due. The donee is secondarily responsible for payment of the gift tax should the donor fail to pay the tax. § 6324(b). The donee's liability, however, is limited to the value of the gift. Ibid. This responsibility of the donee is analogous to a lien or security. Ibid.

49. The existence of the "condition" that the gift will be made only if the donee assumes the gift tax consequences precludes any characterization that the payment of the taxes was simply a gift from the donee back to the donor.

A conditional gift not only relieves the donor of the gift tax liability, but also may enable the donor to transfer a larger sum of money to the donee than would otherwise be possible due to such factors as differing income tax brackets of the donor and donee.

Finally, the benefit realized by the taxpayer is not diminished by the fact that the liability attaches during the course of a donative transfer. It cannot be doubted that the donors were aware that the gift tax obligation would arise immediately upon the transfer of the property; the economic benefit to the donors in the discharge of the gift tax liability is indistinguishable from the benefit arising from discharge of a preexisting obligation. Nor is there any doubt that had the donors sold a portion of the stock immediately before the gift transfer in order to raise funds to pay the expected gift tax, a taxable gain would have been realized. § 1001. The fact that the gift tax obligation was discharged by way of a conditional gift rather than from funds derived from a pregift sale does not alter the underlying benefit to the donors.

C

Consistent with the economic reality, the Commissioner has treated these conditional gifts as a discharge of indebtedness through a part gift and part sale of the gift property transferred. The transfer is treated as if the donor sells the property to the donee for less than the fair market value. The "sale" price is the amount necessary to discharge the gift tax indebtedness; the balance of the value of the transferred property is treated as a gift. The gain thus derived by the donor is the amount of the gift tax liability less the donor's adjusted basis in the entire property. Accordingly, income is realized to the extent that the gift tax exceeds the donor's adjusted basis in the property. This treatment is consistent with § 1001 of the Internal Revenue Code, which provides that the gain from the disposition of property is the excess of the amount realized over the transferor's adjusted basis in the property.

III

We recognize that Congress has structured gift transactions to encourage transfer of property by limiting the tax consequences of a transfer. See, e.g., § 102 (gifts excluded from donee's gross income). Congress may obviously provide a similar exclusion for the conditional gift. Should Congress wish to encourage "net gifts," changes in the income tax consequences of such gifts lie within the legislative responsibility. Until such time, we are bound by Congress' mandate that gross income includes income "from whatever source derived." We therefore hold that a donor who makes a gift of property on condition that the donee pay the resulting gift taxes realizes taxable income to the extent that the gift taxes paid by the donee exceed the donor's adjusted basis in the property.

The judgment of the United States Court of Appeals for the Eighth Circuit is affirmed.

[The dissenting opinion of Mr. Justice REHNQUIST is omitted.]

NOTES AND QUESTIONS

1. *The amount of the gain.* (a) At the end of the opinion the Court states that the amount of gain to be taxed is the excess of "the gift taxes paid by the donee [over] the donor's adjusted basis in the property." Is this formula for computing the amount of gain consistent with the theory of the case? See the last two sentences of Part IIB of the Court's opinion. Consider the following hypothetical facts: *P* owns 1,000 shares of common stock with a basis of $15,000 and a fair market value of $100,000. She transfers the shares to *C*, who agrees to pay the gift tax of $20,000. Under the *Diedrich* formula the gain recognized is $5,000. What would the gain have been if *P* had sold enough shares to pay the tax herself? What if the basis of the shares had been $25,000? The Court's reasoning in *Diedrich* seems to suggest that *P* should be allowed to claim a loss of $5,000. Regs. § 1.1001-1(e), however, hold otherwise.

(b) By way of comparison, in the case of a transfer to a charitable organization that is part sale and part gift (that is, where the transfer is for an amount less than the fair market value of the property), the basis of the property is allocated between the portion deemed to have been sold and the portion deemed to have been given. § 1011(b). For example, suppose that *T* transfers to a charitable organization property with a basis of $20 and a fair market value of $100, in return for a payment of $20. The transaction is treated as if *T* had sold $20 worth, or one-fifth, of the property and had given the other $80 worth. Thus, one-fifth of the basis, or $4, is allocated to the sale and *T* has a taxable gain of $16. *T* will also be entitled to a charitable deduction of $80, to the extent allowed by § 170.

2. *Theory.* What is the correct result and the most sensible theory in each of the following hypotheticals?

(a) Parent, *P*, transfers to child, *C*, shares of stock with a value of $10,000 and a basis of $1,000. No gift tax is payable. *P* tells *C* that *C* is free to do what she wants with the property. *C* sells the shares.

(b) *P* transfers the shares to *C* and tells *C* to sell the shares for her and use the proceeds to pay *P*'s $10,000 bill at the country club.

(c) *P* transfers the shares to *C* and tells *C* that she can do as she wishes with them provided that she pays *P*'s $10,000 bill at the country club.

(d) Same as (c) except that *C* must pay *P*'s $10,000 debt to the United States Treasury for income taxes.

3. *Donor's liability.* As the court in *Diedrich* points out, the gift tax is imposed on the donor. Would the result have been different if the tax had been imposed on the donee? Would it matter whether the donee had funds with which to pay the tax without selling any of the shares?

4. *Time of recognition.* In Estate of Weeden v. Commissioner, 685 F.2d 1160 (9th Cir. 1982), the taxpayer near the end of 1968 made a gift of property subject to an obligation on the part of the donees to pay the gift tax, which exceeded the donor's basis in the property. The donees paid the tax in 1969. The court held that the gain should be recognized in 1969, pointing out that the donor remained personally liable for the tax until paid, that he was a cash-basis taxpayer, and that what he had received from the donees was only an

unsecured promise to pay, which it said was not "the equivalent of cash." (The same result might now be reached under § 453, relating to installment sales (see infra page 268).)

5. *The* Old Colony *case.* The facts of *Old Colony*, a leading case relied on by the Court in Diedrich (see discussion supra page 175), were simple. In 1918, Mr. William M. Wood earned and received, as president of the American Woolen Company, salary and commissions of approximately $1 million. The company decided to pay his income tax liability of approximately $680,000, though it had no obligation to do so. The Court held that Mr. Wood was taxable on the $680,000 as well as the $1 million. Putting aside the possibility of gift, which the Court easily rejected, the result is obviously correct. At the time the case arose there was no withholding tax, but the $680,000 is comparable to withheld taxes and it is plain that the income subject to taxation is the full amount earned before withholding, not the net amount after withholding. What is interesting about *Old Colony*, by the standards of the present day, is that it was litigated at all, especially all the way to the Supreme Court. The taxpayer relied on a very narrow definition of "income" and emphasized that the $680,000 payment had been made by the corporation not in fulfillment of any contractual obligation but voluntarily (apparently out of sympathy for the plight of its president, whose expectations of earning enough to be able to lead a comfortable life had been frustrated by the imposition of an income tax on his $1 million earnings).

6. *Substance and form in tax law.* It is worth emphasizing that the analytic technique encountered in this note, and in *Diedrich* — the technique of reconstructing or restating a transaction to fully and accurately reflect its underlying economic reality — is encountered throughout tax (and other) law. Sometimes (though not here) it may be difficult to determine what the reality is or how it may best be fit into the descriptive modes with which we are familiar.

5.   Transfer of Property Subject to Debt

The *Diedrich* case is a relatively simple instance of an assumption of debt in connection with a transfer of property. We turn now to somewhat more complex instances of that phenomenon.

Before turning to the next case, it will be helpful to explain some basic tax principles in the context of a simple example. These principles are explained again, and developed further, in other examples in the notes following the case.

Suppose *T* buys commercial property (land and building) for $2 million using her own funds, and that she rents the property out for a net of $300,000 a year after all expenses. The $300,000 will be *T*'s cash in pocket each year, but it will not be her income for tax purposes. For tax purposes she will be allowed a deduction called ACRS (for accelerated cost recovery system), sometimes called depreciation, which is intended as an allowance for the decline in the value of the building due to wear and tear and obsolescence. See infra page 565. The deduction may not be consistent with economic reality; it is allowed even if in fact there is no decline in the value of the property. Suppose that the ACRS deduction is $100,000 per year and that this deduction is taken, against the income of $300,000, each year for five years. Each year the taxable income will be $200,000, and T's basis in the property will be reduced by the amount of the ACRS deduction ($100,000). At the end of the fifth year the total reduction in basis will be $500,000, and the remaining, or adjusted, basis will be $1.5 million. If the ACRS deduction is consistent with economic reality, the property will have declined in value to $1.5 million, and if it is sold at that price there will be no gain or loss. Assume, however, that the property has not declined (or risen) in value and that at the end of the five years it is sold for $2 million. The gain for tax purposes will be $500,000, which is the difference between the amount realized, $2 million, and the adjusted basis, $1.5 million.[50] See § 1001(a). The $500,000 corresponds to the difference between the total amount of cash that T has received as rent ($1.5 million) and the total amount of income she has reported ($1 million) in connection with the ownership of the property. It can also be thought of as the amount by which the ACRS deduction exceeded the economic decline in the value of the property.

Now suppose that instead of using her own funds, T borrows the $2 million that she invests in the property, that the lender takes a mortgage on the property in that amount, and that the interest on the loan is at a rate of 10 percent or $200,000 per year. Suppose that the loan is nonrecourse, which means that in the event of default the lender can foreclose on the mortgage but has no recourse against T personally. We have already seen (see supra pages 159-160) that the amount T receives by loan is not included in her income. Nonetheless, her basis in the property will be $2 million. Regardless of the formalities of the entire transaction, she is treated as if she had received the $2 million in cash (a nontaxable receipt) and had then invested what is now her $2 million in the property (an investment giving rise to basis). Suppose again that T receives rent net of expenses of $300,000 per year for five years and that each year she takes an ACRS deduction of $100,000 and a deduction for the interest payment of $200,000, so that her taxable income each year is zero. At the end of the fifth year her basis in the property is

---

50. These facts may be summarized as follows:

	(a) One year	(b) Five years cumulative	(c) End of fifth year
1. Purchase price	$2,000,000	—	—
2. Net annual rent	300,000	$1,500,000	—
3. ACRS	100,000	500,000	—
4. Taxable income	200,000	1,000,000	—
5. Sale price	—	—	$2,000,000
6. Adjusted basis[a]	—	—	1,500,000
7. Gain	—	—	500,000

a. 1(a) minus 3(b).

$1.5 million.[51] Suppose that at the end of the fifth year she abandons the property, which is taken by foreclosure by the lender. What tax consequences to T? Note that she has received $500,000 over the five years of her ownership of the property and has paid no tax. She ought to be taxable on an additional $500,000. But what is the proper theory?

CRANE v. COMMISSIONER
331 U.S. 1 (1947)

Mr. Chief Justice VINSON delivered the opinion of the Court.

The question here is how a taxpayer who acquires depreciable property subject to an unassumed mortgage, holds it for a period, and finally sells it still so encumbered, must compute her taxable gain.

[In 1932, Mrs. Beulah Crane inherited land and a building from her husband. The property was subject to a nonrecourse mortgage, or one that she was not personally liable to repay, with an unpaid balance of $262,042.50. An appraisal conducted for federal estate tax purposes determined that the property's value was also exactly $262,042.50.

Between 1932 and 1938, Mrs. Crane claimed depreciation deductions for the building in the amount of $25,500. In 1938, with the lender threatening foreclosure, Mrs. Crane transferred the property, still subject to the mortgage, to a third party in return for a cash payment (net of sale expenses) of $2,500.

In reporting this transaction, Mrs. Crane took the position that, for income tax purposes, the "property" she acquired in 1932 and sold in 1938 consisted only of the "equity," or excess in value of the land plus building over the mortgage that encumbered them. Thus, her amount realized on the sale was $2,500 and her basis was zero. This suggested that she had previously erred in claiming that the building had a depreciable basis, but the statute of limitations prevented any adjustment.

---

51. These facts may be summarized as follows:

	(a) One year	(b) Five years cumulative	(c) End of fifth year
1. Purchase price	$2,000,000	—	—
2. Loan proceeds	2,000,000	—	—
3. Net cash outlay	-0-	—	—
4. Net annual rent	300,000	$1,500,000	—
5. ACRS	100,000	500,000	—
6. Interest paid	200,000	1,000,000	—
7. Net cash	100,000[a]	500,000	—
8. Taxable income	-0-	-0-	—
9. Sale price	—	—	$2,000,000
10. Loan discharge	—	—	2,000,000
11. Net cash	—	—	-0-
12. Adjusted basis[b]	—	—	1,500,000
13. Gain	—	—	500,000

a. 4(a) minus 6(a).
b. 1(a) minus 5(b).

The government argued that her "property" was not limited to her "equity" interest. It thus recomputed her basis as $233,997.40 (the original appraised value of the land and building minus a slightly revised measure of the proper depreciation). And it included in her amount realized the principal amount of the mortgage to which the property remained subject, thus increasing the amount realized to $257,500.

Accordingly, under the government's approach, Mrs. Crane's gain from selling the property was $23,502.60, rather than $2,500 as reported. The difference was mainly attributable to the fact that, under its view but not hers, depreciation deductions that reduced the basis of the property had been properly allowable between 1932 and 1938.]

[Section 1001(a)] defines the gain from "the sale or other disposition of property" as "the excess of the amount realized therefrom over the adjusted basis provided in section [1011(a)]. . . ." It proceeds, [§ 1001(b)], to define "the amount realized from the sale of other disposition of property" as "the sum of any money received plus the fair market value of the property (other than money) received." Further, in [§ 1016(a)(2)], the "adjusted basis for determining the gain or loss from the sale or other disposition of property" is declared to be "the basis determined under subsection (a), adjusted . . . for exhaustion, wear and tear, obsolescence, amortization . . . to the extent allowed (but not less than the amount allowable). . . ." The basis under subsection (a) "if the property was acquired by . . . devise . . . or by the decedent's estate from the decedent," [§ 1014], is "the fair market value of such property at the time of such acquisition."

Logically, the first step under this scheme is to determine the unadjusted basis of the property, under [§ 1014], and the dispute in this case is as to the construction to be given the term "property." If "property," as used in that provision, means the same thing as "equity," it would necessarily follow that the basis of petitioner's property was zero, as she contends. If, on the contrary, it means the land and building themselves, or the owner's legal rights in them, undiminished by the mortgage, the basis was $262,042.50.

We think that the reasons for favoring one of the latter construction are of overwhelming weight. In the first place, the words of statutes — including revenue acts — should be interpreted where possible in their ordinary, everyday senses. The only relevant definitions of "property" to be found in the principal standard dictionaries are the two favored by the Commissioner, i.e., either that "property" is the physical thing which is a subject of ownership, or that it is the aggregate of the owner's rights to control and dispose of that thing. "Equity" is not given as a synonym, nor do either of the foregoing definitions suggest that it could be correctly so used. Indeed, "equity" is defined as "the value of a property . . . above the total of the liens. . . ." The contradistinction could hardly be more pointed. Strong countervailing considerations would be required to support a contention that Congress, in using the word "property," meant "equity," or that we should impute to it the intent to convey that meaning.

In the second place, the Commissioner's position [accorded with long-standing administrative practice]. . . .

Moreover, in the many instances in other parts of the Act in which Congress has used the word "property," or expressed the idea of "property" or "equity," we find no instances of a misuse of either word or of a confusion of the ideas.

In some parts of the Act other than the gain and loss sections, we find "property" where it is unmistakably used in its ordinary sense. On the other hand, where either Congress or the Treasury intended to convey the meaning of "equity," it did so by the use of appropriate language.

A further reason why the word "property" in [§ 1001(a)] should not be construed to mean "equity" is the bearing such construction would have on the allowance of deductions for depreciation and on the collateral adjustments of basis.

Section [167(a)] permits deduction from gross income of "a reasonable allowance for the exhaustion, wear and tear of property. . . ." Section [167(i)] declare[s] that the "basis upon which exhaustion, wear and tear . . . are to be allowed" is the basis "provided in section [1001] for the purpose of determining the gain upon the sale" of the property, which is the [§ 1001(a)] basis "adjusted . . . for exhaustion, wear and tear . . . to the extent allowed (but not less than the amount allowable). . . ."

Under these provisions, if the mortgagor's equity were the [§ 1001(a)] basis, it would also be the original basis from which depreciation allowances are deducted. If it is, and if the amount of the annual allowances were to be computed on that value, as would then seem to be required, they will represent only a fraction of the cost of the corresponding physical exhaustion, and any recoupment by the mortgagor of the remainder of that cost can be effected only by the reduction of his taxable gain in the year of sale. If, however, the amount of the annual allowances were to be computed on the value of the property, and then deducted from an equity basis, we would in some instances have to accept deductions from a minus basis or deny deductions altogether.[52] The Commissioner also argues that taking the mortgagor's equity as the [§ 1001(a)] basis would require the basis to be changed with each payment on the mortgage, and that the attendant problem of repeatedly recomputing basis and annual allowances would be a tremendous accounting burden on both the Commissioner and the taxpayer. Moreover, the mortgagor would acquire control over the timing of his depreciation allowances.

Thus it appears that the applicable provisions of the Act expressly preclude an equity basis, and the use of it is contrary to certain implicit principles of income tax depreciation, and entails very great administrative difficulties. It may be added that the Treasury has never furnished a guide through the maze of problems that arise in connection with depreciating an equity basis, but, on the contrary, has consistently permitted the amount of depreciation allowances to be computed on the full value of the property, and subtracted from it as a basis. Surely, Congress' long-continued acceptance of this situation gives it full legislative endorsement.

We conclude that the proper basis under [§ 1014] is the value of the property, undiminished by mortgages thereon, and that the correct basis here was $262,042.50. The next step is to ascertain what adjustments are required under [§ 1016]. As the depreciation rate was stipulated, the only question at

---

52. So long as the mortgagor remains in possession, the mortgagee can not take depreciation deductions, even if he is the one who actually sustains the capital loss, as [§167(a)] allows them only on property "used in the trade or business."

this point is whether the Commissioner was warranted in making any depreciation adjustments whatsoever.

Section [1016] provides that "proper adjustment in respect of the property *shall in all cases be made* . . . for exhaustion, wear and tear . . . to the extent allowed (but not less than the amount allowable). . . ." (Italics supplied.) The Tax Court found on adequate evidence that the apartment house was property of a kind subject to physical exhaustion, that it was used in taxpayer's trade or business, and consequently that the taxpayer would have been entitled to a depreciation allowance under [§ 167], except that, in the opinion of that Court, the basis of the property was zero, and it was thought that depreciation could not be taken on a zero basis. As we have just decided that the correct basis of the property was not zero, but $262,042.50, we avoid this difficulty, and conclude that an adjustment should be made as the Commissioner determined.

Petitioner urges to the contrary that she was not entitled to depreciation deductions, whatever the basis of the property, because the law allows them only to one who actually bears the capital loss, and here the loss was not hers but the mortgagee's. We do not see, however, that she has established her factual premise. There was no finding of the Tax Court to that effect, nor to the effect that the value of the property was ever less than the amount of the lien. Nor was there evidence in the record, or any indication that petitioner could produce evidence, that this was so. The facts that the value of the property was only equal to the lien in 1932 and that during the next six and one-half years the physical condition of the building deteriorated and the amount of the lien increased, are entirely inconclusive, particularly in the light of the buyer's willingness in 1938 to take subject to the increased lien and pay a substantial amount of cash to boot. Whatever may be the rule as to allowing depreciation to a mortgagor on property in his possession which is subject to an unassumed mortgage and clearly worth less than the lien, we are not faced with that problem and see no reason to decide it now.

At last we come to the problem of determining the "amount realized" on the 1938 sale. Section [§ 1001(b)], it will be recalled, defines the "amount realized" from "the sale . . . of property" as "the sum of any money received plus the fair market value of the property (other than money) received," and [§ 1001(a)] defines the gain on "the sale . . . of property" as the excess of the amount realized over the basis. Quite obviously, the word "property," used here with reference to a sale, must mean "property" in the same ordinary sense intended by the use of the word with reference to acquisition and depreciation in [§ 1014], both for certain of the reasons stated heretofore in discussing its meaning in [§ 1014], and also because the functional relation of the two sections requires that the word mean the same in one section that it does in the other. If the "property" to be valued on the date of acquisition is the property free of liens, the "property" to be priced on a subsequent sale must be the same thing.

Starting from this point, we could not accept petitioner's contention that the $2,500.00 net cash was all she realized on the sale except on the absurdity that she sold a quarter-of-a-million dollar property for roughly one percent of its value, and took a 99 percent loss. Actually, petitioner does not urge this. She argues, conversely, that because only $2,500.00 was realized on the sale, the "property" sold must have been the equity only, and that consequently we are forced to accept her contention as to the meaning of "property" in [§ 1014]. We adhere, however, to what we have already said on the meaning of "property," and we find that the absurdity is avoided by our conclusion that the amount of the mortgage is properly included in the "amount realized" on the sale.

Petitioner concedes that if she had been personally liable on the mortgage and the purchaser had either paid or assumed it, the amount so paid or assumed would be considered a part of the "amount realized" within the meaning of [§ 1001(b)]. The cases so deciding have already repudiated the notion that there must be an actual receipt by the seller himself of "money" or "other property," in their narrowest senses. It was thought to be decisive that one section of the Act must be construed so as not to defeat the intention of another or to frustrate the Act as a whole, and that the taxpayer was the "beneficiary" of the payment in "as real and substantial [a sense] as if the money had been paid it and then paid over by it to its creditors."

Both these points apply to this case. The first has been mentioned already. As for the second, we think that a mortgagor, not personally liable on the debt, who sells the property subject to the mortgage and for additional consideration, realizes a benefit in the amount of the mortgage as well as the boot.[53] If a purchaser pays boot, it is immaterial as to our problem whether the mortgagor is also to receive money from the purchaser to discharge the mortgage prior to sale, or whether he is merely to transfer subject to the mortgage — it may make a difference to the purchaser and to the mortgagee, but not to the mortgagor. Or put in another way, we are no more concerned with whether the mortgagor is, strictly speaking, a debtor on the mortgage, than we are with whether the benefit to him is, strictly speaking, a receipt of money or property. We are rather concerned with the reality that an owner of property, mortgaged at a figure less than that at which the property will sell, must and will treat the conditions of the mortgage exactly as if they were his personal obligations. If he transfers subject to the mortgage, the benefit to him is as real and substantial as if the mortgage were discharged, or as if a personal debt in an equal amount had been assumed by another.

Therefore we conclude that the Commissioner was right in determining that petitioner realized $257,500.00 on the sale of this property. . . .

Petitioner contends that the result we have reached taxes her on what is not income within the meaning of the Sixteenth Amendment. If this is because only the direct receipt of cash is thought to be income in the constitutional sense, her contention is wholly without merit. If it is because the entire transaction is thought to have been "by all dictates of common sense . . . a ruinous disaster," as it was termed in her brief, we disagree with her premise. She was entitled to depreciation deductions for a period of nearly seven years,

---

53. [This is the well-known footnote 37 in the original opinion. — EDS.] Obviously, if the value of the property is less than the amount of the mortgage, a mortgagor who is not personally liable cannot realize a benefit equal to the mortgage. Consequently, a different problem might be encountered where a mortgagor abandoned the property or transferred it subject to the mortgage without receiving boot. That is not this case.

and she actually took them in almost the allowable amount. The crux of this case, really, is whether the law permits her to exclude allowable deductions from consideration in computing gain. We have already showed that, if it does, the taxpayer can enjoy a double deduction, in effect, on the same loss of assets. The Sixteenth Amendment does not require that result any more than does the Act itself.

Affirmed.

Mr. Justice JACKSON, dissenting.

The Tax Court concluded that this taxpayer acquired only an equity worth nothing. The mortgage was in default, the mortgage debt was equal to the value of the property, any possession by the taxpayer was forfeited and terminable immediately by foreclosure, and perhaps by a receiver pendente lite. Arguments can be advanced to support the theory that the taxpayer received the whole property and thereupon came to owe the whole debt. Likewise it is argued that when she sold she transferred the entire value of the property and received release from the whole debt. But we think these arguments are not so conclusive that it was not within the province of the Tax Court to find that she received an equity which at that time had a zero value. The taxpayer never became personally liable for the debt, and hence when she sold she was released from no debt. The mortgage debt was simply a subtraction from the value of what she did receive, and from what she sold. The subtraction left her nothing when she acquired it and a small margin when she sold it. She acquired a property right equivalent to an equity of redemption and sold the same thing. It was the "property" bought and sold as the Tax Court considered it to be under the Revenue Laws. We are not required in this case to decide whether depreciation was properly taken, for there is no issue about it here.

We would reverse the Court of Appeals and sustain the decision of the Tax Court.

Mr. Justice FRANKFURTER and Mr. Justice DOUGLAS join in this opinion.

NOTES AND QUESTIONS

1. Whose view of how to treat acquisitions and dispositions of property subject to nonrecourse debt is more favorable to taxpayers in the long run: that of Mrs. Crane or that of the Commissioner? Note that under Mrs. Crane's view, if applied consistently throughout her period of ownership, she acquired the property with a zero basis, should not have deducted any depreciation, and then sold it for $2,500. The Commissioner's view gives her a higher basis and amount realized, by reason of including on both sides the amount of the nonrecourse debt. In practice, the main difference between the two views is that the Commissioner's permits the taxpayer to claim depreciation deductions, which are then offset by recapture gain upon disposition of the property. Why does this matter?

2. *Basis and tax shelters.* Despite its somewhat homely facts, the *Crane* decision turned out to be highly significant to the development of U.S. tax law.

Boris Bittker, the original author of this casebook, once observed that *Crane* "laid the foundation stone of most tax shelters." The term "tax shelter" is typically used to describe certain investments entered into largely for the sake of their tax benefits, such as accelerated depreciation for real estate and other assets. Because these and other annual deductions often exceeded any allowance that would be consistent with economic reality, taxpayers investing in tax shelters commonly reported losses for tax purposes. Before the adoption in 1986 of the "passive loss" limitations (see infra 594), those losses could be used to offset, or "shelter," income from other sources (such as compensation for services as a doctor, a lawyer, a movie star, or an athlete). Tax shelters will be examined at some length, after we have examined deductions, but a simple illustration may be helpful here. Suppose that S is a surgeon earning $300,000 per year. He has saved $100,000, which he uses to buy an office building that is worth $1 million and is subject to a mortgage of $900,000. Suppose that the rents from the building are just equal to the interest and all other expenses, but that S is entitled to depreciate the building at a rate of $50,000 per year. He will show a loss of $50,000 a year on his investment, even if (as is likely in many instances) the property is not in fact declining in value. Before 1987, the $50,000 loss could have been deducted on his personal income tax return and thus would have "sheltered" $50,000 of income from his medical practice. In other words, he would have received $50,000 of income tax free because of the tax loss. Suppose that he kept the building for five years and then sold it, subject to the $900,000 mortgage, for $100,000 — the amount he initially invested. His basis would be $750,000 (for the land and building), so he would have a gain for tax purposes of $250,000, which is, as it should be, precisely equal to the deductions he had taken in earlier years. He would come out even except that he would have had the advantage of deferral and of long-term capital gain treatment of the $250,000 gain.

3. When a mortgage is nonrecourse, the lender rather than the borrower bears the risk that, on the maturity date, the security's value will be less than the amount due. For example, suppose Beulah owes a bank $1 million under a nonrecourse mortgage on Blackacre that bears 10 percent annual interest ($100,000) and is due in ten years. If, on the maturity date, Blackacre is worth, say, $850,000, Beulah can default, leaving the bank with no further right to repayment on its million-dollar loan.

However, the use of nonrecourse debt provides only one of an array of distinctive legal forms that can be used to make the bank, rather than Beulah, bear this risk of loss. Alternatively, the parties could, for example:

- Make Beulah personally liable to repay the loan, but have the bank give her the legal right to require it to buy Blackacre from her for $1 million on the loan maturity date. How can this lead to the same result as the use of a nonrecourse mortgage if Blackacre is worth only $850,000 on the loan maturity date?
- Structure the transaction so that the bank, rather than Beulah, is Blackacre's legal owner during the ten-year period, but give her the legal right to require it to sell her Blackacre for $1 million at the end of this period. In the interim, if she is occupying the property (or collecting rent from a third

party for using it), her annual $100,000 payments to the bank can be called rent for Blackacre, rather than interest on a loan.

Can you think of any other ways (e.g., with "default insurance") to replicate the economic substance of a *Crane*-style transaction without formally using nonrecourse debt? What does the variety of ways in which the same economic transaction can be arranged tell you about the wisdom of (as Mrs. Crane proposed) treating nonrecourse debt differently from recourse debt?

4. If nonrecourse borrowers were denied depreciation deductions by the exclusion of nonrecourse debt from basis, might Congress decide that such deductions should go to the lender? Critics of the *Crane* rule sometimes argue that this is the correct result, on the ground that the lender, rather than the owner, bears the economic loss if the property's value declines to less than the face amount of the outstanding nonrecourse debt. In fact, however, this is not entirely correct, even to the extent that the deductions correctly measure an actual decline in value of the property. Rather, if the property's value is volatile (it might go back up) or its rental value declines along with its sale value, the economic loss is split between the owner and lender. As for depreciation that exceeds any real economic decline in the property's value, it does not represent an economic loss that anyone has suffered, and thus arguably there is no "correct" taxpayer to claim the deduction. See Shaviro, Risk and Accrual: The Tax Treatment of Nonrecourse Debt, 44 Tax L. Rev. 401, 433-437 (1989).

5. In *Crane*, it was stipulated that, when the taxpayer acquired the property, the face amount of the nonrecourse debt precisely equaled the value of the property. What if the face amount of the nonrecourse debt had been greater? Fully including it in basis might seem to fly in the face of the decreased likelihood that the taxpayer would ever pay the debt in full, and would increase the tax shelter advantages of the investment by increasing depreciation deductions (which generally are determined as a percentage of basis).

In Estate of Franklin v. Commissioner, 544 F.2d 1045 (9th Cir. 1976) (infra page 588), the taxpayer had purchased a motel (which was simultaneously leased back to the seller/lender) for nonrecourse debt in an amount that substantially exceeded the hotel's fair market value. The court held that the nonrecourse debt lacked economic substance since it was unlikely ever to be repaid, and that the purported buyer was not the owner of the property for tax purposes. Even had ownership been transferred for tax purposes, the court's analysis suggests that the nonrecourse debt might have been completely excluded from the new owner's basis.

By contrast, in Pleasant Summit Land Corp. v. Commissioner, 863 F.2d 263 (3d Cir. 1988), cert. denied, 493 U.S. 901 (1989), the court permitted nonrecourse debt that exceeded the value of the property to be included in basis to the extent of such value at the time of acquisition. The case involved preexisting nonrecourse debt, provided by a third-party lender rather than by the seller, to which the property was subject when acquired by the taxpayer. The court defended its departure from the approach in *Estate of Franklin* by noting the possibility that the taxpayer might end up agreeing with the lender to settle the debt for this amount. Subsequent cases have generally either rejected *Pleasant Summit* in favor of *Estate of Franklin*, or else reconciled the two on the ground that *Pleasant Summit* applies in nonabusive situations, such as those involving preexisting or third-party financing, rather than seller financing and a sale-leaseback as in *Estate of Franklin*. Lukens v. Commissioner, 945 F.2d 92 (5th Cir. 1991); Regents Park Partners v. Commissioner, 63 T.C.M. 3131 (1992).

Thus, if one paid $5,000 in cash for property that was worth $400,000 and subject to a $1 million nonrecourse debt, one's basis for the property would be either $5,000 under *Estate of Franklin*, or else $405,000 under *Pleasant Summit*. However, it plainly would not be $1,005,000, as seemingly suggested by the *Crane* rule.

Why would a taxpayer, as in *Estate of Franklin*, purport to purchase property for nonrecourse debt in excess of the property's value and simultaneously lease the property back to the seller? How do *Pleasant Summit*–type transactions, where the nonrecourse debt that exceeds the property's value upon acquisition by the taxpayer either is preexisting and did not at its inception exceed the property's value, and/or is provided by a third-party lender, differ from *Estate of Franklin*–type seller financing transactions in the tax planning opportunities that they present?

6. *Crane's* famous footnote 37 (appearing in this chapter as footnote 53) expressly reserves the question of how to treat a sale of property that is worth less than the amount of a nonrecourse mortgage to which it is subject. Thus, suppose a taxpayer purchases depreciable property for $1 million of nonrecourse debt, over time claims $1 million of depreciation deductions (reducing adjusted basis to zero), and then abandons the property. If the property is worth zero upon abandonment, the footnote seems to suggest that the taxpayer need not include any gain to offset the previously deducted loss, although the last paragraph of the Court's opinion is seemingly to the contrary.

For many years, a belief among taxpayers that they were entitled to rely upon the favorable implications of footnote 37 helped to make tax shelters even more appealing than otherwise. After all, permanently deducting depreciation that one never bears economically is even more advantageous than the deferral described in our Note 2 above. This practice, and the correct tax treatment of situations described in footnote 37, finally received the Supreme Court's attention in the following case.

COMMISSIONER v. TUFTS
461 U.S. 300 (1983)

Justice BLACKMUN delivered the opinion of the Court.

Over 35 years ago, in Crane v. Commissioner, 331 U.S. 1 (1947), this Court ruled that a taxpayer, who sold property encumbered by a nonrecourse mortgage (the amount of the mortgage being less than the property's value), must include the unpaid balance of the mortgage in the computation of the amount the taxpayer realized on the sale. The case now before us presents the question whether the same rule applies when the unpaid amount of the nonrecourse mortgage exceeds the fair market value of the property sold.

I

On August 1, 1970, respondent Clark Pelt, a builder, and his wholly owned corporation, respondent Clark, Inc., formed a general partnership. The purpose of the partnership was to construct a 120-unit apartment complex in Duncanville, Tex., a Dallas suburb. Neither Pelt nor Clark, Inc., made any capital contribution to the partnership. Six days later, the partnership entered into a mortgage loan agreement with the Farm & Home Savings Association (F&H). Under the agreement, F&H was committed for a $1,851,500 loan for the complex. In return, the partnership executed a note and a deed of trust in favor of F&H. The partnership obtained the loan on a nonrecourse basis: neither the partnership nor its partners assumed any personal liability for repayment of the loan. Pelt later admitted four friends and relatives, respondents Tufts, Steger, Stephens, and Austin, as general partners. None of them contributed capital upon entering the partnership.

The construction of the complex was completed in August 1971. During 1971, each partner made small capital contributions to the partnership; in 1972, however, only Pelt made a contribution. The total of the partners' capital contributions was $44,212. In each tax year, all partners claimed as income tax deductions their allocable shares of ordinary losses and depreciation. The deductions taken by the partners in 1971 and 1972 totalled $439,972. Due to these contributions and deductions, the partnership's adjusted basis in the property in August 1972 was $1,455,740.

In 1971 and 1972, major employers in the Duncanville area laid off significant numbers of workers. As a result, the partnership's rental income was less than expected, and it was unable to make the payments due on the mortgage. Each partner, on August 28, 1972, sold his partnership interest to an unrelated third party, Fred Bayles. As consideration, Bayles agreed to reimburse each partner's sale expenses up to $250; he also assumed the nonrecourse mortgage.

On the date of transfer, the fair market value of the property did not exceed $1,400,000. Each partner reported the sale on his federal income tax return and indicated that a partnership loss of $55,740 had been sustained.[54] The Commissioner of Internal Revenue, on audit, determined that the sale resulted in a partnership capital gain of approximately $400,000. His theory was that the partnership had realized the full amount of the nonrecourse obligation.[55]

Relying on Millar v. Commissioner, 577 F.2d 212, 215 (C.A.3), cert. denied, 439 U.S. 1046 (1978), the United States Tax Court, in an unreviewed decision, upheld the asserted deficiencies. 70 T.C. 756 (1978). The United States Court of Appeals for the Fifth Circuit reversed. 651 F.2d 1058 (1981). That court expressly disagreed with the *Millar* analysis, and, in limiting Crane v.

---

54. The loss was the difference between the adjusted basis, $1,455,740, and the fair market value of the property, $1,400,000. On their individual tax returns, the partners did not claim deductions for their respective shares of this loss. In their petitions to the Tax Court, however, the partners did claim the loss.

55. The Commissioner determined the partnership's gain on the sale by subtracting the adjusted basis, $1,455,740, from the liability assumed by Bayles, $1,851,500. . . .

Commissioner, *supra*, to its facts, questioned the theoretical underpinnings of the *Crane* decision. We granted certiorari to resolve the conflict. . . .

II

Section 752(d) of the Internal Revenue Code of 1954 specifically provides that liabilities incurred in the sale or exchange of a partnership interest are to "be treated in the same manner as liabilities in connection with the sale or exchange of property not associated with partnerships." Section 1001 governs the determination of gains and losses on the disposition of property. Under § 1001(a), the gain or loss from a sale or other disposition of property is defined as the difference between "the amount realized" on the disposition and the property's adjusted basis. Subsection (b) of § 1001 defines "amount realized." "The amount realized from the sale or other disposition of property shall be the sum of any money received plus the fair market value of the property (other than money) received." At issue is the application of the latter provision to the disposition of property encumbered by a nonrecourse mortgage of an amount in excess of the property's fair market value.

A

In Crane v. Commissioner, *supra*, this Court took the first and controlling step toward the resolution of this issue. . . .
[T]he Court concluded that Crane obtained an economic benefit from the purchaser's assumption of the mortgage identical to the benefit conferred by the cancellation of personal debt. Because the value of the property in that case exceeded the amount of the mortgage, it was in Crane's economic interest to treat the mortgage as a personal obligation; only by so doing could she realize upon sale the appreciation in her equity represented by the $2,500 boot. The purchaser's assumption of the liability thus resulted in a taxable economic benefit to her, just as if she had been given, in addition to the boot, a sum of cash sufficient to satisfy the mortgage.

In a footnote, pertinent to the present case, the Court observed:

> Obviously, if the value of the property is less than the amount of the mortgage, a mortgagor who is not personally liable cannot realize a benefit equal to the mortgage. Consequently, a different problem might be encountered where a mortgagor abandoned the property or transferred it subject to the mortgage without receiving boot. That is not this case.

Id., at 14, n.37.

B

This case presents that unresolved issue. We are disinclined to overrule *Crane*, and we conclude that the same rule applies when the unpaid amount of the nonrecourse mortgage exceeds the value of the property transferred.

Crane ultimately does not rest on its limited theory of economic benefit; instead, we read *Crane* to have approved the Commissioner's decision to treat a nonrecourse mortgage in this context as a true loan. This approval underlies *Crane's* holdings that the amount of the nonrecourse liability is to be included in calculating both the basis and the amount realized on disposition. That the amount of the loan exceeds the fair market value of the property thus becomes irrelevant.

When a taxpayer receives a loan, he incurs an obligation to repay that loan at some future date. Because of this obligation, the loan proceeds do not qualify as income to the taxpayer. When he fulfills the obligation, the repayment of the loan likewise has no effect on his tax liability.

Another consequence to the taxpayer from this obligation occurs when the taxpayer applies the loan proceeds to the purchase price of property used to secure the loan. Because of the obligation to repay, the taxpayer is entitled to include the amount of the loan in computing his basis in the property; the loan, under § 1012, is part of the taxpayer's cost of the property. Although a different approach might have been taken with respect to a nonrecourse mortgage loan,[56] the Commissioner has chosen to accord it the same treatment he gives to a recourse mortgage loan. The Court approved that choice in *Crane*, and the respondents do not challenge it here. The choice and its resultant benefits to the taxpayer are predicated on the assumption that the mortgage will be repaid in full.

When encumbered property is sold or otherwise disposed of and the purchaser assumes the mortgage, the associated extinguishment of the mortgagor's obligation to repay is accounted for in the computation of the amount realized. . . . Because no difference between recourse and nonrecourse obligations is recognized in calculating basis,[57] *Crane* teaches that the Commissioner may ignore the nonrecourse nature of the obligation in determining the amount realized upon disposition of the encumbered property. He thus may include in the amount realized the amount of the nonrecourse mortgage assumed by the purchaser. The rationale for this treatment is that the original inclusion of the amount of the mortgage in basis rested on the assumption that

56. The Commissioner might have adopted the theory, implicit in Crane's contentions, that a nonrecourse mortgage is not true debt, but, instead, is a form of joint investment by the mortgagor and the mortgagee. On this approach, nonrecourse debt would be considered a contingent liability, under which the mortgagor's payments on the debt gradually increase his interest in the property while decreasing that of the mortgagee. . . . Because the taxpayer's investment in the property would not include the nonrecourse debt, the taxpayer would not be permitted to include that debt in basis. . . .

We express no view as to whether such an approach would be consistent with the statutory structure and, if so, and *Crane* were not on the books, whether that approach would be preferred over *Crane's* analysis. We note only that the *Crane* Court's resolution of the basis issue presumed that when property is purchased with proceeds from a nonrecourse mortgage, the purchaser becomes the sole owner of the property. . . .

57. The Commissioner's choice in *Crane* "laid the foundation stone of most tax shelters," Bittker, Tax Shelters, Nonrecourse Debt, and the *Crane* Case, 33 Tax L. Rev. 277, 283 (1978), by permitting taxpayers who bear no risk to take deductions on depreciable property. Congress recently has acted to curb this avoidance device by forbidding a taxpayer to take depreciation deductions in excess of amounts he has at risk in the investment. . . . § 465(a) [see infra 596]. . . . Although this congressional action may foreshadow a day when nonrecourse and recourse debts will be treated differently, neither Congress nor the Commissioner has sought to alter *Crane's* rule of including nonrecourse liability in both basis and the amount realized.

the mortgagor incurred an obligation to repay. Moreover, this treatment balances the fact that the mortgagor originally received the proceeds of the nonrecourse loan tax-free on the same assumption. Unless the outstanding amount of the mortgage is deemed to be realized, the mortgagor effectively will have received untaxed income at the time the loan was extended and will have received an unwarranted increase in the basis of his property.[58] The Commissioner's interpretation of § 1001(b) in this fashion cannot be said to be unreasonable.

C

The Commissioner in fact has applied this rule even when the fair market value of the property falls below the amount of the nonrecourse obligation. Treas. Reg. § 1.1001-2(b); Rev. Rul. 76-111, 1976-1 Cum. Bull. 214. Because the theory on which the rule is based applies equally in this situation, . . . we have no reason, after *Crane*, to question this treatment.[59]

Respondents received a mortgage loan with the concomitant obligation to repay by the year 2012. The only difference between that mortgage and one on which the borrower is personally liable is that the mortgagee's remedy is limited to foreclosing on the securing property. This difference does not alter the nature of the obligation; its only effect is to shift from the borrower to the lender any potential loss caused by devaluation of the property. If the fair market value of the property falls below the amount of the outstanding obligation, the mortgagee's ability to protect its interests is impaired, for the mortgagor is free to abandon the property to the mortgagee and be relieved of his obligation.

This, however, does not erase the fact that the mortgagor received the loan proceeds tax-free and included them in his basis on the understanding that he had an obligation to repay the full amount. . . . When the obligation is canceled, the mortgagor is relieved of his responsibility to repay the sum he originally received and thus realizes value to that extent within the meaning of § 1001(b). From the mortgagor's point of view, when his obligation is assumed by a third party who purchases the encumbered property, it is as if the

58. Although the *Crane* rule has some affinity with the tax benefit rule; . . . the analysis we adopt is different. Our analysis applies even in the situation in which no deductions are taken. It focuses on the obligation to repay and its subsequent extinguishment, not on the taking and recovery of deductions. . . .

59. Professor Wayne G. Barnett, as amicus in the present case, argues that the liability and property portions of the transaction should be accounted for separately. Under his view, there was a transfer of the property for $1.4 million, and there was a cancellation of the $1.85 million obligation for a payment of $1.4 million. The former resulted in a capital loss of $50,000, and the latter in the realization of $450,000 of ordinary income. Taxation of the ordinary income might be deferred under § 108 by a reduction of respondents' bases in their partnership interests. [Deferral under § 108 was broadly available at the time this case was decided. It is now available only for insolvent debtors and farmers and the relief mechanism is slightly different from the one applied under the now-repealed provision referred to by the Court. — EDS.]

Although this indeed could be a justifiable mode of analysis, it has not been adopted by the Commissioner. Nor is there anything to indicate that the Code requires the Commissioner to adopt it. We note that Professor Barnett's approach does assume that recourse and nonrecourse debt may be treated identically. . . .

mortgagor first had been paid with cash borrowed by the third party from the mortgagee on a nonrecourse basis, and then had used the cash to satisfy his obligation to the mortgagee.

Moreover, this approach avoids the absurdity the Court recognized in *Crane*. Because of the remedy accompanying the mortgage in the nonrecourse situation, the depreciation in the fair market value of the property is relevant economically only to the mortgagee, who by lending on a nonrecourse basis remains at risk. To permit the taxpayer to limit his realization to the fair market value of the property would be to recognize a tax loss for which he has suffered no corresponding economic loss. Such a result would be to construe "one section of the Act . . . so as . . . to defeat the intention of another or to frustrate the Act as a whole." 331 U.S., at 13.

In the specific circumstances of *Crane*, the economic benefit theory did support the Commissioner's treatment of the nonrecourse mortgage as a personal obligation. The footnote in *Crane* acknowledged the limitations of that theory when applied to a different set of facts. *Crane* also stands for the broader proposition, however, that a nonrecourse loan should be treated as a true loan. We therefore hold that a taxpayer must account for the proceeds of obligations he has received tax-free and included in basis. Nothing in either § 1001(b) or in the Court's prior decisions requires the Commissioner to permit a taxpayer to treat a sale of encumbered property asymmetrically, by including the proceeds of the nonrecourse obligation in basis but not accounting for the proceeds upon transfer of the encumbered property. . . .

Justice O'CONNOR, concurring.

I concur in the opinion of the Court, accepting the view of the Commissioner. I do not, however, endorse the Commissioner's view. Indeed, were we writing on a slate clean except for the *Crane* decision, I would take quite a different approach—that urged upon us by Professor Barnett as amicus.

Crane established that a taxpayer could treat property as entirely his own, in spite of the "coinvestment" provided by his mortgagee in the form of a nonrecourse loan. That is, the full basis of the property, with all its tax consequences, belongs to the mortgagor. That rule alone, though, does not in any way tie nonrecourse debt to the cost of property or to the proceeds upon disposition. I see no reason to treat the purchase, ownership, and eventual disposition of property differently because the taxpayer also takes out a mortgage, an independent transaction. In this case, the taxpayer purchased property, using nonrecourse financing, and sold it after it declined in value to a buyer who assumed the mortgage. There is no economic difference between the events in this case and a case in which the taxpayer buys property with cash; later obtains a nonrecourse loan by pledging the property as security; still later, using cash on hand, buys off the mortgage for the market value of the devalued property; and finally sells the property to a third party for its market value.

The logical way to treat both this case and the hypothesized case is to separate the two aspects of these events and to consider, first, the ownership and sale of the property, and, second, the arrangement and retirement of the loan. Under *Crane*, the fair market value of the property on the date of acquisition—the purchase price—represents the taxpayer's basis in the property, and the fair market value on the date of disposition represents the proceeds on sale. The benefit received by the taxpayer in return for the property is the cancellation of a mortgage that is worth no more than the fair market value of the property, for that is all the mortgagee can expect to collect on the mortgage. His gain or loss on the disposition of the property equals the difference between the proceeds and the cost of acquisition. Thus, the taxation of the transaction in *property* reflects the economic fate of the *property*. If the property has declined in value, as was the case here, the taxpayer recognizes a loss on the disposition of the property. The new purchaser then takes as his basis the fair market value as of the date of the sale. . . .

In the separate borrowing transaction, the taxpayer acquires cash from the mortgagee. He need not recognize income at that time, of course, because he also incurs an obligation to repay the money. Later, though, when he is able to satisfy the debt by surrendering property that is worth less than the face amount of the debt, we have a classic situation of cancellation of indebtedness, requiring the taxpayer to recognize income in the amount of the difference between the proceeds of the loan and the amount for which he is able to satisfy his creditor. 26 U.S.C. § 61(a)(12). The taxation of the financing transaction then reflects the economic fate of the loan.

The reason that separation of the two aspects of the events in this case is important is, of course, that the Code treats different sorts of income differently. A gain on the sale of the property may qualify for capital gains treatment, while the cancellation of indebtedness is ordinary income, but income that the taxpayer may be able to defer. Not only does Professor Barnett's theory permit us to accord appropriate treatment to each of the two types of income or loss present in these sorts of transactions, it also restores continuity to the system by making the taxpayer-seller's proceeds on the disposition of property equal to the purchaser's basis in the property. Further, and most important, it allows us to tax the events in this case in the same way that we tax the economically identical hypothesized transaction.

Persuaded though I am by the logical coherence and internal consistency of this approach, I agree with the Court's decision not to adopt it judicially. We do not write on a slate marked only by *Crane*. The Commissioner's long-standing position, Rev. Rul. 76-111, 1976-1 C.B. 214, is now reflected in the regulations. Treas. Reg. § 1.1001-2, 26 C.F.R. § 1.1001-2 (1982). In the light of the numerous cases in the lower courts including the amount of the unrepaid proceeds of the mortgage in the proceeds on sale or disposition, . . . it is difficult to conclude that the Commissioner's interpretation of the statute exceeds the bounds of his discretion. As the Court's opinion demonstrates, his interpretation is defensible. . . .

NOTES AND QUESTIONS

1. *Taking debt into account on disposition of property.* (a) The Court in *Tufts* requires the taxpayer to recognize income upon the disposition of the apartment complex. The following simplified version of the facts in the case should help illuminate the logic behind that aspect of the decision. Assume

Tufts put up $45,000 of his own funds and used $1,850,000 of borrowed funds to acquire an apartment complex for $1,895,000. Tufts deducted $440,000 depreciation and then "sold" the complex for a nominal sum (which we will ignore). Tufts's total dollar loss, then, was $45,000. His prior tax loss, however, was $440,000. Clearly, something is amiss here. Tufts deducted $440,000 depreciation but lost only the cash contribution of $45,000. In order for the tax consequences to match the economic consequences, the taxpayer must, in effect, "give back" the $395,000 of depreciation that represented a loss he did not incur.

The Court in *Tufts* reaches the correct result (as to income recognized) by including the buyer's assumption of the nonrecourse debt as part of the sales proceeds. The taxpayer is thus treated as having received $1,850,000 upon sale of the property. The depreciation reduced the taxpayer's basis in the property from $1,895,000 (the invested loan proceeds plus the $45,000 of the taxpayer's own funds) to $1,455,000 (basis less depreciation). The difference between that basis and the $1,850,000 sales proceeds yields a gain of $395,000. There is a nice symmetry to the way the Court derives the proper result: If nonrecourse debt is treated as cash for the purposes of determining basis, perhaps it should be treated as cash for the purposes of determining sales proceeds.

The approach favored in Justice O'Connor's concurrence reaches the same result (as to amount recognized), but by a different means. Under that approach, property is treated as sold for its fair market value. If property purchased with, and secured by, a nonrecourse loan declines in value to zero and is abandoned (or foreclosed upon by the lender, or deeded over to the lender in lieu of foreclosure) the sales proceeds are zero. The taxpayer recognizes no property gain and, depending on the basis of the property at the time the proposed is disposed of, may well recognize a loss. The taxpayer does, however, recognize cancellation of indebtedness income equal to the difference between the amount of outstanding debt secured by the property and its fair market value at time of disposal. The intuition behind this "bifurcated" approach is that the taxpayer has not repaid the full amount it has borrowed and must recognize cancellation of indebtedness income under *Kirby Lumber*, supra page 161.

(b) While the dictates of logic are clear, the language of the Code, at least in the case of nonrecourse debt, is not. The relevant provisions are §§ 61(a)(3), 61(a)(12), and 1001(a) and (b). Section 61(a)(12) does not quite fit because it focuses on the debt alone and not on the transfer of property. Moreover, in the case of many transfers subject to debt there will be no reason to suppose that there is a gain from a favorable loan, such as was encountered in *Kirby Lumber*. Application of § 1001 (with § 61(a)(3)) requires that an assumption of debt by the transferee of the property be treated as an "amount realized," which requires a strained interpretation of that language, but that is the approach taken by the Court in *Tufts*. This approach seems to foreclose the application of § 108 and the treatment of any portion of the gain as ordinary income (which is the possibility associated with bifurcation).

2. *Comparison to the tax benefit rule.* *Tufts* provides a kind of tax benefit rule, whereby "a taxpayer must account for the proceeds of obligations he has

received tax-free and included in basis." Is inclusion in basis necessary for its tax benefit rationale to apply? Suppose one owned property with a basis and value of $1 million, and then borrowed $900,000 in cash under a nonrecourse mortgage of the property. If the property's value subsequently declined below $900,000 and one abandoned the property rather than repay the loan, *Tufts* presumably would require treating the abandonment as a sale of the property for $900,000. Here, however, it is the receipt of $900,000 in cash tax free, rather than inclusion in basis, that triggers application of the tax benefit rationale.

3. *Amount of recapture income.* Note 5 following the *Crane* case, supra, described the situation where the face amount of nonrecourse debt exceeds the fair market value of the property at the time of acquisition, causing the nonrecourse debt either to be entirely excluded from basis, as in Estate of Franklin v. Commissioner, or to be included to the extent of the property's value under Pleasant Summit Land Corp. v. Commissioner. Thus, if one paid $5,000 in cash for property that was worth $400,000 and was subject to a $1 million nonrecourse debt, one's basis for the property would be either $5,000 under *Estate of Franklin*, or $405,000 under *Pleasant Summit.*

In either case, if the taxpayer subsequently abandoned the property subject to the nonrecourse debt, what would be the amount realized under the tax-benefit-like reasoning of the Supreme Court in *Tufts*? Does the value of the property at the time of such abandonment make any difference for this purpose?

4. *Bifurcation.* The Supreme Court in *Tufts* respectfully rejected a "bifurcation" approach, under which the taxpayer would be treated at disposition as selling the property for its fair market value at that time, but would have cancellation of indebtedness income (subject to § 108) to the extent that such value was less than the face amount of the nonrecourse debt. However, bifurcation is the rule with respect to transactions in which property is transferred to a creditor in satisfaction of *recourse* debt. See Regs. § 1.1001-2(a)(2), (b), and Ex. 8; Gehl v. Commissioner, 102 T.C. 784 (1994), aff'd without op., 50 F.3d 12 (8th Cir. 1995); Rev. Rul. 90-16, 1990-1 Cum. Bull. 12; Danenberg v. Commissioner, 73 T.C. 370 (1979). Should this have affected the Supreme Court's willingness to consider adopting the bifurcation approach in *Tufts*?

H.   ILLEGAL INCOME

GILBERT v. COMMISSIONER
552 F.2d 478 (2d Cir. 1977)

Lumbard, Circuit Judge.

The taxpayer Edward M. Gilbert appeals from a determination by the tax court that he realized taxable income on certain unauthorized withdrawals of corporate funds made by him in 1962. We reverse.

Until June 12, 1962, Gilbert was president, principal stockholder, and a director of the E. L. Bruce Company, Inc., a New York corporation which was engaged in the lumber supply business. In 1961 and early 1962 Gilbert acquired on margin [that is, in large part with borrowed money] substantial personal and beneficial ownership of stock in another lumber supply company, the Celotex Corporation, intending ultimately to bring about a merger of Celotex into Bruce. To this end, he persuaded associates of his to purchase Celotex stock, guaranteeing them against loss, and also induced Bruce itself to purchase a substantial number of Celotex shares. In addition, on March 5, 1962, Gilbert granted Bruce an option to purchase his Celotex shares from him at cost. By the end of May 1962, 56% of Celotex was thus controlled by Gilbert and Bruce, and negotiations for the merger were proceeding; agreement had been reached that three of the directors of Bruce would be placed on the board of Celotex. It is undisputed that this merger would have been in Bruce's interest.

The stock market declined on May 28, 1962, however, and Gilbert was called upon to furnish additional margin [that is, individual funds] for the Celotex shares purchased by him and his associates. Lacking sufficient cash of his own to meet this margin call, Gilbert instructed the secretary of Bruce to use corporate funds to supply the necessary margin. Between May 28 and June 6 a series of checks totalling $1,958,000 were withdrawn from Bruce's accounts and used to meet the margin call. $5,000 was repaid to Bruce on June 5. According to his testimony in the tax court, Gilbert from the outset intended to repay all the money and at all times thought he was acting in the corporation's best interests as well as his own. He promptly informed several other Bruce officers and directors of the withdrawals; however, some were not notified until June 11 or 12.

On about June 1, Gilbert returned to New York from Nevada, where he had been attending to a personal matter. Shortly thereafter he consulted with Shearman, Sterling & Wright, who were outside counsel to Bruce at the time, regarding the withdrawals. They, he, and another Bruce director initiated negotiations to sell many of the Celotex shares to Ruberoid Company as a way of recouping most of Bruce's outlay.

On June 8, Gilbert went to the law offices of Shearman, Sterling & Wright and executed interest-bearing promissory notes to Bruce for $1,953,000 secured by an assignment of most of his property. The notes were callable by Bruce on demand, with presentment and notice of demand waived by Gilbert. The tax court found that up through June 12 the net value of the assets assigned for security by Gilbert substantially exceeded the amount owed.

After Gilbert informed other members of the Bruce board of directors of his actions, a meeting of the board was scheduled for the morning of June 12. At the meeting the board accepted the note and assignment but refused to ratify Gilbert's unauthorized withdrawals. During the meeting, word came that the board of directors of the Ruberoid Company had rejected the price offered for sale of the Celotex stock. Thereupon, the Bruce board demanded and received Gilbert's resignation and decided to issue a public announcement the next day regarding his unauthorized withdrawals. All further attempts on June 12 to arrange a sale of the Celotex stock fell through and in the evening Gilbert flew to Brazil, where he stayed for several months. On June 13 the market price of Bruce and Celotex stock plummeted, and trading in those shares was suspended by the Securities and Exchange Commission.

On June 22 the Internal Revenue Service filed tax liens against Gilbert based on a [claim of tax liability of] $1,720,000 for 1962. Bruce, having failed to file the assignment from Gilbert because of the real estate filing fee involved,[60] now found itself subordinate in priority to the IRS and, impeded by the tax lien, has never since been able to recover much of its $1,953,000 from the assigned assets.[61] For the fiscal year ending June 30, 1962, Bruce claimed a loss deduction on the $1,953,000 withdrawn by Gilbert. Several years later Gilbert pled guilty to federal and state charges of having unlawfully withdrawn the funds from Bruce.

On these facts, the tax court determined that Gilbert realized income when he made the unauthorized withdrawals of funds from Bruce, and that his efforts at restitution did not entitle him to any offset against this income.

The starting point for analysis of this case is James v. United States, 366 U.S. 213 (1961), which established that embezzled funds can constitute taxable income to the embezzler.

> When a taxpayer acquires earnings, lawfully or unlawfully, without the consensual recognition, express or implied, of an obligation to repay and without restriction as to their disposition, "he has received income which he is required to return, even though it may still be claimed that he is not entitled to the money, and even though he may still be adjudged liable to restore its equivalent." . . .

Id. at 219.

The Commissioner contends that there can never be "consensual recognition . . . of an obligation to repay" in an embezzlement case. He reasons that because the corporation — as represented by a majority of the board of directors — was unaware of the withdrawals, there cannot have been *consensual* recognition of the obligation to repay at the time the taxpayer Gilbert acquired the funds. Since the withdrawals were not authorized and the directors refused to treat them as a loan to Gilbert, the Commissioner concludes that Gilbert should be taxed like a thief rather than a borrower.

In a typical embezzlement, the embezzler intends at the outset to abscond with the funds. If he repays the money during the same taxable year, he will not be taxed. See James v. Commissioner, supra at 220; Quinn v. Commissioner, 524 F.2d 617, 624-625 (7th Cir. 1975); Rev. Rul. 65-254, 1965-2 Cum. Bul. 50. As we held in Buff v. Commissioner, 496 F.2d 847 (2d Cir. 1974), if he spends the loot instead of repaying, he cannot avoid tax on his embezzlement

---

60. When attempting to file in the New York County Clerk's office on June 13 or 14, Bruce was told that it would have to pay a mortgage tax of at least $10,000 because the assignment included real property. Since the net value of the real property was negligible, Bruce sought to perfect only the personal property portion, but the clerk still demanded the mortgage tax on the ground that the real property assignment and the personal property assignment were contained in the same document.

61. As of the date of trial in the tax court, less than $500,000 had been raised through sales of the assigned assets. Pursuant to an agreement reached between Bruce and the government in 1970, 35% of these proceeds have been paid over to the government pending the outcome of this lawsuit.

income simply by signing promissory notes later in the same year. See also id. at 849-850 (Oakes, J., concurring).

This is not a typical embezzlement case, however, and we do not interpret *James* as requiring income realization in every case of unlawful withdrawals by a taxpayer. There are a number of facts that differentiate this case from *Buff* and *James*. When Gilbert withdrew the corporate funds, he recognized his obligation to repay and intended to do so.[62] The funds were to be used not only for his benefit but also for the benefit of the corporation; meeting the margin calls was necessary to maintain the possibility of the highly favorable merger. Although Gilbert undoubtedly realized that he lacked the necessary authorization, he thought he was serving the best interests of the corporation and he expected his decision to be ratified shortly thereafter. That Gilbert at no time intended to retain the corporation's funds is clear from his actions.[63] He immediately informed several of the corporation's officers and directors, and he made a complete accounting to all of them within two weeks. He also disclosed his actions to the corporation's outside counsel, a reputable law firm, and followed its instructions regarding repayment. In signing immediately payable promissory notes secured by most of his assets, Gilbert's clear intent was to ensure that Bruce would obtain full restitution. In addition, he attempted to sell his shares of Celotex stock in order to raise cash to pay Bruce back immediately.

When Gilbert executed the assignment to Bruce of his assets on June 8 and when this assignment for security was accepted by the Bruce board on June 12, the net market value of these assets was substantially more than the amount owed. The Bruce board did not release Gilbert from his underlying obligation to repay, but the assignment was nonetheless valid and Bruce's failure to make an appropriate filing to protect itself against the claims of third parties, such as the IRS, did not relieve Gilbert of the binding effect of the assignment. Since the assignment secured an immediately payable note, Gilbert had as of June 12 granted Bruce full discretion to liquidate any of his assets in order to recoup on the $1,953,000 withdrawal. Thus, Gilbert's net accretion in real wealth on the overall transaction was zero: he had for his own use withdrawn $1,953,000 in corporate funds but he had now granted the corporation control over at least $1,953,000 worth of his assets.

We conclude that where a taxpayer withdraws funds from a corporation which he fully intends to repay and which he expects with reasonable certainty he will be able to repay, where he believes that his withdrawals will be approved by the corporation, and where he makes a prompt assignment of assets sufficient to secure the amount owed, he does not realize income on the withdrawals under the *James* test. When Gilbert acquired the money, there was an express consensual recognition of his obligation to repay: the secretary of the corporation, who signed the checks, the officers and directors to whom

---

62. Quinn v. Commissioner, relied on by the Commissioner, involved taxation of funds received without any contemporaneous recognition of the obligation to repay, and it is therefore distinguishable from the present case.

63. If Gilbert had been intending to abscond with the $1,953,000, it is difficult to see how he could have hoped to avoid detection in the long run. Since his equity in the corporation itself was worth well over $1,953,000, it would have been absurd for him to attempt such a theft.

Gilbert gave contemporaneous notification, and Gilbert himself were all aware that the transaction was in the nature of a loan. Moreover, the funds were certainly not received by Gilbert "without restriction as to their disposition" as is required for taxability under *James*; the money was to be used solely for the temporary purpose of meeting certain margin calls and it was so used. For these reasons, we reverse the decision of the tax court.

NOTES AND QUESTIONS

1. *Analysis.* The court says, "In a typical embezzlement, the embezzler intends at the outset to abscond with the funds." That may well be true, but in many instances the embezzler fully intends to repay, as soon as his or her horse, lottery ticket, or high-tech stock investment pays off. If misfortune becomes evident within two weeks and an embezzler confesses, and promises repayment, are the proceeds of the embezzlement nontaxable?

2. *The special status of embezzlers.* The decision of the Supreme Court in James v. United States, relied on by the court in *Gilbert*, overruled an earlier decision of the Court in Commissioner v. Wilcox, 327 U.S. 404 (1946), in which it had held that embezzled funds were not income because of the obligation to restore the funds to the victim. This decision was at odds with a later decision in Rutkin v. United States, 343 U.S. 130 (1952), in which the Court held an extortionist liable for tax on the amount extorted, but the Rutkin Court had expressly refused to overrule *Wilcox*. *James* was thought to have laid to rest the confusion and inconsistency created by the *Rutkin-Wilcox* distinction. Does the *Gilbert* decision revive the confusion and uncertainty to some degree?

3. *Dirty business?* Is it unseemly for the government, by taxing the proceeds of an embezzlement, to share in the profits of an illegal activity? This was the view expressed by Judge Martin T. Manton of the Second Circuit Court of Appeals in a concurring opinion in Steinberg v. United States, 14 F.2d 564, 569 (1926). Judge Manton also expressed his dismay over the thought of the government allowing deductions for bribes. In an O. Henry ending, Judge Manton was convicted in 1939 of accepting bribes of more than $66,000 over a three-year period when he was senior circuit judge of the Second Circuit and in 1948, after his death, was held liable for fraud penalties for failing to report the bribes on his tax returns. 7 T.C.M. 937.

4. *Borrowing versus swindling.* A taxpayer who purports to borrow funds, or to receive them as investments, may in fact be a swindler. The line between the two possibilities may in some instances be difficult to draw. See In re Diversified Brokers Co., 487 F.2d 355 (8th Cir. 1973) (receipts in "Ponzi" pyramiding scheme treated as loans to corporate borrower rather than as embezzled funds); Moore v. United States, 412 F.2d 974 (5th Cir. 1969) (money received in complex scheme involving purported purchase of equipment that did not exist held to be the fruits of a swindle, not a loan). Would it be best in situations of this sort to wait and see how a person uses the funds, instead of examining the circumstances of receipt?

5. *Nontax objectives.* The use of selective tax enforcement to punish political enemies is plainly intolerable. But what about selective enforcement against

"known" crime figures who cannot be convicted of other crimes? Al Capone, the Chicago mob leader who was reportedly guilty of a host of serious crimes, was ultimately sent to jail for tax evasion. Is it wrong to use the tax system deliberately to punish people like Capone?

6. *Adding injury to injury.* As the *Gilbert* case illustrates, the taxes collected from an embezzler (or other wrongdoer) by the IRS generally will come from funds that otherwise would be returned (or paid) to the victim; generally the IRS's claim for taxes comes before the victim's claim for recovery of the stolen money.[64]

An interesting example of the IRS attitude toward victims of embezzlement is found in Letter Ruling 8604003. The embezzler, a bank employee, had disguised his defalcation by making false book entries showing wage payments (in amounts reaching a total of about $1 million). As part of his scheme he paid Social Security taxes (FICA) and withholding taxes. The bank, on discovering that it had been victimized, sought to recover the taxes. The IRS refused. It defended this result by arguments in the alternative. On the one hand, it reasoned, if the amounts were wages to the embezzler, the taxes were properly withheld. On the other hand, if the wage payments and the corresponding tax payments were unauthorized, then the bank did not make any payments, the embezzler did; so the bank is not entitled to a recovery on the theory of a mistaken payment. Moreover, the IRS is entitled to keep the money as long as the amount does not exceed what the embezzler owes. As far as the IRS is concerned, once money is stolen, that money belongs to the thief and the thief must pay his or her taxes before returning anything to the victim.

I. INTEREST ON STATE AND LOCAL BONDS

1. Basic Concepts

Section 103 exempts from taxation the interest on certain state, municipal, and other such bonds. This exemption serves as a good model of some general tax principles.

One of the most important observations to be made about tax-exempt bonds is that the holders of such bonds pay what may be called a "putative" tax. Tax-exempt bonds pay a lower rate of interest than taxable bonds because people buying tax-exempts are willing to accept a lower rate in order to obtain the exemption. The relationship between the taxable and the tax-exempt rate varies from time to time, but the tax-exempt rate is always lower than the taxable rate. Suppose that the interest rate on taxable bonds is 10 percent and the rate on comparable tax-exempts is 8 percent. A taxpayer in the 20 percent

---

64. Under § 6321 the United States has a lien for unpaid taxes after demand for the tax owed. The lien is against all the property of the taxpayer, which, in the case of an embezzler, will include the embezzled funds. This lien will take priority over any claim of the victim unless the victim is able to file a judgment lien (that is, obtain a judgment against the embezzler and then file a lien on the embezzled funds) before the IRS files its lien. See § 6323. As a practical matter, the IRS will be able to file its lien before the victim will be able to file its lien.

marginal tax bracket should then be indifferent between taxable and tax-exempt alternatives.

If such a person were to invest $100,000 in a taxable bond the annual interest earned would be $10,000 and the tax would be $2,000, leaving a net return after tax of $8,000, which is the same as the return on an investment of the same amount in a tax-exempt. The $2,000 of additional pretax interest that the investor forgoes by investing in the tax-exempt may be thought of as a putative tax. The federal government loses $2,000 of tax that it would have received if the investor had bought a taxable bond, but the state or local entity that issued the tax-exempt bond saves $2,000, the difference between the interest it pays ($8,000) and the interest it would have to pay if the interest were taxable to the recipient ($10,000). There is simply a shift from the federal to the state or local treasury. The investor receives no windfall; there is no violation of either horizontal or vertical equity. The putative tax is equal in amount to the actual tax that is avoided. One might object that if funds are in effect to be shifted from federal to state or local coffers, the federal government should be allowed to decide on the kinds of projects or activities on which the money is to be spent and on the total amount that is to be made available. But the lack of control from Washington is precisely the reason why some people like the exemption. And if controls are thought to be desirable, they can be imposed as a condition for qualifying bonds for exemption, as recent legislative development has amply demonstrated. See §§ 103(b), 142-151.

The picture changes, however, when purchasers have incomes such that their marginal rates are greater than the spread between the tax-exempt and the taxable rate (in our hypothetical 20 percent). For a person taxed at a marginal rate of 30 percent, if the taxable rate is 10 percent and the tax-exempt rate is 8 percent, then on an investment of $100,000, the after-tax return on the taxable investment will be $7,000 while the after-tax return on the tax-exempt investment will be $8,000. Such an investor pays a putative tax of $2,000 by buying a tax-exempt instead of an actual tax of $3,000 on a taxable investment and therefore saves $1,000 in taxes by buying the tax-exempt. The putative tax is at a rate of only 20 percent, while the nominal rate is 30 percent. The federal government loses $3,000, while the state or local government gains only $2,000. Since most individual investors are in fact in the higher brackets, many analysts argue that the exemption is an inefficient method of federal subsidy to state and local government and that it confers indefensible benefits on investors. As to the latter objection (windfalls to investors), however, one should add the qualification that horizontal equity among *investors* is not the issue, since tax-exempt investment is equally available to all high-bracket investors. One should be concerned only about the effects of the exemption on vertical equity and on horizontal equity between investors and people with incomes from salaries. Suppose, for example, that two taxpayers, Adele and Bernardo, both have inherited $1 million. Adele invests in U.S. Treasury bonds that pay 10 percent or $100,000 per year. She pays an income tax of $28,000 on this amount, and has no other income, so she is left with a spendable $72,000. Bernardo invests his $1 million in state general obligation bonds that pay 8 percent or $80,000, and he, too, has no other income. He pays no tax so his spendable amount is the full $80,000. If Adele were to complain about her treatment relative to that of Bernardo, it might be sufficient to respond that she is free to sell her Treasury bonds and buy state bonds. But now let's add another taxpayer, Carlos, who earns $100,000 in salary and has no investments. He pays tax at a rate of 28 percent, or $28,000, and is left with $72,000. When he complains of his treatment relative to that of Bernardo, there is no easy answer.

These observations about the effects of the exemption of interest on state and municipal bonds are relevant to other tax-favored investments. Investors in certain kinds of real estate projects, in oil and gas drilling ventures, and in various other kinds of tax shelters generally have been forced to accept a lower before-tax rate of return than they could have earned in fully taxed investments (though the complexity of tax shelter investments makes clear-cut comparisons with taxable alternatives difficult). Such investors have paid a putative tax. Similarly, investors in the common stock of corporations that have paid little tax could expect to earn no greater return than investors in the common stock of corporations that have been heavily taxed. The lightly taxed corporations pay a putative tax. Generally, tax subsidies do not raise problems of horizontal equity, but they do raise problems of vertical equity and of efficiency.

2. Limitations on Exempt Status

Increasingly over the past two decades, state and local governments used their ability to borrow at low rates to finance projects having little or nothing to do with traditional governmental activities. The most important manifestation of this trend was the "industrial revenue bond" (IRB),[65] a bond whose proceeds were used to finance private investment, generally in an effort to lure industry to a community (in competition, often, with other communities offering the same financial incentive). The payment of interest and principal on such bonds is solely the responsibility of the user of the property bought or built with the proceeds; the local government unit that is the purported borrower is strictly an intermediary, with no financial risk.

Congress has responded by imposing limitations on the use of tax-exempt financing for private purposes. For example, some limitations are based on the purpose for which the proceeds are used and require specific provisions defining permissible purposes. The result is that the law, once simple, has become detailed and complex. See §§ 103, 142-151. Exemption continues to be available, without limit, for bonds whose proceeds are used for traditional governmental purposes such as financing schools, roads, and sewers. All other bonds are called "private-activity bonds" and are not exempt unless they fit within a specific exception. One major exception is for "exempt-facility bonds." These include bonds used to finance airports, docks and wharves, mass commuting facilities, water and sewage disposal facilities, qualified hazardous waste facilities, and certain electric and gas facilities. Other categories of private-activity

65. Also sometimes referred to as industrial development bonds (IDBs).

bonds that qualify for exemption include qualified mortgage bonds (for financing home purchases by middle- and low-income people) and qualified veterans' mortgage bonds, qualified small-issue (not more than $1 million) bonds, and bonds used for certain charitable purposes. The income on certain private-activity bonds, though exempt from the regular tax, may be subject to the alternative minimum tax (see infra page 611).

In addition to the purpose-related limitations, there is an overall, or aggregate, dollar volume limit, or "cap," on most categories of newly issued private-activity bonds for which exemption is available. Beginning in 1988, the limit in each state is the greater of (1) $50 per resident or (2) $150 million. The states may allocate the total among their subdivisions and agencies. If they fail to do so, the allocation is made according to rules set forth in the Code (§ 146).

There are also rules designed to prevent "arbitrage" — that is, to prevent a state or local government from borrowing at tax-exempt rates and investing in taxable obligations with the expectation of profiting on the spread in interest rates. § 148. It is easier to describe the problem than to prescribe a solution. A state or local government, with no intention of engaging in arbitrage, may issue bonds for an exempt purpose and collect the proceeds before it is ready to spend those proceeds. In the interim the proceeds will, of course, be invested at the highest available rate. The question presented is at what point this process calls for the application of the arbitrage rules.

3. Constitutional Barrier?

In South Carolina v. Baker, 485 U.S. 505 (1988), the Court upheld the requirement (now in § 149(a)) that interest on otherwise qualifying bonds is not tax exempt unless the bonds are registered and subject to certain reporting requirements. In so holding, the Court rejected the notion that there is a constitutional barrier to the imposition of a federal income tax on the interest earned on obligations issued by a state or one of its instrumentalities. In a study published in 1989, economist James Poterba showed that municipal bond futures prices dropped sharply in the hour following the announcement of the Supreme Court's decision in South Carolina v. Baker, presumably because of the new legal risk that the tax-exemption might actually be repealed. As Poterba noted, however, "[i]n the hours immediately following the decision, key Congressional leaders indicated support for retaining tax-exempt treatment for interest . . . and by the end of the trading day the rapid decline in municipal bond prices had been reversed." See James Poterba, Tax Reform and the Market for Tax-Exempt Debt, 19 Regional Science and Urban Economics 537, 556 (1989).

4. Tax Arbitrage

Tax-exempt bonds offer a good vehicle for describing a general tax strategy called "arbitrage" and to examine its effects. Suppose an individual taxpayer, T, has taxable income from a salary of $90,000 per year, pays tax at a marginal rate of 33 percent, and has no investments. *T* borrows $100,000 at 10 percent, or $10,000, per year, and uses the loan proceeds to buy tax-exempt bonds that pay 9 percent, or $9,000, per year. Suppose that the annual $10,000 interest payment is deductible (in fact, under § 265(2), it is not). The transaction—the loan and the investment—would cost *T* $1,000 before taxes (the difference between the interest paid and the interest received), but the $10,000 deduction would reduce *T*'s taxes by $3,300, so *T* would be ahead by $2,300. The tax savings arise, of course, because *T*'s interest expense is deductible, while *T*'s interest income is tax exempt.

The transaction described above would not have changed *T*'s net asset position. The $100,000 investment in the tax-exempt bond would be offset by the $100,000 loan liability, so net assets would still be zero. *T* could be thought of as having "bought" an asset (the borrowed funds) in one market (the taxable market) and as having "sold" a virtually identical asset (the funds loaned to the state or local government) in another market (the tax-exempt market) with the sole objective of taking advantage of the differing tax regimes in the two markets. Assuming that the loan and the investment are of the same duration, it is plain that the transaction would not have taken place but for its tax effects. That is tax arbitrage.

If permitted to do so, the states might also engage in purely tax-motivated transactions involving the interplay between taxable and tax-exempt obligations. For example, a state might issue its tax-exempt bonds at an interest rate of 9 percent and invest the proceeds in Treasury bonds paying 10 percent. This would be another form of tax arbitrage and, again, as we have just seen, is not permitted.

Now we are ready to consider some of the possible economic consequences of arbitrage. Suppose that arbitrage by issuers of state and local bonds is prohibited. There is a limited need for funds for the purposes for which tax-exempt bonds can be issued, so the supply of such bonds is limited. Now suppose we repeal § 265(2) and allow a deduction for interest incurred on loans whose proceeds are used to purchase tax-exempt bonds. More people would now be able to buy such bonds. The demand would increase. The probable effect would be that investors would compete for the bonds by accepting lower and lower interest rates until only people in the highest marginal tax brackets would be willing to buy them and all the advantage of the tax exemption would be eliminated. In other words, the putative tax discussed above (page 201) would equal the actual tax that would be avoided and the effect of the exemption would be to reduce state and local borrowing costs by the full amount of the revenue lost by the U.S. Treasury. Some tax experts argue that this would be a good thing and that § 265(2) should be repealed.

Suppose we retain the § 265(2) restrictions on purchasers, but allow state and local governments to engage in arbitrage. Presumably they would issue more and more tax-exempt bonds and buy more and more U.S. Treasury (or other taxable) bonds. As they did so, the rate the states and local governments would be required to pay on the bonds they issued would rise and the rates paid on taxable bonds would fall until the two rates would be the same and all the advantage of arbitrage would be eliminated. Taxpayers could then buy tax-exempt bonds without paying any putative tax.

Suppose we allow both purchasers and issuers to engage in arbitrage. The arbitrage of purchasers would tend to increase demand and price; the arbitrage of issuers would tend to increase supply and decrease price. The final outcome, or equilibrium position, would be difficult to predict, but fortunately we need not worry about that. What is important, for people who want to understand the workings of the tax system, is a general understanding of the process of arbitrage.

One final point: The proposition that state and local governments should be allowed to engage in arbitrage may seem so dangerous and so inconsistent with the purposes of exemption as to be unthinkable, and it probably is. But thinking the unthinkable may cast light on underlying principles. Consider two hypothetical states, A and B. A relies heavily on borrowing and by virtue of doing so in effect receives a large subsidy from the U.S. Treasury in the form of reduced interest costs attributable to the exemption from federal income taxation of the interest it pays on its obligations. B does not borrow at all. Its citizens, believing that borrowing is unfair to future generations, are proud of their pay-as-you-go tradition. B receives no benefits from the U.S. Treasury comparable to A's interest-rate subsidy. If we were prepared to allow arbitrage (with, perhaps, a dollar limit on total debt), we could allow B to obtain the same subsidy that A receives — a possibility that seems to have some appeal to a sense of fairness and that recognizes the importance of allowing states to adopt the fiscal policies they prefer without unwarranted interference from the federal government. But if we were prepared to allow B to obtain a subsidy by engaging in arbitrage, would it not be more effective for the federal government simply to write out a check and save all the transactions costs? If so, what are the implications for the treatment of A?

5.   U.S. Treasury Bonds

Section 135, added by the 1988 act, exempts from taxation the interest on certain U.S. Treasury savings bonds if the proceeds of the redemption of the bonds do not exceed tuition and fees for higher education for the taxpayer and her or his spouse or dependents. The exclusion is phased out as income rises above $40,000 ($60,000 for a joint return), with the phaseout levels to be adjusted for inflation. There is no tracing of funds, so even if other funds are in fact used to pay the education expenses, the exemption is available. One may wonder why education is singled out, as compared, for example, with medical expenses or the down payment on a house.

J.   GAIN ON THE SALE OF A HOME

According to the U.S. Census Bureau, more than two-thirds of Americans own their homes. While the homeownership rate has declined slightly in the past few years, having peaked at 69 percent in 2004, at no time since 1960 have fewer than 62 percent of Americans owned their own homes. Moreover, for the typical American family the principal residence is by far the most valuable asset they own, dominating the household's investment portfolio. It is perhaps not surprising, therefore, that Congress has turned to the tax code to curry favor with America's homeowners. We have already seen that the non-taxation of imputed rental income is one of the key benefits available for owner-occupied housing. We now turn to a more explicit benefit available for the American homeowner — the exclusion of gain from the sale of one's principal residence.

Section 121 excludes from income certain gain on the sale or exchange of a home. In order for the exclusion to apply, the taxpayer must have owned the home and used it as a principal residence for periods aggregating at least two years over the five-year period ending on the date the taxpayer sold it. § 121(a). Thus, the sale of a vacation home generally would not qualify for the exclusion.

The amount of gain that § 121 excludes from income on a given home sale is generally limited to $250,000. Section 121(b)(1). Thus, suppose a taxpayer sold for $400,000 a home that she had bought for $100,000. Assuming that the sale otherwise qualified under § 121, $50,000 of the gain (the excess of the overall gain of $300,000 over the exclusion limit) would be taxable.

For married taxpayers filing a joint return, the exclusion limit is $500,000 rather than $250,000, so long as both spouses have used the home as a principal residence for two of the prior five years. § 121(b)(2). Exclusion at the $500,000 level is also available for surviving spouses, provided that the sale takes place within two years of the date of death of the deceased spouse and the ownership and holding period requirements were satisfied as of that date. § 121(b)(4).

Section 121 generally cannot apply to any taxpayer more than once every two years. § 121(b)(3)(A). Thus, if on January 25 of Year 1 a taxpayer made a qualifying sale of a principal residence for an amount that was at least 1 cent greater than her basis for the property, the exclusion could not apply again until January 25 of Year 3.[66] However, this limitation is called off if the sale or exchange was "by reason of a change in place of employment, health, or, to the extent provided in regulations, unforeseen circumstances." § 121(c)(2)(B).

These same grounds also permit exclusion up to a reduced dollar ceiling for taxpayers who failed to meet the two-year use requirement. For example, if an unmarried taxpayer lived in a principal residence for exactly one year before moving, due to a transfer from the New York to the California office of her employer, § 121 would permit exclusion of up to $125,000 of gain upon its sale.

NOTES AND QUESTIONS

1. Section 121 was added to the Code in 1997. Prior to its enactment, gain upon the sale of a home could be "rolled over" (and thus not currently

---

66. This limitation is not merely redundant of the two-year use requirement because taxpayers can move into new principal residences before selling previous ones.

included in income) to the extent that the sale proceeds were reinvested within a two-year period through the purchase of a new home. (§ 1034, repealed in 1997.) In addition, a repealed prior version of § 121 provided a limited one-time exclusion of gain on the sale of a principal residence to taxpayers who were age 55 or older. This rule was apparently designed to help "empty-nesters," who sold their homes and bought smaller ones (thus potentially failing to reinvest fully) when their children moved out.

2. What policy arguments, if any, support the current version of § 121? Is the exclusion supported by the fact that losses on the sale of a home are considered personal in character and thus are not deductible? If so, should the exclusion be unlimited? And should gambling gains be excluded from income on the same rationale?

3. Section 121 arguably creates various incentives for taxpayers to alter their behavior so they can take full advantage of it. For example, if you have a vacation home that has appreciated significantly and that you plan to sell soon, the provision can motivate using it as a principal residence for two years even if you otherwise would not have chosen to do so. Or, if your home has appreciated to about the full statutory limit and you expect homes in general to continue appreciating, the provision creates an incentive to sell now and buy a new home so that you can start excluding appreciation all over again.

Are these incentives likely to have much effect on people's behavior? Even if not, do the disparities in tax treatment that give rise to them tell you anything about § 121?

K.   SPECIAL RATE FOR DIVIDENDS

Dividends (that is, distributions by corporations to their shareholders) are included in gross income. See § 61(a)(7). In 2003, however, Congress added § 1(h)(11), which applies to dividends the same tax rate as is applied to capital gains. This is accomplished in a somewhat peculiar, but effective, way by adding dividends to net capital gain. See § 1(h)(11)(A). The result is that, for taxpayers with income above the exempt threshold, dividends are taxed at a rate of 5 percent for those whose ordinary income is taxed at a rate of 25 percent or less and at a rate of 15 percent for those whose income is taxed at a higher rate. Thus, there is a 20 percent spread between the top individual rate (35 percent beginning in 2003) and the dividend rate for people in that bracket.[67]

In addition to the obvious reduction in tax burden, particularly for people in high marginal tax brackets and with substantial dividend income, the effect

---

67. Under § 1(h), however, dividend income is added to taxable income and then taxed at the special rate. The addition to taxable income can increase the effective rate above 15 percent for people subject to the Alternative Minimum Tax (AMT). Moreover, for such people, because the AMT disallows a deduction for state and local income taxes, the dividend income will pay the full state rate with no offsetting federal tax benefit.

of the lowered rate will be to reduce tax disincentives to the payment of dividends and to reward certain investment strategies by individuals. For example, suppose an individual has $200,000 in a qualified pension trust and $200,000 in ordinary savings, and wishes to hold half of the total in common stocks that pay dividends and half in bonds that pay interest. The tax-efficient strategy is to hold all the bonds in the pension trust and all the common stock in the ordinary, taxable, account. This is the preferred strategy because the income of the pension trust is nontaxable, but the ultimate distributions from the trust to its individual owner are taxable as ordinary income, so the favorable rate on dividends does the owner/taxpayer no good. It is worth noting, however, that the same strategy would have been advisable before the 2003 reduction in the rate of tax on dividends, to the extent that the taxpayer anticipated (as typically would be the case) that most of the return on the holdings of common stock would be in the form of capital appreciation, which would escape taxation until the stock was sold and would then be taxed at the lower rates applicable to capital gain.

The principal rationale relied upon by the members of Congress and the White House to support the favorable treatment of dividends was that income earned by corporations and paid out as dividends is taxed twice — once as earned by the corporation and again as distributed to shareholders as dividends. This double taxation, it was claimed, resulted in unfairness and economic distortion. The lowered rate (as opposed to complete elimination of the double taxation) reflected a compromise with those who challenged the rationale (on various grounds) or who considered that the lost revenue was either unaffordable or could have been put to better use.

3

PROBLEMS OF TIMING

The previous chapter examined the question, "What is income?" Whether your role is advising a client or advocating tax reform, understanding the scope of the tax base is obviously important. Yet another question—"*When* is it income?"—is often just as important. Indeed, the question of when a tax liability arises is one of the most significant issues in all of tax law. At first blush, this may seem somewhat surprising. To the uninitiated, questions of timing appear to be decidedly second-order. After all, if a taxpayer knows that she must eventually pay tax on *x* amount of income, isn't the timing of that payment just a minor ancillary detail? The answer, depending on your tolerance for exclamation marks, is either (a) No!, (b) No!!, or (c) No!!! As it turns out, what looks to the unschooled like a collateral issue undeserving of serious attention is in fact a core concern of tax planning and tax policy. Understanding why is a critical step toward developing a professional expertise in tax law.

Timing is important for at least two reasons. First, and most obviously, tax rates may vary from year to year. One source of tax rate variation is the system of progressive marginal tax rates. For example, consider a farmer with fluctuating income who is subject to a top marginal tax rate of 35 percent in Year 1 and 15 percent in Year 2. Any set of tax rules that allows taxpayers the flexibility to manipulate the timing of income recognition will obviously give the farmer an incentive to shift income to Year 2 to enjoy the benefit of the lower tax rate. In this example, shifting the timing of income recognition by one year is the equivalent of avoiding a 20 percent tax. Tax rate variation may also arise from legislative changes in the tax rate schedule. Historically, year-over-year variation in tax rates has been a significant feature of the U.S. tax system, especially in those years immediately preceding, during, and immediately following the country's major wars.

Even leaving aside tax rate variation, however, timing issues are important because of the time value of money. Because money can generally earn interest, taxpayers almost always prefer to defer tax liability (subject to the sometimes countervailing incentive to exploit rate differentials, just discussed), while the IRS, at least when revenue-conscious, may want to accelerate it. Consider the issue from the perspective of a taxpayer who knows that she must include $5,000 in income at some point and that, no matter which year the amount is included in income, the tax rate will be 20 percent for a tax liability of $1,000. If she can earn interest at an after-tax rate of, say, 5 percent, then postponing a $1,000 tax liability for one year reduces its present value from $1,000 to $952. That is, she would need to set aside (and invest at 5 percent) only $952 today in order to have $1,000 to pay in a year, whereas it would obviously cost her $1,000 to pay $1,000 of tax today. Permit the deferral of a $1,000 tax liability to last for, say, ten years instead of one, and its present value declines to $641.

As the materials that follow demonstrate, U.S. tax law provides ample opportunity for taxpayers to shift the timing of their tax liabilities from one year to another. The tax lawyer who understands the importance of timing will always be a step ahead of those who don't.

A.   GAINS AND LOSSES FROM INVESTMENT IN PROPERTY

Perhaps the most important timing issues in the federal income tax are those relating to the realization and recognition of gains and losses from investment in property. In general, gain or loss resulting from a change in the value of an asset held by the taxpayer is not taken into account under the income tax until a "realization" event occurs (such as sale), and even then only in the absence of an applicable "nonrecognition" statute (one that provides that the gain or loss from the realization event can, at least for the present, be ignored).

To illustrate, consider taxpayer *A* who buys for $100,000 an asset that rises in value by $20,000 during the year. The asset is not sold, so the gain is not "realized" and is not taxed. Taxpayer *B* buys for $100,000 a similar asset that also rises in value; he sells for a profit of $20,000. Under the realization approach, *B*'s profit is taxable, even if *B* reinvests the $20,000, along with the $100,000, in some other asset. Taxpayer *C* receives a salary of $20,000, which he invests, along with $100,000 previously saved, in some asset. Like *B*'s profit, *C*'s $20,000 salary will be fully taxed. In the end, each taxpayer experiences a similar $20,000 increase in wealth, yet *B* and *C* are taxed, while *A* escapes taxation (at least for now). Fairness and economic rationality argue for treating all three taxpayers the same. Practicality, however, is generally thought to argue for nontaxation of *A*'s gain, largely because that gain may be difficult to measure and because *A* may not have easy access to cash with which to pay a tax.

1.   Legal Origins of the Realization Doctrine

Our first case, Eisner v. Macomber, is one of the most famous and significant decisions in the history of U.S. tax law. As noted in the previous chapter, the opinion's notoriety derives in part from its now-disparaged definition of income. See supra page 48. The case is also important, however, for its enthusiastic adoption of the requirement, as a condition for taxing gain, that the gain be "realized" — that is, that there be something more than a mere increase in value. The Court holds, in fact, that the realization requirement is embedded in the Sixteenth Amendment. This use of the Constitution to constrain congressional authority in tax matters is not consonant with modern theories of the proper role of the judiciary in the development of the tax law. Most analysts believe that the present-day Court would decide the case differently. Still, study of the case is important not only because of its contribution to the concept of income, and as a part of the history of taxation and of American attitudes toward taxation, but also because of the insights it offers into problems of realization and recognition.

EISNER v. MACOMBER
252 U.S. 189 (1920)

Mr. Justice PITNEY delivered the opinion of the Court.

This case presents the question whether, by virtue of the Sixteenth Amendment, Congress has the power to tax, as income of the stockholder and without apportionment, a stock dividend made lawfully and in good faith against profits accumulated by the corporation since March 1, 1913.

It arises under the Revenue Act of September 8, 1916, c.463, 39 Stat. 756, et seq., which, in our opinion . . . plainly evinces the purpose of Congress to tax stock dividends as income.[1]

[In 1916, the taxpayer, Mrs. Myrtle H. Macomber, owned 2,200 shares of the common stock of Standard Oil Company of California. Each of her shares had a "par value" of $100 per share. In the era in which this case arose, par value was a significant financial and accounting concept; generally, it reflected the amount initially paid to the company for each share, or at least a minimum amount that could be paid; in the aggregate, the amounts paid as par value were labeled, on the company's books, "capital" or "capital stock," with any excess paid, over par value, called "capital surplus" or "paid in surplus" or something of the sort. The company over the years had earned profits substantially in excess of the amounts paid out as dividends on the common stock. Such retained earnings are recorded on the books of a company under a heading such as "earned surplus." By strict accounting convention, the company must show on its books assets corresponding in value to the par value

---

1. TITLE I. INCOME TAX *Part I. On Individuals.* Sec. 2(a) That, subject only to such exemptions and deductions as are hereinafter allowed, the net income of a taxable person shall include gains, profits, and income derived . . . , also from interest, rent, dividends, securities, or the transaction of any business carried on for gain or profit, or gains or profits and income derived from any source whatever: Provided, That the term "dividends" as used in this title shall be held to mean any distribution made or ordered to be made by a corporation, . . . out of its earnings or profits accrued since March first, nineteen hundred and thirteen, and payable to its shareholders, whether in cash or in stock of the corporation, . . . which stock dividend shall be considered income, to the amount of its cash value.

plus the earned surplus (though this book value might be different from market value). Generally, dividends can be paid only to the extent of the earned surplus. In 1916, the company declared a 50 percent stock dividend. This meant that the company issued to each and every existing shareholder one new share for each two old shares, without cost to the shareholders. Accordingly, Mrs. Macomber received 1,100 new shares to add to her 2,200 original shares. The issuance of the new shares required a bookkeeping adjustment by the company: For each new share issued, the par value of that share, $100, was transferred from the earned surplus account to the par value, or capital, account. That amount of earned surplus (undistributed profits) was then said to have been "capitalized." In some instances such an adjustment might improve the creditworthiness of the company by limiting its freedom to pay dividends, though lenders of large sums can bargain for contractual limitations on dividend payments. Otherwise, the adjustment is purely a matter of changing bookkeeping labels. It has no effect whatsoever on underlying economic values or on operations.

According to the record in the case (at pages 4-5), the market value of Mrs. Macomber's shares before the stock dividend was $360 to $382 per share and after the stock dividend was $234 to $268 per share. In other words, the price of each share fell by about 30 to 35 percent, so that Mrs. Macomber's wealth was not significantly altered by the stock dividend. This is what one would expect, since the total value of the company, and her pro rata share of that total value, both remained the same. (Modern studies confirm the hypothesis that stock dividends do not increase wealth.)

The government sought to impose a tax on Mrs. Macomber based on the par value of the new shares, rather than the market value. However, of the amounts transferred by the company from earned surplus to capital, only 18.07 percent had arisen after the imposition of an income tax in 1913, and it was only this portion of the total that the government claimed to be taxable. Accordingly, the amount the government included in income was 18.07 percent of $100 multiplied by 1,100 shares, or $19,877. — Eds.]

[In Towne v. Eisner, 245 U.S. 418,] we rejected the reasoning of the District Court, saying (245 U.S. 426):

> Notwithstanding the thoughtful discussion that the case received below we cannot doubt that the dividend was capital as well for the purposes of the Income Tax Law as for distribution between tenant for life and remainderman. What was said by this court upon the latter question is equally true for the former. "A stock dividend really takes nothing from the property of the corporation, and adds nothing to the interests of the shareholders. Its property is not diminished, and their interests are not increased. . . . The proportional interest of each shareholder remains the same. The only change is in the evidence which represents that interest, the new shares and the original shares together representing the same proportional interest that the original shares represented before the issue of the new ones." Gibbons v. Mahon, 136 U.S. 549, 559, 560. In short, the corporation is no poorer and the stockholder is no richer than they were before. . . .

. . . We ruled at the same term, in Lynch v. Hornby, 247 U.S. 339, that a cash dividend extraordinary in amount, and in Peabody v. Eisner, 247 U.S.

347, that a dividend paid in stock of another company, were taxable as income although based upon earnings that accrued before adoption of the Amendment. In the former case, concerning "corporate profits that accumulated before the Act took effect," we declared (pp. 343-344):

> Just as we deem the legislative intent manifest to tax the stockholder with respect to such accumulations only if and when, and to the extent that, his interest in them comes to fruition as income, that is, in dividends declared, so we can perceive no constitutional obstacle that stands in the way of carrying out this intent when dividends are declared out of a preexisting surplus. . . . Congress was at liberty under the Amendment to tax as income, without apportionment, everything that became income, in the ordinary sense of the word, after the adoption of the Amendment, including dividends received in the ordinary course by a stockholder from a corporation, even though they were extraordinary in amount and might appear upon analysis to be a mere realization in possession of an inchoate and contingent interest that the stockholder had in a surplus of corporate assets previously existing. . . .

The Sixteenth Amendment must be construed in connection with the taxing clauses of the original Constitution and the effect attributed to them before the Amendment was adopted. In Pollock v. Farmers' Loan & Trust Co., 158 U.S. 601, under the Act of August 27, 1894, c.349, § 27, 28 Stat. 509, 553, it was held that taxes upon rents and profits of real estate and upon returns from investments of personal property were in effect direct taxes upon the property from which such income arose, imposed by reason of ownership; and that Congress could not impose such taxes without apportioning them among the States according to population, as required by Art. I, § 2, cl. 3, and § 9, cl. 4, of the original Constitution.

Afterwards, and evidently in recognition of the limitation upon the taxing power of Congress thus determined, the Sixteenth Amendment was adopted, in words lucidly expressing the object to be accomplished:

> The Congress shall have power to lay and collect taxes on incomes, from whatever source derived without apportionment among the several States, and without regard to any census or enumeration.

As repeatedly held, this did not extend the taxing power to new subjects, but merely removed the necessity which otherwise might exist for an apportionment among the States of taxes laid on income. . . .

A proper regard for its genesis, as well as its very clear language, requires also that this Amendment shall not be extended by loose construction, so as to repeal or modify, except as applied to income, those provisions of the Constitution that require an apportionment according to population for direct taxes upon property, real and personal. This limitation still has an appropriate and important function, and is not to be overridden by Congress or disregarded by the courts.

In order, therefore, that the clauses cited from Article I of the Constitution may have proper force and effect, save only as modified by the Amendment, and that the latter also may have proper effect, it becomes essential to distinguish between what is and what is not "income," as the term is there used; and to apply the distinction, as cases arise, according to truth and substance, without regard to form. Congress cannot by any definition it may adopt conclude the matter, since it cannot by legislation alter the Constitution, from which alone it derives its power to legislate, and within whose limitations alone that power can be lawfully exercised.

The fundamental relation of "capital" to "income" has been much discussed by economists, the former being likened to the tree or the land, the latter to the fruit or the crop; the former depicted as a reservoir supplied from springs, the latter as the outlet stream, to be measured by its flow during a period of time. For the present purpose we require only a clear definition of the term "income," as used in common speech, in order to determine its meaning in the Amendment; and, having formed also a correct judgment as to the nature of a stock dividend, we shall find it easy to decide the matter at issue.

After examining dictionaries in common use (Bouv. L.D.; Standard Dict.; Webster's Internat. Dict.; Century Dict.), we find little to add to the succinct definition adopted in two cases arising under the Corporation Tax Act of 1909 (Stratton's Independence v. Howbert, 231 U.S. 399, 415; Doyle v. Mitchell Bros. Co., 247 U.S. 179, 185) — "income may be defined as the gain derived from capital, from labor, or from both combined," provided it be understood to include profit gained through a sale or conversion of capital assets, to which it was applied in the *Doyle* case (pp. 183, 185).

Brief as it is, it indicates the characteristic and distinguishing attribute of income essential for a correct solution of the present controversy. The Government, although basing its argument upon the definition as quoted, placed chief emphasis upon the word "gain," which was extended to include a variety of meanings; while the significance of the next three words was either overlooked or misconceived. "*Derived — from — capital*"; — "the *gain — derived — from — capital*," etc. Here we have the essential matter: not a gain accruing to capital, not a *growth* or *increment* of value in the investment; but a gain, a profit, something of exchangeable value *proceeding from* the property, *severed from* the capital however invested or employed, and *coming in*, being "*derived*," that is, *received or drawn by* the recipient (the taxpayer) for his *separate use*, benefit and disposal; — *that is* income derived from property. Nothing else answers the description.

The same fundamental conception is clearly set forth in the Sixteenth Amendment — incomes *from* whatever *source derived* — the essential thought being expressed with a conciseness and lucidity entirely in harmony with the form and style of the Constitution.

Can a stock dividend, considering its essential character, be brought within the definition? To answer this, regard must be had to the nature of a corporation and the stockholder's relation to it. We refer, of course, to a corporation such as the one in the case at bar, organized for profit, and having a capital stock divided into shares to which a nominal or par value is attributed.

Certainly the interest of the stockholder is a capital interest, and his certificates of stock are but the evidence of it. They state the number of shares to which he is entitled and indicate their par value and how the stock may be transferred. . . . Short of liquidation, or until dividend declared, he has no right to withdraw any part of either capital or profits from the common enterprise; on the contrary, his interest pertains not to any part, divisible or indivisible, but to the entire assets, business, and affairs of the company. Nor is it the interest of an owner in the assets themselves, since the corporation has full title, legal and equitable, to the whole. The stockholder has the right to have the assets employed in the enterprise, with the incidental rights mentioned; but, as stockholder, he has no right to withdraw, only the right to persist, subject to the risks of the enterprise, and looking only to dividends for his return. If he desires to dissociate himself from the company he can do so only by disposing of his stock.

For bookkeeping purposes, the company acknowledges a liability in form to the stockholders equivalent to the aggregate par value of their stock, evidenced by a "capital stock account." If profits have been made and not divided they create additional bookkeeping liabilities under the head of "profit and loss," "undivided profits," "surplus account," or the like. None of these, however, gives to the stockholders as a body, much less to any one of them, either a claim against the going concern for any particular sum of money, or a right to any particular portion of the assets or any share in them unless or until the directors conclude that dividends shall be made and a part of the company's assets segregated from the common fund for the purpose. The dividend normally is payable in money, under exceptional circumstances in some other divisible property; and when so paid, then only (excluding, of course, a possible advantageous sale of his stock or winding-up of the company) does the stockholder realize a profit or gain which becomes his separate property, and thus derive income from the capital that he or his predecessor has invested.

In the present case, the corporation had surplus and undivided profits invested in plant, property, and business, and required for the purposes of the corporation, amounting to about $45,000,000, in addition to outstanding capital stock of $50,000,000. In this the case is not extraordinary. The profits of a corporation, as they appear upon the balance sheet at the end of the year, need not be in the form of money on hand in excess of what is required to meet current liabilities and finance current operations of the company. Often, especially in a growing business, only a part, sometimes a small part, of the year's profits is in property capable of division; the remainder having been absorbed in the acquisition of increased plant, equipment, stock in trade, or accounts receivable, or in decrease of outstanding liabilities. . . .

A "stock dividend" shows that the company's accumulated profits have been capitalized, instead of distributed to the stockholders or retained as surplus available for distribution in money or in kind should opportunity offer. Far from being a realization of profits of the stockholder, it tends rather to postpone such realization, in that the fund represented by the new stock has been transferred from surplus to capital, and no longer is available for actual distribution.

The essential and controlling fact is that the stockholder has received nothing out of the company's assets for his separate use and benefit; on the contrary, every dollar of his original investment, together with whatever accretions and accumulations have resulted from employment of his money and that of the other stockholders in the business of the company, still remains the property of the company, and subject to business risks which may result in wiping out the entire investment. Having regard to the very truth of the matter, to substance and not to form, he has received nothing that answers the definition of income within the meaning of the Sixteenth Amendment. . . .

We are clear that not only does a stock dividend really take nothing from the property of the corporation and add nothing to that of the shareholder, but that the antecedent accumulation of profits evidenced thereby, while indicating that the shareholder is the richer because of an increase of his capital, at the same time shows he has not realized or received any income in the transaction.

It is said that a stockholder may sell the new shares acquired in the stock dividend; and so he may, if he can find a buyer. It is equally true that if he does sell, and in doing so realizes a profit, such profit, like any other, is income, and so far as it may have arisen since the Sixteenth Amendment is taxable by Congress without apportionment. The same would be true were he to sell some of his original shares at a profit. But if a shareholder sells dividend stock he necessarily disposes of a part of his capital interest, just as if he should sell a part of his old stock, either before or after the dividend. What he retains no longer entitles him to the same proportion of future dividends as before the sale. His part in the control of the company likewise is diminished. Thus, if one holding $60,000 out of a total $100,000 of the capital stock of a corporation should receive in common with other stockholders a 50 percent stock dividend, and should sell his part, he thereby would be reduced from a majority to a minority stockholder, having six-fifteenths instead of six-tenths of the total stock outstanding. A corresponding and proportionate decrease in capital interest and in voting power would befall a minority holder should he sell dividend stock; it being in the nature of things impossible for one to dispose of any part of such an issue without a proportionate disturbance of the distribution of the entire capital stock, and a like diminution of the seller's comparative voting power — that "right preservative of rights" in the control of a corporation. Yet, without selling, the shareholder, unless possessed of other resources, has not the wherewithal to pay an income tax upon the dividend stock. Nothing could more clearly show that to tax a stock dividend is to tax a capital increase, and not income, than this demonstration that in the nature of things it requires conversion of capital in order to pay the tax. . . .

We have no doubt of the power or duty of a court to look through the form of the corporation and determine the question of the stockholder's right, in order to ascertain whether he has received income taxable by Congress without apportionment. But, looking through the form, we cannot disregard the essential truth disclosed; ignore the substantial difference between corporation and stockholder; treat the entire organization as unreal; look upon stockholders as partners, when they are not such; treat them as having in equity a right to a partition of the corporate assets, when they have none; and indulge the fiction that they have received and realized a share of the profits of the company which in truth they have neither received nor realized. We must treat the corporation as a substantial entity separate from the stockholder, not only because such is the practical fact but because it is only by recognizing such separateness that any dividend — even one paid in money or property—can be regarded as income of the stockholder. Did we regard corporation and stockholders as altogether identical, there would be no income except as the corporation acquired it; and while this would be taxable against the corporation as income under appropriate provisions of law, the individual stockholders could not be separately and additionally taxed with respect to their several shares even when divided, since if there were entire identity between them and the company they could not be regarded as receiving anything from it, any more than if one's money were to be removed from one pocket to another.

Conceding that the mere issue of a stock dividend makes the recipient no richer than before, the Government nevertheless contends that the new certificates measure the extent to which the gains accumulated by the corporation have made him the richer. There are two insuperable difficulties with this: In the first place, it would depend upon how long he had held the stock whether the stock dividend indicated the extent to which he had been enriched by the operations of the company; unless he had held it throughout such operations the measure would not hold true. Secondly, and more important for present purposes, enrichment through increase in value of capital investment is not income in any proper meaning of the term.

The complaint contains averments respecting the market prices of stock such as plaintiff held, based upon sales before and after the stock dividend, tending to show that the receipt of the additional shares did not substantially change the market value of her entire holdings. This tends to show that in this instance market quotations reflected intrinsic values—a thing they do not always do. But we regard the market prices of the securities as an unsafe criterion in an inquiry such as the present, when the question must be, not what will the thing sell for, but what is it in truth and in essence.

It is said there is no difference in principle between a simple stock dividend and a case where stockholders use money received as cash dividends to purchase additional stock contemporaneously issued by the corporation. But an actual cash dividend, with a real option to the stockholder either to keep the money for his own or to reinvest it in new shares, would be as far removed as possible from a true stock dividend, such as the one we have under consideration, where nothing of value is taken from the company's assets and transferred to the individual ownership of the several stockholders and thereby subjected to their disposal.

Upon the second argument,[2] the Government, recognizing the force of the decision in Towne v. Eisner, supra, and virtually abandoning the contention that a stock dividend increases the interest of the stockholder or otherwise enriches him, insisted as an alternative that by the true construction of the Act of 1916 the tax is imposed not upon the stock dividend but rather upon the stockholder's share of the undivided profits previously accumulated by the corporation; the tax being levied as a matter of convenience at the time such profits become manifest through the stock dividend. If so construed, would the act be constitutional?

---

2. [Eisner v. Macomber was argued in 1919 and reargued by order of the Court in 1920. — EDS.]

That Congress has power to tax shareholders upon their property interests in the stock of corporations is beyond question; and that such interest might be valued in view of the condition of the company, including its accumulated and undivided profits, is equally clear. But that this would be taxation of property because of ownership, and hence would require apportionment under the provisions of the Constitution, is settled beyond peradventure by previous decisions of this court.

The Government relies upon Collector v. Hubbard (1870), 12 Wall. 1, 17, which arose under § 117 of the Act of June 30, 1864, c.173, 13 Stat. 223, 282, providing that "the gains and profits of all companies, whether incorporated or partnership, other than the companies specified in this section, shall be included in estimating the annual gains, profits, or income of any person entitled to the same, whether divided or otherwise."

The court held an individual taxable upon his proportion of the earnings of a corporation although not declared as dividends and although invested in assets not in their nature divisible. Conceding that the stockholder for certain purposes had no title prior to dividend declared, the court nevertheless said (p. 18):

> Grant all that, still it is true that the owner of a share in a corporation holds the share with all its incidents, and that among those incidents is the right to receive all future dividends, that is, his proportional share of all profits not then divided. Profits are incident to the share to which the owner at once becomes entitled provided he remains a member of the corporation until a dividend is made. Regarded as an incident to the shares, undivided profits are property of the shareholder, and as such are the proper subject of sale, gift, or devise. Undivided profits invested in real estate, machinery, or raw material for the purpose of being manufactured are investments in which the stockholders are interested, and when such profits are actually appropriated to the payment of the debts of the corporation they serve to increase the market value of the shares, whether held by the original subscribers or by assignees.

In so far as this seems to uphold the right of Congress to tax without apportionment a stockholder's interest in accumulated earnings prior to dividend declared, it must be regarded as overruled by Pollock v. Farmers' Loan & Trust Co., 158 U.S. 601, 627, 628, 637. Conceding Collector v. Hubbard was inconsistent with the doctrine of that case, because it sustained a direct tax upon property not apportioned among the States, the Government nevertheless insists that the Sixteenth Amendment removed this obstacle, so that now the *Hubbard Case* is authority for the power of Congress to levy a tax on the stockholder's share in the accumulated profits of the corporation even before division by the declaration of a dividend of any kind. Manifestly this argument must be rejected, since the Amendment applies to income only, and what is called the stockholder's share in the accumulated profits of the company is capital, not income. As we have pointed out, a stockholder has no individual share in accumulated profits, nor in any particular part of the assets of the corporation, prior to dividend declared.

Thus, from every point of view, we are brought irresistibly to the conclusion that neither under the Sixteenth Amendment nor otherwise has Congress power to tax without apportionment a true stock dividend made lawfully and in good faith, or the accumulated profits behind it, as income of the stockholder. The Revenue Act of 1916, in so far as it imposes a tax upon the stockholder because of such dividend, contravenes the provisions of Article I, § 2, cl. 3, and Article I, § 9, cl. 4, of the Constitution, and to this extent is invalid notwithstanding the Sixteenth Amendment.

Judgment affirmed.

Mr. Justice HOLMES, dissenting. . . .

I think that the word "incomes" in the Sixteenth Amendment should be read in "a sense most obvious to the common understanding at the time of its adoption." . . . For it was for public adoption that it was proposed. McCulloch v. Maryland, 4 Wheat. 316, 407. The known purpose of this Amendment was to get rid of nice questions as to what might be direct taxes, and I cannot doubt that most people not lawyers would suppose when they voted for it that they put a question like the present to rest. I am of opinion that the Amendment justifies the tax. . . .

Mr. Justice DAY concurs in this opinion.

Mr. Justice BRANDEIS, dissenting, delivered the following opinion, in which Mr. Justice CLARKE concurred.

Financiers, with the aid of lawyers, devised long ago two different methods by which a corporation can, without increasing its indebtedness, keep for corporate purposes accumulated profits, and yet, in effect, distribute these profits among its stockholders. One method is a simple one. The capital stock is increased; the new stock is paid up with the accumulated profits; and the new shares of paid-up stock are then distributed among the stockholders pro rata as a dividend. If the stockholder prefers ready money to increasing his holding of the stock in the company, he sells the new stock received as a dividend. The other method is slightly more complicated. Arrangements are made for an increase of stock to be offered to stockholders pro rata at par and, at the same time, for the payment of a cash dividend equal to the amount which the stockholder will be required to pay to the company, if he avails himself of the right to subscribe for his pro rata of the new stock. If the stockholder takes the new stock, as is expected, he may endorse the dividend check received to the corporation and thus pay for the new stock. In order to ensure that all the new stock so offered will be taken, the price at which it is offered is fixed far below what it is believed will be its market value. If the stockholder prefers ready money to an increase of his holdings of stock, he may sell his right to take new stock pro rata, which is evidenced by an assignable instrument. In that event the purchaser of the rights repays to the corporation, as the subscription price of the new stock, an amount equal to that which it had paid as a cash dividend to the stockholder.

Both of these methods of retaining accumulated profits while in effect distributing them as a dividend had been in common use in the United States for many years prior to the adoption of the Sixteenth Amendment. They were recognized equivalents. Whether a particular corporation employed one or the other method was determined sometimes by requirements of the law under which the corporation was organized; sometimes it was determined by preferences of the individual officials of the corporation; and sometimes by stock market conditions. Whichever method was employed the resultant distribution of the new stock was commonly referred to as a stock dividend. . . .

It is conceded that if the stock dividend paid to Mrs. Macomber had been made by the more complicated method . . . , that is, issuing rights to take new stock pro rata and paying to each stockholder simultaneously a dividend in cash sufficient in amount to enable him to pay for this pro rata of new stock to be purchased — the dividend so paid to him would have been taxable as income, whether he retained the cash or whether he returned it to the corporation in payment for his pro rata of new stock. But it is contended that, because the simple method was adopted of having the new stock issued direct to the stockholders as paid-up stock, the new stock is not to be deemed income, whether she retained it or converted it into cash by sale. If such a different result can flow merely from the difference in the method pursued, it must be because Congress is without power to tax as income of the stockholder either the stock received under the latter method or the proceeds of its sale; for Congress has, by the provisions in the Revenue Act of 1916, expressly declared its purpose to make stock dividends, by whichever method paid, taxable as income. . . .

It surely is not clear that the enactment exceeds the power granted by the Sixteenth Amendment. And, as this court has so often said, the high prerogative of declaring an act of Congress invalid, should never be exercised except in a clear case. "It is but a decent respect due to the wisdom, the integrity and the patriotism of the legislative body, by which any law is passed, to presume in favor of its validity, until its violation of the Constitution is proved beyond all reasonable doubt." Ogden v. Saunders, 12 Wheat. 213, 270.

Mr. Justice CLARKE concurs in this opinion.

NOTES AND QUESTIONS

1. *Introduction.* The government sought to justify the taxation of Mrs. Macomber's stock dividend on at least three related grounds. First, the government argued that the distribution of the stock dividend increased Mrs. Macomber's wealth. Second, the government argued that the company's accumulation of profits increased Mrs. Macomber's wealth and that part of that increase was realized through the distribution of the stock dividend. Finally, the government argued that the company's accumulation of profits increased Mrs. Macomber's wealth and that the increase in wealth could be taxed at any time. Broadly construed, the last argument would allow an annual tax on all property appreciation, whether or not such appreciation had been realized in the form of a sale or a cash distribution.

Most of the Court's opinion deals with the first two arguments, which are explored in Notes 2 and 3. The larger question raised by the case — the possibility of an annual tax on unrealized appreciation — is discussed in Note 4.

2. *Analysis of stock dividends.* (a) If the government had prevailed in Eisner v. Macomber, what effect do you suppose the decision would have had on the

policies of corporations on the issuance of stock dividends? What do you suppose Justice Brandeis, who, in his days as a practitioner, had been an expert on matters of this sort, would have advised his corporate clients? If he had been asked how to advise Congress on the advisability of taxing stock dividends, what do you suppose he would have said?

(b) One reason often given for issuing stock dividends is to reduce the price of the shares to facilitate trading. For example, if the value of one share rose to $10,000, many people who wished to invest a lesser amount would be precluded from doing so. Can you think of any devices by which this problem might be solved, other than issuing stock dividends? Another reason sometimes given for issuing stock dividends is to provide shareholders with tangible evidence of the success of the corporation. Wouldn't a piece of parchment entitled "declaration of success," with a gold seal and a blue ribbon, do just as well?

(c) The Court refers to the fact that if Mrs. Macomber had sold her dividend shares she would have reduced her fractional voting power (control) in the company. How important do you suppose this would have been to her?

3. *Stock dividends versus cash dividends.* Suppose that Mrs. Macomber's shares had been worth $300 each and that the company had paid a cash dividend of $100, after which the shares were worth $200 each. Would the $100 distribution be taxable, assuming that the company had an earned surplus in excess of that amount? See §§ 61(a)(7) and 316(a). Is this fair? Would it matter whether she had bought the shares the day before the declaration of the dividend?

4. *Policy: taxing unrealized appreciation.* (a) What are the objections to taxing shareholders on amounts earned by the corporation, regardless of distribution? This is how partners are taxed. In a partnership, the decision whether to distribute profits is one that is made by a majority of the partners, but in the absence of an agreement to the contrary, any partner can withdraw from the partnership (and be paid his or her pro rata share of the value of the partnership) at any time. Should this freedom to withdraw matter? If so, what if the partnership agreement makes withdrawal very costly? If the law were to provide for taxation of shareholders on corporate profits regardless of distribution of dividends, how do you suppose corporations would adjust?

(b) Another possibility would be to tax people like Mrs. Macomber on their "paper" profits — that is, on the unrealized appreciation in the market value of their shares of stock — with a corresponding deduction for unrealized losses. The principal objections to taxing unrealized gains have been (i) the potential difficulties of valuation and (ii) the fact that the taxpayer might have difficulty raising the cash to pay the tax. How forceful are these objections as applied to Mrs. Macomber and people like her? Would it have been difficult to value the appreciation in her holdings? Do you think she would have found it difficult to obtain the cash to pay the tax?

(c) The principle that unrealized appreciation should not be taxed is no longer thought to be embedded in the Constitution, but it is thoroughly embedded in present tax rules. Those rules, which will be examined in the remainder of this chapter, create serious problems of tax fairness, or equity, of economic incentive, and of administration. The problem of horizontal equity is illustrated by comparison of a person whose wealth increases by $100,000 from receipt of a salary, and who must pay a tax on that amount, with a person whose wealth increases by the same amount through a rise in the value of her property holdings and who pays no tax on that increase. The discrepancy in tax treatment is particularly disturbing where the property can easily be sold or can serve as collateral for a loan. Nontaxation of appreciation may also distort investment decisions. At the margin, taxpayers will prefer investments that produce gain in the form of unrealized appreciation. Finally, the current regime raises serious definitional issues: At what point has appreciation been realized? As you read the cases in this chapter you may find it useful to think about how a regime that taxed unrealized appreciation might simplify the law.

5. *The present law.* The rule of Eisner v. Macomber is now embodied in § 305(a) ("gross income does not include the amount of any distribution of the stock of a corporation made by such corporation to its shareholders with respect to its stock."), with several important limitations set forth in § 305(b). The most easily understood limitation is that a stock dividend is taxable if the shareholder had the option to take cash or other property in lieu of that dividend. § 305(b)(1). Other rules in § 305(b) cover situations in which the distribution results in some change in the nature of the shareholder's initial investment or proportional interest. These statutory provisions are typically covered in detail in more advanced courses on the taxation of corporations and their shareholders.

6. *Basis and holding period.* Under Regs. § 1.307-1(a), the taxpayer's total basis of the old shares is allocated between the old and the new shares in accordance with relative fair market values after the distribution of the stock dividend. In a case like *Macomber* (where the new shares were identical to the old shares), this means simply that the total basis is allocated equally to all shares, so each share, old and new, winds up with the same basis. The holding period is important in distinguishing between long-term and short-term capital gains. See Chapter 8.B. The rule, under § 1223(5), is that the new shares will be deemed to have been acquired at the time when the old shares were acquired.

7. *Statutory provisions ignoring the decision.* Despite the assertion in the penultimate paragraph of the majority opinion of Eisner v. Macomber that "what is called the stockholder's share in the accumulated profits of the company is capital, not income," Congress requires the U.S. shareholders of foreign personal holding companies and of certain other foreign corporations to report their proportionate share of corporate income even though it is accumulated by the corporation rather than distributed to them. The relevant provisions are § 551 (foreign personal holding companies) and § 951 (controlled foreign corporations). For an extensive discussion of the constitutional validity of requiring shareholders to report their shares of undistributed corporate income, see Whitlock's Estate v. Commissioner, 59 T.C. 490, 506 et seq. (1972) (upholding constitutionality of § 951), 494 F.2d 1297 (10th Cir. 1974) (aff'g on this issue). Under § 1366, the undistributed income of so-called S corporations is also taxed directly to the shareholders, but this result is elective rather than compulsory. And under § 1256, certain taxpayers are

required to "mark to market" (that is, "treat as sold for . . . fair market value") at the end of the year various publicly traded options.

Also of relevance are § 83 (taxing the gain on property previously transferred for services, on the occurrence of events such as the lapse or cancellation of certain restrictions) and § 84 (treating the donation of appreciated property to a political organization as a sale by the contributor on the date of transfer). See also Regs. § 1.471-4 (elective valuation of inventories at cost or market, whichever is lower) and § 1.471-5(c) (security dealers allowed to value their inventory of securities at market value), both of which allow unrealized depreciation, and the latter, unrealized appreciation as well, to be taken into account each year.

8. *The constitutional issue.* As to the impact of the constitutional "realization" concept, see Surrey, The Supreme Court and the Federal Income Tax: Some Implications of the Recent Decisions, 35 Ill. L. Rev. 779, 782 (1941): "Each succeeding opinion paid its respects to the principle of realization which was the core of the Court's pronouncement in Eisner v. Macomber, but went on to a result which never matched the rigor of that pronouncement." Does the case that follows, Helvering v. Bruun, retreat from the "rigor" of Eisner v. Macomber? See also J. Sneed, The Configurations of Gross Income 125 (1967), suggesting that whatever "rusty remnant" of Eisner v. Macomber remains "be consigned to the junk yard of judicial history."

9. *The "realization" concept today.* Notwithstanding general rejection of the constitutional principle of Eisner v. Macomber, the realization requirement remains important in our tax law. We do not generally tax unrealized gains in property values, perhaps because annual property appraisals are difficult; or because the taxpayer may not have the money to pay the tax on such gains; or because unrealized gains in one year may turn into unrealized losses in another year. For better or for worse, the current U.S. income tax depends on "transactions" or "taxable events" and thus is not strictly a tax on "income" as an economist might define that term.

COMPARATIVE FOCUS: The Dutch System of Presumptive Capital Income Taxation

Like the United States, most countries with income taxes take property gains and losses into account only upon the occurrence of a realization event, such as a sale, exchange or other disposition of the property. Beginning in 2001, the Netherlands adopted a different approach under which owners of certain assets are taxed on an imputed return without regard to the receipt of cash or the occurrence of a realization event.

Under the Dutch approach, taxpayers are presumed to earn a return equal to 4 percent of the market value (minus liabilities) of certain capital assets, a category defined to include things such as deposits, stocks, bonds, and real estate other than owner-occupied housing. A tax rate of 30 percent is then applied to that imputed return. For example, assume that Vincent owns a tulip field worth $1 million. Under the 2001 reforms, a return of $40,000 would be imputed to Vincent and he would be required to pay a 30 percent tax (i.e., $12,000) on that amount. Note that the Dutch presumptive return system is equivalent to a wealth tax at a nominal tax rate of 1.2 percent (i.e., 30 percent of 4 percent). In fact, the presumptive return regime replaced the Dutch wealth tax, which dated back to 1892.

In addition to taxing the imputed return from capital assets, Dutch tax law also requires taxpayers to pay tax on the net imputed rental income from owner-occupied housing. Net imputed rental income is calculated by multiplying the value of the taxpayer's home (determined by municipal authorities) by a specified percentage and then allowing a deduction for any mortgage interest and certain other expenses. Unlike imputed capital income, the taxpayer's net imputed rental income from owner-occupied housing is subject to a progressive tax rate schedule.

2. The Decline of Realization as a Constitutional Requirement

Understanding the role of the realization requirement in the U.S. tax system requires understanding the interplay between Congress and the judiciary, as well as having some sense of the political history of the U.S. Supreme Court. In the same way that the New Deal Court in the late 1930s began chipping away at the Court's more conservative constitutional jurisprudence from the *Lochner* era, so too did the Court begin to depart from its restrictive understanding of "income" within the meaning of the Sixteenth Amendment. The case reproduced below, Helvering v. Bruun, was decided at a time when a majority of the Court's members had been appointed by President Franklin Roosevelt. It marks an important midway point in the Court's march away from its constitutional holding in Eisner v. Macomber (1920) and toward the view of congressional primacy in tax matters endorsed in *Glenshaw Glass* (1955). Significantly, however, the decline of realization *as a constitutional requirement* did not translate into a decline of realization principles in U.S. tax law. Indeed, as is further discussed in Note 6 following the case, two years after the Court's decision Congress passed legislation overruling *Bruun*.

HELVERING v. BRUUN
309 U.S. 461 (1940)

Mr. Justice ROBERTS delivered the opinion of the Court.

The controversy had its origin in the petitioner's [the tax collector's] assertion that the [taxpayer/lessor] realized taxable gain from the forfeiture of a leasehold, the tenant having erected a new building upon the premises. The court below held that no income had been realized. . . .

The Board of Tax Appeals made no independent findings. The cause was submitted upon a stipulation of facts. From this it appears that on July 1, 1915, the respondent, as owner, leased a lot of land and the building thereon for a term of ninety-nine years.

The lease provided that the lessee might, at any time, upon giving bond to secure rentals accruing in the two ensuing years, remove or tear down any building on the land, provided that no building should be removed or torn down after the lease became forfeited, or during the last three and one-half years of the term. The lessee was to surrender the land, upon termination of the lease, with all buildings and improvements thereon.

In 1929 the tenant demolished and removed the existing building and constructed a new one which had a useful life of not more than fifty years. July 1, 1933, the lease was cancelled for default in payment of rent and taxes and the respondent regained possession of the land and building.

The parties stipulated

> that as at said date, July 1, 1933, the building which had been erected upon said premises by the lessee had a fair market value of $64,245.68 and that the [lessor's] unamortized cost of the old building, which was removed from the premises in 1929 to make way for the new building, was $12,811.43, thus leaving a net fair market value [net "gain"] as at July 1, 1933, of $51,434.25, for the aforesaid new building erected upon the premises by the lessee.

On the basis of these facts, the petitioner determined that in 1933 the respondent realized a net gain of $51,434.25. The Board overruled his determination and the Circuit Court of Appeals affirmed the Board's decision.

The course of administrative practice and judicial decision in respect of the question presented has not been uniform. In 1917 the Treasury ruled that the adjusted value of improvements installed upon leased premises is income to the lessor upon the termination of the lease. The ruling was incorporated in two succeeding editions of the Treasury Regulations. In 1919 the Circuit Court of Appeals for the Ninth Circuit held in Miller v. Gearin, 258 F. 225, that the regulation was invalid as the gain, if taxable at all, must be taxed as of the year when the improvements were completed.

The regulations were accordingly amended to impose a tax upon the gain in the year of completion of the improvements, measured by their anticipated value at the termination of the lease and discounted for the duration of the lease. Subsequently the regulations permitted the lessor to spread the depreciated value of the improvements over the remaining life of the lease, reporting an aliquot part each year, with provision that, upon premature termination, a tax should be imposed upon the excess of the then value of the improvements over the amount theretofore returned.

In 1935 the Circuit Court of Appeals for the Second Circuit decided in Hewitt Realty Co. v. Commissioner, 76 F.2d 880, that a landlord received no taxable income in a year, during the term of the lease, in which his tenant erected a building on the leased land. The court, while recognizing that the lessor need not receive money to be taxable, based its decision that no taxable gain was realized in that case on the fact that the improvement was not portable or detachable from the land, and if removed would be worthless except as bricks, iron, and mortar. . . .

This decision invalidated the regulations then in force.

In 1938 this court decided M. E. Blatt Co. v. United States, 305 U.S. 267. There, in connection with the execution of a lease, landlord and tenant mutually agreed that each should make certain improvements to the demised premises and that those made by the tenant should become and remain the property of the landlord. The Commissioner valued the improvements as of the date they were made, allowed depreciation thereon to the termination of the leasehold, divided the depreciated value by the number of years the lease had to run, and found the landlord taxable for each year's aliquot portion thereof. His action was sustained by the Court of Claims. The judgment was reversed on the ground that the added value could not be considered rental accruing over the period of the lease; that the facts found by the Court of Claims did not support the conclusion of the Commissioner as to the value to be attributed to the improvements after a use throughout the term of the lease; and that, in the circumstances disclosed, any enhancement in the value of the realty in the tax year was not income realized by the lessor within the Revenue Act.

The circumstances of the instant case differentiate it from the *Blatt* and *Hewitt* cases; but the petitioner's contention that gain was realized when the respondent, through forfeiture of the lease, obtained untrammeled title, possession and control of the premises, with the added increment of value added by the new building, runs counter to the decision in the *Miller* case and to the reasoning in the *Hewitt* case.

The respondent insists that the realty, — a capital asset at the date of the execution of the lease, — remained such throughout the term and after its expiration; that improvements affixed to the soil became part of the realty indistinguishably blended in the capital asset; that such improvements cannot be separately valued or treated as received in exchange for the improvements which were on the land at the date of the execution of the lease; that they are, therefore, in the same category as improvements added by the respondent to his land, or accruals of value due to extraneous and adventitious circumstances. Such added value, it is argued, can be considered capital gain only upon the owner's disposition of the asset. The position is that the economic gain consequent upon the enhanced value of the recaptured asset is not gain derived from capital or realized within the meaning of the Sixteenth Amendment and may not, therefore, be taxed without apportionment.

We hold that the petitioner was right in assessing the gain as realized in 1933.

We might rest our decision upon the narrow issue presented by the terms of the stipulation. It does not appear what kind of a building was erected by the tenant or whether the building was readily removable from the land. It is not stated whether the difference in the value between the building removed and that erected in its place accurately reflects an increase in the value of land and building considered as a single estate in land. On the facts stipulated, without more, we should not be warranted in holding that the presumption of the correctness of the Commissioner's determination has been overborne.

The respondent insists, however, that the stipulation was intended to assert that the sum of $51,434.25 was the measure of the resulting enhancement in value of the real estate at the date of the cancellation of the lease. The petitioner seems not to contest this view. Even upon this assumption we think that gain in the amount named was realized by the respondent in the year of repossession.

The respondent can not successfully contend that the definition of gross income in [§ 61(a) of the 1986 Code] is not broad enough to embrace the gain in question. That definition follows closely the Sixteenth Amendment. Essentially the respondent's position is that the Amendment does not permit the taxation of such gain without apportionment amongst the states. He relies upon what was said in Hewitt Realty Co. v. Commissioner, supra, and upon expressions found in the decisions of this court dealing with the taxability of stock dividends to the effect that gain derived from capital must be something of exchangeable value proceeding from property, severed from the capital, however invested or employed, and received by the recipient for his separate use, benefit, and disposal. He emphasizes the necessity that the gain be separate from the capital and separately disposable. These expressions, however, were used to clarify the distinction between an ordinary dividend and a stock dividend. They were meant to show that in the case of a stock dividend, the stockholder's interest in the corporate assets after receipt of the dividend was the same as and inseverable from that which he owned before the dividend was declared. We think they are not controlling here.

While it is true that economic gain is not always taxable as income, it is settled that the realization of gain need not be in cash derived from the sale of an asset. Gain may occur as a result of exchange of property, payment of the taxpayer's indebtedness, relief from a liability, or other profit realized from the completion of a transaction. The fact that the gain is a portion of the value of property received by the taxpayer in the transaction does not negative its realization.

Here, as a result of a business transaction, the respondent received back his land with a new building on it, which added an ascertainable amount to its value. It is not necessary to recognition of taxable gain that he should be able to sever the improvement begetting the gain from his original capital. If that were necessary, no income could arise from the exchange of property; whereas such gain has always been recognized as realized taxable gain.

Judgment reversed.

THE CHIEF JUSTICE concurs in the result in view of the terms of the stipulation of facts.

Mr. Justice McREYNOLDS took no part in the decision of this case.

NOTES AND QUESTIONS

1. *The original lease transaction.* When Mr. Bruun leased the land in 1915, did he have rental income in the amount of the present value of the expected future rental payments to be made during the entire term of the lease? Why?

2. *The events of 1929.* When the tenant in 1929 tore down the old building and constructed the new one, why did Bruun not have income for tax purposes in an amount equal to the difference between the value of the new

building and his basis in the old one? Apart from taxes, is it likely that the
construction of the building increased the value of his investment? Why?

3. *Buildings intended as rent.* (a) Suppose that the owner of land agrees to
allow a tenant to occupy the land "rent free" for ten years if the tenant con-
structs a building with an expected life of twenty years, a value at the completion of construction of $400,000, and an expected value at the end of the
ten-year lease of $200,000. If income is realized in this situation, when and
how much? Which of the possibilities discussed by the Court in *Bruun* makes
most sense? See Regs. § 1.61-8(c). Cf. Code § 109.

(b) If an owner of land enters into a lease under which an oil company is
permitted to drill for oil, in return for a royalty on any oil that is discovered
and sold, does the landowner have income at the time the oil company con-
structs a rig and begins drilling? When oil is found? Why?

4. *The events of 1933.* The Court holds that Bruun realized a big chunk of
income in 1933. (a) Does this accord with economic reality? Though the
tenant no doubt added considerable value to the property by constructing
the new building in 1929, presumably this added value was not reflected in the
rent, since the lease did not require the tenant to build and the cost was borne
by the tenant. Thus, as of 1929, presumably the rental value of the property,
with its new building, was higher than the amount of rent that the tenant was
required to pay to Bruun. (b) If so, why do you suppose that the tenant "threw
up" the lease in 1933? (c) What do you suppose had happened to the value of
the land? (d) If the value of the land fell, does it follow that Bruun had a loss in
a tax sense? See § 1001(a). (e) Even if he did have a loss, was it realized? See
Trask v. Hoey, 177 F.2d 940 (2d Cir. 1949) (lessor taxed on fair market value
at the time of forfeiture of tenant's improvements but can claim no offsetting
loss for decline in value of lessor's improvements; taxable gain or loss with
respect to lessor's improvements will be realized only on a disposition of the
property).

5. *Realization doctrine.* (a) Where does this case leave Eisner v. Macomber (on
which the taxpayer heavily relied) and the constitutional doctrine of realization adopted in that case? (b) Considering the reasons that might be given for
the result in *Macomber*, and for the requirement of realization in general, does
Mr. Bruun seem to have a stronger or a weaker case for nonrealization than
Mrs. Macomber? (c) The Court in *Bruun says*, "it does not appear . . . whether
the building was readily removable from the land." The building was in
Kansas City, Missouri, where, one presumes, buildings have basements and
are firmly attached to the ground. Note the interesting discussion of the nature of the taxpayer's stipulation as to the amount of gain at issue. What's this
all about? If you had represented Bruun, how would you have written the
stipulation?

6. *Statutory relief.* Congress ultimately accepted the arguments for nontaxation in cases like *Bruun* with legislation enacted in 1942. See §§ 109 and
1019. Note that the effect of the statutory relief is not to exclude or exempt
income but to defer or postpone its recognition. Suppose, for example, that in
1933, when the property was abandoned by the tenant, the building was worth
$50,000 and had a ten-year remaining life and that Mr. Bruun was able to

lease the property to a new tenant for $7,000 per year net of all expenses, beginning in 1933. Disregard any unrecovered cost of the demolished building. Under the decision in the case, Bruun would have income of $50,000 in 1933. This means that he would have a basis in the building of $50,000; for tax purposes it is as if he had received $50,000 in cash and had used that money to buy the building. Thus, he would have been entitled to a depreciation deduction. If we assume that he would have used straightline depreciation, the deduction would have been $5,000 per year. Thus, the income to be reported from the new rental of the property for the period 1933 through 1942 would have been $2,000 per year, or a total of $20,000. The total income would have been $50,000 in 1933 from the abandonment plus the $20,000 from 1933 through 1942 from the rental, or a total of $70,000. If §§ 109 and 1019 had been applied, there would have been no income from the abandonment in 1933. Since Bruun paid nothing for the building, his basis in it would have been zero, so there would have been no depreciation deduction. His rental income would therefore have been $7,000 per year or a total of $70,000 over the ten-year term of the new lease. Table 3-1 summarizes this illustration.

TABLE 3-1
Illustration of Mr. Bruun's Income Under *Bruun* and Under §§ 109 and 1019

Outcome under Bruun	
Income from abandonment in 1933	$50,000
Income from rental, 1933-1942	20,000
Total	$70,000
Outcome under §§ 109 and 1019	
Income from abandonment in 1933	$ -0-
Income from rental, 1933-1942	70,000
Total	$70,000

3. The Limits of Realization: Nonrecourse Borrowing in Excess of Basis

The tax law has developed to treat a broad range of transactions as "realization" events. It is now widely understood that any sale or other disposition of an asset will be regarded as a realization event, thus requiring the taxpayer (in the absence of an applicable nonrecognition provision) to report any gain or loss from the sale on her federal income tax return. But *why* should a sale of an asset be regarded as a realization event? Common sense suggests that there must be something about the change in the taxpayer's economic circumstances that makes it an appropriate time for the tax system to take account of the taxpayer's gain or loss. But what if the taxpayer's economic circumstances change in some manner very closely approximating a sale but the taxpayer has not actually parted with legal title to the property? Keep this question in mind when reading the following case.

WOODSAM ASSOCIATES, INC. v. COMMISSIONER
198 F.2d 357 (2d Cir. 1952)

CHASE, Circuit Judge.

OPINION

The petitioner paid its income . . . taxes for 1943 as computed upon returns it filed which included as part of its gross income . . . gain realized upon the mortgage foreclosure sale in that year of improved real estate which it owned and which was bid in by the mortgagee for a nominal sum. It filed a timely claim for refund on the ground that its adjusted basis for the property had been understated and its taxable gain, therefore, was less than that reported. The refund claim was denied and a deficiency . . . was determined which was affirmed, without dissent, in a decision reviewed by the entire Tax Court. The decisive issue now presented is whether the basis for determining gain or loss upon the sale or other disposition of property is increased when, subsequent to the acquisition of the property, the owner receives a loan in an amount greater than his adjusted basis which is secured by a mortgage on the property upon which he is not personally liable. If so, it is agreed that part of the income taxes . . . paid for 1943 should be refunded.

A comparatively brief statement of the admitted facts and their obvious, and conceded, tax consequences will suffice by way of introduction.

On December 29, 1934, Samuel J. Wood and his wife organized the petitioner and each transferred to it certain property in return for one-half of its capital stock. One piece of property so transferred by Mrs. Wood was the above mentioned parcel of improved real estate consisting of land in the City of New York and a brick building thereon divided into units suitable for use, and used, in retail business. The property was subject to a $400,000 mortgage on which Mrs. Wood was not personally liable and on which the petitioner never became personally liable. [Under applicable statutory nonrecognition rules] the petitioner took the basis of Mrs. Wood for tax purposes. . . . Upon the final disposition of the property at the foreclosure sale there was still due upon the mortgage the principal amount of $381,000. . . .

Turning now to the one item whose effect upon the calculation of the petitioner's adjusted basis is disputed, the following admitted facts need to be stated. Mrs. Wood bought the property on January 20, 1922 at a total cost of $296,400. [The acquisition was partly financed by mortgage debt, which she increased through further mortgage borrowing post-acquisition. The various mortgages were then refinanced into a single consolidated mortgage debt in the amount of $325,000. Up to this point, Mrs. Wood had been personally liable to repay the mortgage debt. In 1931, however, she borrowed an additional $75,000 from the bank that now held the mortgage and refinanced again to create a second, replacement consolidated mortgage in the amount of $400,000. This second consolidated mortgage was nonrecourse; she was not personally liable to repay it upon default even if the value of the property was insufficient to pay it off in full.]

The contention of the petitioner may now be stated quite simply. It is that, when the borrowings of Mrs. Wood subsequent to her acquisition of the property became charges solely upon the property itself [in 1931], the cash she received for the repayment of which she was not personally liable was a gain then taxable to her as income to the extent that the mortgage indebtedness exceeded her adjusted basis in the property. That being so, it is argued that her tax basis was, under familiar principles of tax law, increased by the amount of such taxable gain. . . .

While this conclusion would be sound if the premise on which it is based were correct, we cannot accept the premise. It is that the petitioner's transferor made a taxable disposition of the property . . . when the second consolidated mortgage was executed, because she had, by then, dealt with it in such a way that she had received cash, in excess of her basis, which, at that time, she was freed from any personal obligation to repay. Nevertheless, whether or nor personally liable on the mortgage, "The mortgagee is a creditor, and in effect nothing more than a preferred creditor, even though the mortgagor is not liable for the debt. He is not the less a creditor because he has recourse only to the land." . . . Mrs. Wood merely augmented the existing mortgage indebtedness when she borrowed each time and, far from closing the venture, remained in a position to borrow more if and when circumstances permitted and she so desired. And so, she never "disposed" of the property to create a taxable event which [§ 1001(a)] makes a condition precedent to the taxation of gain. "Disposition," within the meaning of [§ 1001(a)], is the "getting rid, or making over, of anything; relinquishment." . . . Nothing of that nature was done here by the mere execution of the second consolidated mortgage; Mrs. Wood was the owner of this property in the same sense after the execution of this mortgage that she was before. As was pointed out in our decision in the *Crane* case, [supra page 180], [a nonrecourse borrower] . . . has all the income from the property; he manages it; he may sell it; any increase in its value goes to him; any decrease falls on him, until the value goes below the amount of the lien. Realization of gain was, therefore, postponed for taxation until there was a final disposition of the property at the time of the foreclosure sale. . . . Therefore, Mrs. Wood's borrowings did not change the basis for the computation of gain or loss.

Affirmed.

NOTES AND QUESTIONS

1. How could Mrs. Wood have persuaded the mortgage lender (a bank that was an unrelated party) to execute a $400,000 nonrecourse mortgage on land that she had purchased for only $296,400? Was there any reason for the bank to care about her original purchase price? Why would it have agreed to waive her personal liability to repay the mortgage in the event that the land's value declined to less than the amount of the outstanding loan?

2. Under the taxpayer's theory, executing a $400,000 nonrecourse mortgage in 1931 with respect to property that had a basis of $296,400 (ignoring, for simplicity, any depreciation deductions with respect to the building) was

tantamount, for income tax purposes, to selling the property for the amount of the mortgage. Thus, the taxpayer argued that in 1931 Mrs. Wood should have reported taxable gain in the amount of $103,600 (the excess of the "sale price" over basis), whereupon the basis increased to $400,000 — just as if she had received that amount outright and used it to purchase new property — so that the property's appreciation from the sale price to the amount she borrowed would not be taxed twice. This argument was to her benefit because the 1931 taxable year, unlike 1943, was no longer open to review due to the statute of limitations.

3. To understand the taxpayer's theory in *Woodsam Associates*, you need to ask: Why is the mere appreciation of property generally not taxed in the absence of an event such as a sale or exchange? The usual rationales for not taxing unrealized appreciation are threefold: It is hard to measure; the taxpayer may not have the cash in hand to pay the tax; and the taxpayer still faces a risk of loss if the property subsequently declines in value. Upon the execution of a nonrecourse mortgage in excess of basis, are these rationales still persuasive?

4. The court rejects the taxpayer's theory on straight statutory interpretation grounds: A nonrecourse loan is not a sale or exchange under the existing Code, particularly in the aftermath of cases such as *Crane* that, in other settings, ignore nonrecourse debt's arguably distinctive features. Plainly, however, there is no constitutional issue regarding whether Congress *could* tax appreciation in these circumstances.

5. Would accepting the taxpayer's theory in *Woodsam Associates* have been in the government's long-run revenue interest even though, in this case, it was too late to reopen the 1931 taxable year? Why?

6. Would a rule treating the execution of a nonrecourse mortgage in excess of basis as a taxable event be difficult to enforce? How easy or hard would taxpayers find the challenge of avoiding the realization of taxable gain under such a rule?

4. Contemporary Understandings of the Realization Doctrine

In most cases where a taxpayer owns property that has appreciated in value, the incentive is to avoid experiencing a realization event so that recognition of the built-in gain can be deferred as long as possible. With respect to property that has declined in value, however, the incentive is generally the opposite. That is, taxpayers usually prefer to accelerate the recognition of losses in order to claim the valuable tax deductions that realized losses generate. Of course, in all cases the taxpayer may have nontax reasons for wanting to retain or dispose of particular property. It is a happy coincidence if the taxpayer's nontax objectives happen to match her tax objectives. For example, a taxpayer who owns appreciated property that she would prefer not to sell can simply hold that property and simultaneously satisfy her tax and nontax objectives. Likewise, a taxpayer who is hoping to sell property that has declined in value faces no particular dilemma; she should simply sell the property and take the loss. The hard cases are those where the tax objective is at variance with the nontax objective — i.e., the taxpayer wants to sell appreciated property but prefers to avoid a realization event or the taxpayer wants to recognize a loss for tax purposes but would prefer not to sell the property.

The following case, Cottage Savings Association v. Commissioner, shows these dynamics at play in the context of so-called Memorandum R-49 transactions entered into by thrift institutions at the height of the savings and loan crisis in the 1980s. Motivating these transactions was the dramatic increase in interest rates during the 1970s. The rise in interest rates reduced the value of existing fixed-rate mortgages held by thrift institutions. To understand why this is so, imagine that a thrift institution had made a $100,000 loan in 1965 at 7 percent annual interest. Assume (somewhat unrealistically) that the loan required the borrower to make interest payments only for thirty years and then to repay the full amount of the principal. In 1980, the thrift would hold an asset — the mortgage — that amounted to a promise to repay $100,000 in fifteen years and in the meantime to pay interest of $7,000 a year. The prevailing interest rate on home loans in 1980, however, was approximately 14 percent. No one in 1980 would pay $100,000 for a debt obligation that paid only 7 percent interest. Why invest at 7 percent when you could make a similar investment at 14 percent? The fair market value of the 7 percent mortgage as of 1980 might be as low as $60,000. That is, the thrift would be holding an asset with a basis of $100,000 (the amount originally extended as a loan) and fair market value of $60,000 — i.e., a built-in loss of $40,000.

By 1980, when the events at issue in *Cottage Savings* took place, the fair market value of mortgages held by the nation's savings and loan institutions had declined by over a trillion dollars. Recognizing these losses for tax purposes would generate valuable loss deductions for the thrifts, but an outright sale of the mortgages was off the table for accounting reasons. To have their cake and eat it too, the thrifts would have to find a way to "sell" their mortgages for tax purposes without "selling" their mortgages for accounting purposes.

COTTAGE SAVINGS ASSOCIATION v. COMMISSIONER
499 U.S. 554 (1991)

Justice MARSHALL delivered the opinion of the Court.

The issue in this case is whether a financial institution realizes tax-deductible losses when it exchanges its interests in one group of residential mortgage loans for another lender's interests in a different group of residential mortgage loans. We hold that such a transaction does give rise to realized losses.

I

Petitioner Cottage Savings Association (Cottage Savings) is a savings and loan association (S&L) formerly regulated by the Federal Home Loan Bank

Board (FHLBB). Like many S&L's, Cottage Savings held numerous long-term, low-interest mortgages that declined in value when interest rates surged in the late 1970's. These institutions would have benefited from selling their devalued mortgages in order to realize tax-deductible losses. However, they were deterred from doing so by FHLBB accounting regulations, which required them to record the losses on their books. Reporting these losses consistent with the then-effective FHLBB accounting regulations would have placed many S&L's at risk of closure by the FHLBB.

The FHLBB responded to this situation by relaxing its requirements for the reporting of losses. In a regulatory directive known as "Memorandum R-49," dated June 27, 1980, the FHLBB determined that S&L's need not report losses associated with mortgages that are exchanged for "substantially identical" mortgages held by other lenders.[3] The FHLBB's acknowledged purpose for Memorandum R-49 was to facilitate transactions that would generate tax losses but that would not substantially affect the economic position of the transacting S&L's.

This case involves a typical Memorandum R-49 transaction. On December 31, 1980, Cottage Savings sold "90% participation" in 252 mortgages to four S&L's. It simultaneously purchased "90% participation interests" in 305 mortgages held by these S&L's. All of the loans involved in the transaction were secured by single-family homes, most in the Cincinnati area. The fair market value of the package of participation interests exchanged by each side was approximately $4.5 million. The face value of the participation interests Cottage Savings relinquished in the transaction was approximately $6.9 million.

On its 1980 federal income tax return, Cottage Savings claimed a reduction for $2,447,091, which represented the adjusted difference between the face value of the participation interests that it traded and the fair market value of the participation interests that it received. As permitted by Memorandum R-49, Cottage Savings did not report these losses to the FHLBB. After the Commissioner of Internal Revenue disallowed Cottage Savings' claimed deduction, Cottage Savings sought a redetermination in the Tax Court. The Tax Court held that the deduction was permissible.

---

3. Memorandum R-49 listed 10 criteria for classifying mortgages as substantially identical.

1) involve single-family residential mortgages,
2) be of similar type (e.g., conventionals for conventionals),
3) have the same stated terms to maturity (e.g., 30 years),
4) have identical stated interest rates,
5) have similar seasoning (i.e., remaining terms to maturity),
6) have aggregate principal amounts within the lesser of 2-1/2% or $100,000 (plus or minus) on both sides of the transaction, with any additional consideration being paid in cash,
7) be sold without recourse,
8) have similar fair market values,
9) have similar loan-to-value ratios at the time of the reciprocal sale, and
10) have all security properties for both sides of the transaction in the same state.

Record, Exh. 72-BT.

On appeal by the Commissioner, the Court of Appeals reversed. 890 F.2d 848 (C.A.6 1989). The Court of Appeals agreed with the Tax Court's determination that Cottage Savings had realized its losses through the transaction. See id., at 852. However, the court held that Cottage Savings was not entitled to a deduction because its losses were not "actually" sustained during the 1980 tax year for purposes of § 165(a). See 890 F.2d at 855.

Because of the importance of this issue to the S&L industry and the conflict among the Circuits over whether Memorandum R-49 exchanges produce deductible tax losses, we granted certiorari. We now reverse.

II

Rather than assessing tax liability on the basis of annual fluctuations in the value of a taxpayer's property, the Internal Revenue Code defers the tax consequences of a gain or loss in property value until the taxpayer "realizes the gain or loss." The realization requirement is implicit in § 1001(a) of the Code, which defines "[t]he gain [or loss] from the sale or other disposition of property" as the difference between "the amount realized" from the sale or disposition of the property and its "adjusted basis." As this Court has recognized, the concept of realization is "founded on administrative convenience." Helvering v. Horst, 311 U.S. 112, 116 (1940). Under an appreciation-based system of taxation, taxpayers and the Commissioner would have to undertake the "cumbersome, abrasive, and unpredictable administrative task" of valuing assets on an annual basis to determine whether the assets had appreciated or depreciated in value. See 1 B. Bittker & L. Lokken, Federal Taxation of Income, Estates and Gifts ¶5.2, pp. 5-16 (2d ed. 1989). In contrast, "[a] change in the form or extent of an investment is easily detected by a taxpayer or an administrative officer." R. Magill, Taxable Income 79 (rev. ed. 1945).

Section 1001(a)'s language provides a straightforward test for realization: to realize a gain or loss in the value of property, the taxpayer must engage in a "sale or other disposition of [the] property." The parties agree that the exchange of participation interests in this case cannot be characterized as a "sale" under § 1001(a); the issue before us is whether the transaction constitutes a "disposition of property." The Commissioner argues that an exchange of property can be treated as a "disposition" under § 1001(a) only if the properties exchanged are materially different. The Commissioner further submits that, because the underlying mortgages were essentially economic substitutes, the participation interests exchanged by Cottage Savings were not materially different from those received from the other S&L's. Cottage Savings, on the other hand, maintains that any exchange of property is a "disposition of property" under § 1001(a), regardless of whether the property exchanged is materially different. Alternatively, Cottage Savings contends that the participation interests exchanged were materially different because the underlying loans were secured by different properties.

We must therefore determine whether the realization principle in § 1001(a) incorporates a "material difference" requirement. If it does, we must further decide what that requirement amounts to and how it applies in this case. We consider these questions in turn.

A

Neither the language nor the history of the Code indicates whether and to what extent property exchanged must differ to count as a "disposition of property" under § 1001(a). Nonetheless, we readily agree with the Commissioner that an exchange of property gives rise to a realization even under § 1001(a) only if the properties exchanged are "materially different." The Commissioner himself has by regulation construed § 1001(a) to embody a material difference requirement:

> Except as otherwise provided...the gain or loss realized from the conversion of property into *cash, or from the exchange of property for other property differing materially either in kind or in extent*, is treated as income or as loss sustained.

Treas. Reg. § 1.1001-1 (1990) (emphasis added). Because Congress has delegated to the Commissioner the power to promulgate "all needful rules and regulations for the enforcement of [the Internal Revenue Code]," § 7805(a), we must defer to his regulatory interpretations of the Code so long as they are reasonable. . . .

We conclude that Treasury Regulation § 1.1001-1 is a reasonable interpretation of § 1001(a). Congress first employed the language that now comprises § 1001(a) of the Code in § 202(a) of the Revenue Act of 1924, ch. 234, 43 Stat. 253; that language has remained essentially unchanged through various reenactments. And since 1934, the Commissioner has construed the statutory term "disposition of property" to include a "material difference" requirement. As we have recognized, " 'Treasury regulations and interpretations long continued without substantial change, applying to unamended or substantially reenacted statutes, are deemed to have received congressional approval and have the effect of law.' " United States v. Correll, 389 U.S. 299, 305-306 (1967), quoting Helvering v. Winmill, 305 U.S. 79, 83 (1938).

Treasury Regulation § 1.1001-1 is also consistent with our landmark precedents on realization. In a series of early decisions involving the tax effects of property exchanges, this Court made clear that a taxpayer realizes taxable income only if the properties exchanged are "materially" or "essentially" different. . . . Because these decisions were part of the "contemporary legal context" in which Congress enacted § 202(a) of the 1924 Act, . . . and because Congress has left undisturbed through subsequent reenactments of the Code the principles of realization established in these cases, we may presume that Congress intended to codify these principles in § 1001(a). . . . The Commissioner's construction of the statutory language to incorporate these principles certainly was reasonable.

B

Precisely what constitutes a "material difference" for purposes of § 1001(a) of the Code is a more complicated question. The Commissioner argues that properties are "materially different" only if they differ in economic substance. To determine whether the participation interests exchanged in this case were "materially different" in this sense, the Commissioner argues, we should look to the attitudes of the parties, the evaluation of the interests by the secondary mortgage market, and the views of the FHLBB. We conclude that § 1001(a) embodies a much less demanding and less complex test.

Unlike the question *whether* § 1001(a) contains a material difference requirement, the question of *what constitutes* a material difference is not one on which we can defer to the Commissioner. For the Commissioner has not issued an authoritative, prelitigation interpretation of what property exchanges satisfy this requirement. Thus, to give meaning to the material difference test, we must look to the case law from which the test derives and which we believe Congress intended to codify in enacting and reenacting the language that now comprises § 1001(a). . . .

We start with the classic treatment of realization in Eisner v. Macomber [supra page 213]. In *Macomber*, a taxpayer who owned 2,200 shares of stock in a company received another 1,100 shares from the company as part of a pro rata stock dividend meant to reflect the company's growth in value. At issue was whether the stock dividend constituted taxable income. We held that it did not, because no gain was realized. . . . We reasoned that the stock dividend merely reflected the increased worth of the taxpayer's stock, . . . and that a taxpayer realizes increased worth of property only by receiving "something of exchangeable value *proceeding from* the property." . . .

In three subsequent decisions—United States v. Phellis, [257 U.S. 156 (1921)]; Weiss v. Stearn, [265 U.S. 242 (1924)]; and Marr v. United States, [268 U.S. 536 (1925)]—we refined *Macomber*'s conception of realization in the context of property exchanges. In each case, the taxpayer owned stock that had appreciated in value since its acquisition. And in each case, the corporation in which the taxpayer held stock had reorganized into a new corporation, with the new corporation assuming the business of the old corporation. While the corporations in *Phellis* and *Marr* both changed from New Jersey to Delaware corporations, the original and successor corporations in *Weiss* both were incorporated in Ohio. In each case, following the reorganization, the stockholders of the old corporation received shares in the new corporation equal to their proportional interest in the old corporation.

The question in these cases was whether the taxpayers realized the accumulated gain in their shares in the old corporation when they received in return for those shares stock representing an equivalent proportional interest in the new corporations. In *Phellis* and *Marr*, we held that the transactions were realization events. We reasoned that because a company incorporated in one State has "different rights and powers" from one incorporated in a different State, the taxpayers in *Phellis* and *Marr* acquired through the transactions property that was "materially different" from what they previously had. . . . In contrast, we held that no realization occurred in *Weiss*. By exchanging stock in the predecessor corporation for stock in the newly reorganized corporation, the taxpayer did not receive "a thing really different from what he theretofore had." Weiss v. Stearn, supra, 265 U.S., at 254. As we explained in *Marr*, our determination that the reorganized company in *Weiss* was not "really different" from its predecessor turned on the fact that both companies were incorporated in the same State. . . .

Obviously, the distinction in *Phellis* and *Marr* that made the stock in the successor corporations materially different from the stock in the predecessors was minimal. Taken together, *Phellis, Marr,* and *Weiss* stand for the principles that properties are "different" in the sense that is "material" to the Internal Revenue Code so long as their respective possessors enjoy legal entitlements that are different in kind or extent. Thus, separate groups of stock are not materially different if they confer "the same proportional interest of the same character in the same corporation." Marr v. United States, 268 U.S., at 540. However, they *are* materially different if they are issued by different corporations, id., at 541; United States v. Phellis, supra, 257 U.S., at 173, or if they confer "differen[t] rights and powers" in the same corporation, Marr v. United States, supra, 268 U.S., at 541. No more demanding a standard than this is necessary in order to satisfy the administrative purposes underlying the realization requirement in § 1001(a). . . . For, as long as the property entitlements are not identical, their exchange will allow both the Commissioner and the transacting taxpayer easily to fix the appreciated or depreciated values of the property relative to their tax bases.

In contrast, we find no support for the Commissioner's "economic substitute" conception of material difference. According to the Commissioner, differences between properties are material for purposes of the Code only when it can be said that the parties, the relevant market (in this case the secondary mortgage market), and the relevant regulatory body (in this case the FHLBB) would consider them material. Nothing in *Phellis, Weiss,* and *Marr* suggests that exchanges of properties must satisfy such a subjective test to trigger realization of a gain or loss.

Moreover, the complexity of the Commissioner's approach ill serves the goal of administrative convenience that underlies the realization requirement. In order to apply the Commissioner's test in a principled fashion, the Commissioner and the taxpayer must identify the relevant market, establish whether there is a regulatory agency whose views should be taken into account, and then assess how the relevant market participants and the agency would view the transaction. The Commissioner's failure to explain how these inquiries should be conducted further calls into question the workability of his test.

Finally, the Commissioner's test is incompatible with the structure of the Code. Section 1001(c) provides that a gain or loss realized under § 1001(a) "shall be recognized" unless one of the Code's nonrecognition provisions applies. One such nonrecognition provision withholds recognition of a gain or loss realized from an exchange of properties that would appear to be economic substitutes under the Commissioner's material difference test. This provision, commonly known as "like kind" exception, withholds recognition of a gain or loss realized "on the exchange of property held for productive use in a trade or business or for investment . . . for property of like kind which is to be held either for productive use in a trade or business or for investment." § 1031. If Congress had expected that exchanges of similar properties would not count as realization events under § 1001(a), it would have had no reason to bar recognition of a gain or loss realized from these transactions.

C

Under our interpretation of § 1001(a), an exchange of property gives rise
to a realization event so long as the exchanged properties are "materially
different" — that is, so long as they embody legally distinct entitlements.
Cottage Savings' transactions at issue here easily satisfy this test. Because the
participation interests exchanged by Cottage Savings and the other S&L's
derived from loans that were made to different obligors and secured by different homes, the exchanged interests did embody legally distinct entitlements. Consequently, we conclude that Cottage Savings realized its losses at
the point of the exchange.

The Commissioner contends that it is anomalous to treat mortgages
deemed to be "substantially identical" to the FHLBB as "materially different."
The anomaly, however, is merely semantic; mortgages can be substantially
identical for Memorandum R-49 purposes and still exhibit "differences" that
are "material" for purposes of the Internal Revenue Code. Because Cottage
Savings received entitlements different from those it gave up, the exchange
put both Cottage Savings and the Commissioner in a position to determine
the change in the value of Cottage Savings' mortgages relative to their tax
bases. Thus, there is no reason not to treat the exchange of these interests as a
realization event, regardless of the status of the mortgages under the criteria
of Memorandum R-49.

III

Although the Court of Appeals found that Cottage Savings' losses were realized, it disallowed them on the ground that they were not sustained under
§ 165(a) of the Code. Section 165(a) states that a deduction shall be allowed for
"any loss sustained during the taxable year and not compensated for by insurance or otherwise." Under the Commissioner's interpretation of § 165(a),

> To be allowable as a deduction under section 165(a), a loss must be evidenced by
> closed and completed transactions, fixed by identifiable events, and, except as
> otherwise provided in section 165(h) and § 1.165-11, relating to disaster losses,
> actually sustained during the taxable year. Only a bona fide loss is allowable.
> Substance and not mere form shall govern in determining a deductible loss.

Treas. Reg. § 1.165-1(b).

The Commissioner offers a minimal defense of the Court of Appeals'
conclusion. The Commissioner contends that the losses were not sustained
because they lacked "economic substance," by which the Commissioner seems
to mean that the losses were not bona fide. We say "seems" because the
Commissioner states the position in one sentence in a footnote in his brief
without offering further explanation. The only authority the Commissioner
cites for this argument is Higgins v. Smith, 308 U.S. 473 (1940).

In *Higgins*, we held that a taxpayer did not sustain a loss by selling securities
below cost to a corporation in which he was the sole shareholder. We found
that the losses were not bona fide because the transaction was not conducted at

arm's length and because the taxpayer retained the benefit of the securities through his wholly owned corporation. . . . Because there is no contention that the transactions in this case were not conducted at arm's length, or that Cottage Savings retained de facto ownership of the participation interests it traded to the four reciprocating S&L's, *Higgins* is inapposite. In view of the Commissioner's failure to advance any other arguments in support of the Court of Appeals' ruling with respect to § 165(a), we conclude that, for purposes of this case, Cottage Savings sustained its losses within the meaning of § 165(a).

IV

For the reasons set forth above, the judgment of the Court of Appeals is reversed, and the case is remanded for further proceedings consistent with this opinion.

So ordered.

Justice BLACKMUN with whom Justice WHITE joins . . . dissenting. . . .

The exchanges, as the Court acknowledges, were occasioned by the Federal Home Loan Bank Board's (FHLBB) Memorandum R-49 of June 27, 1980, and by that Memorandum's relaxation of theretofore-existing accounting regulations and requirements, a relaxation effected to avoid placement of "many S&L's at risk of closure by the FHLBB" without substantially affecting the "economic position of the transacting S&L's." . . . But the Memorandum, the Court notes, also had as a purpose "the facilit[ation of] transactions that would generate tax losses. . . ." I find it somewhat surprising that an agency not responsible for tax matters would presume to dictate what is or is not a deductible loss for federal income tax purposes. I had thought that that was something within the exclusive province of the Internal Revenue Service, subject to administrative and judicial review. Certainly, the Bank Board's opinion in this respect is entitled to no deference whatsoever. . . .

That the mortgage participation partial interests exchanged in these cases were "different" is not in dispute. The materiality prong is the focus. A material difference is one that has the capacity to influence a decision. . . .

The application of this standard leads, it seems to me, to only one answer—that the mortgage participation partial interests released were not materially different from the mortgage participation partial interests received. Memorandum R-49, as the Court notes, . . . lists 10 factors that, when satisfied, as they were here, serve to classify the interests as "substantially identical." These factors assure practical identity; surely, they then also assure that any difference cannot be of consequence. Indeed, nonmateriality is the full purpose of the Memorandum's criteria. The "proof of the pudding" is in the fact of its complete accounting acceptability to the FHLBB. Indeed, as has been noted, it is difficult to reconcile substantial identity for financial accounting purposes with a material difference for tax accounting purposes.

This should suffice and be the end of the analysis. Other facts, however, solidify the conclusion: The retention by the transferor of 10% interests, enabling it to keep on servicing its loans; the transferor's continuing to collect the payments due from the borrowers so that, so far as the latter were concerned, it was business as usual, exactly as it had been; the obvious lack of concern or dependence of the transferor with the "differences" upon which the Court relies (as transferees, the taxpayers made no credit checks and no appraisals of collateral . . .); the selection of the loans by computer programmed to match mortgages in accordance with the Memorandum R-49 criteria; the absence of even the names of the borrowers in the closing schedules attached to the agreements; Centennial's receipt of loan files only six years after its exchange; the restriction of the interests exchanged to the same State; the identity of the respective face and fair market values; and the application by the parties of common discount factors to each side of the transaction — all reveal that any differences that might exist made no difference whatsoever and were not material. This demonstrates the real nature of the transactions, including nonmateriality of the claimed differences.

We should be dealing here with realities and not with superficial distinctions. As has been said many times, and as noted above, in income tax law we are to be concerned with substance and not with mere form. When we stray from that principle, the new precedent is likely to be a precarious beacon for the future.

I respectfully dissent on this issue.

NOTE

Although the subject of the *Cottage Savings* litigation was the tax treatment of S&L mortgage portfolio swaps, the opinion, like most court decisions, had much broader and far-reaching consequences. Most commentators came to view the case as establishing a "hair-trigger" standard for interpreting § 1001 and regulations thereunder. As a result, certain transactions not considered as triggering realization prior to *Cottage Savings* were regarded, after the decision, as taxable events. Perhaps the most important impact of the Court's decision was in the area of debt workouts, where distressed borrowers and their creditors agreed to certain modifications of the underlying debt instruments. Post–*Cottage Savings*, the question arose whether certain debt modifications would require the parties to such transactions to treat the modification as a "sale or other disposition" of the original obligation, triggering recognition of gain or loss and, in some cases, of income from cancellation of indebtedness. Regs. § 1.1001-3. The so-called *Cottage Savings* regulations cover a wide variety of possible modifications. In general, the key is whether a "significant modification" has occurred in yield, timing or amounts of payments, the obligor, or the nature of the instrument. Some of the rules are specific. For example, if the interest rate is changed by more than ¼ of 1 percent, the change is significant and a recognition event has occurred, but in the case of a variable-rate obligation, a change in the rate resulting from a change in the index used to compute the rate is not a modification. § 1.1001-3(e)(1). An extension of the final maturity date is significant if it is greater than the lesser of five years or 50 percent of the original term.

§ 1.1001-3(e)(2). Other rules are stated more generally. For example, a change in the collateral is "a significant modification if a substantial portion of the collateral is released or replaced with other property," but not where fungible property is replaced by similar property (for example, "government securities of a particular type and rating"). Regs. § 1.1001-3(e)(3)(iv).

The result of modifying a debt instrument can be surprising potential tax liability for taxpayers who buy distressed debt at a discount and thereafter modify the terms. Bear in mind that a significant modification results in an exchange — a recognition event — for both the debtor and the holder of the debt. Suppose, for example, that debt, owed by Debtor Co., has a face amount of $10 million and an interest rate of 10 percent, but that Debtor Co., subsequent to the issuance of the debt, has experienced financial reverses. Because of an increased risk of default, the market value of the debt has declined. Suppose Holder Co. buys the debt for $7 million and shortly thereafter, seeking to give Debtor Co. an improved chance of survival, reduces the interest rate to 9 percent. This is a significant modification. Suppose the applicable federal rate of interest (which is, essentially, the market rate for debt with comparable terms) is 8 percent. Debtor Co. will not have any cancellation of debt income. See § 108(e)(10). Holder Co., on the other hand, despite having no economic gain, will be treated as having exchanged a debt instrument with a basis of $7 million for a new debt instrument with a value of $10 million and will realize a gain of $3 million. If Holder Co. is not a dealer in such instruments it may be able to defer recognition of gain by use of the installment method (under § 453, described infra at pages 273-276), but even then would be liable for a special interest charge designed to offset the advantage of deferral (see § 453A).

QUESTIONS

1. Is the loss in a case like *Cottage Savings* properly claimed under § 165 or under § 1001? What is the role of each of these provisions?

2. Before the swap described in *Cottage Savings*, had the taxpayer experienced a true economic loss on the loans that it swapped? If so, when was that loss incurred?

3. If the taxpayer had a true economic loss (with or without the swap), why did the FHLBB not require that the loss be recognized for nontax accounting purposes?

4. Should the fact that the FHLBB did not recognize the loss for nontax accounting purposes have had any bearing on whether the loss was recognized for tax purposes? Why?

5. If the taxpayer had a true economic loss, was there any tax policy justification for the Commissioner's resistance to allowing the loss to be recognized once the swap occurred?

6. What is the legal test for recognition of loss? What is meant by "legal entitlements"? Is it fair to describe the test as "formalistic"? If so, what is the advantage, if any, of such a test?

7. Was there any reason for the taxpayer in *Cottage Savings* to enter into a Memorandum R-49 transaction other than a reduction in its federal income tax liability? If not, should the Court's opinion be viewed as support for the proposition that taxpayer efforts to structure transactions for the sake of tax benefits should be respected even if the taxpayer has no independent business purpose for undertaking the transaction?

PROBLEMS

1. Jim and Barbara are both cotton dealers and are business acquaintances of one another. Each is in the business of buying cotton from farmers and selling it to manufacturers. Recently each bought large quantities of cotton and stored it in a warehouse in the town where both of them live. The cotton was all grown in the same area and is considered to be identical in grade and quality. The end of the year is approaching. The price of cotton has fallen and Jim and Barbara both have substantial unrealized losses on the cotton they hold in storage. Jim and Barbara both believe that the price of cotton will rise in a month or so and would like to avoid selling, but each has large gains from transactions earlier in the year and would like to be able to deduct their losses. Will each of them be entitled to recognize his or her loss if they swap their cotton holdings? (Ignore § 1031.)

2. Susan and Josh are both dealers in high-priced, high-performance, "exotic" sports cars. Susan has her showroom and office in New York City, and Josh has his showroom and office in Miami. Two years ago Machorari Automobile Company, which is located in Italy, announced that it had plans to build a new sports car, to be called the Streaker, and that it would take orders at $500,000 each, with $100,000 payable on placing the order. Only thirty of the cars were to be built. Susan and Josh each placed orders. Machorari's cars are essentially hand made. When an order is placed, a particular car is assigned to the buyer. Susan was assigned Streaker No. 13 and Josh was assigned Streaker No. 14. The cars were recently finished, paid for by Susan and Josh, and shipped to them. Unfortunately, a mistake was made in the shipping and Susan's Streaker No. 13 was shipped to Miami while Josh's Streaker No. 14 was shipped to New York. Susan and Josh each have documents establishing their ownership of their cars. The cars are as close to being identical as cars can be when they are not made on an assembly line. Demand is so intense that the cars can be sold without effort for $750,000. Susan has several potential buyers in New York at that price. In Miami, several people have come to Josh's showroom with suitcases full of cash ($750,000), seeking to buy a Streaker. Certain modifications must be made, however, before the cars can meet federal regulations and be sold. The modifications will take several months. Josh calls Susan and suggests that they swap titles, which can be accomplished easily, so they don't need to ship cars to each other. If they do so, must they recognize their gain at the time of the swap? Would it matter if the colors of the cars were different and colors were of great importance to particular buyers?

B. STATUTORY NONRECOGNITION PROVISIONS

Section 1001(c) of the Internal Revenue Code reads as follows: "Except as otherwise provided in this subtitle, the entire amount of the gain or loss, determined under this section, on the sale or exchange of property shall be recognized." In most cases, this language ensures an automatic connection between realization and recognition. That is, a taxpayer who *realizes* a gain or loss from the disposition of property must *recognize* such gain or loss for tax purposes. As is often the case with the tax code, however, there is a great deal riding on the first few seemingly innocuous words of this subsection — "except as otherwise provided in this subtitle." These seven words open up the possibility that realized gains and losses may not, in some instances, be recognized for federal tax purposes. The statutory provisions that produce this result are known as "nonrecognition" rules. Students who go on to take advanced tax courses, especially those relating to the taxation of corporations and partnerships, typically devote a great deal of time mastering highly sophisticated nonrecognition provisions in subchapters C (relating to corporations and their shareholders) and K (relating to partnerships and their partners).

1. Introduction to Nonrecognition Rules

The chief function of a nonrecognition rule is to ensure that a taxpayer disposing of property in a manner that would otherwise be a taxable event will not recognize gain or loss on the disposition of the property. Significantly, nonrecognition rules typically do not provide for the permanent exclusion of gain or disallowance of loss but rather defer that gain or loss for recognition at some later time. In most transactions involving nonrecognition provisions, the taxpayer maintains some sort of property interest following the disposition upon which nonrecognition treatment has been conferred. Thus, preservation of any realized but unrecognized gain or loss is accomplished through adjustments to the basis of the taxpayer's ongoing property interest.

To illustrate, imagine a provision allowing for the tax-free exchange of baseball memorabilia. Gianna owns a vintage New York Yankees jersey worth $1,000 that she bought several years ago for $300. She plans to exchange it for a Los Angeles Dodgers jersey, also worth $1,000, which Nora purchased for $800. It should be clear that, in the absence of a nonrecognition provision, the jersey exchange would trigger $700 of gain for Gianna and $200 of gain for Nora. Both taxpayers have experienced a realization event. Under § 1001(c), any gain from the sale or other disposition of an asset must generally be recognized and reported on the taxpayer's federal income tax returns for the year of the exchange. Assuming that a nonrecognition rule applies, however, neither taxpayer would be required to recognize gain from the exchange. In order to preserve each taxpayer's realized but unrecognized gain from the transaction, Gianna would take a basis in her newly acquired Dodgers jersey equal to her basis in the Yankees jersey ($300), while Nora would take a basis in her newly acquired Yankees jersey equal to her basis in the Dodgers jersey ($800).

What is the rationale for nonrecognition rules? Consider the following arguments: (a) Gain should not be recognized if the transaction does not generate cash with which to pay the tax. (b) Gain or loss should not be recognized if the transaction is one in which the gain or loss is or might be difficult to measure — that is, in which there is or might be a serious problem of valuation. (c) Gain or loss should not be recognized if the nature of the taxpayer's investment does not significantly change. (d) Gain should not be recognized (but loss should be) in order to encourage (or avoid discouraging) mobility of capital (that is the movement of investments from less valuable to more valuable uses).

Arguments (a) and (b) respond to the goal of practicality or administrative feasibility in the operation of the tax system. As noted earlier, the realization concept is rooted, at least in part, in precisely such practical considerations. Perhaps nonrecognition rules are justified in those transactions where a realization event has occurred yet liquidity and valuation concerns still obtain because of the nature of the transaction. Argument (c) seems to respond to the goal of fairness; it compares the taxpayer who sells and reinvests, or who swaps, with an otherwise similar taxpayer who holds on to an existing investment. If continuity of investment justifies not taxing those who simply hold on to existing investments, then perhaps the same rationale justifies extending nonrecognition treatment to those who continue in a similar investment. Finally, argument (d) speaks to economic considerations. To the extent that the realization doctrine discourages the transfer of property that has appreciated in value, then perhaps nonrecognition rules can be justified as a means of mitigating that lock-in effect.

2.   Like-Kind Exchanges

Apart from certain rules that relate to acquiring newly issued corporate stock or partnership interests, the most prominent nonrecognition rule in the Code is § 1031, which applies to exchanges of certain business or investment property (such as real estate and personal property, but not financial instruments such as stocks and bonds) that are held to be "of a like kind." Taxpayers have relied upon § 1031 across a broad range of business and investment settings. Indeed, an entire industry has grown up around this one provision of the Internal Revenue Code. To get some sense of the players in this industry and the types of transactions being done, take a moment and Google "section 1031 like-kind exchanges." The sources you will discover are no substitute for actually reading the statute and regulations (and this casebook!). Nonetheless, spending ten minutes online — perhaps reviewing the IRS website or the National Association of Realtors' "Field Guide to 1031 Exchanges" — can give you a quick "lay of the land" that will help put the materials that follow into context.

Section 1031(a)(1) provides that "[n]o gain or loss shall be recognized on the exchange of property held for productive use in a trade or business or for investment if such property is exchanged solely for property of a like kind which is to be held either for productive use in a trade or business or for investment." At first blush, this provision seems extraordinarily broad, potentially conferring nonrecognition treatment on all property exchanges other than those involving personal use assets. However, § 1031(a)(2) sets forth several important exceptions. Read these provisions and consider the tax consequences of the following transactions.

(a) Long ago *A* bought shares of stock of Texaco for $10,000. He swaps them for shares of stock of Exxon worth $60,000. Is the swap a taxable event?

(b) Long ago *B* bought *X* Farm for $10,000 and has held it as an investment. He swaps *X* Farm for *Y* Farm, worth $60,000. Is the swap a taxable event?

(c) Long ago *C* bought *M* Farm for $10,000 and has held it as an investment. She sells it for $60,000 and uses the proceeds to buy *N* Farm the next week. Is the sale a taxable event?

(d) Long ago *D* bought *S* Farm for $10,000 and has used it in his farming business. He swaps it for a fleet of tractors worth $60,000 that he will also use in his farming business. Is the sale a taxable event?

Is it possible to reconcile the outcomes in the hypotheticals (a) through (d) by reference to the alternative rationales for nonrecognition treatment discussed above?

a. The Like-Kind Requirement

As noted above, § 1031(a) applies only if qualifying property is exchanged "for property of a *like-kind*" (emphasis added), but the statute itself offers no guidance whatsoever regarding how to make the like-kind determination. As a result, the taxpayer must turn to other sources of legal authority to glean the meaning of the term. Regulations section 1.1031(a)-1(b) notes that "the words 'like-kind' have reference to the nature or character of the property and not to its grade or quality." The following private letter ruling illustrates the application of that standard.

PLR 200203033

Internal Revenue Service

Private Letter Ruling
January 18, 2002

Dear _____:

This responds to the letter written in your behalf, dated January 26, 2001, requesting a ruling on the proper treatment of an exchange, under § 1031 of the Internal Revenue Code, of a Perpetual Conservation Easement (PCE) in real property for a fee interest in other real estate that will also be burdened with a PCE upon receipt. These are the applicable facts:

. . .

Taxpayers and other co-owners wish to engage in a like-kind exchange with ConOrg, a § 501(c)(3) organization. Under an agreement entered into by Taxpayers and the other co-owners with ConOrg, Taxpayers and the other co-owners will convey a PCE on the Old Ranch to ConOrg in exchange for the fee estate of New Ranch, in State X, which will also be burdened with a PCE when received by Taxpayers and the other co-owners.

The planned transaction will be a simultaneous, two-sided exchange (i.e., involving no accommodation parties, third party sellers of replacement property or third party buyers of relinquished property). Following the exchange, New Ranch will be held by Taxpayers and the other co-owners in the exact same proportions as the interests they now hold and will retain in Old Ranch burdened with the PCE.

The State X Civil Code provides at Citation X.1 that the purpose of a conservation easement is to retain land predominantly in its natural, scenic, historical, agricultural, forested, or open space condition. Citation X.2 provides that a conservation easement is an interest in real property voluntarily created and freely transferable in whole or in part for the purposes stated in Citation X.1 by any lawful method for the transfer of interest in real property in State X. Citation X.2 further provides that a conservation easement shall be perpetual in duration and shall constitute an interest in real property notwithstanding the fact that it is negative in character.

Section 1031(a)(1) of the Code provides generally that no gain or loss shall be recognized on the exchange of property held for productive use in a trade or business or for investment if such property is exchanged solely for property of like kind which is to be held either for productive use in a trade or business or for investment.

Section 1031(b) states that if an exchange would be within the provisions of section 1031(a) if it were not for the fact that the property received in exchange consists not only of property permitted by such provisions to be received without the recognition of gain, but also of other property or money, then the gain, if any, to the recipient shall be recognized, but in an amount not in excess of the sum of such money and the fair market value of such other property.

Section 1.1031(a)-1(b) of the Income Tax Regulations provides that, as used in section 1031(a), the words "like kind" have reference to the nature or character of the property and not to its grade or quality. One kind or class of property may not, under that section, be exchanged for property of a different kind or class. The fact that any real estate involved is improved or unimproved is not material, for that fact relates only to the grade or quality of the property and not to its kind or class. Unproductive real estate held by one other than a dealer for future use or future realization of the increment in value is held for investment and not primarily for sale.

Section 1.1031(a)-1(c) of the regulations, as an example, provides that no gain or loss is recognized if a taxpayer who is not a dealer in real estate exchanges city real estate for a ranch or farm, or exchanges a leasehold of a fee with 30 years or more to run for real estate, or exchanges improved real estate for unimproved real estate.

Rev. Rul. 55-749, 1955-2 C.B. 295 holds that where, under applicable state law, water rights are considered real property rights, the exchange of perpetual water rights for a fee interest in land constitutes a nontaxable exchange of property of like kind within the meaning of § 1031(a).

Rev. Rul. 72-549, 1972-2 C.B. 472, holds that an easement and right-of-way, which were permanent, granted to an electric power company, were properties of like kind with real property with nominal improvements and real property improved with an apartment building.

Under the regulations cited, the types of real estate interests that are within the same kind or class as fee interests in real estate is broad. Both revenue rulings cited demonstrate that perpetual easements in the form of water rights and right-of-ways are of the same kind or class of property to which a fee interest in real estate belongs. The PCE at issue is also an easement. Under State X law, a PCE is an interest in real estate which, like a fee, is of a perpetual nature.

Therefore, based upon the above authorities and the facts and representations submitted, and assuming the proposed PCE is, by virtue of state law, an interest in real property, Taxpayers' exchange of a PCE in real property, under § 1031(a), for a fee interest in other real estate that is also subject to a PCE will qualify as a tax deferred exchange of like-kind property, provided that the properties are held for productive use in a trade or business or for investment. If Taxpayers receive money or other nonlike-kind property in the exchange, gain will be recognized to the extent of the such money received and the fair market value of such other property. Also, Taxpayers (and each of the co-owners) must recognize whatever gain is realized with respect to the fair market value of the replacement property received attributable to the transfer of the PCE as to that portion of the Old Ranch used for residential purposes and not for use in a trade or business or for investment.

No determination is made by this letter as to whether the described transaction otherwise qualifies for deferral of gain realized under § 1031. Except as specifically ruled above, no opinion is expressed as to the federal tax treatment of the transaction under any other provisions of the Code and the Income Tax Regulations that may be applicable or under any other general principles of federal income taxation. No opinion is expressed as to the tax treatment of any conditions existing at the time of, or effects resulting from, the transaction that are not specifically covered by the above ruling.

This ruling is directed only to the taxpayer(s) who requested it. Section 6110(k)(3) of the Code provides that it may not be cited as precedent.

Sincerely yours,

Office of Associate Chief Counsel (Income Tax & Accounting)

This document may not be used or cited as precedent. Section 6110(j)(3) of the Internal Revenue Code.

NOTES AND QUESTIONS

1. PLR 200203033 is the first and only "private letter ruling" included in this casebook. Among alternative sources of legal authority, the private letter ruling is perhaps the weakest. Indeed, as you can see from the final sentence of this ruling, the IRS expressly notes that it "may not be used or cited as precedent." Still, tax attorneys regularly consult IRS letter rulings for guidance regarding the tax effects of various transactions, especially in the absence of clear answers from the statute, regulations, court decisions or revenue rulings. The procedures for requesting a letter ruling are set forth in the first revenue procedure (also known as a "Rev. Proc.") of each calendar year. Rev. Proc. 2008-1 defines a "letter ruling" as "a written determination issued to a taxpayer by an Associate office in response to the taxpayer's written inquiry, filed prior to the filing of returns or reports that are required by the tax laws, about its status for tax purposes or the tax effects of its acts or transactions." The user fee charged for providing a letter ruling varies depending on the nature of the question asked and the gross income of the requesting taxpayer. Standard user fees can range from $10,000 on up. These fees are typically set forth in an Appendix to the Revenue Procedure containing the procedures for requesting a ruling. For example, see Appendix A, Rev. Proc. 2008-1.

2. Suppose that when ConOrg initially approached the owners of Old Ranch, ConOrg had proposed paying cash for the PCE. Suppose further that the owners had in turn proposed that ConOrg buy New Ranch and then exchange it with them for the PCE. Would the result be the same?

3. Suppose that X Corp. exchanges a computer for a printer and an airplane for a bus. Is either of these exchanges entitled to nonrecognition treatment? See Regs. § 1.1031(a)-2(b).

4. Section 1033 provides for nonrecognition where property is compulsorily or involuntarily converted (e.g., by theft, destruction, or condemnation) and is replaced with property that is "similar or related in service or use." Nonrecognition of gain is mandatory where there is a direct conversion. Where the taxpayer receives cash and then buys the replacement property, nonrecognition is optional. The period in which replacement must occur is generally two years. Note the contrasts with § 1031. Under § 1033, (a) the replacement property must be "similar or related in service or use" as opposed to "like kind" (but see § 1033(g), allowing reliance on the "like kind" standard in the case of certain conversions of real property); (b) if cash is received, the taxpayer has two years in which to find replacement property; (c) if cash is received, the taxpayer may choose to recognize gain; and (d) losses are recognized.

b. *Boot and Basis in Like-Kind Exchanges*

Boot. As you might suspect, most transactions qualifying as like-kind exchanges involve the transfer of property without identical values. Unless the party transferring the more valuable property is willing to accept property of a lesser value (which is very unlikely), the other party to the exchange will have to pay some additional amount to even out the deal. Tax lawyers use the word "boot" to refer to money, and property other than money, that, under a provision like § 1031, is transferred as part of the like-kind exchange but is not like-kind property. The transfer of boot will affect basis and may result in the recognition of gain.

For example, if a farmer exchanges a farm for another farm and receives some cash and a tractor to boot (that is, in addition), the amount of the money plus the value of the tractor is the boot. The transaction qualifies for non-recognition despite the boot, but if there is *gain*, it *is recognized to the extent of the boot*. See § 1031(b). Thus, the amount of *gain recognized* is the *lesser* of the amount of *gain realized* or the amount of the *boot*. See also § 1031(c), relating to loss situations. Note that if there is no *gain* to be recognized, the boot is not taxable; it is the gain that is recognized (and taxable), to the extent of boot, not the boot itself. For example, suppose that S exchanges X Farm, with a basis of $10,000, for Y Farm, which is worth $100,000, and that in addition S receives $15,000 cash and a tractor worth $8,000, or a total of $123,000 in property and cash. His total *gain* would be $113,000, the difference between his proceeds ($123,000) and his basis ($10,000). Of this realized gain of $113,000, $23,000, the fair market value of the boot, would be *recognized*. The remaining $90,000 gain would not be recognized. What amount of gain or loss would be recognized if the basis for X Farm had been $110,000? $130,000?

Basis. Section 1031(d) sets forth the rule for determining the basis of property received in an exchange covered by § 1031. Generally, there will be a "substituted" basis (see § 7701(a)(42)) — that is, the basis for the property received will be the same as the basis of the property relinquished. The rule becomes slightly more complicated when there is boot. The calculation of basis when there is boot involved can be made by following the directions in § 1031(d) mechanically, but the following principles should explain why those directions produce a correct result. First, in a simple exchange of like-kind properties with no boot, the property received must take on the basis of the property relinquished so that when the property received is ultimately disposed of in a recognition transaction, any previously realized but unrecognized gain or loss will be taken into account for tax purposes. For example, if S exchanges X Farm, with a basis of $10,000, for Y Farm, worth $100,000, and there is no boot, and no gain is recognized, S's basis for Y Farm must be $10,000 so that if it is later sold for $100,000 the previously unrecognized gain of $90,000 will be recognized.

Second, when gain is recognized because of boot, basis must be increased in the amount recognized so that that gain will not be taxed again; the basis of the like-kind property received plus the basis of the boot must therefore equal the basis of the original property plus the amount of gain recognized. For example, if S exchanges his X Farm, with a basis of $10,000, for Y Farm, worth $100,000, and receives $15,000 cash to boot, he must recognize his gain to the extent of the $15,000, and his basis must be increased by that amount. The basis of the property received plus the basis of the cash must therefore be $25,000.

Third, of the total basis thus calculated, a portion equal to the fair market value of the boot must be allocated to that boot, with the remainder being

allocated to the like-kind property received. Thus, in the immediately preceding example, $15,000 of the total basis must be allocated to the cash (which
always must receive a basis equal to its face amount). If the boot had consisted
of a tractor worth $15,000, rather than cash, $15,000 of basis would be allocated to the tractor; because there is no justification for attaching nonrecognition basis attributes to the tractor, S is treated as if he had received cash equal
to the tractor's fair market value and had used that cash to buy the tractor.

Fourth, if boot is *paid*, rather than received, the amount of the boot is added
to basis. See Regs. § 1.1031(d)-1(a). For example, if T owns Y farm, with a basis
of $10,000, and exchanges it, plus $15,000 cash, for X farm, in an exchange
that qualifies under § 1031, T's basis in the X farm will be $25,000.

The rules described above can be expressed algebraically—though we
emphasize that algebra is hardly necessary to understand the basic approach
just described. Nevertheless, for those who are algebraically inclined, note that
where A is the original basis, B is the amount of gain recognized, and C is the
total basis to be allocated between the like-kind property received and the boot,

$$(1)\ A + B = C$$

Where D is the portion of the basis allocated to the boot (which always receives
a basis equal to its fair market value (FMV), so D is the fair market value of the
boot) and E is the new, or substituted, basis of the like-kind property received,

$$(2)\ C - D = E.$$

Thus, if there is no boot (B and D are both zero), the like-kind property
received will have the same basis as the property surrendered ($E = A$). If there
is boot, the first step is to increase the original basis by the amount of the gain
recognized to determine the total basis to be allocated (see equation (1) above).
Then the boot receives a basis equal to its fair market value ($D = $ FMV) and the
basis left for the like-kind property received (E) is the total basis (C) reduced by
the basis allocated to the boot (D), so $E = C - D$. If the gain recognized is equal
to the amount of the boot ($B = D$), then the basis of the like-kind property
received equals the basis of the like-kind property surrendered.

c. Multiparty Transactions

Section 1031 is an important element in the planning of transactions involving farms and real estate investments. Many transactions have taken the
form of complex three-party or four-party exchanges. By its terms, § 1031
(unlike § 1033) would seem to be available only in the relatively unusual circumstance where owners of two like-kind properties happen to want to swap
with one another, but it has been extended beyond that situation, in a series of
cases dealing with complex, multiparty transactions. These cases offer valuable insights into a basic problem in tax, and other, law—the problem of
distinguishing between substance and form and of deciding when outcomes
should be governed by form and when by substance.

Suppose that S (seller) owns the X Farm, which has risen in value because of its potential for residential real estate development. B (buyer) offers to buy the farm for $1 million in cash. S would be happy to sell and use the proceeds to buy a bigger and better farm, but his basis is only $10,000 and he can't stand the thought of sharing any of his gain with the Treasury. (He has held the farm so long that he thinks of it as entirely his, almost as part of his person. He has come to think of himself as a person worth $1 million and has forgotten, or never recognized, that for years he has managed to escape tax on his gradual increase in wealth.) R, a real estate broker, who will earn a commission of $60,000 if the sale is made, proposes that the tax barrier to the transaction can be avoided if the parties are prepared to pay a modest fee for a lawyer to construct a somewhat complex, and obviously artificial, legal arrangement. Following R's advice, S finds another farm, the Y Farm, whose owner, O, is willing to sell for $1 million. The lawyer then devises the following transaction: B will buy the Y Farm for $1 million cash. Since B does not want to be stuck with that farm, there will be a previous agreement between S and B that will require S to swap the X Farm for the Y Farm once B has acquired the Y Farm. S, B, and O all follow the plan. B buys the Y Farm from O for $1 million and swaps it with S for the X Farm. S winds up with the Y Farm, B with the X Farm, and O with $1 million. S is so happy that he scarcely quibbles over the $70,000 that he must borrow in order to be able to pay $60,000 to R and $10,000 to the lawyer. The relationships and transactions may be depicted as in Figure 3-1.

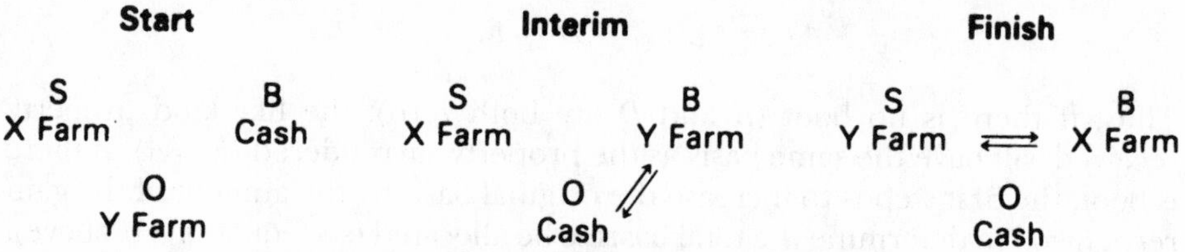

FIGURE 3-1
Illustration of Three-Party Transactions Under § 1031 (part I)

(a) What is the substance of the transactions? Bear in mind that B never wanted the Y Farm. He wanted to buy the X Farm for cash and bought the Y Farm only to help S exchange his farm for another farm he wanted. In fact, his purchase of the Y Farm is contingent on S's agreement to swap the X Farm for it. In the end, B winds up paying out cash and owning the X Farm. If tax considerations had played no role in the transactions, the easy, natural way for the three parties to have accomplished their objective would have been for B to pay $1 million for the X Farm and for S to use the $1 million to buy the Y Farm. We know as much not just from logic but from experience as well. Thus, one might argue that while the form of the transaction was a swap, the substance was a sale for cash and a reinvestment of the cash (though perhaps that is true to some degree of all swaps). Beyond that, the argument for granting relief under § 1031 is weakened by the fact that the calculation of the gain to S is not a problem and cash was available to him. Given the substance versus form issue and the policy considerations, will the effort to achieve nonrecognition succeed? Many tax lawyers, if confronted with this question, in the absence of any authority on which to rely, might predict that it would not. The Service is quite capable of seeing through artificially devised transactions and taxing them according to their underlying substance. And the courts often uphold the Service in this kind of effort. But not always, and the three-corner exchange is one instance where they did not. See, e.g., Alderson v. Commissioner, 317 F.2d 790 (9th Cir. 1963), where the court held in favor of the taxpayer even though he had initially agreed to sell for cash and later modified the agreement to follow the three-corner-exchange model.

(b) One explanation for why taxpayers prevailed in the three-corner-exchange cases may be seen by considering the following slightly modified form of our hypothetical transaction. Suppose that S was adamant in refusing to sell unless he could be assured of nonrecognition under § 1031. S finds O's Y Farm and offers to swap his X Farm for O's Y Farm. O is anxious to sell for cash; he does not want S's farm. So O finds B, who does want S's farm. O then enters into an agreement with B under which B agrees that if O acquires the X Farm, B will buy it from O for $1 million cash. O and S thereupon swap farms, and O sells the X Farm to B. (See Figure 3-2.) Now, from S's perspective, what is the substance? Is the net effect of this transaction any different from the one initially hypothesized? Formally, perhaps the most significant difference is that in the modified form S does not agree to swap with B before B has the Y Farm. S has no connection with the cash transaction between B and O. Does this make the case for nonrecognition by S seem stronger? Should § 1031 be construed to require ownership of the properties by both parties to the swap for some substantial period following the swap? Should it be construed to be inapplicable in any situation in which it is clearly contemplated, or required by the terms of the arrangement viewed in its entirety, that the property initially owned by the taxpayer is to be purchased at some point for cash?

Start		Interim		Finish	
S X Farm	B Cash	S Y Farm	B Cash	S Y Farm	B X Farm
O Y Farm		O X Farm		O Cash	

FIGURE 3-2
Illustration of Three-Party Transactions Under § 1031 (part II)

(c) In Biggs v. Commissioner, 69 T.C. 905 (1978), aff'd, 632 F.2d 1171 (5th Cir. 1980), the court allowed nonrecognition in a situation involving convolutions even more strained than those involved in the typical, "straightforward" three-corner exchange of the sort described above. The Service argued, in effect, that the taxpayer had failed to follow the transactional form that had been approved for three-corner exchanges. The court conceded the point but concluded that the transaction was in substance equivalent to the approved form of the three-corner exchange and that therefore the taxpayer was entitled to nonrecognition treatment. In explaining the basis for its conclusion the court stated (69 T.C. at 913):

> The purpose of section 1031 (and its predecessors) was to defer recognition of gain or loss on transactions in which, although in theory the taxpayer may have realized a gain or loss, his economic situation is in substance the same after, as it was before, the transaction. Stated otherwise, if the taxpayer's money continues to be invested in the same kind of property, gain or loss should not be recognized.

If that is indeed the purpose of the provision, how might it be amended to permit the objective to be achieved without forcing people to adopt convoluted forms? Would such a change be sensible?

It is worth noting that in support of the statements quoted above, the *Biggs* opinion cites H.R. Rep. 704, 73d Cong., 2d Sess. (1934), 1939-1 C.B. (Pt. 2) 554, 564. The report contains language similar to that used by the court but goes on to say:

> The Treasury Department states that its experience indicates that this provision does not in fact result in tax avoidance. If all exchanges were made taxable, it would be necessary to evaluate the property received in exchange in thousands of horse trades and similar barter transaction each year, and for the time being, at least, claims for theoretical losses would probably exceed any profits which could be established. The committee does not believe that the net revenue which could thereby be collected, particularly in these years, would justify the additional administrative expense.

(d) What if, in our initial example, S could not find property that he wanted by the time B insisted on acquiring the X Farm? Is there a way of structuring the transaction so that S can find suitable property later and still achieve nonrecognition under § 1031? In Starker v. United States, 602 F.2d 1341 (9th Cir. 1979), the sellers transferred property in exchange for cash that was paid into an escrow fund (with a 6 percent annual "growth factor") that was to be used to acquire like-kind property if any was identified within five years, and otherwise paid out to the sellers in cash. Like-kind replacement properties were indeed identified, and transferred to the sellers upon being purchased through the escrow fund, over a two-year period. The court held that § 1031 could apply under these circumstances. In 1984, however, Congress amended § 1031 by adding § 1031(a)(3). Under this provision, nonrecognition is available if, and only if, after property has been relinquished by the taxpayer, the like-kind property is *identified* within forty-five days thereafter and is *received* within the earlier of (a) 180 days or (b) the due date of the taxpayer's return. Thus, delayed three-corner exchanges are permitted, but the transaction in the *Starker* case itself would not be entitled to nonrecognition treatment under § 1031 because the new time limits were exceeded. Do those requirements seem to you to be too harsh? too generous?

In 2000 the IRS issued a ruling creating a safe harbor for "reverse-Starker" exchanges — that is, exchanges in which the replacement property is acquired before the relinquished property is transferred. Rev. Proc. 2000-37. To avoid recognition of gain, the transaction must be accomplished through a qualified titleholding intermediary, and the final transfers must occur within 180 days after the initial transfer to the intermediary.

(e) Note that while delayed exchanges are permitted, § 1031 still requires an "*exchange.*" A person relinquishing property is not permitted to receive cash even if the cash is reinvested within the time limits specified in § 1031(a)(3). That is all well and good if the person relinquishing the property is willing to rely on the promise of the person to whom the property is transferred. If, however, the transferor insists, for example, that the agreed amount be paid into an escrow account, protected from the claims of the transferee's creditors, the exchange requirement will be met if and only if the terms of the escrow comply with the rules of Regs. § 1.1031(k)-1(g).

3. Nonrecognition Rules for Certain Corporate Transactions

As discussed above, § 1031 provides a useful introduction to nonrecognition provisions for the basic federal income tax course. Once you have a basic understanding of the tax treatment of like-kind exchanges, you have taken an important first step toward mastering more sophisticated transactions involving corporations, partnerships, and limited liability companies. In this section we will examine briefly, and only at the most rudimentary level, some of the basic rules relating to the taxation of exchanges arising in the corporate context. The objective here is in part to offer a glimpse into the law in this area and in part to examine, in still another context, problems of realization and recognition.

a. Formation of a Corporation

Incorporation of a sole proprietorship. Suppose that T owns and operates as a sole proprietorship a business whose assets have a fair market value of $100,000 and a basis of $30,000. She has decided, for a variety of reasons, that she wants to operate in corporate form. In order to incorporate, typically T would form the corporation (draft and file the necessary documents, etc.) and transfer to the corporation the assets of the business in exchange for shares of the corporation's common stock. She would then be the sole shareholder, but she would no longer own the assets, any more than a shareholder of IBM owns the assets of that corporation. The assets would be owned by the corporation. At least this is how the matter is perceived in our legal system, both for tax and nontax purposes. The corporation is treated as a separate entity, one having an existence separate from that of its shareholders; it is reified. Of course, T would have the power as sole shareholder to elect all the directors of the corporation, and the directors would have the power to control its operation. The directors might appoint T president of the corporation, in which case she would have day-to-day control, but in the eyes of the law (and of the tax system) her control would be as an employee, an agent of the corporation, not as an owner.

Once one appreciates the notion of the separate entity status of corporations, one can begin to grasp the realization/recognition problem. When *T* exchanges her assets for shares of common stock of the corporation, that exchange results in a realization of the gain of $70,000. Should that gain be recognized? Using our common sense and ignoring conceptualisms, we can see that all that has happened is that *T* has changed the legal form in which she is doing business. That does not seem like the kind of change that should give rise to the recognition of gain by *T*. Congress, having accepted that common-sense view, enacted a nonrecognition provision, § 351,[4] and a corollary provision, § 1032, under which the corporation does not recognize gain on the exchange of its shares for *T*'s assets. It is important to recognize, however, that without § 351, gain would be recognized by *T* under §§ 61(a) and 1001(c). One must therefore look to the language of § 351 to determine the circumstances in which gain is or is not recognized in the case of particular corporate formations.

Amalgamations. What happens if twenty people, all with assets used in their separate unincorporated businesses, decide to pool their assets and form a single firm, using the corporate form? Each contributes assets to the newly formed corporation and each receives in return a pro rata share of the common stock of the corporation. Now what do you think about the arguments in favor of nonrecognition? Under § 351, would this be a nontaxable transaction?

Basis. Return to the initial facts, with one person, *T*, contributing to a corporation assets with a fair market value of $100,000 and a basis of $30,000. What must *T*'s basis be for her shares? If you have mastered the material in the earlier parts of this chapter, your instinct should be to suppose that *T*'s shares must take a substituted basis of $30,000. That is in fact the result dictated by the Code, in § 358. The only plausible alternative would be a basis of $100,000. But if this were the rule, and if *T* had decided to sell her unincorporated business assets, she could instead incorporate and sell the shares of stock in the corporation and thereby avoid taxation on her gain.

What about the basis of the assets held by the corporation? Under § 362(a) the corporation will take a basis in the contributed assets of $30,000. Again, this rule is required in order to prevent tax avoidance. Suppose that the corporation's basis were $100,000. Now suppose that *T* had decided to sell her unincorporated business assets and reinvest the proceeds in a different kind of business, but that there was no nonrecognition provision (such as § 1031) available that would allow her to escape tax on the gain. If the rule were that the corporation took a basis of $100,000 for the assets, she could transfer the assets to a corporation and have it sell them and reinvest in the new business,

---

4. See also § 721, which provides for nonrecognition in the case of contributions of property to partnerships.

thereby escaping tax on the gain. That possibility is foreclosed by § 362(a). But do § 358 and § 362(a), combined, go too far? What happens if T sells her shares and then the corporation sells the assets? What is the total amount of gain recognized? Does this seem right?

Transfer of property subject to debt. Suppose that T, as sole proprietor of the business, had borrowed $40,000 nonrecourse on the security of its assets and later transferred the assets, subject to the debt, to a corporation in return for its shares. We have previously seen that loan proceeds are not taxable, but that when debt is discharged gain may be recognized. See Chapter 2.H. In the case of transfers to a corporation, a specific Code provision, § 357(c), provides for recognition of gain to the extent that liabilities ($40,000) exceed basis ($30,000). T would recognize a gain of $10,000. Her basis for the shares would then be zero. See § 358(a) and (d). The basis outcome accords with tax logic. T started out with a basis of $30,000; that was her investment for tax purposes. She previously received $40,000 as a loan and has put this money in her pocket, so she is ahead $10,000; that $10,000 was recognized when she transferred the assets to the corporation, but the addition to basis to which she is entitled by virtue of this recognition of gain ($10,000), plus the original basis ($30,000), must be assigned to the cash that she previously received ($40,000) and did not transfer to the corporation. So there is no basis left for the shares of stock of the corporation. By contrast, if she had transferred the $40,000 to the corporation, she would have that much less cash and her basis for her shares would be $40,000.

Contributions of services. Suppose that at the time she decides to incorporate, T decides to hire M to manage the business for her. Suppose further that T and M agree that T will contribute her assets to the corporation in return for seventy shares of common stock and M will serve as its manager and will receive thirty shares. What are the tax consequences to T and to M? How might T and M structure their arrangement so that M still winds up with 30 percent of the common shares but the tax effects are more favorable?

b. Tax-Free Reorganizations

Changing the state of incorporation. Suppose that a corporation was initially formed in and under the laws of California but it has grown into a worldwide conglomerate and its directors have decided to shift the state of incorporation to Delaware. This cannot be done by simply writing to the authorities in each state and asking them to arrange for a transfer. In the eyes of the law, what must happen is that a new corporation must be organized under Delaware law, the assets or shares of the California corporation must be transferred to the new Delaware corporation, and the shareholders must receive shares of the Delaware corporation in exchange for their shares of the California corporation. The California corporation would probably be liquidated; it would then cease to exist. This is clearly a situation in which there should be a nonrecognition provision to relieve the shareholders from recognition of gain (and preclude recognition of loss); there is not a sufficient change in the nature of the investment to justify recognition. In fact there is, as one would expect, a nonrecognition provision. See §§ 354(a) and 368(a)(1)(F). Substituted basis is provided for both the shareholders and the corporation under §§ 358 and 362, the same provisions applying to § 351 transfers.

Mergers and acquisitions. (a) Suppose that an individual, *A*, owns 100 shares of *X* Corp. stock, with a fair market value of $10,000 and a basis of $1,000, and another individual, *B*, owns 100 shares of *Y* Corp. stock, with a fair market value of $10,000 and a basis of $2,000. Now suppose that *A* and *B* decide to combine their investments, with each becoming an equal cotenant in the shares of each of the two corporations. That transaction would require the recognition of gain by each of the two individuals; no nonrecognition provision applies. *A* would be treated as having exchanged half her interest in *X* Corp., with a basis of $500 (for the half interest), for a half interest in *B*'s shares of *Y* Corp., worth $5,000 (for the half interest) and would recognize a gain of $4,500. *B*'s recognized gain would be $4,000.

(b) Suppose that the directors of two corporations, *X* and *Y*, with the approval of the shareholders, decide to merge them into a single corporation. This can be done in a number of ways. *X* can be merged into *Y* or vice versa; both can be merged into a newly formed corporation; shares can be exchanged for shares or assets can be exchanged for shares. No matter how it is done, if *A* and *B* receive shares of the new firm (or if one of them receives new shares and the other keeps her old shares), and if the appropriate formats have been adopted, the amalgamation can be achieved, under § 354, with no recognition of gain to either *A* or *B*. This is true, moreover, even if one of the corporations is huge (a "whale") and the other is tiny (a "minnow").

(c) Can the results in the situations described in the two preceding paragraphs be reconciled according to any sound principle of tax policy? nontax policy?

C. DEEMED REALIZATION — CONSTRUCTIVE SALES

In late 1996, less than a month after President Bill Clinton won reelection in his campaign against Republican presidential nominee Bob Dole, the *New York Times* published a front page special report titled "Wealthy, Helped by Wall St., Find New Ways to Escape Tax on Profits." The article described "several exotic Wall Street strategies" designed to allow large shareholders "to raise cash and lock in their stock market profits without actually selling their shares." Among the numerous transactions described in the article was the so-called short-against-the-box strategy that members of the Estée Lauder family had reportedly used to avoid paying $95 million in federal income taxes that would have been owed had they chosen to simply sell their stock. The article quoted then–Deputy Treasury Secretary Lawrence H. Summers (who was later appointed Treasury Secretary by President Clinton) as saying, "What are functionally capital gains realizations should be taxed." Congress agreed, adopting the administration's "constructive sale" provision — now § 1259 — as part of the Taxpayer Relief Act of 1997. The story behind § 1259 provides a fascinating illustration of our tax system's ongoing struggle to manage the realization concept.

The transactions at which § 1259 was aimed were designed principally for individuals with large blocks of low basis, high value stock — typically company founders. In most cases, these individuals had a disproportionately large share of their overall net worth invested in a single company. Absent tax considerations, the desired strategy would be to sell the company stock and reinvest the proceeds in a diversified pool of assets in order to minimize exposure to company-specific risk. However, that approach would clearly trigger a realization event for tax purposes, causing the taxpayer to recognize a large amount of taxable gain. The trick then was to devise transactions that would allow the taxpayer to monetize her appreciated financial position without triggering a realization event. One such transaction was the so-called short against the box.

To understand how these transactions work, imagine that Eileen owns 1,000 shares of ABC stock with a basis of $10,000 ($10 per share) and a fair market value of $90,000 ($90 per share). Eileen obviously cannot sell the stock without recognizing gain. Suppose, however, that Eileen borrows 1,000 shares of ABC from Bob for a period of one year and then immediately sells those shares. The sale of borrowed stock is called a "short sale." It is a strategy commonly used by investors who believe the stock is going to decline in value. For example, assume that Jake borrows 1,000 shares of ABC stock from his broker, agreeing to deliver the same number of ABC shares a year later, and sells those borrowed shares $90,000 cash ($90 per share). If ABC drops to $50 per share, it will cost Jake only $50,000 to come up with the replacement shares, leaving him with a $40,000 profit.

In Eileen's case, however, the short sale serves a somewhat different function. Like Jake, Eileen will benefit from a decline in value of the ABC stock because that decline will reduce the cost of acquiring the shares she must deliver to Bob a year later. But because Eileen still owns her original ABC shares, a decline in the value of ABC stock also hurts her. In fact, any benefit she enjoys with respect to her short position is precisely offset by the loss she suffers with respect to her long position, and vice versa. In other words, by entering into a short sale of ABC stock, Eileen (i) gets $90,000 cash up front, and (ii) completely insulates herself from fluctuations in value of the ABC stock. Is it accurate to say that Eileen still "owns" the ABC stock? In a superficial legal sense, the answer is yes; after all, she still has title to her ABC stock. In an economic sense, however, these transactions have a great deal in common with an outright sale. As is true for an outright sale, Eileen has completely transformed her economic exposure to fluctuations in value of the ABC stock.

Section 1259 now treats this transaction as a sale. More precisely, the statute provides that if there is a "constructive sale" of an "appreciated financial position" the taxpayer must "recognize gain as if such position were sold. . . ." § 1259(a)(1). A taxpayer is treated as having made a constructive sale of an appreciated financial position if she "enters into a short sale of the same or substantially identical property." § 1259(c)(1)(A). Thus, the statute directly targets the "short against the box transaction" described above. However, the statute doesn't stop there. It also treats certain other transactions — including "offsetting notional principal contracts" (§ 1259(c)(1)(B)) and "futures or forward contracts" (§ 1259(c)(1)(C)) — as constructive sales.

As is often the case in the development of the tax law, § 1259 has not put an end to the types of transactions that it targeted but rather has turned attention to whether particular transactions not expressly described by the statute should be treated as "constructive sales." The ongoing ambiguity of § 1259's scope is perhaps best illustrated by reference to a transaction known as a "zero-cost collar." Like the short against the box transaction, the zero-cost collar is designed to allow investors to replicate the economic effects a sale without parting with legal title to the appreciated stock. For example, assume that XYZ founder Ahmed owns XYZ stock with a basis of $10,000 and a value of $500 million. In a typical collar transaction, Ahmed might (i) sell a call option (i.e., an option to purchase the shares from him on some future date for, say $510 million), and (ii) buy a put option (i.e., an option to sell the shares on some future date for, say, $490 million). By entering into these two transactions — called a *zero-cost* collar because the cost of acquiring the put option can be financed by the proceeds of the sale of the call option — Ahmed has effectively eliminated his exposure to upside potential over and above $510 million as well as any downside risk should the stock decline in value below $490 million.

Should Ahmed's zero-cost collar be treated as a "constructive sale" within the meaning of § 1259? As a first cut, note that these transactions are not described in § 1259(c)(1)(A), (B), (C) or (D). However, this is not the end of the analysis. The statute further provides that a taxpayer will be treated as having made a constructive sale of an appreciated financial position if he, or a related person, "to the extent prescribed by the Secretary in regulations, enters into 1 or more other transactions (or acquires 1 or more positions) that have substantially the same effect as" any of the other constructive sale transactions described in the statute. § 1259(c)(1)(E). Given this language, it might be tempting to examine the Treasury regulations under § 1259. As of mid-2008, however, regulations under § 1259 have not yet been promulgated.

The absence of regulatory guidance leaves taxpayers and their advisors with some uncertainty regarding the appropriate tax treatment of the transaction in question. Oftentimes, tax lawyers will consult legislative history in an effort to get some comfort with a particular transaction. With respect to collar transactions, consider the following passage from the "General Explanation of Tax Legislation Enacted in 1997" prepared by the staff of the Joint Committee on Taxation (December 17, 1997):

JOINT COMMITTEE ON TAXATION
GENERAL EXPLANATION OF TAX LEGISLATION
ENACTED IN 1997
(December 17, 1997)

. . .

TITLE X. REVENUE-INCREASE PROVISIONS

A. FINANCIAL PRODUCTS

1. Require Recognition of Gain on Certain Appreciated Financial Positions in Personal Property (sec. 1001(a) of the Act and sec. 1259 of the Code)

. . .

Treasury Guidance

The Act provides regulatory authority to the Treasury to treat as constructive sales certain transactions that have substantially the same effect as those specified (i.e., short sales, offsetting notional principal contracts and futures or forward contracts to deliver the same or substantially similar property).

. . .

The Congress anticipated that the Treasury regulations, when issued, will provide specific standards for determining whether several common transactions will be treated as constructive sales. One such transaction is a "collar." In a collar, a taxpayer commits to an option requiring him to sell a financial position at a fixed price (the "call strike price") and has the right to have his position purchased at a lower fixed price (the "put strike price"). For example, a shareholder may enter into a collar for a stock currently trading at $100 with a put strike price of $95 and a call strike price of $110. The effect of the transaction is that the seller has transferred the rights to all gain above the $110 call strike price and all loss below the $95 put strike price; the seller has retained all risk of loss and opportunity for gain in the price range between $95 and $110. A collar can be a single contract or can be effected by using a combination of put and call options. In order to determine whether collars have substantially the same effect as the transactions specified in the provision, the Congress anticipated that Treasury regulations will provide specific standards that take into account various factors with respect to the appreciated financial position, including its volatility. It is expected that several aspects of the collar transaction will be relevant, including the spread between the put and call prices, the period of the transaction, and the extent to which the taxpayer retains the right to periodic payments on the appreciated financial position (e.g., the dividends on collared stock). The Congress intended that the Treasury regulations with respect to collars will be applied prospectively, except in cases to prevent abuse.

QUESTIONS

1. Recall that Company XYZ founder Ahmed is considering entering into a zero-cost collar transaction. His basis in the XYZ stock is $10,000. The fair market value of the stock is $500 million. Under the terms of the proposed transaction, Ahmed will (i) sell to a third party an option to purchase his XYZ shares on December 31, 2015 for $510 million, and (ii) buy from a third party an option to sell his XYZ shares on December 15, 2015 for $490 million. Based on your understanding of § 1259 and the foregoing legislative history, what advice would you give Ahmed regarding the federal income tax treatment of the proposed transaction? Are there any changes to the proposed transaction that you might suggest in order to minimize the likelihood that it will be treated as a constructive sale?

2. Recall that Woodsam Associates, Inc. v. Commissioner held that a taxpayer who borrows money on a nonrecourse basis, pledging appreciated property as security for the loan, does not experience a realization event for tax purposes. In what sense is borrowing nonrecourse against appreciated property any different from the types of transactions covered by § 1259? Should the statute be amended to treat borrowing nonrecourse against appreciated property as a constructive sale?

D. ORIGINAL ISSUE DISCOUNT AND RELATED RULES

The rules on original issue discount (OID) provide that to the extent that a "debt instrument" does not provide for current payment of an adequate amount of interest, interest must be accrued (that is, included currently in income) by the obligee regardless whether the obligee is a cash-method or accrual-method taxpayer. See §§ 1272-1275. The obligor is entitled to deduct the amount that the obligee is required to accrue. The OID rules apply to debt instruments issued for cash or for property, with certain exceptions for relatively small transactions. The concept of original issue discount (OID) refers to the unstated interest in a deferred payment. When a bond is sold for cash, the OID is the difference between the issue price (that is, the price at which the bond is sold) and the redemption price (the price required to be paid by the issuer/borrower when the term of the loan ends and the bond must be paid off (redeemed)). For example, suppose that a bond is issued (sold) for $600,000 and that it is to be redeemed five years later for $1 million, with no interest payments in the interim. The amount of the OID is the difference between the redemption price ($1 million) and the issue price ($600,000), or $400,000. § 1273(a). This amount is treated as interest earned ratably over the five-year term of the loan with semi-annual compounding. The amount of interest to be reported by the lender and deducted by the borrower each year is shown below:

Redemption price		$1,000,000
Issue price		600,000
OID		400,000
Term		5 years

Annual interest amounts:		New basis (end of year):
Year 1	$64,540	$664,540
Year 2	71,482	736,022
Year 3	79,171	815,193
Year 4	87,687	902,880
Year 5	97,120	1,000,000
Total	$400,000	

Here the effect of the OID rules is to treat the purchaser of the bond as if she had simply placed the $600,000 issue price in a bank or money market account that paid interest at a rate sufficient to generate the redemption price in five years. Each year the amount in the account would rise and the interest income would increase.

Section 1275(a)(1)(A) provides that "the term 'debt instrument' means a bond, debenture, note, or certificate or other evidence of indebtedness." The OID rules provide an economically accurate reporting of income and deductions. The main purpose of their adoption was to prevent the tax avoidance that occurred when an accrual-method obligor deducted accrued interest while the cash-method obligee reported no interest income.

The application of the OID concept in the above example of a sale of a bond for cash is relatively simple and straightforward since there is no question about the amount of the original issue discount: It is simply the difference between the price paid for the bond at the time of issuance and the redemption price. Where a promissory obligation is issued in return for property, the application of the OID rules is more complex because there is no readily determinable issue price. The counterpart of the receipt and payment of an issue price is the transfer of property; the value of the property often will be difficult to determine. The approach of the OID rules, therefore, is to apply discount rates to the expected payments. In other words, the issue price is determined by discounting the expected payments to present value. Obviously, the key element in the process is the selection of an appropriate interest rate. The Code calls for the Treasury to publish periodically interest rates for obligations of various durations. § 1274(d). These interest rates, called the "applicable federal rates," are based on the current rates paid on U.S. Treasury obligations. If the amount of interest stated by the parties is adequate, as compared with the applicable federal rate, then that stated rate is accepted in determining the amount of interest deducted by the obligor and reported by the obligee. Otherwise, the applicable federal rate is used.

To illustrate, assume that on January 1 of Year 1, T buys an apartment building for an amount stated to be $5 million. T pays no cash but instead executes a promissory note for $5 million, due ten years later, with interest payable at the rate of 8 percent per year. Assume that the annualized "applicable federal rate" at the time the note is issued is 10 percent.[5] The payments of $400,000 per year for nine years, plus $5,400,000 in the tenth year, are discounted to present value using the 10 percent rate. The result is a present value, or "imputed principal amount" (§ 1274(b)(1)), of $4,385,543, which is treated as the issue price. The difference between this amount and the $5,000,000 redemption price is $614,457, which is the OID. A portion of this total amount of OID must be reported each year along with the $400,000 annual cash payment called for in the obligation.

How much OID is recognized each year? In the first year, the total interest earned on the note is equal to the present value of the amount owed ($4,385,543) multiplied by the applicable federal rate of 10 percent. That comes to $438,554. The stated interest is only $400,000, so the OID is the difference, $38,554. This $38,554, along with the $400,000 cash payment, is reported as income by the holder of the obligation and is deducted by the obligor in the first year. The $38,554 has not in fact been paid, however, and is in effect added to the principal amount owed, which produces a principal amount at the beginning of the second year of $4,424,097 (with an error of $1 due to rounding). (The same result is reached by discounting the remaining payments to present value.) The interest on the debt in the second year is equal to the new principal amount ($4,424,097) multiplied by the applicable federal rate of 10 percent, or $442,410. Again, the stated interest is $400,000, so the OID is $42,410. These numbers and the corresponding numbers for the remaining years are shown in Table 3-2.

The OID concept is also applied to rents, under § 467. To illustrate, suppose Lessor agrees to rent property to Lessee for three years in return for a single payment of $1 million at the end of the three-year term. Before the adoption of § 467, an accrual-method lessee might accrue and treat as a deduction each year one-third of the total amount due at the end of the three

TABLE 3-2

Year	Value of debt obligation[a]	Total interest earned	Annual stated interest	Annual OID[b]	Principal payment
1	$4,385,543	$438,554	$400,000	$38,554	
2	4,424,098	442,410	400,000	42,410	
3	4,466,507	446,651	400,000	46,651	
4	4,513,158	451,316	400,000	51,316	
5	4,564,474	456,447	400,000	56,447	
6	4,620,921	462,092	400,000	62,092	
7	4,683,013	468,301	400,000	68,301	
8	4,751,315	475,131	400,000	75,131	
9	4,826,446	482,645	400,000	82,645	
10	4,909,091	490,909	400,000	90,909	$5,000,000

[a]Principal and interest payments discounted at applicable federal rate of 10 percent.
[b]This amount is added to principal.

5. The rates published by the Treasury include rates with a slight upward adjustment that may be used for compounding on an annual, rather than semiannual, basis to achieve the same annual result that would be reached using the semiannual rate with semiannual compounding.

years. At the same time, a cash-method lessor would not include any amount in income until the $1 million was received. Section 467 is intended to put an end to such mismatching. Here is how it would work on the hypothetical facts.

First, one computes the present value of the $1 million payment at the end of the third year, using 110 percent of the applicable federal rate. Assume that the applicable federal rate is 9.09 percent and that 110 percent of that rate is therefore (almost) 10 percent. The present value (with semiannual compounding) is $746,237. One then computes (on a computer) the annual rent, payable at the end of each year, that would have the same present value. That annual rental amount, which turns out to be $301,389, is called the "constant rental amount." See § 467(e)(1). The lessee is allowed to deduct, and the lessor is required to include in gross income, this $301,389 at the end of each year. Because that amount of rent is not in fact paid, however, it is treated as if it were a loan from the lessor to the lessee, and unstated interest must be attributed to the parties. Thus, at the end of the first year, the lessee is treated as owing $301,389 and at the end of the second year is treated as owing interest on this amount (again, at 110 percent of the applicable federal rate, compounded semiannually). The interest at the end of the second year is $30,889. In addition, at the end of the second year, lessee is treated as owing the second year's rent of $301,389. In the third year, interest continues to accrue on the first year's unpaid rent (plus the unpaid interest on that rent) and begins to accrue on the second year's unpaid rent. Thus, the total interest at the end of the third year is $64,944. The constant rental amounts, the interest, and the total amounts to be included in income by the lessor and deducted by the lessee are as follows:

Year	Rent	Interest	Total
1	$301,389	—	$ 301,389
2	301,389	30,889	332,278
3	301,389	64,944	366,333
Total	$904,167	$95,833	$1,000,000

There are also rules for taxation of "market discount." These rules do not alter the normal rules on timing of recognition of gain. Their purpose and function was to prevent the conversion of ordinary income into capital gain. To illustrate their operation, suppose a bond was issued many years ago and bears interest at a rate of 3 percent on a face value of $1,000 (this being the amount that must be paid at maturity), with four years to maturity. If the present market rate of interest is 12 percent, the present value of the bond is $727. A buyer of such a bond would receive annual interest payments of $30. These would be taxable as received as ordinary income. At maturity, the buyer would receive $1,000 and would report a gain of $273. This $273 is called "market discount"; under §§ 1276 and 1278 the gain is treated as ordinary income, rather than as capital gain (which is the way it was treated before the adoption of these provisions in 1984). If the bond is sold before the maturity date, a ratable portion of the market discount (determined on a linear daily basis) is treated as ordinary income.

There are exceptions to the application of the OID rules, including exceptions for sales of principal residences, sales of farms for less than $1 million, and sales for payments totaling less than $250,000. § 1274(c)(3). In these situations, where the OID rules do not apply, § 483 applies. Section 483 does not affect the timing of the recognition of the imputed interest income, but ensures that that income is treated as ordinary income rather than as capital gain. In other words, § 483 determines the character or nature of the gain from certain sales transactions, whereas the OID rules determine not just the character of the gain but the time of its recognition. For example, suppose that a personal residence with a basis of $400,000 is sold for a single payment of $1 million to be made at the end of five years, and that the applicable federal rate is 10 percent. At the time of sale the present value of the future payment is $620,921 and the "unstated interest" is the difference between that present value amount and the $1 million payment, or $379,079. When the $1,000,000 is collected at the end of five years, the seller will report a total gain of $600,000, the difference between the basis, $400,000, and the amount received, $1 million. Of the $600,000, $379,079 is reported as ordinary interest income and the remaining $220,921 is reported as capital gain.

E. OPEN TRANSACTIONS AND INSTALLMENT SALES

1. Open Transaction Doctrine

The case that follows, Burnet v. Logan, has little if any remaining importance for the rule it adopts. The case continues to be of interest, however, because it establishes what one may think of as one end of a spectrum of possible recovery-of-basis rules and because of its discussion of the justification for the approach it adopts.

BURNET v. LOGAN
283 U.S. 404 (1931)

Mr. Justice McReynolds delivered the opinion of the Court.

[The facts in the case are complicated and confusing. The following simplified and modified version of the facts reveals the essence of the transaction and the issues raised.

Mrs. Logan, the taxpayer, owned 1,000 shares of stock of Andrews and Hitchcock Mining Company. Her basis in these shares was $180,000. Andrews and Hitchcock owned the right to a part of the ore mined from a rich iron deposit. In 1916 Youngstown Sheet & Tube Company bought all the shares of Andrews and Hitchcock owned by Mrs. Logan and her fellow shareholders. As consideration for the purchase, Youngstown made a cash payment and agreed to make additional payments in the future based on the amount of ore that it would receive as a result of its acquisition of the Andrews and Hitchcock rights in the iron mine. There was considerable uncertainty about what the amount of the future payments would turn out to be.

Mrs. Logan's share of the cash payment was $120,000. The government estimated that she would receive future payments, based on the amount of ore going to Youngstown, of $9,000 per year for twenty-five years, with a present value of $100,000.

The position taken by the government was that in 1916 Mrs. Logan sold her shares for $220,000 (the cash of $120,000 plus the present value of the promise of future payments, $100,000) and should have reported a gain of $40,000. In other words, the government claimed that the transaction was a "closed transaction" in 1916. Mrs. Logan would then have a basis of $100,000 in the right to receive the future payments and, according to the government, would be allowed to recover this basis at the rate of $4,000 per year over the twenty-five years in which she expected to receive payments.

Mrs. Logan argued for "open transaction" treatment. There were two separate aspects to her position. The first was that the promise to make future payments did not have an ascertainable value in 1916 and should be ignored in that year. The second aspect of Mrs. Logan's tax position was that she should be allowed to recover her entire basis before reporting any gain. Thus, she claimed that she was not required to report any gain in 1916, since she received only $120,000 in cash and her basis was $180,000, and that she was not required to treat any of the future payments from Youngstown as income until the total of such payments had exceeded her remaining basis ($60,000).

The Court, without separating the two aspects of Mrs. Logan's position, held in her favor. Its opinion follows.]

The 1916 transaction was a sale of stock—not an exchange of property. We are not dealing with royalties or deductions from gross income because of depletion of mining property. Nor does the situation demand that an effort be made to place according to the best available data some approximate value upon the contract for future payments. This probably was necessary in order to assess the mother's estate. As annual payments on account of extracted ore come in they can be readily apportioned first as return of capital and later as profit. The liability for income tax ultimately can be fairly determined without resort to mere estimates, assumptions and speculation. When the profit, if any, is actually realized, the taxpayer will be required to respond. The [total] consideration for the sale [realized by all the shareholders] was $2,200,000.00 in cash and the promise of future money payments wholly contingent upon facts and circumstances not possible to foretell with anything like fair certainty. The promise was in no proper sense equivalent to cash. It had no ascertainable fair market value. The transaction was not a closed one. Respondent might never recoup her capital investment from payments only conditionally promised. Prior to 1921, all receipts from the sale of her shares amounted to less than their value on March 1, 1913. She properly demanded the return of her capital investment before assessment of any taxable profit based on conjecture.

"In order to determine whether there has been gain or loss, and the amount of the gain if any, we must withdraw from the proceeds an amount sufficient to restore the capital value that existed at the commencement of the period under consideration." Doyle v. Mitchell Bros. Co., 247 U.S. 179, 184, 185. . . . Ordinarily, at least, a taxpayer may not deduct from gross receipts a supposed loss which in fact is represented by his outstanding note. . . . And, conversely, a promise to pay indeterminate sums of money is not necessarily taxable income. "Generally speaking, the income tax law is concerned only with realized losses, as with realized gains." Lucas v. American Code Co., 280 U.S. 445, 449.

From her mother's estate, Mrs. Logan obtained [by inheritance] the right to [additional payments from Youngstown Steel by virtue of the mother's ownership of Andrews and Hitchcock stock]. The value of this [right] was assumed [for estate tax purposes] to be $277,164.50. . . . Some valuation — speculative or otherwise — was necessary in order to close the estate. It may never yield as much, it may yield more. If a sum equal to the value thus ascertained had been invested in an annuity contract, payments thereunder would have been free from income tax until the owner had recouped his capital investment.[6] We think a like rule should be applied here. The statute definitely excepts bequests from receipts which go to make up taxable income. . . .

The judgments below are affirmed.

NOTES AND QUESTIONS

1. The *"open transaction."* Burnet v. Logan is said to stand for the "open transaction" concept or doctrine — the notion that where the total value of the consideration to be received by a taxpayer is sufficiently uncertain (not "equivalent to cash" because of "no ascertainable fair market value") gain is not recognized until the payments actually received exceed basis. The key sentence in the opinion is, "The transaction was not a closed one." The case may be compared with Inaja Land Co. v. Commissioner, supra page 120, where the taxpayer sold an easement affecting a river that crossed its property and the court treated the entire proceeds as a recovery of basis. There the uncertainty related to what was sold, and in Burnet v. Logan it related to what was received. In both cases the courts adopted a "wait and see" attitude. This is highly favorable to the taxpayer, much more so in an era of high interest rates than in the era of low interest rates when these cases were decided.

The taxpayer had another, unused string to her bow in Burnet v. Logan. Even if the value of the expected payments in the case had been ascertainable, the taxpayer might have argued that the transaction should not result in recognition or gain because what she received was a "mere" promise to pay, which is not treated as a receipt for cash-method taxpayers. For example, if a lawyer performs services for a client and the client agrees to pay $1,000 to the lawyer next year, the lawyer (assuming she or he uses the cash method) is not required to report the $1,000 until received. If, on the other hand, the promise to pay takes the form of negotiable promissory notes, such notes generally are considered "property," the value of which must be included in income.

---

6. [This was the rule for annuities before 1934. — EDS.]

2. *Three possible approaches.* Consider three possible approaches to recognition of gain or loss and recovery of basis where property has been sold in return for the right to a series of cash payments (installments) to be received in the future. For present purposes, let us assume that each installment payment is to bear interest at the market rate, so we need not be concerned about the rules relating to unstated interest or original issue discount. (1) One possible rule for recovery of basis is the *open transaction* approach. In Burnet v. Logan this was combined with a rule under which all payments received were treated as recovery of basis until the full amount of the basis was recovered and then all payments are treated as gain. Thus, the case may be said to reflect a *basis first* rule. (2) A second possibility is to determine the *present value* of the expected payments and treat this sum as if it were cash received on the date of the sale. Gain or loss is then determined by comparing this amount with basis.[7] This is the *closed transaction* approach. (3) A third possibility is to use an open transaction approach but to allocate some portion of basis to each expected payment received, so that some portion of the gain or loss is recognized as each payment is received. This is the approach of the *installment method*, discussed infra at page 273.

What are the advantages of and objections to each approach? What are the circumstances to which each approach may be best suited?

3. *The present rule.* (a) In 1980, Congress expanded the availability of the installment method of reporting, under which gain or loss is reported as payments are received. See infra page 273. In explaining the revised rules, the Senate Finance Committee Report (No. 96-1000, 96th Cong., 2d Sess. (1980)) had this to say:

> The creation of a statutory deferred payment option for all forms of deferred payment sales significantly expands the availability of installment reporting to include situations where it has not previously been permitted. By providing an expanded statutory installment reporting option, the Committee believes that in the future there should be little attempt to obtain deferred reporting. In any event, the effect of the new rules is to reduce substantially the justification for treating transactions as "open" and permitting the use of the cost-recovery method sanctioned by Burnet v. Logan [supra page 268]. Accordingly, it is the Committee's intent that the cost-recovery method not be available in the case of sales for a fixed price (whether the seller's obligation is evidenced by a note, contractual promise, or otherwise), and that its use be limited to those rare and extraordinary cases involving sales for a contingent price where the fair market value of the purchaser's obligation cannot reasonably be ascertained.

(b) Even before 1980, the Regulations relating to gain or loss on disposition of property had provided that "only in rare and extraordinary cases will property be considered to have no fair market value." Regs. § 1.1001-1(a).

(c) In Warren Jones Co. v. Commissioner, 524 F.2d 788 (9th Cir. 1975), the taxpayer sold a building by land sale contract for $153,000, receiving $20,000 in cash and a contract calling for payment of the balance, $133,000, over

---

7. If the payments bear interest at the market rate, the present value will be equal to the total stated amount of the payments, before interest.

fifteen years. In the year of sale, the taxpayer received $24,000, and since it had a basis of $61,913.34, it deferred reporting gain until it recovered its basis. Evidence was presented that the $133,000 contract could have been sold in the marketplace for only $76,980. The Tax Court held that the taxpayer properly deferred reporting gain, that the contract was not "property (other than money)" under § 1001(b), and that it was not the equivalent of cash since with a fair market value of $76,980, it could not be sold for anywhere near its $133,000 face amount. The circuit court reversed, interpreting the legislative history of § 1001(b) to mean that Congress intended to establish a definite rule that if the fair market value received in an exchange can be ascertained, the fair market value must be reported as the amount realized, rejecting the argument that cash equivalency close to face amount of an obligation was an element to be considered in determining whether fair market value could be ascertained. The court reasoned that § 453, providing for installment reporting and discussed infra page 273, was Congress's way of providing relief from the rigors of § 1001(b). Compare material on economic benefit and cash equivalents in Chapter 2A.

(d) Cf. Bolles v. Commissioner, 69 T.C. 342 (1977), where members of the Piper family agreed in 1969 to an exchange offer of their shares of Piper Corp. stock for Bangor Punta Corp. stock if Bangor Punta could acquire more than half of the Piper Corp. outstanding shares, with the consideration to be determined by a third party. During 1969, Bangor Punta had not acquired the requisite number of shares and the final price had not been set by the third party. The court, following Burnet v. Logan, held that due to the contingencies involved, the rights had no ascertainable fair market value and the taxpayer need not recognize any gain from receipt of the rights in 1969. Should the reason for deferral in this case be the lack of ascertainable value or the inappropriateness of the time to tax, given the substantial contingencies still unresolved? Can't everything be valued if necessary?

4. *The capital gain issue.* Under present law, whenever we are confronted with deferred payments we must be concerned about unstated interest (§ 483) or original issue discount (OID). The § 483 and OID rules have the important effect of ensuring that the interest element in any deferred payment is treated as ordinary income rather than capital gain. Before § 483 and the OID rules were adopted, and to some extent even now, judicially developed rules relating to open versus closed transactions affected the characterization of gain as ordinary or capital and the timing of the recognition of gain. If, as in Burnet v. Logan, a transaction was treated as open, payments received were treated as nontaxable recovery of basis until basis was exhausted and, if, as in that case, the transaction involved the sale of a capital asset, all subsequent payments were treated as capital gain. Thus, the seller had two advantages, maximum deferral and maximum capital gain treatment.

If the transaction had been treated as closed, the seller not only would have lost the advantage of deferral but also could have lost some of the benefit of capital gain treatment. For example, in Waring v. Commissioner, 412 F.2d 800 (3d Cir. 1969), the taxpayer in 1946 had in effect sold a license to use the name "Waring" on the Waring blender, in return for royalties. In his 1946 tax return, he treated the transaction as closed. He valued the right to the royalties at $300,000, deducted his basis of $93,000, and reported a capital gain of $207,000. This meant that his basis for the right to receive the royalties became $300,000. As royalties were received in subsequent years, he treated them as recovery of capital, reducing basis.[8] By the end of 1952, all the basis was exhausted and at that point all subsequent payments were treated as ordinary income (since they were not received as a result of a "sale or exchange"). In time, Waring obviously realized that he would have been better off if, in 1946, he had treated the transaction as open, under Burnet v. Logan. If he had done so, after recovery of basis, all payments would have been treated as capital gain as long as he received them. In 1960 and 1961, he filed returns claiming capital gain treatment for the royalties received in those years; his position was that his original decision to treat the transaction as closed was an error as to a continuing transaction and that he was entitled to correct that error as it affected years not closed by the statute of limitations. Unfortunately for him, open-transaction treatment depends on the taxpayer's ability to establish that the value of the rights received is not ascertainable. In light of the fact that in 1946 his accountant had valued the rights at $300,000, the court had little difficulty in concluding that no error had been made in treating the transaction as closed in 1946.

2. The Installment Method

The installment method (§§ 453, 453A, and 453B) is a set of accounting rules that permit nonrecognition of gain in transactions involving the sale of property. The principal congressional objective in allowing this method is to provide relief from the harshness of an obligation to pay taxes when the taxpayer has not received cash with which to pay those taxes, but the benefits are enjoyed by many taxpayers who have no problem of cash availability but who prefer, as do most taxpayers, to pay taxes later rather than sooner.

The basic approach. The basic approach is simple. First, the rules relating to unstated interest (§ 483) or OID (original issue discount) are applied. The installment method applies to what remains. See Regs. § 15a.453-1(b)(2)(ii). For purposes of illustration, let us assume that all payments bear interest at an adequate rate; thus, we can focus on the amount of the payment, before interest, and illustrate the installment method without concern for the interest

---

8. Note that the taxpayer treated the initial sale as a closed transaction. The result was that he had a basis of $300,000 in the right to receive the royalty payments. The standard treatment then would have been to amortize this basis over the expected duration of the payments. For example, if that expected duration was ten years, the taxpayer should have deducted $30,000 per year. Instead, he was allowed to follow the basis-first approach of Burnet v. Logan, allocating basis to the payments thereafter received until all of his basis was recovered, with subsequent payments fully taxed. That basis-first approach was justified in Burnet v. Logan by the difficulty of determining the duration and amount of the payments. In *Waring*, however, the valuation difficulties were not considered too serious to prevent treating the original transaction as closed. That being so, it seems inconsistent to use basis-first cost recovery, which can be thought of as a form of open-transaction treatment. In other words, in *Waring* the open-transaction issue arises not just once but twice. The first time, we get closed-transaction treatment and the second time we get open-transaction treatment on the same facts.

element in any total amount received. The taxpayer computes a ratio of gain to total expected payments and applies this ratio to each payment. See § 453(c). For example, suppose a taxpayer sells property with a basis of $100,000 in return for a total stated amount of $300,000 in the form of payments to be received at the end of each of the subsequent five years of $30,000, $60,000, $30,000, $60,000, and $120,000 (plus adequate interest on each payment). Since the basis is $100,000 and the total to be received is $300,000, two-thirds of each payment received is treated as gain; the other one-third is a recovery of basis. For the results, see Table 3-3.

TABLE 3-3
BASIS: $100,000

Year	Amount received	Gain recognized	Basis used	Basis remaining
1	$ 30,000	$ 20,000	$ 10,000	$ 90,000
2	60,000	40,000	20,000	70,000
3	30,000	20,000	10,000	60,000
4	60,000	40,000	20,000	40,000
5	120,000	80,000	40,000	-0-
Totals	$300,000	$200,000	$100,000	—

The taxpayer is permitted to elect not to use the installment method. See § 453(d). In that case, the transaction is treated as closed and gain is recognized at the outset in an amount equal to the difference between the fair market value of the installment payments and the basis (except for the highly unlikely possibility that the taxpayer can establish the right to open-transaction treatment).

A loophole closed. Here is a nice example of a substance-versus-form issue. Suppose that Maria holds property with a basis of $100,000 and wants to sell it now for its fair market value of $300,000 and receive cash from the prospective buyer. Maria hopes to defer the recognition of gain. Rather than selling the property directly to the buyer, Maria sells it first to her daughter, Dora, for a total of $300,000, in the form of five annual payments of $60,000 over the next five years. Dora then sells the property to the buyer for $300,000 cash. Dora has no gain since her basis is her purchase price of $300,000. She holds the $300,000 in an interest-bearing account and at the end of each year, for five years, pays $60,000 plus the interest earned in that year. If the form of the transaction is respected, Maria's gain is deferred even though there is no justification for deferral (since cash was paid and is in the family). Section 453(e) closes this loophole by requiring Maria to treat the $300,000 as an amount realized by her if the property is later sold by a "related person." Under § 267(b)(1), the term "related person" includes "members of a family," which is later defined as an individual's "brothers and sisters (whether by the whole or half blood), spouse, ancestors, and lineal descendants."

A loophole still open? Assume the same facts as above, except that Maria, instead of transferring the property to her daughter—who is plainly a "related person" within the meaning of the statute—transfers the property to her same-sex partner, Frida, under the same terms as those described above (i.e., a total of $300,000, in the form of five annual payments of $60,000 over the next five years). Are Frida and Maria "related persons" for purposes of §§ 267 and 453? It would appear that the answer is no. In fact, even if Frida and Maria happen to be married (in a state permitting same-sex couples to wed) and thus "spouses" as a matter of state law, the federal Defense of Marriage Act provides that "[i]n determining the meaning of any Act of Congress, . . . the word 'spouse' refers only to a person of the opposite sex who is a husband or wife." (1 U.S.C. § 7). Does this mean that the loophole that § 453(e) was designed to close may actually still be open, so long as the initial transfer is to someone who fails to satisfy the statutory definition of a "related person"? Perhaps—though presumably the IRS would still challenge the transaction on general economic substance grounds, perhaps contending that Frida's receipt of the sale proceeds in the subsequent sale was in substance a receipt by Maria herself.

Limitation. The installment method is not available for sales of personal property under a revolving credit plan, for sales of publicly traded property, or for sales of inventory items by dealers in real or personal property. § 453(b)(2), (k)(1). There is an interesting exception for sellers of time-share units and residential lots. § 453(l). They are permitted to use the installment method, but when payment is received they must pay the government interest on the amount of tax deferred. Thus, any cash-flow problems are solved, but the tax advantage of deferral is eliminated. The advantage of deferral has been described as equivalent to an interest-free loan from the government (in the amount of the tax); here the loan is no longer interest free. A similar approach is taken with respect to sales of all nonfarm property where the sales price is greater than $150,000. See § 453A. If the aggregate face amount of the installment obligations arising from such sales exceeds $5 million, tax that is deferred on the excess is subject to an interest charge.

In the case of certain installment obligations, if a taxpayer uses the obligation to secure a loan, the loan is treated as payment of the installment obligation. § 453A(d). The installment method does not apply to recapture gain (§ 453(i)), nor does it apply for purposes of computing the alternative minimum tax (§ 56(a)(6)).

Permissible consideration. Since the installment method is designed to provide relief where the taxpayer has not received cash, it is not available where the consideration received is thought to be readily convertible into cash. Thus, demand notes and publicly tradable debt obligations are treated the same as cash payments (in an amount equal to their fair market value). See § 453(f)(4). The fact that a promise to pay is guaranteed does not, however, transform that promise into a "payment" that must be treated as cash. See § 453(f)(3). This rule extends to guarantees by banks in the form of standby letters of credit. (Regs. § 15a.453-1(b)(3)(iii) defines a "standby letter of credit" as a "non-negotiable nontransferable (except with the evidence of indebtedness which it secures) letter of credit, issued by a bank or other financial institution, which serves as a guarantee of the evidence of indebtedness which is secured by the letter of credit.")

Sales with contingent payments. In Burnet v. Logan, since the amount of the payments to be received was contingent on the output of a mine, the total consideration was uncertain. In this situation, how does one apply the installment method? How does one allocate basis to the payments? The regulations provide different solutions for three different situations. Regs. § 15a.453-1(c). First, if it is possible to determine a maximum amount that may be paid, basis is allocated by treating that maximum as the selling price (that is, the amount to be received by the seller). Second, where a maximum selling price cannot be determined, but it is possible to determine a maximum period of time over which payments will be made, basis is allocated in equal annual amounts over that time period. Third, if it is not possible to determine either a maximum price or a maximum time period (as, for example, in Burnet v. Logan), basis is recovered in equal annual amounts over a period of fifteen years.

F.   CONSTRUCTIVE RECEIPT AND RELATED DOCTRINES

One should not be surprised that some of the most important issues of timing in taxation relate to the taxpayer's method of accounting. Recall from the introduction that cash method taxpayers generally take income into account when it is received and take deductions into account when they are paid. This is in contrast to accrual method taxpayers, who generally take income into account when earned and take deductions into account when incurred. With respect to both categories of taxpayers, there are some important exceptions. The materials that follow cover some of the most significant exceptions relevant to cash method taxpayers.

1.   Basic Principles

Under case law and longstanding Treasury regulations, cash method taxpayers must take income into account in the first year in which it is either actually or constructively received. Treasury regulations provide that "[i]ncome although not actually reduced to a taxpayer's possession is constructively received by him in the taxable year during which it is credited to his account, set apart for him, or otherwise made available so that he may draw upon it at any time, or so that he could have drawn upon it during the taxable year if notice of intention to withdraw had been given." Treas. Reg. § 1.451-2(a). A key to understanding some of the subtler aspects of the doctrine of constructive receipt is to remember that constructive receipt results in taxation of amounts that are set aside or available—amounts to which the taxpayer has a legal claim—not amounts that would have been available if the taxpayer had made some other deal. The following case nicely illustrates this point.

AMEND v. COMMISSIONER
13 T.C. 178 (1949), acq., 1950-1 C.B. 1

BLACK, Judge.

We have two taxable years before us for decision, 1944 and 1946. . . .

In each of the taxable years there is one common issue and that is whether the doctrine of constructive receipt should be applied to certain payments which petitioner received from the sale of his wheat. There is no controversy as to the amounts which petitioner received or as to the time when he actually received them. Petitioners, being on the cash basis, returned these amounts as part of their gross income in the years when petitioner actually received them. . . .

In applying the doctrine of constructive receipt, the Commissioner relies upon Regulations 111, section 29.42-2. . . .[9]

In Loose v. United States, 74 Fed. (2d) 147, the rule providing for the taxation of income constructively received is stated as follows:

the strongest reason for holding constructive receipt of income to be within the statute is that for taxation purposes income is received or realized when it is made subject to the will and control of the taxpayer and can be, except for his own action or inaction, reduced to actual possession. So viewed, it makes no difference why the taxpayer did not reduce to actual possession. The matter is in no wise dependent upon what he does or upon what he fails to do. It depends solely upon the existence of a situation where the income is fully available to him. . . .

Respondent, in his brief, relies upon the *Loose* case, from which the above quotation is taken, and several other cases which deal with the doctrine of constructive receipt. Needless to say, each of those cases depends upon its own facts. In the *Loose* case, for example, interest coupons had matured prior to the decedent's death. The decedent had not presented them for payment because of his physical condition. It was held that, even though the decedent had not cashed them, the interest coupons represented income to him in the year when they matured, under the doctrine of constructive receipt.

---

9. "Sec. 29.42-2. *Income Not Reduced to Possession.* Income which is credited to the account of or set apart for a taxpayer and which may be drawn upon by him at any time is subject to tax for the year during which so credited or set apart, although not then actually reduced to possession. To constitute receipt in such a case the income must be credited or set apart to the taxpayer without any substantial limitation or restriction as to the time or manner of payment or condition upon which payment is to be made, and must be made available to him so that it may be drawn at any time, and its receipt brought within his own control and disposition. . . ."

It seems clear to us that the facts in the instant case do not bring it within the doctrine of Loose v. United States, supra, and the other cases cited by respondent dealing with constructive receipt.

In discussing the situation which we have in the instant case, we turn our attention first to the contract of sale which petitioner made of his 1944 wheat crop to Burrus. The testimony was that 1944 was a bumper wheat crop year and that petitioner produced and harvested about 30,000 bushels, some of which was lying out on the ground and some of which was stored on the farm. Petitioner, through his attorney in fact, Paul Higgs, sold his wheat to Burrus for January 1945 delivery at $1.57 per bushel. It was the understanding that petitioner would ship his wheat to Burrus at once and that Burrus would pay him for it in January of the following year. The contract was carried out. Some time during the month of August 1944, after August 2, petitioner shipped the 30,000 bushels to Burrus. Burrus received it, put it in its elevator, and paid petitioner for it by check dated January 17, 1945.

Respondent's contention seems to be based primarily on the fact that petitioner could have sold Burrus the wheat at the same price for immediate cash payment in August 1944 and that although he did not do so, he should be treated in the same manner as if he had and the doctrine of constructive receipt should be applied to the payments received. We do not think the doctrine of constructive receipt goes that far. Porter Holmes, who was the manager of the Burrus Panhandle Elevator in Amarillo at the time of the 1944 transaction, testified at the hearing. He testified that it was the usual custom of Burrus to pay cash for wheat soon after it was delivered and that the transaction between Burrus and petitioner for January 1945 delivery and settlement was unusual and that he telephoned the manager at Dallas, Texas, for authority to make the deal that way and secured such authority and the deal was made. He testified that when Burrus' check for $40,164.08 was mailed to petitioner January 17, 1945, it was done in pursuance of the contract. So far as we can see from the evidence, petitioner had no legal right to demand and receive his money from the sale of his 1944 wheat until in January 1945. Both petitioner and Burrus understood that to be the contract. Such is the substance of the testimony of both petitioner, who was the seller of the wheat, and Holmes, who acted for the buyer. Such also is the testimony of Paul Higgs, who represented the seller in the negotiations for the sale. During 1944 all that petitioner had in the way of a promise to pay was Burrus' oral promise to pay him for that wheat in January 1945. Burrus was a well known and responsible grain dealer and petitioner testified that he had not the slightest doubt that he would receive his money in January 1945, as had been agreed upon in the contract. Such a situation, however, does not bring into play the doctrine of constructive receipt. See Bedell v. Commissioner, 30 Fed. (2d) 622, wherein the court said:

> While, therefore, we do not think that the case is like a promise to pay in the future for a title which passes at the time of contract, we would not be understood as holding by implication that even in that case the profit is to be reckoned as of the time of sale. If a company sells out its plant for a negotiable bond issue payable in the future, the profit may be determined by the present market value

of the bonds. But if land or a chattel is sold, and title passes merely upon a promise to pay money at some future date, to speak of the promise as property exchanged for the title appears to us a strained use of language, when calculating profits under the income tax. . . . [I]t is absurd to speak of a promise to pay in the future as having a "market value," fair or unfair. . . .

The doctrine that a cash basis taxpayer can not be deemed to have realized income at the time a promise to pay in the future is made was reiterated by the Circuit Court of Appeals for the Eighth Circuit in the more recent case of Perry v. Commissioner, 152 Fed. (2d) 183. In that case it was stated:

These cases seem to be predicated upon the fact that in a contract of sale of property containing a promise to pay in the future, but not accompanied by notes or other unqualified obligations to pay a definite sum on a day certain, the obligation to pay and the obligation to pass title both being in the future, there is an element of uncertainty in the transaction and the promise has no "market value," fair or unfair. This theory is supported by the decision of the Supreme Court in Lucas v. North Texas Co. . . .

The Commissioner in the instant case is not contending that Burrus' contract to pay petitioner for his wheat in January 1945 had a fair market value equal to the agreed purchase price of the wheat when the contract was made in August 1944. What he is contending is that petitioner had the unqualified right to receive his money for the wheat in 1944; that all he had to do to receive his money was to ask for it; and that, therefore, the doctrine of constructive receipt applies as defined in section 29.42-2, Regulations 118.

For reasons already stated, we do not think the Commissioner's determination to this effect can be sustained. If petitioner had begun this method of selling his wheat in 1944, when he had a bumper crop, there might be reason to doubt the bona fides of the contract, but what we have said about the 1944 transaction between Burrus and petitioner is based upon the finding that the contract between Burrus and petitioner was bona fide in all respects, though it was initiated by petitioner, and each party was equally bound by its terms. Petitioner did not begin this method of selling his wheat in 1944 — he began it in 1942 and continued it through 1946. No doubt his taxes were more in some years and less in others than they would have been if petitioner had sold and delivered his wheat for cash in the year when it was produced. To illustrate this we need only point out that under the method which petitioner used he reported income in 1945 upon which he paid a tax of $2,672.64. His wife Eva also reported income and paid a tax of about the same amount. By treating petitioner's proceeds from the sale of his 1944 wheat as constructively received in 1944, the Commissioner determined over-assessments as to each petitioner for 1945 and deficiencies against each petitioner for 1944.

Petitioner was asked at the hearing why he adopted the manner of selling his wheat which has been detailed in our findings of fact. His answer was as follows:

Well, that had been my practice, to handle that wheat that way since 1942 and I have handled my wheat that way, '42, '43, '44, '45, '46, '47 and into 1948. It is still my practice to do that and there have been some years in that interval that

I would certainly have paid less income had I handled it the other way, but that is a semi-arid country and we are uncertain about our wheat crops and our expenses are always pretty well set and we know they are going to be high and we need our own protection to carry part of this wheat forward. . . .

As I have already explained, it's been a matter of making my income more uniform and even; about five of those years had it all been set back and sold in the year that it was supposed to have been sold in, my income tax would have been less and in the other two it would have been more. I merely emphasize that to show the consistency of my policy and not as a matter of paying any tax.

Whether the reasons advanced by petitioner in his testimony quoted above are good or bad as a business policy, we do not undertake to decide. The question we think we have to decide is whether the contracts detailed in our findings of fact were bona fide arm's-length transactions and whether under them the petitioner had the unqualified right to receive the money for his wheat in the year when the contracts were made and whether petitioner's failure to receive his money was of his own volition. Our conclusion, as already stated, is that the contracts were bona fide arm's-length transactions and petitioner did not have the right to demand the money for his wheat until in January of the year following its sale. This being true, we do not think the doctrine of constructive receipt applies. See Howard Veit, first point decided, 8 T.C. 809.

Petitioner, in each of the years before us, returned as a part of his gross income the checks which he actually received in payment for his wheat. This being so, we think he complied with the income tax laws governing a taxpayer who keeps his accounts and makes his returns on the cash basis. . . .

NOTES

1. *Current rules.* Amend's sale of the wheat would now be an installment sale (see § 453(b)(1)), and unless he elected out, he would use the installment method. Under the installment method, Amend would report his entire gain in 1945 since he received 100 percent of the payment for the wheat in 1945. So the result would not be changed.[10] If, however, Amend elected out of the installment method (pursuant to § 453(d)), he would be required to report in 1944 the fair market value of the obligation of the buyer, Burrus.[11] This result is required by the present rule for sales of property not reported under the installment method. See supra page 271, Note 3, describing the adoption of new rules for the installment method and the effort to limit the "open

10. Because of the exception for farmers in § 453(1)(2), Amend's sale is not a "dealer disposition," so it is not excluded from installment sale treatment under § 453(b)(2)(A). The exception for inventories in § 453(b)(2)(B) would not be applicable because Amend would not be required to, and presumably would not, use an inventory method of accounting. See Regs. § 1.471-6.

11. An accrual method taxpayer who elects out of the installment method is required to report the total amount payable (not including interest or OID) rather than the fair market value of the obligation. Regs. § 15a.453-1(d)(2)(ii)(A).

transaction" approach of Burnet v. Logan (supra page 268), and the following language from Temporary Regs. § 15a.453-1(d)(2):

> (i) Receipt of an installment obligation shall be treated as a receipt of property, in an amount equal to the fair market value of the obligation, whether or not such obligation is the equivalent of cash. An installment obligation is considered to be property and is subject to valuation, [using fair market value], without regard to whether the obligation is embodied in a note, an executory contract, or any other instrument, or as an oral promise enforceable under local law.
>
> (ii) Under no circumstances will an installment sale for a fixed amount be considered an "open" transaction.

The doctrine of constructive receipt would still be relevant, however. If the payment by Burrus had been constructively received by Amend in 1944 (for example, if the contract had given Amend the legal right to demand cash payment at any time), then Amend would have been required to report the amount to which he was entitled in 1944. He could not have deferred recognition under the installment method. The installment method permits a taxpayer to avoid recognition of gain under the rule limiting open transactions, or under the cash equivalence doctrine, not under the doctrine of constructive receipt.

The installment method is available only for sales of property, not for sales of services. With respect to services, as soon will be seen (infra pages 283-289), a right to payment is not currently treated as income by a cash-method taxpayer, at least as long as it is embodied in a "mere promise to pay."

2. *Consistency and clear reflection of income.* Note the court's reference to the fact that the taxpayer had been consistent in his practice. Thus, there was no distortion of income. Had there been such distortion, the Service could have invoked the forerunner of § 446(b), which allows the Service to impose a method of accounting if the taxpayer's method does not "clearly reflect income."

3. *The relevance of delivery.* Amend delivered his wheat to Burrus in 1944, but apparently he was not legally required by contract to do so. If the contract had required delivery (and transfer of title) in 1944, would the result have been different?

The next case tests the distinction between constructive receipt and economic benefit.

PULSIFER v. COMMISSIONER
64 T.C. 245 (1975)

HALL, Judge.

Respondent determined a deficiency of $2,449.41 against each of the three petitioners for 1969. The sole issue for decision is whether petitioners, who were minors in 1969, must include in gross income in 1969 their winnings from the 1969 Irish Hospital Sweepstakes which were deposited with the Irish court.

FINDINGS OF FACT

All of the facts have been stipulated and are so found.

The petitioners, Stephen W. Pulsifer, Susan M. Pulsifer, and Thomas O. Pulsifer, are brothers and sister who lived in Medford, Mass., when they filed their petitions. . . . They are the minor children of Gordon F. Pulsifer and Theodora T. Pulsifer of Medford, Mass., who together are petitioners' counsel herein.

Mr. Pulsifer acquired an Irish Hospital Sweepstakes ticket in his name and the names of his three minor children. On March 21, 1969, he and petitioners received a telegram from the Hospital Trust advising them that their ticket would be represented by Saratoga Skiddy, a horse which would run on their behalf in the Lincolnshire Handicap. Saratoga Skiddy placed second, winning $48,000.

When he applied for the winnings, Mr. Pulsifer was advised that three-fourths of the amount would not be released to him because the ticket stub reflected three minor co-owners. He was further advised that, pursuant to Irish law, the withheld portion together with interest earned to date would be deposited with the Bank of Ireland at interest to the account of the Accountant of the Courts of Justice for the benefit of each of the petitioners. The money would not be released until petitioners reached 21 or until application on their behalf was made by an appropriate party to the Irish court for release of the funds. Mr. Pulsifer was sent his share of the prize.

The amounts paid over and credited to each of the petitioners were principal of $11,925 plus interest of $250.03, or $12,175.03. Mr. Pulsifer, as petitioners' next friend and legal guardian, has since filed for release of those funds, and he has an absolute right to obtain them.[12]

OPINION

Both parties agree the prize money is income to the petitioners. The only question is in what year must it be included in income. Petitioners contend that they should not be required to recognize the Irish Hospital Sweepstakes winnings held for them by the Irish court in 1969. They reason that neither the constructive-receipt nor the economic-benefit doctrines apply, and that all they had in 1969 was a nonassignable chose in action. Respondent argues that the economic-benefit doctrine applies, thereby dictating recognition of the prize money in 1969. . . . We agree with respondent.

Under the economic-benefit theory, an individual on the cash receipts and disbursements method of accounting is currently taxable on the economic and financial benefit derived from the absolute right to income in the form of a fund which has been irrevocably set aside for him in trust and is beyond the reach of the payor's [creditors]. E. T. Sproull, 16 T.C. 244 (1951), affd. per curiam, 194 F.2d 541 (6th Cir. 1952). Petitioners had an absolute, non-

12. The record does not disclose whether he had already received the funds at the time of trial.

forfeitable right to their winnings on deposit with the Irish court. The money had been irrevocably set aside for their sole benefit. All that was needed to receive the money was for their legal representative to apply for the funds, which he forthwith did. See Orlando v. Earl of Fingall, Irish Reports 281 (1940). We agree with respondent that this case falls within the legal analysis set out in *E. T. Sproull*, supra.

In the *Sproull* case the employer-corporation unilaterally and irrevocably transferred $10,500 into a trust in 1945 for taxpayer's sole benefit in consideration for prior services. In 1946 and 1947, pursuant to the trust document, the corpus was paid in its entirety to taxpayer. In the event of his death the funds were to have been paid to his administrator, executor, or heirs. The Court held that the entire $10,500 was taxable in 1945 because Sproull derived an economic benefit from it in 1945. The employer had made an irrevocable transfer to the trust, relinquishing all control. Sproull was given an absolute right to the funds which were to be applied for his sole benefit. The funds were beyond the reach of the employer's creditors. Sproull's right to those funds was not contingent, and the trust agreement did not contain any restrictions on his right to assign or otherwise dispose of that interest.

The record does not show whether the right to the funds held by the Bank of Ireland was assignable. Petitioner claims they were not, but cites no authority for his position. However, the result is the same whether or not the right to the funds is assignable. See Renton K. Brodie, 1 T.C. 275 (1942) (deferred annuity contract held currently taxable even though nonassignable and without surrender value).

In order to reflect our conclusion, decisions will be entered for the respondent.

QUESTION

Could the court have reached the same result under the doctrine of constructive receipt? What if the funds could not be obtained until the person entitled to them reached age 21?

2. Nonqualified Deferred Compensation

In Revenue Ruling 60-31, 1960-1 C.B. 174, the IRS set forth some basic rules for the taxation of deferred compensation (that is, compensation whose receipt is deferred to a future taxable year). The types of arrangements covered by this ruling are referred to as *nonqualified* deferred compensation planes, as distinguished from *qualified* deferred compensation plans, which are discussed in the next section. For nonqualified plans there is essentially no limit on the amount of current compensation that can be deferred to, and become taxable in, future years. Such plans are generally used for senior corporate executives and other high-income people, while qualified plans, as we shall see, generally must be made available to all employees and are limited in the amounts that can be deferred. One important principle stated in

Revenue Ruling 60-31 is that a cash-method employee is not taxable currently by virtue of an employer's "mere promise to pay" some amount of compensation in the future, even if the promise is unqualified (that is, without contingencies). Citing the *Amend* case (supra page 277), the ruling observes that "the statute cannot be administered by speculating whether the payor would have been willing to agree to an earlier payment." On the other hand, where money is set aside in a trust or an escrow account for the benefit of the employee, out of the control of the employer, the employee is taxed at the time when the money is paid by the employer to the trustee or escrow agent. The case that follows applies these principles.

MINOR v. UNITED STATES

772 F.2d 1472 (9th Cir. 1985)

The government appeals a tax refund judgment holding that contributions to a deferred compensation plan are not currently taxable. We affirm.

Ralph H. Minor is a physician practicing in Snohomish County, Washington. In 1959, he entered into an agreement with the Snohomish County Physicians Corporation (Snohomish Physicians) under which he agreed to render medical services to subscribers of Snohomish Physicians' prepaid medical plan in exchange for fees to be paid by Snohomish Physicians according to its fee schedule.

In 1967, Snohomish Physicians adopted a deferred compensation plan for its participating physicians. Under the voluntary plan, a physician who desired deferred compensation entered into a "Supplemental Agreement" in which the physician and Snohomish Physicians agree that for future services the physician would be paid a designated percentage of the fee he or she would receive under the fee schedule if not participating in the plan. The physician could elect any percentage from 10 per cent to 90 per cent. The balance would go into the deferred compensation fund. Minor's agreement with Snohomish Physicians provided that he would be paid 50 per cent of the scheduled fees through November 30, 1971, and 10 per cent thereafter.

To provide for its obligations under the Supplemental Agreement, Snohomish Physicians established a trust. Snohomish Physicians was the settlor, three physicians, including Minor, were trustees, and Snohomish Physicians was the beneficiary. The trustees, pursuant to instructions from Snohomish Physicians, purchased retirement annuity policies to provide for the payment of benefits under the plan. These benefits would become payable to the physician or to his beneficiaries when he or she retires, dies, becomes disabled, or leaves the Snohomish Physicians service area to practice medicine elsewhere. The physician agrees to continue to provide services to Snohomish Physicians patients until the benefits become payable, to limit his or her practice after retirement, to continue to provide certain emergency and consulting services at Snohomish Physicians' request, and to refrain from providing medical services to competing groups.

On his federal income tax returns for 1970, 1971, and 1973, Minor included in gross income only the 10 per cent of the scheduled fees which he actually received. The remaining 90 per cent, which Minor did not receive, went into the deferred compensation plan trust.

The IRS argues that Minor should have included in his gross income that portion of the fees Snohomish Physicians placed in trust for his future benefit. The IRS relies on the economic benefit doctrine, which is an exception to the well-settled rule that a taxpayer pays income tax only on income which is actually or constructively received by him. In this case, Minor did not actually receive the income the IRS attributes to him nor, the IRS has conceded, did he constructively receive the income. The IRS argues, however, that the economic benefit doctrine applies here because an economic benefit was presently conferred on Minor, although he did not receive and had no right to receive the deferred compensation benefits during the tax year.

Minor argues that the participants in the deferred compensation plan have no right to compel Snohomish Physicians to execute the trust agreement, or even to cause it to be created, implemented or continued. The participants have no right, title or interest in the trust agreement or any asset held by the trust. He argues that his right to receive payments of currently earned compensation in the future is contingent, and therefore does not vest any interest in him.

Recent cases from a number of courts provide useful guidelines for determining when a taxpayer is entitled to defer his tax obligations by participating in a deferred compensation plan. The cases fall into two general groups.

(1) *Constructive Receipt.* The constructive receipt doctrine holds that income, although not actually reduced to the taxpayer's possession, is constructively received by the taxpayer during any year in which it is credited to his account or otherwise set apart so that it is available to him without "substantial limitations or restrictions." Regs. § 1.451-2(a) (1985). . . . If a corporation merely credits funds to an employee on its books but does not make those funds available to the employees, there has been no constructive receipt. [Regs.] § 1.451-2(a). Similarly, an employer's mere promise to pay funds, not represented by notes or otherwise secured, cannot constitute constructive receipt by the employee to whom the promise is made. Rev. Rul. 60-31, 1960-1 C.B. 174, 177.

The IRS has conceded that Minor did not constructively receive the proceeds of Snohomish Physicians' deferred compensation plan. Because the IRS has acknowledged that the doctrine does not apply, we need not decide whether, under the constructive-receipt doctrine, Snohomish Physicians' promise to pay deferred compensation is anything more than a "naked, unsecured promised to pay compensation in the future." Goldsmith v. United States, 586 F.2d 810, 816, 218 Ct. Cl. 387 (1978).

(2) *Economic Benefit.* Although taxation of deferred compensation plans is generally analyzed under the constructive receipt doctrine, the economic benefit doctrine provides an alternate method of determining when a taxpayer receives taxable benefits. Under that doctrine, an employer's promise to pay deferred compensation in the future may itself constitute a taxable economic benefit if the current value of the employer's promise can be given an appraised value. The concept of economic benefit is quite different from that of constructive receipt because the taxpayer must actually receive the property or currently receive evidence of a future right to property. . . .

The economic benefit doctrine is applicable only if the employer's promise is capable of valuation. . . . A current economic benefit is capable of valuation where the employer makes a contribution to an employee's deferred compensation plan which is nonforfeitable, fully vested in the employee and secured against the employer's creditors by a trust arrangement.

In cases where courts or the IRS have found a current economic benefit to have been conferred, the employer's contribution has always been secured or the employee's interest has been nonforfeitable. See United States v. Basye, 410 U.S. 441, 445-446 (1973) (because trust was established, partnership's interest was nonforfeitable even though individual partner's share of the trust monies was not capable of valuation); *Goldsmith*, 586 F.2d at 821 (life insurance benefits were a nonforfeitable current economic benefit although other unsecured elements of deferred compensation plan did not constitute currently taxable economic benefit); Reed v. Commissioner, 723 F.2d 138, 147 (1st Cir. 1983) (economic benefit for a cash basis taxpayer requires that taxpayer's contractual right to future payment be evidenced by an instrument which is not only nonforfeitable but also readily assignable); United States v. Drescher, 179 F.2d 863, 865 (2d Cir.) (non-assignable annuity confers an economic benefit because annuity was nonforfeitable), cert. denied, 340 U.S. 821 (1950), McEwen v. Commissioner, 6 T.C. 1018, 1026 (1946) (deferred compensation secured by trust in which employee was the beneficiary). If the employee's interest is unsecured or not otherwise protected from the employer's creditors, the employee's interest is not taxable property, see [Regs.] § 1.83-3(e) (1985), so the forfeitability of the employee's interest is irrelevant.

Superficially, the Snohomish Physicians' deferred compensation plan establishes a trust arrangement which protects the plan against Snohomish Physicians' creditors but also establishes conditions upon Minor's receipt of the deferred compensation which makes his benefits forfeitable. We examine separately the trust arrangement and risk of forfeiture.

Trust Arrangement. Neither Minor nor any other participants in the deferred compensation plan has any right, title or interest in the trust which holds the annuity contract. The trust, which was established to hold the assets of the deferred compensation plan, was not established pursuant to Minor's Supplemental Agreement, but was created at the initiative of Snohomish Physicians which is both the settlor and beneficiary of the trust. Although Minor incidentally benefits from the trust, he is not a beneficiary. See Restatement (Second) of Trusts § 126 (1959). Because Snohomish Physicians has not established any trust in favor of Minor or the other participants, the assets of the trust remain solely those of Snohomish Physicians and subject to the claims of its general creditors. . . .

Minor has pointed out several provisions of the trust agreement which show that the participating physicians had no vested, funded right to the assets of the trust. The IRS in response has cited Sproull v. Commissioner, 16 T.C. 244 (1951), aff'd, 194 F.2d 541 (6th Cir. 1952), in which a corporation paid over to a trustee compensation for past services rendered by petitioner. The trustee was directed to hold, invest, and pay over this sum to petitioner or his estate in two installments. The Tax Court held the entire trust fund was income to the petitioner in the year it was paid to the trustee. In *Sproull*, the settlor of the trust was the corporation and the beneficiary was the petitioner or his estate. The petitioner exercised substantial control over the money because he could assign or otherwise alienate the trust, had standing to bring an action against the trustee, if needed, and other powers under the trust. See id. at 247-248. In this case Snohomish Physicians is both the settlor and the beneficiary of the trust. Minor's only involvement is as one of the trustees. Because Snohomish Physicians' trust was not established in favor of Minor or the other plan participants, the deferred compensation plan is unfunded. Unfunded plans do not confer a present taxable economic benefit. . . .

Risk of Forfeiture. Minor's receipt of benefits under the deferred compensation plan is contingent upon his agreement to limit his practice after retirement to consulting services and to refrain from competing with Snohomish Physicians if he leaves its practice. The district court found that this restriction subjected Minor's benefits to a risk of forfeiture. The Code requires a taxpayer to include in his gross income any property transferred in connection with the performance of services unless the taxpayer's rights in such property are subject to a "substantial risk of forfeiture." § 83(a) (1982). The district court did not enter a finding on the substantiality of the risk that Minor's benefits could be forfeited. See § 83(c)(1) (1982).

If a recipient must perform or refrain from performing further acts as a condition to payment of benefits, the recipient's rights are regarded as forfeitable. . . . If Minor's Supplemental Agreement requires him to perform substantial post-retirement services or imposes substantial conditions upon his receipt of benefits, the economic benefit doctrine is inapplicable. . . .

From the record before us, we are unable to determine whether the restrictions on Minor's receipt of benefits satisfy the substantiality requirement of § 83. We need not, however, invade the province of the trial court by inferring either substantiality or insubstantiality. We conclude that the deferred compensation plan is unsecured from Snohomish Physicians' creditors and therefore incapable of valuation. Thus, Minor's benefits do not constitute property under § 83 (1982) and [Regs.] § 1.83-3.

While Minor's deferred compensation plan severely stretches the limits of a non-qualified deferred compensation plan, we conclude that the Snohomish Physicians' plan is an unfunded, unsecured plan subject to a risk of forfeiture. We need not examine the substantiality of that risk.

Affirmed.

NOTES

1. *Constructive receipt.* In *Minor* it was clear that the taxpayer could have contracted for payment to him of the amounts that were in fact, pursuant to the actual contract, credited to his account in the deferred compensation fund. This being so, why was the amount set aside for the taxpayer not constructively received?

2. *The importance of looking at both sides of the transaction.* The attractiveness of deferred compensation plans of the sort approved by Rev. Rul. 60-31 is limited by the fact that the employer will not receive a deduction for the

amount to be paid in the future until the year in which the employee recognizes income. See § 404(a)(5). If, in a given situation, a deferred payment is not taxed to the employee until ten years from now, the deferred payment will not generate a deduction for the employer until ten years from now. If the parties are in the same tax bracket, the advantage to the employee of deferral of the income will be exactly offset by the disadvantage to the employer of deferral of the deduction for the amount to be paid.

If the employer is in a lower tax bracket than the employee, deferral can be advantageous. To understand why this is so, imagine an employee who works for a tax-exempt employer, such as a private university. Suppose the employee's marginal tax rate is 40 percent (combined federal and state) and she is able to earn a 10 percent before-tax rate of return on her money. Her after-tax rate of return is 6 percent. The employer, on the other hand, pays no tax and is able to earn a before-tax and after-tax rate of return of 10 percent. The employee obviously would be better off if she were able to invest a portion of her salary at her employer's after-tax rate of return.

In the past, employees who worked for tax-exempt institutions managed to achieve this result through deferred compensation arrangements. The amount of currently deferred compensation would be invested by the employer and would increase in value at the employer's after-tax (that is, no-tax) rate — in our example, 10 percent. Eventually, the deferred funds, together with the interest earned on the funds, would be distributed to the employee.[13]

Concern over the use of such plans led to the adoption of § 457, which places dollar limitations on such plans when used by state agencies. A less strict limitation applies to charitable organizations described in § 501(c)(3) (such as schools and churches) and to public educational institutions. See § 403(b). An employer such as a professional sports team might be nontaxable because it has substantial tax losses, but may be sufficiently well financed so that the promise of future payment is acceptable consideration. Employees of this kind of organization may therefore find it advantageous to defer unlimited amounts of their income, as long as the deferred arrangement meets the guidelines described in the *Minor* case.

We shall soon see (infra page 290) that Congress has established a form of deferred compensation arrangement, known as a qualified pension or profit-sharing plan, that offers the same sort of tax advantage that is described in this note. Qualified pension and profit-sharing plans must, however, cover a broad

---

13. A numerical example may help illuminate this point. Suppose, under the above facts, that the employee decides to save the after-tax portion of $10,000 of her salary. Since she is taxed at a rate of 40 percent, the initial amount of her after-tax investment is $6,000. If that sum is invested at an after-tax rate of 6 percent, the total amount at the end of the year is $6,360 (1.06($6,000)). Suppose instead that the employee enters into a deferred compensation agreement under which $10,000 of her salary, plus the 10 percent annual interest that the employer can earn on that amount, is deferred for one year — that is, is not paid until a year later. The amount initially in the hands of the employer, held for payment to the employee, is $10,000. At the end of a year that amount increases to $11,000. (Recall that the employer earns 10 percent and pays no tax.) At the end of the year the $11,000 is paid to the employee. The employee pays a tax at a rate of 40 percent, so the tax is $4,400 and the after-tax amount is $6,600. This $6,600 is $240 more than the $6,360 that the employee would have wound up with if she had taken immediate payment and had invested the proceeds herself for a year. In other words, the employee increases her after-tax amount by 4 percent of the $6,000 she would have received had she taken immediate payment. Her total return on that $6,000 is $600, or 10 percent.

spectrum of the employer's workforce and are subject to a number of other restrictions.

Section 409A

From an employee's point of view, the obvious downside to nonqualified deferred compensation is that the employer may be financially unable to make the future payment, since the assets in the control of the employer are not safe from its creditors. In the past, some aggressive lawyers structured plans that limited that risk, but still purported to provide the benefits of deferral. For example, some plans provided that if the company's financial health deteriorated, deferred amounts would be funded in a manner that would be secure from the company's creditors (and presumably, would be subject to taxation when and if that occurred). This removed the danger that bargained-for compensation would be lost; the worst that could happen is that bargained-for compensation would become taxable prior to receipt. Other plans allowed employees to elect to accelerate plan benefits in the event of unspecified financial hardship. Under § 409A, adopted in 2004, these sorts of plans will no longer provide the benefits of deferral. In general, § 409A provides that amounts payable in the future are taxable when bargained for if the plan allows employees to accelerate benefits or provides that upon a deterioration of the employer's financial health, assets are shielded from outside creditors. Section 409A applies, with some significant exceptions, to grants of restricted stock and stock options. It does not apply to qualified deferred compensation plans, discussed in the next section.

Section 409A may represent good tax policy but was adopted in response to a failure in corporate governance. A prime example was Enron Corporation, a large natural resources and trading company that had enjoyed great success with investors, based in large part on phony transactions and misleading accounting. Enron eventually collapsed, with huge losses to investors and employees. By late 2001, top executives in Enron had claims to over $150 million in nonqualified deferred compensations plans. Under those plans, executives were allowed to petition for acceleration of payment in the event of financial hardship. As the collapse of Enron became more and more likely, executives petitioned the plan administrator (another Enron executive) for acceleration of payment, and the administrator granted the petitions. In the weeks before bankruptcy, over $50 million of previously deferred compensation left the company in the form of accelerated payments to executives.

PROBLEM

Suppose you represent a superstar college football player who was selected first in the National Football League draft, by a newly established team (an "expansion" team). The team has offered to pay your client a signing bonus of $1 million, payable at the end of five years. This is in addition to salary and performance bonuses and is not contingent on any aspect of performance other than signing the contract. You are satisfied with the amount of the signing bonus, but are concerned about the financial ability of the team to continue to pay the $1 million at the end of the five years, since it will presumably operate at a loss for at least five years and the losses may turn out to be greater than expected. The team is operated as a corporation. All the shares of stock of the corporation are held by a real estate tycoon who is active in management of the team and who is extremely anxious that your client sign. Your client is anxious not to pay tax on money that he has not received and wants to avoid any substantial risk of not being paid. What is your advice about each of the following possible ways of structuring the deal?

(a) The corporation buys an annuity policy from an insurance company. The policy names the player as the annuitant and provides for payment of $1 million to the player at the end of five years. The corporation pays $600,000 for the policy. It is nonassignable and the payment cannot be accelerated.

(b) The corporation contributes $600,000 to a trust. The trustee is directed to invest the $600,000 in U.S. Treasury bonds. The interest that will be earned on these bonds (and on the interest received) over the next five years will total $400,000. The trustee is directed at the end of the five years to pay the $1 million to the player. The corporation retains no interest in the trust.

(c) The facts are the same as in (b) except that at the end of the five years the $1 million is to be paid to the corporation to provide funds that it can use to meet its own contractual obligation to the player.

(d) The corporation signs an unconditional agreement to pay $1 million to the player at the end of five years. The real estate tycoon who owns all the shares of the corporation signs a guarantee of its obligation.

3. Qualified Employee Plans

Basic choices and rules. Even without tax considerations, employers often have good reason to establish employee retirement plans. For example, such plans may increase employee loyalty if benefits are subjects to forfeiture upon leaving the employer prematurely or moving to a competing firm. Or the plans may be thought to improve employees' incentives to increase shareholder value if the benefits are linked to the value of company stock. Well-run retirement plans may also simply be a benefit that prospective employees value in deciding where to work.

From an economic perspective, employee retirement plans generally take either of two forms. First, they may be defined benefit plans, in which the employer agrees to provide fixed retirement benefits to each employee based on factors such as the employee's pre-retirement salary and number of years of employment. Second, they may be defined contribution plans, in which the employer's annual contribution to the plan, rather than the amount of ultimate benefit, is fixed by a formula, and the amount a retiree ultimately gets depends on the investment return that was earned on the contributions.

There also are two basic choices for tax planning. Nonqualified plans, or those not covered by special statutory rules, are taxable to employees based on generally applicable tax rules, such as § 83, along with the doctrines of constructive receipt and economic benefit that were discussed in the previous section. The employer's deduction generally is not allowed until the benefit is taxable to the employee. See § 83(h). Thus, even if taxability is deferred relative to the treatment of current salary payments, there is no overall tax benefit to the parties from the deferral unless the employee's marginal tax rate exceeds that of the employer.

Taxpayers can do better than this, however, by using qualified pension, profit-sharing, or stock bonus plans, which have the following set of highly attractive features:

(a) Amounts paid into the plan (that is, paid to the plan's trustee) are not taxed to those employees who become entitled to future benefits by virtue of such payments, even if the employee rights are vested (that is, are payable even if the employee quits or is fired before retirement). Employees are taxed only when they actually receive payments on retirement.[14] Under so-called 401(k) plans (after Code § 401(k), which provides the legal authority), employees are not taxable on amounts up to $11,000 per year set aside for retirement (rising gradually to $15,000 in 2006) even if they had the option to take cash.

(b) Employers are entitled to an immediate deduction for amounts paid into the plan. Thus, disregarding the tax and nontax effects on the employee, the employer should be indifferent as between a payment into a plan and a payment of an equal amount as part of the employee's current wage or salary; the employer gets the same deduction either way.

(c) Earnings on funds paid into the plan and invested by it are not taxed (except to the extent that they are taxed to employees when paid to them).

(d) Employers are also allowed to provide "Roth 401(k)" plans. Under these plans, the employee is taxed on amounts paid into the retirement fund by the employer, but distributions are tax free — including earnings on the initial contributions. Thus, the tax advantage of deferral in the traditional 401(k) plan is sacrificed in return for the later advantage of tax-free distributions. See further description below.

Amount of tax benefit. The following hypothetical figures illustrate the tax advantage of qualified plans (including traditional, tax-deferred 401(k) plans). Suppose that an employer pays into a qualified defined-contribution plan, on behalf of an employee, $10,000 per year for twenty-five years, and these funds earn an annual return of 10 percent. At the end of twenty-five years, on these assumptions, the total of the contributions and the earnings will be $983,471. Assume that at this point the employee retires and begins to collect benefits for life; that his life expectancy is fifteen years; and that the amounts to be paid to him are calculated on the assumption that the funds held in the plan will continue to earn 10 percent per year. The annual payment to the employee will be $129,301,[15] all of which is taxable. Assume that the employee

---

14. At retirement, the employee normally will receive payments spread over his or her remaining life, but in some circumstances may be allowed to choose a single lump-sum payment.

15. This figure is not quite accurate. In calculating it, the assumption was made that each year of life expectancy is weighed equally. In the real world this assumption is not accurate. The deviation from reality is not important for our purposes, however, since it is relatively minor and since the same method of calculation is used in the next paragraph.

pays a tax on this amount at a rate of 35 percent on the entire amount. The amount left after tax will be $84,045.

Now consider what happens if we remove all the tax benefits. The employer pays $10,000 each year to the employee as a bonus. Assume that the employee is taxed on this amount at a rate of 35 percent. After tax, the amount available for investment is $6,500. Assume that this sum is invested each year at 10 percent before tax. The after-tax rate of return will be 6.5 percent. Assuming, then, an investment of $6,500 per year with a return of 6.5 percent per year, the total accumulated at the end of twenty-five years will be $382,770. Assume that this fund is used to buy an annuity whose payout is calculated based on an assumption of a rate of return of 10 percent. Again, assume a life expectancy of fifteen years. The annual payment will be $50,324. Of this, $24,810 will be taxed.[16] Assuming a tax rate of 35 percent, the tax will be $8,684, leaving, after tax, $41,640 per year. This is 49.5 percent of the after-tax amount ($84,045) available where the qualified plan is used.[17]

Note that in this hypothetical a constant tax rate of 35 percent has been assumed and that consequently the entire advantage of the qualified plan is from deferral. The comparison probably overstates somewhat the advantage of the use of qualified plans, however, because it assumes that a taxpayer whose salary and investment returns are not sheltered by such a plan would fail to find some form of investment with a tax advantage (e.g., investment in common stocks with growth potential, where there is deferral on unrealized appreciation). Note that tax-favored investment returns are of no advantage in a qualified plan.

Antidiscrimination rules. Congress has conditioned the availability of the tax benefits associated with qualified plans on compliance with certain rules. The most important of these are rules prohibiting discrimination in favor of highly paid employees. The purpose of the antidiscrimination rules may be understood by first examining the interests of highly paid and of rank-and-file employees. Rank-and-file employees are generally in the lower tax brackets and benefit less than highly paid employees from the tax savings associated with qualified pension plans. Moreover, rank-and-file employees generally are inclined to save only a small portion of their salaries. Highly paid employees, on the other hand, benefit more substantially from the tax savings associated with qualified plans and generally are more inclined to save a higher portion of their salaries than are low-paid employees. Absent a rule to the contrary, highly paid employees might bargain with employers to receive a large percentage of their salaries in the form of tax-favored pension benefits, while

---

16. See § 72(e). The exclusion ratio is the investment in the contract ($382,770) divided by the expected return ($50,324 × 15 = $754,860), or 0.507. The amount excluded is 0.507 × $50,324, which is $25,514. The amount taxed is the $50,324 received, less the $25,524 excluded under § 72(e), or $24,810.

17. The calculation ignores Social Security taxes, which would be relevant for a taxpayer whose other income is below the social security maximum. For such taxpayers, the cash bonus will be subject to the social security tax, but neither contributions to qualified plans nor retirement benefits received from such plans are. The additional social security taxes will, however, result in increased social security retirement benefits.

rank-and-file employees might bargain with employers for low pension benefits or none at all or might not be offered the option of taking a pension benefit in lieu of wages.

The antidiscrimination rules prevent this outcome by requiring that qualified plans must provide reasonably comparable benefits to all employees. At the heart of the antidiscrimination rules is the requirement that, in general, the ratio of pension benefits to salary for highly paid employees must be no greater than the ratio of such benefits to the wages of rank-and-file employees. Thus, if highly paid employees receive benefits equal to 50 percent of their immediate preretirement salary, rank-and-file employees must also receive benefits equal to 50 percent of their preretirement wages. This requirement tends to limit the use of qualified plans by highly paid employees, while at the same time helping to ensure that rank-and-file employees receive some form of pension benefits. It is important to understand, however, that the benefits do not necessarily represent a "gift" to rank-and-file employees. Some portion of the benefits is most likely paid for by a reduction in the cash wages received by those employees.

The other major condition for qualification is compliance with the so-called ERISA rules (after the Employee Retirement Income Security Act of 1974), which impose obligations designed to ensure the safety of investments by the plan and which impose vesting requirements. The vesting rules are designed to ensure that after specified periods of service an employee's retirement benefit becomes nonforfeitable (that is, it is not lost if the employee quits or is fired). See §§ 401(a)(7), 411.

The ERISA rules and the antidiscrimination rules are extremely complex; partly because of these rules, the role of adviser on qualified plans has become a full-time specialty.

The rules on qualified plans also contain provisions designed to protect the interest of an employee's spouse in the retirement benefits earned by the employee. See §§ 401(a)(11), 417.

Individuals. There are special rules under which self-employed individuals are permitted to set up qualified plans, called H.R. 10 (formerly "Keogh") plans. For many years, self-employed doctors, lawyers, actors, and other highly paid individuals formed corporations, of which they became the sole (or at least the major) employee, in order to take advantage of the more generous rules available to employees (as compared with self-employed individuals). The Tax Equity and Fiscal Responsibility Act of 1982 (TEFRA) removed most of the advantage of this artificial use of the corporate form, partly by increasing the maximum amount that can be set aside each year by self-employed individuals and partly by reducing to the same level the maximum amount that can be set aside in corporate plans.

Individuals may also set up for themselves qualified plans called individual retirement accounts (IRAs). See § 408. An individual may set aside in the IRA account, and claim as a deduction, up to $5,000 ($6,000 for a person over 50 years of age), with inflation adjustments after 2008, but not more than the amount of his or her compensation. Additional "catch-up contributions" may be made, in limited amounts, by people age 50 or over. The income earned on

IRAs is not taxed as long as it is accumulated. The amounts put into the account each year are deductible if the taxpayer is not covered by an employer plan or, if covered, has adjusted gross income below certain limits, with a phaseout as income rises above these levels. Amounts ultimately withdrawn as retirement benefits are included in income, with an exclusion to take account of amounts for which there was no deduction.

Instead of contributing funds to a "normal" IRA, described above, individuals filing a joint return whose adjusted gross income is below $150,000 can elect to contribute to a "Roth IRA." § 408A. Contributions to a Roth IRA are nondeductible but there is no annual tax on the income earned by funds in an IRA and "qualified distributions" are tax free. A "qualified distribution" is a distribution that takes place more than five years after the year of contribution, and that is made after age 59½, is made after the contributor becomes disabled or dies, or is made for certain higher education or first-time home buyer expenses of up to $10,000. Any other distribution, to the extent that it (along with prior distributions) exceeds the nondeductible contributions to the Roth IRA, is taxable as ordinary income and is subject to a 10 percent penalty.

A Roth IRA will be more advantageous than a normal IRA for taxpayers who wish to save for college or first-time home purchase expenses, or who are in a lower tax bracket in the time of contribution than in the time of withdrawal. Otherwise, under reasonable assumptions, the value of deducting the contribution (as in the case of a normal IRA) is exactly equal to the value of not paying tax on the distribution (as in the case of a Roth IRA), but since the Roth IRA is established with after-tax dollars, the amount sheltered from taxation, as compared with an ordinary IRA, in effect includes the amount of tax already paid.

In addition to adding the new Roth IRA, the 1997 Taxpayer Relief Act added new section 530, which provides for tax-exempt education IRAs. These IRAs are trusts created for the purpose of paying a beneficiary's higher education expenses. Contributions to the trust are nondeductible, cannot exceed $500 per year, and must be made before the beneficiary reaches age 18. No tax is payable on income by the trust and distributions from the trust are tax free to the extent of the beneficiary's higher education expenses in the year of distribution. Again, the education IRA is phased out as income rises above $190,000 (joint return) or $95,000 (individual return).

Penalty for early withdrawal. Amounts withdrawn from a qualified plan before reaching age 59½, in addition to being includable in gross income, are subject to a penalty of 10 percent. § 72(t). The penalty does not apply if the employee has retired after age 55, has died, or has become disabled; or if the distribution is one of a series of periodic payments for the life of the employee or the joint lives of the employee and a designated beneficiary; or if the distribution does not exceed deductible medical expenses; or to distributions used, after separation from employment, to pay medical insurance premiums; or, in the case of an IRA (normal or Roth), if the distribution is used for higher education or a limited amount (typically, $10,000) of first-time home-purchase costs. The penalty tax is consistent with the purpose of the favorable treatment of retirement plans—encouragement of saving for retirement. Some of the exceptions, however, have the effect of transforming retirement plans into college, home-buying, or medical savings plans, and move the income tax in the direction of a consumption tax.

Mandatory distributions. Since the purpose of the favorable treatment of retirement plans is to encourage or support saving for retirement, not to allow accumulation of wealth for future generations, qualified plans are subject to rules specifying minimum distributions, which generally must begin in the calendar year following the year in which the employee reaches age 70½.

Limitations on contributions and benefits. The Code imposes limitations on contributions to and benefits from qualified plans, including a rule under which the maximum benefit under any plan may not exceed $160,000 adjusted for inflation after 2001. See § 415.

4. Stock Options and Other Restricted Property

For certain corporate employees, especially high-level executives, a significant portion of overall compensation may be provided in the form of "compensatory" or "employee" stock options—that is, options that are granted in consideration of services to the employer, with the option entitling the employee to buy a specified number of shares of the employer's common stock at a specified price during or at the end of some defined period of time (usually two to five years after the date of the grant). Employee stock options should be distinguished from ordinary options on common stock that are sold by the owner of that stock to some other person in consideration of an immediate cash payment. Ordinary options are mere "side bets" by shareholders and others on the movement of the corporation's stock price, not directly affecting the corporation itself. Employee stock options, by contrast, can lead to the issuance of new stock at a price that is favorable to the option-holder, thus potentially diluting the old stock.

One obvious reason for issuing an employee stock option is to provide compensation that will induce the recipient to agree to work for the issuing corporation. In addition, however, the receipt of a stock option may improve an employee's incentive to provide the corporation with her best efforts, since now she stands to benefit directly if the stock price goes up. This incentive effect may be especially valuable to the employer if the stock price reliably indicates how well the corporation is doing, the employee's true performance level is hard to observe directly, and the employee can affect the stock price significantly through her poorly observable efforts.

An initial income tax question raised by the issuance of an employee stock option is whether the employee should be taxed at all. In Commissioner v. LoBue, 351 U.S. 243 (1956), the taxpayer, who had received such options from his employer, had succeeded in persuading the Tax Court that they were excludable from income. The Tax Court had reasoned that the options were granted to give the taxpayer "a proprietary interest in the corporation, and not as compensation for services," and that this made them excludable. This line of reasoning brings to mind the *Benaglia* case, supra page 54, in which meals and lodging provided to a hotel manager were deemed excludable (before the enactment of § 119) because they were provided for the "convenience of the employer" rather than with compensatory intent. (In *Benaglia*, however, there may have been a better argument that the noncompensatory motive was evidence of a limited value to the recipient.)

The Supreme Court in *LoBue* reversed the Tax Court and held that employee stock options were taxable notwithstanding the Tax Court's factual finding about intent. Since the transfer was not a gift motivated by detached generosity, and "[t]he company was not giving away something for nothing . . . , it seems impossible to say that it was not compensation. . . . *LoBue* received a very substantial economic and financial benefit from his employer prompted by the employer's desire to get better work from him. This is 'compensation for personal service' within the meaning of [§ 61(a)]." 351 U.S. at 247.

This portion of the Supreme Court decision in *LoBue* left only the question of how and when to tax employee stock options. This is a much harder question, complicated by the fact that such options generally result in a combination of compensation for services and return to investment in a capital asset and therefore raise issues both of timing and of capital gain versus ordinary income.

There are three main approaches to the taxation of an employee stock option (assuming it cannot be transferred and can be exercised only at the end of its term). As it happens, the Internal Revenue Code utilizes all three of these approaches in different circumstances. They are best explained through the use of a hypothetical example, before we turn to the provisions that determine which applies in a given case.

Example

Gordon is a high-level executive in the Sodor Train Corporation (STC). In Year 1, STC gives Gordon an option to buy one share of STC stock in Year 5 for an exercise price of $8. At the time of issuance, STC stock is selling for $20 per share. In Year 5, Gordon exercises the option, using it to buy for the $8 option price a share of STC stock, now selling at $25 per share. In Year 10, Gordon sells the share for $35.

Over the ten-year period, Gordon's income from the grant of the stock option is $27, or the excess of his ultimate receipt ($35) over his outlay ($8). However, both the timing and the character (ordinary income versus capital gain) of his outlay can be viewed three different ways. This reflects the fact that three different events could be viewed as taxable realizations: his receipt of the option in Year 1, his exercise of the option to buy the stock for a bargain price in Year 5, and his sale of the stock for a profit in Year 10.

(1) Income upon receipt of the option. Under this approach, Gordon is treated as if he received cash in Year 1 in the amount of the option's fair market value and used this cash to buy the option. STC is entitled to a deduction of the

amount that Gordon includes in income. Gordon, like any other arm's-length purchaser of an option, then has no further income upon exercise in Year 5. Instead, he simply adds the amount deemed to have been paid for the option in Year 1 to the amount actually paid for the stock in Year 5 in order to determine the basis of the stock. He then has gain or loss upon selling the stock in Year 10.

To apply this approach to the above example, one would have to determine the option's fair market value in Year 1. If similar options are publicly traded in observable markets, then determining this value should be easy. Otherwise, it may be difficult. Is the value $12? This is the excess of the stock's $20 value at the time of issuance over the $8 exercise price. Other factors complicate the analysis, however. The fact that it is an *option* indicates that the value is greater than $12. Gordon can exercise it if the stock price still exceeds the exercise price in Year 5, but simply walk away (unlike an owner of the stock) if the stock price at that time has declined below $8. On the other hand, any restrictions on exercise of the option—for example, a provision that Gordon cannot exercise it unless he is still employed by STC in Year 5—would tend to reduce its value.

Suppose, for arithmetical convenience, that the option is worth exactly $12 in Year 1. If so, then in Year 1 Gordon has $12 of ordinary income, and STC has a $12 deduction for the payment of employee compensation. There are no tax consequences in Year 5, but Gordon holds the share of STC stock with a basis of $20 ($12 basis of option after including it as that amount of income plus $8 outlay for the stock). He then has $15 of capital gain in Year 10 upon selling the stock for $35.

(2) Income upon exercise of the option. Under this approach, there are no tax consequences in Year 1, perhaps on the rationale that nothing definite has happened yet. After all, Gordon might forfeit the option before exercise (depending on its terms), or he might end up not exercising it because the stock price declines, or its fair market value may be hard to ascertain. Gordon is, however, treated as receiving cash in Year 5, when he exercises the option, in the amount of the difference between the STC stock price and the option exercise price at that time. STC is entitled to a deduction of the same amount.

Applying this approach to the above example, in Year 5 Gordon has $17 of ordinary income ($25 stock value minus $8 exercise price). In addition, STC has a $17 deduction in Year 5 for the payment of employee compensation if otherwise allowable. He now holds the stock with a basis of $25. In Year 10, he has $10 of capital gain upon selling the stock for $35.

(3) Gain recognized upon sale of the stock. The third approach is slower still to treat Gordon as having realized a gain. Under this approach, the events not only of Year 1 but also of Year 5 have no immediate tax consequences. After all, who knows (the argument might go) whether Gordon will ultimately make or lose money on his purchase of the share of STC stock. He has merely been fortunate enough to make a bargain purchase of the stock. Only when he sells the stock in Year 10 for an amount that exceeds the exercise price does he have taxable gain.

Applying this approach to the above example, Gordon has no taxable income and STC no deduction either in Year 1 or in Year 5. Gordon holds the share of STC stock with a basis of $8, and he has $27 of capital gain upon selling it for $35 in Year 10. STC therefore never claims any deduction with respect to the transaction.

QUESTIONS

1. Which of these three approaches most accurately reflects economic reality? Which makes the most sense, taking account of all the goals of the income tax, including administrative convenience? What factors might affect the administrative convenience of the alternative approaches?

2. Which of the three approaches is most favorable, and least favorable, to Gordon? To STC? To Gordon and STC considered together, if we assume that their marginal tax rates for ordinary income are the same and that the capital gains rate is somewhat below the tax rate on ordinary income?

3. If, in advance of any transaction, Gordon and STC could simply file an election with the Internal Revenue Service stating which of the three approaches they had chosen to apply consistently to both of them, what would be the best way for them to choose between the approaches they respectively preferred? Assume that the terms of the transaction (including the exercise price and the amount of stock covered by the option) are still malleable.

Statutory Rules for Determining the Tax Treatment of Employee Stock Options

The Court in Commissioner v. LoBue, supra page 295, picked the second of the above approaches (income upon exercising the option). The precedential authority of this holding has been largely superseded by two statutes, however: §§ 422 and 83.

Incentive Stock Options

Section 422, covering what are called "incentive stock options" (ISOs) applies the third approach (capital gain upon sale of stock) to taxpayers who meet specified statutory requirements. Among other things, a stock option that gets ISO treatment must require the employee to retain the stock for at least two years after the grant of the option and one year after receiving the stock under the option (§ 422(a)(1)). Also, the option price must be no less than the fair market value of the stock at the time the option is granted (§ 422(b)(4)). Moreover, the option must be granted pursuant to a plan that stockholders of the granting corporation approve after receiving information about how many shares and which employees the plan covers (§ 422(b)(1)).

A final important limitation on application of the ISO rules is that, for each individual, there is a $100,000 ceiling on the value of the stock that as yet unexercised options constituting ISOs can cover (§ 422(d)). The value of the stock is determined as of the time the option is granted. In illustration, suppose that, on each of five consecutive days, an employer issues a stock option to a given employee for the purchase of stock that, as of the issue date, was worth $25,000, and otherwise meets all the terms of § 422. Given the $100,000 ceiling, only the first four days' options receive ISO treatment. The $100,000 ceiling makes the ISO rules relatively insignificant as a factor in the overall compensation of really high-paid employees, such as the chief executives at many major corporations.

The requirements for ISO treatment other than the $100,000 ceiling can make the application of § 422 in effect elective. While not literally elective, since it automatically applies if all its terms are met, taxpayers who want to deliberately fail to meet its terms may find this easy. For example, the option price can simply be set slightly below the stock price at the time when the option is granted, perhaps with an offsetting adjustment to the employee's other compensation.

Congress's stated reason for enacting § 422 was to "provide an important incentive device for corporations to attract new management . . . retain the services of executives who might otherwise leave . . . [and e]ncourag[e] the management of a business to have a proprietary interest in its successful operation. . . ." General Explanation of the Economic Recovery Tax Act of 1981, prepared by the Staff of the Joint Committee on Taxation, 97th Cong., 1st Sess., at 157 (1981).

QUESTIONS

1. Do corporations need a special tax incentive to provide compensation in whatever form is most favorable to superior management performance? Or should one expect them to make the best compensation decisions for themselves?

2. Given the fact that § 422 results in the denial of any corporate deduction for compensation provided through incentive stock options, is it really an incentive provision? In circumstances where it is not tax favorable, might there be any other reasons why companies would prefer to provide compensation this way despite (or because of) the lack of any tax deduction?

Nonstatutory Stock Options

The parties to employee stock option arrangements sometimes prefer to avoid § 422, for reasons that range from preserving the corporate-level deduction to discomfort with various of its requirements, such as the need to submit for shareholder approval the details of option arrangements with senior management. Thus, "nonstatutory" stock options, or those that fail (perhaps deliberately) to meet the terms of § 422 or its predecessors, have long been popular. They were initially governed by *LoBue*, and thus taxable upon exercise of the option. In the 1960s, however, companies started using nonstatutory options and outright stock transfers that, due to the difficulty of valuing the stock when it was acquired, the employees claimed were taxable in the same manner as is now prescribed by § 422. That is, despite *LoBue*'s formal applicability, the taxpayers claimed that nothing was includable in income at the time of option exercise, thus leading the employee's entire gain (relative to the option exercise price) to be taxed only upon ultimate sale of the stock. These claims to a zero inclusion upon option exercise could be based either on the difficulty of valuing the stock itself (where, for example, the stock was not publicly traded), or on valuation difficulties created by restrictions that the options at least initially placed on the employee's ownership of the underlying stock.

In particular, stock that was thus transferred might be subject to restrictions on transferability and to a risk of forfeiture. To illustrate both, suppose an employer sells to an employee, for $5, shares of its common stock that at the time of the sale are selling in a public exchange for $30, but that the sale is subject to two conditions: (1) the employee cannot sell the shares for five years, and (2) if the employee is fired for cause or quits within the next two years, he must sell the shares back to the company for $5 per share.

Restrictions of this kind may serve good business purposes of the employer. In addition, however, they provide a ground for the employee to argue that the bargain acquisition not only is worth less than $25 (the difference between the stock's public price and the amount for which it was purchased), but indeed has no ascertainable value. One doubts that very many of the employees who relied on this argument actually believed that what they had received had zero value, yet the argument had some success in the courts.

In 1969, Congress responded to the growth of restricted nonstatutory stock options by enacting § 83 (which, however, applies far more generally, to all transfers of property as compensation for services). Under § 83, if property is transferred to a person (generally, but not necessarily, an employee) as compensation for services, the tax consequences can be summarized as follows:

(1) Income upon receipt of the option:

(a) Mandatory includability. When a stock option is issued to an employee, if it has a "readily ascertainable fair market value" (which will rarely be the case), its value must be included in the income of the employee (and may be deducted by the employer). § 83(a); Regs. § 1.83-3(a)(2) and 1.83-7T. The value of such an option is not includable, however, if the option is (a) nontransferable and (b) subject to a "substantial risk of forfeiture" — in which case the value is includable when either of these two conditions lapses. § 83(a)(2). The same two conditions determine the time when a transfer of other property, such as the company's stock (rather than just an option on the stock), is included (and deducted). These rules also apply to the transfer of options or other property to people other than employees.

Ordinarily, compensatory stock options will not have a fair market value at the time of issuance. In that case, there are no tax consequences at the time of issuance of the option. See Regs. § 1.83-3. When the option is exercised, the employee is taxed on the spread between the exercise price and the value of the stock (assuming the stock is transferable or is not subject to substantial risk of forfeiture), and the corporation is entitled to a corresponding deduction.

A substantial risk of forfeiture exists where the employee's "rights to full enjoyment of such property are conditioned upon the future performance of substantial services by any individual." § 83(c)(1).

(b) *Elective includability.* Even if taxation of the employee is not required at the time of issuance of an option (or transfer of other property), because of nontransferability and substantial risk of forfeiture, the employee is allowed to elect taxation. In the event of such an election, the fair market value of the property is determined without regard to any restrictions other than those that will never lapse. The amount included in income becomes the employee's basis in the stock, but an employee who ultimately forfeits the property cannot claim a subsequent deduction by reason of the forfeiture. § 83(b).

(c) *Prerequisite to both mandatory and elective includability.* Neither of the above two rules applies, and the receipt of an option therefore is not immediately taxable after all, if, when granted, the option "lacks a readily ascertainable fair market value." § 83(e)(3).

(2) *Income subsequent to receipt of the option:*

(a) *Income when the option becomes nonforfeitable or transferable.* Where the employee could have made the election in (b) above but did not, the option is included in income (and deductible by the employer) when it either ceases to be nontransferable or ceases to be subject to a substantial risk of forfeiture. § 83(a).

(b) *Income upon exercise of the option.* An option that lacked a "readily ascertainable fair market value" when granted is not taxed until it is exercised, even if the value becomes ascertainable after it is granted but before it is exercised.

In recent years, many employees of high technology companies received nonstatutory options as a substantial part of their compensation. Most of these options had no "readily ascertainable fair market value." Under the rule described above, income was recognized when these options were exercised. The difference between the exercise price and the fair market value of the stock was treated as salary compensation. For example, an employee who exercised an option and paid an exercise price of $5 per share to purchase 1,000 shares of stock trading at $100 per share would recognize income of $95,000 ($100,000 market value less $5,000 purchase price). When the technology bubble burst in 2000 and 2001, such employees were often left with stock that was either worthless or worth much less than the $100,000 that had been used in computing their income (and quite possibly with a substantial loan incurred to pay the tax on the $95,000 income). In some cases, the employer was bankrupt and the employee lost not only the value of the stock but her job as well. The employee could not, however, deduct the loss on the stock against her salary income since the stock is a capital asset, and, as explained above (page 35), capital losses are fully deductible only against capital gains. Only $3,000 of the excess of capital losses over capital gains may be deductible in any given year against ordinary income. The moral of the story is that employees who exercise nonstatutory options run the risk of recognizing ordinary income on the exercise and sustaining a largely unusable capital loss on sale. The risk can be avoided only by immediately selling the shares received on exercise of the options.

NOTES AND QUESTIONS

1. *Broader rule of inclusion?* Why not mandate inclusion of the option's value (if ascertainable) upon receipt even if it is forfeitable or nontransferable, treating any such restrictions as simply affecting value? Would such a rule of immediate inclusion be unfair to taxpayers? Pose insuperable administrative difficulties? Permit taxpayer manipulation?

2. *Tax planning and business planning.* Taxpayers often prefer to ensure that the employee need not recognize income upon receipt of an option, even though the employer deduction provides an offsetting tax benefit that seemingly might induce the employer to increase the before-tax value of compensation provided. In cases where the employer actually wants to limit transferability and impose forfeiture risks to maximize the employee's motivation to stay on the job and work hard, this can create a happy coincidence between the employer's business planning aims and the employee's tax planning aims. While the employee might still prefer, all else equal, to receive an unrestricted option, at least the restrictions serve her tax planning aims. If the employer is just trying to provide valuable compensation, however, the parties may try to structure the deal so that the forfeiture risk and restrictions on transferability are as weak as they can possibly be without leading to mandatory inclusion upon receipt.

3. *Not for the timid.* One common but often questionable tax planning technique is to elect immediate inclusion of a stock option when granted, but claim it has zero value. For example, an employee of a speculative start-up company may claim that the company is such a long-shot that no one would pay anything for the option even if it were unrestricted. In such a case, one often may wonder if the taxpayer (or others in the know) really think that the option has zero value. If the treatment is allowable, however, its consequence is that, in the guise of immediate inclusion, the taxpayer has actually received treatment equivalent to that afforded ISOs under § 422. After all, including zero upon receipt of the option is equivalent to treating the receipt as not a taxable event!

One way the government has attempted to combat this technique is through Regs. § 1.83-7, which provides that in many situations an option's fair market value will be treated as nonascertainable. The result, under *LoBue*, is income inclusion when the option is exercised (rather than zero upon receipt followed by nothing further until the stock is sold). The following case discusses this regulation and a taxpayer claim that it was invalid due to inconsistency with legislative intent.

CRAMER v. COMMISSIONER
64 F.3d 1406 (9th Cir. 1995)

. . .

In 1972, Richard Cramer founded IMED Corp., a company that designed, manufactured, and sold electronic medical instruments. Cramer served as president and chief executive officer of IMED from its inception until 1982.

During that time, Warren Boynton served as vice-president, and Kevin Monaghan, an attorney, served as outside general counsel. All three also served at various times on the board of directors of IMED.

From 1978 to 1981, the stock of IMED was neither publicly traded on an established exchange, nor registered with the Securities and Exchange Commission. During that time, that stock was held by approximately 150 to 250 shareholders. In 1978, IMED issued to Cramer an option to purchase 50,000 shares of IMED stock at $50 per share. The terms of the option provided certain vesting restrictions: Cramer could only exercise the option in 20% increments in each of the next five years, and only so long as he remained employed by IMED. The terms also provided certain transfer restrictions: Cramer could only transfer the option to persons approved by the board as "qualified offerees," and any transferee would take the option subject to the vesting restrictions.

In 1979, IMED issued to Cramer an option to purchase 4390 shares of IMED stock at $8 per share, to Boynton an option to purchase 30,000 shares of IMED stock at $13 per share, and to Monaghan an option to purchase 4500 shares at $13 per share. All of these options provided for a five year vesting schedule and were subject to the same vesting and transfer restrictions as Cramer's 1978 option. . . .

IMED issued all of these options in recognition of the services Cramer, Boynton and Monaghan provided to the company. The delayed vesting schedules and restrictions were intended to induce their continued employment with IMED. Appellants never exercised any part of the options.

In 1978, Dan Hendrickson, the corporate comptroller and treasurer of IMED, consulted with an accountant at Arthur Young & Co. regarding the tax treatment of these options. The accountant did not actually review the IMED options. Nonetheless, he informed Hendrickson that as a general matter, § 83(b) elections could be filed to include the value of so-called "nonstatutory options" (options not subject to § 422), such as the IMED options, in ordinary income at the time of grant, even if they were not publicly traded, and that the options would then receive capital gains treatment upon later disposition.

On the basis of that information, as well as his own research, Hendrickson advised Cramer, Boynton and Monaghan that on the one hand, statements in the legislative history of the 1976 Tax Reform Act arguably supported treating the IMED options in this manner. He told them that in order to have a chance at receiving capital gain treatment upon future disposition of the options, they would have to file § 83(b) elections with the Internal Revenue Service to include their value in ordinary income in the year of grant. But he told them that on the other hand, under Treasury regulations, he believed that the value of the options could not be readily ascertained upon grant. If that were the case, § 83 would not apply at grant at all. He advised them that pursuant to those regulations, the IRS could take the position that the options would not receive capital gains treatment upon future disposition. He further informed them that acting contrary to or overturning a Treasury regulation "is very difficult."

In an attempt to ensure capital gain treatment upon future disposition of the options, appellants filed § 83(b) elections with the IRS for Cramer's 1978

option, Boynton's 1979 option and Monaghan's 1979 option. The elections
stated that the fair market value of the options at the date of grant was zero.
No such elections were filed either for Cramer's 1979 option. . . . Appellants
reported no taxable income in the year of grant from the receipt of any of the
options.

Despite filing elections declaring that the options had zero value, Cramer
believed that the options had a value greater than zero upon grant. Boynton
believed that the options had value upon grant, but that it was not "readily
recognizable value." Appellants did not consult an expert on options or valuation before they claimed that value as zero.

In 1981, John Stine of Arthur Young began handling IMED's tax matters.
At that time, appellants inquired whether the statute of limitations on their
treatment of the options would run from the time when they filed the § 83(b)
elections. Stine determined that it would not, and also sent a letter to
Monaghan stating:

> IMED currently takes the position that its stock options are governed by Section
> 83 and therefore the present tax treatment is . . . no income to the employee on
> grant or exercise and no compensation deduction to IMED. However, Regula-
> tion 1.83-7 states that an option must have a "readily ascertainable fair market
> value" before § 83 will apply. Since the definition of "readily ascertainable fair
> market value" is virtually impossible to meet, IMED's present position is subject
> to challenge.

He suggested that IMED consider changing its position in light of the potential exposure to exercising employees, should the IRS successfully assert
the nonapplication of § 83 at grant. Monaghan discussed Stine's letter with
Cramer.

In 1982, Warner-Lambert Corp. purchased all of the stock of IMED for
approximately $163 per share.[18] As part of the agreement, the officers and
directors of IMED resigned. Warner-Lambert also agreed to buy all outstanding vested and nonvested options on IMED stock. Warner-Lambert paid
appellants approximately $163 less the exercise price for each option. Cramer
received $25,945,506 for all of his options; Boynton received $7,714,800 for
his options; and Monaghan received $2,274,895 for his.

Tax professionals prepared all of appellants' 1982 federal income tax
returns. Those professionals informed appellants that they had a plausible
position that gain on the options was capital gain, but that Treasury regulations were to the contrary. They said that there was a risk the IRS would reach
a contrary conclusion.

Richard and Alice Cramer's joint 1982 income tax return reported all but
$1.3 million of the receipts from the options as long-term capital gain. The
sale of the options was set out in a section of the return designated for stocks
and bonds, even though the return contained another section for options.
Furthermore, even though Richard Cramer knew they had no basis in the

---

18. [By the time of the purchase, the number of shares covered by the options had increased at the
result of a stock split. — EDS.]

options, the return misreported the options as having a basis of $7,535,620 and sales proceeds of $32,191,126.

Warren and Susi Boynton's joint 1982 income tax return declared all receipts from sale of the options as long-term capital gain. It listed the options as "IMED stock" with a zero basis. Kevin and Dina Monaghan's joint 1982 return also declared all receipts from the sale of the options as long-term capital gain. Even though Kevin Monaghan knew they had no basis in the options, their return misreported the options as having a basis of $2,558,500 and sales proceeds of $4,832,395.

None of the returns disclosed that the options were subject to transfer and vesting restrictions; that § 83(b) elections had been filed with respect to some of the options; that the options were not traded on an established market; or on what authority appellants relied to support their treatment of the options.

The IRS audited appellants' 1982 returns. It determined that the sale of the options produced ordinary income in 1982, not capital gain, and calculated deficiencies accordingly. It also assessed penalties against appellants for intentional disregard of tax rules and regulations, pursuant to § 6653(a) (now § 6652(b)(1) and (2)), and for substantial understatement of tax, pursuant to § 6661(a).

Appellants challenged these determinations in United States Tax Court. After a full trial, in a published decision, Cramer v. Commissioner, 101 T.C. 255 (1993), the Tax Court upheld Treas. Reg. § 1.83-7(b)(2) as a valid interpretation of § 83. Under that regulation, because the IMED options were subject to various restrictions at the time of grant, they did not have a "readily ascertainable fair market value" within the meaning of § 83(e)(3). Section 83(a) and (b) therefore did not apply to the options at grant, and thus their value was not includable in ordinary income in the year of grant. Accordingly, none of the gain from their subsequent sale in 1982 was taxable as capital gain, and the court upheld the Commissioner's determination of deficiency. The court also found that appellants had intentionally disregarded Reg. § 1.83-7(b)(2), and therefore upheld the penalty assessed pursuant to § 6653(a) [now § 6662(b)(1)]. It also found that appellants had substantially understated their tax, that they had no substantial authority to support their tax treatment of the options, that they had not disclosed the facts relevant to that treatment on their returns, and that they had not acted in good faith. On those grounds, it upheld the penalty assessed pursuant to § 6661(a) [now § 6662(b)(2)]. The Cramers, Boyntons, and Monaghans timely appeal.

DISCUSSION

I. The Deficiencies in Appellants' 1982 Tax Payments . . .

[T]he issue presented by this case is whether, at the time of the original transfer, the options had a "readily ascertainable fair market value," within the meaning of § 83(e)(3). Treasury has issued a regulation defining this standard. That regulation provides that an option that is not traded on an established market, such as the IMED options, does not have a readily ascertainable fair market value when granted unless the taxpayer can show that all of the following conditions exist:

  i.   The option is transferable by the optionee;
  ii. The option is exercisable immediately in full by the optionee;
  iii. The option or the property subject to the option is not subject to any restriction or condition . . . which has a significant effect upon the fair market value on the option; and
  iv. The fair market value of the option privilege is readily ascertainable in accordance with paragraph (b)(3) of this section.

Treas. Reg. § 1.83-7(b)(2) (emphasis added).

The 1978 and 1979 IMED options clearly did not meet all four of these conditions at the time of transfer, and therefore did not have a "readily ascertainable fair market value" according to this regulation. Because the options could not be exercised unless the original recipient remained employed at IMED, the options were subject to "substantial risk of forfeiture." See § 83(c)(1). The terms of the options also required that if they were transferred, the transferee must take the options subject to this risk. Thus, the options were no "transferable" within the meaning of the statue. See § 83(c)(2). Moreover, the five year vesting schedule rendered them not "exercisable immediately in full" upon grant. Finally, appellants do not seriously challenge the Tax Court's factual finding that the transfer and vesting restrictions had a "significant effect upon the fair market value on the option[s]." We need not address whether the fourth condition was satisfied, because, even though appellants presented evidence below that the value of each IMED "option privilege" was ascertainable, these options so clearly failed the first three conditions. Therefore, according to Reg. § 1.83-7(b)(2), the value of the options was not readily ascertainable at the time of transfer, § 83 did not apply to that transfer, and the gain from the 1982 sale of those options was ordinary income, not capital gain.

Rather than contest this analysis, appellants argue that Reg. § 1.83-7(b)(2) is simply an invalid interpretation of § 83. They point out that § 83(a) and (b) both require that all lapsing restrictions, such as those listed in Reg. § 1.83-7(b)(2) (I-iii), be disregarded when valuing an option for purposes of calculating the tax. They argue that such restrictions should also be disregarded when determining whether an option has a "readily ascertainable fair market value" within the meaning of § 83(e)(3). Since, rather than disregarding those restrictions, Reg. § 1.83-7(b)(2) mandates that such restrictions prevent an option from satisfying the § 83(e)(3) test, appellants argue it is invalid.

The Tax Court determined that the regulation was valid. . . . We conclude that Reg. § 1.83-7(b)(2) is neither plainly inconsistent with, nor an unreasonable interpretation of, § 83. The plain meaning of the statute supports Treasury's interpretation. Section 83(a) and (b) both contain language requiring that the value of transferred property be "determined without regard to any restriction. . . ." This language is conspicuously absent from § 83(e)(3). Adoption of appellants' argument would require us to read that language in § 83(e)(3). It is a fundamental rule of statutory construction that "[w]hen Congress includes a specific term in one section of a statute but omits it in another section of the same Act, it should not be implied where it is excluded." Arizona Elec. Power Co-op., Inc. v. United States, 816 F.2d 1366, 1375 (9th Cir. 1987) (citing Russello v. United States, 464 U.S. 16, 23 (1983)).

Furthermore, Congress has had opportunity to include such language in § 83(e)(3), or otherwise to amend the statute in order to insure that § 83 applies to options subject to restrictions, but it has failed to do so. . . .

Appellants cite legislative history from the 1976 Tax Reform Act to argue that Reg. § 1.83-7(b)(2), which had only been proposed at that time, is invalid. The 1976 Conference Report explaining that Act states:

> The conferees intend that in applying these rules for the future, the Service will make every reasonable effort to determine a fair market value for an option . . . where the employee irrevocably elects . . . to have the option valued at the time it is granted (particularly in the case of an option granted for a new business venture). The conferees intend that the Service will promulgate regulations and rulings setting forth as specifically as possible the criteria which will be weighed in valuing an option which the employee elects to value at the time it is granted. . . .

This legislative history does not demonstrate that the Reg. § 1.83-7(b)(2) interpretation of § 83 is unreasonable. First, "an analysis of legislative history is proper only to solve, not to create ambiguity." . . . This legislative history, on the other hand, provides at best an ambiguous directive regarding § 83(e)(3): It is unclear whether the conferees intended that the Commissioner should henceforth disregard the restrictions listed in then-proposed Reg. § 1.83-7(b)(2)(i-iii), or whether she should relax the rules on valuing the "option privilege" proposed in Reg. § 1.83-7(b)(3), or neither. . . . Second, the 1976 Tax Reform Act in no way amended the language of § 83, which was enacted in 1969. We hesitate to rely entirely on the views of a later Congress to interpret an earlier enactment. . . . Finally, this statement . . . at most invited, but did not require Treasury to adopt rules that Congress did not enact. . . .

Treasury reasonably concluded that § 83(e)(3) allows restrictions to be considered when determining whether an option has a "readily ascertainable fair market value."

In sum, because the 1978 and 1979 options clearly did not have a "readily ascertainable fair market value" upon transfer according to Reg. § 1.83-7, § 83 did not apply until the sale of those options in 1982, see § 83(e)(3); Reg. § 1.83-7(a), and that sale therefore produced only ordinary income. We affirm the Tax Court's decision upholding the deficiency with respect to these options. . . .

II. The Penalty Under § 6653(a) for Intentional Disregard of Rules and Regulations

The version of § 6653(a) [now § 6662(a)(1)] applicable to appellants provides: "If any part of any underpayment . . . is due to negligence or intentional disregard of rules and regulations . . . there shall be added to the tax . . ." various penalties. We have established that "[i]ntentional disregard occurs when a taxpayer who knows or should know of a rule or regulation chooses to ignore its requirements." Hansen v. Commissioner, 820 F.2d 1464, 1469 (9th Cir. 1987).

In this case, the Tax Court found that appellants learned from their various tax advisors that capital gain treatment of the 1982 options sale was contrary to Reg. § 1.83-7(b)(2). Nonetheless, appellants, together with their advisors, concluded that there was a plausible argument that the regulation was invalid. On the basis of that argument, they decided to claim capital gain treatment of their returns. Under these circumstances, the Tax Court upheld the penalties assessed pursuant to § 6653(a).

We review that decision for clear error. . . . Appellants bear the burden of proving that § 6653(a) did not apply. Id. Appellants do not challenge the Tax Court's basic finding of fact. Rather, they argue that because they had a reasonable basis to believe that the regulation was invalid, and because they were so advised by tax professionals, they should not be subject to the penalty.

The Second Circuit has rejected such a "reasonable basis" exception to § 6653(a). Durker v. Commissioner, 697 F.2d 46, 53-55 (2d Cir. 1982), cert. denied, 461 U.S. 957 (1983). After exhaustively tracing the legislative history of the statute as well as the relevant caselaw, that court stated:

> The statutory language "there shall be added," could hardly be clearer. The reasonableness of a taxpayer's action may indeed be relevant when he is charged with negligence but not when he admittedly has flouted applicable rules and regulations which he fully understood.

Id. at 53. That court went on to describe favorably a Board of Tax Appeals case: " '[h]arsh though the conclusion may seem,' the 5 percent addition was mandatory even where the taxpayer had reasonably believed, on the advice of counsel, that a regulation issued by the Commissioner was invalid." Id. at 54 (citing The Journal Co. v. Commissioner, 46 B.T.A. 841, 845-46 (1942), rev'd on other grounds, 134 F.2d 165 (7th Cir. 1943)).

We too reject appellants' "reasonable basis" argument. Appellants are sophisticated businessmen, one of whom is himself an attorney. After carefully reviewing the matter with their tax advisers, they decided to ignore Reg. § 1.83-7(b)(2), because they thought it invalid. As the court in *Durker* explained, the proper course, by which they would have avoided the risk of penalty, was to file their returns in accordance with the regulation, and then to challenge the validity of the regulation in a suit for a refund. See 697 F.2d at 54. Instead, appellants chose to play the audit lottery. They lost. The Tax Court did not clearly err by upholding their penalty pursuant to § 6653(a).

III. The Penalty Under § 6661(a) for Substantial Understatement of Tax

The version of the Code that applies to appellants' 1982 returns provides: "If there is a substantial understatement of income tax for any taxable year, there shall be added to the tax an amount equal to 25 percent of the amount of any underpayment attributable to such understatement." § 6661(a) (1986) [now § 6662(b)(2)]. It is undisputed that the deficiencies that we have affirmed in Section I of this opinion were "substantial understatements" of tax as defined by § 6661(b). Nonetheless, the statute provides that the amount of an understatement shall be reduced by the portion of the understatement which is attributable either, 1) to tax treatment that was supported by "substantial authority," or, 2) to tax treatment about which the relevant facts were "adequately disclosed in the return or in a statement attached to the return." § 6661(b)(2)(B). Furthermore, the Commissioner may waive any such penalty on a showing by the taxpayer that there was reasonable cause for the understatement and that the taxpayer acted in good faith. § 6661(c).

The Tax Court concluded that appellants' tax treatment of the options was not supported by substantial authority. We review this conclusion of law de novo. . . . "Substantial authority" supports a position "only if the weight of the authorities supporting the treatment is substantial in relation to the weight of authorities supporting contrary positions." Treas. Reg. § 1.6661-3(b)(1). Appellants' treatment of the options does not meet this test. They have relied heavily upon ambiguous legislative history from 1976 Tax Reform Act that was created subsequent to the enactment of § 83. The principal authorities supporting the contrary position include the plain meaning of the statute, and a regulation promulgated by Treasury interpreting that statute. These authorities far outweigh those cited by appellants. The Tax Court properly refused to reduce appellants' penalties pursuant to the substantial authority exception.

The Tax Court also found that appellants did not adequately disclose the facts relevant to their tax treatment of the options. We review this finding of fact for clear error. See Fed. R. Civ. P. 52(a). Appellants do not even challenge the Tax Court's finding that rather than disclosing the relevant facts, their 1982 returns actually concealed the true nature of the option proceeds. Cramer and Monaghan both claimed basis in the options, even though they knew they had none. Also, Cramer and Boynton both listed the options in sections labeled for stock, even though the returns contained separate sections for options. These unexplained misrepresentations appear designed to avoid audit. Furthermore, we reject appellants' argument that their filing of § 83(b) elections in 1978 and 1979 provided adequate disclosure. Section 6661(b)(2)(B)(iii) explicitly requires that the disclosure be attached to the return itself. Therefore, the Tax Court properly refused to reduce appellants' penalties pursuant to the disclosure exception.

The Tax Court also found that appellants did not act in good faith. We review this finding of fact for clear error. See Fed. R. Civ. P. 52(a). The concealment described in the previous paragraph, coupled with appellants' decision to ignore Reg. § 1.83-7(b)(2), amply supports this finding. Therefore, the Tax Court correctly concluded that the good faith/reasonable cause waiver did not apply in this case.

Accordingly, we affirm the Tax Court's decision to uphold the entire penalty for substantial understatement of tax.

Affirmed.

NOTES AND QUESTIONS

1. Sections 6653 and 6661 have now been consolidated in § 6662, which imposes a single penalty of 20 percent for either "negligence or disregard of rules or regulations" or "substantial understatement." See § 6662(a), (b)(1)

and (2). Does 20 percent seem to you to be a reasonable level of penalty? If you were now in a position similar to that of Cramer, filing your return for the year in which you sold the options, would the penalty be sufficient to deter you from filing the type of return that Cramer filed?

2. The court states that the issue in the case is the applicability of § 83(e)(3), which turns on whether the options had a "readily ascertainable fair market value." What is the consequence of the failure to meet that standard?

3. Does Reg. § 1.83-7(b)(2) seem to be a reasonable elaboration of § 83(e)(3)?

4. Should Richard Cramer have been charged with criminal fraud? See § 7201, discussed at page 27. What about civil fraud under § 6663 (with a 75 percent penalty)? What about Boynton?

5. Suppose Cramer had asked you to write an opinion letter on the applicability of § 83. What would you have written?

6. Suppose that Cramer had decided that he would file a § 83(b) election in 1979 and sought your advice on what how to value the options. What would you have advised?

G. TRANSFERS INCIDENT TO MARRIAGE AND DIVORCE

1. Introduction

Transfers incident to marriage and divorce raise an interesting set of issues. Suppose, for example, that pursuant to a divorce, Linda transfers to her ex-spouse, Martin, stock with a basis of $40,000 and a fair market value of $100,000. One question raised by such a transfer is whether, by virtue of the transfer, Martin should be required to include $100,000 in his income and Linda should be allowed to deduct $100,000. That is the "alimony" issue, to which we will return later in this section. (The answer under current law is that Linda would not be entitled to a deduction and Martin would not be required to include any amount in his income, but it is by no means obvious that that result is consistent with sound principles of tax policy.) At this point we address the narrower question — the "recognition" question — of whether the transfer should be treated as a realization event for Linda, an appropriate time at which to recognize Linda's gain of $60,000. Should Linda be treated as if she had sold the property and transferred the proceeds? Should it matter whether the transfer is of community property? Whether the transfer is made pursuant to a divorce decree or an antenuptial agreement?

As we have just suggested, transfers incident to marriage and divorce raise income and deduction issues as well. Suppose that, in addition to the stock transfer described above, Linda makes cash alimony payments of $1,000 a month for three years to Martin. Those payments would be deductible by Linda and taxable to Martin, but we will see that there are complex rules distinguishing between alimony and other types of transfers that are not deductible by the payor and not taxable to the payee. The income and deduction issues that arise with transfers of both appreciated and non-appreciated property might be discussed in Chapter 2, in connection with other characteristics of income, or in Chapter 4, in connection with other personal deductions. Instead, in the pages that follow, we provide an introduction to all tax issues raised by transfers incident to marriage and divorce, but we begin with the recognition issue, which plainly fits in this chapter.

2. Property Settlements

The next two cases, *Davis* and *Farid-Es-Sultaneh*, are included because of their historical importance and usefulness in setting forth some the key issues raised by property transfers incident to marriage and divorce. As we will see, their current legal significance is affected, and in some respects eliminated, by the subsequent enactment of § 1041.

a. Transfers Incident to a Divorce or Separation Agreement

UNITED STATES v. DAVIS
370 U.S. 65 (1962)

Mr. Justice CLARK delivered the opinion of the Court.

These cases involve the tax consequences of a transfer of appreciated property by Thomas Crawley Davis to his former wife pursuant to a property settlement agreement executed prior to divorce. . . .

In 1954 the taxpayer and his then wife made a voluntary property settlement and separation agreement calling for support payments to the wife and minor child in addition to the transfer of certain personal property to the wife. Under Delaware law all the property transferred was that of the taxpayer, subject to certain statutory marital rights of the wife including a right of intestate succession and a right upon divorce to a share of the husband's property. Specifically as a "division in settlement of their property" the taxpayer agreed to transfer to his wife, inter alia, 1,000 shares of stock in the E. I. duPont de Nemours & Co. The then Mrs. Davis agreed to accept this division "in full settlement and satisfaction of any and all claims and rights against the husband whatsoever (including but not by way of limitation, dower and all rights under the laws of testacy and intestacy). . . ."

I

The determination of the income tax consequences of the stock transfer described above is basically a two-step analysis: (1) Was the transaction a taxable event? (2) If so, how much taxable gain resulted therefrom? Originally the Tax Court (at that time the Board of Tax Appeals) held that the accretion to property transferred pursuant to a divorce settlement could not be taxed as capital gain to the transferor because the amount realized by the satisfaction of the husband's marital obligations was indeterminable and because, even if such benefit were ascertainable, the transaction was a nontaxable division of property.... However, upon being reversed in quick succession by the Courts of Appeals of the Third and Second Circuits, ... the Tax Court accepted the position of these courts and has continued to apply these views in appropriate cases since that time.... [T]he Courts of Appeals reasoned that the accretion to the property was "realized" by the transfer and that this gain could be measured on the assumption that the relinquished marital rights were equal in value to the property transferred. The matter was considered settled until the Court of Appeals for the Sixth Circuit, in reversing the Tax Court, ruled that, although such a transfer might be a taxable event, the gain realized thereby could not be determined because of the impossibility of evaluating the fair market value of the wife's marital rights.... In so holding that court specifically rejected the argument that these rights could be presumed to be equal in value to the property transferred for their release. This is essentially the position taken by the Court of Claims in the instant case.

II

We now turn to the threshold question of whether the transfer in issue was an appropriate occasion for taxing the accretion to the stock. There can be no doubt that Congress, as evidenced by its inclusive definition [in § 61(a)] of income subject to taxation, i.e., "all income from whatever source derived, including ... [g]ains derived from dealings in property," intended that the economic growth of this stock be taxed. The problem confronting us is simply when is such accretion to be taxed. Should the economic gain be presently assessed against taxpayer, or should this assessment await a subsequent transfer of the property by the wife? The controlling statutory language, which provides [§ 1001] that gains from dealings in property are to be taxed upon "sale or other disposition," is too general to include or exclude conclusively the transaction presently in issue. Recognizing this, the Government and the taxpayer argue by analogy with transactions more easily classified as within or without the ambient [sic] of taxable events. The taxpayer asserts that the present disposition is comparable to a nontaxable division of property between two co-owners,[19] while the Government contends it more resembles a

19. Any suggestion that the transaction in question was a gift is completely unrealistic. Property transferred pursuant to a negotiated settlement in return for the release of admittedly valuable rights is not a gift in any sense of the term. To intimate that there was a gift to the extent the value of the property exceeded that of the rights released not only invokes the erroneous premise that every exchange not precisely equal involves a gift but merely raises the measurement problem discussed in Part III [of this opinion]. Cases in which this Court has held transfers of property in exchange for the release of marital rights subject to gift taxes are based not on the premise that such transactions are inherently gifts but on the concept that in the contemplation of the gift tax statute they are to be taxed as gifts. Merrill v. Fahs, 324 U.S. 308 (1945); Commissioner v. Wemyss, 324 U.S. 303 (1945); see Harris v. Commissioner, 340 U.S. 106 (1950). In interpreting the particular income tax provisions here involved, we find ourselves unfettered by the language and considerations ingrained in the gift and estate tax statutes. See Farid-Es-Sultaneh v. Commissioner [infra page 316].

taxable transfer of property in exchange for the release of an independent legal obligation. Neither disputes the validity of the other's starting point.

In support of his analogy the taxpayer argues that to draw a distinction between a wife's interest in the property of her husband in a common-law jurisdiction such as Delaware and the property interest of a wife in a typical community property jurisdiction would commit a double sin; for such differentiation would depend upon "elusive and subtle casuistries which . . . possess no relevance for tax purposes," Helvering v. Hallock, 309 U.S. 106, 118 (1940), and would create disparities between common-law and community property jurisdictions in contradiction to Congress' general policy of equality between the two. The taxpayer's analogy, however, stumbles on its own premise, for the inchoate rights granted a wife in her husband's property by the Delaware law do not even remotely reach the dignity of co-ownership. The wife has no interest — passive or active — over the management or disposition of her husband's personal property. Her rights are not descendable, and she must survive him to share in his intestate estate. Upon dissolution of the marriage she shares in the property only to such extent as the court deems "reasonable." 13 Del. Code Ann. § 1531(a). What is "reasonable" might be ascertained independently of the extent of the husband's property by such criteria as the wife's financial condition, her needs in relation to her accustomed station in life, her age and health, the number of children and their ages, and the earning capacity of the husband. See, e.g., Beres v. Beres, 52 Del. 133, 154 F.2d 384 (1959).

This is not to say it would be completely illogical to consider the shearing off of the wife's rights in her husband's property as a division of that property, but we believe the contrary to be the more reasonable construction. Regardless of the tags, Delaware seems only to place a burden on the husband's property rather than to make the wife a part owner thereof. In the present context the rights of succession and reasonable share do not differ significantly from the husband's obligations of support and alimony. They all partake more of a personal liability of the husband than a property interest of the wife. The effectuation of these marital rights may ultimately result in the ownership of some of the husband's property as it did here, but certainly this happenstance does not equate the transaction with a division of property by co-owners. Although admittedly such a view may permit different tax treatment among the several States, this Court in the past has not ignored the differing effects on the federal taxing scheme of substantive differences between community property and federal taxing systems. E.g., Poe v. Seaborn [infra page 626]. To be sure Congress has seen fit to alleviate this disparity in many areas, . . . but in other areas the facts of life are still with us. . . .

III

Having determined that the transaction was a taxable event, we now turn to the point on which the Court of Claims balked, viz., the measurement of the taxable gain realized by the taxpayer. The Code defines the taxable gain from the sale or disposition of property as being the "excess of the amount realized therefrom over the adjusted basis. . . ." § 1001(a). The "amount realized" is further defined as "the sum of any money received plus the fair market value of the property (other than money) received." § 1001(b). In the instant case the "property received" was the release of the wife's inchoate marital rights. The Court of Claims, following the Court of Appeals for the Sixth Circuit, found that there was no way to compute the fair market value of these marital rights and that it was thus impossible to determine the taxable gain realized by the taxpayer. We believe this conclusion was erroneous.

It must be assumed, we think, that the parties acted at arm's length and that they judged the marital rights to be equal in value to the property for which they were exchanged. There was no evidence to the contrary here. Absent a readily ascertainable value it is accepted practice where property is exchanged to hold, as did the Court of Claims in Philadelphia Park Amusement Co. v. United States, 130 Ct. Cl. 166, 172, 126 F. Supp. 184, 189 (1954), that the values "of the two properties exchanged in an arm's-length transaction are either equal in fact, or are presumed to be equal." . . . To be sure there is much to be said of the argument that such an assumption is weakened by the emotion, tension and practical necessities involved in divorce negotiations and the property settlements arising therefrom. However, once it is recognized that the transfer was a taxable event, it is more consistent with the general purpose and scheme of the taxing statutes to make a rough approximation of the gain realized thereby than to ignore altogether its tax consequences. . . .

Moreover, if the transaction is to be considered a taxable event as to the husband, the Court of Claims' position leaves up in the air the wife's basis for the property received. In the context of a taxable transfer by the husband,[20] all indicia point to a "cost" basis for this property in the hands of the wife [under § 1012]. Yet under the Court of Claims' position her cost for this property, i.e., the value of the marital rights relinquished therefor, would be indeterminable, and on subsequent disposition of the property she might suffer inordinately over the Commissioner's assessment which she would have the burden of proving erroneous. . . . Our present holding that the value of these rights is ascertainable eliminates this problem; for the same calculation that determines the amount received by the husband fixes the amount given up by the wife, and this figure, i.e., the market value of the property transferred by the husband, will be taken by her as her tax basis for the property received.

Finally, it must be noted that here, as well as in relation to the question of whether the event is taxable, we draw support from the prior administrative practice and judicial approval of that practice. See supra. We therefore conclude that the Commissioner's assessment of a taxable gain based upon the value of the stock at the date of its transfer has not been shown erroneous.

---

20. Under the present administrative practice, the release of marital rights in exchange for property or other consideration is not considered a taxable event as to the wife. For a discussion of the difficulties confronting a wife under a contrary approach, see Taylor and Schwartz, Tax Aspects of Marital Property Agreements, 7 Tax L. Rev. 19, 30 (1951); Comment, The Lump Sum Divorce Settlement as a Taxable Exchange, 8 U.C.L.A. L. Rev. 593, 601-602 (1961).

IV

[Discussion of attorney fee question omitted.]

Reversed in part and affirmed in part.

Mr. Justice FRANKFURTER took no part in the decision of these cases.

Mr. Justice WHITE took no part in the consideration or decision of these cases.

NOTES AND QUESTIONS

1. *Analysis of* Davis. (a) Assume that the general approach of the Court was correct and that the outcome of *Davis* should turn on whether Mrs. Davis owned an "interest" in property held in Mr. Davis's name, as opposed to a "mere expectancy"; on whether Mrs. Davis received property that she previously owned in some sense, as opposed to a payment in discharge of a debt owed to her by Mr. Davis. How should the issue be decided? By reference to one's common-sense judgment about how married people in Delaware are likely to think of the property rights of husbands and wives? By reference to what sociologists can tell us about the question? By trying to count the ways in which Delaware marital property law is like or unlike community property law? Or by reference to rules of law defining what is an interest in property for purposes of resolving other legal issues? Which approach did the Court adopt?

(b) Compare the outcome of this case with the rules adopted by Congress in provisions such as §§ 1031, 1033, and 109. What does this comparison tell you about the wisdom and fairness of the rule applied in the case?

(c) What was Mrs. Davis's basis in the property received? What is the conceptual foundation for that result? If the Court had held that the transfer did not result in the realization of gain by Mr. Davis, what should Mrs. Davis's basis have been? Under what Code provision can that result be reached?

2. *Belated congressional response.* The *Davis* decision gave rise to a substantial amount of litigation and complexity in the law. Ultimately, Congress altered the result in *Davis* and simplified the law by adopting § 1041. Section 1041 provides that no gain or loss shall be recognized on transfers of property between spouses or incident to a divorce. Thus, most spousal transfers of appreciated or depreciated property are not treated as sales that generate gain or loss to the transferor. Consistent with nonrecognition treatment, the property transferred has a substituted basis in the hands of the transferee. Section 1041 works together with the alimony rule, in § 71(b)(1), discussed below (see infra page 320), that provides that only cash transfers are considered alimony. Alimony is deductible by the payor and included in the income of the payee; other transfers incident to divorce are not deductible by the payor or included in the income of the payee. The results are that a transfer of property, other than cash, incident to divorce (a) does not result in the recognition of gain and (b) does not give rise to a deduction by the transferor or income to the transferee. This combination of rules may offend other goals of the tax system but it does simplify administration.

3. *The limits of § 1041.* In Rev. Rul. 87-112, 87-2 C.B. 207, the taxpayer, *A*, transferred to the taxpayer's former spouse, *B*, U.S. Series E and EE savings bonds that had been bought in an earlier year entirely with *A*'s separate funds. *A*, pursuant to § 454(c) and Regs. § 1.454-1(a), had not included in income the interest on these bonds; taxpayers are allowed to defer tax on such interest until the bonds are cashed in. The Ruling holds that § 1041(a) does not apply to the gain from the accrued interest and that the deferred, accrued interest from the date of original issuance of the bonds to the date of transfer of the bonds to *B* is includable in *A*'s gross income.

4. *Unmarried couples.* Section 1041 substantially reduces the problems of dividing the economic interests of married couples. It is not available to un-married couples who split up, no matter how long they have lived together, how deep and sincere their sharing and mutual commitment has been, and how tangled and intertwined their economic interests — and regardless of the fact that, if they were a same-sex couple, they had no legal opportunity to marry.

PROBLEMS

1. Henry and Wilma, when they were married, jointly owned a house with a fair market value of $400,000 and a basis of $100,000. Pursuant to their recent divorce, Henry took title to the house and executed a promissory note for $200,000 payable to Wilma and secured by the house.

(a) What amount of gain, if any, is recognized by Wilma? What is Wilma's basis for the note?

(b) What is Henry's basis for the house?

(c) What would your answer to the above questions be in the absence of § 1041?

2. Herb and Wanda were divorced six years ago. Herb was awarded custody of their two children. The decree of divorce provided that Herb was to remain in the family home until the younger child reached age 18 and that the house would then be sold, with the proceeds equally divided between Herb and Wanda. Last month, when the younger child turned 18, the house was sold for $400,000. Its basis was $100,000. Can Wanda, who currently lives in an apartment, exclude the $150,000 from income under § 121?

b.   *Antenuptial Settlements*

FARID-ES-SULTANEH v. COMMISSIONER
160 F.2d 812 (2d Cir. 1947)

Before SWAN, CHASE, and CLARK, Circuit Judges.

CHASE, Circuit Judge. . . .

[In 1924, S. S. Kresge, in contemplation of his marriage to taxpayer (petitioner) Farid-Es-Sultaneh, transferred to her some shares of stock of the S. S. Kresge Co. worth a total of about $800,000. Shortly thereafter they entered into an antenuptial agreement under which she acknowledged receipt of the shares "as a gift . . . pursuant to this indenture, and as an antenuptial settlement" and in consideration thereof released all her dower and other marital rights, including the right to support. Kresge and Farid-Es-Sultaneh were married in 1924 and divorced in 1928. She did not claim or receive alimony. Kresge's basis for the shares transferred in 1924 was fifteen cents per share; their value at that time was about $10 per share. In 1938, Farid-Es-Sultaneh sold some of the shares for $19 per share].[21]

When the petitioner and Mr. Kresge were married he was 57 years old with a life expectancy of 16½ years. She was then 32 years of age with a life expectancy of 33 years. He was then worth approximately $375,000,000 and owned real estate of the approximate value of $100,000,000.

The Commissioner determined [a deficiency for the year 1938] on the ground that the petitioner's stock . . . was acquired by gift . . . and [that under § 1015(a) she must thus use] as the basis for determining the gain on her sale of it the basis it would have had in the hands of the donor. This was correct if [§ 1015(a)] is applicable, and the Tax Court held it was on the authority of Wemyss v. Commissioner, 324 U.S. 303 (1945) and Merrill v. Fahs, 324 U.S. 308 (1945).

The issue here presented cannot, however, be adequately dealt with quite so summarily. The *Wemyss* case determined the taxability to the transferor as a gift, under [§§ 2511(a) and 2512(b)], of property transferred in trust for the benefit of the prospective wife of the transferor pursuant to the terms of an antenuptial agreement. It was held that the transfer, being solely in consideration of her promise of marriage, and to compensate her for loss of trust income which would cease upon her marriage, was not for an adequate and full consideration in money or money's worth within the meaning of [§ 2512(b)], the Tax Court having found that the transfer was not one at arm's length made in the ordinary course of business. But we find nothing in this decision to show that a transfer, taxable as a gift under the gift tax, is ipso facto to be treated as a gift in construing the income tax law.

In Merrill v. Fahs [supra], it was pointed out that the estate and gift tax statutes are in pari materia and are to be so construed. . . . Although Congress in 1932 also expressly provided that the release of marital rights should not be treated as a consideration in money or money's worth in administering the estate tax law [see § 2043(b)] and failed to include such a provision in the gift tax statute, it was held that the gift tax law should be construed to the same effect.

We find in this decision no indication, however, that the term "gift" as used in the income tax statute should be construed to include a transfer which, if made when the gift tax were effective, would be taxable to the transferor as a

___

21. [After her divorce from Kresge (her second husband), the taxpayer "sailed in luxury to Europe. An extremely attractive woman who just missed beauty," she met and married Prince Farid of Sadri-Azam, a nephew of a former Shah of Iran, and acquired the title Princess Farid-Es-Sultaneh. Her marriage to the prince ended in 1936, but for the rest of her life she continued to use the name Farid-Es-Sultaneh and, despite the published declaration of the prince that she was not entitled to do so, the title "princess." N.Y. Times, Aug. 13, 1963, at 31, col. 3 (obituary). — EDS.]

gift merely because of the special provisions in the gift tax statute defining and restricting consideration for gift tax purposes.[22]

In our opinion the income tax provisions are not to be construed as though they were in pari materia with either the estate tax law or the gift tax statutes. They are aimed at the gathering of revenue by taking for public use given percentages of what the statute fixes as net taxable income. Capital gains and losses are . . . factors in determining net taxable income. What is known as the basis for computing gain or loss on transfers of property is established by statute in those instances when the resulting gain or loss is recognized for income tax purposes. . . . When Congress provided that gifts should not be treated as taxable income to the donee, there was, without any correlative provisions fixing the basis of the gift to the donee, a loophole which enabled the donee to . . . take as the basis for computing gain or loss its value when the gift was made. Thus it was possible to exclude from taxation any increment in value during the donor's holding and the donee might take advantage of any shrinkage in such increment after the acquisition by gift in computing gain or loss upon a subsequent sale or exchange. It was to close this loophole that Congress provided that the donee should take the donor's basis when property was transferred by gift. . . . Because of this we think that a transfer which would be classed as a gift under the gift tax law is not necessarily to be treated as a gift income-tax-wise. Though such a consideration as this petitioner gave for the shares of stock she acquired from Mr. Kresge might not have relieved him from liability for a gift tax, had the present gift tax then been in effect, it was nevertheless a fair consideration which prevented her taking the shares as a gift under the income tax law since it precluded the existence of a donative intent.

Although the transfers of the stock made . . . to this taxpayer are called a gift in the ante-nuptial agreement later executed and were to be for the protection of his prospective bride if he died before the marriage was consummated, the "gift" was contingent upon his death before such marriage, an event that did not occur. Consequently, it would appear that no absolute gift was made before the ante-nuptial contract was executed and that she took title to the stock under its terms, viz.: in consideration for her promise to marry him coupled with her promise to relinquish all rights in and to his property which she would otherwise acquire by the marriage. Her inchoate interest in the property of her affianced husband greatly exceeded the value of the stock transferred to her. It was a fair consideration under ordinary legal concepts of that term for the transfers of the stock by him. . . . She performed the contract under the terms of which the stock was transferred to her and held the shares not as a donee but as a purchaser for a fair consideration. . . .

Decision reversed.

CLARK, Circuit Judge (dissenting). . . .

It is true that Commissioner v. Wemyss and Merrill v. Fahs, supra, which would require the transactions here to be considered a gift, dealt with estate

---

22. [See the suggestion of Judge Jerome N. Frank that the terms "gift," "gaft," and "geft" be used, depending upon whether the gift, income, or estate tax meaning is implied. Commissioner v. Beck's Estate, 129 F.2d 243 (2d Cir. 1942). — EDS.]

and gift taxes. But no strong reason has been advanced why what is a gift under certain sections of the Revenue Code should not be a gift under yet another section. . . . The Congressional purpose would seem substantially identical — to prevent a gap in the law whereby taxes on gifts or on capital gains could be avoided or reduced by judicious transfers within the family or intimate group.

But decision on that point might well be postponed. . . . Kresge transferred the stock to petitioner more than three months before their marriage. Part was given when Kresge was married to another woman. At these times petitioner had no dower or other rights in his property. If Kresge died before the wedding, she could never secure dower rights in his lands. Yet she would nevertheless keep the stock. Indeed the specifically stated purpose of the transfer was to protect her against his death prior to marriage. It is therefore difficult to perceive how her not yet acquired rights could be consideration for the stock. . . .

If the transfer be thus considered a sale, as the majority hold, it would seem to follow necessarily that this valuable consideration (equivalent to one-third for life in land valued at one hundred million dollars) should have yielded sizable taxable capital gains to Kresge, as well as a capital loss to petitioner when eventually she sold. I suggest these considerations as pointing to the unreality of holding as a sale what seems clearly only intended as a stimulating cause to eventual matrimony.

QUESTIONS

1. What were the tax consequences to Kresge in 1924? Note the court's statement (last paragraph of majority opinion) about the value of the rights released by Farid-Es-Sultaneh.

What would have been the tax consequences of the transfer in 1924 if § 1041 had been enacted? What if the antenuptial agreement provided that the transfer would not be made until after the marriage? What do these questions suggest about negotiating and drafting antenuptial settlements?

2. Was Farid-Es-Sultaneh taxable in 1924? If not, on what theory? Whatever your theory, is it better than viewing the transfer as a gift?

3. In Marvin v. Marvin, 18 Cal. 3d 660, 557 F.2d 106, 134 Cal. Rptr. 815 (1976), the plaintiff alleged an agreement with the defendant by which they would live together as husband and wife and the plaintiff would "devote her full time to defendant . . . as a companion, homemaker, housekeeper and cook" and in return defendant would "provide for all of plaintiff's financial support and needs for the rest of her life." 18 Cal. 3d at 666. The court held that the complaint stated a cause of action. What is the proper tax treatment of any amount ultimately recovered by the plaintiff? Is the defendant entitled to a deduction? If the final judgment were to order the defendant to transfer a house to the plaintiff, what would be the tax consequences to the defendant? See Green v. Commissioner, and Reynolds v. Commissioner, described supra page 102. In the *Reynolds* case, the court assumed, without much evidence, that the property received as gifts by the woman during the years of cohab-

itation, and relinquished by her in return for a cash settlement, had a basis equal at least to the amount that she received, so she did not realize any gain. The court noted that the woman did not claim a loss deduction (which probably would have been useless to her); thus, there was no need to determine the actual basis.

3. Alimony, Child Support, and Property Settlements

a. The Basic Scheme

The Code establishes a coordinated system in which, following divorce, certain payments received by the payee spouse are taxable to him or her under § 71(a) and those payments become deductible by the payor spouse under § 215. Other payments are not taxable to the payee spouse and are not deductible by the payor spouse. Very roughly speaking, alimony (and separate maintenance) is taxable to the payee and deductible by the payor, while child support and "property settlements" are not taxable to the payee and are not deductible by the payor. To some significant degree, however, the terms "alimony" (and separate maintenance) and "child support" have special meanings for tax purposes. The phrase "property settlement" is not used in the Code. It has some historical foundation and is used to help describe certain specific rules; the technical language is "excess front loading rules." The alimony deduction is an adjustment in arriving at AGI (adjusted gross income), so it is available to payors who do not itemize deductions. See § 62(a)(10).

b. The Rules

"Alimony," and "separate maintenance payments," are payments that meet certain conditions specified in § 71. First, the payment must be in cash. § 71(b)(1). This rule jibes with the rule of § 1041 (see supra page 315) that no gain or loss is recognized on certain transfers of property between spouses and former spouses. The two rules together serve the goal of simplicity. Putting aside that goal, it is difficult to see why a transfer of property in satisfaction of periodic support-type obligations should not be treated as alimony.

Second, the payment must be received under an "instrument" of divorce or separate maintenance. §§ 71(b)(1)(A), 71(b)(2). Oral agreements will not do. Unmarried couples are not covered.

Third, the parties must not have agreed that the payment will be nontaxable to the payee and nondeductible by the payor. This rule simply gives the parties an election as to payments that would, but for the election, be treated as alimony. Note, however, that the election goes only one way. There is no election available to treat as deductible by the payor and taxable to the payee payments that are not alimony or separate maintenance within the rules of § 71.

Fourth, the parties must not be members of the same household. § 71(b)(1)(C). This rule will remove some or all of the tax incentive for friendly divorces by couples who seek to take advantage of the favorable single-person (or head-of-household) rates. A tax advantage will still be available to unmarried couples (either never-married or divorced from one another) whose marginal rates on their individual incomes would be about the same. But for couples with unequal incomes the advantage of the more favorable rates for single taxpayers will be offset by the disadvantage of having more income taxed at the higher end of the rate structure and they will not be able to equalize the individual incomes by alimony payments — unless they are prepared to live apart.

Fifth, the payments cannot continue after the death of the payee spouse. § 71(b)(1)(D). This rule is consistent with a notion that alimony and separate maintenance are payments for support of the payee. If the payments continue after the death of the payee, they cannot have been intended purely as support; they must be in the nature of a property settlement or, at least in part, for the support of some other person. The nondeductibility of property settlements seems to be based on the idea that because such payments do not represent a diversion of income there is no justification for a deduction.

Sixth, the payments must not be for child support. The relevant provision, § 71(c), attempts to ensure that substance prevails over form. Thus, a payment that is called "alimony" but terminates when a child of the marriage dies or reaches age 18 will be treated as child support. This is an important change from prior law. The idea behind the denial of a deduction for child support is that if the payor had custody of, and supported, the children, there would be no deduction for the cost of the support, so there is no justification for deduction of similar amounts when paid to a former spouse. Obviously this rule does not take account of the expense of maintaining two households. Perhaps the lack of sympathy for that circumstance is a reflection of a moral (or moralistic) sense that people should not expect the tax system to relieve them of burdens of their own making.

Finally, there is a set of rules that deals broadly, and arbitrarily, with the problem of distinguishing between alimony and cash "property settlements." Roughly speaking, § 71(f) provides that only payments that are substantially equal for the first three years will be treated as alimony. This requirement of "periodicity" reflects a long-held notion of a distinction between, on the one hand, once-and-for-all settlements ("property settlements"), in one payment or a few installments, and, on the other hand, regular support payments (alimony).

Under § 71(f)'s arbitrary implementation of this distinction, if the first three yearly payments are "front-loaded" — that is, unequal, with larger amounts in the first or second year — some portion of the amount paid will not be treated as alimony. (Section 71(f) does not recharacterize alimony payments that are unequal but "back-loaded" — that is, payments that increase in size over the first three years.) Specifically, if the payments in the first year exceed the average payments in the second and third years by more than $15,000, the payments initially are treated as alimony but the excess amounts are "recaptured" in the third year. "Recaptured" means that the payor must include the excess in income. A similar rule applies to the extent that the payments in the second year exceed the payments in the third year by more than $15,000. In effect the payor is required to include in income an amount previously deducted as alimony, on the ground that in retrospect, because the payments did not continue in a manner consistent with the concept of alimony, the purported alimony was in fact a property settlement. When the payor is required to include an excess amount in income, the payee, who will have taken the full amount into income in the first or second year, is allowed a deduction in the same amount.

To illustrate the mechanics of the basic rule, suppose the payor makes and deducts an alimony payment of $50,000 in the first year and makes no payments in the second and third years. The amount recaptured in the third year is $35,000 (the $50,000 payment in the first year less the $15,000 threshold amount); $35,000 of the $50,000 payment that was deducted by the payor in the first year is included in the payor's income in the third year. The payee, who has included the $50,000 first-year payment in income, is allowed a $35,000 deduction in the third year. Timing differences aside, the net effect of the payment structure is that only $15,000 of the payment is treated as alimony.

The primary and intended effect of the recapture rule is on the planning process; it deprives people of the opportunity and incentive to convert property settlements into alimony.[23] It has the potential for harshness, however, when payments are reduced not by design but by virtue of changed circumstances. To minimize such harshness, recapture is not required if either party dies or if the payee spouse remarries by the end of the calendar year that is two years after the payments began and payments end because of the remarriage. Also, the recapture rule does not apply to temporary support payments or to payments based on an obligation to pay a fixed portion of the payor's income for at least three years.

c. Policy Questions

Is the deduction for alimony a subsidy to marriage? to divorce? Can it sensibly be defended as an effort to encourage support of ex-spouses? to remove obstacles to remarriage? Or is it just part of a proper definition of income, based on notions of involuntariness and lack of consumption? In Gould v. Gould, 245 U.S. 151 (1917), involving an attempt to tax a spouse receiving alimony, the Supreme Court held that alimony was not encompassed by the phrase "gains or profits and income derived from any source whatever" as used in the Revenue Act of 1917.

---

23. If the payor spouse has income-producing assets, however, those assets can be placed in trust, with the income payable to the payee spouse, for any time period desired. The income from the trust is taxable to the payee spouse. See § 682. For example, assume that A wishes to make payments to B of $25,000 per year for two years and no longer and that A owns bonds that pay interest of $25,000 a year. A can create a trust with a duration of two years, with B as the income beneficiary and with the reversion to A, and fund the trust with the bonds. The $25,000 interest on the bonds will be paid, and taxed, to B each year for the two years and then the bonds will be returned to A.

d.   The Tax Incentive

To understand the effect of the rules it is useful to begin with a sense of the tax saving that can be achieved, and shared by the payor and the payee, when a payment is treated as alimony. Suppose that the payor is taxed at a marginal rate of 35 percent (state and federal tax combined) and the payee is taxed at a marginal rate of 15 percent, and that the payor is obligated to make a payment of $2,000 that will not be treated as alimony for tax purposes. The net after-tax cost to the payor, and the benefit to the payee, obviously, will be the amount of the payment — the $2,000. Now suppose we are able to transform the payment into alimony and that we raise the amount to $2,700. The net after-tax cost to the payor will be $1,755 (65 percent of $2,700). He or she will be $245 to the good ($2,000 less $1,755). The net after-tax amount in the hands of the payee will be $2,295; he or she will be $295 to the good ($2,295 less $2,000). The total gain to the payor and the payee combined is $540 ($245 plus $295), which results from reducing the tax on $2,700 by 20 percent, the difference between the payor's rate of 35 percent and the payee's rate of 15 percent.

Under the rate structure effective in 2008, the potential gain from transforming a payment from nondeductible child support or property settlement into deductible alimony can be significant. The maximum difference between the rates is 20 percentage points (from 15 percent to 35 percent). Where the former spouses' tax rates are similar, however, the tax benefit of the deduction to the payor will be roughly offset by the tax owed by the payee. The total tax savings available through transforming child support or property settlements into alimony will rarely rise above several thousand dollars. That is nothing to be sniffed at, but it is scarcely in the realm of big-time tax avoidance.

e.   A Final Question

Is the game worth the candle? Considering the amounts of tax saving at issue, would it be better either to (a) deny any deduction for alimony or (b) allow the parties complete freedom to decide whether any payment is alimony?

PROBLEMS

1. Max and Winifred were divorced last year. The divorce decree has no provision for spousal support. Max, who has never been steadily employed, has not been able to hold a job for several months and asks Winifred, who is a successful personal injury lawyer, to help him out. Max threatens to go to court to seek spousal support. To avoid a hassle, and out of some lingering concern for Max, Winifred agrees orally to pay him $2,000 per month as spousal support. Will Winifred be allowed a deduction for the payments? Must Max report the payments as income?

2. Suppose Manuel and Wanda have decided to dissolve their marriage. Manuel is a successful surgeon. Wanda has just finished her first year of law school. Manuel and Wanda have decided that for each of the next two years Manuel should pay Wanda $60,000, while she finishes law school; that he should pay her $5,000 per year for the succeeding two years; and that at the end of four years there should be no more payments. If the terms of this agreement are incorporated in a decree of divorce, what will be the tax consequences to Manuel and Wanda? Are these tax results objectionable? If so, what suggestion would you make?

3. Suppose the facts are the same as in Problem 2, except that Wanda has a father, Fred, who lives with Manuel and Wanda and is dependent on them, and that the agreement provides that if Wanda dies during the four-year period in which payments are required, the payments will be made to Fred. Moreover, during the four years, Manuel is required to pay for an insurance policy on Wanda's life, with Fred as beneficiary. What are the tax consequences to Manuel, Wanda, and Fred?

4. Suppose Mike and Wilma have a son, Carlos, who is two years old. Mike is a successful lawyer. Wilma was also a successful lawyer, but quit practice when Carlos was born, with the understanding that she would care for him until he reached age 12 and then would return to work. Mike and Wilma have decided to end their marriage and have agreed that Mike will pay Wilma $40,000 a year for ten years, but with the obligation to terminate if Carlos should die sooner. What will be the tax consequences to Mike and Wilma?

5. Suppose that the marriage of Nancy and John is dissolved by a judicial decree that requires that Nancy pay John spousal support (alimony) of $10,000 per year. When the payment becomes due in the first year after the decree is entered, Nancy offers to transfer to John, in settlement of her obligation to pay the spousal support, shares of stock of IBM with a fair market value of $10,000 and a basis in her hands of $1,000. Suppose that John would be legally entitled to insist on payment in cash and that no other form of payment had been contemplated at the time of the dissolution. If John accepts the IBM stock in satisfaction of Nancy's obligation, what are the tax consequences to him and to Nancy? What if the same events occur in the second year following the dissolution of the marriage? Regs. § 1.1041-1T, A-7 provides that "[a] transfer of property is treated as related to the cessation of the marriage if the transfer is pursuant to a divorce or separation instrument . . . and the transfer occurs not more than 6 years after the date on which such marriage ceases."

4.   Child Support Obligations in Default

Child support is not deductible by the payor and is not taxed to the payee (usually the custodial parent). Suppose that child support payments are not made, and the expense of child support is borne entirely by the custodial parent. The custodial parent is clearly poorer. Should the tax burden of the custodial parent reflect the loss?

DIEZ-ARGUELLES v. COMMISSIONER
48 T.C.M. 496 (1984)

FINDINGS OF FACT . . .

In 1972, petitioner, Christina Diez-Arguelles ("Christina"), was divorced from her former husband, Kevin Baxter, and was granted custody of their two minor children. Pursuant to a property settlement agreement, which was incorporated into the divorce decree, Mr. Baxter agreed to pay Christina $300 per month for child support. Mr. Baxter failed to make full payment of his obligation for child support during the years 1972 through 1978 and by the end of 1978 he was in arrears by the amount of $4,325.00. During 1979 he paid only $600.00 in child support and consequently at the end of 1979 was in arrears by another $3,000.00. On their 1978 return the petitioners treated the $4,325.00 then due from Mr. Baxter as a nonbusiness bad debt and deducted the amount from their gross income as a short-term capital loss. On their 1979 return they deducted the $3,000.00 in the same manner. Respondent disallowed both deductions in their entirety.

Because of Mr. Baxter's failure to meet his support obligations, the petitioners had to bear the entire support of the two children from the date of the divorce in 1972 through 1979. The amount of such support borne by the petitioners through the end of 1978 exceeded the support payments made by Mr. Baxter during that period by at least $4,325.00. The amount of such support borne by them during 1979 exceeded the support payments made by Mr. Baxter in that year by more than $3,000.00.

Over the years Christina has diligently attempted to collect the support payments from Mr. Baxter. She has returned to the divorce court on several occasions and has received judgments and supplemental orders against him but to the date of trial she had been unable to collect the amount deducted on the joint returns for 1978 and 1979.

OPINION . . .

Under § 166(d) a noncorporate taxpayer may deduct nonbusiness bad debts as a short-term capital loss in the year such debts become completely worthless. However, the nonbusiness bad debts are deductible only to the extent of the taxpayer's basis in the debts. Section 166(b); Long v. Commissioner, 35 B.T.A. 479 (1937), affd., 96 F.2d 270 (9th Cir. 1938), cert. denied, 305 U.S. 616 (1938). In Long v. Commissioner, supra, the Board of Tax Appeals held that the uncollectible obligation of a taxpayer's ex-husband to pay her a fixed amount for maintenance was not deductible as a bad debt because the taxpayer was not "out of pocket" anything as the result of the ex-husband's failure to pay the support obligation. In other words, the taxpayer had no basis in the debt. Swenson v. Commissioner, 43 T.C. 897 (1965).

In the case before us, petitioners argue that they are "out of pocket" the amounts they expended for the support of Christina's children in excess of the support payments received from Mr. Baxter. We have considered and rejected this argument in similar cases. Swenson v. Commissioner, supra; Imeson v. Commissioner, T.C. Memo. 1969-180, affd., 487 F.2d 319 (9th Cir. 1973), cert. denied, 417 U.S. 917 (1974).

In *Imeson* the Ninth Circuit affirmed our decision but stated by way of dictum that the taxpayer might have a basis in the debt up to the amount she had expended from her capital or income to support the children, 487 F.2d at 321. Because of this dictum we subsequently reexamined our position on this issue and concluded that the cases cited by the Ninth Circuit were distinguishable. Williford v. Commissioner, T.C. Memo. 1975-65. Consequently, our position on this issue is still the same as set forth in Swenson v. Commissioner, supra, and Imeson v. Commissioner, supra. Respondent's determination that the amounts due Christina by Mr. Baxter for child support are not deductible under section 166 as nonbusiness bad debts is sustained.

Accord, Pierson v. Commissioner, 48 T.C.M. 954 (1984).

NOTES AND QUESTIONS

1. *Analysis.* Is the result in *Diez-Arguelles* consistent with principles of taxation previously examined? Does it seem fair? In answering these questions, consider the following hypotheticals. What are the tax consequences to Ann and Bob in each? Why? In each of the hypotheticals, assume that Ann is obligated to pay Bob $10,000 pursuant to a court order for child support issued on their divorce.

(a) In lieu of $10,000 cash, Bob accepts from Ann shares of stock of IBM for which she had paid $1,000 and that are worth $10,000 at the time of transfer. Bob later sells the shares for $9,000. See §§ 1001, 1012. (Assume that § 1041 does not apply.)

(b) Ann borrows $10,000 from Thelma and pays Bob. Ann defaults on the debt to Thelma. Bob invests the $10,000 in IBM stock, which he later sells for $9,000. What are the tax consequences not only to Ann and Bob but also to Thelma? See § 166.

(c) Ann pays Bob $10,000. Two days later, pleading a medical emergency, Ann borrows the $10,000 back from Bob. Shortly thereafter, Ann dies, totally destitute (though she had a good job at the time of her death).

(d) Ann, having failed to pay Bob the $10,000 child support obligation when it became due, executes, and delivers to Bob a negotiable promissory note, payable in three months and bearing interest at the market rate of 1 percent per month. Shortly thereafter, Ann dies, totally destitute.

(e) Same as (d), except that before Ann dies, Bob sells the note to Thelma for $9,000.

(f) What are the implications of the court's statement that "the taxpayer had no basis in the debt"? Suppose, again, that Ann owes Bob $10,000 for child support. If she pays him the $10,000, it is excluded from Bob's gross income under § 71(c). Basis seems to be irrelevant because of the statutory exclusion.

But what if Bob sells or assigns his claim against Ann to a third party for $9,000?

2. *Public policy.* (a) In Perry v. Commissioner, 92 T.C. 470 (1989), aff'd, 912 F.2d 1466 (5th Cir. 1990), the Tax Court again rejected a claim for a bad debt deduction for nonpayment of child support. After addressing a variety of legal arguments, the court concluded with the following:

> Petitioner insists that she ought to be allowed to deduct the shortfall in Perry's support payment obligations. If this were to be viewed as an appeal to public policy, i.e., the public failed to see to it that Perry satisfied his legal obligations and so the public ought to make up for this to some extent by reducing petitioner's tax obligations, then we have two responses.
>
> Firstly, the statute for the years in issue does not embody that policy; to get that policy into the law, petitioner should go to the Congress, in which has been "vested" "All legislative Powers herein granted." U.S. Const., art. 1, § 1.
>
> Secondly, since the tax benefit of such a deduction relates directly to the taxpayer's marginal tax bracket, it would appear that this claimed public policy would provide the greatest relief to those who have the greatest amount of other income and little or no relief to those who truly depended on the fulfillment of the support obligations. The Congress, of course, may enact any public policy it chooses (unless otherwise limited by the Constitution), but the policy that would be advanced by allowing such a deduction may fairly be viewed as topsy-turvy.
>
> In any event, this Court will not so legislate in the guise of filling in gaps in the statute, or whatever other judicial power it is that petitioner would have us exercise.

(b) Why does the court in the *Diez-Arguelles* case refer to Kevin Baxter as Mr. Baxter and to Christina Diez-Arguelles as Christina?

3. *A bad trip.* Compare Garber v. Commissioner, 48 T.C.M. 959 (1984), in which the taxpayer signed up for a two-year, around-the-world sailing trip with seven other people. Each of the eight contributed $16,000 toward the cost of the boat. Their agreement with the captain provided that if any of them were required to leave, there would be no refund, but if the boat were destroyed there would be a pro rata refund. The taxpayer became ill and left the boat for several months. He recovered from his illness and would have returned to the boat for the remainder of the cruise, but it was destroyed by fire. He was unable to obtain a refund and claimed a deduction for a bad debt. The court denied the deduction, relying on Regs. § 1.166-1(c), which requires a "valid and enforceable obligation to pay a fixed or determinable sum of money." The court said, "Generally, a claim which arises out of breach of contract prior to being reduced to judgment does not create a debtor-creditor relationship because the injured party has only an unliquidated claim to damages." Suppose the captain had written a letter to the taxpayer saying, "I have collected insurance proceeds from the loss of the boat and clearly I owe you $5,000. I will put a check in the mail tomorrow." Suppose the check never arrives and the captain dies following a drunken binge on which he spent all the insurance money. What if the captain had sent a check for $5,000, but it bounced (i.e., proved uncollectible)?

Was the claim in the *Diez-Arguelles* case a "valid and enforceable obligation to pay a fixed or determinable sum of money"?

4. *Legal fees.* In McClendon v. Commissioner, T.C. Mem. 1986-416, legal fees incurred to obtain child support payments were held to be nondeductible personal expenses. The court relied on United States v. Gilmore, infra page 500.

H. THEORETICAL ISSUES

Compare the tax treatment of the individuals in each of the four following situations:

(a) Charlie Carpenter last year earned $35,000. This year he reduced the number of hours he worked, earned $20,000, and devoted himself to building a house that he intends to hold for rental to others. He used $30,000 of savings from earlier years to buy the land and materials. When he completed the building of the house, for which he supplied all the labor, its fair market value was $45,000.

(b) Tom Trucker this year earned $35,000 driving a truck. He took $30,000 of savings from earlier years and $15,000 of this year's earnings and bought, for $45,000, a house that he intends to hold for rental.

(c) Ann Accountant earned $35,000 last year. This year she reduced the number of hours she worked, earned $20,000, and went to law school.

(d) Perry Player was born with exceptional coordination and by the time he graduated from UCLA this year was over seven feet tall and an all-American center on its basketball team. He has played and practiced basketball almost incessantly since he was old enough to hold the ball. Everyone agrees that he will be the number one draft choice in the National Basketball Association and will be able to sign a contract that will be certain to make him a multimillionaire. In a recent article in a leading sports magazine, a highly respected actuary estimated that the present value of Player's expected future earnings is $30 million. It has been clear since he was a senior in high school that he was an exceptional basketball player.

Under an income tax, should Player be taxed at some point in his amateur career on the expected value of his future earnings or, if you will, on the value of his genetic inheritance and the rewards for his investment of time in self-improvement? How about Carpenter? Should he be taxed on the $15,000 increment to his wealth that can be attributed to the performance of services for himself? If Carpenter is to be taxed on only $20,000, how about Trucker? If both Trucker and Carpenter are to be taxed on $35,000, what about Accountant (and other future professionals)? Is it not clear that she has invested $15,000 worth of her time in creating "human capital"? If Accountant is to be taxed on $35,000, again, how about Player? If Player is to be taxed on the benefit of what some call his "genetic windfall," should Accountant be taxed similarly — that is, on some amount reflecting the full value of her law degree, not just the value of the time she invested in it? If you think that Ann or Perry should be taxed on the value of their human capital, as reflected in their prospective earnings, how, if at all, would you take account of their prospective tax liabilities? In answering these questions, be sure to take account of the Simons definition of income (supra page 14) and the arguments in support of it. See W. Klein, Timing in Personal Taxation, 6 J. Legal Stud. 461 (1977).

I. CONSUMPTION TAX

We have seen that a core concept of our income tax laws, reflected in cases like Eisner v. Macomber though not in any express provision of the Code, is that unrealized gain is not taxable. Congress has extended this core concept generously in provisions like § 1031. Unrealized appreciation can be thought of as a form of saving; it is a gain that has, in a sense, been reinvested in the same property. Congress has also favored other forms of saving — most notably retirement savings held in qualified pension plans. No one has ever seriously suggested that we should tax savings in the nature of investment in human capital. The tax system that we wind up with thus falls far short of a tax on income as it is defined by Simons and other purists. Suppose we took these departures a step further and permitted all savings to be excluded from taxable income. The result would be a tax on consumption. Symbolically,

$$Y = C + S$$

where Y is income, C is consumption, and S is saving (investment). It follows that

$$C = Y - S$$

which tells us that a tax on consumption is the same as a tax on income minus saving, which tells us in turn that if we want to tax consumption we need not measure it directly.

What would be the reasons for wanting to tax consumption rather than income? One argument might be that, even if you would prefer a comprehensive income tax, the practical or political difficulty of taxing all returns to saving suggests (on grounds of fairness or economic rationality) exempting them altogether. But some people argue that even a comprehensive income tax would be less desirable than a comprehensive consumption tax. These arguments are best approached by returning to the point (briefly discussed in Chapter 1 and the beginning of Chapter 2) that what we really want to tax is something that is hard to observe directly, but that might be called "ability" or "ability to pay." Various possible tax bases, including income, consumption, and wealth, are merely imperfect implementations of this underlying idea, which we should evaluate based on how well they identify relevant taxpaying ability.

A key issue in choosing between income, consumption, and wealth as tax bases goes to the choice of time frame for evaluating ability to pay. For "snapshot" comparisons of how well off people are at a given moment, wealth may seem the most appropriate measure. The ease with which one can pay tax at a given moment may depend on one's entire bank account (and other assets), not just the interest income that the account earned during the current year, or the year's spending out of the account to pay for currently consumed market goods and services. However, taxing wealth results in higher tax burdens for those who save for future consumption than for those who do not; it punishes those who provide for their own or their heirs' futures. A tax on consumption, imposed annually, avoids this effect. It thus may provide a better measure than does a wealth tax of economic well-being over a lifetime. The income tax is intermediate between a wealth tax and a consumption tax; it imposes a tax on the return to invested savings (the so-called double tax) but not directly on the investments as such.

Advocates of consumption taxation argue that economic well-being over a lifetime is the right way to look at ability to pay. Suppose that Alice and Bert earn the same amount each year through work but that Alice saves more than Bert during her working years because she would like to have more money to spend during her retirement, whereas he places a greater value on consumption when young. An income tax will penalize Alice relative to Bert because her saving will generate extra capital income that is subject to tax as earned, rather than when it is spent later on consumption. If you think that Alice and Bert are relevantly the same — for example, because they had the same opportunities and merely made different choices due to differences in personal taste — you may consider it unfair to tax Alice more than Bert. Or you may be concerned that the income tax will unduly discourage saving.

Advocates of income taxation might respond that Alice and Bert are not relevantly the same if Alice's greater saving makes her wealthier than Bert for much of her life and that economists have struggled in vain to find strong empirical evidence that the income tax reduces saving significantly, or even moderately. In addition, income tax advocates argue that a consumption tax typically is less progressive than an income tax, mainly because people with higher incomes tend to save a greater percentage of what they earn than people with lower incomes. This, however, depends on the two taxes' rate structures. A consumption tax with sufficient extra rate graduation could be as progressive as one might wish.

For a long time, people thought that a consumption tax could not easily be imposed with graduated rates. The consumption taxes that we observe, such as sales taxes imposed by various state and local governments and the similar value-added taxes (VATs) imposed by most industrialized nations, are collected from businesses. This makes it impossible to adjust their rates based on the circumstances of the individual consumer. (Imagine telling a convenience store owner to impose different sales taxes on customers with different annual earnings.) One response by many governments has been to give exemptions or lower rates to "necessities" such as food that are thought to make up a higher proportion of low-income households' total expenditure. These special rates, however, tend to have a disappointing distributional payoff, while also distorting consumer choices and increasing the taxes' administrative costs.

COMPARATIVE FOCUS: The Value-Added Tax—A Primer on the Most Common Tax in the World

Perhaps the most significant tax policy development of the past half century is the adoption of value-added taxes (VAT) by nearly every country in the world. If you've ever traveled abroad, chances are that you've paid VAT on some of your purchases. Not so for those who limit their travels to the United States. Among the world's major economies, the United States stands alone in not having adopted a VAT. To be sure, there are some explicit consumption taxes in the United States, most notably the retail sales taxes imposed by many states. Yet these taxes account for only 8.2 percent of government revenues in the United States, while taxes on personal consumption make up 19.1 percent of all tax revenue in other OECD countries.

The intended base of the VAT is the same as that of the retail sales tax (RST)—i.e., household consumption. However, the two taxes are collected in a very different manner. While RSTs apply to sales made at retail, the VAT applies at each stage of production to the "value added" by each firm. For example, assume that Firm X pays $100 for goods and services acquired from other firms and then sells its own goods and services for $180. Assuming a tax rate of 25 percent, Firm X will owe a VAT of $20. Under a so-called credit invoice VAT, the tax may be calculated as 25 percent of Firm X's revenues (i.e., 25 percent of $180, or $45) reduced by a credit for VAT amounts shown on the invoices for goods and services acquired by Firm X (i.e., 25 percent of $100, or $25).

Various commentators have urged the adoption of a value-added tax at the federal level in the United States. Some have suggested that a federal VAT could replace the current income tax, while others have argued that it should supplement an income tax on the wealthy. Still others have advocated a modified VAT that would allow a deduction for wages (which are not typically deductible in a VAT), combined with a separate free-standing wage tax paid at the household level. One benefit of this last approach would be the flexibility to apply a separate rate schedule to the wage base, something that the standard VAT design does not accommodate.

But the accounting equivalence stated above, $C = Y - S$, suggests another route to the same end. Suppose we allow a deduction for all saving. This requires that amounts dissaved (taken out of savings, or borrowed and spent on consumption) be included in taxable "income." As a result of the savings deduction, the assets bought with savings will have a zero basis. When such assets are sold, income is increased by the full proceeds (though it may be reduced again if those proceeds are invested elsewhere). The result is a variety of consumption tax, often called a cash-flow or consumed income tax, that lends itself perfectly well to the kind of graduated rate structure existing in the present income tax. See W. Andrews, A Consumption-Type or Cash Flow Personal Income Tax, 87 Harv. L. Rev. 1113 (1974).

To illustrate, suppose that an individual in a given year earns a salary of $100,000, borrows $50,000, and invests $85,000 in an apartment building. Under a consumption tax, the salary plus the loan, a total of $150,000, would be treated as "income." From this amount would be deducted the $85,000 invested in the apartment building, leaving a net of $65,000. The $65,000 is presumably the amount used for consumption and would be taxed (at progressive rates). Since the entire cost of the building is deducted at the time of purchase, its basis would be zero and there would be no depreciation deduction. Suppose that in the next year the building is sold for $70,000, the salary is again $100,000, and the individual's bank account increases by $50,000. The taxable amount (consumption) would be $120,000 ($70,000 + $100,000 − $50,000).

Under this system of taxation, any amounts earned by a corporation and not distributed by it would, at least from the shareholder perspective, be saved and invested. Corporations cannot have consumption; only individuals can. Thus, under a consumption tax there would be no need for a corporation income tax to prevent tax avoidance by shareholders.

Much scholarly writing has examined how such a tax system could be implemented as a practical matter. No nation in the world has ever tried it more than briefly, but provisions for allowing exclusions or deductions for saving (e.g., qualified employee pension plans and individual retirement accounts (IRAs)) shift the income tax toward a consumption base. And the wisdom of such a move is of course hotly debated, even assuming its political and administrative feasibility. The relative merit of income versus consumption taxation remains a subject on which there is little consensus.

J.   CASH RECEIPTS AND PAYMENTS OF ACCRUAL-METHOD TAXPAYERS

The two major systems of accounting are the cash method and the accrual method. The cash method focuses on actual receipts and disbursements, while the accrual method focuses on amounts earned (though not necessarily received) and obligations incurred (though not necessarily paid). The accrual method attempts to match income with the expense of earning it. While this method results in a more accurate annual measurement of income than does the cash method, it requires more sophisticated bookkeeping and accounting. Therefore most individuals and small businesses use the cash method if possible.

Almost all businesses of any substantial size report on the accrual method of accounting.[24] The accrual method, however, is not a matter of mathematical certainty; it has its infirmities and is constantly evolving and often contro-

---

24. Most large-scale firms are required to use the accrual method. See § 448.

versial. Moreover, the Treasury has consistently opposed certain aspects of normal accrual accounting such as the deferral of prepaid income or accrual of estimated future expenses.

For nontax purposes a good accounting system should organize and present the underlying data of a business in a way that permits its managers to make sound decisions and investors to make sound judgments about its condition. It is by no means clear, however, that the rules that are appropriate for nontax purposes are also appropriate for tax purposes. It does seem plain that tax accounting rules can have significant effects on behavior. For example, if tax rules allow the immediate deduction of a particular investment that has an expected life of five years, people will tend to prefer that investment over one whose cost must be written off over its five-year life. If income from an activity must be reported earlier than is consistent with economic reality, the effect will be to discourage that activity as compared with other activities in which income is more accurately reported. To the extent that income for purposes of tax accounting differs from true economic income, we will tend to discourage some activities and encourage others, often for no good reason.[25]

1. Delay in the Receipt of Cash

GEORGIA SCHOOL-BOOK DEPOSITORY v. COMMISSIONER
1 T.C. 463 (1943)

KERN, Judge.

The question is whether petitioner, which was on an accrual basis, should have accrued certain school book commissions at the time the books were sold by the publishers to the state, or should have returned them as income only when the books were paid for by the state, as petitioner contends.

Petitioner was a broker which received an 8 percent commission on all school books purchased by the State of Georgia through it. For this commission it performed certain services of advantage to both parties, such as executing the contracts of the state board of education with various publishers, taking care of the books as a central depository until final distribution, seeing that enough were on hand to meet the state's demands, distributing them, and

---

25. Similarly, a system that allows deductions for depreciation at a rate faster than the actual decline in the value of the asset will favor investment in long-lived assets over short-lived assets and investment in capital (plant, machinery, etc.) over investment in current labor inputs. In other words, if an income tax is to be neutral among different types of investments and inputs, it must be accurate in its measurement of income. A deduction for depreciation greater than the actual decline in value of the asset in the taxable year introduces inaccuracy. See P. Samuelson, Tax Deductibility of Economic Depreciation to Insure Invariant Valuations, 72 J. Pol. Econ. 604 (1964). This is not to say, however, that an income tax is to be preferred to a consumption tax, even though a consumption tax allows an immediate write-off of all investments. It is merely a statement about neutrality once the decision has been made to adopt an income tax. Some economists believe that an income tax unduly burdens all investment and that a consumption tax is preferable for that reason. If one accepts this position, then it is the consumption tax that produces neutrality among investments, as well as between investment and consumption. In any event, all arguments based on the desirability of a neutral tax system are confounded by the reality of pervasive nontax governmental intervention in the allocation of resources.

collecting the moneys in payment from the state and holding them in trust until paid over to the publishers. It was responsible for the return in salable condition of any books not used. It had no title to the books at any time, and (except in the case of one publisher) posted a bond with each publisher to guarantee performance of its duties. Petitioner also carried on a somewhat similar business as a book broker of college books not on the state list and under these contracts was responsible for the collection of all accounts.

Petitioner did not accrue its commissions on the state books but did accrue its commissions on the college books at the same time that its liability for the books to the publishers was accrued. Under the contracts for state school books it was provided that petitioner should receive its brokerage "at the time of settlement" and this term is explained by the provision that the petitioner shall make quarterly reports "so as to show the exact balance due" the publisher by the petitioner, and shall remit "its pro rata share of all cash received from the collection of warrants issued by the State of Georgia for books sold to the state when and as such warrants are received."

The publishers could look for payment from the state, and, consequently, petitioner could look for its commissions only from the "Free Textbook Fund," which was renewed only from the excise laid on beer.[26] During the taxable years 1938 and 1939 this fund was insufficient to pay the petitioner in full. The state, in its accounting, did not treat these large deficits as present liabilities except to the extent that funds were already on hand to meet them, the remainder being considered an encumbrance on the textbook fund in the next year. The "accounts ripen," the auditor reported, "for payment when and as funds become available in the Textbook Fund."

Petitioner contends, first, that the brokerage was not earned until payment, and, secondly, that there was no reasonable expectancy that payment ever would be made; and for these reasons, it urges its ultimate contention that the commissions here involved were not properly accruable in the respective taxable years.

In so far as appears, all acts which were required of petitioner to earn its brokerage, save one, had been done in the taxable year. It had received the books from the publishers, stored them, and later distributed them to the several schools. All it had not done was to receive the money from the state and pay it out to the publishers. On this account the actual payment of the brokerage may not have been due to petitioner until this money was received,

---

26. [The court's findings of fact describe the textbook fund as follows:

On March 4, 1937, the State of Georgia enacted a Free Textbook Act, under which the state board of education was directed to inaugurate and administer a system of free textbooks for the public schools of Georgia, and to execute contracts therefor. The act provides that the cost of administering the free textbook system and purchasing the books shall be paid by the state from such funds as may be provided by the General Assembly for that purpose. . . . The Legislature thereupon created a free textbook fund, made up solely from excise taxes on the sale of malt beverages in the state. The act provides that funds derived from taxes on malt beverages shall be apportioned as follows: Not over 3 percent shall be paid to the revenue commission for enforcing the malt beverage act and "the remainder shall be set aside and devoted for the support of the common schools of the state and used for the purpose of furnishing free textbooks to the children attending the common schools, any excess to be used for other school purposes."

—EDS.]

but the right to it had accrued by the performance of its duties. United States v. Anderson, 269 U.S. 422. It is the *right* to receive money which in accrual accounting justifies the accrual of money receivable and its return as accrued income.

The Supreme Court said in Spring City Foundry Co. v. Commissioner, 292 U.S. 182 (p.184):

> ... Keeping accounts and making returns on the accrual basis, as distinguished from the cash basis, import that it is the right to receive and not the actual receipt that determines the inclusion of the amount in gross income. When the right to receive an amount becomes fixed, the right accrues. . . .

The receipt of the money from the state, the deduction of petitioner's commission, and the transmission of the balance to the publishers were the least of its duties and can not be made the criterion of the arisal of the right. Paragraph 9 of the contract assumes that the publisher's right to payment had arisen, for it requires that the quarterly reports which petitioner was to submit should "show the exact balance due the first party by the second party [petitioner]. . . ."

We pass, then, to the second question, whether there was a reasonable expectancy that the claim would ever be paid. Where there is a contingency that may preclude ultimate payment, whether it be that the right itself is in litigation or that the debtor is insolvent, the right need not be accrued when it arises. This rule is founded on the old principle that equity will not require a suitor to do a needless thing. The taxpayer need not accrue a debt if later experience, available at the time that the question is adjudged, confirms a belief reasonably held at the time the debt was due, that it will never be paid. . . . On the other hand, it must not be forgotten that the alleviating principle of "reasonable expectancy" is, after all, an exception, and the exception must not be allowed to swallow up the fundamental rule upon which it is engrafted requiring a taxpayer on the accrual basis to accrue his obligations, Spring City Foundry Co. v. Commissioner, supra. If this were so, the taxpayer might at his own will shift the receipt of income from one year to another as should suit his fancy. . . . To allow the exception there must be a definite showing that an unresolved and allegedly intervening legal right makes receipt contingent or that the insolvency of his debtor makes it improbable. Postponement of payment without such accompanying doubts is not enough. . . .

Applying these principles to the instant case, we must conclude that, despite the condition of the treasury of the State of Georgia when the free schoolbook fund was inaugurated and for several years thereafter, there was no reasonable expectation that the sums owed by the state to petitioner's publishers and, consequently, the commissions to petitioner itself, would not ultimately be paid. It would naturally take a few years to establish in full working order a system of such magnitude, but a comparison of the two years before us shows that Georgia was gradually reducing its schoolbook obligations. Georgia is a state possessing great resources and a fine record of fiscal probity, and undoubtedly it can and will meet its obligations. The fact that petitioner, on behalf of its principals, continued to sell and deliver school books to the state indicates that there was no serious doubt as to the ultimate collection of the accounts here involved.

We conclude, therefore, that petitioner's commissions on all books purchased by the state through it in the taxable years should have been accrued and returned as income in those years.

Judgment will be entered for the respondent.

NOTES AND QUESTIONS

1. *Analysis.* (a) Under *Georgia School-Book Depository*, delay in the receipt of cash in the absence of doubt about ultimate payment is not enough to prevent accrual of income. Collectibility has nothing to do with accruability unless the obligor is insolvent. The "reasonable expectancy" language in *Georgia School-Book Depository* goes to the issue of solvency. It is important to distinguish between a contingent receivable, which will not accrue since it is uncertain whether the taxpayer has earned it as yet, and an earned determinable amount, which must be accrued even if there is some question as to whether it will ultimately be collected. In defense of its rule, the court says that if "reasonable expectancy" is interpreted too favorably to taxpayers, "a taxpayer might at his own will shift the receipt of income from one year to another as should suit his fancy." Do you agree? See § 446(b).

(b) In Hallmark Cards, Inc. v. Commissioner, 90 T.C. 26 (1988), Hallmark, in order to maintain a level production schedule and to avoid warehousing costs, shipped Valentine cards to retailers in December. After the customers objected to including the cards in their inventory (which resulted, among other things, in their becoming liable for personal property taxes), Hallmark adopted a policy under which it retained title to the cards until January 1. The court held that Hallmark was not required to accrue income from the sale of the cards in December, because the "all events" test was not satisfied until title passed in January.

2. *Other accrual methods.* Section 446(c) speaks of "the" cash receipts and disbursements method of accounting for taxable income, but in sanctioning accrual accounting, it uses the more expansive phrase "an accrual method." The principal variations are the installment method of reporting income from installment sales (supra page 273) and the "completed-contract" and "percentage-of-completion" methods of reporting income from building, installation, construction, or manufacturing contracts not completed within one taxable year (supra page 142).

2. Prepaid Income

The following case involves income of an automobile club operated by the American Automobile Association. For purposes of analysis it may be helpful to refer to the following hypothetical facts.

Suppose that the club is on the calendar year and that a particular member joins on October 1 of 1982 for one year and pays upon joining a fixed fee of $60. The member is entitled, among other things, to towing services and maps, on demand. The club has hundreds of thousands of members and has kept good records of its costs. Its fixed costs (for offices, staff, etc.) are $3 per month per member and vary only insignificantly from month to month and year to year. Its variable costs (for towing, etc.) are (on average) $3 per month per member in the six months of October through March and $1 per month per member in the other six months, but they vary from member to member.

How was AAA reporting these kinds of receipts and outlays before being challenged? How was it required to report under the decision in the case? Why?

AMERICAN AUTOMOBILE ASSOCIATION v. UNITED STATES
367 U.S. 687 (1961)

Mr. Justice CLARK delivered the opinion of the Court.

In this suit for refund of federal income taxes the petitioner, American Automobile Association, seeks determination of its tax liability for the years 1952 and 1953. Returns filed for its taxable calendar years were prepared on the basis of the same accrual method of accounting as was used in keeping its books. The Association reported as gross income only that portion of the total prepaid annual membership dues, actually received or collected in the calendar year, which ratably corresponded with the number of membership months covered by those dues and occurring within the same taxable calendar year. The balance was reserved for ratable monthly accrual over the remaining membership period in the following calendar year as deferred or unearned income reflecting an estimated future service expense to members. The Commissioner contends that petitioner should have reported in its gross income for each year the entire amount of membership dues actually received in the taxable calendar year without regard to expected future service expense in the subsequent year. The sole point at issue, therefore, is in what year the prepaid dues are taxable as income.

In auditing the Association's returns for the years 1952 through 1954, the Commissioner, in the exercise of his discretion under [§ 446(b)], determined not to accept the taxpayer's accounting system. As a result, adjustments were made for those years principally by adding to gross income for each taxable year the amount of prepaid dues which the Association had received but not recognized as income, and subtracting from gross income amounts recognized in the year although actually received in the prior year. . . .

The Association is a national automobile club organized as a nonstock membership corporation with its principal office in Washington, D.C. It provides a variety of services to the members of affiliated local automobile clubs and those of ten clubs which taxpayer itself directly operates as divisions, but such services are rendered solely upon a member's demand. Its income is derived primarily from dues paid one year in advance by members of the clubs. Memberships may commence or be renewed in any month of the year. For many years, the association has employed an accrual method of accounting and the calendar year as its taxable year. It is admitted that for its purposes the method used is in accord with generally accepted commercial accounting principles. The membership dues, as received, were deposited in the Association's bank accounts without restriction as to their use for any of its corporate purposes. However, for the Association's own accounting purposes, the dues were treated in its books as income received ratably[27] over the 12-month membership period. The portions thereof ratably attributable to membership months occurring beyond the year of receipt, i.e., in a second calendar year, were reflected in the Association's books at the close of the first year as unearned or deferred income. Certain operating expenses were chargeable as prepaid membership cost and deducted ratably over the same periods of time as those over which dues were recognized as income.

The Court of Claims bottomed its opinion on Automobile Club of Michigan v. Commissioner, 1957, 353 U.S. 180, finding that "the method of treatment of prepaid automobile club membership dues employed [by the Association here was,] . . . for Federal income tax purposes, 'purely artificial.'" 181 F. Supp. 255, 258. It accepted that case as "a rejection by the Supreme Court of the accounting method advanced by plaintiff in the case at bar." Ibid. The Association does not deny that its accounting system is substantially identical to that used by the petitioner in *Michigan*. It maintains, however, that *Michigan* does not control this case because of a difference in proof, i.e., that in this case the record contains expert accounting testimony indicating that the system used was in accord with generally accepted accounting principles; that its proof of cost of member service was detailed; and that the correlation between that cost and the period of time over which the dues were credited as income was shown and justified by proof of experience. The holding of *Michigan*, however, that the system of accounting was "purely artificial" was based upon the finding that "substantially all services are performed only upon a member's demand and the taxpayer's performance was not related to fixed dates after the tax year." 353 U.S. 180, 189, note 20. That is also true here. . . .

Whether or not the Court's judgment in *Michigan* controls our disposition of this case, there are other considerations requiring our affirmance. . . . In 1954 the Congress found dissatisfaction in the fact that

> as a result of court decisions and rulings, there have developed many divergencies between the computation of income for tax purposes and income for business purposes as computed under generally accepted accounting principles. The areas of difference are confined almost entirely to questions of when certain

27. In 1952 and 1953 dues collected in any month were accounted as income to the extent of one-twenty-fourth for that month (on the assumption that the mean date of receipt was the middle of the month), one-twelfth for each of the next eleven months, and again one-twenty-fourth in the anniversary month. In 1954, however, guided by its own statistical average experience, the Association changed its system so as to more simply reach almost the same result by charging to year of receipt, without regard to month of receipt, one-half of the entire dues payment and deferring the balance to the following year.

types of revenue and expenses should be taken into account in arriving at net income.

House Ways and Means Committee Report, H.R. Rep. No. 1337, 83d Cong., 2d Sess. 48. As a result, it introduced into the Internal Revenue Code of 1954 § 452 and § 462 which specifically permitted essentially the same practice as was employed by the Association here. Only one year later, however, in June, 1955, the Congress repealed these sections retroactively.... [T]he repeal of the section the following year, upon insistence by the Treasury that the proposed endorsement of such tax accounting would have a disastrous impact on the Government's revenue, was ... clearly a mandate from the Congress that petitioner's system was not acceptable for tax purposes.... We are further confirmed in this view by consideration of the even more recent action of the Congress in 1958, subsequent to the decision in *Michigan*, supra. In that year § 455 was added to the Internal Revenue Code of 1954. It permits publishers to defer receipt as income of prepaid subscriptions of newspapers, magazines and periodicals. An effort was made in the Senate to add a provision in § 455 which would extend its coverage to prepaid automobile club membership dues. However, in conference the House Conferees refused to accept this amendment....

The validity of the long established policy of the Court in deferring, where possible, to congressional procedures in the tax field is clearly indicated in this case. Finding only that, in light of existing provisions not specifically authorizing it, the exercise of the Commissioner's discretion in rejecting the Association's accounting system was not unsound, we need not anticipate what will be the product of further "study of this entire problem."

Affirmed.

Mr. Justice STEWART, whom Mr. Justice DOUGLAS, Mr. Justice HARLAN, and Mr. Justice WHITTAKER join, dissenting....

The effect of the Court's decision is to allow the Commissioner to prevent an accrual basis taxpayer from making returns in accordance with the accepted and clearly valid accounting practice of excluding from gross income amounts received as advances until the right to such amounts is earned by rendition of the services for which the advances were made. To permit the Commissioner to do this, I think, is to ignore the clear statutory command that a taxpayer must be allowed to make his returns in accord with his regularly employed method of accounting, so long as that method clearly reflects his income....

I can find nothing in *Automobile Club of Michigan* which controls disposition of this case. And the legislative history upon which the Court alternatively relies seems to me upon examination to be singularly unconvincing.

In *Michigan* there was no offer of proof to show the rate at which the taxpayer fulfilled its obligations under its membership contracts. The deferred reporting of prepaid dues was, therefore, rejected in that case simply because there was no showing of a correlation between the amounts deferred and the costs incurred by the taxpayer in carrying out its obligations to its members. Until today, that case has been recognized as one that simply held that, in the absence of proof that the proration used by the taxpayer reasonably matched actual expenses with the earning of related revenue, the Commissioner was justified in rejecting the taxpayer's proration....

As to the enactment and repeal of § 452 and § 462, upon which the Court places so much reliance, . . .I think that the enactment and subsequent repeal of § 452 and § 462 give no indication of Congressional approval of the position taken by the Commissioner in this case. If anything, the legislative action leads to the contrary impression....

To my mind, this legislative history shows that Congress made every effort to dissuade the courts from doing exactly what the Court is doing in this case — drawing from the repeal of § 452 an inference of Congressional disapproval of deferred reporting of advances. But even if the legislative history on this point were hazy, the same conclusion would have to be reached upon examination of Congressional purpose in repealing § 452 and § 462.... Sections 452 and 462 were repealed *solely* because of a prospective loss of revenue during the first year in which taxpayers would take advantage of the new sections. Insofar as the reporting of advances was concerned, that loss of revenue would have occurred solely as a consequence of taxpayers changing their method of reporting, without the necessity of securing the Commissioner's consent, to that authorized under § 452 and § 462. The taxpayer who shifted his basis for reporting advances would have been allowed what was commonly termed a "double deduction" during the transitional year. Under § 462, deductions could be taken in the year of change for expenses attributable to advances taxed in prior years under a claim of right theory, as well as for reserves for future expenditures attributable to advances received and reported during that year. Similarly, under § 452, pre-payments received during the year of transition would be excluded from gross income while current expenditures attributable to past income would still be deductible.

The Congressional purpose in repealing § 452 and § 462 — maintenance of the revenues — does not, however, require disapproval of sound accounting principles in cases of taxpayers who, like the petitioner, have customarily and regularly used a sound accrual accounting method in reporting advance payments. No transition is involved, and no "double deduction" is possible. Moreover, taxpayers formerly reporting advances as income in the year of receipt can now shift to a true accrual system of reporting only with the approval of the Commissioner. See . . . § 446(e). Before giving his approval the Commissioner can be expected to insist upon adjustments in the taxpayer's transition year to forestall any revenue loss which would otherwise result from the change in accounting method....

The net effect of compelling the petitioner to include all dues in gross income in the year received is to force the petitioner to utilize a hybrid accounting method — a cash basis for dues and an accrual basis for all other items. Schlude v. Commissioner, 8 Cir., 283 F.2d 234, 239. Cf. Commissioner of Internal Revenue v. South Texas Lumber Co., 333 U.S. 496, 501. For taxpayers generally the enforcement of such a hybrid accounting method may result in a gross distortion of actual income, particularly in the first and last years of doing business. On the return for the first year in which advances are received, a taxpayer will have to report an unrealistically high net income, since he will have to include unearned receipts, without any offsetting deductions for the future cost of earning those receipts. On subsequent tax returns, each year's unearned prepayments will be partially offset by the deduction of current expenses attributable to prepayments taxed in prior years. Even then, however, if the taxpayer is forbidden to correlate earnings with related expenditures, the result will be a distortion of normal fluctuations in the taxpayer's net income. For example, in a year when there are low current expenditures because of fewer advances received in the preceding year, the result may be an inflated adjusted gross income for the current year. Finally, should the taxpayer decide to go out of business upon fulfillment of the contractual obligations already undertaken, in the final year there will be no advances to report and many costs attributable to advances received in prior years. The result will be a grossly unrealistic reportable net loss.

The Court suggests that the application of sound accrual principles cannot be accepted here because deferment is based on an estimated rate of earnings, and because this estimate, in turn, is based on average, not individual, costs. It is true, of course, that the petitioner cannot know what service an individual member will require or when he will demand it. Accordingly, in determining the portion of its outstanding contractual obligations which have been discharged during a particular period (and hence the portion of receipts earned during that period), the petitioner can only compare the total expenditures for that period against estimated average expenditures for the same number of members over a full contract term. But this use of estimates and averages is in no way inconsistent with long-accepted accounting practices in reflecting and reporting income. . . .

Finally, it is to be noted that the regulations under both the 1939 and 1954 Codes permit various methods of reporting income which require the use of estimates.[28] In the absence of any showing that the estimates used here were faulty, I think the law did not permit the Commissioner to forbid the use of standard accrual methods simply upon the ground that estimates were necessary to determine what the rate of deferral should be. . . .

NOTES AND QUESTIONS

1. *The deduction side.* One of the principal objectives of accrual accounting is to match income with the costs of producing that income. The good sense of such an approach is obvious in the case of a firm like American Automobile Association. Imagine the first year of its operations. If it reports as income the fees received during the year from members, without taking into account the cost of the services that it will be required to render to those members in the following year, it will overstate its income. Thus, assuming that the

---

28. See, e.g., Treas. Reg. § 1.451-3 (1975) (providing for the percentage of completion method of reporting income on long-term contracts); Treas. Reg. § 1.451-4 (1957) (providing for [a] deduction for redemption of trading stamps based upon "the rate, in percentage, which the stamps redeemed in each year bear to the total stamps issued in such year"). . . .

decision in the *AAA* case is controlling as to income, should the taxpayer be allowed to claim a deduction for the expected costs of providing services?

2. *Other cases.* The *AAA* case is but one of many that consider the includability of prepaid income upon receipt. In Schlude v. Commissioner, 372 U.S. 128 (1963), the Supreme Court, relying on *AAA* along with the limited scope of the subsequently enacted § 456, held (five to four) that a dancing school was taxable in the year of receipt on amounts paid by students for lessons to be provided in the future. However, some appellate decisions reflect greater sympathy for the use of accrual principles (requiring deferral of prepaid but unearned income).

For example, Artnell Co. v. Commissioner, 400 F.2d 981 (7th Cir. 1968), rev'g 48 T.C. 411 (1967), permits income recognition to be deferred for prepaid admissions to baseball games to be played in the following taxable year. The court stated that, where the time and extent of the future services are sufficiently specific, the Commissioner would abuse his discretion under § 446 by refusing to permit deferral. The three Supreme Court decisions (*Automobile Club of Michigan, American Automobile Association,* and *Schlude*) were distinguished as involving greater uncertainty.

A similar sympathy for accrual principles is found in Boise Cascade Corp. v. United States, 530 F.2d 1367 (Ct. Cl.), cert. denied, 429 U.S. 867 (1976), where the taxpayer had performed engineering services. In *Boise Cascade*, the taxpayer sometimes performed services before being paid, and other times was paid before performing services. It followed a consistent practice of reporting the income when services were performed. The Commissioner sought to require that the income be reported when the services were performed or when the payment was collected, whichever came first. This was too much for the court to swallow. It concluded that "the inconsistency within the Commissioner's method is strident," and that "his method would appear to the ordinary mind to distort income instead of clearly reflecting it" (530 F.2d at 1378). *American Automobile Association* and *Schlude* were distinguished — although how convincingly is open to dispute — on the ground that here the services to be performed by the taxpayer were "fixed and definite," and "in no sense . . . dependent solely upon the demand or request of its clientele" (530 F.2d at 1377).

3. *The legislative sequel to the* AAA *case.* Following the decision in *American Automobile Association,* Congress enacted § 456 to permit membership organizations reporting on the accrual method to elect to spread prepaid dues over the period of responsibility for the performance of services. The provision has much in common with § 455 (prepaid subscription income), to which both the majority and the dissenters in the *AAA* case referred.

4. *Limited deferral by administrative action.* Modest relief from the full force of the all events test — and from the divergence between financial (nontax) accounting and tax accounting — is made available by Revenue Procedure 2004-34 and Regs. § 1.451-5. The former applies to advance payments received for services, for certain sales of goods, for the use of intellectual property, and for various other specified types of payments. The taxpayer is allowed to include, for tax purposes, the portion of such payments properly allocable to the year of receipt, provided that this is consistent with the taxpayer's financial

reporting. The remainder of the advance payment must be included in the following year. To illustrate, drawing on Examples 1 and 2 of the Revenue Procedure, suppose that in 2004 Taxpayer (*T*), which is in the business of providing dance lessons, receives $6,000 as full advance payment for 100 lessons. The expectation is that there will be twenty lessons in 2004, forty in 2005, and forty in 2006. Assuming consistency with its financial reports, and assuming that in fact twenty lessons are provided in 2004, *T* may report for tax purposes, in 2004, $1,200, rather than the entire $6,000. The remaining $4,800 must be reported in 2005, even if a total of only sixty lessons have been provided by the end of that year. Similar tax treatment is available under Regs. § 1.451-5, which applies generally to sales of goods.

5. *An observation.* Suppose that *T*, an individual accrual-method taxpayer, performs services for the U.S. Treasury Department and receives in return a promise by the Treasury to pay her $1,500 at the end of twenty years. Consider the implications of a rule that requires the inclusion of $1,500 in *T*'s income in the year the services are performed. Assume that *T* pays taxes at a rate of 33 percent and that as a result the Treasury collects $500 in taxes from her. Suppose that that amount is invested by the Treasury at 10 percent. At the end of twenty years it would grow to $3,364 and the Treasury would be ahead $1,864 by virtue of having incurred the obligation to pay the $1,500. Or suppose *T* decides to accept no payment for her services. She will pay $500 less in taxes in the year the services are performed. If she invests this amount at 6.7 percent after taxes, she will have $1,829 at the end of twenty years, $329 more than if she had agreed to accept payment. Compare the discussion of deduction of amounts of damages a taxpayer is obligated to pay in the future under a structured settlement, supra page 157.

3. Deposits Versus Advance Payments

When is an advance payment not an advance payment? This question will naturally occur to any taxpayer that is paid in advance of performing services and wishes to avoid the *American Automobile Association* line of cases. The answer, apparently, is to characterize and structure the payment as merely a security deposit that is made in advance to protect the recipient against the risk of being paid late or not at all.

In Commissioner v. Indianapolis Power & Light Co., 493 U.S. 203 (1990), the taxpayer (IPL), an electrical utility, succeeded on this ground in avoiding inclusion upon receipt of advance payments that it demanded from customers whose credit it determined was suspect. In practice, these payments usually ended up being credited against the customers' monthly electric bills. Customers earned interest on the payments, but at what the Court noted was a relatively modest rate, below what IPL could expect to earn by investing the money. IPL did not place the deposits in escrow or segregate them from its other funds, and thus could use the money without restriction.

Under these circumstances, the Supreme Court held for IPL, finding that the payments were analogous to loans by the customers rather than to advance payments of the sort discussed in *AAA*. The Court mainly relied on the fact that customers could demand repayment of the deposits if service was terminated or upon establishing good credit. Earlier Tax Court decisions had come out the same way for lease deposits that secure the tenant's obligations under the lease. The main difference from prepaid rent, apparently, was the landlord's legal obligation to return lease deposits if the tenant met all obligations, such as by paying all rent when due and not damaging the premises.

QUESTIONS

1. Suppose you have just bought a rental apartment building. In accordance with local practice, you expect that at the time you rent an apartment you will collect the first month's rent in advance plus an amount equal to the last month's rent, with the latter intended to provide security for any damages to the apartment and for the payment of the rent. Is it possible to contract with your lessees so that the "last month's rent" will be treated as a security deposit rather than as advance rent? What might you do, both at the outset of the lease and thereafter?

2. Suppose you are counsel to the American Automobile Association, which wants to know if it can restructure its membership practices to take advantage, if possible, of the cases concerning the tax treatment of security deposits. What, if anything, would you suggest?

3. Is there a better way to handle advance payment issues in general than by distinguishing between "true" advance payments and security deposits?

WESTPAC PACIFIC FOOD v. COMMISSIONER
457 F.3d 970 (9th Cir. 2006)

KLEINFELD, Circuit Judge.

We must decide whether cash paid in advance by a wholesaler to a retailer, in exchange for a volume commitment, is "gross income" under § 61. In the grocery trade, these are called "advance trade discounts."

It is hard to think of a way to make money by buying things. A child may think buying things is how one makes money: he sees his father give a clerk a single piece of paper money, and receive in exchange the goods purchased, several pieces of paper money, and a number of coins. And a person may jokingly say to a spouse "I made $100 today" after buying something on sale for $100 off. But everyone knows these are merely amusing remarks, not real ways to make money.

The facts outlined below sound more complicated than they are, so imagine a simple hypothetical. Harry Homeowner goes to the furniture store, spots just the right dining room chairs for $500 each, and says "I'll take four, if you give me a discount." Negotiating a 25% discount, he pays only $1,500 for the chairs. He has not made $500, he has spent $1,500. Now suppose Harry Homeowner is short on cash, and negotiates a deal where the furniture store gives him a 20% discount as a cash advance instead of the 25% off. This means the store gives him $400 "cash back" today, and he pays $2,000 for the four chairs when they are delivered shortly after the first of the year. Harry cannot go home and say "I made $400 today" unless he plans to skip out on his obligation to pay for the four chairs. Even though he receives the cash, he has not made money by buying the chairs. He has to sell the chairs for more than $1,600 if he wants to make money on them. The reason why the $400 "cash back" is not income is that, like a loan, the money is encumbered with a repayment obligation to the furniture store and the "cash back" must be repaid if Harry does not perform his obligation.

This case is that simple, except that it involves a little more math and a lot more money. The taxpayer promised to buy a lot of items and received cash in advance as its discount on its future, high-volume purchases. Using accrual accounting, the taxpayer treated the up front cash discount as a liability when it was received, just like a loan. As goods were sold, the taxpayer applied the discount pro rata to the full purchase price it paid. The net effect was that Westpac reduced its cost of goods sold and increased its reported profit (and thus its taxable income). The taxpayer reported pro rata amounts without matching sales as miscellaneous or other income.

The government concedes, and the Tax Court agreed, that Westpac's method was consistent with generally accepted accounting principles. . . . Nevertheless, the Tax Court concluded that the cash discount received in advance was income, noting that tax principles do not serve the same purposes as accounting principles, such as reflecting to shareholders how their company is performing.

A company would indeed have a major problem if it accounted to its shareholders as the Tax Court would have it account to the government. Were a company to get very significant amounts of up front cash discounts on its obligation to purchase goods in the future and tell stockholders and prospective stock purchasers that it had "made" this much "income," investors would be sorely disappointed to learn that all the money had to be paid back if their company did not sell all the goods it had promised to sell in the future. The company would be like Harry Homeowner claiming to have "made" $400 when he received his cash advance discount on the four chairs. Harry might have to spend the night on the couch, but the CEO could spend the night in jail.

FACTS

Three grocery store chains — Raley's, Save Mart, and Bel Air — organized the taxpayer, Westpac, as a partnership to purchase and warehouse inventory. Westpac is an accrual basis taxpayer.

During 1990 and 1991, Westpac made four contracts to buy inventory and receive cash in advance: (1) lightbulbs from GTE Sylvania; (2) Hallmark cards from Ambassador; (3) bows, wrapping paper, and other products from American Greetings; and (4) spices from McCormick. Under each contract, Westpac promised to buy a minimum quantity of merchandise and received a volume discount in the form of cash up front. If Westpac bought too few lightbulbs, spices, greeting cards, etc., then it was obligated to pay back the cash advance pro rata. Conversely, Westpac's obligation to repay the cash advance was extinguished if Westpac purchased the required volume. Westpac made other promises as well, such as exclusivity and shelf space, but the volume purchased determined whether it had to refund the cash advance and, if so, how much it had to refund.

GTE Sylvania Contract

In July of 1990, Westpac made a deal with the Sylvania Lighting division of GTE Products Corp. to (1) make GTE Sylvania its exclusive lightbulb supplier for Westpac and its member stores for four years; (2) "aggressively and regularly" advertise and promote GTE Sylvania's products; (3) dedicate on average at least 12 lineal feet of shelf space to GTE Sylvania's products in its member stores; and (4) purchase $17 million in lightbulbs during the term of the agreement. Given Westpac's volume purchase commitment, GTE Sylvania agreed to pay Westpac $1.1 million as an "unearned advance allowance." GTE Sylvania paid this to Westpac by check, and agreed to pay Westpac another $200,000 on the first, second, and third anniversaries of the agreement, provided that GTE Sylvania was satisfied with Westpac's warehouse distribution arrangement. The contract refers to the total $1.7 million in payments as the "Westpac Allowance" and contains the following clause:

> Upon termination of this Agreement, Westpac will reimburse GTE Sylvania on a pro-rated basis for any portion of the Westpac Allowance advanced to Westpac but not earned due to the failure by Westpac to purchase at least $17.0 million in lamps.

During Westpac's 1991 tax year, GTE Sylvania paid the first $200,000 to Westpac.

Westpac could not resell enough lightbulbs to meet the minimum volume the contract called for, so it terminated the arrangement in October of 1994. Westpac's termination letter acknowledged its obligation to pay back a prorated portion of the Westpac Allowance, and it repaid $861,857 to GTE Sylvania in December.

[The court provides details of three other such contracts. — EDS.]

Westpac's Tax Reporting

In accord with standard accounting principles, Westpac accounted for the up front cash as a liability at the time it received the cash. The cash advance got translated into taxable income through Westpac's inventory accounting. As Westpac purchased the goods for which it had the volume obligations, it subtracted pro rata portions of the advance cash discounts from what it paid. This had the effect of reducing the cost of goods sold (and increasing the taxable profits from sales) by the amount of the cash advances attributable to the goods sold.

The government took the position that Westpac and Save Mart underreported over $5.5 million in gross income for 1990 and over $4.9 million for 1991 because they did not report the cash advances as gross income. Westpac filed a petition for readjustment and the government opposed it. Relying on

Commissioner of Internal Revenue v. Glenshaw Glass Co., [348 U.S. 426 (1955), casebook page 85], the Tax Court held that the cash advance discounts were "income" under [§ 61]. Westpac timely filed this appeal.

The sole issue before us is whether advance trade discounts constitute gross income when received. We hold that they do not and reverse the Tax Court.

ANALYSIS

. . .

B. IS A DISCOUNT IN THE FORM OF A CASH ADVANCE INCOME WHEN RECEIVED?

There appears to be no circuit court authority on point, but the Supreme Court authorities bracketing the question compel our answer: Cash advances in exchange for volume purchase commitments, subject to pro rata repayment if the volume commitments are not met, are not income when received.

The statutory definition of gross income is expansive. Commissioner v. Glenshaw Glass Co. held that punitive damages received by a successful litigant were "income" because they were "accessions to wealth, clearly realized, and over which the taxpayers have complete dominion." The government argues that the cash advances in this case fit that definition because Westpac had "complete dominion" over the money. It did not have to put the cash in a trust account and could spend the money as it chose. But that leaves out sine qua non of income: that it be an "accession to wealth." One may have "complete dominion" over money but it does not become income until it is an "accession to wealth." That is why borrowed money is not income, even though the borrower has "complete dominion" over the cash. . . .

The Supreme Court decisions bracketing this case are Commissioner v. Indianapolis Power & Light Co., [493 U.S. 203 (1990)], on one side, and Automobile Club of Michigan v. Commissioner, [353 U.S. 180 (1957)], and Schlude v. Commissioner, [372 U.S. 128 (1963)], on the other.

Indianapolis Power held that utility customers' security deposits are not income to the utility because of the obligation to repay the money when service ended. The decision analogizes the security deposits to loans because of the repayment obligation.

Automobile Club of Michigan holds that prepaid membership dues are income when received, despite the association's obligation to provide membership services — maps, tire repair and the like — during the subsequent year. The reason was that pro rata application of the dues to each month "bears no relation to the services" the club had to perform. Drivers do not call AAA once a month to repair a flat or send a map, and AAA is entitled to keep the membership dues regardless of whether the member ever requests any goods or services. *Schlude* held that cash paid to a dance studio for ballroom dancing lessons was income when received, not when the lessons were provided. The Court applied *Automobile Club of Michigan,* because the money was not refundable and the studio could keep it even if the student did not show up for dance lessons.

This case is like *Indianapolis Power*, not *Automobile Club of Michigan* or *Schlude*. The cash advance trade discounts are like the security deposits in that they are subject to repayment, and unlike the membership dues in that the recipient cannot keep the money regardless of what happens after receipt. Westpac could only retain the full, up front trade discount if it met the volume requirements. Like the security deposit, the cash advance is subject to repayment. The only difference is that the repayment amount in this case may not be the full amount advanced by the vendor, but that is because the repayment amount is reduced pro rata to the extent Westpac fails to fulfill its volume commitment.

Because the taxpayer here has to pay the money back if the volume commitments are not met, it is not an "accession to wealth" as required by *Glenshaw Glass*. Westpac either has to buy a specified volume of goods for more than it would otherwise pay or pay back the money, just like Harry Homeowner. Thus the cash advance discounts are, like a loan or customer security deposit, liabilities rather than income when received.

The Tax Court found that Westpac's accounting for the cash advances as affecting cost of goods sold complied with generally accepted accounting principles, but correctly held that accounting rules are not necessarily controlling for tax purposes. The regulations require that inventory accounting conform to best accounting practices and clearly reflect income. But that does not go far enough to transform the cash into "income" in the face of *Indianapolis Power*. We cannot agree with the government that Westpac's "unfettered use" of the money makes it income, because it was not an accession to wealth. Rather, it was merely an advance against an obligation, repayable if the obligation was not performed.

Our decision in Milenbach [v. Commissioner, 318 F.3d 924 (9th Cir. 2003),] is more analogous to this case than *Schlude* or *Automobile Club of Michigan*. In *Milenbach*, a Los Angeles entity loaned the Oakland Raiders $6.7 million, repayable only out of revenue from the luxury suites to be built in the future, to induce the team to move to Los Angeles. Even though it was a non-recourse loan with no certain repayment date, and even though the Raiders neither built the suites nor made any payments, we held that the $6.7 million was not income because the repayment obligation was genuine. The case at bar is easier than *Milenbach* because the cash advances here are more plainly subject to repayment in calculable amounts by a set date. Westpac not only had a duty to repay the discounts, it actually did repay them when it did not meet the volume commitments. When Westpac did buy the required volume of goods, it paid list price rather than a discounted price, and realized the income for tax purposes.

It works out about the same as with Harry Homeowner: He has to sell the chairs for more than he paid in order to make money on them. Westpac had to sell the lightbulbs, ribbons, greeting cards, and such for more than they paid in order to make money on them. It remains exceedingly difficult to make money merely by buying things. Westpac did not get any richer when it received its volume discount in the form of cash up front than Harry

Homeowner did when he got the $400 from the furniture store. There was no accession to wealth when Westpac got the cash, just an increase in cash assets offset by an equal liability for the advance trade discounts.

REVERSED.

QUESTIONS

1. How can this case be reconciled with American Automobile Association v. United States?

2. Suppose the court had upheld the IRS, and ruled that the payments constituted income in the year they were received. What effect would that have on income Westpac would recognize in future years?

3. Is it relevant to know how GTE Sylvania or the other suppliers treated the payments? If the payments do not constitute income because of Westpac's obligation to repay, presumably they are not deductible to GTE Sylvania. Nondeductibility could be justified on the grounds that the payments constitute a sort of a loan, or that the payments are a capital expense, designed to produce income in a future year when Westpac actually orders the light bulbs, and ought to be deductible only in that future year. The treatment of capital expenditures is discussed in Chapter 6, beginning on page 511.

Suppose, though, that GTE Sylvania deducted the payments, on the premise that it was paying for Westpac to give its product shelf space in the present year. Would that change your mind as to whether Westpac ought to report the payments as income?

4. Current Deduction of Future Expenses

The accrual method of accounting relies on circumstances other than when cash changes hands. Thus, just as it may support deferring the inclusion of a cash receipt by the taxpayer, so it may support allowance of a deduction before the taxpayer actually pays out a liability. Not surprisingly, the deduction side, like the inclusion side, is covered by detailed rules and has been the subject of ongoing controversy.

If the accrual method actually aimed to make the timing of taxable income depend purely on "true" economic accrual, then a future obligation (assuming its ultimate deductibility) would give rise to a deduction as soon as it had a positive expected present value, though only in the amount of the present value (or the yearly increase in such value). Reduction in the expected value of an obligation from a decline in the likelihood of its being paid would trigger an inclusion, in effect "recapturing" some or all of the deduction.

Given the tax system's need for greater certainty, however, we are very far from having any such system. Thus, accrual method taxpayers, like those on the cash method, cannot deduct before payment liabilities that are uncertain or contested. Deductions under the accrual method are subject to the "all events" test. Under this test, which dates back to early case law, a future obligation is not deductible unless (a) the fact of liability is firmly established and (b) the amount of the liability can be determined with reasonable accuracy.

In United States v. General Dynamics Corp., 481 U.S. 239 (1987), the taxpayer provided medical benefits to its employees by reimbursing qualifying medical expenses that they incurred. It claimed deductions for its obligations to pay for medical services that, as of the close of the taxable year, had been rendered but as to which the employee had not yet submitted a claim. These deductions were based on estimates from past experience. The Supreme Court (by a six-to-three vote) denied the deductions on the ground that the all events test was not satisfied until employees actually submitted their reimbursement claims. Such filing was not a "mere technicality" because some employees might fail to submit claims for reimbursement to which they were plainly entitled out of "oversight, procrastination, confusion over the coverage provided, or fear of disclosure to the employer of the extent or nature of the services received" (481 U.S. at 244).

Section 461(h), enacted in 1984, put the all events test in the statute and added a further requirement of "economic performance" with respect to any item that the taxpayer seeks to deduct under the all events test. In general, economic performance occurs as the property or services to which an obligation relates are provided. Thus, a fixed and determinate obligation to pay an employee a definite amount for work that she will perform next year, or a lessor for the use of property next year, generally cannot be deducted this year.

QUESTIONS

1. Does the suggestion by the Supreme Court in *General Dynamics* that procrastinators might never file claims to reimbursable medical expenses seem a bit strained? Other language in the decision suggests that the Court was partly motivated by its discomfort with deduction claims that are based on mere estimates, "no matter how statistically certain" or defensible as an "appropriate conservative accounting measure" (481 U.S. at 244, 246).

2. The taxable year at issue in *General Dynamics* predated the enactment of the economic performance requirement. How would this test have applied to the case if the taxpayer had satisfied the all events test?

3. Under the all events test and substantial performance requirement, would the American Automobile Association be able to claim deductions for the expected cost of providing future services to members whose fees were currently includable?

4

PERSONAL DEDUCTIONS, EXEMPTIONS, AND CREDITS

A. INTRODUCTION

In the previous chapters, we have focused primarily on questions relating to specific inclusions and exclusions from gross income, as well as questions of timing. In this chapter, as well as the next two, we will turn our attention to the various deductions that are allowed in arriving at taxable income. As you might imagine, certain deductions are necessary to ensure that what is ultimately taxed is indeed "income" and not something else, like "revenue" or "gross receipts." For example, few would argue that businesses should not be allowed a deduction for the cost of goods sold or wages paid to an employee. Expenditures on such items represent the cost of earning income and thus are appropriately deductible under an income tax. We will examine those deductions in Chapters 5 and 6.

But what about expenditures that are unrelated to the production of income? Is there any place in an income tax for deductions for those types of expenses? And if so, what is the rationale for such deductions? In the materials that follow, we will refer to these deductions somewhat generically as "personal deductions," though note that this is not a legal term but rather just shorthand for deductions that are unrelated to the cost of producing income.

1. The Mechanics of Personal Deductions

Most of the deductions covered in this chapter are "itemized" deductions, meaning that they are generally available only to taxpayers who elect to itemize and file a Schedule A with their Form 1040. Take a moment to review the Schedule A on the next page.

| SCHEDULES A&B
(Form 1040)
Department of the Treasury
Internal Revenue Service
Name(s) shown on Form 1040 | **Schedule A - Itemized Deductions**
(Schedule B is on page 2)
▶ Attach to Form 1040.   ▶ See Instructions for Schedules A&B (Form 1040). | OMB No. 1545-0074
2007
Attachment
Sequence No. 07
Your social security number |

BARACK H. & MICHELLE L. OBAMA

Medical and Dental Expenses		**Caution:** Do not include expenses reimbursed or paid by others.			
	1	Medical and dental expenses (see page A-1)		1	
	2	Enter amount from Form 1040, line 38	2		
	3	Multiply line 2 by 7.5% (.075)		3	
	4	Subtract line 3 from line 1. If line 3 is more than line 1, enter -0-			4

Taxes You Paid (See page A-2.)	5	State and local (check only one box): a [X] Income taxes, or b [ ] General sales taxes SEE STATEMENT 7		5	133,309.
	6	Real estate taxes (see page A-5)		6	22,162.
	7	Personal property taxes		7	
	8	Other taxes. List type and amount ▶ _____		8	
	9	Add lines 5 through 8		9	155,471.

Interest You Paid (See page A-5.) Note. Personal interest is not deductible.	10	Home mortgage interest and points reported to you on Form 1098		10	57,838.
	11	Home mortgage interest not reported to you on Form 1098. If paid to the person from whom you bought the home, see page A-6 and show that person's name, identifying no., and address ▶ _____		11	
	12	Points not reported to you on Form 1098.		12	
	13	Qualified mortgage insurance premiums (See page A-7)		13	
	14	Investment interest. Attach Form 4952 if required. (See page A-7.)		14	
	15	Add lines 10 through 14		15	57,838.

Gifts to Charity If you made a gift and got a benefit for it, see page A-8.	16	Gifts by cash or check. SEE STATEMENT 8		16	240,370.
	17	Other than by cash or check. If any gift of $250 or more, see page A-8. You **must** attach Form 8283 if over $500		17	
	18	Carryover from prior year		18	
	19	Add lines 16 through 18		19	240,370.

Casualty and Theft Losses	20	Casualty or theft loss(es). Attach Form 4684. (See page A-9.)		20	

Job Expenses and Certain Miscellaneous Deductions (See page A-9.)	21	Unreimbursed employee expenses - job travel, union dues, job education, etc. Attach Form 2106 or 2106-EZ if required. (See page A-9.) ▶ _____		21	
	22	Tax preparation fees		22	
	23	Other expenses - investment, safe deposit box, etc. List type and amount ▶ _____		23	
	24	Add lines 21 through 23		24	
	25	Enter amount from Form 1040, line 38	25		
	26	Multiply line 25 by 2% (.02)		26	
	27	Subtract line 26 from line 24. If line 26 is more than line 24, enter -0-			27

Other Miscellaneous Deductions	28	Other - from list on page A-10. List type and amount ▶ _____		28	

Total Itemized Deductions	29	Is Form 1040, line 38, over $156,400 (over $78,200 if married filing separately)? [ ] **No.** Your deduction is not limited. Add the amounts in the far right column for lines 4 through 28. Also, enter this amount on Form 1040, line 40. } STMT 9 ▶		29	374,008.
		[X] **Yes.** Your deduction may be limited. See page A-10 for the amount to enter.			
	30	If you elect to itemize deductions even though they are less than your standard deduction, check here ▶ [ ]			

LHA 719501 11-08-07   **For Paperwork Reduction Act Notice, see Form 1040 instructions.**   Schedule A (Form 1040) 2007

8

15330410 131470 4OC01F   2007.05051 OBAMA, BARACK H.   4OC01F_1

Lawyers, accountants, and others who work in the tax field sometimes refer to itemized deductions as "below the line" deductions, meaning that they are taken from "adjusted gross income" (i.e., the "line" in "below the line") in arriving at "taxable income." Deductions taken from gross income in arriving at adjusted gross income are thus referred to as "above the line" deductions. Thus, the basic structure of the income tax can be portrayed as follows:

Gross Income (§ 61)

minus

Above the Line Deductions (§ 62(a))

equals

------ **Adjusted Gross Income** (§ 62) ------

minus

Below the Line Deductions

(i.e., either the standard deduction, § 63(c), or itemized deductions, § 63(d))

and

Deduction for Personal Exemptions (§ 151)

equals

Taxable Income (§ 63)

Note that taxpayers must choose between claiming the standard deduction and electing to itemize. Typically taxpayers will only elect to itemize their deductions if the aggregate amount of those deductions exceeds the amount of the standard deduction, which varies with the taxpayer's filing status. In 2009, single individuals who were not heads of households were eligible for a standard deduction of $5,700, while married individuals filing a joint return were eligible for a standard deduction of $11,400. § 63(c)(2). The amount of the standard deduction is adjusted annually to reflect increases in the Consumer Price Index (CPI). § 63(c)(4).

In addition to itemizing or claiming the standard deduction, all taxpayers are entitled to a personal exemption deduction for themselves and for each of their dependents. § 151. In 2009, the amount of the personal exemption was $3,650; that amount too is adjusted for annual increases in the CPI. The personal exemption, in combination with the standard deduction, can be viewed as providing a "zero-bracket" amount, so that no income tax will be imposed on income below a certain level. For a family of four for the taxable year 2009, the standard deduction and personal exemptions combine to provide a zero-bracket amount of $26,000 (i.e., $11,400 + [$3,650 × 4]). These provisions, along with the earned income tax credit (discussed infra) help to explain why the bottom 60 percent of the income distribution paid less than 1 percent of all individual income taxes for 2005.[1]

Under current law, both the personal exemption and itemized deductions are reduced as adjusted gross income rises above certain threshold amounts. § 151(d)(3), § 68. These "phaseout" provisions have been the subject of some controversy, mostly because they amount to little more than back-door increases in marginal tax rates (perhaps benefiting politicians who would like to claim that marginal rates are lower than they actually are).[2] It bears noting that both the phaseout of the personal exemptions and the overall limitation on itemized deductions have an uncertain future. In 2001, Congress enacted a gradual repeal of both provisions. The repeal began in 2006 and will be complete for years beginning with 2010. Pending further legislation, however, both provisions will then be fully restored in 2011, since all provisions in the 2001 Act are officially scheduled to expire at that point.

2. The Rationale for Personal Deductions

What justifies allowing personal deductions within an income tax? On the one hand, a deduction may be a proper allowance in arriving at a definition of income that accords with our sense of justice; it may be a proper refinement of the concept of income as a measure of ability to pay. On the other hand, a deduction may be intended as an express approval of, or encouragement to, particular kinds of expenditures, in which case the deduction can sensibly be analogized to a direct subsidy. The use of deductions as subsidies is often attacked on the ground that the amount of the subsidy increases as income rises, since a deduction is worth nothing to a poor person and more to a high-bracket person than to a low-bracket person. For this reason, certain personal

---

1. According to the Congressional Budget Office, the top two quintiles of households (as measured by comprehensive household income) accounted for 99.4 percent of all individual income taxes for 2005. See Congressional Budget Office, Historical Effective Federal Tax Rates: 1979-2005 (December 2007).

2. To illustrate, consider the operation of § 68. For single individuals for the tax year 2004, itemized deductions were required to be reduced by 3 percent of the excess of adjusted gross income over $142,700. Thus, an individual with an adjusted gross income of $192,700 would lose $1,500 of her itemized deductions. (The excess of adjusted gross income over the threshold amount is $50,000; 3 percent of $50,000 is $1,500.) The loss cannot exceed 80 percent of the otherwise allowable itemized deductions, and deductions allowable for medical care, casualty losses, and investment interest expense are not subject to the limitation. For taxpayers who do not lose enough deductions to bring the 80 percent limitation into play, the § 68 phaseout is arithmetically identical to a marginal tax rate increase. The marginal tax rate increase equals the product of 3 percent and the taxpayer's officially stated marginal tax rate. Thus, suppose you earn an extra $100 and have income subject to the 35 percent bracket. Due to the operation of § 68, your taxable income increases by $103, rather than $100. Applying a 35 percent marginal tax rate to this amount, your tax liability increases by $36.05. Thus, your true marginal tax rate on the extra $100 of earnings was 36.05 percent, not 35 percent. Once one's adjusted gross income over the threshold is high enough (relative to one's itemized deductions) for the 80 percent limitation to take effect, § 68 functions like a 20 percent disallowance rule for those deductions.

deductions are sometimes labeled "upside-down" subsidies—subsidies that benefit most those who need them least.

One should be cautious, however, about embracing the notion of personal deductions (and exclusions, exemptions, and credits) as subsidies and the implicit argument that such deductions and exclusions, exemptions, and credits, are offensive to fairness, to economic rationality, and to simplicity. The argument may lead further than one might expect. A proponent of reform may begin with an attack on the personal deductions—for example, the deductions for interest on home mortgages, for individual state income and property taxes, for extraordinary medical expenses, and for charitable contributions. But then one is entitled to ask about such items as the deduction for alimony and the credit for child-care expenses. And what about business deductions and special investment credits (e.g., for investment in low-income housing)? Some proposals, though vaguely stated, seem to contemplate a tax on gross receipts, with no deduction for wages, rent, or even for the cost of goods sold, but this is inconsistent with the income concept.

In the materials that follow, we will examine the most significant personal deductions allowed under the U.S. federal income tax. Bear in mind, however, that the availability of a deduction for a particular expenditure does not necessarily reflect a stable consensus in favor of the allowance. In fact, for a number of years the Code has contained a set of tax rules—the Alternative Minimum Tax (AMT)—that treats certain of these expenses differently. The history and operation of the AMT will be discussed in further detail later in the book; at this point, we note only that the AMT's differential treatment of certain expenditures perhaps suggests some ambivalence regarding what sort of adjustments are appropriate within an "income" tax.

B. CASUALTY LOSSES

We begin with the deduction under § 165(c)(3) for losses from "fire, storm, shipwreck, or other casualty, or from theft." Imagine that a lawyer receives, from a client for whom he was able to obtain an acquittal in a narcotics case, a fee of $10,000, in cash, and that on the way home he is robbed of this amount. He will never have the opportunity to use the $10,000 for consumption. It is not available to pay taxes. A strong case can therefore be made for a deduction. Yet robberies are all too common. Perhaps the loss should be seen as part of the ordinary vicissitudes of life, part of the cost of living. These observations suggest a possible distinction between "casualties" and the day-to-day misfortunes that we must all learn to bear without tax relief.

In some respects, allowing the lawyer to deduct his $10,000 loss would be equivalent to offering him free insurance. If he is in the 35 percent tax bracket, the deduction would save him $3,500 in taxes, thus reducing his after-tax loss to $6,500. It therefore has the same economic effect on him as robbery insurance with no deductible and a 65 percent "co-payment" (the term for the portion of the loss that the insurance company does not cover). In addition, since 1983 the deduction has been limited to losses that exceed in the aggregate, for the year, 10 percent of adjusted gross income, after reduction by a $100 "floor" for each individual loss. Continuing with the insurance analogy, this provision can be viewed as the equivalent of an AGI-related "deductible." That is, no deduction is allowed until losses in the aggregate exceed the specified threshold.

The implicit cost of the Code's casualty "insurance" is not really free, of course, since all taxpayers bear it via the revenue cost of allowing the deduction. It would, however, be free to our hypothetical lawyer in the sense that he would receive it without paying an arm's-length premium. In cases where the deduction is available, therefore, it discourages people from purchasing insurance (the premium for which is not deductible if it is a personal rather than a business expense). Note § 165(h)(4)(e), under which deductions for losses covered by insurance are allowed only if a timely claim was filed.

Does the availability of private insurance affect your view as to whether casualty losses ought to be deductible? Why offer mandatory insurance via the income tax if (a) it is sufficiently available in the marketplace at an actuarially fair price, and (b) people can make good decisions for themselves regarding whether they want to be insured?

DYER v. COMMISSIONER
20 T.C.M. 705 (1961)

On their income tax return for the year 1955, petitioners claimed a casualty loss deduction[3] of $100 for damages to a vase broken by their household pet, a Siamese cat. The vase was one of a pair given to Jean by her father prior to her marriage to petitioner and was bought by him in France. The vase was one of a matched pair, the pair having a value when acquired by petitioner of $250, and singly a value of $100 each. One of the vases was broken by petitioners' Siamese cat in the course of having its first fit. The cat had developed a neurosis and thereafter had other fits; within a month it was pronounced incurable by the veterinarian and had to be destroyed. Immediately after the accident the broken vase had no value at all. The broken vase was repaired at a cost of $33.49; the value of the two vases was then $133.49. The vases were insured under a comprehensive insurance policy covering loss from fire, theft, tornado, malicious mischief, etc., up to $200 in value but the company refused to reimburse petitioners for any loss arising from damage to the vase. . . .

Manifestly, petitioners' loss was not from fire, storm, or shipwreck. They, of course, make no claim that it was. But was it a casualty loss at all? In construing the term "other casualty" the rule of ejusdem generis is applicable and in order that a loss may be deductible as a casualty loss it must appear that the casualty was of a similar character to a fire, storm, or a shipwreck. Of course, it goes without saying that it does not have to be exactly the same. The breakage of ordinary household equipment such as china or glassware

---

3. [The taxpayer relied on § 165(c)(3), which, at the time the case arose, permitted the deduction of the entire amount of the loss (but not more than the taxpayer's basis). — EDS.]

through negligence of handling or by a family pet is not a "casualty loss" under section 165(c)(3) in our opinion. Petitioners do not question the soundness of the foregoing statement as a general proposition. In their brief they state as follows:

> Petitioners admit that breakage of the vase, if occasioned by its ordinary handling by their servant, or by their cat, would not entitle them to a casualty loss deduction. . . . But that was not the situation here. The breakage of the vase was not occasioned by the cat's ordinary perambulations on the top of the particular piece of furniture, but by its extraordinary behavior there in the course of having its first fit.

We are not persuaded that the distinction which petitioners endeavor to draw in the foregoing quotation from their brief is a sound one and it is, therefore, not sustained. Doubtless, petitioners' "kitty cat" was having its first fit as petitioner testified at the trial. We have no reason to doubt the truth of his testimony to that effect. We do not think, however, such fact would make the loss a "casualty loss" within the meaning of the applicable statute. . . .

[W]e hold in favor of respondent.

NOTES AND QUESTIONS

1. *The threshold of 10 percent of AGI.* The rule limiting deductions to those that exceed 10 percent of adjusted gross income has rid the courts of pesky little cases like this one. Indeed, the prior $100 threshold would have been enough to avoid this particular case. Are those thresholds enough to dispose of the "ordinary wear and tear" argument?

2. *Analysis of the case.* Was the decision in *Dyer* correct? What if the cat had recently been purchased for $1,000 and had been struck by lightning? run over by a car? died of heart failure? Do you think that a deduction is required by the statutory language in any of these situations? If the answer is yes to one or more and no to the others, is there any sensible policy justification for the difference in outcome?

3. *The "suddenness" requirement: termites, dry rot, and lost rings.* The Service has ruled that termite damage is not deductible because scientific data establishes that it does not occur "with the suddenness comparable to that caused by fire, storm, or shipwreck." Rev. Rul. 63-232, 1963-2 C.B. 97. Similarly, a deduction has been denied for damage due to dry rot. Hoppe v. Commissioner, 42 T.C. 820 (1964), aff'd, 354 F.2d 988 (9th Cir. 1965). The suddenness requirement has led to differing results in cases involving lost rings. In Stevens v. Commissioner, 6 T.C.M. 805 (1947), the taxpayer was duck hunting. While he was retrieving a decoy, his ring "slipped off his finger and dropped into muddy water several feet deep." The taxpayer recovered from his insurance company for part of the loss and claimed a casualty loss deduction for the rest. The deduction was denied because there was no "intervention of any sudden or destructive force." In Keenan v. Bowers, 91 F. Supp. 771 (E.D.S.C. 1950), a husband and wife stayed at a motel one night. Before going to sleep the wife

wrapped her diamond ring in a tissue and put it on the night stand. During the night the husband used tissues to blow his nose and in the morning gathered up all the tissues on the nightstand, including the one with the ring, and flushed them down the toilet. Held: no deduction; not sudden. In Carpenter v. Commissioner, 25 T.C.M. 1186 (1966), the wife put her diamond ring in a glass of water and ammonia for the purpose of cleaning it and placed the glass on the kitchen counter next to the sink. The husband, while washing the dishes, emptied the glass, with the ring, into the garbage disposal unit and turned it on. The ring was a total loss. Held: deduction allowed. In White v. Commissioner, 48 T.C. 430 (1967), the wife's ring was lost when the husband slammed a car door on her hand. Held: deduction allowed. And, finally, in Kielts v. Commissioner, 42 T.C.M. 238 (1981), the wife lost her diamond ring with no help from her husband. It was simply found to be missing from its setting one day. There was evidence, however, that good care had been taken of the setting and that the loss had been the result of a "sudden, unexpected, destructive blow to the ring" — though not so violent as to have been noticed by the wife. Held: deduction allowed.

Is a deduction in any of these cases consistent with the language of the statute? with sound tax policy? It appears that Congress reacted to some concrete situations and failed to develop a rule reflecting general principles. What should those principles be? If you were responsible for drafting a new provision, how would it read? If insurance was reasonably available and the taxpayer failed to buy it, should the government provide relief through the tax system when a loss occurs? On the other hand, if insurance was not reasonably available, does that tell us something about the nature of the loss that should affect our attitude toward tax relief?

CHAMALES v. COMMISSIONER
T.C. Memo. 2000-33

MEMORANDUM FINDINGS OF FACT AND OPINION

Respondent determined a Federal income tax deficiency for petitioners' 1994 taxable year in the amount of $291,931. Respondent also determined an accuracy-related penalty of $58,386 for 1994, pursuant to § 6662(a).

The issues for decision are as follows:

(1) Whether petitioners are entitled to deduct a net casualty loss of $751,427 for the taxable year 1994; and

(2) whether petitioners are liable for the § 6662(a) accuracy-related penalty on account of negligence. . . .

FINDINGS OF FACT

. . .

Gerald and Kathleen Chamales (petitioners) are married and resided in Los Angeles, California, at the time of filing their petition in this case. In the spring of 1994, petitioners became interested in purchasing a residence in Brentwood Park, an exclusive Los Angeles neighborhood. They were attracted to the beautiful, parklike setting and the quiet peacefulness of the area. Subsequently, on June 2, 1994, petitioners opened escrow on property located in Brentwood Park, at 359 North Bristol Avenue. . . .

At the time petitioners opened escrow, O.J. Simpson (Simpson) owned and resided at the property located directly west of and adjacent to that being purchased by petitioners. Simpson's address was 360 North Rockingham Avenue. Both parcels were corner lots, bounded on the north by Ashford Street. The rear or westerly side of petitioners' land abutted the rear or easterly side of the Simpson property.

During the escrow period, on June 12, 1994, Nicole Brown Simpson and Ronald Goldman were murdered at Ms. Brown Simpson's condominium in West Los Angeles. Simpson was arrested for these murders shortly thereafter. Following the homicides and arrest, the Brentwood Park neighborhood surrounding the Simpson property became inundated with media personnel and equipment and with individuals drawn by the area's connection to the horrific events. The media and looky-loos[4] blocked streets, trespassed on neighboring residential property, and flew overhead in helicopters in their attempts to get close to the Simpson home. Police were summoned to the area for purposes of controlling the crowds, and barricades were installed at various Brentwood Park intersections to restrict traffic. This police presence, however, had little practical effect. Significant media and public attention continued throughout 1994 and 1995. Although Simpson was acquitted on October 4, 1995, civil proceedings in 1996 reignited public interest.

Petitioners closed escrow on June 29, 1994, purchasing the residence on North Bristol Avenue for $2,849,000. Petitioners had considered canceling the escrow and had discussed this possibility with their attorney, but upon being advised that liability would result from a cancellation, they decided to go through with the transaction. Later that summer, as the crowds and disruption persisted, Gerald Chamales (petitioner) inquired of his broker Solton whether the value of his property had declined. Solton indicated that she estimated a decrease in value of 20 to 30 percent.

Petitioners' 1994 tax return was prepared by Ruben Kitay (Kitay), a certified public accountant. In the course of preparing this return, Kitay and petitioner discussed the possibility of claiming a deduction for casualty loss. After preliminary research in the regulations addressing casualty loss, Kitay spoke with two area real estate agents regarding the amount by which petitioners' property had decreased in value. The agents estimated the decline at 30 to 40 percent. Kitay and petitioner decided to use the more conservative 30 percent figure in calculating the deduction to be taken on petitioners' return. An expert appraisal was not obtained at this time, as Kitay felt that a typical appraisal based on values throughout the Brentwood Park area would be

---

4. As explained by petitioners' counsel, "looky-loo" is a term developed in Hollywood to describe individuals who gather at places and events in hopes of glimpsing celebrities. The phrase is apparently used in California to denote those who frequent a location not because of its status as a conventional tourist sight but because of its association with a famous or notorious person. . . .

inconclusive as to the loss suffered by the few properties closest to the Simpson home.

Kitay and petitioner also recognized and discussed the fact that there existed a substantial likelihood of an audit focusing on petitioners' 1994 return. Hence, to clarify the position being taken and the reasons underlying petitioners' deduction, an explanatory supplemental statement labeled "Casualty Loss" was attached to the return. After indicating the location of petitioners' property in relation to that of Simpson, it stated that the casualty loss was premised on "the calamity of the murder & trial, which was sudden & unavoidable & which resulted in a permanent loss to value of property." . . .

At the time petitioners purchased their property, they were aware that the existing home required remodeling and repair. In the fall of 1994, petitioners demolished most of the house. Then, in March of 1995, they began a reconstruction project costing approximately $2 million. This reconstruction was completed in December of 1996, and petitioners moved into the residence. Petitioners continued to reside at 359 North Bristol Avenue up to and through the date of trial.

Other residents of Brentwood Park have undertaken similar reconstruction projects in recent years. The Nebekers, who own the property across Ashford Street from the former Simpson residence, are proceeding with a $1 million remodeling of their home. Likewise, the property owned by Simpson was sold after he moved out in 1998, the existing house was demolished, and a new residence is currently being constructed.

As of early 1999, the area surrounding the former Simpson home was no longer inundated with media personnel or equipment. The police barricades restricting traffic in the immediate vicinity of petitioners' property had been removed. Looky-loos, however, continued to frequent the neighborhood, often advised of the location of Simpson's former residence by its inclusion on "star maps" published for the Los Angeles area. Anniversaries of the murders were also typically accompanied by periods of increased media and public attention.

OPINION

We must decide whether petitioners are entitled to a casualty loss deduction based upon a postulated decline in the value of their residential property and, if not, whether they are liable for the § 6662(a) accuracy-related penalty.

Petitioners contend that the media and onlooker attention following the murders and focusing on Simpson's home has decreased the value of their adjacent property. They argue that because the homicides were a sudden, unexpected, and unusual event, and because aspects of the public interest precipitated thereby continued at least to the time of trial in this case, they have suffered a permanent casualty loss. Petitioners further allege that the proximity of their residence to that of Simpson has stigmatized their property and rendered it subject to permanent buyer resistance.

Conversely, respondent asserts that public attention over the course of a lengthy murder trial is not the type of sudden and unexpected event that will qualify as a casualty within the meaning of the Code. Respondent additionally contends that the Court of Appeals for the Ninth Circuit, to which appeal in this case would normally lie, has limited the amount that may be claimed as a casualty loss deduction to the loss suffered as a result of physical damage to property. According to respondent, since petitioners have failed to substantiate any such damage, they are entitled to no deduction. In respondent's view, any decline in market value represents merely a temporary fluctuation and not a permanent, cognizable loss.

We agree with respondent that petitioners have not established their entitlement to a casualty loss deduction. The difficulties suffered by petitioners as a consequence of their proximity to the Simpson residence do not constitute the type of damage contemplated by § 165(c)(3). However, because we find that petitioners acted reasonably and in good faith in the preparation of their tax return, no additional liability for the § 6662(a) accuracy-related penalty will be imposed.

ISSUE 1. CASUALTY LOSS

Regulations promulgated under § 165 . . . provide that, to be allowable as a deduction, a loss must be both "evidenced by closed and completed transactions" and "fixed by identifiable events." § 1.165-1(b). As interpreted by case law, a casualty loss within the meaning of § 165(c)(3) arises when two circumstances are present. First, the nature of the occurrence precipitating the damage to property must qualify as a casualty. . . . Second, the nature of the damage sustained must be such that it is deductible for purposes of § 165. . . .

A. *Nature of Occurrence Constituting a Casualty*

The word "casualty" as used in § 165(c)(3) has been defined, through application of the principle of ejusdem generis, by analyzing the shared characteristics of the specifically enumerated casualties of fire, storm, and shipwreck. . . . As explained by this Court:

Wherever unexpected, accidental force is exerted on property and the taxpayer is powerless to prevent application of the force because of the suddenness thereof or some disability, the resulting direct and proximate damage causes a loss which is like or similar to losses arising from the causes specifically enumerated in § 165(c)(3). . . .

Hence, casualty for purposes of the Code denotes " 'an undesigned, sudden and unexpected event,' " Durden v. Commissioner, supra at 3 (quoting Webster's New International Dictionary), or " 'an event due to some sudden, unexpected or unusual cause,' " id. (quoting Matheson v. Commissioner, 54 F.2d 537, 539 (2d Cir. 1931), affg. 18 B.T.A. 674 (1930)). Conversely, the term " 'excludes the progressive deterioration of property through a steadily operating cause.' " Id. (quoting Fay v. Helvering, 120 F.2d 253, 253 (2d Cir. 1941), affg. 42 B.T.A. 206 (1940)). The sudden and unexpected occurrence, however, is not limited to those events flowing from forces of nature and may be a product of human agency. See id. at 4.

Here, we cannot conclude that the asserted devaluation of petitioners' property was the direct and proximate result of the type of casualty contemplated by

§ 165(c)(3). While the stabbing of Nicole Brown Simpson and Ronald Goldman was a sudden and unexpected exertion of force, this force was not exerted upon and did not damage petitioners' property. Similarly, the initial influx of onlookers, although perhaps sudden, was not a force exerted on petitioners' property and was not, in and of itself, the source of the asserted decrease in the home's market value. Rather, petitioners base their claim of loss on months, or even years, of ongoing public attention. If neither media personnel nor looky-loos had chosen to frequent the Brentwood Park area after the murders, or if the period of interest and visitation had been brief, petitioners would have lacked grounds for alleging a permanent and devaluing change in the character of their neighborhood.

Hence, the source of their difficulties would appear to be more akin to a steadily operating cause than to a casualty. Press and media attention extending for months bears little similarity to a fire, storm, or shipwreck and is not properly classified therewith as an "other casualty."

B. Nature of Damage Recognized as Deductible

With respect to the requisite nature of the damage itself, this Court has traditionally held that only physical damage to or permanent abandonment of property will be recognized as deductible under § 165. . . . In contrast, the Court has refused to permit deductions based upon a temporary decline in market value. . . .

For example, in Citizens Bank v. Commissioner, supra at 720, the Court stated that "physical damage or destruction of property is an inherent prerequisite in showing a casualty loss." When again faced with taxpayers seeking a deduction premised upon a decrease in market value, the Court further explained in Pulvers v. Commissioner, supra at 249 (quoting Citizens Bank v. Commissioner, 252 F.2d at 428): "'The scheme of our tax laws does not, however, contemplate such a series of adjustments to reflect the vicissitudes of the market, or the wavering values occasioned by a succession of adverse or favorable developments.'" Such a decline was termed "a hypothetical loss or a mere fluctuation in value." Id. at 250. . . .

Moreover, the Court of Appeals for the Ninth Circuit, to which appeal in the present case would normally lie, has adopted this rule requiring physical damage. See, e.g., Kamanski v. Commissioner, 477 F.2d at 452; Pulvers v. Commissioner, 407 F.2d 838, 839 (9th Cir. 1969), affg. 48 T.C. 245 (1967). In Pulvers v. Commissioner, supra at 839, the Court of Appeals reviewed the specific casualties enumerated in § 165(c)(3) and concluded: "Each of those surely involves physical damage or loss of the physical property. Thus, we read 'or other casualty,' in para materia, meaning 'something like those specifically mentioned.'" Even more explicitly, the Court of Appeals based affirmance in Kamanski v. Commissioner, supra at 452, on the following grounds:

The Tax Court ruled that the loss sustained was a nondeductible personal loss in disposition of residential property and not a casualty loss; that the drop in market value was not due to physical damage caused by the [earth]slide, but to "buyer resistance"; that casualty loss is limited to damage directly caused by the casualty. We agree. . . .

In Caan v. United States, 83 AFTR 2d 99-1640, 99-1 USTC par. 50,349 (C.D. Cal. 1999), the District Court dismissed for failure to state a claim the complaint of taxpayers alleging facts nearly identical to those at issue here. The Caans, residents of Brentwood Park, argued that they were entitled to a § 165(c)(3) casualty loss deduction for the decline in market value and permanent buyer resistance to which they asserted their property became subject as a result of the " 'O.J. Simpson double murders.' " Id. at 99-1641 n.2, 99-1 USTC par. 50,349, at 87,829 n.2. The court, however, reiterated that "the Ninth Circuit only recognizes casualty losses arising from physical damage caused by enumerated or other similar casualties" and held that "[b]ecause the Caans have not alleged any physical damage to their property due to the murders and subsequent media frenzy, they have not alleged a casualty loss that is a proper basis for a deduction." Id. at 99-1641, 99-1 USTC par. 50,349, at 87,829.

Given the above decisions, we conclude that petitioners here have failed to establish that their claimed casualty loss is of a type recognized as deductible for purposes of § 165(c)(3). They have not proven the extent to which their property suffered physical damage, and their attempt to base a deduction on market devaluation is contrary to existing law. . . .

[P]etitioners' efforts to circumvent the established precedent repeatedly rejecting deductions premised on market fluctuation, through reliance on Finkbohner v. United States, 788 F.2d 723 (11th Cir. 1986), are misplaced. In Finkbohner v. United States, supra at 727, the Court of Appeals for the Eleventh Circuit permitted a deduction based on permanent buyer resistance in the absence of physical damage. The Finkbohners lived on a cul-de-sac with 12 homes, and after flooding damaged several of the houses, municipal authorities ordered 7 of the residences demolished and the lots maintained as permanent open space. See id. at 724. Such irreversible changes in the character of the neighborhood were found to effect a permanent devaluation and to constitute a casualty within the meaning of § 165(c)(3). See id. at 727.

However, as explicated above, this Court has long consistently held that an essential element of a deductible casualty loss is physical damage or, in some cases, physically necessitated abandonment. Furthermore, under the rule set forth in Golsen v. Commissioner, 54 T.C. 742, 756-757 (1970), affd., 445 F.2d 985 (10th Cir. 1971), we are in any event constrained to apply the law of the court in which an appeal would normally lie. Since the Court of Appeals for the Ninth Circuit has adopted and has not diverged from a requirement of physical damage for a § 165(c)(3) deduction, to hold otherwise would contravene Golsen.

Moreover, we further note that petitioners' circumstances do not reflect the type of permanent devaluation or buyer resistance which would be analogous to that held deductible in Finkbohner v. United States, supra. The evidence in the instant case reveals that media and onlooker attention has in fact lessened significantly over the years following the murders. Access to petitioners' property is no longer restricted by media equipment or police barricades. Residents of Brentwood Park have continued to invest substantial funds in remodeling and upgrading their homes. Hence, petitioners' difficulties are more akin to a temporary fluctuation in value, which no court has found to support a deduction under § 165(c)(3). We therefore hold that petitioners have failed to establish their entitlement to a casualty loss deduction. Respondent's determination of a deficiency is sustained. . . .

ISSUE 2. ACCURACY-RELATED PENALTY

Section 6662(a) and (b)(1) imposes an accuracy-related penalty in the amount of 20 percent of any underpayment that is attributable to negligence or disregard of rules or regulations. "Negligence" is defined in § 6662(c) as "any failure to make a reasonable attempt to comply with the provisions of this title," and "disregard" as "any careless, reckless, or intentional disregard." . . .

An exception to the § 6662(a) penalty is set forth in § 6664(c)(1) and provides: "No penalty shall be imposed under this part with respect to any portion of an underpayment if it is shown that there was a reasonable cause for such portion and that the taxpayer acted in good faith with respect to such portion." The taxpayer bears the burden of establishing that this reasonable cause exception is applicable, as the Commissioner's determination of an accuracy-related penalty is presumed correct. See Rule 142(a).

Regulations interpreting § 6664(c) state:

> The determination of whether a taxpayer acted with reasonable cause and in good faith is made on a case-by-case basis, taking into account all pertinent facts and circumstances. . . . Generally, the most important factor is the extent of the taxpayer's effort to assess the taxpayer's proper tax liability. . . . [§ 1.6664-4(b)(1).]

Furthermore, reliance upon the advice of an expert tax preparer may, but does not necessarily, demonstrate reasonable cause and good faith in the context of the § 6662(a) penalty. . . . Such reliance is not an absolute defense, but it is a factor to be considered. . . . In order for this factor to be given dispositive weight, the taxpayer claiming reliance on a professional such as an accountant must show, at minimum, that (1) the accountant was supplied with correct information and (2) the incorrect return was a result of the accountant's error. . . .

Applying these principles to the instant case, we conclude that petitioners have sustained their burden of establishing reasonable cause and good faith for the deduction taken on their return. Petitioner first inquired of his real estate agent, an experienced broker, regarding a potential decline in value as a result of events stemming from the alleged Simpson murders. He then sought advice from his accountant Kitay concerning the propriety of a casualty loss deduction. Kitay, in turn, discussed devaluation with two additional real estate brokers. Kitay's opinion that a typical appraisal would be inconclusive as to petitioners' property also appears to have played a significant role in the decision not to seek such an evaluation.

Moreover, the explanatory statement prepared by Kitay and attached to petitioners' return indicates, on the part of petitioners, both communication to the accountant of relevant information and good faith. Petitioners supplied Kitay with factual data related to the nature of the loss, and they chose to make full disclosure rather than to obscure the reasons for their deduction.

We therefore conclude that petitioners did not exhibit the type of unreasonableness or imprudence that would support imposition of the § 6662(a) accuracy-related penalty.

We further observe that on brief respondent alternatively contends that petitioners should be held liable for the § 6662(a) penalty on the grounds of a substantial understatement of income tax. See § 6662(b)(2). We note, however, that the notice of deficiency sent to petitioners reads, in explaining the accuracy-related penalty: "Underpayment due to negligence 291,931," followed by "Underpayment due to substantial understatement 0." As respondent has not amended his pleadings to assert an underpayment due to substantial understatement, this issue was not properly raised. In addition, we also observe that the § 6664(c) reasonable cause exception is equally applicable in the case of a § 6662(a) penalty attributed to a substantial understatement of income tax. Respondent's determination of an accuracy-related penalty is denied. . . .

QUESTIONS

1. What would the outcome of the case have been if it had arisen in the Eleventh Circuit?

2. If you had been lawyer for the taxpayers, would you have advised inclusion in their tax return of an "explanatory statement"?

PROBLEMS

After a successful career in television, Gary Gilligan and his wife Ginger retired to a house they bought for $2 million on an idyllic broad sandy beach on the Kona coast of the island of Hawaii. Immediately adjacent to their house was a little-used public beach that stretched for about a mile.

1. A hurricane hit the area where the Gilligan house is located, damaged the house, and washed away all the sand from the Gilligans' beach, from the public beach next to it, and from the beach of the house owned by an impecunious professor on the other side of the Gilligans' house. The hurricane also destroyed palm trees and washed up on the professor's property a yacht owned by an incompetent skipper who, despite adequate warnings, had failed to seek a safe harbor. Following the storm, the Gilligans brought in several barge loads of sand and restored their beach. They also planted new palm trees and repaired their house, all at a cost of $250,000 (of which $100,000 was recovered on an insurance policy). The professor, however, lacked the funds, and the inclination, to restore his property. Rather than repair his badly damaged house (which was uninsured), he chose to start living in the washed-up and no-longer-seaworthy yacht. The state of Hawaii decided that since hurricanes are natural phenomena, no effort would be made to restore the public beach. Consequently, the Gilligan property became, in effect, a sumptuous island surrounded by desolation and ugliness. A real estate agent advised the Gilligans that the highest price they could expect to receive for the

sale of their house would be $1 million. Are they entitled to any casualty loss deductions?

2. Assume the same initial facts—no hurricane. The state decides to develop the public beach and begins by building a large paved parking lot and rest rooms directly adjacent to the Gilligans' property. The beach soon begins to attract large crowds of tourists, and the state builds a refreshment stand that plays, on loudspeakers, all day long and into the evening, the type of "Hawaiian" music loved only by tourists. The Gilligans complain, but the parking lot and refreshment stand concessions are controlled by Thurston Howell III and his wife Lovey Howell, who is a niece of a leading member of the Hawaiian legislature, and the Gilligans' complaints are ignored. The Gilligans try to sell their house. The highest bid is $800,000. Before long, Gary, unable to block the music from his consciousness, loses his sanity. Ginger commits him to a home for senile movie stars, sells the house for $800,000, and moves back to Los Angeles, where she accepts a role as permanent chaperone on a television series in which a group of demented men and women agree to be cast away on a desert island for as long as they can stand to be with one another. Are the Gilligans entitled to any casualty loss deductions?

BLACKMAN v. COMMISSIONER
88 T.C. 677 (1987)

FINDINGS OF FACT

. . . At the time of the filing of the petition in this case, the petitioner, Biltmore Blackman, resided in Billerica, Massachusetts. He and his wife filed their joint Federal income tax return for 1980 on April 28, 1981, with the Internal Revenue Service Center, Atlanta, Georgia.

The petitioner's employer transferred him from Baltimore, Maryland, to South Carolina. The petitioner relocated his wife and children to South Carolina. Mrs. Blackman was dissatisfied with South Carolina and returned, with the couple's five children, to Baltimore. During the 1980 Labor Day weekend, the petitioner returned to Baltimore, hoping to persuade his wife to give South Carolina another chance. When he arrived at his Baltimore home, he discovered that another man was living there with his wife. The neighbors told the petitioner that such man had been there on other occasions when the petitioner had been out of town on business.

On September 1, 1980, the petitioner returned to his former home to speak to his wife. However, Mrs. Blackman was having a party; her guests refused to leave despite the petitioner's request that they do so. He returned to the house several times, repeating his request, and emphasizing it by breaking windows. Mrs. Blackman's guests did not leave the house until about 3 A.M. September 2, 1980.

Later, on September 2, 1980, the petitioner again went to his former home. He wanted to ask his wife whether she wanted a divorce. They quarreled, and Mrs. Blackman left the house. After she left, the petitioner gathered some of Mrs. Blackman's clothes, put them on the stove, and set them on fire.

The petitioner claims that he then "took pots of water to dowse the fire, put the fire totally out" and left the house. The fire spread, and the fire department was called. When the firefighters arrived, they found some of the clothing still on the stove. The house and its contents were destroyed.

The petitioner was arrested later that day and charged with one count of Setting Fire while Perpetrating a Crime, a violation of Md. Ann. Code art. 27, sec. 11 (Repl. vol. 1982), and one count of Destruction of Property (Malicious Mischief), a violation of Md. Ann. Code art. 27, sec. 111 (Repl. vol. 1982). The arson charge was based on the allegation that the petitioner "had set fire to and burned . . . [the house] while perpetrating the crime of Destruction of Property" and the malicious destruction charge was based on the allegation that he "did willfully and maliciously destroy, injure, deface and molest clothing, the property of" Mrs. Blackman. The petitioner pleaded not guilty to both charges. On November 5, 1980, by order of the District Court of Baltimore County, the arson charge was placed on the "stet" docket. The petitioner was ordered to serve 24 months unsupervised probation without verdict on the malicious destruction charge.

The petitioner filed a claim for the fire damage with his insurer, State Farm Fire & Casualty Co. of Baltimore, Maryland. The company refused to honor the claim due to the cause of the fire.

On his 1980 Federal income tax return, the petitioner deducted as a casualty loss $97,853 attributable to the destruction of his residence and its contents. In his notice of deficiency, the Commissioner disallowed the deduction. . . .

OPINION

The primary issue for our decision is whether the petitioner is allowed to deduct the loss resulting from the fire started by him. Section 165(a) allows a deduction for "any loss sustained during the taxable year and not compensated for by insurance or otherwise." Section 165(c)(3) provides, in pertinent part, that in the case of an individual, the deduction allowed in subsection (a) is to be limited to "losses of property not connected with a trade or business, if such losses arise from fire, storm, shipwreck, or other casualty, or from theft." The Commissioner concedes that the petitioner sustained a loss through fire. However, the Commissioner argues that the petitioner intentionally set the fire which destroyed his home in violation of Maryland's public policy, that allowing the deduction would frustrate that public policy, and that, therefore, under the doctrine of Commissioner v. Heininger, 320 U.S. 467 (1943), and subsequent cases, the petitioner is not entitled to a deduction for the damage caused by his fire.

Courts have traditionally disallowed business expense and casualty loss deductions under section 162 or 165 where national or state public policies would be frustrated by the consequences of allowing the deduction. Commissioner v. Heininger, supra. "[T]he test of non-deductibility always is the severity and immediacy of the frustration resulting from allowance of the deduction." Tank Truck Rentals v. Commissioner, 356 U.S. 30, 35 (1958).

"From the cases, it is clear that the question of illegality to frustrate public policy is, in the last analysis, *one of degree, to be determined from the peculiar facts of each case.*" Fuller v. Commissioner, 213 F.2d 102, 106 (10th Cir. 1954), aff'g 20 T.C. 308 (1953); emphasis supplied. . . .

Conviction of a crime is not essential to a showing that the allowance of a deduction would frustrate public policy. . . .

Moreover, it is well settled that the negligence of the taxpayer is not a bar to the allowance of the casualty loss deduction. . . . On the other hand, gross negligence on the part of the taxpayer will bar a casualty loss deduction. . . . "Needless to say, the taxpayer may not knowingly or willfully sit back and allow himself to be damaged in his property or willfully damage the property himself." White v. Commissioner, 48 T.C. 430, 435 (1967).

In our judgment, the petitioner's conduct was grossly negligent, or worse. He admitted that he started the fire. He claims that he attempted to extinguish it by putting water on it. Yet, the firemen found clothing still on the stove, and there is no evidence to corroborate the petitioner's claim that he attempted to dowse the flame. The fact is that the fire spread to the entire house, and we have only vague and not very persuasive evidence concerning the petitioner's attempt to extinguish the fire. Once a person starts a fire, he has an obligation to make extraordinary efforts to be sure that the fire is safely extinguished. This petitioner has failed to demonstrate that he made such extraordinary efforts. The house fire was a foreseeable consequence of the setting of the clothes fire, and a consequence made more likely if the petitioner failed to take adequate precautions to prevent it. We hold that the petitioner's conduct was grossly negligent and that his grossly negligent conduct bars him from deducting the loss claimed by him under section 165(a) and (c)(3).

In addition, allowing the petitioner a deduction would severely and immediately frustrate the articulated public policy of Maryland against arson and burning. Maryland's policy is clearly expressed. Article 27, section 11, of the Maryland Annotated Code (Repl. vol. 1982), makes it a felony to burn a residence while perpetrating a crime. The petitioner admits that he set fire to his wife's clothes, and he has not denied that the residence burned as a result of the fire started by him. The petitioner was charged with violating that section, but that charge was placed on the "stet" docket. As we understand Maryland practice, such action merely postponed any action on the charge. . . . However, the mere fact that the petitioner was never brought to trial for burning the house does not foreclose a finding by this Court that the petitioner acted in violation of that policy. . . . We are mindful, also, that Maryland has an articulated public policy against domestic violence. We refuse to encourage couples to settle their disputes with fire. We hold that allowing a loss deduction, in this factual setting, would severely and immediately frustrate the articulated public policies of Maryland against arson and burning, and against domestic violence. . . .

The remaining issue concerns the addition, under section 6653(a), for negligence or intentional disregard of rules and regulations. The Commissioner argues that the petitioner is liable for the addition because he claimed a substantial deduction to which he was not entitled and that such a claim justifies imposing the addition. We cannot agree in this case. Under the circumstances of this case, it was not negligent for the petitioner to claim a deduction for his loss by fire.... Imposition of the addition is therefore not warranted in this case.

QUESTIONS

1. *Ordinary versus gross negligence.* Imagine that Carol was building a cabinet in the living room of her house, left a cigarette burning while she went to answer the telephone, and returned to find that the cabinet was burning. She ran to the kitchen, filled a bucket with water, and emptied the bucket of water on the fire. Satisfied in her own mind that the fire was out, she left the house. In fact, the fire had not been thoroughly extinguished and started up again. The house burned down and was not adequately insured. Carol had invested $100,000 in the house and recovered only $40,000 from her insurance company. Is her $60,000 loss deductible under § 165(c)(3)? On the question of the role of negligence in casualty loss cases, how is her situation any different from that of Blackman? What if Carol had been smoking marijuana, rather than tobacco?

2. *Public policy.* Why is it that allowing Blackman a deduction would frustrate public policy? Suppose an arsonist sets fire to a house owned by someone else. The possibility of a casualty loss deduction for the arsonist simply does not arise; the arsonist has no casualty loss. The arsonist will presumably be subject to whatever penalties are imposed by the state for arson. Blackman, in addition to whatever penalties are imposed on him under state law, will lose his tax deduction. Is that because we assume that, for Blackman, whatever criminal penalty is imposed by the state is inadequate to effectuate its policies? Then what about the arsonist who sets fire to someone else's house?

3. *Intentional conduct.* Before the clothes-burning incident, Blackman broke some windows in his house. Suppose the house had not caught fire and burned down. Would Blackman have been entitled to deduct the loss resulting from the broken windows?

C. EXTRAORDINARY MEDICAL EXPENSES

1. Overview

Under § 213(a), medical expenses are deductible to the extent that they exceed 7.5 percent of adjusted gross income (AGI). For purposes of the alternative minimum tax the threshold is increased to 10 percent. Thus, like the deduction for casualty losses, the medical expense deduction is akin to mandatory "free" insurance, with a "co-payment" equal to 100 percent minus the taxpayer's marginal rate and with an AGI-related "deductible" that applies on an annual rather than a per-event or per-family-member basis.

The 7.5 (or 10) percent threshold seems to reflect the same kind of effort to distinguish between extraordinary misfortunes and the ordinary vicissitudes of life that is reflected in the casualty loss deduction. The threshold also has the desirable effect of reducing both the number of taxpayers who need to figure out each year precisely how much they spent on medical care and the resources the service and the courts must devote to the process of verifying medical expense deductions.

The deduction threshold under § 213 creates a tax disincentive for individuals to buy medical insurance. Even though the premium is treated as a medical expense, most or all of the deduction will be eliminated by the operation of the threshold. At the same time, in the absence of insurance, medical expenses will tend to be high in some years and low in others, and the high-expense years will generate deductions. So taxpayers who buy no insurance will likely wind up with some deductions, in some years, while those who do buy insurance will probably have no deductions. This tax reality is unlikely to deter many taxpayers from buying insurance, but there is another tax incentive that has led to greater congressional concern and to a legislative reaction, as described immediately below.

Recall that § 106(a) excludes from gross income the value of employer-provided health insurance (see Chapter 2.A.3). In combination with the § 213 threshold, the exclusion for employer-provided health insurance provides a strong incentive for employers to offer medical coverage, rather than to pay higher taxable compensation and allow employees to seek their own policies. This may be all well and good, since the result of pushing people into group plans has the possibly desirable effect of spreading risk by including high-risk people in an insured pool. But the combination also encourages employees to seek, and employers to provide, "first dollar" coverage, as opposed to coverage with a significant deductible (and a higher cash wage), since the full coverage is excluded while the amounts paid by employees as deductibles would probably not exceed the threshold for deduction. Significant deductibles are thought by some observers, and apparently by many members of Congress, to be a good thing, since people spending their own money will, so the thinking goes, avoid wasteful trips to the doctor and other wasteful use of medical resources and will pay attention to the prices they are asked to pay. In other words, significant deductibles may bring market discipline to bear on at least some of the soaring cost of medical care.

This reasoning may or may not be persuasive, but Congress accepted it and, in 2003, enacted § 223, providing for the Health Savings Account (HSA). The focus of the HSA is on employer-provided coverage. The coverage must have a deductible of at least $1,000 and not more than $5,000 for self-only coverage and twice those amounts for family coverage, with an annual adjustment for inflation. § 223(c)(2). An employee with coverage falling within this range is allowed to claim a tax deduction for a contribution to an HSA up to the lesser of (a) the amount of the deductible or (b) $2,250 (self-only coverage) or $4,500 (family coverage); additional deductible contributions are allowed for people who are 55 years old or older. § 223(b). The deduction is treated as an adjustment to gross income under § 62(a)(19) and therefore may be claimed by taxpayers who do not itemize their deductions. The deduction is not phased out under § 62 and is not subject to the Alternative Minimum Tax. Instead of paying cash to the employee and allowing the employee to contribute to an HSA, the employer may contribute directly to the HSA on behalf of the employee and the contribution is deductible by the employer and nontaxable to the employee. Amounts earned in the account are nontaxable (§ 223(e)), and amounts paid from the account to reimburse the employee for medical expenses are nontaxable to the employee. § 223(f)(1). Amounts paid out that are not for medical expenses are taxable to the employee, with a 10 percent penalty — except that amounts paid out upon death or disability or upon reaching retirement age are taxable but with no penalty. § 223(f)(2) and (4). The idea behind this program is that people with money in an HSA account will be relatively careful in incurring medical expenses because they will be spending their own money.

The deduction is allowed each year even though amounts are left over from prior years. Additional amounts may be contributed each year even though the balance in the account from prior years exceeds the annual maximum contribution amount. Thus, the account may grow in amount and serve as a retirement-savings account (without some of the limitations on other retirement-savings accounts). In fact, this could turn out to be the principal function of HSAs for high-bracket taxpayers, who are the ones who benefit the most from using such accounts and who are most likely to be able to afford to contribute to them. For an individual at retirement age with a substantial balance in an HSA account, the incentive effects seem inconsistent with the apparent goal of the law. Amounts withdrawn from an HSA account for ordinary living expenses are taxable as ordinary income, while amounts used to pay medical expenses are nontaxable. Thus, there is a tax incentive for profligacy rather than frugality in incurring medical costs.

HSA accounts may also encourage increased medical outlays for another reason. The medical expenses that may be reimbursed tax free from an HSA account are all those covered, quite broadly, by § 213, including, for example, laser vision correction, eyeglasses, and dental care. Most insurance policies have more limited coverage. For expenses covered by § 213 and not by insurance, § 223 permits the use of tax-free dollars rather than the after-tax dollars that people were spending before the adoption of § 223.

The efficacy of § 223 in reducing aggregate use of medical services is quite limited. The great bulk of medical outlays are incurred for expensive procedures. Such outlays will exceed the HSA deductible amount, so the tax incentive becomes irrelevant. What remains is the moral hazard — that is, the tendency of people with insurance to demand, and use, "excessive" medical services because they do not incur the cost.

One interesting sidelight: An employer plan may provide for preventive care, not subject to a deductible, without disqualifying it from being treated as a high-deductible plan eligible for HSA treatment. This provision reflects the plausible theory that it may be a good idea to encourage people to be frugal in most of their medical spending decisions, but not in their decisions with respect to preventive care, which may reduce medical costs in the long run.

2.   What Is "Medical Care"?

Most of the legal issues concerning medical expenses relate to the question of what is "medical care" as it is defined in § 213(d). The cases that follow raise some puzzling aspects of that question.

TAYLOR v. COMMISSIONER
54 T.C.M. 129 (1987)

. . . Due to a severe allergy, petitioner's doctor instructed him not to mow his lawn. Petitioner in 1982 paid a total of $178 to have his lawn mowed and claimed a medical expense deduction in that amount for lawn care.

. . . Petitioner contends that since his doctor had advised him not to mow his lawn, he is entitled to a deduction for amounts he paid someone else to do his lawn mowing. Respondent contends the amounts paid by petitioner for lawn mowing are nondeductible personal expenses under section 262 rather than section 213 medical expenses.

Except as otherwise specifically provided, section 262 disallows deductions for personal, living or family expenses. Section 213, however, specifically authorizes a deduction for medical care expenses paid during the taxable year which are not compensated for by insurance or otherwise. . . .

In this case, petitioner, bearing the burden of proof . . . must establish that the apparently personal expense of lawn care is a medical expense. Petitioner has cited no authority to support his position either in general or with respect to lawn care expenses specifically. Petitioner testified that due to a severe allergy his doctor had directed him not to perform lawn care activities but there was no showing why other family members could not undertake these activities or whether petitioner would have paid others to mow his lawn even absent his doctor's direction not to do so himself.

Doctor recommended activities have been held in a number of cases not to constitute deductible medical expenses where the expenses did not fall within the parameters of "medical care." For example, in Altman v. Commissioner, 53 T.C. 487 (1969), this Court held that the expense of playing golf was not a deductible medical expense even though this activity was recommended by the taxpayer's doctor as treatment for his emphysema and provided therapeutic benefits. On this record we conclude that petitioner has not carried his burden of proof with respect to the deduction of lawn care costs as a medical expense and is thus not entitled to include the $178 expended for lawn care in his medical expense deductions.

Decision will be entered for the respondent.

HENDERSON v. COMMISSIONER
T.C. Memo. 2000-321

. . . [Petitioners] David A. and Paula J. Henderson['s] . . . son, Bradley, suffers from spina bifida and is confined to a wheelchair.

In 1991, petitioners purchased a van for the sole purpose of transporting Bradley. The purchase price of the van was approximately $26,000. In 1992, Bradley's physician believed that, due to Bradley's increasing weight and size and his prolonged medical condition, a wheelchair lift was necessary. Petitioners modified the van specifically for Bradley's medical needs by installing an automatic wheelchair lift and raising the roof of the van. Such modifications cost petitioners an additional $4,406.

During 1994 and 1995, petitioners lived in eastern Oregon and, on a weekly basis, transported Bradley to and from hospitals and doctors' appointments in Spokane and Seattle, Washington. The specially modified van was the only means of transportation for Bradley. Petitioners used two other vehicles for their own transportation.

The van was also used to transport Bradley to and from school every day. The van was used because the school bus in the town where they lived was not equipped with a wheelchair lift. Petitioners wrote to the superintendent of schools to request that the school district purchase a wheelchair lift for the school bus, but the request was denied due to the low budget of the small community.

Petitioners also used the van whenever they needed to take Bradley on trips with them. Petitioners used the van for a trip in 1994 to drive to Missouri for a family emergency. They decided to take the van to Missouri in order to accommodate Bradley's medical condition at the time. The doctors advised petitioners that Bradley, who was then in a full body cast, could not travel by air. Petitioners also could not find a child care person who was willing to care for a child in a body shell.

On the recommendation of their certified public accountant, petitioners deducted the cost of the van and the conversions at a rate of $5,500 per year for 1991, 1992, 1993, 1994, and 1995. Respondent audited petitioners' 1994 and 1995 tax returns and denied petitioners' depreciation deduction for both years.

OPINION

The issue presented is whether depreciation is deductible as a medical expense under § 213. Petitioners argue that the total cost of the van is deductible and is depreciable over 5 years as medical expense under § 213.

Respondent concedes that petitioners' expense of $4,406 to convert the van to meet the medical needs of their son was deductible for 1992, the year in which it was paid. Petitioners claimed medical expense deductions of $5,500 in 1992, which is in excess of the cost of the modifications of $4,406. Neither the deduction taken for medical expense on petitioners' 1992 tax return nor the equivalent depreciation deductions taken on their 1991 and 1993 tax returns were audited or disallowed, and they are not in issue in this case. Respondent's position is that only the cost of the modifications was deductible, but, in any event, depreciation is not an "expense paid" and, thus, is not deductible as a medical expense under § 213.

In general, deductions are not allowed for personal, living, or family expenses. See § 262(a). Section 213, however, creates an exception to this general rule and provides a deduction for medical expenses. Section 213 provides in part: "There shall be allowed as a deduction the *expenses paid* during the taxable year . . . for medical care of the taxpayer, his spouse, or a dependent . . . to the extent that such expenses exceed 7.5 percent of adjusted gross income." (Emphasis added.) Medical expense is defined as "*amounts paid* . . . for transportation primarily for and essential to medical care." § 213(d). (Emphasis added.) The Court has previously addressed the issue of whether depreciation is a deductible medical expense and held that depreciation is not an "expense paid" within the meaning of § 213. See Weary v. United States, 510 F.2d 435 (10th Cir. 1975); Elwood v. Commissioner, 72 T.C. 264 (1979); Gordon v. Commissioner, 37 T.C. 986 (1962). In Pfersching v. Commissioner, T.C. Memo. 1983-34, we explained our holding in language equally applicable here:

> We have great sympathy for petitioners and their conscientious efforts to deal with the unfortunate illness of their son. We are, however, compelled to conclude that the van depreciation is not allowable because it does not meet the requirements of the statute. . . . Depreciation is not an "expense paid" or "amount paid" within the meaning of § 213. Therefore, petitioner's claim cannot be allowed. . . .

QUESTIONS

1. Can § 213 fairly be read to allow the deduction of the depreciation — or of the entire purchase price of the van? If so, should it be so read? If not, should the Code be amended to allow the deduction?

2. Why did the IRS fight this case? Does the Commissioner have no heart? No compassion? No judgment? Or is the problem the *next* case that might arise if the taxpayer wins here?

OCHS v. COMMISSIONER
195 F.2d 692 (2d Cir. 1952)

Before AUGUSTUS N. HAND, CHASE and FRANK, Circuit Judges.
AUGUSTUS N. HAND, Circuit Judge. . . .
The Tax Court made the following findings:

> During the taxable year petitioner was the husband of Helen H. Ochs. They had two children, Josephine age six and Jeanne age four.
> On December 10, 1943, a thyroidectomy was performed on petitioner's wife. A histological examination disclosed [cancer]. . . . During the taxable year [1946] the petitioner maintained his two children in day school during the first half of the year and in boarding school during the latter half of the year at a cost of [$1450]. Petitioner deducted this sum from his income for the year 1946 as a medical expense under [§ 213].

During the taxable year . . . [efforts by Helen] to speak were painful, required much of her strength, and left her in a highly nervous state. . . . Petitioner and his wife consulted a reputable physician and were advised by him that if the children were not separated from petitioner's wife she would not improve and her nervousness and irritation might cause a recurrence of the cancer. Petitioner continued to maintain his children in boarding school [until 1948] . . . having been advised that if there was no recurrence . . . during that time his wife could be considered as having recovered from the cancer.

During the taxable year petitioner's income was between $5,000 and $6,000. Petitioner's two children have not attended private school but have lived at home and attended public school since [1948]. . . .

In our opinion the expenses incurred by the taxpayer were nondeductible family expenses within the meaning of [§ 262] rather than medical expenses. Concededly the line between the two is a difficult one to draw, but this only reflects the fact that expenditures made on behalf of some members of a family unit frequently benefit others in the family as well. . . . If, for example, the husband had employed a governess for the children, or a cook, the wages he would have paid would not be deductible. Or, if the wife had died, and the children were sent to a boarding school, there would certainly be no basis for contending that such expenses were deductible. The examples given serve to illustrate that the expenses here were made necessary by the loss of the wife's services, and that the only reason for allowing them as a deduction is that the wife also received a benefit. We think it unlikely that Congress intended to transform family expenses into medical expenses for this reason. . . .

The decision is affirmed.

FRANK, Circuit Judge (dissenting). . . .

The Commissioner, the Tax Court, and now my colleagues, are certain Congress did not intend relief for a man in this grave plight. The truth is, of course, no one knows what Congress would have said if it had been faced with these facts. The few paltry sentences of Congressional history for [§ 213] do not lend strong support — indeed any support at all — to a strict construction theory:

> This allowance is granted in consideration of the heavy tax burden that must be borne by industry during the existing emergency [1942] and of the desirability of maintaining the present high level of public health and morale. . . . The term "medical care" is broadly defined to include amounts paid for the diagnosis, cure, mitigation, treatment, or prevention of disease, or for the purpose of affecting any structure or function of the body. It is not intended, however, that a deduction should be allowed for any expense that is not incurred primarily for the prevention or alleviation of a physical or mental defect or illness.[5]

I think that Congress would have said that this man's expense fell within the category of "mitigation, treatment, or prevention of disease," and that it was

---

5. Sen. Rep. 1631, 77th Cong., 2d Sess. 95-96 (1942).

for the "purpose of affecting [a] structure or function of the body." . . . The Commissioner seemingly admits that the deduction might be a medical expense if the wife were sent away from her children to a sanitarium for rest and quiet, but asserts that it never can be if, for the very same purpose, the children are sent away from the mother—even if a boarding-school for the children is cheaper than a sanitarium for the wife. "I cannot believe that Congress intended such a meaningless distinction. . . ."[6] The cure ought to be the doctor's business, not the Commissioner's. . . .

In the final analysis, the Commissioner, the Tax Court and my colleagues all seem to reject Mr. Ochs' plea because of the nightmarish spectacle of opening the floodgates to cases involving expense for cooks, governesses, baby-sitters, nourishing food, clothing, frigidaires, electric dish-washers—in short, allowances as medical expenses for everything "helpful to a convalescent housewife or to one who is nervous or weak from past illness." I, for one, trust the Commissioner to make short shrift of most such claims. The tests should be: Would the taxpayer, considering his income and his living standard, normally spend money in this way regardless of illness? Has he enjoyed such luxuries or services in the past? Did a competent physician prescribe this specific expense as an indispensable part of the treatment? Has the taxpayer followed the physician's advice in the most economical way possible? Are the so-called medical expenses over and above what the patient would have to pay anyway for his living expenses, i.e., room, board, etc.? Is the treatment closely geared to a particular condition and not just to the patient's general good or well-being?

My colleagues . . . would classify the children's schooling here as a family expense, because, they say, it resulted from the loss of the wife's services. . . . The Tax Court specifically found that the children were sent away so they would not bother the wife, and not because there was no one to take care of them. Ochs' expenditures fit into the Congressional test for medical deductions because he was compelled to go to the expense of putting the children away primarily for the benefit of his sick wife. Expenses incurred solely because of the loss of the patient's services and not as a part of his cure are a different thing altogether. . . . I would limit the deductible expense to the care of the children at the times when they would otherwise be around the mother. . . .

___

6. The Commissioner has, in the past, shown more liberal tendencies in sanctioning somewhat unorthodox kinds of treatment as contemplated by the statute: He has allowed the deduction of fees paid to chiropractors and Christian Science practitioners. I.T. 3598, 1943 C.B. 157. He should not, in this context, lag behind the progress of the medical art. Especially in this case should the Commissioner realize the growing emphasis placed by medical practitioners upon peace of mind as a major factor in the recovery of patients from what were formerly thought to be entirely organic diseases. If the wife here had been recovering from a nervous breakdown, it could not be sensibly argued that the cure did not fit the disease. Are we ready now to discount the uncontroverted evidence of the doctor in this case that peace of mind and body (it takes not only mental but physical gymnastics to keep up with two children aged four and six) was essential to recovery from, and prevention of, a throat cancer?

[See Ring v. Commissioner, 23 T.C. 950 (1955) (disallowing cost of trip to shrine at Lourdes). — EDS.]

Line-drawing may be difficult here as everywhere, but that is what courts are for. See Lavery v. Purssell, 399 Ch. D. 508, 517: ". . . courts of justice ought not to be puzzled by such old scholastic questions as to where a horse's tail begins and where it ceases. You are obliged to say, this is a horse's tail at some time."

NOTES AND QUESTIONS

1. *Causation.* (a) The expenditure in *Ochs* would not have been incurred but for the illness, which suggests that it should be deductible. It is equally true, however, that the expenditure would not have been incurred but for the children, which suggests that it should not be deductible. (Cf. W. Prosser, The Law of Torts 236 (4th ed. 1971): "In a philosophical sense, the consequences of an act go forward to eternity, and the causes back to the discovery of America and beyond.") Is it relevant to ask whether Mr. and Mrs. Ochs made a conscious decision to have children; in the language of torts, whether the children were "preventable"? What about the *Taylor* case? What were the significant necessary antecedents to the expense incurred in that case?

(b) In some cases, of course, a court may reject entirely the taxpayer's claimed causative link. In Jacobs v. Commissioner, 62 T.C. 813 (1974), the taxpayer claimed a deduction under § 213 for the lawyer's fees and settlement costs for his divorce, claiming that his psychiatrist had recommended the divorce after the taxpayer had experienced severe depression and suicidal tendencies. The Tax Court concluded that the divorce would have been obtained regardless of the psychiatric problems and denied the deduction. The court distinguished Gerstacher v. Commissioner, 414 F.2d 448 (6th Cir. 1969), which allowed a deduction under § 213 of legal fees for a commitment proceeding that was necessary in order to render medical treatment, on the ground that there the expenses would not have been incurred but for the illness.

2. *The language of the Code.* The claim for a deduction in *Ochs* may appeal strongly to one's sense of compassion or fairness, but how strong is the statutory basis for the deduction? Was the expenditure for the "cure, mitigation, treatment, or prevention of disease, or for the purpose of affecting any structure or function of the body"? § 213(d)(1)(A). Or was it only for dealing with the consequences of disease? If you interpret § 213 to allow a deduction in *Ochs*, would a deduction also be allowed in *Taylor*?

3. *Statutory drafting.* How would you draft the language of a Code provision intended to ensure a deduction in a case like *Ochs*? Would you favor extending the deduction to expenses that would have been incurred by someone like Mr. Ochs in raising his children if Mrs. Ochs had died? If so, what about the child-rearing expenses of other single parents? What about a deduction for all expenses incurred as a result of any physical or mental impairment, illness, or disability, including additional living expenses? Would such a provision promote the goal of fairness? If your answer is yes, what does that imply as to

societal obligations to people with an impairment, illness, or disability and no income?

4. *Drawing the line.* (a) Rev. Rul. 75-318, 1975-2 C.B. 88, holds that a taxpayer may deduct as a medical expense the excess of the cost of Braille books and magazines, for his blind child, over the cost of regular printed editions. And Rev. Rul. 64-173, 1964-1 C.B. (Pt. 1) 121, allows a deduction for the cost of hiring a person to accompany the taxpayer's blind child while at school "for the purpose of guiding the child in walking throughout the school day." The rationale is that the purpose of the outlay is to "alleviate the child's physical defect of blindness." Has the Service had a change (addition) of heart since *Ochs*?

(b) Deductions were also allowed for face-lifts (Rev. Rul. 76-332, 76-2 C.B. 81) and for electrolysis but not for tattoos and ear piercing (Rev. Rul. 82-111, 1982-1 C.B. 48). Deductions for "cosmetic surgery" are now limited under § 213(d)(9).

(c) Outlays for elevators, swimming pools in one's house, etc., are currently deductible if they are necessitated by illness, though only to the extent that they do not add to the value of the house. Regs. § 1.213-1(e)(1)(iii).

(d) Sometimes Congress discharges its lawmaking function by inserting into the legislative history of a current enactment language that purports to "clarify" existing law. The attraction of this approach is that it avoids the necessity of facing the difficult task of drafting appropriate language and of cluttering up the Code. The effect may also be to delegate lawmaking discretion to the Treasury. An example is reflected in the following excerpt from Rev. Rul. 87-106, 1987-2 C.B. 67:

> In S. Rep. No. 99-313, 99th Cong., 2d Sess. 59 (1986), 1986-3 (Vol. 3) C.B. 59, and 2 H.R. Rep. No. 99-841 (Conf. Rep.), 99th Cong., 2d Sess. II-22 (1986), 1986-3 (Vol. 4) C.B. 22, Congress expressed a desire to clarify that certain capital expenditures generally do not increase the value of a personal residence and thus generally are deductible in full as medical expenses. These expenditures are those made for removing structural barriers in a personal residence for the purpose of accommodating it to the handicapped condition of the taxpayer or the taxpayer's spouse or dependents who reside there.
>
> The Internal Revenue Service has determined that expenditures for the following purposes generally do not increase the fair market value of a personal residence and thus generally are eligible in full for the medical expense deduction when made for the primary purpose of accommodating a personal residence to the handicapped condition of the taxpayer, the taxpayer's spouse, or dependents who reside there:
>
> 1. constructing entrance or exit ramps to the residence;
> 2. widening doorways at entrances or exits to the residence;
> 3. widening or otherwise modifying hallways and interior doorways;
> 4. installing railing, support bars, or other modifications to bathrooms;
> 5. lowering of or making other modifications to kitchen cabinets and equipment;
> 6. altering the location of or otherwise modifying electrical outlets and fixtures;
> 7. installing porch lifts and other forms of lifts (Generally, this does not include elevators, as they may add to the fair market value of the residence and any deduction would have to be decreased to that extent. See section 1.213-1(e)(1)(iii) of the regulations.);

8. modifying fire alarms, smoke detectors, and other warning systems;
9. modifying stairs;
10. adding handrails or grab bars whether or not in bathrooms;
11. modifying hardware on doors;
12. modifying areas in front of entrance and exit doorways; and
13. grading of ground to provide access to the residence.

The above list of expenditures is not exhaustive.

The first six items listed in this Ruling are taken almost verbatim from the Senate Report.

(e) In 1996, Congress expressly provided that the costs of long-term care for the "chronically ill," including the cost of "maintenance or personal care services," if provided by a "licensed health care practitioner," are treated as medical expenses under § 213, as are premiums paid for insurance for such care, subject to certain dollar limits. See §§ 213(d)(1)(C), 213(d)(10), 7702B(c).

3. Policy

It seems reasonable to suppose that a significant portion of total medical deductions is for expenses that tend to be incurred only by the affluent—for example, for private-duty nurses, private rooms at hospitals, outpatient psychiatric care, orthodonture, and a variety of other benefits that tend not to be covered by insurance and that middle- and low-income people tend to find they can do without. Should the line be drawn to deny deductions for such outlays?

Consider the strength of each of the following policy rationales for deductions for extraordinary medical expenses and the implications of each for the scope of the deduction:

(i)   Amounts spent for extraordinary medical expenses do not provide consumption in the ordinary sense and therefore are simply not part of income.

(ii) Individuals who pay their own medical costs relieve the government of an expense that it would otherwise be obliged to bear.

(iii) The deduction is a proper encouragement to people to take good care of themselves; it is a useful subsidy for medical care.

(iv) In many instances, an injury or illness stems from work (e.g., a professional athlete's bad knee) or interferes with the ability to work (e.g., a truck driver's bad back), so the cost of medical care should be regarded as a cost of producing income.

Finally reconsider the *Blackman* case, supra page 366. Suppose Blackman had been badly burned in the fire he had set and had incurred substantial medical expenses. Would he be allowed to deduct those expenses? Should he be allowed to deduct those expenses? If a deduction is denied to Blackman, on the rationale that his expenses were caused by his own misfeasance, what about expenses arising out of alcohol or other drug dependencies? Smoking?

D. CHARITABLE CONTRIBUTIONS

1. Overview

The Code allows individuals and corporations to claim as itemized deductions any "charitable contribution . . . payment of which is made within the taxable year." § 170(a)(1). The term "charitable contribution" is defined to be a "contribution or gift to or for the use of" certain enumerated eligible donees. § 170(c). These include the United States and any political subdivisions of it or any of the states, organizations that are "organized and operated exclusively for religious, charitable, scientific, literary, or educational purposes," and certain other enumerated donees, including veterans organizations, fraternal-lodge organizations (but only if the gift is to be used for charitable purposes), and cemetery companies. In general, these organizations must operate on a nonprofit basis, and none of their profits can "inure to the benefit of any private shareholder or individual."

Section 170 limits allowable deductions for individuals for gifts made to churches, educational organizations, medical institutions, and certain publicly supported organizations, as listed in § 170(b)(1), to 50 percent of the taxpayer's "contribution base" (which is generally adjusted gross income). In the case of contributions to other organizations, principally "private foundations," and gifts "for the use of" an organization, the allowable deductions for individuals are limited to a maximum 30 percent of adjusted gross income.[7] § 170(b)(1)(B). Special rules apply to the contributions of capital gain property. Corporations may deduct charitable contributions only to the extent such contributions do not exceed 10 percent of taxable income. § 170(b)(2). If the taxpayer makes gifts that exceed any of these limits, the excess may be carried over to the succeeding five years. See §§ 170(d), 170(b)(1)(B), 170(b)(1)(C)(ii), and 170(b)(1)(D)(ii).

Section 170(c) specifies the organizations that qualify as recipients of deductible contributions. However, the organization's own immunity from taxation on receipts from donors, from its investments, and from its activities is determined not by § 170(c), but by §§ 501 et seq. For some organizations, the same characteristics that permit donors to deduct contributions also serve to confer tax exemption on the organization. Thus, the charitable, religious, and educational organizations that are described by § 170(c)(2) also enjoy tax exemption by virtue of identical language in § 501(c)(3). However, the overlap is far from complete. Many organizations that are tax exempt under § 501 (e.g., pension plans, social welfare groups, foreign charities, labor unions, social clubs, chambers of commerce, etc.) do not meet the requirements of § 170(c); conversely, but much less frequently, organizations (e.g., posts of war veterans and fraternal lodges) may be qualified donees under § 170(c) without meeting all of the standards for tax exemption prescribed by § 501. Section 527 provides separate and detailed rules for the tax treatment of political

---

7. Such deductions are also reduced to the extent that deductions to organizations listed in § 170(b)(1) exceed 20 percent of adjusted gross income.

organizations, making them taxable on their income, but excluding from their income such items as political contributions, income from fund-raising events, etc.

If an organization engages in lobbying, it may lose its status as an organization to which tax-deductible contributions may be made, though it may remain exempt from taxation. See §§ 170(c)(2)(D), 501(c)(3), 501(h). Some organizations have coped with the prohibition on lobbying by setting up separate but related organizations that limit their activities to such matters as nonpartisan education or litigation.

2. Contributions of Capital Gain Property

When a taxpayer makes a gift of property whose sale would produce long-term capital gain, the amount allowed as a deduction is generally the full fair market value of the property. If, for example, a person owns shares of common stock with a fair market value of $10,000 and a basis of $1,000, has held them for the requisite holding period (generally more than one year) and gives the shares to a charitable organization, no tax is paid on the gain and the deduction is for the full $10,000 value. Obviously, then, the gift of the property itself is more advantageous than the sale of the property followed by a gift of the proceeds. In the case of a gift of property whose sale would produce short-term capital gain or ordinary income, the deduction is limited to the taxpayer's basis in the property; there is also a limit on the deductibility of the value of tangible personal property (e.g., a painting, except when given to certain kinds of organizations). § 170(e)(1).

Deductions for gifts of property the sale of which would have generated long-term capital gain are limited to 30 percent of adjusted gross income, or 20 percent if the gift is to a private foundation or for the use of the charitable organization.

3. Policy

Review the list of possible objectives of the deduction for medical expenses, supra page 379. Which of these objectives — or some other objective — best supports the deduction for charitable contributions? In answering this question, it may be helpful to refer to four kinds of contributions.

1. A contribution to a charity such as the United Fund, the Red Cross, the American Cancer Society, or the Boy or Girl Scouts
2. An ordinary contribution to a church or other religious organization
3. A contribution to a church by a person who feels bound by a religiously based obligation to tithe, where the person genuinely believes that 10 percent of one's income belongs not to oneself but to God
4. A contribution to New York's Metropolitan Opera by a wealthy opera lover.

Suppose we take as given the desirability of government support for the type of organizations listed in § 170(c). Is a tax deduction for charitable gifts a cost effective way to support those organizations? The charitable deduction reduces tax revenues by billions of dollars a year. Does the deduction stimulate charitable giving? Or is the deduction just a (deserved?) windfall to those who would give (and give the same amount) anyway? One way to answer these questions is to look at how charitable giving changes as tax rates change. A decline in the marginal tax rates of donors reduces the value of the tax deduction. If the tax deduction is an important factor in charitable giving, then donations should decline with falling marginal rates. Conversely, donations should rise as marginal rates rise, as the deduction becomes more valuable. Economists who have studied the issue have generally concluded that the "dollar efficiency" of the deduction is quite high. Deductions stimulate donations, and most studies find the dollar gain to the supported organizations equals and in some cases exceeds the dollar loss to the fisc. See Auten, Cilke, & Randolph, The Effects of Tax Reform on Charitable Contributions, XLV National Tax Journal 266 (1993).

Still, even if the evidence shows that charitable giving is in fact responsive to changes in marginal tax rates, this alone may not be enough to justify the full cost of the current deduction. One way of reducing that cost, while maintaining the incentive for charitable giving, would be to introduce a floor similar to the provisions we have already examined in connection with the casualty loss and medical expense deductions. For example, Congress could decide to make charitable contributions deductible only to the extent that they exceed, say, 3 percent of the taxpayer's adjusted gross income. Because it is a floor, such a change would not affect incentives to give at the margin, yet it would reduce the overall cost of the deduction. For example, assume that Olivia has adjusted gross income of $100,000 and is subject to a marginal tax rate of 25 percent. Assume further that she typically makes $10,000 of donations each year. Under the new law, Olivia would be allowed a deduction of only $7,000 instead of $10,000, the $3,000 difference having been disallowed by the 3 percent floor. In effect, Olivia would face a sliding scale subsidy rate for charitable giving, with a 0 percent subsidy rate for donations up to 3 percent of her AGI, and a subsidy rate equal to her marginal tax rate for donations above that amount. This precise change may or may not strike the right balance between maximizing the incentive for charitable giving at the lowest possible revenue cost, but the example should get you thinking about different alternatives for accomplishing that result.

COMPARATIVE FOCUS: Canada's Charitable Contribution Credit

In 1988, Canada converted its longstanding deduction for charitable contributions to a credit. Under pre-1988 Canadian law, individuals were allowed to claim a deduction for charitable contributions as they are in the United States. The 1988 law eliminated the deduction and enacted in its place a "two tier credit" under which taxpayers would be allowed a credit equal to 17 percent for the first $250 in charitable donations and 29 percent for all donations in excess of $250. Because these initial credit percentages were keyed to statutory tax rates in place at the time, the change had little effect on aggregate charitable giving. Note, however, that the credit device allows policymakers substantially greater flexibility in crafting a subsidy. In effect, a credit allows the government subsidy for charitable contributions to be "unhitched" from the marginal rate structure. Subsidy rates can then be modified depending upon any number of factors, including, for example, the amount of the taxpayer's total donations or the nature of the donee institutions.

4. Gifts with Private Objectives or Benefits

One of the most important legal issues surrounding the deduction for charitable contributions concerns situations where the donor receives something in return for her gift. In many cases, getting something in return has clear and obvious effects. For example, assume that Ava gives $100 to PBS and gets a PBS tote bag, with a value of $20, in exchange for her donation. It is clear that Ava's deduction is $80, not $100. It is as though she purchased a tote bag for $20 and made a donation of $80. In other cases, however, a charitable donation may provide the donor with more indirect benefits. If these benefits are significant, they may even call into question the characterization of the transfer as a charitable gift. The case below offers a good example.

OTTAWA SILICA CO. v. UNITED STATES
699 F.2d 1124 (Fed. Cir. 1983)

[The taxpayer, Ottawa, was in the business of mining, processing, and marketing silica, also known as quartzite. Beginning in 1956 the taxpayer acquired various ranch properties in Oceanside, California, a town located on the ocean, north of San Diego, with a major U.S. Marine Corps base, Camp Pendleton, on its northern border. Initially Ottawa acquired properties for their quartzite deposits; those deposits were found only on a portion of the land, and the rest was of relatively little interest to Ottawa. Before many years had passed, however, it became apparent that the land would ultimately be valuable for residential or commercial development. Silica mining is a dirty process that cannot be carried on close to residential areas, so Ottawa was in no hurry with the development, but in 1965 it hired William L. Pereira & Associates to produce a plan for the use of the properties that Ottawa had acquired. On the recommendation of Pereira, Ottawa bought two additional ranches (the Jones and Talone ranches) for the purpose of permitting it to maximize its land development opportunities; these ranches contained no quartzite deposits.

In the mid-1960s it became apparent that a new high school would be needed for the school district that included Oceanside and its neighbor to the south, Carlsbad. The Oceanside-Carlsbad Union High School District (OCUHSD), after a survey of possible sites, asked Ottawa whether it would be willing to donate to it about fifty acres on a portion of its property known as the Freeman Ranch. It was plain that if the OCUHSD did build the high school on the taxpayer's site, it would be required to build access roads that would be of benefit to Ottawa. In 1970, after long negotiations, Ottawa contributed the fifty-acre site, plus twenty acres for right-of-way for two access roads, to OCUHSD, and claimed a deduction of $415,000 for the value of the property contributed. It was conceded that OCUHSD was a political subdivision of the State of California within the meaning of § 170(c)(1). The government argued that no deduction was allowable because Ottawa had received a substantial benefit from the transfer of the property. The court of appeals agreed, affirming per curiam the Claims Court decision on the basis of the opinion of Judge Colaianni. Portions of that opinion follow.]

The case law dealing with this aspect of a § 170 deduction makes clear that a contribution made to a charity is not made for exclusively public purposes if the donor receives, or anticipates receiving a substantial benefit in return. . . .

In Singer [Co. v. United States, 196 Ct. Cl. 90, 449 F.2d 413 (1972)], this court considered whether discount sales of sewing machines to schools and other charities entitled Singer to a charitable deduction. The court found that Singer, which at the time of the sales was in the business of selling sewing machines, had made the discount sales to the schools for the predominant purpose of encouraging the students to use and, in the future, to purchase its sewing machines, thereby increasing Singer's future sales. This purpose colored the discount sales, making them business transactions rather than charitable contributions. Accordingly, the court disallowed the deduction for the sales to the schools. The court allowed deductions for the discount sales made to other charities, however, because Singer had no expectation of increasing its sales by making the contributions and benefited only incidentally from them.

The *Singer* court noted that the receipt of benefits by the donor need not always preclude a charitable contribution. The court stated its reasoning as follows:

> [I]f the benefits received, or expected to be received, [by the donor] are substantial, and meaning by that, benefits greater than those that inure to the general public from transfers for charitable purposes (which benefits are merely *incidental* to the transfer), then in such case we feel that the transferor has received, or expects to receive, a quid pro quo sufficient to remove the transfer from the realm of deductibility under section 170.

Singer Co. v. United States, 196 Ct. Cl. at 106, 449 F.2d 423. The parties to the present case disagree as to the meaning of the above quotation. The plain language clearly indicates that a "substantial benefit" received in return for a contribution constitutes a quid pro quo, which precludes a deduction. The court defined a substantial benefit as one that is "greater than those that inure to the general public from transfers for charitable purposes." Id. at 106, 449 F.2d at 423. Those benefits that inure to the general public from charitable contributions are incidental to the contribution, and the donor, as a member of the general public, may receive them. It is only when the donor receives or expects to receive additional substantial benefits that courts are likely to conclude that a quid pro quo for the transfer exists and that the donor is therefore not entitled to a charitable deduction. . . .

Plaintiff argues that it received no benefits, except incidental ones as defined by *Singer*, in return for its contribution of the site, and it is therefore entitled to a § 170 deduction for the transfer of its land to the school district. After having considered the testimony and the evidence adduced at trial, I conclude that the benefits to be derived by plaintiff from the transfer were substantial enough to provide plaintiff with a quid pro quo for the transfer and thus effectively destroyed the charitable nature of the transfer.

To begin, although plaintiff is correct in arguing that it was not the moving party in this conveyance, and that the school district sought plaintiff out for a donation of a high school site, that alone fails to justify a § 170 deduction. The record clearly establishes that following the passage of a bonding referendum, which authorized the building of a new high school by the city of Oceanside in 1968, as many as nine sites had been evaluated. Because of the eastward growth of the city, Mr. LaFleur, the superintendent of the OCUHSD, felt that the ideal location for the new high school would be near El Camino Real [the road on the western boundary of plaintiff's property]. Following careful consideration, the city and school district decided that the best location for a high school would be on plaintiff's land. Thus, during the summer of 1968, John Steiger, the vice-mayor of Oceanside, and Mr. LaFleur approached Mr. Thomas Jones to see if plaintiff would consider making a site on the Freeman Ranch available for the new high school.

On September 20, 1968, Mr. LaFleur wrote to plaintiff's president, Mr. Thornton, to ask if plaintiff would be willing to donate 50 acres of its land for a school site. The record also establishes, however, that plaintiff was more than willing to oblige Mr. LaFleur on the basis of its own self-interest. Indeed, the evidence shows that on that same September 20, Mr. Jones also wrote to Mr. Thornton to advise him of the discussions he had participated in regarding a high school site. In his letter Mr. Jones stated that he had met with John Steiger and Larry Bagley, Oceanside's planning director, and had learned that the school district's first choice for a high school site was on land owned by plaintiff. In a most revealing statement, Mr. Jones went on to say:

> I was pessimistic when talking to John and Larry, but this actually could trigger and hasten the development of the whole eastern end of [the] Freeman and Jones [ranches] at no cost to us. The increase in these property values should be substantial if this should go through. . . . In any event, nothing more is to be done on this until the school board writes to you and asks to open negotiations. On the other hand, I recommend that [Ottawa] actively pursue this, since a high school in this location would probably trigger the early development of El Camino Real from the May Co. to Mission Road.

The exact meaning of Mr. Jones' statement will be better understood following a full development of the prevailing circumstances at the time of the transfer. It should be recalled that plaintiff had amassed some 2,300 acres in eastern Oceanside, but only 481 acres had silica reserves. . . . While a portion of the western boundary of the Freeman Ranch ran along El Camino Real, its northernmost boundary was about a mile from all of the major roads. The unavailability of major roads to service the northernmost reaches of the Cubbison and Freeman Ranches ultimately led Pereira to recommend that plaintiff purchase the Jones and Talone Ranches. . . .

The only thing frustrating the implementation of the plan was the inaccessibility of the Jones Ranch from Mission Boulevard. . . .

The construction of a high school on the Freeman Ranch, however, alleviated this problem for plaintiff. State and local officials required that the high school be serviced by two separate access roads. After some discussions, the school district and plaintiff agreed on the general direction of Mesa Drive which would provide the school with access to El Camino Real, and the surrounding topography dictated that the second road run north to Mission Boulevard through the Jones Ranch and parcels of property owned by Mr. Ivey and the Mission of San Luis Rey. This road, Rancho Del Oro Drive, provided plaintiff with access to the Jones Ranch directly from Mission Boulevard. Plaintiff could not have obtained such access to Mission Boulevard on its own unless both Mr. Ivey and the fathers at the mission had agreed to convey part of their land or easements to plaintiff. There is no evidence suggesting that either party was interested in doing so. Mr. Ivey, in fact, had resisted plaintiff's overtures about selling or developing his land. . . .

It is thus quite apparent that plaintiff conveyed the land to the school fully expecting that as a consequence of the construction of public access roads through its property it would receive substantial benefits in return. In fact, this is precisely what happened. Plaintiff obtained direct access to the Jones Ranch via Rancho Del Oro Drive and ultimately sold the ranch to a developer. Plaintiff also sold two parcels of the Freeman Ranch, lying north of Mesa Drive, to other developers. . . . It is my opinion that the plaintiff knew that the construction of a school and the attendant roads on its property would substantially benefit the surrounding land, that it made the conveyance expecting its remaining property to increase in value, and that the expected receipt of these benefits at least partially prompted plaintiff to make the conveyance. Under *Singer*, this is more than adequate reason to deny plaintiff a charitable contribution for its conveyance.

NOTES AND QUESTIONS

1. *What's at stake in* Ottawa Silica Co.? Had the taxpayer won, it would have recognized a current deduction equal to the fair market value of the contributed property. Instead, the taxpayer received no current deduction and could only add the basis of the contributed property to its other land. See discussion of capital expenditures in Chapter 6, infra. The taxpayer would, in effect, be able to deduct that basis when and if it sold its other land. The effect of the government victory was twofold. First, the taxpayer was forced to defer any tax benefit for what might turn out to be many years. Second, the eventual

tax benefit would be limited to the basis of the contributed property, rather than the fair market value of the contributed property.

(a) *Business versus nonbusiness benefits.* The taxpayer in *Ottawa Silica* received a business-related benefit from its transfer of property to a charity. In the business-related setting, the rule applied by the court was that no charitable deduction was allowable if the business benefit was substantial. An alternative might have been to allow a charitable deduction for the value of the property transferred to the charity reduced by the value of the benefit received by the taxpayer. This alternative would more accurately reflect the amount of the charitable gift and is in fact the approach used for "quid pro quo" contributions that are not business related — as described immediately below.

(b) In DuVal v. Commissioner, T.C. Memo. 1994-603, DuVal was a real estate developer who needed rezoning for a parcel of property he intended to develop. The county authorities from whom DuVal sought the rezoning had in the past "solicited" developers to dedicate land for public use. There was some doubt as to the legal authority to require such dedications, but the county "assumed that it did have such authority." The county's representatives asked DuVal to contribute a portion of his property as a site for a library. DuVal did so. He claimed that his motivation was a desire "to give something back" to the community and his commitment to education. The court found that the gift of the library site was not a "condition precedent to the county's approval of Mr. DuVal's rezoning request." In holding that DuVal was entitled to a charitable deduction for the gift of the land for the library site, the court stated:

> To resolve the question of whether a transfer is a gift for purposes of § 170(c), we must determine the taxpayer's primary or dominant intent or purpose in making the transfer. . . . To resolve this question, we do not examine only the taxpayer's statements of his or her subjective intent. Rather, we must make an objective inquiry into the nature of the transaction to determine whether what is labeled a gift is in substance a gift.

How does this test differ from the test applied in *Ottawa Silica*? To what extent, if at all, is the outcome in a case like *DuVal* or *Ottawa Silica* likely to change depending on which test is applied?

5. More on Private Benefits

(a) *Quid pro quo contributions.* As noted above, it has long been the rule that the amount of any non-business-related deduction for a charitable contribution is limited to the excess of the payment to the charity over the value of any benefit (other than trivial ones) received by the donor. In determining the amount of the reduction, it is the value to the donor that counts. The value to the donor is assumed to be the fair market value of whatever is received by the donor — that is, what the item or service would cost the donor if purchased. The cost to the donee organization is irrelevant. See Rev. Rul. 67-246, 1967-2 C.B. 104; Rev. Proc. 90-12, 1990-1 C.B. 471; Rev. Proc. 92-49, 1992-1 C.B. 987.

The rule is entirely reasonable. Suppose you attend a charity's fund-raising auction and make a winning bid of $500 for the use of a condominium at the beach for a weekend. Suppose the use of the condominium was contributed to the charity, so the cost to the charity is nothing, but the condominium would normally rent for $300 for the relevant period. Certainly it is not fair to say that you have made a gift of $500, even though the charity benefits by that amount. You have in part made a gift and in part paid for a weekend at the beach. To be sure, in some circumstances you might plausibly claim that the value to you of the use of the condominium was not its market value of $300. But if you in fact use it, could you plausibly claim that it was worth nothing? And could you plausibly argue that the IRS should attempt to administer a rule based on your subjective valuation?

As one can easily imagine, charitable organizations and their supporters do not much like the rule requiring a quid pro quo reduction in the amount of deductions. For years, the level of compliance was low; the amount of cheating (or innocent disregard) was substantial. Finally, in 1993, Congress enacted § 6115, which requires that for any quid pro quo contribution over $75 the charity must provide the donor with a written statement that the entire amount is not deductible and must provide a "good faith estimate of the value of [the] goods or services" received. The $75 threshold for a written statement does not change the rule for contributions of lesser amounts. The deduction is still limited to the excess over the value of any goods or services received, but the charity has no statutory obligation to provide an estimate of that value and the level of compliance with the law seems to be low.

The quid pro quo rationale has never been applied to psychic returns. If an individual contributes money to a university in return for the university's agreement to name a building after him or her, it is plain that the contribution is deductible, despite the obvious psychic benefit to the taxpayer.

(b) *The complicitous role of some charitable organizations.* The problem of disentangling individual benefit from charitable donation is exacerbated by the tendency of many § 170(c) organizations to adopt fee structures that blur the distinction between donations and the costs of services. As a result, individuals deduct amounts that might be more accurately described as nondeductible fees for services. Consider, for example, the fee structure at one West Coast opera company. The nominal cost of a "Series A" box seat is $1,585. However, such seats are available only after a major donation. The amount of donation that will secure such a box is said to be $20,000—down from $100,000 in the 1980s. In addition, holders of Series A boxes are requested to make a "minimum contribution" of $4,500 a year. It is virtually certain that holders of Series A seats deduct the major donation necessary to get the seats and the annual minimum contribution associated with the seats. Suppose, instead, that the opera company charged (continued to charge?) what the market would bear for the seats but did not tie the seats to donations or term any of the amount paid as a donation. It would then be clear that no portion of the ticket price could be deducted. The after-tax cost of the seats would rise. This would disadvantage ticket holders. It would also make it harder to sell seats and, in that sense, disadvantage the opera company. (Indeed, the most likely result is that the opera company would have to reduce the price of the seats.)

6. Overvaluation of Contributed Property

One of the major problems with charitable contributions has been the overvaluation of works of art. A good illustration is provided by the case of Isbell v. Commissioner, 44 T.C.M. 1143 (1982). The taxpayer contributed to a public television station, for its annual fund-raising auction, a Han dynasty jar with a crack on one side and a hole in its bottom (made for the purpose of converting the jar to a lamp). Isbell had received the jar as a gift. Initially he claimed a deduction of $15,000 and later, in an amended return, raised this to $50,000, based on an appraisal of all his valuables, done at his request two years before the gift, by a firm that appraised interior furnishings, that had no experience in appraising Asian art objects, whose representatives were not called as witnesses, and whose appraisal was "incorrect in several respects." The jar sold at the auction for $360. A "very impressive" expert who testified for the government placed the value at $800, which the court accepted as the fair market value. The amount of the deduction was further reduced under § 170(e)(1)(B). It does not appear that the Service sought to impose fraud or negligence penalties. In response to the abuse and the enforcement difficulties suggested by this case, the Tax Reform Act of 1984 imposed a requirement that the Treasury issue regulations for substantiation of the amount of the deduction in the case of gifts of property with a value greater than $5,000 (or $10,000 in the case of nonpublicly traded stock). See § 155 of the act, which was not made part of the Code. Substantiation is not required, however, for publicly traded stock. To meet the substantiation requirement, the donor must obtain a qualified appraisal and attach to his or her return a signed appraisal summary. The appraisal must come from an independent person, not, for example, the seller of the property or any person regularly employed by the seller. If the donee sells the property within two years of receipt, it must report the selling price and identify the donor.

In response to more garden variety forms of noncompliance, Congress added further substantiation provisions as part of the Revenue Reconciliation Act of 1993. Under those provisions, taxpayers who claim a deduction for any form of contribution in excess of $250 must be able to substantiate the deduction with a written acknowledgment of the donation by the donee organization. The acknowledgment must state the fair market value, if any, of any services or goods provided by the organization in return for the donation. § 170(f)(8). A cancelled check is not sufficient. As an alternative to providing a written acknowledgment to the donor for each gift, the donee organization is permitted to file with the IRS a form containing the information that otherwise is required to be supplied to the donor. § 170(f)(8)(D). The reporting requirement of § 170(f)(8) does not supplant the rules described in the preceding paragraph.

In 2004, Congress added § 170(f)(11), which provides that for contributions of property that is not "readily valued" and for which the deduction is more than $500, the taxpayer must include with the return "a description of such property and such other information as the Secretary [of the Treasury] may require." If the claimed deduction is for more than $5,000, the taxpayer must attach to return a "qualified appraisal." Congress also added special rules for contributions of motor vehicles, boats, and airplanes. See § 170(f)(12), which requires that the return include an acknowledgment of the gift from the donee and, more important, where the vehicle, boat, or airplane, is sold; provided that the deduction is limited to the proceeds of the sale.

7.   The Special Case of Collegiate Athletics

In Rev. Rul. 86-63, 86-1 C.B. 88, the IRS ruled on the politically sensitive issue of deductions for contributions to the athletic scholarship programs of colleges and universities, where the contributor becomes entitled to buy tickets for seating at athletic events. The holding, relying on Rev. Rul. 67-246, supra, was that where reasonably comparable seating would not have been available in the absence of the contribution, there is a presumption that the contribution was the price of a substantial benefit to the taxpayer and no deduction is allowable unless the taxpayer can establish that the amount of the contribution exceeded the value of the benefit received. After considerable whining by universities and the supporters of their athletic (and other) programs, Congress, in 1988, adopted § 170(l). This provision allows a deduction for 80 percent of any amount paid to an "institution of higher learning" if the deduction would be allowable "but for the fact that the taxpayer receives (directly or indirectly) as a result of paying such amount the right to purchase tickets for seating at an athletic event in an athletic stadium of such institution." Why are athletic events treated differently from, say, musical or dramatic performances?

8.   Religious Benefits and Services

Rev. Rul. 70-47, 1970-1 C.B. 49, states that "pew rents, building fund assessments, and periodic dues paid to a church . . . are all methods of making contributions to the church, and such payments are deductible as charitable contributions within the limitations set out in section 170 of the Code." Similarly, the IRS has never challenged the deductibility of specified amounts required to be paid for attendance at Jewish High Holy Day services. (The principle underlying these rules is now reflected in § 170(f)(8)(B), relating to the $250 substantiation rule described above.) On the other hand, fees for attendance at parochial schools providing mostly secular education are not deductible.

In Hernandez v. Commissioner, 490 U.S. 680 (1989), the Supreme Court upheld the Commissioner's disallowance of a deduction for amounts paid by members of the Church of Scientology for individual "training" (learning of doctrine) and "auditing" (development of "spiritual awareness"). The amounts to be paid were determined by a schedule of prices based on the length of the sessions and their level of "sophistication." A central tenet of the Church was the "doctrine of exchange," under which a person receiving something must pay something in return. Free auditing or training sessions were "categorically barred." For the purposes of the case, the IRS stipulated that the Church was a bona fide religious organization, contributions to which were deductible. The IRS's argument was that the fees at issue were not "contributions." The majority concluded, "As the Tax Court found, these payments were part of a quintessential quid pro quo exchange: in return for their money, petitioners received an identifiable benefit, namely, auditing and training sessions." In reaching this result, the majority rejected the taxpayers' argument that the receipt of consideration in the form of religious or spiritual services is not inconsistent with the notion of gift or contribution. Justice O'Connor, in a dissent joined by Justice Scalia, argued that the disallowance of the deductions was inconsistent with the IRS's "70-year practice of allowing [deduction of] fixed payments indistinguishable from those made by petitioners." The majority attempted to avoid this argument by stating that the record was unclear on the precise facts in the allegedly similar situations — "for example, whether payments for other faiths' services are truly obligatory or whether any or all of these services are generally provided whether or not the encouraged 'mandatory' payment is made."

The *Hernandez* decision seemed to resolve the question of whether payments by members of the Church of Scientology for training and auditing could be deducted as charitable contributions. Yet despite the Supreme Court's ruling, the controversy has continued. The taxpayers in the *Hernandez* case were individuals who had made payments to the Church of Scientology in exchange for training and auditing courses, but the Church itself also had several open tax controversies with the IRS. In 1997, the Wall Street Journal reported that the IRS had entered into a settlement agreement with the Church of Scientology regarding these disputes. Among other things, the Journal reported that the agreement "lets Scientologists deduct on their individual tax returns 'auditing' fees as donations, [superseding] the IRS's earlier rule denying such deductions — a position that was backed by the Supreme Court." See Elizabeth MacDonald, Scientologists and IRS Settled for $12.5 Million, Wall Street Journal (December 30, 1997). Perhaps not surprisingly, these reports have prompted allegations of unfairness and inconsistency in the administration of the tax law since members of other religions are presumably subject to the Supreme Court's decision in *Hernandez*.

The ongoing drama over the *Hernandez* issue has centered on the case of Michael and Marla Sklar, an Orthodox Jewish couple who claimed deductions on their 1994 tax return for a portion of the tuition expenses for sending their children to a religious private school. The Sklars based their deduction on the assumption that 55 percent of the school day was allocated to religious education. Citing the IRS's closing agreement with the Church of Scientology, the Sklars argued that not allowing them a similar deduction would violate the Establishment Clause by conferring preferential treatment on members of one religion. While expressing some sympathy for this view, the Ninth Circuit nonetheless chose not to reach the Establishment Clause claim, instead denying the deduction on the grounds that the Sklars had failed to show that the total tuition paid was greater than the value of the secular education their children received, Sklar v. Commissioner, 282 F.3d 310 (9th Cir. 2002). Undeterred by the outcome, the Sklars have continued pressing the issue, challenging the government's disallowance of the same deduction on their

1995 tax return. Once again, the Tax Court denied the deductions, Sklar v. Commissioner, 125 T.C. No. 14 (2005), and once again the Sklars have appealed the Tax Court's decision to the Ninth Circuit. In February 2008, the Ninth Circuit heard oral arguments, but as of December 2008 no decision had been issued.

9. Voluntariness

In Lombardo v. Commissioner, 50 T.C.M. 1374 (1985), the taxpayer pleaded guilty to a state-law charge of felonious sale and delivery of marijuana. Incident to the taxpayer's arrest, the police seized fourteen tons of marijuana, $148,000 in cash, the land (with improvements) on which he was operating, and various other property. The taxpayer was placed on probation and was able to stay out of prison under an order that required him to pay $145,000 to the county school fund. He made the required payments, over two years, and claimed charitable deductions. His tax returns for the years at issue (during which he was on probation) showed income from "Business or Profession," without elaboration; in response to a question on the return about the nature of his business, he relied on the Fifth Amendment. The Tax Court upheld the Commissioner's denial of the charitable deduction. It observed that the taxpayer made the payments in order to avoid going to prison and stated, "It would strain our credulity to the breaking point to conclude that petitioner's contributions proceeded even remotely from a charitable impulse." The court viewed as irrelevant the possibility that the state court might have exceeded its authority by requiring a payment of $145,000 for violation of a statute with a maximum fine of $5,000.

10.   What Is Charitable?

BOB JONES UNIVERSITY v. UNITED STATES
461 U.S. 574 (1983)

Chief Justice BURGER delivered the opinion of the Court.

We granted certiorari to decide whether petitioners, nonprofit private schools that prescribe and enforce racially discriminatory admissions standards on the basis of religious doctrine, qualify as tax-exempt organizations under § 501(c)(3) of the Internal Revenue Code of 1954.

I . . .

Bob Jones University is a nonprofit corporation located in Greenville, South Carolina. Its purpose is "to conduct an institution of learning . . . , giving special emphasis to the Christian religion and the ethics revealed in the Holy Scriptures." . . . The corporation operates a school with an enrollment of approximately 5,000 students, from kindergarten through college and graduate school. Bob Jones University is not affiliated with any religious denomination, but is dedicated to the teaching and propagation of its fundamentalist Christian religious beliefs. It is both a religious and educational institution. Its teachers are required to be devout Christians, and all courses at the University are taught according to the Bible. Entering students are screened as to their religious beliefs, and their public and private conduct is strictly regulated by standards promulgated by University authorities.

The sponsors of the University genuinely believe that the Bible forbids interracial dating and marriage. To effectuate these views, Negroes were completely excluded until 1971. From 1971 to May 1975, the University accepted no applications from unmarried Negroes, but did accept applications from Negroes married within their race.

Following the decision of the United States Court of Appeals for the Fourth Circuit in McCrary v. Runyon, 515 F.2d 1082 (C.A. 4 1975), aff'd, 427 U.S. 160 (1976), prohibiting racial exclusion from private schools, the University revised its policy. Since May 29, 1975, the University has permitted unmarried Negroes to enroll; but a disciplinary rule prohibits interracial dating and marriage. That rule reads:

There is to be no interracial dating

1. Students who are partners in an interracial marriage will be expelled.

2. Students who are members of or affiliated with any group or organization which holds as one of its goals or advocates interracial marriage will be expelled.

3. Students who date outside their own race will be expelled.

4. Students who espouse, promote, or encourage others to violate the University's dating rules and regulations will be expelled.

The University continues to deny admission to applicants engaged in an interracial marriage or known to advocate interracial marriage or dating.

Until 1970, the IRS extended tax-exempt status to Bob Jones University under § 501(c)(3). By the letter of November 30, 1970, that followed the injunction issued in Green v. Kennedy [309 F. Supp. 1127 (D.D.C.), app. dismissed sub nom. Cannon v. Green, 398 U.S. 956 (1970)] the IRS formally notified the University of the change in IRS policy, and announced its intention to challenge the tax-exempt status of private schools practicing racial discrimination in their admissions policies.[8]

The United States District Court for the District of South Carolina held that revocation of the University's tax-exempt status exceeded the delegated powers of the IRS, was improper under the IRS rulings and procedures, and

---

8. Revenue Ruling 71-447, 1971-2 Cum. Bull. 230, defined "racially nondiscriminatory policy as to students" as meaning that:

[T]he school admits the students of any race to all the rights, privileges, programs, and activities generally accorded or made available to students at that school and that the school does not discriminate on the basis of race in administration of its educational policies, admissions policies, scholarship and loan programs, and athletic and other school-administered programs.

violated the University's rights under the Religion Clauses of the First Amendment. 468 F. Supp. 890, 907 (D.S.C. 1978). . . .

The Court of Appeals for the Fourth Circuit, in a divided opinion, reversed, 639 F.2d 147 (C.A. 4 1980). Citing Green v. Connally, supra, with approval, the Court of Appeals concluded that § 501(c)(3) must be read against the background of charitable trust law. To be eligible for an exemption under that section, an institution must be "charitable" in the common law sense, and therefore must not be contrary to public policy. In the court's view, Bob Jones University did not meet this requirement, since its "racial policies violated the clearly defined public policy, rooted in our Constitution, condemning racial discrimination and, more specifically, the government policy against subsidizing racial discrimination in education, public or private." Id., at 151. The court held that the IRS acted within its statutory authority in revoking the University's tax-exempt status. Finally, the Court of Appeals rejected petitioner's arguments that the revocation of the tax exemption violated the Free Exercise and Establishment Clauses of the First Amendment. The case was remanded to the District Court with instructions to dismiss the University's claim for a refund and to reinstate the Government's counter-claim. . . .

Goldsboro Christian Schools is a nonprofit corporation located in Goldsboro, North Carolina. Like Bob Jones University, it was established "to conduct an institution of learning . . . , giving special emphasis to the Christian religion and the ethics revealed in the Holy scriptures." . . . The school offers classes from kindergarten through high school, and since at least 1969 has satisfied the State of North Carolina's requirements for secular education in private schools. The school requires its high school students to take Bible-related courses, and begins each class with prayer.

Since its incorporation in 1963, Goldsboro Christian Schools has maintained a racially discriminatory admissions policy based upon its interpretation of the Bible.[9] Goldsboro has for the most part accepted only Caucasians. On occasion, however, the school has accepted children from racially mixed marriages in which one of the parents is Caucasian.

[A district court decision in favor of the government's denial of exemption was affirmed by the Fourth Circuit on the authority of Bob Jones University.][10]

---

9. According to the interpretation espoused by Goldsboro, race is determined by descendance from one of Noah's three sons — Ham, Shem and Japheth. Based on this interpretation, Orientals and Negroes are Hamitic, Hebrews are Shemitic, and Caucasians are Japhethitic. Cultural or biological mixing of the races is regarded as a violation of God's command. . . .

10. After the Court granted certiorari, the Government filed a motion to dismiss, informing the Court that the Department of Treasury intended to revoke Revenue Ruling 71-447 and other pertinent rulings and to recognize § 501(c)(3) exemptions for petitioners. The Government suggested that these actions were therefore moot. Before this Court ruled on that motion, however, the United States Court of Appeals for the District of Columbia Circuit enjoined the Government from granting § 501(c)(3) tax-exempt status to any school that discriminates on the basis of race. Wright v. Regan, No. 80-1124 (C.A.D.C. Feb. 18, 1982) (per curiam order). Thereafter, the Government informed the Court that it would not revoke the revenue rulings and withdrew its request that the actions be dismissed as moot. The Government continues to assert that the IRS lacked authority to promulgate Revenue Ruling 71-447, and does not defend that aspect of the rulings below. [The Court appointed special counsel to argue in support of the Court of Appeals decision.]

II

In Revenue Ruling 71-447, the IRS formalized the policy first announced in 1970, that § 170 and § 501(c)(3) embrace the common law "charity" concept. Under that view, to qualify for a tax exemption pursuant to § 501(c)(3), an institution must show, first, that it falls within one of the eight categories expressly set forth in that section, and second, that its activity is not contrary to settled public policy.

Section 501(c)(3) provides that "[c]orporations . . . organized and operated exclusively for religious, charitable . . . or educational purposes" are entitled to tax exemption. Petitioners argue that the plain language of the statute guarantees them tax-exempt status. They emphasize the absence of any language in the statute expressly requiring all exempt organizations to be "charitable" in the common law sense, and they contend that the disjunctive "or" separating the categories in § 501(c)(3) precludes such a reading. Instead, they argue that if an institution falls within one or more of the specified categories it is automatically entitled to exemption, without regard to whether it also qualifies as "charitable." The Court of Appeals rejected that contention and concluded that petitioners' interpretation of the statute "tears section 501(c)(3) from its roots." United States v. Bob Jones University, supra, 639 F.2d, at 151. . . .

Section 501(c)(3) . . . must be analyzed and construed within the framework of the Internal Revenue Code and against the background of the Congressional purposes. Such an examination reveals unmistakable evidence that, underlying all relevant parts of the Code, is the intent that entitlement to tax exemption depends on meeting certain common law standards of charity — namely, that an institution seeking tax-exempt status must serve a public purpose and not be contrary to established public policy.

This "charitable" concept appears explicitly in § 170 of the Code. That section contains a list of organizations virtually identical to that contained in § 501(c)(3). It is apparent that Congress intended that list to have the same meaning in both sections. In § 170, Congress used the list of organizations in defining the term "charitable contributions." On its face, therefore, § 170 reveals that Congress' intention was to provide tax benefits to organizations serving charitable purposes. The form of § 170 simply makes plain what common sense and history tell us: in enacting both § 170 and § 501(c)(3), Congress sought to provide tax benefits to charitable organizations, to encourage the development of private institutions that serve a useful public purpose or supplement or take the place of public institutions of the same kind.

Tax exemptions for certain institutions thought beneficial to the social order of the country as a whole, or to a particular community, are deeply rooted in our history, as in that of England. The origins of such exemptions lie in the special privileges that have long been extended to charitable trusts.[11] . . .

---

11. The form and history of the charitable exemption and deduction sections of the various income tax acts reveal that Congress was guided by the common law of charitable trusts. See Simon, The Tax-Exempt Status of Racially Discriminatory Religious Schools, 36 Tax L. Rev. 477, 485-489 (1981) (hereinafter Simon).

A corollary to the public benefit principle is the requirement, long recognized in the law of trusts, that the purpose of a charitable trust may not be illegal or violate established public policy. . . .

When the Government grants exemptions or allows deductions all taxpayers are affected; the very fact of the exemption or deduction for the donor means that other taxpayers can be said to be indirect and vicarious "donors." Charitable exemptions are justified on the basis that the exempt entity confers a public benefit — a benefit which the society or the community may not itself choose or be able to provide, or which supplements and advances the work of public institutions already supported by tax revenues. History buttresses logic to make clear that, to warrant exemption under § 501(c)(3), an institution must fall within a category specified in that section and must demonstrably serve and be in harmony with the public interest.[12] The institution's purpose must not be so at odds with the common community conscience as to undermine any public benefit that might otherwise be conferred.

We are bound to approach these questions with full awareness that determinations of public benefit and public policy are sensitive matters with serious implications for the institutions affected; a declaration that a given institution is not "charitable" should be made only where there can be no doubt that the activity involved is contrary to a fundamental public policy. But there can no longer be any doubt that racial discrimination in education violates deeply and widely accepted views of elementary justice. Prior to 1954, public education in many places still was conducted under the pall of Plessy v. Ferguson, 163 U.S. 537 (1896); racial segregation in primary and secondary education prevailed in many parts of the country. See, e.g., Segregation and the Fourteenth Amendment in the States (B. Reams & P. Wilson, eds. 1975). This Court's decision in Brown v. Board of Education, 347 U.S. 483 (1954), signalled an end to that era. Over the past quarter of a century, every pronouncement of this Court and myriad Acts of Congress and Executive Orders attest a firm national policy to prohibit racial segregation and discrimination in public education.

An unbroken line of cases following Brown v. Board of Education establishes beyond doubt this Court's view that racial discrimination in education violates a most fundamental national public policy, as well as rights of individuals. . . . In Norwood v. Harrison, 413 U.S. 455, 468-469 (1973), we dealt with a nonpublic institution:

> [A] private school — even one that discriminates — fulfills an important educational function; *however, . . . [that] legitimate educational function cannot be isolated from discriminatory practices. . . . [D]iscriminatory treatment exerts a pervasive influence on the entire educational process.*

---

12. The Court's reading of § 501(c)(3) does not render meaningless Congress' action in specifying the eight categories of presumptively exempt organizations, as petitioners suggest. See Brief of Petitioner Goldsboro Christian Schools 18-24. To be entitled to tax-exempt status under § 501(c)(3), an organization must first fall within one of the categories specified by Congress, and in addition must serve a valid charitable purpose.

(Emphasis added.) See also Runyon v. McCrary, 427 U.S. 160 (1976); Griffin v. County School Board, 377 U.S. 218 (1964)....

Petitioners contend that, regardless of whether the IRS properly concluded that racially discriminatory private schools violate public policy, only Congress can alter the scope of § 170 and § 501(c)(3). Petitioners accordingly argue that the IRS overstepped its lawful bounds in issuing its 1970 and 1971 rulings.

Yet ever since the inception of the tax code, Congress has seen fit to vest in those administering the tax laws very broad authority to interpret those laws. In an area as complex as the tax system, the agency Congress vests with administrative responsibility must be able to exercise its authority to meet changing conditions and new problems....

The actions of Congress since 1970 leave no doubt that the IRS reached the correct conclusion in exercising its authority. It is, of course, not unknown for independent agencies or the Executive Branch to misconstrue the intent of a statute; Congress can and often does correct such misconceptions, if the courts have not done so. Yet for a dozen years Congress has been made aware — acutely aware — of the IRS rulings of 1970 and 1971. As we noted earlier, few issues have been the subject of more vigorous and widespread debate and discussion in and out of Congress than those related to racial segregation in education. Sincere adherents advocating contrary views have ventilated the subject for well over three decades. Failure of Congress to modify the IRS rulings of 1970 and 1971, of which Congress was, by its own studies and by public discourse, constantly reminded; and Congress' awareness of the denial of tax-exempt status for racially discriminatory schools when enacting other and related legislation make out an unusually strong case of legislative acquiescence in and ratification by implication of the 1970 and 1971 rulings....

The evidence of Congressional approval of the policy embodied in Revenue Ruling 71-447 goes well beyond the failure of Congress to act on legislative proposals. Congress affirmatively manifested its acquiescence in the IRS policy when it enacted the present § 501(i) of the Code....

III

Petitioners contend that, even if the Commissioner's policy is valid as to nonreligious private schools, that policy cannot constitutionally be applied to schools that engage in racial discrimination on the basis of sincerely held religious beliefs. As to such schools, it is argued that the IRS construction of § 170 and § 501(c)(3) violates their free exercise rights under the Religion Clauses of the First Amendment. This contention presents claims not heretofore considered by this Court in precisely this context....

The governmental interest at stake here is compelling.... [T]he Government has a fundamental, overriding interest in eradicating racial discrimination in education[13] — discrimination that prevailed, with official approval,

---

13. We deal here only with religious *schools* — not with churches or other purely religious institutions; here, the governmental interest is in denying public support to racial discrimination in education....

for the first 165 years of this Nation's history. That governmental interest substantially outweighs whatever burden denial of tax benefits places on petitioners' exercise of their religious beliefs. The interests asserted by petitioners cannot be accommodated with that compelling governmental interest, . . . and no "less restrictive means" . . . are available to achieve the governmental interest.

The judgments of the Court of Appeals are, accordingly,

Affirmed.

Justice POWELL concurring in part and concurring in the judgment. . . .

I . . . concur in the Court's judgment that tax-exempt status under §§ 170(c) and 501(c)(3) is not available to private schools that concededly are racially discriminatory. I do not agree, however, with the Court's more general explanation of the justifications for the tax exemptions provided to charitable organizations. . . .

With all respect, I am unconvinced that the critical question in determining tax-exempt status is whether an individual organization provides a clear "public benefit" as defined by the Court. Over 106,000 organizations filed § 501(c)(3) returns in 1981. Internal Revenue Service, 1982 Exempt Organization/Business Master File. I find it impossible to believe that all or even most of those organizations could prove that they "demonstrably serve and [are] in harmony with the public interest" or that they are "beneficial and stabilizing influences in community life." Nor am I prepared to say that petitioners, because of their racially discriminatory policies, necessarily contribute nothing of benefit to the community. It is clear from the substantially secular character of the curricula and degrees offered that petitioners provide educational benefits.

Even more troubling to me is the element of conformity that appears to inform the Court's analysis. The Court asserts that an exempt organization must "demonstrably serve and be in harmony with the public interest," must have a purpose that comports with "the common community conscience," and must not act in a manner "affirmatively at odds with [the] declared position of the whole government." Taken together, these passages suggest that the primary function of a tax-exempt organization is to act on behalf of the Government in carrying out governmentally approved policies. In my opinion, such a view of § 501(c)(3) ignores the important role played by tax exemptions in encouraging diverse, indeed often sharply conflicting, activities and viewpoints. . . .

The Court's decision upholds IRS Revenue Ruling 71-447, and thus resolves the question whether tax-exempt status is available to private schools that openly maintain racially discriminatory admissions policies. There no longer is any justification for Congress to hesitate — as it apparently has — in articulating and codifying its desired policy as to tax exemptions for discriminatory organizations. Many questions remain, such as whether organizations that violate other policies should receive tax-exempt status under § 501(c)(3). These should be legislative policy choices. . . . The contours of public policy should be determined by Congress, not by judges or the IRS.

Justice REHNQUIST, dissenting.

The Court points out that there is a strong national policy in this country against racial discrimination. To the extent that the Court states that Congress in furtherance of this policy could deny tax-exempt status to educational institutions that promote racial discrimination, I readily agree. But, unlike the Court, I am convinced that Congress simply has failed to take this action and, as this Court has said over and over again, regardless of our view on the propriety of Congress' failure to legislate we are not constitutionally empowered to act for them. . . .

With undeniable clarity, Congress has explicitly defined the requirements for § 501(c)(3) status. An entity must be (1) a corporation, or community chest, fund, or foundation, (2) organized for one of the eight enumerated purposes, (3) operated on a nonprofit basis, and (4) free from involvement in lobbying activities and political campaigns. Nowhere is there to be found some additional, undefined public policy requirement.

I have no disagreement with the Court's finding that there is a strong national policy in this country opposed to racial discrimination. I agree with the Court that Congress has the power to further this policy by denying § 501(c)(3) status to organizations that practice racial discrimination. But as of yet Congress has failed to do so. Whatever the reasons for the failure, this Court should not legislate for Congress.

NOTES AND QUESTIONS

1. *Drawing the line.* The actions by the government described in n.10 of *Bob Jones* reflected the Reagan Administration's discomfort with the exercise of IRS discretionary authority to withhold tax-exempt status on public policy grounds. It offered legislation that would have provided express statutory authority for the result in the case, by denying § 501(c)(3) treatment to any school that practiced racial discrimination. The legislation was effectively mooted by the Supreme Court's decision in *Bob Jones*.

During Senate Finance Committee hearings to consider this legislation, the question arose whether the legislation would deny tax-exempt status to a yeshiva (an Orthodox Jewish religious school) that had no black students as a foreseeable consequence of its admitting only Orthodox Jews. Everyone seemed to agree that the legislation would not deny tax-exempt status to the yeshiva, by reason of the absence of an intent to discriminate against blacks.

Is this distinction persuasive? Does the decision in *Bob Jones* permit such a yeshiva to be tax exempt?

2. *Public policy.* Once the Court in *Bob Jones* decides that §§ 501(c)(3) and 170 include a public policy limitation, it turns to the question whether racial discrimination in private schools violates public policy. The Court cites Brown v. Board of Education. How is that case relevant to racial discrimination in private education? Note that if the Court had been willing to treat tax deductibility as a form of governmental support or subsidy, Brown v. Board of Education would have been not only relevant but dispositive. But what would

that approach have done to the deduction for contributions to religious organizations?

Norwood v. Harrison, also cited by the Court, held that the equal protection and due process rights of minority citizens were violated by a state textbook lending program for private schools to the extent that it included schools that engaged in racial discrimination. And Runyon v. McCrary, also cited, held that the protection of the right of contract under the Civil Rights Act of 1866 (now 42 U.S.C. § 1981) applied to private schools.

3. *"Charitable" versus "educational."* Given the Court's interpretation of § 170(c)(2)(B), does the word "educational" have any function? That is, could the provision be amended, without losing anything, to cover "charitable purposes" as opposed to "charitable or educational purposes"?

4. *Where there's a will.* Examine § 501(i). Note its limited applicability and its failure to include discrimination based on gender. What does that tell us about public policy concerning such discrimination?

5. *Loss of exemption due to private inurement.* Bob Jones University lost its tax-exempt status because the relevant statutory provisions were held to incorporate the requirement that an organization's activities be consistent with public policy. A more common reason for loss (or denial) of tax-exempt status is that an organization benefits donors, or employees, or other persons and therefore serves a private, rather than public purpose. See § 503; Regs. § 1.501(c)(3).

E. INTEREST

1. The Rules

Interest is the cost of borrowing money. Imagine a taxpayer who expects to have $10,000 in cash one year from now, but wants to be able to use that $10,000 today. By borrowing $10,000, he can make current use of money he expects to receive later. Thus, interest can be thought of as the price one pays for accelerating access to financial resources that would otherwise only be available in the future. Should interest costs be deductible within an income tax? U.S. tax law offers a familiar answer: It depends.

Business or investment interest — that is, interest incurred in a trade or business or for the production of income — has always been allowed as a deduction, albeit subject to certain limitations designed to curb tax avoidance. See § 163(a), (d). We will examine these rules in more detail in Chapter 6. By contrast, the tax treatment of interest on debt incurred for personal purposes has undergone some important changes over the past quarter century. Before 1987, *all* personal interest was deductible. This remarkable rule was changed as part of the Tax Reform Act of 1986; but rather than making a wholesale break with the past, Congress decided to retain the deduction in some circumstances. Today, personal interest is deductible only if it is "qualified residence interest" within the meaning of § 163(h)(3). All other interest not incurred for business or investment purposes is nondeductible "personal interest." § 163(h)(2).

"Qualified residence interest" is interest on loans falling within either of two categories. First, there is "acquisition indebtedness," which is debt incurred to buy, build, or improve a personal residence, and which is secured by the residence. There is a limit of $1 million on such debt. § 163(h)(3)(B). Second, there is "home equity indebtedness," which is any debt (without limitation as to the use of the proceeds) secured by a personal residence. The amount of home equity indebtedness with respect to which a deduction is allowed is limited to the lesser of $100,000 or the fair market value of the residence minus the amount of any outstanding acquisition indebtedness. § 163(h)(3)(C). Along with the nontaxation of imputed rent from living in one's own home, these rules form the core of the U.S. tax system's subsidy for homeownership.

The following examples illustrate the operation of these rules. In each example assume that the house is used as the taxpayer's personal residence.

Example A. *A* buys a house for $1.5 million, with a down payment of $300,000 and a loan of $1.2 million. Acquisition indebtedness accounts for $1 million (which is the limit) of the loan. An additional $100,000 of the debt qualifies as home equity indebtedness. Thus, the qualified residence interest (that is, the amount of interest that can be deducted) is the interest allocable to $1.1 million of the $1.2 million loan.

Example B. *B* buys a house for $300,000, with a loan of $115,000 and the remaining $185,000 from her savings. A month later she borrows $125,000, secured by the house. The entire amount of the first loan ($115,000) is acquisition indebtedness. The second loan ($125,000) is a home equity loan and qualifies only up to $100,000. If *B* had borrowed the entire $240,000 at the time of the purchase of the house, the entire amount of the loan would have been acquisition indebtedness. Can you think of any sound justification for this difference in result?

Example C. *C* bought a house many years ago for $50,000. It is now worth $300,000. The debt incurred at the time of the original purchase was paid off several years ago. *C* takes out a loan of $140,000; the loan is secured by the house. Since the loan was not used to buy, build, or improve the house, the qualified residence interest is limited to the home equity indebtedness amount, $100,000. Note that home equity indebtedness may exceed basis. Note also that if *C* had sold her present house for $300,000 and had bought another house for the same price, but with a loan of $140,000 secured by the house, she would have wound up with $140,000 in cash from the transaction (just as if she had borrowed that amount on the security of the first house), but the entire loan would have qualified as acquisition indebtedness. (The same possibility arises in Example B.) Why would Congress create that kind of incentive?

2.   Policy Issues

One widely held view of interest on personal indebtedness is that it is a cost of consuming sooner rather than later, part of the cost of achieving personal satisfaction, and as such represents a form of consumption expense and should not be deductible. Thus, the Senate Finance Committee Report on the 1986 bill (S. Rep. No. 313, 99th Cong., 2d Sess. 804 (1986)), in justifying the denial of a deduction for consumer interest, states that allowing the deduction would provide "an incentive to consume rather than save." It notes, moreover, that a deduction for consumer interest "allows consumers to avoid the tax that would apply if funds were invested in assets producing taxable income."

This view is in considerable tension with the rationale for an income tax, under which your tax burden evidently is supposed to be lower if you consume sooner rather than later. Thus, suppose that the Grasshopper and the Ant, who are subject to a 40 percent income tax, both earn $100,000 in Year 1. Both pay $40,000 of income tax. The Grasshopper immediately spends the remaining $60,000, and thus owes no further tax (other than on subsequent earnings). The Ant, by contrast, invests his $60,000 for a year at 10 percent interest. He therefore has $6,000 of taxable interest income in Year 2, and pays an additional $2,400 of income tax. The Ant therefore pays more tax than the Grasshopper, notwithstanding that the Grasshopper got the personal satisfaction of consuming sooner.

Doesn't the taxation of interest income, no less than the allowance of consumer interest deductions, provide an incentive to consume rather than save? And doesn't consuming sooner rather than later, even without consumer borrowing, allow one to avoid the tax that would apply if the funds used to pay for the consumption were instead invested in assets producing taxable income?

In the same Senate report, the favorable treatment of loans secured by personal residences is justified on the ground that "encouraging home ownership is an important policy goal." Do you agree? Why should Congress encourage people to own rather than rent their homes, or to buy homes rather than cars, other consumer durables, or for that matter, local restaurant meals?

Many reformers believe the home mortgage interest deduction ought to be eliminated. One difficulty with this reform is persons have purchased homes on the assumption that they would be able to deduct their mortgage interest. Such individuals might find it difficult to keep up their mortgage payments without the benefit of the tax deduction. It would be possible, of course, to grandfather persons with existing loans but repeal the deduction for new mortgage indebtedness. This more limited reform would not affect current homeowners who keep their present homes and do not increase the size of their mortgages. The reform would, however, reduce the value of homes to new purchasers, who could no longer deduct mortgage interest. This in turn would reduce the price existing homeowners could get when and if they decide to sell their home. Do the reliance interests of current homeowners offer a persuasive argument against reform? Would you take a different view of the reliance interests if the reason existing homes lost value was that the Federal Reserve Board had raised interest rates? If so, then on what ground?

If the home mortgage interest deduction were newly enacted, should the benefit of the deduction be denied either to existing mortgages or to existing homes? If not, does this imply a "one-way ratchet," whereby the taxpayers directly affected by a tax law change are allowed to reap transition gain if it is favorable but are protected against transition loss if it is unfavorable?

3. Tracing

The differing treatment of interest on personal and business loans raises a number of difficult tracing issues. Suppose, for example, that business property is used to secure a loan that is used for personal purposes. Is the loan a personal or a business loan? Under proposed Treasury Regulation § 1.163-8T, interest generally is allocated according to the *use* of the loan proceeds. Thus, interest on a loan that is used for personal purposes is characterized as personal interest; the fact that the loan may be secured by business property is irrelevant. Regs. § 1.163-8T(c). As noted earlier, however, special rules apply to interest incurred in connection with a principal residence.

Suppose borrowed funds are commingled with nonborrowed funds, and some of the commingled funds are used for business purposes, and some of the funds are used to finance personal consumption. No portion of the loan is incurred in connection with a principal residence. Is the loan a business loan, a personal loan, or a combination of both? What portion of interest on the loan is deductible? Treas. Reg. § 1.163-8 provides a complicated set of tracing rules for that situation. A review of those rules is left to the curious student.

PROBLEMS

1. Jennifer has $50,000 in a savings account. She uses the $50,000 to buy a Mercedes and the next day borrows $50,000 to finance the purchase of a fast-food franchise that she intends to operate. Will the interest on the $50,000 loan be deductible?

2. Barbara owns her personal residence free and clear. Its value is $100,000. She borrows $50,000 on a "home equity" loan, secured by the residence. (a) She uses the proceeds to buy a Mercedes. Is the interest deductible? Under what Code section? (b) She uses the proceeds instead to buy a tax-exempt bond. Is the interest deductible? See § 265(a)(2), § 163(h)(2)(D), § 163(a). (c) She uses the proceeds of the loan to buy taxable bonds, but at the time she holds $50,000 of tax-exempt bonds. Is the interest deductible?

3. Joe has a portfolio of stocks and bonds worth $200,000. The annual income from the portfolio is $12,000. Joe borrows $50,000 on a margin loan and uses the proceeds to buy a Mercedes. Since the proceeds are used to buy the Mercedes, the interest on the loan is personal interest. See Regs. § 1.163-8T(c)(1). What might he do to achieve a better tax result?

4. Interest on Student Loans

Section 221 allows a deduction for interest on indebtedness used to pay higher education expenses of the taxpayer, the taxpayer's spouse, or a dependent of the taxpayer. The maximum amount deductible is $2,500. Beginning in 2002, the deduction is phased out for taxpayers with modified adjusted gross income in excess of $50,000 ($100,000 in the case of a joint return). The phaseout ranges are adjusted annually for inflation after 2002, and were lower ($40,000 for singles and $60,000 for joint returns) for taxable years before 2002.

F. TAXES

Under § 164, a taxpayer may claim a deduction for certain taxes paid to state, local, and foreign governments. Our focus here will be on the deduction for taxes paid to state and local governments. Like the various provisions already discussed above, the deduction for state and local taxes (SALT) is an itemized deduction that appears on Schedule A. Thus, with one minor exception, the deduction is not available to those who choose to claim the standard deduction instead of itemizing their deductions. The exception is a temporary above-the-line deduction available for property taxes paid by non-itemizers for tax years 2008 and 2009.

1. Rationale for the SALT Deduction

The policy issue presented by § 164 is similar in many ways to the issue raised by other deductions considered in this chapter — should the deduction be regarded as a necessary adjustment in order to arrive at a proper definition of net income or, if not, is it simply a device for achieving some desirable goal extraneous to the income tax system, in this case support of state and local governmental operations?

On the question of properly defining income, one argument commonly offered in favor of the § 164 deduction is that taxes are involuntary and do not buy personal consumption. In the most extreme version, one might even equate the payment of taxes to theft, for which a deduction is allowable under § 165(c)(3). But surely this is taking the argument too far. Consider Justice Holmes's observation that "Taxes are what we pay for civilized society. . . ." *Compania General de Tobacos de Filipinas v. Collector*, 275 U.S. 87, 100 (1927). In the case of state and local governments, the benefits that make up the "civilized society" include police and fire protection, education, medical benefits, a legal infrastructure for the enforcement of contracts, etc. While individual taxpayers may not provide direct consent for each one of these collective purchases, only the most extreme libertarian would deny that state and local governments provide *some* benefits to their residents.

What then is the proper income tax rule when individuals are not simply paying taxes, but also receiving benefits? The answer is not obvious. Part of the difficulty lies in the fact that the amount of taxes paid by any one individual is unlikely to equal the amount of benefits received. If these amounts could be determined, then one (admittedly hypothetical) solution does seem to suggest itself. Taxpayers who pay more in taxes than they receive in services (net payors) might be allowed a deduction for the excess of taxes paid over benefits received, while taxpayers whose benefits exceed their taxes (net payees) would be taxed on that excess. On balance, this approach should result in no net revenue gain or loss for the federal government, except insofar as the tax rate at which deductions are taken differs from the tax rate at which benefits are included in income.

Of course, such an approach is not likely to materialize any time soon, for all the obvious practical and political reasons. But consider the following alternative. Rather than taxing net payees and allowing a deduction for net payors, perhaps we should simply ignore both the income and the deduction. Here the outcome would be similar to the current tax treatment of intra-family gifts, where the donor is allowed no deduction and the donee recognizes no income. In the same way that we thought of the nondeductibility of gift transfers as a form of surrogate taxation of the donee, we can think of the nondeductibility of net payments to state and local governments as a form of surrogate taxation of net payees.

These two hypothetical approaches are of course only that. As noted above, the actual tax law allows a deduction for tax payments to state and local governments and does not require the inclusion of state and local government benefits in income. Nevertheless, a comparison of the actual law to these hypothetical approaches helps to illustrate the extent to which current law deviates from a pure income tax model. A better rationale for the deduction derives not from income measurement principles, but rather from the broader policy objective of encouraging (or reducing the resistance to) state and local government spending. In effect, by providing the SALT deduction, the federal government has committed to reimbursing taxpayers up to 35 percent of the taxes they pay to state and local governments.

2. The Basic Structure of U.S. State and Local Taxation

The most important of the taxes listed as personal deductions in § 164 are state and local income, sales, and real property taxes. The deduction for sales taxes was actually repealed as part of the Tax Reform Act of 1986. In 2004, however, Congress reintroduced the deduction for sales taxes in a modified form primarily for the benefit of people in states with no income tax. § 164(b)(5). Under this new provision, taxpayers may elect to deduct state and local general sales taxes in lieu of state and local income taxes. These three taxes—income taxes, property taxes, and sales taxes—make up the vast majority of state and local governments' tax revenues in the United States. As shown in the figure below, revenues from these three sources accounted for 91 percent of all state and local tax revenue for 2005-2006.

Of course, not all taxes paid to state and local governments will be deducted on a federal income tax return. The deduction is available only to itemizers and, as noted above, those who do itemize must choose between deducting either income or sales taxes. Because of these features, the amount of the federal subsidy available under § 164 varies greatly depending on the type of tax. For example, note from the figure above that approximately $412 billion in sales taxes were paid in 2005-2006. According to IRS data, however, taxpayers claimed only $18 billion of sales taxes on individual tax returns in

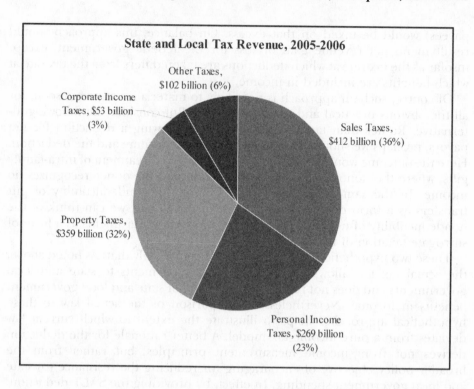

State and Local Tax Revenue, 2005-2006

Other Taxes,
$102 billion (6%)

Corporate Income
Taxes, $53 billion
(3%)

Sales Taxes,
$412 billion (36%)

Property Taxes,
$359 billion (32%)

Personal Income
Taxes, $269 billion
(23%)

2006. The disparity between these two numbers is likely due to the fact that those paying sales taxes are either not itemizing their deductions or are claiming the deduction for income taxes instead of the deduction for sales taxes. By contrast, taxpayers claimed $159 billion in property tax deductions and $251 billion in income tax deductions for tax year 2006.

In addition, because § 164 is a deduction, the value of the federal subsidy is a function of the taxpayer's marginal tax rate. Not surprisingly, the same individuals who face the highest federal marginal tax rates also tend to bear the largest share of state and local tax burdens. The result is that the tax benefit of § 164 flows mostly to high-income households. For tax year 2007, the Joint Committee on Taxation estimated that approximately 80 percent of the value of the SALT deduction went to taxpayers with adjusted gross income of $100,000 or higher, which is roughly the breakpoint for the top 20 percent of the household income distribution. In other words, like all itemized deductions, the deduction for state and local taxes is a regressive subsidy embedded within a progressive income tax.

One final note regarding state and local taxes deserves mention, in part because of its potential relevance to the point just made. For purposes of the alternative minimum tax, no deduction is allowed for state and local taxes. In fact, the deduction for state and local taxes is by far the largest AMT "preference" item, accounting for more than 70 percent of all AMT preference items for tax year 2006. Thus, how (or whether) Congress decides to reform the AMT will have a direct bearing on the deduction for state and local taxes.

In effect, by letting the AMT continue to grow in significance, Congress is undertaking a gradual (de facto) repeal of the deduction for state and local taxes.

G. PERSONAL AND DEPENDENCY EXEMPTIONS

Section 151 grants each taxpayer a deduction for a personal exemption. The amount was $3,650 in 2009, and is annually adjusted for inflation. If a joint return is filed by a married couple, there are two taxpayers and, consequently, two exemptions. If a married individual files a separate return, one personal exemption is allowed for the taxpayer and a second for the spouse if the spouse has no gross income and is not another's dependent. § 151(b).

Section 151(c) provides an exemption for each "dependent," as defined in § 152. To qualify, the person must be either a "qualifying child" or a "qualifying relative." These two terms are defined in some detail in § 152. Essentially, a "qualifying child" is a person who:

1. is a child, a child's descendant, or a sibling of the taxpayer;
2. is less than 19 years old or, if a student, less than 24 years old;
3. has not provided more than half of his or her own support; and
4. "has the same principal place of abode as the taxpayer for more than one-half of [the] taxable year."

A "qualifying relative" is a person who:

1. is a child or a child's descendant, parent or parent's ancestor, sibling, aunt, uncle, cousin, or in-law, or "has the same principal place of abode as the taxpayer and is a member of the taxpayer's household";
2. has a gross income less than the exemption amount;
3. receives more than half his or her support from the taxpayer; and
4. is not a qualifying child of the taxpayer.

As between two (or more?) parents not filing a joint return, the exemption for a qualifying child goes to the parent "with whom the child resided for the longest period of time," and, in case of a tie, to the one with the higher adjusted gross income. However, divorced or legally separated parents are allowed, by agreement between them, to assign the exemption to the non-custodial parent. In other situations, the exemption goes to the parent or, if none, to the taxpayer with the highest adjusted gross income.

The deduction for dependents offers an interesting case study of tax evasion. For many years, audits revealed fraudulent dependency deductions, with anecdotal evidence of taxpayers claiming their pets as dependents (and succeeding by escaping audit). In the mid-1980s, a clever IRS employee named John Szilagyi came up with the idea of requiring Social Security numbers for dependents. The year the reform was implemented, the number of dependents dropped by seven million, increasing tax revenues by nearly $3 billion, or almost $30 a taxpayer! (This story is recounted in the insightful book by J. Slemrod & J. Bakija, Taxing Ourselves: A Citizen's Guide to the Great Debate Over Tax Reform (1996).)

The personal and dependency exemptions are available in addition to the standard deduction amount. § 63.

KING v. COMMISSIONER
121 T.C. No. 12 (2003)

. . .

FINDINGS OF FACT

. . .

Mr. Lopez and Mrs. King are the biological parents of Monique Desiree Vigil (Monique), who was born on January 17, 1986. Mr. Lopez and Mrs. King have never been married to each other. Mr. Lopez and Mrs. King lived apart at all times during 1998 and 1999.

For 1987, Mr. Lopez timely filed his Federal income tax return and claimed a dependency exemption deduction for Monique. In a letter dated April 20, 1988, respondent requested that Mr. Lopez complete a Form 8332, Release of Claim to Exemption for Child of Divorced or Separated Parents. On April 30, 1998, Mrs. King executed a Form 8332 in favor of Mr. Lopez for the taxable year 1987 and all years thereafter.[14] Mr. Lopez claimed a dependency exemption deduction for Monique for the taxable years 1987 through 1999. Mr. Lopez attached a copy of the Form 8332 executed by Mrs. King to his tax returns for the years in issue.

Beginning with the taxable year 1993, the year they were married, the Kings began claiming a dependency exemption deduction for Monique on each of their Federal income tax returns. Monique resided with the Kings at all times during the calendar years 1998 and 1999. The Lopezes and the Kings provided all of Monique's financial support in 1998 and 1999. On the basis of the expenditures for Monique established by the record, the Kings provided over half of Monique's support during these years. Mr. Lopez and Mrs. King have had only sporadic and brief contact with each other since

---

14. The Form 8332 Mrs. King executed was the December 1987 version of the form. Pt. I of the form was entitled "Release of Claim to Exemption for Current Year." Mrs. King completed and signed Pt. I, thereby releasing her claim to the exemption deduction for Monique for 1987. Pt. II was entitled "Release of Claim to Exemption for Future Years." In the space specified "for the tax year(s)," the words "future years" were written. Mrs. King signed the space in Pt. II releasing her claim to exemption deductions. The general instructions to that version of the Form 8332 stated that a parent who might be entitled to claim an exemption deduction for a child could agree to release the claim for the current calendar year or for future years, or both. In December 2000, the Commissioner revised Form 8332 and inserted cautionary language stating that the special support test "does not apply to parents who never married each other."

1987, and at no time did she inform him that she wanted or otherwise intended to revoke the release contained in the Form 8332 that she executed on April 30, 1988.

On July 29, 2002, respondent issued notices of deficiency to the Kings and the Lopezes for their taxable years 1998 and 1999. In order to protect the Government from a potential whipsaw, respondent determined that neither the Kings nor the Lopezes were entitled to dependency exemption deductions under section 151.[15] The Kings and the Lopezes timely filed petitions to this Court seeking redeterminations. Because of the common issues presented, the cases were consolidated for purposes of trial, briefing, and opinion.

OPINION

The issue for decision is which petitioners are entitled to dependency exemption deductions for Monique for the years in issue. As explained below, we hold that the Lopezes are entitled to the deductions because Mr. Lopez and Mrs. King lived apart at all times during the last 6 months of 1998 and 1999 and Mrs. King released her claim to the dependency exemption deductions for the years in issue.

Section 151 provides exemption deductions for qualified dependents of a taxpayer in computing taxable income. A child of a taxpayer is generally a dependent of the taxpayer only if the taxpayer provides over half of the child's support during the taxable year. § 152(a). A special support test applies to certain parents. Section 152(e) provides:

§ 152(e) Support Test in Case of Child of Divorced Parents, Etc. —
(1) Custodial parent gets exemption. — Except as otherwise provided in this subsection, if —
(A) a child (as defined in section 151(c)(3)) receives over half of his support during the calendar year from his parents —
(i) who are divorced or legally separated under a decree of divorce or separate maintenance,
(ii) who are separated under a written separation agreement, or
(iii) who live apart at all times during the last 6 months of the calendar year, and
(B) such child is in the custody of one or both of his parents for more than one-half of the calendar year,
such child shall be treated, for purposes of subsection (a), as receiving over half of his support during the calendar year from the parent having custody for a greater portion of the calendar year (hereinafter in this subsection referred to as the "custodial parent").
(2) Exception where custodial parent releases claim to exemption for the year. — A child of parents described in paragraph (1) shall be treated

15. [The denial of the exemption resulted in denial of the child tax credit (§ 24) for Monique for the Lopezes and the Kings and in a downward adjustment in the earned income credit (§ 32) for the Kings. — EDS.]

as having received over half of his support during a calendar year from
the noncustodial parent if—

>   (A) the custodial parent signs a written declaration (in such manner
>   and form as the Secretary may by regulations prescribe) that such
>   custodial parent will not claim such child as a dependent for any tax-
>   able year beginning in such calendar year, and
>   (B) the noncustodial parent attaches such written declaration to the
>   noncustodial parent's return for the taxable year beginning during
>   such calendar year.

For purposes of this subsection, the term "noncustodial parent" means
the parent who is not the custodial parent.

If the requirements of § 152(e)(1) are met, the child is treated as having
received over half of his support from the custodial parent, and the custodial
parent is entitled to the dependency exemption deduction. The noncustodial
parent can gain entitlement to the deduction if the custodial parent executes a
valid written declaration under § 152(e)(2) releasing the claim to the deduction. The declaration may apply to 1 year, a set number of years, or all future
years.... A validly executed Form 8332 satisfies the written declaration
requirement.

The Lopezes argue that they are entitled to the dependency exemption
deductions because Mr. Lopez and Mrs. King lived apart at all times during the
years in issue and Mrs. King signed a written declaration stating that she would
not claim Monique for 1987 and future years. Respondent and the Kings
contend that the special support test of § 152(e) does not apply to parents who
have never married each other.[16] If the special support test can apply to parents
who have never married each other, respondent and the Kings, for different
reasons, claim that the Form 8332 Mrs. King executed in 1988 did not release
her claim to the exemption deductions for the years in issue.

This case presents an issue that has not been squarely addressed by the
Court.[17] Additionally, it appears that the Commissioner has at times taken
inconsistent positions on the matter.[18] Resolution of the issue requires us to

---

16. Because we have found as a fact that the Kings provided over half of Monique's support during
the years in issue, they would be entitled to the dependency exemption deductions if § 152(e)(1) did
not apply to parents who have never married each other.

17. In Hughes v. Commissioner, T.C. Memo. 2000-143, and Brignac v. Commissioner, T.C.
Memo. 1999-387, we applied, without discussion of this point, § 152(e)(1) to parents who had never
married each other. It does not appear that the Commissioner argued in those cases that the statute
did not apply.

18. On brief, respondent explained that his current position is based on a Litigation Guideline
Memorandum issued in 1999. Chief Counsel Advice 1999-49-033 (Dec. 10, 1999). However, the
Commissioner previously issued a Field Service Advisory in 1997 taking the same position. Field
Service Advice 1997392 (Apr. 2, 1997). The 1997 advisory stated that a copy of then-current training
materials reflected the position taken in 1990 that the special support test did not apply to parents who
have never married each other, and that the Commissioner's opinion had not changed. However, in
1996 the Commissioner issued a Field Service Advisory concluding that the special support test under
§ 152(e)(1) could apply to parents who had never married each other. Field Service Advice 1996442
(Apr. 22, 1996). Additionally, the version of the Form 8332 provided by the Commissioner from
December 1987 until December 2000 did not state that the special support test did not apply to
parents who had never married each other.

interpret the language of § 152(e)(1). In interpreting a statute, our purpose is to give effect to Congress's intent. . . . Usually, the plain meaning of the statutory language is conclusive. . . . If the statute is silent or ambiguous, then we may look to the legislative history to determine congressional intent. . . . The legislative history of a statute is secondary when we can apply the plain meaning of unambiguous text; however, unequivocal evidence of clear legislative intent may sometimes override a plain meaning interpretation and lead to a different result. . . .

Section 152(e)(1) provides that the special support test applies to "parents" in three different situations. The statute specifically provides that the test applies not only to divorced and certain separated parents, but to parents "who live apart at all times during the last 6 months of the calendar year." There is no requirement in the statute that parents have married each other before the special support test can apply. Section 152(e)(1) applies to any parents, regardless of marital status, as long as they lived apart at all times for at least the last 6 months of the calendar year.

Respondent contends that the legislative history of § 152(e) supports the interpretation that § 152(e)(1)(A)(iii) applies only to parents who are married but who live apart. Although we find the statute unambiguous, we have examined the legislative history, and we disagree with respondent regarding its import.

Section 152(e) was amended in 1984 to add current paragraphs (1)(A)(iii) and (2). Deficit Reduction Act of 1984, Pub. L. 98-369, sec. 423(a), 98 Stat. 799. Before the 1984 amendment, the special support test applied only to parents who were divorced or separated under a written separation agreement.[19] The conference report accompanying the Deficit Reduction Act of 1984 states that the special support test was being extended to parents living apart at all times during the last 6 months of the calendar year. H. Conf. Rept. 98-861, at 1118-1119 (1984), 1984-3 C.B. (Vol.2) 1, 372–373. The reason for the change was to resolve disputes without the involvement of the Commissioner between parents who both claim the dependency exemption deduction based on providing support over the applicable thresholds. H. Rept. 98-432 (Part II), at 1498 (1984).[20]

Contrary to respondent's assertions, the legislative history of § 152(e) does not provide support for deviating from the plain meaning of the statute that the special support test can apply to parents who have never married each other. Neither the House bill nor the conference report state that the amendment to § 152(e) was intended to apply only to married parents. Indeed, applying § 152(e)(1)(A)(iii) to both married parents and parents who have never married each other is consistent with the stated purpose of resolving dependency disputes without the Commissioner's involvement in cases where parents both claim the dependency exemption deductions.

19. This meant that under former § 152(e) "only parents previously united in marriage [came] within its ambit." Radin v. Commissioner, T.C. Memo. 1987-348.

20. See also Bramante v. Commissioner, T.C. Memo. 2002-228, citing the legislative history and stating that the pre-1985 version was often subjective and presented difficult problems of proof and substantiation.

Therefore, we hold that the special support test in § 152(e)(1) applies in this case. This means that Mrs. King is treated as having provided over half of Monique's support for 1998 and 1999 and will be entitled to the dependency exemption deductions unless, pursuant to § 152(e)(2), she released her claim to the exemption deductions for Monique for these years.

Stipulation 10 of the stipulation of facts states that Mrs. King executed a Form 8332 in favor of Mr. Lopez "for taxable year 1987 and all years thereafter." Despite this stipulation, respondent claimed for the first time at trial, and subsequently argued on brief, that the Form 8332 is ambiguous because Mrs. King "did not specify particular future years" or write "all" future years.[21] The Kings also dispute the stipulation, claiming that Mrs. King did not release her claim to the exemption deductions because the Form 8332 was signed under duress and she was not aware what the form was until the instant proceeding began.

Rule 91(a)(1) generally requires the parties to stipulate to the fullest extent all matters not privileged which are relevant to the case, regardless of whether such matters involve fact or opinion or the application of the law to fact. Stipulations are binding on the parties to the stipulation, unless the parties agree otherwise or the court relieves a party from the binding effect "where justice requires." Rule 91(e). The parties have not otherwise agreed to be relieved from the binding effect of stipulation 10. Additionally, as explained below, justice does not require us to disregard the stipulation.

Stipulation 10 states that the release contained in the Form 8332 was not just for 1987; it was for each and every year after 1987. The Form 8332 itself clearly demonstrates that Mrs. King intended to release her claim to exemptions for 1987 and all subsequent years, and we reject respondent's new argument that the omission of the word "all" renders the release ineffective.[22]

The Kings are also bound by the stipulation. However, we briefly discuss why their arguments are not grounds for finding that the Form 8332 was invalid with respect to the years in issue. Mrs. King's overall testimony at trial indicates that she was not under duress at the time she signed the Form 8332. Mrs. King testified that Mr. Lopez did not threaten her on the day she executed the Form 8332 or otherwise force her to sign the document. Mrs. King's allegations of abuse involve isolated incidents not contemporaneous with her signing of the Form 8332 and do not support a finding under either federal or state law that there was an unlawful threat or pattern of abuse or mental intimidation that caused her to sign the form under duress. . . . Additionally, it was Mrs. King's duty to make the appropriate inquiries before she signed the

---

21. The notices of deficiency do not discuss the validity of the Form 8332 executed by Mrs. King. Additionally, respondent did not raise this issue in either the answer or the trial memorandum as a ground for denying the dependency exemption deductions to the Lopezes. Indeed, in the trial memorandum, respondent indicates that if the special support test can apply to unmarried parents, then Mr. Lopez is entitled to the dependency exemption deductions unless Mrs. King can establish that she signed the Form 8332 under duress. Respondent has consistently taken the position that the form was not signed under duress.

22. In any event, we find respondent's argument that the Form 8332 is ineffective because it lacks the word "all" strained and unpersuasive. The words "future years" written on the form clearly indicate that the claim for the exemption deduction was intended to be released not just for 1987 but for each and every year thereafter.

Form 8332 permanently releasing her claim to exemption deductions for Monique, and we will not ignore the properly executed form because she now contends that she did not intend to release her claim for the years in issue. . . . Therefore, we find that Mrs. King validly released her claim to the exemption deductions for Monique for the years in issue and, as a result, the Kings are not entitled to dependency exemption deductions under § 151 for Monique for the years in issue. Accordingly, the Lopezes are entitled to the deductions for the years in issue. . . .

QUESTIONS

1. What is the best evidence of legislative intent?
2. Do you agree with the court that the language of the statute is "unambiguous"? If so, does it seem well drafted and coherent?
3. The court states, "it was Mrs. King's duty to make the appropriate inquiries before she signed the Form 8332 permanently releasing her claim to exemption deductions for Monique. . . ." Where does this "duty" come from? Is there any specific basis for it in the Code or is it an invention of the court? Does it seem to be reasonable burden to impose on someone like Mrs. King?
4. Does the outcome of the case seem fair to both parties? If not, should the court be faulted for not finding a way to reach a different outcome? Section 152 was revised in 2004, with § 152(e) now reading as follows:

> (e) Special Rule for Divorced Parents. —
> (1) In general. — Notwithstanding subsection (c)(1)(B), (c)(4), or (d)(1) (C), if —
> > (A) a child receives over one-half of the child's support during the calendar year from the child's parents —
> > > (i) who are divorced or legally separated under a decree of divorce or separate maintenance,
> > > (ii) who are separated under a written separation agreement, or
> > > (iii) who live apart at all times during the last 6 months of the calendar year, and
> > (B) such child is in the custody of 1 or both of the child's parents for more than one-half of the calendar year,
> > such child shall be treated as being the qualifying child or qualifying relative of the noncustodial parent for a calendar year if the requirements described in paragraph (2) are met.
> (2) Requirements. — For purposes of paragraph (1), the requirements described in this paragraph are met if —
> > (A) a decree of divorce, a separate maintenance or written separation agreement between the parents applicable to the taxable year beginning in such calendar year provides that —
> > > (i) the noncustodial parent shall be entitled to any deduction allowable under section 151 for such child, or
> > > (ii) the custodial parent will sign a written declaration (in such manner and form as the Secretary may prescribe) that such parent

will not claim such child as a dependent for such taxable
year, or

* * *

For purposes of subparagraph (B), amounts expended for the support of
a child or children shall be treated as received from the noncustodial
parent to the extent that such parent provided amounts for such support.

Does this new language change the result?

H. CREDITS BASED ON PERSONAL CIRCUMSTANCES

1. The Earned Income Tax Credit

The "earned income tax credit" (or EITC), set forth in § 32, has become an
important part of the federal system for relief of poverty. Originally enacted
in 1975, the EITC was substantially expanded during the Reagan and Clinton
years. In 2007, the EITC generated payments of about $47 billion to low-
income households, which is significantly more than is paid in total state and
federal cash welfare benefits under Temporary Assistance to Needy Families
(TANF), formerly AFDC. The credit is sometimes referred to as a wage subsidy or, more broadly, as form of "negative income tax."

Under § 32, a taxpayer is entitled to claim a credit equal to a specified
percentage of "earned income" up to a certain level. Several features of the
EITC deserve mention:

- The amount of the credit depends on the number of children. Taxpayers
  with no children receive a very small credit (maximum of $428 for 2007),
  while substantially larger maximum amounts are available for taxpayers
  with one child ($2,853) or two or more children ($4,716).
- The EITC is a "refundable" credit, which means that it does not just offset
  any tax liability but, far more important, results in a payment from the
  government to the extent that the credit exceeds tax liability.
- The credit is phased in — that is, over a certain income range, the credit
  rises as earned income rises, so it can be thought of as a form of wage
  subsidy or supplement.
- At a specified higher level of adjusted gross income (or earned income, if
  higher) the credit is phased out as income rises, which is consistent with the
  objective of providing benefits only to people with low incomes.
- The point at which the credit begins to phase out is slightly higher for a
  married couple than it is for a single taxpayer, reflecting an effort to
  reduce the marriage penalty inherent in the credit's design.

Each of these features can be seen in the graph below, which shows the amount of the EITC available to taxpayers in different circumstances for the tax year 2007.[23]

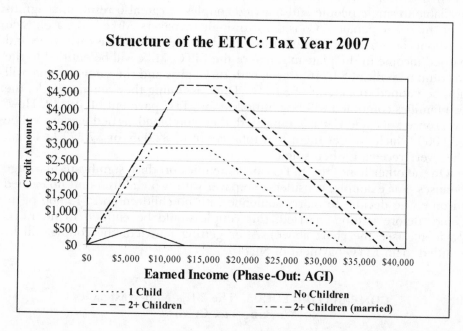

Structure of the EITC: Tax Year 2007

This figure helps to illustrate the EITC's chief incentive effects. First, take note of the steep line that represents the phase-in range of the credit for taxpayers with two or more children. In that income range, the taxpayer can very substantially increase her EITC payment by increasing her earned income. More specifically, for every one dollar increase in earned income over the phase-in range (up to $11,750), the taxpayer's EITC benefit increases by 40 cents. Thus, an increase in earned income from, say, $5,000 to $15,000 will increase the EITC payment from $2,000 to the maximum credit allowable of $4,716.

The credit amount remains the same over the range of $11,750 to $15,400 and then begins to phase out as the taxpayer's adjusted gross income or earned income (whichever is higher) exceeds $15,400 ($17,400 for married taxpayers filing a joint return). Note that in this phaseout range, the declining credit amount has incentive effects similar to the imposition of a positive tax. That is, for every one dollar increase in income over the range from $15,400 to $37,800, the taxpayer loses 21 cents of the credit. Here the incentive effects are exactly the opposite as those in the phase-in range. The more the taxpayer earns, the smaller the credit she will receive. This work disincentive is in addition to numerous other taxes and phaseouts that create work disincentives in this same range—e.g., payroll taxes (7.65 percent), the federal income tax (15 percent), housing subsidy phaseouts (27.9 percent). This kind of "piling

23. Please note that, with respect to married taxpayers, we have included a dotted line only for taxpayers with two or more children. Lines showing the amounts available for married taxpayers with no children or one child were omitted to avoid excessive clutter in the graph.

on" of taxes and benefit reductions, resulting in high marginal rates of "taxation" of earnings, is common in welfare programs.

Finally, it should be noted that, because of the way the EITC is made available to single people and married couples, it can also result in a significant "marriage penalty." Consider two single taxpayers, Mike and Carol, each of whom earns $15,000 and has three children. Because he has three boys and earned income in the plateau range of the EITC, Mike will be entitled to the maximum credit of $4,716. Carol, with three girls and the same income, will also be entitled to a credit of $4,716. Thus, assuming they remain single, the two families combined will be entitled to an EITC payment of $9,432. However, once Mike and Carol get married, their combined earned income will be $30,000, which entitles them to a total credit of $2,055, or $7,377 less than they were receiving when single.

On the other hand, the EITC can sometimes produce significant marriage bonuses. For example, consider a taxpayer with two children and no earned income who decides to marry someone with no children and $15,000 of income. Before getting married, this couple would be entitled to no EITC payments (see the chart above). After getting married, the couple will be entitled to an EITC payment of $4,716.

COMPARATIVE FOCUS: The UK's Non-Wasteable Working Tax Credit

The United Kingdom has a provision in its income tax law similar to the EITC called the "Working Tax Credit." Like the EITC, the Working Tax Credit phases out over a certain income range, thus creating work disincentives for individuals with income in that range. In addition, like the EITC, the Working Tax Credit is refundable, though the British use the term "non-wasteable." However, unlike the EITC, the Working Tax Credit does not phase in but instead features an "hours worked" threshold for eligibility. For example, in order to claim the credit, taxpayers age 16 and over with at least one child must work at least 16 hours per week in order to claim the credit. Once the hours worked threshold is satisfied, the taxpayer is entitled to the full amount of the credit, which is substantially more generous than the EITC. Taxpayers with children may also claim a separate Child Tax Credit, as in the United States.

Once eligibility for the credit is established, Her Majesty's Revenue and Customs will remit payment to the taxpayer's bank or building society account. Those desiring further information may contact an HMRC Enquiry Centre (closed on Boxing Day).

---

2. Credit for the Elderly and the Permanently and Totally Disabled

Section 22, providing a credit for retirement income, was initially designed to equalize the tax burden on people over 65 receiving federal Social Security benefits, which until 1983 were wholly tax exempt (see supra page 109), and people who provided for their own retirement with pension, annuities, or other investments. In 1976, however, the law was changed to apply the credit to income from any source, including earnings from services currently performed. Unlike § 151, § 22 retains in its title (though not in text) the now-suspect term "the elderly," which a sensitive person might wish to replace with "senior citizens," or, better yet, "persons who through no fault of their own have attained age sixty-five." In order to limit the credit to low-income taxpayers, § 22(d) reduces the "section 22 amount" as income rises above $7,500 (single persons), $10,000 (joint returns), or $5,000 (separate return filed by married individual).

3.   Child Tax Credit

Section 24 allows each taxpayer a $1,000 credit for each dependent "child" under age 17. ("Child" is defined under § 152 to include certain other relatives living with the taxpayer.) The credit is reduced by $50 for every $1,000 that income rises above certain threshold amounts. There are rules that apply in special circumstances (for example, for certain taxpayers with three or more qualifying children). It is limited by interactions with other credits and with the alternative minimum tax. The credit is refundable (that is, payable to the taxpayer to the extent it exceeds the amount of tax owed), but only under limited circumstances. In general, the rules are so complicated and difficult to apply that in many cases even professional tax preparers are likely to have difficulty filling out the forms and calculating the amount of the credit. The credit is scheduled to revert to $500 in 2011.

4.   Credits, Phaseouts, and Effective Marginal Tax Rates

Many individual credits are intended to provide relief for low-income families and are phased out as income rises above specified levels. An unwanted but unavoidable consequence is an often very high "tax" rate (since the reduction of a credit is functionally equivalent to the imposition of a tax). To illustrate hypothetically, suppose you want to provide that a couple with children and an income of $15,000 will receive a credit (that is, a payment from the Treasury) of $5,000. But suppose you also want to begin imposing taxes when income reaches $25,000. As income rises from $15,000 to $25,000, the payment from the Treasury must decline to zero. That is, for every dollar of earnings there must be a reduction of 50 cents in benefits, so the net effect of earning a dollar will be an additional 50 cents in pocket. The marginal "tax" rate is 50 percent.

If you think this rate is too high (don't forget that the people earning the income will also be paying Social Security taxes, may be losing other benefits, and are likely to have some work-related expenses), you might think that the solution is to increase the level at which the credit is finally phased out — to, say, $35,000. The problem with that solution is that the resulting loss of revenue is likely to be substantial. The lost revenue could, of course, be replaced by increasing (substantially) the rates for people earning above $35,000, but that might result in unacceptably high actual tax rates.

Consider, for example, a family with income of $45,000 that pays a tax at a rate of 15 percent on income above the $25,000 "breakeven" point, for a tax of $3,000 (15 percent of the difference of $20,000). Now suppose you raise the breakeven point from $25,000 to $35,000 but you want to raise the same $3,000 in revenue. The tax rate then must be raised to 30 percent. If you want to keep the $45,000 family's tax rate at 15 percent, you lose revenue and you just keep moving the problem up the income ladder, and the further up the ladder you go the fewer are the people available to make up for the lost revenue and the higher are the rates to begin with.

This observation is not fanciful. It reflects a central problem of welfare, whether the welfare takes the form of traditional cash payments, benefits in kind (e.g., food stamps and medical care), or tax credits designed to relieve financial hardship. The problem is exacerbated where there are multiple benefit programs with overlapping phaseouts.

5

ALLOWANCES FOR MIXED
BUSINESS AND
PERSONAL OUTLAYS

The allowances examined in the previous chapter were associated with purely personal circumstances or objectives. In Chapter 6 we will examine allowances associated with purely business or investment circumstances or objectives. In this chapter we examine the somewhat perplexing intermediate ground.

There are two basic provisions under which individuals may claim deductions for expenses that may be thought of as the cost of generating income. The first is § 162(a), which allows a deduction for "ordinary and necessary expenses paid or incurred . . . in carrying on any trade or business." It is under this provision, for example, that a practicing lawyer who heads her own office would claim deductions for office expenses, salaries paid to associates, automobile expenses, entertainment expenses, etc.[1] The other basic deduction provision for individuals is § 212,[2] which covers expenses of generating income from sources other than a trade or business. Under this provision a person with investments in stocks and bonds would claim deductions for fees paid to investment advisors, the cost of a subscription to the Wall Street Journal, and expenses incurred in attending investment seminars.

Much of the material in this chapter concerns instances where a taxpayer's expense is defined not only in § 162 or § 212 but also in § 262, which provides that "no deduction shall be allowed for personal, living, or family expenses." For better or for worse (usually the latter), it takes very little imagination to concoct a business rationale for even the most routine personal living expenses. Take the case of Pennel Irwin, the taxpayer in Irwin v. Commissioner, 72 T.C.M. 1148 (1996). Mr. Irwin had a "day job" with the Defense

---

1. These deductions are taken in arriving at "adjusted gross income" (see § 62(a)(1)) and are sometimes called "above-the-line" deductions.

2. Deductions under § 212 are "itemized" deductions, which are deducted from adjusted gross income to arrive at taxable income.

Department. He was also the author of five unpublished novels, and took the position that "[f]or fiction writing all personal experiences and observations are all business experiences and observations." Consistent with this position, Mr. Irwin deducted all purchases that, in his opinion, would yield interesting observations for his novels. These purchases included a washing machine and microwave oven, as well as the items discussed in the colloquy below, between Mr. Irwin and Judge Panuthos of the Tax Court.

The Court: Mr. Irwin, please explain your research expenses.

Irwin: Materials for research are items I am purchasing so that I can research their use and then relay that in literary form. Interview research expenses are incurred when I am trying to gain information. . . . For instance, Scott Keithley is listed under interview research materials. Scott Keithley happens to be a dentist, and I was getting information on dental hygiene and dental practices, which I learned about firsthand.

The Court: Was he your dentist?

Irwin: Scott Keithley? Yes. So, part of the service I'm paying for—

The Court: What was the fifteen dollars for? What did Scott Keithley do for you? Did he clean your teeth?

Irwin: For the fifteen dollars?

The Court: Yeah.

Irwin: Okay, well, when I'm paying for a service, I prefer—I pay both for the physical service as well as for the information that person provides. The fifteen dollars, geez, right offhand, I can't remember if that was for cleaning. . . .

The Court: Okay. How about education expenses?

Irwin: For 1990, the main part of the education expenses involved renting dormitory space for my research assistant. In the course of my research I realized I would love to find out what dormitory experiences were like in California. So my daughter agreed to move into a dormitory at California State University, Sacramento. I paid for the dormitory, both to get her in there and so I would have direct access to dormitory life and she could also, by living there, report back to me her impression as about dormitory living.

The Court: Okay.

Irwin: Because it was not necessarily required for her education that she live in the dormitory.

The Court: Okay. How about supplies?

Irwin: Uh-hmm. Yes. Okay. These supplies basically fell under the material research expenses. . . .

The Court: So, many of these expenses related to the purchase of books? For example, "Costco: novel writing research materials. . . ." What does that mean?

Irwin: Ah, they, hm . . . They could be any number of items. . . .

The Court: The court's not really clear. What is it that you purchased? Did you purchase an item, a commodity, a piece of clothing, and then write about it?

Irwin: Oh. You mean as in—

The Court: What did you get? What did you physically get for $148.17 on February 9, 1990 at Costco?

Irwin: Okay. It can involve any number of materials that I would be purchasing at Costco. It could be clothes, it could be tools, it could be fixtures. . . .

The Court: So you buy a kitchen chair. That would be listed as a research material?

Irwin: If I'm using it in the research toward one of my writing projects, yes. Anything, basically, that I purchase is being used for my writing.

The Court: So on April 19, 1990, when you buy something at Lockeford County Flower, do you think you, for $42.50, do you think you bought flowers?

Irwin: Physically, I probably did. However, what I am purchasing is an item I can research.

Not surprisingly, the Court disallowed deductions for each of the items mentioned in this exchange.

For a tax return featuring considerably less drama, take a look at the Schedule C on the next page. The types of expenses for which deductions are typically allowed are set forth in Part II, lines 8-27.

In some cases, even if a deduction is allowed by § 162 or § 212, some other provision operates to reduce or even eliminate the deduction. One such provision is § 67, which allows certain itemized deductions only to the extent that they exceed 2 percent of the taxpayer's adjusted gross income. The most notable deductions covered by § 67 are deductions claimed under § 212 and deductions claimed by employees under § 162. Thus, for example, a self-employed practicing lawyer or a self-employed salesperson may claim deductions under § 162 without regard to § 67. The § 162 expenses of a lawyer or salesperson who works as an employee, however, are covered by § 67, though the burden may be avoided to a considerable extent, with the co-operation of the employer, by establishing a "reimbursement or other expense allowance arrangement with [the] employer." § 62(a)(2)(A). Another limitation on the deduction under § 212 of the expenses of earning income is that it is not allowed under the Alternative Minimum Tax (AMT). § 56(b)(1)(A)(i). We will discuss the AMT in further detail in Chapter 6.

The § 67 threshold, the § 68 phaseout (discussed in Chapter 4A), and the AMT all come into play with respect to attorneys' fees paid where a taxpayer sues and recovers for taxable lost income. For example, suppose an employee is fired, sues for wrongful discharge, and recovers $1 million, of which $400,000 goes to his or her attorney pursuant to a contingent fee arrangement. Although the legal fee is deductible, it is a miscellaneous itemized deduction under § 212 and is therefore subject to §§ 67 and 68. Even worse for the taxpayer, for purposes of the AMT the fee cannot be deducted at all. Thus, the taxpayer would be taxed on the full $1 million recovery with no offset for the amount remitted to the attorney.

In such situations, the taxpayer faces a clear incentive to treat the attorneys' fees as having been paid directly by the employer to the employee's lawyer, so as to avoid the issue of deductibility altogether. Unfortunately for taxpayers, the Supreme Court rejected this attempt to bypass the problem in its 2005 decision in Commissioner v. Banks, concluding that the plaintiff in a similar case had dominion over the entire amount of the recovery and could not avoid taxation via an "anticipatory assignment of income." See Commissioner v.

SCHEDULE C
(Form 1040)
Department of the Treasury
Internal Revenue Service (99)

Profit or Loss From Business
(Sole Proprietorship)
▶ Partnerships, joint ventures, etc., must file Form 1065 or 1065-B.
▶ Attach to Form 1040, 1040NR, or 1041.   ▶ See Instructions for Schedule C (Form 1040).

OMB No. 1545-0074

2007
Attachment
Sequence No. **09**

Name of proprietor

Social security number (SSN)

BARACK H. OBAMA

A   Principal business or profession, including product or service (see page C-2)

AUTHOR

B Enter code from pages C-8, 9, & 10
▶ 711510

C   Business name. If no separate business name, leave blank.

BARACK H. OBAMA

D Employer ID number (EIN), if any

E   Business address (including suite or room no.) ▶ _____
    City, town or post office, state, and ZIP code

F   Accounting method: (1) [X] Cash   (2) [ ] Accrual   (3) [ ] Other (specify) ▶ _____

G   Did you "materially participate" in the operation of this business during 2007? If "No," see page C-3 for limit on losses .... [X] Yes [ ] No

H   If you started or acquired this business during 2007, check here .... ▶ [ ]

Part I	**Income**		
1	Gross receipts or sales. **Caution.** If this income was reported to you on Form W-2 and the "Statutory employee" box on that form was checked, see page C-3 and check here .... ▶ [ ]	1	
2	Returns and allowances	2	
3	Subtract line 2 from line 1	3	
4	Cost of goods sold (from line 42 on page 2)	4	
5	**Gross profit.** Subtract line 4 from line 3	5	
6	Other income, including federal and state gasoline or fuel tax credit or refund (see page C-3) SEE STATEMENT 10	6	4,094,690.
7	**Gross income.** Add lines 5 and 6 .... ▶	7	4,094,690.

Part II	**Expenses.** Enter expenses for business use of your home **only** on line 30.						
8	Advertising	8		18	Office expense	18	432.
9	Car and truck expenses (see page C-4)	9		19	Pension and profit-sharing plans	19	
10	Commissions and fees	10	139,792.	20	Rent or lease (see page C-5):		
11	Contract labor (see page C-4)	11		a	Vehicles, machinery, and equipment	20a	
				b	Other business property	20b	
12	Depletion	12		21	Repairs and maintenance	21	
13	Depreciation and section 179 expense deduction (not included in Part III) (see page C-4)	13		22	Supplies (not included in Part III)	22	
				23	Taxes and licenses	23	
				24	Travel, meals, and entertainment:		
14	Employee benefit programs (other than on line 19)	14		a	Travel	24a	
15	Insurance (other than health)	15		b	Deductible meals and entertainment (see page C-6)	24b	
16	Interest:			25	Utilities	25	
a	Mortgage (paid to banks, etc.)	16a		26	Wages (less employment credits)	26	
b	Other	16b		27	Other expenses (from line 48 on page 2)	27	
17	Legal and professional services	17	11,088.				
28	**Total expenses** before expenses for business use of home. Add lines 8 through 27 in columns .... ▶					28	151,312.
29	Tentative profit (loss). Subtract line 28 from line 7					29	3,943,378.
30	Expenses for business use of your home. Attach Form 8829					30	
31	**Net profit or (loss).** Subtract line 30 from line 29.						
	• If a profit, enter on both **Form 1040, line 12,** and on **Schedule SE, line 2** or on Form 1040NR, line 13 (statutory employees, see page C-7). Estates and trusts, enter on **Form 1041, line 3.**					31	3,943,378.
	• If a loss, you **must** go to line 32.						
32	If you have a loss, check the box that describes your investment in this activity (see page C-7).						
	• If you checked 32a, enter the loss on both **Form 1040, line 12,** and **Schedule SE, line 2** or on Form 1040NR, line 13 (statutory employees, see page C-7). Estates and trusts, enter on **Form 1041, line 3.**					32a	[ ] All investment is at risk.
	• If you checked 32b, you **must** attach Form 6198. Your loss may be limited.					32b	[ ] Some investment is not at risk.

LHA   For Paperwork Reduction Act Notice, see page C-8 of the instructions.

Schedule C (Form 1040) 2007

720001 11-05-07

10

15330410 131470 4OC01F   2007.05051 OBAMA, BARACK H.   4OC01F_1

Banks, 543 U.S. 426 (2005). The "anticipatory assignment" doctrine is based largely on the case of Lucas v. Earl, 281 U.S. 111 (1930), which is covered in Chapter 7.A. In apparent sympathy with the taxpayer's plight in such situations, Congress enacted § 62(a)(19), which allows an "above the line" deduction (that is, a deduction in arriving at adjusted gross income) for attorneys' fees and court costs for claims of "unlawful discrimination" under the civil rights law, and for various other claims. Because of the limited scope of this provision, however, taxpayers may still, in some situations, experience a dramatic reduction in the after-tax recovery (and even, in extreme cases, a tax liability exceeding the amount of the litigant's net recovery).

As the *Irwin* and *Banks* cases illustrate, the question of how to treat expenses on the business-personal borderline surfaces in many diverse contexts. In reviewing the materials below, you may find that our tax system's approach to this general problem has been somewhat ad hoc. The challenge, therefore, is to see if it is possible to discern any overarching themes or general principles that reconcile the many different outcomes.

A. CONTROLLING THE ABUSE OF BUSINESS DEDUCTIONS

1. Hobby Losses

NICKERSON v. COMMISSIONER
700 F.2d 402 (7th Cir. 1983)

PELL, Circuit Judge.

Petitioners appeal the judgment of the United States Tax Court finding that profit was not their primary goal in owning a dairy farm. Based on this finding the tax court disallowed deductions for losses incurred in renovating the farm. The sole issue presented for our review is whether the tax court's finding regarding petitioners' motivation was clearly erroneous.

I. FACTS

Melvin Nickerson (hereinafter referred to as petitioner) was born in 1932 in a farming community in Florida. He worked evenings and weekends on his father's farm until he was 17. Petitioner entered the field of advertising after attending college and serving in the United States Army. During the years relevant to this case he was self-employed in Chicago, serving industrial and agricultural clients. His wife, Naomi W. Nickerson, was a full-time employee of the Chicago Board of Education. While petitioners were not wealthy, they did earn a comfortable living.

At the age of forty, petitioner decided that his career in the "youth oriented" field of advertising would not last much longer, and he began to look for an alternative source of income for the future. Petitioners decided that dairy farming was the most desirable means of generating income and examined a number of farms in Michigan and Wisconsin. After several years of searching, petitioners bought an 80-acre farm in Door County, Wisconsin for $40,000. One year later they purchased an additional 40 acres adjoining the farm for $10,000.

The farm, which had not been run as a dairy for eight years, was in a run-down condition. What little equipment was left was either in need of repair or obsolete. The tillable land, about 60 acres, was planted with alfalfa, which was at the end of its productive cycle. In an effort to improve this state of affairs petitioners leased the land to a tenant farmer for $20 an acre and an agreement that the farmer would convert an additional ten acres a year to the cultivation of a more profitable crop. At the time of trial approximately 80 acres were tillable. The rent received from the farmer was the only income derived from the farm.

Petitioner visited the farm on most weekends during the growing season and twice a month the rest of the year. Mrs. Nickerson and the children visited less frequently. The trip to the farm requires five hours of driving from petitioners' home in Chicago. During these visits petitioner and his family either worked on their land or assisted neighboring farmers. When working on his own farm petitioner concentrated his efforts on renovating an abandoned orchard and remodeling the farm house. In addition to learning about farming through this experience petitioner read a number of trade journals and spoke with the area agricultural extension agent.

Petitioners did not expect to make a profit from the farm for approximately 10 years. True to their expectations, petitioners lost $8,668 in 1976 and $9,872.95 in 1977. Although they did not keep formal books of account petitioners did retain receipts and cancelled checks relating to farm expenditures. At the time of trial, petitioners had not yet acquired any livestock or farm machinery. The farm was similarly devoid of recreational equipment and had never been used to entertain guests.

The tax court decided that these facts did not support petitioners' claim that the primary goal in operating the farm was to make a profit. We will examine the tax court's reasoning in more detail after setting out the relevant legal considerations.

II.   THE STATUTORY SCHEME

Section 162(a) of the Code allows deduction of "all the ordinary and necessary expenses paid or incurred during the taxable year in carrying on any trade or business." Section 183, however, limits the availability of these deductions if the activity "is not engaged in for profit" to deductions that are allowed regardless of the existence of a profit motive and deductions for ordinary and necessary expenses "only to the extent that the gross income derived from such activity for the taxable year exceeds [otherwise allowable deductions]." § 183(b)(2). The deductions claimed by petitioners are only allowable if their motivation in investing in the farm was to make a profit.

Petitioners bear the burden of proving that their primary purpose in renovating the farm was to make a profit.[3] . . . In meeting this burden, however, "it is sufficient if the taxpayer has a bona fide expectation of realizing a profit, regardless of the reasonableness of such expectation." . . . Although petitioners need only prove their sincerity rather than their realism the factors considered in judging their motivation are primarily objective. In addition to the taxpayer's statements of intent, which are given little weight for obvious reasons, the tax court must consider "all facts and circumstances with respect to the activity," including the following:

(1) *Manner in which the taxpayer carries on the activity.* The fact that the taxpayer carries on the activity in a businesslike manner and maintains complete and accurate books and records may indicate that the activity is engaged in for profit. . . .

(2) *The expertise of the taxpayer or his advisors.* Preparation for the activity by extensive study of its accepted business, economic, and scientific practices, or consultation with those who are expert therein, may indicate that the taxpayer has a profit motive where the taxpayer carries on the activity in accordance with such practices. . . .

(3) *The time and effort expended by the taxpayer in carrying on the activity.* The fact that the taxpayer devotes much of his personal time and effort to carrying on the activity, particularly if the activity does not have substantial personal or recreational aspects, may indicate an intention to derive a profit. . . . The fact that the taxpayer devotes a limited amount of time to an activity does not necessarily indicate a lack of profit motive where the taxpayer employs competent and qualified persons to carry on such activity.

(4) *Expectation that assets used in activity may appreciate in value.* . . .

(5) *The success of the taxpayer in carrying on other similar or dissimilar activities.* . . .

(6) *The taxpayer's history of income or losses with respect to the activity.* . . .

(7) *The amount of occasional profits, if any, which are earned.* . . .

(8) *The financial status of the taxpayer.* . . .

(9) *Elements of personal pleasure or recreation.* The presence of personal motives in [the] carrying on of an activity may indicate that the activity is not engaged in for profit, especially where there are recreational or personal elements involved. On the other hand, a profit motivation may be indicated where an activity lacks any appeal other than profit. It is not, however, necessary that an activity be engaged in with the exclusive intention of deriving a profit or with the intention of maximizing profits. . . .

Treas. Reg. § 1.183-2(b)(1)-(9). None of these factors is determinative, nor is the decision to be made by comparing the number of factors that weigh in the taxpayer's favor with the number that support the Commissioner. Id. There is no set formula for divining a taxpayer's true motive, rather "[o]ne struggles in vain for any verbal formula that will supply a ready touchstone. The standard

3. The Code does provide a presumption that a taxpayer engaged in an activity with a bona fide profit motive when a profit is realized two of five consecutive years. § 183(d). Because of petitioners' consistent losses this is not available. [The rule has now been changed from two of five to three of five consecutive years. — Eds.]

set by the statute is not a rule of law; it is rather a way of life. Life in all its fullness must supply the answer to the riddle." Welch v. Helvering [infra page 545]. Nonetheless, we are given some guidance by the enumerated factors and by the Congressional purpose in enacting section 183.

> The legislative history surrounding section 183 indicates that one of the prime motivating factors behind its passage was Congress' desire to create an objective standard to determine whether a taxpayer was carrying on a business for the purpose of realizing a profit or was instead merely attempting to create and utilize losses to offset other income.

Jasionowski v. Commissioner, 66 T.C. 312, 321 (1976). Congressional concern stemmed from a recognition that

> [w]ealthy individuals have invested in certain aspects of farm operations solely to obtain "tax losses"—largely bookkeeping losses—for use to reduce their tax on other income. . . . One of the remarkable aspects of the problem is pointed up by the fact that persons with large nonfarm income have a remarkable propensity to lose money in the farm business.

S. Rep. No. 91-552, 91st Cong., 1st Sess., reprinted in 1969 U.S. Code Cong. & Ad. News 2027, 2376. With this concern in mind we will now examine the decision of the tax court.

III. DECISION OF THE TAX COURT

The tax court analyzed the relevant factors and determined that making a profit was not petitioners' primary goal in engaging in farming. The court based its decision on a number of factors that weighed against petitioners. The court found that they did not operate the farm in a businesslike manner and did not appear to have a concrete plan for improving the profitability of the farm. The court believed that these difficulties were attributable to petitioners' lack of experience, but did not discuss the steps actually taken by Melvin Nickerson to gain experience in farming.

The court found it difficult to believe that petitioners actually believed that the limited amount of time they were spending at the farm would produce a profit given the dilapidated condition of the farm. Furthermore, the court found that petitioners' emphasis on making the farm house habitable rather than on acquiring or repairing farm equipment was inconsistent with a profit motive. These factors, combined with the consistent history of losses borne by petitioners, convinced the court that "petitioner at best entertains the hope that when he retires from the advertising business and can devote his complete attention to the farming operation, he may at that time expect to produce a profit." The court did not think that this hope rose to the level of a bona fide expectation of profit.

IV. REVIEW OF THE COURT'S FINDINGS

Whether petitioners intended to run the dairy farm for a profit is a question of fact, and as such our review is limited to a determination of whether the tax court was "clearly erroneous" in determining that petitioners lacked the requisite profit motive. . . . This standard of review applies although the only dispute is over the proper interpretation of uncontested facts. . . . This is one of those rare cases in which we are convinced that a mistake has been made.

Our basic disagreement with the tax court stems from our belief that the court improperly evaluated petitioners' actions from the perspective of whether they sincerely believed that they could make a profit from their current level of activity at the farm. On the contrary, petitioners need only prove that their current actions were motivated by the expectation that they would later reap a profit, in this case when they finished renovating the farm and began full-time operations. It is well established that a taxpayer need not expect an immediate profit; the existence of "start up" losses does not preclude a bona fide profit motive. . . . We see no basis for distinguishing petitioners' actions from a situation in which one absorbs larger losses over a shorter period of time by beginning full-time operations immediately. In either situation the taxpayer stands an equal chance of recouping start-up losses. In fact, it seems to us a reasonable decision by petitioners to prepare the farm before becoming dependent upon it for sustenance. Keeping in mind that petitioners were not seeking to supplement their existing incomes with their current work on the farm, but rather were laying the ground work for a contemplated career switch, we will examine the facts relied upon by the tax court.

The tax court found that the amount of time petitioners devoted to the farm was inadequate. In reaching this conclusion the court ignored petitioners' agreement with the tenant-farmer under which he would convert 10 acres a year to profitable crops in exchange for the right to farm the land. In this situation the limited amount of time spent by petitioners, who were fully employed in Chicago, is not inconsistent with an expectation of profit. . . .

The court also rested its decision on the lack of a concrete plan to put the farm in operable condition. Once again, this ignores petitioners' agreement with the tenant-farmer concerning reclamation of the land. Under this agreement the majority of the land would be tillable by the time petitioners were prepared to begin full-time farming. The tax court also believed that petitioners' decision to renovate the farm house and orchard prior to obtaining farm equipment evidenced a lack of profit motive. As petitioners planned to live on the farm when they switched careers refurbishing the house would seem to be a necessary first step. The court also failed to consider the uncontradicted testimony regarding repairs made to the hay barn and equipment shed, which supported petitioners' contention that they were interested in operating a farm rather than just living on the land. Additionally, we fail to understand how renovating the orchard, a potential source of food and income, is inconsistent with an expectation of profit.

The tax court took into account the history of losses in considering petitioners' intentions. While a history of losses is relevant, in this case little weight
should be accorded this factor. Petitioners did not expect to make a profit for a
number of years, and it was clear from the condition of the farm that a financial
investment would be required before the farm could be profitable. . . .

The court believed that most of petitioners' problems were attributable to
their lack of expertise. While lack of expertise is relevant, efforts at gaining
experience and a willingness to follow expert advice should also be considered. Treas. Reg. § 1.183-2(b)(2). The court here failed to consider the uncontradicted evidence that Melvin Nickerson read trade journals and
Government-sponsored agricultural newsletters, sought advice from a state
horticultural agent regarding renovation of the orchard and gained experience by working on neighboring farms. In addition, petitioners' agreement
with the tenant-farmer was entered into on the advice of the area agricultural
extension agent. To weigh petitioners' lack of expertise against them without
giving consideration to these efforts effectively precludes a bona fide attempt
to change careers. We are unwilling to restrict petitioners in this manner and
believe that a proper interpretation of these facts supports petitioners' claims.

The tax court recognized that the farm was not used for entertainment and
lacked any recreational facilities, and that petitioners' efforts at the farm were
"prodigious," but felt that this was of little importance. While the Commissioner need not prove that petitioners were motivated by goals other than
making a profit, we think that more weight should be given to the absence of
any alternative explanation for petitioners' actions. As we previously noted the
standard set out by the statute is to be applied with the insight gained from a
lifetime of experience as well as an understanding of the statutory scheme.
Common sense indicates to us that rational people do not perform hard
manual labor for no reason, and if the possibility that petitioners performed
these labors for pleasure is eliminated the only remaining motivation is profit.
The Commissioner has argued that petitioner was motivated by a love of
farming that stems from his childhood. We find it difficult to believe that he
drove five hours in order to spend his weekends working on a dilapidated
farm solely for fun, or that his family derived much pleasure from the experience. Furthermore, there is no support for this contention in the record. At
any rate, that petitioner may have chosen farming over some other career
because of fond memories of his youth does not preclude a bona fide profit
motive. Treas. Reg. § 1.183-2(b)(9). We believe that the absence of any recreational purpose strongly counsels in favor of finding that petitioners' prodigious efforts were directed at making a profit. . . .

If this were a case in which wealthy taxpayers were seeking to obtain tax
benefits through the creation of paper losses we would hesitate to reverse.
Before us today, however, is a family of modest means attempting to prepare
for a stable financial future. The amount of time and hard work invested by
petitioners belies any claim that allowing these deductions would thwart
Congress' primary purpose, that of excluding "hobby" losses from permissible
deductions. Accordingly, we hold that the tax court's finding was clearly erroneous and reverse.

NOTES AND QUESTIONS

1. *Hobby losses and tax losses.* Since the court in *Nickerson* holds that the Nickersons' farm activity was a business and not a hobby, the losses incurred in running the farm are deductible — that is, those losses can be used to offset the Nickersons' salary and other income. Assuming that the Nickersons reasonably and realistically viewed their cash outlays on the farm not as money down the drain (a true economic loss) but rather as an investment in what they hoped would be a valuable asset, their loss can be thought of as an artifact of the tax system, a "tax loss" that is not a true economic loss.

2. *Start-up costs.* Although the Tax Court opinion in *Nickerson* does not describe the outlays that gave rise to the deductible losses, it seems clear that on the court's view of the taxpayers' primary objective, those outlays were made for the purpose of creating a productive farm; they were part of the farm's start-up costs. For purposes of normal accounting, such outlays should be treated as capital expenditures; they are part of the cost of acquisition of a productive farm, not current expenses. For tax purposes, however, the outlays are treated as deductible expenses, at least for a cash-method farmer. (The distinction between capital expenditures and current expenses is explored in Chapter 6.) On the government's view of the case, the distinction between capital and current outlays was irrelevant to the outcome of the case it was litigating, since the outlays were simply the personal cost of indulging a desire to play farmer. The distinction would, however, be relevant to basis and thus to gain on disposition. If a person buys a farm for purely personal purposes, the acquisition cost becomes the farm's basis, which affects gain or loss on ultimate disposition. Though a loss would not be deductible, a gain would be taxable. Expenses of maintaining the farm (current outlays) would not be added to basis and thus would not reduce any gain that might otherwise be realized on disposition, but even for a farm owned for personal purposes, capital outlays would increase basis.

In McCarthy v. Commissioner, 164 F.3d 618 (2d Cir. 1998), the Tax Court had held that, because of a lack of profit motive, McCarthy was not entitled to deduct losses incurred in "managing and promoting his 13-year-old son's motocross racing career." The Second Circuit reversed and remanded on the ground that the Tax Court had improperly reasoned that since the son was an amateur and could not earn prize or endorsement money, no profit motive was possible. The Second Circuit, citing *Nickerson*, stated that "the inability to make a profit in a particular tax year is not dispositive," and held that all the facts bearing on long-term profit motive must be weighed. It went on to state, however, that on remand the Tax Court should consider the "pre-opening expense" doctrine, under which "expenses incurred before a taxpayer begins business operations [must] be capitalized." The court noted that this possibility had been "mentioned in the Commissioner's brief on this appeal." *Nickerson* is distinguishable on this issue because farmers are allowed to deduct currently many outlays that would be treated as capital expenditures in other businesses.

3. *Imputed income.* One other source of some possible confusion in *Nickerson* is that Mr. Nickerson appears to have performed valuable services in

improving the farm. As we have seen, the value of those services is a form of imputed income that escapes taxation. See supra page 77. (In this situation, however, even if income were imputed, that income would be offset by a deduction — as if Mr. Nickerson had paid himself wages, which would then be part of the costs that the court considered he was entitled to deduct.) The value of the services was an element that made the prospect for profit better by far than it would otherwise have been and thus helped establish that the Nickersons' primary purpose was economic gain, not personal pleasure. Suppose that Mr. Nickerson had hired someone else to perform all the services that he in fact performed himself. Would that have weakened or strengthened his argument that he was seeking primarily profit rather than pleasure in operating the farm?

4. *Primary purpose.* (a) The *Nickerson* court follows the typical approach in cases involving activities with both business and personal elements: It seeks to determine the taxpayer's primary purpose. The objectively observed facts reviewed by the court are indirect evidence of purpose. The court insists, however, that the taxpayers "need only prove their sincerity rather than their realism." In other words, a person might establish a sincere intent to make a profit even though the hope or expectation of profit is unrealistic. How likely do you suppose it is that a person with an unrealistic expectation will be able to prove a sincere intent to make a profit? See infra Note 7. How important are the nine factors listed in the regulations (§ 1.183-2(b)) and cited by the court? See the last sentence of Regs. § 1.183-2(a).

(b) Is the court's decision too trusting and generous? Why do you suppose the farm had been abandoned eight years before the Nickersons bought it?

5. *An alternative approach.* Is primary purpose the best test? Why not focus on benefit? Suppose, for example, that it could be established that the Nickersons had lost (and had expected to lose) $10,000 per year, that the farm was not as good an investment as other alternatives available to them, but that it became a good investment when they took account of the fact that it provided $6,000 worth of pleasure each year. How much deduction, if any, would you allow? What if the pleasure had been worth only $4,000 per year? Is it feasible to determine the value of the pleasure element? Less so than to determine primary purpose? If you don't like either approach because of the difficulty of the factual determinations, what objective approach would you prefer?

6. *The role of § 183.* (a) Does § 183 provide much guidance with respect to the basic question of deductibility in cases like *Nickerson?*

(b) Note the presumption rule in § 183(d). Where applicable, this rule overcomes the normal presumption of correctness of the Commissioner's determination. Did that presumption seem important in *Nickerson?*

(c) Section 183(b) allows income generated by a hobby venture to be offset by the expenses of that venture (after reduction of the income by the amount of any deductions, such as for interest and taxes, allowed without regard to profit-seeking motive), but, since 1987, only to the extent that those expenses, plus other miscellaneous expenses, exceed 2 percent of AGI. See §§ 67, 183(b).

7. *Results in other hobby cases.* Commenting on country estate and racing stable cases, long ago Randolph Paul said: "The American businessman has never appeared so indefatigably optimistic as in some of the cases on this

point." Paul, Motive and Intent in Federal Tax Law, in Selected Studies in Federal Taxation 281-282 (2d ser. 1938).

Horse breeding and racing, though the sport of kings, have been held in a surprising number of cases to be the business of taxpayers. See, e.g., Farish v. Commissioner, 103 F.2d 63 (5th Cir. 1939). In that case, the possibility of geographical and occupational discrimination was suggested (103 F.2d at 65):

> It is common for a man in the oil business, of sound judgment, to expend thousands of dollars in exploring the land and drilling for oil in "wild cat" territory. Sometimes, this results in dry holes and the costs of drilling and development are totally lost. On other occasions, producing wells are brought in and the profits are enormous. The breeding of horses would not be considered merely a fad in Texas. It is not at all improbable that men in the oil business, having ample capital, would engage in the enterprises here involved with the hope and expectation of ultimately making a fair return on the investment.

In Dailey v. Commissioner, 44 T.C.M. 1352 (1982), the taxpayers, husband and wife, who were knowledgeable and experienced antique collectors, were denied deductions of $4,050 for the cost of a trip to Europe to visit museums, $926 for travel to museums in this country for the same purpose, and $201 for subscriptions to art and antique journals. The court observed (44 T.C.M. at 1353):

> Petitioners collected art and antique items for fun and profit, much like a philatelist might collect stamps, or a numismatist coins. Over a period of more than three decades, petitioners never advertised any item for sale, never offered an item for sale, and in fact never sold an item. A comprehensive inventory was first prepared in connection with this trial. They hoped to make a profit through appreciation, but so does the numismatist or philatelist. This floating expectation does not make the trip to Europe or to museums in this country deductible.

Do you think that the Nickersons had more than a "floating expectation" of profit? Is antique collecting basically different from farming in ways that should affect tax results? If you represented a couple like the Daileys before the Tax Court, what kind of evidence would you want to introduce?

2. Home Offices and Vacation Homes

Many people have offices in their homes, or at least claim that they do, even though their principal place of work is elsewhere. Where a person does in fact use part of his home exclusively, or even primarily, for business, the costs of that part of the home (including a pro rata share of utility bills and depreciation on that part) might properly be regarded as a deductible business expense. It is not difficult, however, to see the opportunities for abuse of any opportunity for deduction. For many years, the Service and the courts tried to curb the abuses, but that was a losing effort. The problem was that it was easy for a dishonest, or at least self-serving, taxpayer to offer his or her own testimony in support of a primary business purpose or use and difficult for the government to rebut that testimony. Not only were some taxpayers winning doubtful cases at the administrative level (within the IRS) and in the courts, but many more were playing, and winning, the audit lottery. Congress finally intervened, in 1976, adopting the stringent restrictions found in § 280A. The approach of § 280A is to begin with a general rule denying deductions for any use of a home for business purposes (§ 280A(a)) and then to list specific, concrete exceptions (§ 280A(c)), which you should examine briefly.

At the same time it addressed offices in the home, Congress dealt with vacation homes, again a source of considerable abuse. There are, of course, taxpayers who have bought resort-area houses and condominiums strictly as investments. Often these investments showed losses for tax purposes because deductions for interest, taxes, depreciation, utilities, condominium fees, and so forth exceeded rental returns. In other words, a resort-area house or condominium could have been acquired as a "tax shelter," with no element of personal use. The 1986 act substantially reduced the attractiveness of such investments by disallowing deductions for "passive losses." See § 469, described infra page 594. People may continue to hold, or acquire, such investments despite the passive loss limitations. They should be, and are, allowed to offset any income from renting such units by claiming all the ordinary deductions, including depreciation (ACRS). But there is another tax issue. In the past many people acquired resort-area dwelling units largely for personal use, while claiming that the purpose of the acquisition was to make a profit and that the personal use was purely incidental. Since a profit-making objective depends on the investor's state of mind, the opportunity for abuse was, as with offices in the home, great. Real estate developers aggressively exploited the opportunity to sell vacation units intended for mostly personal use by pointing to the tax advantages that could be achieved by claiming investor status. Section 280A deals with this problem, with an arbitrary approach that is severe, though somewhat less so than the approach taken with respect to offices in the home.

(a) Vacation homes. Section 280A covers both vacation homes and home offices; we begin our discussion with the rules governing vacation homes. These rules listed below are quite complex. We present them to illustrate the downside of adopting a rules, rather than standards, based approach. Students should not attempt to memorize these rules. Instead, as you read the rules, imagine yourself to be a taxpayer with a vacation home who is trying to do his or her own taxes. Here, then, are the rules:

(1) The statute covers any "dwelling unit" that is used by the taxpayer for more than a specified amount of time during the year for personal purposes. See § 280A(a) and (d). The specified amount of time is the greater of "14 days, or 10 percent of the number of days during [the] year for which [the] unit is rented at a fair rental." See § 280A(d)(1).

(2) If the unit is not used at all for personal purposes, the taxpayer is allowed to deduct expenses (utilities, repairs, condominium fees, etc.), depreciation (cost recovery), interest, and taxes, subject to the limitation on deduction of passive activity losses.

(3) If the unit is used for personal purposes for more than the specified amount of time, but is rented out for less than fifteen days, then the owner

excludes the rental income and may not claim deductions other than for interest and taxes (which are deductible without regard to profit motive, subject to the § 163(h) limits on the interest deduction). See § 280A(g), (b). This is obviously intended to be a de minimis exception but has allowed tax windfalls for people who have been able to rent their homes for short periods, at high rents.

(4) If the unit is used for personal purposes for less than the specified amount of time, the disallowance rule of § 280A(a) does not apply, but the deduction other than for taxes is allowed only on a pro rata basis (comparing rental and personal use) (§ 280A(e)) and, again, is subject to the limitation on deduction of passive activity losses. (Interest cannot be deducted without regard to profit because the unit is not a "second home," since it is occupied less than the required number of days. If a profit motive is lacking, the interest becomes "personal interest," which is not deductible. See § 163(h)(1), (h)(3), and (h)(4)(A).)

(5) If the unit is used for personal purposes for more than the specified amount of time, then expenses other than interest and taxes must still be prorated, but the deduction for such prorated expenses cannot exceed the rent received, reduced by an allocable share of the interest and taxes. See § 280A(c)(5). This rule is comparable to that found in § 183(b), which limits deductions for hobby activities to the income from the activity (see Regs. § 1.183-1(d)(3)).

(b) Offices in the home. To curb the abuse of deductions for offices in the home, Congress used broad language denying a deduction (§ 280A(a)), followed by a set of specific, relatively concrete exceptions (§ 280A(c)). Thus, taxpayers cannot base home office deduction claims on general assertions regarding business use, but instead must show that they meet the terms of one of the exceptions.

PROBLEMS

1. (a) Susan is an associate at a large law firm. On nights and weekends, Susan often works at home in her study. Susan and her family also use the study for personal purposes. The use of the study is divided about equally between personal and work activities. May Susan deduct half of the cost of the study as a business expense? See § 280A(c).

(b) The facts are the same as in (a) except that the study is used exclusively for work. May Susan deduct the cost of the study as a business expense?

(c) The facts are the same as in (b) except that Susan sees clients in the study. May Susan deduct the cost of the study as a business expense?

2. Sharon uses her vacation home sixty days a year and rents it out ten days a year. What portion, if any, of the depreciation and rental expenses may Sharon deduct? See § 280A(g). (For this and the following questions, you may assume that otherwise deductible losses will not be limited by the passive loss rules of § 469.)

3. (a) Anne uses her vacation home five days a year and rents it out 95 days a year. Rental income from the property is $8,000, real estate taxes are $2,000,

and annual depreciation and maintenance for the property amounts to $10,000. There are no other expenses associated with the property. How much, if any, of the annual depreciation and maintenance expense may Anne deduct? See § 280A(e).

(b) The facts are the same as in (a) except that Anne uses her vacation home fifteen days a year and rents it out eighty-five days a year. How much, if any, of the annual depreciation and maintenance expense may Anne deduct? See § 280A(c)(5), (e).

POPOV v. COMMISSIONER
246 F.3d 1190 (9th Cir. 2001)

This case concerns the continuing problem of the home office deduction. We conclude, on the facts of this case, that a professional musician is entitled to deduct the expenses from the portion of her home used exclusively for musical practice.

FACTS AND PROCEDURAL BACKGROUND

Katia Popov is a professional violinist who performs regularly with the Los Angeles Chamber Orchestra and the Long Beach Symphony. She also contracts with various studios to record music for the motion picture industry. In 1993, she worked for twenty-four such contractors and recorded in thirty-eight different locations. These recording sessions required that Popov be able to read scores quickly. The musicians did not receive the sheet music in advance of the recording sessions; instead, they were presented with their parts when they arrived at the studio, and recording would begin shortly thereafter. None of Popov's twenty-six employers provided her with a place to practice.

Popov lived with her husband Peter, an attorney, and their four-year-old daughter Irina, in a one-bedroom apartment in Los Angeles, California. The apartment's living room served as Popov's home office. The only furniture in the living room consisted of shelves with recording equipment, a small table, a bureau for storing sheet music, and a chair. Popov used this area to practice the violin and to make recordings, which she used for practice purposes and as demonstration tapes for orchestras. No one slept in the living room, and the Popovs' daughter was not allowed to play there. Popov spent four to five hours a day practicing in the living room.

In their 1993 tax returns, the Popovs claimed a home office deduction for the living room and deducted forty percent of their annual rent and twenty percent of their annual electricity bill. The Internal Revenue Service ("the Service") disallowed these deductions, and the Popovs filed a petition for redetermination in the Tax Court.

The Tax Court concluded that the Popovs were not entitled to a home office deduction. Although "practicing at home was a very important component to [Popov's] success as a musician," the court found that her living room was not her "principal place of business." In the court's view, her principal places of business were the studios and concert halls where she recorded and performed, because it was her performances in these places that earned her income. . . .[4]

ANALYSIS

The Internal Revenue Code allows a deduction for a home office that is exclusively used as "the principal place of business for any trade or business of the taxpayer." § 280A(c)(1)(A). The Code does not define the phrase "principal place of business."

A. THE *SOLIMAN* TESTS

Our inquiry is governed by Commissioner v. Soliman, 506 U.S. 168 (1993), the Supreme Court's most recent treatment of the home office deduction. In *Soliman*, the taxpayer was an anesthesiologist who spent thirty to thirty-five hours per week with patients at three different hospitals. None of the hospitals provided Soliman with an office, so he used a spare bedroom for contacting patients and surgeons, maintaining billing records and patient logs, preparing for treatments, and reading medical journals.

The Supreme Court denied Soliman a deduction for his home office, holding that the "statute does not allow for a deduction whenever a home office may be characterized as legitimate." Id. at 174. Instead, courts must determine whether the home office is the taxpayer's principal place of business. Although the Court could not "develop an objective formula that yields a clear answer in every case," the Court stressed two primary considerations: "the relative importance of the activities performed at each business location and the time spent at each place." Id. at 174-75. We address each in turn.

1. *Relative Importance*

The importance of daily practice to Popov's profession cannot be denied. Regular practice is essential to playing a musical instrument at a high level of ability, and it is this level of commitment that distinguishes the professional from the amateur.[5] Without daily practice, Popov would be unable to perform in professional orchestras. She would also be unequipped for the peculiar demands of studio recording: The ability to read and perform scores on sight requires an acute musical intelligence that must be constantly developed and

---

4. The Popovs also challenge the Tax Court's denial of their deductions for long-distance phone calls, meal expenses, and clothing. We find no merit in these claims. The Popovs did not adequately establish the business purpose of the phone calls or the meal expenses. See Welch v. Helvering, 290 U.S. 111, 115 (1933). The Tax Court did not err in finding that most of Katia Popov's concert attire was adaptable to general usage as ordinary clothing. See Pevsner v. Comm'r, 628 F.2d 467, 469 (5th Cir. 1980).

5. One who doubts this might consult George Bernard Shaw's famous observation that "hell is full of musical amateurs." George Bernard Shaw, Man and Superman act 3 (1903).

honed. In short, Popov's four to five hours of daily practice lay at the very heart of her career as a professional violinist.

Of course, the concert halls and recording studios are also important to Popov's profession. Without them, she would have no place in which to perform. Audiences and motion picture companies are unlikely to flock to her one-bedroom apartment. In *Soliman*, the Supreme Court stated that, although "no one test is determinative in every case," "the point where goods and services are delivered must be given great weight in determining the place where the most important functions are performed." Id. at 175. The Service places great weight on this statement, contending that Popov's performances should be analogized to the "service" of delivering anesthesia that was at issue in *Soliman*; these "services" are delivered in concert halls and studios, not in her apartment.

We agree with Popov that musical performance is not so easily captured under a "goods and services" rubric. The German poet Heinrich Heine observed that music stands "halfway between thought and phenomenon, between spirit and matter, a sort of nebulous mediator, like and unlike each of the things it mediates—spirit that requires manifestation in time, and matter that can do without space."[6] Heinrich Heine, Letters on the French Stage (1837), quoted in *Words about Music: A Treasury of Writings 2* (John Amis & Michael Rose eds., 1989). Or as Harry Ellis Dickson of the Boston Symphony Orchestra explained more concretely:

> A musician's life is different from that of most people. We don't go to an office every day, or to a factory, or to a bank. We go to an empty hall. We don't deal in anything tangible, nor do we produce anything except sounds. We saw away, or blow, or pound for a few hours and then we go home. It is a strange way to make a living!

Harry Ellis Dickson, *Gentlemen, More Dolce Please* (1969), quoted in Drucker v. Comm'r, 715 F.2d 67, 68-69 (2d Cir. 1983).

It is possible, of course, to wrench musical performance into a "delivery of services" framework, but we see little value in such a wooden and unblinking application of the tax laws. *Soliman* itself recognized that in this area of law "variations are inevitable in case-by-case determinations." 506 U.S. at 175. We believe this to be such a case. We simply do not find the "delivery of services" framework to be helpful in analyzing this particular problem. Taken to extremes, the Service's argument would seem to generate odd results in a variety of other areas as well. We doubt, for example, that an appellate advocate's primary place of business is the podium from which he delivers his oral argument, or that a professor's primary place of business is the classroom, rather than the office in which he prepares his lectures.

We therefore conclude that the "relative importance" test yields no definitive answer in this case, and we accordingly turn to the second prong of the *Soliman* inquiry.

---

6. Although not, perhaps, without practice space.

2. *Amount of Time*

Under *Soliman*, "the decisionmaker should . . . compare the amount of time spent at home with the time spent at other places where business activities occur." Id. at 177. "This factor assumes particular significance when," as in this case, "comparison of the importance of the functions performed at various places yields no definitive answer to the principal place of business inquiry." Id.[7] In *Soliman*, the taxpayer spent significantly more time in the hospitals than he did in his home office. In this case, Popov spent significantly more time practicing the violin at home than she did performing or recording.[8]

This second factor tips the balance in the Popovs' favor. They are accordingly entitled to a home office deduction for Katia Popov's practice space, because it was exclusively used as her principal place of business.

B. DRUCKER

The result we reach in this case harmonizes with that of the Second Circuit in Drucker v. Comm'r, 715 F.2d 67 (2d Cir. 1983). *Drucker* involved concert musicians employed by the Metropolitan Opera Association, which did not provide its musicians with practice facilities. Each musician instead devoted a portion of his or her apartment exclusively to musical study and practice, and spent approximately thirty hours a week practicing. Id. at 68. The musicians sought to deduct a portion of the rent and electricity allocable to the practice area. The Service denied the deduction. The Tax Court agreed with the Service, holding that off-premises practice was not a requirement of the musicians' jobs and that the musicians' principal place of business was Lincoln Center.

The Second Circuit reversed. The court first rejected as clearly erroneous the Tax Court's conclusion that practice was not a "requirement or condition of employment." Id. at 69. The court then concluded that the musicians' principal place of business was their home practice studios, finding that this was "the rare situation in which an employee's principal place of business is not that of his employer." Id. Both "in time and in importance, home practice was the 'focal point' of the appellant musicians' employment-related activities." Id. Accordingly, the musicians were entitled to a deduction for home

---

7. Justices Thomas and Scalia concurred in *Soliman*, but noted that the Court provided no guidance if the taxpayer "spent 30 to 35 hours at his home office and only 10 hours" at the hospitals. 506 U.S. at 184 (Thomas, J., concurring) "Which factor would take precedence? The importance of the activities undertaken at home . . . ? The number of hours spent at each location? I am at a loss, and I am afraid the taxpayer, his attorney, and a lower court would be as well." Id.

8. The Service argues that the evidence is unclear as to "how much time Mrs. Popov spent practicing at home as opposed to the time she spent performing outside of the home." It is true that the evidence is not perfectly clear and that the Tax Court made no specific comparative findings. However, the Tax Court found that she practiced four to five hours a day in her apartment. If we read this finding in the light most generous to the Service and assume that she only practiced four hours a day 300 days a year, Popov would still have practiced 1200 hours in a year. She testified that she performed with two orchestras for a total of 120-140 hours. If she spent a similar amount of time recording, she would still be spending about five hours practicing for every hour of performance or recording. The only plausible reading of the evidence is that Popov spent substantially more time practicing than she did performing or recording.

office expenses. The facts in this case are even more compelling. In *Drucker*, the musicians had only one employer; here Popov worked for twenty-six different employers and recorded in thirty-eight different locations.

We are unpersuaded by the Service's contention that *Drucker* is no longer good law. The Service has not directed us to any decision that has ever called *Drucker* into question. The Supreme Court cited *Drucker* twice in *Soliman*, but never suggested that it was overruling *Drucker*'s result. *Soliman*, 506 U.S. at 171, 172. Although the particular "focal point test" employed by the Second Circuit may no longer be valid, we are unwilling to conclude that the Supreme Court sub silentio overruled a long-standing precedent of the Second Circuit. "Uniformity of decision among the circuits is vitally important on issues concerning the administration of tax laws. Thus the tax decisions of other circuits should be followed unless they are demonstrably erroneous or there appear cogent reasons for rejecting them." Unger v. Comm'r, 936 F.2d 1316, 1320 (D.C. Cir. 1991) (quoting Keasler v. United States, 766 F.2d 1227, 1233 (8th Cir. 1985)).

C.   CONCLUSION

For the foregoing reasons, the Tax Court's denial of the Popovs' home office deduction is reversed.

QUESTIONS

1. Is it likely that the living room in a one-bedroom apartment where three people lived was used exclusively as a place of business, as § 280A(c)(1) requires?

2. Why is it, according to the court, that "musical performance is not so easily captured under a 'goods or services' rubric"? Did Judge Hawkins's evident fondness for classical music improperly influence his application of the *Soliman* test?

3. Is there any reasonable basis for denying that the first prong of the *Soliman* test (where services are rendered or goods delivered) supported the Commissioner's position? Wouldn't it also support the Commissioner's position (whatever the overall outcome given the second prong, relative time spent) in the case of an appellate advocate or professor who had no office other than a home office?

4. Given that the first prong of the *Soliman* test supported the Commissioner but the second prong supported the taxpayer, how should the court have tried to resolve the case? Is this indeterminacy the Supreme Court's fault?

5. Justices Thomas and Scalia, whose concurrence in *Soliman* the court mentions in footnote 7 (originally n. 5), would have adopted a test under which the first prong would be determinative unless "the home office is one of several locations where goods or services are delivered, and thus also one of the multiple locations where income was generated." Would this test have yielded clearer answers than the one the Supreme Court adopted in *Soliman*? Would it have been less fair?

6. Imagine you are a musician who must spend hours at home practicing and that you are looking for a house or apartment. Would your practice-related needs influence your choice of residence? Lead you to spend more for a residence? If so, why shouldn't the tax law allow you to deduct those extra costs? Which of the following considerations is persuasive?

a) It is difficult to determine extra costs.

b) It is difficult to determine who must in fact work at home and to what degree.

c) Allowing deductions in cases such as *Popov* will encourage other taxpayers to take wildly aggressive positions. The expected financial return for these taxpayers will be positive, due to low audit rates, low penalty rates, and the unlikelihood of penalty assessments.

How would you resolve this issue?

3. Income Unconnected to a Trade or Business

The following case, decided in 1983, arises under § 280A, but the outcome turns on whether the taxpayers were engaged in a "trade or business." The "trade or business" concept arises in a variety of contexts and has taken on increased importance recently because of the adoption in 1986 of § 67. Section 67, as we have seen, imposes a 2 percent threshold on deductions for expenses claimed by investors, under § 212, but not for expenses claimed, under § 162, as trade or business expenses. Indeed, in the case itself there is a reference to substantial expenses that were deducted without challenge under § 212 and that would now be subject to § 67's partial disallowance.

MOLLER v. UNITED STATES
721 F.2d 810 (Fed. Cir. 1983)

Before KASHIWA, Circuit Judge, NICHOLS, Senior Circuit Judge, and NIES, Circuit Judge.

KASHIWA, Circuit Judge.

This is an appeal by the United States from a judgment of the Claims Court granting taxpayers, Joseph A. and Dorothy D. Moller, a tax refund for the years 1976 and 1977. 1 Cl. Ct. 25, 553 F. Supp. 1071 (1982). The Claims Court concluded that taxpayers were active investors engaged in the "trade or business" of making investments and held that taxpayers were entitled to deduct the expenses of two home offices under I.R.C. § 280A. For the reasons stated below, we reverse.

FACTS

Since 1965 taxpayers have relied almost entirely on the income derived from their investments for their support. Their only other sources of income have been two small pensions and social security payments.

The Mollers' investments consist of four portfolios of stocks and bonds. Mr. and Mrs. Moller own an investment portfolio individually and each receives income from a portfolio held in trust. However, they have full management control of all four portfolios, including those held in trust.

In 1976 and 1977 taxpayers devoted their full time to their investment activities. Each spent approximately forty to forty-two hours per week in connection with these activities. They kept regular office hours and monitored the stock market on a daily basis. They made all their investment decisions on their own. The total value of the four portfolios was $13,500,000 in 1976 and $14,500,000 in 1977.

The Mollers engaged in a variety of activities in managing their portfolios. They maintained a "watch list" listing their portfolios. They maintained a "watch list" listing all stocks on the New York Stock Exchange that were considered to be potential purchases. They kept detailed records of the stocks in their portfolios. They also subscribed to and regularly studied a number of financial publications and services.

The Claims Court concluded that taxpayers engaged in 83 security purchase transactions and 41 sales transactions in 1976 and 76 purchase and 30 sales transactions in 1977. Eight of the security purchase transactions in 1976 and nine in 1977 consisted of deposits to secure shares in interest-bearing common trust accounts; three transactions in 1976 and 23 in 1977 consisted of invasions by Mrs. Moller of her trust corpus; and 14 transactions in 1976 and nine in 1977 consisted of stocks acquired through splits and dividends. Twenty-two of the sales transactions in 1976 and seven in 1977 were withdrawals from common trust accounts. The stocks which taxpayers sold in 1976 and 1977 had been held for an average of more than 3½ and 8 years, respectively.

The taxpayers did not purchase stocks for speculative purposes. They were primarily interested in long-term growth potential and the payment of interest and dividends. Interest and dividend income was over 98% of their gross income in 1976 and 1977. In 1976 their income from the sale of securities was only $612, while in 1977 their sales resulted in a loss of $223.

The taxpayers also invested in Treasury Bills but they did so to maintain liquidity and earn interest. Of the taxpayers' 46 Treasury Bill transactions in 1976 and 1977, only 7 involved bills sold before maturity.

The Mollers maintained a summer and a winter residence. Each house had quarters in which the taxpayers conducted their investment activities. The taxpayers kept regular hours and used the quarters exclusively for investment activities.

In managing their portfolios, the taxpayers incurred expenses of $22,659.91 in 1976 and $29,561.69 in 1977, and deducted these on their joint income tax returns. The expenses attributable to maintaining the taxpayers' two home-offices amounted to $7,439.65 in 1976 and $7,247.21 in 1977.[9]

The Internal Revenue Service disallowed that portion of the claimed deductions based on the home-office expenses for both offices and asserted

9. The home-office expenses included depreciation, utilities, insurance, and various maintenance expenses attributable to the offices.

deficiencies against the taxpayers for the years 1976 and 1977.[10] The tax-payers paid the deficiencies and filed claims for refunds. After these claims were disallowed, the taxpayers brought this action seeking recovery of the taxes paid, plus interest.

The Claims Court held that taxpayers were investors, not traders, but were nevertheless engaged in the trade or business of making investments and therefore entitled to deduct their home-offices expenses under section 280A of the Internal Revenue Code.

OPINION

I

Section 280A was added to the Internal Revenue Code of 1954 by the Tax Reform Act of 1976, Pub. L. No. 455, 90 Stat. 1520, to provide "definitive rules . . . governing the deductibility of expenses attributable to the mainte-nance of an office in the taxpayers' personal residence." S. Rep. No. 938, 94th Cong., 2d Sess. 144, 147, reprinted in 1976 U.S. Code Cong. & Admin. News 2897, 3576, 3579; H.R. Rep. No. 658, 94th Cong., 2d Sess. 157, 160, rep-rinted in 1976 U.S. Code Cong. & Admin. News 2897, 3050, 3053. Section 280A generally disallows all deductions for a taxpayer's use of a residence. Section 280A(c)(1)(A), however, provides an exception to this rule for that portion of the residence used as "the principal place of business for any trade or business of the taxpayer."

In order to get a deduction under section 280A, a taxpayer must conduct an activity which is a trade or business, the principal office of which is in his home.[11] Prior to the enactment of section 280A, home-office expenses could have been deducted either under I.R.C. § 162(a), if incurred in carrying on a trade or business, or under I.R.C. § 212 if incurred for the production of income. The legislative history of section 280A makes clear that a taxpayer can no longer take a home-office deduction for an activity where it is for the production of income within the meaning of section 212 but is not a "trade or business" under section 162. . . .

The principal question in the instant case is whether the taxpayers' in-vestment activity was a trade or business.

II

Neither the Internal Revenue Code nor the regulations define "trade or business." However, the concept of engaging in a trade or business, as dis-tinguished from other activities pursued for profit, has been in the Internal Revenue Code since its inception and has generated much case law.

---

10. The other investment expenses, amounting to $15,220.26 for 1976 and $22,314.48 for 1977 included subscriptions, office supplies, accounting and legal services, and other similar items. There is no dispute that taxpayers are entitled to deduct these expenses under I.R.C. § 212.

11. There is also the statutory requirement that the office be "exclusively used on a regular basis." The government concedes that this requirement has been met.

In determining whether a taxpayer who manages his own investments is engaged in a trade or business, the courts have distinguished between "traders," who are considered to be engaged in a trade or business, and "investors," who are not. See e.g., Levin v. United States, 597 F.2d 760, 765 (Ct. Cl. 1979). Contrary to the holding of the trial court, investors are considered to be merely engaged in the production of income. See Purvis v. Commissioner, 530 F.2d 1332 (9th Cir. 1976).

This court's predecessor, the Court of Claims, has defined a trader as one whose profits are derived from the "direct management of purchasing and selling." *Levin*, 597 F.2d at 765. The Ninth Circuit has adopted a similar test to distinguish between investment and trading accounts:

> In the former, securities are purchased to be held for capital appreciation and income, usually without regard to short-term developments that would influence the price of securities on the daily market. In a trading account, securities are bought and sold with reasonable frequency in an endeavor to catch the swings in the daily market movements and profit thereby on a short term basis.

Purvis, 530 F.2d at 1334, quoting Liang v. Commissioner, 23 T.C. 1040, 1043 (1955).

Therefore, in order to be a trader, a taxpayer's activities must be directed to short-term trading, not the long-term holding of investments, and income must be principally derived from the sale of securities rather than from dividends and interest paid on those securities. In determining whether a taxpayer who manages his own investments is a trader, and thus engaged in a trade or business, relevant considerations are the taxpayer's investment intent, the nature of the income to be derived from the activity, and the frequency, extent, and regularity of the taxpayer's securities transactions. See *Purvis*, 530 F.2d at 1334.

The Claims Court concluded that taxpayers were investors and not traders because they were primarily interested in the long-term growth potential of their stocks. We agree. Mr. Moller testified that he was looking for long-term growth and the payment of dividends. In addition, the taxpayers did not derive their income from the relatively short-term turnover of stocks, nor did they derive any significant profits through the act of trading. Interest and dividend income was over 98% of taxpayers' gross income for 1976 and 1977, and in 1976 their profit from the sale of securities was only $612, while in 1977 their sales resulted in a loss of $223.

The number of sales transactions made by the taxpayers also leads to the conclusion that they were not traders in securities. In the cases in which taxpayers have been held to be in the business of trading in securities for their own account, the number of their transactions indicated that they were engaged in market transactions on an almost daily basis. At most, the Mollers engaged in 83 security purchase transactions and 41 sales transactions in 1976 and 76 purchase and 30 sales transactions in 1977.

Moreover, taxpayers did not "endeavor to catch the swings in the daily market movements and profit thereby on a short term basis." *Purvis*, 530 F.2d at 1334. The stocks owned by taxpayers, which they sold during 1976 and 1977, had been held for an average of over 3 1/2 and 8 years, respectively.

The Mollers were investors and not traders. The Claims Court so concluded and we agree.

III

The Claims Court, however, went on to hold that despite the fact that the Mollers were investors, they were in the trade or business of making investments. The court distinguished between passive and active investors and concluded that the Mollers were active investors engaged in a trade or business because their investment activities were regular, extensive, and continuous, and they involved the active and constant exercise of managerial and decision-making functions. We disagree.

A taxpayer who merely manages his investments seeking long-term gain is not carrying on a trade or business. This is so irrespective of the extent or continuity of the transactions or the work required in managing the portfolio. Higgins v. Commissioner, 312 U.S. 212 (1941). The fact that the Mollers spent much time managing a large amount of money is not determinative of the question whether they were engaged in a trade or business.

In *Higgins* a taxpayer who resided abroad maintained an office in the United States to handle bookkeeping and other details of his extensive security transactions. The taxpayer directed these activities from abroad. He sought primarily permanent investments but did make changes in his portfolio. Despite the fact that the taxpayer devoted a considerable amount of time to overseeing his securities, the Court held that his securities activities did not constitute a trade or business:

> The petitioner merely kept records and collected interest and dividends from his securities, through managerial attention for his investments. No matter how large the estate or how continuous or extended the work required may be, such facts are not sufficient as a matter of law to permit the courts to reverse the decision of the Board.

312 U.S. at 218.

The Claims Court, relying on Kales v. Commissioner, 101 F.2d 35 (6th Cir. 1939), distinguished the *Higgins* case on the basis that the taxpayer's activities in *Higgins* "were not at all comparable to the regular, extensive, and continuous activities of the plaintiffs in this case." In *Kales*, the Sixth Circuit held that a taxpayer was engaged in the trade or business of managing her own investments because her management activities were "extensive, varied, regular and continuous." 101 F.2d at 39. However, in a subsequent case, the Sixth Circuit recognized that the decision in *Kales* was impliedly if not expressly disapproved in *Higgins*. . . . Goodyear Investment Corp. v. Campbell, 139 F.2d 188, 191.

The Claims Court erred in relying on the *Kales* case. The "regular, extensive, and continuous" test is not in itself the correct test for determining whether a taxpayer is engaged in the trade or business of managing his own investments. In *Higgins*, the Court stated that continuity and extent of in-vestment activity were not determinative of the question of whether a taxpayer who manages his own investment is engaged in a trade or business. In a subsequent case, Whipple v. Commissioner, 373 U.S. 193 (1963), the Court stated that it had established a definition of trade or business in *Higgins* and went on to explain the import of the case:

> In response to the *Higgins* case and to give relief to *Higgins*-type taxpayers . . . Section 23(a) (now I.R.C. § 162) was amended not by disturbing the Court's definition of "trade or business" but by following the pattern that had been established since 1916 of "[enlarging] the category of incomes with reference to which expenses were deductible" . . . to include [in new § 212] expenses incurred in the production of income.

373 U.S. at 200.

The Internal Revenue Code, however, does not provide that all expenses incurred in the production of income are deductible expenses. In *Whipple*, section 166, which restricts bad debt deductions to those incurred in a trade or business, as section 280A restricts home-office deductions to expenses incurred in a trade or business, was at issue. In denying the taxpayer a deduction because the bad debt was incurred in an activity entered into for profit, and not in a trade or business, the Court stated: "[w]hen the only return is that of an investor, the taxpayer has not satisfied his burden of demonstrating that he is engaged in a trade or business since investing is not a trade or business. . . ." 373 U.S. at 202.

The Court of Claims, relying on *Higgins*, has also stated: "Managing one's own investments in securities is not the carrying on of a trade or business, irrespective of the extent of the investments or the amount of time required to perform the managerial functions." Wilson v. United States, 376 F.2d 280, 293 (1967).

In the instant case, taxpayers were not engaged in a trade or business. They were active investors in that their investment activities were continuous, reg-ular, and extensive. However, this is not determinative of the issue and it is not the correct test. What is determinative is the fact that the taxpayers' return was that of an investor: they derived the vast majority of their income in the form of dividends and interest; their income was derived from the long-term holding of securities, not from short-term trading; and they were interested in the capital appreciation of their stocks, not short-term profits. Merely because taxpayers spent much time managing their own sizeable investments does not mean that they were engaged in a trade or business.

CONCLUSION

Although taxpayers' investment activity was entered into for the production of income, it did not rise to the level of a trade or business. Section 280A restricts home-office deductions to expenses incurred in the carrying on of a trade or business. Therefore, taxpayers were not entitled to a deduction under this section.

Because we decide this case on the grounds that taxpayers were not en-gaged in the trade or business of making investments, we need not and do not reach the issue of whether they could deduct the expenses of both their home-offices as their "principal place of business."

Accordingly, the judgment of the Claims Court is reversed.

QUESTIONS

1. Under the *Moller* decision, deductions are allowed under § 280A for traders but not for investors like the Mollers. What is the difference between a trader and an investor?

2. Does the deduction claimed by the Mollers seem to have strong personal elements? In general, are the expenses of investors more likely to be personal than those of traders?

3. Reconsider the *Nickerson* case. Why do you suppose Congress might be unwilling or unable to adopt arbitrary rules for denial of deductions for hobby farmers? Can you think of how such a rule might be framed?

NOTE

Specific, arbitrary rules sometimes offer clever tax advisors the opportunity to devise or find "creative" tax plans (also less respectfully referred to as tax avoidance schemes or loopholes). Where the statutory language is specific and clear, judges, responding to the notion that taxpayers should be able to rely on the plain meaning of such language, may be required to validate a tax-reduction plan that seems to undercut the abuse-curbing objectives of the provision at issue. The process is illustrated in Feldman v. Commissioner, 791 F.2d 781 (9th Cir. 1986). The taxpayer in that case was an accountant and was one of the principals (a shareholder and managing director) in the incorporated accounting firm at which he performed his services. He had good business reasons for doing some of his work at home and for that purpose used one room of his house exclusively as an office. If the firm had simply made an adjustment in his salary and he had borne the cost of the office, he would not have been entitled to any deduction for his office expense (a pro rata share of utilities and other expenses and depreciation). See the plain language of § 280A(c)(1). Instead, he rented the office to the firm (technically, his employer) and claimed a deduction under § 280A(c)(3). The Commissioner disallowed the deduction, claiming that the taxpayer's arrangement was an artificial scheme designed to avoid the strict limitations of § 280A(c)(1). The Tax Court held in favor of the taxpayer. 84 T.C. 1 (1985). The Ninth Circuit affirmed, stating that the taxpayer "draws his support from the plain meaning of the statute" and that "we are content to await the action of Congress." The wait was not long. In the 1986 act, Congress added § 280A(c)(6), adopting plain language reversing the result in the case. The new provision adds to the bulk of the Code and to its apparent complexity. It does not significantly increase taxpayer compliance burdens, since its effect is simply that people will not engage in artificial transactions that only a clever person intent on reducing his taxes would have thought of in the first place. Still, it is one more provision that many lawyers and accountants will be required to be aware of.

WHITTEN v. COMMISSIONER
T.C. Memo. 1995-508

[The taxpayers appeared pro se.]

This case is before the Court on the parties' cross-motions for summary judgment. The issue for decision concerns the proper characterization of expenses incurred by petitioner Stanley B. Whitten in attending and participating in the television game show "Wheel of Fortune." . . .

BACKGROUND

Stanley B. and Rose M. Whitten (petitioners) are husband and wife who filed a joint Federal income tax return for 1991. At the time that their petition was filed in this case, petitioners resided in Northbrook, Illinois. Stanley B. Whitten (petitioner) is a criminal investigator with the United States Securities and Exchange Commission. He is also a nationally recognized cruciverbalist who has constructed crossword puzzles that have appeared in newspapers and magazines throughout the United States, including the Chicago Tribune, the New York Times, and the Washington Post.

In early 1990, petitioner learned that the staff of the "Wheel of Fortune" television game show was coming to Chicago, Illinois, to interview and select contestants to appear on the program. Petitioner applied for and received an invitation to compete to be a contestant. The selection process began with a written examination that served to eliminate many of the applicants from consideration, followed by a personal interview and a mock session of the game. At the conclusion of this process, petitioner was one of approximately 30 applicants who were selected to appear on the program.

In mid-January 1991, petitioner was contacted by the "Wheel of Fortune" game show and arrangements were made for petitioner to take part in the taping of the program to be conducted in Los Angeles, California, on February 8, 1991. In anticipation of his appearance on the program, petitioner watched "Wheel of Fortune" nearly every night and acquired both a computerized and manual version of the game with which to practice.

Because the producers of the "Wheel of Fortune" program film 8 shows in one day, contestants are required to bring additional changes of clothing so that the winner of one show can reappear on the next show in a different outfit and thereby simulate different days. Contestants who win three games in a row are not permitted to return for a fourth show.

"Wheel of Fortune" contestants are required to sign a document entitled "CONTESTANT RELEASE FORM" which states in part:

> I have not paid or accepted any money or other valuable consideration (including a division of prizes) in connection with my appearance on the Program, or authorized anyone else to do so. I am aware that payment or acceptance of or

agreement to pay or accept any money or valuable consideration for the appearance of any person or the mention of anything on the Program without disclosure to NBC prior to broadcast is a federal offense punishable by fine and/or imprisonment. I agree that if anyone tries to induce me to do any such act, I shall immediately notify a NBC Program Practices representative.

The release form further states that any travel undertaken by a contestant in connection with the contestant's appearance on the program shall be at the contestant's sole risk and expense.

Petitioner, as well as his wife and three of his children, flew to Los Angeles on February 7, 1991, and petitioner appeared for the taping of "Wheel of Fortune" as scheduled. Petitioner won three consecutive games and was awarded cash prizes in the total amount of $14,850 and a 1991 Chevrolet Geo Tracker automobile. The "Wheel of Fortune" programs that petitioner appeared on were televised nationally on February 18, 19, and 20, 1991.

As indicated, petitioners filed a joint 1991 Federal income tax return (Form 1040). Petitioner's winnings from the "Wheel of Fortune" game show were reported as "other income" on line 22 of Form 1040 in the amount of $19,830. The $19,830 entry represents the sum of the value of the GEO Tracker and petitioner's cash winnings of $14,850, reduced by the expenses that petitioner and his family purportedly incurred, namely $1,820, for transportation, meals, and lodging in order to participate as a contestant on the show in Los Angeles. Petitioners' reporting position is premised on the theory that the foregoing expenses represent "gambling losses" that may be offset directly against petitioner's "gambling winnings" from the program.

Respondent determined a deficiency in the amount of $582 in petitioners' Federal income tax for 1991. Specifically, respondent determined that petitioners failed to report $1,820 in income from petitioner's winnings on the "Wheel of Fortune" game show. In respondent's view, the $1,820 in expenses that petitioner purportedly incurred in attending and participating in the game show are properly characterized either as nondeductible personal expenses under section 262 or as miscellaneous itemized deductions that may only be deducted subject to the 2-percent floor prescribed by § 67(b). . . .

During the course of the hearing in Washington, D.C., petitioner conceded that he is not in the trade or business of either gambling or appearing as a contestant on television game shows. In addition, petitioner stated that his theory of the case rests solely on § 165.

DISCUSSION

. . .

The parties have devoted a substantial amount of time and effort debating the issue of whether a contestant's appearance on the "Wheel of Fortune" game show constitutes wagering transaction governed by the provisions of § 165(d). In our opinion it does not. However, we need not definitively decide this because such issue begs the question regarding the proper characterization of the expenses incurred by petitioner in attending and participating in the "Wheel of Fortune" game show. Consequently, we will focus our attention on the more pertinent issue of whether the expenses in dispute can be characterized as wagering losses within the meaning of § 165(d).

Section 165(d) was originally codified as § 23(g) of the Revenue Act of 1934. Notwithstanding the long history of the section, the term "wagering losses" is not defined in either the Internal Revenue Code or the regulations. Nor is the term defined in the legislative history underlying § 165(d).

It is within this relative vacuum of authority that petitioners rely on Kozma v. Commissioner, T.C. Memo. 1986-177, as support for their position that the expenses disputed herein constitute wagering losses under section 165(d). As explained below, petitioners' reliance on *Kozma* is misplaced.

In *Kozma* the taxpayer, an individual engaged in the trade or business of gambling, enjoyed gross gambling winnings (gross receipts) of $9,750 and $15,191 for 1980 and 1981, respectively. However, after combining the amounts that he paid for wagering tickets with business expenses for transportation, depreciation, meals and lodging, admission fees, and office supplies, the taxpayer reported net losses in respect of his gambling business for both 1980 and 1981. The Commissioner issued a notice of deficiency disallowing the losses claimed by the taxpayer on the ground that gambling losses are allowable only to the extent of gambling winnings under § 165(d).

In proceedings before this Court, the taxpayer argued that the expenses incurred for transportation, depreciation, meals and lodging, admission fees, and office supplies constitute business expenses under § 162(a), rather than wagering losses under § 165(d), and that such expenses are deductible by virtue of § 162(a) notwithstanding the limitation imposed by § 165(d).

Focusing on the tension between sections 162(a) and 165(d), we held that the Commissioner was correct in disallowing the taxpayer's business expenses to the extent that those expenses generated an overall loss from the taxpayer's gambling business. . . .

Unlike the taxpayer in *Kozma*, petitioner admits that he is not in the trade or business of gambling and that he did not incur losses or expenses in excess of his "wagering winnings." In this light, it is evident that *Kozma* can be distinguished on its facts from the present case.

Nor are we persuaded that the legal holding in *Kozma* is controlling in the present case. Rather, *Kozma* stands for the narrow proposition that, in the case of a professional gambler, the limitation imposed under § 165(d) limiting wagering losses to wagering winnings overrides the deduction otherwise allowable under § 162(a) for ordinary and necessary business expenses. . . . Petitioners apparently believe that *Kozma*, together with the cases cited therein, stand[s] for the proposition that all expenses related to a wagering activity are properly characterized as wagering losses under § 165(d). However, we do not glean from those cases any intention to eliminate the distinction between wagering losses, i.e., the amount of wagers or bets lost on wagering transactions, and expenses related thereto, e.g., expenses for transportation, meals, and lodging incurred to engage in wagering transactions. . . .

Consistent with the foregoing, we conclude that wagering losses must be accounted for and reported separately from the expenses incurred by the taxpayer in order to engage in the underlying wagering transaction. In applying this rule to the facts presented herein, we hold that the expenses incurred by petitioner in order to attend and participate in the "Wheel of Fortune" game show are at best expenses, deductible as a miscellaneous itemized deduction under § 67, rather than wagering losses under § 165(d). In so holding, we reject petitioners' contention that the expenses in issue are tantamount to a bet or wager. Unlike a wager or bet, petitioner incurred the expenses in question in exchange for specific goods and services, such as transportation, meals, and lodging. Further, we doubt that Congress ever intended to allow casual gamblers to treat expenses for transportation, meals, and lodging as anything other than either miscellaneous itemized deductions or non-deductible personal expenses. Consequently, we shall deny petitioners' motion for Summary Judgment and grant respondent's cross motion.

In order to reflect the foregoing,

An order denying petitioners' Motion for Summary Judgment . . . and granting respondent's Motion for Summary Judgment will be entered.

QUESTIONS

1. Is there a connection between Stanley Whitten's success as a cruciverbalist and his success on Wheel of Fortune?

2. Assuming that Whitten was paid for crossword puzzles that were published, was he entitled to deduct any expenses incurred in producing those puzzles? If so, under what Code section?

3. Was Whitten misguided in his concession that the expenses incurred in appearing on Wheel of Fortune were not deductible as trade or business expenses?

PROBLEM

Gena is a successful tax lawyer and an avid sports fan. About twenty weekends each year, for many years, she has driven from her home in Los Angeles to Las Vegas (a distance of about 300 miles). She spends her time in Las Vegas (when not sleeping) in one of the casino sports gambling arenas, watching the action, studying sporting news and data, and gambling on sports events. She is reasonably skillful and has managed, every year, to win about $10,000. Suppose the travel and lodging expense is about $6,000 per year. Is the $6,000 deductible from gross income under §§ 162 and 62? What if the average amount won each year is $4,000 and the expenses are $6,000?

4. Office Decoration

HENDERSON v. COMMISSIONER
46 T.C.M. 566 (1983)

Petitioners, Hoke F. Henderson, Jr., and Karen L. Henderson (hereinafter petitioner), resided at Columbia, S.C., at the time the petition was filed.

Petitioner was employed in 1977 by the State of South Carolina as an assistant attorney general. As an employee of the State of South Carolina, petitioner was provided an office with furniture and furnishings that consisted of a desk, a desk chair, a work table, a telephone, a dictaphone, a bookcase, a filing cabinet, law books, and two chairs for visitors. Her duties included consulting with public officials and attorneys and others from the private sector, which at times took place in her office.

During 1977, petitioner purchased a framed print for $35 and a live plant for $35 for the purpose of decorating her office. In addition, petitioner paid a total of $180 to rent a parking space located across the street from her office. Petitioner occasionally used her automobile for business purposes when an automobile from the pool of State automobiles was not available.

In the statutory notice of deficiency, respondent disallowed the deduction for the framed print, live plant, and parking fees in their entirety.

OPINION

The only issue is whether petitioner is entitled to a deduction under § 162(a) for amounts paid for a framed print and live plant used to decorate her office, and for amounts paid to rent a parking space. Petitioner contends that the expenses were all ordinary and necessary business expenses deductible under § 162(a). Respondent counters that the expenses were not ordinary and necessary, and that the expenses are nondeductible personal expenses under § 262. We agree with respondent that the expenses constitute nondeductible personal expenses under § 262.

Section 162(a) allows a deduction for all the ordinary and necessary expenses paid or incurred during the taxable year in carrying on any trade or business. However, even assuming an expense meets the requirements of § 162(a), it still may be disallowed if the amount was expended for a personal, living, or family expense. § 262. The essential inquiry here is whether a sufficient nexus existed between petitioner's expenses and the "carrying on" of petitioner's trade or business to qualify the expenses for the deduction under § 162(a), or whether they were in essence personal or living expenses and non-deductible by virtue of § 262. . . . Moreover, where both sections 162(a) and 262 may apply, the latter section takes priority over the former. . . .

We find that the amounts paid for the framed print and live plant were expended to improve the appearance of petitioner's office, a personal expense, and only tangentially, if at all, aided her in the performance of her duties as an employee of the State of South Carolina. Her employer had provided her with all the furnishings considered necessary to do her job. No evidence was presented to prove that the presence of the print and plant in her office were either necessary or helpful in performing her required services. "It is not enough that there may be some remote or incidental connection" with the taxpayer's business to support the deduction. Larrabee v. Commissioner, 33 T.C. 838, 843 (1960).

The two cases primarily relied on by petitioners, Gillis v. Commissioner, T.C. Memo. 1973-96, and Judge v. Commissioner, T.C. Memo. 1976-283, are distinguishable. In *Gillis* the Court relied on the fact that the circumstances were very unusual. In *Judge*, which involved a pediatrician who furnished his own office, the Court found that the paintings in issue were of subjects "intended to be of interest to children," the taxpayer's patients, and were used solely for the purpose of decoration of petitioner's business offices and not for any personal or non-business use. Accordingly, we deny the deduction for these two expenditures.

QUESTIONS

1. Suppose that Ms. Henderson had been in private practice and had bought the plant and the print for her office. Would she have been entitled to treat the cost as a business outlay?

2. Suppose that Ms. Henderson had installed a carpet in her office and had donated it to the state of South Carolina. Would she have been entitled to a charitable deduction? See supra pages 380-392.

5. Automobiles, Computers, and Other Listed Property

The 1984 act provides special rules for "listed property," which includes computers kept in the home, automobiles, cellular telephones, "any property of a type generally used for purposes of entertainment, recreation, or amusement," or "any other property of a type specified by the Secretary by regulations." § 280F(d)(4). Where listed property is used 50 percent or less for business purposes, depreciation (as to the portion of the cost allocable to business use) is limited to straightline using the normal useful life (as opposed to the shorter life available under ACRS). § 280F(b). Moreover, where an employee (such as a professor of law) acquires and uses listed property (such as a computer in his or her home), the business use requirement of this provision is not met except by use that is "for the convenience of the employer and required as a condition of employment." § 280F(d)(3). Does that seem fair? Even as applied to a professor who is single and uses the computer exclusively for writing articles and books? If not, how can the denial of the deduction be justified? What about the possibility of having the university "require" that the professor buy the computer? The House Conference Report on the Tax Reform Act of 1984, H.R. Rep. No. 861, 98th Cong., 2d Sess. 1027 (1984), says that the "condition of employment" language will not be "satisfied merely by an employer's statement that the property is required as a condition of employment. The conferees intend that the principles of Dole v. Commissioner, 43 T.C. 697, aff'd, 351 F.2d 308 (1st Cir. 1965) apply." In *Dole*, the Tax Court said (at 706) that the test is "objective"; it does not turn on the employer's "state of mind." Is it likely that a law professor could show that he or she was required by objectively observable circumstances to have the tools of the teaching and writing trade in his or her home rather than at the office supplied by the law school?

B.   TRAVEL AND ENTERTAINMENT EXPENSES

1.   Question Presented

If a person must go to another city on business, the cost of getting there and back is deductible. If the person stays overnight, the cost of food and lodging also is deductible. In most instances these rules are easily reconciled with sound tax policy objectives, but such reconciliation can become difficult where there are significant personal as well as business benefits from the trip. We properly ignore the fact that a person traveling on business may enjoy traveling. The fact that one enjoys one's job is not a reason for denying a deduction of the costs of getting that job done; purely psychic benefits are not part of the income tax base. But suppose that a self-employed consultant is going to another city on business, that the person's mother happens to live there, and that the person is anxious to see her. Now we have a substantial personal benefit that is not an inextricable part of the business activity. Suppose that the air fare for the trip is $400, that the person would have been willing to pay this much for the purely business objectives, but that he or she would also have been willing to pay that amount to travel to the same place just to see his or her mother. An appealing argument can be made for including in income the value of the personal satisfaction or (what amounts to the same thing) denying a deduction for the $400. But the practical difficulty of such an approach should be obvious. The rule that the courts purport to apply is that the cost of a trip, or of other activities such as dinner with a customer at a restaurant, is deductible if the "primary purpose" is business. The primary purpose test is based on unrealistic assumptions about how people think and about the ability of the tax authorities to get at the true facts. For example, if you travel to another city on business and see your mother while you're there, do you necessarily engage in a mental process in which you weigh the value of the business objective against that of the personal objective? Of course not. And even if you did, the IRS employee who examines your return would have no practical way of verifying or challenging your assertions about that mental process. Thus, one can reasonably surmise that in practice some other test must be used. In all probability that test is that if there is a *sufficient* business justification for the trip, the deduction will be allowed. Even that test leaves considerable opportunity for cheating, since the tax authorities are properly reluctant, and limited in their ability, to challenge the business judgments of taxpayers.

The business versus personal issue often arises when an individual pays her own expenses and then tries to deduct the outlay. In the example above, a self-employed consultant flies somewhere to attend a business meeting and see her mother. In other cases, an employee might pay an expense that has mixed business and personal motives and that is not reimbursable by her employer, and deduct the outlay.

Suppose, though, that an employer pays expenses associated with an employee's travel. The trip has some business rationale, and therefore some benefit to the employer; it also provides some personal benefits to the employee. If the trip is characterized for tax purposes as business related, the value of the trip is not treated as income to the employee. Employees are not taxed on whatever personal benefit they receive out of employer-provided business travel. Statutory support for nontaxation is found in § 132(d), discussed supra at page 62. Section 132 provides that an employer-provided benefit is not included in employee income if the benefit would have been deductible as a business expense and the employee paid for it out of her own pocket. If, instead, the trip is characterized as non-business related, then it is treated as a form of salary, and included in the employee's gross income. What about the employer? Obviously, the cost of employee business travel is deductible.[12] A non-business-related trip the employer pays for is also deductible for the employer,[13] because such a trip is treated as salary to the employee, and salary is a deductible business expense.

Thus, outlays by an employer that have business benefits to the employer and personal benefits to an employee raise the same question that is raised by outlays of a self-employed person that provide business and personal benefits: whether the outlay is properly characterized as business related. Employer-provided outlays that would have been deductible if paid for directly by the employee do not constitute income to the employee. Outlays that would not have been deductible if paid for by the employee are treated as taxable salary to the employee.

RUDOLPH v. UNITED STATES
370 U.S. 269 (1962)

PER CURIAM. . . .

An insurance company provided a trip from its home office in Dallas, Texas, to New York City for a group of its agents and their wives. Rudolph and his wife were among the beneficiaries of this trip, and the Commissioner assessed its value to them as taxable income. It appears to be agreed between the parties that the tax consequences of the trip turn upon the Rudolphs' "dominant motive and purpose" in taking the trip and the company's in offering it. In this regard, the District Court, on a suit for a refund, found that the trip was provided by the company for "the primary purpose of affording a pleasure trip . . . in the nature of a bonus reward, and compensation for a job well done" and that from the point of view of the Rudolphs it "was primarily a pleasure trip in the nature of a vacation. . . ." 189 F. Supp. 2, 4-5. The Court of Appeals approved these findings. 291 F.2d 841. Such ultimate facts are subject to the "clearly erroneous" rule, cf. Comm'r v. Duberstein [supra page 90], and their review would be of no importance save to the litigants themselves.

---

12. If the expense creates or improves a long-term asset, it must be capitalized. See Chapter 6 infra, at 511.

13. Occasionally, deductions will be denied because the expense fails the "ordinary and necessary" test of § 162. See *Danville Plywood* infra, at 464.

The appropriate disposition in such a situation is to dismiss the writ as improvidently granted. . . .

Mr. Justice FRANKFURTER took no part in the decision of this case.

Mr. Justice WHITE took no part in the consideration or decision of this case.

Separate opinion of Mr. Justice HARLAN. . . .

[N]ow that the case is here I think it better to decide it, two members of the Court having dissented on the merits. . . .

Petitioners, husband and wife, reside in Dallas, Texas, where the home office of the husband's employer, the Southland Life Insurance Company, is located. By having sold a predetermined amount of insurance, the husband qualified to attend the company's convention in New York City in 1956 and, in line with company policy, to bring his wife with him. The petitioners, together with 150 other employees and officers of the insurance company and 141 wives, traveled to and from New York City on special trains, and were housed in a single hotel during their two-and-one-half-day visit. One morning was devoted to a "business meeting" and group luncheon, the rest of the time in New York City to "travel, sightseeing, entertainment, fellowship or free time." The entire trip lasted one week.

The company paid all the expenses of the convention-trip . . . petitioner's allocable share being $560. . . . The District Court held that the value of the trip being "in the nature of a bonus, reward, and compensation for a job well done," was income to Rudolph, but being "primarily a pleasure trip in the nature of a vacation," the costs were personal and nondeductible.

I

Under § 61 . . . was the value of the trip to the taxpayer-husband properly includable in gross income? . . .

[I]t was surely within the Commissioner's competence to consider as "gross income" a "reward, or a bonus given to . . . employees for excellence in service," which the District Court found was the employer's primary purpose in arranging this trip. . . .

II

There remains the question whether, though income, this outlay for transportation, meals, and lodging was deductible by petitioners as an "ordinary and necessary" business expense under § 162. . . .

[T]he crucial question is whether . . . the purpose of the trip was "related primarily to business" or was rather "primarily personal in nature." . . . [T]hat certain doctors, lawyers, clergymen, insurance agents or others have or have not been permitted similar deductions only shows that in the circumstances of those cases, the courts thought that the expenses were or were not deductible as "related primarily to business."

The husband places great emphasis on the fact that he is an entrapped "organization man," required to attend such conventions, and that his future promotions depend on his presence. Suffice it to say that the District Court did not find any element of compulsion; to the contrary, it found that the petitioners regarded the convention in New York City as a pleasure trip in the nature of a vacation. . . .

Mr. Justice DOUGLAS, with whom Mr. Justice BLACK joins, dissenting.

I

It could not, I think, be seriously contended that a professional man, say a Senator or a Congressman, who attends a convention to read a paper or conduct a seminar *with all expenses paid* has received "income." . . . Income has the connotation of something other than the mere payment of expenses. . . .

The formula "all expenses paid" might be the disguise whereby compensation "for services" is paid. Yet it would be a rare case indeed where one could conclude that a person who gets only his expenses for attendance at one convention gets "income" in the statutory sense. If this arrangement were regular and frequent or if it had the earmarks of a sham device as a cloak for remuneration, there would be room for fact-finders to conclude that it was evasive. But isolated engagements of the kind here in question have no rational connection with compensation "for services" rendered.

It is true that petitioner was an employee and that the expenses for attending the convention were paid by his employer. He qualified to attend the convention by selling an amount of insurance that met a quota set by the company. Other salesmen also qualified, some attending and some not attending. They went from Dallas, Texas, to New York City, where they stayed two and a half days. One day was given to a business session and a luncheon; the rest of the time was left for social events.

On this record there is no room for a finding of fact that the "expenses paid" were "for services" rendered. They were apparently a proper income tax deduction for the employer. The record is replete with evidence that from management's point of view it was good business to spend money on a convention for its leading agents — a convention that not only kept the group together in New York City, but in transit as well, giving ample time for group discussions, exchanges of experience, and educational training. It was the exigencies of the employment that gave rise to the convention. There was nothing dishonest, illegitimate, or unethical about this transaction. No services were rendered. New York City may or may not have been attractive to the agents and their wives. Whether a person enjoys or dislikes the trip that he makes "with all expenses paid" has no more to do with whether the expenses paid were compensation "for services" rendered than does his attitude toward his job. . . .

III

The wife's expenses are, on this record, also deductible.[14] The Treasury Regulations state in § 1.162-2(c):

> Where a taxpayer's wife accompanies him on a business trip, expenses attributable to her travel are not deductible unless it can be adequately shown that the wife's presence on the trip has a bona fide business purpose. The wife's performance of some incidental service does not cause her expenses to qualify as deductible business expenses. . . .

The civil law philosophy, expressed in the community property concept, attributes half of the husband's earnings to the wife — an equitable idea that at long last was reflected in the idea of income splitting under the federal income tax law. The wife's contribution to the business productivity of the husband in at least some activities is well known. . . . Business reasons motivated the inclusion of wives in this particular insurance convention. An insurance executive testified at this trial:

Q: I hand you Plaintiff's Exhibit 15, and you will notice it is a letter addressed to "John Doe"; also a bulletin entitled "A New Partner Has Been Formed." Will you tell us what that consists of?
A: This is a letter addressed to the wife of an agent, a new agent, as we make the contract with him. This letter is sent to his wife within a few days after the contract, enclosing this booklet explaining to her how she can help her husband in the life insurance business.
Q: Please tell us, as briefly as you can and yet in detail, how you as agency director for Southland attempt to integrate the wives' performance with the performance of agents in the life insurance business.
A: One of the important functions we have in mind is the attendance at these conventions. In addition to that communication, occasionally there are letters that will be written to the wife concerning any special sales effort that might be desired or promoted. The company has a monthly publication for the agents and employees that is mailed to their homes so the wife will have a convenient opportunity to see the magazine and read it. At most of our convention program[s], we have some specific references to the wife's work, and in quite a few of the convention programs we have had wives appear on the program.
Q: Suppose you didn't have the wives and didn't seek to require their attendance at a convention, would there be some danger that your meetings and conventions would kind of degenerate into stag affairs, where the whole purpose of the meeting would be lost?
A: I think that would definitely be a tendency.

I would reverse the judgments below and leave insurance conventions in the same category as conventions of revenue agents, lawyers, doctors, businessmen,

---

14. This case arose before the adoption of § 274(m)(3), which, beginning in 1994, would expressly deny a deduction by Rudolph's employer of the travel expenses of the spouses.

accountants, nurses, clergymen and all others, until and unless Congress decides otherwise.

2. Section 274

In 1962, Congress, responding to the uncertainty produced by decisions such as *Rudolph*, enacted § 274, which superimposes on the basic requirements of § 162 additional rules for travel and entertainment (often referred to as T and E). Congress has amended § 274 at various times since then. Section 274 is specific and detailed; the regulations, which to a considerable extent pick up ideas and language found in congressional committee reports, are even more so. The principal features of § 274 are described below.

Required relationship between expense and business purpose. Section 274(a)(1)(A) allows taxpayers to deduct the cost of "any activity which is of a type generally considered to constitute entertainment, amusement, or recreation" only if the activity is "directly related" to business. This language is intended to rule out deductions for entertainment intended merely to establish goodwill. See Regs. § 1.274-2(c). It is true, of course, that expenditures to establish goodwill might be incurred for sound business reasons, but in this instance the opportunity for abuse proved to be so great as to justify a blanket denial of deductions. The direct relationship standard of § 274(a) is weakened considerably, however, by another part of that same section, which allows deductions for expenses that are "associated with" business and directly precede or follow a "substantial and bona fide business discussion." Thus, for example, not only is the cost of a dinner at which business is discussed treated as a business expense, but the cost of a dinner or sporting or other entertainment event that directly precedes or follows a business discussion is also treated as a business expense. That provides plenty of scope for expense-account living for taxpayers who are willing to stretch the truth or who genuinely believe that their entire lives are business. And it may help explain why, if you must pay your own way, with no help from the government by way of a tax deduction, you may find you cannot afford good seats at professional basketball or football games.[15]

Fifty percent limitation on meal and entertainment deduction. Section 274(n), first adopted in 1986, limits the otherwise allowable deduction for meals and entertainment to 50 percent of the cost. The remaining 50 percent of the cost is treated as a nondeductible personal expense. The reasons given in Congress in 1986 for the original version of this provision, which limited the deduction to 80 percent of the amount otherwise allowable, are noted in the Report of

---

15. Some relief may be experienced by beleaguered nonbusiness sports and entertainment enthusiasts as a result of a provision adopted in 1986 that limits deductions for tickets to sports and entertainment events to the face value of the ticket (except in case of certain charitable events). § 274(l)(1)(A). The 1986 act also limited deductions for the cost of renting a "skybox." § 274(l)(1)(B). These expenses are also subject to § 274(n), which allows a deduction of only 50 percent of outlays for business meals and entertainment.

the Senate Finance Committee in its discussion of the 1986 act (S. Rep. No. 313, 99th Cong., 1st Sess. 68 (1986)):

> The committee believes that present law, by not focusing sufficiently on the personal-consumption element of deductible meal and entertainment expenses, unfairly permits taxpayers who can arrange business settings for personal consumption to receive, in effect, a Federal tax subsidy for such consumption that is not available to other taxpayers. The taxpayers who benefit from deductibility under present law tend to have relatively high incomes, and in some cases the consumption may bear only a loose relationship to business necessity. For example, when executives have dinner at an expensive restaurant following business discussions and then deduct the cost of the meal, the fact that there may be some bona fide business connection does not alter the imbalance between the treatment of those persons, who have effectively transferred a portion of the cost of their meal to the Federal Government, and other individuals, who cannot deduct the cost of their meals.
>
> The significance of this imbalance is heightened by the fact that business travel and entertainment often may be more lavish than comparable activities in a nonbusiness setting. For example, meals at expensive restaurants and season tickets at sporting events are purchased to a significant degree by taxpayers who claim business deductions for these expenses. This disparity is highly visible, and contributes to public perceptions that the tax system is unfair. Polls indicate that the public identifies the deductibility of normal personal expenses such as meals to be one of the most significant elements of disrespect for and dissatisfaction with the present tax system.

Expenses of spouse. Where a person is on a legitimate tax-deductible business trip, no deduction is allowed for the additional travel expenses of the person's spouse (or dependent, or any other person accompanying that person), unless (i) the spouse (etc.) is an employee of the person claiming the deduction, (ii) the spouse (etc.) had a bona fide business purpose for going on the trip, *and* (iii) the additional expenses would otherwise be deductible. § 274(m)(3) (added by the 1993 act). This provision overrules cases allowing deductions of a spouse's expenses if there was a valid reason for the spouse to come along (such as assisting with the entertainment of clients).

Section 274's substantiation requirements. By virtue of § 274(d), no deduction may be taken for traveling expenses, entertainment, or business gifts unless the taxpayer "substantiates by adequate records or by sufficient evidence corroborating the taxpayer's own statement" the amount, the time and place of the travel or entertainment or the date and description of the gift, the business purpose of the expense, and the business relationship to the person entertained or the donee. The substantiation requirement may have been the most significant aspect of the 1962 T and E legislation.

The Treasury is authorized to dispense with some or all of the substantiation requirements, and this power has been exercised as to some expenditures. For example, the amount of expenditures under $75 (other than for lodging) need not be substantiated by receipts (Regs. § 1.274-5T(c)(2)(iii)); per diem and mileage allowances paid by an employer to an employee need not be substantiated if they do not exceed maximum amounts specified from time to time by the Commissioner (Regs. § 1.274-5T(g)); employees are not required to substantiate expenses to the Service if they have substantiated those expenses to their employers for purposes of obtaining reimbursement (Regs. § 1.274-5T(f)(2)); and taxpayers may claim fixed per diem amounts for meals without substantiation if the time, place, and business purpose of the travel are properly substantiated (but subject to § 274(n)'s 50 percent limitation on the deduction for meals). See Rev. Proc. 92-17, 92-1 C.B. 679.

No deduction is allowed for "amounts paid or incurred for membership in any club organized for business, pleasure, recreation, or other social purpose." § 274(a)(3).

Exceptions. Examine briefly § 274(e), which contains exceptions that are relatively straightforward and easy to understand.

Foreign travel. Section 274(c) provides that in certain circumstances, where a person combines business and pleasure on a trip to a foreign country, the air fare is partially disallowed. This provision seems to look to benefit rather than to primary purpose or to the sufficiency of the business objective. As initially adopted in 1962 it applied to domestic as well as foreign travel but in 1964 was repealed as to domestic travel. The moral of this bit of history would seem to be that one should not underestimate the political power of the hotel and travel industry and the unions representing all the people who work in that industry.

Cruises and foreign conventions. Section 274(h) now contains rules, not part of the original 1962 legislation, that disallow deductions for conventions held outside the "North American area" unless "it is as reasonable for the meeting to be held outside the North American area as within." Again, this was a response to widespread abuses such as deduction of the expenses of attending an annual American Bar Association convention held in London and, more so, to the adverse effects of the prior law on the owners and employees of domestic hotels and restaurants. There is also a special rule for conventions and seminars on cruise ships (§ 274(h)(2)) and a rule, added in 1986, denying deductions for "luxury water transportation" (§ 274(m)(1)).

PROBLEMS

1. (a) A law firm with offices in six cities holds an annual three-day "retreat" for partners at an exclusive warm-weather resort in February. The firm sponsors the following activities: Friday and Saturday night banquets; Saturday and Sunday golf and tennis tournaments; and Sunday horseback riding. A two-hour firm meeting is held from noon to 2 P.M. on Saturday. The firm's leading partners believe that the annual meetings enable partners in different offices to become acquainted with one another and share views about the firm. Attendance at the retreat is encouraged but not required. All expenses are paid by

the firm. Are the expenses deductible? See § 274(a)(1)(A), § 274(e)(4), (5); Regs. § 1.274-2(f)(2)(vi).

(b) The facts are the same as in (a) except that associates are also invited to the retreat and many associates believe that attendance will further their chances of making partner. Are the associates taxable on the value of the room, meals, and entertainment?

2. Lawyer Lopez's law firm invites promising law students to interview with members of the firm. After the interview, the students are taken out to dinner. Lopez often takes his wife (not a lawyer) along on such dinners. Is the cost of Lopez's wife's dinner deductible? See Regs. § 1.274-2(d)(2).

3. (a) Lawyer Friedman is a partner in an urban law firm. The law firm buys season tickets for the local professional baseball team's games. Lawyers at the firm generally give the tickets to clients, or use the tickets to take clients to the games. About one-fourth of the time, however, the tickets are not claimed by lawyers who wish to give them to clients or take clients to games. In that case, the tickets are used by the firm's partners and their families and friends. Should the firm be allowed to deduct the entire cost of the season tickets?

(b) The facts are the same as in (a) except that tickets not given to clients or used to take clients to games are used by associates and their families or friends. Are the associates taxed on the value of the tickets?

3.   Business Lunches

MOSS v. COMMISSIONER
758 F.2d 211 (7th Cir. 1985)

POSNER, Circuit Judge.

The taxpayers, a lawyer named Moss and his wife, appeal from a decision of the Tax Court disallowing federal income tax deductions of a little more than $1,000 in each of two years, representing Moss's share of his law firm's lunch expense at the Cafe Angelo in Chicago. The Tax Court's decision in this case has attracted some attention in tax circles because of its implications for the general problem of the deductibility of business meals. . . .

Moss was a partner in a small trial firm specializing in defense work, mostly for one insurance company. Each of the firm's lawyers carried a tremendous litigation caseload, averaging more than 300 cases, and spent most of every working day in courts in Chicago and its suburbs. The members of the firm met for lunch daily at the Cafe Angelo near their office. At lunch the lawyers would discuss their cases with the head of the firm, whose approval was required for most settlements, and they would decide which lawyer would meet which court call that afternoon or the next morning. Lunchtime was chosen for the daily meeting because the courts were in recess then. The alternatives were to meet at 7:00 A.M. or 6:00 P.M. and these were less convenient times. There is no suggestion that the lawyers dawdled over lunch, or that the Cafe Angelo is luxurious.

The framework of statutes and regulations for deciding this case is simple, but not clear. Section 262 of the Internal Revenue Code (Title 26) disallows, "except as otherwise expressly provided in this chapter," the deduction of "personal, family, or living expenses." Section 119 excludes from income the value of meals provided by an employer to his employees for his convenience, but only if they are provided on the employer's premises; and § 162(a) allows the deduction of "all the ordinary and necessary expenses paid or incurred during the taxable year in carrying on any trade or business, including — ... (2) traveling expenses (including amounts expended for meals...) while away from home...." Since Moss was not an employee but a partner in a partnership not taxed as an entity, since the meals were not served on the employer's premises, and since he was not away from home (that is, on an overnight trip away from his place of work, see United States v. Correll, 389 U.S. 299 (1967)), neither § 119 nor § 162(a)(2) applies to this case. The Internal Revenue Service concedes, however, that meals are deductible under § 162(a) when they are ordinary and necessary business expenses (provided the expense is substantiated with adequate records, see § 274(d)) even if they are not within the express permission of any other provision and even though the expense of commuting to and from work, a traveling expense but not one incurred away from home, is not deductible. Treasury Regulations on Income Tax § 1.262-1(b)(5); Fausner v. Commissioner, 413 U.S. 838 (1973) (per curiam).

The problem is that many expenses are simultaneously business expenses in the sense that they conduce to the production of business income and personal expenses in the sense that they raise personal welfare. This is plain enough with regard to lunch; most people would eat lunch even if they didn't work. Commuting may seem a pure business expense, but is not; it reflects the choice of where to live, as well as where to work. Read literally, § 162 would make irrelevant whether a business expense is also a personal expense; so long as it is ordinary and necessary in the taxpayer's business, thus bringing section 162(a) into play, an expense is (the statute seems to say) deductible from his income tax. But the statute has not been read literally. There is a natural reluctance, most clearly manifested in the regulation disallowing deduction of the expense of commuting, to lighten the tax burden of people who have the good fortune to interweave work with consumption. To allow a deduction for commuting would confer a windfall on people who live in the suburbs and commute to work in the cities; to allow a deduction for all business-related meals would confer a windfall on people who can arrange their work schedules so they do some of their work at lunch.

Although an argument can thus be made for disallowing *any* deduction for business meals, on the theory that people have to eat whether they work or not, the result would be excessive taxation of people who spend more money on business meals because they are business meals than they would spend on their meals if they were not working. Suppose a theatrical agent takes his clients out to lunch at the expensive restaurants that the clients demand. Of course he can deduct the expense of their meals, from which he derives no pleasure or sustenance, but can he also deduct the expense of his own? He can, because he cannot eat more cheaply; he cannot munch surreptitiously on a peanut butter and jelly sandwich brought from home while his client is wolfing down tournedos Rossini followed by soufflé au grand marnier. No doubt our theatrical agent, unless concerned for his longevity, derives personal utility from his fancy meal, but probably less than the price of the meal. He would not pay for it if it were not for the business benefit; he would get more value from using the same money to buy something else; hence the meal confers on him less utility than the cash equivalent would. The law could require him to pay tax on the fair value of the meal to him; this would be (were it not for costs of administration) the economically correct solution. But the government does not attempt this difficult measurement; it once did, but gave up the attempt as not worth the cost. . . . The taxpayer is permitted to deduct the whole price, provided the expense is "different from or in excess of that which would have been made for the taxpayer's personal purposes." Sutter v. Commissioner, 21 T.C. 170, 173 (1953).

Because the law allows this generous deduction, which tempts people to have more (and costlier) business meals than are necessary, the Internal Revenue Service has every right to insist that the meal be shown to be a real business necessity. This condition is most easily satisfied when a client or customer or supplier or other outsider to the business is a guest. Even if Sydney Smith was wrong that "soup and fish explain half the emotions of life," it is undeniable that eating together fosters camaraderie and makes business dealings friendlier and easier. It thus reduces the costs of transacting business, for these costs include the frictions and the failures of communication that are produced by suspicion and mutual misunderstanding, by differences in tastes and manners, and by lack of rapport. A meeting with a client or customer in an office is therefore not a perfect substitute for a lunch with him in a restaurant. But it is different when all the participants in the meal are coworkers, as essentially was the case here (clients occasionally were invited to the firm's daily luncheon, but Moss has made no attempt to identify the occasions). They know each other well already; they don't need the social lubrication that a meal with an outsider provides — at least don't need it daily. If a large firm had a monthly lunch to allow partners to get to know associates, the expense of the meal might well be necessary, and would be allowed by the Internal Revenue Service. . . . But Moss's firm never had more than eight lawyers (partners and associates), and did not need a daily lunch to cement relationships among them.

It is all a matter of degree and circumstance (the expense of a testimonial dinner, for example, would be deductible on a morale-building rationale); and particularly of frequency. Daily — for a full year — is too often, perhaps even for entertainment of clients, as implied by Hankenson v. Commissioner, 47 T.C.M. 1567, 1569 (1984), where the Tax Court held nondeductible the cost of lunches consumed three or four days a week, 52 weeks a year, by a doctor who entertained other doctors who he hoped would refer patients to him, and other medical personnel.

We may assume it was necessary for Moss's firm to meet daily to coordinate the work of the firm, and also, as the Tax Court found, that lunch was the most convenient time. But it does not follow that the expense of the lunch was a necessary business expense. The members of the firm had to eat somewhere, and the Cafe Angelo was both convenient and not too expensive. They do not claim to have incurred a greater daily lunch expense than they would have incurred if there had been no lunch meetings. Although it saved time to combine lunch with work, the meal itself was not an organic part of the meeting, as in the examples we gave earlier where the business objective, to be fully achieved, required sharing a meal.

The case might be different if the location of the courts required the firm's members to eat each day either in a disagreeable restaurant, so that they derived less value from the meal than it cost them to buy it, . . . or in a restaurant too expensive for their personal tastes, so that, again, they would have gotten less value than the cash equivalent. But so far as appears, they picked the restaurant they liked most. Although it must be pretty monotonous to eat lunch the same place every working day of the year, not all the lawyers attended all the lunch meetings and there was nothing to stop the firm from meeting occasionally at another restaurant proximate to their office in downtown Chicago; there are hundreds.

An argument can be made that the price of lunch at the Cafe Angelo included rental of the space that the lawyers used for what was a meeting as well as a meal. There was evidence that the firm's conference room was otherwise occupied throughout the working day, so as a matter of logic Moss might be able to claim a part of the price of lunch as an ordinary and necessary expense for work space. But this is cutting things awfully fine; in any event Moss made no effort to apportion his lunch expense in this way.

Affirmed.

NOTE

In Christey v. United States, 841 F.2d 809 (8th Cir. 1988), cert. denied, 489 U.S. 1016 (1989), the court allowed a deduction for the meal expenses of a state highway patrol officer. See description of the case supra page 59. In footnote 7 of the case, the court stated that the government in the *Moss* case had "conceded that meals are deductible under § 162(a) when they are ordinary and necessary business expenses" but noted that the court in that case had concluded that the expenses were not "necessary."

QUESTIONS

1. Is the court's decision in *Moss* grounded on the theory that a taxpayer should only be able to deduct business meals that are more expensive than the meals the taxpayer would otherwise have consumed? On the theory that a taxpayer should only be able to deduct business meals with clients? On the theory that Congress could not have intended to allow a taxpayer to deduct lunch every day?

2. Do you agree with Judge Posner that eating with clients "reduces the costs of transacting business" by lessening the "frictions and the failures of communication that are produced by suspicion and mutual misunderstanding"? Do you think that disallowance of a deduction for all business meals would significantly reduce business efficiency? How do you suppose it would affect the restaurant business and the people employed in that activity?

3. In which, if any, of the following circumstances will the lunch be deductible?

(a) A lawyer takes her client to lunch to discuss her firm's handling of the client's case.
(b) A client takes her lawyer to lunch to discuss the lawyer's firm's handling of the client's case.
(c) A lawyer takes her client to lunch in order to retain the client's goodwill.
(d) A partner in a law firm takes an associate to lunch to discuss the associate's future with the firm.
(e) A partner in a law firm takes an associate to lunch to discuss a pending case.
(f) Two partners go to lunch once a week to talk about an ongoing case.

4. More on Entertaining Customers

DANVILLE PLYWOOD CORPORATION v. UNITED STATES
899 F.2d 3 (8th Cir. 1990)

I. Facts . . .

Danville is a closely held Virginia corporation owned by George Buchanan, his wife, and their relatives. At all relevant times Buchanan has served as Danville's president.

Danville manufactures custom plywood for use in kitchen cabinets, store fixtures, furniture, wall panels, wall plaques, and similar items. Danville sells to wholesale distributors who in turn sell to architects, mill work houses, and cabinet shops. Each order Danville receives is filled to customer specifications and thus Danville does not maintain a fixed inventory of finished products.

During the years at issue, Danville maintained its books and filed its returns using the accrual method of accounting with a fiscal year ending November 30. On its returns for 1980 and 1981 Danville claimed deductions totaling $103,444.51[16] in connection with a weekend trip for 120 persons to the Super Bowl in New Orleans, Louisiana, from January 23 through January 26, 1981.

To decide who [sic] to invite to the Super Bowl weekend, Danville looked at the current and potential income from each customer. Danville did not invite specific individuals; instead, it sent two invitations to the selected customer and instructed the customer to decide whom to send. Buchanan asserts that Danville asked the customer to send individuals with "decision making authority." The majority of the customers sent one individual who was accompanied by that individual's spouse.

16. Of this amount $27,151.00 constituted payment for Super Bowl tickets; $30,721.51 for airfare for Danville's employees and guests; $45,300.00 to a tour agency for accommodations and related services; and $272.00 to General Aviation to pick up football tickets. Of the amount claimed the Commissioner disallowed $98,297.83. Of this amount $64,467.51 was disallowed on the 1980 return and $33,380.32 on the 1981 return.

Of the people attending the Super Bowl, six were employees of Danville (including Buchanan), five were spouses of the employees, one was the daughter of a shareholder, three were Buchanan's children, and four were Buchanan's friends. The remaining individuals were 58 of Danville's customers, 38 spouses of those customers, two children of one of Danville's customers, and three customers of one of Danville's customers.

In making arrangements for the Super Bowl weekend, Danville sent a letter on June 5, 1980, to Abbott Tours, a New Orleans travel agency. In the letter Danville requested accommodations for three nights, Super Bowl tickets, banquet facilities for one night, and a Mississippi River cruise. Notably, Danville did not indicate that the trip was in any way business related and failed to request access to meeting rooms or other facilities appropriate for a business trip. As finalized, the weekend included accommodations at the Sheraton Hotel, a Saturday evening dinner in the hotel's dining room, and an outing to the French Quarter on Saturday night.

On January 13, 1981, Danville sent a letter to the selected customers stating that "Super Bowl weekend is just around the corner." This letter also failed to contain any reference to business meetings or discussions of any kind. Shortly before Super Bowl weekend, Buchanan distributed a memorandum to the Danville employees who would be going to New Orleans. In the memorandum, Buchanan told his employees they should promote certain types of wood, inform the customers Danville could supply 10 ft. panels, and survey the customers regarding their need for Danville to purchase a "cut-to-size" saw.

Upon arrival at the hotel, Danville's customers were met at a hospitality desk in the lobby staffed by family members of Danville's employees. Danville also displayed some of its products in an area adjacent to the lobby. During the weekend Danville's employees met informally with customers.

During the dinner on Saturday evening Danville's customers shared the dining room with other hotel guests, although the customers were segregated in one section of the dining room. There were no speakers or general announcements made at the dinner. Buchanan and Danville's other employees circulated among the tables to speak with their guests. None of the customers placed orders during the weekend although some promised to contact Danville's employees in the future. The only scheduled activity on Sunday was the Super Bowl game and by Monday the guests were preparing to leave.

During an audit of the 1980 and 1981 returns the Commissioner disallowed the deductions claimed by Danville for the expenses incurred relating to Super Bowl weekend. . . .

II. STATUTORY SCHEME

Prior to 1961, § 162 was the sole statutory provision regulating the deduction of entertainment expenses. In response to what was perceived as widespread abuse of expense accounts and entertainment expenses Congress enacted § 274.[17] This provision is referred to as a "disallowance provision" and its effect is to disallow certain deductions for entertainment expenses which would otherwise be properly deductible under § 162.

Under the stricter limitations of § 274, no deduction for business expenses allowable under § 162 shall be allowed unless the taxpayer establishes that the item was "directly related to" or "associated with" the active conduct of the taxpayer's trade or business. In the case of the latter situation the item for which the deduction is claimed must directly precede or follow a substantial and bona fide business discussion. § 274(a)(1)(A).

Therefore, to be deductible, an entertainment expense must meet the requirements of both § 162 and § 274. First, the expense must be an ordinary and necessary business expense under § 162. Second, the expense must be either "directly related to" or "associated with" the active conduct of the taxpayer's business.

III. Standard of Review

The Claims Court held that the expenses surrounding the Super Bowl weekend were neither "ordinary and necessary" business expenses of Danville's trade or business under § 162 nor "directly related to" or "associated with" the active conduct of Danville's business under § 274. Danville acknowledges that both of these findings are factual and must be sustained on appeal unless clearly erroneous. . . .

The ruling of the Commissioner enjoys a presumption of correctness and a taxpayer bears the burden of proving it to be wrong. . . . This means that the taxpayer must come forward with enough evidence to support a finding contrary to the Commissioner's determination. . . . Even after satisfying this burden, the taxpayer must still carry the ultimate burden of proof. . . .

IV. Section 162

A. Children and Shareholder

Three of Buchanan's children and two children of Danville's customers as well as a shareholder of Danville attended Super Bowl weekend at Danville's expense. In its brief on appeal, Danville concedes that the expenses of these six individuals were not deductible and thus we need not address this class of attendees.

---

17. See H.R. Rep. No. 1447, 87th Cong., 2d Sess. 16-19 (1962-63 Cum. Bull. 405, 423); S. Rep. No. 1881, 87th Cong., 2d Sess., U.S. Code Cong. & Admin. News 1962, p.3297 (1962-63 Cum. Bull. 707, 731). Section 274 was also enacted in response to Cohan v. Commissioner, 39 F.2d 540 (2d Cir. 1930), which allowed a taxpayer to estimate the amount of his entertainment expenses. Today, § 274(d) of the code contains strict substantiation requirements. Because of our disposition of this appeal it is not necessary for us to reach the issue of adequate substantiation.

B. EMPLOYEES' SPOUSES

Five spouses of Danville employees also attended Super Bowl weekend.[18] Danville argues that these individuals "manned the hospitality desk all day Saturday and Sunday morning, and otherwise assisted by handling other tasks which needed attention." Danville also argues that Buchanan was aware that a significant number of the customer representatives would bring their wives and thus he "deemed it appropriate and helpful to have five wives of Danville employees" there to meet and entertain the spouses of the customer representatives.

Treasury regulations provide that when a taxpayer's wife accompanies him on a business trip, her expenses are not deductible unless the taxpayer can adequately show that her presence has a bona fide business purpose. The wife's performance of an incidental service does not meet this requirement. § 1.162-2c(c). This regulation does not directly apply because the taxpayer here is a corporation and the deductibility involved the expenses not of the corporation president's wife, but of the wives of other employees. The principle upon which that regulation rests, however, is no less applicable to the wives of employees of a corporate taxpayer than it is to the wife of an individual taxpayer.

Under the standards of this regulation, the Claims Court concluded that the wives of Danville's employees performed at best a social function and thus their expenses were not deductible. . . .

Danville cites United States v. Disney, 413 F.2d 783, 788 (9th Cir. 1969), and Wilkins v. United States, 348 F. Supp. 1282, 1284 (D. Neb. 1972), as examples of cases which allowed a taxpayer to deduct his wife's expenses. In *Disney*, the court stated that the "critical inquiries are whether the dominant purpose of the trip was to serve her husband's business purpose in making the trip and whether she actually spent a substantial amount of her time in assisting her husband in fulfilling that purpose." *Disney*, 413 F.2d at 788. The court in *Disney* went on to state that "the result reached in an individual case is so dependent upon the peculiar facts of that case, that the decisions called to our attention are of only limited assistance." Id.

In the case at bar, Danville simply did not present enough evidence to the Claims Court to sustain its burden of establishing that the spouses of Danville's employees performed a bona fide business purpose and not merely incidental services. Meridian Wood Prod. Co. v. United States, 725 F.2d 1183 (9th Cir. 1984) (expenses of corporation's president's spouse not deductible because her primary purpose was to socialize with other wives of business associates). The record leaves one with the overall impression that the wives of the employees went along for fun and merely helped out when they could.

---

18. [The deductions claimed for spouses would now be disallowed under § 274(m)(3). The court's discussion of prior law and of the facts of this case illustrates the potential for abuse and the problem of enforcement. — EDS.]

C.   CUSTOMER REPRESENTATIVES AND SPOUSES

As stated previously, to qualify as an "ordinary and necessary" business expense under § 162(a) an expenditure must be both "common and accepted" in the community of which Danville is a part as well as "appropriate" for the development of Danville's business. . . . The Claims Court found that Danville failed to carry its burden of proof to establish that the expenses for the customer representatives met these requirements. In support of this conclusion the Court cited the testimony of Will Gregory, General Manager for Central Wholesale Supply, one of Danville's customers. Mr. Gregory testified that he had attended seminars hosted by the National Building Materials Distributors Association which consisted of booths manned by vendors where the attendees could talk privately about the company's products.

Danville argues that nothing could be more "ordinary, necessary, usual, customary, common or important in a manufacturing business than efforts to promote products and increase sales." We agree that this is true as a general proposition. However, what is at issue in this case is the manner in which Danville attempted to promote its products and increase sales. The Claims Court stated that the "record inescapably demonstrates that the entertainment . . . was the *central* focus of the excursion, with all other activities running a distant second in importance." (Emphasis in original.)

We cannot say the Claims Court finding is clearly erroneous. What business discussions that occurred were incidental to the main event, i.e., entertainment for Danville's customers. Similarly, expenses for the customers of one of Danville's customers who attended Super Bowl weekend are not deductible under § 162.

D.   DANVILLE'S EMPLOYEES

The treasury regulations provide that only traveling expenses which are reasonable and necessary to the conduct of the taxpayer's business and which are directly attributable to it may be deducted. § 1.162-2(a). The Claims Court held that Danville failed to establish that the expenses of its employees were attributable to its business, and that the trip was undertaken primarily for business purposes. The court found that none of the correspondence between Danville and Abbott Tours referred to the business nature of the trip. Furthermore, the Claims Court described the agenda distributed by Danville to its employees as little more than a "bootstrapping afterthought."

Danville argues that its employees met with customer representatives throughout the weekend and discussed business. As indicated by the Claims Court, only two of the six Danville employees who attended the Super Bowl weekend testified. Thus, the Court could not ascertain how the other four employees spent their time. In addition, the three customer representatives who testified indicated that the discussions which did occur took place "whenever we found [Buchanan] . . . and whenever we could catch him." In light of this evidence the Claims Court concluded that Danville had failed to carry its burden of proof of demonstrating that the trip was undertaken for bona fide business purposes or that the expenses were directly attributable to Danville's business.

Danville argues that these quotes of the customer representatives were taken out of context and the full quotes indicate that the representatives talked to Buchanan whenever he was not engaged in discussions with other customers. Accepting Danville's version as true, once again we must agree with the Claims Court that Danville failed to present sufficient evidence to satisfy its burden of proof. The Super Bowl weekend appears to have been little more than a group social excursion with business playing a subsidiary role.

On the narrow facts of this case, we hold that the decision of the Claims Court that Danville failed to satisfy its burden of proof that the Super Bowl expenses were "ordinary and necessary" business expenses under § 162(a) of the Code is not clearly erroneous.

In view of our holding that Danville has not met its burden relative to § 162(a), any discussion of § 274 is unnecessary. . . .

NOTES AND QUESTIONS

1. *The ordinary and necessary test.* The court in *Danville* based its opinion in large part on the fact that the expenses in question did not meet the "ordinary and necessary" test of § 162. The requirement that a deduction be "ordinary," if interpreted literally, would rule out deductions for many expenses that are deductible, and should be deductible. Suppose, for example, an urban department store suffers an unheard-of infestation of locusts. The locusts swarm around the entrance and drive away customers. The store responds by purchasing other insects to feed upon the locusts. That expense may properly be characterized as extraordinary and would not be deductible under a literal interpretation of the ordinary and necessary test. It is quite clear, however, that the expense is and should be deductible.

The requirement that a deduction be "necessary" is rarely invoked. To understand why this is so, suppose that a company decides to greatly expand its advertising budget. So long as the company purchases advertising from an unrelated party, the IRS will not inquire as to whether the expense is necessary. This seems correct. A tax deduction offsets only part of the real cost of a business expense. (For example, a taxpayer in the 40 percent combined state and federal tax bracket saves only 40 cents in taxes for every dollar spent.) It will never be worthwhile for a business to make unnecessary payments to an unrelated party. There does not seem to be any reason, then, for the IRS to second-guess the "necessity" of payments to unrelated parties.

What distinguishes *Danville* from the cases described above? Are there other tests the court might rely on to determine the deductibility of these sorts of expenses? What about primary purpose?

2. *The expense of sending customers and their spouses to the Super Bowl.* The court in *Danville* disallowed costs incurred to purchase tickets and the like for Danville's customers and their spouses. The court reasoned that these expenses were not "ordinary and necessary." Suppose that instead of providing travel and entertainment, Danville had simply sent its customers a

rebate, or lowered its prices on future goods. The rebate or price reduction would have reduced taxable income in much the same way and same amount as the cost of the Super Bowl tickets. As stated in Note 1, supra, the IRS would not have inquired as to the necessity for the rebate or reduction.

What if Danville had simply mailed its best customers Super Bowl tickets and travel vouchers for free air fare to the Super Bowl but had not sent any of its own employees to the Super Bowl? Could Danville have then deducted the expense as an advertising or promotional expense? Could Danville have argued that, because the tickets went solely to unrelated parties, it was inappropriate for the IRS to inquire as to the business necessity for the expense?

Danville argued that the expense of both customer and employee tickets should be deducted because the trip made it possible for Danville employees to pitch products to Danville customers. Under this theory, the presence of Danville employees supported the deduction for Danville customers. Consistent with this theory, Danville deducted the cost of sending its employees to the Super Bowl. It also deducted the cost of sending spouses and, in one case, children of its employees. Danville did not treat the cost as salary to the employees and thus did not withhold employment taxes from that sum or report that sum as salary to the IRS. Danville's employees in turn treated the travel and entertainment they (and their spouses and, in one case, children) received as a non-taxable — an incidental benefit received in connection with a business trip. Is it possible that the court regarded the whole affair as an excuse to provide a tax-free fringe benefit to Danville employees, and that the presence of such employees (and their relations) tainted the deduction otherwise allowable for Danville customers? Or did the cost of the travel and entertainment provided to Danville's customers simply offend the IRS and the court?

3. *The costs of sending its own employees and their spouses to the Super Bowl*. Had Danville simply given its employees cash equal to the cost of the travel and entertainment, the expense would clearly have been deducted as salary. Indeed, had Danville given its employees (and their relations) a free vacation and reported that expense as salary to the employees it is virtually certain it would have been deductible under § 162. Seen from this perspective, the "offending" aspect of the Super Bowl trip was not the deduction to the employer, but the fact that the employee did not report the value of the travel and entertainment as income, and that the employees did not pay tax on that income. Provided that the employer and employees are in roughly the same tax bracket, the disallowance of the deduction has much the same effect as allowing deduction of the salary but taxing the employees on the value of the trip.

4. *Planning*. With hindsight, what advice would you have given to Danville about the conduct of the trip to the Super Bowl to increase the odds of the deduction being sustained? Would you advise that spouses of employees not be invited? See § 274(m)(3). What about hiring the spouses as temporary employees of Danville?

CHURCHILL DOWNS, INC. v. COMMISSIONER
307 F.3d 423 (6th Cir. 2002)

Petitioner Churchill Downs, Incorporated and its subsidiaries (together "Churchill Downs") appeal the United States Tax Court's judgment that they were entitled to deduct only 50 percent of certain expenses they incurred in 1994 and 1995 because the expenses qualified as "entertainment" for purposes of Internal Revenue Code § 274(n)(1)(B). For the reasons stated below, we AFFIRM.

I

The facts of this case are not in dispute. Churchill Downs owns and operates the Churchill Downs race track in Louisville, Kentucky, and three other race tracks. Churchill Downs conducts horse races at these tracks, and earns revenues from wagering, admissions and seating charges, concession commissions, sponsorship revenues, licensing rights, and broadcast fees. Although Churchill Downs does not compete directly with other race tracks due to differences in the timing of race events, it competes for patrons with other sports, entertainment, and gaming operations.

Churchill Downs' biggest race is the Kentucky Derby, held each year on the first Saturday in May. Churchill Downs hosts the following events in connection with the race: (1) a "Sport of Kings" gala, (2) a brunch following the post position drawing for the race, (3) a week-long hospitality tent offering coffee, juice, and donuts to the press, and (4) the Kentucky Derby Winner's Party. The Sport of Kings Gala includes a press reception/cocktail party, dinner, and entertainment. The Kentucky Derby items and amounts at issue in this case are:

Item	1994 Expenditure	1995 Expenditure
Sport of King Gala	$114,375	$88,571
Hospitality Tent	-0-	$ 7,803
Derby Winner's Party	17,500	-0-
Total	$131,875	$93,374

In 1994, Churchill Downs also agreed to host another race, the Breeders' Cup, at the Churchill Downs racetrack. Its contract with Breeders' Cup Limited ("BCL") obligated it to host certain promotional events designed to enhance the significance of the Breeders' Cup races as a national and international horse racing event. These events included: (1) a press reception cocktail party and dinner, (2) a brunch, and (3) a press breakfast. The Breeders' Cup items and amounts at issue in this case are:

	1994
	Expenditure
Item	
Breeders' Cup Dinner	$116,000
Breeders' Cup Brunch	$21,885
Press Breakfast	$7,500
Total	$145,385

Finally, Churchill Downs hosted a number of miscellaneous dinners, receptions, cocktail parties and other events indirectly associated with one or both of these races, at an expense of $4,940 in 1994 and $21,619 in 1995.

Churchill Downs deducted the full amount of these Kentucky Derby and Breeder's Cup expenses on its 1994 and 1995 federal income tax returns as "ordinary and necessary business expenses" pursuant to § 162. . . . [T]he Commissioner . . . rejected this treatment and concluded that Churchill Downs was entitled to deduct only 50 percent of these expenses. The Tax Court agreed. . . .

II

This court reviews the Tax Court's factual findings for clear error and its conclusions of law de novo. . . . In particular, this court reviews the Tax Court's interpretation of Internal Revenue Code provisions and related Treasury regulations de novo. . . .

Section 162(a) allows a taxpayer to deduct "all the ordinary and necessary expenses paid or incurred during the taxable year in carrying on any trade or business." § 162(a). Section 274(a) disallows certain deductions otherwise permitted by § 162, and provides that:

> No deduction otherwise allowable under this chapter shall be allowed for any item . . . [w]ith respect to an activity which is of a type generally considered to constitute entertainment, amusement, or recreation, unless the taxpayer establishes that the item was directly related to, or, in the case of an item directly preceding or following a substantial and bona fide business discussion (including business meetings at a convention or otherwise), that such item was associated with, the active conduct of the taxpayer's trade or business.

Section 274(n)(1) further limits deductions for entertainment expenses, providing that:

> The amount allowable as a deduction under this chapter for—
> (A) any expense for food or beverages, and
> (B) any item with respect to an activity which is of a type generally considered to constitute entertainment, amusement, or recreation, or with respect to a facility used in connection with such activity,
> shall not exceed 50 percent of the amount of such expense or item which would (but for this paragraph) be allowable as a deduction under this chapter.

The Commissioner does not dispute that all of the expenses at issue qualify as "ordinary and necessary" business expenses "directly related" to the "active conduct" of Churchill Downs' business, and thus that some deduction of these expenses is allowed. However, he argues that § 274(n)(1) applies to limit deduction of these expenses because they qualify as items associated with activity generally considered entertainment.

Section 274(o) gives the Commissioner the power to promulgate "such regulations as he may deem necessary" to enforce § 274. Here the Commissioner has promulgated a regulation in connection in § 274(n), which provides that:

> An objective test shall be used to determine whether an activity is of a type generally considered to constitute entertainment, it will constitute entertainment for purposes of this section and section 274(a) regardless of whether the expenditure can also be described otherwise, and even though the expenditure relates to the taxpayer alone. This objective test precludes arguments such as that *entertainment* means only entertainment of others or that an expenditure for entertainment should be characterized as an expenditure for advertising or public relations. However, in applying this test the taxpayer's trade or business shall be considered. Thus, although attending a theatrical performance would generally be considered entertainment, it would not be so considered in the case of a professional theater critic, attending in his professional capacity. Similarly, if a manufacturer of dresses conducts a fashion show to introduce his products to a group of store buyers, the show would not be generally considered to constitute entertainment. However, if an appliance distributor conducts a fashion show for the wives of his retailers, the fashion show would be generally considered to constitute entertainment.

Regs. § 1.274-2(b)(1)(ii) (emphasis in original). Each party relies on this language as support for its position. Churchill Downs argues that the Derby and Breeders' Cup expenses at issue should not be considered entertainment expenses because these pre- and post-race events "showcased" its "entertainment product." Specifically, it contends that the Sport of Kings Gala and the other invitation-only events generated publicity and media attention which introduced its races to the public in the same manner that a dress designer's fashion show introduces its product to clothing buyers. In response, the Commissioner relies on § 1.274-2(b)(1)(ii)'s statement that an item generally considered to be entertainment is subject to the 50 percent limitation even where it may be otherwise characterized as an advertising or public relations expense. The Commissioner argues that the brunches, dinners, galas, and parties at issue qualify on their face as items "generally considered entertainment" and, following § 1.274-2(b)(1)(ii), that they are not saved from this classification by the fact that these amounts were spent to publicize Churchill Downs' racing events.

These arguments expose an inherent tension in § 1.274-2(b)(1)(ii). On the one hand, § 1.274-2(b)(1)(ii) states that an item generally considered to be entertainment is subject to the 50 percent limitation even if it may be described otherwise, in particular as advertising or public relations. At the same time, the regulation suggests that certain expenses generally considered entertainment but somehow instrumental to the conduct of a taxpayer's business do not qualify as "entertainment" for purposes of § 274(n). The regulation draws the line between pure publicity and entertainment events integral to the conduct of the taxpayer's business by providing the contrasting examples of a fashion show offered by a dress designer to store buyers (not entertainment) and a fashion show offered by an appliance manufacturer to the spouses of its buyers (entertainment). See Regs. § 1.274-2(b)(1)(ii). In the first example, the event is attended by the taxpayer's primary customers, and the taxpayer's product is present at the event and is the focus of it. In contrast, the second example reflects a purely social event focused on something unrelated to the taxpayer's product, held to generate good will among selected third parties with the expectation that they will influence the taxpayer's primary customers into buying its product.

Here, as the Tax Court found, Churchill Downs is in the business of staging horse races and makes its money primarily from selling admission to the races accepting wagers on them. However, no horse racing was conducted at the dinners and other events at issue. Nor did the events, held away from the track at rented facilities, provide attendees with an opportunity to learn more about the races—for example, the horses that would appear, the odds associated with each horse, the types of wagers available, track conditions, etc.—similar to the product information store buyers might acquire at a fashion show. Rather, Churchill Downs concedes that the events were planned simply as social occasions. Nor were the events open to the gaming public that attends Churchill Downs races and wagers on them. Instead, Churchill Downs invited selected dignitaries and members of the media to these private receptions, not with the expectation that they would later consume significant amounts of its product, but rather in the hopes that they would influence its primary customer base, the general public, to do so, either through the example of their attendance or through favorable reporting. As Churchill Downs explained, the attendance of the celebrities at these pre-race events was "essential" because "the presence of those individuals in Louisville for two or more days before the races gave rise to related publicity and media attention that helped sustain and advance the glamour and prestige of the races." In other words, the purpose of the galas and dinners was not to make Churchill Downs' product directly available to its customers or to provide them with specific information about it, but rather to create an aura of glamour in connection with the upcoming races and generally to arouse public interest in them. In this regard, the dinners, brunches, and receptions at issue most closely resemble the example given above of a fashion show held for the wives of appliance retailers, and are best characterized not as a product introduction event used to conduct the taxpayer's business, but as pure advertising or public relations expenses. Accordingly, we conclude that the Kentucky Derby and Breeders' Cup expenses at issue qualify as "entertainment" under § 1.274-2(b)(1)(ii)'s objective standard.

As an alternative argument, Churchill Downs contends that, under the objective test, an event generally considered entertainment should not be deemed "entertainment" for purposes of § 274 where the event itself is the product the taxpayer is selling. In support of this position, it relies on a statement in the legislative history of § 274(n)(1) that:

> The trade or business of the taxpayer will determine whether an activity is of the type generally considered to constitute entertainment.... For example, with respect to taxpayer who is a professional hunter, a hunting trip would not generally be considered a recreation-type activity.

S. Rep. No. 87-1881 (1962), 1962 WL 4862, at *3330. Churchill Downs argues that its entertainment products, the Kentucky Derby and the Breeders' Cup, necessarily include the Spot of Kings Gala and the other brunches, dinners and receptions at issue as integral parts of unified entertainment experience.

We disagree. Unlike the hunter in the example above, who earns his money by hosting recreational hunting trips, Churchill Downs did not make any money from hosting the Sport of Kings Gala or the other events for which it seeks a deduction. Indeed, these events are easily separable from Churchill Downs' business because its primary customers, the gaming public, were not permitted to attend them, either by purchasing tickets or otherwise.... The Commissioner puts it succinctly: "taxpayers were in the horse racing business, not the business of throwing parties." ...

Finally, Churchill Downs offers two additional rationales for allowing a full deduction of these items. Section 274(e) provides that:

> [§ 274(a)] shall not apply to—
>
> ***
>
> (7) **Items available to public.**—Expenses for goods, services, and facilities made available by the taxpayer to the general public.
> (8) **Entertainment sold to customers.**—Expenses for goods or services (including the use of facilities) which are sold by the taxpayer in a bona fide transaction for an adequate and full consideration in money or money's worth.

§ 274(e) (emphasis in original). Churchill Downs argues that the Gala expenses and other items at issue are exempt from § 274(a) pursuant to this section either because these events were available to the general public or because they qualify as entertainment sold to customers.

Churchill Downs does not dispute that these events were by invitation only, or that such invitations were offered only to a small number of individuals. However, it argues that amount spent on these events meet the requirements of § 274(e)(7) because the expenditures were incurred to promote other events, the Kentucky Derby and Breeders' Cup races, which were open to the general public. We reject this argument....

Churchill Downs also relies on an Internal Revenue Service ("IRS") technical advice memorandum holding that food, beverages, lodging, and entertainment offered free by a casino to "high rollers" qualified as "items available to the public" for purposes of § 274(e)(7). See Tech. Advice Mem. 9641005, 1996 WL 584428 (July 27, 1996) ("TAM"). The IRS reasoned that all of the benefits provided were items the casino routinely offered to the paying public as part of its stock in trade. As such, the IRS concluded, this practice of "comping" favored customers was akin to providing free product samples, a practice Congress previously had characterized as making goods available to the general public. The agency also concluded that the fact that a customer was required to engage in some amount of gaming activity in order to receive this benefit did not prevent it from being "available to the public" for purposes of § 274(e)(7).... Here Churchill Down argues that invitations to the Sport of Kings Gala and the other non-race events were akin to the "comps" provided to favored customers at a casino.

We reject this argument. As an initial matter, written determinations like the TAM have no precedential value to parties other than the taxpayer they are issued to, and § 6110(k)(3) prohibits taxpayers from relying on them in proceedings before the agency.... Furthermore, unlike the "comps" offered to casino patrons, the dinners and galas at issue here are not the products that members of the general public routinely purchase from Churchill Downs, namely, admission to horse races or wagers. Indeed, Churchill Downs does not sell admission to these non-race dining events at all....

In regards to its "entertainment sold to customers" argument, Churchill Downs concedes that those invited to the Sport of Kings Gala and the other occasions did not pay for the privilege of attending these events. Nevertheless, Churchill Downs once again argues that these dinners and brunches were integral parts of an encompassing entertainment event — the races — which members of the public did in fact pay to attend. For the reasons already discussed above, this argument is unpersuasive.

As a final matter, it would seem that, even if these events were deemed not to constitute "entertainment" for purposes of §§ 274(a) and (n)(1)(B) § 274(n)(1)(A) would preclude full deduction of many of the expenses at issue here. See § 274(n)(1)(A). That section, read in conjunction with the rest of § 274(n)(1), provides that "[t]he amount allowable as a deduction under this chapter for . . . any expense for food or beverages . . . shall exceed 50 percent of the amount of such expense or item which would (but for this paragraph) be allowable as a deduction under this chapter." Id. This limitation does not appear to be contingent on a classification of the expenses as "entertainment." Given that the events at issue are mainly dinners, brunches, breakfasts, and receptions, it seems likely that a significant portion of the expenses for which Churchill Downs seeks deduction are for food and beverages. However, we need not resolve this issue, which the parties have not briefed, because we conclude that the expenses associated with these events already are subject to the 50 percent limitation as items "generally considered entertainment."

QUESTIONS

1. What is the rationale for the 50 percent limitation? Is the outcome of this case consistent with that limitation? What about the Treasury position (in the Regulations) on fashion shows? Suppose that the taxpayer had been able to establish that 40 percent of the people at the "Sport of Kings Gala" had been

invited because they were big-time bettors and that 10 percent were people who owned horses that had been entered in various races at Churchill Downs, including the Kentucky Derby.

2. Suppose the taxpayer provides free food and drinks to people in the prime boxes on the day of the Kentucky Derby. Full deduction or only 50 percent?

3. Suppose that at the "Sport of Kings Gala" the taxpayer had had large video screens with pictures of prior races, pictures of the horses in the current Kentucky Derby, and the early betting odds on each horse, and that it was possible for people at the event to make off-track bets.

C. CHILD-CARE EXPENSES

The case that follows arose before the adoption of express statutory provisions allowing a credit for certain child- and household-care expenses of working parents. See infra Note 4. It is still controlling on the question of deductibility of child-care expenses and interesting in that it reflects an effort to grapple with the question whether such expenses should be regarded as costs of earning income.

SMITH v. COMMISSIONER
40 B.T.A. 1038 (1939), aff'd without opinion, 113 F.2d 114 (2d Cir. 1940)

OPPER, J.

[The Commissioner] determined a deficiency ... in petitioners' 1937 income tax ... due to the disallowance of a deduction claimed by petitioners, who are husband and wife, for sums spent by the wife in employing nursemaids to care for petitioners' young child, the wife, as well as the husband, being employed....

Petitioners would have us apply the "but for" test. They propose that but for the nurses, the wife could not leave her child; but for the freedom so secured, she could not pursue her gainful labors, and but for them, there would be no income and no tax. This thought evokes an array of interesting possibilities. The fee to the doctor, but for whose healing service, the earner of the family income could not leave his sickbed; the cost of the laborer's raiment, for how can the world proceed about its business unclothed; the very home which gives us shelter and rest and the food which provides energy, might all by an extension of the same proposition be construed as necessary to the operation of business and to the creation of income. Yet these are the very essence of those "personal" expenses the deductibility of which is expressly denied. [§ 262.]

We are told that the working wife is a new phenomenon. This is relied on to account for the apparent inconsistency that the expenses in issue are now a commonplace, yet have not been the subject of legislation, ruling, or adjudicated controversy. But if that is true, it becomes all the more necessary to apply accepted principles to the novel facts. We are not prepared to say that the care of children, like similar aspects of family and household life, is other than a personal concern. The wife's services as custodian of the home and protector of its children are ordinarily rendered without monetary compensation. There results no taxable income from the performance of this service and the correlative expenditure is personal and not susceptible of deduction. . . . Here the wife has chosen to employ others to discharge her domestic function and the services she performs are rendered outside the home. They are a source of actual income and taxable as such. But that does not deprive the same work performed by others of its personal character. . . .

We are not unmindful that, as petitioners suggest, certain disbursements normally personal may become deductible by reason of their intimate connection with an occupation carried on for profit. In this category fall entertainment, . . . traveling expenses, . . . and the cost of an actor's wardrobe. . . . The line is not always an easy one to draw nor the test simple to apply. But we think its principle is clear. It may for practical purposes be said to constitute a distinction between those activities which, as a matter of common acceptance and universal experience, are "ordinary" or usual as the direct accompaniment of business pursuits, on the one hand; and those which, though they may in some indirect and tenuous degree relate to the circumstances of a profitable occupation, are nevertheless personal in their nature, of a character applicable to human beings generally, and which exist on that plane regardless of the occupation, though not necessarily of the station in life, of the individuals concerned. See Welch v. Helvering [infra page 545].

In the latter category, we think, fall payments made to servants or others occupied in looking to the personal wants of their employers. . . . And we include in this group, nursemaids retained to care for infant children.

NOTES AND QUESTIONS

1. *Causation.* The court's rejection of the taxpayers' "but for" argument is not convincing: The other expenses to which the court refers would be incurred by people even if they were not employed. It is clear in the *Smith* case that the child-care expense would not have been incurred but for the job. It is equally clear, however, that the expense would not have been incurred but for the child. Where does this kind of analysis leave you? See discussion of the *Ochs* case, supra page 374, Note 1. The Smiths would have you compare them with another couple with a child but with one parent staying home to care for it. The court would have you compare them with another couple with both spouses employed but with no children. Where does this kind of observation leave (or lead) you?

2. *The statutory language.* However appealing the taxpayers' claim may be, can their outlays sensibly be characterized as "ordinary and necessary expenses paid or incurred . . . in carrying on a trade or business"?

3. *Policy.* (a) Which of the following arguments for some sort of allowance for child-care expenses do you find most appealing?

(i)   In our society, since most married people have children, children should be taken as given. From the perspective of a potential job seeker with children the return from taking a job is the amount available after deduction for unavoidable child-care expenses. "Income" must therefore be defined as the net amount after child-care expenses, both in the interests of fairness and in order to avoid distorting job-taking decisions.

(ii) Our tax system discourages job-taking by the person who is the secondary worker in a marriage. It does this by taxing the secondary worker's earned income at rates determined by piling that income on top of the income of the primary worker (see supra page 22), while at the same time imposing no tax on imputed income from performing household and child-care services (see supra page 77). The secondary worker also pays Social Security taxes and incurs a variety of work-related expenses. Most secondary workers are women. Thus, the system tends to discourage job-taking by women. It may at the same time impose psychological and other burdens on women by depreciating the value of services performed outside the home as compared with those performed in the home. An allowance for child-care expenses mitigates these effects.

(iii) Child-care allowances are necessary in order to permit low-income people to take jobs.

(iv) Child-care allowances will encourage people to have more children.

(v)   Child-care allowances will lead to child-care jobs and will provide employment to people who might otherwise be unemployed.

(b) What implications does each of these arguments have for whether the allowance should be a deduction of the entire outlay, a deduction of some part of the outlay, or a credit?

4. *Congressional response.* (a) In 1954, Congress responded to the claims of people like the Smiths with a new deduction that had some interesting limitations, reflecting the attitudes of the time toward working mothers. The deduction was initially limited to $600 per year. (Even in 1954 it must have been difficult at best to hire babysitters for $12 a week.) It was available to unmarried women, widows, and divorced men but not to unmarried men. The deduction was liberalized in 1963, 1964, and 1971, and finally in 1976 changed to a credit, which is what we find today in § 21. The credit is a percentage of the amount spent for household services, up to $2,400 for one child (or other "qualifying individual") and $4,800 for two or more children (or qualifying individuals). The percentage used in determining the amount of the credit declines as income rises. In a household with a wife and husband, both employed, with a total income of $30,000, two children, and expenses of $4,800 or more, the credit (which reduces the amount of tax payable dollar-for-dollar) would be $960.

(b) Examine § 21. Consider the possible rationale for each of the following features:

(i)   The phase-down of the credit from 30 percent to 20 percent of expenses as income rises above $10,000 (§ 21(a)(2));

(ii)   The importance of having in the home a "qualifying individual" (§ 21(a)(1) and (b)(1));

(iii)   The availability for "expenses for household services" (§ 21(b)(2)(A)(i));

(iv)   The limitation on the dollar amount of the credit (§ 21(c)); and

(v)   The limitation of expenses that may be taken into account, in the case of a husband and wife, to the income of the lower earner (§ 21(d)(1)(B)).

(c) Compare § 129, which permits an employer to make available to employees, free of tax, up to $5,000 per year for child-care expenses through a dependent care assistance program, or DCAP. This benefit may be part of a § 125 cafeteria plan (see supra page 65), so the employee can be allowed, in effect, to treat up to $5,000 of salary as a nontaxable DCAP benefit. But under § 21(c), the amount of child-care expenses that can be used to calculate the § 21 tax credit is reduced by amounts paid through a DCAP and excluded under § 129. Taxpayers are therefore confronted with a tax-planning choice. When the marginal rate of tax on their income is lower than the credit rate on their expenses (which, as we have just seen, ranges from 30 percent to 20 percent), they are better off to forgo the DCAP exclusion and use their expenses to claim a credit under § 21. For example, suppose a couple has two children and qualified expenses of $4,000 and a taxable income of $15,000. Their marginal rate is 15 percent. If they take the $4,000 under a DCAP plan and avoid tax on that amount, they save $600. Suppose their adjusted gross income is $19,000. The credit rate for them is 25 percent. If they forgo the DCAP exclusion and claim a credit for the $4,000 of expenses, the amount of their credit will be $1,000, or $400 more than they would save by using the DCAP. On the other hand, if their taxable income were $50,000, their marginal rate would be 28 percent and a DCAP exclusion would save them $1,120. If their adjusted gross income were $60,000, their credit rate would be 20 percent and the amount of the credit would be $800, which is $320 less than what they could save under the DCAP.

5. *What is an "employment-related" expense?* In Zoltan v. Commissioner, 79 T.C. 490 (1982), the taxpayer, who worked fifty-five hours a week as an accountant, sent her eleven-year-old son to an eight-week summer camp costing $1,100. Alternative forms of child care for the same period would have cost about the same amount. The Tax Court allowed the taxpayer to treat the entire $1,100 as a child-care expense within the contemplation of § 21(c)(2)(A). After this case became a news item, Congress amended § 21(b)(2)(A) to provide that "employment expenses" do not include the costs of "a camp where the [child] stays overnight." The Senate Committee on Finance explanation (see Report on the Omnibus Budget Reconciliation Act of 1987, 100th Cong., 1st Sess. 165 (1987)) states that "overnight camp expenses are a personal consumption expenditure that is not a necessary cost of being able to go to work." Do you agree?

In the *Zoltan* case the taxpayer also sent her son on a school trip to Washington, D.C., during the week of his Easter vacation. The cost, including transportation and lodging, was $116, which was less than what the taxpayer would have been required to pay for his care if he had remained home. The court disallowed all but $35 of this because of the educational value of the trip. What if the Easter trip had been to Disneyland?

D. COMMUTING EXPENSES

COMMISSIONER v. FLOWERS
326 U.S. 465 (1945)

Mr. Justice Murphy delivered the opinion of the Court.

This case presents a problem as to the meaning and application of the provision of [the predecessor of § 162(a)(2)], allowing a deduction for income tax purposes of "traveling expenses (including the entire amount expended for meals and lodging) while away from home in the pursuit of a trade or business."

The taxpayer, a lawyer, has resided with his family in Jackson, Mississippi, since 1903. There he has paid taxes, voted, schooled his children and established social and religious connections. He built a house in Jackson nearly thirty years ago and at all times has maintained it for himself and his family. He has been connected with several law firms in Jackson, one of which he formed and which has borne his name since 1922.

In 1906 the taxpayer began to represent the predecessor of the Gulf, Mobile & Ohio Railroad, his present employer. He acted as trial counsel for the railroad throughout Mississippi. From 1918 until 1927 he acted as special counsel for the railroad in Mississippi. He was elected general solicitor in 1927 and continued to be elected to that position each year until 1930, when he was elected general counsel. Thereafter he was annually elected general counsel until September, 1940, when the properties of the predecessor company and another railroad were merged and he was elected vice president and general counsel of the newly formed Gulf, Mobile & Ohio Railroad.

The main office of the Gulf, Mobile & Ohio Railroad is in Mobile, Alabama, as was also the main office of its predecessor. When offered the position of general solicitor in 1927, the taxpayer was unwilling to accept it if it required him to move from Jackson to Mobile. He had established himself in Jackson both professionally and personally and was not desirous of moving away. As a result, an arrangement was made between him and the railroad whereby he could accept the position and continue to reside in Jackson on condition that he pay his traveling expenses between Mobile and Jackson and pay his living expenses in both places. This arrangement permitted the taxpayer to determine for himself the amount of time he would spend in each of the two cities and was in effect during 1939 and 1940, the taxable years in question.

The railroad company provided an office for the taxpayer in Mobile but not in Jackson. When he worked in Jackson his law firm provided him with office space, although he no longer participated in the firm's business or shared in its profits. He used his own office furniture and fixtures at this office. The railroad, however, furnished telephone service and a typewriter and desk for his secretary. It also paid the secretary's expenses while in Jackson. Most of the legal business of the railroad was centered in or conducted from Jackson, but this business was handled by local counsel for the railroad. The taxpayer's participation was advisory only and was no different from his participation in the railroad's legal business in other areas.

The taxpayer's principal post of business was at the main office in Mobile. However, during the taxable years of 1939 and 1940, he devoted nearly all of his time to matters relating to the merger of the railroads. Since it was left to him where he would do his work, he spent most of his time in Jackson during this period. In connection with the merger, one of the companies was involved in certain litigation in the federal court in Jackson and the taxpayer participated in that litigation.

During 1939 he spent 203 days in Jackson and 66 in Mobile, making 33 trips between the two cities. During 1940 he spent 168 days in Jackson and 102 in Mobile, making 40 trips between the two cities. The railroad paid all of his traveling expenses when he went on business trips to points other than Jackson or Mobile. But it paid none of his expenses in traveling between these two points or while he was at either of them.

The taxpayer deducted $900 in his 1939 income tax return and $1,620 in his 1940 return as traveling expenses incurred in making trips from Jackson to Mobile and as expenditures for meals and hotel accommodations while in Mobile.[19] The Commissioner disallowed the deductions. . . .

The portion of [§ 162(a)] authorizing the deduction of "traveling expenses (including the entire amount expended for meals and lodging) while away from home in the pursuit of a trade or business" is one of the specific examples given by Congress in that section of "ordinary and necessary expenses paid or incurred during the taxable year in carrying on any trade or business." It is to be contrasted with the provision of [§ 262]. [The Regulations provide] that

> Traveling expenses, as ordinarily understood, include railroad fares and meals and lodging. If the trip is undertaken for other than business purposes, the railroad fares are personal expenses and the meals and lodging are living expenses. If the trip is solely on business, the reasonable and necessary traveling expenses, including railroad fares, meals, and lodging, are business expenses. . . . Only such expenses as are reasonable and necessary in the conduct of the business and directly attributable to it may be deducted. . . . Commuters' fares are not considered as business expenses and are not deductible.

Three conditions must thus be satisfied before a traveling expense deduction may be made under [§ 162(a)(2)]:

(1) The expense must be a reasonable and necessary traveling expense, as that term is generally understood. This includes such items as transportation fares and food and lodging expenses incurred while traveling.

(2) The expense must be incurred "while away from home."

(3) The expense must be incurred in pursuit of business. This means that there must be a direct connection between the expenditure and the carrying on of the trade or business of the taxpayer or of his employer. Moreover, such an expenditure must be necessary or appropriate to the development and pursuit of the business or trade.

---

19. No claim for deduction was made by the taxpayer for the amounts spent in traveling from Mobile to Jackson. . . .

Whether particular expenditures fulfill these three conditions so as to entitle a taxpayer to a deduction is purely a question of fact in most instances. . . . And the Tax Court's inferences and conclusions on such a factual matter, under established principles, should not be disturbed by an appellate court. . . .

In this instance, the Tax Court without detailed elaboration concluded that "The situation presented in this proceeding is, in principle, no different from that in which a taxpayer's place of employment is in one city and for reasons satisfactory to himself he resides in another." It accordingly disallowed the deductions on the ground that they represent living and personal expenses rather than traveling expenses incurred while away from home in the pursuit of business. The court below accepted the Tax Court's findings of fact but reversed its judgment on the basis that it had improperly construed the word "home" as used in the second condition precedent to a traveling expense deduction under [§ 162(a)(2)]. The Tax Court, it was said, erroneously construed the word to mean the post, station or place of business where the taxpayer was employed—in this instance, Mobile—and thus erred in concluding that the expenditures in issue were not incurred "while away from home." The court below felt that the word was to be given no such "unusual" or "extraordinary" meaning in this statute, that it simply meant "that place where one in fact resides" or "the principal place of abode of one who has the intention to live there permanently." 148 F.2d at 164. Since the taxpayer here admittedly had his home, as thus defined, in Jackson and since the expenses were incurred while he was away from Jackson, the court below held that the deduction was permissible.

The meaning of the word "home" in [§ 162(a)(2)] with reference to a taxpayer residing in one city and working in another has engendered much difficulty and litigation. . . . The Tax Court and the administrative rulings have consistently defined it as the equivalent of the taxpayer's place of business. . . . On the other hand, the decision below and Wallace v. Commissioner, 144 F.2d 407 (C.C.A.9), have flatly rejected that view and have confined the term to the taxpayer's actual residence. . . .

We deem it unnecessary here to enter into or to decide this conflict. The Tax Court's opinion, as we read it, was grounded neither solely nor primarily upon that agency's conception of the word "home." Its discussion was directed mainly toward the relation of the expenditures to the railroad's business, a relationship required by the third condition of the deduction. Thus even if the Tax Court's definition of the word "home" was implicit in its decision and even if that definition was erroneous, its judgment must be sustained here if it properly concluded that the necessary relationship between the expenditures and the railroad's business was lacking. Failure to satisfy any one of the three conditions destroys the traveling expense deduction.

Turning our attention to the third condition, this case is disposed of quickly. There is no claim that the Tax Court misconstrued this condition or used improper standards in applying it. And it is readily apparent from the facts that its inferences were supported by evidence and that its conclusion that the expenditures in issue were non-deductible living and personal expenses was fully justified.

The facts demonstrate clearly that the expenses were not incurred in the pursuit of the business of the taxpayer's employer, the railroad. Jackson was his regular home. Had his post of duty been in that city the cost of maintaining his home there and of commuting or driving to work concededly would be non-deductible living and personal expenses lacking the necessary direct relation to the prosecution of the business. The character of such expenses is unaltered by the circumstance that the taxpayer's post of duty was in Mobile, thereby increasing the costs of transportation, food and lodging. Whether he maintained one abode or two, whether he traveled three blocks or three hundred miles to work, the nature of these expenditures remained the same.

The added costs in issue, moreover, were as unnecessary and inappropriate to the development of the railroad's business as were his personal and living costs in Jackson. They were incurred solely as the result of the taxpayer's desire to maintain a home in Jackson while working in Mobile, a factor irrelevant to the maintenance and prosecution of the railroad's legal business. The railroad did not require him to travel on business from Jackson to Mobile or to maintain living quarters in both cities. Nor did it compel him, save in one instance, to perform tasks for it in Jackson. It simply asked him to be at his principal post in Mobile as business demanded and as his personal convenience was served, allowing him to divide his business time between Mobile and Jackson as he saw fit. Except for the federal court litigation, all of the taxpayer's work in Jackson would normally have been performed in the headquarters at Mobile. The fact that he traveled frequently between the two cities and incurred extra living expenses in Mobile, while doing much of his work in Jackson, was occasioned solely by his personal propensities. The railroad gained nothing from this arrangement except the personal satisfaction of the taxpayer.

Travel expenses in pursuit of business within the meaning of [§ 162(a)(2)] could arise only when the railroad's business forced the taxpayer to travel and to live temporarily at some place other than Mobile, thereby advancing the interests of the railroad. Business trips are to be identified in relation to business demands and the traveler's business headquarters. The exigencies of business rather than the personal conveniences and necessities of the traveler must be the motivating factors. Such was not the case here.

It follows that the court below erred in reversing the judgment of the Tax Court.

Reversed.

Mr. Justice JACKSON took no part in the consideration or decision of this case.

Mr. Justice RUTLEDGE, dissenting.

I think the judgment of the Court of Appeals should be affirmed. When Congress used the word "home" in [§ 162] of the Code, I do not believe it meant "business headquarters." And in my opinion this case presents no other question. . . .

Respondent's home was in Jackson, Mississippi, in every sense, unless for applying [§ 162]. There he maintained his family, with his personal, political and religious connections; schooled his children; paid taxes, voted, and resided over many years. There too he kept hold upon his place as a lawyer, though not substantially active in practice otherwise than to perform his work as general counsel for the railroad. . . .

I agree with the Court of Appeals that if Congress had meant "business headquarters," and not "home," it would have said "business headquarters." When it used "home" instead, I think it meant home in everyday parlance, not in some twisted special meaning of "tax home" or "tax headquarters." . . .

Congress gave the deduction for traveling away from home on business. The commuter's case, rightly confined, does not fall in this class. One who lives in an adjacent suburb or city and by usual modes of commutation can work within a distance permitting the daily journey and return, with time for the day's work and a period at home, clearly can be excluded from the deduction on the basis of the section's terms equally with its obvious purpose. But that is not true if "commuter" is to swallow up the deduction by the same sort of construction which makes "home" mean "business headquarters" of one's employer. If the line may be extended somewhat to cover doubtful cases, it need not be lengthened to infinity or to cover cases as far removed from the prevailing connotation of commuter as this one. Including it pushes "commuting" too far, even for these times of rapid transit.[20] . . .

By construing "home" as "business headquarters"; by reading "temporarily" as "very temporarily" into [§ 162]; by bringing down "ordinary and necessary" from its first sentence into its second; by finding "inequity" where Congress has said none exists; by construing "commuter" to cover long-distance, irregular travel; and by conjuring from the "statutory setting" a meaning at odds with the plain wording of the clause, the Government makes over understandable ordinary English into highly technical tax jargon. There is enough of this in the tax laws inescapably, without adding more in the absence of either compulsion or authority. The arm of the tax-gatherer reaches far. In my judgment it should not go the length of this case. . . .

NOTES AND QUESTIONS

1. Flowers *and commuting costs.* The deductions at issue in *Flowers* were in large part for the expenses of living in Mobile, but the case has been treated as authority primarily for the proposition that a person cannot deduct transportation costs incurred in commuting to and from work. The view of the majority in *Flowers* was that Mr. Flowers's trips to Mobile and back (usually via New Orleans) were just a long commute. As an employee of the railroad on which he traveled, Mr. Flowers "had a railroad pass [and] paid no train fare but did have to pay seat or berth fare." Flowers v. Commissioner, 3 T.C.M. 803, 805 (1944). The Commissioner did not treat the value of the free train fare as income to Mr. Flowers, though logic would suggest that such treatment would have been appropriate.

---

20. Conceivably men soon may live in Florida or California and fly daily to work in New York and back. Possibly they will be regarded as commuters when that day comes. But, if so, that is not this case and, in any event, neither situation was comprehended by Congress when [§ 162] was enacted.

2. *Causative analysis.* In *Flowers*, the Court says that the expenses at issue "were incurred solely as a result of the taxpayer's desire to maintain a home in Jackson while working in Mobile." In other words, the expenses would not have been incurred but for the personal decision to live in Jackson. It is equally clear, however, that the expenses would not have been incurred but for the business decision to take the job in Mobile. Compare the earlier discussion of "but for" analysis in connection with the deductions for medical expenses (supra page 377, Note 1) and for child-care expenses (supra page 478, Note 1). Does it help to try to identify a "proximate" cause of the expenses? Should it be relevant that the necessary business condition (the job in Mobile) arose after the necessary personal condition (the home in Jackson?) As between the two necessary conditions, which seems relatively more fixed and which relatively more variable in each case? Does this depend on the strength of each of the taxpayer's marriages?

3. *Two places of employment or business.* What if Mr. Flowers had continued to practice law in Jackson after he took the job in Mobile? The Tax Court would apparently permit his expenses in Mobile to be deducted if the business activity in Jackson were substantial, even though the income therefrom was less than the Mobile income. The Service generally takes the position that the "home" of a taxpayer having two widely separated posts of duty is the "principal business" post, so that the taxpayer is not "away from home" while there but may deduct living expenses while at the minor post. See, e.g., Rev. Rul. 75-432, 1975-2 C.B. 60. This ruling is also applicable to seasonal workers such as baseball players.

COMPARATIVE FOCUS: The Controversy over Germany's Deduction for Commuting Expenses

Most countries with an income tax follow the U.S. approach of disallowing deductions for commuting expense on the theory that it represents personal consumption rather than a cost of earning income. One notable exception is Germany, which has long allowed such a deduction. The amount of the deduction a set amount per kilometer for travel between the home and workplace, multiplied by the number of days worked. The deduction has long been criticized for its environmental effects—the farther the taxpayer lived from her place of work, the larger the deduction she would be allowed.

In 2007, Germany limited the commuting deduction to distances traveled in excess of 20 kilometers. The ostensible rationale for the limitation was that commuting expenses of 20 kilometers or less were inherently personal in nature, though it is hard to see why one's commute becomes more business-related the farther one lives from home. In any event, the limitation was promptly challenged in court, with taxpayers alleging that it was contrary to the ability-to-pay principle and Article 3(1) of the German constitution, providing that all persons shall be equal before the law. Germany's *Bundesfinanzhof* sided with the taxpayer, concluding that commuting expenses are an unavoidable cost of earning income. The case has now been referred to the Federal Constitutional Court.

HANTZIS v. COMMISSIONER
638 F.2d 248 (1st Cir.), cert. denied, 452 U.S. 962 (1981)

CAMPBELL, Circuit Judge. . . .

In the fall of 1973 Catharine Hantzis (taxpayer), formerly a candidate for an advanced degree in philosophy at the University of California at Berkeley, entered Harvard Law School in Cambridge, Massachusetts, as a full-time student. During her second year of law school she sought unsuccessfully to obtain employment for the summer of 1975 with a Boston law firm. She did, however, find a job as a legal assistant with a law firm in New York City, where she worked for ten weeks beginning in June 1975. Her husband, then a member of the faculty of Northeastern University with a teaching schedule for that summer, remained in Boston and lived at the couple's home there. At the time of the Tax Court's decision in this case, Mr. and Mrs. Hantzis still resided in Boston.

On their joint income tax return for 1975, Mr. and Mrs. Hantzis reported the earnings from taxpayer's summer employment ($3,750) and deducted [under § 162(a)(2)] the cost of transportation between Boston and New York, the cost of a small apartment rented by Mrs. Hantzis in New York and the cost of her meals in New York ($3,204). . . .

The Commissioner disallowed the deduction on the ground that taxpayer's home for purposes of section 162(a)(2) was her place of employment and the cost of traveling to and living in New York was therefore not "incurred . . . while away from home." The Commissioner also argued that the expenses were not incurred "in the pursuit of a trade or business." Both positions were rejected by the Tax Court, which found that Boston was Mrs. Hantzis' home because her employment in New York was only temporary and that her expenses in New York were "necessitated" by her employment there. The court thus held the expenses to be deductible under § 162(a)(2).[21]

In asking this court to reverse the Tax Court's allowance of the deduction, the Commissioner has contended that the expenses were not incurred "in the pursuit of a trade or business." We do not accept this argument; nonetheless, we sustain the Commissioner and deny the deduction, on the basis that the expenses were not incurred "while away from home." . . .

---

21. The court upheld the Commissioner's disallowance of a deduction taken by Mr. and Mrs. Hantzis on their 1975 return for expenses incurred by Mrs. Hantzis in attending a convention of the American Philosophical Association. Mr. and Mrs. Hantzis do not appeal that action.

II

The Commissioner has directed his argument at the meaning of "in pursuit of a trade or business." He interprets this phrase as requiring that a deductible traveling expense be incurred under the demands of a trade or business which predates the expense, i.e., an "already" existing trade or business. Under this theory, § 162(a)(2) would invalidate the deduction taken by the taxpayer because she was a full-time student before commencing her summer work at a New York law firm in 1975 and so was not continuing in a trade or business when she incurred the expenses of traveling to New York and living there while her job lasted. The Commissioner's proposed interpretation erects at the threshold of deductibility under section 162(a)(2) the requirement that a taxpayer be engaged in a trade or business before incurring a travel expense. Only if that requirement is satisfied would an inquiry into the deductibility of an expense proceed to ask whether the expense was a result of business exigencies, incurred while away from home, and reasonable and necessary.

Such a reading of the statute is semantically possible and would perhaps expedite the disposition of certain cases.[22] Nevertheless, we reject it as unsupported by case law and inappropriate to the policies behind § 162(a)(2).

The two cases relied on by the Commissioner do not appear to us to establish that traveling expenses are deductible only if incurred in connection with a preexisting trade or business. . . .

Nor would the Commissioner's theory mesh with the policy behind § 162(a)(2). [T]he travel expense deduction is intended to exclude from taxable income a necessary cost of producing that income. Yet the recency of entry into a trade or business does not indicate that travel expenses are not a cost of producing income. To be sure, the costs incurred by a taxpayer who leaves his usual residence to begin a trade or business at another location may not be truly travel expenses, i.e., expenses incurred while "away from home," see infra, but practically, they are as much incurred "in the pursuit of a trade or business" when the occupation is new as when it is old.

An example drawn from the Commissioner's argument illustrates the point. The Commissioner notes that if a construction worker, who normally works in Boston for Corp. *A*, travels to New York to work for Corp. *B* for six months, he is traveling . . . in the pursuit of his own trade as a construction worker. Accordingly, the requirement that travel expenses be a result of business exigencies is satisfied. Had a construction worker just entering the labor market followed the same course his expenses under the Commissioner's reasoning would not satisfy the business exigencies requirement. Yet in each case, the taxpayer's travel expenses would be costs of earning an income and

22. We do not see, however, how it would affect the treatment of this case. The Commissioner apparently concedes that upon starting work in New York the taxpayer engaged in a trade or business. If we held — as we do not — that an expense is deductible only when incurred in connection with an already existing trade or business, our ruling would seem to invalidate merely the deduction of the cost of taxpayer's trip from Boston to New York to begin work (about $64). We would still need to determine, as in any other case under section 162(a)(2), whether the expenses that arose *subsequent* to the taxpayer's entry into her trade or business were reasonable and necessary, required by business exigencies and incurred while away from home.

not merely incidents of personal lifestyle. Requiring that the finding of business exigency necessary to deductibility under section 162(a)(2) be predicated upon the prior existence of a trade or business would thus captiously restrict the meaning of "in pursuit of a trade or business." . . .

III

Flowers [v. Commissioner, supra page 481], construed section 162(a)(2) to mean that a traveling expense is deductible only if it is (1) reasonable and necessary; (2) incurred while away from home; and (3) necessitated by the exigencies of business. Because the Commissioner does not suggest that Mrs. Hantzis' expenses were unreasonable or unnecessary, we may pass directly to the remaining requirements. Of these, we find dispositive the requirement that an expense be incurred while away from home. As we think Mrs. Hantzis' expenses were not so incurred, we hold the deduction to be improper.

The meaning of the term "home" in the travel expense provision is far from clear. When Congress enacted the travel expense deduction now codified as § 162(a)(2), it apparently was unsure whether, to be deductible, an expense must be incurred away from a person's residence or away from his principal place of business. . . . This ambiguity persists and courts, sometimes within a single circuit, have divided over the issue. . . . It has been suggested that these conflicting definitions are due to the enormous factual variety in the cases. . . . We find this observation instructive, for if the cases that discuss the meaning of the term "home" in § 162(a)(2) are interpreted on the basis of their unique facts as well as the fundamental purposes of the travel expense provision, and not simply pinioned to one of two competing definitions of home, much of the seeming confusion and contradiction on this issue disappears and a functional definition of the term emerges.

We begin by recognizing that the location of a person's home for purposes of § 162(a)(2) becomes problematic only when the person lives one place and works another. Where a taxpayer resides and works at a single location, he is always home, however defined; and where a taxpayer is constantly on the move due to his work, he is never "away" from home. (In the latter situation, it may be said either that he has no residence to be away from, or else that his residence is always at his place of employment. . . .) However, in the present case, the need to determine "home" is plainly before us, since the taxpayer resided in Boston and worked, albeit briefly, in New York.

We think the critical step in defining "home" in these situations is to recognize that the "while away from home" requirement has to be construed in light of the further requirement that the expense be the result of business exigencies. The traveling expense deduction obviously is not intended to exclude from taxation every expense incurred by a taxpayer who, in the course of business, maintains two homes. Section 162(a)(2) seeks rather "to mitigate the burden of the taxpayer who, *because of the exigencies of his trade or business, must* maintain two places of abode and thereby incur additional and duplicate living expenses." . . . Consciously or unconsciously, courts have effectuated this policy in part through their interpretation of the term "home" in § 162(a)(2). Whether it is held in a particular decision that a taxpayer's home is his residence or his principal place of business, the ultimate allowance or disallowance of a deduction is a function of the court's assessment of the reason for a taxpayer's maintenance of two homes. If the reason is perceived to be personal, the taxpayer's home will generally be held to be his place of employment rather than his residence and the deduction will be denied. . . . If the reason is felt to be business exigencies, the person's home will usually be held to be his residence and the deduction will be allowed. . . . We understand the concern of the concurrence that such an operational interpretation of the term "home" is somewhat technical and perhaps untidy, in that it will not always afford bright line answers, but we doubt the ability of either the Commissioner or the courts to invent an unyielding formula that will make sense in all cases. The line between personal and business expenses winds through infinite factual permutations; effectuation of the travel expense provision requires that any principle of decision be flexible and sensitive to statutory policy.

Construing in the manner just described the requirement that an expense be incurred "while away from home," we do not believe this requirement was satisfied in this case. Mrs. Hantzis' *trade or business* did not require that she maintain a home in Boston as well as one in New York. Though she returned to Boston at various times during the period of her employment in New York, her visits were all for personal reasons. It is not contended that she had a business connection in Boston that necessitated her keeping a home there; no professional interest was served by maintenance of the Boston home—as would have been the case, for example, if Mrs. Hantzis had been a lawyer based in Boston with a New York client whom she was temporarily serving. The home in Boston was kept up for reasons involving Mr. Hantzis, but those reasons cannot substitute for a showing by *Mrs.* Hantzis that the exigencies of *her* trade or business required *her* to maintain two homes. Mrs. Hantzis' decision to keep two homes must be seen as a choice dictated by personal, albeit wholly reasonable, considerations and not a business or occupational necessity. We therefore hold that her home for purposes of § 162(a)(2) was New York and that the expenses at issue in this case were not incurred "while away from home."

We are not dissuaded from this conclusion by the temporary nature of Mrs. Hantzis' employment in New York. Mrs. Hantzis argues that the brevity of her stay in New York excepts her from the business exigencies requirement of § 162(a)(2) under a doctrine supposedly enunciated by the Supreme Court in Peurifoy v. Commissioner, 358 U.S. 59 (1958) (per curiam).[23] The Tax Court here held that Boston was the taxpayer's home because it would have

---

23. In *Peurifoy* the Court stated that the Tax Court had "engrafted an exception" onto the requirement that travel expenses be dictated by business exigencies, allowing "a deduction for expenditures . . . when the taxpayer's employment is 'temporary', as contrasted with 'indefinite' or 'indeterminate.'" 358 U.S. at 59. Because the Commissioner did not challenge this exception, the Court did not rule on its validity. It instead upheld the circuit court's reversal of the Tax Court and disallowance of the deduction on the basis of the adequacy of the appellate court's review. The Supreme Court agreed that the Tax Court's finding as to the temporary nature of taxpayer's employment was clearly erroneous. Id. at 60-61.

Despite its inauspicious beginning, the exception has come to be generally accepted. Some uncertainty lingers, however, over whether the exception properly applies to the "business exigencies" or the "away from home" requirement. . . . In fact, it is probably relevant to both. . . .

been unreasonable for her to move her residence to New York for only ten weeks. At first glance these contentions may seem to find support in the court decisions holding that, when a taxpayer works for a limited time away from his usual home, § 162(a)(2) allows a deduction for the expense of maintaining a second home so long as the employment is "temporary" and not "indefinite" or "permanent." . . . This test is an elaboration of the requirements under § 162(a)(2) that an expense be incurred due to business exigencies and while away from home. . . . Thus it has been said:

> Where a taxpayer reasonably expects to be employed in a location for a substantial or indefinite period of time, the reasonable inference is that his choice of a residence is a personal decision, unrelated to any business necessity. Thus, it is irrelevant how far he travels to work. The normal expectation, however, is that the taxpayer will choose to live near his place of employment. Consequently, when a taxpayer reasonably expects to be employed in a location for only a short or temporary period of time and travels a considerable distance to the location from his residence, it is unreasonable to assume that his choice of a residence is dictated by personal convenience. The reasonable inference is that he is temporarily making these travels because of a business necessity.

Frederick [v. United States], 603 F.2d at 1294-95 (citations omitted).

The temporary employment doctrine does not, however, purport to eliminate any requirement that continued maintenance of a first home have a business justification. We think the rule has no application where the taxpayer has no business connection with his usual place of residence. If no business exigency dictates the location of the taxpayer's usual residence, then the mere fact of his taking temporary employment elsewhere cannot supply a compelling business reason for continuing to maintain that residence. Only a taxpayer who lives one place, works another and has business ties to *both* is in the ambiguous situation that the temporary employment doctrine is designed to resolve. In such circumstances, unless his employment away from his usual home is temporary, a court can reasonably assume that the taxpayer has abandoned his business ties to that location and is left with only personal reasons for maintaining a residence there. Where only personal needs require that a travel expense be incurred, however, a taxpayer's home is defined so as to leave the expense subject to taxation. See supra. Thus, a taxpayer who pursues temporary employment away from the location of his usual residence, but has no business connection with that location, is not "away from home" for purposes of § 162(a)(2). . . .

On this reasoning, the temporary nature of Mrs. Hantzis' employment in New York does not affect the outcome of her case. She had no business ties to Boston that would bring her within the temporary employment doctrine. By this holding, we do not adopt a rule that "home" in § 162(a)(2) is the equivalent of a taxpayer's place of business. Nor do we mean to imply that a taxpayer has a "home" for tax purposes only if he is already engaged in a trade or business at a particular location. Though both rules are alluringly determinate, we have already discussed why they offer inadequate expressions of the purposes behind the travel expense deduction. We hold merely that for a taxpayer in Mrs. Hantzis' circumstances to be "away from home in the pursuit of a trade or business," she must establish the existence of some sort of business relation both to the location she claims as "home" and to the location of her temporary employment sufficient to support a finding that her duplicative expenses are necessitated by business exigencies. This, we believe, is the meaning of the statement in *Flowers* that "[b]usiness trips are to be identified *in relation to* business demands and the traveler's business headquarters." 326 U.S. at 474 (emphasis added). On the uncontested facts before us, Mrs. Hantzis had no business relation to Boston; we therefore leave to cases in which the issue is squarely presented the task of elaborating what relation to a place is required under § 162(a)(2) for duplicative living expenses to be deductible.

Reversed.

KEETON, District Judge, concurring in the result.

Although I agree with the result reached in the court's opinion, and with much of its underlying analysis, I write separately because I cannot join in the court's determination that New York was the taxpayer's home for purposes of § 162(a)(2). In so holding, the court adopts a definition of "home" that differs from the ordinary meaning of the term and therefore unduly risks causing confusion and misinterpretation of the important principle articulated in this case. . . .

A word used in a statute can mean, among the cognoscenti, whatever authoritative sources define it to mean. Nevertheless, it is a distinct disadvantage of a body of law that it can be understood only by those who are expert in its terminology. Moreover, needless risks of misunderstanding and confusion arise, not only among members of the public but also among professionals who must interpret and apply a statute in their day-to-day work, when a word is given an extraordinary meaning that is contrary to its everyday usage.

The result reached by the court can easily be expressed while also giving "home" its ordinary meaning, and neither Congress nor the Supreme Court has directed that "home" be given an extraordinary meaning in the present context. . . .

NOTES AND QUESTIONS

1. *The motivation in* Hantzis. Hantzis earned $3,750 and spent $3,204, which means she netted $546 for her ten weeks of work. She could have netted more working part time at a menial job in Boston. So why did she go to New York, and what does your answer tell you about how people like her should be taxed?

2. *Temporary versus indefinite jobs.* The court in *Hantzis* refers to the rule, cited by the Supreme Court in Peurifoy v. Commissioner, 358 U.S. 59 (1958) (per curiam), under which a person who takes a *temporary* job away from his or her home area is allowed to deduct travel and living costs (as, for example, would a lawyer from New York who must spend three months in Chicago

trying a case). The costs are not deductible, however, where the job away from the area of the taxpayer's residence is of *indefinite* duration. A new job with an indefinite duration is treated as if it were a permanent new job, like Mr. Flowers's job in Mobile. The temporary-versus-indefinite distinction has given rise to a great deal of litigation. Many of the cases involve construction workers. The legal uncertainty that gave rise to much of this litigation was ended in 1992, when Congress, as part of comprehensive energy legislation, added the final sentence of § 162(a), which limits "temporary" jobs to those lasting a year or less.

The IRS applied the one-year rule in Rev. Rul. 93-86, 1993-2 C.B. 71, which provides in part:

Situation 1. Taxpayer *A* is regularly employed in city *CI-1*. In 1993, *A* accepted work in city *CI-2*, which is 250 miles from *CI-1*. *A* realistically expected the work in *CI-2* to be completed in six months and planned to return to *CI-1* at that time. In fact, the employment lasted ten months, after which time *A* returned to *CI-1*.

Situation 2. The facts are the same as in Situation 1, except that Taxpayer *B* realistically expected the work in *CI-2* to be completed in eighteen months, but in fact it was completed in ten months.

Situation 3. The facts are the same as in Situation 1, except that Taxpayer *C* realistically expected the work in *CI-2* to be completed in nine months. After eight months, however, *C* was asked to remain for seven more months (for a total actual stay of fifteen months).

. . . In Situation 1, *A* realistically expected that the work in *CI-2* would last only six months, and it did in fact last less than one year. Because *A* had always intended to return to *CI-1* at the end of *A*'s employment in *CI-2*, the *CI-2* employment is temporary. Thus, *A*'s travel expenses paid or incurred in *CI-2* are deductible.

In Situation 2, *B*'s employment in *CI-2* is indefinite because *B* realistically expected that the work in *CI-2* would last longer than one year, even though it actually lasted less than one year. Thus, *B*'s travel expenses paid or incurred in *CI-2* are nondeductible.

In Situation 3, *C* at first realistically expected that the work in *CI-2* would last only nine months. However, due to changed circumstances occurring after eight months, it was no longer realistic for *C* to expect that the employment in *CI-2* would last for one year or less. Therefore, *C*'s employment in *CI-2* is temporary for eight months, and indefinite for the remaining seven months. Thus, *C*'s travel expenses paid or incurred in *CI-2* during the first eight months are deductible, but *C*'s travel expenses paid or incurred thereafter are nondeductible.

3. *Split summers.* Catharine Hantzis was not allowed to deduct the travel, meals, and lodging expenses she incurred in connection with her summer employment at a New York law firm because, for tax purposes, her "home" was considered to be the place of her principal employment, New York. Suppose Hantzis had spent the first six weeks of her summer working in New York and then had spent the last five weeks of the summer working in the Los Angeles office of the same New York law firm. Would her expenses in connection with the Los Angeles job have been deductible? What if the job in Los Angeles had been with a firm not affiliated with the New York firm?

4. *Parking.* In the *Henderson* case, supra page 449, the court denied the taxpayer's deduction of $180 for parking across the street from her office, despite her statement that she "occasionally used her automobile for business purposes when an automobile from the pool of State automobiles was not available." The court said that "petitioner has offered no evidence to establish that her employer required her to have her car at her place of employment or that she would not have driven to work in any event." Similarly, in Fillerup v. Commissioner, 1988-103 T.C.M., where the taxpayer, a doctor, was allowed to deduct the cost of driving his car (a 6.9 Mercedes-Benz) from one hospital to another but not from home to the first hospital or from the last hospital back home. The court in this case rested its partial disallowance on the ground that the taxpayer would have driven to work even if he had not needed the car to get from one hospital to another. In Croughan v. Commissioner, 1988-303 T.C.M., the court disallowed a deduction for commuting expenses despite its finding that if the taxpayer, a microbiologist, "had not been required to have her car available at work [to transport specimens from her place of work to other public health facilities], she would have commuted to work by bus." The court reasoned that the taxpayer was required to have a car available at work but not to take it home at night, and that the commuting use was therefore personal.

5. *Moving expenses.* Examine briefly § 217, which allows a deduction for the moving expenses (as defined in § 217(b)) of a taxpayer who takes a new job, if, roughly speaking, the new job would add at least fifty miles to his or her commute and in the year following the move the taxpayer works at least thirty-nine weeks at the new job (§ 217(c)). Is it not clear that moving expenses above a minimal amount would not be incurred but for personal decisions relating to the acquisition of a family and of possessions? Where does that observation lead you?

Section 217 was in large part a response to the unfairness of prior law, under which payments or reimbursements by an employer for an employee's moving expenses were not income, but amounts paid by an employee or a self-employed person to meet such expenses were not deductible. Congress finds it easier to eliminate unfairness of this sort by extending benefits than by contracting them. Its statement of the reasons for the adoption of the provision is, however, an interesting illustration of the application of principles of tax policy. See Staff of the Joint Committee on Internal Revenue Taxation, General Explanation of the Tax Reform Act of 1969, 91st Cong., 2d Sess. 101 (1970):

> *General reasons for change.* The mobility of labor is an important and necessary part of the nation's economy, since it reduces unemployment and increases productive capacity. It has been estimated that approximately one-half million employees are requested by their employers to move to new job locations each year. In addition, self-employed individuals relocate to find more attractive or useful employment. Substantial moving expenses often are incurred by taxpayers in connection with employment-related relocations, and these expenses may be regarded as a cost of earning income.
>
> The Congress believed that more adequate recognition should be given in the tax law to expenses connected with job-related moves. In addition, the Congress

concluded that equity required that the moving expense deduction be made available on a comparable basis for self-employed persons who move to a new work location. Finally, it was desired to equalize fully the tax treatment for the moving expenses of new employees and unreimbursed transferred employees with the treatment accorded reimbursed employees.

Deductions under § 217 are not subject to the 2 percent threshold found in § 67. See § 67(b)(6). Moreover, for the years after 1993, the deduction is an above-the-line item that can be claimed by people who use the standard deduction. § 62(a)(15).

6. *Daily transportation expenses.* In Revenue Ruling 99-7, 1999-1 C.B. 361, the IRS held (modifying various earlier rulings) that daily transportation expenses incurred in going between a taxpayer's residence and a work location, while generally nondeductible, may be deducted in the following circumstances:

(a) if the work location is temporary and located outside the metropolitan area where she lives and normally works.

(b) if the work location is temporary and she has one or more regular work locations, away from her residence, in the same trade or business. (Same as (a), except that the distance to the temporary work location does not matter.)

(c) if the taxpayer's residence is her principal place of business and the work location is in the same trade or business. (Same as (b), except that the work location need not be temporary.)

In Walker v. Commissioner, 101 T.C. 537 (1993), the Tax Court permitted a taxpayer to deduct daily transportation expenses incurred in going between his residence and numerous temporary work sites. The taxpayer was a self-employed professional "faller" or "cutter" who, using his own truck and equipment, cut trees at various locations in the Black Hills National Forest and delivered them to a lumber mill. The case fit none of the above three exceptions, but the court allowed the deduction on the ground (coming close to both (b) and (c) above) that recurring work by the taxpayer at his residence made it a "regular," albeit not "principal," place of business. The IRS has announced that it does not accept and will not follow this decision.

What might be the IRS's reason for drawing so fine a distinction? Ought it to allow the deduction in such cases?

PROBLEMS: TESTING THE RATIONALE

The usual rationale for disallowing a deduction for commuting expenses is that the taxpayer is expected to move as near as possible to the job location. If that is done, the expense is trivial. If the taxpayer chooses to live far from the job, that is regarded as a personal choice. Consider the soundness of that rationale in each of the following hypotheticals. Would a deduction be allowed in any of them (disregarding the effect of § 67)? Consider whether the tax outcome in each case seems fair and how that outcome might affect family harmony, job-taking decisions by women, and the rationality of job-taking choices in general.

(a) Taxpayer *A* is a woman who lives on a farm with her husband. She drives each day to town, where she earns $50 per day teaching school. The distance is thirty miles each way and the cost of driving is $10 per day. There is no public transportation.

(b) Taxpayer *B* is a poor woman who lives in the central city and works as a maid in an affluent suburb. The distance from her home to the place where she works is twenty miles. Public transportation is available but would take about two hours each way because of the need to make several transfers and to walk substantial distances. *B*'s employer pays $10 a day to a driver of a van who picks *B* up near her home each morning and drops her off at the place where she works. Her pay is $30 per day. She supports her two young children as well as herself. For purposes of determining eligibility for Medicaid, food stamps, and other welfare, what seems to you to be the proper amount of income? What is the rule for income tax purposes? See § 132(f). What do you suppose is the practice? Note that even though the worker is probably below the income threshold for paying taxes, the amount of her income is relevant to calculation of her earned income tax credit.

(c) *C* is a tax lawyer who works in the central business district and lives in the suburbs, twenty-five miles from work. When he first took his job, he lived in an apartment about two miles from the office but later decided that he preferred the ambience and the recreational opportunities in the suburbs. He earns $150,000 per year and commutes in a Mercedes that costs $20 a day to drive to and from work each day. On rare occasions he uses the car during the day to drive to a meeting with a client.

(d) *D* is a trial lawyer who lives next door to *C*, works in the same firm, earns the same amount, and drives to work in the same model car. *D* needs his car most days in order to get to the various courts in which he must make appearances or to places where he takes depositions.[24] He says that he brings the car to work only in order to have it available for these business uses, but in fact he drives to work even on those days when he will almost certainly spend the entire day in the office. He could take the bus, which would add about forty-five minutes each way to his commuting time and would cost $4 per day round trip.

(e) *E* is a lawyer who is just like *D* in all respects except that his reason for moving to the suburbs was the "better" schools available there. At the time he moved, a federal court had just issued a desegregation order requiring busing in the city schools. In the suburb where he lives, there are very few minority children, and there is no school busing. He denies that his move to the suburbs had anything to do with desegregation and every year contributes $100 to the NAACP Legal Defense Fund.

(f) *F* is also a lawyer, working at the same firm as *C*, *D*, and *E*. *F* is married to *E*. She would prefer to live in the city and to have her children go to the city schools or to a private school in the city but acquiesced in *E*'s decision to move

---

24. The costs of driving to court or to take depositions plainly are deductible, under § 162(a), as "ordinary and necessary expenses." Section 162(a)(2) is irrelevant to this expense, though even in cases where it is relevant it is only an elaboration on the basic operative rule stated in the opening clause of § 162(a).

to the suburbs. Because *E* and *F* have different schedules, they cannot drive to work together.

(g) *G* is a construction worker. He has lived in the same home, in the central city, for many years. He works at various job sites, for periods ranging from a month to a year. His commutes range in distance from ten to forty miles each way. Rarely is public transportation available, but when it is *G* takes it (largely because he is an avid reader and likes to have the time on the bus or train for reading).

(h) *H* is a construction worker who cannot find a job in the area in which he has lived and worked for the past twenty years. He takes a job in another city, 200 miles away. He expects that job to last about three months, which it does. His cost of traveling to and from the new job location is $100. His living costs while he is there, including food and lodging, are $25 per day. In addition, he spends $5 per day driving back and forth between the job site and his temporary dwelling place.

(i) *I* is just like *H* except that the new job is expected to last three years.

(j) *J* is a civilian employee at an air force base. He is not allowed to live on the base. The nearest habitable community is twenty miles from the workplace. The cost of driving the forty miles to and from work each day in his own car is $8. No other means of transportation is available. (Held, on similar facts: no deduction. Sanders v. Commissioner, 439 F.2d 296 (9th Cir.), cert. denied, 404 U.S. 864 (1971).)

E. CLOTHING EXPENSES

PEVSNER v. COMMISSIONER
628 F.2d 467 (5th Cir. 1980)

JOHNSON, Circuit Judge.

This is an appeal by the Commissioner of Internal Revenue from a decision of the United States Tax Court. The tax court upheld taxpayer's business expense deduction for clothing expenditures in the amount of $1,621.91 for the taxable year 1975. We reverse.

Since June 1973 Sandra J. Pevsner, taxpayer, has been employed as the manager of the Sakowitz Yves St. Laurent Rive Gauche Boutique located in Dallas, Texas. The boutique sells only women's clothes and accessories designed by Yves St. Laurent (YSL), one of the leading designers of women's apparel. Although the clothing is ready to wear, it is highly fashionable and expensively priced. Some customers of the boutique purchase and wear the YSL apparel for their daily activities and spend as much as $20,000 per year for such apparel.

As manager of the boutique, the taxpayer is expected by her employer to wear YSL clothes while at work. In her appearance, she is expected to project the image of an exclusive lifestyle and to demonstrate to her customers that she is aware of the YSL current fashion trends as well as trends generally.

Because the boutique sells YSL clothes exclusively, taxpayer must be able, when a customer compliments her on her clothes, to say that they are designed by YSL. In addition to wearing YSL apparel while at the boutique, she wears them while commuting to and from work, to fashion shows sponsored by the boutique, and to business luncheons at which she represents the boutique. During 1975, the taxpayer bought, at an employee's discount, the following items: four blouses, three skirts, one pair of slacks, one trench coat, two sweaters, one jacket, one tunic, five scarves, six belts, two pairs of shoes and four necklaces. The total cost of this apparel was $1,381.91. In addition, the sum of $240 was expended for maintenance of these items.

Although the clothing and accessories purchased by the taxpayer were the type used for general purposes by the regular customers of the boutique, the taxpayer is not a normal purchaser of these clothes. The taxpayer and her husband, who is partially disabled because of a severe heart attack suffered in 1971, lead a simple life and their social activities are very limited and informal. Although taxpayer's employer has no objection to her wearing the apparel away from work, taxpayer stated that she did not wear the clothes during off-work hours because she felt that they were too expensive for her simple everyday lifestyle. Another reason why she did not wear the YSL clothes apart from work was to make them last longer. Taxpayer did admit at trial, however, that a number of the articles were things she could have worn off the job and in which she would have looked "nice."

On her joint federal income tax return for 1975, taxpayer deducted $990 as an ordinary and necessary business expense with respect to her purchase of the YSL clothing and accessories. However, in the tax court, taxpayer claimed a deduction for the full $1,381.91 cost of the apparel and for the $240 cost of maintaining the apparel. The tax court allowed the taxpayer to deduct both expenses in the total amount of $1,621.91. The tax court reasoned that the apparel was not suitable to the private lifestyle maintained by the taxpayer. This appeal by the Commissioner followed. . . .

The generally accepted rule governing the deductibility of clothing expenses is that the cost of clothing is deductible as a business expense only if: (1) the clothing is of a type specifically required as a condition of employment, (2) it is not adaptable to general usage as ordinary clothing, and (3) it is not so worn. . . .

In the present case, the Commissioner stipulated that the taxpayer was required by her employer to wear YSL clothing and that she did not wear such apparel apart from work. The Commissioner maintained, however, that a deduction should be denied because the YSL clothes and accessories purchased by the taxpayer were adaptable for general usage as ordinary clothing and she was not prohibited from using them as such. The tax court, in rejecting the Commissioner's argument for the application of an objective test, recognized that the test for deductibility was whether the clothing was "suitable for general or personal wear" but determined that the matter of suitability was to be judged subjectively, in light of the taxpayer's lifestyle. Although the court recognized that the YSL apparel "might be used by some members of society for general purposes," it felt that because the "wearing of YSL apparel outside work would be inconsistent with . . . [taxpayer's] lifestyle," sufficient reason was shown for allowing a deduction for the clothing expenditures. . . .

[T]he Circuits that have addressed the issue have taken an objective, rather than subjective, approach. . . . Under an objective test, no reference is made to the individual taxpayer's lifestyle or personal taste. Instead, adaptability for personal or general use depends upon what is generally accepted for ordinary streetwear.

The principal argument in support of an objective test is, of course, administrative necessity. The Commissioner argues that, as a practical matter, it is virtually impossible to determine at what point either price or style makes clothing inconsistent with or inappropriate to a taxpayer's lifestyle. Moreover, the Commissioner argues that the price one pays and the styles one selects are inherently personal choices governed by taste, fashion, and other unmeasurable values. Indeed, the tax court has rejected the argument that a taxpayer's personal taste can dictate whether clothing is appropriate for general use. . . . An objective test, although not perfect, provides a practical administrative approach that allows a taxpayer or revenue agent to look only to objective facts in determining whether clothing required as a condition of employment is adaptable to general use as ordinary streetwear. Conversely, the tax court's reliance on subjective factors provides no concrete guidelines in determining the deductibility of clothing purchased as a condition of employment.

In addition to achieving a practical administrative result, an objective test also tends to promote substantial fairness among the greatest number of taxpayers. As the Commissioner suggests, it apparently would be the tax court's position that two similarly situated YSL boutique managers with identical wardrobes would be subject to disparate tax consequences depending upon the particular manager's lifestyle and "socio-economic level." This result, however, is not consonant with a reasonable interpretation of Sections 162 and 262.

For the reasons stated above, the decision of the tax court upholding the deduction for taxpayer's purchase of YSL clothing is reversed. Consequently, the portion of the tax court's decision upholding the deduction for maintenance costs for the clothing is also reversed.

NOTE

In Nelson v. Commissioner, 1966-224 T.C.M., the taxpayers, husband and wife, were allowed to deduct the cost of the clothing they wore in the television series *The Adventures of Ozzie and Harriet*. The annual costs ranged from $12,341 in 1957 to $6,037 in 1962. In the series, the taxpayers "portrayed an average American family, with certain reasonable exaggerations." While the clothing was suitable for personal use, the court found that some of it was too heavy for use in southern California, where the Nelsons lived, it was subject to heavy wear and tear in production of the show, the Nelsons worked such long hours that they had little chance to wear the clothing off the set, and in fact the personal use was de minimis.

In Mella v. Commissioner, T.C.M. 1986-594, the taxpayer was a tennis professional. He was head professional at two tennis clubs and a nationally ranked player who played in at least a dozen tournaments in the year at issue. He claimed deductions for tennis clothes and shoes. The shoes lasted only two or three weeks. The court denied the deductions, stating:

> The Court observes that it is relatively commonplace for Americans in all walks of life to wear warm-up clothes, shirts, and shoes of the type purchased by the petitioner while engaged in a wide variety of casual or athletic activities. The items are fashionable, and in some cases have the name or logo of designers that have become common in America. Indeed, at trial, it was stated that tennis professionals, such as the petitioner, are clothing style setters for their students.

In Williams v. Commissioner, T.C. Memo. 1991-317, the taxpayer rode a motorcycle in his business as an Amway distributor. He was allowed to deduct the cost of his "leather uniform," which he wore while riding the motorcycle in connection with his business, and which bore the Amway label, but not the cost of the helmet and steel-toe boots that he also wore and that the court considered to be suitable for nonbusiness use.

QUESTIONS

1. (a) Do you think the result in *Pevsner* is unfair to the taxpayer? (b) If so, can you suggest a rule that would allow her a deduction, would be feasible for the Service to administer, and would not lead to abuse?

2. Is the present rule that allows a deduction for the cost of uniforms not suitable for ordinary wear subject to significant abuse?

F. LEGAL EXPENSES

UNITED STATES v. GILMORE
372 U.S. 39 (1963)

Mr. Justice HARLAN. . . .

In 1955, the California Supreme Court confirmed the award to the respondent taxpayer of a decree of absolute divorce. . . . The case before us involves the deductibility for federal income tax purposes of that part of the husband's legal expense incurred in such proceedings as is attributable to his successful resistance of his wife's claim to certain of his assets asserted by her to be community property under California law. The claim to such deduction, which has been upheld by the Court of Claims, 290 F.2d 942, is founded on [§ 212(2)], which allows as deductions from gross income: . . . ordinary and necessary expenses . . . incurred during the taxable year . . . for the . . . conservation . . . of property held for the production of income.

At the time of the divorce proceedings, instituted by the wife but in which the husband also cross-claimed for divorce, respondent's property consisted primarily of controlling stock interests in three corporations [General Motors dealerships]. . . . As president . . . of the three corporations, he received salaries from them aggregating about $66,800 annually, and in recent years his total annual dividends had averaged about $83,000. . . . His income from other sources was negligible.

As found by the Court of Claims the husband's overriding concern in the divorce litigation was to protect these assets against the claims of his wife. Those claims had two aspects: *First,* that the earnings accumulated and retained by these three corporations during the Gilmores' marriage (representing an aggregate increase in corporate net worth of some $600,000) were the product of respondent's personal services, and not the result of accretion in capital values, thus rendering respondent's stockholdings in the enterprises pro tanto community property under California law; *second,* that to the extent that such stockholdings were community property, the wife, allegedly the innocent party in the divorce proceeding, was entitled under California law to more than a one-half interest in such property.

The respondent wished to defeat those claims for two important reasons. *First,* the loss of his controlling stock interests, particularly in the event of their transfer in substantial part to his hostile wife, might well cost him the loss of his corporate positions, his principal means of livelihood. *Second,* there was also danger that if he were found guilty of his wife's sensational and reputation-damaging charges of marital infidelity, General Motors Corporation might find it expedient to exercise its right to cancel these dealer franchises.

The end result of this bitterly fought divorce case was a complete victory for the husband. He, not the wife, was granted a divorce on his cross-claim; the wife's community property claims were denied in their entirety; and she was held entitled to no alimony.

Respondent's legal expenses in connection with this litigation amounted to . . . a total of $40,611.36. . . . The Commissioner found all of these expenditures "personal" or "family" expenses and as such none of them deductible. [§ 262.] In the ensuing refund suit, however, the Court of Claims held that 80 percent of such expense (some $32,500) was attributable to respondent's defense against his wife's community property claims respecting his stockholdings and hence deductible under [§ 212(2)] as an expense "incurred . . . for the . . . conservation . . . of property held for the production of income." . . .

The Government['s] . . . sole contention here is that the court below misconceived the test governing [§ 212(1) and (2)] deductions, in that the deductibility of these expenses turns, so it is argued, not upon the *consequences* to respondent of a failure to defeat his wife's community property claims but upon the origin and *nature* of the claims themselves. . . . [W]e think the Government's position is sound and that it must be sustained.

I

For income tax purposes, Congress has seen fit to regard an individual as having two personalities: "one is [as] a seeker after profit who can deduct the expenses incurred in that search; the other is [as] a creature satisfying his needs as a human and those of his family but who cannot deduct such consumption and related expenditures."[25] The Government regards [§ 212(1) and (2)] as embodying a category of expenses embraced in the first of these roles.

Initially, it may be observed that the wording of [§ 212(2)] more readily fits the Government's view of the provision than that of the Court of Claims. For in context "conservation of property" seems to refer to operations performed with respect to the property itself, such as safeguarding or upkeep, rather than to a taxpayer's retention of ownership in it. But more illuminating than the mere language of [§ 212(1) and (2)] is the history of the provision.

Prior to 1942 [the Code] allowed deductions only for expenses incurred "in carrying on any trade or business," the deduction presently authorized by [§ 162(a)]. In Higgins v. Comm'r, 312 U.S. 212, this Court gave that provision a narrow construction, holding that the activities of an individual in supervising his own securities investments did not constitute the "carrying on of a trade or business," and hence that expenses incurred in connection with such activities were not tax deductible. . . . The Revenue Act of 1942 . . . by adding what is now [§ 212(1) and (2)], sought to remedy the inequity inherent in the disallowance of expense deductions in respect of such profit-seeking activities, the income from which was nonetheless taxable.

As noted in McDonald v. Comm'r, 323 U.S. 57, 62, the purpose of the 1942 amendment was merely to enlarge "the category of incomes with reference to which expenses were deductible." And committee reports make clear that deductions under the new section were subject to the same limitations and restrictions that are applicable to those allowable under [§ 162(a)]. Further, this Court has said that [§ 212(1) and (2)] "is comparable and in pari materia with [§ 162(a)]," providing for a class of deductions "coextensive with the business deductions allowed by [§ 162(a)], except for" the requirement that the income-producing activity qualify as a trade or business. Trust of Bingham v. Comm'r, 325 U.S. 365, 373, 374.

A basic restriction upon the availability of a [§ 162(a)] deduction is that the expense item involved must be one that has a business origin. That restriction not only inheres in the language of [§ 162(a)] itself, confining such deductions to "expenses . . . incurred . . . in carrying on any trade or business," but also follows from [§ 262], expressly rendering nondeductible "in any case . . . [p]ersonal, living, or family expenses." In light of what has already been said with respect to the advent and thrust of [§ 212(1) and (2)], it is clear that the "[p]ersonal . . . or family expenses" restriction of [§ 262] must impose the same limitation upon the reach of [§ 212(1) and (2)]—in other words that the only kind of expenses deductible under [§ 212(1) and (2)] are those that relate to a "business," i.e., profit-seeking, purpose. The pivotal issue in

---

25. Surrey and Warren, Cases on Federal Income Taxation, 272 (1960).

this case then becomes: was this part of respondent's litigation cost a "business" rather than a "personal" or "family" expense?

The answer to this question has already been indicated in prior cases. In Lykes v. U.S., 343 U.S. 118, the Court rejected the contention that legal expenses incurred in contesting the assessment of a gift tax liability were deductible. The taxpayer argued that if he had been required to pay the original deficiency he would have been forced to liquidate his stockholdings, which were his main source of income, and that his legal expenses were therefore incurred in the "conservation" of income-producing property and hence deductible under [§ 212(2)]. The Court first noted that the "deductibility [of the expenses] turns wholly upon the nature of the activities to which they relate" (343 U.S. at 123), and then stated (id. at 125-126):

> Legal expenses do not become deductible merely because they are paid for services which relieve a taxpayer of liability. That argument would carry us too far. It would mean that the expense of defending almost any claim would be deductible by a taxpayer on the ground that such defense was made to help him keep clear of liens whatever income-producing property he might have. For example, it suggests that the expense of defending an action based upon personal injuries caused by a taxpayer's negligence while driving an automobile for pleasure should be deductible. Section [212(1) and (2)] never has been so interpreted by us. . . .
>
> [T]he threatened deficiency assessment . . . related to the tax payable on petitioner's gifts. . . . The expense of contesting the amount of the deficiency was thus at all times attributable to the gifts, as such, and accordingly was not deductible.
>
> If, as suggested, the relative size of each claim, in proportion to the income-producing resources of a defendant, were to be a touchstone of the deductibility of the expense of resisting the claim, substantial uncertainty and inequity would inhere in the rule.

In Kornhauser v. U.S., 276 U.S. 145, this Court considered the deductibility of legal expenses incurred by a taxpayer in defending against a claim by a former business partner that fees paid to the taxpayer were for services rendered during the existence of the partnership. In holding that these expenses were deductible even though the taxpayer was no longer a partner at the time of suit, the Court formulated the rule that "where a suit or action against a taxpayer is directly connected with, or . . . proximately resulted from, his business, the expense incurred is a business expense. . . ." 276 U.S. at 153. Similarly, in a case involving an expense incurred in satisfying an obligation (though not a litigation expense), it was said that "it is the origin of the liability out of which the expense accrues" or "the kind of transaction out of which the obligation arose . . . which [is] crucial and controlling." Deputy v. duPont, 308 U.S. 488, 494, 496.

The principle we derive from these cases is that the characterization, as "business" or "personal," of the litigation costs of resisting a claim depends on whether or not the claim *arises in connection with* the taxpayer's profit-seeking activities. It does not depend on the *consequences* that might result to a taxpayer's income-producing property from a failure to defeat the claim, for, as

Lykes teaches, that "would carry us too far"[26] and would not be compatible with the basic lines of expense deductibility drawn by Congress.[27] Moreover, such a rule would lead to capricious results. If two taxpayers are each sued for an automobile accident while driving for pleasure, deductibility of their litigation costs would turn on the mere circumstance of the character of the assets each happened to possess, i.e., whether the judgments against them stood to be satisfied out of income- or non-income-producing property. We should be slow to attribute to Congress a purpose producing such unequal treatment among taxpayers, resting on no rational foundation. . . .

We turn then to the determinative question in this case: did the wife's claims respecting respondent's stockholdings arise in connection with his profit-seeking activities?

II

In classifying respondent's legal expenses the court below did not distinguish between those relating to the claims of the wife with respect to the *existence* of community property and those involving the *division* of any such property. . . . Nor is such a break-down necessary for a disposition of the present case. It is enough to say that in both aspects the wife's claims stemmed entirely from the marital relationship, and not, under any tenable view of things, from income-producing activity. This is obviously so as regards the claim to more than an equal division of any community property found to exist. For any such right depended entirely on the wife's making good her charges of marital infidelity on the part of the husband. The same conclusion is no less true respecting the claim relating to the existence of community property. For no such property could have existed but for the marriage relationship.[28] Thus, none of respondent's expenditures in resisting these claims can be deemed "business" expenses, and they are therefore not deductible under [§ 212(2)]. . . .

Mr. Justice BLACK and Mr. Justice DOUGLAS believe that the Court reverses this case because of an unjustifiably narrow interpretation of the 1942 amendment to the Internal Revenue Code and would accordingly affirm the judgment of the Court of Claims.

---

26. The Treasury Regulations have long provided:

An expense (not otherwise deductible) paid or incurred by an individual in determining or contesting a liability asserted against him does not become deductible by reason of the fact that property held by him for the production of income may be required to be used or sold for the purpose of satisfying such liability.

Treas. Regs. (1954 Code) § 1.212-1(m); see Treas. Regs. 118 (1939 Code) § 39.23(a)-15(k).

27. Expenses of contesting tax liabilities are now deductible under § 212(3) of the 1954 Code. This provision merely represents a policy judgment as to a particular class of expenditures otherwise nondeductible, like extraordinary medical expenses, and does not cast any doubt on the basic tax structure set up by Congress.

28. The respondent's attempted analogy of a marital "partnership" to the business partnership involved in the *Kornhauser* case, supra, is of course unavailing. The marriage relationship can hardly be deemed an income-producing activity.

NOTES AND QUESTIONS

1. *Causative analysis revisited.* (a) Is the "origins" test in *Gilmore* different from the "but for" test that we have encountered earlier in connection with deductions for medical expenses (supra page 377, Note 1), child-care expenses (supra page 478, Note 1), and commuting costs (supra page 486, Note 2)?

(b) Would and should the result in *Gilmore* have been different if Mr. Gilmore had first met Mrs. Gilmore when she came to work for his business?

(c) The Court would presumably have us compare Mr. Gilmore with a taxpayer who had the same property interests but who never married or, having married, never got divorced. Does the Court offer any explanation of why we should not compare Mr. Gilmore with a man who gets divorced but who has no property in jeopardy?

(d) What was Mr. Gilmore's "primary purpose" in incurring the expenses he sought to deduct? Would primary purpose be a better test than "origins"?

(e) Are Mr. Gilmore's fees like casualty losses? medical expenses? commuting expenses? Does the answer depend on the incidence of divorce among people like the Gilmores?

2. *The scope of* Gilmore. In a companion case, United States v. Patrick, 372 U.S. 53 (1963), the Supreme Court held nondeductible a husband's payments to his and his wife's attorneys for services in connection with another divorce where there was a private settlement of various property interests. The Court held that *Gilmore* was controlling:

> We find no significant distinction in the fact that [in *Patrick*] the legal fees for which the deduction is claimed were paid for arranging a transfer of stock interests, leasing real property, and creating a trust rather than for conducting litigation. These matters were incidental to litigation brought by respondent's wife, whose claims arising from respondent's personal and family life were the origin of the property arrangements.

372 U.S. at 57. Do you agree that *Gilmore* is controlling?

3. *Addition to basis.* In a subsequent year, Mr. Gilmore sold some of the stock that had been contested in the divorce actions. He added disallowed attorneys' fees to the basis of his stock as capitalized costs of defending title. Prior cases had allowed the addition of such costs to basis. See Gilmore v. United States, 245 F. Supp. 383, 384 (N.D. Cal. 1965). The government contended that the reasoning of the Supreme Court in United States v. Gilmore should also be applied to basis questions. The District Court held for the taxpayer, finding that costs of defending title are capital expenses whether arising in suits primarily business or personal in character. The court conceded that legal expenses may not be added to basis in some personal suits because "as a factual matter, the expenses would not have been primarily to defend title." Suppose that a taxpayer is sued for alleged personal debts and a lien is placed on his personal residence, which is his only asset. May the cost of defending against the suit be added to his basis for the house?

4. *Criminal defense*. In Accardo v. Commissioner, 942 F.2d 444 (7th Cir. 1991), the taxpayer, Anthony Accardo, had successfully defended himself in a criminal prosecution for violation of the Racketeer Influenced and Corrupt Organizations Act (RICO). Accardo was "the reputed head of the Chicago organized crime family." See United States v. Guzzino, 810 F.2d 687, 690 (7th Cir. 1987), cert. denied, 481 U.S. 1030. He was accused of having taken "kickbacks from a union insurance program." Some of his codefendants were convicted and were allowed to deduct their legal fees as ordinary and necessary business expenses, under § 162. Accardo could not claim a deduction under § 162 because he was acquitted (and presumably was not willing to argue that the acquittal was a mistake or an artifact of the rules for establishing criminal liability). Because of the acquital he was not in the trade or business of racketeering, so his legal expenses could not be trade or business expenses. Thus, the guilty criminal defendants were treated better by the tax system than innocent defendants. In reaching this result, which it calls "paradoxical," the Seventh Circuit opinion relies in part on *Gilmore*. The deduction under § 162 is considered further in Chapter 6, infra pages 558-564.

Accardo in effect conceded that he was not entitled to a deduction under § 162 and claimed instead that the cost of his legal defense was deductible under § 212 as the cost of protecting certain assets from seizure by the government under provisions of RICO for forfeiture of the fruits of criminal activity. The court rejected this claim on the ground that the assets that Accardo claimed he sought to protect were not in fact traceable to any criminal activity and therefore were not subject to forfeiture. The court found Accardo's argument so lacking in merit that it sustained a penalty for negligence and a penalty for substantial underpayment of tax (two separate penalties that are now combined in § 6662).

What if the government had alleged that Accardo's assets were in fact traceable to the racketeering activity of which he was accused, but, as in the actual case, he was acquitted?

G.   EXPENSES OF EDUCATION

CARROLL v. COMMISSIONER
418 F.2d 91 (7th Cir. 1969)

CASTLE, Chief Judge. . . .

James A. Carroll (hereinafter referred to as the petitioner) was employed by the Chicago Police Department as a detective during the year in question. In his 1964 federal income tax return, he listed as a deduction $720.80 which represented his cost of enrollment in DePaul University. The course of study entered into by plaintiff was stated by him to be in preparation for entrance to law school and consisted of a major in Philosophy. The six courses in which plaintiff was enrolled included two English, two Philosophy, one History and one Political Science course. Petitioner justified the deduction under

§ 162(a), . . . as an expense "relative to improving job skills to maintain [his] position as a detective."

During 1964, the Police Department had in effect General Order No. 63-24, which encouraged policemen to attend colleges and universities by arranging their schedules of duties so as to not conflict with class schedules. Petitioner availed himself of the benefits of this order when he enrolled in DePaul University. . . .

[Regs. § 1.162-5] abolished the primary purpose test and established a more objective standard for determining whether the cost of education may be deducted as a business expense. . . . Thus, petitioner in the instant case must justify his deduction under § 1.162-5(a)(1), as maintaining or improving skills required by him in his employment. . . .

While the Commissioner concedes that a general college education "hold[s] out the potential for improved performance as a policeman," he argues that petitioner has failed to demonstrate a sufficient relationship between such an education and the particular job skills required by a policeman. Thus, although a college education improves the job skills of all who avail themselves of it, this relationship is insufficient to remove the expense of such education from the realm of personal expenses which are disallowed under § 262. Many expenses, such as the cost of commuting, clothing, and a babysitter for a working mother, are related and even necessary to an individual's occupation or employment, but may not be deducted under § 162(a) since they are essentially personal expenditures. See Smith v. Commissioner [supra page 477]. We are of the opinion that plaintiff's educational expenditure is even more personal and less related to his job skills than the expenditures enumerated above.

Of course, not all college courses may be so classified as nondeductible. Thus, the cost of a course in Industrial Psychology was properly deducted from the income of an Industrial Psychologist, although it led to an advanced degree and the potential of new job opportunities. . . . Similarly, a housing administrator was allowed to deduct the cost of courses in housing administration, . . . and a professional harpist was allowed to deduct the cost of music lessons. . . . The difference between those cases and the instant case is that petitioner's courses were general and basically unrelated to his duties as a policeman. As the Commissioner notes in his brief, a currently employed taxpayer such as petitioner might be allowed to deduct the cost of college courses which directly relate to the duties of his employment. If such courses were taken along with other, more general courses, their cost, or that part of the tuition representing their cost, would be deductible under § 162(a). In the instant case, however, petitioner does not claim that any particular course in which he was enrolled in 1964 bears any greater relationship to his job skills than the others.

Therefore, while tax incentives might be employed as an effective tool to encourage such valuable public servants as policemen, as well as others, to acquire a college education so as to improve their general competence, we feel that such a decision should be made by the Congress rather than the courts. To allow as a deduction the cost of a general college education would surely go beyond the original intention of Congress in its enactment of the Internal Revenue Code of 1954. Accordingly, we affirm the judgment of the Tax Court.

Affirmed.

NOTES AND QUESTIONS

1. *Personal expenses.* The cost of a college education, according to the orthodox rationale relied on in *Carroll*, is a personal expense. It seems even more clearly personal than the commuting and child-care costs to which the court analogizes. Of course, some philistines may go to college only to enhance their future earning capacity, but surely we cannot countenance a rule under which self-professed philistines are allowed a deduction and seekers of wisdom and culture are not. Mr. Carroll tried to avoid the rule that college expenses are nondeductible by arguing that his education was helpful to him in his job as a detective. Do you agree that this kind of argument must be rejected?

2. *Personal versus capital expenditures.* The best rationale for nondeductibility of the cost of a law school (or other professional) education is not that it is a personal expense (despite the potential personal rewards) but rather that it is a capital, as opposed to current, expenditure. That is, it creates an asset, the ability (or at least the essential credential) to practice law, that will produce income over many years. The distinction between capital and current expenditures is examined further in the next chapter. Infra page 511. Mr. Carroll said that he went to college in order to prepare to go to law school. Should this objective take his college costs out of the category of personal expenses? See infra page 547.

3. *Travel by school teachers.* A frequent source of litigation has been the deduction by school teachers of the travel costs for trips that they claim to be useful to them in their role as teachers. For example, in Krist v. Commissioner, 483 F.2d 1345 (2d Cir. 1973), the taxpayer taught first grade and deducted the cost of a trip to Europe and the Far East while she was on sabbatical leave. Her itinerary was approved by school authorities in connection with her application for the leave. During her six months of travel she visited schools on five days. Her argument for the claimed deduction was summarized by the court as follows (483 F.2d at 1350):

> Appellee claims that if she had been on vacation, as opposed to a business trip, she would not have used freighters, would have stayed at better hotels, and her activities would have been geared to swimming and skating rather than the travel and visits she made which she said tired her each day. But the fact that she used a freighter for travel and didn't go to "the best hotels" doesn't indicate a thing one way or the other as to whether her travel was related to her teaching. Economy travel and travel accommodations are as consistent with a personal as with an educational trip. She was six weeks on one freighter trip itself, and while there did no specific reading directed toward her teaching although she did read Louis Nizer and How to Tour Japan on Five Dollars a Day.
>
> When Mrs. Krist returned from her trip she did use in her teaching some of the pictures, costumes, dolls and games that she had acquired during the trip. She also acquired one technique abroad, the use of an individual slate and abacus at each child's desk, which she learned in Japan. Mrs. Krist was also required to write a report and make a presentation to the faculty regarding her trip on her return. The superintendent of the district certified that Mrs. Krist had "completed the program for which she was granted leave" and that "[t]he

travel was undertaken for professional improvement in order to enhance her teaching skills."

In upholding the Commissioner's denial of the deduction, the court said (483 F.2d at 1351):

> All travel has some educational value, but the test is whether the travel bears a direct relationship to the improvement of the traveler's particular skills. Such a relationship must be substantial, not ephemeral; the trip must be more than . . . "sightseeing." . . . We do not have to say here whether a trip abroad or two-thirds around the world for a first grade teacher could ever directly and substantially relate to educational skills. Suffice it to say here that taxpayer's trip in 1967 was not sufficiently so related as a matter of law.

The 1986 act added § 274(m)(2), which disallows deductions for "travel as a form of education" and thereby puts an end to deductions in cases like *Krist*. Do you approve of this congressional action? Why do you suppose it was thought to be necessary? What does that tell you about tax administration? About school teachers?

4. *Above-the-line deduction for qualified higher education expenses.* Section 222, originally enacted in 2001 and recently extended through 2009 via the "bailout" legislation enacted in September 2008, provides an above-the-line deduction for "qualified higher education expenses," such as tuition, paid by the taxpayer during a taxable year. The maximum deduction is $4,000, and is only allowed to taxpayers with adjusted gross income of $65,000 or less ($130,000 for joint returns).[30] Taxpayers with adjusted gross income between $65,000 and $80,000 ($130,000 and $160,000 for joint returns) may claim a maximum deduction of $2,000. Note that, unlike many other tax benefits, the deduction under § 222 is not gradually phased out but rather is subject to a "notch" and a "cliff." In other words, the amount of the deduction drops from $4,000 to $2,000 as the taxpayer's income reaches $65,001 (the "notch") and then drops to zero as the taxpayer's income reaches $80,001 (the "cliff"). As with all notches and cliffs, the effective marginal tax rate on the one dollar above the threshold is extraordinarily high. The rationale for these peculiar features is unclear, though sensible statutory design seems not to have played a significant role.

5. *Additional benefits for education.* Section 222 one of several tax benefits for college costs that have been enacted since 1996. The other provisions are the Hope scholarship credit (§ 25A(a)(1)), the lifetime learning credit (§ 25A(a)(2)), the deduction for interest on education loans (§ 221), the tax exemption for qualified state tuition programs (§ 529), and the tax exemption for Coverdell education savings accounts (§ 530). These provisions employ a bewildering array of income phaseouts, definitions of eligible individuals, and other special features. A felony drug conviction, for example, deprives one of the Hope scholarship credit but not the other benefits.

---

30. For purposes of the rule, adjusted gross income is computed without regard to this deduction, even though it is allowed above the line.

The § 529 "qualified tuition program" has proved to be especially attractive, particularly because it is available to high-income taxpayers while many of the other programs are phased out as income rises above modest levels. The so-called 529 plans are set up by the states and each of the fifty states has its own plan. Any person can invest in the plan of any state, creating an account for the benefit of a designated beneficiary to pay educational expenses, including room, board, tuition, and certain other expenses. Thus, for example, a wealthy couple living in Maine with grandchildren living in Massachusetts can set up a plan under Colorado law (and it can in effect be administered by their broker in New York). The state plans vary as to the types of available investments, fees, and various other matters, and as to the state income tax treatment of distributions (see www.savingforcollege.com). The amounts contributed to these plans are not deductible, but the income earned while the funds are held in the plan is not taxed and the distributions are tax free if made for "qualified educational expenses" (otherwise, they are taxable and subject to a 10 percent penalty). The person setting up and funding the plan can retain substantial control over the disposition of the funds by virtue of the freedom to change the beneficiary at any time, so long as the recipient is a member of the "family" of the original designated beneficiary. For this purpose, "family" is broadly defined to include the beneficiary's spouse, siblings, first cousins, descendants, and various other relations identified in § 152(a)(1) through (8).

529 plans have attracted billions of dollars in investment, which generates fees for the states, which in turn has generated competition among the states. The competition has encouraged some states to engage in anti-competitive measures such as imposition of a state income tax on distributions from plans set up under the laws of another state. The 529 plans compete with, but have proved far more popular than, the "Coverdell Educational Savings Accounts" (§ 530), which limit contributions to $2,000 per year.

Evidently, the members of Congress are more concerned about being able to crow to constituents about the brand new tax breaks they have added to the Code than about the actual effects on taxpayers who incur college costs.

6

DEDUCTIONS FOR THE COSTS
OF EARNING INCOME

A. CURRENT EXPENSES VERSUS CAPITAL EXPENDITURES

As noted in previous chapters, one of the fundamental precepts of an income tax is that taxpayers should be allowed to deduct the costs of earning income. Chapter 5 considered how this principle, which is codified in § 162 of the tax code, sometimes comes into conflict with the competing notion, reflected in § 262, that no deduction should be allowed for personal expenses. In this chapter, we continue our focus on deductions for the cost of earning income by highlighting an additional tension regarding the proper scope of § 162, one with special significance to the question of timing.

Like the section that immediately precedes it, § 263 operates to disallow certain deductions; in this case, however, the target is "any amount paid out for new buildings or for permanent improvements or betterments made to increase the value of any property or estate." The rationale for this rule is perhaps best understood by considering the different role that different types of expenditures play in producing income. Whereas certain expenditures generate largely current benefits, and thus can be thought of as appropriate offsets against current income, other expenditures help to produce income over longer periods of time. For example, salary expenses are usually seen as a current cost of doing business and are deductible under § 162 against current income. Thus, a restaurant that pays its cook $50,000 in a given year receives a deduction of $50,000 in that same year. On the other hand, a company must capitalize, rather than currently deduct, the amount it pays for a new factory. The idea behind not allowing a current deduction is that a new factory is more in the nature of an investment, rather than a current expense.

The fact that an expenditure is described in § 263 does not necessarily mean that the tax system will completely ignore its role in the production of income. In many cases, costs that must be capitalized under § 263 will be "recovered" (i.e., deducted) via some other provision, such as §§ 167-168 concerning the allowance for depreciation. Thus, unlike § 262, the effect of § 263 is typically not complete disallowance, but rather a spreading of the cost recovery over a longer period of time or perhaps even postponement until a sale of the asset.

1.   Which Expenditures Must Be Capitalized?

Controversies abound regarding which expenditures can be currently deducted and which must be capitalized. For example, suppose that a company spends $1 million not on a factory but on a product such as an atlas or encyclopedia with a long useful life. Is the cost deductible? Does it matter whether the product is developed in house, and the $1 million is paid out as salaries to employees, or whether the developed product is purchased from another company? Consider the views of Judge Richard Posner from the U.S. Court of Appeals for the Seventh Circuit.

ENCYCLOPAEDIA BRITANNICA v. COMMISSIONER

685 F.2d 212 (7th Cir. 1982)

POSNER, Circuit Judge.

Section 162(a) of the Internal Revenue Code allows the deduction of "all the ordinary and necessary expenses paid or incurred during the taxable year in carrying on any trade or business . . .," but this is qualified (see § 161) by section 263(a) of the Code, which forbids the immediate deduction of "capital expenditures" even if they are ordinary and necessary business expenses. We must decide in this case whether certain expenditures made by Encyclopaedia Britannica, Inc. to acquire a manuscript were capital expenditures.

Encyclopaedia Britannica decided to publish a book to be called The Dictionary of Natural Sciences. Ordinarily it would have prepared the book in-house, but being temporarily shorthanded it hired David-Stewart Publishing Company "to do all necessary research work and to prepare, edit and arrange the manuscript and all illustrative and other material for" the book. Under the contract David-Stewart agreed "to work closely with" Encyclopaedia Britannica's editorial board "so that the content and arrangement of the Work (and any revisions thereof) will conform to the idea and desires of [Encyclopaedia Britannica] and be acceptable to it"; but it was contemplated that David-Stewart would turn over a complete manuscript that Encyclopaedia Britannica would copyright, publish, and sell, and in exchange would receive advances against the royalties that Encyclopaedia Britannica expected to earn from the book.

Encyclopaedia Britannica treated these advances as ordinary and necessary business expenses deductible in the years when they were paid, though it had not yet obtained any royalties. The Internal Revenue Service disallowed the deductions and assessed deficiencies. Encyclopaedia Britannica petitioned the Tax Court for a redetermination of its tax liability, and prevailed. The Tax Court held that the expenditures were for "services" rather than for the acquisition of an asset and concluded that therefore they were deductible immediately rather than being, as the Service had ruled, capital expenditures. "The agreement provided for substantial editorial supervision by [Encyclopaedia Britannica]. Indeed, David-Stewart's work product was to be the embodiment of [Encyclopaedia Britannica's] ideas and desires. David-Stewart was just the vehicle selected by [Encyclopaedia Britannica] to assist . . . with the editorial phase of the Work." Encyclopaedia Britannica was "the owner of the Work at all stages of completion" and "the dominating force associated with the Work." The Service petitions for review of the Tax Court's decision pursuant to § 7482.

As an original matter we would have no doubt that the payments to David-Stewart were capital expenditures regardless of who was the "dominating force" in the creation of The Dictionary of Natural Sciences. The work was intended to yield Encyclopaedia Britannica income over a period of years. The object of sections 162 and 263 of the Code, read together, is to match up expenditures with the income they generate. Where the income is generated over a period of years the expenditures should be classified as capital, contrary to what the Tax Court did here. From the publisher's standpoint a book is just another rental property; and just as the expenditures in putting a building into shape to be rented must be capitalized, so, logically at least, must the expenditures used to create a book. It would make no difference under this view whether Encyclopaedia Britannica hired David-Stewart as a mere consultant to its editorial board, which is the Tax Court's conception of what happened, or bought outright from David-Stewart the right to a book that David-Stewart had already published. If you hire a carpenter to build a tree house that you plan to rent out, his wage is a capital expenditure to you. See Commissioner of Internal Revenue v. Idaho Power Co., 418 U.S. 1, 13 (1974).[1]

We are not impressed by Encyclopaedia Britannica's efforts to conjure up practical difficulties in matching expenditures on a book to the income from it. What, it asks, would have been the result if it had scrapped a portion of the manuscript it received from David-Stewart? Would that be treated as the partial destruction of a capital asset, entitling it to an immediate deduction? We think not. The proper analogy is to loss or breakage in the construction of our hypothetical tree house. The effect would be to increase the costs of construction, which are deductible over the useful life of the asset. If the scrapped portion of the manuscript was replaced, the analogy would be perfect. If it was not replaced, the tax consequence would be indirect: an increase or decrease in the publisher's taxable income from the published book.

What does give us pause, however, is a series of decisions in which authors of books have been allowed to treat their expenses as ordinary and necessary business expenses that are deductible immediately even though they were incurred in the creation of long-lived assets — the books the authors were writing. The leading case is Faura v. Commissioner, 73 T.C. 849 (1980); it

---

1. [In *Idaho Power*, the taxpayer claimed current deductions for depreciation on the trucks and other such equipment it used in constructing capital assets such as transmission lines. The Court upheld the Commissioner's disallowance of such deductions, reasoning that the cost of the trucks was simply part of the cost of creating the capital asset itself. — Eds.]

was discussed with approval just recently by a panel of the Tenth Circuit in Snyder v. United States, 674 F.2d 1359, 1365 (10th Cir. 1982), and was relied on heavily by the Tax Court in the present case.

We can think of a practical reason for allowing authors to deduct their expenses immediately, one applicable as well to publishers though not in the circumstances of the present case. If you are in the business of producing a series of assets that will yield income over a period of years—which is the situation of most authors and all publishers—identifying particular expenditures with particular books, a necessary step for proper capitalization because the useful lives of the books will not be the same, may be very difficult, since the expenditures of an author or publisher (more clearly the latter) tend to be joint among several books. Moreover, allocating these expenditures among the different books is not always necessary to produce the temporal matching of income and expenditures that the Code desiderates, because the taxable income of the author or publisher who is in a steady state (that is, whose output is neither increasing nor decreasing) will be at least approximately the same whether his costs are expensed or capitalized. Not the same on any given book—on each book expenses and receipts will be systematically mismatched—but the same on average. Under these conditions the benefits of capitalization are unlikely to exceed the accounting and other administrative costs entailed in capitalization.

Yet we hesitate to endorse the *Faura* line of cases: not only because of the evident tension between them and *Idaho Power*, supra, where the Supreme Court said that expenses, whatever their character, must be capitalized if they are incurred in creating a capital asset, but also because *Faura*, and cases following it such as *Snyder*, fail in our view to articulate a persuasive rationale for their result. *Faura* relied on cases holding that the normal expenses of authors and other artists are deductible business expenses rather than nondeductible personal expenses, and on congressional evidence of dissatisfaction with the Internal Revenue Service's insistence that such expenses be capitalized. See 73 T.C. at 852-861. But most of the cases in question (including all those at the court of appeals level), such as Doggett v. Burnett, 65 F.2d 191 (D.C. Cir. 1933), are inapposite, because they consider only whether the author's expenditures are deductible at all—not whether, if they are deductible, they must first be capitalized. . . .

[But] we need not decide whether *Faura* is good law, and we are naturally reluctant to precipitate a conflict with the Tenth Circuit. The Tax Court interpreted *Faura* too broadly in this case. As we interpret *Faura* its principle comes into play only when the taxpayer is in the business of producing a series of assets that yield the taxpayer income over a period of years, so that a complex allocation would be necessary if the taxpayer had to capitalize all his expenses of producing them. This is not such a case. The expenditures at issue are unambiguously identified with The Dictionary of Natural Sciences. We need not consider the proper tax treatment of any other expenses that Encyclopaedia Britannica may have incurred on the project—editorial expenses, for example—as they are not involved in this case. Those expenses would be analogous to author Faura's office and travel expenses; they are the normal, recurrent expenses of operating a business that happens to produce capital assets. This case is like *Idaho Power*, supra. The expenditure there was on transportation equipment used in constructing capital facilities that Idaho Power employed in its business of producing and distributing electricity, and was thus unambiguously identified with specific capital assets, just as Encyclopaedia Britannica's payment to David-Stewart for the manuscript of The Dictionary of Natural Sciences was unambiguously identified with a specific capital asset.

It is also relevant that the commissioning of the manuscript from David-Stewart was somewhat out of the ordinary for Encyclopaedia Britannica. Now the word "ordinary" in section 162 of the Internal Revenue Code has two different uses: to prevent the deduction of certain expenses that are not normally incurred in the type of business in which the taxpayer is engaged ("ordinary" in this sense blends imperceptibly into "necessary"), . . . and to clarify the distinction between expenses that are immediately deductible and expenses that must first be capitalized. . . . (A merging of these two distinct senses of the word is a possible explanation for the result in *Faura*.) Most of the "ordinary," in the sense of recurring, expenses of a business are noncapital in nature and most of its capital expenditures are extraordinary in the sense of nonrecurring. Here, as arguably in *Idaho Power* as well — for Idaho Power's business was the production and distribution of electricity, rather than the construction of buildings — the taxpayer stepped out of its normal method of doing business. In this particular project Encyclopaedia Britannica was operating like a conventional publisher, which obtains a complete manuscript from an author or in this case a compiler. The conventional publisher may make a considerable contribution to the work both at the idea stage and at the editorial stage but the deal is for a manuscript, not for services in assisting the publisher to prepare the manuscript itself. Yet we need not consider whether a conventional publisher should be permitted to deduct royalty advances made to its authors as current operating expenses, merely because those advances are for its recurring business expenses because its business is producing capital assets. *Idaho Power*, though factually distinguishable, implies one answer to this question (no), [and] *Faura* another (yes). . . . But the principle of *Faura*, whatever its soundness, comes into play only when the expenditure sought to be immediately deducted is a normal and recurrent expense of the business, as it was not here. . . .

There is another point to be noted about the distinction between recurring and nonrecurring expenses and its bearing on the issue in this case. If one really takes seriously the concept of a capital expenditure as anything that yields income, actual or imputed, beyond the period (conventionally one year . . .) in which the expenditure is made, the result will be to force the capitalization of virtually every business expense. It is a result courts naturally shy away from. . . . It would require capitalizing every salesman's salary, since his selling activities create goodwill for the company and goodwill is an asset yielding income beyond the year in which the salary expense is incurred. The administrative costs of conceptual rigor are too great. The distinction between recurring and nonrecurring business expenses provides a very crude but perhaps serviceable demarcation between those capital expenditures that can feasibly be capitalized and those that cannot be. Whether the distinction breaks down where, as in the case of the conventional publisher, the firm's entire business is the production of capital assets, so that it is literally true that all of its business expenses are capital in nature, is happily not a question we have to decide here, for it is clear that Encyclopaedia Britannica's payments to David-Stewart were of a nonnormal, nonrecurrent nature.

In light of all that we have said, the contention that really what David-Stewart did here was to render consulting services to Encyclopaedia Britannica no different from the services of a consultant whom Encyclopaedia Britannica might have hired on one of its in-house projects, which if true would make the payments more "ordinary" in the *Faura* sense, is of doubtful relevance. But in any event, if that is what the Tax Court meant when it said that David-Stewart was not the "dominating force," its finding was, we think, clearly erroneous. We deprecate decision by metaphor. If the concept of a dominating force has any relevance to tax law, which we doubt, an attempt should have been made to operationalize it, as by computing the ratio of Encyclopaedia Britannica's in-house expenditures on The Dictionary of Natural Sciences to its payments to David-Stewart. If the ratio was greater than one, then Encyclopaedia Britannica could fairly be regarded as the dominant force in the enterprise. Although this computation was never made, we have no doubt that Encyclopaedia Britannica was dominant in the sense that, as the buyer, it was calling the tune; and it was buying a custom-made product, built to its specifications. But what it was buying was indeed a product, a completed manuscript. This was a turnkey project, remote from what is ordinarily understood by editorial consultation. While maybe some creators or buyers of capital goods — some authors and publishers — may deduct as current expenses what realistically are capital expenditures, they may not do so . . . when the expense is tied to producing or acquiring a specific capital asset.

Encyclopaedia Britannica urges, as an alternative ground for sustaining the Tax Court's decision, that the payments to David-Stewart were immediately deductible as research and experimental expenditures under § 174(a). This ground was not considered by the Tax Court, and it would be premature for us to consider it without the benefit of that court's views. The Tax Court can on remand consider it and any other unresolved issues.

Reversed and remanded.

NOTES AND QUESTIONS

1. *True reflection of income.* As the court in *Encyclopaedia Britannica* observes, "The object of sections 162 and 263 of the Code, read together, is to match up expenditures with the income they generate." This objective, though often ignored both by Congress and by the courts in shaping the rules of tax accounting, is consistent with the basic goal of sound accrual accounting principles, which is to provide a true reflection of income. To appreciate the importance of the point, imagine that the contract in the *Encyclopaedia Britannica* case had represented a large part of the total operations of Encyclopaedia Britannica for the year at issue. If the entire cost of the contract had been treated as an expense of the year in which the payment was made,

the result could well have been a huge loss for that year. Surely it would be misleading for the managers or the shareholders of the company to conclude that in fact they had a very bad year and that drastic changes might be required. The amounts spent are obviously the price of acquiring a capital asset, not money down the drain. It seems quite likely, therefore, that for the purposes of making investment decisions and of reporting to shareholders (assuming the item was significant), the outlay was not treated as an offset to current income.

Corporate scandals in the early part of this decade help to illustrate, from the financial accounting side, the importance of the distinction between expensing and capitalization. In June 2002, WorldCom, a leading telecommunications company with more than 20 million customers and $100 billion of assets, disclosed that, for accounting purposes, it had improperly capitalized nearly $4 billion of expenditures that ought to have been expensed, thereby inflating its reported earnings. The market reaction was so intense that, within a month, WorldCom was forced to file for bankruptcy.

2. *Capitalization of inventory, construction, and development costs.* The court in *Encyclopaedia Britannica* states that "if you hire a carpenter to build a tree house that you plan to rent out, his wage is a capital expenditure to you." The court cites Commissioner v. Idaho Power Co., 418 U.S. 1 (1974), which is described in footnote 1, supra. The principle underlying the court's tree-house metaphor, and *Idaho Power*, is now generalized in § 263A, which was adopted in 1986 and is described in further detail below.

3. *Depreciation and amortization.* When an outlay is treated as the cost of acquiring a capital asset, traditional accounting principles require that that cost be recovered over the useful life of the asset — that is, over the time in which the asset is expected to contribute to the production of the firm's income. In the case of an intangible asset like a copyright for a book, the label given to the annual deductions is "amortization." In the case of a tangible asset like a factory building or a truck, the deduction has traditionally been called "depreciation." See § 167. Under the present Code, the deduction is called "ACRS" (accelerated cost recovery system). See § 168, which is described infra page 565. Under ACRS, the time over which deductions are claimed in some cases is shorter than the expected useful lives of the assets. This favorable tax treatment may be the result of a conscious decision to use the tax system to encourage investments in plant and equipment.

4. *Scrapping part of the manuscript.* If a taxpayer buys four trucks in a single transaction, the cost is allocated among them. If one is destroyed in a fire, the cost of that truck is deductible as a loss under § 165(a). (Even though the loss is attributable to a "casualty," § 165(c)(3) is irrelevant because its function is to permit deductions of certain nonbusiness losses.) On the other hand, if Encyclopaedia Britannica had scrapped a portion of the manuscript that it had acquired, presumably, as the court suggests, there would be no loss deduction. The amount paid for the original manuscript would be treated as the cost of what was ultimately used. What if a publisher commissions the preparation of a set of four books and ultimately decides to sell only three of them?

5. *Cash-method versus accrual-method of accounting.* Note that § 263 applies to both cash- and accrual-method taxpayers. Thus, it is irrelevant that individual

authors are likely to be cash-method taxpayers while Encyclopaedia Britannica no doubt used the accrual method.

6. *The value of deferral.* In distinguishing the *Faura* case, the court in *Encyclopaedia Britannica* observes that "the taxable income of the author or publisher who is in a steady state ... will be at least approximately the same whether his costs are expensed or capitalized." This is true only in the long run. Imagine an author, with income from other sources, who begins to write books in 1999 and to receive royalties in 2000. Suppose he is allowed to begin deducting research expenses in 1999, rather than in 2000, and continues this practice until he retires forty years later. He will have the advantage of deferral to the extent of one year's deductions not just for one year but for forty. That is, he will reduce his income in 1999 and the effects will not catch up with him until forty years later. To put that still another way, he has the advantage of a premature deduction of expense attributable to the next year's income not just in the first year (1999) but in every year until retirement. What is the relative burden of a tax paid now as compared with one paid forty years from now? What does this tell you about the significance of the *Encyclopaedia Britannica* decision?

7. *Economic consequences.* How do you suppose the holding in *Encyclopaedia Britannica* affected the decisions of firms like Encyclopaedia Britannica about contracting out manuscript-preparation work to other firms? Was that a sensible economic outcome?

8. *Exceptions to the requirement of capitalization and some tax shelter fundamentals.* One important exception to the requirement of capitalization of expenditures expected to produce revenues in future years is § 174, covering research and development (R&D) expenditures. Another important exception is found in Regs. § 1.162-12, which permits expensing of the costs of developing farms, orchards, and ranches. This rule led to a substantial amount of investment by high-bracket people seeking tax shelters. For example, a person with a high income from a medical practice would buy a parcel of undeveloped land and develop an orange grove. The cost of the land itself was a capital expenditure, but most of the costs of developing the land into a productive orange grove were currently deductible. Thus, in the years before the grove reached a productive state, the investment showed losses for tax purposes. These tax losses offset income from the medical practice, though in an economic sense they were not losses but, instead, the cost of acquiring a capital asset. When the grove reached a productive state, it was sold, and the gain, which was largely attributable to deducted expenditures for development, was realized. But that gain was capital gain, and so received favorable tax treatment. Thus, even if the venture lost money apart from taxes, it could turn out to be profitable after taxes were taken into account. The tax avoidance possibility described here has now largely been foreclosed by the denial of deductions for passive activity losses (§ 469) and by a requirement of capitalization of the cost of property produced by a taxpayer (§ 263A).

9. *Prepaid expenses.* In Commissioner v. Boylston Market Association, 131 F.2d 966 (1st Cir. 1942), a cash-basis taxpayer was required to capitalize prepaid insurance premiums covering a three-year period. The court cited similar results in cases involving prepaid rent, bonuses for the acquisition of leases, and commissions for negotiating leases. Under § 461(g), a taxpayer

must capitalize most forms of prepaid interest. Note, however, the special treatment of "points" in § 461(g)(2).

2. The Uniform Capitalization Rules of Section 263A

Before 1986 the rules governing capitalization of costs incurred in creating inventory or other long-lived assets produced by the taxpayer were inconsistent. This inconsistency is apparent on a careful reading of the *Encyclopaedia Britannica* case. In that case, the court held that the cost of purchasing a completed manuscript from an unrelated company must be capitalized and amortized against sales. The court noted, however, that the in-house costs of producing such a manuscript would be currently deductible. One reason why in-house publishing expenses have in the past been deductible is administrative. An in-house employee's time may be spent on many different projects. Allocating that time among projects may be quite difficult. As the court in *Encyclopaedia Britannica* concluded, "[t]he administrative costs of conceptual rigor are too great." (Note, however, that allocation of costs may be vital to making sound business decisions. How can a business person decide whether a project will be or has been profitable without knowing what it cost?)

In 1986, Congress decided that conceptual rigor and, probably more important, revenue needs outweighed administrative concerns in this area, and adopted § 263A, the uniform capitalization (UNICAP) rules. Under that provision, the costs of producing inventory and other self-created assets, such as the in-house production of a manuscript, must be capitalized. See § 263A(b); General Explanation of the Tax Reform Act of 1986, Staff of the Joint Committee on Taxation (May 4, 1987) at 509 n.58; Temp. Regs. § 1.263A-2(a)(2). These costs include not only the salaries of people writing the manuscript, but such indirect expenses as the allocable share of the salaries of supervisory and administrative people.

The UNICAP rules extend to virtually all manufacturers. All the costs of producing the goods to be sold, including such items as the cost of insurance on the manufacturing plant, must be added to the cost of the inventory and deducted at the time the inventory is sold. Regs. § 1.263A-1(e). Similar rules apply to large wholesalers and retailers of inventory. For example, the salaries of purchasing agents must be allocated to inventory and recovered at the time the inventory is sold.

Costs incurred by sellers or producers of long-lived assets that do not require capitalization include marketing and advertising costs, and costs of general and administrative expenses that do not relate to sale or production. In this latter category are costs of general business planning, costs of shareholder or public relations, and other costs removed from sale or production. Regs. § 1.263A-1(e)(4).

As is perhaps evident from the preceding discussion, the rules governing uniform capitalization under § 263A are complicated and require many difficult determinations. For example, it will often be unclear whether a particular employee's time is spent on matters that relate to production or to general business planning. Congress has limited the scope of § 263A somewhat by excluding from its ambit retailers and wholesalers with annual gross receipts of less than $10,000,000. § 263A(b)(2)(B). Congress has also excluded from § 263A costs incurred by freelance writers, artists, and photographers. § 263A(h). Other producers and sellers will have to learn to live with the complexity (and conceptual rigor) of UNICAP.

3. The *INDOPCO* Decision and the Capitalization Regulations

Section 263A applies only to real or tangible personal property produced or acquired by the taxpayer or to inventory or property acquired for resale. See § 263A(b). After the adoption of § 263A, uncertainty and litigation persisted over intangibles that produce long-term benefits. In a landmark decision in 1992, INDOPCO, Inc. v. Commissioner, 503 U.S. 79, the Supreme Court, resolving a conflict among the circuits, held that investment banking fees incident to a merger must be capitalized. Prior case law had left open the possibility that such fees could be currently deducted since they typically did not "create or enhance . . . a separate and distinct additional asset." See Commissioner v. Lincoln Savings & Loan Ass'n, 403 U.S. 345, 354 (1971).

The *INDOPCO* Court rejected the taxpayer's argument that capitalization was required only in instances involving the creation or enhancement of a separate and distinct asset, holding instead that "the realization of benefits beyond the year in which the expenditure is incurred is undeniably important in determining whether the appropriate tax treatment is immediate deduction or capitalization." Since the fees at issue in the case generated a host of long-term benefits for the taxpayer, the Supreme Court concluded that the amounts could not be deductions under § 162 as ordinary and necessary business expenses.

The highly general language of the Court in *INDOPCO* left considerable uncertainty, which gave rise to controversy and litigation over tax-accounting practices of widespread and significant impact. The Treasury responded by proposing and ultimately, in 2004, adopting lengthy, detailed regulations under § 263 (as distinguished from § 263A). See T.D. 9107, publishing and explaining Regs. § 1.263A(a)-4 and (a)-5.

These so-called *INDOPCO* regulations cover a broad range of expenses, including amounts incurred in creating or acquiring various intangibles, such as goodwill, customer lists, covenants not to compete, an assembled workforce, an ownership interest in a corporation or partnership, or a license to practice law. The regulations eschew the approach of stating general principles and concepts; instead, they are replete with highly detailed rules for specific types of expenditures. For example, Regs. § 1.263(a)-4(e)(5), Example 8, states that a commercial bank "is not required to capitalize any portion of the compensation paid to the employees in its loan acquisition department or any portion of its overhead allocable to the loan acquisition department." Regs. § 1.263(a)-5 covers "amounts paid or incurred to facilitate an acquisition of a trade or business, a change in the capital structure of a business entity, and certain other transactions," such as bankruptcy reorganization costs. Under Regs. § 1.167(a)-3, many capitalized expenses are amortizable over a fifteen-year period.

The rules found in the *INDOPCO* regulations are in some respects more favorable to taxpayers than the more stringent rules that might have been imposed under existing precedent, leading one commentator to suggest that a more apt moniker would be the "anti-*INDOPCO* regulations."[2] The Treasury's explanation states that the "regulations strike an appropriate balance between the capitalization provisions of the Code and the ability of taxpayers and IRS personnel to administer the law." T.D. 9107, 68 Fed. Reg. 436, 436-437. One important general principle is that expenses must be capitalized if they create, or facilitate the creation of, a "separate and distinct intangible" — one that has a "measurable value in money's worth," is legally protected, and is "capable of being sold, transferred or pledged . . . separate and apart from a trade or business." § 1.263(a)-4(b)(3). There is a de minimis rule (excluding expenses under $5,000) — with an interesting cell-phone example: Where a tele-communications company provides a "free" telephone worth $300 to induce a customer to sign a multi-year contract, the company may deduct the $300 currently under the de minimis rule. In another concession to practicality, expenses for benefits that extend beyond the current year may be deducted currently if they provide benefits that do not extend beyond twelve months. The regulations' detailed rules and extensive examples quite plainly respond to issues raised in the administrative process by particular industries and types of business activity.

The broader lesson of *INDOPCO* and its regulatory aftermath is that administrative practicalities often set the basic parameters for the development of the law. Even if right on the merits, the Supreme Court's *INDOPCO* decision triggered an avalanche of new legal controversies. According to a GAO study published in 1995, within a few years of the Supreme Court's opinion the *INDOPCO* issue had come to dominate the portfolio of cases involving large corporate taxpayers before the IRS Office of Appeals, accounting "for about 42 percent of the issues they contested" and "$1.1 billion of the total $1.9 billion in proposed adjustments."[3] In some ways, then, the final regulations may be viewed as a white flag of sorts, with the government trading in its victory in *INDOPCO* for greater certainty in the law and a reduced likelihood of perpetual litigation.

B. REPAIR AND MAINTENANCE EXPENSES

Another area of frequent controversy concerns the tax treatment of repair and maintenance expenses. Under Treasury regulations in place since 1960, the "cost of incidental repairs which neither materially add to the value of the

---

2. See Ethan Yale, The Final INDOPCO Regulations, Tax Notes (October 25, 2004).
3. Government Accounting Office, Tax Administration: Recurring Issues in Tax Disputes Over Business Expense Deductions 2 (Sept. 1995) (available at http://www.gao.gov/archive/1995/gg95232.pdf).

property nor appreciably prolong its life" are generally allowed as current deductions. Treas. Regs. § 1.162-4. Does this legal standard produce clear results in specific cases? Consider the following case.

MIDLAND EMPIRE PACKING CO. v. COMMISSIONER
14 T.C. 635 (1950), acq., 1950-2 C.B. 3

ARUNDELL, Judge.

The issue in this case is whether an expenditure for a concrete lining in petitioner's basement to oil-proof it against an oil nuisance created by a neighboring refinery is deductible as an ordinary and necessary expense under [§ 162(a)], on the theory it was an expenditure for a repair, or, in the alternative, whether the expenditure may be treated as the measure of the loss sustained during the taxable year and not compensated for by insurance or otherwise within the meaning of [§ 165(a)].

The respondent has contended, in part, that the expenditure is for a capital improvement and should be recovered through depreciation charges and is, therefore, not deductible as an ordinary and necessary business expense or as a loss.

[Regs. § 1.162-4] is helpful in distinguishing between an expenditure to be classed as a repair and one to be treated as a capital outlay. In Illinois Merchants Trust Co., Executor, 4 B.T.A. 103, at p.106, we discussed this subject in some detail and in our opinion said:

> It will be noted that the first sentence of the article [now Regs. § 1.162-4] relates to repairs, while the second sentence deals in effect with replacements. . . . To repair is to restore to a sound state or to mend, while a replacement connotes a substitution. A repair is an expenditure for the purpose of keeping the property in an ordinarily efficient operating condition. It does not add to the value of the property, nor does it appreciably prolong its life. It merely keeps the property in an operating condition over its probable useful life for the uses for which it was acquired. Expenditures for that purpose are distinguishable from those for replacements, alterations, improvements, or additions which prolong the life of the property, increase its value, or make it adaptable to a different use. The one is a maintenance charge, while the others are additions to capital investment which should not be applied against current earnings.

It will be seen from our findings of fact that for some 25 years prior to the taxable year petitioner had used the basement rooms of its plant as a place for the curing of hams and bacon and for the storage of meat and hides. The basement had been entirely satisfactory for this purpose over the entire period in spite of the fact that there was some seepage of water into the rooms from time to time. In the taxable year it was found that not only water, but oil, was seeping through the concrete walls of the basement of the packing plant and, while the water would soon drain out, the oil would not, and there was left on the basement floor a thick scum of oil which gave off a strong odor that permeated the air of the entire plant, and the fumes from the oil created a fire hazard. It appears that the oil which came from a nearby refinery had also gotten into the water wells which served to furnish water for petitioner's plant, and as a result of this whole condition the Federal meat inspectors advised petitioner that it must discontinue the use of the water from the wells and oil-proof the basement, or else shut down its plant.

To meet this situation, petitioner during the taxable year undertook steps to oil-proof the basement by adding a concrete lining to the walls from the floor to a height of about four feet and also added concrete to the floor of the basement. It is the cost of this work which it seeks to deduct as a repair. The basement was not enlarged by this work, nor did the oil-proofing serve to make it more desirable for the purpose for which it had been used through the years prior to the time that the oil nuisance had occurred. The evidence is that the expenditure did not add to the value or prolong the expected life of the property over what they were before the event occurred which made the repairs necessary. It is true that after the work was done the seepage of water, as well as oil, was stopped, but, as already stated, the presence of the water had never been found objectionable. The repairs merely served to keep the property in an operating condition over its probable useful life for the purpose for which it was used.

While it is conceded on brief that the expenditure was "necessary," respondent contends that the encroachment of the oil nuisance on petitioner's property was not an "ordinary" expense in petitioner's particular business. But the fact that petitioner had not theretofore been called upon to make a similar expenditure to prevent damage and disaster to its property does not remove that expense from the classification of "ordinary" for, as stated in Welch v. Helvering [infra page 545]:

> ordinary in this context does not mean that the payments must be habitual or normal in the sense that the same taxpayer will have to make them often. . . . [T]he expense is an ordinary one because we know from experience that payments for such a purpose, whether the amount is large or small, are the common and accepted means of defense against attack. . . . The situation is unique in the life of the individual affected, but not in the life of the group, the community, of which he is a part.

Steps to protect a business building from the seepage of oil from a nearby refinery, which had been erected long subsequent to the time petitioner started to operate its plant, would seem to us to be a normal thing to do. . . .

In American Bemberg Corporation, 10 T.C. 361, we allowed as deductions, on the ground that they were ordinary and necessary expenses, extensive expenditures made to prevent disaster, although the repairs were of a type which had never been needed before and were unlikely to recur. In that case the taxpayer, to stop cave-ins of soil which were threatening destruction of its manufacturing plant, hired an engineering firm which drilled to the bedrock and injected grout to fill the cavities where practicable. . . . We found that the cost [of the drilling and grouting] did not make good the depreciation previously allowed, and stated in our opinion:

[T]he . . . program was intended to avert a plant-wide disaster and avoid forced abandonment of the plant. The purpose was not to improve, better, extend or increase the original plant, nor to prolong its original useful life. Its continued operation was endangered; the purpose of the expenditures was to enable petitioner to continue the plant in operation not on any new or better scale, but on the same scale and, so far as possible, as efficiently as it had operated before.

The petitioner here made the repairs in question in order that it might continue to operate its plant. Not only was there danger of fire from the oil and fumes, but the presence of the oil led the Federal meat inspectors to declare the basement an unsuitable place for the purpose for which it had been used for a quarter of a century. After the expenditures were made, the plant did not operate on a changed or larger scale, nor was it thereafter suitable for new or additional uses. The expenditure served only to permit petitioner to continue the use of the plant, and particularly the basement for its normal operations.

In our opinion, the expenditure of $4868.81 for lining the basement walls and floor was essentially a repair and, as such, it is deductible as an ordinary and necessary business expense. This holding makes unnecessary a consideration of petitioner's alternative contention that the expenditure is deductible as a business loss. . . .

NOTES AND QUESTIONS

1. *Repairs and losses.* (a) An interesting aspect of the *Midland Empire* opinion is its reference at the beginning and end to the possible alternative of a deduction for a loss, which would be claimed under § 165(a). A problem with deductions for losses is they must be "realized." There must be some identifiable event that justifies a current accounting. A decline in value due to wear and tear, to changes in the economic environment, or to other circumstances does not give rise to a loss deduction; such a decline is recognized only through ACRS (formerly, and for nontax purposes, called depreciation) or as a loss when the property is sold. Does the oil-seepage problem confronted by the taxpayer in *Midland Empire* seem to you to justify a loss deduction? If so, what is the best way to measure the amount of the loss? If no loss deduction is available, is a deduction for repair a sensible substitute?

(b) If a deduction for a loss is allowed, a deduction for any repair to restore the property to the preloss condition must be denied. See Regs. § 1.161-1 ("Double deductions are not permitted").[4] To illustrate this principle, suppose a farmer builds a new barn for $50,000. The cost is a capital expenditure, even for a cash-method farmer. See Regs. § 1.162-12(a). The basis for the barn is its cost, $50,000. This cost is deducted over time through ACRS. Suppose that in the first year of its existence, the roof of the barn is destroyed by a tornado and is replaced at a cost of $10,000. The farmer has two tax alternatives. One

---

4. The same conclusion seems to be supported by § 263(a)(2), but Regs. § 1.263(a)-1(a)(2) refers only to deductions for "depreciation, amortization, or depletion."

alternative is to claim a deduction for a loss. The amount, quite plainly, would be $10,000. The loss deduction would reduce basis by $10,000, to $40,000. § 1016(a)(1). The cost of the replacement, or repair, would not be deducted. It would be treated as a capital cost, increasing basis by $10,000, back to $50,000. § 1016(a)(1). The other alternative is to forgo any deduction for a loss and deduct instead the cost of the repair, $10,000, as a current expense. The basis of the barn would not change. Under either alternative we get the same net result: a current deduction of $10,000 and a basis of $50,000, which properly reflects what happened.

(c) But what if the roof wears out over a period of several years, because of shoddy initial construction or because of some unusually harsh weather, or both? Is a loss deduction still available? Should the replacement be treated as a repair or as a capital expenditure? What if the barn had been fully depreciated and thus had a basis of zero? See Regs. §§ 1.162-4 and 1.263(a)-1.

In Mt. Morris Drive-In Theatre Co. v. Commissioner, 238 F.2d 85 (6th Cir. 1956), a taxpayer, whose actions in clearing land to build a drive-in theater caused substantial increase of water drainage onto an adjacent landowner's property, installed a correction drainage system under threat of litigation. Held: The cost of the drainage system had to be capitalized since the need for it was foreseeable and was part of the process of completing taxpayer's initial investment for its original intended use. See also United States v. Times-Mirror Co., 231 F.2d 876 (9th Cir. 1956) (cost of microfilming a set of back issues as protection against loss by enemy bombing deductible; amount spent allowed "business to be operated on the same scale and not to increase"); Jones v. Commissioner, 242 F.2d 616 (5th Cir. 1957) (taxpayer reconstructed decrepit building in French Quarter of New Orleans because he could not get permission to raze it; held: costs of general rehabilitation must be capitalized).

What if a taxpayer is required to install a sprinkler system in a hotel, in order to comply with a city fire code? That issue was presented in Hotel Sulgrave v. Commissioner, 21 T.C. 619 (1954), where the court said (at 621):

> We do not agree that the installation of the sprinkler system constituted a repair made "for the purpose of keeping the property in an ordinarily efficient operating condition." . . . It was a permanent addition to the property ordered by the city of New York to give the property additional protection from the hazard of fire. It was an improvement or betterment having a life extending beyond the year in which it was made and which depreciates over a period of years. While it may not have increased the value of the hotel property or prolonged its useful life, the property became more valuable for use in the petitioner's business by reason of compliance with the city's order. The respondent did not err in determining that the cost of this improvement or betterment should be added to petitioner's capital investment in the building, and recovered through depreciation deductions in the years of its useful life.

2. *Repairs and accounting theory.* Apart from the connection to a loss, what justification is there for treating any repair as a current expense, except where the amount is so small that an addition to basis would not be worth the trouble? Consider the example, discussed in Note 1 above, of a farmer whose roof is destroyed by a tornado. When she decides to replace the roof, will she look to the

benefits that the replacement will provide for this year only or to the benefits over many years in the future? What about the taxpayer in *Midland Empire*?

3. *Maintenance of a business versus creating a new capability.* The concept of a repair is widely recognized and fairly easily grasped. It serves therefore as a useful analogy in approaching other problems that are conceptually similar. One of these is the distinction between efforts to maintain an existing business in the face of changing conditions and efforts to expand into new, related lines of business.

REVENUE RULING 94-38

1994-1 C.B. 35

ISSUE

Are the costs incurred to clean up land and to treat groundwater that a taxpayer contaminated with hazardous waste from its business deductible by the taxpayer as business expenses under § 162 of the Internal Revenue Code, or must they be capitalized under § 263?

FACTS

X, an accrual basis corporation, owns and operates a manufacturing plant. *X* built the plant on land that it had purchased in 1970. The land was not contaminated by hazardous waste when it was purchased by *X*. *X*'s manufacturing operations discharge hazardous waste. In the past *X* buried this waste on portions of its land.

In 1993, in order to comply with presently applicable and reasonably anticipated federal, state, and local environmental requirements ("environmental requirements"), *X* decided to remediate the soil and groundwater that had been contaminated by the hazardous waste, and to establish an appropriate system for the continued monitoring of the groundwater to ensure that the remediation had removed all hazardous waste. Accordingly, *X* began excavating the contaminated soil, transporting it to appropriate waste disposal facilities, and backfilling the excavated areas with uncontaminated soil. These soil remediation activities started in 1993 and will be completed in 1995. *X* also began constructing groundwater treatment facilities which included wells, pipes, pumps, and other equipment to extract, treat, and monitor contaminated groundwater. Construction of these groundwater treatment facilities began in 1993, and the facilities will remain in operation on *X*'s land until the year 2005. During this time, *X* will continue to monitor the groundwater to ensure that the soil remediation and groundwater treatment eliminate the hazardous waste to the extent necessary to bring *X*'s land into compliance with environmental requirements.

The effect of the soil remediation and groundwater treatment will be to restore *X*'s land to essentially the same physical condition that existed prior to the contamination. During and after the remediation and treatment, *X* will continue to use the land and operate the plant in the same manner as it did prior to the cleanup except that X will dispose of any hazardous waste in compliance with environmental requirements.

LAW AND ANALYSIS

Section 162 generally allows a deduction for the ordinary and necessary expenses paid or incurred during the taxable year in carrying on any trade or business. . . .

Section 263 generally prohibits deductions for capital expenditures. . . .

Section 263A provides that the direct costs and indirect costs properly allocable to real or tangible personal property produced by the taxpayer shall be capitalized. Section 263A(g)(1) provides that, for purposes of section 263A, "the term 'produce' includes construct, build, install, manufacture, develop, or improve."

. . . Through provisions such as §§ 162(a), 263(a), and related sections, the Internal Revenue Code generally endeavors to match expenses with the revenues of the taxable period to which the expenses are properly attributable, thereby resulting in a more accurate calculation of net income for tax purposes. See, e.g., INDOPCO, Inc. v. Commissioner, 112 S. Ct. 1039 (1992); Commissioner v. Idaho Power Co., 418 U.S. 1, 16 (1974). Moreover, as the Supreme Court has specifically recognized, the "decisive distinctions [between capital and ordinary expenditures] are those of degree and not of kind," and a careful examination of the particular facts of each case is required. Welch v. Helvering, 290 U.S. [111], at 114 [(1933)]. . . . In determining whether current deduction or capitalization is the appropriate tax treatment for any particular expenditure, it is important to consider the extent to which the expenditure will produce significant future benefits. See INDOPCO, Inc. v. Commissioner, 112 S. Ct. at 1044-45.

The groundwater treatment facilities constructed by X have a useful life substantially beyond the taxable year in which they are constructed and, thus, the costs of their construction are capital expenditures under §§ 263(a) and 1.263(a)-2(a). Moreover, because the construction of these facilities constitutes production within the meaning of § 263A(g)(1), X is required to capitalize under § 263A the direct costs and a proper share of allocable indirect costs of constructing these facilities. The costs of the groundwater treatment facilities are recoverable under applicable law (e.g., § 168).

Under these facts, X's soil remediation expenditures and ongoing groundwater treatment expenditures (i.e., the groundwater treatment expenditures other than the expenditures to construct the groundwater treatment facilities) do not produce permanent improvements to X's land within the scope of § 263(a)(1) or otherwise provide significant future benefits. Under the facts of this ruling, the appropriate test for determining whether the expenditures increase the value of property is to compare the status of the asset after the expenditure with the status of that asset before the condition arose that necessitated the expenditure (i.e., before the land was contaminated by X's hazardous waste). See Plainfield-Union Water Co. v. Commissioner, 39 T.C.

333, 338 (1962), nonacq. on other grounds, 1964-2 C.B. 8. X's soil remediation and ongoing groundwater treatment expenditures do not result in improvements that increase the value of X's property because X has merely restored its soil and groundwater to their approximate condition before they were contaminated by X's manufacturing operations.

No other aspect of § 263 requires capitalization of X's ongoing soil remediation or ongoing groundwater treatment expenditures. These expenditures do not prolong the useful life of the land, nor do they adapt the land to a new or different use. Moreover, since the land is not subject to an allowance for depreciation, amortization, or depletion, the amounts expended to restore the land to its original condition are not subject to capitalization under § 263(a)(2). Accordingly, the expenses incurred by X for the soil remediation and ongoing groundwater treatment do not constitute capital expenditures under § 263.

The soil remediation and ongoing groundwater treatment expenditures incurred by X represent ordinary and necessary business expenses within the scope of § 162. They are appropriate and helpful in carrying on X's business and are commonly and frequently required in X's type of business. Therefore, the costs incurred by X to evaluate and remediate its soil and groundwater contamination (other than the costs of constructing the groundwater treatment facilities) constitute ordinary and necessary business expenses that are deductible under § 162.

NOTES AND QUESTIONS

1. How, if at all, can one reconcile this Ruling's conclusion as to the soil remediation with its conclusion as to the groundwater treatment facilities? Is the difference in result consistent with the *INDOPCO* "future benefits" test? With the *Plainfield-Union* "before and after" test? Should it be relevant that the soil remediation expenditures do not produce a new, separate, tangible asset? Compare the description, infra page 572, of the *Newark Morning Ledger* case.

2. In Private Letter Ruling (PLR) 9240004, the taxpayer was a manufacturer that used equipment insulated with asbestos. In response to state and federal law, it decided to remove the asbestos. It then replaced the asbestos with other insulating material, which was about 10 percent less thermally efficient than the asbestos. The Ruling holds that the removal and replacement costs were capital expenditures. Among other reasons, the Ruling states that the removal and replacement made the taxpayer's equipment more valuable by decreasing the risk of liability, by making the equipment more marketable, and by saving the costs of protecting employees when they maintained the equipment. Can this Ruling be reconciled with Rev. Rul. 94-38 or has PLR 9240004 been overruled?

3. In the situation described in Rev. Rul. 94-38 or in PLR 9240004 could the taxpayer have claimed a loss deduction when it determined that it had a serious contamination problem?

4. Suppose the soil contamination had been caused not by the taxpayer but by the prior owner of the land. Would the cost of soil remediation and ongoing groundwater treatment have been deductible?

5. *Qualified environmental remediation expenditures*. Section 198 allows a taxpayer to deduct an expenditure that otherwise must be capitalized if it is incurred in connection with the abatement or control of hazardous substances at a qualified containment site. Hazardous substances are those described in the Comprehensive Environmental Response, Compensation and Liability Act of 1980, often referred to by its acronym, CERCLA. A qualified containment site is defined most notably as a site within a census tract with a poverty rate of not less than 20 percent. Is it sensible to make deductibility dependent upon the local poverty rate? What might you imagine is the theory behind this provision?

TREATMENT OF ENVIRONMENTAL REMEDIATION EXPENSES UNDER SECTION 263A

Revenue Ruling 2004-18 2004-8 I.R.B. 509

. . .

ISSUE

Are costs incurred to clean up land that a taxpayer contaminated with hazardous waste by the operation of the taxpayer's manufacturing plant includible in inventory costs under § 263A of the Internal Revenue Code?

FACTS

X, a corporation using an accrual method of accounting, owns and operates a manufacturing plant that produces property that is inventory in *X*'s hands. *X*'s manufacturing operations discharge hazardous waste. In the past, *X* buried this waste on portions of *X*'s land. The land was not contaminated by hazardous waste when purchased by *X*.

In order to comply with applicable federal, state, and local environmental requirements, *X* incurs costs (within the meaning of § 461(h)) to remediate the soil and groundwater that had been contaminated by the hazardous waste, and to establish an appropriate system for the continued monitoring of the groundwater to ensure that the remediation removes all hazardous waste. The costs *X* incurs are not research and experimental expenditures within the meaning of § 174 or environmental management policy costs. The soil remediation and groundwater treatment restores *X*'s land to essentially the same physical condition that existed prior to the contamination. During and after the remediation and treatment, *X* continues to use the land and operate the plant in the same manner as *X* did prior to the cleanup except that *X* disposes of any hazardous waste in compliance with environmental requirements.

LAW

Section 263A(a) provides that the direct costs and indirect costs properly allocable to property that is inventory in the hands of the taxpayer shall be included in inventory costs.

Section 1.263A-1(a)(3)(ii) of the Income Tax Regulations provides, in part, that taxpayers that produce tangible personal property must capitalize (1) all direct costs of producing the property, and (2) the property's allocable share of indirect costs.

Section 1.263A-1(e)(3)(i) provides, in part, that indirect costs are properly allocable to property produced when the costs directly benefit or are incurred by reason of the performance of production activities. Cost recovery, production facility repair and maintenance costs, and scrap and spoilage costs, such as waste removal costs, are examples of indirect costs that must be capitalized to the extent the costs are properly allocable to produced property. See § 1.263A-1(e)(3)(ii)(I), (O) and (Q).

Section 1.263A-1(e)(4)(iv)(I) provides that costs incurred for environmental management policy generally are not allocated to production or resale activities (except to the extent that the costs of any system or procedure benefit a particular production or resale activity).

. . .

Rev. Rul. 94-38, 1994-1 C.B. 35, analyzes whether costs incurred to clean up land and to treat groundwater that a taxpayer contaminated with hazardous waste from the taxpayer's manufacturing business are capital expenditures. The ruling holds that the costs to clean up land used in the taxpayer's manufacturing process and to treat groundwater are not capital expenditures because these costs do not prolong the useful life of the land or adapt the land to a new or different use. Therefore, costs incurred to clean up land and to treat groundwater that a taxpayer contaminated with hazardous waste from the taxpayer's business are deductible by the taxpayer as business expenses under § 162. Costs properly allocable to constructing groundwater treatment facilities, however, are capital expenditures under § 263.

Rev. Rul. 98-25, 1998-1 C.B. 998, holds that costs incurred to replace underground storage tanks containing waste by-products under the circumstances in the ruling are not capital expenditures under § 263, but are ordinary and necessary expenses under § 162.

ANALYSIS

The discussion in Rev. Rul. 94-38 of Plainfield-Union Water Co. v. Commissioner, 39 T.C. 333 (1962), nonacq., 1964-2 C.B. 8, demonstrates that the revenue ruling was intended to address whether the costs to clean up the land and to treat the groundwater are capital expenditures that must be capitalized into the basis of the land under § 263(a) or whether the costs are ordinary and necessary repair expenses under § 162. Rev. Rul. 94-38 does not address the treatment of these costs as inventory costs under § 263A. Similarly, Rev. Rul. 98-25 does not address whether amounts incurred to replace underground storage tanks must be included in inventory costs under § 263A.

The holdings of Rev. Rul. 94-38 that the costs to construct a groundwater treatment facility must be capitalized under §§ 263(a) and 263A rather than deducted under § 162 demonstrates the distinction between capital expenditures and costs that are more in the nature of repairs than capital improvements. As with other types of deductible business costs, such as labor costs, taxes, rent, and supplies, once repair costs are determined to be deductible under § 162, a taxpayer with inventories must still apply the rules of § 263A to determine whether the repair costs must be included in inventory. . . . In addition, if repair costs must be capitalized under §§ 263(a) and 263A to a depreciable asset, a taxpayer with inventories must still apply the rules of § 263A to determine whether the depreciation expenses must be included in inventory. . . .

In this situation, *X* incurs environmental remediation costs to clean up land that was contaminated as part of the ordinary business operations of *X*'s manufacturing of inventory. *X*'s environmental remediation costs are incurred by reason of *X*'s production activities within the meaning of § 1.263A-1(e)(3)(i). The costs are properly allocable to property produced by *X* that is inventory in *X*'s hands under § 1.263A-1(e)(3)(i). Accordingly, *X* must capitalize the otherwise deductible environmental remediation costs by including the costs in inventory costs in accordance with § 1.263A-1(c)(3). Similarly, costs incurred to replace underground storage tanks and depreciation cost recoveries of the groundwater treatment facility must be included in inventory costs to the extent properly allocable to inventory.

HOLDING

Environmental remediation costs are subject to capitalization under § 263A. Therefore, costs incurred . . . to clean up land that a taxpayer contaminated with hazardous waste by the operation of the taxpayer's manufacturing plant must be included in inventory costs under § 263A. . . .

QUESTIONS

What are relative functions of §§ 263 and 263A? What is the continuing significance of Revenue Ruling 94-38?

NORWEST CORPORATION AND SUBSIDIARIES v. COMMISSIONER
108 T.C. 265 (1997)

I

Norwest Bank Nebraska, N.A., a subsidiary of petitioner, removed asbestos-containing materials from its Douglas Street building in connection with the building's renovation and remodeling. On its 1989 return, petitioner claimed a $902,206 ordinary and necessary business deduction with respect to the asbestos-removal expenditures. In the notice of deficiency, respondent disallowed the deduction.

Held: The costs of removing the asbestos-containing materials must be capitalized because they were part of a general plan of rehabilitation and renovation that improved the Douglas Street building. . . .

OPINION

JACOBS, Judge: . . .

GENERAL FINDINGS . . .

The . . . issue is whether petitioner is entitled to deduct the costs of removing asbestos-containing materials from its Douglas Street bank building. Petitioner argues that the expenditures constitute 162(a) ordinary and necessary expenses. Respondent, on the other hand, contends that the expenditures must be capitalized pursuant to 263(a)(1). Alternatively, respondent contends that the expenditures must be capitalized pursuant to the "general plan of rehabilitation" doctrine.

A. The Douglas Street Building

One of petitioner's subsidiaries, Norwest Bank Nebraska, N.A. (Norwest Nebraska), owns a building at 1919 Douglas Street in Omaha, Nebraska (the Douglas Street building or building). The Douglas Street building is a three-story commercial office building that occupies half a square block and has a lower level parking garage. Norwest Nebraska constructed the building in 1969 at a $4,883,232 cost. During all relevant periods, Norwest Nebraska used the Douglas Street building as an operations center as well as a branch for serving customers.

B. Remodeling Plans

In 1985 and 1986, Norwest Nebraska consolidated its "back room" operations at the Douglas Street building. Pursuant to that process, Norwest Nebraska undertook to determine the most efficient means for providing more space to accommodate the additional operations personnel within the building. The planning process indicated that the building needed a major remodeling. (The building had not been remodeled since its construction; Norwest Nebraska usually remodels its banks every 10 to 15 years.) Thus, by the end of 1986, petitioner and Norwest Nebraska had decided to completely remodel the Douglas Street building. In December 1986, both petitioner and Norwest Nebraska approved a preliminary budget of $2,738,000 for carpet, furniture, and improvements.

C. Use of Asbestos-Containing Materials in the Douglas Street Building

The Douglas Street building was constructed with asbestos-containing materials as its main fire-retardant material. (The local fire code required that buildings contain fire-proofing material.) Asbestos-containing materials were sprayed on all columns, steel I-beams, and decking between floors. The health dangers of asbestos were not widely known when the Douglas Street building was constructed in 1969, and asbestos-containing materials were generally used in building construction in Omaha, Nebraska.

A commercial office building's ventilation system removes existing air from a room through a return air plenum as new air is introduced. The returned air is subsequently recycled through the building. The area between the decking and the suspended ceiling in the Douglas Street building functioned as the return air plenum. The top part of the return air plenum, the decking, was one of the components of the building where asbestos-containing materials had been sprayed during construction.

Over time, the decking, suspended ceiling tiles, and light fixtures throughout the building became contaminated. This contamination occurred because the asbestos-containing fireproofing had begun to delaminate, and pieces of this material reached the top of the suspended ceiling.

D. Federal Asbestos Guidelines

In the 1970's and 1980's, research confirmed that asbestos-containing materials can release fibers that cause serious diseases when inhaled or swallowed. Diseases resulting from exposure to asbestos can reach the incurable stage before detection and can cause severe disability or death. Asbestosis is a progressive and disabling lung disease caused by inhaling asbestos fibers that become lodged in the lungs. Persons exposed to asbestos may develop lung cancer or mesothelioma, an extremely rare form of cancer.

On March 29, 1971, the Environmental Protection Agency (EPA) designated asbestos a hazardous substance. The parties have stipulated that Federal, State, and local laws and regulations at all relevant times did not require asbestos-containing materials to be removed from commercial office buildings if they could be controlled in place. Nevertheless, building owners had to take precautions against the release of asbestos fibers.

The presence of asbestos in a building does not necessarily endanger the health of building occupants. The danger arises when asbestos-containing materials are damaged or disturbed, thereby releasing asbestos fibers into the air (when they can be inhaled). . . .

Asbestos removal must be performed by specially trained professionals wearing protective clothing and respirators. The work area must be properly contained to prevent release of fibers into other areas. Containment typically requires barriers of polyethylene plastic sheets with folded seams, complete with air locks and negative air pressure systems. Asbestos-containing materials that are removed must be wetted to reduce fiber release. Once removed, the materials must be disposed of in leak-tight containers in special landfills.

E. Testing at the Douglas Street Building and Decision to Remove Asbestos-Containing Materials

In October 1985, petitioner's general liability and property damage insurer, the St. Paul Property and Liability Insurance Co. (St. Paul), tested a bulk sample of fire-retardant material from the Douglas Street building's steel I-beams to determine whether the building contained asbestos. The results indicated that the material contained 8 to 10 percent chrysotile asbestos, the most common type of asbestos.

. . . [Further tests revealed] that the airborne asbestos fiber concentrations present during normal occupancy of the Douglas Street building . . . did not exceed either the EPA or OSHA guidelines. There was, however, the expectation that the airborne asbestos-fiber concentrations would continue to increase. Moreover, the asbestos-containing fire-proofing at the Douglas Street Building had characteristics that the EPA had identified as warranting removal of the material, such as evidence of delamination, presence of debris, proximity to an air plenum, and necessity of access for maintenance.

After considering the circumstances, petitioner decided to remove the asbestos-containing materials from the Douglas Street building (other than the parking garage) in coordination with the overall remodeling project. Indeed, the remodeling could not have been undertaken without disturbing the asbestos-containing fireproofing. Thus, because petitioner and Norwest Nebraska chose to remodel, it became a matter of necessity to remove the asbestos-containing materials. Petitioner essentially decided that "managing the asbestos in place" was not a viable option, given the extent of remodeling that would disturb the asbestos.

Removing the asbestos-containing materials from the Douglas Street building at the same time as, and in connection with, the remodeling was more cost efficient than conducting the removal and renovations as two separate projects at different times. It also minimized the amount of inconvenience to building employees and customers.

As late as May 1988 (approximately 6 months after asbestos removal began) petitioner and Norwest Nebraska did not intend to remove the parking garage asbestos-containing materials. No remodeling was planned for the garage, and the materials were in sound condition. However, petitioner and Norwest Nebraska subsequently decided to remove the garage asbestos-containing materials as well, on the basis of their expectation that the garage tiles would eventually deteriorate, as well as the fact that it was financially advantageous to conduct this removal in connection with the ongoing abatement activity.

F.   Contractors and Work Performed

. . .

The asbestos removal and remodeling were basically performed in 13 phases; each phase involved a defined area of the Douglas Street building. For each phase, the asbestos-removal contractor removed the asbestos-containing materials before the general contractor began remodeling. . . .

Removing all the asbestos-containing materials from the Douglas Street building was a large project, entailing an enormous amount of work. . . .

The removal of the asbestos-containing materials from the Douglas Street building was substantially completed by the end of May 1989. . . .

The removal of the asbestos-containing materials from the Douglas Street building did not extend the building's useful life.

G.   Health Concerns

In addition to removing the asbestos-containing materials on account of the remodeling, petitioner also considered the health and welfare of its employees and customers. Even though the level of airborne asbestos fiber concentrations in the Douglas Street building did not exceed OSHA or EPA standards for exposure, the presence of asbestos-containing materials in the return air plenum nonetheless increased the possibility for release of asbestos fibers into the air. . . .

Petitioner intended to create a safer and healthier environment for the building employees by removing the asbestos-containing materials. The building indeed became safer after the asbestos-containing materials were removed.

H. Liability Issues

By removing the asbestos-containing materials from the Douglas Street building, petitioner also intended to avoid or minimize its potential liability for damages from injuries to employees, customers, and workers resulting from asbestos exposure. Petitioner's general liability insurance policies in effect at all relevant times contained an exclusion for damages attributable to the discharge of pollutants. . . .

Furthermore, by removing the asbestos-containing materials from the building, petitioner intended to avoid or minimize a potential increase in its premiums for workmen's [sic] compensation insurance. . . .

I. Tax and Accounting Matters

The total cost of renovating the Douglas Street building was close to $7 million, comprising nearly $4,998,749 in remodeling costs and approximately $1.9 million in asbestos removal costs. Petitioner considered the cost of all demolition done by the asbestos removal contractors (including the cost of removing the asbestos tiles) as a removal cost for both book and tax purposes. Petitioner considered the cost of any demolition done by the general contractor or one of the subcontractors a remodeling cost for both book and tax purposes.

All construction-related remodeling costs were added to the basis of the building and depreciated on a straight-line basis over 31.5 years. The portion of the remodeling costs for furniture and fixtures was written off over 7 years. . . .

DISCUSSION

At issue is whether petitioner's costs of removing the asbestos-containing materials are currently deductible pursuant to § 162 or must be capitalized pursuant to § 263 or as part of a general plan of rehabilitation.

L. Capital Expenditures vs. Current Deductions

Section 263 requires taxpayers to capitalize costs incurred for permanent improvements, betterments, or restorations to property. In general, these costs include expenditures that add to the value or substantially prolong the life of the property or adapt such property to a new or different use. Regs. § 1.263(a)-l(b). In contrast, § 162 permits taxpayers to currently deduct the costs of ordinary and necessary expenses (including incidental repairs) that neither materially add to the value of property nor appreciably prolong its life but keep the property in an ordinarily efficient operating condition. See Regs. § 1.162-4. . . .

The Court in Plainfield-Union Water Co. v. Commissioner, 39 T.C. 333, 338, (1962), articulated a test for determining whether an expenditure is capital by comparing the value, use, life expectancy, strength, or capacity of the property after the expenditure with the status of the property before the condition necessitating the expenditure arose (the *Plainfield-Union* test). Moreover, the Internal Revenue Code's capitalization provision envisions an inquiry into the duration and extent of the benefits realized by the taxpayer. See INDOPCO, Inc. v. Commissioner, 503 U.S. 79, 88 (1922).

Whether an expense is deductible or must be capitalized is a factual determination. . . . Courts have adopted a practical case-by-case approach in applying the principles of capitalization and deductibility. . . .

M. General Plan of Rehabilitation Doctrine

Expenses incurred as part of a plan of rehabilitation or improvement must be capitalized even though the same expenses if incurred separately would be deductible as ordinary and necessary. . . . Unanticipated expenses that would be deductible as business expenses if incurred in isolation must be capitalized when incurred pursuant to a plan of rehabilitation. . . .

An asset need not be completely out of service or in total disrepair for the general plan of rehabilitation doctrine to apply. For example, in Bank of Houston v. Commissioner, T.C. Memo. 1960-110, the taxpayer's 50-year-old building was in "a general state of disrepair" but still serviceable for the purposes used (before, during, and after the work) and was in good structural condition. The taxpayer hired a contractor to perform the renovation (which included nonstructural repairs to flooring, electrical wiring, plaster, window frames, patched brick, and paint, as well as plumbing repairs, demolition, and cleanup). Temporary barriers and closures were erected during work in progress. The Court recognized that each phase of the remodeling project, removed in time and context, might be considered a repair item, but stated that "The Code, however, does not envision the fragmentation of an overall project for deduction or capitalization purposes." The Court held that the expenditures were not made for incidental repairs but were part of an overall plan of rehabilitation, restoration, and improvement of the building.

N. The Parties' Arguments

. . .

The parties . . . disagree as to whether the *Plainfield-Union* test is appropriate for determining whether petitioner's asbestos removal expenditures are capital. Petitioner contends that it is the appropriate test because the condition necessitating the asbestos removal was the discovery that asbestos is hazardous to human health. Accordingly, until the danger was discovered, petitioner argues that the physical presence of the asbestos had no effect on the building's value. Only after the danger was perceived could the contamination affect the building's operations and reduce its value.

Petitioner points to Rev. Rul. 94-38, 1994-1 C.B. 35, which cites *Plainfield-Union* in addressing the proper treatment of costs to remediate soil and treat groundwater that a taxpayer had contaminated with hazardous waste from its business. The ruling treats such costs (other than those attributable to the construction of ground-water treatment facilities) as currently deductible.

Respondent, on the other hand, argues that the discovery that asbestos is hazardous and that the Douglas Street building contained that substance is not a relevant or satisfactory reference point. Respondent contends that the *Plainfield-Union* test does not apply herein because a comparison cannot be made between the status of the building before it contained asbestos and after the asbestos was removed; since construction, the building has always contained asbestos. In cases where the *Plainfield-Union* test has been applied . . . , respondent continues, the condition necessitating the repair resulted from a physical change in the property's condition. In this case, no change occurred to the building's physical condition that necessitated the removal expenditures. The only change was in petitioner's awareness of the dangers of asbestos. Accordingly, respondent argues that the *Plainfield-Union* test is inapplicable, and the Court must examine other factors to determine whether an increase in the building's value occurred.

Respondent also disagrees with petitioner's reliance on Rev. Rul. 94-38, supra, arguing that the present facts are distinguishable. The remediated property addressed in the ruling was not contaminated by hazardous waste when the taxpayer acquired it. The ruling permits a deduction only for the costs of remediating soil and water whose physical condition has changed during the taxpayer's ownership of the property. Under this analysis, the taxpayer is viewed as restoring the property to the condition existing before its contamination. Thus, respondent contends, unlike Rev. Rul. 94-38, petitioner's expenditures did not return the property to the same state that existed when the property was constructed because there was never a time when the building was asbestos free. Rather, the asbestos-abatement costs improved the property beyond its original, unsafe condition.

O. Analysis

We believe that petitioner decided to remove the asbestos-containing materials from the Douglas Street building beginning in 1987 primarily because their removal was essential before the remodeling work could begin. The extent of the asbestos-containing materials in the building or the concentration of airborne asbestos fibers was not discovered until after petitioner decided to remodel the building and a budget for the remodeling had been approved. Because petitioner's extensive remodeling work would, of necessity, disturb the asbestos fireproofing, petitioner had no practical alternative but to remove the fireproofing. Performing the asbestos removal in connection with the remodeling was more cost effective than performing the same work as two separate projects at different times. (Had petitioner remodeled without removing the asbestos first, the remodeling would have been damaged by subsequent asbestos removal, thereby creating additional costs to petitioner.) We believe that petitioner's separation of the removal and remodeling work is artificial and does not properly reflect the record before us. The parties have stipulated that the asbestos removal did not increase the useful life of the Douglas Street building. We recognize (as did petitioner) that removal of the asbestos did increase the value of the building compared to its value when it was known to contain a hazard. However, we do not find, as respondent advocates, that the expenditures for asbestos removal materially increased the value of the building so as to require them to be capitalized. We find, however, that had there been no remodeling, the asbestos would have remained in place and would not have been removed until a later date. In other words, but for the remodeling, the asbestos removal would not have occurred.

The asbestos removal and remodeling were part of one intertwined project, entailing a full-blown general plan of rehabilitation, linked by logistical and economic concerns. . . . Clearly, the purpose of removing the asbestos-containing materials was first and foremost to effectuate the remodeling and renovation of the building. Secondarily, petitioner intended to eliminate health risks posed by the presence of asbestos and to minimize the potential liability for damages arising from injuries to employees and customers.

In sum, based on our analysis of all the facts and circumstances, we hold that the costs of removing the asbestos-containing materials must be capitalized because they were part of a general plan of rehabilitation and renovation that improved the Douglas Street building.

QUESTIONS

1. If the taxpayer had removed the asbestos without doing any remodeling, would it have been entitled to a current deduction for the cost of the removal?

2. Assume that the answer to the first question is yes and that the taxpayer first decides to remodel and then becomes aware of the asbestos problem. It then receives bids for the asbestos removal and the remodel as a combined project and determines that the best price is $1.9 million for the asbestos removal and $5 million for the remodel. After consulting with a tax lawyer it then obtains new bids for each project separately, which would require restoring damage done by the asbestos removal and removing this restoration after the completion of the asbestos project. On this separate-project basis the best price for the asbestos removal is $2.2 million and for the remodel is $5.1 million. Suppose you are the official of the taxpayer corporation who must decide which approach to take and obtain approval from the corporation's board of directors. Which approach will you recommend, and how will you explain your decision? What if the corporation is a nontaxable entity? What do your answers to these two questions tell you about how the tax rule applied by the court in the *Norwest* case affects economic behavior?

3. Suppose that the taxpayer had not had any asbestos problem in its own building but discovered that airborne asbestos was being carried into its building from an abandoned mine nearby. If it installs an air filtration system to protect its employees, is it entitled to a current deduction for the capital cost and the yearly operating cost?

C.   INVENTORY ACCOUNTING

If a taxpayer buys machinery that will produce income over several years, its costs must be capitalized and depreciated over such period. If a taxpayer buys pencils, stationery, and other supplies, they are usually currently deductible even if some may last beyond the present tax year. But what of goods that the taxpayer will sell to the public? What if the owner of a clothing store buys dresses, suits, and other goods during the year, sells some, and has some on hand at the end of the year? Or what if a manufacturer of clothing buys cloth, thread, and other materials, some of which is on hand at the end of the year in its original form and some of which has been embodied in finished product that has not yet been shipped out? Inventory accounting methods are used to match costs with revenues in such cases.

The use of authorized methods of inventory accounting is required in every situation where the production, purchase, or sale of merchandise is an income-producing factor (except in farming). This means, for example, that a retailer does not simply deduct the cost of the goods and materials purchased during the year. Instead, the purchases are added to "inventory" and their cost is treated as if it were a capital expenditure; the ultimate disposition of the goods and materials, as reflected in changes in the quantity of physical goods in the inventory after taking account of additions to it during the year, is treated as the event giving rise to a deduction for that cost. See Regs. § 1.471.

The inventory account includes all finished or partly finished goods and those raw materials and supplies acquired for sale or that will become part of merchandise intended for sale. Regs. § 1.471-1. Merchandise is included in inventory if title to it is vested in the taxpayer, even though the merchandise may be in transit or otherwise may not be in the physical possession of the taxpayer. The accrual method of accounting is required with regard to purchases and sales whenever the use of an inventory is necessary. Regs. § 1.446-1(c)(2).

Cost of goods sold. Gross profit from a business operation is found by deducting the cost of goods sold from gross receipts. The cost of goods sold is found by adding the beginning inventory to the cost of goods purchased or produced during the year and subtracting the total inventory still on hand at the end of the year. (See Table 6-1.)

Valuation of inventories. It is necessary to both identify and value the particular goods in inventory so that proper costs can be applied. Regs. § 1.471-2(b) states that in the valuation of inventories greater weight is to be given to consistency in practice than to any particular method of inventorying. The two common bases of valuing inventories are (1) cost (Regs. § 1.471-3) and (2) cost or market, whichever is lower (Regs. § 1-471-4).

When inventory is valued at cost, for merchandise on hand at the beginning of the year, cost is the amount at which it was included in the closing inventory

TABLE 6-1
Illustration of Cost of Goods Sold

Beginning inventory	$ 40,000
Purchases during year	200,000
Total	240,000
Less ending inventory	60,000
Cost of goods sold	$180,000

of the preceding taxable year. For merchandise purchased after the beginning of the year, cost is invoice price plus transportation and other acquisition charges less certain trade discounts. For merchandise produced during the year, cost is the total of direct costs (e.g., raw materials, labor, and supplies) and indirect production costs (e.g., depreciation computed under the full absorption method of Regs. § 1.471-11).

Any change in valuation method is a change of accounting requiring consent from the Commissioner.

Inventory cost. Inventory accounting requires that the taxpayer determine the cost of items in inventory. Often there will be many identical items in inventory, such items will have been purchased in more than one year, the cost of the items will have changed over time, and it may be impractical to determine when items now on hand were acquired. In that situation, in order to arrive at a cost figure for the items currently on hand, some assumption must be made about how items move into and out of inventory. The general rule is that a first-in-first-out (FIFO) assumption, or method, should be used. However, last-in-first-out (LIFO) may be used if the taxpayer so elects under § 472.

FIFO assumes that goods first acquired are sold first and therefore the goods in the closing inventory are those most recently purchased. Either method of valuing inventory — *cost* or *cost or market, whichever is lower* — may be used with FIFO. The use of cost with FIFO often presents a profit or loss picture closest to the actual results of the physical flow of goods through a business. In a rising market there is usually no difference between cost and cost or market, whichever is lower, since market will rarely be lower than cost. But in a falling market, the lower of cost or market tends to reduce income; the value of the closing inventory is reduced to market, creating a higher cost of goods sold, resulting in lower gross income. So cost or market, whichever is lower, anticipates losses in a falling market but not additional profits in a rising market.

Under LIFO, since items purchased last are considered sold first, closing inventory is valued as if composed of the earliest purchases. Under LIFO, inventories must be valued at cost. The Treasury has consistently opposed efforts to permit LIFO in conjunction with the lower of cost or market. Overall, the LIFO method tends to have a stabilizing effect on the measurement and reporting of income during periods of fluctuating prices, since current receipts tend to be matched with current costs. Since LIFO results in lower reported profits in a rising market, it generally produces the best tax results for taxpayers during periods of rising prices; tax liability is deferred on inventory gains as long as the firm maintains the inventory. In a period of declining prices, by the same token, LIFO would not be advantageous since losses inherent in earlier high-cost inventory are not realized.

Section 472(c) contains a requirement that LIFO must be used for reports to investors and for credit purposes if it is used for tax purposes.[5] Because LIFO reduces taxes in periods of rising prices, and because prices have risen persistently in recent decades, one might expect that almost all businesses

---

5. This is in contrast to accounting for depreciation, where a taxpayer may (and most do) claim a higher deduction for tax purposes than for purposes of reporting to shareholders.

would use LIFO. Bear in mind that choice of an accounting method does not in any way change underlying economic realities. Economic profit is the same regardless of what method of accounting is used. But managers of businesses generally are anxious to issue reports that show the highest possible profit. This may explain why many businesses still use FIFO despite the fact that their decision to do so results in their paying higher taxes than they would pay under LIFO. Is the conformity requirement of § 472(c) desirable? If so, should it be extended to ACRS deductions?

PROBLEMS

1. In December 2001, Products Inc. begins business and buys 100,000 widgets for $200,000. It has no sales in 2001. In January 2002, Products Inc. buys another 100,000 widgets for $300,000. In June 2002, Products Inc. sells 100,000 widgets for $350,000. Assume that there are no costs allocable to the widget inventory under § 263A. (a) Assume Products Inc. uses the LIFO method of inventory valuation. What is the cost of the goods sold and the gross profit on the June 2002 sale? (b) What is the answer to the same question if Products Inc. uses FIFO instead of LIFO?

2. In March 2001, Products Inc. begins business and buys 40,000 widgets for $120,000. In May 2001, Products Inc. sells 20,000 widgets for $80,000. Developments in the second half of 2001 cause the value of the widgets to fall. At the close of the year, the 20,000 widgets left in inventory have a value of $20,000. Assume that Products Inc. is able to value closing inventory at the lower of cost or market. Determine the company's 2001 cost of goods sold deduction and gross profit on widget sales.

D. RENT PAYMENT VERSUS INSTALLMENT PURCHASE

STARR'S ESTATE v. COMMISSIONER

274 F.2d 294 (9th Cir. 1959)

CHAMBERS, Circuit Judge.

Yesterday's equities in personal property seem to have become today's leases. This has been generated not a little by the circumstance that one who leases as a lessee usually has less trouble with the federal tax collector. At least taxpayers think so.

But the lease still can go too far and get one into tax trouble. While according to state law the instrument will probably be taken (with the consequent legal incidents) by the name the parties give it, the [IRS] is not always bound and can often recast it according to what the service may consider the practical realities.[6] . . . The principal case concerns a fire sprinkler system

---

6. Thus, it shifts rental payments of a business (fully deductible) to a capital purchase for the business. If the nature of the property is wasting, then depreciation may be taken, but usually not all in one year.

installed at the taxpayer's plant.... The "lessor" was "Automatic" Sprinklers of the Pacific, Inc.... The instrument entitled "Lease Form of Contract" (hereafter "contract") is just about perfectly couched in terms of a lease for five years with annual rentals of $1,240. But it is the last paragraph thereof, providing for nominal rental for five years, that has caused the trouble. It reads as follows:

> 28. At the termination of the period of this lease, if Lessee has faithfully performed all of the terms and conditions required of it under this lease, it shall have the privilege of renewing this lease for an additional period of five years at a rental of $32.00 per year. If Lessee does not elect to renew this lease, then the Lessor is hereby granted the period of six months in which to remove the system from the premises of the Lessee.

Obviously, one renewal for a period of five years is provided at $32.00 per year, if Starr so desired. Note, though, that the [contract] is silent as to [the] status of the system beginning with the eleventh year....

The tax court sustained the [Commissioner], holding that the five payments of $1,240, or the total of $6,200, were capital expenditures and not pure deductible rental. Depreciation of $269.60 was allowed for each year. Generally, we agree....

The law in this field for this circuit is established in Oesterreich v. Commissioner, [226 F.2d 798].... There we held that for tax purposes form can be disregarded for substance and, where the foreordained practical effect of the rent is to produce title eventually, the rental agreement can be treated as a sale.

In this, Starr's case, we do have the troublesome circumstance that the contract does not by its terms ever pass title to the system to the lessee. Most sprinkler systems have to be tailor-made for a specific piece of property and, if removal is required, the salvageable value is negligible. Also, it stretches credulity to believe that the "lessor" ever intended to or would "come after" the system. And the "lessee" would be an exceedingly careless businessman who would enter into such contract with the practical possibility that the "lessor" would reclaim the installation. He could have believed only that he was getting the system for the rental money. And we think the commissioner was entitled to take into consideration the practical effect rather than the legal, especially when there was a record that on other such installations the "lessor," after the term of the lease was over, had not reclaimed from those who had met their agreed payments. It is obvious that the nominal rental payments after five years, of $32.00 per year, were just a service charge for inspection.

Recently the Court of Appeals for the Eighth Circuit had decided Western Contracting Corporation v. Commissioner, 1959, 271 F.2d 694, reversing the tax court in its determination that the commissioner could convert leases of contractor's equipment into installment purchases of heavy equipment....

There are a number of facts there which make a difference. For example, in the contracts of Western there is no evidence that the payments on the substituted basis of rent would produce for the "lessor" the equivalent of his normal sales price plus interest. There was no right to acquire for a nominal amount at the end of the term as in *Oesterreich* and the value to the "lessor" in the personalty had not been exhausted as in Starr's case. And there was no basis for inferring that Western would just keep the equipment for what it had paid. It appears that Western paid substantial amounts to acquire the equipment at the end of the term. There was just one compelling circumstance against Western in its case: What it had paid as "rent" was apparently always taken into full account in computing the end purchase price. But on the other hand, there was almost a certainty that the "lessor" would come after his property if the purchase was not eventually made for a substantial amount. This was not even much of a possibility in *Oesterreich* and not a probability in Starr's case.

In Wilshire Holding Corporation v. Commissioner, 9 Cir., 262 F.2d 51, we referred the case back to the tax court to consider interest as a deductible item for the lessee. We think it is clearly called for here. Two yardsticks are present. The first is found in that the normal selling price of the system was $4960 while the total rental payments for five years were $6200. The difference could be regarded as interest for the five years on an amortized basis. The second measure is in clause 16 (loss by fire) where the figure of six percent per annum discount is used. An allowance might be made on either basis, division of the difference (for the five years) between "rental payments" and "normal purchase price" of $1240, or six percent per annum on the normal purchase price of $4960, converting the annual payments into amortization. We do not believe that the "lessee" should suffer the pains of a loss for what really was paid for the use of another's money, even though for tax purposes his lease collapses.

We do not criticize the commissioner. It is his duty to collect the revenue and it is a tough one. If he resolves all questions in favor of the taxpayers, we soon would have little revenue. However, we do suggest that after he has made allowance for depreciation, which he concedes, and an allowance for interest, the attack on many of the "leases" may not be worthwhile in terms of revenue.

Decision reversed for proceedings consistent herewith.

NOTES AND QUESTIONS

1. *Advance rent.* Suppose a taxpayer becomes a tenant in property, used for business, under a lease with a ten-year term and a single rental payment of $7,000 at the beginning of the term. As we have seen (see discussion of *Boylston Market*, supra page 518), the advance payment cannot be deducted in the year of payment. The taxpayer would be required to take deductions in the form of amortization at the rate of $700 per year over the ten-year term. What does this suggest as to an alternative approach to *Starr's Estate*?

2. *Distinguishing leases from installment purchases.* What are the critical elements supporting the conclusion that a transaction such as the one in *Starr's Estate* is an installment purchase rather than a true lease? The taxpayer's objective in the case was to bunch deductions as much as possible in the early

years of the use of the asset.[7] How would you advise a taxpayer in similar circumstances to structure a transaction so as to be successful in this objective (bearing in mind that what the seller has in mind is pinning down a sale)?

3. *Changing times.* At the time this case arose, depreciation deductions were at a rate substantially lower than what is now available under ACRS. At present, because of ACRS, the kind of transaction at issue in *Starr's Estate* would offer little, if any, advantage over ownership. These days, it may be advantageous for the seller (or some other person or entity) to purport to retain (or acquire) ownership in order to take advantage of ACRS deductions, which, for any of a variety of reasons, may not be of benefit to the user of the property. At the same time, however, the user might want the ordinary economic incidents of ownership. This state of affairs has led to complex transactions in which the user purported to lease property from the seller (or some third person) and to correspondingly complex judicial, administrative, and statutory developments, which are explored later in this chapter (infra pages 608-610).

4. *The interest element.* At the end of the opinion in *Starr's Estate*, the court points out that if the transaction is treated as an installment purchase, the taxpayer is entitled to an interest deduction, as well as depreciation. The normal selling price of the system, says the court, is $4,960. The actual payments are $1,240 per year for five years. The implicit interest rate turns out to be 7.93 percent (assuming the first payment is at the end of the first year). That means that the interest for the first year, on the $4,960, would be $393. The allowable depreciation deduction, according to the court, was $269. Thus, the total deductions should be $662. The total dollar amounts are not large, but $662 is only 53 percent of the $1,240 claimed by the taxpayer. For a tax planner, that is a dramatic difference.

5. *Substance versus form. Starr's Estate* presents one of many situations in which, in an effort to achieve tax benefits, a transaction's substance (here, an installment sale) is different from the form in which it has been cast (a lease). Why is it that here the court insists on treating the transaction for tax purposes according to its substance?

PROBLEM

Suppose Seller owns farmland with a basis of $100,000 and a fair market value of $1,000,000. Buyer is willing to pay $1,000,000, with an immediate cash payment of $300,000 and a promissory note (secured by a mortgage on the property) for the remaining $700,000, with interest at 10 percent (the prevailing market rate), payable one year after closing. (Thus, the total payable at the end of the year would be $770,000.) Just before Buyer and Seller

---

7. In order to accomplish this objective, the taxpayer was required to pay out the cash in the year in which the deduction was sought and thereby to forgo the interest that could have been earned on part of the cash if a slower rate of payment had been called for; but presumably the value of the payments of cash (i.e., of the forgone interest) was reflected in the total amount of payments called for under the contract.

are about to sign a contract of purchase and sale, Buyer's sister-in-law, Lois (an accountant who fancies herself an expert in finding loopholes in the tax law) suggests to Buyer that the promissory note be in the principal amount of $600,000, with interest of $170,000. Lois points out that Buyer will benefit by accelerating or increasing her deductions.

(a) Is Lois right?

(b) Suppose that Lois was able to convince Buyer that her plan would work and that the transaction was in fact structured as she suggested. A year has now passed, the promissory note has been paid in full, and Buyer asks you for your legal opinion on whether she can deduct the full $170,000 of "interest" that she has paid. What is your response? What if the interest element had been $270,000? $90,000?

E. "ORDINARY AND NECESSARY"

In reading the language of § 162, one is immediately struck by the use of the words "ordinary and necessary." What is meant by these words? Is the limitation designed to prevent deductions for unusual or needless expenses? Or do these words serve some other function? The following two cases touch on these questions.

1. Payments for "Goodwill" and Other Assets

WELCH v. HELVERING
290 U.S. 111 (1933)

Mr. Justice CARDOZO delivered the opinion of the Court.

The question to be determined is whether payments by a taxpayer, who is in business as a commission agent, are allowable deductions in the computation of his income if made to the creditors of a bankrupt corporation in an endeavor to strengthen his own standing and credit.

In 1922, petitioner was the secretary of the E. L. Welch Company, a Minnesota corporation, engaged in the grain business. The company was adjudged an involuntary bankrupt, and had a discharge from its debts. Thereafter, the petitioner made a contract with the Kellogg Company to purchase grain for it on a commission. In order to reestablish his relations with customers whom he had known when acting for the Welch Company and to solidify his credit and standing, he decided to pay the debts of the Welch business so far as he was able. In fulfillment of that resolve, he made payments of substantial amounts during five successive years. In 1924, the commissions were $18,000,[8] the payments $4000; in 1925, the commissions $31,000, the payments $12,000; in 1926, the commissions $21,000, the payments $13,000;

---

8. [Amounts have been rounded. — EDS.]

in 1927, the commissions $22,000, the payments $7,000; and in 1928, the commissions $26,000, the payments $11,000. The Commissioner ruled that these payments were not deductible from income as ordinary and necessary expenses, but were rather in the nature of capital expenditures, an outlay for the development of reputation and goodwill. . . . [The Tax Court and Eighth Circuit sustained the Commissioner.]

We may assume that the payments to creditors of the Welch Company were necessary for the development of the petitioner's business, at least in the sense that they were appropriate and helpful. . . . He certainly thought they were, and we should be slow to override his judgment. But the problem is not solved when the payments are characterized as necessary. Many necessary payments are charges upon capital. There is need to determine whether they are both necessary and ordinary. Now, what is ordinary, though there must always be a strain of constancy within it, is none the less a variable affected by time and place and circumstance. Ordinary in this context does not mean the payments must be habitual or normal in the sense that the same taxpayer will have to make them often. A lawsuit affecting the safety of a business may happen once in a lifetime. The counsel fees may be so heavy that repetition is unlikely. None the less, the expense is an ordinary one because we know from experience that payments for such a purpose, whether the amount is large or small, are the common and accepted means of defense against attack. . . . The situation is unique in the life of the individual affected, but not in the life of the group, the community, of which he is a part. At such times there are norms of conduct that help to stabilize our judgment, and make it certain and objective. The instance is not erratic, but is brought within a known type.

The line of demarcation is now visible between the case that is here and the one supposed for illustration. We try to classify this act as ordinary or the opposite, and the norms of conduct fail us. No longer can we have recourse to any fund of business experience, to any known business practice. Men do at times pay the debts of others without legal obligation or the lighter obligation imposed by the usages of trade or by neighborly amenities, but they do not do so ordinarily, not even though the result might be to heighten their reputation for generosity and opulence. Indeed, if language is to be read in its natural and common meaning . . . we should have to say that payment in such circumstances, instead of being ordinary, is in a high degree extraordinary. There is nothing ordinary in the stimulus evoking it, and none in the response. Here, indeed, as so often in other branches of the law, the decisive distinctions are those of degree and not of kind. One struggles in vain for any verbal formula that will supply a ready touchstone. The standard set up by the statute is not a rule of law; it is rather a way of life. Life in all its fullness must supply the answer to the riddle.

The Commissioner of Internal Revenue resorted to that standard . . . and found that the payments in controversy came closer to capital outlays than to ordinary and necessary expenses in the operation of a business. His ruling has the support of a presumption of correctness, and the petitioner has the burden of proving it to be wrong. . . . Unless we can say from facts within our knowledge that these are ordinary and necessary expenses according to the ways of conduct and the forms of speech prevailing in the business world, the tax must be confirmed. But nothing told us by this record or within the sphere of our judicial notice permits us to give that extension to what is ordinary and necessary. Indeed, to do so would open the door to many bizarre analogies. One man has a family name that is clouded by thefts committed by an ancestor. To add to his own standing he repays the stolen money, wiping off, it may be, his income for the year. The payments figure in his tax return as ordinary expenses. Another man conceives the notion that he will be able to practice his vocation with greater ease and profit if he has an opportunity to enrich his culture. Forthwith the price of his education becomes an expense of the business, reducing the income subject to taxation. There is little difference between these expenses and those in controversy here. Reputation and learning are akin to capital assets, like the good will of an old partnership. . . . For many, they are the only tools with which to hew a pathway to success. The money spent in acquiring them is well and wisely spent. It is not an ordinary expense of the operation of a business.

Many cases in the federal courts deal with phases of the problem presented in the case at bar. To attempt to harmonize them would be a futile task. They involve the appreciation of particular situations, at times with border-line conclusions. . . .

The decree should be affirmed.

NOTES AND QUESTIONS

1. *Analysis. Welch* is a famous and often-cited decision. This reflects its showy, relentless phrasemaking and the fame of its author rather than its capacity to aid in the analysis of subsequent fact patterns, which (to put it as kindly as possible) is extremely limited. Pompous and needlessly Delphic, it has generated considerable confusion. The issue presented by the Commissioner was simply whether the payments were capital expenditures or current expenses. This being so, what is the relevance, if any, of "uniqueness" (of litigation expenses) or of payments to establish "reputation for generosity and opulence," to "protect a family name," or to "enrich [one's] culture"? Does Justice Cardozo confuse the distinction between capital and current with the distinction between personal and business?[9] Is it clear that "one struggles in vain for any verbal formula that will apply a ready touchstone"? See the opinion in the *Encyclopaedia Britannica* case, supra page 512. If your authorities were limited to the principal cases in this chapter, on which one would you place your principal reliance if you were representing Mr. Welch? What facts would you emphasize?

2. *Other debt-repayment cases.* In Dunn & McCarthy v. Commissioner, 139 F.2d 242 (2d Cir. 1943), a corporation was permitted to deduct amounts it

9. In Commissioner v. Tellier, 383 U.S. 687, 689-690 (1966) (see infra page 559), the Court said,

The principal function of the term ordinary in § 162(a) is to clarify the distinction, often difficult, between those expenses that are currently deductible and those that are in the nature of capital expenditures, which, if deductible at all, must be amortized over the useful life of the asset. Welch v. Helvering. . . .

paid to certain employees who had lent funds to its former president; he had lost the money gambling at the race track and had died insolvent. The court did not think the payments were "extraordinary": "It was the kind of outlay which we believe many corporations would make, and have made, under similar circumstances." The *Welch* case was distinguished: "Welch made a capital outlay to acquire goodwill for a new business. In the present case the payment was an outlay to retain an existing goodwill, that is, to prevent loss of earnings that might result from destroying such goodwill by failing to recognize the company's moral obligation." In M. L. Eakes Co. v. Commissioner, 686 F.2d 217 (4th Cir. 1982), the court allowed a current deduction of the debts of a predecessor corporation that had become insolvent. The court concluded that the payments were made to establish credit and thereby preserve an existing business rather than to establish a new one and, after quoting extensively from the *Welch* discussion of "ordinary and necessary," referred to testimony to the effect that the repayment of debts of a liquidated corporation was not unusual in the business in which the taxpayer was engaged.

3. *Recovery of cost of goodwill.* As suggested in Note 1, supra, the holding in *Welch* is best justified on the rationale that the expenditure at issue produced benefits beyond the current year and for that reason was capital in nature. If the cost of acquiring goodwill is a capital expenditure, can a taxpayer receive a deduction for amortization of that cost over the expected life of the asset? Historically, the answer to this question has been "no." Amounts paid to produce goodwill have been recoverable for tax purposes only upon sale or other taxable disposition of the business. The same treatment has applied to the portion of the purchase price paid for a business that is allocable to goodwill: No current deduction, no amortization, recovery only upon disposition of the business. Understandably, taxpayers have gone to great length to avoid characterizing expenditures as having been for goodwill. Section 197, added to the tax law in 1993, provides for a fifteen-year amortization of goodwill acquired through purchase. Self-created goodwill, such as that at issue in *Welch*, is still unamortizable. See § 197(c)(2)(B), (d)(1)(A), (d)(1)(C)(iv), (d)(1)(C)(v), (d)(2), (d)(3). See also discussion of "Goodwill and Other Intangibles," infra page 572.

In Steger v. Commissioner, 113 T.C. 227 (1999), the taxpayer, a lawyer who had just retired from practice, paid $3,168 for a malpractice policy that had an indefinite duration but covered only malpractice that occurred before the date of retirement. The IRS took the position that Steger was entitled to deduct only 10 percent of the cost of the policy each year for ten years; there is no explanation in the Tax Court opinion of where the 10 percent came from. The Tax Court — relying on language from INDOPCO, Inc. v. Commissioner, supra page 520 — held that Steger was entitled to deduct the entire amount in the year of purchase, reasoning that even if the policy was a capital asset (as opposed to a current cost of closing the business), the cost was deductible in full on dissolution of his business.

4. *Advertising.* The Regulations under § 263A allow current deductions for "marketing, selling, advertising, and distribution costs." Regs. § 1.263A-1(e)(iii)(A). Would this rule change the outcome in Welch v. Helvering?

5. *Education*. We have already seen that the cost of a college education is nondeductible because it is a "personal" expense. See supra page 506. For education that relates more directly to the production of income, the regulations (Regs. § 1.162-5) adopt a set of objective tests (as opposed to tests dependent on motive or purpose) that rely on the distinction between capital expenditures and current expenses. No deduction is allowed for the expense of meeting "the minimum educational requirements for qualification in [an] employment or other trade or business." Regs. § 1.162-5(b)(2)(i). This rule is most widely applied to people who, while holding jobs as schoolteachers, complete or continue their education. Deductions are also denied for the expenses of "a program of study being pursued by [a person] which will lead to qualifying [the person] in a new trade or business." Regs. § 1.162-5(b)(3)(i). This rule precludes deductions for the cost of a law school education, even by people working as, say, engineers, accountants, or police officers, who claim that they never intend to practice law and that the law school education is intended only to enhance their performance in their present occupations.

If the taxpayer is already qualified to practice an occupation or profession but incurs expenses for additional training, the regulations allow deductions for two overlapping categories of education. The first is education that "maintains or improves skills required by the individual in his employment or other trade or business." Regs. § 1.162-5(a)(1). A refresher course to bring a lawyer or doctor up to date on new developments is most typical of this category. The second is education that meets the "express requirements of the individual's employer, or the requirements of applicable law or regulations, imposed as a condition to the retention by the individual of an established employment relationship, status or rate of compensation." Regs. § 1.162-5(a)(2). Covered under this category are annual graduate course credits that public school teachers are often required to obtain as a condition of retaining their positions.

Sharon v. Commissioner, 66 T.C. 515 (1976), aff'd, 591 F.2d 1273 (9th Cir. 1978), cert. denied, 442 U.S. 941 (1979), held that a lawyer could not amortize the costs of a legal education or of a bar preparation course but could (under § 167) amortize registration, test, and bar admission fees over his expected life. In Kohen v. Commissioner, 44 T.C.M. 1518 (1982), the court denied a deduction of the cost of obtaining an LLM in taxation at NYU immediately following graduation from law school but before entering into practice in any way other than giving free advice to family members. Presumably the costs of a legal education cannot be deducted as a loss when one's legal career ends. See Regs. § 1.162-5(b)(1), indicating that the costs "constitute an inseparable aggregate of personal and capital expenditures." Do you agree?

6. *The cost of finding a new business or job*. Rev. Rul. 77-254, 1977-2 C.B. 63, 64 holds:

Expenses incurred in the course of a general search for or preliminary investigation of a business or investment include those expenses related to the decisions *whether* to enter a transaction and *which* transaction to enter. Such expenses are personal [!] and are not deductible under section 165 of the Code. Once the taxpayer has focused on the acquisition of a specific business or investment, expenses that are related to an attempt to acquire such business or investment are capital in nature and, to the extent that the expenses are allocable to an asset the cost of which is amortizable or depreciable, may be amortized as part of the asset's cost if the attempted acquisition is successful. If the attempted acquisition fails, the amount capitalized is deductible in accordance with section 165(c)(2). The taxpayer need not actually enter the business or purchase the investment in order to obtain the deduction.

Do you agree that the costs of a "general search" for a business or investment opportunity are personal? If not, does the language of the Code require the result that some outlays of this sort will never give rise to a deduction? Compare the treatment of the costs of a law school education. In some circumstances, the costs of investigating a business opportunity may be amortizable under § 195, enacted in 1980, but this provision does not appear to be relevant to the costs of "general search."

Regs. § 1.212-1(f) denies current deductions under § 212 for "expenses such as those paid or incurred in seeking employment or in placing oneself in a position to begin rendering personal services for compensation. . . ." In Cremona v. Commissioner, 58 T.C. 219 (1972), acq., a taxpayer who was employed as an "administrator" paid $1,500 for job counseling and referral services that had not led to a new position by the time of hearing of the case. The Court held the expenses deductible under § 162 since the taxpayer was in "the trade or business of being an administrator." Rev. Rul. 77-16, 1977-1 C.B. 37, allowed deduction of the expenses of looking for a new position in the taxpayer's present trade or business, a limit that is quite broad since the Service, like the Tax Court, recognizes such a broad trade or business as being a corporate executive or administrator. See also Rev. Rul. 78-93, 1978-1 C.B. 38, permitting the deduction of expenses for career counseling when the taxpayer, engaged in the businesses of being both a full-time practicing attorney and part-time law school lecturer, after receiving the counseling secured a position of full-time assistant professor of law. The Service held that since the taxpayer had been engaged in two trades or businesses, he was not changing his trade or business by seeking a full-time teaching job.

7. *Two percent threshold.* Recall that business expenses of *employees*, including the cost of employment-related education, can be deducted only to the extent that in the aggregate they exceed 2 percent of adjusted gross income (AGI). See § 67, which is described supra page 421 at the beginning of Chapter 5. In addition, such miscellaneous itemized deductions ARE NOT allowed at all for purposes of calculating a taxpayer's alternative minimum tax liability. § 56(b).

2. Extraordinary Behavior

GILLIAM v. COMMISSIONER

51 T.C.M. 515 (1986)

When the petition was filed in the instant case, petitioners Sam Gilliam, Jr. (hereinafter sometimes referred to as "Gilliam"), and Dorothy B. Gilliam, husband and wife, resided in Washington, D.C.

Gilliam was born in Tupelo, Mississippi, in 1933, and raised in Louisville, Kentucky. In 1961, he received a master of arts degree in painting from the University of Louisville.

Gilliam is, and was at all material periods, a noted artist. His works have been exhibited in numerous art galleries throughout the United States and Europe, including the Corcoran Gallery of Art, Washington, D.C., the Philadelphia Museum of Art, Philadelphia, Pennsylvania, the Karl Solway Gallery, Cincinnati, Ohio, the Phoenix Gallery, San Francisco, California, and the University of California, Irvine, California. His works have also been exhibited and sold at the Fendrick Gallery, Washington, D.C. In addition, Gilliam is, and was at all material periods, a teacher of art. On occasion, Gilliam lectured and taught art at various institutions.

Gilliam accepted an invitation to lecture and teach for a week at the Memphis Academy of Arts in Memphis, Tennessee. On Sunday, February 23, 1975, he flew to Memphis to fulfill this business obligation.

Gilliam had a history of hospitalization for mental and emotional disturbances and continued to be under psychiatric care until the time of his trip to Memphis. In December 1963, Gilliam was hospitalized in Louisville; Gilliam had anxieties about his work as an artist. For periods of time in both 1965 and 1966, Gilliam suffered from depression and was unable to work. In 1970, Gilliam was again hospitalized. In 1973, while Gilliam was a visiting artist at a number of university campuses in California, he found it necessary to consult an airport physician; however, when he returned to Washington, D.C., Gilliam did not require hospitalization.

Before his Memphis trip, Gilliam created a 225-foot painting for the Thirty-fourth Biennial Exhibition of American Painting at the Corcoran Gallery of Art (hereinafter sometimes referred to as "the Exhibition"). The Exhibition opened on Friday evening, February 21, 1975. In addition, Gilliam was in the process of preparing a giant mural for an outside wall of the Philadelphia Museum of Art for the 1975 Spring Festival in Philadelphia. The budget plans for this mural were due on Monday, February 24, 1975.

On the night before his Memphis trip, Gilliam felt anxious and unable to rest. On Sunday morning, Gilliam contacted Ranville Clark (hereinafter sometimes referred to as "Clark"), a doctor Gilliam had been consulting intermittently over the years, and asked Clark to prescribe some medication to relieve his anxiety. Clark arranged for Gilliam to pick up a prescription of the drug Dalmane on the way to the airport. Gilliam had taken medication frequently during the preceding 10 years. Clark had never before prescribed Dalmane for Gilliam.

On Sunday, February 23, 1975, Gilliam got the prescription and at about 3:25 he boarded American Airlines flight 395 at Washington National Airport, Washington, D.C., bound for Memphis. Gilliam occupied a window seat. He took the Dalmane for the first time shortly after boarding the airplane.

About one and one-half hours after the airplane departed Washington National Airport, Gilliam began to act in an irrational manner. He talked of bizarre events and had difficulty in speaking. According to some witnesses, he appeared to be airsick and held his head. Gilliam began to feel trapped, anxious, disoriented, and very agitated. Gilliam said that the plane was going to crash and that he wanted a life raft. Gilliam entered the aisle and, while going from one end of the airplane to the other, he tried to exit from three different doors. Then Gilliam struck Seiji Nakamura (hereinafter sometimes referred to as "Nakamura"), another passenger, several times with a telephone receiver. Nakamura was seated toward the rear of the airplane, near one of the exits. Gilliam also threatened the navigator and a stewardess, called for help, and cried. As a result of the attack, Nakamura sustained a one-inch laceration above his left eyebrow which required four sutures. Nakamura also suffered ecchymosis of the left arm and pains in his left wrist. Nakamura was treated for these injuries at Methodist Hospital in Memphis.

On arriving in Memphis, Gilliam was arrested by Federal officials. On March 10, 1975, Gilliam was indicted. He was brought to trial in the United States District Court for the Western District of Tennessee, Western Division, on one count of violation of 49 U.S.C. § 1472(k) (relating to certain crimes aboard an aircraft in flight) and two counts of violating 49 U.S.C. § 1472(j) (relating to interference with flight crew members or flight attendants). Gilliam entered a plea of not guilty to the criminal charges. The trial began on September 9, 1975, and ended on September 10, 1975. After Gilliam presented all of his evidence, the district court granted Gilliam's motion for a judgment of acquittal by reason of temporary insanity.

Petitioners paid $9,250 and $9,600 for legal fees in 1975 and 1976, respectively, in connection with both the criminal trial and Nakamura's civil claim. In 1975, petitioners also paid $3,900 to Nakamura in settlement of the civil claim.

Petitioners claimed deductions for the amounts paid in 1975 and 1976 on the appropriate individual income tax returns. Respondent disallowed the amounts claimed in both years attributable to the incident on the airplane.

Gilliam's trip to Memphis was a trip in furtherance of his trades or businesses.

Petitioners' expenses for the legal fees and claim settlement described, supra, are not ordinary expenses of Gilliam's trades or businesses.

OPINION

Petitioners contend that they are entitled to deduct the amounts paid in defense of the criminal prosecution and in settlement of the related civil claim under section 162.[10] Petitioners maintain that the instant case is directly controlled by our decision in Dancer v. Commissioner, 73 T.C. 1103 (1980). According to petitioners, "[t]he clear holding of Dancer is . . . that expenses for litigation arising out of an accident which occurs during a business trip are deductible as ordinary and necessary business expenses." Petitioners also

---

10. At trial, petitioners asserted that the amounts paid were deductible under section 162 and section 212. On brief, petitioners do not address the deductibility of the amounts paid under section 212. Whether this constitutes a concession by petitioners is unclear; however, it does not affect the analysis herein, since the same criteria apply to the deduction of expenses under section 162 and section 212 . . . .

contend that Clark v. Commissioner, 30 T.C. 1330 (1958), is to the same effect as *Dancer*.

Respondent maintains that *Dancer* and *Clark* are distinguishable. Respondent contends that the legal fees paid are not deductible under either section 162 or section 212 because the criminal charges against Gilliam were neither directly connected with nor proximately resulted from his trade or business and the legal fees were not paid for the production of income. Respondent maintains that "the criminal charges which arose as a result of . . . [the incident on the airplane], could hardly be deemed 'ordinary,' given the nature of [Gilliam's] profession." Respondent contends "that the provisions of section 262 control this situation." As to the settlement of the related civil claim, respondent asserts that since Gilliam committed an intentional tort, the settlement of the civil claim constitutes a nondeductible personal expense.

We agree with respondent that the expenses are not ordinary expenses of Gilliam's trade or business.

Section 162(a) allows a deduction for all the ordinary and necessary expenses of carrying on a trade or business. In order for the expense to be deductible by a taxpayer, it must be an ordinary expense, it must be a necessary expense, and it must be an expense of carrying on the taxpayer's trade or business. If any one of these requirements is not met, the expense is not deductible under section 162(a). Deputy v. du Pont, 308 U.S. 488 (1940); Welch v. Helvering, [supra page 545]; Kornhauser v. United States, 276 U.S. 145 (1928). In Deputy v. du Pont, the Supreme Court set forth a guide for application of the statutory requirement that the expense be "ordinary," as follows (308 U.S. at 494-497)[11]:

> In the second place, these payments were not "ordinary" ones for the conduct of the kind of business in which, we assume arguendo, respondent was engaged. The District Court held that they were "beyond the norm of general and accepted business practice" and were in fact "so extraordinary as to occur in the lives of ordinary business men not at all" and in the life of the respondent "but once." Certainly there are no norms of conduct to which we have been referred or of which we are cognizant which would bring these payments within the meaning of ordinary expenses for conserving and enhancing an estate. We do not doubt the correctness of the District Court's finding that respondent embarked on this program to the end that his beneficial stock ownership in the du Pont Company might be conserved and enhanced. But that does not make the cost to him an "ordinary" expense within the meaning of the Act. Ordinary has the connotation of normal, usual, or customary. To be sure, an expense may be ordinary though it happen but once in the taxpayer's lifetime. Cf. Kornhauser v. United States, supra. Yet the transaction which gives rise to it must be of common or frequent occurrence in the type of business involved. Welch v. Helvering, supra. Hence, the fact that a particular expense would be an ordinary or common one in the course of one business and so deductible under [§ 162(a)]

11. [In Deputy v. du Pont, the taxpayer had claimed a deduction for certain expenses arising from his sale of stock in the du Pont Corporation to a group of young executives. The purpose of the sale was to give these executives a financial interest in the corporation; because the corporation was prevented by legal restrictions from doing so, the taxpayer stepped in "to the end that his beneficial stock ownership in the du Pont Company might be conserved and enhanced." — EDS.]

does not necessarily make it such in connection with another business. . . . As stated in Welch v. Helvering, supra, pp.113-114: ". . . What is ordinary, though there must always be a strain of constancy within it, is none the less a variable affected by time and place and circumstance." One of the extremely relevant circumstances is the nature and scope of the particular business out of which the expense in question accrued. The fact that an obligation to pay has arisen is not sufficient. It is the kind of transaction out of which the obligation arose and its normalcy in the particular business which are crucial and controlling.

Review of the many decided cases is of little aid since each turns on its special facts. But the principle is clear. And on application of that principle to these facts, it seems evident that the payments in question cannot be placed in the category of those items of expense which a conservator of an estate, a custodian of a portfolio, a supervisor of a group of investments, a manager of wide financial and business interests, or a substantial stockholder in a corporation engaged in conserving and enhancing his estate would ordinarily incur. We cannot assume that they are embraced within the normal overhead or operating costs of such activities. There is no evidence that stockholders or investors, in furtherance of enhancing and conserving their estates, ordinarily or frequently lend such assistance to employee stock purchase plans of their corporations. And in absence of such evidence there is no basis for an assumption, in experience or common knowledge, that these payments are to be placed in the same category as typically ordinary expenses of such activities, e.g., rental of safe deposit boxes, cost of investment counsel or of investment services, salaries of secretaries and the like. Rather these payments seem to us to represent most extraordinary expenses for that type of activity. Therefore, the claim for deduction falls, as did the claim of an officer of a corporation who paid its debts to strengthen his own standing and credit. Welch v. Helvering, supra. And the fact that the payments might have been necessary in the sense that consummation of the transaction with the Delaware Company was beneficial to respondent's estate is of no aid. For Congress has not decreed that all necessary expenses may be deducted. Though plainly necessary they cannot be allowed unless they are also ordinary. Welch v. Helvering, supra.

Petitioners bear the burden of proving entitlement to a deduction under section 162. Welch v. Helvering, 290 U.S. at 115; Rule 142(a), Tax Court Rules of Practice & Procedure. Gilliam is a noted artist and teacher of art. It undoubtedly is ordinary for people in Gilliam's trades or businesses to travel (and to travel by air) in the course of such trades or businesses; however, we do not believe it is ordinary for people in such trades or businesses to be involved in altercations of the sort here involved in the course of any such travel. The travel was not itself the conduct of Gilliam's trades or businesses. Also, the expenses here involved are not strictly a cost of Gilliam's transportation. Finally, it is obvious that neither the altercation nor the expenses were undertaken to further Gilliam's trades or businesses.

We conclude that Gilliam's expenses are not ordinary expenses of his trades or businesses.

It is instructive to compare the instant case with Dancer v. Commissioner, supra, upon which petitioners rely. In both cases, the taxpayer was travelling on business. In both cases, the expenses in dispute were not the cost of the travelling, but rather were the cost of an untoward incident that occurred in the course of the trip. In both cases, the incident did not facilitate the trip or otherwise assist the taxpayer's trade or business. In both cases, the taxpayer was responsible for the incident; in neither case was the taxpayer willful. In *Dancer*, the taxpayer was driving an automobile; he caused an accident which resulted in injuries to a child. The relevant expenses were the taxpayer's payments to settle the civil claims arising from the accident. 73 T.C. at 1105. In the instant case, Gilliam was a passenger in an airplane, he apparently committed acts which would have been criminal but for his temporary insanity, and he injured a fellow passenger. Gilliam's expenses were the costs of his successful legal defense, and his payments to settle Nakamura's civil claim.

In *Dancer*, we stated as follows (73 T.C. at 1108-1109):

> It is true that the expenditure in the instant case did not further petitioner's business in any economic sense; nor is it, we hope, the type of expenditure that many businesses are called upon to pay. Nevertheless, neither factor lessens the direct relationship between the expenditure and the business. Automobile travel by petitioner was an integral part of this business. *As rising insurance rates suggest, the cost of fuel and routine servicing are not the only costs one can expect in operating a car. As unfortunate as it may be, lapses by drivers seem to be an inseparable incident of driving a car.* . . . Costs incurred as a result of such an incident are just as much a part of overall business expenses as the cost of fuel. [Emphasis supplied.]

Dancer is distinguishable.

In Clark v. Commissioner, supra, also relied on by petitioners, the expenses consisted of payments of (a) legal fees in defense of a criminal prosecution and (b) amounts to settle a related civil claim.[12] In this regard, the instant case is similar to *Clark*. In *Clark*, however, the taxpayer's activities that gave rise to the prosecution and civil claim were activities directly in the conduct of Clark's trade or business. In the instant case, Gilliam's activities were not directly in the conduct of his trades or businesses. Rather, the activities merely occurred in the course of transportation connected with Gilliam's trades or businesses. And, as we noted in Dancer v. Commissioner, 73 T.C. at 1106, "in cases like this, where the cost is an adjunct of and not a direct cost of transporting an

---

12. [In *Clark*, the taxpayer, as branch manager of a company that solicited magazine subscriptions, was responsible for hiring people to go out and do the soliciting. "If an applicant for an outside solicitor's job was a married female, [taxpayer's] policy was always to interview the applicant's husband, have him understand the conditions under which the wife would be working, and get his approval before employing the applicant." Pursuant to this policy, the taxpayer made an appointment with an applicant to interview the applicant's husband at the applicant's and her husband's home at 8 A.M., before the husband went to work. When the taxpayer arrived for the interview, the husband was not at home. The taxpayer spent a few minutes in the house and left. According to the tax court, the taxpayer "did not assault the . . . applicant." Nonetheless, the applicant later the same day "swore out a warrant against [the taxpayer] charging him with assault with intent to rape," and this was followed by a warrant served by the county sheriff. Nine days later a court order was issued stating that "after hearing evidence [it appears] that the offense is Assault and Battery instead of Assault with Intent to Rape." Thereafter the criminal action was dismissed "upon the request of the prosecutrix." The taxpayer thereafter paid $1,250 as fees to his lawyers and "turned over to them $1,500 which they paid over to [the] applicant and her husband in consideration for a release to [the taxpayer] of any claim of civil liability which might arise." The Tax Court allowed deductions for both the $1,250 and the $1,500. As to the $1,500, the court relied on the statement of doctrine, "Expenditures incurred by a taxpayer to protect his business reputation or avoid unfavorable business or commercial publicity have been regarded as deductible." — EDS.]

individual, we have not felt obliged to routinely allow the expenditure as a transportation costs deduction."

Petitioners also rely on Commissioner v. Tellier, 383 U.S. 687 (1966), in which the taxpayer was allowed to deduct the cost of an unsuccessful criminal defense to securities fraud charges. The activities that gave rise to the criminal prosecution in *Tellier* were activities directly in the conduct of Tellier's trade or business. Our analysis of the effect of Clark v. Commissioner, applies equally to the effect of Commissioner v. Tellier.

In sum, Gilliam's expenses were of a kind similar to those of the taxpayers in *Tellier* and *Clark*; however the activities giving rise to Gilliam's expenses were not activities directly in the conduct of his trades or businesses, while Tellier's and Clark's activities were directly in the conduct of their respective trades or businesses. Gilliam's expenses were related to his trades or businesses in a manner similar to those of the taxpayer in *Dancer;* however Gilliam's actions giving rise to the expenses were not shown to be ordinary, while Dancer's were shown to be ordinary. *Tellier, Clark*, and *Dancer* all have similarities to the instant case, however, *Tellier, Clark*, and *Dancer* are distinguishable in important respects. The expenses are not deductible under section 162(a).

We hold for respondent.

NOTES AND QUESTIONS

1. *Precedent.* The court in *Gilliam* relies on Welch v. Helvering (supra page 545) and Deputy v. du Pont (quoted at length in the court's opinion). Disregarding the language of those two cases, how might they be distinguished?

2. *Appropriate time and place?* Suppose Gilliam's anxiety attack had occurred while he had been lecturing to a room full of students and he had injured one of them. Would his expenses then have been deductible?

3. *Causation.* (a) Is it the assumption of the court that the anxiety attack was brought on by the business trip — that is, that it would not have occurred but for the pressures associated with that trip? Or is the assumption that it was only a coincidence that the attack occurred while Gilliam was on a business trip? Should it matter? Compare our prior encounters with the problem of causation, supra at pages 377 and 478.

(b) Suppose that Gilliam had hired an attendant to accompany him on the trip, to soothe and, if necessary, restrain him. Would the cost have been deductible?

4. *The scrupulous lawyer and other extraordinary taxpayers.* (a) In Friedman v. Delaney, 171 F.2d 269 (1st Cir. 1948), cert. denied, 336 U.S. 936 (1949), the taxpayer, Friedman, was a lawyer. After one of his clients had become insolvent, Friedman met with creditors to work out a settlement and finally reached an agreement under which the client would pay $5,000 to the creditors. Friedman, relying on prior representations by the client, gave his word that this money would be forthcoming, but when Friedman asked for it, the client (who had anticipated cashing in an insurance policy to produce the money) had a change of heart and refused. Thereupon, Friedman paid the $5,000

himself. Claiming that the ethics of his profession and his own conscience required that he keep his word, he deducted the $5,000 as a business loss. The court denied the deduction on the ground that the payment was "voluntary." The court said that "it is obviously no part of a lawyer's business to take on a personal obligation to make payments which should come from his client, unless in pursuance of a previous understanding or agreement to do so."

(b) On the other hand, in Pepper v. Commissioner, 36 T.C. 886 (1961), another lawyer paid up when his client misbehaved and a deduction was allowed. The taxpayer had helped a client find financing for a business by approaching other clients, friends, and business acquaintances and by drafting the necessary loan and security arrangements. On discovering that the client was engaged in fraudulent manipulations and that the business was bankrupt, the taxpayer and his law partner paid about $65,000 to the victims after concluding that the payments were "imperative" in order to save their law practice. Welch v. Helvering, supra page 545, was distinguished on the ground that there the expenditures were made to *acquire*, and not to *retain or protect*, the taxpayer's business. *Friedman* was distinguished on the ground that in that case "there was no contention that the money involved was paid to protect or promote Friedman's business." Does this mean that if Friedman had proved that his conduct had been a response not to moral scruple, but rather to profit-maximization goals, the deduction would have been allowed? If a payment is not unlawful, if its deduction would not contravene public policy in some fashion (a problem dealt with infra at page 558), and if it is made in a taxpayer's business judgment for profit-making reasons, should a deduction be denied merely because it is unusual, extraordinary, or unique?

In Goedel v. Commissioner, 39 B.T.A. 1, 12 (1939), a stock dealer was denied a deduction for premiums paid on insurance on the life of the President of the United States, whose death, he feared, would disrupt the stock market:

> Where, as here, the expenditure is so unusual as never to have been made, so far as the record reveals, by other persons in the same business, *when confronted with similar conditions,* . . . then we do not think the expenditure was ordinary or necessary, so as to be a deductible business expense within the intendment and meaning of the statute.

In Trebilcock v. Commissioner, 64 T.C. 852 (1975), aff'd, 557 F.2d 1226 (6th Cir. 1977), a deduction was denied for the cost of hiring an ordained minister "to minister spiritually to petitioner and his employees [and to conduct] prayer meetings, at which he tried to raise the level of spiritual awareness of the participants." The court said that such "benefits . . . are personal in nature." Suppose an employer who is a physical-fitness addict hires a physical education instructor to come to her place of business each morning and lead her employees in exercises. "Ordinary"? Deductible? If not, what if the employer hates all forms of physical exercise but thinks it might make her employees work better? What if an employer hires a yoga instructor to lead his employees in meditation each morning?

3. Reasonable Compensation

Section 162(a)(1) provides expressly for the deduction of a "reasonable allowance for salaries or other compensation for personal services actually rendered." This language seems to add little, if anything, to the basic requirement of § 162 that deductible payments must be for genuine business expenses. The language was originally intended to *permit* taxpayers to deduct reasonable amounts "allowed" for salaries, even though not paid, for purposes of computing the World War I excess profits tax, but it has been relied on by the Service and the courts in *denying* deductions for salaries thought to be unreasonable. The instances of denial of deductions, however, almost always involve situations in which the salary is not truly a salary but rather a nondeductible payment masquerading as a salary. Probably the most common situation giving rise to denial is that of the closely held corporation where it is found that what purports to be a deductible salary is in fact a nondeductible dividend. The recipient of the payment may be either an employee who is a principal shareholder or an employee who is a child, parent, or other relation of a principal shareholder. The purported salary in these cases is referred to as a "disguised dividend." In the past decade, most closely held corporations have elected to be taxed as so-called S corporations. An S corporation is treated very much like a partnership for tax purposes. It pays no tax; instead, its income is taxed to its shareholders. Whether a payment is characterized as a dividend or salary makes no difference to an S corporation, which pays no tax, and little difference to its shareholders, who are taxed on both dividends and salary.[13]

In addition to the reasonable compensation limit of § 162(a)(1), deductions for compensation are subject to a number of additional limitations. Under § 162(m), added to the Code in 1993, publicly held corporations cannot deduct more than $1 million a year in pay to a chief executive officer or any other of its four highest paid employees. The $1 million limit on deductible compensation does not apply to performance-based compensation. Provided certain conditions are met, the term "performance-based compensation" includes stock options and other stock appreciation rights.

Of somewhat lesser importance, §§ 280G and 4999, added in 1984, restrict deductions for so-called golden parachute payments and impose an excise tax on such payments. Roughly speaking, golden parachute payments are substantial bonuses paid to corporate executives on termination of employment following a change in control of the corporation.

4. Costs of Illegal or Unethical Activities

Pre-1970 judicial doctrine. Before 1970 the courts, generally relying on the "ordinary and necessary" language of § 162(a), disallowed deductions whose

---

13. The characterization may matter for reasons unrelated to the reasonable compensation limitation of § 162. For example, amounts paid as salary are subject to Social Security and related payroll taxes.

allowance, it was thought or assumed, would frustrate public policy. The state of the law was uncertain and controversial. In Tank Truck Rentals v. Commissioner, 356 U.S. 30 (1958), the Court held that fines paid by a trucking company for violations of state maximum-weight laws were nondeductible. At the same time, in Commissioner v. Sullivan, 356 U.S. 27 (1958), it permitted the deduction of the rent and wages paid in operating an illegal bookmaking establishment in Chicago, Illinois, even though payment of the rent was itself an illegal act under Illinois law. In Commissioner v. Tellier, 383 U.S. 687 (1966), a securities dealer was allowed to deduct legal expenses incurred when he was convicted of violating the Securities Act of 1933 and mail fraud statutes. Citing United States v. Gilmore, supra page 500, the Court said that the source of the expenses was business. (Why was the source not the taxpayer's purely personal, and extraordinary, defect of character, which led him down the path of crime?) The Court observed, "No public policy is offended when a man faced with serious criminal charges employs a lawyer to help in his defense."

Tellier seemed to limit the relevance of "ordinariness" and the frustration-of-public-policy doctrine, saying (383 U.S. at 694):

> Only where the allowance of a deduction would "frustrate sharply defined national or state policies proscribing particular types of conduct" have we upheld its disallowance. Commissioner v. Heininger, 320 U.S., at 473. Further, the "policies frustrated must be national or state policies evidenced by some governmental declaration of them." Lilly v. Commissioner, 343 U.S., at 97. Finally, the "test of non-deductibility always is the severity and immediacy of the frustration resulting from allowance of the deduction." Tank Truck Rentals v. Commissioner, 356 U.S. 30, 35.

Despite the language quoted in this passage, in United Draperies v. Commissioner, 340 F.2d 936 (7th Cir. 1964), the court had disallowed the deduction (in the years 1957 through 1960) of kickbacks from a drapery company to officers and employees of customers in the business of manufacturing mobile homes. The taxpayer had been extremely successful and its practices did not violate any state law. Distinguishing the *Lilly* case on the ground that there the practice was widespread, the court stated, "As a matter of common knowledge we are convinced that the mores of the marketplace of this nation is not such that 'kickbacks' by vendor-suppliers to the officers or employees of customers, while they do occur, are an ordinary means of securing or promoting business." 340 F.2d at 938.

The Tax Reform Act of 1969 amendments to § 162. In 1969 Congress responded to complaints about the murkiness of the law and about the fact that the Internal Revenue Service was making decisions about what did and did not violate public policy[14] by adding to § 162 three new subsections, § 162(c), (f), and (g).

---

14. Compare this objection to the objection to the decision in the Bob Jones University case, supra page 392. See supra page 399, Note 2.

Section 162(f) flatly prohibits the deduction of "any fine or similar penalty paid to a government for violation of any law."

Section 162(c) covers bribes and kickbacks. Section 162(c)(1) prohibits the deduction of any illegal bribe or kickback to a government employee and (as amended in 1982) bribes or kickbacks to employees of foreign governments "if the payment is unlawful under the Foreign Corrupt Practices Act of 1977."[15] Section 162(c)(2) covers illegal payments to people other than government employees, "but only if [the] law is generally enforced." And § 162(c)(3), added in 1971, disallows deductions for kickbacks, rebates, or bribes by physicians, suppliers, and other providers of services or goods in connection with Medicare or Medicaid, regardless whether the payment is illegal.

Section 162(g) disallows deductions for the punitive two-thirds portion of damages paid for criminal violations of the antitrust provisions found in the Clayton Act.

The Senate report on these amendments states that the statute "is intended to be all-inclusive" and that "[p]ublic policy, in other circumstances, generally is not sufficiently clearly defined to justify the disallowance of the deductions." S. Rep. No. 91-552, 91st Cong., 1st Sess. 274 (1969), 1969-3 C.B. 423, 597.

See also § 280E, denying deductions for expenses incurred in drug trafficking. The Senate Report on this provision states, "To preclude challenges on constitutional grounds, the adjustment to gross receipts with respect to effective costs of goods sold is not affected by this provision of the bill." Thus, for example, a cocaine dealer is allowed an "adjustment to gross receipts" for the cost of the cocaine but not for other costs. The constitutional basis for this rule is that the Sixteenth Amendment authorizes a tax on "income," not on gross receipts. See supra page 10.

What would be the outcome under present law in each of the pre-1970 cases summarized supra at pages 558-559?

Taxes paid to disfavored nations. In general, persons that pay income taxes to foreign countries but are subject to United States income tax on their worldwide income may credit the foreign tax payments against their United States income tax liability. See § 901. This credit is subject to a number of limitations, but in its most simple form the credit allows United States taxpayers to reduce their tax liability by the amount of the foreign tax paid. This credit is not available, however, for taxes paid to countries the United States does not recognize, to countries with which the United States does not have current diplomatic relations, and to countries that the Secretary of State designates as supporters of international terrorism. § 901(j)(2). Taxes that do not qualify for the credit can still be deducted against income. A deduction, however, is worth less than a credit (which reduces taxes dollar for dollar).

---

15. The pre-1982 version of this provision was in part the basis in 1976 for a large-scale and well-publicized attack by the IRS and the SEC on "questionable foreign payments" and secret "slush funds" used to make such payments.

STEPHENS v. COMMISSIONER
905 F.2d 667 (2d Cir. 1990)

BACKGROUND

In September of 1981, Stephens and other defendants were indicted for participating in a scheme to defraud Raytheon, a Delaware corporation doing business in the United States and in foreign countries. Following a jury trial, Stephens was convicted in December of 1982 of four counts of wire fraud . . . ; one count of transportation of the proceeds of fraud in interstate commerce . . . ; and one count of conspiracy. . . .

Stephens was sentenced on December 3, 1982. . . .

In pronouncing sentence, the sentencing judge agreed [with a recommendation of the U.S. Attorney] that Stephens ought to make restitution to Raytheon. After emphasizing that she "believe[d] a period of imprisonment is absolutely necessary in this case not only for the protection of the public but because we cannot ignore the seriousness of the crimes for which you stand convicted," and "that [Stephens was among] the most culpable," the judge added, "Now, this Court does believe that Raytheon must get its money back. I'm just firmly convinced of that. . . . I can and shall require restitution from the principals of the [corporate defendant] because you, in my view, the principals . . . defrauded Raytheon. . . . I'm going to see to it that you give Raytheon its money back."

On each of the counts of wire fraud, Stephens was sentenced to a concurrent 5-year prison term and a $1,000 fine. On the conspiracy count, he was sentenced to a concurrent prison term of 5 years and a $10,000 fine. On the count of interstate transportation of the proceeds of fraud, Stephens was sentenced to a consecutive 5-year prison term and a $5,000 fine; execution of this consecutive prison term, but not the fine, was suspended, and Stephens was placed on 5 years of probation, on the condition that he make restitution to Raytheon in the amount of $1,000,000.

The $1,000,000 represented $530,000 in principal, the amount which was initially embezzled from Raytheon, and $470,000 in interest. Stephens was taxed upon his receipt of the $530,000 in 1976. In 1984, as part of a settlement agreement with Raytheon in connection with two civil actions Raytheon had brought against Stephens, Stephens turned over to Raytheon the $530,000 fund, and executed a $470,000 promissory note, representing the interest. In an Amended 1984 Tax Return, Stephens claimed as a deduction the $530,000 restitution payment. . . .

DISCUSSION

As Stephens and the Commissioner agree, Stephens' restitution payment is deductible, if at all, pursuant to Section 165(c)(2) of the Tax Code, which permits an individual to deduct any uncompensated loss sustained during the taxable year, incurred in any transaction entered into for profit, though not connected with a trade or business. . . . Deductions under Section 165 have been disallowed by the courts, however, where "the allowance of a deduction would 'frustrate sharply defined national or state policies proscribing particular types of conduct.' . . . " Commissioner v. Tellier, 383 U.S. 687, 694 (1966) (quoting Commissioner v. Heininger, 320 U.S. 467, 473, (1943)). Thus, "the 'test of nondeductibility always is the severity and immediacy of the frustration resulting from allowance of the deduction.' " Id. (quoting Tank Truck Rentals, Inc. v. Commissioner, 356 U.S. 30, 35 (1958)).

For example, in *Tellier*, the Tax Court disallowed a deduction for expenses incurred in the successful defense of a criminal prosecution. This Court reversed, and the Supreme Court affirmed. Emphasizing that "the 'policies frustrated must be national or state policies evidenced by some governmental declaration of them,'" id. (quoting Lilly v. Commissioner, 343 U.S. 90, 97 (1952)), the Court concluded that "[n]o public policy is offended when a man faced with serious criminal charges employs a lawyer to help in his defense." Id. On the other hand, in Tank Truck Rentals, Inc. v. Commissioner, 356 U.S. 30 (1958), the Supreme Court affirmed the disallowance of a deduction of fines paid by a trucking company for violations of state maximum weight laws. Id. at 35-36. . . .

Although *Tellier* and *Tank Truck Rentals* were both decided pursuant to Tax Code provisions relating to business expenses, the test for nondeductibility enunciated in those opinions is applicable to loss deductions under Section 165. Accordingly, the issue before us is whether a deduction for Stephens' restitution payment of embezzled funds to Raytheon so sharply and immediately frustrates a governmentally declared public policy that the deduction should be disallowed.

We note at the outset that . . . taxpayers who repay embezzled funds are ordinarily entitled to a deduction in the year in which the funds are repaid. . . . Clearly, no public policy would be frustrated if a restitution payment unrelated to a criminal prosecution were at issue; Stephens would be entitled to a deduction for repaying the embezzled funds to Raytheon.

The Commissioner, however, argues that because Stephens made the restitution payment in lieu of punishment, the deduction should be disallowed. Emphasizing that the sentencing judge suspended the consecutive 5-year sentence on the condition that Stephens make restitution to Raytheon, the Commissioner contends that allowing Stephens a deduction for the restitution payment would take "the sting" out of Stephens' punishment, and therefore would sharply and immediately frustrate public policy. See *Tank Truck Rentals*, 356 U.S. at 35-36. Because Stephens has already paid taxes on the embezzled funds in his 1976 tax return, however, disallowing the deduction for repaying the funds would in effect result in a "double sting." . . . The sentencing judge made no reference to these tax consequences at the sentencing hearing. Moreover, Stephens received a stern sentence: he was sentenced to five years in prison, and fined a total of $16,000 — the $5,000 fine which accompanied the suspended consecutive sentence was not, as we have noted, suspended. We believe that allowing Stephens a deduction for his restitution payment would not severely and immediately frustrate public policy.

However, having reviewed the cases that have sought to elucidate the meaning and scope of the public policy exception under Section 165, and finding them insufficiently decisive, we turn next to Section 162, the Tax Code provision on deductibility of business expenses, as an aid in applying Section 165. Prior to the codification of the public policy exception to deductibility of business expenses, the test for nondeductibility of business expenses and losses was the same: whether the deduction would severely and immediately frustrate a sharply defined national or state policy proscribing particular types of conduct, evidenced by some governmental declaration thereof. In 1969, Congress codified this public policy exception to deductibility of expenses in Section 162 of the Code, limiting the exception to: illegal bribes, kickbacks, and other illegal payments (subsection 162(c)); fines or similar penalties paid to a government for the violation of any law (subsection 162(f)); and a portion of treble damage payments under the anti-trust laws (subsection 162(g)). Congress intended these "provision[s] for the denial of the deduction for payments in these situations which are deemed to violate public policy . . . to be all inclusive. Public policy, in other circumstances, generally is not sufficiently clearly defined to justify the disallowance of deductions." S. Rep. No. 552, 91st Cong., 1st Sess., reprinted in 1969 U.S. Code Cong. & Admin. News 2027, 2311 (hereinafter S. Rep. 552).

The public policy exception to deductibility under Section 165 was not explicitly affected by the amendments to Section 162. The Internal Revenue Service summarized its view on the impact of the amendments in a Revenue Ruling:

> Congress codified and limited the public policy doctrine in the case of ordinary and necessary business expenses by amending section 162(c) of the Code, adding section 162(f) and (g) in the Tax Reform Act of 1969 . . . , and amending section 162(c) in the Revenue Act of 1971. . . .
>
> However, the rules for disallowing a deduction under section 165 of the Code on the grounds of public policy were not limited by Congress but remain the same as they were before 1969. Therefore, disallowance of deductions under section 165 is not limited to amounts of a type for which deduction would be disallowed under section 162(c), (f), and (g) and the regulations thereunder in the case of a business expense.

Rev. Rul. 77-126, 1977-1 C.B. 47, 48. The Tax Court, however, announced a different view: "[t]here is some question whether the public policy doctrine retains any vitality since the enactment of sec. 162(f)." Medeiros v. Commissioner, 77 T.C. 1255, 1262 n.8 (1981). The court observed that "[i]f sec. 162(f) was intended to supplant the public policy doctrine, in all likelihood it would disallow deductions under sec. 165(c)(1) as well as sec. 162(a), as both involved an expenditure incurred in a trade or business." Id.

Though Congress, in amending Section 162, did not explicitly amend Section 165, we believe that the public policy considerations embodied in Section 162(f) are highly relevant in determining whether the payment to Raytheon was deductible under Section 165. Congress can hardly be considered to have intended to create a scheme where a payment would not pass muster under Section 162(f), but would still qualify for deduction under Section 165. It is arguable that the converse is also true, that a payment imposed in the course of a criminal prosecution that does pass muster under Section 162(f) will escape the public policy limitations of Section 165. However, we need not decide in this case whether that is so.

Reference to Section 162(f) supports our conclusion that allowing Stephens a deduction for his restitution payment would not severely and immediately frustrate public policy. Two considerations drawn from Section 162(f) and the cases construing that provision combine to support our conclusion in this case. Whether either consideration alone would suffice is a matter we need not decide.

First, Stephens' restitution payment is primarily a remedial measure to compensate another party, not a "fine or similar penalty," even though Stephens repaid the embezzled funds as a condition of his probation. . . .

Our review of the proceedings at Stephens' sentencing convinces us that Stephens' restitution payment was more compensatory than punitive in nature. . . .

Second, Stephens' payment was made to Raytheon, and not "to a government." . . .

We conclude that Stephens' restitution payment was neither a fine or similar penalty, nor paid to the government. Thus, we hold that neither the public policy exception to Section 165, precluding a deduction when it would severely and immediately frustrate public policy to allow it, nor the codification of the public policy exception to deductibility of expenses pursuant to Section 162, bars deduction of Stephens' restitution payment. Accordingly, we reverse and remand to the Tax Court for further proceedings not inconsistent with this opinion.

QUESTIONS

1. In 2001, Jim had gross income of $100,000. All of his income was realized from the sale of stolen goods. Discuss whether the following expenses are, or should be, deductible:

   (a) Payment to "get-away" driver used in four burglaries

   (b) Three-hundred-dollar gift to "fence" who purchases stolen goods from Jim

   (c) Costs of purchasing locksmith tools from retiring burglar

   (d) Bribe to local police officer

   (e) Cost of gun carried on burglaries

2. Tom, Dick, and Mary are college students. Last summer each saved $4,000, which they pooled and used to buy marijuana that they intended to sell to other students at a substantial profit. After they brought the marijuana to their dormitory, Tom got cold feet and flushed it all down the toilet. Tom also turned himself in to the police. All three pled guilty to possession with intent to distribute a controlled substance and were sentenced to probation. Can Dick and Mary deduct the $4,000 that they lost? How about Tom?

3. In Lincoln v. Commissioner, 50 T.C.M. 185 (185), the court denied a deduction for theft loss for a person who had put up $140,000 in a scheme in which he thought he was buying $600,000 of stolen money; in fact, the scheme was a ruse devised by his confederates to bilk him of his own money. How would the *Stephens* court decide this case?

F. DEPRECIATION

1. General Principles

The basic idea. The economic or accounting concept underlying the allowance for depreciation is that there should be an offset against revenues for the cost of "wasting" assets that are used for the production of those revenues but have a life extending beyond the current tax year.[16] For example, suppose a farmer buys a tractor that she expects to use for five years. To properly determine her income from operation of the farm, we must take account of the cost of the tractor, since it is a "wasting asset." The full cost should not be treated as a cost of earning income in the year of purchase, since the tractor will have a substantial value at the end of that year. Allowing a deduction of the full cost in the first year would result in an understatement of income. On the other hand, allowing no deduction until the year in which the tractor is disposed of (sold, exchanged, or scrapped) would result in an overstatement of income until the year of disposition and, in that year, an understatement. What is needed is some allocation of a portion of the cost of the tractor to each year of its use. If the farmer buys land, there is no deduction for depreciation because it is not expected that the land will decline in value; it is not a wasting asset.

Economic depreciation and economic incentives. The economically accurate method for allocating the cost of the tractor, or any other asset, would be to treat as a cost of each year's operations the difference between the value of the asset at the beginning of the year and the value at the end of the year. This is often referred to as "economic depreciation." For example, suppose the farmer buys the tractor for $10,000, puts it to use on the farm, and at the end of the first year of use could sell it for $8,000. The cost of use for the year, then, would be $2,000. While economic depreciation is, by definition, accurate, it is also nearly impossible to determine. No one has ever seriously suggested that taxpayers, or the government, measure the annual decline in value of each asset, or even each category of asset. In recent years, economic depreciation has not even been a goal of the tax system. Instead, the depreciation provisions are designed to overstate the decline in value of business property, and, in so doing, understate taxable income. See discussion, infra at 569. This taxpayer-friendly approach is intended to encourage business investment.

The "building blocks" of depreciation rules. Any depreciation system revolves around the spreading, or allocation, of cost over time and has three elements: (a) the determination of useful life; (b) taking account of salvage value; and (c) the application of a method of allocating the cost, in excess of salvage value,

---

16. No deduction is allowed for a decline in the value of an asset used for personal purposes, such as an automobile used for personal purposes or a personal residence. The decline in the value of such assets is a nondeductible personal expense.

over the useful life. For example, if the farmer buys the tractor for $10,000, expects to use it for five years and then sell it for scrap for $2,000, the useful life is five years, the salvage value is $2,000, and the amount to be allocated over the five years is $8,000. One possible method of allocation would be to assign equal amounts of $1,600 to each year; this is called the "straightline" method. Other methods are described below.

Useful lives. The basic idea of determining the expected useful life of an asset is simple enough that it requires no discussion. The application of the idea, however, has proved to be difficult, particularly in the case of certain long-lived assets (e.g., factory buildings), complex, specialized machinery and equipment, and unique assets such as customer lists.

Salvage value. Salvage value is of much less importance than useful lives and method of allocation. Under the Modified Accelerated Cost Recovery System (MACRS) that now applies to all tangible assets, salvage value is disregarded; that is, salvage value is assumed to be zero. This rule obviously favors taxpayers. It sacrifices accuracy for simplicity.

Methods of allocation. As indicated above, under the *straightline* method an equal portion of the total cost of the asset is allocated to each year. The deduction can be expressed as an annual percentage: for an asset with a useful life of five years, 20 percent a year; for an asset with a useful life of ten years, 10 percent a year; and so forth. This percentage is applied to the original cost (unadjusted basis). There are various accelerated methods, by which greater amounts are allocated to early years than to later years. Most taxpayers prefer to use accelerated methods since the effect is to increase deductions, and reduce income, in the early years of the life of an asset, at the price of reduced deductions, and increased income, in the later years. The advantage is deferral.

The currently most significant accelerated method is the *declining balance* method. Under this method, the straightline percentage is determined and then this percentage is increased by a specified factor. The resulting percentage is applied to the cost of the asset reduced by the amounts previously deducted. For example, suppose an asset costs $10,000 and has an expected life of ten years and a zero salvage value. Under the straightline method, the annual deduction would be 10 percent of $10,000, or $1,000. Suppose the declining balance factor is 200 percent (which is referred to as the double, or 200 percent, declining balance method). The amount of the deduction in the first year would be double the straightline method, or 20 percent, or $2,000. The next year the same percentage is used, but it is applied to the balance of the original $10,000 cost after subtracting the $2,000 already deducted. The balance would be $8,000 and the deduction would be $1,600. The balance the next year would be $6,400 and 20 percent of that would be $1,280. And so forth. At some point, this method produces a deduction less than would be produced by straightline; and it never reaches zero. Under the present system, however, when the point is reached where the straightline amount exceeds the declining balance amount, the taxpayer switches to straightline.

It would be possible, of course, to use a method under which deductions are lower in the early years of an asset than in the later years. In fact, if an asset produces a steady stream of income over its useful life, the method that corresponds with economic depreciation has this characteristic (that is, the characteristic of rising each year). The possibility of a "decelerated" (sometimes referred to as "sinking fund") method as a basic or general method of cost recovery is only of theoretical importance. In recent years, it has not been thought of as a serious basic alternative for tax purposes.

Other methods are also possible, including the "income forecast" method, under which the current year's depreciation deduction is derived from a projection of future income — specifically, that portion of basis equal to a fraction of which the numerator is the current year's income and the denominator is the estimated total income to be derived from the asset for its entire useful life. See Rev. Rul. 60-358, 1960-2 C.B. 68. This method is used for films, sound recordings, and video recordings. See Rev. Rul. 89-62, 1989-1 C.B. 62.

Rapid amortization and current deduction. The Code allows rapid amortization for certain investments (e.g., § 169 relating to pollution control facilities) and current deductions for various other investments (e.g., § 174 relating to research and experimental expenditures).

The first year of service. There is a practical problem of how much of a deduction to allow for an asset that is first used during a taxable year but is not used for the whole year. The question is, just how accurate does one want to be? One possibility would be to prorate the deduction on a daily basis, but that could be more trouble than it is worth. The practical compromise under present law is described below; the rules are referred to as the "applicable convention."

Component depreciation. Another problem of practicality is how far to go in allowing, or requiring, different rates of depreciation for different components of an asset. For example, in the case of a building, should there be separate rates for the structure, the roof, the elevators, the plumbing and wiring, the air-conditioning equipment, etc.?

Basis and gain or loss on disposition. The deduction for depreciation, or cost recovery, results, for tax purposes, in a reduction of basis. In fact, the basis is reduced if depreciation is allowable, even if the deduction is not taken. See § 1016(a)(2). If the depreciation deduction happens to correspond exactly with economic reality, adjusted basis will correspond exactly with market value. Otherwise there will be a gain or loss that will be reported on disposition of the asset.

Recapture. Generally, when a business asset is disposed of, any gain is treated as capital gain. See infra page 701. But the depreciation deduction is an offset to ordinary income. For example, suppose that a farmer buys a tractor for $10,000 and over the first three years of its use claims depreciation deductions of $6,000, leaving an adjusted basis of $4,000. Now suppose the tractor is sold for $5,000. The gain is $1,000. But for the "recapture" rule, adopted in 1962, that gain would be treated as capital gain. Capital gain treatment seems wrong since the gain is in a sense a recovery of what turned out to be an excess reduction of ordinary income by virtue of depreciation deductions. In the case of personal property such as tractors (and other equipment and machinery), the Code now provides that any gain on disposition is treated as ordinary income to the extent of prior deductions for depreciation. § 1245. Thus, in our example, the gain of $1,000 would be treated as ordinary income. If the tractor had been sold for $11,000, the gain would consist of $6,000 of ordinary income (the amount of depreciation previously taken) and $1,000 of capital gain. For real property the recapture amount is the excess of accelerated depreciation over straightline depreciation (with a phaseout for certain specialized property as the property is held for more than a specified number of months). § 1250. This is not an issue for real property acquired after 1986, which only gets straightline depreciation. See § 168(b)(3). However, a special capital gains rate of 25 percent, rather than the usual 20 percent, applies to the recapture of such straightline depreciation. § 1(h)(1)(D).

Investment tax credit. The depreciation deduction has been supplemented, from time to time, by a series of investment tax credits. As the term implies, an investment tax credit gives a taxpayer a one-time credit upon purchase of a qualifying asset. Perhaps the most important investment tax credit was adopted in 1981 and generally applied to tangible depreciable property other than real estate. Taxpayers purchasing such property received a tax credit equal to 10 percent of the purchase price. In effect, the government paid 10 percent of the cost of all qualifying property. (Recall that while a deduction simply reduces taxable income, a credit produces a dollar-for-dollar reduction in taxes owed.) This was repealed in 1986.

2. History

The depreciation deduction has been part of the modern income tax since its inception. In the early years of the tax, the debate over the deduction was cast in terms of what was a realistic allowance — one that accorded with economic reality. The basic rule was that useful lives were determined on an individual basis, according to all the "facts and circumstances" relating to particular assets as they were used by each taxpayer. The tax law now deviates from that ideal in two important respects. First, the useful life of tangible assets is no longer determined on an individualized basis; instead, each tangible asset falls within a specific category of assets and must be depreciated over the recovery period applicable to that category. For example, automobiles fall within the category of five-year property and are depreciated over that period. Second, and more important, for tangible assets at least, tax depreciation is no longer intended to mirror economic depreciation. Instead, Congress has deliberately provided taxpayers with a deduction that is generally in excess of the anticipated decline in value of the asset, in the hope of thereby stimulating investment. This favorable treatment has been brought about by assigning each category of assets a useful life for tax purposes below the actual useful lives, so that, for example, an asset that might be expected to last eight years is given a five-year useful life. In addition, within the prescribed recovery period, taxpayers have been allowed to use methods of depreciation that concentrate deductions in the early years of that period. Finally, the depreciation deduction has been supplemented, from time to time, by investment tax credits, described supra on this page.

Increasingly favorable cost of recovery rules were passed in the Eisenhower, Kennedy, and Nixon administrations. The trend toward generous depreciation allowances and investment tax credits reached its zenith in the 1981 Economic Recovery Tax Act, passed in the first year of the Reagan administration. This Act combined short useful lives, accelerated methods of depreciation that concentrated the deduction in the first years of that useful life, and investment tax credits. The net effect was as favorable, for some capital investments, as a rule that allowed the taxpayer to deduct the entire amount of the investment in the first year of service. Again, the motive for the generous cost of recovery rules was the desire to stimulate investment. Since 1981, fiscal pressures have led to a scale-back of depreciation and the investment tax credit. After a series of minor downward adjustments to the cost recovery system, Congress in 1986 repealed the investment tax credit, increased the useful lives for many assets, and changed the method of depreciation to lessen the deductions available in the first few years of service. Depreciation has been the subject of further, albeit minor, reductions in more recent years.

3. Basic Rules

a. *Tangible assets depreciable under § 168.* Tangible assets placed in service after 1980 are depreciated under the rules of § 168, described below.

Recovery period. The useful life or (to use the statutory term) recovery period for many assets is stated directly in the statute. For example, automobiles are subject to a five-year recovery period. § 168(e)(3). Cost recovery begins not when property is acquired but when it is "placed in service." The useful life for more specialized assets is determined by reference to class life tables published by the IRS. § 168(e).

Personal property: basic recovery periods. For personal property there are now recovery periods for six different classes of property — three-year property (e.g., certain special tools and racehorses more than two years old when placed in service); five-year property (e.g., computers, typewriters, copiers, trucks, cargo containers, and semiconductor manufacturing equipment); seven-year property (e.g., office furniture, fixtures and equipment, railroad tracks, and single-purpose agricultural and horticultural structures); ten-year property (e.g., assets used in petroleum refining); fifteen-year property (e.g., sewage treatment plants and telephone distribution plants); and twenty-year property (e.g., municipal sewers).

Personal property: basic method. The method prescribed for personal property is 200 percent declining balance for three-, five-, seven-, and ten-year property and 150 percent for fifteen- and twenty-year property, shifting to straightline when that produces larger deductions. A half-year convention is used for the first year of service; that is, for the first year the rate is half of what it would be for a full year (as if the asset were placed in service exactly in the middle of the year, without regard to when it was actually placed in service). If, however, more than 40 percent of all property is placed in service in the last quarter of the taxable year, a mid-quarter convention applies. A half-year's deduction is allowed in the year of disposition. There are, however, special rules for automobiles and other "listed" property (see supra page 451); for patents and copyrights (straightline under Regs. § 1-167(a)(6)); and for films, sound recordings, and certain other assets (§ 168(f)(3) and (4); see supra page 567).

Personal property: optional recovery periods and method. Taxpayers have the option of using certain recovery periods and methods that tend to delay deductions.

Real property: basic recovery periods. The recovery periods for real property are 27.5 years for residential rental property and 39 years for other real property.

Real property: basic method. The method for real property is straightline. The first-year applicable convention is that the full-year deduction is prorated according to the number of months during which the property is in service during the year. Similarly, in the year of disposition, the deduction is prorated according to months of service. Component depreciation is not permitted; the recovery period and method used for a building as a whole must be used for all its components that are real property.

Real property: optional recovery periods and method. Taxpayers may use optional longer useful lives.

Recapture. There are complex rules for recapture for both real and personal property. The recapture rule transforms capital gain, which can be offset by capital losses, into ordinary gain, which cannot be offset by capital losses (except for $3,000 per year for individuals). See supra page 567. Recapture also is significant in two other situations. First, recapture gain is not eligible for the installment method. § 453(i). Second, the amount of recapture gain reduces the amount of the deduction in the case of a gift of property to a charity. § 170(e).

Limited expensing. A limited amount of the cost of certain property (roughly, all personal property) used in a trade or business may be treated as a current expense. § 179. For 2006 through 2010, the amount is $125,000; thereafter, it is $25,000. This deduction may not exceed the income from the business and is phased out, dollar for dollar, as total investment exceeds $500,000. The $125,000 and $500,000 amounts are to be adjusted for inflation.

Investment credit. The investment credit was repealed in 1986.

Intangible assets. Intangible assets, such as patents and copyrights, are subject to § 167 and are not eligible for the accelerated statutory methods of depreciation described above. In general, such assets must be depreciated on a straightline basis. Intangible assets that are purchased rather than created "in-house" are generally subject to § 197, discussed immediately below.

COMPARATIVE FOCUS: The U.K. "Industrial Buildings Allowance"

Recall that under U.S. law, depreciation deductions are allowed with respect to the "exhaustion, wear and tear" of "property used in the trade or business" or "property held for the production of income." § 167(a). In the United Kingdom, the scope of tax depreciation is substantially narrower, especially with respect to buildings.

As part of the Income Tax Act of 1945, the UK adopted what came to be known as the "industrial buildings allowance" (IBA) as a means of encouraging post-war reconstruction by certain industries. Under the original IBA scheme, depreciation deductions were allowed for the cost of constructing buildings and structures, but only for firms engaged in manufacturing and processing. Over time, the buildings allowance was broadened to incorporate depreciation for certain other types of structures (e.g., qualifying hotels, tunnels, bridges); however, the IBA regime was never extended to buildings and structures used in connection with a retail establishment. The distinction naturally resulted in litigation, especially in cases where the taxpayer had constructed a building used for both qualifying and non-qualifying purposes (see, e.g., Kilmarnock Equitable Co-operative Society Ltd. v. CIR, 42 TC 675).

Beginning in April 2008, the UK initiated a "phased withdrawal" of the industrial buildings allowance regime over four years. The change, which was adopted as part of a broader package of business tax reforms, was motivated in part by a desire to eliminate the preferential treatment of industrial buildings. Despite a storm of protest over the IBA repeal, the government stuck to its guns, noting that IBAs had become a "poorly focused subsidy" and that "the tax system already recognises the depreciation of buildings and structures in other ways: through tax relief for the costs of repairs and insurance, and by directly recognising any actual depreciation (or appreciation) through the capital gains tax system at the point of a building's sale." For more information, see HM Revenue & Customs, Business Tax Reform: Capital Allowance Changes, Technical Note (Dec. 2007) (available at http://www.hmrc.gov.uk/legislation/pu451.pdf.).

4. Goodwill and Other Intangibles

An individual who acquires more than one asset in a single transaction must allocate a portion of the purchase price to each asset. The allocation is made on the basis of the relative fair market value of the assets as of the date of purchase. Under this rule, the purchase of a business is treated as the purchase of the individual assets of the business. In many cases, tangible assets and intangible assets such as copyrights or patents will account for the entire purchase price. In some cases, however, some portion of the purchase price will be attributable to a different sort of intangible, such as the enterprise's reputation, loyal customers, or skilled work force. These sorts of intangibles are sometimes referred to collectively as the enterprise's going concern value or goodwill. A business with a high going concern value may be worth far more than the sum of its tangible assets and discrete intangible assets, such as copyrights.

The treatment of going concern value, goodwill, and similar intangibles for purposes of depreciation has long been a bone of contention. For many years, the government has contended that such assets are nondepreciable goodwill. Taxpayers, on the other hand, have estimated useful lives for some of these assets and have depreciated the portion of the purchase price allocated to them over their useful lives. In 1993, the Supreme Court attempted to resolve a conflict among the circuits over the treatment of such assets in its decision in Newark Morning Ledger Co. v. United States, 507 U.S. 546 (1993). The taxpayer in that case had paid $328 million to acquire a chain of newspapers and had allocated $67.8 million of that amount to an intangible asset denominated "paid subscribers." The $67.8 million was the taxpayer's estimate of the present value of future profits to be derived from the newspaper's current subscribers, most of whom were expected to continue to subscribe after the acquisition. The taxpayer presented experts who testified that, using generally accepted statistical techniques, they were able to estimate how long the average subscriber would continue to subscribe. The taxpayer then depreciated the $67.8 million on a straightline basis over the estimated life of the asset. The government denied the deduction on the ground that the concept of "paid subscribers" was indistinguishable from goodwill, which had long been treated as nondepreciable. The Court (in a five-to-four decision) held that the taxpayer had in fact shown the asset had a determinable useful life and allowed the deduction.

The decision in *Newark Morning Ledger Co.* threatened to embroil taxpayers, the Service, and the courts in a never-ending wave of fact-specific litigation. To understand why this is so, suppose you represent a client who in 1992 paid $2,000,000 for a well-regarded and highly successful restaurant. The restaurant's tangible assets were worth only $500,000; the remaining value was attributable to the reputation and skill of the current employees, the presumed loyalty of the current clientele, and the restaurant's reputation apart from its current employees. Under *Newark Morning Ledger Co.*, the remaining $1,500,000 is in theory depreciable. But how would one go about assigning values to the different intangibles described above? And how would one determine the useful life of those intangibles?

To end unproductive litigation, and to limit the damage to the fisc from aggressive taxpayer positions, Congress in 1993 passed § 197, which provides for a fifteen-year amortization of a long list of intangibles. These intangibles include goodwill, going concern value, the value of work force in place, and the value of current relationships with customers or suppliers, provided that such assets are acquired by purchase rather than self-created. Under § 197, then, it no longer matters whether the premium paid in connection with a business is called by a general term such as goodwill or going concern value or is divided among its component parts and allocated to work force in place or customer relationships. The premium will in any event be depreciable over fifteen years.

Section 197 applies to purchased patents, copyrights, films, sound recordings, etc. (but only if they are acquired as part of the acquisition of a trade or business or a substantial portion thereof) (§ 197(e)(4)). What about self-created assets? Certain assets, such as trademarks and covenants not to compete, qualify for fifteen-year amortization under § 197. The assets in these categories that are not covered by § 197 are subject to the various other tax rules relating to capitalization (see, e.g., § 174) and are depreciable under § 167 rather than under the fifteen-year, straightline rule of § 197.

G. DEPLETION AND INTANGIBLE DRILLING COSTS

Cost and percentage depletion. Although the Court in *Baltic Mining Co.*, 240 U.S. 103 (1916), stated that an "adequate allowance . . . for the exhaustion of the ore body" resulting from mining operations is not required by the Constitution, Congress has always allowed depletion to be deducted in computing taxable income from mining and other extractive activities.

Originally, the deduction was based on the cost of the property being depleted, and cost depletion is still authorized. § 611. When this method is employed, the taxpayer allocates adjusted basis equally among the estimated recoverable units and deducts an appropriate amount as the units are sold. Thus, if the cost to be allocated is $100,000 and there are 100,000 recoverable tons, the depletion allowance will be $1 per ton, deducted as the ore is sold. This method of depletion, cost depletion, may simply be viewed as another method of depreciation. The provision considered in the *Baltic Mining Co.* case, providing that the depletion allowance might not in any circumstances exceed 5 percent of gross income, was repealed in 1916.

The second method available for recovering the cost of most depletable deposits is percentage depletion. The percentage depletion method ignores both the taxpayer's cost and the number of recoverable units. Instead, the taxpayer is permitted to deduct a given percentage of gross income (but not to exceed 50 percent of taxable income calculated before depletion is taken) as a depletion allowance. This method avoids the problem in cost depletion of estimating the number of recoverable units in the deposit—an estimate that may be only the wildest of guesses.[17] For the taxpayer, percentage depletion has the special attraction of an increasing depletion allowance as income rises, which ordinarily is when the deduction will save most in taxes. But percentage depletion just keeps rolling along, even after the taxpayer's full cost has been recovered. This is not an essential feature of percentage depletion, since the total depletion deductions could have been limited to the tax cost of the deposit, but the statute does not contain such a limitation.

Percentage depletion rates. The percentage of annual gross income that may be deducted as depletion ranges from 22 percent for certain minerals (such as sulfur and uranium) to 5 percent for other minerals (such as clay used in the manufacture of drainage and roofing tile). § 613(b). The percentage depletion rates reflect the political clout of the various extractive industries. As the political influence of an industry changes, the percentage depletion rates sometimes change. For example, soon after the oil blockade was carried out by Arab members of OPEC, percentage depletion was eliminated for major oil and gas producers, but was retained for the relatively small, independent producers and royalty owners (though even for them it was reduced from 22 percent to 15 percent). Many explanations have been given for these changes, but the most cogent appears to be that independent producers and royalty owners were an effective lobbying group and were not as unpopular as the major oil and gas producers, whose images were tarnished by charges of collaboration with the blockading OPEC nations.

The concept of an "economic interest" in the depletable mineral. There are many problems in determining which of the many persons with a financial stake in the extraction of a mineral are entitled to a deduction for depletion. Since the grant of depletion rights to one taxpayer may deny it to another in the chain of production, many cases have been litigated. The Supreme Court early formulated the notion of an economic interest in the mineral extracted as the touchstone. To have an economic interest, the taxpayer must have acquired an interest in the mineral in place and must look only to the mineral for return of his or her capital. Palmer v. Bender, 287 U.S. 551 (1933). For example, a landowner who allows another the right to drill for and extract oil in exchange for a royalty based on production has such an economic interest. See Thomas v. Perkins, 301 U.S. 655 (1937), and Kirby Petroleum Co. v. Commissioner, 326 U.S. 599 (1946). Thus, if the gross income is $100 and the royalty is 16½ percent, the operator uses $83.50 as the base for percentage depletion while the landowner takes percentage depletion on the $16.50.

Income subject to percentage depletion. The appropriate percentage depletion rate for a mineral (other than oil or gas) is applied to the "gross income from mining" to determine the taxpayer's percentage depletion deduction. In United States v. Cannelton Sewer Pipe Co., 364 U.S. 76 (1960), the taxpayer

---

17. Despite this, the taxpayer may have to compute depletion on a cost basis for some purposes (e.g., for purposes of the alternative minimum tax, discussed infra page 611), even though percentage depletion is used in determining taxable income.

mined clay, processed it, and manufactured clay pipes and other related products. It claimed percentage depletion on its gross income from the sale of manufactured sewer pipe. The Court found that it was entitled to a percentage depletion only on the value of the clay up to the cutoff point of processes used by a nonintegrated miner before sale. The range of choice in *Cannelton* was from $1.60 (the going price for fire clay) to $40 per ton, the value of the finished pipe product, but for some other minerals the range is even more dramatic; for example, salt worth $10 at an early point in the extractive process might be worth $1,800 after it has been purified for table use and packaged in small containers for sale to consumers.

Today, gross income from mining is defined in § 613(c) to include income from certain technical processes and from transportation. Section 613(c)(4)(G) now contains an explicit statement of the processes that qualify for sewer pipe clay.

Limits on percentage depletion. Section 613 limits the percentage depletion deduction to 50 percent of the taxable income from the property. The importance of this limitation may be illustrated as follows: Suppose that X Corp. sells 10,000 tons of a certain mineral for $100,000; that X Corp. has labor and other mining costs (exclusive of depletion) of $90,000; and that the depletion percentage for the mineral is 22 percent. X Corp.'s gross income from mining is $100,000 and its depletion deduction would therefore be 22 percent of that amount, or $22,000. But X Corp.'s taxable income from mining is only $10,000 and its percentage depletion deduction is limited to half of that amount, or $5,000.

Intangible drilling costs. Section 263(c) allows taxpayers that develop an oil, gas, or geothermal deposit (as opposed to buying a deposit from someone else) to deduct as current expenses the "intangible drilling and development costs."[18] These costs, roughly speaking, include materials that are used up in the drilling or development process and labor. See Regs. § 1.612-4. Section 263(c) is a dramatic exception to the general rule that the costs of acquiring a capital asset must be treated as a capital expenditure; it is an important element in the economics of the extractive industries and in tax-shelter planning. To the same general effect as § 263(c) are §§ 616 and 617, applying to other deposits.[19]

Percentage depletion is particularly beneficial to taxpayers that take advantage of § 263(c). Such taxpayers will have deducted virtually all the costs of development before production of the mineral deposit and will have a cost basis in the deposit of zero (or close to it). Cost depletion will therefore be of no value. Percentage depletion, however, will be unaffected by the low basis.

18. For large, "integrated" producers, however, 30 percent of intangible drilling and development costs must be amortized over a five-year period. See § 291(b).
19. In the case of foreign mines, however, exploration and development costs are recovered by either (a) ten-year straightline amortization or (b) at the election of the taxpayer, as part of basis for cost depletion. See § 616(d).

Foreign natural resource interest. While the tax benefits provided the natural resource industries are often justified on the ground that they stimulate increased supplies of such resources in the United States, the benefits in the past normally applied to foreign activities also. Increasingly, this has changed. See, e.g., limitations to U.S. deposits in § 613(b)(1)(B) and (b)(2); § 613A(c); § 616(d); § 617(h)(1); § 901(e).

The environment and natural resource tax benefits. It is interesting to speculate on the effect of the tax benefits to our natural resource industries on some of our current environmental problems. For example, have these benefits led to a lower price for gasoline and encouraged the use of more and larger automobiles than would otherwise have been the case? If so, has this contributed to the demise or stillbirth of public transportation in many parts of our country and substantial reliance on automobile transportation to the detriment of the quality of our air? Has this contributed to or created patterns of suburban living that might otherwise not have occurred? Does the fact that new metals and some virgin oil receive percentage depletion make recycling of used metals or used oil relatively less economical and therefore accelerate the exhaustion of natural resources and exacerbate waste disposal problems? As previously noted, the tax benefits to promote home ownership may also have had a role in creating some of the present living and community habits. The federal and state highway trust funds, which pour a steady stream of gasoline tax and other revenues into highway construction, must also be given a leading role in such speculation.

H. TAX AVOIDANCE

People regularly make investments and engage in other activities that are motivated by, and result in, substantial tax savings. For example, suppose that you can buy either a U.S. Treasury bond that pays interest at a rate of 9 percent or a tax-exempt bond with virtually identical characteristics except that the interest rate is 7 percent. If you buy the tax-exempt bond, your sole reason must be to save taxes. Purchase of the tax-exempt bond would make no sense whatsoever but for tax considerations. Yet most informed people would not view the investment as inappropriate or describe it, pejoratively, as a "tax shelter." They might even be uncertain about use of the less pejorative, but still disapproving, term "tax avoidance." Nor would the IRS or the courts hold (as they have done with other tax-motivated investments) that the tax benefit (exemption) is lost because the sole motive was tax reduction. The same observation can be made about a purchase of common stocks by a person who is clear in his or her own mind that but for the tax advantages of that investment (deferral of recognition of gain and capital gain), he or she would have bought bonds.

Where do we draw the line between "legitimate" tax savings and "abusive" tax avoidance? More precisely, what does it mean to describe a particular investment as a "tax shelter"? Unfortunately, there is no quick and easy answer to these questions, in part because of a more general disagreement regarding the propriety of tax planning. Clearly some types of tax planning are almost universally regarded as legitimate (e.g., contributions to a § 401(k) plan), while certain other types of "tax planning" are likely to invite the scorn of tax experts and laypersons alike. Given the difficulty of the drawing a line between these two categories, you should not expect the ensuing materials to reveal a detailed roadmap of "legitimate" versus "abusive" tax planning; however, a careful attention to legal developments in this area should bring nuance and sophistication to the way you think about tax avoidance.

1.   The Tax Shelter Problem

In general, the term "tax shelter" is used to describe an investment that is unrelated to a taxpayer's trade or business or a taxpayer's "normal" investments and is certain to produce a tax loss but is not expected to produce an economic loss. Some (but by no means all) tax shelters use statutes and regulations in a manner inconsistent with the intent of the representatives who enacted the statutes or the bureaucrats who wrote and approved the regulations.

Most of the tax shelters described in the following pages generated paper losses that are used to offset income from other sources. Over the years a variety of rules have been adopted to prevent such tax avoidance, culminating in 1986 in the passive activity loss (PAL) rules, described infra at page 594. A description of tax shelters is important, however, for an understanding of the development of the law and the role of the various limitations that one now encounters.

The elements of a tax shelter. Tax shelters attempt to achieve some combination of (a) deferral, (b) conversion, and (c) tax arbitrage. Deferral consists of pushing income into the future by incurring costs that are currently deductible and receiving the corresponding return from the investment in some future year. The tax advantage arises from the use of the funds that would otherwise be paid in taxes for the period of deferral.

Conversion consists of converting ordinary income into tax-favored income, such as capital gain.

Tax arbitrage involves incurring expenses that are deductible in order to generate income that is tax favored, thus creating a tax loss in excess of any economic loss. In illustration, suppose that you borrow to hold municipal bonds. If not for § 265, the transaction might generate deductible interest expense on the one hand and excludable income on the other. The tax loss it generated would therefore exceed any real economic loss. While § 265 blocks this particular tax arbitrage transaction (assuming the interest expense is indeed allocated to the bonds for tax purposes), the basic idea of pairing deductible expense against tax-favored income can be implemented in a variety of ways.

The real estate tax shelter. The operation of a typical real estate tax shelter in the heyday of such transactions may be illustrated by the following simplified example. Assume that before the enactment of the anti–tax shelter legislation described below, and at a time that depreciation rates for real estate were far more generous than they are today, an investor borrowed $100,000 at 9 percent and used the proceeds to buy an apartment building. In the first year, the investor paid $9,000 interest. Assume further that during the first year, the apartment building produced net rental income of $9,000. The net rental income represented profit after taking into account all expenses except that of the $9,000 interest payment on the loan used to purchase the building. Finally, assume that the building neither increased nor decreased in value. The rental income therefore exactly offset the interest expense and left the investor's wealth unchanged. For tax purposes, the investor recognized rental income and deducted interest expense. In addition, however, the investor was able to deduct approximately $12,000 depreciation. Thus, a break-even economic investment produced a $12,000 tax loss. The investor could use this loss as a deduction to offset income from other sources.

Eventually, the tax and economic consequences of the investment would converge. The $12,000 depreciation deduction taken in the first year would reduce the basis of the building to $88,000. If the building were sold on the first day of the second year for its fair market value of $100,000, the taxpayer would recognize $12,000 gain. In effect, the taxpayer was required to "give back" the $12,000 of depreciation taken in the previous year.

The investment was nonetheless advantageous because the loss in the first year allowed the investor to defer taxes payable on income from other sources. The investment was even more advantageous if, as was generally the case, the gain recognized on sale qualified for favorable capital gain treatment.

Financial and other tax shelters. Real estate was not the only source of tax-shelter investments. Many tax shelters were based on financial investments. For example, an individual might borrow at 9 percent to buy a deferred annuity (that is, an annuity policy that did not start making payments until some time in the future) that provided a return of 8 percent. The 9 percent interest would be currently deductible, while the 8 percent appreciation would not be taxed until the payments on the annuity began. The loan might be secured by the annuity and made by the company that sold the annuity. A variant of this kind of tax shelter is discussed in the *Knetsch* case, immediately below.

Overvaluation. The attractiveness of many tax shelters depended on overvaluation of an asset and the use of nonrecourse debt. For example, Rev. Rul. 77-110, 1977-1 C.B. 58, describes a motion picture tax shelter in which the investors purported to buy the picture for $2 million with $200,000 in cash and $1.8 million in the form of a nonrecourse promissory note payable out of the proceeds of its exploitation. The promoter of this tax shelter had bought the picture a few months earlier for $200,000, and there was nothing to suggest that it was worth more than that amount. The investors presumably were little concerned about the fact that they "overpaid" for the picture; they expected to recover their investment from depreciation deductions on an asset with a claimed basis of $2 million. Eventually, of course, the investors would default on the note and recognize gain from discharge of indebtedness, but the value of deferral would nonetheless have made the transaction advantageous. The motion picture scheme was thwarted by an IRS decision that "an obligation, the payment of which is so speculative as to create [only] contingent liability, cannot be included in the basis of the property." But other, less egregious shelters based on overvaluation were more successful. The use of overvaluation in tax shelters is illustrated by the *Estate of Franklin* case, infra at page 588.

2. The Judicial Response to Tax Shelters

KNETSCH v. UNITED STATES
364 U.S. 361 (1960)

Mr. Justice BRENNAN delivered the opinion of the Court.

This case presents the question of whether deductions . . . of $143,465 in 1953 and of $147,105 in 1954, for payments made by petitioner, Karl F. Knetsch, to Sam Houston Life Insurance Company, constituted "interest paid . . . on indebtedness" within the meaning of . . . § 163(a). . . .

On December 11, 1953, the insurance company sold Knetsch ten 30-year maturity deferred annuity bonds, each in the face amount of $400,000 and bearing interest at two and one-half percent compounded annually. The purchase price was $4,004,000. Knetsch gave the Company his check for $4,000, and signed $4,000,000 of nonrecourse annuity loan notes for the balance. The notes bore 3½% interest and were secured by the annuity bonds. The interest was payable in advance, and Knetsch on the same day prepaid the first year's interest, which was $140,000. Under the Table of Cash and Loan Values made part of the bonds, their cash or loan value at December 11, 1954, the end of the first contract year, was to be $4,100,000. The contract terms, however, permitted Knetsch to borrow any excess of this value above his indebtedness without waiting until December 11, 1954. Knetsch took advantage of this provision only five days after the purchase.[20] On December 16, 1953, he received from the company $99,000 of the $100,000 excess over his

20. [The following summary of the basic transaction may be helpful:

Loan to Knetsch from Ins. Co.	$4,000,000	
Interest on loan (at 3½%)		$140,000
Investment by Knetsch in annuity	4,000,000	
Tax-free return (at 2½%)*		100,000
Net before tax effects		(40,000)
Tax saving from interest deduction, at tax rate of:		
90%		126,000
70		98,000
50		70,000
25		35,000
Net after-tax effects at tax rate of:		
90%		86,000
70		58,000
50		30,000
25		(5,000)

*In the form of loan based on increased value of annuity.

—EDS.]

$4,000,000 indebtedness, for which he gave his notes bearing 3½% interest. This interest was also payable in advance and on the same day he prepaid the first year's interest of $3,465. In their joint return for 1953, the petitioners deducted the sum of the two interest payments, that is $143,465, as "interest paid . . . within the taxable year on indebtedness." . . .

The second contract year began on December 11, 1954, when interest in advance of $143,465 was payable by Knetsch on his aggregate indebtedness of $4,099,000. Knetsch paid this amount on December 27, 1954. Three days later, on December 30, he received from the company cash in the amount of $104,000, the difference less $1,000 between his then $4,099,000 indebtedness and the cash or loan value of the bonds of $4,204,000 on December 11, 1955. He gave the company appropriate notes and prepaid the interest thereon of $3,640. In their joint return for the taxable year 1954 the petitioners deducted the sum of the two interest payments, that is $147,105. . . .

[Roughly the same procedure was followed in December 1955.]

Knetsch did not go on with the transaction for the fourth contract year beginning December 11, 1956, but terminated it on December 27, 1956. His indebtedness at that time totalled $4,307,000. The cash or loan value of the bonds was the $4,308,000 value at December 11, 1956. . . . He surrendered the bonds and his indebtedness was canceled. He received the difference of $1000 in cash.

The contract called for a monthly annuity of $90,171 at maturity (when Knetsch would be 90 years of age) or for such smaller amount as would be produced by the cash or loan value after deduction of the then existing indebtedness. It was stipulated that if Knetsch had held the bonds to maturity and continued annually to borrow the net cash value less $1,000, the sum available for the annuity at maturity would be . . . enough to provide an annuity of only $43 per month.

The trial judge made findings that "[t]here was no commercial economic substance to the . . . transaction," that the parties did not intend that Knetsch "become indebted to Sam Houston," that "[n]o indebtedness of [Knetsch] was created by any of the . . . transactions," and that "[n]o economic gain could be achieved from the purchase of these bonds without regard to the tax consequences. . . ." His conclusion of law . . . was that "[w]hile in form the payments to Sam Houston were compensation for the use or forbearance of money, they were not in substance. As a payment of interest, the transaction was a sham."

We first examine the transaction between Knetsch and the insurance company to determine whether it created an "indebtedness." . . . We put aside a finding by the District Court that Knetsch's "only motive in purchasing these 10 bonds was to attempt to secure an interest deduction."[21] As was said in Gregory v. Helvering [infra page 781]: "The legal right of a taxpayer to decrease the amount of what otherwise would be his taxes, or altogether avoid them, by means which the law permits, cannot be doubted. . . . But the

---

21. We likewise put aside Knetsch's argument that, because he received ordinary income when he surrendered the annuities in 1956, he has suffered a net loss even if the contested deductions are allowed, and that therefore his motive in taking out the annuities could not have been tax avoidance.

question for determination is whether what was done, apart from the tax motive, was the thing which the statute intended."

When we examine "what was done" here, we see that Knetsch paid the insurance company $294,540 during the two taxable years involved and received $203,000 back in the form of "loans." What did Knetsch get for the out-of-pocket difference of $91,570? In form he had an annuity contract . . . which would produce monthly annuity payments of $90,171, or substantial life insurance proceeds in the event of his death before maturity. This, as we have seen, was a fiction, because each year Knetsch's annual borrowings kept the net cash value, on which any annuity or insurance payments would depend, at the relative pittance of $1,000. . . . What he was ostensibly "lent" back was in reality only the rebate of a substantial part of the so-called "interest" payments. The $91,570 difference retained by the company was its fee for providing the facade of "loans" whereby the petitioners sought to reduce their 1953 and 1954 taxes in the total sum of $233,298 [about 80 percent of the "interest deduction"]. . . .

The petitioners contend, however, . . . that § 264(a)(2) denies a deduction for amounts paid on indebtedness incurred to purchase or carry a single-premium annuity contract, but only as to contracts purchased after March 1, 1954. The petitioners thus would attribute to Congress a purpose to allow the deduction of pre-1954 payments under transactions of the kind carried on by Knetsch with the insurance company without regard to whether the transactions created a true obligation to pay interest. Unless that meaning plainly appears we will not attribute it to Congress. "To hold otherwise would be to exalt artifice above reality and to deprive the statutory provision in question of all serious purpose." Gregory v. Helvering [infra page 781]. . . .

Congress . . . in 1942 denied a deduction for amounts paid on indebtedness incurred to purchase single-premium life insurance and endowment contracts . . . "to close a loophole" in respect of interest allocable to partially exempt income.

The 1954 provision extending the denial to amounts paid on indebtedness incurred to purchase or carry single-premium annuities appears to us simply to expand the application of the policy in respect of interest allocable to partially exempt income.[22]

Moreover the provision itself negates any suggestion that sham transactions were the congressional concern, for the deduction denied is of certain interest payments on actual "indebtedness." And we see nothing . . . to suggest that Congress is exempting pre-1954 annuities intended to protect sham transactions. . . .

The judgment of the Court of Appeals is affirmed.

Mr. Justice DOUGLAS, with whom Mr. Justice WHITTAKER and Mr. Justice STEWART concur, dissenting. . . .

22. [In 1964, Congress acted again in this field, by enacting § 264(a)(3), which disallows (subject to certain exceptions) any deduction for interest on indebtedness incurred or continued to purchase or carry a life insurance, endowment, or annuity contract pursuant to a plan which "contemplates the systematic direct or indirect borrowing of part or all of the increases in the cash value of such contract." — EDS.]

It is true that in this transaction the taxpayer was bound to lose if the annuity contract is taken by itself. At least, the taxpayer showed by his conduct that he never intended to come out ahead on that investment apart from his income tax deduction. . . . Yet as long as the transaction itself is not hocus-pocus, the interest . . . seem[s] to be deductible . . . as respects annuity contracts made prior to March 1, 1954, the date Congress selected for terminating this class of deductions. . . . The insurance company existed; it operated under Texas law; it was authorized to issue these policies and to make these annuity loans. . . .

Tax avoidance is a dominating motive behind scores of transactions. It is plainly present here. Will the Service that calls this transaction a "sham" today not press for collection of taxes arising out of the surrender of the annuity contract? I think it should, for I do not believe any part of the transaction was a "sham." . . . The remedy is legislative. Evils or abuses can be particularized by Congress. . . .

NOTES AND QUESTIONS

1. *Expenses.* Knetsch's decision to terminate the transaction in 1956 may have reflected his receipt, earlier in that year, of an IRS statutory notice of deficiency covering 1953 and 1954. On his 1956 tax return, he claimed a deduction for his out-of-pocket losses, which totaled $137,000. This appears to have been a fallback position, protecting his deduction claim lest 1956 "close" for tax purposes before litigation concerning the earlier years was resolved. Had he computed his taxable income for 1956 in a manner that was consistent with his previous three years' reporting positions, he would instead have reported gain in the amount of $304,000.[23]

His attempt to deduct the out-of-pocket losses, as a loss under § 165(c)(2) or an expense under § 212, subsequently failed, on the ground that he had lacked the requisite profit motive. In effect, he was treated as if the expenses had been for personal consumption—which they surely were not, unless one imagines that he expected and enjoyed the IRS audit and subsequent litigation. Denial of the deduction might, however, be rationalized as an implicit penalty for engaging in a sham transaction (as subsequently held) that presumably was unlikely to be detected on audit.

2. *Turning pretax straw into after-tax spun gold.* For 1953, the first year of the transaction, Knetsch paid the company $140,000 of interest and earned $100,000 in the form of a nontaxable increase in the value of his policy. He was able, in effect, to draw down the $100,000 increase in value by "borrowing" from the insurance company. Thus, he paid out $140,000, received $100,000, and was $40,000 out-of-pocket (leaving aside the $4,000 fee). However, by deducting the $140,000 interest paid without currently including the $100,000 of loan proceeds, he was able (he thought) to reduce his tax

---

23. Under Knetsch's view of the transaction, $304,000 was the excess of his amount realized (($1,000 cash plus $4,307,000 discharge of indebtedness) over his cost basis ($4,004,000)) in the annuity contracts.

liability for the year by about $110,000. (Marginal rates in 1953 were far higher than today, with a top rate of 91 percent; $110,000 was the tax saving from the $140,000 deduction.) He thus—assuming the transaction worked—converted a $40,000 pretax loss into a $70,000 after-tax gain ($110,000 tax saving less $40,000). While this ignores his expected future tax liability when he would have to take all the deferred income into account, this was not scheduled to happen for at least thirty years. It therefore seemingly made sense for him to borrow $4 million at 3½ percent in order to invest the same amount at 2½ percent. Indeed, had he needed the deductions (so long as he had the requisite out-of-pocket cash), he presumably could have borrowed $40 million, $400 million, or for that matter $4 billion with the same spread between his borrowing and lending rates.

3. *Private and not-so-private letter rulings.* Knetsch apparently invested in reliance on a private letter ruling that the IRS had issued to one R.C. Salley, the President and Treasurer of the company that sold him the annuity contract. The IRS issues such rulings at its discretion to taxpayers who apply for them, stating that a given transaction, if it conforms to the stipulated facts, will be taxed in a specified way. Private rulings always state on their face that they are not precedent and that no other taxpayer may rely on them, thus permitting the IRS to feel safe in issuing them without high-level review. They nonetheless are frequently treated by taxpayers as precedent, or at the least as evidence of IRS administrative practice.

The IRS refused to publish its private rulings, even with the identity of the taxpayer redacted, until publication was compelled in the 1970s following the enactment of the Freedom of Information Act. Even before publication was compelled, however, the IRS could not prevent enterprising taxpayers such as Mr. Salley from using private rulings in their possession to their advantage and profit.

A Supreme Court amicus brief in *Knetsch* (on behalf of taxpayers who were litigating similar transactions) argued that the IRS practice of allowing the taxpayer who received a private ruling, but no other taxpayer, to rely on it was "monstrous" and equivalent to racial discrimination. The Court declined to address this argument, however, noting that Knetsch had not raised it.

4. *Economic substance.* The trial judge's finding that the transaction offered no prospect of pre-tax economic gain overlooked the possibility that market interest rates would decline substantially. Knetsch had the right to earn 2½ percent annually, but was free to pay off his 3½ percent loan to the insurance company and borrow the funds elsewhere. Thus, had the market rate at which he could borrow declined sufficiently below 2½ percent, he theoretically could have made money on the deal. He apparently was not aware of this possibility, however, since it was not raised during the litigation.

Arguably, this prospect of pretax profit would have been deemed too remote to change the outcome even if Knetsch's attorneys had raised it. It is highly likely, however, that Knetsch would have won the case if interest rates had recently been fluctuating enough for him to point to a plausible upside, and he had left a "paper trail" suggesting that this upside was relevant to him.

Why wasn't the deal structured to involve greater economic risk? A key reason may be that the insurance company could not have offered Knetsch a greater "upside" without either charging him more for the transaction or requiring him to bear a greater "downside" as well. Taxpayers are often reluctant to accept a significant "downside" in their tax shelter investments, for reasons that are easy to understand. In illustration, suppose you could buy, for $49,000, a chance to win either $100,000 or nothing, depending on the outcome of a fair coin toss. Since you would have a 50 percent probability of winning $100,000, the odds would be in your favor. But if you are like most people, you would not want to do this (even assuming you had the $49,000) by reason of being risk-averse. That is, you might mind losing $49,000 a lot more than you would value winning a slightly greater amount.

The economic substance requirement therefore deters taxpayers from making tax-favored investments unless they are willing to accept some economic risk (including "downside" risk if they are reluctant to pay extra for being given just the "upside"). Why, however, should taxpayers be rewarded with tax benefits for accepting a given risk? Why not let their risk positions depend purely on their own preferences as investors? Would Knetsch have benefited the public fisc in any way by betting on changes in the market interest rate? So what might be the point of the economic substance requirement?

5. *Statutory response.* As the Court observed, after 1954, § 264 expressly denied deductions for interest on debt of the sort involved in *Knetsch*. The case nonetheless remains important as a broader precedent that the IRS can deploy in combating what it regards as unacceptable tax avoidance.

SUBSEQUENT DEVELOPMENTS

In Goldstein v. Commissioner, 364 F.2d 734 (2d Cir. 1966), cert. denied, 385 U.S. 1005 (1967), the taxpayer, having won $140,000 in the Irish Sweepstakes in 1958, in that year borrowed $465,000 from a bank at 4 percent and prepaid $52,000 of interest. She used the proceeds of the loan to buy (for $465,000) U.S. Treasury notes with a face value of $500,000, bearing interest at 1½ percent and due in October 1961. She also entered into another transaction of the same sort with another bank. Her projected economic loss on these two transactions, assuming the bonds were held to maturity, was $18,500. Her expected tax saving was from two sources. First, the interest deduction would reduce her income in 1958 and returns on the Treasury notes would arise in later years. Thus, she would push part of her income from the sweepstakes into later years when it would be taxed at lower rates than if it were all taxed in 1958. Second, the interest deduction was to be an offset to the ordinary income from the sweepstakes, while a large part of the return would be capital gain (the difference between the purchase price of the bonds and notes and proceeds received at maturity). The taxpayer was a retired garment worker living on a modest pension and was totally unsophisticated in financial affairs. She followed the advice of her son, a certified public accountant (whose computation of the projected $18,500 economic loss was introduced by the government). The court upheld the Commissioner's denial of an interest deduction for the loans used to finance these transactions. It refused to follow *Knetsch* and characterize the transactions as "shams," pointing out that the loans were made by independent financial institutions, that the "two loan transactions did not within a few days return all the parties to the position from which they started," that the banks could demand payment at any time, and that the notes were with recourse. In holding for the Commissioner, the court relied instead on the fact that the taxpayer's sole motive (given her son's careful computation) was tax avoidance. The court said that § 163 "does not permit a deduction for interest paid or accrued in loan arrangements, like those now before us, that cannot with reason be said to have purpose, substance, or utility apart from their anticipated tax consequences." The court went on to opine (364 F.2d at 741):

> In order fully to implement [the] Congressional policy of encouraging purposive activity to be financed through borrowing, Section 163(a) should be construed to permit the deductibility of interest when a taxpayer has borrowed funds and incurred an obligation to pay interest in order to engage in what with reason can be termed purposive activity, even though he decided to borrow in order to gain an interest deduction rather than to finance the activity in some other way. In other words, the interest deduction should be permitted whenever it can be said that the taxpayer's desire to secure an interest deduction is only one of mixed motives that prompt the taxpayer to borrow funds; or, put a third way, the deduction is proper if there is some substance to the loan arrangement beyond the taxpayer's desire to secure the deduction. After all, we are frequently told that a taxpayer has the right to decrease the amount of what otherwise would be his taxes, or altogether avoid them, by any means the law permits. E.g., Gregory v. Helvering [infra page 781]. On the other hand, and notwithstanding Section 163(a)'s broad scope, this provision should not be construed to permit an interest deduction when it objectively appears that a taxpayer has borrowed funds in order to engage in a transaction that has no substance or purpose aside from the taxpayer's desire to obtain the tax benefit of an interest deduction; and a good example of such purposeless activity is the borrowing of funds at 4% in order to purchase property that returns less than 2% and holds out no prospect of appreciation sufficient to counter the unfavorable interest rate differential. Certainly the statutory provision's underlying purpose, as we understand it, does not require that a deduction be allowed in such a case. Indeed, to allow a deduction for interest paid on funds borrowed for no purposive reason, other than the securing of a deduction from income, would frustrate Section 163(a)'s purpose; allowing it would encourage transactions that have no economic utility and that would not be engaged in but for the system of taxes imposed by Congress....

Goldstein differs from *Knetsch* because the *Goldstein* transaction concededly was not a "sham." Rather than borrowing and lending the same amount and thus inviting the critique that the transaction amounted to no more than paper-shuffling, the taxpayer actually bought Treasury notes with the proceeds of her own personal debt. At least, she did so if (like the IRS and the court) we ignore the narrower argument that, under the facts of the case, the bank or broker really owned the bonds.

The case therefore establishes that even a non-sham transaction (i.e., one involving more than just paper-shuffling) may be ineffective for tax purposes if it is designed to generate a tax loss and otherwise lacks "purpose, substance, or utility," and thus does not constitute "purposive activity."

In *Knetsch* and *Goldstein* transactions that fit within the literal language of the statute were held invalid because of lack of economic substance. Other courts made similar rulings in cases involving other tax shelters. In time, these rulings produced the so-called economic substance doctrine, which was used to invalidate transactions that have no significant nontax purpose or effect. See Winn-Dixie v. Commissioner, infra page 601.

Not all courts have embraced the economic substance doctrine. In Coltec Industries v. United States, 62 Fed. Cl. 716 (2004), the court held that using the doctrine to trump the language of the statute would usurp the legislature's place and violate the separation of powers clause of the Constitution.

Coltec involved a so-called contingent liability tax shelter. In that shelter, Parent Corporation would contribute $50x in cash to its newly formed Subsidiary Corporation. It would also have Subsidiary Corporation assume $50x of Parent's liabilities. The liabilities were such that they would give rise to a deduction when paid. (In *Coltec*, they were for asbestos-related damages.) The net amount contributed to Subsidiary was 0, since the $50x of liabilities offset the $50x of cash contributed. Subsidiary used the cash to pay the liabilities and claimed a $50x deduction. That deduction flowed through to Parent's tax return. That, in itself, was unproblematic since Parent could have taken the deduction had it paid the liabilities itself. What was problematic was that Parent also took the position that it had a basis of $50x in the Subsidiary stock that it held; it gave itself a basis equal to the cash it contributed but did not reduce its basis by the liabilities it dropped into Subsidiary. Parent sold the stock for its fair market value and claimed a loss of $50x. The net result was that the $50x in liabilities was deducted twice—once by Subsidiary when it paid the amounts owed and once when Parent sold its Subsidiary stock. Parent's position was, alas, supported by badly worded language of the relevant statute. Contingent liability shelters were used by corporations to reduce aggregate tax liability by billions of dollars within a relatively brief (five-year) time period.

In *Coltec*, the government challenged the taxpayer's claimed loss, arguing that the transaction (setting up the subsidiary, transferring liabilities, and so on) had no nontax effect or purpose, and therefore no substance.

The court rejected government's argument, stating:

> In A Matter of Interpretation: Federal Courts and the Law (1997), Justice Scalia presents a compelling argument that the courts must interpret statutes as Congress wrote them, rather than what they "ought to mean." Id. at 3-37 . . .
>
> The public must be able to rely on clear and understandable rules established by Congress to ascertain their federal tax obligations. If federal tax laws are applied in an unpredictable and arbitrary manner, albeit by federal judges for the "right" reasons in the "right case," public confidence in the Code and tax enforcement system surely will be further eroded. . . . Moreover, as a legal scholar cited by the Government, observed:
>
> > The economic substance test is dizzyingly complex. . . . This complexity arises from a number of interrelated factors. First, the test is best seen as a

technique of statutory interpretation, which poses open-ended and unanswerable questions. Second, the test must be applied to a near-infinite variety of economic activities and transactions. Third, the present treatment of capital is inconsistent and to some extent incoherent. Taxpayers can exploit this incoherence by structuring transactions that produce tax benefits out of thin air. And conflicting rules make it difficult . . . sometimes . . . to determine the "correct" treatment of a particular transaction. Finally, only a few cases have been decided under the economic substance test, leaving open multiple interpretations of the doctrine.

Joseph Bankman, The Economic Substance Doctrine, 74 S. Cal. L. Rev. 5, 29 (2000-01); see Gov't Post-Trial Memorandum at 38, 40 (citing Bankman). This candid assessment of the deficiencies of "economic substance" doctrine certainly does not suggest a compelling case for the court to jump into to "fill in some of the lacunae and resolve some of the [doctrine's] ambiguities." Bankman, 74 S. Cal. L. Rev. at 29. . . .

Under our time-tested system of separation of powers, it is Congress, not the court, that should determine how the federal tax laws should be used to promote economic welfare. . . . Accordingly, the court has determined that where a taxpayer has satisfied all statutory requirements established by Congress, as Coltec did in this case, the use of the "economic substance" doctrine to trump "mere compliance with the Code" would violate the separation of powers.

Id. at 755-756.

The use of the economic substance and similar doctrines has been defended as follows:

Should we . . . ditch the whole non-literalist project? The answer is no, for three reasons — two minor and one overwhelming. First, and least important, the costs of ambiguity entailed in applying the economic substance doctrine to tax-related transactions fall disproportionately on promoters and others who plan to approach (and in many cases step over) whatever line the tax law draws. The sad truth, known to economists, is that all else equal, tax planning is a deadweight loss to the system. Reducing the payoff to aggressive tax planning is hardly a social evil. Second, it is not impossible to apply the tax law in a manner consistent with underlying purpose and intent. Indeed, many of the same lawyers who argue for literal interpretation in the shelter context argue for purposive interpretation in cases in which the literal language disadvantages their clients. To be sure the[se] are close questions, but literal interpretation raises close questions as well.

The third and most important reason to retain the doctrine is this: without the doctrine, plus a wide array of somewhat narrow doctrines, and willingness to engage in non-literal interpretation, we cannot raise significant revenue from capital, and possibly not from labor either. This seems like it must be an overstatement, but it is not. The tax law is enormously complex, and has been cobbled together, over the years, by tens of thousands of legislators, legislative aides, and administrators. Some of these drafters were wordsmiths, others were not. Some sections were sensibly worded for the time in which they were drafted but must be reinterpreted in light of more recent developments. The short of it is our tax law is absolutely riddled with what literal interpretation would reveal to be legal tax shelters which for purposes of exposition I will refer to as "loopholes."

Making the law loophole free is like retrofitting all of the buildings in California to make them earthquake-proof. There aren't the resources in the world to do it. Or perhaps a better analogy is to land mines buried within a field. It is prohibitive or unfeasible to remove all the mines and removing most of them is not enough. All it takes is a few loopholes to siphon off most of the tax revenues.

Joseph Bankman, The Tax Shelter Battle in The Crisis in Tax Administration (Aaron & Slemrod, eds. Brookings 2004), at 19-20.

ESTATE OF FRANKLIN v. COMMISSIONER
544 F.2d 1045 (9th Cir. 1976)

SNEED, Circuit Judge.

This case involves another effort on the part of the Commissioner to curb the use of real estate tax shelters.[24] In this instance he seeks to disallow deductions for the taxpayers' distributive share of losses reported by a limited partnership[25] with respect to its acquisition of a motel and related property. These "losses" have their origin in deductions for depreciation and interest claimed with respect to the motel and related property. These deductions were disallowed by the Commissioner on the ground either that the acquisition was a sham or that the entire acquisition transaction was in substance the purchase by the partnership of an option to acquire the motel and related property on January 15, 1979. The Tax Court held that the transaction constituted an option exercisable in 1979 and disallowed the taxpayers' deductions. Estate of Charles T. Franklin, 64 T.C. 752 (1975). We affirm this disallowance although our approach differs somewhat from that of the Tax Court.

The interest and depreciation deductions were taken by Twenty-Fourth Property Associates (hereinafter referred to as Associates), a California limited partnership of which Charles T. Franklin and seven other doctors were the limited partners. The deductions flowed from the purported "purchase" by Associates of the Thunderbird Inn, an Arizona motel, from Wayne L. Romney and Joan E. Romney (hereinafter referred to as the Romneys) on November 15, 1968.

Under a document entitled "Sales Agreement," the Romneys agreed to "sell" the Thunderbird Inn to Associates for $1,224,000. The property would

---

24. An early skirmish in this particular effort appears in Manuel D. Mayerson, 47 T.C. 340 (1966) which the Commissioner lost. The Commissioner attacked the substance of a nonrecourse sale, but based his attack on the nonrecourse and long-term nature of the purchase money note, without focusing on whether the sale was made at an unrealistically high price. In his acquiescence to *Mayerson*, 1969-2 Cum. Bull. xxiv, the Commissioner recognized that the fundamental issue in these cases generally will be whether the property has been "acquired" at an artificially high price, having little relation to its fair market value.

The Service emphasizes that its acquiescence in *Mayerson* is based on the particular facts in the case and will not be relied upon in the disposition of other cases except where it is clear that the property has been acquired at its fair market value in an arm's length transaction creating a bona fide purchase and a bona fide debt obligation.

Rev. Rul. 69-77, 1969-1 Cum. Bull. 59.

25. [For a description of the taxation of partners and partnerships, see supra page 692. — EDS.]

be paid for over a period of ten years, with interest on any unpaid balance of seven and one-half percent per annum. "Prepaid interest" in the amount of $75,000 was payable immediately; monthly principal and interest installments of $9,045.36 [$108,544 per year] would be paid for approximately the first ten years, with Associates required to make a balloon payment at the end of the ten years of the difference between the remaining purchase price, forecast as $975,000, and any mortgages then outstanding against the property.

The purchase obligation of Associates to the Romneys was nonrecourse; the Romneys' only remedy in the event of default would be forfeiture of the partnership's interest. The sales agreement was recorded in the local county. A warranty deed was placed in an escrow account, along with a quitclaim deed from Associates to the Romneys, both documents to be delivered either to Associates upon full payment of the purchase price, or to the Romneys upon default.

The sale was combined with a leaseback of the property by Associates to the Romneys; Associates therefore never took physical possession. The lease payments were designed to approximate closely the principal and interest payments with the consequence that with the exception of the $75,000 prepaid interest payment no cash would cross between Associates and [the] Romneys until the balloon payment. The lease was on a net basis; thus, the Romneys were responsible for all of the typical expenses of owning the motel property including all utility costs, taxes, assessments, rents, charges, and levies of "every name, nature and kind whatsoever." The Romneys also were to continue to be responsible for the first and second mortgages until the final purchase installment was made; the Romneys could, and indeed did, place additional mortgages on the property without the permission of Associates. Finally, the Romneys were allowed to propose new capital improvements which Associates would be required to either build themselves or allow the Romneys to construct with compensating modifications in rent or purchase price.[26]

26. [The expected tax benefits are revealed in the following table taken from the Tax Court opinion (64 T.C. 752, 760):

| | Lease income | *Depreciation* | | | Contract interest | Indicated income (loss) |
		Building	Furnishings	Total		
1968 (2 months)	$ 2,800	$8,000	$16,300	$24,300	$75,000	($96,500)
1969	48,800	47,500	92,900	140,400	31,300	(122,900)
1970	108,550	44,700	65,000	109,700	89,550	(90,700)
1971	108,550	42,000	53,600	95,600	88,250	(75,300)
1972	108,550	39,500	53,600	93,100	86,550	(71,100)
1973	108,550	37,100	44,600	81,700	84,850	(58,000)
1974	108,550	34,900		34,900	83,050	(9,400)
1975	108,550	32,800		32,800	81,050	(5,300)
1976	108,550	30,800		30,800	78,950	(1,200)
1977	108,550	29,000		29,000	76,650	2,900
1978 (10 months)	90,500	22,700		22,700	62,000	5,800

During this time period, the only cash changing hands was the $75,000 of interest in 1968; rents precisely equaled debt service (interest and principal), and the lessee paid all expenses and taxes. — EDS.]

In holding that the transaction between Associates and the Romneys more nearly resembled an option than a sale, the Tax Court emphasized that Associates had the power at the end of ten years to walk away from the transaction and merely lose its $75,000 "prepaid interest payment." It also pointed out that a deed was never recorded and that the "benefits and burdens of ownership" appeared to remain with the Romneys. Thus, the sale was combined with a leaseback in which no cash would pass; the Romneys remained responsible under the mortgages, which they could increase; and the Romneys could make capital improvements.[27] The Tax Court further justified its "option" characterization by reference to the nonrecourse nature of the purchase money debt and the nice balance between the rental and purchase money payments.

Our emphasis is different from that of the Tax Court. We believe the characteristics set out above can exist in a situation in which the sale imposes upon the purchaser a genuine indebtedness within the meaning of section 167(a), Internal Revenue Code of 1954, which will support both interest and depreciation deductions.[28] They substantially so existed in Hudspeth v. Commissioner, 509 F.2d 1224 (9th Cir. 1975) in which parents entered into sale-leaseback transactions with their children. The children paid for the property by executing nonnegotiable notes and mortgages equal to the fair market value of the property; state law proscribed deficiency judgments in case of default, limiting the parents' remedy to foreclosure of the property. The children had no funds with which to make mortgage payments; instead, the payments were offset in part by the rental payments, with the difference met by gifts from the parents to their children. Despite these characteristics this court held that there was a bona fide indebtedness on which the children, to the extent of the rental payments, could base interest deductions. . . .

In none of these cases, however, did the taxpayer fail to demonstrate that the purchase price was at least approximately equivalent to the fair market value of the property. Just such a failure occurred here. The Tax Court explicitly found that on the basis of the facts before it the value of the property could not be estimated. 64 T.C. at 767-768.[29] In our view this defect in the taxpayers' proof is fatal.

---

27. There was evidence that not all of the benefits and burdens of ownership remained with the Romneys. Thus, for example, the leaseback agreement appears to provide that any condemnation award will go to Associates.

28. Counsel differed as to whether the Tax Court's decision that the transaction was not a sale, but at best only an option, is reviewable by this court as a question of law or of fact. We agree with other circuits that, while the characteristics of a transaction are questions of fact, whether those characteristics constitute a sale *for tax purposes* is a question of law. . . .

29. The Tax Court found that appellants had "not shown that the purported sales price of $1,224,000 (or any other price) had any relationship to the actual market value of the motel property. . . ." 64 T.C. at 767.

Petitioners spent a substantial amount of time at trial attempting to establish that, whatever the actual market value of the property, Associates acted in the good faith *belief* that the market value of the property approximated the selling price. However, this evidence only goes to the issue of sham and does not supply substance to this transaction. "Save in those instances where the statute itself turns on intent, a matter so real as taxation must depend on objective realities, not on the varying subjective beliefs of individual taxpayers." Lynch v. Commissioner, 273 F.2d 867, 872 (2d Cir. 1959). . . . On the other side, there existed cogent evidence indicating that the fair market value was substantially less than the purchase price. This evidence included (i) the Romneys' purchase of the stock of two

Reason supports our perception. An acquisition such as that of Associates if at a price approximately equal to the fair market value of the property under ordinary circumstances would rather quickly yield an equity in the property which the purchaser could not prudently abandon. This is the stuff of substance. It meshes with the form of the transaction and constitutes a sale.

No such meshing occurs when the purchase price exceeds a demonstrably reasonable estimate of the fair market value. Payments on the principal of the purchase price yield no equity so long as the unpaid balance of the purchase price exceeds the then existing fair market value. Under these circumstances the purchaser by abandoning the transaction can lose no more than a mere chance to acquire an equity in the future should the value of the acquired property increase. While this chance undoubtedly influenced the Tax Court's determination that the transaction before us constitutes an option, we need only point out that its existence fails to supply the substance necessary to justify treating the transaction as a sale ab initio. It is not necessary to the disposition of this case to decide the tax consequences of a transaction such as that before us if in a subsequent year the fair market value of the property increases to an extent that permits the purchaser to acquire an equity.[30]

Authority also supports our perception. It is fundamental that "depreciation is not predicated upon ownership of property *but rather upon an investment in property*. Gladding Dry Goods Co., 2 BTA 336 (1925)." *Mayerson*, supra at 350 (italics added). No such investment exists when payments of the purchase price in accordance with the design of the parties yield no equity to the purchaser. . . . In the transaction before us and during the taxable years in question the purchase price payments by Associates have not been shown to constitute an *investment in the property*. Depreciation was properly disallowed. Only the Romneys had an investment in the property.

Authority also supports disallowance of the interest deductions. This is said even though it has long been recognized that the absence of personal liability for the purchase money debt secured by a mortgage on the acquired property does not deprive the debt of its character as a bona fide debt obligation able to support an interest deduction. *Mayerson*, supra at 352. However, this is no longer true when it appears that the debt has economic significance only if the property substantially appreciates in value prior to the date at which a very large portion of the purchase price is to be discharged. Under these circumstances the purchaser has not secured "the use or forbearance of money." See Norton v. Commissioner, 474 F.2d 608, 610 (9th Cir. 1973). Nor has the seller advanced money or forborne its use. . . . Prior to the date at which the balloon payment on the purchase price is required, and assuming no substantial increase in the fair market value of the property, the absence of

---

corporations, one of which wholly-owned the motel, for approximately $800,000 in the year preceding the "sale" to Associates ($660,000 of which was allocable to the sale property, according to Mr. Romney's estimate), and (ii) insurance policies on the property from 1967 through 1974 of only $583,200, $700,000, and $614,000. 64 T.C. at 767-768.

Given that it was the appellants' burden to present evidence showing that the purchase price did not exceed the fair market value and that he had a fair opportunity to do so, we see no reason to remand this case for further proceedings.

30. These consequences would include a determination of the proper basis of the acquired property at the date the increments to the purchaser's equity commenced.

personal liability on the debt reduces the transaction in economic terms to a mere chance that a genuine debt obligation may arise. This is not enough to justify an interest deduction. To justify the deduction the debt must exist; potential existence will not do. For debt to exist, the purchaser, in the absence of personal liability, must confront a situation in which it is presently reasonable from an economic point of view for him to make a capital investment in the amount of the unpaid purchase price. . . .

Our focus on the relationship of the fair market value of the property to the unpaid purchase price should not be read as premised upon the belief that a sale is not a sale if the purchaser pays too much. Bad bargains from the buyer's point of view—as well as sensible bargains from buyer's, but exceptionally good from the seller's point of view—do not thereby cease to be sales. . . . We intend our holding and explanation thereof to be understood as limited to transactions substantially similar to that now before us.

Affirmed.

NOTES AND QUESTIONS

1. *Treatment of the seller.* The transaction in *Estate of Franklin* might have been highly disadvantageous to the Romneys, from a tax standpoint, had they been required to report the supposed gain from the sale. However, due to the installment method of accounting for gain on the sale of property (discussed at page 268, supra), they did not have to do so. The inconsistency between giving Franklin immediate basis for amounts not yet paid (if the transaction worked) while permitting the Romneys to defer treating the same amounts as recognized was crucial to the tax planning opportunity that the transaction was designed to exploit.

2. *A lost tax planning opportunity?* Suppose that law students could deduct the cost of pens that they buy for use in class, and that *Estate of Franklin* had come out the other way, so that nonrecourse debt was included in basis without regard to the value of the property. (Assume as well that there is no economic substance requirement or sham transaction doctrine.) If you otherwise anticipated having $100,000 of taxable income for the year, you could eliminate this income at the stroke of a pen (so to speak) by buying a pen from your neighbor for $5 cash plus $100,000 in nonrecourse debt. You would not mind overpaying for the pen, since you never would actually have to repay the "loan." (Your neighbor would have to settle for taking back the pen.) Your neighbor would not mind making such a bad loan, since he or she could not otherwise have gotten even $5 for the pen. You would at some future time have income of $100,000 from cancellation of indebtedness (or gain from the "sale" of the pen subject to the debt), but you would have deferred the tax liability until that time.

While this example is fanciful, the underlying point about the tax planning potential of seller-provided nonrecourse financing (if automatically respected for tax purposes) is not. Would addressing in across-the-board fashion the underlying asymmetry in tax treatment of the buyer and seller, described in Note 1 above, be preferable to attacking aggressive transactions with an array of judicial doctrines (as well as statutes that are discussed infra)? Note, however, that, if the response involved denying use of the installment method, *Franklin*-style deals could still be done by sellers who were "tax indifferent" (for example, by reason of having huge expiring losses).

3. *The option theory.* How important is the difference between the Tax Court's option theory and the Court of Appeals' equity theory? Suppose that you have negotiated to buy a house for $30,000 payable at the time you take title and possession and $70,000 payable one year later. The buyer insists that the transaction take the form of a payment of $30,000 for an option to buy the house one year hence for $70,000. Is this what we would normally think of as a true option? Why?

4. *Precedent.* Could the court in *Estate of Franklin* have cited *Knetsch* (supra page 579) and forgone further analysis?

3. The Congressional Response to Tax Shelters

While judicial responses to tax shelters helped knock out some of the most egregious (or at least aesthetically unappealing) cases, they were widely perceived as falling short of an adequate response to the tax shelter boom of the 1970s and early 1980s. Part of the problem was that taxpayers could satisfy the judicial standard (to the extent there was such a thing) by simply folding in enough actual or at least apparent nontax content when engaging in transactions that were mainly designed to generate tax losses. A second part of the problem was that uncertainty concerning how the courts would evaluate a given case encouraged taxpayers who knew they were unlikely to be audited to take aggressive "reporting positions" on their tax returns, by acting under the undisclosed assumption that a questionable transaction actually was legitimate under the judicial standard.

Congress therefore responded with a number of statutory provisions designed to defeat or discourage tax sheltering activity. One mode of response was to make various deduction rules less favorable across the board — that is, without regard to whether a given taxpayer was engaged in aggressive sheltering. In addition, congressional concern with tax shelters led to the adoption of a new set of enforcement tools in the 1982 act (TEFRA). In an effort to attack abusive tax shelters at their source, Congress imposed a penalty, equal to the greater of $1,000 or 10 percent of the gross income derived or to be derived from a tax shelter activity, on promoters, organizers, or sellers who make statements that they know or have reason to know are false, about the availability of tax benefits or statements that consist of a "gross overvaluation" (more than 200 percent of the correct value). § 6700.

The 1982 act also imposed a new tax equal to 20 percent of any "substantial understatement of income tax." § 6662. A substantial understatement is one that exceeds the greater of 10 percent of the proper tax or $5,000. The amount of the understatement is reduced by amounts attributable to tax treatment for which there was substantial authority, but, in the case of a tax shelter, only if the taxpayer "reasonably believed that the tax treatment of [the] item . . . was more likely than not" proper. § 6662(d)(2)(C)(i).

In addition to these new penalties, the 1982 act added a penalty for aiding and abetting the understatement of a tax liability (§ 6701), provided for injunctions against promoters of abusive tax shelters (§ 7408), added or increased other penalties, and added other procedural devices.

In 1984, Congress added provisions requiring that tax shelters register with the IRS (§§ 6111, 6707) and that an organizer of a "potentially abusive tax shelter" maintain a list of investors (§§ 6112, 6708). Congress also imposed a new penalty on tax shelter promoters who provide false or fraudulent statements about tax effects or who provide a "gross valuation overstatement" (§ 6700).

Apart from changing deduction rules across the board and imposing new penalties, Congress's main response to tax sheltering activity was to adopt several provisions using an approach that might be called "basketing." Under this approach, deductions from items in a group of transactions (colloquially, a "basket") are allowed only against income from other items in the same group, thus preventing the use of net losses from the basket to offset other taxable income such as wages. We saw an earlier example of a basketing rule in Chapter 2, concerning gambling losses, which (under § 165(d)) are deductible only to the extent of gambling gains from the same taxable year.

Many of the basketing rules that Congress adopted to discourage tax shelter activity are hard to understand other than as responses to specific taxpayer practices that had come to its attention. In addition, these rules may in some cases either overlap or leave gaps in their application. For some taxpayers (including those engaged in straightforward business activity that is not primarily designed to generate tax losses), the result is to make tax planning and compliance more complicated than ever, given the need to steer one's way through the various basketing rules or at least to apply them accurately in tax returns. For other taxpayers, the result is to make tax planning simpler, as sheltering becomes too difficult to justify the effort.

The main basketing rules that Congress has adopted to discourage tax sheltering activity by individuals are the following.

Passive activity loss rules. The classic tax shelter investor often is someone who has a lot of taxable income that unmistakably is earned from work. Consider, for example, a doctor or lawyer who gets a salary, service fees from patients or clients, or a share of the income for services earned by her group medical practice or law partnership. Such a taxpayer may be eager to generate tax losses that are deductible against this income. One way to seek these losses is by investing in some sort of business or rental enterprise (say, an apartment building, cattle farm, or oil well) that can be structured to generate large tax losses in excess of any real economic loss. An investor of this sort is unlikely, however, to be eager or even able to spend a lot of time working on the loss-producing enterprise. Few lawyers in New York or Los Angeles, for example, are likely, even for a sizeable tax advantage, to consider spending a significant portion of the free time that is left to them shoveling cattle manure or handling an oil drill in Texas.

The fact that many tax shelter investors were generating taxable income from businesses in which they did substantial work while trying to deduct losses from those in which they did little or no work encouraged Congress to enact § 469, which limits deductions for passive activity losses. A passive activity loss is a loss on an investment (a) that constitutes a trade or business and (b) in which the taxpayer does not "materially participate." See § 469(d)(1). In addition, rental activities are passive activities without regard to material participation. See § 469(e)(2). A passive loss from one investment may be used to offset passive income from another investment, and net passive losses may be carried forward indefinitely and deducted when the investment that generates the loss is sold, but passive losses may not be used to offset other income from nonpassive investments or activities, wages and salaries, or "portfolio income" (dividends, interest, etc.).

The passive loss rules may be illustrated by again considering the investor who borrows $100,000 at 9 percent and uses the proceeds to buy an apartment building that appreciates at 8 percent a year. (Assume that the rental income is offset by taxes, maintenance costs, and other expenses.) Absent special limitations, in the first year the taxpayer would be able to deduct interest and depreciation. The taxpayer would not pay tax on the appreciation since it is not realized gain. If, however, the investor does not materially participate in the activity and does not qualify for special relief provisions discussed below, the loss from the building will be a passive loss. That loss will be deductible against current or future passive activity income from other sources, or from the building itself (in future years), or it may be deducted at the time the building is sold, but the loss will not be deductible against other current income such as salary or portfolio income.

The concept of material participation is central to the passive loss rules. "Material participation" is statutorily defined as participation that is "regular, continuous, and substantial." § 469(h). Under the regulations, a taxpayer will be deemed to materially participate in an activity only if he or she meets one of seven tests. Under one test, the taxpayer must personally spend more than 500 hours on the activity. Under another test, the taxpayer must spend at least 100 hours on the activity and must spend at least as much time on the activity as any other individual. A third test is qualitative: An individual materially participates in an activity if (unspecified) facts and circumstances show material participation. Regs. § 1.469-5(a). Section 469 contains many exceptions, special rules, and exceptions to the special rules. For example, limited partnership interests and rental activities are considered passive activities. Rental activities, however, are not passive for individuals in the real property business who meet certain tests (such as performing more than 750 hours of service in connection with a real property rental activity). § 469(c)(7). In addition, up to $25,000 of annual losses may be deducted from real estate rental activities of certain individuals who meet a lesser standard of participation, but this exemption is phased out as income rises from $100,000 to $150,000. § 469(i)(6)(A). An apartment building with monthly or annual tenants typically is a rental activity, but a hotel typically is not, due to the higher turnover rate and greater services provided in connection with the occupants' use of the property.

Some observers credit the passive loss rules with a major role in reducing tax shelter activity by individuals other than the super-rich (whose income may come from investments rather than work). The rules may apply, however, to people who do not think of themselves as engaged in tax shelter activity. Suppose, for example, that you decide to invest money in a restaurant that you think (or hope) will be profitable, but you will be little if at all involved in the restaurant's operations. If this is your only passive activity, you may face a "heads the IRS wins, tails I lose" scenario, whereby your share of the profits will be taxable if the restaurant is a success, but, if it loses money, the deductions will be suspended until you sell your interest or the restaurant closes.

Under the passive loss rules, taxpayers benefit from seeking passive status for investments that generate positive taxable income (so the income can be sheltered by other passive losses) and nonpassive status for investments that generate tax losses (so the deductions will not be limited). The IRS, if trying to maximize revenues, has an opposite incentive. Struggle concerning passive versus nonpassive classification typically centers on determining the scope of a distinct "activity" that needs to be tested for passive status, whether the taxpayer has materially participated, and whether a given activity is a rental activity.

Limitations on the deduction of interest on "investment indebtedness." The passive loss rules only restrict losses from investments that constitute a trade or business or a rental activity. Section 163(d), which was adopted in 1969, applies a similar restriction on the deduction of interest on "investment indebtedness" — that is, on debt tied to any investment, including stocks and bonds and undeveloped real estate. The role of this provision may be illustrated as follows: Assume that an investor borrows $100,000 at 10 percent and uses the proceeds to buy shares of common stock of a growing electronics company. In the first year, consistent with expectations, the shares increase in value by 15 percent but pay no dividends. There has been an economic gain, but no gain or income for tax purposes. Absent special rules, the $10,000 interest expense would be deductible. Section 163(d) prevents a tax advantage by limiting the amount of the interest deduction to "net investment income." Net investment income includes non-capital gain income from all portfolio investments, so that interest payments incurred in holding one such investment can be deducted to the extent of income from another such investment. Net investment income includes capital gain income only if the taxpayer elects to forgo the lower maximum rate on such income and, in effect, treat capital gain income as ordinary income. Interest disallowed as a deduction by reason of § 163(d) may be deducted, subject to the same limitations, in succeeding taxable years. In the present example, there is no investment income, so the $10,000 interest expense would not be currently deductible.

Limitations on deductions to amount of "at risk" investment. Another broad-scale approach is the "at risk" rules of § 465, first introduced in 1976 and broadened in application in 1978 and 1986. These rules are another form of attack on the leverage (use of borrowed funds) that has been vital to most tax shelters. Section 465 disallows deductions for *"losses"* (that is, the excess of deductions over income) of an investment in excess of the amount that the taxpayer has at risk in that investment. The amount at risk includes cash invested plus amounts of debt for which the taxpayer is personally liable or which is secured by assets of the taxpayer (other than assets of the tax shelter investment). Thus, if a person purports to buy a motion picture for $2 million but puts up only $200,000 in cash and signs a nonrecourse note for the balance, the maximum loss that can be deducted is $200,000. Losses not currently deductible may be carried forward and deducted against income in later years as the investment produces taxable income, or as the at-risk amount increases. Section 465 applies to all investments and business activities except that in the case of real estate it does not apply to "qualified non-recourse financing" (which includes loans from banks and certain other loans; see § 465(b)(6)). Section 465 overlaps with the passive loss rules of § 469 since both may apply to investments that constitute a trade or business. Losses on trade or business investments will not be deductible unless they pass muster under both § 465 and § 469.

The reason for addressing tax sheltering via the at-risk approach was apparently twofold. First, as shown by cases such as *Estate of Franklin*, the use of nonrecourse financing that is provided by the purchaser in a sale of property encourages overvaluation. For example, you could hypothetically buy a paper clip for $1 billion without concern about economic loss from the transaction if your liability were confined to a nonrecourse loan secured only by the paper clip. And the seller of the paper clip could make this loan without concern about your defaulting on it, given that all she would "lose" is the opportunity to collect on a bogus sale price. *Estate of Franklin* does not wholly foreclose transactions of this sort since, at least in cases less extreme than the paper clip example, taxpayers can claim that the property's value matches the face amount of the nonrecourse loan. However, the "qualified nonrecourse financing" rule for real estate is probably sufficient to take care of this problem. After all, a bank presumably would not be willing to lend you $1 billion secured only by a paper clip that an unrelated party had sold to you.

Thus, the fact that the at-risk rules' qualified nonrecourse financing exception applies only to real estate suggests some additional reason for attacking tax sheltering activity via a requirement of personal liability. The reason apparently was that Congress observed the frequent use of nonrecourse debt and similar devices in transactions in tax shelter transactions. Overvaluation aside, such use probably reflected the fact that many tax shelter investors were reluctant to accept much downside economic risk from these investments. This, in turn, may have resulted both from a general aversion to large financial gambles and from the investors' grasping how little they really knew either about the investments' true economic prospects or about the reputability of the promoters and managers. The at-risk rules may put such investors in a bind: The price of larger deductions may be accepting an unpalatable risk of actually losing a lot of money in a worst-case scenario. And even then all the investor may get for her pains is disallowance by the passive loss rules anyway!

Debt used to purchase or carry tax-favored investments. One of the earliest responses to tax avoidance was to deny deductions for "interest on indebtedness incurred or continued to purchase or carry" tax-exempt bonds. § 265(a)(2).

See also § 265(a)(1), denying deductions for certain expenses "allocable to" tax-exempt income. Absent § 265(2), a taxpayer might borrow at 8 percent to buy tax-exempt bonds that pay 7 percent. Interest paid on the loan would be deductible, while the interest on the bonds would be tax free. Under § 265, the interest on the loan would be nondeductible.

In a similar vein, § 264 denies deductions for interest on indebtedness "incurred or continued to purchase or carry" certain insurance and annuity policies. Section 264, among other things, now expressly covers the type of transaction engaged in by the taxpayer in the *Knetsch* case (supra page 579).

NOTES AND QUESTIONS

1. What do you think of the statutory approach of causing the allowance of a deduction to depend on such considerations as whether the taxpayer spends at least 500 hours working on a given activity, or whether she would be personally liable for certain economic losses if they occurred? Are there better ways of trying to discourage unduly tax-motivated investment? Are the passive loss and at-risk rules better than doing nothing?

2. (a) On January 1, 1999, Stan obtains a recourse loan of $200,000 and uses the proceeds to buy shares of common stock. Stan pays $20,000 interest on the loan in 1999 and receives $10,000 in dividends. Stan has no other investments or loans. How much, if any, of the 1999 interest payment is deductible?

(b) The facts are the same as in (a) except that Stan also receives $5,000 of dividends from another stock that he bought with nonborrowed funds. How much, if any, of the 1999 interest payment is deductible?

3. On January 1, 2000, Jamie invests $250,000 of nonborrowed funds in a widget manufacturing enterprise. Jamie does not materially participate in the enterprise, which shows a taxable loss of $50,000 for the year. Jamie is the sole owner of the enterprise.

(a) If Jamie has no other investments, how much, if any, of the loss may she deduct?

(b) Assume Jamie has another trade or business investment in which she does materially participate, and in 2000, this produces taxable income of $40,000. How much, if any, of the loss from the widget enterprise may Jamie deduct for the year?

(c) Assume Jamie has net dividend income of $20,000 from common stocks in 2000. How much, if any, of the loss from the widget enterprise may Jamie deduct?

(d) Assume that in 2001 Jamie has no income or loss from the widget enterprise, but that in 2001 she has income of $30,000 from a different trade or business in which she materially participates. How much, if any, of the 2000 loss from the widget enterprise may Jamie deduct?

4. On January 1, 1999, Rafael borrows $200,000 and uses the proceeds to buy a restaurant. The loan is nonrecourse and does not require repayment of any of the principal until 2002. Rafael rents the building in which the restaurant operates. In 1999, the restaurant shows a net loss of $40,000. In 2000,

the restaurant shows a net income of $25,000. Also in 2000, Rafael obtains a recourse loan of $10,000 and uses the proceeds to improve the restaurant. In all years, Rafael materially participates in the management of the restaurant. Is any portion of the 1999 loss deductible? When?

5. On January 1, 1999, Sarah obtains a recourse loan of $100,000 and uses the proceeds to buy Fly Co. common stock. In 1999, Sarah pays $10,000 interest on the loan and the stock pays dividends of $15,000. Sarah pays $10,000 interest on the loan in 2000 and in 2001. The stock pays no dividends in 2000 and dividends of $15,000 in 2001. Sarah has no other investments. What portion, if any, of Sarah's $30,000 interest expense is deductible? When?

4. The New Market in Corporate and Individual Tax Shelters

The 1986 tax reforms, particularly the passive rules, have largely put an end to the real estate and other tax shelters designed to provide ordinary losses to individual investors. The passive loss rules and other anti–tax shelter measures do not apply to corporate taxpayers, however. Nor do those rules limit the ability of individual investors to deduct capital losses against capital gains. It is therefore not surprising that, over time, a new market in tax shelters has emerged — one in which corporations and wealthy individuals, with capital gains to shelter are the primary investors.

The new tax shelter is much more sophisticated than the older individual tax shelters. It is much more likely to involve financial assets than real assets, and much more likely to be based on a hypertechnical (and some might say hyperaggressive) reading of a relevant statute or regulation. The shelters revolve around tax rules governing business entities; in-depth analysis of the corporate tax shelter market is beyond the scope of an introductory casebook. However, a brief (and simplified) description of one of the more typical shelters, the "lease-strip" shelter, may prove instructive.

The lease-strip shelter was built around two sets of tax rules. The first, discussed in some detail in connection with the *AAA* case, supra at page 337, is that prepaid services are taxed as current income to the recipient. Thus, a company that in 2000 leases its property out for five years for $1 million and receives the entire sum upon the signing of the lease in 2000 is taxed on the entire $1 million in 2000. The second set of tax rules, discussed in connection with *Tufts*, supra at page 188, is that partnerships are not subject to tax. Instead, partnership income is taxed to the partners.

The lease-strip shelter involved a Fortune 500 company and a zero-bracket taxpayer. The zero-bracket taxpayer was either a foreign person not subject to U.S. taxes, a nonprofit organization or Native American tribe, or a corporation with net operating loss carryovers. The partnership purchased $1 billion of equipment and immediately leased the equipment for substantially all of its useful life for approximately $1 billion. The nontax consequences of the transaction were insignificant.

In the first year, the partnership recognized $1 billion of prepaid rental income, less the depreciation deductions attributable to the equipment. In later years, the partnership recognized no income, and received $1 billion in depreciation deductions, less the depreciation taken the first year. The partnership agreement allocated virtually all of the income and deductions to the zero-bracket party. However, after being allocated the income in year one, the zero-bracket party was bought out of the partnership by a subsidiary of the Fortune 500 company. The zero-bracket party had stayed in just long enough to "soak up" all the income. In tax shelter vernacular, that party was (and in newer tax shelters is) sometimes referred to as "Sponge Co." The net result? The Fortune 500 company and its subsidiary were left to realize most of the $1 billion of cost recovery deductions. The income in the lease-strip had been "stripped-out" by the zero-bracket party. The market for these kinds of corporate and individual shelters was fueled by the boom years of the 1990s (which left companies and individuals with income to shelter) and by the perception that the government would never find out about most shelters.

How could a corporate taxpayer, which is always audited, hope to hide a $100 million loss on a tax return? The answer is that the loss would be listed in a schedule alongside dozens of equally large gains and losses and given a deceptively innocent description. Some taxpayers would go further, and net the loss against a larger gain, and report only the net gain on the tax return. The government has taken a number of steps to increase detection. Sections 6011 and 6111 now require taxpayers and material advisers to disclose so-called reportable transactions — transactions with shelter-like characteristics. For example, a transaction that provides a corporate taxpayer a loss of at least $10 million in any single taxable year or $20 million overall must be disclosed. Regs. § 1.6011-4. In addition, "material advisers" are required to keep a list of investors in reportable transactions. § 6112. The term "material adviser" is defined generally to include any person who receives more than $250,000 in connection with the promotion of a corporate reportable transaction or more than $50,000 in connection with a reportable transaction carried out by a natural person. Tax shelter promoters will fall under the category of material advisers, as will some outside lawyers and advisors. The IRS has redesigned tax forms to make shelters easier to spot. The IRS has also established an Office of Tax Shelter Analysis and generally increased resources devoted to ferreting out shelters.

Lawyers and other advisors played an important (and not entirely reputable) role in shelter development and sales. For example some lawyers were paid astronomical sums to opine that it was more likely than not that a particular transaction would be upheld in court if challenged by the IRS. These opinion letters were thought to provide insurance against penalties and helped provide legitimacy to the shelter. Congress responded by changing the standards for penalty relief; the IRS has responded by establishing new guidelines for tax practice. Perhaps more significantly, the Justice Department has charged some lawyers and accountants who helped sell a class of shelters with conspiracy to commit tax fraud. The role of the lawyer and the standards for tax practice are discussed in Section I(5) of this chapter.

Congress sought to tilt the cost-benefit calculus away from shelter purchase by increasing shelter penalties, albeit only slightly, and by making it harder for a taxpayer to avoid penalties. See § 6662A.

Finally, the IRS has denied taxpayer claims for shelter losses and, when challenged, has litigated the matter. In this litigation, the government has sought not only to sustain its position in the individual case, but to establish principles or guidelines (such as business purpose or economic substance) that could be used to attack (and therefore deter the development of) future shelters. The government won nearly all the first set of cases, which were litigated mostly in the Tax Court, and all of its victories were upheld on appeal. Since that time, taxpayers with shelter-related deficiencies have chosen to litigate in district court or claims court. (See previous discussion of forum shopping.) Only a few decisions have been handed down by those courts; most of those decisions have gone for the taxpayer. There are hundreds of more cases awaiting trial and while most will settle, some will not. The government's success in the earlier cases, together with the other measures described above, has almost eliminated shelter sales. However, if taxpayers continue to find success in the district and claims court, the tax shelter market will surely bounce back.

We close this discussion with the decision in Winn-Dixie Stores, Inc. v. Commissioner, a multi-billion-dollar shelter built around the favorable treatment of life insurance. Students should compare this case with *Knetsch*, an earlier case involving life insurance, supra at page 579, and with *Coltec Industries*, supra at page 586, a recent case that holds for the taxpayer and rejects the economic substance doctrine as a usurpation of legislative power.

WINN-DIXIE STORES, INC. v. COMMISSIONER

254 F.3d 1313 (11th Cir. 2001), cert. denied, 535 U.S. 986 (2002)

PER CURIAM.

Winn-Dixie Stores, Inc. appeals the tax court's judgment resting on the conclusion that Winn-Dixie was not entitled to deduct interest and fees incurred in borrowing against insurance policies that it owned on the lives of more than 36,000 Winn-Dixie employees. We affirm.

BACKGROUND

In summary, the tax court found the following facts: In 1993, Winn-Dixie embarked on a broad-based company-owned life-insurance (COLI) program whose sole purpose, as shown by contemporary memoranda, was to satisfy Winn-Dixie's "appetite" for interest deductions. Under the program, Winn-Dixie purchased whole life insurance policies on almost all of its full-time employees, who numbered in the tens of thousands. Winn-Dixie was the sole beneficiary of the policies. Winn-Dixie would borrow against those policies' account value at an interest rate of over 11%. The high interest and the administrative fees that came with the program outweighed the net cash surrender value and benefits paid on the policies, with the result that in pretax terms Winn-Dixie lost money on the program. The deductibility of the interest and fees post-tax, however, yielded a benefit projected to reach into the billions of dollars over 60 years. Winn-Dixie participated until 1997, when a change in tax law jeopardized this tax arbitrage, and it eased its way out.

The IRS determined a deficiency because of the interest and fee deductions taken in Winn-Dixie's 1993 tax year. Winn-Dixie challenged the determination before the tax court. The tax court rejected Winn-Dixie's assertions that the COLI program had a business purpose, or that Congress had expressly authorized its tax benefits. See Winn-Dixie Stores, Inc. v. Comm'r, 113 T.C. 254 (1999). The court held that the loans against the policies were substantive shams, and that Winn-Dixie was therefore not entitled to deductions for the interest and fees paid for the loans. Winn-Dixie appeals.

Winn-Dixie's two core arguments here are the same as those it made to the tax court. The first is that Congress, through the Internal Revenue Code, explicitly authorized the deduction of interest and fees incurred in certain borrowing against whole life-insurance policies' account value. This explicit permission, Winn-Dixie says, makes application of the sham-transaction doctrine inappropriate. In the alternative, Winn-Dixie argues that even if the sham-transaction doctrine properly applies here, the tax court misinterpreted the economic-substance and business-purpose prongs of that doctrine and thus "shammed" a transaction that was due respect. Winn-Dixie does not dispute any finding of historical fact; these issues are exclusively ones of law, and our consideration of them is accordingly de novo....

Discussion

Winn-Dixie starts its argument by invoking the special treatment afforded life insurance contracts (as defined in § 7702) in general, whose benefits are generally untaxed and whose appreciation is tax-deferred. See §§ 101(a)(1), 72(e). That treatment extends to loans made against a policy, whose interest... is generally not deductible. See § 264(a)(3). ... [Under the law in effect until 1997, however, § 264(a)(3) was subject to a special exception permitting the interest on such loans to be deducted.] Winn-Dixie's loans fell within ... [this] exception, all agree. Because they qualify for the exception, and because the loans are within the specially treated world of life insurance that has obviously been the subject of congressional attention, Winn-Dixie contends, there is no room for application of the sham-transaction doctrine.

This argument may have some force, but it runs into binding precedent. The Supreme Court was faced with a materially similar argument decades ago by a taxpayer who sought to deduct interest payments on loans taken against an annuity contract. Knetsch v. United States, 364 U.S. 361 (1960). Because, as here, the annuity contract was obviously being used as a tax shelter, and as used offered the taxpayer no financial benefit other than its tax consequences, the Court held that the indebtedness was not bona fide, and the interest not deductible under § 163(a) See id. at 366. ... Along the way, the Court rejected an argument based on § 264 that is at least a cousin of Winn-Dixie's present contention. Knetsch argued that Congress's failure to close a loophole in § 264 (that section's prohibition of deductions on indebtedness to purchase life-insurance policies did not extend to annuities until 1954, the year after the tax year in question) equated to blessing the loophole. The Court declined to attribute such an intention to Congress, because that would "exalt artifice above reality." Id. at 367. . . . *Knetsch* holds, therefore, that the sham-transaction doctrine does apply to indebtedness that generates interest sought to be deducted under § 163(a), even if the interest deduction is not yet prohibited by § 264. . . .

Winn-Dixie tries to get around *Knetsch* with the argument that we have 33 more years (as of 1993) of congressional regulation of interest deductions in this context, and that 33-year history shows that Congress does not want to look behind facial compliance with, for instance, the . . . exception [relied on by Winn-Dixie]. It may well be that *Knetsch* was then, and this is now, but we are not the court to make that call. *Knetsch*'s holding is at best undermined by congressional action (or inaction) in the intervening decades, and it is up to the Supreme Court, not us, to determine when the Court's holdings have expired. . . . We therefore must conclude that the tax court properly examined the transaction under the sham-transaction doctrine.

That doctrine provides that a transaction is not entitled to tax respect if it lacks economic effects or substance other than the generation of tax benefits, or if the transaction serves no business purpose. . . . The doctrine has few bright lines, but "[i]t is clear that transactions whose sole function is to produce tax deductions are substantive shams." . . . That was, as we read the tax court's opinion, the rule the tax court followed. Nor did the court misapply the rule in concluding that the broad-based COLI program had no "function" other than generating interest deductions.

The tax court found, without challenge here, that the program could never generate a pretax profit. That was what Winn-Dixie thought as it set up the program, and it is the most plausible explanation for Winn-Dixie's withdrawal after the 1996 changes to the tax law threatened the tax benefits Winn-Dixie was receiving. No finding of the tax court suggests, furthermore, that the broad-based COLI program answered any business need of Winn-Dixie, such as indemnifying it for the loss of key employees. Nor could it have been conceived as an employee benefit, because Winn-Dixie was the beneficiary of the policies. . . . [T]herefore, the broad-based COLI program lacked sufficient economic substance to be respected for tax purposes, and the tax court did not err in so concluding.

CONCLUSION

For the foregoing reasons, the judgment of the tax court is affirmed.

NOTES

1. Corporate-owned life insurance, or COLI, policies have long been used to cover key employees, such as high-ranking executives, whose untimely death might disrupt a company's operations. By the early 1990s, tax planners had come up with the idea of using debt-financed policies to cover rank-and-file

workers, even though these individuals' deaths would have little impact on operations. They sought the tax benefit available, at little out-of-pocket cost, through a *Knetsch*-style arbitrage (borrowing deductibly in order to generate tax-free income). These policies were known in the business as "dead peasants' insurance" or "janitors' insurance."

2. Not surprisingly, given *Knetsch*, the IRS has been quite successful in arguing that COLI transactions are shams. See In re CM Holding, Inc., 254 B.R. 578 (D. Del. 2000); American Electric Power, Inc. v. United States, 136 F. Supp. 2d 762 (S.D. Ohio 2001). Its fortunes in other prominent "corporate tax shelter" cases, particularly on appeal from the Tax Court, have been more mixed.

While there is as yet no clearcut circuit split in corporate tax shelter cases, the differences between the approaches taken in different circuits create a possibility of Supreme Court intervention at some point. There is also a possibility of legislation addressing the scope and character of economic substance doctrine. However, until either the Supreme Court or Congress clarifies the state of the law, taxpayers that engage in transactions having little nontax economic effect or prospect of pretax profit must bear significant tax law risk, whether or not they need bear other economic risk.

3. Suppose Winn-Dixie had financed its purchase of the insurance policies by borrowing from a bank on its general credit, or using property other than the insurance policy to secure the loans. Would the interest paid on the loans still be nondeductible?

Similarly, suppose Winn-Dixie had used spare cash generated by its operations to buy the insurance policies. Suppose further that an internal memorandum showed the investment in the insurance policies made economic sense, compared with other alternatives, solely because of the favorable tax treatment of the insurance. Would the IRS have any way to attack the tax consequences?

Why do you think Winn-Dixie (and other COLI purchasers) engaged in *Knetsch*-like transactions that amounted to little more than paper-shuffling, rather than using separate borrowing or spare cash?

4. Is a "sham" transaction one that amounts to little or nothing more than paper-shuffling? Why should tax-motivated paper-shuffling be treated less favorably than investment decisions that have at least minimal economic consequences and pretax profit potential, but that are every bit as tax motivated?

5. Rules Aimed at the Tax Lawyer

Tax lawyers play a crucial role in the tax shelter world. Tax lawyers (together with tax accountants and investment bankers) develop tax shelters, and prospective shelter investors often ask their tax lawyer to evaluate a particular shelter. Finally, tax lawyers are often asked by a shelter promoter to opine that the tax benefits offered by the shelter are more likely than not to be upheld if challenged by the IRS. The more-likely-than-not tax opinion is then circulated with the offering materials.

The tax opinion obviously serves as a source of information for purchasers and as a marketing tool for promoters. A carefully drafted tax opinion serves another function as well. In the past, at least, taxpayers who relied on tax opinions, even those opinions solicited and paid for by tax shelter promoters, were protected against the 20 percent accuracy-related penalty. See Sections 6662, 6664. Consider the following: description of the role of the tax lawyer at the height of the shelter boom of the 1990s.

The most prominent role for tax lawyers acting in capacity as lawyers (rather than promoters) in the shelter industry is as opinion writers. Most shelters come with more-likely-than-not opinions. As noted above, the opinion provides insurance against tax penalties; more speculatively, it also provides psychological support to executives and their advisors.

The opinion writing process is by all accounts odd, in large part because the law is so ill-defined. Virtually all tax shelters comply with the literal language of a relevant (and perhaps the most relevant) statute, administrative ruling, or case. The issue presented is whether the result is so at odds with economic reality and/or tax theory that it ought to be trumped by a competing legal rule. Frequently, the only competing legal rule is one encapsuled, perhaps, in common law doctrines such as business purpose, substance over form, step transaction, and sham transaction.

Adding to the difficulty of opinion writing is the required translation of legal analysis into the language of the more-likely-than-not opinion. "Deciding whether a close question is 51% likely to go to a client or 49% can drive you crazy," says one practitioner.

Given the ambiguity in law and standards, it is not surprising that tax lawyers vary dramatically in their estimation of a given shelter. One might imagine that the variance would primarily be a function of the lawyer's implicit interpretive theory: A literalist would find the opinions easy to write; a lawyer who believes in a more purposive interpretation of legal rules would find the task harder. In fact, attorneys with similar interpretive theories and therefore similar levels of "tax aggressiveness" often have different estimations of the possibility of success of a given tax shelter. Attorneys from one firm may refuse to give a more-likely-than-not opinion, while attorneys from another firm find the same opinion easy to write. The firm that gives the opinion may generally have the reputation of a more aggressive firm, but not always. The legal ambiguity and hence variance in perception of a given shelter, together with the different attitudes lawyers bring to interpretive issues makes it easy for a shelter promoter to obtain a more-likely-than-not opinion: All the promoter has to do is to "shop" the opinion to more than one firm. Eventually, the promoter will find a lawyer who will give the opinion.

Some lawyers offer a more cynical explanation for the ease by which promoters get more-likely-than-not opinions on the more aggressive tax shelters. Opinion writing is interesting work, and promoters generally don't question how many hours it takes to get a desired opinion. For lawyers under billing pressure, tax shelter work can be a godsend. "You break your back for a firm, month after month," one partner reports, "and next month the firm is going to ask 'What have you done for me lately?' Then a Merrill Lynch comes to you—maybe for the first time—to ask you for an opinion. You know that if you give the client what it wants, there is more work in the future. It's a real temptation."

More commonly, lawyers report that the pressure to "deliver" an opinion comes from the dynamics of the promotion and opinion writing process. A lawyer might first write an opinion on a tax product that assumes some genuine nontax business purpose or investment. The product, with opinion, is then pitched to clients who like the tax results but wish to reduce the real investment and business risk. The promoter wishes to accommodate the client, and the lawyer is asked to modify the opinion to bless the revised deal. At that point, the lawyer is aware that a number of parties have already sunk considerable time and expense into considering the deal. The lawyer knows as well that the business purpose doctrine is analytically elusive and that there is no sharp dividing line between sufficient and insufficient business purpose. The temptation to at least compromise, giving the revised opinion if the parties will accept some business risk (but less risk than in the deal as originally envisioned) is strong.

Lawyers who wrote the kinds of opinions described in that passage were well compensated. Some lawyers associated with promoters wrote identical opinions for scores of taxpayers and received $50,000 for each opinion. In other cases, lawyers charged and received $500,000 and more for an opinion on a particular shelter and, again, sold the same opinion to many taxpayers. This state of affairs led Congress to amend the "reasonable cause" exception to the accuracy-related penalty. That section now prevents a taxpayer from relying on opinion from a "disqualified advisor" to establish reasonable cause for its position. A disqualified advisor is defined to include attorneys who write opinions for the use of shelter promoters, or who are referred to clients by shelter promoters. § 6662A.

Perhaps more significantly, in August 2005, the Justice Department indicted eight members of the large accounting firm KMPG for conspiracy to commit criminal tax fraud. The actions taken in furtherance of the alleged conspiracy, as set forth in indictment, included writing opinion letters known to include mistakes of both fact and law. The indictment marked a sea change in governmental policy toward shelters. Previously, nearly all enforcement efforts had been civil, rather than criminal, and directed only against taxpayers. The fact that the government has shown itself willing to adopt this approach is certain to affect behavior of future opinion writers.

Finally, Treasury has changed the rules governing tax practice to require higher standards for so-called covered opinions. Under those rules, adopted in a document known as Circular 230 and made part of the code of federal regulations (31 C.F.R. § 10.35), a covered opinion includes any more-likely-than-not opinion on a transaction a significant purpose of which is the evasion or avoidance of tax. The rules specify in considerable detail what types of opinions are covered and what types are not. They then impose standards, including the following:

(c) *Requirements for covered opinions.* A practitioner providing a covered opinion must comply with each of the following requirements.

(1) *Factual matters.*

(i) The practitioner must use reasonable efforts to identify and ascertain the facts, which may relate to future events if a transaction is prospective or proposed, and to determine which facts are relevant. The opinion must identify and consider all facts that the practitioner determines to be relevant.

(ii) The practitioner must not base the opinion on any unreasonable factual assumptions (including assumptions as to future events). An unreasonable factual assumption includes a factual assumption that the practitioner knows or should know is incorrect or incomplete. For example, it is unreasonable to assume that a transaction has a business purpose or that a transaction is potentially profitable apart from tax benefits. A factual assumption includes reliance on a projection, financial forecast or appraisal. It is unreasonable for a practitioner to rely on a projection, financial forecast or appraisal if the practitioner knows or should know that the projection, financial forecast or appraisal is incorrect or incomplete or was prepared by a person lacking the skills or qualifications necessary to prepare such projection, financial forecast or appraisal. The opinion must identify in a separate section all factual assumptions relied upon by the practitioner.

(iii) The practitioner must not base the opinion on any unreasonable factual representations, statements or findings of the taxpayer or any other person. An unreasonable factual representation includes a factual representation that the practitioner knows or should know is incorrect or incomplete. For example, a practitioner may not rely on a factual representation that a transaction has a business purpose if the representation does not include a specific description of the business purpose or the practitioner knows or should that the representation is incorrect or incomplete. The opinion must identify in a separate section all factual representations, statements or findings of the taxpayer relied upon by the practitioner.

(2) *Relate law to facts.*

(i) The opinion must relate the applicable law (including potentially applicable judicial doctrines) to the relevant facts.

(ii) The practitioner must not assume the favorable resolution of any significant Federal tax issue except as provided in paragraphs (c)(3)(v) and (d) of this section, or otherwise base an opinion on any unreasonable legal assumptions, representations, or conclusions.

(iii) The opinion must not contain internally inconsistent legal analyses or conclusions.

(3) *Evaluation of significant Federal tax issues.*

(i) *In general.* The opinion must consider all significant Federal tax issues except as provided in paragraphs (c)(3)(v) and (d) of this section.

(ii) *Conclusion as to each significant Federal tax issue.* The opinion must provide the practitioner's conclusion as to the likelihood that the taxpayer will prevail on the merits with respect to each significant Federal tax issue considered in the opinion. If the practitioner is unable to reach a conclusion with respect to one or more of those issues, the opinion must state that the practitioner is unable to reach a conclusion with respect to those issues. The opinion must describe the reasons for the conclusions, including the facts and analysis supporting the conclusions, or describe the reasons that the practitioner is unable to reach a conclusion as to one or more issues. If the practitioner fails to reach a conclusion at a confidence level of at least more likely than not with respect to one or more significant Federal tax issues considered, the opinion must include the appropriate disclosure(s) required under paragraph (e) of this section.

(iii) *Evaluation based on chances of success on the merits.* In evaluating the significant Federal tax issues addressed in the opinion, the practitioner must not take into account the possibility that a tax return will not be audited, that an issue will not be raised on audit, or that an issue will be resolved through settlement if raised.

(iv) *Marketed opinions.* In the case of a marketed opinion, the opinion must provide the practitioner's conclusion that the taxpayer will prevail on the merits at a confidence level of at least more likely than not with respect to each significant Federal tax issue. If the practitioner is unable to reach a more likely than not conclusion with respect to each significant Federal tax issue, the practitioner must not provide the marketed opinion, but may provide written advice that satisfies the requirements in paragraph (b)(5)(ii) of this section.

* * *

Attorneys who do not meet these requirements face monetary fines or suspension from practice before the IRS.

6. Sale and Leaseback Transactions

Overview. The favorable depreciation rules are designed to, and do, stimulate business investment. Suppose, though, that a taxpayer in a low bracket (or one that pays no tax at all) wishes to expand a trade or business and requires additional depreciable property. Is there any way such a taxpayer can take advantage of the generous depreciation allowance?

One alternative for the low-bracket taxpayer is to lease the depreciable property from a high-bracket taxpayer. The high-bracket taxpayer will enjoy the tax advantages associated with the investment and can pass on part of those advantages to the low-bracket taxpayer in the form of lower rent.

In some cases, finding a high-bracket lessor of the desired property is difficult. In that situation, the low-bracket taxpayer may itself buy or construct the depreciable property. Before the property is placed in service, however, a suitable high-bracket lessor may be found, in which case the property may be sold to the high-bracket taxpayer, which in turn leases it back to the low-bracket taxpayer. The high-bracket taxpayer receives the tax benefits of ownership and the low-bracket taxpayer receives either some up front cash in addition to the amount of its investment or rental payments that are less than they would otherwise be.

The following simplified example may help illustrate the sale-leaseback transaction. Suppose Yaba Company requires $1 million of depreciable property for its business. Yaba has past operating losses that can be carried over to present and future years; as a result, Yaba is in a zero percent marginal tax bracket and will not benefit from the depreciation deduction on the new investment. Yaba buys the property for $1 million and then sells it to Xenon Corporation for $1 million. Xenon pays $200,000 cash and gives Yaba a note for the remaining $800,000. Xenon then leases the property back to Yaba at an annual rent that is exactly equal to the payments Xenon must make on the $800,000 purchase note. The only money that ever changes hands between Yaba and Xenon is the $200,000 purchase payment.

When the smoke has cleared, Xenon has paid $200,000 for the legal ownership of $1 million of business property. Xenon must make payments on its $800,000 purchase money note, but those payments will be offset by the rental payments it receives from Yaba. If the transaction is respected for tax purposes, Xenon will receive the tax benefits associated with the property. Yaba, on the other hand, receives the property it needs for a net outlay of $800,000 instead of $1 million. Yaba will be required to make annual rental payments to Xenon, but these will be offset by the payments to which it will be entitled on the purchase money note.

Will the transaction be respected for tax purposes? The answer to that question will depend on many considerations, including the motivation of the parties and the incidents of ownership borne by the purported lessor. In Frank Lyon Co. v. United States, 435 U.S. 561 (1978), the Supreme Court upheld a transaction which was a lot like the Yaba-Xenon example except that the lessee, a bank, could point to a business reason for the form of the transaction — essentially, to circumvent banking regulations (with the approval of the regulators) that would have applied if it held legal title to the property. Other cases, however, have emphasized the business purpose of the lessor, and disallowed its depreciation deductions if it had no chance of earning a before-tax profit. See Hilton v. Commissioner, 74 T.C. 305 (1980), aff'd per curiam, 671 F.2d 316 (9th Cir. 1982); James v. Commissioner, 87 T.C. 905 (1986).

The IRS has promulgated guidelines under which it will issue advance rulings that certain equipment leases will be respected for tax purposes. These guidelines are set forth in Revenue Procedures 75-21, 1975-1 C.B. 715, and 75-28, 1975-1 C.B. 752. The guidelines are not intended to represent the IRS's position on audit and do not apply to many forms of leases, such as the leases of real property. Nonetheless, the guidelines are generally taken into account when structuring a lease transaction. The guidelines have been summarized as follows by the Joint Committee on Taxation (General Explanation of the Revenue Provisions of the Tax Equity and Fiscal Responsibility Act of 1982 — Safe Harbor Leasing, 97th Cong., 2d Sess. 45-63 (1982)):

1. *Minimum investment.* The lessor must have a minimum 20 percent unconditional at-risk investment in the property. This rule represents an attempt to ensure that the lessor suffers some significant loss if the property declines in value.

2. *Purchase options.* In general, the lessee may not have an option to purchase the property at the end of the lease term unless, under the lease agreement, the option can be exercised only at fair market value (determined at the time of exercise). This rule precludes fixed price purchase options, even at a bona fide estimate of the projected fair market value of the property at the option date. In addition, when the property is first placed in service by the lessee, the lessor cannot have a contractual right to require the lessee or any other party to purchase the property, even at fair market value (a put).

The fair market value purchase option requirement fulfills three purposes related to the determination of the economic substance of the transaction. First, it ensures that the lessor bears the risk implicit in ownership that no market will exist at the end of the lease. The owner of depreciable property is the person who bears any decline in value of the asset. Second, it ensures that the lessor has retained an equity interest in the property. Any fixed price option represents a limitation on the lessor's right of full enjoyment of the property's value. Third, it limits the ability of the parties to establish an artificial rent structure to avoid the cash flow test (described below). However, several courts have held that the mere existence of a fixed price purchase option does not prevent lease treatment so long as the lessor retains other significant burdens and benefits of ownership.

3. *Lessee investment precluded.* Neither the lessee nor a party related to the lessee may furnish any part of the cost of the property. The rationale is that a lessee investment may suggest that the lessee is in substance a co-owner of the property.

4. *No lessee loans or guarantees.* As a corollary to the prior rule, the lessee must not loan to the lessor any of the funds necessary to acquire the property. In addition, the lessee must not guarantee any lessor loan.

5. *Profit and cash flow requirements.* The lessor must expect to receive a profit from the transaction and have a positive cash flow from the transaction independent of tax benefits. As mentioned previously, a profitability requirement is based on the requirement that lease transactions must have a business purpose independent of tax benefits.

6. *Limited use property.* Under Revenue Procedure 76-30, 1976-2 C.B. 647, property that can be used only by the lessee (limited use property) is not eligible for lease treatment. The rationale is that if the lessee is the only person who could realistically use the property, the lessor has not retained any significant ownership interest.

The safe-harbor leasing experiment. In the 1981 act, Congress adopted "safe-harbor leasing" provisions, which allowed arrangements to be treated as leases even though the substance of ownership (by the lessor) was plainly lacking. Under the safe-harbor leasing rules, the transaction between Yaba and Xenon, described in the first part of this section, would have been treated as a genuine sale and leaseback. The effect of this law was to permit firms that did not pay tax (e.g., Chrysler Corp., which had suffered huge operating losses) to gain the advantage of accelerated depreciation and the investment credit by arranging for a firm with a profit (e.g., IBM) to buy the assets that the no-tax firm needed and lease those assets to the no-tax firm. The tax benefits of ownership by the profit firm (IBM) were passed on to the no-tax firm (Chrysler) (at least in large part, depending on the outcome of the bargain between the parties) in the form of relatively low rent payments by the latter. The effect was akin to a sale of tax benefits, which was the characterization given to these transactions in newspaper accounts. Huge deals were reported, and the public became outraged. Do you think the outrage was justified? If Congress wanted to allow no-tax firms to be able to take advantage of incentives to investment, is safe-harbor leasing the best way to do it?[31] In any event, in 1982 Congress repealed the 1981 rules.

---

31. It would be possible to provide that where a firm is not subject to taxation, the investment credit (or even the ACRS deduction) would entitle the firm to a check from the Treasury. This possibility has

7. The Alternative Minimum Tax

The alternative minimum tax (AMT) imposes a tax at a reduced rate on a broader base. Its original objective was to ensure that a taxpayer (corporate or individual) could not take advantage of certain preferences (deductions, exclusions, accounting methods, etc.) to avoid all tax liability. This objective is achieved, roughly speaking, by taking taxable income, adding to it the amount of the preferences, and imposing a tax on this amount,[32] at a reduced rate (presently between 10 and 28 percent, depending on the type of income for individuals and 20 percent for corporations); but the resulting tax is payable only to the extent that it exceeds the normal tax. To the extent that the amount of the AMT tax attributable to timing rules (as opposed to exclusions such as tax-exempt interest) exceeds the regular tax, the excess is treated as a credit that can be used in subsequent years to reduce the excess of the regular tax over the AMT. The credit provides relief where an AMT timing rule results in an item being included in AMT income in one year and the same item is included in regular income under the regular-tax rules in a later year.

The AMT reflects an uneasy compromise over the role of tax preferences. Preferences are not part of the tax law by accident and their revenue costs are substantial. Congress seems ready to accept that they may be used by certain taxpayers to save millions of dollars in taxes. Yet Congress refuses to allow a taxpayer to use one or more preferences to reduce taxes too far, even though that taxpayer's total tax saving may be only a few thousand dollars rather than millions.[33]

While its original purpose was preventing overuse of certain preferences, the AMT has been broadened (particularly in 1986) to the point where it may now be thought of as creating a second concept of taxable income that

---

been referred to as refundability. The arguments against it are summarized in the following passage from Sunley, Safe Harbor Leasing, 43 Tax Found. Tax Rev. 17 (April 1982):

> Refundability would tend to increase further the enormous power of the tax-writing committees. Refundability also might further erode the perception that the tax system is fair, since some companies will be paying what will be viewed as a negative income tax. Nonrefundability may also help keep the investment credit from entities not subject to the income tax, such as state and local governments, charities, and schools. Finally, the business community may fear that if the investment credit is made refundable, Congress will view it not as a reduction in tax, but as a subsidy program for business, thereby endangering the basic credit itself.
>
> Refundability of the investment tax credit would not be as generous as leasing, since the ACRS benefits would not be cashed out. . . .

32. There is, however, an exemption of $40,000 for corporations and $45,000 for married taxpayers filing a joint return ($33,750 for single taxpayers). The 2009 stimulus legislation increased the individual AMT exemption amount to $70,950 for taxpayers filing joint returns ($46,700 for single taxpayers), solely for the year 2009. This exemption is phased out at the rate of 25 cents per dollar as alternative minimum taxable income (AMTI) rises above $150,000 ($112,500 for single taxpayers). The AMT does not apply to "small business corporations," which generally are defined as those with annual gross receipts below $5,000,000.

33. The AMT was first adopted in 1969 after the Treasury had brought to public attention a small number of cases of individuals with substantial incomes who had used various preferences to reduce their taxable incomes to zero and thereby avoid paying any tax. It was never made clear why one should be concerned about a few people saving relatively small amounts of taxes, when the source of their saving was a set of provisions that cost the Treasury billions of dollars each year and that Congress seemed to consider essential to the well-being of the economy. Nonetheless, the thought of rich people paying no taxes seemed to be sufficiently disturbing to force Congress to take some action.

operates alongside the basic concept of the normal tax. The concept of the normal tax is narrow; it allows a wide variety of preferences. Since Congress is not entirely confident of that concept, it adopts the AMT, which defines a broader one, with fewer preferences. But Congress reflects its continuing, though uncertain, fidelity to the narrower concept by imposing a tax on the broader base only at a lower rate and collecting that tax only to the extent it exceeds the tax imposed on the narrower base. While the AMT represents an attack on preferences in general, it may deflect attention from particular preferences and the objectives served by each; the tax imposed under it is a function of the aggregate effect of all listed preferences.

By no means all tax provisions that might be regarded as sources of deviation from an accurate definition of income are treated as preferences under the AMT. For example, among the most significant sources of AMT liability for individuals are the AMT's denial of any deduction for state and local income tax paid, for personal exemptions with respect to one's children, and for business or investment expenses that are allowed only as itemized deductions. To say the least, these items could hardly be described as the prototypical tax shelter deductions. As one can easily imagine, the legislative process for prescribing tax preferences for purposes of the AMT involves intense lobbying and debate, and the resulting list may tell us more about political power than it does about sound principles of taxation.

The preferences are not entirely the same for individuals and corporations. The main preferences for individuals (many of which also apply to corporations) are:

1. *Tax-exempt interest.* The interest on certain newly issued private activity bonds is a preference.

2. *Percentage depletion.* The amount of the percentage depletion allowance in excess of cost depletion is a preference.

3. *Intangible drilling costs.* The preference is the excess of expensing over ten-year amortization or cost depletion, to the extent in excess of 65 percent of net oil and gas income.

4. *Research and experimentation expenses.* The preference is the excess of the amount claimed as a current expense over the amount allowable with ten-year amortization.

5. *Incentive stock options.* The preference is the spread between the fair market value of the stock and the exercise price, at the time of exercise.

6. *Itemized deductions.* The amount of the preference is determined by disallowing certain itemized deductions, including the deduction for state and local taxes and the deduction for interest on home equity loans, and certain job-related outlays and by limiting the deduction for medical expenses to the excess over 10 percent of AGI (as opposed to 7.5 percent for the normal tax).

7. *Credits denied.* Certain tax credits, though technically not listed as preferences, are "lost" for purposes of computing the AMT. This result is accomplished by disallowing these credits when computing the regular tax as a prelude to computing the AMT. The limitations are found not in the AMT rules but in the rules relating to the credits. See, e.g., § 26. Beginning in 2002 the lost credits will include child and education credits, unless the current suspension of the limitations on those credits is extended.

8. *Heads of households.* In the regular tax there is a rate schedule for heads of households that is not as favorable as that for married couples but more favorable than that for single persons. Under the AMT there is a $45,000 exemption for married couples ($70,950 for 2009) and a $33,750 exemption for single persons ($46,700 for 2009) with heads of households treated as single persons.

NOTES AND QUESTIONS

1. *Planning.* The AMT creates opportunities for tax advisers to earn their fees by recommending tax-minimization strategies. For example, suppose a corporation in the current year will have normal income of $1 million and alternative minimum taxable income (AMTI) of $5 million, but expects that in the next year its normal income and its AMTI will both be $5 million. Suppose that the income expected for next year includes a $1 million fee for services and that it may be possible to arrange for advance payment of that fee, so that it can be included in the current year's income. At what rate will the fee be taxed if it is received in the current year? At what rate will it be taxed if it is received in the next year? Do you get the point? Suppose there is a repair expense that can be incurred this year or deferred until next year. What do tax considerations suggest should be done?

2. *Disparate effects of the AMT.* The AMT gives some taxpayers but not others the full benefit of a given tax preference. For example, suppose that Alice and Bert each have a $100,000 AMT preference as a result of using incentive stock options to purchase stock that is worth more than the exercise price at the time of exercise. However, because Alice is paid a higher salary than Bert, only Bert owes AMT in the year of exercise. (Increasing the amount of income, such as salary, that is taxable under both the regular tax and the AMT reduces the application of the AMT since the inclusion increases regular tax liability more than AMT liability.)

Is this disparate effect of the AMT unfair? If you believe that the regular tax exclusion that applies to Alice and Bert is itself unfair, does reducing the tax benefit for Bert but not Alice increase or diminish overall unfairness?

3. *Impact and prospects.* While Congress has scaled back the AMT several times in recent years, the number of individuals to whom the AMT applies has been increasing rapidly, mainly because its exemption amount (in 2009, $70,950 for married taxpayers filing a joint return and $46,700 for single taxpayers) is not indexed for inflation and thus has been losing value in real terms. Tax legislation enacted in the early 2000s made this problem considerably worse by reducing most people's regular tax liability without adjusting the AMT.

Until 2000, less than 1 percent of taxpayers paid the AMT in any given year. Under current law, however, the Tax Policy Center (TPC) estimates that the number of taxpayers paying AMT will grow from just over 1 million in 2001 to over 33 million in 2010. The TPC also estimates that, in 2010, AMT will be paid by (a) approximately 27 percent of taxpayers earning between $50,000 and $100,000, (b) nearly 80 percent of taxpayers earning between $100,000 and $200,000, and (c) roughly 95 percent of taxpayers earning between

$200,000 and $500,000. (The percentage paying the AMT then drops as income continues to rise.)

This level of AMT application seems likely to be politically intolerable given the compliance burdens of having to function under two parallel tax systems. Unfortunately, however, it is unclear how the problem can be solved. The difficulty here is not administrative, since it would be simple enough to raise the AMT's exemption amounts and thereafter index them for inflation. Rather, the problem concerns revenues and the annual federal budget deficit. As of June 2008, it was estimated that repealing the AMT would result in a reduction of federal revenues in the amount of $960 billion through 2018 if the 2001-2006 tax cuts are allowed to expire, and $1.8 trillion if those tax cuts are extended beyond their scheduled expiration of January 1, 2011. For 2008 alone, the TPC estimated that repealing the AMT would cost $87.6 billion, while repealing the regular income tax (but retaining the AMT) would cost only $51.7 billion. It seems clear, therefore, that the AMT is a ticking time bomb with no solution in sight that is both politically appealing and fiscally responsible.

4. *Are all of the AMT preferences really preferences?* Not everyone would agree that all of the items identified as tax preferences by the AMT deserve that label. The following case helps to illustrate this point, plus the fact that the AMT can apply to people other than the wealthy tax avoiders typically emphasized in political discussion of it.

KLAASSEN v. COMMISSIONER

182 F.3d 932, 1999 WL 197172 (10th Cir. 1999) (unpublished opinion)

. . . David R. and Margaret J. Klaassen appeal from the Tax Court's ruling that they are liable for an alternative minimum tax (AMT) in the amount of $1,085 for the 1994 tax year. The Klaassens contend that the tax court erred (1) by applying the AMT provisions, §§ 55-59, to them in violation of congressional intent; or, alternatively (2) by applying the AMT provisions to them in violation of their First and Fifth Amendment rights. We affirm.

BACKGROUND

The facts are undisputed. During the 1994 tax year, the Klaassens were the parents of ten dependent children. According to their 1994 joint tax return, they earned an adjusted gross income (AGI) of $83,056. On Schedule A, the Klaassens claimed deductions for medical expenses and for state and local taxes in the respective amounts of $4,767 and $3,264. Including their claimed deductions for interest and charitable contributions, their total Schedule A itemized deductions equaled $19,564. Therefore, they subtracted that amount from their AGI, and on line 35 of their Form 1040, they showed a balance of $63,492. On line 36, they entered a total of $29,400 for twelve personal exemptions—one each for themselves and their ten children. After subtracting that amount, they showed a taxable income of $34,092 on line 37 of their Form 1040, and a resulting regular tax of $5,111 on line 38. They did not provide any computations for AMT liability.

Following an audit, the IRS issued a notice of deficiency, advising the Klaassens that they were liable for a $1,085.43 AMT pursuant to §§ 55-59. Specifically, the IRS concluded that, in the Klaassens' case, §§ 55-56 required three specific adjustments, or increases, to the taxable income which they showed on line 37 of their Form 1040. According to the IRS's interpretation, § 56(b)(1)(A)(ii) required the entire $3,263.56 deduction for state and local taxes to be added back. Next, § 56(b)(1)(B) reduced the deduction allowable for medical expenses by setting a 10% floor in lieu of the 7.5% floor normally allowed under § 213(a) — resulting in a net adjustment of $2,076.41. Finally, § 56(b)(1)(E) deprived the Klaassens of the entire $29,400 deduction they claimed on line 36 of their Form 1040. After adjusting the taxable income by these three amounts, the IRS set the alternative minimum taxable income at $68,832. After deducting the $45,000 exemption, the tentative minimum tax was computed on the excess: 26% × $23,832 = $6,196. The difference between that figure and the Klaassens' regular tax was $1,085. The Tax Court upheld the IRS's position. . . .

DISCUSSION

The Klaassens do not dispute the numbers or the mechanics used to calculate the AMT deficiency. Rather, they claim that, as a matter of law, the AMT provisions should not apply to them. . . .

A.

Section 56(b)(1)(E) plainly states that, in computing the alternative minimum taxable income, "the deduction for personal exemptions under § 151 . . . shall not be allowed." Nonetheless, the Klaassens argue that Congress intended the AMT to apply only to very wealthy persons who claim the types of tax preferences described in § 57. Essentially, the Klaassens contend that Congress did not intend to disallow personal exemptions for taxpayers at their income level when no § 57 preferences are involved. Although they cite no legislative history to support their contention, the Klaassens argue that their entitlement to their personal exemptions is mandated by §§ 151-153. In particular, they note that for 1994, § 151(d) allowed taxpayers filing joint returns to claim the full exemption so long as their AGI was less than $167,700. They then argue that the § 151(d) threshold amount should be interpolated as a threshold for the AMT provisions. We disagree.

In the absence of exceptional circumstances, where a statute is clear and unambiguous our inquiry is complete. . . . The AMT framework establishes a precise method for taxing income which the regular tax does not reach. In creating this framework, Congress included several provisions, "marked by a high degree of specificity," by which deductions or advantages which are allowed in computing the regular tax are specifically disallowed for purposes of computing the AMT. Huntsberry v. Commissioner, 83 T.C. 742, 747-48 (1984). . . . Instead of permitting those separate "regular tax" deductions, Congress specifically substituted the $45,000 fixed exemption for purposes of

AMT computations. § 55(d)(1). If, as the Klaassens claim, Congress had intended the AMT to apply only to taxpayers whose incomes reached a certain threshold, or only to taxpayers with § 57 tax preferences, it could have easily drafted the statute to achieve that result. Instead, as the tax court correctly held, the statute's plain language unequivocally reaches the Klaassens, and our inquiry is therefore complete. While the law may result in some unintended consequences, in the absence of any ambiguity, it must be applied as written. It is therefore from Congress that the Klaassens should seek relief.

B.

As their second, alternative, point of error, the Klaassens contend that applying the AMT provisions to them violates their First Amendment rights, as well as their equal protection and due process rights. First, the Klaassens contend that, by disallowing the personal exemptions for their children, the statute impermissibly burdens their free exercise of religion.[34] Second, they contend that their equal protection and due process rights are violated, because the statute deprives them of full deductions for medical and local taxes, whereas those deductions are allowed for families with similar incomes, but fewer than eight children.

Tax legislation carries a "presumption of constitutionality," Regan v. Taxation With Representation of Washington, 461 U.S. 540, 547 (1983) (citations omitted). . . . [T]he fact that a generally applicable — but neutral — law "may have the effect of making the observance of some religious beliefs more expensive does not render the statute unconstitutional under the First Amendment." Black v. Commissioner, 69 T.C. 505, 510 (1977) (citing Braunfeld v. Brown, 366 U.S. 599, 605-07 (1961)). . . . [A] taxpayer may overcome the presumption of constitutionality "only by the most explicit demonstration that a classification is a hostile and oppressive discrimination against particular persons and classes." Madden v. Kentucky, 309 U.S. 83 (1940).

In the present case, the Klaassens do not contend that the AMT's classification are grounded in religion. Rather, they contend that one of the effects of the statute is to burden their exercise of religion in violation of the First Amendment. However, the Supreme Court has clearly instructed that such contentions must be viewed with great care. . . .

Accordingly, we agree with the tax court's ruling. The uniform application of the AMT provisions furthers a compelling governmental interest, and we therefore conclude that it does not violate the Free Exercise Clause of the First Amendment. For similar reasons, . . . we find no equal protection or due process violation.

Affirmed.

KELLY, Circuit Judge, concurring.

Although I agree with the court that the taxpayers cannot prevail on the theories advanced, we are not precluded from examining the legislative

---

34. The Klaassens are members of the Reformed Presbyterian Church of North America. As part of their religious beliefs, they are opposed to any form of birth control.

history of the alternative minimum tax (AMT), despite the clarity of the statute. . . . The legislative history supports an argument that the original purpose of the AMT, one of the more complex parts of the Internal Revenue Code, was to insure that taxpayers with substantial economic income pay a minimum amount of tax on it. . . .

For a variety of reasons, the number of moderate income taxpayers subject to the AMT has been steadily increasing. From a tax compliance and administration perspective, many of these taxpayers simply are unaware of their AMT obligations. If aware, they probably would need the assistance of a tax professional to comply with the separate rules and computations (apart from regular tax) and additional record keeping essential for the AMT. From a fairness perspective, many of these taxpayers have not utilized § 57 preferences (or other more arcane AMT adjustment items) to reduce regular taxable income but are caught up in the AMT's attempt to impose fairness. That certainly seems to be the case here. In the interest of progressivity, the regular tax already reduces or phases out itemized deductions and personal exemptions based upon income, see, e.g., § 67(a) (miscellaneous itemized deductions), § 68 (overall reduction of itemized deductions), § 151(d)(3) (phaseout of personal exemptions), § 213(a) (medical and dental expenses deduction only for amounts beyond 7.5% floor); surely Congress never intended a family of twelve that still qualified for these items under the regular tax to partly forfeit them under the AMT.

That said, we must apply the law as it is plainly written, despite what appears to be the original intent behind the AMT. . . . The solution to this inequity, whether it be (1) eliminating itemized deductions and personal exemptions as adjustments to regular taxable income in arriving at alternative minimum taxable income, (2) exempting low and moderate income taxpayers from the AMT, (3) raising and indexing the AMT exemption amount, or (4) some other measure, must come from Congress, as the tax court rightly concluded. . . .

QUESTIONS

1. Did the court have any choice but to decide the case in favor of the government?
2. Do you agree with the taxpayers and the concurring judge that the result is inequitable? If so, which of the changes in the law listed in the concurring opinion would you recommend and why?

PROSMAN v. COMMISSIONER
T.C. Memo. 1999-87

. . . Respondent determined a deficiency in petitioners' Federal income tax for 1995 in the amount of $2,688. The issue for decision is whether petitioners are subject to the alternative minimum tax (AMT) under § 55. . . .

FINDINGS OF FACT

During the year in issue, petitioner was employed as a computer consultant by Command Systems, Inc. (Command Systems). As a consultant, petitioner bid on different projects using a formula which included both a standard hourly base rate and a "per diem allowance" amount. Petitioner included a "per diem allowance" amount in his bid formula because most of his projects were out of town and petitioner incurred substantial meal and lodging expenses while away from home. Accordingly, petitioner requested that Command Systems separate petitioner's "per diem allowance" amount, which petitioner used to pay for employee business expenses, from his base rate. Command Systems refused and included both amounts as wages on petitioner's 1995 Form W-2. On their Federal income tax return for 1995, petitioners reported adjusted gross income (AGI) in the amount of $83,143. On Schedule A of their 1995 return, petitioners claimed, among other deductions, the following itemized deductions:

Expense	Amount
Taxes paid	$ 8,824.82
Job expenses and other miscellaneous deductions, above the 2-percent floor	$28,589.63
Total	$37,414.45

For 1995, petitioners reported income prior to the deduction for exemptions of $37,843, taxable income of $32,843, and total tax of $4,924. There is no dispute that petitioners incurred expenses as claimed on their 1995 return. In the notice of deficiency, respondent determined that petitioners were subject to the AMT for the tax year in issue. Respondent computed an AMT in the amount of $7,612 for petitioners' 1995 tax year, and determined a deficiency in petitioners' tax in the amount of $2,688.

OPINION

Petitioners contend that respondent's application of § 55 is inequitable. Section 55(a) imposes a tax equal to the excess of the tentative minimum tax over the regular tax. The tentative minimum tax for noncorporate taxpayers is equal to 26 percent of the amount (the taxable excess), as does not exceed $175,000, by which the alternative minimum taxable income (AMTI) exceeds the exemption amount, plus 28 percent of such taxable excess as exceeds $175,000. See § 55(b)(1)(A). The exemption amount for married couples filing a joint return is $45,000. See § 55(d). AMTI equals the taxpayer's taxable income for the year with the adjustments provided in §§ 57 and 58 and increased by the amount of tax preference items described in § 57. See § 55(b)(2). In calculating AMTI, no deduction is allowed for miscellaneous itemized deductions and State and local taxes paid, unless such amounts are deductible in determining AGI. See § 56(b)(1). Also, no deduction for personal exemptions under § 151 is allowed. See § 56(b)(1)(E).

In computing petitioners' AMTI for the year in issue, respondent disallowed petitioners' deductions for taxes paid and for job expenses and other miscellaneous itemized deductions. We have reviewed respondent's computations of the AMT and find that they comport with the provisions of §§ 55 and 56.

Petitioners, however, contend that the AMT was intended to apply to high income earners rather than to lower income taxpayers, such as themselves. Petitioners contend that if Command Systems had separated petitioner's "per diem allowance" amount from petitioner's base rate, petitioner would not have been subject to the AMT. We are not persuaded by petitioners' argument. While we may sympathize with petitioners, under the plain meaning of the statute they are subject to the AMT. Furthermore, this Court has considered and rejected equitable arguments like those of petitioners. . . .

Petitioner may be correct in asserting that the AMT would not apply if Command Systems had designated certain amounts paid to petitioner as reimbursed employee business expenses rather than as wages. Petitioner, however, negotiated the best contract that he could, and his remuneration must be taxed based on the manner in which it was received.

Respondent's determination is sustained. . . .

QUESTIONS

1. Did the court have any more choice here than in *Klaassen* regarding whether to decide this case in favor of the government? How could Congress change the result in future cases resembling this one if it accepted the taxpayer's equitable argument?

2. Given their adjusted gross income of $83,143, were the Prosmans really "lower income taxpayers"? Under the facts stated, is that the right number to use in determining their "true" income level (assuming the question to be of interest for its own sake)?

3. Should state and local taxes paid be an item of AMT preference? What about miscellaneous itemized deductions such as employee business expenses?

PROBLEMS

1. Herman and Wanda are husband and wife. In 2009 they file a joint return, reporting regular taxable income of $100,000. Under the tax schedule in effect for 2009 their regular tax is $17,375. Because of various preferences their alternative minimum taxable income (AMTI) is $150,000. What is their AMT? What is their total tax?

2. Wendy and Hiram are wife and husband. In 2009 their regular taxable income is $200,000, which includes $100,000 of net capital gain. Under the tax schedules in effect for 2009, their regular tax is $32,375 ($17,375 on the ordinary income and $15,000 on the net capital gain). If all the income had been ordinary income, the tax would have been $44,263. On their tax return, they claimed deductions of $15,000 for state taxes and $10,000 for interest on

a home equity loan. In 2009, Wendy exercised an incentive stock option (ISO) and was not liable for any regular tax on the spread of $25,000 between the stock's fair market value ($40,000) and the amount she paid for it ($15,000).

(a) What is the amount of the AMT? What is the total tax?

(b) What would the total tax have been if the ISO had not been exercised?

(c) Suppose Wendy and Hiram could have deferred the recognition of their $100,000 capital gain. How much did it cost them to recognize the gain in 2009? To answer this question, figure out what their total tax would have been in 2009 if they had not recognized the gain and compare this number with the total calculated in part (a) above.

7

THE SPLITTING OF INCOME

Recall that the U.S. federal income tax is progressive. That is, as an individual's taxable income rises, her tax liability also increases — not only in absolute terms but as a percentage of income as well. This result is accomplished primarily through the application of a rate schedule featuring increasing marginal tax rates. The 2009 tax rate table for single individuals is shown below:

If taxable income is	The tax is
Not over $8,350	10% of the taxable income
Over $8,350 but not over $33,950	$835 plus 15% of the excess over $8,350
Over $33,950 but not over $82,250	$4,675 plus 25% of the excess over $33,950
Over $82,250 but not over $171,550	$16,750 plus 28% of the excess over $82,250
Over $171,550 but not over $372,950	$41,754 plus 33% of the excess over $171,550
Over $372,950	$108,216 plus 35% of the excess over $372,950

To get comfortable with the operation of this rate structure, you may wish to take a few moments to calculate the average and marginal tax rates for individuals at different income levels. For example, consider a taxpayer, Jamal, who has taxable income for 2009 of $100,000. Because Jamal's taxable income is "over $82,250 but not over $171,550," the amount of federal income tax that Jamal owes is "$16,750 plus 28% of the excess over $82,250." Since the excess of $100,000 over $82,250 is $17,750, and 28 percent of $17,750 is $4,970, Jamal will owe a total of $21,720 (i.e., $16,750 + $4,970). Note that this figure implies an average tax rate of 21.7 percent. However, Jamal's marginal tax rate is 28 percent. This is the tax rate that applies to Jamal's last and next dollar of income and the most relevant figure for purposes of tax planning. For example, if Jamal is considering taking a part-time job for an extra $10,000, he may wish to know that an additional $10,000 of income will net him only $7,200 after income taxes (i.e., $10,000 minus $2,800). Alternatively, if Jamal is considering making a charitable contribution of $1,000, he may wish to know that a deduction of that amount would reduce his tax liability by $280.

It bears noting that, in a tax system featuring marginal rate progressivity, even taxpayers subject to the highest tax brackets enjoy the benefit of the lower tax rates. For example, consider Latika, who has total taxable income of $1 million. Since her taxable income is "over $372,950" her tax is "$108,216 plus 35% of the excess over $372,950." Since the excess of $1 million over $372,950 is $627,050, and 35 percent of $627,050 is $219,467, Latika will owe a total of $327,683 (i.e., $108,216 + $219,467). Latika's average tax rate is 32.8 percent — i.e., a blend of all six of the statutory tax rates. Although her marginal tax rate is 35 percent, she still benefits from having her first $8,350 of income taxed at the 10 percent rate, her next $25,600 taxed at 15 percent, and so on. Though obvious on reflection, this point is often misunderstood by those who lack familiarity with the basic operation of progressive marginal tax rates.

The U.S. income tax has always been progressive, though the degree of progressivity has varied dramatically. The top marginal tax rate started out quite low at 7 percent (1913-1915) and has risen as high as 94 percent (1944-1945) and fallen as low as 24 percent (1929) and, more recently, 28 percent (1988-1989). In the first thirty-five years of the post-WWII era, the top marginal tax rate remained relatively high, ranging from 92 percent in 1952 to just over 69 percent in 1981. Perhaps not surprisingly, this period was the heyday of tax shelters, as the payoff for reducing one's taxable income was extraordinarily high.

In this chapter, we will focus on another type of incentive created by the system of progressive marginal tax rates — i.e., the shifting of income from high-income individuals to low-bracket family members. This effort is often referred to as the "splitting" or "assignment" of income. The basic objective is to get as many "starts from the bottom" as possible. To take a simple example, consider two sisters, Meg and Jo, with aggregate taxable income of $16,700, which is exactly twice the amount of income taxed at the lowest 10 percent bracket for unmarried individuals. If Jo earns the entire amount herself, only half of it will be taxed at 10 percent and the other half will be subject to the 15 percent bracket. However, if Meg and Jo each earn $8,350, then the entire $16,700 would be taxed at 10 percent.

The incentive to split income is greatest where two taxpayers face a large marginal tax rate differential and would otherwise share economic resources. Thus, much of the law in this area concerns the treatment of individuals within a family or household, such as a husband and wife, parents and their children, etc. However, taxpayers have also sought to shift income to entities such as trusts and corporations. The tax system's response to these efforts has not been uniform. Much of the law of income splitting has come in the form of judicial decisions, though Congress has periodically intervened to limit specific income-splitting strategies. For example, the ability to shift income to children is limited by § 1(g), which taxes unearned income of certain children at their parents' marginal tax rate. Other sections, such as the trust and family partnership rules described later in this chapter, also limit income splitting.

A. INCOME FROM SERVICES: DIVERSION BY PRIVATE AGREEMENT

Our first case, Lucas v. Earl, arose at a time when there was only one rate schedule used by all taxpayers and when husband and wife were treated as separate taxpayers. Since 1948 we have had a system of joint returns and split income for husband and wife and as a result no advantage can be achieved (except in rare circumstances) by shifting income from one spouse to another, but the legal principles developed in early husband/wife cases are still relevant to efforts to shift income to other family members and to entities. In addition, this case and the one that follows (Poe v. Seaborn) are essential to understanding contemporary controversies over the "marriage penalty" and broader issues of how to tax the family unit.

LUCAS v. EARL
281 U.S. 111 (1930)

Mr. Justice HOLMES delivered the opinion of the Court.

This case presents the question whether the respondent, Earl, could be taxed for the whole of the salary and attorney's fees earned by him in the years 1920 and 1921, or should be taxed for only a half of them in view of a contract with his wife which we shall mention. The Commissioner of Internal Revenue and the Board of Tax Appeals imposed a tax upon the whole, but their decision was reversed by the Circuit Court of Appeals, 30 F.2d 898. . . .

By the contract, made in 1901, Earl and his wife agreed

> that any property either of us now has or may hereafter acquire . . . in any way, either by earnings (including salaries, fees, etc.), or any rights by contract or otherwise, during the existence of our marriage, or which we or either of us may receive by gift, bequest, devise, or inheritance, and all the proceeds, issues, and profits of any and all such property shall be treated and considered, and hereby is declared to be received, held, taken, and owned by us as joint tenants, and not otherwise, with the right of survivorship.

The validity of the contract is not questioned, and we assume it to be unquestionable under the law of the State of California,[1] in which the parties lived. Nevertheless we are of opinion that the Commissioner and Board of Tax Appeals were right.

The Revenue Act of 1918 . . . imposes a tax upon the net income of every individual including "income derived from salaries, wages, or compensation for personal service . . . of whatever kind and in whatever form paid," [§ 61(a)]. . . .

---

1. [Under the community property law of California at the time this case arose, Mrs. Earl's rights in Mr. Earl's salary and fees were less substantial than the rights she acquired under the contract. In 1927, in response to Poe v. Seaborn, infra page 626, California changed its law to give wives greater community-property rights. — EDS.]

A very forcible argument is presented to the effect that the statute seeks to tax only income beneficially received, and that taking the question more technically the salary and fees became the joint property of Earl and his wife on the very first instant on which they were received. We well might hesitate upon the latter proposition, because however the matter might stand between husband and wife he was the only party to the contracts by which the salary and fees were earned, and it is somewhat hard to say that the last step in the performance of those contracts could be taken by anyone but himself alone. But this case is not to be decided by attenuated subtleties. It turns on the import and reasonable construction of the taxing act. There is no doubt that the statute could tax salaries to those who earned them and provide that the tax could not be escaped by anticipatory arrangements and contracts however skillfully devised to prevent the salary when paid from vesting even for a second in the man who earned it. That seems to us the import of the statute before us and we think that no distinction can be taken according to the motives leading to the arrangement by which the fruits are attributed to a different tree from that on which they grew.

Judgment reversed.

NOTES AND QUESTIONS

1. *Fruit and tree.* The fruit-and-tree metaphor in the last sentence of Justice Holmes's opinion is widely known among tax experts and is frequently cited but, like many metaphors, is more colorful than helpful. For example, if two unrelated lawyers form a partnership and agree to split equally any net income, the income will be taxed according to the rights created by the agreement, regardless whose efforts happen to generate the income. The fruit-and-tree metaphor is simply inaccurate as applied to such a case. In other cases, it is often more puzzling to try to figure out what is tree and what is fruit than to reach a decision by using more direct analysis.

2. *Mrs. Earl's tax status.* Was Mrs. Earl also taxable on the income in question? Why (not)?

3. *Tax avoidance.* Was *Earl* a tax avoidance case?

4. *Theory of the case.* (a) Is it fair to say that in the era in which this case arose, Mr. Earl probably gave up nothing of significance when he entered into the contract with Mrs. Earl? Would the result have been different if the agreement had been for the life of Mr. Earl rather than "during the existence of [the] marriage"? If the income in question had gone into a trust for the benefit of impoverished relatives of Mrs. Earl, to be selected by her, would it still have been taxable to Mr. Earl?

(b) What if Mrs. Earl had paid for Mr. Earl's legal education, his law library, etc., in return for an assignment of 50 percent of his professional earnings either for a stated period or for life? Would the income then be taxed to Mr. Earl? See Hundley v. Commissioner, 48 T.C. 339 (1967), in which the taxpayer, a teenager, agreed in 1958 in exchange for his father's coaching, business management, and agent services, to share with his father equally any bonus he might receive for signing a professional baseball contract. The taxpayer signed with a professional team in 1960 and was allowed to deduct as a business expense

$55,000 (one-half of his $110,000 bonus) paid to his father. But compare Allen v. Commissioner, 50 T.C. 466 (1968), aff'd per curiam, 410 F.2d 398 (3d Cir. 1969), where a similar effort failed since the taxpayer shared his bonus with his mother, whom the Tax Court found to be ignorant of baseball.

(c) In some instances splitting may be attempted by creation of a partnership between, say, a father and his sons. This possibility is explored later in this chapter (page 669).

5. *Gratuitous performance of services.* Suppose that a famous actress plays the lead role in a movie produced by her son and is not paid for her services. Should and would the mother be taxed on some reasonable compensation? How would you determine the appropriate amount? It may be difficult to draw the line between this kind of service performed for one's child and other, presumably nontaxable, benefits that a parent may bestow on a child, such as investment advice by an investment advisor or legal advice by a lawyer.

When it comes to services performed for charities, the rules are more generous to taxpayers than the rules relating to services performed for an employer, customer, or client. Ordinarily any income that might be attributed to a taxpayer from performance of services for a charity would be offset by a deduction of the same amount. The issue becomes significant, however, where the deduction would be limited by the percentage limitations in § 170, by the phaseout of § 68, or by the alternative minimum tax. The regulations provide that no income arises where services are rendered directly to a charitable organization (Regs. § 1.61-2(c)), and this includes services rendered to a charity as promoter of public entertainment (G.C.M. 27026, 1951-2 C.B. 7). But despite the scorn expressed by Justice Holmes for "attenuated subtleties," the regulations distinguish between services rendered directly to the charity and services rendered to a third person with payment going to the charity. This is the kind of distinction that invites manipulation of the forms of transactions to achieve desirable tax results.

It may be difficult to work up concern about the shifting of income to charities. The principles applied to charities have been extended, however, to services rendered for the benefit of political organizations. See Rev. Rul. 68-503, 1968-2 C.B. 44, issued during the heat of the 1968 presidential campaign and holding that a featured performer at a political fund-raising event, for which admission was charged, was not taxable on any amount of income. Is this result consistent with *Earl*? with sound principles of taxation? with sound principles of campaign funding? If income should be taxed to the performer at a political fund-raising event, what if a famous actor appears in a television "spot" on behalf of a candidate (with no direct effort to raise money)?

6. *Attorneys' fees.* In Commissioner v. Banks, 543 U.S. 426 (2005), the U.S. Supreme Court cited Lucas v. Earl in support of its conclusion that a taxpayer who sued and recovered damages for employment discrimination must include in gross income the amount paid to his attorney as a contingent fee. The Court rejected an argument by the taxpayer that *Earl* applies only to gratuitous transfers. The result is that both the client and the attorney include in gross income the amount of the attorneys' fee. The client can deduct the fee, but subject to the limitations § 67 (2 percent floor) and § 68 (phaseout of itemized deductions) and not at all for purpose of the AMT. But see § 62(a)(19), which provides relief to the client in many, but not all, situations.

B. INCOME FROM SERVICES: DIVERSION BY OPERATION OF LAW

Lucas v. Earl dealt with private agreements to divert income from the person who earned it to someone else. But what about situations where income is diverted not via some "skillfully devised" arrangement but rather by operation of law?

1. State Community Property Law Applied to Husband and Wife

The following case, decided approximately eight months after Lucas v. Earl, deals with the division of income between a couple whose rights are determined under state community property law. As noted in Justice Roberts's opinion, *Earl* presented "quite a different question" from Poe v. Seaborn. See if you agree.

POE v. SEABORN
282 U.S. 101 (1930)

Mr. Justice ROBERTS delivered the opinion of the Court.

Seaborn and his wife, citizens and residents of the State of Washington, made for the year 1927 separate income tax returns. . . .

During and prior to 1927 they accumulated property comprising real estate, stocks, bonds and other personal property. While the real estate stood in [the husband's] name alone, it is undisputed that all of the property real and personal constituted community property and that neither owned any separate property or had any separate income.

The income comprised Seaborn's salary, interest on bank deposits and on bonds, dividends, and profits on sales of real and personal property. He and his wife each returned one-half the total community income as gross income and each deducted one-half of the community expenses to arrive at the net income returned.

The Commissioner of Internal Revenue determined that all of the income should have been reported in the husband's return. . . .

The case requires us to construe Sections 210(a) and 211(a) of the Revenue Act of 1926,[2] and apply them, as construed, to the interests of husband and wife in community property under the law of Washington. These sections lay a tax upon the net income of every individual. The Act goes no farther, and furnishes no other standard or definition of what constitutes an individual's income. The use of the word "of" denotes ownership. . . .

---

2. [These sections provided that the normal tax and the surtax "shall be levied, collected, and paid for each taxable year upon the net income of every individual." Substantially the same language now appears in § 1(a) of the Code. — EDS.]

The Commissioner concedes that the answer to the question involved in the cause must be found in the provisions of the law of the State, as to a wife's ownership of or interest in community property. What, then, is the law of Washington as to the ownership of community property and of community income including the earnings of the husband's and wife's labor?

The answer is found in the statutes of the State, and the decisions interpreting them.

These statutes provide that, save for property acquired by gift, bequest, devise or inheritance, all property however acquired after marriage, by either husband or wife, or by both, is community property. On the death of either spouse his or her interest is subject to testamentary disposition, and failing that, it passes to the issue of the decedent and not to the surviving spouse. While the husband has the management and control of community personal property and like power of disposition thereof as of his separate personal property, this power is subject to restrictions which are inconsistent with denial of the wife's interest as co-owner. The wife may borrow for community purposes and bind the community property. . . . Since the husband may not discharge his separate obligation out of community property, she may, suing alone, enjoin collection of his separate debt out of community property. . . . She may prevent his making substantial gifts out of community property without her consent. . . . The community property is not liable for the husband's torts not committed in carrying on the business of the community. . . .

Without further extending this opinion it must suffice to say that it is clear the wife has, in Washington, a vested property right in the community property, equal with that of her husband; and in the income of the community, including salaries or wages of either husband or wife, or both. . . .

The taxpayer contends that if the test of taxability under Sections 210 and 211 is ownership, it is clear that income of community property is owned by the community and that husband and wife have each a present vested one-half interest therein.

The Commissioner contends, however, that we are here concerned not with mere names, nor even with mere technical legal titles; that calling the wife's interest vested is nothing to the purpose, because the husband has such broad powers of control and alienation, that while the community lasts, he is essentially the owner of the whole community property, and ought so to be considered for the purposes of Sections 210 and 211. He points out that as to personal property the husband may convey it, make contracts affecting it, may do anything with it short of committing a fraud on his wife's rights. And though the wife must join in any sale of real estate, he asserts that the same is true, by virtue of statutes, in most States which do not have the community system. He asserts that control without accountability is indistinguishable from ownership, and that since the husband has this, quoad community property and income, the income is that "of" the husband under Sections 210, 211 of the income tax law.

We think, in view of the law of Washington above stated, this contention is unsound. The community must act through an agent. . . .

The reasons for conferring such sweeping powers of management on the husband are not far to seek. Public policy demands that in all ordinary circumstances, litigation between wife and husband during the life of the community should be discouraged. Law-suits between them would tend to subvert the marital relation. The same policy dictates that third parties who deal with the husband respecting community property shall be assured that the wife shall not be permitted to nullify his transactions. The powers of partners, or of trustees of a spendthrift trust, furnish apt analogies.

The obligations of the husband as agent of the community are no less real because the policy of the State limits the wife's right to call him to account in a court. Power is not synonymous with right. Nor is obligation coterminous with legal remedy. The law's investiture of the husband with broad powers, by no means negatives the wife's present interest as a co-owner.

We are of opinion that under the law of Washington the entire property and income of the community can no more be said to be that of the husband, than it could rightly be termed that of the wife. . . .

The Commissioner urges that we have, in principal [sic], decided the instant question in favor of the Government. He relies on United States v. Robbins, 269 U.S. 315; Corliss v. Bowers, 281 U.S. 376; and Lucas v. Earl [supra page 623].

In the *Robbins* case, we found that the law of California, as construed by her own courts, gave the wife a mere expectancy and that the property rights of the husband during the life of the community were so complete that he was in fact the owner. . . .

The *Corliss* case raised no issue as to the intent of Congress, but as to its power. We held that where a donor retains the power at any time to revest himself with the principal of the gift, Congress may declare that he still owns the income. While he has technically parted with title, yet he in fact retains ownership, and all its incidents. But here the husband never has ownership. That is in the community at the moment of acquisition.

In the *Earl* case a husband and wife contracted that any property they had or might thereafter acquire in any way, either by earnings (including salaries, fees, etc.), or any rights by contract or otherwise, "shall be treated and considered and hereby is declared to be received held taken and owned by us as joint tenants. . . ." We held that, assuming the validity of the contract under local law, it still remained true that the husband's professional fees, earned in years subsequent to the date of the contract, were his individual income, "derived from salaries, wages, or compensation for personal services." . . . The very assignment in that case was bottomed on the fact that the earnings would be the husband's property, else there would have been nothing on which it could operate. That case presents quite a different question from this, because here, by law, the earnings are never the property of the husband, but that of the community. . . .

The District Court was right in holding that the husband and wife were entitled to file separate returns, each treating one-half of the community income as his or her respective income, and its judgment is affirmed.

NOTES AND QUESTIONS

1. *Reconciliation with Lucas v. Earl.* What do you think of the Court's effort to distinguish Lucas v. Earl?

2. *The congressional response.* After the decision in Poe v. Seaborn, couples in community property states enjoyed a significant tax advantage compared with couples in common-law property states. Spouses in common-law property states could split income by transfers of income-producing property but not by diversions of earnings from the performance of services. In the years following the decision in *Seaborn*, particularly as rates rose before and during World War II, some common-law states reacted by adopting the community property system. Congress could have eliminated most of the disparity among the states by rejecting *Seaborn* and taxing spouses in both community and common-law states on their own salaries, wages, fees, etc. *Seaborn* was based on statutory language, not on the Constitution. But rejecting *Seaborn* would have meant taking away from couples in community property states a benefit to which they had become accustomed, and Congress followed the more politically palatable course of extending the benefit of income splitting to all married couples. It did this, in 1948, by allowing married couples in all states to file joint returns and compute the total tax by first computing a tax on half of the total and then doubling that amount, thereby providing two starts at the bottom of the rate structure, regardless of how income was earned and regardless of legal claims to it. As a result, marriage reduced tax liability for all but the (then very unusual) family in which both spouses earned the same amount of income. This phenomenon is typically called a "marriage bonus" but an equally accurate term is "singles penalty." The 1948 regime remained in force until 1969, when Congress responded to complaints of unfair treatment from unmarried individuals. The story is continued in section C below.

3. *Diversions to comply with the law.* Suppose that a politician is offered a bribe and declines to accept it on the ground that bribes are illegal, but suggests that payment to his wife might be appropriate. If the money is then paid to the wife, who is taxable? Would it matter if, somehow, the payment to the wife were legally permissible and the politician argues, "I could not legally take the money, so it cannot be my income"? In Commissioner v. First Security Bank of Utah, 405 U.S. 394 (1972), the taxpayer bank had been earning sales commissions equal to 40 to 55 percent of the premiums paid by its borrowers on credit life, health, and accident insurance business generated by the bank. After having been advised by counsel that it could not lawfully earn such commissions, the bank set up another corporation, which it owned and which in effect received the fees that had previously been received by the bank. This new arrangement apparently was lawful because the subsidiary was regarded as a separate entity, and it, rather than the parent bank, was viewed as the seller of the policies. The Commissioner sought to tax the profits of the subsidiary to the bank under § 482. (Section 482 is, roughly speaking, a statutory embodiment of the assignment of income doctrine that originated in cases like Lucas v. Earl. See section L of this chapter.) The Court held in favor of the bank, saying, among other things (405 U.S. at 403), "We know of no decision of this Court wherein a person has been found to have taxable income which he did not receive and which he was prohibited from receiving." On the other hand, consider United States v. Scott, 660 F.2d 1145 (7th Cir. 1981), cert. denied, 455 U.S. 907 (1982). In that case the taxpayer, Scott, in 1972 was Attorney General of Illinois and had regulatory and enforcement

powers over various businesses owned by a man named Wirtz. Scott called Wirtz and asked Wirtz to find a job for his friend Cooper, a woman whom Scott later married. Wirtz put Cooper on the payroll of one of his corporations, but it was established that Cooper performed no services for the corporation or for any other of Wirtz's businesses. Wirtz also made some payments directly to Scott. The court held Scott taxable on payments of about $11,000 received by Cooper from Wirtz's corporation. The court was not required to consider whether the payments, if made directly to Scott, would have been bribes, though it is difficult to imagine any more appropriate description.

2. State Community Property Law Applied to Domestic Partners

As noted above, the adoption of the joint return and income splitting in 1948 essentially rendered moot the distinction, established in Lucas v. Earl and Poe v. Seaborn, between married couples living in common-law and community property jurisdictions. In 2003, however, California adopted the Domestic Partner Rights and Responsibilities Act, which extended the state's community property regime to same-sex couples (and certain heterosexual couples), raising the question of whether such individuals should, for federal income tax purposes, separately report the amounts that each taxpayer earns (as indicated by Lucas v. Earl) or combine and split their income (as indicated by Poe v. Seaborn). The issue was presented to the Office of the Chief Counsel of the IRS, which released the following memorandum in 2006.

CHIEF COUNSEL ADVISORY 200608038
2006 WL 469500

. . .

ISSUE

For tax year 2005, is a California individual who is a registered domestic partner, under the California Domestic Partner Rights and Responsibilities Act of 2003, required to include in gross income all of his or her earned income for 2005 or one-half of the combined income earned by the individual and his or her domestic partner?

CONCLUSION

An individual who is a registered domestic partner in California must report all of his or her income earned from the performance of his or her personal services.

FACTS

California is one of nine community property states. With respect to the community property rights of married couples in California, California Family Code section 760 and section 751 provide that all property "acquired by a married person during the marriage while domiciled in California is community property" and that the interests of husband and wife in community property during marriage are "present, existing and equal interests." Consequently, a spouse in California who files his or her tax return as married filing separately must include in gross income one-half of the combined earned income of both spouses.

Since 1999, California has extended certain rights of married couples to domestic partners who register their partnership with the California Secretary of State. A registry of such domestic partnerships has been maintained by the California Secretary of State since 2000.

On September 19, 2003, California enacted the California Domestic Partner Rights and Responsibilities Act of 2003 (the California Act). The California Act became effective on January 1, 2005. Section 297.5(a) of the California Act provides as follows:

Registered domestic partners shall have the same rights, protections, and benefits, and shall be subject to the same responsibilities, obligations, and duties under law, whether they derive from statutes, administrative regulations, court rules, government policies, common law, or any other provisions or sources of law, as are granted to and imposed upon spouses.

As proposed, the California Act allowed registered domestic partners to file joint income tax returns for California state tax purposes and to be taxed in the same manner as married couples for state income tax purposes. The enacted version of the California Act, however, deleted the joint return provision and required registered domestic partners to file separate returns. The pertinent provision of the legislation that has significant state tax implications (section 297.5(g)) is as follows:

Notwithstanding this section, in filing their state income tax returns, domestic partners shall use the same filing status as is used on their federal income tax returns, or that would have been used had they filed federal income tax returns. Earned income may not be treated as community property for state income tax purposes.

On June 30, 2005, California enacted Assembly Bill 2580, which also became effective on January 1, 2005. Assembly Bill 2580 reenacted California Family Code section 297.5 with a series of technical amendments and clarifications. Assembly Bill 2580 added California Family Code section 297.5(m)(1), which states, in pertinent part, that with respect to laws, regulations and policies concerning community property, "the date of marriage will be deemed to refer to the date of registration of a domestic partnership with the state." Further, section 297.5(m)(2) gave domestic partners who registered before January 1, 2005, until June 30, 2005, to enter into agreements identical to premarital agreements between prospective spouses to modify or avoid the application of California's community property laws.

LAW AND ANALYSIS

Section 61(a)(1) provides that gross income means all income from whatever source derived including compensation for services such as fees, commissions, fringe benefits, and similar items.

In general, a taxpayer's gross income includes income earned by that taxpayer. As first enunciated in Lucas v. Earl, 281 U.S. 111 (1930), a taxpayer may not shift the tax burden of his or her earned income to another by contractually assigning all or a portion of it to someone else. In Lucas v. Earl, the Supreme Court held that all of a husband's earnings are to be taxed to husband even though husband and wife had previously entered into an agreement under which all earnings of husband and wife "shall be treated and considered and hereby is declared to be received, held, taken, and owned by us as joint tenants, and not otherwise, with the right of survivorship."

Poe v. Seaborn, 282 U.S. 101 (1930), addressed the issue of whether income earned by a husband is rightfully taxed to his wife in a community property state. In Poe v. Seaborn, the Supreme Court concluded that "the wife has, in Washington, a vested property right in the community property, equal with that of her husband; and in the income of the community, including salaries or wages of either husband or wife, or both." Accordingly, the Court held that husband and wife were entitled to file separate returns, each treating one-half of the community income as his or her respective income. See United States v. Malcolm, 282 U.S. 792 (1931), which applied the rule of Poe v. Seaborn to California's community property law.

The case law relating to income-splitting in community property states has always arisen solely in the context of spouses. . . .

In Commissioner v. Harmon, 323 U.S. 44 (1944), the Supreme Court distinguished its decision in Poe v. Seaborn. In Commissioner v. Harmon, a case addressing the tax consequences of an Oklahoma statute allowing married couples to elect community property status, the Court said:

> In Poe v. Seaborn, supra, the court was not dealing with a consensual community but one made an incident of marriage by the inveterate policy of the State. In that case the court was faced with these facts: The legal community system of the States in question long antedated the Sixteenth Amendment and the first Revenue Act adopted thereunder. Under that system, as a result of State policy, and without any act on the part of either spouse, one half of the community income vested in each spouse as the income accrued and was, in law, to that extent, the income of the spouse. The Treasury had consistently ruled that the Revenue Act applied to the property systems of those States as it found them and consequently husband and wife were entitled each to return one half the community income. The Congress was fully conversant of these rulings and the practice thereunder, was asked to alter the provisions of later revenue acts to change the incidence of the tax, and refused to do so. In these circumstances, the court declined to apply the doctrine of Lucas v. Earl. *Harmon*, 323 U.S. at 46-47.

The Court also said: "The important fact is that the community system of Oklahoma is not a system, dictated by State policy, as an incident of matrimony." *Harmon*, 323 U.S. at 48.

The Supreme Court's decision in Poe v. Seaborn dealt with Washington's community property law, which applied to a husband and wife. We do not believe that the Poe v. Seaborn decision applies to the application of a state's community property law outside the context of a husband and wife. In our view, the rights afforded domestic partners under the California Act are not "made an incident of marriage by the inveterate policy of the State." The relationship between registered domestic partners under the California Act is not marriage under California law. Therefore, the Supreme Court's decision in Poe v. Seaborn does not extend to registered domestic partners.

Consequently, an individual who is a registered domestic partner in California must report all of his or her income earned from the performance of his or her personal services, notwithstanding the enactment of the California Act.

This document may not be used or cited as precedent. § 6110(j)(3).

QUESTIONS

1. In Lucas v. Earl (supra page 623), Poe v. Seaborn (supra page 626), and United States v. Robbins (referred to in Poe v. Seaborn at page 628) the taxpayers were all married couples seeking to split earned income. Why was it that only the Poe v. Seaborn taxpayers prevailed? What does this imply as to the tax treatment of domestic partners?

2. Is the Chief Counsel misreading Poe v. Seaborn as primarily a case about marriage, rather than as primarily a case about the effect of state law on property interests that determine federal income tax consequences?

3. Suppose that two law partners agree, at arm's length, to split the net income from their practice fifty-fifty; that one of them, at the beginning of a taxable year, becomes ill and performs no services in that year; and that the net income is split fifty-fifty even though all of it was earned by one partner. (a) How should the income be reported by the two partners? (b) How is this different from the position of domestic partners?

4. The California law was changed in 2006 to provide that, for state tax purposes, domestic partners must file jointly or file separately with each reporting half of the total earned income. Is that change likely to change the conclusion reached by the Chief Counsel?

C. THE MARRIAGE PENALTY (AND BONUS)

1. The Legislative "Solution" — Partial Income Splitting

Recall that in 1948 Congress amended the tax law to allow married couples to split their incomes by filing a joint return, regardless of how the income was earned and regardless of whether the couple lived in a community property state or a common-law jurisdiction. The result was a system of universal marriage bonuses since all married couples would effectively get two "starts from the bottom" of the progressive rate structure. For example, if Don earned a $100,000 salary while Betty stayed home to care for their children, the couple would be taxed as though each earned $50,000. Meanwhile, Dick, who earns the same $100,000 salary but is not married, would get only one start from the bottom of the rate structure. Predictably, single individuals complained that they were paying more than their fair share of the tax burden.

In 1969, Congress responded to the complaints of singles by adjusting the rate structure to reduce, but not completely eliminate, the singles penalty. The net effect of this change was approximately the same as having the single individual rate structure apply to every taxpayer, and to allow some but not complete income shifting within marriage. From 1969 onward, the tax consequences of marriage would depend upon the composition of the couple's total income between the two spouses. Couples with only one wage earner were still better off with marriage, since the effect of the new schedules was to assume that some (though less than half) of the income was earned by the non-wage earner, and thus (with respect to that income), give the couple two starts at the bottom of the rate structure. The change produced the worst outcome for couples where the income was earned evenly by the two spouses, since the two starts from the bottom they enjoyed while single would no longer be available to them when married. Thus, while there remained a "marriage bonus" for some couples, it was reduced, and there was now a "marriage penalty" for many couples with two wage earners.

Present law contains both marriage bonuses and marriage penalties. In 2009, a single individual with taxable income of $200,000 would pay a tax of $51,143. The tax liability for that same amount of taxable income earned by a married couple filing jointly would be $44,264. In other words, if an individual earning $200,000 were to marry someone with no taxable income, there would be a "marriage bonus" of $6,879. Marriage bonuses for couples with one wage earner occur at almost any level of income. For example, if an individual with an income of $500,000 marries an individual with no taxable income, the marriage bonus would be $7,322 based on 2009 tax rates. By contrast, there is sometimes a marriage *penalty* for families with two wage earners with substantial incomes. The penalty has been eliminated for the 10 and 15 percent brackets. Thus, if two individuals who each have taxable income of $50,000 married, tax liability would remain the same. There is no marriage penalty. However, if two individuals who each have taxable incomes of $100,000 get married, their combined tax liability increases by $824 (from $43,440 to $44,264), again based on 2009 tax rates. The amount of the marriage penalty rises as the incomes of two-earner couples increase. For example, where each individual makes $400,000, marriage increases tax liability by $14,995 (from $235,367 to $250,362).

Marriage penalties and bonuses are also built into the earned income tax credit, or EITC. Recall that the amount of EITC to which a taxpayer is entitled is a function of earned income and the number of qualifying children in the household. Marriage can increase either of these figures. The most extreme instances of marriage penalties in the EITC are those where two working single parents decide to get married. For example, if Adam and Melissa each have two children and $30,000 in total earnings, split evenly between them, they would incur a marriage penalty of more than $7,000 in 2009. In this situation, each individual is receiving the maximum credit ($5,028 for 2009) when single and earning $15,000, but their combined income of $30,000 when married pushes them well into the credit's phaseout range. By contrast, an individual with no children and $15,000 in total earnings would receive a bonus exceeding $4,500 upon marrying a nonworking individual with two children. This is a situation where the credit increases because of the coupling of the earned income and the two children into the same taxable unit.

2. Addressing the Marriage Penalty/Bonus

It is sometimes noted that it is mathematically impossible for a tax system to satisfy all three of the following principles: (1) marriage neutrality (i.e., no penalties or bonuses), (2) couple equality (i.e., couples with the same aggregate income bear the same tax burden), and (3) progressivity. As noted above, current law sacrifices marriage neutrality to ensure both couple equality and progressivity. If all income were taxed at a single rate, say 20 percent, then it would be possible to have both marriage neutrality and couple equality, but at the expense of progressivity. Alternatively, a system of individual filing and rising marginal tax rates would ensure marriage neutrality and progressivity, but at the expense of couple equality.

There is one way that a tax system can satisfy all three principles described above. For example, imagine a system of individual filing in which everyone is subject to a flat rate of 20 percent but also entitled to a refundable tax credit of $5,000. Now consider how this regime would apply to Couple A, which consists of one taxpayer with $100,000 of income and another taxpayer with zero income. The taxpayer with $100,000 of income would owe $15,000 in tax for an average tax rate of 15 percent. The taxpayer with no income would owe no tax but would receive a $5,000 check from the government. Unmarried, Couple A would face a total tax liability of $10,000. Married, they would pay the same amount. Thus, the principle of marriage neutrality is satisfied. Now consider Couple B, where each spouse earns $50,000. Like Couple A, this couple would pay a total of $10,000 in federal income taxes ($5,000 each), with the result that the principle of couple equality is also satisfied.

As for progressivity, note that our hypothetical tax regime features rising *average* tax rates. That is, as an individual's income rises, so does the percentage of income that she must pay in taxes. The taxpayer with $50,000 in income has an average tax rate of 10 percent, the taxpayer with $100,000 in income has an average tax rate of 15 percent, the taxpayer with $200,000 in income has an average tax rate of 17.5 percent, and so on. What this system lacks, of course, is rising *marginal* tax rates. In fact, every taxpayer faces the same marginal tax rate of 20 percent. This is where the mathematical impossibility comes in—it is indeed mathematically impossible to have a tax system that features marriage neutrality, couple equality, and *marginal* tax rate progressivity.

In recent years, more attention has been given to reducing the effect of the marriage penalty than in attempting to satisfy all three of the principles described above. It bears noting that the marriage penalty could be completely eliminated by going back to the system that allows all married couples to split their income, or adopting a rate structure that had that same effect. This is in fact what Congress has done with respect to the 10 percent and 15 percent tax brackets. As a result of legislation enacted in 2001, the breakpoints for these two brackets with regard to the married filing jointly rates are now exactly twice the amounts in the rate structure for single individuals. The result of this change has been an increase in marriage bonuses for many couples.

COMPARATIVE FOCUS: Individual Filing in Japan

In the United States, married couples must either file a joint return or use the filing status "married individuals filing separate returns." By contrast, most countries with an income tax rely on individual filing. One example is Japan.

Prior to World War II, the family was the basic tax unit for purposes of income tax filing in Japan. After the war, however, Japan adopted a system of individual filing based on the recommendation of the Shoup mission. The Shoup mission was named for Carl Sumner Shoup, an American lawyer and economist who oversaw a fundamental reform of Japan's tax system during the years of the U.S. occupation.

One of the chief advantages of individual filing is the absence of any marriage penalties or bonuses. Because each individual is taxed on his or her own earnings, married or not, there is no increase or decrease in tax liability as a result of marriage. Moreover, a system of individual filing avoids the problem of high marginal tax rates on secondary earners that accompanies a system of joint filing with progressive marginal tax rates.

On the other hand, individual filing can result in wide disparities in tax liability for married couples with the same combined income. In Japan, for example, married couples with only one wage-earner generally pay higher income taxes than couples with the same total income evenly divided between the spouses. In addition, individual filing requires a system of rules for determining who should claim deductions for joint expenses and who should be taxed on income that might plausibly be allocated to either spouse. Without such rules, taxpayers may seek to shift income to minimize overall taxes. For example, to the extent that family members face different marginal tax rates, an incentive exists for the lower-bracket taxpayer to report investment income. One approach to forestall this type of tax avoidance, employed in Japan until 1988, is to assign investment income to the spouse with the higher income. Another option is to tax investment income at a single flat rate.

---

3. Married Filing Separate and Head of Household

There is a separate rate structure for married persons filing separate returns. However, it generally offers no tax savings and therefore does not enable those couples subject to the marriage penalty to avoid the additional tax burden created by being married. Individuals who use the "married filing separate" status may be separated but not yet divorced. In addition, a spouse may wish to use the married filing separate status in order to avoid the joint and several liability that one is normally subject to when filing a joint return with one's spouse. Finally, there may be some rare instances (e.g., where one spouse incurs large medical expenses) where using this filing status may allow a couple to reduce its overall tax liability.

There is also a separate rate schedule for "heads of households." This schedule may be used by taxpayers who are not married but whose household includes certain dependents, such as children or parents. This schedule has brackets that are more favorable than those for single people but less favorable than those for married couples filing jointly. In other words, heads of household receive some but not all of the advantage of the married persons' joint return schedule. The reasons for this favorable treatment are perhaps easiest to understand in the case of a surviving spouse with continuing obligations to care for young children.

D. MORE ON DIVERTING SERVICE INCOME BY PRIVATE AGREEMENT

ARMANTROUT v. COMMISSIONER
67 T.C. 996 (1977), aff'd per curiam, 570 F.2d 210 (7th Cir. 1978)

. . . Hamlin, Inc., a Delaware corporation (Hamlin), is engaged in the business of manufacturing, distributing, and selling electronic components. During the taxable years 1971 through 1973, petitioner Richard T. Armantrout was employed by Hamlin as vice president in charge of marketing. . . .

Educo, Inc. (Educo), a Delaware corporation, is engaged in the business of designing, implementing, and administering college education benefit plans for corporate employers.

Sometime in 1969, petitioner Llewellyn G. Owens noticed an advertisement in the Wall Street Journal which outlined, in a general way, the potential benefits of the Educo plan. Upon subsequent investigation, Mr. Owens suggested that such a plan be implemented by Hamlin, Inc.

On September 2, 1969, Hamlin entered into an agreement with Funds for Education, Inc., a Delaware corporation. Subsequently, on November 17, 1969, Funds for Education changed its corporate name to Educo, Inc.

Pursuant to the agreement, Educo undertook to administer an Educo education plan to provide funds for college expenses for the children of certain key employees of Hamlin. Hamlin, upon becoming a participant of the Educo plan, agreed to make contributions to the Continental Illinois National Bank & Trust Co. of Chicago which acted as trustee under a trust agreement entered into with Educo on December 9, 1969.

Pursuant to the Educo plan, children of Hamlin's key employees named in the enrollment schedules which formed a part of the plan would be entitled to receive sums from the trustee to defray college education expenses. Upon receipt of the appropriate information from Hamlin, Educo would direct the trustee to pay, in accordance with the enrollment schedule, the expenses incurred by the employees' children in attending a college or university, trade or vocational school. . . .

The Educo plan as implemented by Hamlin provided for a maximum of $10,000 to be made available to the children of any one employee with an upper limit of $4,000 available to any one child. Payments to or on behalf of a child enrolled in the plan were limited during any one year to one-fourth of the total amount scheduled for that child; however, the unused funds of a prior year could be used to defray expenses in a subsequent academic year. Children otherwise qualified who did not utilize any of the available funds before reaching age 21 or within 2 years after completing the 12th grade would be ineligible to participate in the plan.

In adopting the Educo plan, it was Hamlin's intention to make available sufficient funds to enable at least two children of each key employee to attend college. Consonant therewith, the plan was in general administered so that $4,000 was scheduled to be received by each of the employee's two eldest children while $2,000 would be provided to a third younger child; funds not utilized by the older children were in turn made available to younger children, thus it was possible that more than three children of each key employee could ultimately participate in the plan. However, this administrative policy was not required by the terms of the plan and, moreover, prior to the adoption of the first enrollment schedule the employee-parents were given the opportunity to allocate the available funds within the maximum allowed by the plan to their children in amounts different from those described above. . . .

If any child covered by the Educo plan did not utilize the funds scheduled for his benefit within the period prescribed by the plan, Hamlin could enroll a replacement child of the same or younger age to use any unused funds. Moreover, Hamlin could allocate the unused funds to children already enrolled in the plan or it could apply the funds toward the reduction of its future obligation to make payments to the Educo trust. . . .

The Hamlin Educo plan was adopted, in part, to relieve Hamlin's most important employees from concern and trepidation about the cost of providing a college education for their children and, thus, enable those employees to better perform their duties as employees of Hamlin. Moreover, it was felt by Hamlin that the Educo plan was a benefit which the key employees wanted it to provide. The cost of higher education would be defrayed by the Educo trust for all the children enrolled in the plan without regard to any objective scholastic criteria such as admissions test scores, rank in high school class, or financial need.

Children eligible to participate in the Educo plan were those whose parents were regarded as key employees in the Hamlin organization and although the selection of such employees bore a rough correlation to salary, the determinative factor was the employees' value to the company. Compensation of key employees who did not have children was not increased to counterpoise the effect of the Educo plan on those employees with children. Children of lesser employees could be included as the value of the parents to Hamlin increased.

The employees whose children participated in the Educo plan had no right or claim to the benefits which flowed from the trustees in discharge of their children's educational expenses as outlined in the plan. It was, moreover, impossible for the parent of any child enrolled in the plan to receive benefit from any unused portion of the available funds not expended by their children.

Under the terms of the plan, benefits were payable in accordance with the applicable enrollment schedule to defray the costs incurred by the employee's child in attending college. However, should an employee-parent cease to be employed by Hamlin, the plan would become inoperable for each of his children except that education expenses incurred prior to the termination of the parent's employment would continue to be eligible for payment in accordance with the terms of the Educo plan.

Considering the Educo plan to be a unique benefit made available to its most important employees, Hamlin would describe in a general way the nature and advantages offered by the plan to prospective employees. The existence of the plan has enabled Hamlin to be successful in recruiting and retaining key employees and to do so without the assistance of higher salaries competitive with those in larger urban areas.

By statutory notices of deficiency issued to the respective taxpayers in the cases consolidated herein, the Commissioner determined that the amounts distributed by the Educo trust were scholarships which formed a part of the employees' compensation and were directly related to each employee's pattern of employment and, therefore, compensation for services includable in gross income.

OPINION

Respondent contends that the amounts distributed by the Educo trust in discharge of certain of the educational expenses of petitioners' children constitute taxable income to petitioners because the payments were attributable to petitioners' employment relationship with Hamlin rather than on the basis of any competitive criteria such as need, motivation, or merit.

Petitioners in essence argue, however, that while the amounts distributed by the Educo trust were perhaps "generated" by their efforts as employees of Hamlin, they do not constitute gross income because they were neither beneficially received by them nor did they have the right to receive such distributions and, moreover, because they did not possess an ownership interest in such amounts. In addition, petitioners assert that the mere realization of some familial satisfaction is not sufficient to occasion the recognition of income. For reasons which will hereinafter be expressed, we hold that the distributions from Educo trust to petitioners' children were in the nature of deferred compensation to petitioners and, therefore, includable in their gross income according to the provisions of section 83.

Proper analysis of this issue must begin with the notion often called "the first principle of income taxation: that income must be taxed to him who earns it." Commissioner v. Culbertson, 337 U.S. 733, 739-740 (1949). It is also important to recall that the income tax consequences of a particular transaction are not to be accorded by reference to "anticipatory arrangements" or "attenuated subtleties" but rather income must be attributed to the tree upon which it grew. Lucas v. Earl [supra page 623]. In addition, in apportioning the income tax consequence of a particular factual pattern, it is the substance of the transaction which must govern. Gregory v. Helvering [infra page 781]. . . .

While we might agree with petitioners that mere realization of some "familial" satisfaction is perhaps not sufficient to occasion a tax, we must nevertheless take cognizance of the context in which such a benefit accrues. When such a benefit is created in an employment situation and in connection with the performance of services, we are unable to conclude that such a benefit falls outside the broad scope of section 61. . . . This view is especially compelling herein because there is a specific, additional, and identifiable cost incurred by petitioners' employer.

We find Kohnstamn v. Pedrick, 153 F.2d 506 (2d Cir. 1945), to be inapposite to the issue presented. In *Kohnstamn*, the Commissioner sought to charge the husband with income earned on investments made by his wife from income which was paid to her by a trust to support and maintain their children. The Government's theory was that because the mother consulted him in the management of the income, he "generated" it and was, therefore, taxable on that income. The court held that the amounts earned on the trust earnings were not taxable to the husband because the realization of some familial satisfaction, without more, was not sufficient to occasion a tax burden. In our view, the *Kohnstamn* rationale does not extend to amounts paid to family members which are clearly attributable and related to the performance of services by another family member. . . .

In any event, we do not understand respondent's position to be that the mere "generation" of income is sufficient to occasion a tax. Instead, respondent argues that the amounts paid by the Educo trust were "generated" by petitioners in connection with their performance of services for Hamlin and were, therefore, compensatory in nature. We find this view to be amply supported by the record. . . .

Employees eligible to participate were selected on the basis of their value to the company; selection was thus inexorably linked to the quality of the employee's performance of services. Moreover, the eventual payment of benefits by the Educo trust was directly related to petitioners' employment. This is illustrated quite graphically by the fact that only those expenses incurred by petitioners' children while the parent was employed by Hamlin were covered by the plan.

In recruiting new employees, Hamlin would describe the benefits accorded by the plan and how an employee could become entitled to participate upon attaining a level at which he was sufficiently valuable to the company. The plan was successful in aiding the recruitment and retention of key employees. Moreover, the utilization of the Educo plan at the corporate level was clearly a substitute for salary because it enabled Hamlin to compete with employers in more populated areas which paid higher salaries.

It is fundamental that anticipatory arrangements designed to deflect income away from the proper taxpayer will not be given effect to avoid tax liability. United States v. Basye, 410 U.S. 441 (1973) [infra page 685]; Lucas v. Earl [supra page 623]. In substance, by commencing or continuing to be employed by Hamlin, petitioners have allowed a portion of their earnings to be paid to their children. Petitioners have acquiesced in an arrangement designed, at least in part, to shift the incidence of tax liability to third parties unconnected in any meaningful way with their performance of services.

Petitioners arduously suggest, however, that the doctrine of Lucas v. Earl, supra, can have no application herein because they neither received nor possessed a right to receive the amounts distributed to their children by the Educo trust. In support of this contention, petitioners rely on Commissioner v. First Security Bank of Utah, 405 U.S. 394 (1972), and Paul A. Teschner, 38 T.C. 1003 (1962).

In *First Security Bank of Utah*, a holding company organized a subsidiary corporation to engage in the insurance business (Life); another subsidiary corporation was a national bank (Bank). Bank originated credit life insurance which was placed with an independent insurance company; however, pursuant to a treaty of reinsurance, the independent company reinsured the business with Life. The Commissioner sought to allocate a portion of Life's premium income to Bank as compensation for originating and processing the credit life insurance. Court decisions construing 12 U.S.C. section 92, however, prohibited a national bank from acting as an insurance agent, thus distinguishing cases in which the taxpayer had actually received funds in violation of the law, see, e.g., James v. United States, 366 U.S. 213 (1961). The Court held that the assignment-of-income doctrine and section 482 could have no application where a taxpayer has no right as a matter of law to receive the income in question.

The rationale was that a taxpayer who did not actually receive any income did not possess sufficient dominion and control to occasion a tax where he was prevented by law from actual receipt of the income. The factual pattern in *Teschner* is analogous and much the same kind of analysis was applied. The taxpayer entered a contest by submitting two statements on a form supplied by the sponsor of the contest. The contest rules provided that only persons under age 17 were eligible to receive any prize; contestants over that age were required to designate a person under age 17 to receive the prize. The taxpayer, an adult, designated his daughter as recipient should either of his entries be selected. The taxpayer's inability to win a prize for himself was due to the contest rules and was in no way attributable to any action taken by him. One of the taxpayer's entries was selected and a prize was awarded to his daughter. The Commissioner contended that the prize was includable in the taxpayer's gross income under the principles of Lucas v. Earl, supra. This Court held that the taxpayer's mere power to direct the distribution of the prize was not sufficient to tax its value as income to him because he did not possess a right to receive the prize under the contest rules; thus, it was not includable in his gross income.

While the facts in these cases are analogous to those presented herein, there are crucial distinctions which mandate a different result.

Hamlin and petitioners were acting at arm's length in an employment situation. By accepting employment or continuing to be employed by Hamlin, cognizant of the trust payments, petitioners in effect consented to having a portion of their earnings paid to third parties. There is no evidence to indicate that petitioners were unable to bargain with Hamlin about the terms of their employment and the available avenues of compensation. Hamlin could have made available a direct salary benefit to those employees who so desired, and by supplemental enrollment schedule continued to make available the Educo plan to others. We also think significant petitioners' power, whether exercised or not, to designate which of their children would be enrolled in the Educo plan. Under the facts of this case, such power lends substantial compensatory flavor to the Educo arrangement. Petitioners were in a position to influence the manner in which their compensation would be paid; choosing to acquiesce in the payments to the Educo plan was in our view tantamount to an "anticipatory arrangement" prohibited by Lucas v. Earl, supra. By contrast, in neither *First Security Bank of Utah*, supra, nor in Paul A. Teschner, supra, did such a potential for "arm's-length" negotiation exist. Moreover, the prohibition on petitioners' receipt of the payments in this case was not imposed by a rule of law as in *First Security Bank of Utah*, or as the result of a rule imposed by an independent third party as in *Teschner*. Petitioners herein were not prohibited from receiving income within the meaning of *First Security Bank of Utah* or *Teschner*.

To find the rationale of these cases controlling here would be to ignore the consensual nature of the method of compensation adopted by Hamlin and the economic realities existing in an employer-employee situation. It is clear that a taxpayer may not avoid taxation by entering into an anticipatory assignment of income; to allow petitioners to enter into such an arrangement through the back door simply by allowing the employer to make the necessary arrangements would be highly anomalous and inconsistent with the rationale of Lucas v. Earl, supra, and United States v. Basye [supra]. We can only conclude that this arrangement provided petitioners with additional and deferred compensation as determined by the Commissioner and should have been so reported; the plan was, in effect, a clever and skillfully designed arrangement which cannot be given effect for tax purposes. . . .

Although the legislative history is somewhat vague and the parties have chosen not to argue this case based upon interpretation of section 83, we must point out that our decision is supported by the specific language of section 83 which provides:

> (a) GENERAL RULE. If in connection with the performance of services, property is transferred to *any person* other than the person for whom such services are performed the excess of— . . . shall be *included in the gross income of the person who* performed such services. . . . [Emphasis added.]

Accordingly, we hold that the amounts paid by the Educo trust constituted additional compensation to petitioners and, therefore, are includable in gross income.

Decisions will be entered for the respondent.

NOTES AND QUESTIONS

1. *The theory.* Which is the better theory in support of the decision, assignment of income (Lucas v. Earl) or noncash benefit (§ 83, described supra page 287)?

2. *Time for inclusion.* Under each of the two possible theories, what is the proper time for taxation—when funds are paid to the trustee by Hamlin or when funds are paid by the trustee to a child? How does the choice of time for taxation affect the amount to be taxed? When is Hamlin (the employer) entitled to a deduction? See §§ 404(a)(5), 83(h), 419. In Grant-Jacoby, Inc. v. Commissioner, 73 T.C. 700 (1980), on facts like those in *Armantrout*, the court held that the employer could take a deduction for amounts contributed to its educational trust only when distributions from the trust were includable in the employee's income. The court reasoned that the distributions are deferred compensation, which are normally deductible only when actually paid over to the employee under § 404(a)(5). In Greensboro Pathology Associates, P.A. v. United States, 698 F.2d 1196 (Fed. Cir. 1982), however, the court held that amounts paid by an employer into a trust under a plan for college scholarships for the children of employees were deductible under § 162 and Regs. § 1.162-10 (which governs employee welfare plans) when paid irrevocably into the trust, rather than later, when benefits became taxable to the employee, as required by § 404(a)(5) (which governs deferred compensation). In drawing the line, the court said that not all fringe benefits are deferred compensation and emphasized that under the plan of this employer benefits were available to the children of all employees and were not linked to employee salaries. The case arose before the adoption of § 419.

3. *Reconciliation with earlier decisions.* Possibly the result in *First Security Bank of Utah* (discussed by the court in *Armantrout* and in Note 3, supra page 629) can be defended on the authority (such as it is) of Poe v. Seaborn (supra page 626). But what about *Teschner*, also discussed in *Armantrout*?[3] Do you agree that it is more like *Seaborn* and *First Security Bank of Utah* than it is like *Earl* and *Armantrout*?

4. *Implications.* Suppose that the plan adopted by Hamlin were modified to make benefits available to the children of all executives with salaries above a given level after they had been employed for five years and with the benefits not contingent on continued employment by Hamlin after the transfer of the relevant amounts into the trust. Would the result be different? Would Hamlin still be likely to find the plan attractive?

5. *Equal protection.* In Wheeler v. Commissioner, 768 F.2d 1333 (Fed. Cir. 1985), the taxpayer was taxed on funds provided for his children's college expenses under a plan virtually identical to that in *Armantrout*. The court rejected the taxpayer's argument that, in light of the favorable treatment of employees of educational institutions under Regs. § 1.117-3(a), now embodied in Code § 117(d), this outcome led to a denial of his constitutional right of equal protection.

---

3. The lawyer for the taxpayer in *Armantrout* was Paul A. Teschner, who was the taxpayer, and represented himself, in *Teschner*.

6. *Funds received as agent for another.* Suppose a person manages an apartment building, collects rents in cash, and turns over the sums collected, less a 10 percent commission, to the owner of the building. The amounts turned over to the owner are not included in the income of the manager. The legal rationale generally is that the manager receives those amounts as agent for the owner. Similarly, suppose an associate for a law firm performs services for a client of the firm, the client pays cash to the lawyer, and the lawyer turns the money over to the firm, as she is required to do by her implied contract with the firm. Again, the lawyer is not taxable on the payment received as agent for the firm. In Schuster v. Commissioner, 84 T.C. 764 (1985), aff'd, 800 F.2d 672 (7th Cir. 1986), the taxpayer was a member of a religious order of the Roman Catholic Church. Part of her agreement with and commitment to the order was a vow of poverty, which required, among other things, that she turn over to the order any amounts she received for performing services. She was a nurse-practitioner (midwife) and took a job with a clinic funded by the federal government. Before taking the job, she was required to receive approval from the order. She was paid for her services by checks from the clinic and endorsed the checks over to the order. The Tax Court, sitting en banc and dividing ten to seven, held that she was taxable on the amounts received from the clinic. The majority relied on the fact that the obligation to provide services to the clinic was that of the taxpayer, not of the order; that in providing the services the taxpayer did not act as agent for the order; and that the checks satisfied a legal obligation to the taxpayer, not to the order. The majority noted that if the taxpayer had worked in a clinic operated by the order, amounts received from patients in payment for her services would not have been taxable to her, since in that situation the legal obligation of the payor would be to the order. The dissenting opinion, relying in part on Poe v. Seaborn, argued that the taxpayer, consistent with her vow of poverty, in fact acted as agent for the order when she contracted with the clinic and when she received payment from it. In other words, the dissent focused on the relationship between the taxpayer and the order, not on the triangular relationship of the taxpayer, the order, and the clinic. The dissent concluded by accusing the majority of a "blind and indiscriminating application of Lucas v. Earl" (supra page 623). 84 T.C. at 789.[4]

The Seventh Circuit majority accepted the Tax Court majority's result in *Schuster* but rejected as too narrow its "agency triangle" theory, which stresses the relationship (or lack of it) between the payor and the alleged principal of the payee. The appellate court looked to a number of facts indicating that the taxpayer had earned her wages in an individual capacity rather than as an agent, including the facts that she was free to withdraw from the order at any time, that she was not under its day-to-day control, and that she endorsed the

---

4. The taxpayer was entitled to a charitable deduction for the amounts paid to the order, but the deduction is subject to the 50 percent (of AGI) limit in § 170(b)(1)(A). At one time, under a rule popularly known as the "Philadelphia nun" provision, an unlimited deduction was allowed to people who contributed substantially all of their income to charities for an extended period of time. This special rule was repealed, however, after it came to be used, often in combination with other deductions and exclusions, by many wealthy people, not members of religious orders, to reduce their tax liability to zero.

paychecks over to the order. The dissenting judge focused on the order's right to control and direct the taxpayer's activities, on her vow of poverty, and on the fact that her activities were of a type within the mission or purpose of the order.

Both the majority and dissent in the Seventh Circuit drew on the approach of the Federal Circuit in Fogarty v. United States, 780 F.2d 1005 (1986). In that case the taxpayer was a Jesuit priest who became an associate professor at the University of Virginia, where he taught courses in religious thought, development, and history. Like the taxpayer in *Schuster*, he had taken a vow of poverty. Checks for his salary were made payable to him but at his direction were deposited to an account of his order. The court said that the "facts present a very close case" and held that the taxpayer was taxable on amounts paid to the order. Like the Seventh Circuit, the court rejected the "triangle" theory, instead holding that the "question whether a member of a religious order earns income in an individual capacity, or as an agent of the order, is a question of law based on general rules of agency to be established by considering all the underlying facts." Among the facts the court deemed relevant were the degree of control exercised by the order, the purposes or mission of the order and the type of work performed by the member, the dealings between the member and the payor (including "circumstances surrounding job inquiries and interviews, and control or supervision exercised by the employer"), and dealings between the employer and the order.

Recall the statement by Justice Holmes in Lucas v. Earl that the issue of who is to be taxed "is not to be decided by attenuated subtleties." How do you suppose he would have decided *Schuster* and *Fogarty*? How would you decide them? Suppose you are asked by the head of a religious order whether the order should give up on the tax issue or try to change the way in which the orders proceeded in cases like *Schuster* and *Fogarty* and try again. What advice would you give?

E. TRANSFERS OF PROPERTY AND INCOME FROM PROPERTY

Generally, income from property — such as interest, dividends, or rent — is treated for tax purposes as having been received by the owner of the property and thus is taxed to that person, at that person's rate. One notable exception to that rule is the so-called kiddie tax, which provides that the unearned income of a child under age 18 is taxed at his or her parents' marginal rate. § 1(g). Putting that aside, in applying the principle that income from property is taxed to the owner of that property we are confronted with the question of what is meant by "property." As the materials that follow demonstrate, courts have sometimes answered this question in legalistic and even metaphysical ways.

The next two cases can be viewed from a formalistic perspective as efforts to distinguish between gifts of property and gifts of income from property. From a more realistic perspective the two cases can be seen as efforts to draw a line between diversions of income from property that are respected for tax purposes and those that are not, which should depend, in large part at least, on the economic characteristics of what was given away and what was retained. In the first case (*Blair*), the taxpayer had a limited interest (a life estate), but gave away a portion for its entire duration (i.e., part of the income for his life). In the second (*Horst*), the taxpayer owned the entire property (a bond), and gave away a limited interest (the interest income for a brief period of time); he gave away what has come to be called a "carved out" income interest.[5] The challenge in reading the cases is to figure out why the first taxpayer won and the second lost.

BLAIR v. COMMISSIONER
300 U.S. 5 (1937)

Mr. Chief Justice HUGHES delivered the opinion of the Court.

This case presents the question of the liability of a beneficiary of a testamentary trust for a tax upon the income which he had assigned to his children. . . .

The trust was created by the will of [the petitioner's (taxpayer's) father and called for payment of all income to petitioner during his life]. In 1923, . . . petitioner assigned to his daughter . . . an interest amounting to $6,000 for the remainder of that calendar year, and to $9,000 in each calendar year thereafter, in the net income. . . . At about the same time, he made like assignments of interest, amounting to $9,000 in each calendar year, in the net income of the trust to [two other children]. . . . In later years, by similar instruments, he assigned to these children additional interests. . . . The trustees accepted the assignments and distributed the income directly to the assignees. . . .

[After holding that a judgment in an earlier proceeding involving the same trust was not conclusive in this proceeding as res judicata and that the assignments were valid under local law, the Supreme Court turned to the third issue in the case.]

Third. The question remains whether, treating the assignments as valid, the assignor was still taxable upon the income under the federal income tax act. That is a federal question.

Our decisions in Lucas v. Earl [supra page 623] and Burnet v. Leininger, 285 U.S. 136, are cited. In the *Lucas* [sic] case . . . [w]e were of the opinion that the case turned upon the construction of the taxing act. We said that "the statute could tax salaries to those who earned them and provide that the tax could not be escaped by anticipatory arrangements and contracts however skillfully devised to prevent the same when paid from vesting even for a

---

5. An assigned interest that is coextensive in time with the assignor's interest is sometimes called a "horizontal" division or "horizontal slice," as contrasted with an interest for a fixed number of years shorter than the assignor's interest, called a "vertical slice." This assumes that money flows from side to side rather than up and down — or, if you will, west to east rather than south to north.

second in the man who earned it." That was deemed to be the meaning of the statute as to compensation for personal service and the one who earned the income was held to be subject to the tax. In Burnet v. Leininger, supra, a husband, a member of a firm, assigned future partnership income to his wife. We found that the revenue act dealt explicitly with the liability of partners as such. The wife did not become a member of the firm; the act specifically taxed the distributive share of each partner in the net income of the firm; and the husband by the fair import of the act remained taxable upon his distributive share. These cases are not in point. The tax here is not upon earnings which are taxed to the one who earns them. Nor is it a case of income attributable to a taxpayer by reason of the application of the income to the discharge of his obligation. . . . There is here no question of evasion or of giving effect to statutory provisions designed to forestall evasion; or of the taxpayer's retention of control. . . .

The Government points to the provisions of the revenue acts imposing upon the beneficiary of a trust the liability for the tax upon the income distributable to the beneficiary.[6] But the term is merely descriptive of the one entitled to the beneficial interest. . . . If under the law governing the trust the beneficial interest is assignable, and if it has been assigned without reservation, the assignee thus becomes the beneficiary and is entitled to rights and remedies accordingly. We find nothing in the revenue acts which denies him that status.

The decision of the Circuit Court of Appeals turned upon the effect to be ascribed to the assignments. The court held that the petitioner had no interest in the corpus of the estate and could not dispose of the income until he received it. Hence it was said that "the income was *his*" and his assignment was merely a direction to pay over to others what was due to himself. The question was considered to involve "the date when the income became transferable." 83 F.(2d), p.662. The Government refers to the terms of the assignment, — that it was of the interest in the income "which the said party of the first part now is, or may hereafter be, entitled to receive during his life from the trustees." From this it is urged that the assignments "dealt only with a right to receive the income" and that "no attempt was made to assign any equitable right, title or interest in the trust itself." This construction seems to us to be a strained one. We think it apparent that the conveyancer was not seeking to limit the assignment so as to make it anything less than a complete transfer of the specified interest of the petitioner as the life beneficiary of the trust, but that with ample caution he was using words to effect such a transfer. That the state court so construed the assignments appears from the final decree which described them as voluntary assignments of interests of the petitioner "in said trust estate," and it was in that aspect that petitioner's right to make the assignments was sustained.

The will creating the trust entitled the petitioner during his life to the net income of the property held in trust. He thus became the owner of an equitable interest in the corpus of the property. . . . By virtue of that interest he

6. [The provisions stated in general terms that the "beneficiary" of a trust was taxable on the income distributable to him. See §§ 652(a) and 662(a). — EDS.]

was entitled to enforce the trust, to have a breach of trust enjoined and to obtain redress in case of breach. The interest was present property alienable like any other, in the absence of a valid restraint upon alienation.... The beneficiary may thus transfer a part of his interest as well as the whole. See Restatement of the Law of Trusts, §§ 130, 132 et seq. The assignment of the beneficial interest is not the assignment of a chose in action but of the "right, title, and estate in and to property." ... See Bogert, Trusts and Trustees, vol. 1, 183, pp. 516, 517; 17 Columbia Law Review, 269, 273, 289, 290.

We conclude that the assignments were valid, that the assignees thereby became the owners of the specified beneficial interests in the income, and that as to these interests they and not the petitioner were taxable for the tax years in question....

HELVERING v. HORST
311 U.S. 112 (1940)

Mr. Justice STONE delivered the opinion of the Court.

The sole question for decision is whether the gift, during the donor's taxable year, of interest coupons detached from the bonds, delivered to the donee and later in the year paid at maturity, is the realization of income taxable to the donor.[7]

In 1934 and 1935 respondent, the owner of negotiable bonds, detached from them negotiable interest coupons shortly before their due date and delivered them as a gift to his son who in the same year collected them at maturity. The Commissioner ruled that under [§ 61(a)], the interest payments were taxable, in the years when paid, to the respondent donor who reported his income on the cash receipts basis....

The court below thought that as the consideration for the coupons had passed to the obligor, the donor had, by the gift, parted with all control over them and their payment, and for that reason the case was distinguishable from Lucas v. Earl [supra page 623] and Burnet v. Leininger, 285 U.S. 136, where the assignment of compensation for services had preceded the rendition of the services, and where the income was held taxable to the donor.

The holder of a coupon bond is the owner of two independent and separable kinds of right. One is the right to demand and receive at maturity the principal amount of the bond representing capital investment. The other is

7. [Coupon bonds, which were far more common in earlier days than they are now, are "bearer" obligations (that is, payable to the bearer, or holder). The obligation is reflected in a large, sturdy piece of paper, part of which states the borrower's obligation to pay the principal amount on a given date and part of which is divided into segments called coupons, each of which states the borrower's obligation to pay a fixed amount of money, the interest payment, on a particular interest-payment date, with one coupon for each interest payment. Each coupon is a separate negotiable instrument. Ordinarily, the holder of the bond collects interest by cutting off ("clipping") coupons as they mature and cashing them in, usually at a bank, but, as this case reveals, any other holder of the coupons can cash them in on their due date. These days, most corporate bonds are registered; the owner's name is registered with the debtor company, and the interest payment goes in the mail by check to the registered owner. Since 1983, most bonds are in effect required to be registered. See §§ 103(d), 163(f), 165(j), 1232(d), and 4701.—EDS.]

the right to demand and receive interim payments of interest on the investment in the amounts and on the dates specified by the coupons. Together they
are an obligation to pay principal and interest given in exchange for money or
property which was presumably the consideration for the obligation of the
bond. Here respondent, as owner of the bonds, had acquired the legal right to
demand payment at maturity of the interest specified by the coupons and the
power to command its payment to others which constituted an economic gain
to him.

Admittedly not all economic gain of the taxpayer is taxable income. From
the beginning the revenue laws have been interpreted as defining "realization" of income as the taxable event rather than the acquisition of the right to
receive it. And "realization" is not deemed to occur until the income is paid.
But the decisions and regulations have consistently recognized that receipt in
cash or property is not the only characteristic of realization of income to a
taxpayer on the cash receipts basis. Where the taxpayer does not receive
payments of income in money or property realization may occur when the last
step is taken by which he obtains the fruition of the economic gain which has
already accrued to him. . . .

In the ordinary case the taxpayer who acquires the right to receive income
is taxed when he receives it, regardless of the time when his right to receive
payment accrued. But the rule that income is not taxable until realized has
never been taken to mean that the taxpayer, even on the cash receipts basis,
who has fully enjoyed the benefit of the economic gain represented by his
right to receive income, can escape taxation because he has not himself received payment of it from his obligor. The rule, founded on administrative
convenience, is only one of postponement of the tax to the final event of
enjoyment of the income, usually the receipt of it by the taxpayer, and not one
of exemption from taxation where the enjoyment is consummated by some
event other than the taxpayer's personal receipt of money or property. . . .
This may occur when he has made such use of disposition of his power to
receive or control the income as to procure in its place other satisfactions
which are of economic worth. The question here is whether because one who
in fact receives payment for services or interest payments is taxable only on his
receipt of the payments, he can escape all tax by giving away his right to
income in advance of payment. If the taxpayer procures payment directly to
his creditors of the items of interest or earnings due him, see Old Colony
Trust Co. v. Commissioner, 279 U.S. 716; Bowers v. Kerbaugh-Empire Co.,
271 U.S. 170; United States v. Kirby Lumber Co. [supra page 161], or if he
sets up a revocable trust with income payable to the objects of his bounty,
Corliss v. Bowers, 281 U.S. 376, he does not escape taxation because he did
not actually receive the money. . . .

Underlying the reasoning in these cases is the thought that income is
"realized" by the assignor because he, who owns or controls the source of the
income, also controls the disposition of that which he could have received
himself and diverts the payment from himself to others as the means of
procuring the satisfaction of his wants. The taxpayer has equally enjoyed the
fruits of his labor or investment and obtained the satisfaction of his desires
whether he collects and uses the income to procure those satisfactions, or

whether he disposes of his right to collect it as the means of procuring them. . . .

Although the donor here, by the transfer of the coupons, has precluded any possibility of his collecting them himself he has nevertheless, by his act, procured payment of the interest, as a valuable gift to a member of his family. Such a use of his economic gain, the right to receive income, to procure a satisfaction which can be obtained only by the expenditure of money or property, would seem to be the enjoyment of the income whether the satisfaction is the purchase of goods at the corner grocery, the payment of his debt there, or such non-material satisfactions as may result from the payment of a campaign or community chest contribution, or a gift to his favorite son. Even though he never receives the money he derives money's worth from the disposition of the coupons which he has used as money or money's worth in the procuring of a satisfaction which is procurable only by the expenditure of money or money's worth. The enjoyment of the economic benefit accruing to him by virtue of his acquisition of the coupons is realized as completely as it would have been if he had collected the interest in dollars and expended them for any of the purposes named. . . .

In a real sense he has enjoyed compensation for money loaned or services rendered and not any the less so because it is his only reward for them. To say that one who has made a gift thus derived from interest or earnings paid to his donee has never enjoyed or realized the fruits of his investment or labor because he has assigned them instead of collecting them himself and then paying them over to the donee, is to affront common understanding and to deny the facts of common experience. Common understanding and experience are the touchstones for the interpretation of the revenue laws.

The power to dispose of income is the equivalent of ownership of it. The exercise of that power to procure the payment of income to another is the enjoyment and hence the realization of the income by him who exercises it. We have had no difficulty in applying that proposition where the assignment preceded the rendition of the services, Lucas v. Earl, supra; Burnet v. Leininger, supra, for it was recognized in the *Leininger* case that in such a case the rendition of the service by the assignor was the means by which the income was controlled by the donor and of making his assignment effective. But it is the assignment by which the disposition of income is controlled when the service precedes the assignment and in both cases it is the exercise of the power of disposition of the interest or compensation with the resulting payment to the donee which is the enjoyment by the donor of income derived from them.

This was emphasized in Blair v. Commissioner [supra page 646], on which respondent relies, where the distinction was taken between a gift of income derived from an obligation to pay compensation and a gift of income-producing property. In the circumstances of that case the right to income from the trust property was thought to be so identified with the equitable ownership of the property from which alone the beneficiary derived his right to receive the income and his power to command disposition of it that a gift of the income by the beneficiary became effective only as a gift of his ownership of the property producing it. Since the gift was deemed to be a gift of the property the income from it was held to be the income of the owner of the property, who was the donee, not the donor, a refinement which was unnecessary if respondent's contention here is right, but one clearly inapplicable to gifts of interest or wages. Unlike income thus derived from an obligation to pay interest or compensation, the income of the trust was regarded as no more the income of the donor than would be the rent from a lease or a crop raised on a farm after the leasehold or the farm has been given away. . . .

The dominant purpose of the revenue laws is the taxation of income to those who earn or otherwise create the right to receive it and enjoy the benefit of it when paid. . . . The tax laid by the 1934 Revenue Act upon income "derived from . . . wages, or compensation for personal service, of whatever kind and in whatever form paid . . . ; also from interest . . ." therefore cannot fairly be interpreted as not applying to income derived from interest or compensation when he who is entitled to receive it makes use of his power to dispose of it in procuring satisfactions which he would otherwise procure only by the use of the money when received.

It is the statute which taxes the income to the donor although paid to his donee. Lucas v. Earl, supra; Burnet v. Leininger, supra. True, in those cases the service which created the right to income followed the assignment and it was arguable that in point of legal theory the right to the compensation vested instantaneously in the assignor when paid although he never received it; while here the right of the assignor to receive the income antedated the assignment which transferred the right and thus precluded such an instantaneous vesting. But the statute affords no basis for such "attenuated subtleties." The distinction was explicitly rejected as the basis of decision in Lucas v. Earl. It should be rejected here, for no more than in the *Earl* case can the purpose of the statute to tax the income to him who earns, or creates and enjoys it be escaped by "anticipatory arrangements . . . however skillfully devised" to prevent the income from vesting even for a second in the donor.

Nor is it perceived that there is any adequate basis for distinguishing between the gift of interest coupons here and a gift of salary or commissions. The owner of a negotiable bond and of the investment which it represents, if not the lender, stands in the place of the lender. When, by the gift of the coupons, he has separated his right to interest payments from his investment and procured the payment of the interest to his donee, he has enjoyed the economic benefits of the income in the same manner and to the same extent as though the transfer were of earnings and in both cases the import of the statute is that the fruit is not to be attributed to a different tree from that on which it grew. See Lucas v. Earl, supra.

Reversed.

The separate opinion of Mr. Justice MCREYNOLDS.

. . . The unmatured coupons given to the son were independent negotiable instruments, complete in themselves. Through the gift they became at once the absolute property of the donee, free from the donor's control and in no way dependent upon ownership of the bonds. No question of actual fraud or purpose to defraud the revenue is presented. . . .

THE CHIEF JUSTICE and Mr. Justice ROBERTS concur in this opinion.

NOTES AND QUESTIONS

1. *Rationale:* Blair. The Court says that Mr. Blair was "the owner of an equitable interest in the corpus of the property." So what? Is the characterization relevant because of language in the Code? Because of tax policy objectives? Does it help make the law more predictable? If so, at what cost?

2. *Rationale:* Horst. (a) Is realization a problem in *Horst*? (b) What is the relevance of the fact that Mr. Horst may have obtained some satisfaction from the enjoyment of the income by the son? If Mr. Horst had given the entire bond to the son, would his satisfaction in the son's enjoyment of the income over the next several years have been less? Would the father have been taxed on the interest payments received by the son? (c) What if the father had removed some of the coupons and given them to the son and given the rest of the coupons and the bond itself (that is, the claim to the terminal payment at maturity) to his daughter? Who would be taxed on what? (d) Suppose that the father had cut off all the coupons and given them to the son, at the same time had given the bond itself to his daughter, and thereafter the son had given all the coupons to his son (the grandson). Now who is taxed on the interest: son, daughter, or grandson? Should it matter whether the coupons are called "property" or "an equitable interest in the corpus of the property"? (e) What *is* the proper rationale for *Horst*?

3. *Financial analysis.* Suppose that *F* (father) owns a bond with a face value (the amount due at maturity) of $1,000, due in three years, with interest payable annually at the rate of 12 percent or $120 per year, and that the market rate of interest on such bonds is 12 percent and remains at this level throughout the remaining three-year term. *F* assigns the right to collect the interest for the remaining three years to *S* (son). Immediately after the assignment, the value of *S*'s claim to the interest is $288 (the present value of the right to $120 per year for three years, discounted at 12 percent) and the value of *F*'s claim to the $1,000 payable at maturity is $712. These relationships change over time in the manner suggested by the figures in Table 7-1.

Perhaps the most accurate system of taxation would be one in which *S* is taxed each year on the amounts in row (e) and *F* is taxed each year on the amounts in row (f) (assuming that neither *S* nor *F* sells his interest during the

TABLE 7-1
Illustration of Assignment of Bond Interest

	Start	End Year 1	End Year 2	End Year 3
(a) Value of *F*'s claim	$712	$797	$893	$1,000
(b) Value of *S*'s claim	288	203	107	-0-
(c) Interest payment	—	120	120	120
(d) Decline in value of *S*'s claim	—	85	96	107
(e) Economic gain to *S**	—	35	24	13
(f) Increase in value of *F*'s claim	—	85	96	107

*The difference between the interest payment received and the decrease in the value of *S*'s claim during the year.

remaining three-year term of the bond). Note that the total income taxed each year under this approach would be $120, which is the correct total amount. S can be compared to the holder of a life estate and F with the holder of a remainder. We have seen that where a life estate (or term of years) and a remainder have been created by a transfer from a third party, the life tenant (or holder of the term interest) is taxed on the entire payment received each year and the holder of the remainder reports no income until he or she starts collecting income on the termination of the life estate. See, again, Irwin v. Gavit. That approach may not be accurate, but it appeals to one's sense of practicality. In the present example, practicality may dictate that since the lion's share of the gain each year is F's, F should pay tax on all the income. What does this imply as to the limits of *Horst*? If we assume a bond with a remaining life of ten years and an interest rate of 12 percent, and an assignment of the interest payments from F to S for the entire ten-year term, then immediately after the assignment S's claim is worth $678 and F's claim is worth $322. The economic gain to S in the first year is $81, and the increase in the value of F's interest is $39. For the last three years of the ten-year assignment, the relationships would be the same as in Table 7-1.

4. *Stripped bonds.* The analysis suggested by the preceding Note is consistent with the treatment of "stripped" bonds under § 1286(a). A stripped bond is any bond as to which there has been a separation of ownership of "the bond" (the right to the terminal, or principal, payment) and any interest payment. § 1286(e)(2), (5). When a bond has been stripped, purchasers of the bond and of each "coupon" (that is, each right to an interest payment), must treat each such ownership interest as a separate original issue discount (OID) bond, taxed according to the rules applicable to such instruments. See Chapter 3C. These rules do not seem to apply, however, in a situation such as that in *Horst*, where the bond was not purchased as a stripped bond and the coupons were transferred by gift. See § 1286(e)(6) and § 1272(d)(1).

5. *Unrealized appreciation.* Can the result in *Horst* be reconciled with the rule approved in Taft v. Bowers (supra page 112) and reflected in § 1015, that the donee, rather than the donor, is taxed on the unrealized gain on property transferred by gift? See also the discussion of income in respect of a decedent, supra page 116.

F. SERVICES TRANSFORMED INTO PROPERTY

Consider what you've learned so far from the foregoing materials. Lucas v. Earl indicates that income from the provision of personal services should generally be taxed to the person who provided those services. In the previous section, we saw that income from property is generally taxed to the owner of that property. The obvious next question may have already occurred to you—what happens when one person's services result in the creation of property that is then transferred to another person? The following two cases speak to this issue.

HELVERING v. EUBANK
311 U.S. 122 (1940)

Mr. Justice STONE delivered the opinion of the Court.

This is a companion case to Helvering v. Horst [supra page 648], and presents issues not distinguishable from those in that case.

Respondent, a general life insurance agent, after the termination of his agency contracts and services as agent, made assignments in 1924 and 1928 respectively of renewal commissions to become payable to him for services which had been rendered in writing policies of insurance under two of his agency contracts.[8] The Commissioner assessed the renewal commissions paid by the companies to the assignees in 1933 as income taxable to the assignor in that year under [§ 61].

No purpose of the assignments appears other than to confer on the assignees the power to collect the commissions, which they did in the taxable year. The Government and respondent have briefed and argued the case here on the assumption that the assignments were voluntary transfers to the assignees of the right to collect the commissions as and when they became payable, and the record affords no basis for any other.

For the reasons stated at length in the opinion in the *Horst* case, we hold that the commissions were taxable as income of the assignor in the year when paid. The judgment below is reversed.

The separate opinion of Mr. Justice MCREYNOLDS. . . .

The court below declared—

In the case at bar the petitioner owned a right to receive money for past services; no further services were required. Such a right is assignable. At the time of assignment there was nothing contingent in the petitioner's right, although the amount collectible in future years was still uncertain and contingent. But this may be equally true where the assignment transfers a right to income from investments, as in Blair v. Commissioner, [supra page 646], and Horst v. Commissioner, 107 F.2d 906 (C.C.A. 2), or a right to patent royalties, as in Nelson v. Ferguson, 56 F.2d 121 (C.C.A. 3), certiorari denied, 286 U.S. 565. By an assignment of future earnings a taxpayer may not escape taxation upon his compensation in the year when he earns it. But when a taxpayer who makes his income tax return on a cash basis assigns a right to money payable in the future for work already performed, we believe that he transfers a property right, and the money, when received by the assignee, is not income taxable to the assignor.

Accordingly, the Board of Tax Appeals was reversed; and this, I think, is in accord with the statute and our opinions.

The assignment in question denuded the assignor of all right to commissions thereafter to accrue under the contract with the insurance company. He

---

8. [The commissions were assigned to a corporate trustee. The opinion of the Supreme Court and of the lower courts and the record before the Supreme Court all fail to reveal the purposes of the trust or the relationship of the beneficiaries to Mr. Eubank. The record (at page 6) does, however, establish that the assignment was gratuitous. For purposes of analysis, it seems reasonable to treat the case as if the assignee had been Mr. Eubank's wife or children.—EDS.]

could do nothing further in respect of them; they were entirely beyond his control. In no proper sense were they something either earned or received by him during the taxable year. The right to collect became the absolute property of the assignee without relation to future action by the assignor.

A mere right to collect future payments, for services already performed, is not presently taxable as "income derived" from such services. It is property which may be assigned. Whatever the assignor receives as consideration may be his income; but the statute does not undertake to impose liability upon him because of payments to another under a contract which he had transferred in good faith, under circumstances like those here disclosed....

The general principles approved in Blair v. Commissioner, ... are controlling and call for affirmation of the judgment under review.

THE CHIEF JUSTICE and Mr. Justice ROBERTS concur in this opinion.

HEIM v. FITZPATRICK
262 F.2d 887 (2d Cir. 1959)

Before SWAN and MOORE, Circuit Judges, and KAUFMAN, District Judge.
SWAN, Circuit Judge.

This litigation involves income taxes of Lewis R. Heim, for the years 1943 through 1946. On audit of the taxpayer's returns, the Commissioner of Internal Revenue determined that his taxable income in each of said years should be increased by adding thereto patent royalty payments received by his wife, his son and his daughter....

Plaintiff was the inventor of a new type of rod end and spherical bearing. In September 1942 he applied for a patent thereon. On November 5, 1942 he applied for a further patent on improvements of his original invention. Thereafter on November 17, 1942 he executed a formal written assignment of his invention and of the patents which might be issued for it and for improvements thereof to The Heim Company.[9] This was duly recorded in the Patent Office and in January 1945 and May 1946 plaintiff's patent applications were acted on favorably and patents thereon were issued to the Company. The assignment to the Company was made pursuant to an oral agreement, subsequently reduced to a writing dated July 29, 1943, by which it was agreed (1) that the Company need pay no royalties on bearings manufactured by it prior to July 1, 1943; (2) that after that date the Company would pay specified royalties on 12 types of bearings; (3) that on new types of bearings it would pay royalties to be agreed upon prior to their manufacture; (4) that if the royalties for any two consecutive months or for any one year should fall below stated amounts, plaintiff at his option might cancel the agreement and thereupon all rights granted by him under the agreement and under any and all assigned patents should revert to him, his heirs and assigns; and (5) that this agreement is not transferable by the Company.

---

9. The stock of The Heim Company was owned as follows: plaintiff 1%, his wife 41%, his son and daughter 27% each, and his daughter-in-law and son-in-law 2% each.

In August 1943 plaintiff assigned to his wife "an undivided interest of 25 per cent in said agreement with The Heim Company dated July 29, 1943, and in all his inventions and patent rights, past and future, referred to therein and in all rights and benefits of the First Party [plaintiff] thereunder. . . ." A similar assignment was given to his son and another to his daughter. Plaintiff paid gift taxes on the assignments. The Company was notified of them and thereafter it made all royalty payments accordingly. As additional types of bearings were put into production from time to time the royalties on them were fixed by agreement between the Company and the plaintiff and his three assignees. . . .

The appellant contends that the assignments to his wife and children transferred to them income-producing property and consequently the royalty payments were taxable to his donees, as held in Blair v. Commissioner [supra page 646]. Judge Anderson, however, was of opinion that [151 F. Supp. 576]: "The income-producing property, i.e., the patents, had been assigned by the taxpayer to the corporation. What he had left was a right to a portion of the income which the patents produced. He had the power to dispose of and divert the stream of this income as he saw fit." Consequently he ruled that the principles applied by the Supreme Court in Helvering v. Horst [supra page 648], and Helvering v. Eubank [supra page 654], required all the royalty payments to be treated as income of plaintiff. . . .

In the present case more than a bare right to receive future royalties was assigned by plaintiff to his donees. Under the terms of his contract with The Heim Company he retained the power to bargain for the fixing of royalties on new types of bearings, i.e. bearings other than the 12 products on which royalties were specified. This power was assigned and the assignees exercised it as to new products. Plaintiff also retained a reversionary interest in his invention and patents by reason of his option to cancel the agreement if certain conditions were not fulfilled. This interest was also assigned. The fact that the option was not exercised in 1945, when it could have been, is irrelevant so far as concerns the existence of the reversionary interest. We think that the rights retained by plaintiff and assigned to his wife and children were sufficiently substantial to justify the view that they were given income-producing property.

In addition to Judge Anderson's ground of decision appellee advances a further argument in support of the judgment, namely, that the plaintiff retained sufficient control over the invention and the royalties to make it reasonable to treat him as owner of that income for tax purposes. Commissioner v. Sunnen, 333 U.S. 591, is relied upon. There a patent was licensed under a royalty contract with a corporation in which the taxpayer-inventor held 89% of the stock. An assignment of the royalty contract to the taxpayer's wife was held ineffective to shift the tax, since the taxpayer retained control over the royalty payments to his wife by virtue of his control of the corporation, which could cancel the contract at any time. The argument is that, although plaintiff himself owned only 1% of The Heim Company stock, his wife and daughter together owned 68% and it is reasonable to infer from depositions introduced by the Commissioner that they would follow the plaintiff's advice. Judge Anderson did not find it necessary to pass on this contention. But we are satisfied that the record would not support a finding that plaintiff controlled the corporation whose active heads were the son and son-in-law. No inference can reasonably be drawn that the daughter would be likely to follow her father's advice rather than her husband's or brother's with respect to action by the corporation. . . .

For the foregoing reasons we hold that the judgment should be reversed and the cause remanded with directions to grant plaintiff's motion for summary judgment.

So ordered.

NOTES AND QUESTIONS

1. *Analysis.* (a) In *Eubank*, the majority relied on *Horst*. Was there a better case to rely on? The dissent relied on *Blair*. As between *Blair* and *Horst*, which seems more in point?

(b) In *Heim*, the lower court relied on *Horst* and *Eubank*. Again, was there a better case?

(c) In Commissioner v. Olmsted Incorporated Life Agency, 304 F.2d 16 (8th Cir. 1962) the taxpayer surrendered rights to renewal commissions in return for an annuity of $500 per month for fifteen years. The court rejected the Commissioner's argument that the exchange should have been treated as a taxable disposition. It relied heavily on Commissioner v. Oates, 207 F.2d 711 (7th Cir. 1953). In that case the taxpayer had been entitled to renewal commissions and exchanged that right for a right to payments extending over a longer period of time than the expected duration of the renewal commissions. The Commissioner in *Oates* relied in part on Lucas v. Earl (supra page 623), on Helvering v. Horst (supra page 648), and on *Eubank*. The court distinguished those cases by observing that in each of them the "taxpayer had effectually received the income" in that "by assigning it, he took dominion over it, converted it to his own use and treated it as a property right, thus realizing its full economic benefit." What was the economic benefit in *Earl*, in *Horst*, and in *Eubank*? Why was there no similar economic benefit in *Blair* (supra page 646) or in *Heim*?

2. *The pattern.* (a) *A*, an engineer who spends all her time working for herself on ideas for inventions, creates and patents an invention, then gives (assigns) the patent to her son, who licenses it and receives royalties. As is clear from *Heim*, the son, not the mother, is taxable on the royalties.

(b) *B*, an investor, buys a patent from the inventor and gives the patent to her son, who licenses it and receives the royalties. Plainly, the son, not the mother, is taxable on the royalties.

(c) *C*, a lawyer, assists *N*, an inventor, in obtaining financing for *N*'s invention, which *N* patents. *N* licenses the patent to *X* and, in return for *C*'s services, assigns to *C* a portion of the royalties to be paid by *X*. *C* then assigns her rights to the royalties to her son. In a closely analogous case, the Second Circuit, relying on *Earl* and *Eubank*, and on the fact that the assignor (the *C* counterpart) did not receive any part of the patent itself or any right to control its disposition, held that the royalties were taxable to the assignor. Strauss v. Commissioner, 168 F.2d 441 (2d Cir. 1948), cert. denied, 335 U.S. 858, rehearing denied, 335 U.S. 888 (1948).

(d) *D*, an author, copyrights her book and then assigns the copyright to her son, who licenses it and receives royalties. The royalties are taxable to the son. See Rev. Rul. 54-599, 1954-2 C.B. 52.

(e) Do the outcomes in these hypothetical cases form a consistent pattern? a sensible one?

(f) *F*, an architect, agrees with a client to design a building but refuses to set a price for the job. When the plans are completed, *F* gives them to her son, who sells them to the client for a share of the rents from the building for the next twenty years. Who is taxable on the share of the rents received by the son? When?

3. *The interest element.* In *Eubank* the commissions received by the assignees were a form of deferred compensation and must have included an element of interest on the amount initially earned. Suppose that immediately after writing a group of policies, Mr. Eubank had assigned the renewal commissions to a person who paid him the full market value of the rights, $1,000. How would Mr. Eubank have been taxed? What about the assignee? See Chapter 2D. What, if anything, does this tell us about how the amounts collected by the assignee in the actual situation in *Eubank* should be taxed? Should the *amount* taxable to Mr. Eubank be the value of the renewal commissions at the time of the assignment? If so, at what *time* should this amount be taxed, and how should the assignee be taxed?

G. TRUSTS

1. Overview

In the foregoing cases, the courts had to determine which of *two* parties should be taxed on the income. We now turn to more complex situations in which *three* (or more) parties are potential taxpayers: The owner of property (grantor) transfers it to a trustee to administer, with instructions for distributing the income, currently or at a later date, to one or more beneficiaries. Who — the grantor, the trust, or one of the beneficiaries — is taxed on the income? Occasionally there is another possibility: A person who under the trust instrument can get the income or corpus on demand.

To gain a sense of the nature of the problem, suppose George (the grandfather) is a wealthy man with a daughter, Peggy (the parent), who is a lawyer working in the office of the U.S. Attorney, and who is divorced, with two children, Carol (age 19) and Chris (age 15). George establishes a trust, with his friend Tom as trustee, for the benefit of Carol and Chris. The trust provides that the trustee may, at his discretion, accumulate the income or may use it to provide for the "education, support, or welfare" of Carol or Chris, with the principal and any accumulated income to be distributed to them in equal shares, or to the survivor, ten years hence. Assume that the income is substantial; part of it is used to pay for Carol to go to a private college and to buy her a car. Part of it is used to send Chris to a private boarding school and to summer camp and to pay for his tennis lessons. The rest is accumulated. How should the income be taxed? Should George be taxed on the theory that he has not yet sufficiently severed his ties to the property placed in trust? What if he dies? Should Peggy be taxed on the amounts paid out of the trust for Carol and Chris on the theory that she is the effective beneficiary (bearing in mind that George could have given the property to her and allowed her to pay the bills for Carol and Chris, except that such an approach, natural as it might seem, would have resulted in higher taxes than if the income were taxed to Carol and Chris)? Should Carol and Chris be taxed on the income used for their benefit, on the simple theory that it is legally their income from their property? What about the income accumulated by the trust? Should it be taxed to the trust? At what rate? If it is taxed to the trust, what should happen when it is later distributed? Or should it be taxed to Carol and Chris as earned? These are some of the basic issues addressed by the rules described below.

In the ordinary case, where the trust is irrevocable and the grantor reserves little or no control over it, the trust income will be taxed either to the trust or to the beneficiaries.[10] Trusts of this character, ordinary trusts, are governed by §§ 641 through 668 of the Code. However, a grantor who retains power over the economic benefits of the trust property may be taxed as the "substantial owner" thereof. These trusts, sometimes called grantor trusts, are governed by §§ 671 through 677 of the Code, examined infra pages 662-667. Finally, a third person who has the right to get the income or corpus of the trust on demand may be taxed as the substantial owner of the income under § 678. Trusts of this type are sometimes called Mallinckrodt trusts, after a leading case (see infra page 667).

Special rules tax the U.S. grantor of a foreign trust on its income where there is a U.S. beneficiary. § 679. Special rules also govern employees' pension and similar trusts, § 501(a); certain tax-exempt organizations in trust form, § 501(c); alimony trusts, § 682; and certain other trusts.

2. Tax Treatment of (Ordinary) Simple Trusts

The statutory provisions governing ordinary trusts are exceedingly complex. In an effort to make the statutory scheme less formidable, the Code distinguishes between *simple trusts* (those that are required to distribute all income currently, that have made no distributions of corpus, and that claim no charitable deduction in the taxable year) and *complex trusts* (all others). The statutory provisions applicable to simple trusts are found in Subpart B of Subchapter J, §§ 651-652; those applicable to complex trusts in Subparts C and D of Subchapter J, §§ 661-668.

A simple trust is nominally subject to tax on its income. In computing its income, however, a simple trust deducts all the income that is required to be distributed currently. § 651. Since a simple trust is defined as one that is required to distribute all its income currently, a simple trust generally pays no

---

10. Section 102(a), providing that gifts are not included in the donee's gross income, does not protect the beneficiary of trust income because of the last sentence of § 102(b). Thus, the distinction between gifts, which can be received tax free under § 102(a), and gifts of income from property, which are taxable to the recipient, is delegated, so far as trust income is concerned, to the rules of Subchapter J.

tax.[11] Instead, the income of the trust is taxed to the beneficiary. §§ 61(a)(15), 652(a). A simple trust is sometimes described as a mere conduit. The conduit principle extends to the characterization of trust income. Section 652(b) provides that distributed income shall have the same character in the hands of the beneficiary as in the hands of the trust. Thus, tax-exempt interest and capital gains preserve their special character when distributed to the beneficiary. If there is more than one beneficiary, each receives an appropriate share of these items, unless they are allocated differently by local law or the trust instrument. See Regs. § 1.652(b)-1, (b)-2.

3.   Tax Treatment of (Ordinary) Complex Trusts

A complex trust is any trust that is not a simple trust. A complex trust is subject to taxation on its income under a rate schedule similar to that for individuals, but with the brackets changing at much lower income levels, with the result that in 2004 the 35 percent bracket applies to income over $9,500. (Simple trusts are subject to the same rate schedule on their taxable income, but, as noted above, seldom have taxable income.)

The taxable income of a complex trust is computed in about the same manner as an individual's taxable income. The principal differences are that (a) in lieu of the personal exemption and dependency deductions, a trust is allowed a deduction of either $100 or $300 per year (§ 642(b)); (b) the trust is not allowed a standard deduction; and (c) the trust is not subject to the § 170 20-30-50 percent limits on charitable deductions.[12] Most important, a complex trust, like a simple trust, is allowed a deduction for current income distributed to beneficiaries.

Beneficiaries generally are subject to tax on the lesser of the amount of trust distributions and the amount of the trust's "distributable net income." Distributable net income is generally equal to current taxable income and is often referred to as DNI. See § 643(a). However, under a complicated system of "throwback rules," a beneficiary who receives income that has been accumulated by the trust is taxed on that income when it is distributed in later years. The tax that the beneficiary must pay is reduced by the taxes already paid on that income by the trust. See the last sentence of § 667(b)(1), § 668(b). Distributed income has the same character in the hands of the beneficiary as in the hands of the trust.

The operation of the rules for complex trusts is illustrated by the following examples. Suppose a complex trust distributes all of its DNI in its first taxable year. In that case, the trust is entitled to a deduction for the distribution and the deduction is equal to the income, so there is no tax. The income is taxed only once, at the beneficiary's rate.

Suppose, instead, that the first-year distributions of the trust exceed the trust's DNI. In that case, the trust again pays no tax, because it is entitled to

---

11. A simple trust may be taxed on capital gain that is not treated as income for trust purposes and that is retained by the trust. In that case, the trust will be subject to the same rate bracket, and generally subject to the same limitations on personal deductions, etc., as are described below for complex trusts.

12. The same differences apply to simple trusts that have taxable income after distributions to beneficiaries.

deduct the distribution from its income. The beneficiary is taxed only on the lesser of the DNI or the amount of the distribution. The excess of the distribution over the DNI is a tax-free recovery of corpus. Here, again, the income of the trust is taxed only once, and at the beneficiary's rates.

Suppose, finally, that the trust accumulates income during its first taxable year and distributes that income and the trust corpus on the first day of the following year. The trust is taxed on the income during the first year, and under the throwback rules, the beneficiary is taxed again on the income when it is distributed in the second year. However, the tax the beneficiary must pay on the income is reduced by the tax the trust has paid on that income during the previous year. The trust thus acts as sort of withholding agent for the beneficiary.[13] (But if the tax paid by the trust is greater than the tax owed by the beneficiary, the difference is not refunded to the beneficiary or credited against other taxes owed by the beneficiary.) Here, again, the effect of the rules is to tax the trust income only once, and, provided that the beneficiary is not in a lower bracket than the trust, at the beneficiary's rates. If the trust has accumulated income for more than one year, the same basic result applies, although the rules for taxation of the beneficiary are more complex.

The throwback rules were designed to prevent a taxpayer from achieving substantial tax avoidance in an era when the rate schedule applied to trusts taxed more income at low rates than does the rate schedule applicable since 1987. Without the throwback rules, a beneficiary's income could be accumulated by the trust and taxed at low rates and then distributed free of tax. Even with the rules, taxpayers sometimes found it advantageous to accumulate income in the trust, at its lower rates, since the additional tax on the income when it was distributed to the beneficiary was deferred. No interest was (or is) payable on an accumulation distribution. The modest potential advantage of the deferral of part of the tax on accumulated trust income is still available under current rules, but only if the accumulation is small. A modest advantage from accumulation is also available by virtue of the fact that the throwback rules do not apply to amounts accumulated for a beneficiary before age 21 or birth. § 665(b). In general, though, the fact that trusts are now subject to rates equal to the maximum individual tax rates on relatively low amounts of income removes any advantage from accumulation.

4. The Use of Multiple Trusts

It is sometimes necessary to determine whether a single trust instrument creates several trusts or only one, since each trust is entitled to its own $100 or

---

13. In order to tax the beneficiary on the entire amount of the trust income, the distribution must be "grossed up" by the amount of the tax paid by the trust. For example, suppose a complex trust earns and accumulates income of $10,000, pays a tax of $2,000, and in the next year distributes the accumulated income of $8,000. The $8,000 income is grossed up by the $2,000 tax. The beneficiary is treated as having received the entire $10,000 and as having paid a tax of $2,000 on that distribution. This tax treatment follows the same pattern as the taxation of wages subject to withholding. If you earn $10,000 and your employer withholds tax of $2,000 and pays you $8,000, you report income of $10,000 and are entitled to a tax credit of $2,000.

$300 deduction and to a separately calculated tax. The Service may wish to consolidate the income of two or more trusts and tax the combined income to a single entity. The issue may arise, for example, if a grantor creates two (or ten or 100) trusts all in identical terms and for the benefit of the same beneficiary, in an effort to obtain a $100 or $300 exemption for each trust and to compute the tax on each trust's taxable income separately. The courts tended to uphold the use of multiple trusts against the Commissioner's attack. See, e.g., Morris Trusts v. Commissioner, 51 T.C. 20 (1968), aff'd per curiam, 427 F.2d 1361 (9th Cir. 1970), in which each of ten separate declarations of trust was held to create two separate trusts or a total of twenty trusts for the same beneficiaries. However, § 667(c), adopted in 1976, substantially eliminates the advantage of multiple trusts by providing that where there are accumulation distributions to a beneficiary for any prior year from more than two trusts, the taxes paid by the third trust are not imputed to the beneficiary and he or she receives no credit for those taxes. This provision overrides the normal exemption for accumulations before a beneficiary is born or reaches age 21. And § 643(e), added in 1984, gives the Treasury broad rule-making powers to prevent the use of multiple trusts for tax-avoidance purposes.

H. GRANTOR TRUSTS

1. Revocable Trusts

As we have seen, a person who is willing to make an outright gift of property succeeds in shifting income for tax purposes to the donee. But many people whose objective is to shift income are unwilling, or at least reluctant, to make no-strings-attached gifts. In an early decision, the Supreme Court held that a taxpayer who had established a trust to pay the income from property to his wife and at her death to his children, but who had retained the power to revoke the trust (and thereby regain the corpus) at any time, was taxable on the income as if he had made no gift. Corliss v. Bowers, 281 U.S. 376 (1930). This outcome is now reflected in the Code in § 676,[14] which goes further and nullifies the trust, for tax purposes, if the power to revoke (and thereby shift the assets back to the grantor) is held by any "nonadverse party." A nonadverse party is defined in § 672(b) as one who is not an "adverse party," which § 672(a) defines as one "having a substantial beneficial interest in the trust which would be adversely affected by the exercise or nonexercise of the power which he possesses respecting the trust." Thus, if a grantor transfers property to a trust with the income payable to his or her child for life and retains the power to revoke, the grantor is taxable on the income, even though the child is legally entitled to receive it, and the same is true if the power to revoke is given to the grantor's lawyer or a friend. But if the child (the income

---

14. Technically, a grantor with a power of revocation is "treated as the owner" of the trust. This language leads into § 671, under which a person is taxed on the income of a trust of which he or she is treated as owner.

beneficiary) is given the power to revoke, since the child would plainly be an adverse party (that is, one whose interest would be adversely affected by revocation), the grantor would not be taxable under § 676. Since the donee of an outright gift can always return the gift property to the donor, the rule allowing an adverse party to have a power of revocation seems to make sense. Under § 676(b), § 676(a) does not apply to a power of revocation whose effect might be to restore property to the donor only at such time as he or she would be permitted without adverse tax consequences to have a reversionary interest. (See § 673, described below.)

2. Totten Trusts and Similar Arrangements

In Rev. Rul. 62-148, 1962-2 C.B. 153, the Service ruled that the income from funds deposited in a savings account in the depositor's name "as trustee" for another person is taxable income of the depositor if under local law the transaction creates only a revocable trust (sometimes called a Totten trust in New York, also called a tentative trust or a savings bank trust). Income of custodial accounts under state custodial and uniform gifts to minors acts (see infra page 667), however, is taxed to the child and not to the parent-custodian, on the theory that these funds are the property of the child and may not be taken back by the custodian, even though the funds may be available for support of the child (and if so used may result in income to the parent).

3. Trusts for the Benefit of the Grantor

Consistent with the notion reflected in § 676(a) that a shifting of income requires a transfer that genuinely deprives the donor of the beneficial enjoyment of the property, § 677(a) taxes to the grantor trust income that is, or may be, used for the benefit of the grantor or the grantor's spouse. Section 677(b) relieves the grantor of taxation on income that *might be* used to support his or her children "in the discretion of another person, the trustee, or the grantor acting as trustee or co-trustee." Such income is taxable to the grantor only to the extent actually used to discharge his or her obligation of support. On the question of what is a part of the obligation of support and what is not, see Brooke v. United States, infra page 670.

4. Reversions

Before 1987 a grantor to whom the trust corpus was to revert was not taxable on the income if, at the time the trust was established, the reversion could not take effect for at least ten years (or upon the death of the income beneficiary, if sooner). This rule gave rise to the proliferation of ten-year trusts, also known as "Clifford" trusts.[15] The 1986 act repealed the rule allowing reversions at the

---

15. The label came from Helvering v. Clifford, 309 U.S. 331 (1940), in which the Supreme Court, in a case arising before the adoption of the grantor trust rules (§§ 671-679), held that the income of a

end of ten years (or on the death of the income beneficiary) and substituted a rule taxing the grantor on the income of a trust in which he or she has a reversionary interest whose value is greater than 5 percent of the value of the trust (with an exception for reversions after the death of a minor lineal descendant). § 673.

5. Powers of Control

Section 674(a) lays down the general rule that the grantor is to be treated as owner of any portion of a trust if its "beneficial enjoyment" is subject to a "power of disposition," exercisable by the grantor alone, by a nonadverse party, or by the grantor and a nonadverse party acting together, without the approval or consent of any adverse party. Typical provisions covered by § 674(a) are a retention by the grantor of the power to add beneficiaries to those named in the trust instrument, to vary the proportions in which corpus or income is to be paid to specified beneficiaries, or to accelerate or postpone the time when distributions are to be made. A notable exception to this prohibition on retention of a power to change beneficiaries (without losing the tax advantage of splitting off the income from investments), are § 529's "qualified tuition programs." Under these programs, as previously noted in Chapter 5.G, the grantor/owner of the account is allowed, without losing the program's substantial tax advantages, to change the beneficiary at any time, so long as the recipient is a member of the "family" (broadly defined) of the original designated beneficiary.

Section 674 contains some important exceptions to the basic rule of § 674(a) that any power of disposition results in the grantor being treated as owner. Section 674(b) contains a list of powers that can be retained by anyone, including the grantor. Among the powers permitted by § 674(b) are the power to withhold income temporarily (§ 674(b)(6)) and to distribute corpus (§ 674(b)(5)). Under § 674(c) the grantor may vest in an *independent* person an unfettered "sprinkle" or "spray" power as to both income and corpus — that is, a power to choose which of several beneficiaries will receive income or corpus. And under § 674(d) *any* person other than the grantor or the grantor's spouse may have the sprinkle power over income if the power is limited by a "reasonably definite external standard." The regulations provide that standards such as "reasonable support and comfort"; "education, maintenance, or health"; and enabling the beneficiary "to maintain his accustomed standard of living" all qualify as "reasonably definite." See Regs. § 1.674(d)-1 and § 1.674(b)-1(b)(5). With a cooperative holder of the power and a sufficiently large class of beneficiaries, the effect of the § 674 exceptions is to allow the grantor very substantial control over the use of the trust income. See infra section 7.

The powers of disposition permitted under § 674 need not be held by the trustee. For example, a grantor can be the trustee (and thus, among other things, make investment decisions) and still have some other person hold the sprinkle powers permitted under § 674(c) or (d).

---

five-year trust for the benefit of the grantor's wife was taxable to the grantor. After the case was decided, the Treasury issued regulations that contained safe-harbor rules for trusts with reversions to grantors. Those regulations are the source of the present statutory scheme.

6.   Administrative Powers

Section 675(1) and (2) provide that the grantor is to be treated as owner of the trust property if certain unusual powers (e.g., to purchase trust property for less than adequate consideration) may be exercised by the grantor, a nonadverse party, or both, without the consent of any adverse party. Moreover, § 675(3) treats a grantor who has borrowed from the trust as the owner of the trust property unless the loan was repaid before the beginning of the taxable year or was authorized by an independent trustee and provision was made for adequate interest and security. Finally, certain powers of administration (e.g., the power to vote stock of a corporation in which the holdings of the grantor and trust are significant to voting control) are fatal under § 675(4) if exercisable by anyone acting in a nonfiduciary capacity, unless the consent of a person in a fiduciary capacity is required.

The trustee, who may be the grantor, can have broad discretion in making investment decisions. This means that the grantor, within reasonable limits, can choose to invest in common stocks whose dividend yield is quite low or in bonds that pay a high rate of interest. Of course, there is always the possibility that the beneficiaries (e.g., the grantor's children) might take the grantor to court for abuse of discretion. But the beneficiaries may hesitate to do so out of respect, affection, or fear of loss of inheritance or other tangible benefits that the grantor is in a position to bestow on those who remain, by virtue of their good behavior, the natural objects of his or her bounty and affection.

7.   The Obligation of Support

In Braun v. Commissioner, 48 T.C. Memo. 1984-285, a taxpayer who was a New Jersey resident established a trust for the benefit of his children. The income was used in part to pay for the children's college educations. The court held that under New Jersey law the taxpayer had an obligation to provide his children with college educations and that consequently the amounts of trust income used for that purpose were includable in his income under § 677. (This was an alternative holding. The court also found that the taxpayer had a "sprinkle" power that made him taxable under § 674.) What if the trust had been created by the taxpayer's father (that is, by the children's grandfather)? See §§ 652(a), 662(a); Regs. §§ 1.662(a)-4, 1.652(a)-1.

In Stone v. Commissioner, T.C. Memo. 1987-454, aff'd without opinion, 867 F.2d 613 (9th Cir. 1989), the taxpayers, who were California residents, established a trust for the benefit of their minor children. The court held the parents taxable on amounts of trust income used to pay the children's tuition at private schools, on the theory that under California law affluent parents in circumstances such as those found in the case were legally obligated to provide the private school education and that, consequently, they were taxable under § 677. One significant fact bearing on the obligation, according to the court, was that the parents had sent the children to the private schools for several years before the trust began to pay the tuition. The idea seems to have been that once parents start to send their children to private schools, they may have a legal obligation to continue to do so.

In Sharon v. Commissioner, T.C. Memo. 1989-478, the tax court again addressed the obligation of support under California law. Income from property given by parents to their two daughters was used to pay for "private high school and private college tuition, camps, foreign travel, and other items." The court had no difficulty in rejecting the notion that any of the items other than the private high school tuition were part of the obligation of support. As to the college tuition, it was able to rely on Cal. Civ. Code § 196.5, under which the parental obligation of support ends when a child reaches age 19 or completes the twelfth grade, whichever occurs first. As to the private high school tuition, the court summarized the *Stone* decision, supra, as follows:

> If a child had special needs that would only be met by a private school, that would be an item of support. Similarly, if a child had been attending a private school prior to a divorce, continuing the private education could be an item of support. Also important in determining whether private high school tuition is a support item are the parents' financial ability to pay tuition and the background, values, and goals of parents and child.

In the case before it, the court, in support of its conclusion that the private high school tuition was not part of the obligation of support, observed that the father had begun transferring property to the daughters when they were infants. In addition:

> It cannot be said that [the father] transferred property for the specific purpose of using it to pay [the daughters'] private high school tuition. In fact, [the father] testified that the money was [the daughters] to do with as they pleased. Had they not used the money for private high school tuition, they could have used it for other things.

8. Example

G, who has assets worth several million dollars, intends to transfer $300,000 to a trust for the benefit of his children, *S* (age 12) and *D* (age 14). The trustee is to be *B*, *G*'s brother. The trustee is given discretion either to accumulate income or to distribute it to either child, or both, for "their reasonable comfort or support or for their education, health, or maintenance." The trust is to terminate at the end of ten years, at which time the corpus and any previously undistributed income is to be distributed in equal shares to the two children. *B* is given broad discretion as to the kinds of investments to be held by the trust. *G* contemplates that at least initially the corpus will be invested in bonds, which should yield income of about $40,000 per year. He anticipates that each year *B* will make distributions sufficient to pay private school tuition for each of the children, plus the cost of summer camp, music lessons, ski trips, and the like. Income not used for this purpose will be accumulated and held for future distribution to the children for their college educations or upon termination of the trust. (a) Will it work? (b) Suppose that each of the children has exhibited a streak of rebelliousness and *G* wants to be able to cut off either of them without a penny if he or she fails to conform to *G*'s (and *B*'s) ideas about proper behavior (mostly relating to respect for one's elders). What can he do? (c) What if he were to include as potential (discretionary) beneficiaries his mother and father or an impecunious cousin? (d) What, if anything, might be gained by appointing *F*, *G*'s friend, as trustee and giving *F* unfettered discretion to distribute income or corpus to either of the children? (e) If you were *F*, would you accept this kind of power? What if you were *G*'s lawyer and *G* asked you to hold such a power?

9. Nongrantors with Power to Demand Trust Income or Corpus

Under § 678 persons other than the grantor may be taxable on the income of a trust if they have the power to demand the income or corpus or have partially released such a power, retaining such control over the trust as would, if they were grantors, cause them to be treated as its owner under the grantor trust provisions (§§ 671-677). A typical trust affected by § 678 would be one set up by a person with her grandchildren as the income beneficiaries but with her children having the right to demand that the income be paid to them instead. These trusts are sometimes called "demand trusts" or "Mallinckrodt trusts" (after a pre-1954 case, Mallinckrodt v. Nunan, 146 F.2d 1, 5 (8th Cir.), cert. denied, 324 U.S. 871 (1945)). Note that § 678 applies only to powers vested solely in the person to whom the income or corpus may be paid. Thus, if a person has the power to vest the income of a trust in his or her spouse, that power does not result in taxation of either spouse, except to the extent that income is actually distributed to the potential beneficiary spouse. Moreover, it appears that in order to result in taxation under § 678, a power must be unrestricted, as opposed to a power limited by a standard such as "support" or "needs," at least if the standard imposes, as a practical matter, a substantial constraint on the holder of the power. See 3 B. Bittker & L. Lokken, Federal Taxation of Income, Estates, and Gifts ¶80.8.1 (2d ed. 1991).

I. GIFTS TO MINORS UNDER UNIFORM ACTS

REVENUE RULING 59-357
1959-2 C.B. 212

... Uniform laws have been adopted in many states to facilitate gifts to minors. Generally, these laws eliminate the usual requirement that a guardian be appointed or a trust set up when a minor is to be the donee of a gift. Under the Model Gifts of Securities to Minors Act, a donor may appoint either himself or a member of the minor's family as custodian to manage a gift of securities. The Uniform Gifts to Minors Act[16] provides that money as well as

---

16. [The Uniform Gifts to Minors Act has been succeeded, and replaced in most states, by the Uniform Transfers to Minors Act, which is broader in scope. — EDS.]

securities may be the subject of a gift to a minor and that a bank, trust company, or any adult may act as custodian. When a gift is made pursuant to the model or uniform act the property vests absolutely in the minor. The custodian is authorized to apply as much of the income or principal held by him for the benefit of the minor as he may deem advisable in his sole discretion. Income and principal not so applied are to be delivered to the donee when he reaches the age of 21 or, in event of his prior death, to his estate. . . .

Revenue Ruling 56-484, C.B. 1956-2, 23, holds that income, which is derived from property transferred under the Model Gifts of Securities to Minors Act and which is used in the discharge or satisfaction, in whole or in part, of a legal obligation of any person to support or maintain a minor, is taxable to such a person to the extent so used, but is otherwise taxable to the minor donee. . . .

The provision of the Uniform Gifts to Minors Act regarding the powers of the custodian as to distributions differs from the comparable provision of the Model Gifts of Securities to Minors Act in only three respects. First, the "model" act authorizes the custodian to apply so much of the income from the securities

> as he may deem advisable for the support, maintenance, general use and benefit of the minor in such manner, at such time or times, and to such extent as the custodian in his absolute discretion may deem suitable and proper, without court order, without regard to the duty of any person to support the minor and without regard to any funds which may be applicable or available for the purposes.

The "uniform" act does not use the term "absolute discretion," but this provision is otherwise virtually identical.

Second, the "uniform" act differs from the "model" act in that, in lieu of the latter part of the language quoted above, it provides that the income can be applied by the custodian for the minor's support without regard to the duty of himself or of any other person to support the minor or his ability to do so. Thus, the custodian, who may be legally obligated to support the minor, has power to use custodianship income for such support even though he may have adequate funds for this purpose.

Third, the "uniform" act contains a provision not found in the "model" act which gives a parent or guardian of the minor, or the minor himself after he reaches the age of 14, the right to petition the court to order the custodian to spend custodial property for the minor's support, maintenance or education. This provision, coupled with the "uniform" act's omission of the term "absolute" with reference to the discretion vested in the custodian, suggests the existence of a limitation on the custodian's otherwise uncontrolled power to withhold enjoyment of the custodial property from the minor, at least as to a portion of such property. Nevertheless, the custodian's power to withhold enjoyment is not substantially affected by such limitation.

In view of the foregoing, it is the opinion of the Internal Revenue Service that neither these nor other variations between the "model" act and the "uniform" act warrant any departure from the position previously published in . . . Revenue Ruling 56-484, supra, . . . in regard to gifts made under the "model" act. . . .

Income derived from property so transferred which is used in the discharge or satisfaction, in whole or in part, of a legal obligation of any person to support or maintain a minor is taxable to such person to the extent so used, but is otherwise taxable to the minor donee. . . .

QUESTION

Is the tax treatment of transfers under the Uniform Gifts to Minors Act (now the Uniform Transfers to Minors Act) consistent with the tax treatment of similar transfers using trusts?

J. FAMILY PARTNERSHIPS AND S CORPORATIONS

Unlike the trust, the partnership is not a separate taxable entity. A partnership return must be filed for the Treasury's information, reporting all partnership income and deductions, but the firm's net income is taxed to the partners individually, whether withdrawn or not, in accordance with their respective interests. §§ 701-704. Losses and credits of the firm are similarly allocated among the partners and deducted by them on their individual returns.

With the increase in restrictions on the use of the trust for tax splitting came, fortuitously or not, the rise of the family partnership. Typically, the head of the family, doing business as an individual proprietor, would make gifts of portions of his business capital to children or other relatives. Then a partnership would be formed with these relatives, usually with the income of the enterprise to be distributed among the partners according to their interests in the firm's capital. Ordinarily the new partners took no part in the management of the firm, though occasionally they served in clerical or other minor capacities. Sometimes the donor would reserve a salary for his or her own services, to be deducted before the profits accruing to capital were calculated. The highwater mark in this area is Tinkoff v. Commissioner, 120 F.2d 564 (7th Cir. 1941), involving an accountant who took his son into his accounting firm as a partner on the day the boy was born.

In Commissioner v. Culbertson, 337 U.S. 733 (1949), the Supreme Court attempted to resolve the problematic use of family partnerships to shift income by issuing a set of criteria with which to determine whether a partnership "is real within the meaning of the federal revenue laws." These criteria included relationship of the parties, their respective abilities and capital contributions, and the actual control of income. The *Culbertson* criteria produced considerable uncertainty as to the treatment of any given partnership, leading Congress in 1951 to adopt what is now § 704(e).

Under § 704(e), a partner in a partnership in which capital is a material income-producing factor is free to give some or all of his interest in the partnership to a family member. The family member, not the donor, will be taxed on the income attributable to that interest. Thus, a parent who owns a hotel may give a partnership interest to his or her child and the child will be taxed on his or her partnership income. This result is consistent with the tax principles discussed earlier in this chapter. As noted above, taxpayers may shift income from property by transferring ownership of the property. The gift of a partnership interest in which capital is a material income-producing factor represents a gift of the underlying capital of the partnership. On the other hand, suppose a parent gives his or her newborn infant an interest in his or her law partnership in the hope of shifting the income from that partnership. The attempt will fail because capital is not a material income-producing factor in a law partnership. Here it is income from services, rather than property, that the taxpayer is attempting to shift.

Even in cases in which capital is a material income-producing factor, the amount of income shifted is limited by the requirement that the donor receive reasonable compensation for services rendered to the partnership. The statute and accompanying regulations also contain rules designed to ensure that a partner is able to shift partnership income only by making an actual transfer of the partnership interest that is the source of that income. An individual may not, for example, retain voting rights or other indicia of ownership with respect to a partnership interest and succeed in shifting income from that interest through a putative transfer of the interest to a low-bracket family member.

Taxpayers sometimes conduct business affairs through so-called S corporations; that is, corporations governed by Subchapter S of the Code. S corporations, like partnerships, report income but do not pay tax. Instead, S corporation income, like partnership income, is taxed directly to the entity owners — here, the shareholders. The rules governing family S corporations are similar to those governing family partnerships. Section 1366 requires each family member to receive reasonable compensation for services rendered, and thus prevents a high-bracket family member from using an S corporation to shift personal service income.

K. GIFT AND LEASEBACK

BROOKE v. UNITED STATES
468 F.2d 1155 (9th Cir. 1972)

The taxpayer is a physician who practices medicine in Missoula, Montana. His family in 1959 included six children from ages 6 to 14. His income during the years in issue varied between $26,000 and $30,000. As a gift he deeded to his children real estate which was improved by a pharmacy, a rental apartment, and the offices of his medical practice. Following the conveyance the Montana State Probate Court appointed the taxpayer as guardian of the children. In this capacity the taxpayer collected rents from the pharmacy and apartment. Without a written lease, he also paid to himself as guardian for his children the reasonable rental value of his medical offices. The rents so collected were applied to the children's insurance, health and education. Expenditures were made for private school tuition, musical instruments, music, swimming and public speaking lessons. The taxpayer also purchased an automobile for his oldest child, and paid travel expenses to New Mexico for his asthmatic child.

The fundamental issue presented involves the sufficiency of the property interest transferred. The transfer of a sufficient property interest justifies the taxation of the donees and the deduction of the rental payments under § 162(a)(3) as ordinary and necessary business expenses by the donor.

In analyzing gift and leaseback cases, several factors must be considered: (1) the duration of the transfer; (2) the controls retained by the donor; (3) the use of the gift property for the benefit of the donor; and (4) the independence of the trustee. . . . None of the above factors prevents the income from being shifted in the instant case.

No issue is presented here as to the duration of the transfer — it was absolute and irrevocable; it was by warranty deed, unconditioned and unencumbered. . . . The absolute nature of the transfer distinguishes this case from those urged as controlling by the Government. See, e.g., Helvering v. Clifford, 309 U.S. 331 (1940) (five year trust). . . .

The taxpayer in this instance retained few, if any, controls over the trust property. He was obligated to and did pay the reasonable rental value of his medical offices. The fact that there was no written lease dispels any argument that the tenancy actually amounts to a reversion; the guardianship could at any time terminate the month to month tenancy. Likewise the taxpayer could at any time be terminated as guardian. Other controls retained over the trust property were consonant with possession as a tenant. Accordingly the findings of the District Court regarding both the irrevocable nature of transfer and the necessity of making rental payments are not clearly erroneous. This is in marked contrast with Commissioner v. Sunnen, 333 U.S. 591 (1948), where the taxpayer who assigned royalty agreements to his wife retained corporate control over the royalty agreements with the power to determine the amount of interest paid to his wife.

It is also apparent that trust benefits have not inured to the taxpayer as donor. The rental payments were expended solely for the insurance, health and education of the children. As discussed later, the taxpayer was not legally obligated to provide these benefits for his children.

Many decisions pivot on the issue of the independence of the trustee. . . . The necessary independence of the trustee is achieved in a guardianship. The Montana Probate Court administers a guardianship with the same requisite independence of any court-administered trust. See Mont. Rev. Codes §§ 91-4507, 4510, 4520 and 4522. Under the scrutiny of the court rental obligations must be met and accountings made. Mont. Rev. Codes § 91-4907. Guardianship property cannot be sold without court approval. Mont. Rev. Codes

§ 91-4518. Without belaboring the point there should be no lack of confidence in the supervision by our courts. A court appointed trustee — even though the taxpayer — offers sufficient independence.

If the taxpayer should at some future date breach his fiduciary duty toward his children, the government might well renew its challenge to the validity of the gift.

It must be emphasized that this transfer is not a sham or fraud. The Government adamantly asserts that this transfer lacks a business purpose, which therefore disqualifies it for a business deduction. Several leading cases employ such language. See, e.g., Gregory v. Helvering [infra page 781]. . . . Other cases require only that the transfer be grounded in substantial economic reality. . . .

The non-tax motives, as borne out by the record, are abundant and grounded in economic reality. The taxpayer desired to provide for the health and education of his children; avoid friction with partners in his medical practice; withdraw his assets from the threat of malpractice suits; and diminish the ethical conflict arising from ownership of a medical practice with an adjoining pharmacy. Neither substance nor impact denies this transfer professional or economic reality. This finding by the District Court is not clearly erroneous.

The Government further argues that even if deductions under § 162(a) are allowable, expenditures for the children's benefit merely serve to satisfy the taxpayer's legal obligations to support them imposed by § 677(b) and therefore are not allowable. The District Court determined that Rev. Rul. 56-484, 1956-2 Cum. Bul. at 23, establishes the applicability of local law in construing the meaning of support in Section 677(b). Montana law provides:

> The parent entitled to the custody of a child must give him support and education suitable to his circumstances.

Mont. Rev. Codes § 61-104. The District Court held that the expenditures made were not the legal obligations of the taxpayer under Montana law. The only authority cited by the Government which suggests the contrary, Refer v. Refer, 102 Mont. 121, 56 F.2d 750 (1936), is entirely limited to its facts.

The last issue in this appeal is raised by the taxpayer: Does a court administered guardianship constitute a trust under § 677(b)? Section 677 (or any regulation thereunder) does not refer to guardianships. However, the meaning of "trusts" is very broad and is specifically found in Section 641. Montana law, as interpreted by the District Judge, 292 F. Supp. at 572-573, includes guardianships within the meaning of "trusts." While a guardianship does not possess all trust requisites, for the purposes of taxation under Section 677, it must be considered a trust.

Affirmed.

ELY, Circuit Judge (dissenting).

I vigorously, although respectfully, dissent. The majority's opinion disturbs me for two principal reasons. First, I think it disregards the fundamental consideration that we are bound by prior decisions of our very own. See Etcheverry v. United States, 320 F.2d 873, 874 (9th Cir. 1963). Secondly, by creating yet another legal standard under which to assess the tax consequences of "gift and leaseback" transactions, the majority, in my judgment, adds further inconsistency to an area of tax law that is already fraught with too much semantic confusion.

Our decision controlling the tax treatment of a gift and leaseback transaction is Kirschenmann v. Westover, 225 F.2d 69 (9th Cir.), cert. denied, 350 U.S. 834 (1955), wherein we held

> Tax consequences are determined not from the formal aspect of a transaction, but from the actual substance of a piece of business. What is found here lacks *business meaning* for tax purposes. This court's decision in Shaffer Terminals, Inc. v. Commissioner, 9 Cir., 194 F.2d 539 [1952], is controlling.

225 F.2d at 71 (emphasis added).

In *Shaffer Terminals*, which involved a sale and leaseback transaction, we affirmed the Tax Court's disallowance of rental deductions, relying on the decision of the Tax Court and the then recently pronounced decisions of our Brothers of the Second and Fifth Circuits in White v. Fitzpatrick, 193 F.2d 398 (2d Cir. 1951), cert. denied, 343 U.S. 928 (1952) (gift and leaseback), and W. H. Armston Co. v. Commissioner, 188 F.2d 531 (5th Cir. 1951) (sale and leaseback); accord, Van Zandt v. Commissioner, 341 F.2d 440 (5th Cir.), cert. denied, 382 U.S. 814 (1965) (gift and leaseback). The prior law in our Circuit, therefore, as in the Second and Fifth Circuits, has been that both a sale and leaseback and a gift and leaseback transaction will be subjected to scrutiny under the "business purpose" test. Under that test, rentals cannot be treated as a valid business expense under Section 162 unless there is a legitimate business purpose motivating the transfer of the leased property. I have found no subsequent case in this Circuit that eschews the business purpose test, nor have I perceived its erosion in the other Circuits which follow the same standard. . . . Hence, since the District Court here found as a fact that "[t]he transfer did not serve any substantial business purposes" I would, unlike the majority, reverse on the basis of the binding effect of our prior decision in Kirschenmann v. Westover, supra. See Etcheverry v. United States, supra.

Having stated the primary ground for my concern, I would not ordinarily feel compelled to comment further on the composition of the majority's opinion. Yet, I do feel so compelled in this instance. While I do not share their view, I can understand my Brothers' reluctance to apply the business purpose test to a gift and leaseback transaction. Early cases adopting the business purpose test for a gift and leaseback transaction failed to recognize that a gift, unlike a sale of business property, is not motivated by a business purpose. Yet this distinction is important only if the gift and subsequent leaseback are viewed as separate and independent transactions. The bifurcation approach adopted by the majority does find some support in the decisions of other courts. . . . Therefore, I cannot honestly dismiss my Brothers' position on this point as being wholly unreasonable, even though I am convinced that the better approach requires an integration of the gift and leaseback transactions, at least in cases in which the donor-lessor was an occupant of the premises at the time the gift was made. When the transactions are thus integrated, it becomes obvious that the allowance of rental deductions requires satisfaction of the business purpose test at the inception of the transaction, the time when the gift was made. . . .

Even conceding the reasonableness of the majority's acceptance of the bifurcated transaction approach, I cannot acquiesce in its proposal of yet another test under which to judge a gift and leaseback. As I read the majority opinion, the standard formulated is that in order for the transaction to be recognized for tax purposes, the gift must be founded upon economic reality and must divest the donor of substantial control over the property. Such a test is unique in several respects. While my Brothers purport to rely on the Tax Court's rejection of the business purpose test, they do not adopt that court's formulation of the controlling legal standard:

> The mere transfer of legal title to property, however, is not conclusive for Federal income tax purposes, for the "sale" that lacks economic reality and business purpose, and the "gift" that leaves the donor with substantially the same control over the property that he had before, will simply be disregarded.

Penn v. Commissioner, 51 T.C. 144, 149-150 (1968).

In fashioning its new legal standard, the majority has excised one critical element from the appropriate test for the ascertainment of the validity of a sale and leaseback transaction — economic reality. Moreover, the majority directs its crucial inquiry not to the degree of control *retained* by the donor, as required by the Tax Court's analysis in Penn v. Commissioner, supra, but to the amount of control the donor *surrendered* in making the transfer. Here, the taxpayer, as sole guardian, had complete managerial powers over the property. He set the amount of the rentals, determined the terms, if any, of the unwritten lease, and decided when, if ever, the rentals were to be paid. He retained the power to mortgage, sell, or otherwise encumber or convey the property, the only impediment being that any such action on his part required, at some time, the approval of the court which had appointed him as the guardian of the estates of his children. I therefore find the majority opinion wholly at odds with the Tax Court's analysis in *Penn*. Viewed realistically, the situation here is that the taxpayer has retained "substantially the same control over the property that he had before." I cannot stretch my imagination so far as to believe that the taxpayer had an independent role, apart from his fatherhood and consistent occupancy and control, simply by virtue of some speculative degree of state court supervision over his supposed fiduciary operations.

The two standards which I recognize as being applicable to a case of this nature — the business purpose test, which should have bound us, and the standard relating to the donor's retention of control, which is applicable in the Tax Court — represent judicially imposed restrictions on the availability of a gift and leaseback transaction to effectuate a tax avoidance scheme premised upon intra-family income splitting. As I view these standards, they are interrelated. If a transaction is grounded upon economic reality and business purpose, then perhaps the majority's view as to the minimal independence of the fiduciary could, by some, be accepted. If, however, more leeway is given in the first instance by requiring only economic reality to support the transfer, then a much greater degree of independence should be required of the fiduciary. In my opinion, the necessary independence cannot exist when all managerial powers are retained by the transferor-lessor. See, e.g., Penn v. Commissioner, supra at 153-154. It seems obvious to me, under the facts of this case, that neither of the two recognized tests can be applied to the taxpayer's advantage.

NOTES AND QUESTIONS

1. *Guardianship versus other arrangements.* How much, if any, importance should be attached to the fact that a court-appointed guardian is subject to judicial supervision? In the case of a custodianship under the Uniform Gifts to Minors Act, there is no judicial involvement whatsoever, except in the extremely unlikely event that the child (or someone acting on behalf of the child) challenges the actions of the custodian. The same is generally true for trustees of ordinary trusts. Do you suppose that Dr. Brooke used a guardianship, rather than the more convenient device, a trust, in order to ensure that there would be judicial supervision?

The decision in the case was in favor of Dr. Brooke, but it was close. If Dr. Brooke had set up a trust with an independent trustee, he would have been on much safer ground. Do you suppose that this approach would have imposed significant burdens or created barriers to accomplishing the intended objectives?

2. *Nontax motives.* What is the relevance of nontax motives? Is the desire "to provide for the health and education of his children" a proper nontax motive? a proper business motive? If such a motive is sufficient, will there ever be a case in which a well-advised taxpayer fails to meet the motive test?

3. *Substance.* Did the father in *Brooke* substantially change his, and his children's, economic position (apart from taxes) by making the arrangements for the gift and leaseback?

4. *Property used in the business.* Should it matter that the property was used in the father's business? Suppose that an executive of IBM who owns $1 million worth of IBM common shares puts those shares in trust for the benefit of his children but appoints himself as trustee, with the power to vote the shares. How would the dissenting judge react to such a situation?

5. *A trust?* Was the court on sound ground in relying on the rules for taxation of trusts? In Rev. Rul. 56-484, 1956-2 C.B. 23, cited in Rev. Rul. 59-357, supra page 667, the Service ruled that a donor is taxable under § 61 on income used to discharge his or her obligation of support.

6. *Subsequent holdings.* In Rosenfeld v. Commissioner, 706 F.2d 1277 (2d Cir. 1983), the taxpayer had established a trust for the benefit of his children and had contributed to it a building that he owned and that he occupied in conducting his medical practice. The court, after citing conflicting cases in other circuits, concluded that the test of substantial change in the parties' rights and economic interests had been satisfied and refused to uphold the Commissioner's denial of a deduction for rent paid to the trust. The court

rejected the theory that there must be a business purpose for the gift and leaseback together, saying that a business purpose for the leaseback alone is sufficient. The court also indicated that it was important that there was an independent trustee and pointed out that the taxpayer did have a nontax motive in establishing the trust—namely, to guarantee his children's financial well-being.

L. SHIFTING INCOME THROUGH AND TO CORPORATIONS

1. Shifting Income Through a Corporation

If one concentrates on economic substance rather than on legal forms, it is hard to see why efforts to shift income to children or other dependents by use of ordinary corporations should be dealt with differently from similar efforts involving partnerships or S corporations. But the intellectual tradition of treating corporations as separate entities has exerted a strong influence on tax law. Moreover, a taxpayer who uses the ordinary corporation as a vehicle for shifting income must pay a price: a tax at the corporate level. For example, suppose that a person operates in corporate form a business that generates a net income of $250,000 per year, $200,000 of which is attributable to her services; gives 40 percent of the shares of stock of the corporation to her children, retaining the other 60 percent; and takes no compensation for her services. In effect, $80,000 worth of income from the performance of services (40 percent of $200,000) is diverted to the children, in apparent violation of the principle of Lucas v. Earl that income from the performance of services must be taxed to the one who earns it. The income ultimately realized by the children may take the form of dividends and at a highly conceptual level one might argue that their income is from "property" (the shares of common stock that they own) rather than from services. This ignores underlying economic reality, but in the case of ordinary corporations the reality is likely to be ignored; the income is not likely to be attributed to the parent. As suggested, however, the price of achieving the shift in income in our example is a corporation income tax, not just on the $80,000 diverted to the children but on the entire $250,000, plus the individual income tax on dividends paid by the corporation from the amount of corporate earnings left after the corporation income tax. The corporate-level tax can be reduced by paying a deductible salary to the parent, but to that extent the objective of shifting income is defeated.

Notwithstanding the presence of the corporate income tax, individuals sometimes attempt to shift income through corporations and then to family members. A corporation might have an unusable net operating loss and thus not face any corporate tax liability. In the past, corporate rates were sometimes significantly below individual rates, so that an advantage to income shifting remained even after the payment of the corporate income tax. This is still true for corporations with modest amounts of income. See § 11(b)(1)(A), setting the rate for corporate income up to $50,000 at 15 percent. Individuals also may shift income to corporations for other tax-related reasons. These reasons will vary from time to time and in the past have centered around more favorable treatment of pension plans.

FOGLESONG v. COMMISSIONER
621 F.2d 865 (7th Cir. 1980)

CUDAHY, Circuit Judge. . . .

This is an appeal from a decision of the United States Tax Court, 35 T.C.M. 1309 (1976), determining that the bulk of the commission income of a personal service corporation, Frederick H. Foglesong Co., Inc. (the "Corporation"), set up by a steel tubing sales representative, Frederick H. Foglesong (the "taxpayer"), was taxable to the taxpayer and not to the Corporation. The Tax Court for various reasons, which will appear, chose essentially to disregard the corporate form and, under Section 61 of the Internal Revenue Code and the assignment of income doctrine of Lucas v. Earl [supra page 623], to treat the bulk of the commission income as having been earned by, and as taxable to, the taxpayer. . . . We reverse and remand.

I

The facts here are not in substantial dispute. Frederick H. Foglesong, the taxpayer, was a sales representative for the Plymouth Tube division of the Van Pelt Corporation ("Plymouth Tube") and for the Pittsburgh Tube Company ("Pittsburgh Tube"), two manufacturers of cold drawn steel tubing. . . . There was evidence that taxpayer had an impressive reputation as a salesman, and this was one of the principal reasons he was retained as a sales representative by Plymouth Tube and Pittsburgh Tube.

On August 30, 1966, taxpayer incorporated his business as Frederick H. Foglesong Company, Inc. He, his wife and his accountant were listed as the incorporators on the certificate of incorporation. Of the one hundred shares of common stock issued by the Corporation (for a total subscription price of $1,000), taxpayer held 98 shares and his wife and accountant held 1 share each. The Corporation paid no dividends on its common stock during the taxable years in question, 1966 through 1969.

The Corporation also issued preferred stock to the taxpayer's four minor children (for which the total subscription price was $400). The four children received dividends totaling $32,000 over the period beginning September 1, 1966 and ending December 31, 1969. . . . The Corporation made its first salary payment to taxpayer on January 9, 1967, and he received a regular monthly salary after that date during the years which are relevant here. Taxpayer's salary income from the Corporation during calendar year 1967 was $56,500. In that year and in the succeeding relevant calendar years, he reported no personal income from any business as a sole proprietor. The respective net receipts of the Corporation from sales commissions and its deductions for compensation paid to taxpayer for the four taxable years in question are as follows:

Taxable year ending	Net receipts from commissions before payment of compensation to taxpayer[17]	Compensation to taxpayer deducted
August 31, 1967	$148,486.70	$41,500.00
August 31, 1968	100,482.23	55,000.00
August 31, 1969	99,429.35	65,000.00
August 31, 1970	121,018.24	73,700.00

After the formation of the Corporation, all commissions from Plymouth Tube and Pittsburgh Tube were paid to the Corporation. But a written agreement with Pittsburgh Tube was not executed until May 19, 1969, or with Plymouth Tube until January 1, 1971.

Taxpayer testified that he wished to incorporate his business in order to obtain the limited liability protection afforded by a corporate structure and also to provide a better vehicle for his planned expansion into several new business ventures. Subsequent to the formation of the Corporation, taxpayer interviewed a prospective salesman to help him in the New England area, but these negotiations were unsuccessful. The Corporation did, however, employ a secretary during its taxable years ending August 31, 1969 and 1970, paid her a salary and took corresponding deductions. Taxpayer asserted that he had unsuccessfully attempted to expand his sales business into other areas such as steel warehousing, transportation of steel tubing and the exporting of steel tubes to Europe but produced no documentation of these efforts.

The Corporation paid taxpayer a regular salary as a salesman, paid all of taxpayer's expenses incurred in connection with his sales activities, maintained a bank account, carried its own insurance coverage, maintained a company automobile and complied with all the formalities required of corporations in the state of New Jersey. The Corporation adopted bylaws, held an initial meeting of incorporators, at which the board of directors was elected, and conducted periodic board of directors' and stockholders' meetings as required by its bylaws. Taxpayer served as chairman of the board of directors as well as president and treasurer of the Corporation.

During the years in question here taxpayer did not enter into any written employment contracts with the Corporation nor did he enter into a covenant not to compete with the Corporation.

During these years taxpayer's only gainful activity was as an employee of the Corporation. He had no legal rights under the representation contracts with

17. These figures show the total net commission income (before payment of compensation to taxpayer) as reported by the Corporation on its tax returns for the taxable years in issue. They thus include the income generated on certain sales made within the Corporation's exclusive sales territories, but without any selling effort on taxpayer's part. Approximately two percent of the total commissions received by the Corporation during the taxable years in question resulted from these exclusive territorial arrangements.

Plymouth Tube and Pittsburgh Tube subsequent to the formation of the Corporation. Taxpayer testified that during the period at issue he did not engage in any business activity other than as an employee of the Corporation.

The Tax Court, inter alia, concluded on balance that, although there was no attempt by taxpayer to form a corporation to take advantage of losses incurred by a separate trade or business, tax avoidance considerations "far outweighed any genuine business concerns taxpayer may have had in setting up [the Corporation]." Nonetheless, the Commissioner conceded, and the Tax Court found, that the Corporation was a viable, taxable entity and not a mere sham during the years in issue.

But, in spite of its finding of viability (and strongly influenced by the apparent flagrancy of the tax avoidance), the Tax Court, in effect, substantially disregarded the Corporation for tax purposes. It found that during the years in question control over 98% of the commission income remained with taxpayer so as to cause such income to be taxable to him (as the person who earned it through his personal sales efforts) and not to the Corporation. The Tax Court based this result on Section 61 of the Code and the assignment of income doctrine of Lucas v. Earl, supra. With respect to those commissions which were received by taxpayer solely because of the exclusive territorial rights assigned to the Corporation under its agreements with Plymouth Tube and Pittsburgh Tube (amounting to approximately 2% of the total), the Tax Court held that the Corporation, not the taxpayer, was the party earning this income, and, hence, such commissions should be taxed to it.

The Tax Court found it unnecessary to reach the question whether the Commissioner was authorized to allocate the commission income to taxpayer under Section 482 of the Internal Revenue Code, which permits the Commissioner to reallocate income and expenses among commonly controlled "organizations, trades or businesses."

Personal service corporation tax cases reveal a tension between "the principle of a graduated income tax . . . and the policy of recognizing the corporation as a taxable entity distinct from its shareholders in all but extreme cases." Rubin v. Commissioner, 429 F.2d 650, 652 (2d Cir. 1970). The impact of the graduated income tax is eroded when income is split artificially among several entities or over several tax years. The assignment of income doctrine under Section 61 (as formulated in Lucas v. Earl) seeks to recognize "economic reality" by cumulating income diffused among several recipients through "artificial" legal arrangements. The attribution of income to its "true earner" is simply a species of recognizing "substance" over "form." See Rubin, supra, at 653.

But, if the issue is one of attributing the income of a corporation to its sole stockholder-employee who "really" earned it, we encounter the important policy of the law favoring recognition of the corporation as a legal person and economic actor. As Mr. Justice Holmes said in Klein v. Board of Supervisors, 282 U.S. 19, 24 (1930):

> But it leads nowhere to call a corporation a fiction. If it is a fiction it is a fiction created by law with intent that it should be acted on as if true. The corporation is a person and its ownership is a nonconductor that makes it impossible to attribute an interest in its property to its members.

In the instant case, the following circumstances, among others, are present: (1) the Corporation and not the taxpayer is the party to the contracts under which services are performed, (2) the Corporation is recognized to be a viable, taxable entity and not a mere sham, (3) non-tax business purposes are present even though tax avoidance is apparently a major concern,[18] (4) the Corporation has not been formed for the purpose of taking advantage of losses incurred by a separate trade or business, (5) the corporate form (and the status of the Corporation as an actual operating enterprise) has been consistently honored by the taxpayer and other parties to the transactions giving rise to the income, (6) the taxpayer does not render services as an employee to any entity other than the Corporation, (7) the Corporation is not disqualified from performing the Services required of it by contract because the law requires these services to be performed by an individual, (8) the entities paying or providing the income are not controlled or dominated by the taxpayer, and (9) as will appear, other and more appropriate legal bases exist for attacking apparent tax avoidance than broad-scale disregard of the corporate form through application of assignment of income theory. We note especially that the Tax Court did not find the Corporation to be a pure tax avoidance vehicle.

Under the circumstances of the instant case, we think it inappropriate to attempt to weigh "business purposes" against "tax avoidance motives" in a determination whether the assignment of income doctrine of Lucas v. Earl should apply, in effect, to substantially disregard the corporate form. Ostensibly this inquiry has been made in order to question the validity of a *transaction* purportedly entered into by a corporation, rather than the validity of the corporation itself. . . . But to apply Lucas v. Earl in this fashion under the circumstances present here is effectively (and more realistically) to nullify the determination that the Corporation is a viable, taxable entity and not a sham. . . .

The instant case is not unlike the early case of Fontaine Fox v. Commissioner, 37 B.T.A. 271 (1938), where a cartoonist transferred to his corporation his cartoon copyrights and various contracts pursuant to which he earned royalties and entered into an agreement with the corporation to render his services exclusively to it for a fixed salary. The corporation, in turn, made a contract with a distributor, who made payments to the corporation based on the percentage of sales of newspapers carrying taxpayer's cartoons. In *Fontaine Fox*, the Board of Tax Appeals distinguished Lucas v. Earl on the grounds that, rather than an assignment of income, *Fox* involved an assignment of property (the contracts with distributors); subsequent income arising from such property was income not of the assignor but of the assignee. Accord, Laughton v. Commissioner, 40 B.T.A. 101 (1939), rem'd, 113 F.2d 103 (9th Cir. 1940).

Although we do not regard the point as decisive, the Tax Court here found that, with respect to the contracts to perform sales services for Plymouth Tube and Pittsburgh Tube, there had been not only an assignment but a novation, with the corporation's becoming the sole party obligated to perform sales services and entitled to be compensated for such performance. Hence, this

18. Actual or potential purposes served by the Corporation here included the provision of limited liability and the furnishing of a vehicle for subsequent expansion of the business.

case is in essential concept quite distinguishable from Lucas v. Earl, where only income was assigned, and cannot be plausibly distinguished from *Fontaine Fox*, where the service contracts were assigned. Here not only the fruit but the tree itself was transferred to the Corporation.

In Rubin v. Commissioner, 51 T.C. 251 (1968), the Tax Court held that income was taxable to an individual who owned a 70% interest in a personal service corporation, which performed management services for another company. The same individual also controlled the company for which services were to be performed. The Tax Court attempted to analyze the problem both as one in which form differed from substance (the individual being held to work "directly" for the company) and in which the earning of the income was controlled by the individual rather than his corporation and was, therefore, taxable to the individual under the doctrine of Lucas v. Earl. In *Rubin*, the Tax Court suggested that the difference between the form over substance analysis and the assignment of income approach was only semantic. Thus it attempted to determine whether the form of the transaction, involving the personal service corporation, served any economic purpose and also whether the individual, in fact, controlled the earning of the income. The Tax Court found, first, that the income was properly taxable to the individual and distinguished both *Fox* and *Laughton* on the grounds that in *Rubin* the taxpayer was not contractually bound to (and in fact did not) render services exclusively to the personal service corporation (as he was bound to and did in *Fox* and *Laughton*). Second, in *Rubin*, the taxpayer controlled not only the personal service corporation, but also the corporation to which services were rendered; in *Fox* and *Laughton* only the personal service corporations themselves were controlled.

On the second point—taxpayer's control of the company receiving services—the instant case is like *Fox* and *Laughton* in that taxpayer here had no control over Plymouth Tube and Pittsburgh Tube. On the first point, although taxpayer here was not contractually bound to render services exclusively for the Corporation, he did in fact do so.

Rubin was later reversed on appeal by the Second Circuit, through Judge Friendly, who was of the view that "references to 'substance over form' and the 'true earner' of income merely restate the issue in cases like this: Who is the 'true earner'? What is substance and what is form?" Rubin v. Commissioner, 429 F.2d 650, 653 (2d Cir. 1970). Judge Friendly felt that Section 482 (providing for reallocation of the gross income of controlled taxpayers) was a more appropriate tool for use in this kind of case than "common law" tax doctrines such as assignment of income under Lucas v. Earl. In any event, Judge Friendly believed that the two bases on which the Tax Court distinguished *Fox* (and *Laughton*) were not relevant with respect to § 61.

We think that the Tax Court determination in *Rubin* might be easily distinguished here on the grounds that the taxpayer in the instant case worked exclusively for his personal service corporation (although he was not under contract to do so). Further, he did not own or control Pittsburgh Tube or Plymouth Tube, the entities to which services were rendered. Fundamentally, however, we believe that both *Rubin* and the instant case are more like *Fox* and *Laughton* than they are unlike those leading cases. In the resolution of the instant case we accord considerable deference to Judge Friendly's holding in *Rubin*. . . .

Roubik v. Commissioner, 53 T.C. 365 (1969), on which the Tax Court also relies, involved a professional corporation consisting of four radiologists, where the question raised was whether the business of the four principals was carried on by the corporation or outside it. In *Roubik*, the individual radiologists, not the corporation, maintained contractual relationships with the institutions for which services were rendered. The corporation did not own equipment nor did it incur the great bulk of operating expenses. It did not assign its shareholders to institutions or to tasks. In short, the corporate form was repeatedly flouted. . . .

The Tax Court here also places much emphasis on the absence of a written employment contract and/or a covenant not to compete between taxpayer and the Corporation. The elevation of form over substance in this analysis is manifest. If there were an employment contract and/or a covenant not to compete (in a single employee situation) and the employee-shareholder wished to withdraw his services from the corporate engagement, he could simply (as corporate officer) rescind the contract or covenant or decline to enforce it. There is no way of establishing an enforceable legal obligation which would require the sole shareholder-employee in a personal service corporation to work exclusively for the corporation. In the instant case, the employee-shareholder has in fact so worked exclusively. This fact is more significant than any paper obligation which might have been created. We note also that in the essentially meaningless corporate arrangements of *Roubik*, there was a covenant not to compete, which apparently had no realistic impact. *Roubik*, supra.

We believe that, where the issue is application of the assignment of income doctrine to effectively set aside the corporation, under the particular circumstances of this case (which we have carefully delineated), an attempt to strike a balance between tax avoidance motives and "legitimate" business purposes is an unproductive and inappropriate exercise. Such an approach places too low a value on the policy of the law to recognize corporations as economic actors except in exceptional circumstances. This is true whether the analysis used to dismantle the corporation pursues the rubric of assignment of income or substance over form. Here there are other more precise devices for coping with the unacceptable tax avoidance which is unquestionably present in this case. But there is no need to crack walnuts with a sledgehammer. . . .

In the instant case, Section 482 of the Internal Revenue Code appears available to allocate among controlled taxpayers "gross income, deductions, credits, or allowances" to prevent evasion of taxes or to clearly reflect the income of the controlled taxpayers. Other statutory provisions and "common law" doctrines, structured for more limited application, may also be available to remedy potential tax abuse. Thus, the dividends paid to taxpayer's children, . . . may . . . be subject to attack via . . . the assignment of income doctrine. . . . We think that the very aggressive tax avoidance measures which taxpayer employed here are vulnerable, but we express no opinion as to what statutory provisions or "common law" principles may properly address them. . . .

We, therefore, remand to the Tax Court for consideration of the issues surrounding the Commissioner's claim under Section 482 and other claims if available. For those purposes we do not disagree with the Tax Court's basic findings of fact in this case. But we do not intimate any conclusive view on what specific results with respect to these claims should be.

Reversed and remanded.

WOOD, Circuit Judge, dissenting.

As both sides of the issue are fully and fairly set forth in the majority opinion, little need be added in registering my dissent. Although I view it as a close case, I prefer in general the view of the United States Tax Court. In the alternative, I believe Section 482 of the Internal Revenue Code applies.

This corporation is nothing more than a few incorporating papers lying in a desk drawer of no significance except when a tax return is due. Mr. Foglesong continued to conduct his original one-man sales representative business as he always did, except he has become insulated by those incorporating papers from the taxes he should have been paying. For a subscription price of $400 for all the preferred stock, this "should-be" taxpayer accomplished, among other things, the diversion to his children of at least $8,000 of his own income for each of the four taxable years. His make-believe corporation is too transparent for me to accept for tax purposes under Section 61 of the Code. I respectfully dissent.

NOTES AND QUESTIONS

1. *Aftermath.* On remand, the Tax Court applied § 482 and again allocated 98 percent of the income to Mr. Foglesong. 77 T.C. 1102 (1981). Again the taxpayer appealed and again the Court of Appeals reversed and remanded, with the following explanation of the inapplicability of § 482 (691 F.2d 848, 851-852 (1982)):

Virtually all of the cases upholding the application of section 482, many of which the appellee and the Tax Court rely upon to support their position, have done so either in situations involving an attempt to offset the profits of one business with the losses of another or in situations in which the individual performed work other than that he did on behalf of the corporation. A case involving both situations is Borge v. Commissioner, 405 F.2d 673 (2d Cir. 1968), cert. denied, 395 U.S. 933. In that case, the taxpayer was a successful entertainer who also ran a poultry farm that suffered losses. He organized a corporation and transferred to it all of the assets of the poultry business. He then entered into an agreement to work for the corporation as an entertainer and thereby offset the poultry farm's losses by entertainment profits.

The court held that the section 482 dual business requirement was satisfied because despite the entertainment contract between Borge and his corporation, Borge in fact remained in a separate business. Instead of putting all of his entertainment revenues into the corporation, he put in only a percentage. "[Taxpayer] was not devoting his time and energies to the corporation; he was carrying on his career as an entertainer, and merely channeling a part of his entertainment income through the corporation." Id. at 676. An indicium that Borge, not the corporation, was running the entertainment business was that the parties seeking his services as an entertainer required that he, not the corporation, guarantee the contracts. Id. at 675. The court concluded that the only purpose of the arrangement between the taxpayer and his corporation was to offset poultry business losses with profits from the entertainment business. Id. at 677.

The instant case is markedly different. The taxpayer and his corporation were engaged in the identical business and Foglesong worked exclusively for the corporation. He did no consulting on the side nor did he engage in any other business. Furthermore, he instructed everyone to pay the corporation, not him. Finally, there was no attempt to evade taxes by offsetting the profits of one business against the losses of another.

That was not, however, the end of the story. The Court of Appeals remanded "for a consideration of whether assignment of income principles may be employed to allocate dividends and preferred stock received by Foglesong's children to Foglesong." 691 F.2d at 853. And in Haag v. Commissioner, 88 T.C. 604 (1987), the Tax Court reaffirmed its position that § 482 applies to one-person personal service corporations. The court noted that an appeal in *Haag* would go to the Eighth Circuit Court of Appeals, which, according to the Tax Court, in Wilson v. United States, 530 F.2d 772, 777 (1976), "implied" its support of the Tax Court rule. 88 T.C. at 614, n.4.

2. *Assignment of income doctrine versus ignoring the corporate entity.* Do you agree with the majority in *Foglesong* that application of Lucas v. Earl would be tantamount to disregard of the separate existence of the corporation? Did the decision of the Supreme Court in Earl make Mrs. Earl a nonperson? In his dissenting opinion in the Tax Court in Keller v. Commissioner, 77 T.C. 1014, 1042 (1981), aff'd, 723 F.2d 58 (10th Cir. 1983), Judge Wilbur says, "Mere existence — either of Mrs. Earl or petitioner's corporation — does not carry automatic immunity from the assignment of income doctrine."

3. *Motive.* Determination of the motives of a particular individual for engaging in a particular transaction is, of course, a difficult and dangerous undertaking. A rule that makes motive relevant tends to reward and encourage deceit, or at least disingenuousness. Is there an acceptable alternative: an inquiry into rational business basis (that is, whether a rational person might have entered into the transaction for nontax reasons)? In situations of the sort illustrated by *Foglesong*, what effect would such a test be likely to have?

4. *Formalities.* What do you think, judging from the opinion in *Foglesong*, about the importance of observing corporate formalities such as generating minutes of corporate meetings and maintaining a separate corporate bank account?

5. *Duration.* To what extent was Mr. Foglesong committed to the corporate arrangement? How difficult would it have been for him to terminate his relationship with the corporation? If he had done that, what would have been left for the children? Did Mr. Foglesong in effect have a power of termination that would have been fatal under § 676 if he had used a trust rather than a corporation?

6. *The employment contract.* If you were advising someone like Foglesong, would you recommend a written contract between that person and his or her corporation? Is it important that the person agree to work exclusively for the corporation? Why?

7. *"Property."* The court's discussion in *Foglesong* of the *Fontaine Fox* case should be compared with the material earlier in this chapter on assignment of income from copyrights, patents, etc. See supra page 657, Note 2.

M. PENSION TRUST

UNITED STATES v. BASYE
410 U.S. 441 (1973)

Mr. Justice POWELL delivered the opinion of the Court. . . .

Respondents, each of whom is a physician, are partners in a limited partnership known as Permanente Medical Group, which was organized in California in 1949. Associated with the partnership are over 200 partner physicians, as well as numerous nonpartner physicians and other employees. In 1959, Permanente entered into an agreement with Kaiser Foundation Health Plan, Inc., a nonprofit corporation providing prepaid medical care and hospital services to its dues-paying members.

Pursuant to the terms of the agreement, Permanente agreed to supply medical services for the 390,000 member-families, or about 900,000 individuals, in Kaiser's Northern California Region which covers primarily the San Francisco Bay area. In exchange for those services, Kaiser agreed to pay the partnership a "base compensation" composed of two elements. First, Kaiser undertook to pay directly to the partnership a sum each month computed on the basis of the total number of members enrolled in the health program. That number was multiplied by a stated fee, which originally was set at a little over $2.60. The second item of compensation—and the one that has occasioned the present dispute—called for the creation of a program, funded entirely by Kaiser, to pay retirement benefits to Permanente's partner and nonpartner physicians.

The pertinent compensation provision of the agreement did not itself establish the details of the retirement program; it simply obligated Kaiser to make contributions to such a program in the event that the parties might thereafter agree to adopt one.[19] As might be expected, a separate trust agreement establishing the contemplated plan soon was executed by

---

19. The pertinent portion of the Kaiser-Permanente medical service contract states:

Article II
Base Compensation to Medical Group

As base compensation to [Permanente] for Medical Services to be provided by [Permanente] hereunder [Kaiser] shall pay to [Permanente] the amounts specified in this Article H. . . .

Section H-4. Provision for Savings and Retirement Program for Physicians. In the event that [Permanente] establishes a savings and retirement plan or other deferred compensation plan approved by [Kaiser], [Kaiser] will pay, in addition to all other sums payable by [Kaiser] under this Agreement, the contributions required under such plan to the extent that such contributions exceed amounts, if any, contributed by Physicians. . . .

Permanente, Kaiser, and the Bank of America Trust and Savings Association, acting as trustee. Under this agreement Kaiser agreed to make payments to the trust at a predetermined rate, initially pegged at 12 cents per health plan member per month. Additionally, Kaiser made a flat payment of $200,000 to start the fund and agreed that its pro rata payment obligation would be retroactive to the date of the signing of the medical service agreement.

The beneficiaries of the trust were all partner and nonpartner physicians who had completed at least two years of continuous service with the partnership and who elected to participate. The trust maintained a separate tentative account for each beneficiary. As periodic payments were received from Kaiser, the funds were allocated among these accounts pursuant to a complicated formula designed to take into consideration on a relative basis each participant's compensation level, length of service, and age. No physician was eligible to receive the amounts in his tentative account prior to retirement, and retirement established entitlement only if the participant had rendered at least 15 years of continuous service or 10 years of continuous service and had attained age 65. Prior to such time, however, the trust agreement explicitly provided that no interest in any tentative account was to be regarded as having vested in any particular beneficiary.[20] The agreement also provided for the forfeiture of any physician's interest and its redistribution among the remaining participants if he were to terminate his relationship with Permanente prior to retirement.[21] A similar forfeiture and redistribution also would occur if, after retirement, a physician were to render professional services for any hospital or health plan other than one operated by Kaiser. The trust agreement further stipulated that a retired physician's right to receive benefits would cease if he were to refuse any reasonable request to render consultative services to any Kaiser-operated health plan.

The agreement provided that the plan would continue irrespective either of changes in the partnership's personnel or of alterations in its organizational structure. The plan would survive any reorganization of the partnership so long as at least 50% of the plan's participants remained associated with the reorganized entity. In the event of dissolution or of a nonqualifying reorganization, all of the amounts in the trust were to be divided among the participants entitled thereto in amounts governed by each participant's tentative account. Under no circumstances, however, could payments from Kaiser to the trust be recouped by Kaiser: once compensation was paid into the trust it was thereafter committed exclusively to the benefit of Permanente's participating physicians.

---

20. The trust agreement states:

   The tentative accounts and suspended tentative accounts provided for Participants hereunder are solely for the purpose of facilitating record keeping and necessary computations, and confer no rights in the trust fund upon the individuals for whom they are established. . . .

21. If, however, termination were occasioned by death or permanent disability, the trust agreement provided for receipt of such amounts as had accumulated in that physician's tentative account. Additionally, if, after his termination for reasons of disability prior to retirement, a physician should reassociate with some affiliated medical group his rights as a participant would not be forfeited.

Upon the retirement of any partner or eligible nonpartner physician, if he had satisfied each of the requirements for participation, the amount that had accumulated in his tentative account over the years would be applied to the purchase of a retirement income contract. While the program thus provided obvious benefits to Permanente's physicians, it also served Kaiser's interests. By providing attractive deferred benefits for Permanente's staff of professionals, the retirement plan was designed to "create an incentive" for physicians to remain with Permanente and thus "insure" that Kaiser would have a "stable and reliable group of physicians."[22]

During the years from the plan's inception until its discontinuance in 1963, Kaiser paid a total of more than $2,000,000 into the trust. Permanente, however, did not report these payments as income in its partnership returns. Nor did the individual partners include these payments in the computations of their distributive shares of the partnership's taxable income. The Commissioner assessed deficiencies against each partner-respondent for his distributive share of the amount paid by Kaiser. Respondents, after paying the assessments under protest, filed these consolidated suits for refund.

The Commissioner premised his assessment on the conclusion that Kaiser's payments to the trust constituted a form of compensation to the partnership for the services it rendered and therefore was income to the partnership. And, notwithstanding the deflection of those payments to the retirement trust and their current unavailability to the partners, the partners were still taxable on their distributive shares of that compensation. Both the District Court and the Court of Appeals disagreed. They held that the payments to the fund were not income to the partnership because it did not receive them and never had a "right to receive" them. . . . They reasoned that the partnership, as an entity, should be disregarded and that each partner should be treated simply as a potential beneficiary of his tentative share of the retirement fund.[23] Viewed in this light, no presently taxable income could be attributed to these cash basis[24] taxpayers because of the contingent and forfeitable nature of the fund allocations. . . .

We hold that the courts below erred and that respondents were properly taxable on the partnership's retirement fund income. This conclusion rests on two familiar principles of income taxation, first, that income is taxed to the party who earns it and that liability may not be avoided through an anticipatory

22. The agreed statement of facts filed by the parties in the District Court states:

The primary purpose of the retirement plan was to create an incentive for physicians to remain with [Permanente] . . . and thus to insure [Kaiser] that it would have a stable and reliable group of physicians providing medical services to its members with a minimum of turn-over. . . .

23. The Court of Appeals purported not to decide, as the District Court had, whether the partnership should be viewed as an "entity" or as a "conduit." 450 F.2d 109, 113 n.5, and 115. Yet, its analysis indicates that it found it proper to disregard the partnership as a separate entity. After explaining its view that Permanente never had a right to receive the payments, the Court of Appeals stated: "When the transaction is viewed in this light, the partnership becomes a mere *agent* contracting on behalf of its members for payments to the trust for their ultimate benefit, rather than a *principal* which itself realizes taxable income." Id., at 115 (emphasis supplied).

24. Each respondent reported his income for the years in question on the cash basis. The partnership reported its taxable receipts under the accrual method.

assignment of that income, and, second, that partners are taxable on their distributive or proportionate shares of current partnership income irrespective of whether that income is actually distributed to them. The ensuing discussion is simply an application of those principles to the facts of the present case.

II

Section 703 of the Code, insofar as pertinent here, prescribes that "[t]he taxable income of a partnership shall be computed in the same manner as in the case of an individual." § 703(a). Thus, while the partnership itself pays no taxes, § 701, it must report the income it generates and such income must be calculated in largely the same manner as an individual computes his personal income. For this purpose, then, the partnership is regarded as an independently recognizable entity apart from the aggregate of its partners. Once its income is ascertained and reported, its existence may be disregarded since each partner must pay a tax on a portion of the total income as if the partnership were merely an agent or conduit through which the income passed.[25]

In determining any partner's income, it is first necessary to compute the gross income of the partnership. One of the major sources of gross income, as defined in § 61(a)(1) of the Code, is "[c]ompensation for services, including fees, commissions, and similar items." § 61(a)(1). There can be no question that Kaiser's payments to the retirement trust were compensation for services rendered by the partnership under the medical service agreement. These payments constituted an integral part of the employment arrangement. The agreement itself called for two forms of "base compensation" to be paid in exchange for services rendered — direct per-member, per-month payments to the partnership and other, similarly computed, payments to the trust. Nor was the receipt of these payments contingent upon any condition other than continuation of the contractual relationship and the performance of the prescribed medical services. Payments to the trust, much like the direct payments to the partnership, were not forfeitable by the partnership or recoverable by Kaiser upon the happening of any contingency.

Yet the courts below, focusing on the fact that the retirement fund payments were never actually received by the partnership but were contributed directly to the trust, found that the payments were not includable as income in the partnership's returns. The view of tax accountability upon which this conclusion rests is incompatible with a foundational rule, which this Court has described as "the first principle of income taxation: that income must be taxed to him who earns it." Commissioner v. Culbertson, 337 U.S. 733, 739-740

---

25. There has been a great deal of discussion in the briefs and in the lower court opinions with respect to whether a partnership is to be viewed as an "entity" or as a "conduit." We find ourselves in agreement with the Solicitor General's remark during oral argument when he suggested that "[i]t seems odd that we should still be discussing such things in 1972." Tr. of Oral Arg. 14. The legislative history indicates, and the commentators agree, that partnerships are entities for purposes of calculating and filing informational returns but that they are conduits through which the taxpaying obligation passes to the individual partners in accord with their distributive shares.

(1949). The entity earning the income—whether a partnership or an individual taxpayer—cannot avoid taxation by entering into a contractual arrangement whereby that income is diverted to some other person or entity. Such arrangements, known to the tax law as "anticipatory assignments of income," have frequently been held ineffective as means of avoiding tax liability. The seminal precedent, written over 40 years ago, is Mr. Justice Holmes' opinion for a unanimous Court in Lucas v. Earl. . . . There the taxpayer entered into a contract with his wife whereby she became entitled to one-half of any income he might earn in the future. On the belief that a taxpayer was accountable only for income actually received by him, the husband thereafter reported only half of his income. The Court, unwilling to accept that a reasonable construction of the tax laws permitted such easy deflection of income tax liability, held that the taxpayer was responsible for the entire amount of his income.

The basis for the Court's ruling is explicit and controls the case before us today:

> [T]his case is not to be decided by attenuated subtleties. It turns on the import and reasonable construction of the taxing act. There is no doubt that the statute could tax salaries to those who earned them and provide that the tax could not be escaped by anticipatory arrangements and contracts however skillfully devised to prevent the salary when paid from vesting even for a second in the man who earned it. That seems to us the import of the statute before us and we think that no distinction can be taken according to the motives leading to the arrangement by which the fruits are attributed to a different tree from that on which they grew.

Id., at 114-115. The principle of Lucas v. Earl, that he who earns income may not avoid taxation through anticipatory arrangements no matter how clever or subtle, has been repeatedly invoked by this Court and stands today as a cornerstone of our graduated income tax system. . . . And, of course, that principle applies with equal force in assessing partnership income.

Permanente's agreement with Kaiser, whereby a portion of the partnership compensation was deflected to the retirement fund, is certainly within the ambit of Lucas v. Earl. The partnership earned the income and, as a result of arm's-length bargaining with Kaiser,[26] was responsible for its diversion into the trust fund. The Court of Appeals found the *Lucas* [sic] principle inapplicable because Permanente "never had the right itself to receive the payments made into the trust as current income." 450 F.2d, at 114. In support of this assertion, the court relied on language in the agreed statement of facts stipulating that "[t]he payments . . . were paid solely to fund the retirement plan, and were not otherwise available to [Permanente]. . . ." Ibid. Emphasizing that the fund was created to serve Kaiser's interest in a stable source of qualified, experienced physicians, the court found that Permanente could not have received that income except in the form in which it was received.

---

26. The agreed statement of facts states that the contracting parties were separate organizations independently contracting with one another at arm's length.

The court's reasoning seems to be that, before the partnership could be found to have received income, there must be proof that "Permanente agreed to accept less direct compensation from Kaiser in exchange for the retirement plan payments." Id., at 114-115. Apart from the inherent difficulty of adducing such evidence, we know of no authority imposing this burden upon the Government. Nor do we believe that the guiding principle of Lucas v. Earl may be so easily circumvented. Kaiser's motives for making payments are irrelevant to the determination whether those amounts may fairly be viewed as compensation for services rendered.[27] Neither does Kaiser's apparent insistence upon payment to the trust deprive the agreed contributions of their character as compensation. The Government need not prove that the taxpayer had complete and unrestricted power to designate the manner and form in which his income is received. We may assume, especially in view of the relatively unfavorable tax status of self-employed persons with respect to the tax treatment of retirement plans, that many partnerships would eagerly accept conditions similar to those prescribed by this trust in consideration for tax-deferral benefits of the sort suggested here. We think it clear, however, that the tax laws permit no such easy road to tax avoidance or deferment.[28] Despite the novelty and ingenuity of this arrangement, Permanente's "base compensation" in the form of payments to a retirement fund was income to the partnership and should have been reported as such.

III

Since the retirement fund payments should have been reported as income to the partnership, along with other income received from Kaiser, the individual partners should have included their shares of that income in their individual returns. §§ 61(a)(13), 702, 704. For it is axiomatic that each partner must pay taxes on his distributive share of the partnership's income without regard to whether that amount is actually distributed to him. Heiner v. Mellon, 304 U.S. 271 (1938), . . . articulates the salient proposition. After concluding that "distributive" share means the "proportionate" share as determined by the partnership agreement, id., at 280, the Court stated: "The tax is thus imposed upon the partner's proportionate share of the net income of the partnership, and the fact that it may not be currently distributable, whether by agreement of the parties or by operation of law, is not material." Id., at 281. Few principles of partnership taxation are more firmly established

27. Respondents do not contend that such payments were gifts or some other type of nontaxable contribution. . . .

28. Respondents contend in this Court that this case is controlled by Commissioner v. First Security Bank of Utah, 405 U.S. 394 (1972), decided last Term. [See supra page 629.] We held there that the Commissioner could not properly allocate income to one of a controlled group of corporations under § 482 where that corporation could not have received that income as a matter of law. The "assignment-of-income doctrine" could have no application in that peculiar circumstance because the taxpayer had no legal right to receive the income in question. Id., at 403-404. In essence, that case involved a deflection of income imposed by law, not an assignment arrived at by the consensual agreement of two parties acting at arm's length as we have in the present case.

than that no matter the reason for nondistribution each partner must pay taxes on his distributive share.

The courts below reasoned to the contrary, holding that the partners here were not properly taxable on the amounts contributed to the retirement fund. This view, apparently, was based on the assumption that each partner's distributive share prior to retirement was too contingent and unascertainable to constitute presently recognizable income. It is true that no partner knew with certainty exactly how much he would ultimately receive or whether he would in fact be entitled to receive anything. But the existence of conditions upon the actual receipt by a partner of income fully earned by the partnership is irrelevant in determining the amount of tax due from him. The fact that the courts below placed such emphasis on this factor suggests the basic misapprehension under which they labored in this case. Rather than being viewed as responsible contributors to the partnership's total income, respondent-partners were seen only as contingent beneficiaries of the trust. In some measure, this misplaced focus on the considerations of uncertainty and forfeitability may be a consequence of the erroneous manner in which the Commissioner originally assessed the partners' deficiencies. The Commissioner divided Kaiser's trust fund payments into two categories: (1) payments earmarked for the tentative accounts of *nonpartner* physicians; and (2) those allotted to *partner* physicians. The payments to the trust for the former category of nonpartner physicians were correctly counted as income to the partners in accord with the distributive-share formula as established in the partnership agreement. The latter payments to the tentative accounts of the individual partners, however, were improperly allocated to each partner pursuant to the complex formula in the retirement plan itself, just as if that agreement operated as an amendment to the partnership agreement. 295 F. Supp., at 1292.

The Solicitor General, alluding to this miscomputation during oral argument, suggested that this error "may be what threw the court below off the track." It should be clear that the contingent and unascertainable nature of each partner's share under the retirement trust is irrelevant to the computation of his distributive share. The partnership had received as income a definite sum which was not subject to diminution or forfeiture. Only its ultimate disposition among the employees and partners remained uncertain. For purposes of income tax computation it made no difference that some partners might have elected not to participate in the retirement program or that, for any number of reasons, they might not ultimately receive any of the trust's benefits. Indeed, as the Government suggests, the result would be quite the same if the "potential beneficiaries included no partners at all, but were children, relatives, or other objects of the partnership's largesse."[29] The sole operative consideration is that the income had been received by the

---

29. Brief for United States 21. For this reason, the cases relied on by the Court of Appeals, 450 F.2d, at 113, which have held that payments made into deferred compensation programs having contingent and forfeitable features are not taxable until received, are inapposite. . . . Indeed, the Government notes, possibly as a consequence of these cases, that the Commissioner has not sought to tax the *nonpartner* physicians on their contingent accounts under the retirement plan. Brief for United States 21.

partnership, not what disposition might have been effected once the funds were received.

IV

In summary, we find this case controlled by familiar and long-settled principles of income and partnership taxation. There being no doubt about the character of the payments as compensation, or about their actual receipt, the partnership was obligated to report them as income presently received. Likewise, each partner was responsible for his distributive share of that income. We, therefore, reverse the judgments and remand the case with directions that judgments be entered for the United States.

It is so ordered.

Mr. Justice DOUGLAS dissents.

NOTES AND QUESTIONS

1. *Partnership taxation.* To illustrate the tax treatment required by the decision in *Basye*, suppose that Permanente had five doctor partners, with ten nonpartner doctors working as employees of the partnership. Suppose that Kaiser paid to the retirement trust $500 for the partners ($100 per person) and $500 for the nonpartner doctors ($50 per person); that, as in the actual case, none of the doctors had a vested interest in the trust (because all retirement benefits would be forfeited if he or she were to quit before retirement); and that each of the five partners had an equal 20 percent interest in the partnership. Under the holding of the case, the partnership would have income of $1,000 when that amount was paid into the trust by Kaiser; there would be no deduction for the contingent liabilities to the nonpartner doctors; and each partner would be taxable on his or her $200 pro rata share of the partnership's income.

2. *Entity versus aggregate.* There are two possible views of partnerships such as Permanente. Under the entity view, the partnership is, like a corporation, a separate entity, with an existence of its own. Under this view, the partnership can be thought of as the earner of income, as if it were a person. The income of the partnership is then passed along pro rata to the partners, however, so the partners are taxable on it, not the partnership. The entity view of partnerships appears to have been adopted by the *Basye* Court, despite its disparagement of the entity/conduit distinction (see supra footnote 25). It seems also to be consistent with the fact that the partners were cash method taxpayers while the partnership used the accrual method (see footnote 24).

Under the aggregate view (which many people find difficult to understand), the partnership has no separate identity. It can be thought of as an abstract concept used as a shorthand device to reflect an agreement among the partners to act collectively, through designated representatives, in such matters as bargaining with Kaiser over compensation and keeping books and records. Under this view, which was adopted by the Court of Appeals in *Basye*, the partnership itself does not have income; it merely keeps track of the amounts received by some administrator on behalf of the doctors.

3. *Entity theory.* If one adopts the entity perspective, which of the following is the best theory or concept in support of the conclusion that the amounts paid into the trust are taxable currently? (a) Income has accrued, under standard principles of accrual accounting; (b) cash equivalence (see supra page 281); (c) constructive receipt (see supra page 276); (d) assignment of income, under cases like Lucas v. Earl; or (e) § 83 (see supra page 300).[30]

4. *Aggregate theory.* If one adopts the aggregate view of partnerships, what result does one reach on each of the theories or concepts listed in Note 3? In connection with the assignment-of-income concept, does it matter whether the trust is viewed as the agent of Kaiser, rather than the agent of Permanente? See Note 5.

5. *Characterization of the trust.* Suppose that it had been clear that the idea for setting up the retirement trust had originated with Kaiser, which wanted to ensure continuity of service by the doctors; that the doctors had resisted the use of the trust and would have preferred to take all their compensation in present payments; that the trustees had been selected by Kaiser; and that the documents relating to the establishment of the trust had stated that the trust is "an agent of Kaiser to receive certain payments for the benefit of individual doctors who are associated with Permanente." How would that have affected the Court's reliance on Lucas v. Earl? Would the result have been different? Compare Commissioner v. Olmsted Incorporated Life Agency, supra page 657.

---

30. Section 83 was adopted in 1969, after the years at issue in *Basye.* Note that under § 83(h) amounts set aside for employees are not deductible by the employer until they become taxable to the employee. Cf. § 404(a)(5). Such a restriction is irrelevant to a nontaxable, nonprofit organization like Kaiser. See supra page 287, Note 2.

8

CAPITAL GAINS AND LOSSES

In this final chapter, we examine in further detail a topic that has surfaced periodically throughout the book — i.e., the federal income tax treatment of capital gains and losses. Most students taking the basic federal income tax course are generally aware that the U.S. tax system offers preferential treatment of capital gains in some circumstances. The materials that follow are designed to help you supplement that general awareness with substantive and detailed legal knowledge. As you might suspect, the availability of a preferential rate for capital gains, as well as the law's special rules for capital losses, has put substantial pressure on the legal system to define the term "capital asset." The resulting body of law will be the primary focus of this chapter. We begin, however, with some basic background and an introduction to the statutory framework for capital gains and losses.

A. BACKGROUND AND STATUTORY FRAMEWORK

Throughout most of the history of income taxation in this country, a distinction has been drawn between ordinary income (e.g., salaries, interest, and profits from running a business) and "capital gain" — usually for the purpose of taxing the latter at lower rates. In loose, non-legal terms, one might describe "capital gain" as gain from the sale of property such as real estate, stocks, and bonds. As you know by now, however, the Internal Revenue Code rarely relies on loose, non-legal terms. The Code's reputation for linguistic precision is especially well deserved when it comes to capital gains and losses, an area bursting with defined terms.

1. Net Capital Gain

We begin our examination of the statutory framework with § 1(h), the subsection that specifies the maximum statutory capital gains tax rates. In reviewing this provision, take note that it begins with the language, "If a taxpayer has a *net capital gain* for any taxable year, the tax imposed by this section for such taxable year shall not exceed the sum of—" (emphasis added) and then goes on to specify the preferential statutory capital gains rates for different types of capital gain. The key point here for our purposes is that these preferential rates are not available unless the taxpayer has a "net capital gain." Thus, the key to unlocking the preferential rate structure is having "net capital gain," a term defined in § 1221(11) as "the excess of the net long-term capital gain for the taxable year over the net short-term capital loss for such year." But this is just the beginning of the defined terms. Like nesting dolls, the phrases "net long-term capital gain" (§ 1222(7)) and "net short-term capital loss" (§ 1222(6)) themselves contain multiple defined terms, which in turn contain further defined terms. Take a moment to review these provisions and how they fit together.

In a nutshell, these rules require a netting process involving short-term capital gains and losses (i.e., those arising from the sale of capital assets held for one year or less) and long-term capital gains and losses (i.e., those arising from the sale of capital assets held for more than one year). Only after netting the short-term gains with the short-term losses and the long-term gains with the long-term losses will the taxpayer will be able to determine if she has any "net capital gain." If she does, then the preferential rates set forth in § 1(h) will apply.

Once you take the time to master these netting rules, along with the underlying definitions, you may find yourself bristling at casual references by family and friends that "long-term capital gains are taxed at a lower rate." This statement is true as far as it goes. For example, if a taxpayer's sole transaction for the year is the sale for $30,000 of stock purchased several years ago for $20,000, then her "long-term capital gain" (assuming the stock is a capital asset in her hands) is $10,000, as are her "net long-term capital gain" and her "net capital gain." The result would be a lower tax rate—most likely 15 percent under current law—for that portion of the taxpayer's gross income. But this simple outcome requires a simple set of facts (one transaction for the year) and no need to contend with the netting rules.

Here's an example of how the netting rules apply when taxpayers have multiple transactions for the year. Assume that Cathy and her husband John sold the following four blocks of stock during the year: (1) *W* stock at a long-term gain of $10,000, (2) *X* stock at a long-term loss of $3,000, (3) *Y* stock at a short-term gain of $4,000, and (4) *Z* stock at a short-term loss of $9,000. In this scenario, Cathy and John have a net long-term capital gain of $7,000 (after netting the longs with the longs) and a net short-term capital loss of $5,000 (after netting the shorts with the shorts). As a result, assuming that these four transactions make up all of their sales of capital assets for the year, John and Cathy's "net capital gain" would be $2,000. This is the amount that would be taxed at the preferential rate.

But now suppose that it's December 15 and John and Cathy, having sold the four blocks of stock in the manner described above, are deciding whether to sell for $15,000 some *Q* stock that they bought just a few weeks ago for $10,000. In isolation, this transaction would generate $5,000 of short-term capital gain, which, according to a loose, non-legal understanding of the rules, would not benefit from the preferential rate structure. When added to the four transactions above, however, this short-term gain is absorbed by the outstanding net short-term capital loss, resulting in an increase of the couple's "net capital gain" from $2,000 to $7,000. In other words, the sale of an asset giving rise to $5,000 of short-term capital gain increases the amount of income subject to the preferential rate.

2. Statutory Tax Rates for Net Capital Gain

Under current law, the maximum nominal rate for individuals on most types of net capital gain is 15 percent, while ordinary income is now subject to a maximum marginal rate of 35 percent. § 1(a)-(d), (h)(1).[1] Beginning in 2008, for individuals whose income (including their capital gain) would otherwise be taxed at 15 percent or lower, adjusted net capital gain is subject to a zero-percent tax rate. § 1(h)(1)(B). In effect, Congress is attempting to introduce marginal rate progressivity to the taxation of capital gains, but with breakpoints between the brackets determined by reference to the taxpayer's total taxable income. The political impulse underlying these changes is understandable — Republicans generally prefer lower capital gains rates, while Democrats generally favor reducing taxes for lower-income households. However, the resulting rules, together with the rules described below for special categories of capital gain, require a maddeningly complex, difficult to understand, statutory provision (§ 1(h)) and a correspondingly complex tax return form. The fault for the complexity lies not with the IRS but with Congress. Until recent years the rules, as well as the tax form, were far simpler.

As just noted, in addition to applying different capital gains rates for taxpayers of different incomes, Congress has adopted different tax rates for different types of assets. For example, the maximum rate on the sale of certain small business stock is, in effect, 14 percent (as the result of the exclusion of 50 percent of the gain and the taxation of the remainder at a rate of 28 percent). § 1202. In order to qualify for this low rate, the stock must be acquired on initial issuance by the company or its underwriter (rather than from another stockholder) and must be held for more than five years. A small business corporation is defined, generally, as a company that is engaged in an active business and has no more than $50 million in assets immediately before or after it issues the stock. The maximum amount of gain subject to the favorable treatment cannot exceed $10 million or ten times the cost (adjusted basis) of

---

1. However, under § 1(h), net capital gain is added to taxable income and then taxed at the capital gain rates. The increase in taxable income in effect uses up some or all of the AMT exemption (see § 55 (b)(2) and (d)(3)), which in turn results in a higher AMT for other income. The net effect is that, depending on the amount of other income and the amount of net capital gain, the effective rate on capital gain can exceed 20 percent. Also, because the AMT disallows a deduction for state income taxes, the capital gain will be subject to the full state rate of tax on such gain. See Yvonne L. Hinson and Ralph B. Tower, Influence of Long-Term Capital Gains on Individual AMT, Tax Notes, January 19, 2004, p.403.

the stock. Stock in companies engaged in accounting, law, health, farming, banking, mining, and a variety of other activities does not qualify.

In contrast, gain from the sale of collectibles, such as art (or baseball cards) that would otherwise qualify for the 15 percent maximum rate on long-term capital gain is taxed at a maximum rate of 28 percent. Long-term gain from the sale of real property that would otherwise be treated as capital gain is taxed at a maximum rate of 25 percent to the extent of previously taken depreciation. More possible maximum rates are created by the interaction of the capital gain rates and the alternative minimum tax. Because of the different rates for different categories of net long-term gain, § 1(h) must, and does, provide rules for "stacking" the gains—which is part of the reason why that provision is almost impossible to follow with any reasonable amount of effort. Fortunately, the computations can be done by computer programs, but though the tax return itself is ingeniously devised, and yields the correct result to a person with the patience to follow its directions, its logic is beyond the grasp of all but the most sophisticated and experienced tax expert.

For corporations, the maximum rate on capital gain is 35 percent, which is the same as the maximum rate for ordinary income. §§ 11, 1201.

There is an additional advantage, apart from the favorable tax rates, to characterization of income as capital gain. Capital gain is gain from the sale of property. If a transaction is characterized as one involving the sale of property (as opposed, for example, to the rental of property), not only is the gain capital in nature, but before the gain is calculated a deduction is allowed for the basis of the property. In other words, cases focusing on the capital gain issue often decide implicitly what may be a difficult timing question—namely, whether some of the amount received should be treated as a recovery of investment (basis).

3. Net Capital Loss

Of course, taxpayers sometimes have capital losses that exceed their capital gains for the year. If this is the case, the resulting loss may be used to offset $3,000 of ordinary income. Any net loss above this $3,000 figure is defined as a "net capital loss" and may be carried forward to subsequent years, when it may be used to offset capital gains or, again, up to $3,000 of ordinary income. For example, assume that Dev sells stock for $10,000 that he purchased several years ago for $17,000, resulting in a long-term capital loss of $7,000. Assume further that Dev has $50,000 of salary income and no other capital asset sales for the year. Dev may deduct $3,000 of his capital loss from ordinary income as an above-the-line deduction, reducing his gross income to $47,000. The remaining $4,000 of "net capital loss" may be carried forward to the following year.

Capital gains and losses are reported on Schedule D, reproduced on the next two pages. Note that the form asks the taxpayer to list "Short-Term Capital Gains and Losses—Assets Held One Year or Less" in Part I and "Long-Term Capital Gains and Losses—Assets Held More Than One Year" in Part II. This is the "netting" process described above. For taxable year

SCHEDULE D (Form 1040) Department of the Treasury Internal Revenue Service (99)	Capital Gains and Losses ► Attach to Form 1040 or Form 1040NR. ► See Instructions for Schedule D (Form 1040). ► Use Schedule D-1 to list additional transactions for lines 1 and 8.	OMB No. 1545-0074 **2007** Attachment Sequence No. 12

Name(s) shown on return | | Your social security number

BARACK H. & MICHELLE L. OBAMA

Part I Short-Term Capital Gains and Losses - Assets Held One Year or Less

(a) Description of property (Example: 100 sh. XYZ Co.)	(b) Date acquired (Mo., day, yr.)	(c) Date sold (Mo., day, yr.)	(d) Sales price	(e) Cost or other basis	(f) Gain or (loss) Subtract (e) from (d)
1					

2	Enter your short-term totals, if any, from Schedule D-1, line 2	2		
3	Total short-term sales price amounts. Add lines 1 and 2 in column (d)	3		
4	Short-term gain from Form 6252 and short-term gain or (loss) from Forms 4684, 6781, and 8824		4	
5	Net short-term gain or (loss) from partnerships, S corporations, estates, and trusts from Schedule(s) K-1		5	
6	Short-term capital loss carryover. Enter the amount, if any, from line 10 of your **Capital Loss Carryover Worksheet** in the instructions		6	(7,136)
7	Net short-term capital gain or (loss). Combine lines 1 through 6 in column (f)		7	-7,136.

Part II Long-Term Capital Gains and Losses - Assets Held More Than One Year

(a) Description of property (Example: 100 sh. XYZ Co.)	(b) Date acquired (Mo., day, yr.)	(c) Date sold (Mo., day, yr.)	(d) Sales price	(e) Cost or other basis	(f) Gain or (loss) Subtract (e) from (d)
8					

9	Enter your long-term totals, if any, from Schedule D-1, line 9	9		
10	Total long-term sales price amounts. Add lines 8 and 9 in column (d)	10		
11	Gain from Form 4797, Part I; long-term gain from Forms 2439 and 6252; and long-term gain or (loss) from Forms 4684, 6781, and 8824		11	
12	Net long-term gain or (loss) from partnerships, S corporations, estates, and trusts from Schedule(s) K-1		12	
13	Capital gain distributions		13	
14	Long-term capital loss carryover. Enter the amount, if any, from line 15 of your **Capital Loss Carryover Worksheet** in the instructions		14	( )
15	Net long-term capital gain or (loss). Combine lines 8 through 14 in column (f). Then go to Part III on page 2		15	

LHA For Paperwork Reduction Act Notice, see Form 1040 or Form 1040NR instructions. Schedule D (Form 1040) 2007

720511/11-08-07

12

15330410 131470 40C01F 2007.05051 OBAMA, BARACK H. 40C01F_1

Schedule D (Form 1040) 2007   BARACK H. & MICHELLE L. OBAMA   Page 2

Part III | **Summary**

16	Combine lines 7 and 15 and enter the result.	16	-7,136.

If line 16 is:

- **A gain,** enter the amount from line 16 on Form 1040, line 13, or Form 1040NR, line 14. Then go to line 17 below.
- **A loss,** skip lines 17 through 20 below. Then go to line 21. Also be sure to complete line 22.
- **Zero,** skip lines 17 through 21 below and enter -0- on Form 1040, line 13, or Form 1040NR, line 14. Then go to line 22.

17   Are lines 15 and 16 **both** gains?

     ☐ **Yes.** Go to line 18.

     ☐ **No.** Skip lines 18 through 21, and go to line 22.

18   Enter the amount, if any, from line 7 of the **28% Rate Gain Worksheet** on page D-8 of the instructions .... ▶ | 18 |

19   Enter the amount, if any, from line 18 of the **Unrecaptured Section 1250 Gain Worksheet** on page D-9 of the instructions .... ▶ | 19 |

20   Are lines 18 and 19 **both** zero or blank?

     ☐ **Yes.** Complete Form 1040 through line 43, or Form 1040NR through line 40. Then complete the **Qualified Dividends and Capital Gain Tax Worksheet** on page 35 of the Instructions for Form 1040 (or in the Instructions for Form 1040NR). **Do not** complete lines 21 and 22 below.

     ☐ **No.** Complete Form 1040 through line 43, or Form 1040NR through line 40. Then complete the **Schedule D Tax Worksheet** on page D-10 of the instructions. **Do not** complete lines 21 and 22 below.

21   If line 16 is a loss, enter here and on Form 1040, line 13, or Form 1040NR, line 14, the **smaller** of:

- The loss on line 16 or   ⎫   SEE STATEMENT 12 | 21 | (3,000.)
- ($3,000), or if married filing separately, ($1,500)   ⎭

Note. When figuring which amount is smaller, treat both amounts as positive numbers.

22   Do you have qualified dividends on Form 1040, line 9b, or Form 1040NR, line 10b?

     ☐ **Yes.** Complete Form 1040 through line 43, or Form 1040NR through line 40. Then complete the **Qualified Dividends and Capital Gain Tax Worksheet** on page 35 of the Instructions for Form 1040 (or in the Instructions for Form 1040NR).

     ☒ **No.** Complete the rest of Form 1040 or Form 1040NR.

Schedule D (Form 1040) 2007

2007, the Obamas had no capital asset transactions but did carry over a loss of $7,136 from the previous year. Of this amount, $3,000 was available as a deduction against the Obamas' ordinary income. This deduction appears on the Obama Form 1040, line 13.

B. THE DEFINITION OF "CAPITAL ASSET"

As you may have noted from reviewing § 1222, capital gain or loss arises from the "sale or exchange of a capital asset." Note that there are two elements, "sale or exchange" and "capital asset." Most of the problems in distinguishing between capital gain and ordinary income involve interpretation of "capital asset." "Capital asset" is defined in § 1221 as all "property," with eight listed exceptions. "Property" is, of course, a broad and vague term. We will see that the courts have interpreted "property" narrowly in an effort to avoid extending capital gain treatment to transactions for which such treatment seems plainly inappropriate. See infra sections E, F, and G. The major function of the exceptions is to deny capital gain treatment for the ordinary gains and losses from operating a trade or business. The first five statutory exceptions (paraphrased) are:

1. The inventory, or stock in trade, of a business (either retail or manufacturing), and property held primarily for sale to customers in the ordinary course of a trade or business;
2. Real property or depreciable property used in a trade or business;
3. Copyrights and similar property held by their creators (but not copyrights purchased from the creator or patents);
4. Accounts receivable acquired in the ordinary course of a trade or business; and
5. U.S. government publications held by someone who received them free or at reduced cost (e.g., a member of Congress).

There is, however, a limitation on § 1221(2) that virtually swallows it up. The limitation is found in § 1231, which seems more a response to economic or political forces than to tax logic. The rule embodied in § 1221(2) seems logically correct since it is hard to see any good reason for distinguishing, for tax purposes, between gains or losses arising from normal business operations and gains or losses from disposing of assets used in the business. Nonetheless, at the beginning of World War II, Congress became concerned that people were being compelled to sell property for wartime uses, which subjected them to high income and excess-profits taxes on their gains. Apparently it was thought unfair to impose these high taxes on windfalls generated by wartime conditions, at least when other taxpayers were able to escape such taxes by not selling. Moreover, it was feared that the potential tax liability would inhibit people from selling property such as factory buildings, machinery, and ships to others who might be able to put them to better use in the war effort. These concerns led to the adoption of the predecessor of § 1231, which preserves the § 1221(2) taxpayer benefit of ordinary loss treatment where the taxpayer has a net loss but provides for capital gain treatment where there is a net gain. All sales or exchanges of assets described in § 1221(2) (depreciable property and real property used in a business), plus certain other transactions, are covered by § 1231. There is a complex set of rules for netting out of § 1231 gains and losses and for a carryover of losses.

Various other provisions govern whether certain specified assets or transactions are accorded capital-gain or capital-loss treatment. For example, § 1244 provides that loss on the sale of "small business stock" is treated as an ordinary loss even though it is plain that such stock is a capital asset within the contemplation of § 1221 and therefore any gain on its sale is capital gain. Section 631 provides capital-gain treatment for the proceeds of certain sales of timber and coal. In addition, § 1221(b)(3) now allows taxpayers to treat self-created musical works and copyrights in musical works as capital assets.

Sections 165 and 166 contain special provisions dealing with loans made by the taxpayer. If a loan is evidenced by a bond, the bond is a capital asset under § 1221, so its sale gives rise to capital gain or loss. Section 1232 ensures that the result is the same where the bond is retired by the issuer, and § 165(g) does the same where the bond becomes worthless. But suppose that the loan does not take the form of a bond. Suppose, for example, that an individual who is not in the finance business lends money to the corner grocer, as an investment. That is a "nonbusiness debt," and if it is not repaid, the loss is treated as a short-term capital loss under § 166(d). If, on the other hand, a wholesaler sells produce to the grocer on credit and that debt is not repaid, the loss is from a business debt and is treated as an ordinary loss.

C. POLICY CONSIDERATIONS

1. Rationale for Favorable Treatment of Capital Gain

Here is a brief description of the major arguments that have been used to justify favorable treatment of capital gain, with similarly brief responses to each. It should be apparent that some of the arguments had more force in past years when the maximum marginal rate exceeded 50 percent.

Bunching. Capital gains often accrue over many years. The effect of taxing the entire gain in one year may be to subject all, or almost all, of it to the maximum rate even though it might have been taxed at a lower rate if realized ratably during the entire period of ownership of the asset. This argument has little force because under the current rate structure most individuals and corporations realizing substantial capital gains will have been paying tax at the maximum rate at all relevant times.

Lock-in. A tax on capital gains tends to induce people to hold assets when they might otherwise sell and reinvest the proceeds in some other way. This effect is exacerbated by § 1014, under which basis is stepped up to fair market value at death, which has the effect of eliminating the potential tax liability on such gain. Suppose, for example, an elderly entrepreneur owns a business with a fair market value of $1 million and a basis of $10,000. In the absence of taxation, the business might be worth more to another person than the entrepreneur. The entrepreneur might wish to sell her business, use some of the proceeds to purchase an annuity, and give the remainder of the proceeds to her children. Another person might have better ideas (or think she has better ideas) on how to manage the business and might be willing to put more time in the business. Present law discourages sale, since it triggers a tax that can be entirely avoided if the entrepreneur holds onto the business until her death. The lock-in effect leads to immobility of capital and inefficient uses of capital, with assets not being held by those who will put them to best use. Some supporters of preferential treatment for capital gain believe the lock-in effect is so strong that a reduction in tax rates would actually increase tax revenue by dramatically increasing the number of investors who chose to sell appreciated assets.

Inflation. Favorable treatment of capital gain mitigates the possible unfairness of taxing gains that are attributable to inflation and are therefore not "real" gains. Capital-gain treatment is, however, an inaccurate solution to the inflation problem. It provides relief in some cases where inflation may have had little, if any, impact and fails to provide relief in other cases where inflation may have taken a heavy toll. A better solution is indexing — that is, increasing the basis of assets to reflect increases in an index of prices.

General incentive. Favorable rates of taxation of capital gains reduce the aggregate tax burden on returns on investments and thus provide an incentive, or reduce the disincentive, to saving, investment, and economic growth. Of course, to provide constant tax revenue, other forms of taxes must be raised, and these taxes may reduce economic growth. For example, a cut in the capital gain tax rate may require an increase in the tax rate on labor income, and that increase might reduce work effort. Supporters of favorable rates of taxation on capital income believe that the efficiency gains from reducing the tax on investment gains outweigh such efficiency losses. Again, there appear to be other, more accurate (and perhaps fairer) solutions to the problem (if it is one) of excessive tax burdens on returns on investments. Moreover, it may be that collectively we should save and invest less rather than more. Increased saving necessarily implies decreased consumption. This trade-off implies a transfer of consumption from the current generation to subsequent generations. The consumption that is forgone might be the private consumption of taxpayers or that of poor people to whom welfare payments might be made; or it might be public consumption for park services, public television, crime prevention, or national defense; or it might be any other private or public consumption.

Incentive to new industries. Since new industries tend to generate capital gain, favorable treatment of such gain will tend to stimulate such industries, and many people seem to take it for granted that such stimulation is a good thing. One can question whether new industries that need special tax breaks in order to flourish ought to be encouraged. It is one thing to say that the tax structure is too onerous for business and quite another to say that it is too onerous for new businesses and not for established businesses. Moreover, the capital gain preference is not in fact limited to new industries. If such industries do warrant favorable tax treatment, a more narrowly designed measure would be preferable. (In fact, such a measure exists: the § 1202 exclusion for small business stock, discussed supra page 697.)

Unrealized gains are not taxed. The favorable rate of taxation of capital gains reduces the disparity in treatment of realized and unrealized gains. If that disparity is the problem, however, the more appropriate solution would be an expansion of the provisions allowing tax-free exchanges, which takes us down a path that ultimately seems to lead to a consumption tax. See supra page 329.

Double-tax on corporate earnings. Corporate income is in some sense taxed twice: once when earned by the corporation, and once when repatriated to the shareholders in the form of dividends or corporate repurchase of shares. The rationale for this unfavorable tax regimen is unclear. A capital gain preference reduces the tax paid by shareholders on sale of their stock. Many observers support maintaining or expanding the break shareholders get on stock sale as an indirect way of ameliorating the double-tax on corporate income. One difficulty with this argument is that the capital gains preference is not limited to investments in corporate stock, but applies to individual investments in land and other assets.

2. Rationale for Limiting the Deductibility of Capital Losses

As noted above, capital losses are subject to an unfavorable set of tax rules. Individuals may deduct capital losses from capital gain, but individuals with capital losses in excess of capital gain may deduct only $3,000 of such losses in any year. Corporations may only deduct capital losses from capital gain.

The fact that capital losses are treated unfavorably when capital gains are treated favorably may seem odd. The limitation on deductibility of capital losses certainly works against some of the policy goals that support the favorable treatment of capital gain. For example, the limitation on deductions of capital losses presumably discourages, rather than encourages, capital investment, especially in new, innovative, and risky activities. But see § 1244.

Three explanations for the limitation on deduction of capital losses may be suggested. The first explanation, which relates to the realization requirement for recognition of gain or loss, is that the limitation is necessary to prevent taxpayers from manipulating the recognition of gains and losses to recognize "false" losses. Absent the limitation, a taxpayer could buy two sets of investments that are expected to move in opposite directions. For example, the taxpayer could buy some investments (such as gold) that are expected to rise with inflation and other investments (such as long-term bonds) that are expected to decline with inflation. If inflation rose, the decline in the value of one set of investments would be offset by the rise in the value of the other set of investments and the taxpayer would suffer no economic loss. However, the taxpayer could sell the investments that declined in value and retain the appreciated investments and therefore recognize a tax loss. The offsetting gain on the appreciated investments would not be recognized until those assets were sold. One obvious objection to using the capital loss restrictions to prevent manipulation of the realization requirement is that the loss restrictions apply even in cases where the taxpayer owns no appreciated assets and the manipulation of the realization requirement is therefore not possible.

A second explanation, related to the first, is also based on the realization requirement. Suppose a taxpayer has invested over the years in a diversified portfolio of common stocks and that some have risen in value while others have declined. Without the limitation on the deduction of losses, the taxpayer would have a strong incentive to sell the loss assets and retain the gain assets.

In the aggregate, over the long run, the result would be a substantial advantage to investors and a corresponding disadvantage to the Treasury (that is, to other taxpayers, who would be required to pick up the slack). By imposing a limitation on the deduction of losses, Congress in effect says to taxpayers, "If you want to recognize your losses, you should also recognize a similar amount of gains." The difficulty with this explanation, as with the previous explanation, has to do with the effects of the limitation on taxpayers who have losses and no gains. For such taxpayers, the government is in a "heads-I-win-tails-you-lose" position: The government shares in gains but bears none of the burden of losses.

A third, more cynical explanation for the capital loss limitations is that the unrestricted allowance of deductions for capital losses would decrease tax revenue and these days members of Congress are more concerned about revenue than they are about fairness or economic rationality.

COMPARATIVE FOCUS: South Africa's Decision to Tax Capital Gains

With the collapse of Apartheid and the subsequent election of Nelson Mandela as President in April 1994, South Africa embarked on an ambitious reform of its social, political, and legal institutions. The country's new constitution, approved by the Constitutional Court of South Africa in 1996, took effect in February 1997.

Among the many areas of South African law reform in the post-Apartheid era was taxation, including the question of whether and how the country's income tax should treat capital gains. Historically, South Africa had not taxed capital gains, instead explicitly excluding from the definition of gross income "receipts or accruals of a capital nature." As noted by two U.S. economists involved in the South African tax reform process in the late 1990s, the "absence of a capital gains tax provide[d] huge opportunities to avoid tax by characterizing labor or business income as capital gains." See Henry Aaron and Joel Slemrod, The South African Tax System: A Nation in Microcosm, Tax Notes (December 6, 1999).

After extensive study, including an examination of the tax treatment of capital gains and losses in nearly every country in the world, South Africa amended its Income Tax Act in 2001 to include a new "Capital Gains Tax" (CGT). Under the terms of the new CGT law, individual taxpayers must include 25 percent of capital gains (less an annual exclusion of R10,000 $1,000) as taxable income subject to the normal tax rates applicable to other sources of income. With a top marginal rate of 40 percent, the result is an effective rate on capital gains of no more than 10 percent.

Like the United States, South Africa provides for the non-recognition of gain or loss in several situations, known as "roll-overs" — including, for example, involuntary disposals (similar to U.S. § 1033) and transfers between spouses (similar to U.S. § 1041). In addition, South African law includes a provision, similar to § 121, providing for the exclusion of gain from the sale of a primary residence. Unlike the United States, however, South Africa applies its capital gains tax to transfers (other than transfers to a spouse) at death.

D.   PROPERTY HELD "PRIMARILY FOR SALE TO CUSTOMERS"

1.   Sale to "Customers"

BIELFELDT v. COMMISSIONER
231 F.3d 1035 (7th Cir. 2000)

Before POSNER, COFFEY, and KANNE, Circuit Judges.

POSNER, Circuit Judge.

Gary Bielfeldt (and his wife, but she is a party only by virtue of having filed a joint return with her husband), a large trader in U.S. Treasury notes and bonds, seeks to overturn a decision by the Tax Court denying him the right to offset immense trading losses that he incurred in the 1980s against all but $3,000 a year in ordinary income. He claims to be not a trader but a dealer and that the losses he incurred in the sale of the Treasury securities were losses connected with his dealer's "stock in trade"; such losses, even when they result as his did from the sale of a capital asset, are treated as ordinary rather than capital losses and can therefore be fully offset against ordinary income. In contrast, capital losses, while they can be fully offset against capital gains, can be offset against ordinary income only up to $3,000 a year. § 1211(b). Although the amount is arbitrary, the rationale for limiting such offsets is not; it is to reduce taxpayers' incentives to so structure their capital transactions as to realize losses today and defer gains to the future. If Bielfeldt's characterization of his status is sound, he is entitled to some $85 million in refunds of his federal income tax.

The standard distinction between a dealer and a trader is that the dealer's income is based on the service he provides in the chain of distribution of the goods he buys and resells, rather than on fluctuations in the market value of those goods, while the trader's income is based not on any service he provides but rather on, precisely, fluctuations in the market value of the securities or other assets that he transacts in. . . . This is not to deny that a trader, whether he is a speculator, a hedger, or an arbitrageur, serves the financial system by tending through his activities to bring prices closer to underlying values, by supplying liquidity, and by satisfying different preferences with regard to risk; he is not a parasite, as the communists believed. But he is not paid for these services. His income from trading depends on changes in the market value of his securities between the time he acquired them and the time he sells them.

Although one thinks of a dealer's inventory or stock in trade as made up of physical assets, it can be made up of securities instead. A stockbroker who owned shares that he sold to his customers at market price plus a commission would be a bona fide dealer. The example of a recognized "dealer" in securities that is closest to Bielfeldt's self-description because it blurs the distinction between deriving income from providing a service in the purchase or sale of an asset and deriving income from changes in the market value of an asset is a floor specialist on one of the stock exchanges. The specialist maintains an inventory in a specified stock in order to maintain liquidity. If its price soars, indicating that demand is outrunning supply, he sells from his inventory to meet the additional demand, and if the price of the stock plunges, he buys in the open market in order to provide a market for the people who are trying to sell. He is not paid by the stock market for this service, but is compensated by the income he makes from his purchase and sales and by commissions on limit orders (orders contingent on a stock's price hitting a specified level) placed with him by brokers. The Internal Revenue Service treats his gains and losses as ordinary income because the Internal Revenue Code classifies him as a dealer.

Treasury securities, at least the ones in which Bielfeldt transacted, are not sold on an organized exchange, and so there are no floor specialists — there is no floor. The market for Treasury securities is an over-the-counter market, like the NASDAQ. But the economic function that the specialists on the organized exchanges perform is independent of the form of the market, and dealers who specialize in Treasury securities (called "primary dealers," and discussed in the next paragraph) are close analogues of the floor specialists, just as NASD market makers are. There is even a new law that requires the primary dealers in Treasury securities, with some exceptions, to register with the SEC or the NASD.

Bielfeldt claims that he performs this function too, though he is not a registered or primary dealer. The securities in question are used to finance the national debt. During the period in which he incurred losses, there was no talk of paying off the debt — on the contrary, the debt was growing. To finance growth and redemptions, the Treasury would periodically auction large quantities of bonds and notes, which would be underwritten by a relative handful of primary dealers. Bielfeldt would buy in huge quantities from these dealers and resell in smaller batches, often to the same dealers, a few weeks later. His theory, which worked well for a few years and then turned sour, was that the Treasury auctions were so large that each one would create a temporary glut of Treasury securities, driving price down. He would buy at the depressed price and hold the securities off the market until, the glut having disappeared (because he was hoarding the securities), price rose, and then he would sell. He argues that had it not been for this service that he performed in the marketing of Treasury securities, the price the Treasury got at its auctions would have been depressed, with the result that interest on the national debt would be even higher than it is.

What he is describing is simply the social benefit of speculation. Think back to the Biblical story of Joseph. During the seven fat years, years of glut, Joseph "hoarded" foodstuffs so that there would be an adequate supply in the seven lean years that he correctly predicted would follow. In a money economy, he would have financed the program by buying cheap, which would be easy to do in a period of glut, and selling dear, which would be easy to do in a period of scarcity and would help to ration supplies in that period. He would buy cheap yet pay higher prices than people who were buying for consumption, since he would anticipate a profit from the later sale during the period of scarcity. Similarly, Bielfeldt hoarded Treasury securities during the fat weeks immediately after an auction so that there would be an adequate supply in the lean weeks (the weeks between auctions) that followed. That activity may have been socially beneficial, as he argues, but it is no different from the social benefits of speculation generally. His argument if accepted would turn every speculator into a dealer for purposes of the Internal Revenue Code. . . .

Unlike a floor specialist, Bielfeldt undertook no obligation to maintain an orderly market in Treasury securities. He did not maintain an inventory of securities; and because he skipped auctions that didn't seem likely to produce the glut that was the basis of his speculative profits, there were months on end in which he could not have provided liquidity by selling from inventory because he had no Treasury securities. In some of the tax years in question he participated in as a few as 6 percent of the auctions, and never did he participate in more than 15 percent. As a result, he was out of the market for as much as 200 days a year. He was a speculator, period. As the Federal Reserve Bank of New York, which kept track of Bielfeldt's trading in Treasury securities and sent updates to the IRS, put it, "his activities are in most cases outright speculation of interest rate movements."

In saying that Bielfeldt was not a specialist, we don't mean to imply that the Internal Revenue Service would be required to recognize as a dealer a trader who structured his operation to resemble that of a floor specialist but was not a floor specialist as defined in § 1236(d)(2). That issue is not before us. Nor is the bearing of . . . § 475(f), which allows a securities trader to treat paper gains and losses as ordinary rather than capital income by marketing to market the securities he owns at the end of the tax year, that is, by pretending they had been sold then. We note finally that Bielfeldt's alternative argument, that Treasury securities are "notes receivable acquired in the ordinary course of trade or business" and therefore are not capital assets within the meaning of § 1221(4), is frivolous. It implies that no bonds, government or private, are capital assets, since a bond, like a note receivable, is a promise to pay the holder of the instrument.

Affirmed.

NOTES AND QUESTIONS

1. *The general thrust of § 1221(1) — non-capital characterization of ordinary business profits.* As stated in section B, supra, § 1221(1) excludes from the definition of capital asset "stock in trade of the taxpayer or other property of a kind which would properly be included in the inventory of the taxpayer . . . or property held by the taxpayer primarily for sale to customers in the ordinary course of his trade or business." The broad intent of this section is clear (even if the underlying rationale for capital gain and loss treatment is not): Ordinary business activities generate ordinary income and loss. Unfortunately, it is often difficult to determine exactly what constitutes the form of ordinary business activities that should fall into § 1221(1) and out of capital gain and loss. This case, and the remaining cases in this section D, all examine this question.

2. *The meaning of the term "to customers."* The term "to customers" was added to the statute in 1934. It was designed to prevent "a stock speculator trading on his own account" from claiming ordinary losses on his transactions and thus canceling out his income from dividends, interest, etc., by what were apparently thought by Congress often to be economically insignificant transactions. H.R. Rep. No. 1385, 73d Cong., 2d Sess., 1939-1 C.B. (Pt. 2) 627, 632. In enacting the restriction, Congress seems to have overlooked the possibility that, in another part of the business cycle, "traders" might realize profits and would be able to report them as capital gains.

Judge Posner does not refer to the history behind the 1934 amendment in his decision. Does the fact that Congress specifically intended to exclude from capital asset gains from stock speculation support the decision? Relieve the pressure on the "trader v. dealer" distinction that underlies Posner's decision?

3. *Section 475.* Section 475 now requires securities dealers to mark-to-market any securities that are not properly treated as inventory or held for investment. Mark-to-market tax accounting requires a taxpayer to treat each security as if it is sold at the end of the year. Gain or loss is recognized as ordinary income or loss, and basis adjusted. Section 475(e) allows traders in securities (and dealers in commodities) to elect into mark-to-market accounting. The election applies to the taxable year in which it is made and may not be revoked without consent of the Service.

Do you imagine many traders elect mark-to-market? Why or why not? Under what circumstances would such an election be desirable?

4. *Investment securities held by dealers.* Section 1236 provides that if a securities dealer segregates securities in an investment account, those securities are treated as capital assets. This provision was obviously designed to allow firms dealing in securities to take advantage of the favorable treatment of capital gain. May a firm anxious to escape the capital loss restrictions avoid capital

asset treatment simply by avoiding compliance with § 1236? Even if it is clear that some securities are held as investments for the benefit of the members of the firm? What advice would you give to securities dealers on how to handle the firm's investments? See Stephens, Inc. v. United States, 464 F.2d 53 (8th Cir. 1972), cert. denied, 409 U.S. 1119 (1973), holding that an investment company was not a dealer when it acquired shares of corporations, drew off large cash dividends, then sold the stock at a loss because it had reduced the net assets of the companies by the dividends. The court found that the investment house was not entitled to an ordinary loss deduction on the sale of the stock.

2. "Primarily for Sale"

BIEDENHARN REALTY CO. v. UNITED STATES
526 F.2d 409 (5th Cir.), cert. denied, 429 U.S. 819 (1976)

[Before the court, en banc, thirteen judges — seven agreeing with the majority opinion, one concurring, and five dissenting.]

GOLDBERG, Circuit Judge.

[The facts, much abbreviated, are as follows: Taxpayer corporation, organized in 1923 to hold and manage family investments, held in the relevant years substantial investments in commercial real estate, a stock portfolio, a motel, warehouses, a shopping center, residential real property, and farm property. Among the last was a plantation purchased for $50,000 in 1935, totaling 973 acres, which was said to have been bought for farming and as a good investment. It was farmed for a few years and then leased for farming. The land was close to Monroe, Louisiana, and from 1939 through 1966, three basic residential subdivisions covering 185 acres were carved from the plantation. Although the plantation was named "Hardtimes," for Biedenharn Realty it was a good investment; 208 lots were sold in 158 separate sales at an $800,000 profit. In a pre-1964 settlement with the government it was apparently agreed that 60 percent of the gain would be reported as ordinary income and 40 percent as capital gain for the years of the settlement. The taxpayer then reported its gains for the years 1964 through 1966 on the same basis. The IRS asserted a deficiency, arguing that all the gains were ordinary income, and the taxpayer filed for refund claiming all the gains to be capital.

In addition to the subdivision sales, the taxpayer also sold approximately 275 other acres from the plantation in twelve separate sales starting in 1935. From other land that it owned, the company in the years 1923 through 1966 sold 934 lots, 249 before 1935 and 477 in the years 1935 through 1966. Improvements — streets, drainage, water, sewerage, and electricity — were made in the plantation subdivisions, at an aggregate cost of about $200,000.

The District Court found that the plantation was originally bought for investment and that the intent to subdivide arose later when the city of Monroe expanded in the direction of the plantation. Sales by the taxpayer largely resulted from unsolicited approaches by individuals, except that in the years 1964 through 1966 about 75 percent of the sales were induced by independent brokers with which the company dealt. The issue before the court as to all of the 1964 through 1966 sales from the subdivisions was whether the lots constituted property held by the taxpayer primarily for sale to customers in the ordinary course of its trade or business under § 1221(1)].

II . . .

The problem we struggle with here is not novel. We have become accustomed to the frequency with which taxpayers litigate this troublesome question. . . . The difficulty in large part stems from ad-hoc application of the numerous permissible criteria set forth in our multitudinous prior opinions.[2] Over the past 40 years, this case by case approach with its concentration on the facts of each suit has resulted in a collection of decisions not always reconcilable. . . .

Assuredly, we would much prefer one or two clearly defined, easily employed tests which lead to predictable, perhaps automatic, conclusions. However, the nature of the congressional "capital asset" definition and the myriad situations to which we must apply that standard make impossible any easy escape from the task before us. . . .

Yet our inability to proffer a panaceatic guide to the perplexed with respect to this subject does not preclude our setting forth some general, albeit inexact, guidelines for the resolution of many of the § 1221(1) cases we confront. . . . [W]e more precisely define and suggest points of emphasis for the major *Winthrop* delineated factors[3] as they appear in the instant controversy. . . .

III

We begin our task by evaluating in the light of Biedenharn's facts the main *Winthrop* factors—substantiality and frequency of sales, improvements, solicitation and advertising efforts, and brokers' activities—as well as a few miscellaneous contentions. A separate section follows discussing the keenly contested role of prior investment intent. Finally we consider the significance of the Supreme Court's decision in Malat v. Riddell 383 U.S. 569 (1966).

---

2. One finds evidence of the vast array of opinions and factors discussed therein by briefly perusing the 24 small-type, double column pages of Prentice-Hall's Federal Taxation ¶ 32,486 which lists the cases involving subdivided realty. See also 33 Mertens, The Law of Federal Income Taxation §§ 22.138-22.142 (Malone Rev.). The Second Circuit has called these judicial pronouncements "legion." Gault v. Comm'r, 2 Cir. 1964, 332 F.2d 94, 95.

3. In U.S. v. Winthrop, 5 Cir. 1969, 417 F.2d 905, 910, the Court enumerated the following factors: (1) The nature and purpose of the acquisition of the property and the duration of the ownership; (2) the extent and nature of the taxpayer's efforts to sell the property; (3) the number, extent, continuity and substantiality of the sales; (4) the extent of subdividing, developing, and advertising to increase sales; (5) the use of a business office for the sale of the property; (6) the character and degree of supervision or control exercised by the taxpayer over any representative selling the property; and (7) the time and effort the taxpayer habitually devoted to the sales. The numbering indicates no hierarchy of importance.

A. FREQUENCY AND SUBSTANTIALITY OF SALES

Scrutinizing closely the record and briefs, we find that plaintiff's real property sales activities compel an ordinary income conclusion. In arriving at this result, we examine first the most important of *Winthrop*'s factors — the frequency and substantiality of taxpayer's sales. Although frequency and substantiality of sales are not usually conclusive, they occupy the preeminent ground in our analysis. The recent trend of Fifth Circuit decisions indicates that when dispositions of subdivided property extend over a long period of time and are especially numerous, the likelihood of capital gains is very slight indeed. . . .

On the present facts, taxpayer could not claim *isolated* sales or a passive and gradual liquidation. . . .

The frequency and substantiality of Biedenharn's sales go not only to its holding purpose and the existence of a trade or business but also support our finding of the ordinariness with which the Realty Company disposed of its lots. These sales easily meet the criteria of normalcy set forth in *Winthrop*, supra at 912.

Furthermore, . . . one could fairly infer that the income accruing to the Biedenharn Realty Company from its pre-1935 sales helped support the purchase of the Hardtimes Plantation. Even if taxpayer made no significant acquisitions after Hardtimes, the *purpose, system, and continuity* of Biedenharn's efforts easily constitute a business. . . .

[T]he District Court sought to overcome this evidence of dealer-like real estate activities and property *primarily held for sale* by clinging to the notion that the taxpayer was merely liquidating a prior investment. We discuss later the role of former investment status and the possibility of taxpayer relief under that concept. Otherwise, the question of liquidation of an investment is simply the opposite side of the inquiry as to whether or not one is holding property primarily for sale in the ordinary course of his business. In other words, a taxpayer's claim that he is liquidating a prior investment does not really present a separate theory but rather restates the main question currently under scrutiny. . . .

B. IMPROVEMENTS

Although we place greatest emphasis on the frequency and substantiality of sales over an extended time period, our decision in this instance is aided by the presence of taxpayer activity — particularly improvements — in the other Winthrop areas. Biedenharn vigorously improved its subdivisions, generally adding streets, drainage, sewerage, and utilities. . . .

C. SOLICITATION AND ADVERTISING EFFORTS

Substantial, frequent sales and improvements such as we have encountered in this case will usually conclude the capital gains issue against taxpayer. Thus, on the basis of our analysis to this point, we would have little hesitation in finding that taxpayer held "primarily for sale" in the "ordinary course of [his] trade or business." "[T]he flexing of commercial muscles with frequency and continuity, design and effect" of which *Winthrop* spoke, supra at 911, is here a reality. This reality is further buttressed by Biedenharn's sales efforts, including those carried on through brokers. Minimizing the importance of its own sales activities, taxpayer points repeatedly to its steady avoidance of advertising or other solicitation of customers. Plaintiff directs our attention to stipulations detailing the population growth of Monroe and testimony outlining the economic forces which made Hardtimes Plantation attractive residential property and presumably eliminated the need for sales exertions. We have no quarrel with plaintiff's description of this familiar process of suburban expansion, but we cannot accept the legal inferences which taxpayer would have us draw.

The Circuit's recent decisions . . . implicitly recognize that even one inarguably in the real estate business need not engage in promotional exertions in the face of a favorable market. As such, we do not always require a showing of active solicitation where "business . . . [is] good, indeed brisk." . . . In cases such as *Biedenharn*, the sale of a few lots and the construction of the first homes, albeit not, as in *Winthrop*, by the taxpayer, as well as the building of roads, addition of utilities, and staking off of the other subdivided parcels constitute a highly visible form of advertising. Prospective home buyers drive by the advantageously located property, see the development activities, and are as surely put on notice of the availability of lots as if the owner had erected large signs announcing *residential property for sale.* We do not by this evaluation automatically neutralize advertising or solicitation as a factor in our analysis. This form of inherent notice is not present in all land sales, especially where the property is not so valuably located, is not subdivided into small lots, and is not improved. Moreover, inherent notice represents only one band of the solicitation spectrum. Media utilization and personal initiatives remain material components of this criterion. When present, they call for greater Government oriented emphasis on *Winthrop*'s solicitation factor.

D. BROKERAGE ACTIVITIES

In evaluating Biedenharn's solicitation activities, we need not confine ourselves to the . . . *Winthrop* theory of brisk sales without organizational efforts. Unlike in . . . *Winthrop* where no one undertook overt solicitation efforts, the Realty Company hired brokers who, using media and on site advertising, worked vigorously on taxpayer's behalf. We do not believe that the employment of brokers should shield plaintiff from ordinary income treatment. . . . Their activities should at least in discounted form be attributed to Biedenharn. To the contrary, taxpayer argues that "one who is not already in the trade or business of selling real estate does not enter such business when he employs a broker who acts as an independent contractor. Fahs v. Crawford, 161 F.2d 315 (5 Cir. 1947); Smith v. Dunn, 224 F.2d 353 (5 Cir. 1955)." Without presently entangling ourselves in a dispute as to the differences between an agent and an independent contractor, we find the cases cited distinguishable from the instant circumstances. In both *Fahs* and *Smith*, the taxpayer turned the entire property over to brokers, who, having been granted total responsibility, made all decisions including the setting of sales prices. In comparison, Biedenharn determined original prices and general credit policy. Moreover, the Realty Company did not make all the sales in question through brokers as did taxpayers in *Fahs* and *Smith*. Biedenharn sold the Bayou DeSiard and Biedenharn Estates lots and may well have sold some of the Oak Park land. In other words, unlike *Fahs* and *Smith*, Biedenharn's brokers did not so completely take charge of the whole of the Hardtimes sales as to permit the Realty Company to wall itself off legally from their activities.

E.   ADDITIONAL TAXPAYER CONTENTIONS

Plaintiff presents a number of other contentions and supporting facts for our consideration. . . . Taxpayer emphasizes that its profits from real estate sales averaged only 11.1% in each of the years in controversy, compared to 52.4% in *Winthrop*. Whatever the percentage, plaintiff would be hard pressed to deny the substantiality of its Hardtimes sales in absolute terms (the subdivided lots alone brought in over one million dollars) or, most importantly, to assert that its real estate business was too insignificant to constitute a separate trade or business.

The relatively modest income share represented by Biedenharn's real property dispositions stems not from a failure to engage in real estate sales activities but rather from the comparatively large profit attributable to the Company's 1965 ($649,231.34) and 1966 ($688,840.82) stock sales. The fact of Biedenharn's holding, managing, and selling stock is not inconsistent with the existence of a separate realty business. . . .

Similarly, taxpayer observes that Biedenharn's manager devoted only 10% of his time to real estate dealings and then mostly to the company's rental properties. This fact does not negate the existence of sales activities. Taxpayer had a telephone listing, a shared business office, and a few part-time employees. Because, as discussed before, a strong seller's market existed, Biedenharn's sales required less than the usual solicitation efforts and therefore less than the usual time. Moreover, plaintiff . . . hired brokers to handle many aspects of the Hardtimes transaction — thus further reducing the activity and time required of Biedenharn's employees.

Finally, taxpayer argues that it is entitled to capital gains since its enormous profits (74% to 97%) demonstrate a return based principally on capital appreciation and not on taxpayer's "merchandising" efforts. We decline the opportunity to allocate plaintiff's gain between long-term market appreciation and improvement related activities. . . . Even if we undertook such an analysis and found the former element predominant, we would on the authority of *Winthrop*, supra at 856, reject plaintiff's contention which, in effect, is merely taxpayer's version of the Government's unsuccessful argument in that case.

IV

The District Court found that "[t]axpayer is merely liquidating over a long period of time a substantial investment in the most advantageous method possible." 356 F. Supp. at 1336. In this view, the original investment intent is crucial, for it preserves the capital gains character of the transaction even in the face of normal real estate sales activities.

The Government asserts that Biedenharn Realty Company did not merely "liquidate" an investment but instead entered the real estate business in an effort to dispose of what was formerly investment property. Claiming that Biedenharn's activities would result in ordinary income if the Hardtimes Plantation had been purchased with the intent to divide and resell the property, and finding no reason why a different prior intent should influence this outcome, the Government concludes that original investment purpose is irrelevant. Instead, the Government would have us focus exclusively on taxpayer's intent and the level of sales activity during the period commencing with subdivision and improvement and lasting through final sales. Under this theory, every individual who improves and frequently sells substantial numbers of land parcels would receive ordinary income.[4]

While the facts of this case dictate our agreement with the Internal Revenue Service's ultimate conclusion of taxpayer liability, they do not require our acquiescence in the Government's entreated total elimination of *Winthrop's* first criterion, "the nature and purpose of the acquisition."

We reject the Government's sweeping contention that prior investment intent is always irrelevant. There will be instances where an initial investment purpose endures in controlling fashion notwithstanding continuing sales activity. We doubt that this aperture, where an active subdivider and improver receives capital gains, is very wide; yet we believe it exists. We would most generally find such an opening where the change from investment holding to sales activity results from unanticipated, externally induced factors which make impossible the continued preexisting use of the realty.... Acts of God, condemnation of part of one's property, new and unfavorable zoning regulations, or other events forcing alteration of taxpayer's plans create situations making possible subdivision and improvement as a part of a capital gains disposition....

The distinction drawn above reflects our belief that Congress did not intend to automatically disqualify from capital gains bona fide investors forced to abandon prior purposes for reasons beyond their control. At times, the Code may be severe, and this Court may construe it strictly, but neither Code nor Court is so tyrannical as to mandate the absolute rule urged by the Government. However, we caution that although permitting a land owner substantial sales flexibility where there is a forced change from original investment purpose, we do not absolutely shield the constrained taxpayer from ordinary income....

Clearly, under the facts in this case, the distinction just elaborated undermines Biedenharn's reliance on original investment purpose. Taxpayer's

---

4. The Government suggests that taxpayer can avoid ordinary income treatment by selling the undivided, unimproved tract to a controlled corporation which would then develop the land. However, this approach would in many instances create attribution problems with the Government arguing that the controlled corporation's sales are actually those of the taxpayer.... Furthermore, we are not prepared to tell taxpayers that in all cases a single bulk sale provides the only road to capital gains.

change of purpose was entirely voluntary and therefore does not fall within the protected area. Moreover, taxpayer's original investment intent, even if considered a factor sharply supporting capital gains treatment, is so overwhelmed by the other *Winthrop* factors discussed supra, that that element can have no decisive effect. However wide the capital gains passageway through which a subdivider with former investment intent could squeeze, the Biedenharn Realty Company will never fit.

V

The District Court, citing Malat v. Riddell, supra, stated that "the lots were not held . . . primarily for sale as that phrase was interpreted . . . in *Malat*. . . . " 356 F. Supp. at 1335. Finding that Biedenharn's primary purpose became holding for sale and consequently that *Malat* in no way alters our analysis here, we disagree with the District Court's conclusion. *Malat* was a brief per curiam in which the Supreme Court decided only that as used in Internal Revenue Code § 1221(1) the word "primarily" means "principally," "of first importance." The Supreme Court, remanding the case, did not analyze the facts or resolve the controversy which involved a real estate dealer who had purchased land and held it at the time of sale with the dual intention of developing it as rental property or selling it, depending on whichever proved to be the more profitable. . . . In contrast, having substantially abandoned its investment and farming intent, Biedenharn was cloaked primarily in the garb of sales purpose when it disposed of the 38 lots here in controversy. With this change, the Realty Company lost the opportunity of coming within any dual purpose analysis. . . .

VI . . .

We cannot write black letter law for all realty subdividers and for all times, but we do caution in words of red that once an investment does not mean always an investment. A simon-pure investor forty years ago could by his subsequent activities become a seller in the ordinary course four decades later. The period of Biedenharn's passivity is in the distant past; and the taxpayer has since undertaken the role of real estate protagonist. The Hardtimes Plantation in its day may have been one thing, but as the plantation was developed and sold, Hardtimes became by the very fact of change and activity a different holding than it had been at its inception. No longer could resort to initial purpose preserve taxpayer's once upon a time opportunity for favored treatment. The opinion of the District Court is reversed.

[Four judges joined in a dissent written by Judge Gee stating that the majority summarily discounted a critical trial court fact finding that taxpayer was still farming a large part of the land, that neither the plaintiff nor the court claimed any dual purpose, and that the majority placed preeminent emphasis on sales activities and improvements, effectively eliminating the other factors in *Winthrop*.]

NOTES AND QUESTIONS

1. *Standard of review.* In *Biedenharn*, the Fifth Circuit treated the "ultimate" issue of holding purpose as a question of law. In Byram v. United States, 705 F.2d 1418 (1983), however, responding to the Supreme Court decision on standard of review in Pullman-Standard v. Swint, 456 U.S. 273 (1982), the Fifth Circuit changed its position and held that the question of holding purpose is one of fact, subject to the "clearly erroneous" standard of review. In *Byram*, the court sustained a district court judgment for the taxpayer, who had, "during a three-year period, sold 22 parcels of real estate for over $9 million, netting approximately $3.4 million profit." In the taxpayer's favor, the court cited these facts:

> Byram made no personal effort to initiate the sales; buyers came to him. He did not advertise, he did not have a sales office, nor did he enlist the aid of brokers. The properties at issue were not improved or developed by him. The district court found that Byram devoted minimal time and effort to the transactions.

2. *Condominium conversion.* In Gangi v. Commissioner, 1987-561 T.C. Memo., Gangi and Maginn had been partners in the ownership of an apartment building. After a period of time in which they rented out the apartments, they converted the building to a condominium and sold the units. The court held that the gain on the sales of the units was capital gain. Its reasoning is reflected in these excerpts from its opinion:

> We conclude that Gangi and Maginn did not hold the building "primarily" for sale to customers in the ordinary course of business. They purchased the land and built the building as a retirement investment, and for 8 to 9 years rented the units in accordance with their initial investment motive. When for business and personal reasons they determined it was in their best interest to sell, a business judgment was made to convert the building to condominiums. This decision was made in connection with their investment in real estate, and not in the ordinary course of a business. While we are aware that the purpose for which a taxpayer originally holds the property is not determinative of how the gain from a subsequent sale will be treated for tax purposes, it is nevertheless an important factor to be considered. . . . Thus, while we concede that Gangi and Maginn "sold" the condominium units, we do not think that this activity rises to the level of holding property "primarily" for sale to customers. Petitioners' original intent is relevant for our purposes under all the facts and circumstances. . . . [W]e also determine that Gangi and Maginn were not selling units in the ordinary course of their trade or business. . . .
>
> Respondent urges us to conclude that Gangi and Maginn sold the units in the ordinary course of their trade or business. . . . Respondent points to petitioners' activities in connection with the conversion including the substantial sales, the advertising to increase the sales, the model condominium unit, and the overall involvement of the partnership with the conversion process.
>
> Specifically, respondent notes that 1) the partnership sold twenty-six units to twenty-six different purchasers during 1979 and two units to two purchasers in 1980; 2) the partnership expended $129,384.44 to convert the building into condominium units; 3) the partnership advertised the sale of the condominium

units in a local newspaper; 4) the partnership opened a model unit 6 days a week from noon to 5 to facilitate the sales; and, finally, 5) that the partnership received more money as a result of the conversion of the building into condominium units than it would have received had the building been sold intact. Respondent thus argues that Gangi and Maginn's efforts to sell the units rise to the level of producing sales in the ordinary course of a trade or business.

Petitioners view the transaction differently. In 1970, Gangi and Maginn formed a partnership, which constructed the building for investment purposes. From November 1970 to August 1978, the property was held solely as rental property. In June 1977, petitioners no longer wished to remain as partners, and they concluded that a conversion to condominiums would be the most profitable way for them to liquidate their investment. Maginn testified that the Glendale real estate market for rental real property had declined. Moreover, the building was "showing a relatively poor return. . . . " Confronted with the desire to terminate the partnership and a poor market to sell rental real estate, they decided the additional expenditures to convert the building were worthwhile. . . .

In Heller Trust v. Commissioner, 382 F.2d 675, 680 (9th Cir. 1967), the court held that where the facts clearly indicated that the taxpayer held his property as rental/investment property and that "this purpose continued until shortly before the time of a sale, and that the sale is prompted by a liquidation intent, the taxpayer should not lose the benefits provided for by the capital gain provisions."

In *Heller*, the taxpayer sold 169 duplexes (which formerly had been rented) between the years 1955 and 1958. He hired a staff, advertised the sale and opened a model unit in connection with the sales. The Ninth Circuit noted that the situation had changed between the time the taxpayer originally acquired the investment and the time the duplexes were sold. There was a decline in the taxpayer's health and in the economic conditions of the area in general.

The court commented that if it followed the lower court's treatment of the duplexes as being for sale in the ordinary course of business, the court could not conceive of "how persons with an investment such as we have here could bring themselves within the purview of the capital gains provisions of the statute where . . . they had to abandon a disappointing investment by means of a series of sales." The court stated that they did not "believe that such a harsh treatment is warranted under the applicable law and the facts of this case." Heller v. Commissioner, supra at 680.

We find that petitioners' motives were equally as strong for abandoning their investment. Just as declining health is unanticipated, so is the disintegration of a business relationship between two partners. Moreover, from the testimony of Maginn, it is evident that there was a decline in interest for rental buildings in the Glendale real estate market at the time Gangi and Maginn decided to terminate the partnership and sell the building. . . .

. . . Gangi and Maginn placed advertisements in only one newspaper, the Glendale News Press. The extent of the partnership's advertising to promote the sales totalled $4,437. This amount is minimal compared to the gross sales price of the units of $2,114,295. Moreover, petitioners paid a low brokerage commission of 13/4 percent. . . . Gangi and Maginn were not substantially involved with the sales end of the condominiums.

It must also be noted that the majority of the improvements made to the building prior to sale consisted of maintenance such as painting and carpeting that would have been necessary even if petitioners continued to hold the building as rental/investment property. No structural changes were made to the units themselves and no state or local permits were required prior to the conversion. We do not find that these activities rise to the level of being in the ordinary trade or business of holding condominium units for sale to customers. . . .

3. *Real estate "dealers."* (a) Compare the taxpayer in *Biedenharn* with the taxpayer in *Bielfeldt.* Is there any reason of policy why one should realize ordinary income and losses while the other has capital gains and losses? If the persons to whom Biedenharn sold land were "customers," as that term is used in § 1221(1), why were not the persons who bought securities from Bielfeldt also "customers"? Neither taxpayer had a regular clientele of the kind enjoyed by a department store or other dealer in merchandise. How do the taxpayers in each of these two cases compare with a television manufacturer that sells to distributors? with the distributors, which sell to retailers? with an importer of television sets, which buys from distributors in Japan and sells to distributors in the United States?

(b) While the relevance of most of the factors discussed by the court in *Biedenharn* is easy enough to see, the effect of the use of agents may be puzzling. To what extent should the activities of others be attributed to the owner? What if the owner of the property enters into a contract with a real estate firm in which the latter is paid a fixed fee plus a percentage of gain above a certain level and is given complete control of selling price and methods, with permission to subdivide and make improvements out of its fee? What if the owner subdivides and improves and then contracts with an agent to sell the lots, with the owner to receive a fixed price for each lot, regardless of the selling price? See Fahs v. Crawford, 161 F.2d 315 (5th Cir. 1947), distinguished in *Biedenharn* as a case where the broker made all sales and was given full responsibility over the project so that the taxpayer could wall himself off legally from the activities of the broker; Voss v. United States, 329 F.2d 164 (7th Cir. 1964), where the owner of farm land authorized a real estate dealer to arrange for subdividing and selling property for a fee; held, capital gain.

(c) All of the leading real estate development cases are like *Biedenharn* in that the taxpayer realized gain and argued for status as an investor rather than a dealer. For the tax planner, the challenge in such cases is to figure out how far one can go with development and sales activities without becoming a dealer. Roughly speaking, the answer is not far at all. Where real estate prices have declined, by contrast, real estate investors will want to know how much activity is necessary in order to qualify as a dealer so that losses will be ordinary. Suppose you represent a group of investors who bought a parcel of farm land several years ago and intended to hold it for investment until it became attractive to developers. Unfortunately, the value of the land has declined. They are ready to sell. The investors are doctors, lawyers, and other such professionals who have no inclination to become involved in the business of development and sales. Yet they would like to be able to treat their losses as ordinary losses. What advice would you give them?

E. TRANSACTIONS RELATED TO THE TAXPAYER'S REGULAR BUSINESS

While Congress, in § 1221, broadly defined capital assets as *all* "property," the word "property" cannot be given a broad, or even a plain-language, definition without violating informed notions of the congressional purpose in providing special treatment for capital gain or loss, however dimly perceived that purpose may be. For example, even though a landlord's rights to receive rent under a lease or an insurance agent's rights to renewal commissions might be thought of as "property," most knowledgeable people would agree that the landlord's sale of the leasehold or the insurance agent's sale of the rights to the renewal commissions should not produce capital gain. The cases that follow in this section, and most of the cases in the remainder of the chapter, reflect the efforts of the courts to narrow the concept of "capital asset."

The first case is Corn Products Refining Co. v. Commissioner, which appears immediately below. For the purpose of understanding and discussing the case, consider the following hypothetical and its description of the use of corn futures contracts. Suppose that *CP* is in the business of manufacturing corn syrup, which is made from corn, and that *CP* is committed to the sale of $1,200,000 worth of syrup six months hence. Suppose further that the price at which the syrup will be sold, the $1,200,000, will not vary with the price of corn but the price of the corn itself may change considerably between now and five months from now, when it must be acquired in order to make the syrup. *CP* is anxious to avoid the risk associated with a possible rise in the price of corn. Fortunately for *CP*, there is an active market in corn "futures." A corn future is a contract for the purchase (and delivery) of a specified amount of corn at a specified date in the future for a specified price. A person who buys a contract for such future delivery of corn is said to buy futures (that is, corn futures contracts) or to be "long" in futures. The seller of the contract is sometimes said to have taken a "short" position. (The holder of the short position could be a speculator who anticipates a decline in the price of corn or a person who is hedging against such a decline.) Suppose that *CP* buys futures contracts for the amount of corn it needs, that the price to be paid on delivery is $800,000, and that the cost of buying these contracts, plus all other expenses of manufacture of the syrup, will be $220,000, so the total costs of production are $1,020,000 and *CP* can expect to make a profit of $180,000. Now suppose that five months later, when the time has come for *CP* to take delivery of the corn and make the syrup, the price of corn for immediate delivery on the market — the so-called spot price — is $980,000. *CP* can follow either of two routes. Under Route A, *CP* would take delivery of the corn that it has contracted to buy under its futures contracts, paying $800,000. The result would be a total cost of $1,020,000 and a profit of $180,000, which plainly would be ordinary income, from its normal operations. Under Route B, *CP* would not take delivery on the corn but would instead sell the futures contracts. Ordinarily this is the more convenient way to do business. The profit on the sale of the corn futures contracts should be $180,000 — the difference between the spot price of the corn ($980,000) and the price at which the corn can be bought by a person holding the contracts ($800,000). Having sold the contracts, *CP* would buy the corn it needs on the spot market for $980,000. Disregarding the profit on the sale of the futures contracts, the production of the corn syrup would now be a break-even activity. See Table 8-1.

CORN PRODUCTS REFINING CO. v. COMMISSIONER
350 U.S. 46 (1955)

Mr. Justice CLARK delivered the opinion of the Court.

This case concerns the tax treatment to be accorded certain transactions in commodity futures. In the Tax Court, petitioner Corn Products Refining Company contended that its purchases and sales of corn futures in 1940 and 1942 were capital-asset transactions under [§ 1221]. . . .

Petitioner is a nationally known manufacturer of products made from grain corn. It manufactures starch, syrup, sugar, and their byproducts, feeds and oil. Its average yearly grind of raw corn during the period 1937 through 1942 varied from thirty-five to sixty million bushels. Most of its products were sold under contracts requiring shipment in thirty days at a set price or at market price on the date of delivery, whichever was lower.

In 1934 and again in 1936 droughts in the corn belt caused a sharp increase in the price of spot corn. With a storage capacity of only 2,300,000 bushels of corn, a bare three weeks' supply, Corn Products found itself unable to buy at a price which would permit its refined corn sugar, cerealose, to compete successfully with cane and beet sugar. To avoid a recurrence of this situation,

TABLE 8-1
Illustration of Use of Corn Futures Contracts

Route A (CP takes delivery under futures contracts)		
Revenue		$1,200,000
Costs		
Corn	$800,000	
Other	220,000	
		1,020,000
Net profit		$180,000
Route B (CP sells contracts and buys spot corn)		
Revenue		$1,200,000
Costs		
Corn	$980,000	
Other	220,000	
		1,020,000
Net profit, operations		-0-
Gain from sale of futures contracts		$180,000
Total gains and profits		$180,000

petitioner, in 1937, began to establish a long position in corn futures "as a part of its corn buying program" and "as the most economical method of obtaining an adequate supply of raw corn" without entailing the expenditure of large sums for additional storage facilities. At harvest time each year it would buy futures when the price appeared favorable. It would take delivery on such contracts as it found necessary to its manufacturing operations and sell the remainder in early summer if no shortage was imminent. If shortages appeared, however, it sold futures only as it bought spot corn for grinding.[5] In this manner it reached a balanced position with reference to any increase in spot corn prices. It made no effort to protect itself against a decline in prices.

In 1940 it netted a profit of $680,587.39 in corn futures, but in 1942 it suffered a loss of $109,969.38. . . . It now contends that its futures were "capital assets" under [§ 1221] and that gains and losses therefrom should have been treated as arising from the sale of a capital asset. In support of this position, it claims that its futures trading was separate and apart from its manufacturing operations and that in its futures transactions, it was acting as a "legitimate capitalist." U.S. v. New York Coffee & Sugar Exchange, 263 U.S. 611, 619. It denies that its future transactions were "hedges" or "speculative" dealings as covered by the ruling of General Counsel's Memorandum 17322, XV-2 C.B. 151, and claims that it is in truth "the forgotten man" of that administrative interpretation.

Both the Tax Court and the Court of Appeals found petitioner's futures transactions to be an integral part of its business designed to protect its manufacturing operations against a price increase in its principal raw material and to assure a ready supply for future manufacturing requirements. . . .

We find nothing in this record to support the contention that Corn Products' futures activity was separate and apart from its manufacturing operation. On the contrary, it appears that the transactions were vitally important to the company's business as a form of insurance against increases in the price of raw corn. Not only were the purchases initiated for just this reason, but the petitioner's sales policy, selling in the future at a fixed price or less, continued to leave it exceedingly vulnerable to rises in the price of corn. Further, the purchase of corn futures assured the company a source of supply which was admittedly cheaper than constructing additional storage facilities for raw corn. Under these facts, it is difficult to imagine a program more closely geared to a

---

5. The disposition of the corn futures during the period in dispute were as follows:

	Sales of futures thousand bushels	Delivery under futures thousand bushels
1938	17,400	4,975
1939	14,180	2,865
1940	14,595	250
1941	2,545	2,175
1942	5,695	4,460

company's manufacturing enterprise or more important to its successful operation.

Likewise the claim of Corn Products that it was dealing in the market as a "legitimate capitalist" . . . exercising "good judgment" in the futures market, . . . ignores the testimony of its own officers that in entering that market the company was "trying to protect a part of [its] manufacturing costs"; that its entry was not for the purpose of "speculating and buying and selling corn futures" but to fill an actual "need for the quantity of corn [bought] . . . in order to cover . . . what [products] we expected to market over a period of fifteen or eighteen months." It matters not whether the label be that of "legitimate capitalist" or "speculator"; this is not the talk of the capital investor but of the far-sighted manufacturer. For tax purposes, petitioner's purchases have been found to "constitute an integral part of its manufacturing business" by both the Tax Court and the Court of Appeals, and on essentially factual questions the findings of two courts should not ordinarily be disturbed. . . .

Petitioner also makes much of the conclusion by both the Tax Court and the Court of Appeals that its transactions did not constitute "true hedging." It is true that Corn Products did not secure complete protection from its market operations. Under its sales policy petitioner could not guard against a fall in prices. It is clear, however, that petitioner feared the possibility of a price rise more than that of a price decline. It therefore purchased partial insurance against its principal risk, and hoped to retain sufficient flexibility to avoid serious losses on a declining market.

Nor can we find support for petitioner's contention that hedging is not within the exclusions of [§ 1221]. Admittedly, petitioner's corn futures do not come within the literal language of the exclusions set out in that section. They were not stock in trade, actual inventory, property held for sale to customers or depreciable property used in a trade or business. But the capital-asset provision of [§ 1221] must not be so broadly applied as to defeat rather than further the purpose of Congress. Burnet v. Harmel, 287 U.S. 103, 108. Congress intended that profits and losses arising from the everyday operation of a business be considered as ordinary income or loss rather than capital gain or loss. The preferential treatment provided by [§ 1221] applies to transactions in property which are not the normal source of business income. It was intended "to relieve the taxpayer from . . . excessive tax burdens on gains resulting from a conversion of capital investments, and to remove the deterrent effect of those burdens on such conversions." Burnet v. Harmel, 287 U.S., at 106. Since this section is an exception from the normal tax requirements of the Internal Revenue Code, the definition of a capital asset must be narrowly applied and its exclusions interpreted broadly. This is necessary to effectuate the basic congressional purpose. This Court has always construed narrowly the term "capital assets" in [§ 1221]. See Hort v. Commissioner [infra page 731].

The problem of the appropriate tax treatment of hedging transactions first arose under the 1934 Tax Code revision. Thereafter, the Treasury issued G.C.M. 17322, supra, distinguishing speculative transactions in commodity futures from hedging transactions. It held that hedging transactions were essentially to be regarded as insurance rather than a dealing in capital assets and that gains and losses therefrom were ordinary business gains and losses.

The interpretation outlined in this memorandum has been consistently followed by the courts as well as by the Commissioner. While it is true that this Court has not passed on its validity, it has been well recognized for 20 years; and Congress has made no change in it though the Code has been re-enacted on three subsequent occasions. This bespeaks congressional approval. . . . Furthermore, Congress has since specifically recognized the hedging exception here under consideration in the short-sale rule of § 1233(a) of the 1954 Code.[6]

We believe that the statute clearly refutes the contention of Corn Products. Moreover, it is significant to note that practical considerations lead to the same conclusion. To hold otherwise would permit those engaged in hedging transactions to transmute ordinary income into capital gain at will. The hedger may either sell the future and purchase in the spot market or take delivery under the future contract itself. But if a sale of the future created a capital transaction while delivery of the commodity under the same future did not, a loophole in the statute would be created and the purpose of Congress frustrated.

The judgment is affirmed.

Mr. Justice HARLAN took no part in the consideration or decision of this case.

ARKANSAS BEST CORPORATION v. COMMISSIONER
485 U.S. 212 (1988)

Justice MARSHALL delivered the opinion of the Court.

The issue presented in this case is whether capital stock held by petitioner Arkansas Best Corporation (Arkansas Best) is a "capital asset" as defined in § 1221 of the Internal Revenue Code regardless of whether the stock was purchased and held for a business purpose or for an investment purpose.

I

Arkansas Best is a diversified holding company. In 1968 it acquired approximately 65% of the stock of the National Bank of Commerce (Bank) in Dallas, Texas. Between 1969 and 1974, Arkansas Best more than tripled the number of shares it owned in the Bank, although its percentage interest in the Bank remained relatively stable. These acquisitions were prompted principally by the Bank's need for added capital. Until 1972, the Bank appeared to be prosperous and growing, and the added capital was necessary to

---

6. Section 1233(a) provides that gain or loss from "the short sale of property, other than a hedging transaction in commodity futures," shall be treated as gain or loss from the sale of a capital asset to the extent "that the property, including a commodity future, used to close the short sale constitutes a capital asset in the hands of a taxpayer." The legislative history recognizes explicitly the hedging exception. H.R. Rep. No. 1337, 83d Cong., 2d Sess., p. A278; S. Rep. No. 1622, 83d Cong., 2d Sess., p. 437: "Under existing law bona fide hedging transactions do not result in capital gains or losses. This result is based upon case law and regulations. To continue this result hedging transactions in commodity futures have been specifically excepted from the operation of this subsection."

accommodate this growth. As the Dallas real estate market declined, however, so too did the financial health of the Bank, which had a heavy concentration of loans in the local real estate industry. In 1972, federal examiners classified the Bank as a problem bank. The infusion of capital after 1972 was prompted by the loan portfolio problems of the bank.

Petitioner sold the bulk of its Bank stock on June 30, 1975, leaving it with only a 14.7% stake in the Bank. On its federal income tax return for 1975, petitioner claimed a deduction for an ordinary loss of $9,995,688 resulting from the sale of the stock. The Commissioner of Internal Revenue disallowed the deduction, finding that the loss from the sale of stock was a capital loss, rather than an ordinary loss, and that it therefore was subject to the capital loss limitations in the Internal Revenue Code.[7]

Arkansas Best challenged the Commissioner's determination in the United States Tax Court. The Tax Court, relying on cases interpreting Corn Products Refining Co. v. Commissioner [supra page 721], held that stock purchased with a substantial investment purpose is a capital asset which, when sold, gives rise to a capital gain or loss, whereas stock purchased and held for a business purpose, without any substantial investment motive, is an ordinary asset whose sale gives rise to ordinary gains or losses. . . . The court characterized Arkansas Best's acquisitions through 1972 as occurring during the Bank's "'growth' phase," and found that these acquisitions "were motivated primarily by investment purpose and only incidentally by some business purpose." . . . The stock acquired during this period therefore constituted a capital asset, which gave rise to a capital loss when sold in 1975. The court determined, however, that the acquisitions after 1972 occurred during the Bank's "'problem' phase," . . . and, except for certain minor exceptions, "were made exclusively for business purposes and subsequently held for the same reasons." . . . These acquisitions, the court found, were designed to preserve petitioner's business reputation, because without the added capital the Bank probably would have failed. . . . The loss realized on the sale of this stock was thus held to be an ordinary loss.

The Court of Appeals for the Eighth Circuit reversed the Tax Court's determination that the loss realized on stock purchased after 1972 was subject to ordinary-loss treatment, holding that all of the Bank stock sold in 1975 was subject to capital-loss treatment. 800 F.2d 215 (1986). The court reasoned that the Bank stock clearly fell within the general definition of "capital asset" in Internal Revenue Code § 1221, and that the stock did not fall within any of the specific statutory exceptions to this definition. The court concluded that Arkansas Best's purpose in acquiring and holding the stock was irrelevant to the determination whether the stock was a capital asset. We granted certiorari . . . and now affirm.

---

7. Title 26 U.S.C. § 1211(a) states that "[i]n the case of a corporation, losses from sales or exchanges of capital assets shall be allowed only to the extent of gains from such sales or exchanges." Section 1212(a) establishes rules governing carrybacks and carryovers of capital losses, permitting such losses to offset capital gains in certain earlier or later years.

II

Section 1221 of the Internal Revenue Code defines "capital asset" broadly, as "property held by the taxpayer (whether or not connected with his trade or business)," and then excludes five specific classes of property from capital-asset status. Arkansas Best acknowledges that the Bank stock falls within the literal definition of capital asset in § 1221, and is outside of the statutory exclusions. It asserts, however, that this determination does not end the inquiry. Petitioner argues that in Corn Products Refining Co. v. Commissioner, supra, this Court rejected a literal reading of § 1221, and concluded that assets acquired and sold for ordinary business purposes rather than for investment purposes should be given ordinary-asset treatment. Petitioner's reading of *Corn Products* finds much support in the academic literature and in the courts.[8] Unfortunately for petitioner, this broad reading finds no support in the language of § 1221.

In essence, petitioner argues that "property held by the taxpayer (whether or not connected with his trade or business)" does not include property that is acquired and held for a business purpose. In petitioner's view an asset's status as "property" thus turns on the motivation behind its acquisition. This motive test, however, is not only nowhere mentioned in § 1221, but it is also in direct conflict with the parenthetical phrase "whether or not connected with his trade or business." The broad definition of the term "capital asset" explicitly makes irrelevant any consideration of the property's connection with the taxpayer's business, whereas petitioner's rule would make this factor dispositive.[9]

In a related argument, petitioner contends that the five exceptions listed in § 1221 for certain kinds of property are illustrative, rather than exhaustive, and that courts are therefore free to fashion additional exceptions in order to further the general purposes of the capital-asset provisions. The language of the statute refutes petitioner's construction. Section 1221 provides that "capital asset" means "property held by the taxpayer[,] . . . but does not include" the five classes of property listed as exceptions. We believe this locution signifies that the listed exceptions are exclusive. The body of § 1221 establishes a general definition of the term "capital asset," and the phrase "does not include" takes out of that broad definition only the classes of property that are specifically mentioned. The legislative history of the capital asset definition

8. See, e.g., Campbell Taggart, Inc. v. United States, 744 F.2d 442, 456-458 (C.A.5 1984); Steadman v. Commissioner, 424 F.2d 1, 5 (C.A.6), cert. denied, 400 U.S. 869 (1970); Booth Newspapers, Inc. v. United States, 157 Ct. Cl. 886, 893-896, 303 F.2d 916, 920-921 (1962); W. W. Windle Co. v. Commissioner, 65 T.C. 694, 707-713 (1976).

9. Petitioner mistakenly relies on cases in which this Court, in narrowly applying the general definition of capital asset, has "construed 'capital asset' to exclude property representing income items or accretions to the value of a capital asset themselves properly attributable to income," even though these items are property in the broad sense of the word. United States v. Midland-Ross Corp., 381 U.S. 54, 57 (1965). See, e.g., Commissioner v. Gillette Motor Co., 364 U.S. 130 (1960) ("capital asset" does not include compensation awarded taxpayer that represented fair rental value of its facilities); Commissioner v. P. G. Lake, Inc., [infra page 745] ("capital asset" does not include proceeds from sale of oil payment rights); Hort v. Commissioner, [infra page 724] ("capital asset" does not include payment to lessor for cancellation of unexpired portion of a lease). This line of cases, based on the premise that § 1221 "property" does not include claims or rights to ordinary income, has no application in the present context. Petitioner sold capital stock, not a claim to ordinary income.

supports this interpretation, see H.R. Rep. 704, 73d Cong., 2d Sess., 31 (1934) ("[T]he definition includes all property, except as specifically excluded"); H.R. Rep. 1337, 83d Cong., 2d Sess., A273 (1954) ("[A] capital asset is property held by the taxpayer with certain exceptions"), as does the applicable Treasury regulation, see 26 C.F.R. § 1.1221-1(a) (1987) ("The term 'capital assets' includes all classes of property not specifically excluded by section 1221").

Petitioner's reading of the statute is also in tension with the exceptions listed in § 1221. These exclusions would be largely superfluous if assets acquired primarily or exclusively for business purposes were not capital assets. Inventory, real or depreciable property used in the taxpayer's trade or business, and accounts or notes receivable acquired in the ordinary course of business, would undoubtedly satisfy such a business-motive test. Yet these exceptions were created by Congress in separate enactments spanning 30 years.[10] Without any express direction from Congress, we are unwilling to read § 1221 in a manner that makes surplusage of these statutory exclusions.

In the end, petitioner places all reliance on its reading of Corn Products Refining Co. v. Commissioner [supra page 721]—a reading we believe is too expansive. In Corn Products, the Court considered whether income arising from a taxpayer's dealings in corn futures was entitled to capital-gains treatment. The taxpayer was a company that converted corn into starches, sugars, and other products. After droughts in the 1930's caused sharp increases in corn prices, the company began a program of buying corn futures to assure itself an adequate supply of corn and protect against price increases. . . . The company "would take delivery on such contracts as it found necessary to its manufacturing operations and sell the remainder in early summer if no shortage was imminent. If shortages appeared, however, it sold futures only as it bought spot corn for grinding." . . . The Court characterized the company's dealing in corn futures as "hedging." . . . As explained by the Court of Appeals in Corn Products, "[h]edging is a method of dealing in commodity futures whereby a person or business protects itself against price fluctuations at the time of delivery of the product which it sells or buys." 215 F.2d 513, 515 (C.A.2 1954). In evaluating the company's claim that the sales of corn futures resulted in capital gains and losses, this Court stated:

> Nor can we find support for petitioner's contention that hedging is not within the exclusions of [§ 1221]. Admittedly, petitioner's corn futures do not come within the literal language of the exclusions set out in that section. They were not stock in trade, actual inventory, property held for sale to customers or depreciable property used in a trade or business. But the capital-asset provision of [§ 1221] must not be so broadly applied as to defeat rather than further the purpose of Congress. Congress intended that profits and losses arising from the everyday operation of a business be considered as ordinary income or loss rather

10. The inventory exception was part of the original enactment of the capital-asset provision in 1924. See Revenue Act of 1924, ch. 234, § 208(a)(8), 43 Stat. 263. Depreciable property used in a trade or business was excluded in 1938, see Revenue Act of 1938, ch. 289, § 117(a)(1), 52 Stat. 500, and real property used in a trade or business was excluded in 1942, see Revenue Act of 1942, ch. 619, § 151(a), 56 Stat. 846. The exception for accounts and notes receivable acquired in the ordinary course of trade or business was added in 1954. Internal Revenue Code of 1954, § 1221(4), 68A Stat. 322.

than capital gain or loss.... Since this section is an exception from the normal tax requirements of the Internal Revenue Code, the definition of a capital asset must be narrowly applied and its exclusions interpreted broadly....

The Court went on to note that hedging transactions consistently had been considered to give rise to ordinary gains and losses, and then concluded that the corn futures were subject to ordinary-asset treatment....

The Court in *Corn Products* proffered the oft-quoted rule of construction that the definition of capital asset must be narrowly applied and its exclusions interpreted broadly, but it did not state explicitly whether the holding was based on a narrow reading of the phrase "property held by the taxpayer," or on a broad reading of the inventory exclusion of § 1221. In light of the stark language of § 1221, however, we believe that *Corn Products* is properly interpreted as involving an application of § 1221's inventory exception. Such a reading is consistent both with the Court's reasoning in that case and with § 1221. The Court stated in *Corn Products* that the company's futures transactions were "an integral part of its business designed to protect its manufacturing operations against a price increase in its principal raw material and to assure a ready supply for future manufacturing requirements." ... The company bought, sold, and took delivery under the futures contracts as required by the company's manufacturing needs. As Professor Bittker notes, under these circumstances, the futures can "easily be viewed as surrogates for the raw material itself." 2 B. Bittker, Federal Taxation of Income, Estates and Gifts para. 51.10.3, p.51-62 (1981). The Court of Appeals for the Second Circuit in *Corn Products* clearly took this approach. That court stated that when commodity futures are "utilized solely for the purpose of stabilizing inventory cost[,] ... [they] cannot reasonably be separated from the inventory items," and concluded that "property used in hedging transactions properly comes within the exclusions of [§ 1221]." ... This Court indicated its acceptance of the Second Circuit's reasoning when it began the central paragraph of its opinion, "Nor can we find support for petitioner's contention that hedging is not within the exclusions of [§ 1221]." ... In the following paragraph, the Court argued that the Treasury had consistently viewed such hedging transactions as a form of insurance to stabilize the cost of inventory, and cited a Treasury ruling which concluded that the value of a manufacturer's raw-material inventory should be adjusted to take into account hedging transactions in futures contracts.... This discussion, read in light of the Second Circuit's holding and the plain language of § 1221, convinces us that although the corn futures were not "actual inventory," their use as an integral part of the taxpayer's inventory-purchase system led the Court to treat them as substitutes for the corn inventory such that they came within a broad reading of "property of a kind which would properly be included in the inventory of the taxpayer" in § 1221.

Petitioner argues that by focusing attention on whether the asset was acquired and sold as an integral part of the taxpayer's everyday business operations, the Court in *Corn Products* intended to create a general exemption from capital-asset status for assets acquired for business purposes. We believe petitioner misunderstands the relevance of the Court's inquiry. A business connection, although irrelevant to the initial determination of whether an item is a capital asset, is relevant in determining the applicability of certain of the statutory exceptions, including the inventory exception. The close connection between the futures transactions and the taxpayer's business in *Corn Products* was crucial to whether the corn futures could be considered surrogates for the stored inventory of raw corn. For if the futures dealings were not part of the company's inventory-purchase system, and instead amounted simply to speculation in corn futures, they could not be considered substitutes for the company's corn inventory, and would fall outside even a broad reading of the inventory exclusion. We conclude that *Corn Products* is properly interpreted as standing for the narrow proposition that hedging transactions that are an integral part of a business' inventory-purchase system fall within the inventory exclusion of § 1221.[11] Arkansas Best, which is not a dealer in securities, has never suggested that the Bank stock falls within the inventory exclusion. *Corn Products* thus has no application to this case.

It is also important to note that the business-motive test advocated by petitioner is subject to the same kind of abuse that the Court condemned in *Corn Products*. The Court explained in *Corn Products* that unless hedging transactions were subject to ordinary gain and loss treatment, taxpayers engaged in such transactions could "transmute ordinary income into capital gain at will." . . . The hedger could garner capital-asset treatment by selling the future and purchasing the commodity on the spot market, or ordinary-asset treatment by taking delivery under the future contract. In a similar vein, if capital stock purchased and held for a business purpose is an ordinary asset, whereas the same stock purchased and held with an investment motive is a capital asset, a taxpayer such as Arkansas Best could have significant influence over whether the asset would receive capital or ordinary treatment. Because stock is most naturally viewed as a capital asset, the Internal Revenue Service would be hard pressed to challenge a taxpayer's claim that stock was acquired as an investment, and that a gain arising from the sale of such stock was therefore a capital gain. Indeed, we are unaware of a single decision that has applied the business-motive test so as to require a taxpayer to report a gain from the sale of stock as an ordinary gain. If the same stock is sold at a loss, however, the taxpayer may be able to garner ordinary-loss treatment by emphasizing the business purpose behind the stock's acquisition. The potential for such abuse was evidenced in this case by the fact that as late as 1974, when Arkansas Best still hoped to sell the Bank stock at a profit, Arkansas Best apparently expected to report the gain as a capital gain. . . .

11. Although congressional inaction is generally a poor measure of congressional intent, we are given some pause by the fact that over 25 years have passed since Corn Products Refining Co. v. Commissioner [supra], was initially interpreted as excluding assets acquired for business purposes from the definition of capital asset, see Booth Newspapers, Inc. v. United States [supra], without any sign of disfavor from Congress. We cannot ignore the unambiguous language of § 1221, however, no matter how reticent Congress has been. If a broad exclusion from capital-asset status is to be created for assets acquired for business purposes, it must come from congressional action, not silence.

III

We conclude that a taxpayer's motivation in purchasing an asset is irrelevant to the question whether the asset is "property held by a taxpayer (whether or not connected with his business)" and is thus within § 1221's general definition of "capital asset." Because the capital stock held by petitioner falls within the broad definition of the term "capital asset" in § 1221 and is outside the classes of property excluded from capital-asset status, the loss arising from the sale of the stock is a capital loss. Corn Products Refining Co. v. Commissioner, supra, which we interpret as involving a broad reading of the inventory exclusion of § 1221, has no application in the present context. Accordingly, the judgment of the Court of Appeals is affirmed.

It is so ordered.

Justice KENNEDY took no part in the consideration or decision of this case.

NOTES AND QUESTIONS

1. *What is a hedge?* (a) Despite the Court's restrictive reading of § 1221, limiting the *Corn Products* exception to substitutes for inventory, the Regulations adopted after the decision in *Arkansas Best* allow ordinary gain or loss treatment for a broad variety of hedging transactions, including hedges used to protect against the risk of changes in interest rates or in currency exchange rates. Regs. § 1.1221-2. The Regulations address the potential abuse identified by the Court (that is, taxpayers treating gain as capital and loss as ordinary) by providing for taxpayer advance identification of hedging transactions. Regs. § 1.1221-2(e).

(b) What if the taxpayer in *Corn Products* had been unwilling for some reason to buy corn futures and, as an alternative hedge against a rise in the price of corn, had bought contracts for some other commodity, such as hogs, whose price fluctuations were closely correlated to fluctuations in the price of corn? See Regs. § 1.1221-2(b)(1), (c), (c)(1).

(c) What if the taxpayer had concluded that the price of corn futures contracts was low and had bought contracts for more corn than it normally used in its operations?

2. *Source of supply cases.* Some of the cases applying the *Corn Products* doctrine, or similar analysis, to allow ordinary deductions for losses on investments involved investments made to ensure a source of supply. For example, in *Booth Newspapers*, cited by the Court in *Arkansas Best*, the taxpayer, a newspaper publisher, bought shares of stock of a paper manufacturing corporation to protect its source of newsprint in a time of shortage. How would such a case be decided under the rule of *Arkansas Best*? Under the current Regulations? See Regs. § 1.1221-2(c)(5)(ii). What is the likely effect of taxpayer identification of the transaction as a hedging transaction? See Regs. § 1.1221-2(e), (f). What if an airline hedges against the risk of an increase in the price of jet fuel?

3. *What is inventory?* The regulations provide that the taxpayer's inventory "should include all finished or partly finished goods and, in the case of raw

materials and supplies, only those which have been acquired for sale or which will physically become a part of merchandise intended for sale." Regs. § 1.471-1. Is this provision applicable not only to § 471 (use of inventories in determining income) but also to § 1221(1)? If a business sells an excess stock of supplies that were not to be physically incorporated in its merchandise (e.g., office supplies, cleaning materials, or repair parts for machinery), do they come within § 1221(1)? Should the fact that their cost was deducted (from ordinary income) as a business expense be relevant in determining whether a sale produces ordinary income or capital gain?

F. SUBSTITUTES FOR ORDINARY INCOME

The next two cases (*Hort* and *McAllister*) focus on the question of whether the taxpayer is entitled to a recovery of basis, but also are treated as authority on the issue of capital gain versus ordinary income.

1. Payment for Cancellation of a Lease

HORT v. COMMISSIONER
313 U.S. 28 (1941)

Mr. Justice MURPHY delivered the opinion of the Court.

We must determine whether the amount petitioner received as consideration for cancellation of a lease of realty in New York City was ordinary gross income as defined in [§ 61(a)], and whether, in any event, petitioner sustained a loss through cancellation of the lease which is recognized in [§ 165(a)].

Petitioner acquired the property, a lot and ten-story office building, by devise from his father in 1928. At the time he became owner, the premises were leased to a firm which had sublet the main floor to the Irving Trust Co. In 1927, five years before the head lease expired, the Irving Trust Co. and petitioner's father executed a contract in which the latter agreed to lease the main floor and basement to the former for a term of fifteen years at an annual rental of $25,000, the term to commence at the expiration of the head lease.

In 1933, the Irving Trust Co. found it unprofitable to maintain a branch in petitioner's building. After some negotiations, petitioner and the Trust Co. agreed to cancel the lease in consideration of a payment to petitioner of $140,000. Petitioner did not include this amount in gross income in his income tax return for 1933. On the contrary, he reported a loss of $21,494.75 on the theory that the amount he received as consideration for the cancellation was $21,494.75 less than the difference between the present value of the unmatured rental payments and the fair rental value of the main floor and basement for the unexpired term of the lease. He did not deduct this figure, however, because he reported other losses in excess of gross income.

The Commissioner included the entire $140,000 in gross income, disallowed the asserted loss, made certain other adjustments not material here, and assessed a deficiency. The Board of Tax Appeals affirmed. 39 B.T.A. 922. The Circuit Court of Appeals affirmed per curiam on the authority of Warren Service Corp. v. Commissioner, 110 F.2d 723. 112 F.2d 167. Because of conflict with Commissioner v. Langwell Real Estate Corp., 47 F.2d 841, we granted certiorari limited to the question whether, "in computing net gain or loss for income tax purposes, a taxpayer [can] offset the value of the lease canceled against the consideration received by him for the cancellation." 311 U.S. 641.

Petitioner apparently contends that the amount received for cancellation of the lease was capital rather than ordinary income and that it was therefore subject to [the provisions of the Code] which govern capital gains and losses. Further, he argues that even if that amount must be reported as ordinary gross income he sustained a loss which [§ 165(a)] authorizes him to deduct. We cannot agree.

The amount received by petitioner for cancellation of the lease must be included in his gross income in its entirety. . . . [Section 61(a)] reached the rent paid prior to cancellation just as it would have embraced subsequent payments if the lease had never been canceled. It would have included a prepayment of the discounted value of unmatured rental payments whether received at the inception of the lease or at any time thereafter. Similarly, it would have extended to the proceeds of a suit to recover damages had the Irving Trust Co. breached the lease instead of concluding a settlement. . . . That the amount petitioner received resulted from negotiations ending in cancellation of the lease rather than from a suit to enforce it cannot alter the fact that basically the payment was merely a substitute for the rent reserved in the lease. So far as the application of [§ 61(a)] is concerned, it is immaterial that petitioner chose to accept an amount less than the strict present value of the unmatured rental payments rather than to engage in litigation, possibly uncertain and expensive.

The consideration received for cancellation of the lease was not a return of capital. We assume that the lease was "property," whatever that signifies abstractly. Presumably the bond in Helvering v. Horst [supra page 648] and the lease in Helvering v. Bruun [supra page 226] were also "property," but the interest coupon in Horst and the building in *Bruun* nevertheless were held to constitute items of gross income. Simply because the lease was "property" the amount received for its cancellation was not a return of capital, quite apart from the fact that "property" and "capital" are not necessarily synonymous in the Revenue Act of 1932 or in common usage. Where, as in this case, the disputed amount was essentially a substitute for rental payments which [§ 61(a)(5)] expressly characterizes as gross income, it must be regarded as ordinary income, and it is immaterial that for some purposes the contract creating the right to such payments may be treated as "property" or "capital."

For the same reasons, that amount was not a return of capital because petitioner acquired the lease as an incident of the realty devised to him by his father. Theoretically, it might have been possible in such a case to value realty and lease separately, and to label each a capital asset. . . . But that would not have converted into capital the amount petitioner received from the Trust Co., since [§ 102(b)(1)] would have required him to include in gross income the rent derived from the property, and that section, like [§ 61(a)], does not distinguish rental payments and a payment which is clearly a substitute for rental payments.

We conclude that petitioner must report as gross income the entire amount received for cancellation of the lease, without regard to the claimed disparity between that amount and the difference between the present value of the unmatured rental payments and the fair rental value of the property for the unexpired period of the lease. The cancellation of the lease involved nothing more than relinquishment of the right to future rental payments in return for a present substitute payment and possession of the leased premises. Undoubtedly it diminished the amount of gross income petitioner expected to realize, but to that extent he was relieved of the duty to pay income tax. Nothing in [§ 165(a)] indicates that Congress intended to allow petitioner to reduce ordinary income actually received and reported by the amount of income he failed to realize. . . . We may assume that petitioner was injured insofar as the cancellation of the lease affected the value of the realty. But that would become a deductible loss only when its extent had been fixed by a closed transaction. Regulations [§ 1.165-1(b)]. . . .

The judgment of the Circuit Court of Appeals is affirmed.

NOTES AND QUESTIONS

1. *Background: prepaid leases.* (a) Suppose L buys land for $100,000 and can rent it out for $10,000 per year net of all expenses. For the sake of simplicity, assume further that there is no inflation, that the rent is expected to remain $10,000, and the value of the land $100,000, for the foreseeable future. If L rents the land for one year and receives a rent payment of $10,000 at the end of that year, plainly the $10,000 is fully taxed as ordinary income. Note that there are two elements in this statement of tax consequences. First, no part of L's basis is offset against the $10,000 receipt. This is as it should be, since at the end of the year she still has the land, which is not a wasting asset and which is therefore presumed for tax purposes still to be worth $100,000. (If the land in fact changes in value, that change is unrealized gain or loss.) Second, the $10,000 is ordinary income. It is rent, not the proceeds of the sale of property.

(b) Suppose that L rents the land for two years with the tenant paying $17,355 in advance. ($17,355 is the present value of the right to receive $10,000 at the end of each year for two years, discounted at the rate of 10 percent. Assume here and in the subsequent questions in this note that 10 percent is the appropriate market rate.) Is the entire amount taxable at the time received? Is it still ordinary income?

(c) What if the lease is for ten years and the advance payment is $61,000 (the approximate present value of $10,000 at the end of each year for ten years, discounted at 10 percent)? If the value of the leasehold is $61,000, the value of the reversion should be $39,000. As time passes, the value of the leasehold declines and the value of the reversion rises. See Chapter 2.C.6.

Does this observation help to explain why it may be appropriate to treat the receipt of the advance rent as income, with no basis offset? Does it help explain why the amount received is ordinary income rather than capital gain?

(d) What if the lease is for ninety-nine years and the advance payment is $99,992 (the present value, at a 10 percent discount rate)? Compare Regs. § 1.1031(a)-1(c) (leasehold for thirty years or more is like a fee for purposes of like-kind exchange rules).

(e) By way of review, what are the tax consequences for the tenant in each of the above situations, assuming the property is used in the tenant's business? See Chapter 6.A.

(f) If the property is depreciable, how is L's deduction for depreciation affected by the fact that L receives two or more years' rent in advance?

2. *The legal doctrine of* Hort. Is the holding of *Hort* that there was no "sale or exchange" or that what was sold was not a "capital asset" (that is, "property" not within one of the exceptions of § 1221)?

3. *Inherited property.* Suppose that L owns property worth $100,000, leases it for $10,000 per year (payable at the end of each year) for ten years, and immediately dies, leaving the property, subject to the lease, to her son, S. At the time of L's death the leasehold is worth $61,000, and the remainder $39,000. Before any time passes, S talks the tenant into paying $60,000 to S in full payment for the use of the property for the remaining ten years of the lease. What are the tax consequences to S under *Hort*? Is that result consistent with sound tax policy? Suppose S argues that he inherited a leasehold worth $61,000, sold it immediately for only $60,000, resulting in a loss of $1,000.[12] How would you respond?

4. *Premium leases.* Suppose that L, the owner of land worth $100,000, leases it for $10,000 per year for ten years and that a year later the value of the land has fallen to $60,000 and the rent that could be earned if now leased for nine years would be $6,000 per year. The existing lease for $10,000 per year is a valuable asset; it calls for a premium rent and is called a premium lease. The value of the premium is the present value of the difference, for nine years, between the rent payment called for in the lease ($10,000) and the rent that could be earned if the property were rented at market rates ($6,000). That difference on our facts is $4,000 per year. The present value of $4,000 per year for nine years, discounted at 10 percent, is approximately $23,000. Thus, L's wealth includes the land, independent of the lease, worth $60,000. The $60,000 can be divided into two segments, one consisting of the right to

---

12. In essence this was the position taken by the taxpayer in *Hort*. The taxpayer claimed that the right to receive rent of $25,000 per year for the remaining thirteen years of the lease was worth $257,000, that he received a cash payment of $140,000, plus the right to the use of the property for the fourteen years (worth $96,000), so he gave up $257,000 and received a total of only $236,000 and was entitled to deduct the difference of $21,000. To this, the Court of Appeals (112 F.2d 167 (2d Cir. 1940)) responded by citing its earlier decision in Warren Service Corp. v. Commissioner, 110 F.2d 723 (1940), in which it had said that the taxpayer's claimed loss was "merely a diminution of expected income," which produces "no loss of property in the income-tax sense." 110 F.2d at 724. This may dispose of the taxpayer's claim to a loss deduction but does not resolve the question of how the receipt of the $140,000 should be treated. Apart from the defect in the taxpayer's position noted by the Court of Appeals in *Hort*, it is not the value of the property sold but rather its basis that determines the amount of a gain or loss. See § 1001(a).

$6,000 per year for nine years (worth $34,554), and the other consisting of the right to $60,000 at the end of nine years (worth $25,446). Adding to this the $23,000 (approximate) present value of the right to the $4,000 premium for nine years, we arrive at the total value of $83,000. Suppose that L dies and leaves the land, subject to the lease, to her son, S. The property, with the lease, is worth $83,000. At the end of the remaining nine-year term of the lease it will be worth only $60,000 (all other things equal). The premium lease is a wasting asset. A forceful argument can therefore be made that S should treat the premium value of the lease as a separate asset with a basis of $23,000, to be taken into account in determining gain or loss on disposition, or through a deduction for amortization if S retains the property and collects the annual rent. But see Schubert v. Commissioner, 286 F.2d 573, 580 (4th Cir. 1961), cert. denied, 366 U.S. 960 (1961) (discussing a conflict in other circuits and denying a deduction for failure of proof of premium). The position of a purchaser of property subject to a premium lease is different. See World Publishing Co. v. Commissioner, 299 F.2d 614 (8th Cir. 1962), where the taxpayer bought property subject to a lease with twenty-eight years remaining and a building constructed by the lessee, with a useful life less than twenty-eight years and a value of $300,000. The taxpayer's purchase price was $700,000, and there was testimony that the land was worth $400,000. The court allowed depreciation on the building, with a basis of $300,000. The court commented sympathetically on the alternative possibility, not urged by the taxpayer, that a deduction for the premium value of the lease should be allowed. In any event, in *Hort* it seems unlikely that the lease was a premium lease at the time the property was inherited by the taxpayer.

5. *Leases as capital assets of lessees*. We now turn our attention from the lessor with an advantageous (premium) lease to the lessee with an advantageous (premium) lease.

(a) Suppose T is the tenant under a lease calling for annual rental payments of $10,000 and having a remaining term of ten years and that T is able to sell the leasehold interest to a third person for $25,000. Is the $25,000 capital gain? The answer is yes, regardless whether the property has been used for personal purposes and is therefore covered by §1221 or has been used in the taxpayer's business and thus is §1231 property. See Rev. Rul. 72-85, 1972-1 C.B. 234. How can this result be reconciled with *Hort*? What if T had sold the next three years of the remaining ten years of use of the leasehold for $10,000?

(b) Suppose T pays $60,000 in advance for the use of the land for ten years and one year later sells the leasehold interest for $75,000. What is the amount of gain? Is it capital gain? What if the leasehold had been sold for $40,000? Does the result depend on whether the property was used in T's business? Rev. Rul. 72-85, supra, states that a tenant's leasehold interest in land is "real property."

6. *The relevance of §61(a)*. The reliance in the *Hort* opinion on the fact that §61(a)(5) "expressly characterizes [rental payments] as gross income" reflects a common misunderstanding about capital gain and the meaning of gross income. Section 61(a) defines gross income. Capital gain is part of gross income; §61(a)(3) expressly includes in gross income "gains derived from

dealings in property." Section 61(a) provides no guidance in distinguishing between capital gain and ordinary income.

7. *The "substitute for ordinary income" theory.* The suggestion in the *Hort* opinion that an amount can be characterized as ordinary income because it is a "substitute for" ordinary income such as rental payments is also misguided. If Mr. Hort had sold his entire interest in the land, the amount he received would be a substitute for the rents he otherwise would have received in perpetuity. A fundamental principle of economics is that the value of an asset is equal to the present discounted value of all the expected net receipts from that asset over its life.

What, then, is the rule of the *Hort* case? Does the following case help you in answering this question?

WOMACK v. COMMISSIONER
510 F.3d 1295 (11th Cir. 2007)

This is an appeal by Florida State Lottery winners from the United States Tax Court's decision that proceeds from the sale of the rights to future installment payments from lottery winnings ("Lottery Rights") are taxable as ordinary income, rather than at the lower tax rate applied to the sale of a long term capital asset. The Tax Court specifically held that Lottery Rights are not capital assets as defined in [§ 1221], under the judicially established substitute for ordinary income doctrine. We affirm.

I.   BACKGROUND

Roland Womack won a portion of an $8,000,000 Florida State Lottery ("Florida Lotto") prize on January 20, 1996. At the time, the prize was payable only in twenty annual installments of $150,000. Mr. Womack received four such annual installments from 1996 to 1999, and he reported those payments as ordinary income on the federal tax returns he filed jointly with his wife, Marie Womack.

In 1999, Florida amended its law to permit lottery winners to assign Lottery Rights. . . . Mr. Womack subsequently sold the right to receive the remaining sixteen payments to Singer Asset Finance Company ("Singer") in exchange for a sum of $1,328,000. The total face value of the remaining payments was $2,400,000. The Womacks reported the amount received from Singer on their 2000 joint federal income tax return as proceeds from the sale of a long term capital asset.

[Another couple, the Spiridakoses, who were in essentially the same tax position as the Womacks, were also parties; the two couples are referred to by the court as "Taxpayers." Another 57 "Florida Lotto winners . . . agreed to be bound by the decision in the case."]

. . .

III. DISCUSSION

The question before us is whether Lottery Rights are "capital assets" as defined by . . . § 1221. . . . Taxpayers held their Lottery Rights for more than one year before selling them, so Taxpayers may report the lump sum payment they received in consideration as a [long term] capital gain if Lottery Rights are considered a capital asset.

The Tax Court and the four U.S. Circuit Courts to consider the question have concluded that Lottery Rights are not a capital asset within the definition set forth in § 1221. E.g., Prebola v. Comm'r, 482 F.3d 610 (2d Cir.2007); Watkins v. Comm'r, 447 F.3d 1269 (10th Cir.2006); Lattera v. Comm'r, 437 F.3d 399 (3d Cir.2006), cert. denied, [549] U.S. [1212], 127 S.Ct. 1328 (2007); United States v. Maginnis, 356 F.3d 1179 (9th Cir.2004); Davis v. Comm'r, 119 T.C. 1, 2002 WL 1446631 (2002). These decisions are based on the so-called substitute for ordinary income doctrine, which provides that when a party receives a lump sum payment as "essentially a substitute for what would otherwise be received at a future time as ordinary income" that lump sum payment is taxable as ordinary income as well. Commissioner v. P.G. Lake, Inc., 356 U.S. 260, 265 (1958) [infra page 745]. We agree that the substitute for ordinary income doctrine applies to Lottery Rights, and therefore that proceeds from the sale of Lottery Rights are taxable as ordinary income.

A. THE SUBSTITUTE FOR ORDINARY INCOME DOCTRINE

The statutory definition of capital asset "has . . . never been read as broadly as the statutory language might seem to permit, because such a reading would encompass some things Congress did not intend to be taxed as capital gains." *Maginnis*, 356 F.3d at 1181. Congress intended ordinary income to be the default tax rate, with capital gains treatment an exception applicable only in appropriate cases. In fact, "the term 'capital asset' is to be construed narrowly in accordance with the purpose of Congress to afford capital-gains treatment only in situations typically involving the realization of appreciation in value accrued over a substantial period of time." Commissioner v. Gillette Motor Transp., Inc., 364 U.S. 130, 134 (1960). This interpretation prevents tax-payers from circumventing ordinary income tax rates by selling rights to fu-ture ordinary income payments in exchange for a lump sum. . . .

[Each of the prior circuits to review] the precise legal question we face here [did so] under materially identical circumstances. Each Circuit has concluded that Lottery Rights are substitutes for ordinary income, but came to this conclusion in different ways. The Ninth Circuit used a case-by-case analysis, but focused on two factors in particular: that the taxpayer "(1) did not make any underlying investment of capital in return for the receipt of his lottery right, and (2) the sale of his right did not reflect an accretion in value over cost to any underlying asset [he] held." *Maginnis*, 356 F.3d at 1183. Though the *Maginnis* court noted that these factors would not be dispositive in all cases, the Third Circuit in *Lattera*, 437 F.3d at 404-09, found the factors problematic, and instead formulated its own approach, which it termed the "family re-semblance" test. Within the confines of this test, the Third Circuit analyzed the nature of the sale and the character of the asset, specifically, whether the payment was for the future right to *earn* income or for the future right to *earned* income. Id. at 409. The Second and Tenth Circuits did not explicitly adopt the *Maginnis* reasoning or the *Lattera* test, but held that "whatever the [substitute for ordinary income] doctrine's outer limits, this case falls squarely within them." *Prebola,* 482 F.3d at 612; see *Watkins,* 447 F.3d at 1273 ("[W]e need not formulate any specific test regarding the appropriate limits of the doctrine's application."); Wolman v. Comm'r, 180 Fed.Appx. 830, 831 (10th Cir. 2006) ("For the same reasons stated in *Watkins,* we reject the Wolmans' argument and hold that the lump sum payments were taxable as ordinary income.").

We agree with our sister circuits that Lottery Rights are a clear case of a substitute for ordinary income. A lottery winner who has *not* sold the right to his winnings to a third party must report the winnings as ordinary income whether the state pays him in a lump sum or in installments. . . . Thus, when a lottery winner sells the right to his winnings, he replaces future ordinary income. In defining "capital asset," Congress did not intend for taxpayers to circumvent ordinary income tax treatment by packaging ordinary income payments and selling them to a third party. . . .

There are important differences between Lottery Rights and the typical capital asset. The sale of a capital asset captures the increased value of the underlying asset. Perhaps the most common example occurs when a taxpayer purchases shares of stock, owns the shares for longer than a year, and then sells them at a higher price. The taxpayer makes an underlying investment in a capital asset when he purchases the stock. When he sells the shares at a higher price, the gain represents an increase in the value of the original investment. As the Ninth Circuit noted in *Maginnis,* 356 F.3d at 1183, Lottery Rights lack these characteristics emblematic of capital assets — Lottery Rights involve no underlying investment of capital. Furthermore, any "gain" from their sale reflects no change in the value of the asset. It is simply the amount Taxpayers would have received eventually, discounted to present value.[13]

Furthermore, when a lottery winner sells Lottery Rights, he transfers a right to income that is already earned, not a right to earn income in the future. See *Lattera,* 437 F.3d at 407-09. . . .

A capital asset has the potential to earn income in the future based on the owner's actions in using it. Lottery winners, by contrast, are "entitled to the income merely by virtue of owning the property." Note, Thomas G. Sinclair, Limiting the Substitute-for-Ordinary-Income Doctrine: An Analysis Through

---

13. As they are stated in *Maginnis,* these factors are obviously imperfect. For example, relying on the taxpayer's underlying investment ignores legitimate capital assets obtained through gifts or inheritances, and consideration of accretion in value excludes capital assets that typically depreciate, such as cars. See *Lattera,* 437 F.3d at 405. The *Maginnis* court properly observed that the factors would not be dispositive in every case. *Maginnis,* 356 F.3d at 1183. A court would have no occasion to evaluate these factors where the asset sold is something other than a claim to ordinary income, such as a car. The factors do, however, serve to emphasize the essence of a capital transaction: "that the sale or exchange of an asset results in a return of a capital investment coupled with realized gain or loss." Holt v. Comm'r, 303 F.2d 687, 691 (9th Cir.1962). . . . We also note that the tax treatment of gifts, inheritances, and sales of automobiles is well established and neither relevant to nor affected by the issues in this case.

Its Most Recent Application Involving the Sale of Future Lottery Rights, 56 S.C. L.Rev. 387, 406 (2004). . . . Income need not be accrued for tax purposes to be "earned" in this sense. . . . Thus, income from a lottery payment is earned income despite the fact that it does not accrue until the scheduled annual payment date. Proceeds from the sale of Lottery Rights are a clear substitute for ordinary income and are taxable as ordinary income.

1. Effect of *Arkansas Best*

[The court next addressed the taxpayers' argument that *Arkansas Best* requires construing exceptions to capital gains treatment narrowly. The court rejected this argument on the ground that *Arkansas Best* addresses statutory exceptions to capital gain status and has a footnote expressly distinguishing the "substitute for ordinary income" doctrine from the scope of its analysis. See supra page 726, footnote 9.]

This is not to say that the substitute for ordinary income doctrine applies upon the sale of *every* asset that produces ordinary income. Taken to its logical extreme, the substitute for ordinary income doctrine would obliterate capital gains treatment altogether because a capital asset's present value is often based on its future ability to produce revenue in the form of ordinary income. *Maginnis*, 356 F.3d at 1182. We acknowledge that the doctrine has its outer limits, but we do not define them here. We merely recognize that *Arkansas Best* did not circumscribe the substitute for the ordinary income doctrine. . . .

IV. Conclusion

For the foregoing reasons, we hold that proceeds from the sale of Lottery Rights should be taxed as ordinary income under the substitute for ordinary income doctrine. The Tax Court's decision is AFFIRMED.

QUESTIONS

1. (a) Suppose Lois buys 100 lottery tickets for $1 each, or a total of $100. A week later, one of the tickets proves to be a winner, in the amount of $100,000, payable a week later. She sells the ticket for $99,000. Is the ticket "property" within the meaning of § 1221? If so, could all lottery winnings (including those providing for immediate payment) be transformed into capital gain simply by selling the ticket before collecting the winning amount? (Note that the gain would be short term but would still be capital gain, with the advantage that it could be offset by capital losses.)

(b) Suppose Susan buys 100 shares of stock of an internet start-up company for $1 each, or a total of $100. The company proves to be wildly, and quickly, successful and six months later Susan sells the 100 shares for $100,000. Does she have $99,900 of short-term capital gain?

(c) How can you reconcile your answers to parts (a) and (b)?

2. Imagine a lottery that occurs in two stages, as in the Irish Sweepstakes described in the *Pulsifer* case (supra page 281). Suppose Tyrone buys a ticket for $10 in round one and that his ticket is one of the few that survives to round two. Tyrone then sells the ticket to Ida for $5,000. Ida holds the ticket until the winner is determined, and the ticket is a winner, to the tune of $1,000,000, but a week before she would have been entitled to collect the money, she sells the ticket to Betty for $995,000. A week later Betty receives the $1,000,000. Is Tyrone entitled to treat his $4,990 gain as capital gain? What about Ida's $990,000 gain and Betty's $5,000 gain? Does it, and should it, matter that Betty sells the ticket to Ida rather than turning in the ticket and selling her claim to a payment that is due a week later? Would it matter if the delay between the selection of the winning ticket and the entitlement to payment were a year rather than a week?

3. The court's opinion indicates that the Womacks sold their lottery payments to Singer Asset Finance Company (see http://www.singerasset.com/). In addition to offering lump sum cash payments to lottery winners, Singer describes itself as "an industry leader in buying structured settlements," which are generally excluded from the recipient's gross income under § 104, provided they are received on account of personal physical injury or physical sickness (see discussion at pages 154-157 in Chapter 2). Suppose Katia was injured in a car accident and recovered damages from the negligent driver in the form of a right to receive $20,000 per year for the next ten years. After two years, she sells the remaining payments to Singer in exchange for a lump sum payment of $100,000. How, if at all, should Katia be taxed on the receipt of that $100,000? Does your answer to that question provide any further insight regarding the proper tax treatment of the Womacks? What if the driver defaults on his obligation before Katia is able to sell the remaining payments? Should Katia be entitled to a bad debt deduction under § 166? (See Diez-Arguelles v. Commissioner, at pages 325-326.)

2. Sale of Interest in a Trust

McALLISTER v. COMMISSIONER
157 F.2d 235 (2d Cir. 1946), cert. denied, 330 U.S. 826 (1947), acq.

Before SWAN, CLARK, and FRANK, Circuit Judges.

CLARK, Circuit Judge.

This petition for review presents the question whether the sum of $55,000 received by petitioner on "transfer" or "surrender" of her life interest in a trust to the remainderman constitutes gross income under [§ 61(a)], or receipts from the sale of capital assets as defined in [§ 1221]. . . . Petitioner contends that the life estate was a capital asset, the transfer of which resulted in a deductible capital loss, leaving her with no taxable income for the year. A majority of the Tax Court agreed with the Commissioner that the receipt in question was merely an advance payment of income. . . .

The will of Richard McAllister established a trust fund of $100,000, the income of which was to be paid to his son John McAllister for life and, on the latter's death without children, to John's wife, the petitioner herein. On her death, the trust was to terminate, the residue going to the testator's wife and his son Richard. The testator died in 1926, his widow in 1935, and John in 1937. Except for stock in the R. McAllister corporation, not immediately salable at a fair price, John left assets insufficient to meet his debts; and in order to obtain immediate funds and to terminate extended family litigation according to an agreed plan, petitioner brought suit in the Court of Chancery of New Jersey to end the trust. The parties then agreed upon, and the court in its final decree ordered, a settlement by which the remainderman Richard, in addition to taking over the stock for $50,000, was to pay petitioner $55,000, with accumulated income and interest to the date of payment, in consideration of her release of all interest in the trust and consent to its termination and cancellation. For the year 1940, she reported a capital loss on the transaction of $8,790.20, the difference between the amount received and the value of the estate computed under [Regs. § 1.1014-5].[14]

The issue, as stated by the Tax Court and presented by the parties, reduces itself to the question whether the case is within the rule of Blair v. Commissioner [supra page 646], or that of Hort v. Commissioner [supra page 731]. In the *Blair* case, the life beneficiary of a trust assigned to his children specified sums to be paid each year for the duration of the estate. The Supreme Court held that each transfer was the assignment of a property right in the trust and that, since the tax liability attached to ownership of the property, the assignee, and not the assignor, was liable for the income taxes in the years in question. The continued authority of the case was recognized in Helvering v. Horst [supra page 648], although a majority of the Court thought it not applicable on the facts, and in Harrison v. Schaffner, 312 U.S. 579 (1941), where the Court very properly distinguished it from the situation where an assignor transferred a portion of his income for a single year. We think that its reasoning and conclusion support the taxpayer's position here. . . .

Petitioner's right to income for life from the trust estate was a right in the estate itself. Had she held a fee interest, the assignment would unquestionably have been regarded as the transfer of a capital asset; we see no reason why a different result should follow the transfer of the lesser, but still substantial, life interest. As the Court pointed out in the *Blair* case, the life tenant was entitled to enforce the trust, to enjoin a breach of trust, and to obtain redress in case of breach. The proceedings in the state chancery court completely divested her of these rights and of any possible control over the property. The case is therefore distinguishable from that of Hort v. Commissioner, supra, where a landlord for a consideration cancelled a lease for a term of years, having still some nine years to run. There the taxpayer surrendered his contractual right to the future yearly payments in return for an immediate payment of a lump sum. The statute expressly taxed income derived from rent [§ 61(a)(5)]; and

---

14. [See infra page 744, Note 2. The court apparently uses "value of the estate" to mean "basis." — Eds.]

the consideration received was held a substitute for the rent as it fell due. It was therefore taxed as income.

What we regard as the precise question here presented has been determined in the taxpayer's favor on the authority of the *Blair* case by the Eighth Circuit in Bell's Estate v. Commissioner, 8 Cir., 137 F.2d 454, reversing 46 B.T.A. 484. . . .

The Tax Court and the government have attempted to distinguish both the *Bell* and the *Blair* cases on grounds which seem to us to lack either substance or reality. The principal ground seems to be the form the transaction assumed between the parties. Thus the Court says that petitioner received the payment for "surrendering" her rights to income payments, and "she did not assign her interest in the trust, as did petitioners in the *Bell* case." But what is this more than a distinction in words? Both were cases where at the conclusion of the transaction the remaindermen had the entire estate and the life tenants had a substantial sum of money. . . .

Setting the bounds to the area of tax incidence involves the drawing of lines which may often be of an arbitrary nature. But they should not be more unreal than the circumstances necessitate. Here the line of demarcation between the *Blair* and the *Hort* principles is obviously one of some difficulty to define explicitly or to establish in borderline cases. Doubtless all would agree that there is some distinction between selling a life estate in property and anticipating income for a few years in advance. . . . The distinction seems logically and practically to turn upon anticipation of income payments over a reasonably short period of time and an out-and-out transfer of a substantial and durable property interest, such as a life estate at least is. See 57 Harv. L. Rev. 382; 54 Harv. L. Rev. 1405; 50 Yale L.J. 512, 515. Where the line should be finally placed we need not try to anticipate here. But we are clear that distinctions attempted on the basis of the various legal names given a transaction, rather than on its actual results between the parties, do not afford a sound basis for its delimitation. More rationally, to accept the respondent's contention we ought frankly to consider the *Blair* case as overruled, 50 Yale L.J. 512, 518, a position which, as we have seen, the Supreme Court itself has declined to take.

The parties are in conflict as to the valuation of the life estate; and we are returning the case to the Tax Court for computation, without, of course, assuming that there will necessarily be some tax.

Reversed and remanded.

FRANK, Circuit Judge (dissenting). . . .

We must . . . ascertain the intention of Congress expressed in those provisions—specially [§ 1221]—in the light of the language it employed and the policy there embodied. . . .

My colleagues avoid a direct discussion of that problem. Instead, they rely on Blair v. Commissioner, which they hold to be controlling. But the court in the *Blair* case had no occasion to, and did not, consider [§ 1221]. . . . The only question was whether thereafter the donor, notwithstanding the gift, should be regarded, under [§ 61(a)], as the recipient annually of that part of the income which was the subject of the gift and, consequently, should be taxed each year thereon. In other words, no capital gain or loss was involved, and the one issue was whether the donor or donee was annually taxable.

The policy of the capital gains provisions is not in doubt: Congress believed that the exaction of income tax on the usual basis on gains resulting from dispositions of capital investments would undesirably deter such dispositions. To put it differently, Congress made an exception to [§ 61(a)], in order to give an incentive to the making of such transfers. Having regard to that purpose, the courts have been cautious in interpreting the clauses creating that exception. They have refused to regard as "capital" transactions for that purpose divers sorts of transfers of "property," especially those by which transferors have procured advance payments of future income.

Those cases and Hort v. Commissioner, seem to me to render it somewhat doubtful whether any transfer of a life estate for a valuable consideration is within [§ 1221]. The consideration paid for such a transfer is a substitute for future payments which would be taxable as ordinary income, and resembles the advance payment of dividends, interest or salaries. . . .

I think it most unlikely that Congress intended by [§ 1221] to relieve such a taxpayer of the ordinary tax burdens to supply an incentive for the demolition of such a trust. . . .

NOTES AND QUESTIONS

1. *Treatment of the life tenant.* The court decided two issues in *McAllister*: first, that a life estate is a capital asset falling within the general statutory definition of § 1221, and second, that a life tenant has basis in a life estate. In accord with the characterization of a life estate as a capital asset is Allen v. First National Bank & Trust Co., 157 F.2d 592 (5th Cir. 1946), which held *Hort* not applicable because the taxpayer in Hort did not sell all his rights in the property he owned.

Under the rule applied in Irwin v. Gavit, 268 U.S. 161 (1925), if Mrs. McAllister had retained her life estate and collected the income, she would have been taxable on the entire amount received; no part of the basis of the property held in trust would have been allocated to her in this situation. On the other hand, under the *McAllister* decision, when she in fact sold, part of the basis in the property was allocated to her (see infra Note 2) and she reported a loss. She could then have taken the $55,000 and used it to buy an annuity for her life. Disregarding the costs of servicing the annuity, the payments she should receive under it should be about the same as the payments she would have received from the life estate. But part of the payments received under the annuity would be excluded from income. Meanwhile, the purchaser of the life estate would be entitled to amortize, over Mrs. McAllister's life, the cost of buying it from her,[15] even if the purchaser was also the holder of the

---

15. If the life estate continued past the expected life, the purchaser's entire basis would be exhausted, and the full amounts received would be taxable. If, on the other hand, the life estate terminated before the entire cost had been recovered through amortization deductions, the purchaser would be entitled to a deduction for the remaining basis.

remainder interest. See Bell v. Harrison, 212 F.2d 253 (7th Cir. 1954), and Rev. Rul 62-132, 1962-2 C.B. 73 (acquiescence in Bell v. Harrison, limited to transactions that are bona fide and not for tax avoidance purposes). Even though part of the basis for the property had been used by the life tenant, when the life estate ultimately terminated, the remainder holder's basis would be the entire basis for the property, so the effect is a double use of part of the property's basis. This set of rules gave rise to tax avoidance opportunities that were ended in 1969 with the adoption of § 1001(e), which provides that where a life tenant sells the life interest, unless the remainder holder sells at the same time, the basis for the life interest is zero. Thus, under present law, Mrs. McAllister would have recognized a gain of $55,000. It would still have been capital gain.

2. *Uniform basis.* At the time of *McAllister,* and under present law if the life tenant and the remainder holder sell at the same time, to allocate the total basis in the property between the life interest and the remainder interest, one starts with the adjusted basis for the property (the uniform basis) and allocates that basis between the two interests in accordance with the relative actuarial values of each at the time of sale. Thus, the basis of the life estate declines as the life expectancy of the life tenant declines and the basis of the remainder rises correspondingly. See Regs. § 1.1014-5. The same rule determines the basis for the remainder where the remainder holder sells his or her interest, regardless of whether the life tenant sells at the same time.

3. *The consequences of accelerating income.* Under present law, if a life tenant sells a life interest in a trust and the remainder holder does not sell, the entire amount of the proceeds is taxable, at the capital-gain rate. Suppose that a life tenant sells because of a concern for the nature of the investment held by the trust, and uses the proceeds to buy a life annuity. If the rate of return of the trust and of the company selling the annuity are comparable, it would take the full amount of the proceeds of the sale of the life interest to buy an annuity with annual income equal to the income of the trust. But the proceeds of the sale of the trust will be reduced by the tax on those proceeds, so the life tenant who changes the source of his or her income stream will experience a reduction in income, both before and after tax.[16] Does this outcome argue for allowing the exchange of a life interest for an annuity to be accomplished tax free under a provision like § 1031? If not, does it argue for a favorable rate of taxation of the proceeds of the sale of the life interest?

4. *Sale of a payment from the life estate.* Suppose that in return for a present payment of $30,000, Mrs. McAllister had "sold" the right to the next $30,000 worth of income from the trust plus an increment equal to 5 percent of the unrecovered balance. Assuming that § 1001(e) applies, her gain would be $30,000. Should that be treated as ordinary income or capital gain? Reserve a decision on this question until you have read the next case.

---

16. This effect will be mitigated but not eliminated by the fact that the annuity will have a basis equal to its cost and, consequently, part of each annuity payment will be nontaxable (see supra page 128).

3. Oil Payments

COMMISSIONER v. P. G. LAKE, INC.
356 U.S. 260 (1958)

Mr. Justice DOUGLAS delivered the opinion of the Court.

We have here, consolidated for arguments, five cases involving an identical question of law. . . . The cases are here on petitions for certiorari which we granted because of the public importance of the question presented. 353 U.S. 982.

The facts of the *Lake* case are closely similar to those in the *Wrather* and *O'Connor* cases. Lake is a corporation engaged in the business of producing oil and gas. It has a seven-eighths working interest[17] in two commercial oil and gas leases. In 1950 it was indebted to its president in the sum of $600,000 and in consideration of his cancellation of the debt assigned him an oil payment right in the amount of $600,000, plus an amount equal to interest at 3 percent a year on the unpaid balance remaining from month to month, payable out of 25 percent of the oil attributable to the taxpayer's working interest in the two leases. At the time of the assignment it could have been estimated with reasonable accuracy that the assigned oil payment right would pay out in three or more years. It did in fact pay out in a little over three years.

In its 1950 tax returns Lake reported the oil payment assignment as a sale of property producing a profit of $600,000 and taxable as a long-term capital gain.[18] . . . The Commissioner determined a deficiency, ruling that the purchase price (less deductions not material here) was taxable as ordinary income, subject to depletion.

[The Court here describes the facts in the companion cases, all of which present the same issue raised by the *P. G. Lake* facts.]

[A]s to whether the proceeds were taxable as long term capital gains . . . or as ordinary income subject to depletion, [t]he Court of Appeals started from the premise, laid down in Texas decisions, . . . that oil payments are interests in land.

We too proceed on that basis; and yet we conclude that the consideration received for these oil payment rights (and the sulphur payment right) was taxable as ordinary income, subject to depletion.

---

17. An oil and gas lease ordinarily conveys the entire mineral interest less any royalty interest retained by the lessor. The owner of the lease [that is, the lessee] is said to own "the working interest" because he has the right to develop and produce the minerals. In Anderson v. Helvering, 310 U.S. 404, we described an oil payment as "the right to a specific sum of money, payable out of a specified percentage of the oil, or the proceeds received from the sale of such oil, if, as and when produced." Id., at 410. A royalty interest is "a right to receive a specified percentage of all oil and gas produced" but, unlike the oil payment, is not limited to a specified sum of money. The royalty interest lasts during the entire term of the lease. Id., at 409.

18. [It would seem that the proceeds of the sale of the oil payment would be the amount of debt discharged (see supra pages 159-164) rather than the amount to be received by the assignee. For purposes of analysis, one can assume that the taxpayer sold the oil payment for $600,000 cash. The taxpayer's treatment of the entire $600,000 as capital gain raises the question of why there was no reduction for the adjusted basis of the property. Presumably the answer is that the basis had started out small because of the deduction of intangible drilling costs, and what there was had been exhausted by depletion allowances. — EDS.]

The purpose of [the capital gains provisions] was "to relieve the taxpayer from . . . excessive tax burdens on gains resulting from a conversion of capital investments, and to remove the deterrent effect of those burdens on such conversions." See Burnet v. Harmel, 287 U.S. 103, 106. And this exception has always been narrowly construed so as to protect the revenue against artful devices. See Corn Products Refining Co. v. Commissioner [supra page 721].

We do not see here any conversion of a capital investment. The lump sum consideration seems essentially a substitute for what would otherwise be received at a future time as ordinary income. The pay-out of these particular assigned oil payment rights could be ascertained with considerable accuracy. Such are the stipulations, findings, or clear inferences. In the *O'Connor* case, the pay-out of the assigned oil payment right was so assured that the purchaser obtained a $9,990,350 purchase money loan at 3½ percent interest without any security other than a deed of trust of the $10,000,000 oil payment right, he receiving 4 percent from the taxpayer. Only a fraction of the oil . . . rights were transferred, the balance being retained.[19] [C]ash was received which was equal to the amount of the income to accrue during the term of the assignment, the assignee being compensated by interest on his advance. The substance of what was assigned was the right to receive future income. The substance of what was received was the present value of income which the recipient would otherwise obtain in the future. In short, consideration was paid for the right to receive future income, not for an increase in the value of the income-producing property.

---

19. Until 1946 the Commissioner agreed with the contention of the taxpayers in these cases that the assignment of an oil payment right was productive of a long-term capital gain. In 1946 he changed his mind and ruled that "consideration (not pledged for development) received for the assignment of a short-lived in-oil payment carved out of any type of depletable interest in oil and gas in place (including a larger in-oil payment right) is ordinary income subject to the depletion allowance in the assignor's hands." G.C.M. 24849, 1946-1 C.B. 66, 69. This ruling was made applicable "only to such assignments made on or after April 1, 1946," I.T. 3895, 1948-1 C.B. 39. In 1950 a further ruling was made that represents the present view of the Commissioner. I.T. 4003, 1950-1 C.B. 10, 11, reads in relevant part as follows:

> After careful study and considerable experience with the application of G.C.M. 24849, supra, it is now concluded that there is no legal or practical basis for distinguishing between short-lived and long-lived in-oil payment rights. It is, therefore, the present position of the Bureau that the assignment of any in-oil payment right (not pledged for development), which extends over a period less than the life of the depletable property interest from which it is carved, is essentially the assignment of expected income from such property interest. Therefore, the assignment for a consideration of any such in-oil payment right results in the receipt of ordinary income by the assignor which is taxable to him when received or accrued, depending upon the method of accounting employed by him. Where the assignment of the in-oil payment right is donative, the transaction is considered as an assignment of future income which is taxable to the donor at such time as the income from the assigned payment right arises.
>
> Notwithstanding the foregoing, G.C.M. 24849, supra, and I.T. 3935 supra, do not apply where the assigned in-oil payment right constitutes the entire depletable interest of the assignor in the property or a fraction extending over the entire life of the property.

The pre-1946 administrative practice was not reflected in any published ruling or regulation. It therefore will not be presumed to have been known to Congress and incorporated into the law by reenactment. . . . Moreover, prior administrative practice is always subject to change "through exercise by the administrative agency of its continuing rule-making power." See Helvering v. Reynolds, 313 U.S. 428, 432. . . .

These arrangements seem to us transparent devices. Their forms do not control. Their essence is determined not by subtleties of draftsmanship but by their total effect. See Helvering v. Clifford, 309 U.S. 331; Harrison v. Schaffner, 312 U.S. 579. We have held that if one, entitled to receive at a future date interest on a bond or compensation for services, makes a grant of it by anticipatory assignment, he realizes taxable income as if he had collected the interest or received the salary and then paid it over. That is the teaching of Helvering v. Horst [supra page 648] and Harrison v. Schaffner, supra; and it is applicable here. As we stated in Helvering v. Horst, "The taxpayer has equally enjoyed the fruits of his labor or investment and obtained the satisfaction of his desires whether he collects and uses the income to procure those satisfactions, or whether he disposes of his right to collect it as the means of procuring them." There the taxpayer detached interest coupons from negotiable bonds and presented them as a gift to his son. The interest when paid was held taxable to the father. Here, even more clearly than there, the taxpayer is converting future income into present income. . . .

NOTES AND QUESTIONS

1. *Analysis.* (a) Note that the Court cites *Horst* (supra page 648), in which a father gave bond coupons to his son, and not *Hort* (supra page 731). Which of the two cases seems to you to be more relevant? In its brief (at page 30), the government cited *Hort* (and other cases) for the proposition that "in any case where the lump sum consideration is essentially a substitute for what would otherwise be received in the future as ordinary income, the lump sum consideration is taxable as ordinary income even though, in a sense, a transfer of 'property' is involved." Does this statement go too far? Earlier in its brief (page 25) the government describes *Horst* as holding that even though the coupons given to the son were "property," they were a type of property that "amounted only to a right to receive future income from the income-producing property (the bond)," that the label attached by the state law of property should not be controlling for tax purposes, and that the state-law characterization of oil payments as "interests in land" should be irrelevant for tax purposes. Is this argument sound? Is it dispositive?

(b) Suppose a taxpayer owns a farm whose boundaries are formed in part by streams and ridges and whose size is about 1,000 acres. The taxpayer sells a rectangular portion of the central part of the farm, consisting of 600 acres. Plainly, the taxpayer has sold a capital asset, with the consequence that any gain is treated as capital gain and the taxpayer is entitled to offset against the proceeds of the sale some portion of his or her total basis in the property. (See supra pages 119-122.) If the taxpayer's oil interest in *P. G. Lake* had been valued at $1 million and the taxpayer had sold an undivided 60 percent share in that oil interest for $600,000, the transaction would no doubt have been treated as a sale of a capital asset. How do these transactions differ from the actual transaction in the case?

(c) Suppose a taxpayer owns the right to take half of the water flowing along a river and sells this right for the next ten years for a lump sum payment of $60,000. Has the taxpayer sold a capital asset? How does this case differ from *P. G. Lake*?

(d) Suppose a taxpayer pays $60,000 for the right to use as lessee certain business premises for ten years and then subleases those premises for six years for $40,000 paid in advance. What are the tax consequences? How does this case differ from *P. G. Lake?*

2. *Advantages to taxpayers from* P. G. Lake *and the enactment of § 636.* In certain situations, the *P. G. Lake* decision proved advantageous to taxpayers. For example, if a taxpayer with a producing mineral property had a net loss from other transactions or was restricted in the amount of percentage depletion it could claim by reason of the 50 percent of taxable income limit (§ 613), it could boost current depletable income by carving out and selling an oil payment.

Another taxpayer ploy was called the *ABC* transaction. *A,* the owner of a mineral property, would sell *B* the entire interest less a carved-out, retained mineral payment, which *A* would then sell to *C. A* would have capital gain, having disposed of all that he or she owned. The amounts received by *C* were treated as *C's* income, but *C* was entitled to offset the receipts with an amortization deduction. The payments to *C* were not treated as *B's* income and, to that extent, *B* was able, in effect, to acquire the property with before-tax dollars.

Under § 636, enacted in 1969, these taxpayer opportunities are eliminated by treating the transactions in most instances as a financing device, with the buyer of the oil payment treated as a lender. Thus, in the *ABC* transaction, *B* is treated as the purchaser of both the working interest and the oil payment, with the latter used as security for a nonrecourse loan from *C.*

4.   Bootstrap Sale to Charity

In the next case, the narrow legal issue is one of capital gain versus ordinary income, but the broader issue is substance versus form or, somewhat less broadly, when is a transaction that purports to be a sale not a sale for tax purposes?

COMMISSIONER v. BROWN
380 U.S. 563 (1965)

Mr. Justice WHITE delivered the opinion of the Court.

In 1950, when Congress addressed itself to the problem of the direct or indirect acquisition and operation of going businesses by charities or other tax-exempt entities, it was recognized that in many of the typical sale and leaseback transactions, the exempt organization was trading on and perhaps selling part of its exemption.... For this and other reasons the Internal Revenue Code was accordingly amended in several respects, of principal importance for our purposes by taxing as "unrelated business income" the profits earned by a charity in the operation of a business, as well as the income from long-term leases of the business.[20] The short-term lease, however, of five

---

20. [The Revenue Act of 1950 added what are now §§ 501(b) and 511 to 515. The Tax Reform Act of 1969 further amended these sections. See Note 4, *infra* page 759. — EDS.]

years or less, was not affected and this fact has moulded many of the transactions in this field since that time, including the one involved in this case.

The Commissioner, however, in 1954, announced that when an exempt organization purchased a business and leased it for five years to another corporation, not investing its own funds but paying off the purchase price with rental income, the purchasing organization was in danger of losing its exemption; that in any event the rental income would be taxable income; that the charity might be unreasonably accumulating income;[21] and finally, and most important for this case, that the payments received by the seller would not be entitled to capital gains treatment. Rev. Rul. 54-420, 1954-2 C.B. 128.[22] . . . The basic facts are undisputed. Clay Brown, members of his family and three other persons owned substantially all of the stock in Clay Brown & Company, with sawmills and lumber interests near Fortuna, California. Clay Brown, the president of the company and spokesman for the group, was approached by a representative of California Institute for Cancer Research in 1952, and after considerable negotiation the stockholders agreed to sell their stock to the Institute for $1,300,000, payable $5,000 down from the assets of the company and the balance within 10 years from the earnings of the company's assets. It was provided that simultaneously with the transfer of the stock, the Institute would liquidate the company and lease its assets for five years to a new corporation, Fortuna Sawmills, Inc., formed and wholly owned by the attorneys for the sellers.[23] Fortuna would pay to the Institute 80% of its operating profit without allowance for depreciation or taxes, and 90% of such payments would be paid over by the Institute to the selling stockholders to apply on the $1,300,000 note. This note was noninterest bearing, the institute had no obligation to pay it except from the rental income and it was secured by mortgages and assignments of the assets transferred or leased to Fortuna. If the payments on the note failed to total $250,000 over any two consecutive years, the sellers could declare the entire balance of the note due and payable. The sellers were neither stockholders nor directors of Fortuna but it was provided that Clay Brown was to have a management contract with Fortuna at an annual salary and the right to name any successor manager if he himself resigned.[24]

The transaction was closed on February 4, 1953. Fortuna immediately took over operations of the business under its lease, on the same premises and with practically the same personnel which had been employed by Clay Brown & Company. Effective October 31, 1954, Clay Brown resigned as general manager of Fortuna and waived his right to name his successor. In 1957, because of a rapidly declining lumber market, Fortuna suffered severe reverses and

---

21. [Section 504, dealing with accumulations, was repealed in 1969, but a tougher rule relating only to private foundations was added to the Code. See § 4942. — Eds.]

22. [This rule was declared obsolete by Rev. Rul 77-278, 1977-2 C.B. 485. — Eds.]

23. The net current assets subject to liabilities were sold by the Institute to Fortuna for a promissory note which was assigned to sellers. The lease covered the remaining assets of Clay Brown & Company. Fortuna was capitalized at $25,000, its capital being paid in by its stockholders from their own funds.

24. Clay Brown's personal liability for some of the indebtedness of Clay Brown & Company, assumed by Fortuna, was continued. He also personally guaranteed some additional indebtedness incurred by Fortuna.

its operations were terminated. Respondent sellers did not repossess the properties under their mortgages but agreed they should be sold by the Institute with the latter retaining 10% of the proceeds. Accordingly, the property was sold by the Institute for $300,000. The payments on the note from rentals and from the sale of the properties totaled $936,131.85. Respondents returned the payments received from rentals as the gain from the sale of capital assets.[25] The Commissioner, however, asserted the payments were taxable as ordinary income and were not capital gain. . . .

In the Tax Court, the Commissioner asserted that the transaction was a sham and that in any event respondents retained such an economic interest in and control over the property sold that the transaction could not be treated as a sale resulting in a long-term capital gain. A divided Tax Court, 37 T.C. 461, found that there had been considerable good-faith bargaining at arm's length between the Brown family and the Institute, that the price agreed upon was within a reasonable range in the light of the earnings history of the corporation and the adjusted net worth of its assets, that the primary motivation for the Institute was the prospect of ending up with the assets of the business free and clear after the purchase price had been fully paid, which would then permit the Institute to convert the property and the money for use in cancer research, and that there had been a real change of economic benefit in the transaction.[26]

Having abandoned in the Court of Appeals the argument that this transaction was a sham, the Commissioner now admits that there was real substance in what occurred between the Institute and the Brown family. . . .

Whatever substance the transaction might have had, however, the Commissioner claims that it did not have the substance of a sale within the meaning of §1222(3). His argument is that since the Institute invested nothing, assumed no independent liability for the purchase price and promised only to pay over a percentage of the earnings of the company, the entire risk of the transaction remained on the sellers. . . .

To say that there is no sale because there is no risk-shifting and that there is no risk-shifting because the price to be paid is payable only from the income produced by the business sold, is very little different from saying that because business earnings are usually taxable as ordinary income, they are subject to the same tax when paid over as the purchase price of property. This argument has rationality but it places an unwarranted construction on the term "sale," is contrary to the policy of the capital gains provisions of the Internal Revenue Code, and has no support in the cases. We reject it. "Capital gain" and "capital asset" are creatures of the tax law and the Court has been inclined to give these terms a narrow, rather than a broad, construction. Corn Products Co. v. Commissioner [supra page 721]. A "sale," however, is a common event in the non-tax world; and since it is used in the Code without limiting definition and

---

25. [Currently, the transaction would result in original issue discount under §1272, and, in the absence of §1272, part of the payments would be treated as interest income under §483. — Eds.]

26. The Tax Court found nothing to indicate that the arrangement between the stockholders and the Institute contemplated the Brown family's being free at any time to take back and operate the business. . . .

without legislative history indicating a contrary result, its common and ordinary meaning should at least be persuasive of its meaning as used in the Internal Revenue Code. . . .

As of January 31, 1953, the adjusted net worth of Clay Brown & Company as revealed by its books was $619,457.63. This figure included accumulated earnings of $448,471.63, paid in surplus, capital stock and notes payable to the Brown family. The appraised value as of that date, however, relied upon by the Institute and the sellers, was $1,064,877, without figuring interest on deferred balances. Under a deferred payment plan with a 6% interest figure, the sale value was placed at $1,301,989. The Tax Court found the sale price agreed upon was arrived at in an arm's-length transaction, was the result of real negotiating and was "within a reasonable range in light of the earnings history of the corporation and the adjusted net worth of the corporate assets." 37 T.C. 461, 486.

Obviously, on these facts, there had been an appreciation in value accruing over a period of years . . . and an "increase in the value of the income-producing property." . . . This increase taxpayers were entitled to realize at capital gains rates on a cash sale of their stock; and likewise if they sold on a deferred payment plan taking an installment note and a mortgage as security. Further, if the down payment was less than 30% (the 1954 Code requires no down payment at all) and the transactions otherwise satisfied [§ 453] the gain itself could be reported on the installment basis.

In the actual transaction, the stock was transferred for a price payable on the installment basis but payable from the earnings of the company. Eventually $936,131.85 was realized by respondents. This transaction, we think, is a sale, and so treating it is wholly consistent with the purposes of the Code to allow capital gains treatment for realization upon the enhanced value of a capital asset.

The Commissioner, however, embellishes his risk-shifting argument. Purporting to probe the economic realities of the transaction, he reasons that if the seller continues to bear all the risk and the buyer none, the seller must be collecting a price for his risk-bearing in the form of an interest in future earnings over and above what would be a fair market value of the property. Since the seller bears the risk, the so-called purchase price *must* be excessive and must be simply a device to collect future earnings at capital gains rates. . . .

[The argument] denies what the tax court expressly found — that the price paid was within reasonable limits based on the earnings and net worth of the company; and there is evidence in the record to support this finding. . . .

[T]he Commissioner ignores as well the fact that if the rents payable by Fortuna were deductible by it and not taxable to the Institute, the Institute could pay off the purchase price at a considerably faster rate than the ordinary corporate buyer subject to income taxes, a matter of considerable importance to a seller who wants the balance of his purchase price paid as rapidly as he can get it. . . .

Furthermore, risk-shifting of the kind insisted on by the Commissioner has not heretofore been considered an essential ingredient of a sale for tax purposes. In Le Tulle v. Scofield, 308 U.S. 415, one corporation transferred

properties to another for cash and bonds secured by the properties transferred. The Court held that there was "a sale or exchange upon which gain or
loss must be reckoned in accordance with the provisions of the revenue act
dealing with the recognition of gain or loss upon a sale or exchange," id., at
421, since the seller retained only a creditor's interest rather than a proprietary one. "[T]hat the bonds were secured solely by the assets transferred and
that, upon default, the bondholder would retake only the property sold, [did
not change] his status from that of a creditor to one having a proprietary
stake." Ibid. . . . To require a sale for tax purposes to be to a financially responsible buyer who undertakes to pay the purchase price from sources other
than the earnings of the assets sold or to make a substantial down payment
seems to us at odds with the commercial practice and common understanding
of what constitutes a sale. The term "sale" is used a great many times in the
Internal Revenue Code and a wide variety of tax results hinge on the occurrence of a "sale." To accept the Commissioner's definition of sale would have
wide ramifications which we are not prepared to visit upon taxpayers, absent
congressional guidance in this direction.

The Commissioner relies heavily upon the cases involving a transfer of
mineral interests, the transferor receiving a bonus and retaining a royalty or
other interest in the mineral production. . . . Thomas v. Perkins [301 U.S. 655]
is deemed particularly pertinent. There a leasehold interest was transferred
for a sum certain payable in oil as produced, and it was held that the amounts
paid to the transferor were not includable in the income of the transferee but
were income of the transferor. We do not, however, deem either Thomas v.
Perkins or the other cases controlling.

First, "Congress . . . has recognized the peculiar character of the business of
extracting natural resources." . . .

Second, Thomas v. Perkins does not have unlimited sweep. The Court in
Anderson v. Helvering, [310 U.S. 404], pointed out that it was still possible for
the owner of a working interest to divest himself finally and completely of his
mineral interest by effecting a sale. In that case the owner of royalty interest,
fee interest and deferred oil payments contracted to convey them for
$160,000 payable $50,000 down and the balance from one-half the proceeds
which might be derived from the oil and gas produced and from the sale of
the fee title to any of the lands conveyed. The Court refused to extend
Thomas v. Perkins beyond the oil payment transaction involved in that case.[27]

---

27. Respondents place considerable reliance on the rule applicable where patents are sold or
assigned, the seller or assignor reserving an income interest. In Rev. Rul. 58-353, 1958-2 C.B. 408, the
Service announced its acquiescence in various Tax Court cases holding that the consideration received
by the owner of a patent for the assignment of a patent or the granting of an exclusive license to such
patent may be treated as the proceeds of a sale of property for income tax purposes, even though the
consideration received by the transferor is measured by production, use, or sale of the patented article.
The government now says that the Revenue Ruling amounts only to a decision to cease litigating the
question, at least temporarily, and that the cases on which the rule is based are wrong in principle and
inconsistent with the cases dealing with the taxation of mineral interests. We note, however, that in
Rev. Rul. 60-226, 1960-1 C.B. 26, the Service extended the same treatment to the copyright field.
Furthermore, the Secretary of the Treasury in 1963 recognized the present law to be that "the sale of a
patent by the inventor may be treated as the sale of a capital asset," Hearings before the House
Committee on Ways and Means, 88th Cong., 1st Sess., Feb. 6, 7, 8, and 18, 1963, Pt. I (rev.), on the

These developments in the patent field obviously do not help the position of the Commissioner. Nor does I.R.C. 1954, § 1235, which expressly permits specified patent sales to be treated as sales of capital assets entitled to capital gains treatment. We need not, however, decide here whether the extraction and patent cases are irreconcilable or whether, instead, each situation has its own peculiar characteristics justifying discrete treatment under the sale and exchange language of § 1222. Whether the patent cases are correct or not, absent § 1235, the fact remains that this case involves the transfer of corporate stock which has substantially appreciated in value and a purchase price payable from income which has been held to reflect the fair market value of the assets which the stock represents. . . .

There is another reason for us not to disturb the ruling of the Tax Court and the Court of Appeals. In 1963, the Treasury Department, in the course of hearings before the Congress, noted the availability of capital gains treatment on the sale of capital assets even though the seller retained an interest in the income produced by the assets. The Department proposed a change in the law which would have taxed as ordinary income the payments on the sale of a capital asset which were deferred over more than five years and were contingent on future income. Payments, though contingent on income, required to be made within five years would not have lost capital gains status nor would payments not contingent on income even though accompanied by payments which were. . . . [28]

Congress did not adopt the suggested change but it is significant for our purposes that the proposed amendment did not deny the fact or occurrence of a sale but would have taxed as ordinary income those income-contingent payments deferred for more than five years. If a purchaser could pay the purchase price out of earnings within five years, the seller would have capital gain rather than ordinary income. The approach was consistent with allowing appreciated values to be treated as capital gain but with appropriate safeguards against reserving additional rights to future income. In comparison, the Commissioner's position here is a clear case of "overkill" if aimed at preventing the involvement of tax-exempt entities in the purchase and operation of business enterprises. There are more precise approaches to this problem as well as to the question of the possibly excessive price paid by the charity or foundation. And if the Commissioner's approach is intended as a limitation upon the tax treatment of sales generally, it represents a considerable invasion of current capital gains policy, a matter which we think is the business of Congress, not ours.

The problems involved in the purchase of a going business by a tax-exempt organization have been considered and dealt with by the Congress. Likewise,

---

President's 1963 Tax Message, p. 150, and the Congress failed to enact the changes in the law which the Department recommended.

28. It did, however, accept and enact another suggestion made by the Treasury Department. Section 483, which was added to the Code, provided for treating a part of the purchase price as interest in installment sales transactions where no interest was specified. The provision was to apply as well when the payments provided for were indefinite as to their size, as for example "where the payments are in part at least dependent upon future income derived from the property," S. Rep. No. 830, 88th Cong., 2d Sess., p. 103. This section would apparently now apply to a transaction such as occurred in this case.

it has given its attention to various kinds of transactions involving the payment of the agreed purchase price for property from the future earnings of the property itself. In both situations it has responded, if at all, with precise provisions of narrow application. We consequently deem it wise to "leave to the Congress the fashioning of a rule which, in any event, must have wide ramifications." American Automobile Association v. United States, [supra page 337, 367 U.S. at 697].

Affirmed.

Mr. Justice HARLAN, concurring.

Were it not for the tax laws, the respondents' transaction with the Institute would make no sense, except as one arising from a charitable impulse. However the tax laws exist as an economic reality in the businessman's world, much like the existence of a competitor. Businessmen plan their affairs around both, and a tax dollar is just as real as one derived from any other source. The Code gives the Institute a tax exemption which makes it capable of taking a greater after-tax return from a business than could a nontax-exempt individual or corporation. Respondents traded a residual interest in their business for a faster payout apparently made possible by the Institute's exemption. The respondents gave something up; they received something substantially different in return. If words are to have meaning, there was a "sale or exchange." . . .

One may observe preliminarily that the Government's remedy for the so-called "bootstrap" sale — defining sale or exchange so as to require the shifting of some business risks — would accomplish little by way of closing off such sales in the future. It would be neither difficult nor burdensome for future users of the bootstrap technique to arrange for some shift of risks. If such sales are considered a serious abuse, ineffective judicial correctives will only postpone the day when Congress is moved to deal with the problem comprehensively. Furthermore, one may ask why, if the Government does not like the tax consequences of such sales, the proper course is not to attack the exemption rather than to deny the existence of a "real" sale or exchange.

The force underlying the Government's position is that the respondents did clearly retain some risk-bearing interest in the business. Instead of leaping from this premise to the conclusion that there was no sale or exchange, the Government might more profitably have broken the transaction into components and attempted to distinguish between the interest which respondents retained and the interest which they exchanged. The worth of a business depends upon its ability to produce income over time. What respondents gave up was not the entire business, but only their interest in the business' ability to produce income in excess of that which was necessary to pay them off under the terms of the transaction. The value of such a residual interest is a function of the risk element of the business and the amount of income it is capable of producing per year, and will necessarily be substantially less than the value of the total business. Had the Government argued that it was that interest which respondents exchanged, and only to that extent should they have received capital gains treatment, we would perhaps have had a different case. . . .

Mr. Justice GOLDBERG, with whom THE CHIEF JUSTICE and Mr. Justice BLACK join, dissenting. . . .

. . . In essence respondents conveyed their interest in the business to the Institute in return for 72% of the profits of the business and the right to recover the business assets if payments fell behind schedule.

At first glance it might appear odd that the sellers would enter into this transaction, for prior to the sale they had a right to 100% of the corporation's income, but after the sale they had a right to only 72% of that income and would lose the business after 10 years to boot. This transaction, however, afforded the sellers several advantages. The principal advantage sought by the sellers was capital gain, rather than ordinary income, treatment for that share of the business profits which they received. Further, because of the Tax Code's charitable exemption and the lease arrangement with Fortuna,[29] the Institute believed that neither it nor Fortuna would have to pay income tax on the earnings of the business. Thus the sellers would receive free of corporate taxation, and subject only to personal taxation at capital gains rates, 72% of the business earnings until they were paid $1,300,000. Without the sale they would receive only 48% of the business earnings, the rest going to the Government in corporate taxes, and this 48% would be subject to personal taxation at ordinary rates. In effect the Institute sold the respondents the use of its tax exemption, enabling the respondents to collect $1,300,000 from the business more quickly than they otherwise could and to pay taxes on this amount at capital gains rates. In return, the Institute received a nominal amount of the profits while the $1,300,000 was being paid, and it was to receive the whole business after this debt had been paid off. In any realistic sense the Government's grant of a tax exemption was used by the Institute as part of an arrangement that allowed it to buy a business that in fact cost it nothing. I cannot believe that Congress intended such a result. . . .

In dealing with what constitutes a sale for capital gains purposes, this Court has been careful to look through formal legal arrangements to the underlying economic realities. Income produced in the mineral extraction business, which "resemble[s] a manufacturing business carried on by the use of the soil," Burnet v. Harmel, [287 U.S. 103], at 107, is taxed to the person who retains an economic interest in the oil. Thus, while an outright sale of mineral interests qualifies for capital gains treatment, a purported sale of mineral interests in exchange for a royalty from the minerals produced is treated only as a transfer with a retained economic interest, and the royalty payments are fully taxable as ordinary income. . . .

In Thomas v. Perkins, 301 U.S. 655, an owner of oil interests transferred them in return for an "oil production payment," an amount which is payable only out of the proceeds of later commercial sales of the oil transferred. The Court held that this transfer, which constituted a sale under state law, did not

29. This lease arrangement was designed to permit the Institute to take advantage of its charitable exemption to avoid taxes on payment of Fortuna's profits to it, with Fortuna receiving a deduction for the rental payments as an ordinary and necessary business expense, thus avoiding taxes to both. Though unrelated business income is usually taxable when received by charities, an exception is made for income received from the lease of real and personal property of less than five years. See I.R.C. § 514. . . . Though denial of the charity's tax exemption on rent received from Fortuna would also remove the economic incentive underlying this bootstrap transaction, there is no indication in the Court's opinion that such income is not tax exempt. . . .

constitute a sale for tax purposes because there was not a sufficient shift of economic risk. The transferor would be paid only if oil was later produced and sold; if it was not produced, he would not be paid. The risks run by the transferor of making or losing money from the oil were shifted so slightly by the transfer that no § 1222(3) sale existed, notwithstanding the fact that the transaction conveyed title as a matter of state law, and once the payout was complete, full ownership of the minerals was to vest in the purchaser.

I believe that the sellers have retained an economic interest in the business fully as great as that retained by the seller of oil interests in Thomas v. Perkins. . . .

Moreover, in numerous cases this Court has refused to transfer the incidents of taxation along with a transfer of legal title when the transferor retains considerable control over the income-producing asset transferred. See e.g., . . . Helvering v. Clifford 309 U.S. 331 (1940), Corliss v. Bowers [281 U.S. 376 (1930)]. Control of the business did not, in fact, shift in the transaction here considered. Clay Brown, by the terms of the purchase agreement and the lease, was to manage Fortuna. Clay Brown was given power to hire and arrange for the terms of employment of all other employees of the corporation. The lease provided that "if for any reason Clay Brown is unable or unwilling to so act, the person or persons holding a majority interest in the principal note described in the Purchase Agreement shall have the right to approve his successor to act as general manager of Lessee company." Thus the shareholders of Clay Brown & Co. assured themselves of effective control over the management of Fortuna. Furthermore, Brown's attorneys were the named shareholders of Fortuna and its Board of Directors. The Institute had no control over the business.

I would conclude that on these facts there was not a sufficient shift of economic risk or control of the business to warrant treating this transaction as a "sale" for tax purposes. . . . Moreover, the entire purchase price was to be paid out of the ordinary income of the corporation, which was to be received by Brown on a recurrent basis as he had received it during the period he owned the corporation. I do not believe that Congress intended this recurrent receipt of ordinary business income to be taxed at capital gains rates merely because the business was to be transferred to a tax-exempt entity at some future date.[30]

. . . Even if the Court restricts its holding, allowing only those transactions to be § 1222(3) sales in which the price is not excessive, its decision allows considerable latitude for the unwarranted conversion of ordinary income into capital gain. Valuation of a closed corporation is notoriously difficult. The Tax Court in the present case did not determine that the price for which the corporation was sold represented its true value; it simply stated that the price "was the result of real negotiating" and "within a reasonable range in light of the earnings history of the corporation and the adjusted net worth of the

---

30. The fact that respondents were to lose complete control of the business after the payments were complete was taken into account by the Commissioner, for he treated the business in respondents' hands as a wasting asset, see I.R.C., 1954, § 167, and allowed them to offset their basis in the stock against the payments received. . . .

corporate assets." 37 T.C., at 486. The Tax Court, however, also said that "[i]t may be . . . that petitioner [Clay Brown] would have been unable to sell the stock at as favorable a price to anyone other than a tax-exempt organization." 37 T.C., at 485. Indeed, this latter supposition is highly likely, for the Institute was selling its tax exemption, and this is not the sort of asset which is limited in quantity. Though the Institute might have negotiated in order to receive beneficial ownership of the corporation as soon as possible, the Institute, at no cost to itself, could increase the price to produce an offer too attractive for the seller to decline. . . .

Although the Court implies that it will hold to be "sales" only those transactions in which the price is reasonable, I do not believe that the logic of the Court's opinion will justify so restricting its holding. If this transaction is a sale . . . because it was arrived at after hard negotiating, title in a conveyancing sense passed, and the beneficial ownership was expected to pass at a later date, then the question recurs, which the Court does not answer, why a similar transaction would cease to be a sale if hard negotiating produced a purchase price much greater than actual value. The Court relies upon Kolkey v. Commissioner, 254 F.2d 51 (7th Cir.), as authority holding that a bootstrap transaction will be struck down where the price is excessive. In *Kolkey*, however, the price to be paid was so much greater than the worth of the corporation in terms of its anticipated income that it was highly unlikely that the price would in fact ever be paid; consequently, it was improbable that the sellers' interest in the business would ever be extinguished. Therefore, in *Kolkey*, the Court, viewing the case as one involving "thin capitalization," treated the notes held by the sellers as equity in the new corporation and payments on them as dividends. Those who fashion "bootstrap" purchases have become considerably more sophisticated since *Kolkey*; vastly excessive prices are unlikely to be found and transactions are fashioned so that the "thin capitalization" argument is conceptually inapplicable. Thus I do not see what rationale the Court might use to strike down price transactions which, though excessive, do not reach *Kolkey*'s dimensions, when it upholds the one here under consideration. Such transactions would have the same degree of risk-shifting, there would be no less a transfer of ownership, and consideration supplied by the buyer need be no less than here.

Further, a bootstrap tax avoidance scheme can easily be structured under which the holder of any income-earning asset "sells" his asset to a tax-exempt buyer for a promise to pay him the income produced for a period of years. The buyer in such a transaction would do nothing whatsoever; the seller would be delighted to lose his asset at the end of, say, 30 years in return for capital gains treatment of all income earned during that period. It is difficult to see, on the Court's rationale, why such a scheme is not a sale. . . .

NOTES AND QUESTIONS

1. *The* Clay Brown *case's impact on definition of capital gains transaction.* (a) As noted by the Court, the government finally rested its attack on the ground that a capital gains transaction requires the transfer of a risk-bearing economic

interest to the transferee. Even though the Court rejected the government's argument in *Clay Brown* that there is no sale if the purchase price is to be paid from the earnings of the asset that is sold, the government again advanced that argument in Boone v. United States, 470 F.2d 232 (10th Cir. 1972), where shareholders in a closely held insurance company sold stock for an agreed price that, after a down payment, was payable by the purchasing company only from net premium income on the transferred policies. The court held *Clay Brown* dispositive and in light of the factual evidence found that a sale had occurred.

(b) Would acceptance of the government's theory in *Clay Brown* have invalidated the capital gains eligibility of many real estate sales where the buyer takes subject to — without assuming — an existing mortgage or where under state law there is no personal liability for a purchase money obligation? If *A* sells property to *B*'s newly formed corporation, thus insulating *B* from personal liability for the purchase price, is there a transfer of risk?

(c) In considering these questions, which made the Court hesitate about accepting the government's theory, it should be noted that the government's brief indicated that a down payment or acceptance of personal liability were not the only ways in which a transfer of risk could occur. For example, the performance of significant services by a buyer or other significant changes in his circumstances might have been a sufficient commitment to shift risk.

2. *Transactions where the price is not reasonable*. The *Clay Brown* majority limited its holding that a sale had occurred to transactions in which the purchase price was reasonable. Justice Goldberg, writing for the dissent, was concerned that, under the logic of the majority opinion, this restriction might not be enforceable. On the *Clay Brown* facts, was there any nontax reason why another charity might not have been willing to pay twice the price that was set by the parties in that case? If you had represented the taxpayer in the case, would you have been willing to have your client accept the higher offer? See Estate of Franklin v. Commissioner, supra page 588. In Berenson v. Commissioner, 507 F.2d 262 (2d Cir. 1974), the court considered a transaction similar to the one in *Clay Brown* but concluded that the price was excessive (more than double what would have been paid by a nonexempt purchaser) and that the seller was entitled to capital gain treatment only to the extent of what a nonexempt purchaser would have paid, with the excess treated as ordinary income. (The proceedings following remand are reported at 612 F.2d 695 (2d Cir. 1980).)

As to the reasonableness of the price in *Clay Brown*, note that the transaction called for deferred payments without interest. As a matter of sound financial analysis, it is clear that part of those payments should be treated as interest, but at the time the case arose there was no authority for such treatment for tax purposes. If the market rate of interest on high-quality loans was around 5 percent, what would have been a realistic rate for the purported loan in *Clay Brown*, which was nonrecourse, with a principal amount of $1.3 million and a down payment of $5,000?

3. *The IRS response to* Clay Brown. In Rev. Rul. 66-153, 1966-1 C.B. 187, the Service announced that it would "continue to resist what is in substance an

attempt to convert future business profits to capital gains" but would limit its attacks to cases in which the purchase price was "excessive."

4. *The legislative aftermath.* The Tax Reform Act of 1969 made several changes that eliminated some of the tax advantages available in the tax-exempt bootstrap transactions. Section 514 expanded the definition of unrelated trade or business income, which is taxable to an exempt organization, to include debt-financed income. Under § 514, income is taxed in the proportion in which property is financed by debt, notwithstanding that it otherwise would not be unrelated business income (e.g., dividends, interest, rents, etc.). As the debt is reduced, the percentage taxed diminishes. The provision does not apply to property related in use to the organization's exempt function. The rental income earned by the charity from the operating company in *Clay Brown* would have been taxed under this new provision and the ability of the exempt organization to pay the purchase price considerably impaired as a result. Section 511(a) was also amended to subject churches to the tax imposed on unrelated business income. Charitable organizations that are private foundations are effectively prohibited through severe penalties from owning a controlling interest in a business in any form. § 4943.

G. OTHER CLAIMS AND CONTRACT RIGHTS

1. Termination Payments

BAKER v. COMMISSIONER

118 T.C. 452 (2002)

PANUTHOS, Chief Special Trial Judge:

[T]he issue for decision is whether the termination payment received by petitioner upon retirement as an insurance agent of State Farm Insurance Cos. is taxable as capital gain or ordinary income.

BACKGROUND

I. PETITIONER'S AGREEMENT WITH STATE FARM

A. *General*

[P]etitioner conducted his business as the Warren L. Baker Insurance Agency (the agency). He sold policies exclusively for State Farm. When he began his relationship with State Farm, he was not assigned customers. Instead, he developed a customer base. He selected the location of his office with State Farm's approval. He also hired and paid employees. He was responsible for paying the expenses of an office such as rent, utilities, telephones, and other equipment. He was obligated to establish a trust fund into which he deposited premiums collected on behalf of State Farm.

Petitioner entered into a series of contracts with State Farm known as agent's agreements. The agent's agreement at issue was executed on March 1, 1977. While the agreement contains approximately 6 pages, there are numerous attachments including schedules of payments, amendments, addenda, and memoranda that total 61 pages. The agreement was prepared by State Farm. Petitioner did not have the ability to change the terms of the agreement, but he had the option to refuse a new or revised agreement.

The preamble to the agreement reads, in part, as follows: "The Companies believe that agents operating as independent contractors are best able to provide the creative selling, professional counseling, and prompt and skillful service essential to the creation and maintenance of successful multiple-line companies and agencies."

Section I of the agreement, Mutual Conditions and Duties, provides that petitioner was an independent contractor of State Farm. As a State Farm agent, petitioner agreed to write policies exclusively for State Farm, its affiliates, and government and industry groups. Paragraph C, section I of the agreement states that State Farm "will furnish you, without charge, manuals, forms, records, and such other materials and supplies as we may deem advisable to provide. All such property furnished by us shall remain the property of the Companies [State Farm]." Further, State Farm considered any and all information regarding policyholders to be its property, as follows:

> D. Information regarding names, addresses, and ages of policyholders of the Companies; the description and location of insured property; and expiration or renewal dates of State Farm policies acquired or coming into your possession during the effective period of this Agreement, or any prior Agreement, except information and records of policyholders insured by the Companies pursuant to any governmental or insurance industry plan or facility, are trade secrets wholly owned by the Companies. All forms and other materials, whether furnished by State Farm or purchased by you, upon which this information is recorded shall be the sole and exclusive property of the Companies.

Essentially, any data relating to a policyholder recorded by an agent on any paper was the property of State Farm.

Petitioner's compensation was based on a percentage of the net premiums. . . .

B. Termination

Section III of the agreement addresses termination. Either party could terminate the agreement by written notice. The agreement also provided for termination upon the death of petitioner. Within 10 days after termination of the agreement, "all property belonging to the Companies shall be returned or made available for return to the Companies or their authorized representative."

Petitioner was required to abide by a covenant not to compete for a period of 12 months following termination. The covenant not to compete provides as follows:

E. For a period of one year following termination of this Agreement, you will not either personally or through any other person, agency, or organization (1) induce or advise any State Farm policyholder credited to your account at the date of termination to lapse, surrender, or cancel any State Farm insurance coverage or (2) solicit any such policyholder to purchase any insurance coverage competitive with the insurance coverages sold by the Companies.

Pursuant to section IV of the agreement, petitioner qualified for a termination payment if he met certain requirements. First, he must work for 2 or more continuous years as an agent. Second, within 10 days of termination, he must return or make available for return all property belonging to State Farm.

The amount of the termination payment [depended on the policies in force during the 12 months preceding termination]. . . .

State Farm and petitioner did not negotiate the amount or conditions of the termination payment. State Farm agreed to pay petitioner a termination payment over either a 2- or 5-year period.

Section V of the agreement provides for an extended termination payment if petitioner worked for State Farm for at least 20 years, of which 10 years were consecutive. The extended termination payment would begin 61 months after termination and continue until petitioner's death. The extended termination payment is also based on policies personally produced by petitioner during his last 12 months as an agent for State Farm. . . .

II. PETITIONER'S RETIREMENT

Petitioner retired and terminated his relationship with State Farm on February 28, 1997. At that time, he held approximately 4,000 existing policies generated from 1,800 households. Approximately 90 percent of the policies were assigned to one successor agent. . . .

Petitioner returned State Farm's property, such as policy and policyholder descriptions, which he gathered in master folders that he purchased, claim draft books, rate books, agent's service texts, and a computer. He maintained much of the information regarding the policies and policyholders on the computer. He fully complied with the provision in the agreement for return of property to State Farm.

The successor agent hired the two employees previously employed by petitioner and assumed petitioner's telephone number. The successor agent also worked with petitioner on occasion prior to petitioner's retirement to meet policyholders and to ask questions. The successor agent opened an office in the vicinity of petitioner's office. When the termination was completed, petitioner had returned all of the assets used in the agency to State Farm and the successor agent. . . .

III.   TAX RETURN AND NOTICE OF DEFICIENCY

Petitioners timely filed their 1997 Federal income tax return. They reported the income of $38,622 from the termination payment which petitioner received in 1997 as long-term capital gain on Schedule D, Capital Gains and Losses. . . .

In a notice of deficiency, respondent determined that the termination payment from State Farm was ordinary income and did not qualify for capital gain treatment.

III.   DISCUSSION

I.   POSITIONS OF THE PARTIES

Respondent argues that petitioner did not sell any property to State Farm because all of the property was owned by State Farm and reverted to State Farm when petitioner terminated his relationship with State Farm. Respondent contends that the agreement does not evidence a sale because the contract does not list a seller or purchaser. Respondent also argues that petitioners failed to establish that the termination payment represents proceeds from the sale of a business, business assets, or goodwill. Respondent also suggests that the termination payment is in the nature of income from self-employment, but hedges that position in arguing that the payment is "similar to an annuity" and a "retirement benefit." We note that respondent did not determine that petitioners were liable for self-employment tax with respect to the termination payment.

Petitioners argue that the termination payment was for the sale or buyout of a business resulting in capital gain. They assert that petitioner developed a customer base and the termination payment was designed to protect the existing customer base for the successor agent as well as compensate petitioner for the goodwill and going business concern he developed. Petitioners rely on the concurring opinion in Jackson v. Commissioner, 108 T.C. 130, 141 (1997), which characterizes a termination payment similar to the one at issue as a buyout of the taxpayer's business.

The Coalition of Exclusive Agent Associations, Inc. (CEAA), filed with leave of the Court an amicus brief pursuant to conditions specified in the Court's order. The CEAA's argument is similar to the arguments made by petitioners: State Farm purchased the goodwill generated by petitioner; therefore, petitioner is entitled to capital gain treatment. . . .

[Sections II and III of the discussion, dealing with Burden of Proof and Evidentiary Issues, respectively, are omitted — EDS.]

IV.   SALE OR EXCHANGE OF A CAPITAL ASSET

We must decide the proper characterization of the termination payment made by State Farm to petitioner. We first consider whether petitioner owned a capital asset and whether petitioner sold or exchanged a capital asset for

Federal income tax purposes. We also consider whether petitioner sold a business to which goodwill attached. If petitioner did not sell or exchange a capital asset, then the termination payment is taxable as ordinary income.

Long-term capital gain is defined as gain from the sale or exchange of a capital asset held for more than 1 year. § 1222(3). A "capital asset" means property held by the taxpayer (whether or not connected with his trade or business) that is not covered by one of five specifically enumerated exclusions. § 1221.

In Schelble v. Commissioner, T.C. Memo. 1996-269, aff'd 130 F.3d 1388 (10th Cir. 1997), we considered whether the taxpayer received gain from the sale or exchange of a capital asset. Pursuant to the terms of the agreement with the insurance company for which he was an agent, the taxpayer was required to return all records, manuals, materials, advertising, and supplies or other property of the company. Id. We concluded that there was no evidence of "vendible business assets," and the record did not support a finding of a sale of assets of a business.

The Court of Appeals in Schelble v. Commissioner, 130 F.3d at 1394, held that there was "no evidence in the record of vendible assets to support the sale of Mr. Schelble's insurance business." It observed the following:

By transferring policy records to . . . [the insurance company] pursuant to the Agreement, . . . [the taxpayer] maintains he transferred insurance business goodwill developed by him. . . . [The taxpayer] has failed, however, to show a sale of assets occurred.

Id.

In Foxe v. Commissioner, 53 T.C. 21, 26 (1969), we considered whether payments made to an insurance agent were made pursuant to the sale or exchange of a capital asset to his former insurance company upon the cancellation of his employment contract. The taxpayer claimed that in the course of his business he built up "something of value, an organization" that the insurance company acquired. Moreover, his personal contacts with customers, which were important to the insurance company, were "something of real value."

We concluded that even if the taxpayer had "built up an organization of value," it was not his to sell since . . . [the insurance company] under the contract owned all the property comprising such organization. As to the customer contacts . . . [t]hey were not his to sell. It was held that the taxpayer did not sell or exchange a capital asset, and the payments were taxable as ordinary income.

Section 1001(c) provides that gain is recognized upon the sale or exchange of property. "The word 'sale' means 'a transfer of property for a fixed price in money or its equivalent.'" Schelble v. Commissioner, supra at 1394 (quoting Five Per Cent. Cases, 110 U.S. 471, 478, 28 L. Ed. 198, 4 S. Ct. 210 (1885)); see also Commissioner v. Brown, 380 U.S. 563, 570, 14 L. Ed. 2d 75, 85 S. Ct. 1162 (1965). "Exchange" means an exchange of property for another property that is materially different either in kind or in extent. Regs. § 1.1001-1, Income Tax Regs.

The key to deciding whether there has been a sale for Federal income tax purposes is whether the benefits and burdens of ownership have passed. Highland Farms, Inc. v. Commissioner, 106 T.C. 237 (1996); Grodt & McKay Realty, Inc. v. Commissioner, 77 T.C. 1221, 1237 (1981). Among the many factors we may consider in deciding whether there has been a sale are the following: Whether legal title passes; how the parties treat the transaction; whether an equity was acquired in the property; whether the contract creates a present obligation on the seller to execute and deliver a deed and a present obligation on the purchaser to make payments; whether the right of possession is vested in the purchaser; which party pays the property taxes; which party bears the risk of loss or damage to the property; and which party receives the profits from the operation and sale of the property. Levy v. Commissioner, 91 T.C. 838, 860 (1988); Grodt & McKay v. Commissioner; supra at 1237-1238.

Cases addressing whether there has been a sale or exchange of a capital asset often combine the issue of whether the taxpayer owned a capital asset with the issue of whether the taxpayer sold the asset. For example, in Erickson v. Commissioner, T.C. Memo. 1992-585, aff'd 1 F.3d 1231 (1st Cir. 1993), we concluded that there was no sale of the taxpayer's assets to his former insurance company because there was nothing in the facts showing that there was a sale of "vendible tangible assets" of a business. In *Erickson*, the Court stated:

> [The taxpayers] maintain that . . . certain indicia of a sale exist. They assert that employees who formerly [*24] worked for . . . [the taxpayer] went over to Union Mutual and that all records, supplies, and equipment were turned over to Union Mutual. . . . [H]owever, the individuals who had worked with . . . [the taxpayer] had always been salaried employees of Union Mutual. . . . And by his own admission, . . . [the taxpayer] had owned very little in the way of supplies and equipment. . . .

Id.

Respondent cites Jackson v. Commissioner, 108 T.C. 130 (1997), Milligan v. Commissioner, T.C. Memo. 1992-655, rev'd 38 F.3d 1094 (9th Cir. 1994), and similar cases for the proposition that the taxpayer did not sell or exchange the assets in his business. These cases bear a factual resemblance to the case at hand in that the taxpayer, a former insurance agent, received a termination payment after the termination of his agreement with the insurance company. But these cases focus on whether the taxpayer was subject to self-employment tax under sections 1401 and 1402.

The holdings by the Court of Appeals in *Milligan* and by this Court in *Jackson* do not require a conclusion that the termination payment paid to petitioner represents proceeds from the sale or exchange of a capital asset. Both *Jackson* and *Milligan* left open the question of whether termination payments constitute the sale or exchange of capital assets subject to capital gain treatment or whether they should be treated as ordinary income (other than income subject to self-employment tax).

V. THE CONTROLLING FACTS OF THIS CASE

We now apply the above discussion to the facts before us in this case. Upon his retirement, petitioner returned all assets used in the daily course of business, including a computer, books and records, and customer lists to State Farm pursuant to the agreement. Thus, much like the taxpayers in Foxe v. Commissioner, supra, and Schelble v. Commissioner, 130 F.3d 1388 (10th Cir. 1997), petitioner did not own these assets and, therefore, could not have sold them to State Farm.

Petitioner argues that the successor agent assumed his telephone number and hired the two employees of the agency, and that petitioner taught the successor agent about the agency and introduced him to policyholders, all of which support the argument that he sold the agency to State Farm.

The successor agent obtained the right to use the telephone number utilized by petitioner's agency. Petitioner did not argue, and we do not conclude, that the telephone number was a capital asset in the hands of petitioner. Additionally, there are no facts in the record that indicate that petitioner received any portion of the termination payment as payment for the successor agent's use of the telephone number.

There are no facts in the record that indicate that there was an employment contract between petitioner and the employees who worked for the agency or that the successor agent was required to hire the employees. Petitioner did not argue, and we do not conclude, that the employees constitute capital assets in the hands of petitioner. There is nothing in the record that indicates that petitioner received any portion of the termination payment as payment for the successor agent's hiring of the employees. The fact that the successor agent hired petitioner's former employees does not support petitioner's argument that he sold his agency.

Petitioner may have taught the successor agent about the agency and introduced him to policyholders when the successor agent visited petitioner's office, but there are no facts in the record that indicate that petitioner received the termination payment as payment for teaching the successor agent about the agency and introducing him to policyholders.

We conclude that petitioner did not own a capital asset that he could sell to State Farm. He did not receive the termination payment as payment for any asset. Accordingly, the termination payment does not represent gain from the sale or exchange of a capital asset.

Petitioner also argues that State Farm purchased goodwill. To qualify as the sale of goodwill, the taxpayer must demonstrate that he sold "'the business or a part of it, to which the goodwill attaches.'" Schelble v. Commissioner, 130 F.3d at 1394 (quoting Elliott v. United States, 431 F.2d 1149, 1154 (10th Cir. 1970)). Goodwill is "the expectancy of continued patronage, for whatever reason." Boe v. Commissioner, 307 F.2d 339, 343 (9th Cir. 1962), aff'g 35 T.C. 720 (1961); see also VGS Corp. v. Commissioner, 68 T.C. 563, 590 (1977).

Nevertheless, because petitioner, for the reasons already explained, did not own and sell capital assets in his agency to State Farm, we conclude that petitioner did not sell goodwill.

VI.   NATURE OF ORDINARY INCOME

Respondent does not clearly explain his position as to the nature of the termination payment other than to argue that it is not taxable as capital gain. In the notice of deficiency, respondent determined that the termination payment was ordinary income. In his brief, respondent primarily argues that petitioners did not satisfy their burden of proof to establish that the termination payment was proceeds of a sale and thus subject to capital gain treatment.

Having concluded above that the termination payment was not received for the sale or exchange of a capital asset and is not entitled to treatment as a capital gain, we conclude that the termination payment is taxable as ordinary income. Ordinary income treatment is accorded to a variety of payments. See, e.g., Hort v. Commissioner, 313 U.S. 28, 85 L. Ed. 1168, 61 S. Ct. 757 (1941) (income received upon cancellation of lease derived from relinquishment of right to future rental payments in return for a present substitute payment and possession of premises); Elliott v. United States, supra (payment for termination of insurance agency contract was ordinary income); Foxe v. Commissioner, 53 T.C. at 25 (payment to insurance agent upon cancellation of employment contract was ordinary income); General Ins. Agency, Inc. v. Commissioner, T.C. Memo. 1967-143 (payment for agreement not to compete was ordinary income), aff'd 401 F.2d 324 (4th Cir. 1968).

VII.   COVENANT NOT TO COMPETE

An amount received for an agreement not to compete is generally taxable as ordinary income. Banc One Corp. v. Commissioner, 84 T.C. 476, 490 (1985), aff'd without published opinion 815 F.2d 75 (6th Cir. 1987); Warsaw Photographic Associates, Inc. v. Commissioner, 84 T.C. 21 (1985); Ullman v. Commissioner, 29 T.C. 129 (1957), aff'd 264 F.2d 305 (2d Cir. 1959); General Ins. Agency, Inc. v. Commissioner, supra.

Petitioners reported the sale of a covenant not to compete on Form 8594 attached to the return. The agreement provides that, after retiring, petitioner would not solicit State Farm's policyholders for 1 year, or petitioner would forfeit the termination payment. If petitioner had competed against State Farm after retiring, he would not have received a termination payment. We find that petitioner entered into a covenant not to compete with State Farm and that a portion of the termination payment was paid for the covenant not to compete.

Proceeds allocable to a covenant not to compete are properly classified as ordinary income. . . . Petitioner did not allocate any portion of the termination payment to the covenant not to compete, and it is unnecessary for us to make such an allocation because the termination payment is classified as ordinary income. . . .

NOTES AND QUESTIONS

1. *The importance of legal title.* The court held that no portion of the termination payment constituted capital gain because the taxpayer had neither owned nor sold any capital assets. Suppose that taxpayer had been given title to all books and records connected with the insurance business, but the agreement required the taxpayer to transfer title if for any reason he had ceased performing duties as an agent. Suppose, further, that the agreement between taxpayer and State Farm required a termination payment in exchange for "all assets connected with taxpayers' insurance business, including all books and records and all goodwill." If the court's opinion is taken at face value, the decision would have then gone for the taxpayer. Does that make sense?

2. *Self-employment income and self-employment tax.* Payments similar (and in some cases nearly identical) to the one at issue in this case have engendered a related dispute: whether the payments constitute self-employment income and therefore trigger self-employment tax liability. Section 1401 imposes a 12.4 percent old-age survivors and disability insurance tax on approximately the first $88,000 of self-employment income, and an additional 2.9 percent hospital insurance tax on all the self-employment income. In Jackson v. Commissioner, 108 T.C. 130 (1997), and Milligan v. Commissioner, T.C. Memo. 1992-655, rev'd 38 F.3d 1094 (9th Cir. 1994), nearly identical termination payments from the same insurer were held not to constitute personal service income. On the other hand, termination payments received from other insurers have been held to constitute self-employment income. See Shelble v. Commissioner, 130 F.3d 1338 (10th Cir. 1997), aff'g T.C. Memo. 1996-269; Farnsworth v. Commissioner, T.C. Memo. 2002-29.

The fact that there are a host of recent cases revolving around self-employment tax due on insurance termination payments suggests, correctly, that the self-employment tax generates considerable litigation. The tax requires separating out self-employment income from other sources of income, and this is not an easy task.

3. *Were the payments best characterized as renewal commissions?* The court in the present case characterized part of the termination payment as received in exchange for a covenant not to compete. What about the remaining portion of the payment? There are really only two possibilities: Either that portion of the payment was received in exchange for capital assets or it was received in exchange for personal service income—here, Baker's right to renewal commissions. The court held that no portion of the payments was received in exchange for capital assets. The court did not, however, take what would seem to be the logical step and attribute the remainder of the payment to Baker's right to renewal commissions. It obviously felt that such a holding would be inconsistent with the position it had taken in the employment tax context. See Note 2, supra. Instead, the court simply refused to opine on the source of that portion of the termination payment.

2.   Theatrical Production Rights

COMMISSIONER v. FERRER
304 F.2d 125 (2d Cir. 1962)

FRIENDLY, Circuit Judge.

This controversy concerns the tax status of certain payments received by José Ferrer with respect to the motion picture "Moulin Rouge" portraying the career of Henri de Toulouse-Lautrec. The difficulties Mr. Ferrer must have had in fitting himself into the shape of the artist can hardly have been greater than ours in determining whether the transaction here at issue fits the rubric "gain from the sale or exchange of a capital asset held for more than 6 months," [§ 1221(3)], as the Tax Court held, 35 T.C. 617 (1961), or constitutes ordinary income, as the Commissioner contends. We have concluded that neither party is entirely right, that some aspects of the transaction fall on one side of the line and some on the other, and that the Tax Court must separate the two.

In 1950 Pierre LaMure published a novel, "Moulin Rouge," based on the life of Toulouse-Lautrec. He then wrote a play, "Monsieur Toulouse," based on the novel. On November 1, 1951, LaMure as "Author" and Ferrer, a famous actor but not a professional producer, as "Manager" entered into a contract, called a Dramatic Production Contract, for the stage production of the play by Ferrer.

The contract was largely on a printed form recommended by the Dramatists Guild of the Authors League of America, Inc. However great the business merits of the document, which are extolled in Burton, Business Practices in the Copyright Field, in C.C.H., 7 Copyright Problems Analyzed (1952) 87, 109, for a court, faced with the task of defining the nature of the rights created, it exemplifies what a contract ought not to be. Its first six pages include eleven articles, some introduced by explanatory material whose contractual status is, to say the least, uncertain. Here the last of these pages was preceded by three single-spaced typewritten pages of "Additional Clauses," one with a still further insert. Finally come 15 pages of closely printed "Supplemental Provisions," introduced by explanatory material of the sort noted. We shall thread our way through this maze as best we can.

By the contract the Author "leased" to the Manager "the sole and exclusive right" to produce and present "Monsieur Toulouse" on the speaking stage in the United States and Canada, and gave certain rights for its production elsewhere. Production had to occur on or before June 1, 1952, unless the Manager paid an additional advance of $1500 not later than that date, in which event the deadline was extended to December 1, 1952. Five hundred dollars were paid as an initial advance against Author's royalties; the Manager was required to make further advances of like amount on December 1, 1951, and January 1, 1952. Royalties were to be paid the Author on all box-office receipts, on a sliding scale percentage basis.

Article Seventh said that "In the event that under the terms hereof the Manager shall be entitled to share in the proceeds of the Motion Picture and

Additional Rights hereafter referred to, it is agreed that the Manager shall receive" 40% for the first ten years and diminishing percentages thereafter. Among the additional rights so described were "Radio and Television."

For the beginning of an answer whether the Manager would be so entitled, we turn to Article IV, § 2, of the Supplemental Provisions. This tells us that "In the event the Manager has produced and presented the play for the 'Requisite Performances and Terms,' the Negotiator shall pay the Manager" the above percentages "of the proceeds, from the disposal of the motion picture rights." Article VI, § 3, contains a similar provision as to payment by the Author of the proceeds of the "additional rights" including radio and television. . . .

Further provisions put flesh on these bones. Article IV, § 1(a), says that "The title" to the motion picture rights "vests in the Author, as provided in Article VIII hereof." Article VIII says, even more broadly, "The Author shall retain for his sole benefit, complete title, both legal and equitable, in and to all rights whatsoever (including, but not by way of limitation, the Motion Picture Rights . . . Radio and Television Rights . . .)," other than the right to produce the play. . . .

Finally, . . . [an] "Additional Clause" prescribes that "All dramatic, motion picture, radio and television rights in the novel Moulin Rouge shall merge in and with the play during the existence of this contract," and if the Manager produces and presents the play for a sufficient period, "throughout the copyright period of the play."

Shortly after signature of the Dramatic Production Contract, John Huston called Ferrer to ask whether he would be interested in playing Toulouse-Lautrec in a picture based upon "Moulin Rouge." On getting an affirmative indication, Huston said he would go ahead and acquire the motion picture rights. Ferrer replied, in somewhat of an exaggeration, "When you get ready to acquire them talk to me because I own them."

Both Huston and Ferrer then had discussions with LaMure. Ferrer expressed a willingness "to abandon the theatrical production in favor of the film production, provided that, if the film production were successful, I would be recompensed for my abandoning the stage production." On the strength of this, LaMure signed a preliminary agreement with Huston's corporation. In further negotiations, Huston's attorney insisted on "either an annulment or conveyance" of the Dramatic Production Contract. LaMure's lawyer prepared a letter of agreement, dated February 7, 1952, whereby Ferrer would cancel and terminate the Contract. Ferrer signed the letter but instructed his attorney not to deliver it until the closing of a contract between himself and the company that was to produce the picture; the letter was not delivered until May 14, 1952.

Meanwhile, on May 7, 1952, Ferrer entered into a contract with Huston's company, Moulin Productions, Inc. ("Moulin"), hereafter the Motion Picture Contract. This was followed by an agreement and assignment dated May 12, 1952, whereby LaMure sold Huston all motion picture rights to his novel, including the right to exploit the picture by radio and television. Under this agreement LaMure was to receive a fixed sum of $25,000, plus 5% and 4% of the Western and Eastern Hemisphere motion picture profits, respectively, and 50% of the net profits from exploitation by live television.

The Motion Picture Contract said that Romulus Films Limited, of London, proposed to produce the picture "Moulin Rouge," that Moulin would be vested with the Western Hemisphere distribution rights, and that Moulin on behalf of Romulus was interested in engaging Ferrer's services to play the role of Toulouse-Lautrec. Under clause 4(a), Ferrer was to receive $50,000 to cover 12 weeks of acting, payments to be made weekly as Ferrer rendered his services. Ferrer's performance was to begin between June 1 and July 1, 1952. By clause 4(b), Ferrer was to receive $10,416.66 per week for each additional week, but this, together with an additional $50,000 of salary provided by clause 4(c), was "deferred and postponed" and was payable only out of net receipts. Finally, clauses 4(d) and (e) provided "percentage compensation" equal to stipulated percentages of the net profits from distribution of the picture in the Western and Eastern Hemispheres respectively — 17% of the Western Hemisphere net profits until Ferrer had received $25,000 and thereafter 12¾% (such payments to "be made out of sixty-five (65%) percent of the net profits," whatever that may mean), and 3¾% of the Eastern Hemisphere net profits. If Ferrer's services were interrupted by disability or if production of the picture had to be suspended for causes beyond Moulin's control, but the picture was thereafter completed and Ferrer's "acts, poses and appearances therein" were recognizable to the public, he was to receive a proportion of the compensation provided in clauses 4(c), (d) and (e) corresponding to the ratio of his period of acting to 12 weeks. The same was true if Ferrer failed to "conduct himself with due regard to public conventions and morals" etc. and Moulin cancelled on that account. The absence of any similar provision with respect to termination for Ferrer's wilful refusal or neglect to perform services indicates that all his rights, except that for compensation already due under clause 4(a), would be forfeited in that event. Over objections by the Commissioner, Ferrer offered testimony by Huston's attorney, who was also president of Moulin, that in the negotiation "it was said that the ultimate percentage payment to be made to Ferrer would be his compensation for giving up his interest in the dramatization guild," and a letter from the same attorney, dated March 3, 1953, confirming that in the negotiations with Ferrer's attorney "for the sale of the dramatic rights held by you to the property entitled 'Monsieur Toulouse' and the novel 'MOULIN ROUGE', it was understood that the consideration for such sale price was the payments due, or to become due, to you under Clause 4(d) and Clause 4(e)," and also that LeMure "refused to sell the motion picture rights for the production of the motion picture known as 'MOULIN ROUGE' unless you sold the aforesaid dramatic rights." Ferrer's agent testified, again over objection, that the largest salary Ferrer had previously received for a moving picture appearance was $75,000.

Moulin's books showed $109,027.74 as a salary payment to Ferrer in August, 1953, and $178,751.46 at various later dates in 1953 as the payment of "Participating Interests" under clause 4(d). Ferrer's 1953 return reported the former as ordinary income, and the latter, less expenses of $26,812.72, as a long-term capital gain. The Commissioner determined a deficiency on the basis that the difference, $151,938.74, constituted ordinary income; from the Tax Court's annulment of that determination he has taken this appeal.

Section . . . 1221 tells us, not very illuminatingly, that "capital asset" means property held by the taxpayer (whether or not connected with his trade or business), but does not include four (now five) types of property therein defined. However, it has long been settled that a taxpayer does not bring himself within the capital gains provision merely by fulfilling the simple syllogism that a contract normally constitutes "property," that he held a contract, and that his contract does not fall within a specified exclusion. . . . This is easy enough; what is difficult, perhaps impossible, is to frame a positive definition of universal validity. Attempts to do this in terms of the degree of clothing adorning the contract cannot explain all the cases, however helpful they may be in deciding some, perhaps even this one; it would be hard to think of a contract more "naked" than a debenture, yet no one doubts that is a "capital asset" if held by an investor. Efforts to frame a universal negative, e.g., that a transaction can never qualify if the taxpayer has merely collapsed anticipation of future income, are equally fruitless; a lessor's sale of his interest in a 999 year net lease and an investor's sale of a perpetual bond sufficiently illustrate why. . . .

Two issues can be eliminated before we do this. We need no longer concern ourselves, as at one time we might have been obliged to do, over the alleged indivisibility of a copyright; the Commissioner is now satisfied that sales and exchanges of less than the whole copyright may result in capital gain. . . . Neither do we have in this case any issue of excludability under . . . § 1221(1); Ferrer was not in the "trade or business" of acquiring either dramatic production rights or motion picture rights.

When Huston displayed an interest in the motion picture rights in November 1951, Ferrer was possessed of a bundle of rights, three of which are relevant here. First was his "lease" of the play. Second was his power, incident to that lease, to prevent any disposition of the motion picture rights until June 1, 1952, or, on making an additional $1500 advance, to December 1, 1952, and for a period thereafter if he produced the play, and to prevent disposition of the radio and television rights even longer. Third was his 40% share of the proceeds of the motion picture and other rights if he produced the play. All these, in our view, Ferrer "sold or exchanged," although the parties set no separate price upon them. To be sure, Moulin had no interest in producing the play. But Ferrer did, unless a satisfactory substitute was provided. Hence Moulin had to buy him out of that right, as well as to eliminate his power temporarily to prevent a sale of the motion picture, radio and television rights to liquidate his option to obtain a share of their proceeds.

(1) Surrender of the "lease" of the play sounds like the transactions held to qualify for capital gain treatment in [Commissioner v. Golonsky, 200 F.2d 72 (3d Cir. 1952), cert. denied, 345 U.S. 939 (1953); Commissioner v. McCue Bros. & Drummond, Inc., 210 F.2d 752 (2d Cir.), cert. denied, 348 U.S. 829 (1954)], see § 1241. Such cases as Wooster v. Crane & Co., 147 F. 515 (8 Cir. 1906), . . . are a fortiori authority that courts would have enjoined LaMure, or anyone else, from interfering with this, unless the Dramatic Production Contract dictated otherwise. None of its many negations covered this basic grant. Ferrer thus had an "equitable interest" in the copyright of the play.

The Commissioner did not suggest in the Tax Court, and does not here, that this interest or, indeed, any with which we are concerned in this case, fell within . . . § 1221(3), excluding from the term "capital asset" "a copyright; a literary, musical, or artistic composition; or similar property; held by — (i) a taxpayer, whose personal efforts created such property. . . . " He was right in not doing this. In one sense the lease of the play was "created" simply by the agreed advance of $1500. If it be said that this is too narrow an approach and that we must consider what Ferrer would have had to do in order to make the lease productive, the result remains the same. Although the Dramatic Production Contract demanded Ferrer's personal efforts in the play's production, much else in the way of capital and risk-taking was also required. Yet the legislative history, . . . shows that [§ 1221(3)] was intended to deal with personal efforts and creation in a rather narrow sense. . . . Ferrer's role as producer, paying large sums to the theatre, the actors, other personnel, and the author, is not analogous to that of the writer or even the "creator" of a radio program mentioned by the Committee. Moreover, the dramatic producer does not normally "sell" the production to a single purchaser, as an author or radio program "creator" usually does — he offers it directly to public customers.

We see no basis for holding that amounts paid Ferrer for surrender of his lease of the play are excluded from capital gain treatment because receipts from the play would have been ordinary income. The latter is equally true if a lessee of real property sells or surrenders a lease from which he is receiving business income or subrentals; yet *Golonsky* and *McCue Bros. & Drummond* held such to be the sale or exchange of a capital asset, as § 1241 now provides. Likewise we find nothing in the statute that forbids capital gain treatment because the payment to Ferrer might be spread over a number of years rather than coming in a lump sum; although prevention of the unfairness arising from applying ordinary income rates to a "bunching" of income may be one of the motivations of the "capital gains" provisions, the statute says nothing about this. . . . Finally, with respect to the lease of the play, there was no such equivalence between amounts paid for its surrender and income that would have been realized by its retention as seems to lie at the basis of the Tenth Circuit's recent refusal of capital gain treatment in Wiseman v. Halliburton Oil Well Cementing Co., 301 F.2d 654 (1962), a decision as to which we take no position.

(2) Ferrer's negative power, as an incident to the lease, to prevent any disposition of the motion picture, radio and television rights until after production of the play, was also one which . . . would be protected in equity unless he had contracted to the contrary, and would thus constitute an "equitable interest" in this portion of the copyright. . . . As a practical matter, this feature of the Dramatic Production Contract "clouded" LaMure's title, despite the Contract's contrary assertion. Huston would not conclude with LaMure and LaMure would not conclude with Huston unless Ferrer released his rights; Huston's attorney testified that a contract like Ferrer's "imposes an encumbrance on the motion picture rights." Ferrer's dissipation of the cloud arising from the negative covenant seems analogous to the tenant's relinquishment of a right to prevent his landlord from leasing to another tenant in the same

business, held to be the sale or exchange of a capital asset in *Ray*. What we have said in (1) with respect to possible grounds for disqualification as a capital asset is a fortiori applicable here.

(3) We take a different view with respect to the capital assets status of Ferrer's right to receive 40% of the proceeds of the motion picture and other rights if he produced "Monsieur Toulouse."

We assume, without deciding, that there is no reason in principle why if the holder of a copyright grants an interest in the portion of a copyright relating to motion picture and other rights contingent on the production of a play, or, to put the matter in another way, gives the producer an option to acquire such an interest by producing the play, the option would not constitute a "capital asset" unless the producer is disqualified by . . . § 1221(1). Although the copyright might not be such an asset in the owner's hands because of that section or . . . § 1221(3)(A), the latter disqualification would not apply to the producer for reasons already discussed, and the former would not unless the producer was a professional. However, it is equally possible for the copyright owner to reserve the entire "property" both legal and equitable in himself and agree with the producer that a percentage of certain avails shall be paid as further income from the lease of the play — just as the lessor of real estate might agree to pay a lessee a percentage of what the lessor obtained from other tenants attracted to the building by the lessee's operations. In both instances such payments would be ordinary income. If the parties choose to cast their transaction in the latter mold, the Commissioner may take them at their word.

Here the parties were at some pains to do exactly that. LaMure was to "retain for his sole benefit, complete title, both legal and equitable, in and to all rights whatsoever" other than the right to produce the play. Ferrer was to "have no right, title or interest, legal or equitable, in the motion picture rights, other than the right to receive the Manager's share of the proceeds"; even as to that, he was to have "no recourse, in law or in equity" against a purchaser, a lessee, or the Negotiator, but only a right to arbitration against the Author. We cannot regard all this as mere formalism. The Contract is full of provisions designed to emphasize the Negotiator's freedom to act — provisions apparently stemming from a fear that, without them, the value of the motion picture rights might disintegrate in controversy. . . .

It follows that if Ferrer had produced the play and LaMure had sold the motion picture, radio and television rights for a percentage of the profits, Ferrer's 40% of that percentage would have been ordinary income and not the sale or exchange of a capital asset. The decisions in *Hort* [supra page 731] and [Holt v. Commissioner, 303 F.2d 687 (9 Cir. 1962) (producer receives profit percentage in return for future services; liquidation of claim for lump sum payment treated as ordinary income)] point to what would seem the inevitable corollary that if, on the same facts, Ferrer had then sold his rights to a percentage of the profits for a lump sum, that, too, would have been ordinary income. . . . The situation cannot be better from Ferrer's standpoint because he had merely a contingent right to, or an option to obtain, the 40% interest. . . .

The situation is thus one in which two of the rights that Ferrer sold or exchanged were "capital assets" and one was not. Although it would be easy to say that the contingent contract right to a percentage of the avails of the motion picture, radio and television rights was dominant and all else incidental, that would be viewing the situation with the inestimable advantage of hindsight. In 1952 no one could tell whether the play might be a huge success and the picture a dismal failure, whether the exact opposite would be true, whether both would succeed or both would fail. We cannot simply dismiss out of hand the notion that a dramatic production, presenting an actor famous on the speaking stage and appealing to a sophisticated audience, might have had substantial profit possibilities, perhaps quite as good as a film with respect to a figure, not altogether attractive and not nearly so broadly known then as the success of the picture has made him now, which presumably would require wide public acceptance before returning production costs. At the very least, when Ferrer gave up his lease of the play, he was abandoning his bet on two horses in favor of a bet on only one.

In such instances, where part of a transaction calls for one tax treatment and another for a different kind, allocation is demanded. . . . If it be said that to remand for this purpose is asking the Tax Court to separate the inseparable, we answer that no one expects scientific exactness; that however roughly hewn the decision may be, the result is certain to be fairer than either extreme; and that similar tasks must be performed by the Tax Court in other areas. . . .

Still we have not reached the end of the road. The Commissioner contends that, apart from all else, no part of the payments here can qualify for capital gain treatment, since Ferrer could receive "percentage compensation" only if he fulfilled his acting commitments, and all the payments were thus for personal services. [T]he Commissioner says it was error for the Tax Court to rely on extrinsic evidence to vary the written contract.

Although the parties have taken opposing positions on the applicability of the "parol evidence rule" to a dispute involving a stranger to the contract, . . . no such issue is here presented. No one argued the contract provided anything other than what was plainly said. Huston's attorney did not assert that Ferrer would become entitled to the percentage compensation without fulfilling his acting commitment; what the attorney said in his testimony, as he had earlier in his letter, was that Ferrer was selling two things to Moulin — his services as an actor and his rights under the Dramatic Production Contract — and that the parties regarded the payments under clauses 4(a), (b) and (c) as the consideration for the former and those under clauses 4(d) and (e) as the consideration for the latter.

On the basis of this evidence the Tax Court found that the percentage compensation was not "to any extent the consequence of, or consideration for, petitioner's personal services." In one sense, this is hardly so. Under the Motion Picture Contract, Ferrer would receive no percentage compensation if he wrongfully refused to furnish acting services, and none or only a portion if, for reasons beyond his control, he furnished less than all. Since that must have been as plain to the Tax Court as to us, we read the finding to mean rather that Ferrer and Moulin adopted the percentage of profits formula embodied in clauses 4(d) and (e) as an equivalent and in lieu of a fixed sum payable in all events for the release of the Dramatic Production Contract. If they had first agreed on such a sum and had then substituted the arrangement here made, it would be hard to say that although payments under their initial arrangement would not be disqualified for capital gain treatment, payments under the substituted one would be. Ferrer was already bound to play the role of Toulouse-Lautrec, at a salary implicitly found to constitute fair compensation for his services; adoption of a formula whereby his receipt of percentage compensation for releasing his rights was made contingent on his fulfilling that undertaking does not mean that the percentage compensation could not be solely for his release of the Contract. The Tax Court was not bound to accept the testimony that this was the intent — it could lawfully have found that the percentage compensation was in part added salary for Ferrer's acting services and in part payment for the release. However, it found the contrary, and we cannot say that in doing so it went beyond the bounds to which our review of its fact findings is confined [under] § 7482(a). Since, on the taxpayer's own evidence, the percentage compensation was for the totality of the release of his rights under the Dramatic Production Contract, allocation is required as between rights which did and rights which did not constitute a "capital asset."

We therefore reverse and remand to the Tax Court to determine what portion of the percentage compensation under clauses 4(d) and (e) of the Motion Picture Contract constituted compensation for Ferrer's surrendering his lease of the play and his incidental power to prevent disposition of the motion picture and other rights pending its production, as to which the determination of deficiency should be annulled, and what part for the surrender of his opportunity to receive 40% of the proceeds of the motion picture and other rights as to which it should be sustained. . . .

NOTES AND QUESTIONS

1. *Fragmentation.* Why did the court break up the set of rights for which Ferrer had bargained? Does it seem likely that Ferrer himself saw the rights as independent of one another?

2. *Drafting around the decision.* Could the contract between Ferrer and LaMure have been written so that all of Ferrer's gain would have been capital gain? Would that have required significant changes in LaMure's substantive rights? Would such changes have had any adverse tax effect for LaMure?

3. *The significance of profit sharing.* Note that the fact that Ferrer was to receive a share of the profits of the film, rather than a fixed amount, did not preclude a finding of a "sale" for purposes of allowing capital-gain treatment. This result is consistent with the position taken by the Service (after a long battle) as to licenses of patents (Rev. Rul. 58-353, 1958-2 C.B. 408)[31] and copyrights (Rev. Rul. 60-226, 1960-1 C.B. 26, regardless of whether the amounts "are payable over a period generally coterminus with the grantee's use of the copyrighted work").

---

31. Section 1235, enacted in 1954, allows royalties received by the inventor or other "holder" to be treated as capital gains.

4. *Other favorable contracts.* Perhaps the most intriguing case cited in *Ferrer* is Commissioner v. Pittston Co., 252 F.2d 344 (2d Cir.), cert. denied, 357 U.S. 919 (1958), where the taxpayer had entered into two transactions with Russell. In order to enable Russell to install a coal mining plant on Russell's coal property, it loaned Russell $250,000 and, at the same time, under a second contract, Russell agreed to sell to the taxpayer all of the coal produced by the plant for a period of ten years at a discount below fair market price. Parts of the payments for the coal were to be applied to repay the loan. Russell paid off the loan in four years, and a year later Russell paid the taxpayer $500,000 in consideration of the taxpayer's surrender of its rights under the coal purchase agreement. The taxpayer reported the $500,000 as long-term capital gain and was upheld by the Tax Court. The Circuit Court viewed the two contracts separately and reversed. It held that there was no sale or exchange, but merely the release of "naked" contract rights, which were not property. The court bolstered its position by stating that since Russell could break the contract and respond in damages only, there was no property right that could be specifically enforced; it therefore found that payment was more in the nature of future income (i.e., income Pittston would otherwise earn by buying Russell's coal at a discount and selling it at a higher price) paid in a lump sum. The dissent, viewing the two transactions, the loan and coal purchase agreement, together, concluded that the taxpayer had a property right rather than a mere contract right; that the agreement could have been specifically enforced; that the payment was analogous to payments made to a lessee for voluntary termination of a leasehold prior to expiration; that the payment was not anticipated income because it bore no relationship to future income; and that a surrender of the rights was similar to a sale or exchange. The earlier Second Circuit cases of Commissioner v. Starr Bros., 204 F.2d 673 (2d Cir. 1953) (which found ordinary income on cancellation of an exclusive distributorship), and General Artists Corp. v. Commissioner, 205 F.2d 360 (2d Cir.), cert. denied, 346 U.S. 866 (1953) (which found ordinary income on release of exclusive agency rights), had been distinguished by the Tax Court as cases where a contractual right was not "sold or exchanged" but was "released" and merely vanished.

In Commercial Solvents Corp. v. United States, 427 F.2d 749 (Ct. Cl.), cert. denied, 400 U.S. 943 (1970), a case similar to *Pittston*, the cancellation of a contract giving the taxpayer the right to buy all the production of a certain chemical plant was held to give rise to ordinary income because of the nature of the contract ("a naked contract right"). The government had stipulated that the cancellation of the contract was a sale or exchange.

3. Right of Privacy or of Exploitation

MILLER v. COMMISSIONER
299 F.2d 706 (2d Cir.), cert. denied, 370 U.S. 923 (1962)

Before WATERMAN, KAUFMAN and MARSHALL, Circuit Judges.

KAUFMAN, Circuit Judge.

Petitioner is the widow of Glenn Miller, a band leader who achieved world fame about twenty-five years ago. Although Glenn Miller died in 1944, petitioner has been able to engage in a number of enterprises actively exploiting his continuing popularity. . . .

Thus, in 1952, she entered into a contract with Universal Pictures Company, Inc. (Universal) in connection with the production of a motion picture film entitled "The Glenn Miller Story"; and in the calendar year 1954, she received $409,336.34 as her share of the income derived from that theatrical venture. According to the terms of the 1952 contract, petitioner had purportedly granted to Universal "the exclusive right to produce, release, distribute and exhibit . . . one or more photoplays based upon the life and activities of Glenn Miller throughout the world"; and had warranted that she was "the sole and exclusive owner of all the rights" conveyed by her.

Petitioner now contends that the payment . . . should be considered . . . "gain from the sale or exchange of a capital asset held for more than 6 months. . . . " [T]he conflict is narrowed to the meaning of the word "property" for purposes of [§ 1221].

The Internal Revenue Code does not define "property" as used in § 1221. . . . Therefore, we must look outside the eight corners of the Code for some elucidation. The ordinary technique is to refer to principles of state property law for, if not an answer, at least a hint. Since ultimately it is the Congressional purpose which controls, such nontax definitions are certainly not binding on us. . . . On the other hand, Congress may be presumed to have had ordinary property concepts in mind so they are relevant to our inquiry.

Most people trained in the law would agree that for many purposes one may define "property" as a bundle of rights, protected from interference by legal sanctions. Cf. Restatement, Property §§ 1-5. This concept is behind one prong of petitioner's attack. She cites several cases, claiming they indicate that if Universal had made its motion picture without contracting with her, it would have been the victim of a substantial lawsuit.

Even if this were so, those cases would not compel this court to recognize, for income tax purposes, a "property right" in Glenn Miller himself if he were still alive. However, it is not necessary for us to reach a determination upon such an assertion. Those cases do not even remotely bear on the question whether such a property right, if it existed, could pass to the sole beneficiary under his will; and certainly they lend no support to petitioner's theory that the reputation or fame of a dead person could give rise to such "property rights." In fact, in the only case cited in which the rights of a dead man were considered at all, the court held against the claimant. . . .

Undeterred by her failure to find case authority which would substantiate the existence of "property rights" petitioner invokes the authority of logic. With considerable ingenuity, she argues:

(1) Universal paid petitioner $409,336.34 in 1954, which is a great deal of money.

(2) Universal was a sophisticated corporate being to which donative intent would be difficult to ascribe.

(3) If there was no danger in free use of Glenn Miller material, why did Universal pay?

Petitioner appears to find this question unanswerable unless it is conceded that there was a sale of "property right." Petitioner is wrong.

It is clear to this Court, at least, that many things can be sold which are not "property" in any sense of the word. One can sell his time and experience, for instance, or, if one is dishonest, one can sell his vote; but we would suppose that no one would seriously contend that the subject matter of such sales is "property" as that word is ordinarily understood. Certainly no one would contend that such subject matter was inheritable. We conclude, therefore, that not everything people pay for is "property."

In the instant case, "something" was indeed sold. And the expedient business practice may often be to sell such "things." But the "thing" bought, or more appropriately "bought off," seems to have been the chance that a new theory of "property" might be advanced, and that a lawsuit predicated on it might be successful. . . . Because Universal feared that it might sometime in the future be held to have infringed a property right does not mean, however, that a court presently considering whether that property right *did* exist in 1952 must realize Universal's worst fears. That does not mean that Universal's payment was foolish or illusory. It got what it contracted for in 1952 and what it later paid Mrs. Miller for: freedom from the danger that at a future date a defensible right constituting "property" *would* be found to exist. But it didn't pay for "property."[32]

It may be helpful to compare this situation with one which involves the settlement of a tort claim, e.g., a negligence lawsuit. No one doubts the existence of a legal principle creating liability for negligence. If the facts are as a plaintiff contends, and they come within that principle, the defendant's liability exists. Even if they do not, the defendant, for his own reasons, may agree to make a payment in settlement of his alleged liability. Moreover, the Commissioner, for purposes of taxation, may accept that settlement as an implied affirmation that the *facts* were substantially as the plaintiff contended, and treat the recovery accordingly. But no two individuals can, by agreement between themselves, create a *legal* principle, binding upon everyone else, including the Commissioner, where none existed before. This is the exclusive domain of the legislature and the courts as repository of the public will. . . . Petitioner concedes that at the time of the "sale" there had been no authoritative decision holding that a decedent's successors had any "property right" to the public image of a deceased entertainer; and therefore it follows that their bargain was not, at that time, a bargain that both parties knew involved a "property right." . . . "[I]t is evident that not everything which can be called property in the ordinary sense and which is outside the statutory exclusions qualifies as a capital asset. . . . " Commissioner v. Gillette Motor Transport, Inc., 364 U.S. 130, 134 (1960). . . . Gains which result from the sale or exchange of capital assets receive preferential tax treatment. Therefore, "The definition of a capital asset must be narrowly applied," Corn Products Refining Co. v. Commissioner [supra page 721], in order to effectuate the basic Congressional purpose "to relieve the taxpayer from . . . excessive tax burdens

32. One must remember that, the techniques of advertising and promotion being what they are, timing is very important and a successful motion for a preliminary injunction made by one who *claims* a "property right" might be as disastrous as a final award of damages. One can easily find wisdom in this payment by Universal without finding that it paid for "property."

on gains resulting from a conversion of capital investments, and to remove the deterrent effect of those burdens on such conversions." Burnet v. Harmel, [287 U.S. 103, 106 (1932)]; Corn Products Refining Co. v. Commissioner, supra. We do not believe that for income tax computation purposes beneficiaries of the estate of a deceased entertainer receive by descent a capitalizable "property" in the name, reputation, right of publicity, right of privacy or "public image" of the deceased; or that in this case the petitioner, for tax purposes, owned any "property" which came into existence after Glenn Miller's death. Therefore, income received by Mrs. Miller from contractual arrangements made by her with Universal dealing with deceased's intangible rights of the nature above specified is "ordinary" income as opposed to capital gain or loss under § 1221.

Affirmed.

QUESTIONS

Suppose that at the time of the decision in the *Miller* case there had been clear precedent that a person like Glenn Miller has the exclusive right to exploit his own name and fame and that this right is enforceable by injunction and passes by inheritance to his heirs at his death.[33] Would the result in *Miller* have been different? Should it be? Would Mrs. Miller be entitled to capital gain treatment even if Mr. Miller would not have been? Compare the treatment of holders of copyrights, discussed in the next section.

4. Patents and Copyrights

Before 1950, a patent or copyright was treated as a capital asset if the taxpayer could show that it was neither property held for sale to customers in the regular course of trade or business nor depreciable property used in his or her business. In general, capital-gain treatment was confined to "amateur" authors, and inventors, who had not made more than one or two sales. In 1950, Congress added §§ 1221(3) and 1231(b)(1)(C), depriving authors of the possibility of capital-gain treatment for the fruits of their efforts. This rule does not apply, however, to a person who has bought the copyright. These rules are consistent with the notion that gains from one's efforts are ordinary income while gains or losses from passive investments are capital gains or losses.

---

33. In Lugosi v. Universal Pictures, 25 Cal. 3d 813, 160 Cal. Rptr. 323, 603 P.2d 425 (1979), the California Supreme Court held that the heirs of Bela Lugosi did not have any protected rights in his special depictions of the character Dracula, despite the fact that he might have had such rights during his lifetime. In 1984, the California legislature added Cal. Civ. Code § 990, which provides a cause of action for damages for unauthorized commercial use of "a deceased person's name, voice, signature, or likeness" and stating that the rights established are "property rights, freely transferable." Cal. Civ. Code § 3344 provides a similar cause of action in respect of living persons. Compare Factors, Etc., Inc. v. Creative Card Co., 444 F. Supp. 279 (S.D.N.Y. 1977); Factors, Etc., Inc. v. Pro Arts, Inc., 44 F. Supp. 288 (S.D.N.Y. 1977); and Memphis Dev. Found. v. Factors, Etc., Inc., 441 F. Supp. 1323 (W.D. Tenn. 1977) — all recognizing property rights in the name and likeness of Elvis Presley; the rights had been exploited by him during his lifetime and survived his death.

The "letter or memorandum" language was added to §§ 1221(3) and 1231(b)(1)(C) in 1969, apparently in an effort (in conjunction with § 170(e)(1)(A)) to prevent politicians from claiming charitable deductions for contributions of their papers to libraries, museums, etc. The addition of this language helped bring about the impeachment of President Richard Nixon, who, having signed the legislation, later filed a tax return claiming a deduction based on backdated documents of transfer of his own papers.

The reference in § 1221(3) to "similar property" includes "theatrical productions, a radio program, a newspaper cartoon strip, or any other property eligible for copyright protection but . . . does not include a patent, or an invention, or a design which may be protected only under the patent law and not under the copyright law." Regs. § 1.1221-1(c)(l). The term "similar property" has also been applied to the format of a radio quiz program "Double or Nothing," on which participants could progressively double their winnings by electing to answer an additional question. Cranford v. United States, 338 F.2d 379 (Ct. Cl. 1964). Even if not entitled to copyright protection, the idea was held to be similar to the items explicitly listed in § 1221(3) because it was a type of artistic work resulting from personal effort and skill. The same fate befell the author of "Francis," a talking army mule figuring in a series of novels, when he sold his rights to the character and the novels to a motion-picture company. Stern v. United States, 164 F. Supp. 847 (E.D. La. 1958), aff'd per curiam, 262 F.2d 957 (5th Cir.), cert. denied, 359 U.S. 969 (1959).

The 1950 amendment did not change the treatment of inventors and in 1954 Congress added § 1235, which, when applicable, ensures that income from the transfer of patents will be taxed as long-term capital gain even if received by a professional inventor.

H.   BAILOUT OF CORPORATE EARNINGS

As we have seen before, people sometimes try to use a tax provision to accomplish an objective other than what one would have assumed was intended by the drafters of the statute. Often this kind of effort depends on the use of unnatural and cumbersome legal forms—forms that no sensible lawyer would have used except in the hope of achieving a tax advantage. A notable example of this phenomenon is the set of three-corner like-kind exchange transactions described in Chapter 3.A.7. In those transactions, the taxpayer was successful; form prevailed over substance. In many instances, substance will prevail, and a lawyer must always be sensitive to this possibility, even though reliable prediction of outcomes may be impossible. The case that follows, Gregory v. Helvering, is a classic, taxing the transaction according to its substance while preserving at least an appearance of fidelity to the statutory language by interpreting "reorganization" to require a business purpose for the transaction. The taxpayer owned shares of stock of a corporation that had assets that could have been paid out as a dividend. Dividends, however, are ordinary income. The taxpayer adopted a complex scheme by which she sought to "bail out" the assets in a manner that would produce capital gain rather than ordinary income.

GREGORY v. HELVERING
293 U.S. 465 (1935)

Mr. Justice SUTHERLAND delivered the opinion of the Court.

Petitioner in 1928 was the owner of all the stock of United Mortgage Corporation. That corporation held among its assets 1000 shares of the Monitor Securities Corporation. For the sole purpose of procuring a transfer of these shares to herself in order to sell them for her individual profit, and, at the same time, diminish the amount of income tax which would result from a direct transfer by way of dividend, she sought to bring about a "reorganization" under [a predecessor of § 386(a)(1)(D)]. To that end, she caused the Averill Corporation to be organized under the laws of Delaware on September 18, 1928. Three days later, the United Mortgage Corporation transferred to the Averill Corporation the 1000 shares of Monitor stock, for which all the shares of the Averill Corporation were issued to the petitioner. On September 24, the Averill Corporation was dissolved, and liquidated by distributing all its assets, namely, the Monitor shares, to the petitioner. No other business was ever transacted, or intended to be transacted, by that company. Petitioner immediately sold the Monitor shares for $133,333.33. She returned for taxation, as capital net gain, the sum of $76,007.88, based upon an apportioned cost of $57,325.45. . . .

The Commissioner of Internal Revenue, being of opinion that the reorganization attempted was without substance and must be disregarded, held that petitioner was liable for a tax as though the United Corporation had paid her a dividend consisting of the amount realized from the sale of the Monitor shares. . . .

Section 112 of the Revenue Act of 1928 deals with the subject of gain or loss resulting from the sale or exchange of property. Such gain or loss is to be recognized in computing the tax, except as provided in that section. The provisions of the section, so far as they are pertinent to the question here presented, follow:

> Sec. 112. . . . (g) *Distribution of Stock on Reorganization.* If there is distributed, in pursuance of a plan of reorganization, to a shareholder in a corporation a party to the reorganization, stock or securities in such corporation or in another corporation a party to the reorganization, without the surrender by such shareholder of stock or securities in such a corporation, no gain to the distributee from the receipt of such stock or securities shall be recognized. . . .
>
> (i) *Definition of Reorganization.* As used in this section . . .
>
> (1) The term "reorganization" means . . . (B) a transfer by a corporation of all or a part of its assets to another corporation if immediately after the transfer the transferor or its stockholders or both are in control of the corporation to which the assets are transferred. . . .

It is earnestly contended on behalf of the taxpayer that since every element required by the foregoing subdivision (B) is to be found in what was done, a statutory reorganization was effected; and that the motive of the taxpayer thereby to escape payment of a tax will not alter the result or make unlawful what the statute allows. It is quite true that if a reorganization in reality was effected within the meaning of subdivision (B), the ulterior purpose mentioned will be disregarded. The legal right of a taxpayer to decrease the amount of what otherwise would be his taxes, or altogether avoid them, by means which the law permits, cannot be doubted. . . . But the question for determination is whether what was done, apart from the tax motive, was the thing which the statute intended. The reasoning of the court below in justification of a negative answer leaves little to be said.

When subdivision (B) speaks of a transfer of assets by one corporation to another, it means a transfer made "in pursuance of a plan of reorganization" (section 112(g)) of corporate business; and not a transfer of assets by one corporation to another in pursuance of a plan having no relation to the business of either, as plainly is the case here. Putting aside, then, the question of motive in respect of taxation altogether, and fixing the character of the proceeding by what actually occurred, what do we find? Simply an operation having no business or corporate purpose — a mere device which put on the form of a corporate reorganization as a disguise for concealing its real character, and the sole object and accomplishment of which was the consummation of a preconceived plan, not to reorganize a business or any part of a business, but to transfer a parcel of corporate shares to the petitioner. No doubt, a new and valid corporation was created. But that corporation was nothing more than a contrivance to the end last described. It was brought into existence for no other purpose; it performed, as it was intended from the beginning it should perform, no other function. When that limited function had been exercised, it immediately was put to death.

In these circumstances, the facts speak for themselves and are susceptible of but one interpretation. The whole undertaking, though conducted according to the terms of subdivision (B), was in fact an elaborate and devious form of conveyance masquerading as a corporate reorganization, and nothing else. The rule which excludes from consideration the motive of tax avoidance is not pertinent to the situation, because the transaction upon its face lies outside the plain intent of the statute. To hold otherwise would be to exalt artifice above reality and to deprive the statutory provision in question of all serious purpose.

Judgment affirmed.

NOTE

The following paragraph from the opinion of Judge Learned Hand in the Court of Appeals in the principal case provides another approach (69 F.2d 809, 810-811 (2d Cir. 1934)):

We agree with the Board and the taxpayer that a transaction, otherwise within an exception of the tax law, does not lose its immunity, because it is actuated by a desire to avoid, or, if one choose, to evade, taxation. Any one may so arrange his affairs that his taxes shall be as low as possible; he is not bound to choose that pattern which will best pay the Treasury; there is not even a patriotic duty to increase one's taxes. . . . Therefore, if what was done here, was what was intended by section 112(i)(1)(B), it is of no consequence that it was all an elaborate scheme to get rid of income taxes, as it certainly was. Nevertheless, it does not follow that Congress meant to cover such a transaction, not even though the facts answer the dictionary definitions of each term used in the statutory definition. It is quite true, as the Board has very well said, that as the articulation of a statute increases, the room for interpretation must contract; but the meaning of a sentence may be more than that of the separate words, as a melody is more than the notes, and no degree of particularity can ever obviate recourse to the setting in which all appear, and which all collectively create. The purpose of the section is plain enough; men engaged in enterprises — industrial, commercial, financial, or any other — might wish to consolidate, or divide, to add to, or subtract from, their holdings. Such transactions were not to be considered as "realizing" any profit, because the collective interests still remained in solution. But the underlying presupposition is plain that the readjustment shall be undertaken for reasons germane to the conduct of the venture in hand, not as an ephemeral incident, egregious to its prosecution. To dodge the shareholders' taxes is not one of the transactions contemplated as corporate "reorganizations."

I. FRAGMENTATION VERSUS UNIFICATION OF COLLECTIVE ASSETS

WILLIAMS v. McGOWAN
152 F.2d 570 (2d Cir. 1945)

Before L. HAND, SWAN, and FRANK, Circuit Judges.

L. HAND, Circuit Judge. . . .

Williams, the taxpayer, and one Reynolds, had for many years been engaged in the hardware business in the City of Corning, New York. On the 20th of January, 1926, they formed a partnership, of which Williams was entitled to two-thirds of the profits, and Reynolds, one-third. . . . The business was carried on through the firm's fiscal year, ending January 31, 1940, in accordance with this agreement, and thereafter until Reynolds' death on July 18th of that year. Williams settled with Reynolds' executrix on September 6th in an agreement by which he promised to pay her $12,187.90, and to assume all liabilities of the business. . . . On September 17th of the same year, Williams sold the business as a whole to the Corning Building Company for $63,926.28 — its agreed value as of February 1, 1940 — "plus an amount to be computed by multiplying the gross sales of the business from the first day of February, 1940 to the 28th day of September, 1940," by an agreed fraction. This value was made up of cash of about $8100, receivables of about $7000, fixtures of about $800, and a merchandise inventory of about $49,000 less some $1000 for bills payable. To this was added about $6000 credited to

Williams for profits under the language just quoted, making a total of nearly $70,000. Upon this sale Williams suffered a loss upon his original two-thirds of the business, but he made a small gain upon the one-third which he had bought from Reynolds' executrix; and in his income tax return he entered both as items of "ordinary income," and not as transactions in "capital assets." This the Commissioner disallowed and recomputed the tax accordingly; Williams paid the deficiency and sued to recover it in this action. The only question is whether the business was "capital assets" under [§ 1221].

It has been held that a partner's interest in a going firm is for tax purposes to be regarded as a "capital asset." . . . We too accepted the doctrine in McClellan v. Commissioner, 2 Cir., 117 F.2d 988, although we had held the opposite in Helvering v. Smith, 2 Cir., 90 F.2d 590, 591, where the partnership articles had provided that a retiring partner should receive as his share only his percentage of the sums "actually collected" and "of all earnings . . . for services performed." Such a payment, we thought, was income; and we expressly repudiated the notion that the Uniform Partnership Act had, generally speaking, changed the firm into a juristic entity. . . . If a partner's interest in a going firm is "capital assets" perhaps a dead partner's interest is the same. . . . We need not say. When Williams bought out Reynolds' interest, he became the sole owner of the business, the firm had ended upon any theory, and the situation for tax purposes was no other than if Reynolds had never been a partner at all, except that to the extent of one-third of the "amount realized" on Williams' sale to the Corning Company, his "basis" was different. . . . We have to decide only whether upon the sale of a going business it is to be comminuted into its fragments, and these are to be separately matched against the definition in [§ 1221], or whether the whole business is to be treated as if it were a single piece of property.

Our law has been sparing in the creation of juristic entities; it has never, for example, taken over the Roman "universitas facti";[34] and indeed for many years it fumbled uncertainly with the concept of a corporation. One might have supposed that partnership would have been an especially promising field in which to raise up an entity, particularly since merchants have always kept their accounts upon that basis. Yet there too our law resisted at the price of great and continuing confusion; and even when it might be thought that a statute admitted, if it did not demand, recognition of the firm as an entity, the old concepts prevailed. . . . And so, even though we might agree that under the influence of the Uniform Partnership Act a partner's interest in the firm should be treated as indivisible, and for that reason a "capital asset" within [§ 1221], we should be chary about extending further so exotic a jural concept. Be that as it may, in this instance the section itself furnishes the answer. It starts in the broadest way by declaring that all "property" is "capital assets," and then makes three exceptions. The first is "stock in trade . . . or other property of a kind which would properly be included in the inventory"; next comes "property held . . . primarily for sale to customers"; and finally, property "used in the trade or business of a character which is subject to . . .

---

34. "By universitas facti is meant a number of things of the same kind which are regarded as a whole; e.g., a herd, a stock of wares." Mackeldey, Roman Law § 162.

allowance for depreciation." In the face of this language, although it may be true that a "stock in trade" taken by itself should be treated as a "universitas facti," by no possibility can a whole business be so treated; and the same is true as to any property within the other exceptions. Congress plainly did mean to comminute the elements of a business; plainly it did not regard the whole as "capital assets."

As has already appeared, Williams transferred to the Corning Company "cash," "receivables," "fixtures" and a "merchandise inventory." "Fixtures" are not capital because they are subject to a depreciation allowance; the inventory, as we have just seen, is expressly excluded. So far as appears, no allowance was made for "good-will"; but, even if there had been, we held in Haberle Crystal Springs Brewing Company v. Clarke, Collector, 2 Cir., 30 F.2d 219, that "good-will" was a depreciable intangible.[35] It is true that the Supreme Court reversed that judgment — 280 U.S. 284 — but it based its decision only upon the fact that there could be no allowance for the depreciation of "good-will" in a brewery, a business condemned by the Eighteenth Amendment. There can of course be no gain or loss in the transfer of cash; and, although Williams does appear to have made a gain of $1072.71 upon the "receivables," the point has not been argued that they are not subject to a depreciation allowance.[36] That we leave open for decision by the district court,[37] if the parties cannot agree. The gain or loss upon every other item should be computed as an item in ordinary income.

Judgment reversed.

FRANK, Circuit Judge (dissenting in part). . . .

I do not agree that we should ignore what the parties to the sale, Williams and the Corning Company, actually did. They did not arrange for a transfer to the buyer, as if in separate bundles, of the several ingredients of the business. They contracted for the sale of the entire business as a going concern. Here is what they said in their agreement:

> The party of the first part, agrees to sell and the party of the second part agrees to buy, *all of the right, title and interest* of the said party of the first part *in and of the hardware business* now being conducted by the said party of the first part, *including* cash on hand and on deposit in the First National Bank & Trust Company of Corning in the A. F. Williams' Hardware Store account, in accounts receivable, bills receivable, notes receivable, merchandise and fixtures, including two G.M. trucks, good will and all other assets of every kind and description used in and about said business. . . . Said party of the first part agrees not to engage in the hardware business within a radius of twenty-five miles from the City of Corning, New York, for a period of ten years from the 1st day of October 1940.

To carve up this transaction into distinct sales — of cash, receivables, fixtures, trucks, merchandise, and good will — is to do violence to the realities. I

---

35. [Section 197 now provides for fifteen-year amortization for goodwill acquired by purchase. See supra page 548. — EDS.]

36. [Section 1221(a)(4) would now cover receivables. — EDS.]

37. [The decision on remand is reported at 70 F. Supp. 31 (W.D.N.Y. 1947). — EDS.]

do not think Congress intended any such artificial result. . . . Where a business is sold as a unit, the whole is greater than its parts. Businessmen so recognize; so, too, I think, did Congress. Interpretation of our complicated tax statutes is seldom aided by saying that taxation is an eminently practical matter (or the like). But this is one instance where, it seems to me, the practical aspects of the matter should guide our guess as to what Congress meant. I believe Congress had those aspects in mind and was not thinking of the nice distinctions between Roman and Anglo-American legal theories about legal entities.

NOTES AND QUESTIONS

1. *Analysis.* In Williams v. McGowan, Judge Hand relies on legal history and precedent in approaching the question whether a proprietorship should, for tax purposes, be thought of as an entity. (See the discussion of the entity/aggregate distinction at page 692, Note 2, following the *Basye* case.) Judge Frank, dissenting, relies instead on his perception of how the ordinary business person would think. Which approach seems most likely to be consistent with congressional purpose? with promoting sound tax-policy objectives?

2. *Partnerships and partners; corporations and shareholders.* If a partnership sells the assets of a business it operates (or, if you sympathize with Judge Frank's view in Williams v. McGowan, if it sells "a business") the sale is governed by the fragmentation principle of Williams v. McGowan. If, on the other hand, an individual partner sells his or her interest in the partnership, that sale produces capital gain or loss, except to the extent that the proceeds are attributable to unrealized receivables, recapture property, substantially appreciated inventory items, or certain other ordinary-income property. See §§ 741 and 751. Similarly, a sale of business assets by a corporation is governed by Williams v. McGowan, while a sale of shares by a shareholder ordinarily is treated as the sale of a single capital asset.

J. CORRELATION WITH PRIOR RELATED TRANSACTIONS

MERCHANTS NATIONAL BANK v. COMMISSIONER
199 F.2d 657 (5th Cir. 1952)

STRUM, Circuit Judge. . . .

On January 1, 1941, the petitioner held notes of Alabama Naval Stores Company, representing loans made by the bank to the Naval Stores Company, on which there was an unpaid balance of $49,025.00. In 1941 and 1943, at the direction of national bank examiners, the bank charged these notes off as worthless, thereafter holding them on a "zero" basis. Deductions for the charge-offs, as ordinary losses, were allowed in full by the Commissioner on petitioner's income tax returns in 1941 and 1943. In 1944, petitioner sold the notes to a third party for $18,460.58, which it reported on its return for 1944 as a long term capital gain and paid its tax on that basis. The Commissioner held this sum to be ordinary income. . . .

The rule is well settled, and this Court has held, that when a deduction for income tax purposes is taken and allowed for debts deemed worthless, recoveries on the debts in a later year constitute taxable income for that year to the extent that a tax benefit was received from the deduction taken in a prior year. . . .

When these notes were charged off as a bad debt in the first instance, the bank deducted the amount thereof from its ordinary income, thus escaping taxation on that portion of its income in those years. The amount subsequently recovered on the notes restores pro tanto the amount originally deducted from ordinary income, and is accordingly taxable as ordinary income, not as a capital gain. When the notes were charged off, and the bank recouped itself for the capital loss by deducting the amount thereof from its current income, the notes were no longer capital assets for income tax purposes. To permit the bank to reduce its ordinary income by the amount of the loss in the first instance, thus gaining a maximum tax advantage on that basis, and then permit it to treat the amount later recovered on the notes as a capital gain, taxable on a much lower basis than ordinary income, would afford the bank a tax advantage on the transaction not contemplated by the income tax laws.

The fact that the bank sold these notes to a third party, instead of collecting the amount in question from the maker of the notes does not avoid the effect of the rule above stated. . . .

As the recoveries in question were ordinary income, not capital gains, the 1944 deficiency was properly entered.

Affirmed.

ARROWSMITH v. COMMISSIONER
344 U.S. 6 (1952)

Mr. Justice BLACK delivered the opinion of the Court.

. . . In 1937 two taxpayers, petitioners here, decided to liquidate and divide the proceeds of a corporation in which they had equal stock ownership. Partial distributions made in 1937, 1938, and 1939 were followed by a final one in 1940. Petitioners reported the profits obtained from this transaction, classifying them as capital gains. They thereby paid less income tax than would have been required had the income been attributed to ordinary business transactions for profit. About the propriety of these 1937-1940 returns, there is no dispute. But in 1944 a judgment was rendered against the old corporation. . . . The two taxpayers were required to and did pay the judgment for the corporation, of whose assets they were transferees. . . . Classifying the loss as an ordinary business one, each took a tax deduction for 100% of the amount paid. Treatment of the loss as a capital one would have allowed deduction of a much smaller amount. . . . The Commissioner viewed the 1944 payment as part of the original liquidation transaction requiring classification as a capital loss, just as the taxpayers had treated the original dividends as capital gains. . . .

[Section 165(f)] treats losses from sales or exchanges of capital assets as "capital losses" and [§ 331(a)(1)] requires that liquidation distributions be treated as exchanges. The losses here fall squarely within the definition of "capital losses" contained in these sections. Taxpayers were required to pay the judgment because of liability imposed on them as transferees of liquidation distribution assets. And it is plain that their liability as transferees was not based on any ordinary business transaction of theirs apart from the liquidation proceedings. It is not even denied that had this judgment been paid after liquidation, but during the year 1940, the losses would have been properly treated as capital ones. For payment during 1940 would simply have reduced the amount of capital gains taxpayers received during that year.

It is contended, however, that this payment which would have been a capital transaction in 1940 was transformed into an ordinary business transaction in 1944 because of the well-established principle that each taxable year is a separate unit for tax accounting purposes. United States v. Lewis [supra page 147], North American Oil Consolidated v. Burnet [supra page 143]. But this principle is not breached by considering all the 1937-1944 liquidation transaction events in order properly to classify the nature of the 1944 loss for tax purposes. Such an examination is not an attempt to reopen and readjust the 1937 to 1940 tax returns, an action that would be inconsistent with the annual tax accounting principle. . . .

Affirmed.

Mr. Justice DOUGLAS, dissenting.

I agree with Mr. Justice Jackson that these losses should be treated as ordinary, not capital, losses. There were no capital transactions in the year in which the losses were suffered. Those transactions occurred and were accounted for in earlier years in accord with the established principle that each year is a separate unit for tax accounting purposes. See United States v. Lewis [supra]. I have not felt, as my dissent in the *Lewis* case indicates, that the law made that an inexorable principle. But if it is the law, we should require observance of it — not merely by taxpayers but by the Government as well. We should force each year to stand on its own footing, whoever may gain or lose from it in a particular case. We impeach that principle when we treat this year's losses as if they diminished last year's gains.

Mr. Justice JACKSON, whom Mr. Justice FRANKFURTER joins, dissenting.

This problem arises only because the judgment was rendered in a taxable year subsequent to the liquidation.

Had the liability of the transferor-corporation been reduced to judgment during the taxable year in which liquidation occurred, or prior thereto, this problem, under the tax laws, would not arise. The amount of the judgment rendered against the corporation would have decreased the amount it had available for distribution, which would have reduced the liquidating dividends proportionately and diminished the capital gains taxes assessed against the stockholders. Probably it would also have decreased the corporation's own taxable income.

Congress might have allowed, under such circumstances, tax returns of the prior year to be reopened or readjusted so as to give the same tax results as would have obtained had the liability become known prior to liquidation. Such a solution is foreclosed to us and the alternatives left are to regard the judgment liability fastened by operation of law on the transferee as an ordinary loss for the year of adjudication or to regard it as a capital loss for such year.

I find little aid in the choice of alternatives from arguments based on equities. One enables the taxpayer to deduct the amount of the judgment against his ordinary income which might be taxed as high as 87%, while if the liability had been assessed against the corporation prior to liquidation it would have reduced his capital gain which was taxable at only 25% (now 26%). The consequence may readily be characterized as a windfall (regarding a windfall as anything that is left to a taxpayer after the collector has finished with him).

On the other hand, adoption of the contrary alternative may penalize the taxpayer because of two factors: (1) [limitations on the deductibility of capital losses against ordinary income]; and (2) had the liability been discharged by the corporation, a portion of it would probably in effect have been paid by the Government, since the corporation could have taken it as a deduction, while here the total liability comes out of the pockets of the stockholders.

Solicitude for the revenues is a plausible but treacherous basis upon which to decide a particular tax case. A victory may have implications which in future cases will cost the Treasury more than a defeat. This might be such a case, for anything I know. Suppose that subsequent to liquidation it is found that a corporation has undisclosed claims instead of liabilities and that under applicable state law they may be prosecuted for the benefit of the stockholders. The logic of the Court's decision here, if adhered to, would result in a lesser return to the Government than if the recoveries were considered ordinary income. Would it be so clear that this is a capital loss if the shoe were on the other foot?

Where the statute is so indecisive and the importance of a particular holding lies in its rational and harmonious relation to the general scheme of the tax law, I think great deference is due the twice-expressed judgment of the Tax Court . . . [which] is a more competent and steady influence toward a systematic body of tax law than our sporadic omnipotence in a field beset with invisible boomerangs. I should reverse, in reliance upon the Tax Court's judgment more, perhaps, than my own.

NOTES

In United States v. Skelly Oil Co., 394 U.S. 678 (1969), the taxpayer was required to refund amounts that it had received in an earlier year from the sale of natural gas and that had been the basis for a 27½ percent depletion allowance. The Court held that the deduction for the refund was limited to 72½ percent of the amount refunded, since it was only this amount that had been taxed. In reaching this result, the Court referred to the problems created by the principle of annual accounting (see supra page 138) and, citing *Arrowsmith*, said that "the annual accounting concept does not require us to close our eyes to what happened in prior years." 394 U.S. at 684. The Court went on to say (at 685):

> The rationale for the *Arrowsmith* rule is easy to see; if money was taxed at a special lower rate when received, the taxpayer would be accorded an unfair tax windfall if repayments were generally deductible from receipts taxable at the higher rate applicable to ordinary income. The Court in *Arrowsmith* was unwilling to infer that Congress intended such a result.

Four Circuit Court decisions have addressed the tax problem that arises from the repayment of insider profits. In each case, an employee stockholder made a profit on employer stock purchased and sold (or sold and purchased) allegedly in violation of the securities laws regarding trading restrictions on insiders. None of the employees admitted liability, but each decided to repay the profits to the corporation to preserve his business position and reputation. In all four cases, the Tax Court held the amount repaid was a deduction from ordinary income rather than a capital loss since the taxpayers made the sales in their capacities as shareholders rather than as employees, while the repayments arose from their status as employees. The Circuit Courts reversed all four decisions and held that the deduction must take its character from the income item in which it had its genesis, which was the purchase and/or sale of a capital asset. Mitchell v. Commissioner, 428 F.2d 259 (6th Cir. 1970), cert. denied, 401 U.S. 909 (1971); Anderson v. Commissioner, 480 F.2d 1304 (7th Cir. 1973); Cummings v. Commissioner, 506 F.2d 449 (2d Cir. 1974), cert. denied, 421 U.S. 913 (1975); Brown v. Commissioner, 529 F.2d 609 (10th Cir. 1976).

K. REQUIREMENT OF A SALE OR EXCHANGE

Section 1222 defines capital gains and losses as those recognized from the "sale or exchange" of a capital asset. Suppose a capital asset simply becomes worthless? If the asset is a security, such as stock or a corporate bond, § 165(g)(1) treats the loss as one that arises from sale or exchange. Similarly, under the holding of Helvering v. Hammel, 311 U.S. 504 (1941), the foreclosure of property is treated as a sale or exchange. The sale or exchange requirement is also relaxed in situations that do not involve worthless property. For example, § 1271 treats amounts realized from the retirement of a bond as having been realized from sale or exchange. Insurance or other proceeds from involuntary conversions may generate capital gain under § 1231.

In general, the sale or exchange requirement comes into play in situations in which there is a dispute about whether the taxpayer has parted with ownership. For example, an issue in *Ferrer*, supra at page 768, was whether the taxpayer retained or sold a copyright; an issue in *Baker*, supra at page 759, was whether the taxpayer parted ownership with enough business assets to characterize the proceeds as arising from the sale or exchange of those assets. Occasionally, the sale or exchange requirement comes into play in situations in which there is no dispute about what was retained or transferred. For example, suppose in Year 1 a grocer borrows $10,000 from a commercial lender and then runs into financial difficulties. The commercial lender sells its claim to the taxpayer for $6,000. In Year 2, the grocer regains its financial footing and later that year repays the debt in full. If the taxpayer resells the debt for $10,000 shortly before repayment, any gain recognized will be capital gain. But if the taxpayer retains the debt until it is repaid, the gain recognized will be ordinary income. Capital gain is unavailable because there has been no sale or exchange.

TABLE OF CASES

Italic type indicates principal cases.

TABLE OF INTERNAL REVENUE CODE PROVISIONS

TABLE OF TREASURY
REGULATIONS

TABLE OF REVENUE
RULINGS

TABLE OF MISCELLANEOUS IRS PRONOUNCEMENTS

INDEX